Advances in Computer Communications

Wesley W. Chu

Professor, Computer Science Department
University of California, Los Angeles, California

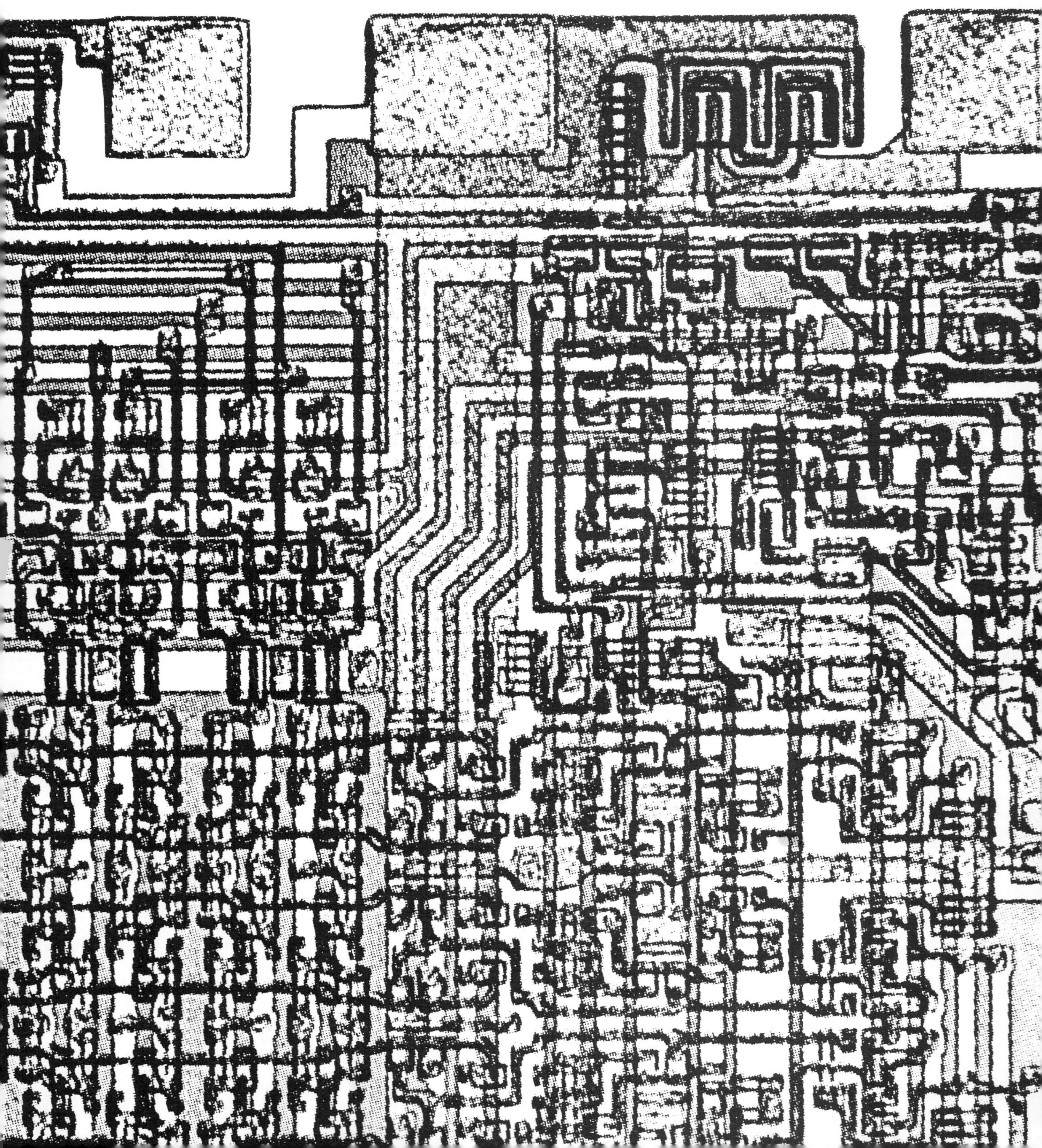

Advances in Computer Communications

Revised Edition

Second Printing

ARTECH HOUSE
610 Washington Street
Dedham, Massachusetts 02026

Printed and bound in the United States of America.

International Standard Book Number: 0-89006-049-5
Library of Congress Catalog Card Number: 75-31381

Since the publication of the first edition of this book in the early part of last year, I have received many favorable comments and responses from students and teachers, as well as practitioners in the computer communications field, both in the United States and abroad. Because of its popularity, the book has gone out of print within a year. In order to reflect the advances in the fast growing computer communications field, we decided to make a second edition of the book. In this second edition, we have added twelve new papers which represent important recent advances in such areas as data link control procedure, flow control, interprocess communications, network performance simulation and measurement, distributed data bases, computer cost and communication cost trends, security in the computer communication environment, and economical and political issues in internetworking. To provide interested readers with further readings relevant to computer communications, we have updated and added many new articles, special books, and publications to the reference list. These references are cited in the introduction to each chapter.

It is our hope that this edition will serve as an up-to-date text or reference book in computer communications, and the information in the book will be interesting and valuable to the readers.

Table of Contents

Computer Traffic Characteristics

Error Control Techniques

Modems

Statistical Multiplexing

Packet Switching via Satellites

Loop Systems

Examples of Computer Communications Networks

Computer Network Design Considerations

Communications Processors for Store-and-Forward Networks

Interprocess Communications

Distributed Data Base Design Considerations

Computer Communications Systems Reliability

Computer Communication Security

Common Carrier Facilities and Services

Social, Regulatory and Legal Issues in Computer Communications

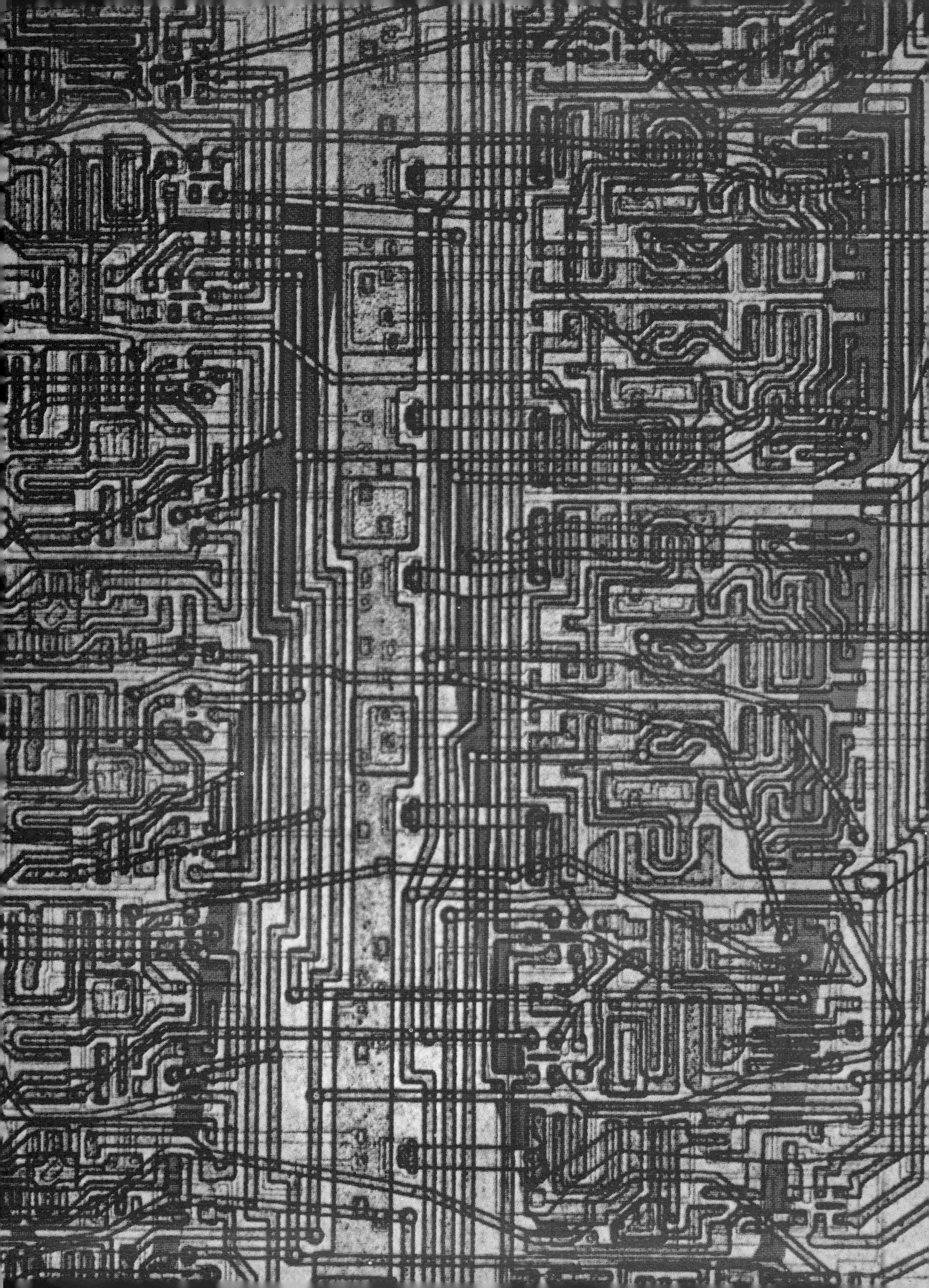

Introduction

The field of Computer Communications has grown rapidly in its applications during the past decade. Remote terminals are now commonly connected to computers for use in time-sharing systems, reservation systems, bank credit checking, inventory systems, business information systems, etc., to achieve resource sharing of hardware, software and data bases. The resource sharing concept has added a new dimension to the capabilities of the user. Under this new environment, he now can benefit from the versatility and power of the interlinking of computers and terminals. However, marriage of the computer and communication equipment also creates many new problems, both in technical and non-technical areas.

The basic technical problems are as follows: to economically and reliably transmit data from one location to another; to handle interface and interprocess communication among the computers, terminals and communication equipment; to control information flow and to predict system behavior; to efficiently share resources such as software and data bases. All of these questions are related to the goal of designing and planning a computer communications system that satisfies a set of user requirements for such parameters as response time, reliability and security, and yet yields a minimum total system cost (for software, firmware, hardware and maintenance).

The non-technical problems are mainly in the areas of the social and legal impact of introducing such computer communications systems into society, and the establishment of government regulating policies for these systems.

A large body of knowledge and techniques concerning computer communications have been developed during the past decades. This information is scattered in various conference proceedings, transactions and journals. A textbook to summarize these results is very desirable, since there is a critical need in the technical community for textbooks as well as reference materials. However, due to the time required to prepare such a text, the time usually required for publication, and the rapid technological changes and growth in this field, publishing a book containing up-to-date information as well as technical depth in computer communications at this time is very difficult, if not impossible. Therefore, we have taken a different approach. We have selected a set of reprints representing significant advances in computer communications during the past decades, and have organized them into a book with the objective of answering some of the questions which have arisen about the planning and designing of computer communications systems.

Chapters 1 to 5 describe computer traffic characterization, error control techniques, modems, statistical multiplexing, and packet switching via satellites. Chapters 6 to 11 present loop systems, examples of computer networks, computer network design considerations, communication processors for store-and-forward networks, interprocess communications and distributed data base design considerations. Chapters 12 to 15 discuss network reliability, computer communication security, common carrier facilities and services, and social, regulatory, and legal issues in computer communications.

This book of reprints is an outgrowth of a summer short course entitled "Recent Advances in Computer Communications," which has been offered at UCLA for a period of five years. Most of the papers in this volume have also been used in a first year graduate course entitled "Data Communications in Computer Systems." Therefore this collection of reprints can be used as a text or reference book for a graduate course in computer communications. It can also be used for reference by engineers or scientists who are engaged in the design and development of computer communications systems.

Considering the large number of fine papers available, and the limited number that we can collect into one book, the selection of the set of papers for this volume has been a difficult task. Many excellent papers that could not be included here are mentioned in the list of references.

Several authors have added comments on and corrections to their papers. This material is appended to their papers.

We wish to express our appreciation to all of the authors and publishers for permission to reprint the papers in this volume. The majority of the papers are publications of the IEEE, AFIPS, and ACM. We have also received helpful comments from W. Chou, P. Green, F. Heart, B. Kahn, L. Kleinrock, J. Postel, and R. Turn in selecting the materials for this book.

WESLEY W. CHU
Westwood, California

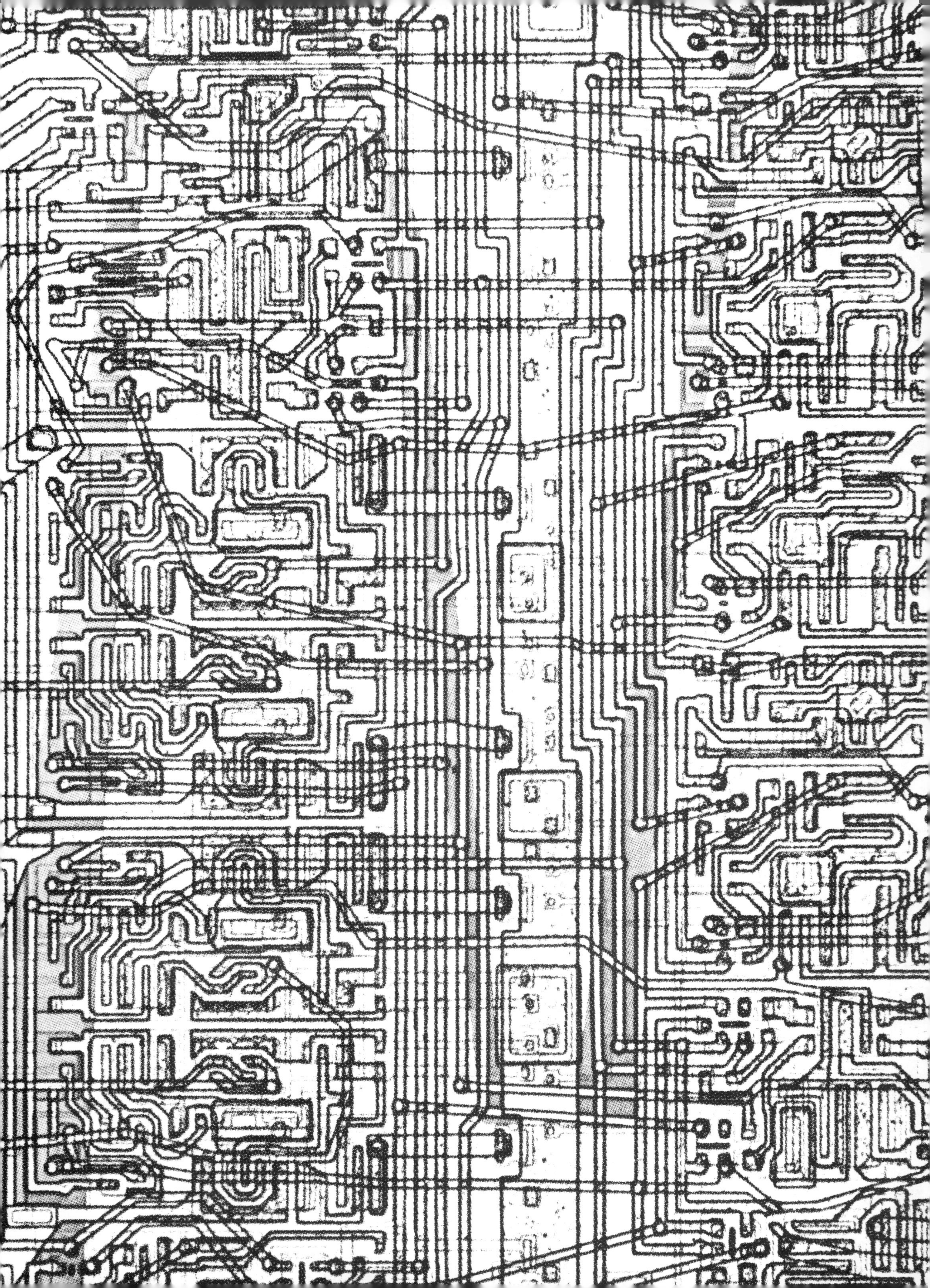

References

AND 72 Andrews, M.C., "New Data Networks in Europe," *Proceedings of the IEEE,* November 1972, p. 1369.

BAL 71 Balkovic, M.D. et al., "1969-70 Connection Survey: High-Speed Voiceband Data Transmission Performance on the Switched Telecommunications Network," *BSTJ,* Vol. 50, No. 4, April 1971, pp. 1349-1384.

BAR 64 Baran, P., "On Distributed Communications: XI. Summary Overview," Mem. RM-3767-PR, The Rand Corporation, August 1964.

BAR72 Barber, D.L.A., "The European Computer Network Project," *The First International Conference on Computer Communications,* Washington, D.C., October 1972, pp. 192-200.

BEC 72 Becher, W.D. and E.M. Aupperle, "The Communications Computer Hardware of the MERIT Computer Network," *IEEE Transactions on Communications,* Vol. COM-20, No. 3, June 1972, pp. 516-526.

BOC 75 Bochmann, Gregor V., "Logical Verification and Implementation of Protocols," *Proceedings of the Fourth Data Communications Symposium*, Quebec City, October 1975, pp. 7-15 to 7-20.

BOE 75 Boesch, F., Chang, S., McHugh, J., "On Characterizing Network Vulnerability by K Component Cuts," *Proceedings of the Fourth Data Communications Symposium,* Quebec City, October 1975, pp. 4-24 to 4-28.

BOU 73 Bouknight, W.J., G.R. Grossman and D.M. Grothe, "The ARPA Network Terminal System--A New Approach to Network Access," *Proceedings of the Third Data Communications Symposium,* St. Petersburg, Florida, November 1973, pp. 73-79.

BRA 75 Bransted, K., "Encryption Protection in Computer Data Communications, *Proceedings of the Fourth Data Communications Symposium*, Quebec City, October 1975, pp. 8-1 to 8-7.

CAR 73 Carter, W., "Reliability Techniques Applicable to Message Processors," *Proceedings of the Third Data Communications Symposium,* St. Petersburg, Florida, November 1973, pp. 157-158.

CAS 72 Casey, R.G., "Allocation of Copies of a File in an Information Network," *AFIPS Conference Proceedings,* SJCC, 1972, pp. 617-625.

CHO 73 Chou, W., H. Frank and R. Van Slyke, "Simulation of Centralized Computer Communications Systems," *Proceedings of the Third Data Communications Symposium,* St. Petersburg, Florida, November 1973, pp. 121-130.

CHU 69 Chu, W.W., "Design Considerations of Statistical Multiplexors," *Proceedings of the ACM Symposium on Problems in the Optimization of Data Communications Systems,* Pine Mountain, Georgia, October 1969, pp. 36-60.

CHU 70 Chu, W.W., "Selection of Optimal Transmission Rate for Statistical Multiplexors," *Proceedings of the ICC,* San Francisco, California, June 1970, pp. 28-22 to 28-25.

CHU 70a Chu, W.W., "Buffer Behavior for Batch Poisson Arrivals and Single Constant Output," *IEEE Transactions on Communication Technology,* Vol. COM-18, No. 5, October 1970, pp. 613-618.

CHU 72 Chu, W.W. and A.G. Konheim, "On the Analysis and Modeling of a Class of Computer Communication Systems," *IEEE Transactions on Communications,* Vol. COM-20, No. 3, June 1972, pp. 645-660.

CHU 75 Chu, W.W. and Nahouraii, E.E., "File Directory Design Considerations for Distributed Data Bases," *Proceedings of the International Conference on Very Large Data Bases*, Framingham, Mass., Sept. 22-24, 1975.

COO 75 Cooper, Stuart, B., "Hardware Considerations for High Level Data Link Control Communications," *Computer Design*, March 1975, pp. 81-87.

COX 72 Cox, J.E., "Western Union Digital Services," *Proceedings of the IEEE,* November 1972, pp. 1350-1357.

CRO 73 Crowther, W., J. McQuillian and D. Walden, "Reliability Issues in the ARPA Network," *Proceedings of the Third Data Communications Symposium,* St. Petersburg, Florida, November 1973, pp. 159-160.

DAN 75 Danthine, A. and Eschenauer, E., "Influence on the Node Behavior of the Node-to-Node Protocol," *Proceedings of the Fourth Data Communications Symposium*, Quebec City, October 1975, pp. 7-1 to 7-8.

DAV 67 Davies, D.W. et al., "A Digital Communication Network for Computers Giving Rapid Response at Remote Terminals," *Proceedings of the ACM Symposium on Operating System Principles,* Gatlinburg, Tennessee, October, 1967.

DOL 72 Doll, D.R., "Multiplexing and Concentration," *Proceedings of the IEEE,* November 1972, pp. 1313-1321.

DON 74 Donnan, R.A., and Kersey, J.R., "Synchronous Data Link Control: A Perspective," *IBM Systems Journal*, Vol. 13, No. 2, 1974, pp. 140-162.

DUN 73 Dunn, D.A. and A.J. Lipinski, "Economic Considerations in Computer-Communication Systems, Chapter 10, *Computer-Communication Networks,* edited by N. Abramson and F.F. Kuo, Prentice-Hall, 1973.

EVA 67 Evans, D.C. and J.Y. Leclerc, "Address Mapping and the Control of Access in an Interactive Computer," *AFIPS Conference Proceedings,* SJCC, Vol. 30, April 18-20, 1967, pp. 23-30.

FAN 72 Fano, R.M., "On the Social Role of Computer Communications," *Proceedings of the IEEE,* November 1972, pp. 1249-1253.

FAR 75 Farber, D. and Larson, K., "Network Security via Dynamic Process Renaming," *Proceedings of the Fourth Data Communications Symposium*, Quebec City, October 1975, pp. 8-13 to 8-18.

FLE 71 Fleming, H.C. and R.M. Hutchinson, Jr., "1969-70 Connection Survey: Low-Speed Data Transmission Performance on the Switched Telecommunications Network," *BSTJ,* Vol. 50, No. 4, April 1971, pp. 1385-1405.

FRA 73 Frank, H., "Providing Reliable Networks with Unreliable Components," *Proceedings of the Third Data Communications Symposium,* St. Petersburg, Florida, November 1973, pp. 161-162.

FRAS 73 Fraser, A.G., "A 10-Wire Interface for Data Communications," *Proceedings of the Third Data Communications Symposium,* St. Petersburg, Florida, November 1973, pp. 113-120.

GAI 56 Gaines, H.F., *Cryptanalysis,* Dover Publications, Inc., New York, 1956.

GER 73 Gerla, M., "Deterministic and Adaptive Routing Policies in Packet-Switched Computer Networks," *Proceedings of the Third Data Communications Symposium,* St. Petersburg, Florida, November 1973, pp. 23-28.

GRA 72 Graham, G.S. and P.J. Denning, "Protection--Principles and Practice," *AFIPS Conference Proceedings,* SJCC, Vol. 40, May 16-18, 1972, pp. 417-429.

GRA 68 Graham, R.M., "Protection in an Information Processing Utility," *CACM,* Vol. 11, No. 5, May 1968, pp. 365-369.

GRE 75 Grenier, E.J., Jr. and Winkler, R.L., "Data Security – Technology and the Regulatory Process," *Proceedings of the Fourth Data Communications Symposium*, Quebec City, October 1975, pp. 3-6 to 3-12.

KAH 67 Kahn, D., *The Code Breakers*, The MacMillan Co., 1967.

KAR 73 Karp, P.M., "Origin, Development and Current Status of the ARPA Network," *Digest of Papers*, COMPCON 73, San Francisco, California, February 1973, pp. 49-52.

KAY 72 Kaye, A.R., "Analysis of a Distributed Control Loop for Data Transmission," *Proceedings of the Symposium on Computer-Communications Networks and Teletraffic*, Polytechnic Institute of Brooklyn, Brooklyn, New York, April 1972, pp. 47-49.

KLE 75 Kleinrock, L. Naylor, W. and Opderbeck, H., "A Study of Line Overhead in the ARPANET," to appear in *CACM*, 1975.

KLE 75a Kleinrock, L. and Opderbeck, H., "Throughput in the ARPANET – Protocols and Measurement," *Proceedings of the Fourth Data Communications Symposium*, Quebec City, October 1975, pp. 6-1 to 6-11.

KON 72 Konheim, A.G., "Service Epochs in a Loop System," *Proceedings of the Symposium on Computer-Communications Networks and Teletraffic*, Polytechnic Institute of Brooklyn, Brooklyn, New York, April 1972, pp. 125-143.

KON 72a Konheim, A.G. and B. Meister, "Service in a Loop System," *JACM*, Vol. 19, No. 1, January 1972, pp. 92-108.

KUO 75 Kuo, F.F., "Public Policy Issues Converning ARPANET," *Proceedings of the Fourth Data Communications Symposium*, Quebec City, October 1975, pp. 3-13 to 3-17.

LAM 69 Lampson, B.W., "Dynamic Protection Structures," *AFIPS Conference Proceedings*, FJCC, Vol. 35, November 18-20, 1969, pp. 27-38.

LAV 75 Lavia, A. and Manning E., "Perturbation Techniques for Topological Optimization of Computer Networks," *Proceedings of the Fourth Data Communications Symposium*, Quebec City, October 1975, pp. 4-16 to 4-23.

LEV 75 Levin, K.D. and Morgan, H.L., "Optimizing Distributed Data Bases: A Frame Work for Research," *AFIPS Proceedings*, Vol. 44, 1975, pp. 473-478.

LIP 75 Lipner, S., "Secure Computer Systems for Network Applications," *Proceedings of the Fourth Data Communications Symposium*, Quebec City, October 1975, pp. 8-8 to 8-12.

MAH 75 Mahmond, S. and Riardon, J.S., "Optimal Allocation of Resources in Distributed Information Networks," *Proceedings of the International Conference on Very Large Data Bases*, Framingham, Mass, Sept. 22-24, 1975.

MAT 75 Mathison, Stuart Jr. and Walker, Phillip, "Value-Added Carriers," *Proceedings of the Fourth Data Communications Symposium*, Quebec City, October 1975, pp. 3-1 to 3-5.

McG 75 McGregor, P. and Shen, D., "Locating Concentration Points in Data Communication Networks," *Proceedings of the Fourth Data Communications Symposium*, Quebec City, October 1975, pp. 4-1 to 4-8.

McK 72 McKenzie, A.A. et al., "The Network Control Center for the ARPA Network," *Proceedings of the First International Conference on Computer Communication, Impacts and Implications*, Washington, D.C., October 1972, pp. 185-191.

McK 75 McKenzie, A., "The ARPA Network Control Center," *Proceedings of the Fourth Data Communications Symposium*, Quebec City, October 1975, pp. 6-1 to 6-11.

McQ 72 McQuillian, J. et al., "Improvements in the Design and Performance of the ARPA Network," *AFIPS Conference Proceedings,* Part II, Vol. 41, 1972, pp. 741-754.

MEI 72 Meister, B., H.R. Mueller and H. Rudin Jr., "On the Optimization of Message-Switching Networks," *IEEE Transactions on Communications,* Vol. COM-20, No. 1, February 1972, pp. 8-14.

PAC 72 Pack, C.D., "The Effect of Multiplexing on a Computer-Communication System," *CACM,* March 1973, pp. 161-168.

PAN 72 Pan, J.W., "Synchronizing and Multiplexing in a Digital Communications Network," *Proceedings of the IEEE,* Vol. 60, No. 5, May 1972, pp. 594-601.

PET 67 Peterson, H.E. and R. Turn, "System Implications of Information Privacy," *AFIPS Conference Proceedings,* Vol. 30, SJCC, April 18-20, 1967, pp. 291-300.

POP 73 Popek, G.J. and R.P. Goldberg," Formal Requirements for Virtualizable Third Generation Architectures", Proceedings of the 4th Symposium on Operating System Principles, Appendix Oct. 1973, New York.

POP 75 Popek, G., "On Data Secure Computer Network," *Proceedings of the ACM Interprocess Communication Workshop,* Santa Monica, Calif., March 1975, pp. 59-62.

PRI 73 Price, W.L., "Simulation of Packet-Switching Networks Controlled on Isarithmic Principles," *Proceedings of the Third Data Communication Symposium,* St. Petersburg, Florida, November 1973, pp. 44-49.

RUB 75 Rubin, P.E., "The T4 Digital Transmission System – Overview," *Conference Record of the International Conference on Communications,* Vol. III, 1975, pp 48-1 to 48-4.

RUD 72 Rudin, H. Jr., "Buffered Packet Switching: A Queue with Clustered Arrivals," *Proceedings of the International Switching Symposium,* Boston, Massachusetts, 1972.

SCH 73 Schwartz, J.W. and M. Muntner, "Multiple-Access Communications for Computer Nets," *Computer-Communication Networks,* Chapter 8, edited by N. Abramson and F.F. Kuo, Prentice-Hall, 1973.

SHA 49 Shannon C., "Communication Theory of Secrecy Systems," *BSTJ,* Vol. 28, No. 4, 1949, pp. 654-715.

SIN 68 Sinkov, A., *Elementary Cryptanalysis--A Mathematical Approach,* Random House, New York, 1968.

SKA 69 Skatrud, R.O., "A Consideration of the Application of Cryptographic Techniques to Data Processing," *AFIPS Conference Proceedings,* FJCC, 1969, Vol. 35, November 18-20, 1969, pp. 111-117.

SPR 72 Spragins, J.D., "Loops Used for Data Collection," *Proceedings of the Symposium on Computer-Communications Networks and Teletraffic,* Polytechnic Institute of Brooklyn, Brooklyn, New York, April 1972, pp. 59-76.

TEN 74 Tenkhoff, P., "The Infonet Remote Teleprocessing Communication Network – Design, Performance, and Operation," *Proceedings of the Second International Conference on Computer Communication,* Stockholm, Sweden, August 1974, pp. 401-412.

VAN 73 Van Slyke, R., W. Chou, and H. Frank, "Avoiding Simulation in Simulating Computer Communication Networks," *AFIPS Conference Proceedings,* NCC, New York, 1973, pp. 165-169.

VIL 72 Villips, V.V., *Data Modem: Selection and Evaluation Guide,* Artech House, Inc., 1972.

WHI 72 Whitney, V.K.M., "Comparison of Network Topology Optimization Algorithms," *Proceedings of the First International Conference on Computer Communication, Impacts and Implications*, Washington, D.C., October 1972, pp. 332-337.

WOO 73 Woo, L.S. and D.T. Tang, "Optimization of Teleprocessing Networks and Concentrators," *Proceedings of the National Telecommunications Conference*, Atlanta, Georgia, November 1973.

WOR 72 Worley, A.R., "The Datran System," *Proceedings of the IEEE*, November 1972, pp. 1357-1368.

ZIM 75 Zimmermann, Hubert, "The CYCLADES End to End Protocols," *Proceedings of the Fourth Data Communications Symposium*, Quebec City, October 1975, pp. 7-21 to 7-26.

SPECIAL PROCEEDINGS AND BOOKS ON COMPUTER COMMUNICATIONS

[1] Proceedings of the ACM/IEEE First Symposium on Problems in the Optimization of Data Communication Systems, Pine Mountain, Georgia, 1969

[2] Proceedings of the ACM/IEEE Second Symposium on Problems in the Optimization of Data Communications Systems, Palo Alto, California, 1971

[3] Proceedings of the Third Data Communications Symposium, St. Petersburg, Florida, 1973

[4] Proceedings of the Fourth Data Communications Symposium, Quebec City, Canada, Oct. 1975

[4A] Proceedings of the Fifth Data Communications Symposium, Snowbird, Utah, 1977.

[5] IEEE Transactions on Communications, Special Issue on Computer Communications, June 1972

[5A] IEEE Transactions on Communications, Special Issues on Computer Communications, January 1977.

[6] Proceedings of the First International Conference on Computer Communications, Washington, D.C. 1972

[7] Proceedings of the Second International Conference on Computer Communications, Stockholm Sweden, Aug. 1974

[7A] Proceedings of the Third International Conference on Computer Communications, Toronto, August 1976.

[8] Proceedings of the IEEE, Special Issue on Computer Communications, November 1972

[9] Proceedings of the Symposium on Computer-Communications Networks and Teletraffic, Polytechnic Press, New York, N.Y., April 1972

[10] Digest of Papers, IEEE Compcon 73, 1973

[11] Proceedings of the ACM Interprocess Communication Workshop, Santa Monica, California, March 1972

[12] S.L. Mathieson and P.M. Walker, "Computer and Telecommunications: Issues in Public Policy," Prentice-Hall, 1970

[13] James Martin, "System Analysis for Data Transmission," Prentice-Hall, 1972

[14] R. Rustin, Ed., "Computer Networks," in 1970 Courant Institute Computer Science Symposium, Englewood Cliffs, N.J., Prentice-Hall, 1972

[15] D.W. Davies and D.L.A. Barber, Communication Networks for Computers, Wiley: New York, 1973

[16] N. Abramson and F. Kuo (Eds.), "Computer-Communication Networks," Prentice-Hall, 1973

[17] P.E. Green, Jr. and R.W. Lucky, Ed., "Computer Communications," IEEE Press, 1975

[17A] R.P. Blanc and I.W. Cotton, Ed., "Computer Networking," IEEE Press, 1976.

[18] L. Kleinrock, Queuing Systems, Vol. II: Computer Applications, Wiley Interscience, 1976

Advances in Computer Communications

Computer Traffic Characteristics

It has become apparent that real progress in modeling and analysis depends upon more than elegant analytical results based upon convenient but unsupported assumptions. Measurement and observation of computer traffic characteristics are needed to obtain estimates of system variables. Computer traffic generally can be divided into two types: long holding time (connect to disconnect) and short holding time. Long holding time is characteristic of business and scientific applications that require extensive computation -- a holding time typically of 15-30 min. Short holding time is characteristic of inquiry-response systems such as on-line banking, credit bureau, checking, and production control -- typically holding times of a few seconds to one or two minutes.

The first paper in this chapter reports the results of studies of long holding time. These studies show that the volume of computer-to-user traffic is an order of magnitude higher than that of user-to-computer traffic. The interarrival time between messages can be approximated by an exponential distribution; that is, the stream of messages can be assumed to constitute a Poisson process. Furthermore, the length of messages can be satisfactorily approximated by the geometrical distribution. During the call interval, the user is active only 5 percent of the time and the computer is active about 30 percent of the time. Thus the channel is idle for a significant portion of the holding time.

The second paper reports traffic characteristics of short holding time. The measured results from four such systems reveal that user send time (the total amount of time during which user characters are being transmitted) is less than 15 percent of the holding time. The character interarrival times can be represented as a sum of two gamma distributions, the number of user segments per call can be represented by a geometrical distribution, and the number of computer segments per call can be represented by a geometrical distribution. These measurements and estimated system variables not only provide us with insight into the behavior of the system and shed light on areas that need improvements, but are essential in the modeling and analysis of computer communication systems.

Estimates of Distributions of Random Variables for Certain Computer Communications Traffic Models

E. Fuchs and P. E. Jackson
Bell Telephone Laboratories, Incorporated, Holmdel, N.J.

A study of multiaccess computer communications has characterized the distributions underlying an elementary model of the user-computer interactive process. The model used is elementary in the sense that many of the random variables that generally are of interest in computer communications studies can be decomposed into the elements of this model. Data were examined from four operational multiaccess systems, and the model is shown to be robust; that is, each of the variables of the model has the same distribution independent of which of the four systems is being examined. It is shown that the gamma distribution can be used to describe each of the continuous variables of the model, and that the geometric distribution can be used to describe the discrete variables. Approximations to the gamma distribution by the exponential distribution are discussed for the systems studied.

KEY WORDS AND PHRASES: computer communications, time-sharing, operating systems, optimization models
CR CATEGORIES: 3.80, 3.81, 6.20

Introduction

Since time-sharing burst on the world some six or seven years ago, many analytical studies have been published of the behavior of such systems [1, 3, 7, 10, 14–17, 21]. In general, the completion of an analytical study of a real process requires several steps to be performed: Construction of a process model, analysis of the model, estimation of the model parameters, and verification of the results. It is sad to report that in almost all of the published studies, the last two steps are omitted.[1] It is evident that the basic reasons for these omissions are: (1) the difficulties encountered in the collection of necessary data due to the complexity of requisite simulations, the potential impairment of the efficiency of real systems by the measurement process, and the problem of avoiding violation of the proprietary constraints of systems applications; (2) the costs in time and dollars for conducting such studies; and (3) the questionable utility of such data in light of the rapid evolution of system capabilities and user characteristics. Nevertheless, as was first pointed out by Sackman [25] in 1967, inferences drawn from such models for the design of systems without empirical determination of parameter values and without testing of the model with the estimated parameters rest on extremely shaky foundations.

Clearly, the third reason is the most difficult to respond to. Many systems are changing so rapidly that a detailed characterization of any one will probably be outdated before it is completed. However, the architecture of computer communication systems has matured to the point that the potential for insight gained from analysis of operational systems for testing models and for forming a basis for research aimed at improvement far outweigh the drawback of obsolescence. Indeed, this situation calls for continued study and review.

If analytical models are to be of value in the design of systems, then the first two problems should be resolved. Efforts have been underway for some time at Bell Telephone Laboratories to model the user-computer interaction process in on-line multiaccess computer systems as an aid in the development of new computer communication systems and services. The studies include extensive efforts at the collection of data from representative working systems to obtain realistic estimates of the parameters of the models. In every case these data are obtained on the premises of the computer service provider and with his full permission and cooperation. To ensure the privacy of the four systems under discussion, however, they are not identified by name.

In a previous paper [13], Jackson and Stubbs reported some of the results of these efforts; specifically, a data stream model of the interaction process was presented, together with estimates of the average values of the basic random variables of the model as obtained from measurements on working systems. In this paper, we report additional results. First, we present the results of goodness of fit tests in which standard probability density functions are fitted to the empirical estimates of the distributions of the random variables of the model. Second, we examine the

[1] The pioneering work of Alan Scherr [26] was supported by extensive measurements on the MIT Project MAC CTSS System, and his results were verified by simulations. Other investigations which were supported by measurements were undertaken for the JOSS system at RAND Corp. [2], the Q-32 Time Sharing System at S.D.C. [6, 18, 19, 27], and additional investigations at Project MAC [11]. Each of these investigations was performed for a specific problem for the system at hand, with no attempt at generalization. However, the results of these studies have been quoted in lieu of measurements by authors of more general studies. An excellent summary and comparisons of these investigations may be found in [25].

significance levels of the fits for the various probability density functions and find that analytically tractable probability density functions can be used for the variables with reasonable significance levels. Third, we note a consistency between systems of widely varying types and applications in characterization of key variables and comment on the significance of this consistency.

In a small way, these analyses are analogous to the early studies of Erlang [8] and others over 70 years ago,[2] in which representative examples of traffic data were collected for the purpose of characterizing local and toll telephone system behavior. The Poisson arrival rate process and exponential interarrival time distribution were the results of some of the earliest of these studies. It is interesting to note that the validity of these characterizations has been retained throughout the years despite the many technological changes in telephone systems and sociological changes in telephone usage.

To provide a framework for presentation of the results, we first give an overview of the study methods and review the data stream model presented in [13]. We then discuss the techniques employed to characterize the variables. Finally, we present the results of the study.

Methods and Models

During the study, we investigated several selected multiaccess computer communication systems in detail. These systems were selected on the basis that they are representative of the advanced state of the art, that the providers of the particular system are knowledgeable in communications, that the systems are fully operational with the initial break-in period accomplished, and that the computer service providers are willing to participate in the study. More detail on the selection procedure is given in [13].

The data which are utilized in the results reported here are the detailed relationships of the flow of message characters to and from users and computers during on-line transactions. The model describes the communications process in terms of random variables which give intercharacter times and the sizes of clusters of characters as they are transmitted through the communication interface. The raw data, then, were collected at the computer ports of active multiaccess computer systems. The model did not require nor did we collect data from internal computer processes such as the length of various internal queues. It is apparent that a model which portrays the interplay of the internal computer processes, such as memory management and processor time scheduling algorithms, with the communication processes would be more satisfactory for joint optimization of computer and communication performance. However, acquisition of data describing the former processes was not within the scope of this study.

Figure 1 illustrates the data stream model. A "call" (or a connect-disconnect time period) is represented as the summation of a sequence of time periods during which the user sends characters without receiving, interleaved with time periods during which he receives characters without sending. (This implies half-duplex operation. Simple modifications to the model would allow the accommodation of full-duplex operation.) The periods during which the user is sending characters to the computer are defined as user burst segments. The periods during which he is receiving characters sent from the computer are computer burst segments. A user burst segment, by definition, begins at the end of the last character of the previous computer burst segment. Similarly, a computer burst segment begins at the end of the last character sent by the user. The first burst segment of a call begins when the call is established, and the last burst segment ends when the call is terminated as measured at the computer interface.

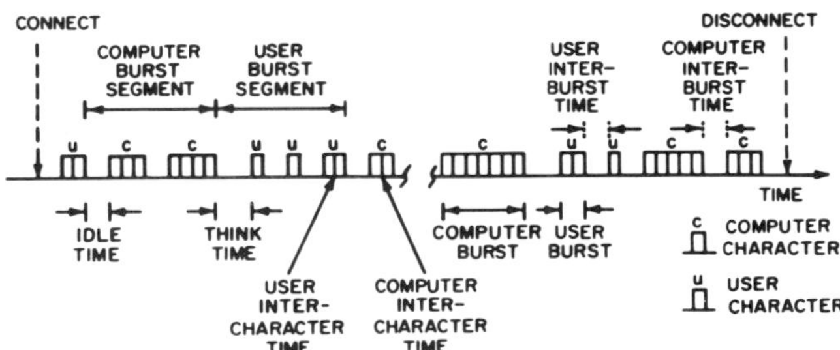

Fig. 1. The data stream model

Within a given burst segment, there are periods of line activity and of line inactivity. The first inactive period of a user burst segment is defined as think time. That is, think time is the time that elapses from the end of the last previous computer character until the beginning of the first user character in that burst segment. In most cases, think time is employed by the user to finish reading the previous computer output and to think about what to do next. The corresponding inactive period in a computer burst segment is called idle time. In some systems idle time represents time during which the user waits for the return of "line feed," after sending "carriage return"; in other systems, idle time represents the time during which the user's program is being processed or is in queue. The remaining inactive periods within a burst segment are called intercharacter times and interburst times. A prerequisite for their definition is the definition of a burst.

Two consecutive characters are defined as belonging to the same burst if the period of inactivity between the characters is less than one-half character width. Thus each burst is the longest string of consecutive characters where the period of inactivity between any two consecutive

[2] Molina [21] reports that G. T. Blood of the AT&T Co in 1898 found a close agreement between the terms of a binomial expansion and the results of the observations on the distribution of busy telephone calls. This is the earliest reference that we have been able to find to empirical studies aimed at verification of assumptions employed in telephone traffic modeling.

characters is less than one-half character width. All of the characters in a burst must, of course, be transmitted from the same party (user or computer). For example, every character of an unbroken string of characters sent at line rate is in the same burst.

For characters within the same user burst, an inactive time between two consecutive characters is called a user intercharacter time. The corresponding variable for computer bursts is computer intercharacter time. For bursts within the same user (computer) burst segment, the inactive time between two consecutive bursts is called a user (computer) interburst time. Five final variables of the data stream model are number of user bursts per burst segment, number of computer bursts per burst segment, number of characters per user burst, number of characters per computer burst, and temporal character width (time from start to end of one character).

TABLE I. Characteristics of Systems Studied

	Systems			
	A	*B*	*C*	*D*
Computer type	Brand X	Brand X	Brand Y	Brand Z
Transmission speed (characters/second)	10	10	15	10
Primary application	Scientific	Scientific	Business	Inquiry/ response
Load*	Moderate	Heavy	Moderate	Light/ moderate

* The term load denotes the relative occupancy of the processor due to on-line demands and background batch work (if any); nothing is implied directly as to the load on the communication channel.

Collected Data and Analysis

During the study, data have been collected for a large number of transactions for each of several multiaccess computer systems. Data from four of the systems are discussed in this paper. These systems are labeled A, B, C, and D. Systems A and B have the same computer equipment and basically the same mix of computer applications (scientific/engineering programming and problem solving), although the average loads supported by the two systems during the study periods were quite different. System C has computer equipment different from each of the others and its mix of user applications is oriented toward business problem solving. System D also has computer equipment different from each of the others, and its applications are data collection and data dissemination in an inquiry/response method of operation. All four systems serve low-speed, half-duplex, teletypewriter-like terminals and fall within the category of "long-holding time systems" as defined by Jackson and Stubbs, i.e. with average holding times or call durations on the order of 20 to 30 minutes. Table I summarizes the salient characteristics of these systems.

The random variables of Figure 1 are of two types. Some are discrete, such as the number of characters per burst. Others are continuous, such as think time. Modeling techniques most commonly used in computer communications studies include queueing processes, renewal processes, birth-death models, Markov processes, and to a limited extent, flow models. Most key random parameters of models used in computer-communication studies are either interevent times such as times between arrivals at a server or burst length counts such as the number of arrivals in a batch arrival process. In solving these types of models, only a very few random functions are tractable and in some cases allowable. In the category of desirable functional forms fall the Poisson, geometric, and binomial distributions for discrete processes, and the gamma distribution family for continuous processes. Hence, we are interested in the extent to which the key variables of such models can be described by these few desirable distributions.

Data collected from the communication lines at the computer ports of the four operating systems described above were used to seek desirable distributions to describe each of the random variables of the data stream model. These data were laundered to remove ambiguities and were then partitioned into sets describing each of the variables. For each set of data for each variable for each system, goodness-of-fit tests were performed to ascertain which standard probability functions could be used to describe the variables. As the existing tests for goodness-of-fit were not satisfactory for our purposes because of their low power or excessive computation time, a new test was devised [12].

The set of distributions used for goodness-of-fit tests included the normal, Cauchy, Laplace, chi-square, exponential, hyperexponential, gamma, and lognormal distributions for continuous variables and the geometric (with and without mass at the origin), uniform, Poisson, compound Poisson and binomial distributions for discrete variables. For each variable, a compound goodness-of-fit test was performed where the parameters of the hypothesized distributions (those being tested) were adjusted so that the mean and variance for a two-parameter distribution were the same as the sample mean and sample variance. For a single-parameter distribution, the mean of the distribution was equated to the sample mean.

Results of the goodness-of-fit tests are shown in Table II. From Table II, we see that the geometric distribution can be used to describe every discrete process but one (the single exception is an impulse function which is a degenerate form of the geometric distribution). Similarly, each of the continuous random variables of the model can be described by the gamma distribution, and the think times, idle times, and interburst times can be described additionally by the lognormal distribution. These results are significant for two reasons.

First, the data stream model, which is elementary in the sense that many of the variables that generally are of in-

Random variable	Systems			
	A	B	C	D
No. of burst segments per call	G	G	G	G,CP
Think time	L,Γ	L,Γ	L,Γ	L,Γ
User interburst time	L,Γ	L,Γ	L,Γ	L,Γ
Computer interburst time	L,Γ	L,Γ	L,Γ	L,Γ
No. bursts/user burst segment	G	G	G	G
No. bursts/computer burst segment	G	G	G	G
No. characters/user burst	G	G	I	G,CP
No. characters/computer burst	G	G	G	G
User intercharacter time	Γ	Γ	N/A	Γ
Computer intercharacter time	Γ	Γ	Γ	Γ

TABLE II. RESULTS OF GOODNESS OF FIT TESTS ACCEPTABLE* DISTRIBUTIONS†

* Acceptable at the 5 percent level.
† Γ—gamma distribution, L—lognormal distribution G—geometric distribution, CP—compound Poisson distribution, I—constant at X = 1.

TABLE III. AVERAGE PARAMETER VALUES

Random Variable	$\hat{\mu}$	$\sigma_{\hat{\mu}}$
No. of burst segments per call	81.	31.
Think time (seconds)	5.0	3.1
Idle time (seconds)	0.81	0.44
User interburst time (seconds)	1.5	0.83
Computer interburst time (seconds)	13.	21.
No. of bursts/user burst segment	11.	2.8
No. of bursts/computer burst segment	2.9	2.4
No. of characters/user burst	1.1	0.1
No. of characters/computer burst	41.	24.
Character width	0.092	
User intercharacter time	0.0	
Computer intercharacter time	0.0	

terest in computer communication studies can be decomposed into the elements of the model, is shown to be robust; that is, each of the variables of the model is described by the same distribution independent of the computer system being examined.[3] These results were obtained in spite of the fact that three different computer types and operating systems were investigated. In addition, the computer loads and programming applications were different.

Table III summarizes the measured values of the model parameters. To insure the privacy of the four systems under discussion, these values are not shown on a per system basis. Rather, for each parameter, a grand mean $\hat{\mu}$ is given where $\hat{\mu}$ is the mean of the four system means for the given parameter. Each number in the column headed σ_{μ} is the standard deviation of the four numbers (system means) averaged to find $\hat{\mu}$. As the character widths are treated in the model as random variables, they are included in Table III for completeness. In the four systems discussed, however, they were constant as can be derived from Table I. The intercharacter times are all zero as the characters occur at line rate. Infrequent, small departures from zero were measured for intercharacter times, but these measurements are attributable to clock slippage between the computer's clock and our clock.

Jackson and Stubbs [13] have examined the mean values of the model variables for the first three systems and make the following observations:

(1) Delays introduced by the computer (primarily idle time and computer interburst delay) can be a large component of holding time and are affected by the number of simultaneous users on the system, probably by the computer scheduling algorithm, and by the characteristics of the communications control unit.

(2) The average number of characters sent by the computer to the user is an order of magnitude greater than the number of characters sent by the user to the computer.

(3) Delays introduced by the user are a significant contributor to average holding time and are remarkably close in absolute values for the four systems studied.

These three observations are examples of information that may be employed by system designers in investigations into improved communications for multiaccess computers. In modeling (probabilistically) the behavior of present and proposed systems to determine their sensitivity to particular elements of the data stream model, the parameters of the distributions need only be changed and not the distributions themselves. These data are equally valuable for investigations into computer operating systems. For example, one might investigate changes in computer scheduling algorithms as reflected in changes in idle time and interburst delay parameters, changes in transmission speed from computer to user and the converse, and changes in terminal characteristics which may influence (hopefully reduce) user delays. Indeed, recently there have been reported many investigations into the performance of scheduling algorithms as measured by response time [1, 3, 7, 10, 14–17, 20]. Almost without exception, these investigations hypothesize arrival rates of requests for CPU time without the support of measurements. Since such arrivals can be approximated from the variables of the data stream model, the above observations as to the efficacy of the results reported in this paper are demonstrated.

Second, the particular distributions obtained in Table II are tractable and are useful in further analytical studies. For example, the geometric distribution was obtained for the discrete distributions and the gamma family for the continuous distributions.

Although the gamma distribution is tractable for some

[3] Although the truth of the statement for the "number of characters per user burst" is artificial, it is made because even for that case the same distributional form can be used in practice with no operational difficulty by choosing appropriate parameters for the distribution.

6

types of analyses, it is interesting to investigate to what degree the gamma distributions obtained in Table II can be approximated by the exponential distribution. We investigated this approximation by examining the coefficients of variation of the gamma-distributed variables. We found that the arrival process is approximately Poisson and thus, assuming independent sources, the large body of queueing theory based upon the Poisson arrival process may be brought to bear for analyses of communications processes in time-sharing systems.

Table IV shows the coefficients of variation, V, for the continuous variables for the four computer systems investigated.[4] The exponential distribution belongs to the gamma distribution family and is the special case where $V = 1$. To illustrate the similarity between the exponential distribution and the gamma distribution with $1.0 \leq V \leq 1.8$, Figure 2 is included.

The error shown in Figure 2 is the difference between the cumulative distributions at the point given. It is apparent that the approximation becomes less accurate as V becomes larger and is less accurate for smaller values of the independent variable than for larger ones. We further observe that even close to the origin, the class of gamma distributions defined by $V \geq 1$ has the same general shape as the exponential distribution. For much analytical work, the behavior of the distribution function in the neighborhood of the mean and in the upper tail are of the most interest. For these types of problems, if errors of the magnitudes shown in Figure 2 are allowable (or alternatively if the relative coefficients of variation shown in Table IV are tolerable), then the exponential distribution may be used in place of the gamma distribution.

The dependencies which exist between the random variables of the model are obvious from the definitions of the variables. In this study no attempt was made to characterize dependencies where they exist. An example of the dependencies which are generated by the computer-user interaction process is the number of characters per computer burst random variable. This variable is a function of such things as the program the user is running, the I/O habit patterns of the user, and the I/O load and CPU load on the computer. Other variables exhibit similar dependencies. No effort was undertaken to test the assumption of independence between sample points of the same process for all of the variables of the model. Rather, the assumption of independence was tested for certain of the variables where the property was required for particular studies.

Conclusions

In analyzing computer communication systems for time-sharing applications, the results of this work have shown that a variety of techniques can be applied to model the processes. Since the input traffic process has been characterized in terms that are usually tractable for analytical models, realistic results may be obtained using standard analytical techniques. In some models where the estimated distributional forms are not amenable to analysis, appropriate approximation techniques are available.

This work has shown that the communication process between a multiaccess computer and a user at a teletypewriter-like terminal can be represented by an elementary model from which more complex models may be constructed. Further, by using real data from operational multiaccess systems, we have shown that the model is robust and that the distributions obtained for each of the variables are tractable. In certain cases, the character arrival process can be approximated by a Poisson process. Thus, in modeling the communication process of long-holding-time multiaccess computer systems only the parameters of the distributions for the variables change for various computer types, applications and system loading.

These observations can be combined with the observa-

TABLE IV. COEFFICIENT OF VARIATION FOR GAMMA DISTRIBUTIONS

	Systems			
	A	*B*	*C*	*D*
Think time	1.56	1.64	0.72	1.61
Idle time	1.09	1.54	1.59	1.45
User interburst time	1.39	1.59	1.49	1.54
Computer interburst time	1.56	1.61	1.59	1.64
User intercharacter time	1.67	1.54	1.67	1.59
Computer intercharacter time	1.67	1.67	1.59	1.56

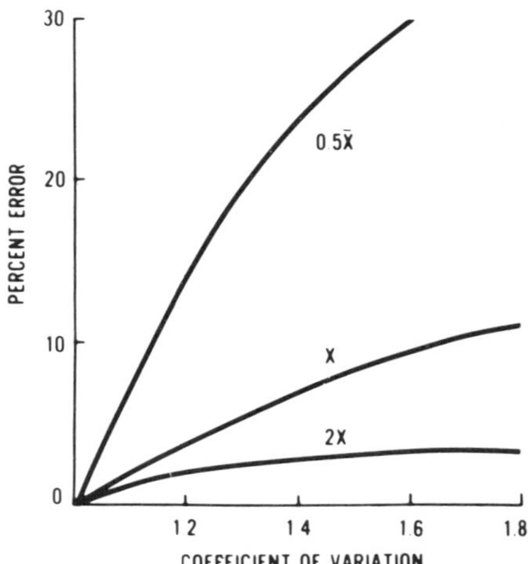

FIG. 2. Difference between gamma and exponential distributions

[4] For one system, the user terminal had an automatic response at the end of a computer burst segment rather than a true user "think time" response. For this system, the estimated value of V for the think time distribution was 0.72, close to that for the hyperexponential distribution ($V = 0.71$).

tions of Jackson and Stubbs [13] on computer-introduced delays, user-introduced delays, and the relative amounts of information flow in each direction on the communication line to give a comprehensive picture of the communication process. For example, these analyses support analytical and simulation studies at Bell Telephone Laboratories which seek solutions to computer access data communications problems, cf. Chu's, Meltzer's and Pilc's studies on asynchronous time division multiplexing [4, 5, 20, 23].

Several authors [9, 24, 28] have suggested that some computer parameters are hyperexponentially distributed or are the sum of exponential variates. In this study, no variable successfully passed the goodness-of-fit test with a significance level of 5 percent under the hyperexponential hypothesis although the coefficient of variation of the think time distribution for System C was close to the coefficient of variation for the hyperexponential distribution. Work is presently under way to investigate the hypothesis of a distribution which is the sum of exponential variates.

Studies of multiaccess computer communications are continuing. Data are being collected from systems with different terminal types, system configurations, average holding times, and user applications. Analyses of data for these new systems will expand our understanding of the computer-communication processes involved as we have a broader base from which to draw conclusions and make comparisons.

Acknowledgments. Many people have contributed their efforts to various parts of this study. Data acquisition was accomplished with the considerable help of the American Telephone and Telegraph Company and the Bell System Operating Companies. Contributions to the model and the analyses and many helpful criticims were made by Messrs. R. J. Roddy and C. D. Stubbs, of Bell Telephone Laboratories, and by Mr. R. J. Price, formerly of Bell Telephone Laboratories.

We would also like to thank Mr. E. Wolman of Bell Telephone Laboratories for carefully reading a draft of this paper.

Our special tanks are extended to the companies whose computer systems are being studied. Without their full permission and very helpful cooperation these analyses would not be feasible.

Received December, 1969; revised April, 1970

REFERENCES

1. Bowden, E. K. Jr. Priority assignment in a network of computers. IEEE Cat. No. 69C30-C, IEEE Comput. Group Conf. Dig., June, 1969.
2. Bryan, G. E. JOSS: 20,000 hours at the console, a statistical summary. RAND Corp. Also in Proc. AFIPS 1967 FJCC, Vol. 31, AFIPS Press, Montvale, N. J., pp. 769–777.
3. Chang, W. A queueing model for a simple case of time sharing. *IBM Syst. J 5.*, 2 (1966).
4. Chu, W. A study of the technique of asynchronous time division multiplexing for time-sharing computer communications. Proc. 2nd Hawaii Int. Conf. on Syst. Sci., Jan. 1969.
5. Chu, W. W. A study of asynchronous time-division multiplexing for time-sharing computer systems. Proc. AFIPS 1969 FJCC, Vol. 35, AFIPS Press, Montvale, N. J., pp. 669–678.
6. Coffman, E. G. Jr., and Wood, R. (1965). Interarrival statistics for TSS. Doc. SP-2161, Syst. Develop. Corp., Santa Monica, Calif. Also in *Comm. ACM 9*, 7 (July 1966), 500–503.
7. Coffman, E. G. Jr., and Kleinrock, L. Computer scheduling measures and their countermeasures. Proc. AFIPS 1968 SJCC, Vol. 32, AFIPS Press, Montvale, N. J., pp. 11–21.
8. Erlang, A. K. Calcul des probabilités et conversations telephoniques. *Revue Generale, de l'Electricité, 18* (Aug. 1925). Previously published in a Danish periodical *Nyt Tidsskrift for Matematick*.
9. Fife, D. W. An optimization model for time-sharing. Proc. AFIPS 1966, SJCC, Vol. 28, Spartan Books. New York, p. 98.
10. Gaver, D. P. Jr., and Lewis, P. A. W. Dynamic buffer storage models. IEEE Cat. No. 69C30-C, IEEE Comput. Group Conf. Dig., June 1969.
11. Hastings, T. Operating statistics of the MAC time-sharing system. Memo. MAC-M-280, MIT Project MAC, Cambridge, Mass., 1965.
12. Jackson, P. E. A Fourier series test of goodness of fit. *J. Amer. Statist. Assoc.* (submitted for publication).
13. Jackson, P. E., and Stubbs, C. D. A study of multiaccess computer communications. Proc. AFIPS 1969 SJCC, Vol. 34, AFIPS Press, Montvale, N. J., pp. 491–504.
14. Kleinrock, L. Analysis of a time-shared processor. *Naval Res. Logistics Quart. 11*, 10 (Mar. 1964) 59–73.
15. Kleinrock, L. Time-shared systems: A theoretical treatment. *J. ACM 14*, 2 (Apr. 1967), 242–261.
16. Kleinrock, L. Certain analytic results for time-shared processors. Proc. IFIP Cong. 1968, Vol. 1, Pt. 2, North Holland Pub. Co., Amsterdam, pp. 838–845.
17. Krishnamoorthi, B., and Wood, R. C. Time-shared computer service with both interarrival and service times exponential. *J. ACM 13*, 3 (July 1966), 317–338.
18. McIsaac, P. V. Time-sharing job descriptions for simulation. TM-2713, Syst. Develop. Corp., Santa Monica, Calif., 1965.
19. McIsaac, P. V. Job description and scheduling in the SDC Q-32 time-sharing system. TM-2996, Syst. Develop. Corp., Santa Monica, Calif., 1966.
20. Meltzer, J. I. (1968). Simulation of an asychronous time division multiplexor for data sources. (Unpublished)
21. Miller, L. W., and Schrage, L. E. The queue M/G/1 with the shortest remaining processing time discipline. Rep. P3263, RAND Corp., Nov. 1965.
22. Molina, E. C. The theory of probabilities applied to telephone trunking problems. *Bell Syst. Tech. J. 1*, (1922), 69–81.
23. Pilc, R. J. (1968). A derivation of buffer occupancy statistics in an asynchronous time division multiplexor used with bursty sources. (Unpublished)
24. Pinkerton, J. B., Program behavior and control in virtual storage computer systems. Tech. Rep. No. 4, Concomp Project, U. of Michigan, Ann Arbor, Michigan, 1968.
25. Sackman, H. Experimental investigation of user performance in time sharing computing systems: Retrospect, prospect and the public interest. AD 654 624, Syst. Develop. Corp., Santa Monica, Calif., May 1967.
26. Scherr, A. L. Joss: Experience with an experimental computing service for users at remote typewriter consoles. P-3149, The RAND Corp., 1965.
27. Totschek, R. A. An empirical investigation into the behavior of the SDC time-sharing system. SP-2191/000/00, Syst. Develop. Corp., Santa Monica, Calif., 1965.
28. Walter, E. S., and Wallace, V. L. Further analysis of a computing center environment. *Comm. ACM 10*, 5 (May 1967), 266–272.

INFORMATION PROCESSING 71 – NORTH-HOLLAND PUBLISHING COMPANY (1972)

DATA TRAFFIC MEASUREMENTS FOR INQUIRY–RESPONSE COMPUTER COMMUNICATION SYSTEMS

A.L. DUDICK, E. FUCHS and P.E. JACKSON

Bell Telephone Laboratories, Holmdel, New Jersey, USA

This paper reports the results of traffic studies of data stream parameters of a class of inquiry–response computer communication systems. Systems in this class employ TOUCH-TONE® telephone signals for input of digital data; responses are generated by voice answerback units under computer control. It is shown that, while traffic models of these systems preserve some of the tailor-made properties of the specific installation studied, we are able to describe the important traffic variables in terms of robust, analytically tractable random variables. In a few cases, where the observed physical behavior of the traffic parameters of interest cannot be described adequately by single random variables, mixtures of analytically tractable random variables are found to yield statistically accurate representations. While such mixtures do not as readily lend themselves to straightforward analytical treatment in system studies, they are easily accommodated in simulation studies.

INTRODUCTION

This is the third of a series of papers that report the results of studies of traffic characteristics of multiaccess computer communication systems. The first two papers [1, 2] described traffic models of systems with long call duration used for on-line programming and problem solving. This paper reports similar results for a limited class of systems with short call durations used for inquiry–response applications. This class of systems employs TOUCH-TONE telephones or TOUCH-TONE pad adjuncts to dial telephones for input of digital data inquiries. Responses are generated by voice answerback units under computer control.

Data for this study were collected from four systems; three of the systems operate in the telephone network while the fourth employs a private switcher. To acquire the data, specially designed logic equipment was placed at the interfaces between two computer communication ports and the data sets (or modems) on the communications lines of each system. The purpose of these logic units was to enable us to capture the communication characteristics and timing relationships of the traffic traversing the lines without violating the privacy of the transaction or the anonymity of the users. The logic units transferred the observed information via private lines to a small, dedicated computer at Bell Laboratories where the captured information and timing relationships were recorded on magnetic tape for further processing.

Each system was monitored continuously (during all hours the system was in service) for two to three weeks. During this period, data describing 5,000 to 10,000 calls were recorded for each system.

The vehicle used for analysis of the data and presentation of results is a data stream model, which is described in the next section. Following that, the relationships among the model variables are presented. Finally the observed data and statistical analyses are presented.

Sufficient data were collected and analyzed to ensure that the distributions presented as descriptive of the model variables are robust in the following senses: First, the distribution forms are stationary over time; scale and location parameters may change but the shapes do not. Second, the forms of the distributions remain the same for different system operating loads, different system applications and for systems employing different computer hardware. Thus only the parameters of the distributions need be changed in system studies and analyses to reflect different operating environments.

DATA STREAM MODEL

The model used to depict the user–computer data stream is illustrated in fig. 1. The first division of the data stream is into user and computer "segments" or "times". Each such segment is the longest period of time during which either the user or computer transmits information to the other party with no intervening periods of reception of information. The user time is composed of an intial inactive period called the "think time" followed by the user input, a succession of distinct characters (TOUCH-TONE signals). The time for each character is represented in the model as a "character width" or "character time," and the associated interval between successive characters as an "inter-character time". The computer time consists of an initial period of inactivity called the "idle time" followed by an "audio response time". In the time from the last audio response of a call to disconnect, one of two distinct events occurs. In a normal call, this time is referred to as "dropoff time". In some calls, the computer program is not equipped to complete the transaction and a credit manager takes over in place of the computer. In this case, the time is called the "referral time". Additional variables necessary to characterize the data stream completely are the length of each call (connect–disconnect) called the "holding time", the "inter-call time",* the "number of characters per user segment", the "number of user segments per call", and the "number of computer segments per call".

RELATIONSHIPS AMONG DATA STREAM MODEL PARAMETERS

Let the following notation be introduced:

τ = holding time of a call (seconds)
W = character width (seconds)
G = intercharacter time or gap (seconds)
N^w= number of characters per user segment
I = idle time (seconds)
T = think time (seconds)
A = audio response time (seconds)
R = referral time (seconds)
D = dropoff time (seconds)
N^c= number of computer segments per call
N^u= number of user segments per call
N^r = number of referrals per call (N^r=0 or 1).

The two indices of sumation to be used are:
i to designate the ith segment (user or computer),
j to designate the jth character in a user segment.

The sum of these components is the holding time for a call:

$$\tau = \sum_{i=1}^{N^u} \left[\sum_{j=1}^{N_i^w} W_{ij} + \sum_{j=1}^{N_i^w-1} G_{ij} + T_i \right] + \sum_{i=1}^{N^c} (I_i+A_i)$$
$$+ N^r R + (1-N^r)D. \qquad (1)$$

Knowing the distributions for the 11 parameters in the expression for holding time, it is theoretically possible to solve directly for the distribution of τ. Except for very restricted cases, however, the mechanics of finding the solution are prohibitive.

One particular case for which a solution is readily obtainable is where the discrete variables used as the limits of summation are geometrically distributed and where the continuous variables being summed are exponential. For this case, Feller [3] has shown that the resulting random variable is exponentially distributed. For the long holding time systems examined earlier [2], it was shown that the discrete random variables were geometrically distributed and that the continuous random variables were gamma distributed but could be approximated by the exponential distribution for many cases of interest. Hence, the holding time was approximately exponentially distributed for those cases.

In later sections of this paper, distributions fitted to samples of each of the important random variables including holding time are displayed. In addition to examining the distributional form of the holding time components, the mean values of these components are of interest in performing systems analyses.

Taking expected values of both sides of (1) where we assume that the random variables are stationary and mutually independent,** we obtain

$$H = N_u\,[N_w W + (N_w-1)G+T] + N_c\,[I+A] + N_r(R-D)+D$$

where H is the average value of holding time and the symbol for each of the other random variables without a subscript of i or j and with u, c, w, and r used as subscripts rather than as superscripts indicates its expected value.

For further analysis, this expression for H may be separated into five parts each having its own functional significance:

(a) User send time, U_s (the total amount of time

* The inter-call time observable at a computer port is a function of the number of ports provided in the system for a given amount of originated traffic. Thus it is a variable that can be changed at the will of the system provider and measurements of it cannot be generalized.

** While this assumption is an obvious approximation to reality, it is a meaningful approximation for the analyses of system behavior discussed in this paper.

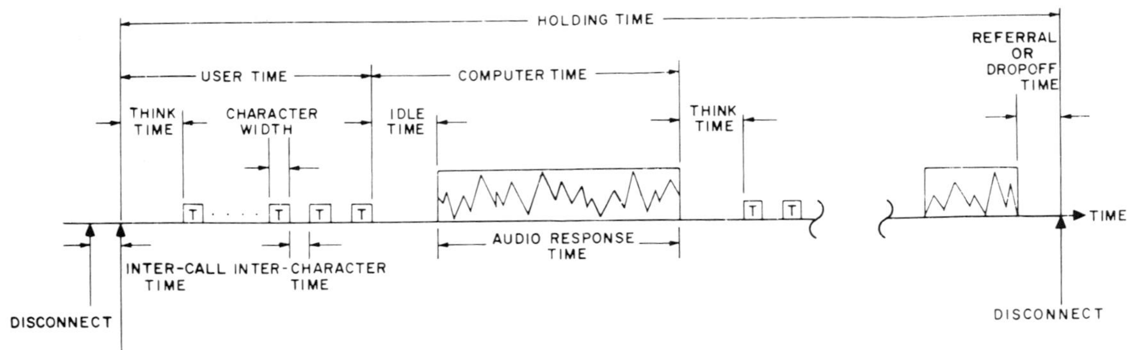

Fig. 1. TOUCH-TONE remote access data stream model.

during which user characters are being transmitted): $U_s = N_u N_w W$

(b) Computer send time, C_s (the total amount of time during which the computer is transmitting): $C_s = N_c A$

(c) User delay time, U_d (the sum of all inactive periods during user segments): $U_d = N_u(T + (N_w - 1)G)$

(d) Computer delay time, C_d (the sum of all inactive periods during computer segments: $C_d = N_c I$

(e) Call termination time: $C_t = N_r R + (1 - N_r)D$

Finally, we can derive expressions for the total send time, S (the total time data is being transmitted during a call) and for total delay time, Δ (the total inactive time during a call) by:

$$S = U_s + C_s$$

$$\Delta = U_d + C_d + C_t$$

OBSERVED DATA AND ANALYSIS

In this section, we present the quantitative results of analyses of data on a large number of calls to each of four short-holding time, multiaccess computer systems. These systems are labelled A, B, C, and D. Systems A and B have the same user applications with different equipment configurations and data input modes. Systems A, C, and D have the same equipment configuration but different applications. Systems A and B serve occasional users relatively unsophisticated in their use of the systems, whereas the users of systems C and D are more proficient from frequent use of the systems. These systems and user characteristics are summarized in table 1. None of these systems were compute-bound or in any way heavily loaded. In fact, the inquiry-response traffic used only a small portion of the real-time of each of the systems.

The data gathered from the four systems were laundered to remove obvious measurement errors and ambiguities (such as two contiguous "connects" with-

Table 1
Monitored systems' characteristics

	System A	System B	System C	System D
Computer Type	IBM 360/40	Honeywell H2206	IBM 360/40	IBM 360/50
Audio Response Unit Type	IBM 7770	Cognitronics 285-8D	IBM 7770	IBM 7770
Primary Application	Credit Bureau	Credit Bureau	On-Line Banking	Production Control
Data Input Mode	Manual TOUCH-TONE and Card Dial	Manual TOUCH-TONE	Manual TOUCH-TONE	Manual TOUCH-TONE
User Proficiency	Low	Low	Moderate	High

Table 2
Mean values of holding time components

	Systems			
	A	B	C	D
H - Holding Time (seconds)	40.	43.	28.	20.
T - Think Time (seconds)	2.1	2.1	.28	1.3
W - Character Width (seconds)	.17	.16	.24	.14
G - Intercharacter Time (seconds)	[illegible]	.41	.37	.31
I - Idle Time (seconds)	1.7	1.8	.22	.89
A - Audio Response Time (seconds)	4.4	8.8	17.	2.0
R - Referral Time (seconds)	77.	33.	N/A	N/A
D - Dropoff Time (seconds)	13.	9.6	0.	.97
N^w - No. Characters/User Segment	28.	20.	18.	5.2
N^u - No. User Segments/Call	1.1	1.5	1.0	3.1
N^c - No. Computer Segments/Call	1.0	1.3	.92	2.9
N^r - No. Referrals/Call	0.13	0.28	N/A	N/A

out an intervening disconnect) and then partitioned into sets describing each of the 11 variables of the model and the holding time. For each variable for each system, means and variances of the variable were estimated and several well-known distribution functions were tested for goodness of fit. Two techniques were used to test goodness of fit. First, the set of unimodal distributions discussed by Fuchs and Jackson [2] were tested using the new goodness of fit test developed by Jackson (see Appendix in [2]), In each case, the parameters of the hypothesized distribution (that distribution being tested) were adjusted so that the mean and variance for a two-parameter distribution were the same as the sample mean and sample variance. For a single-parameter distribution, the mean of the distribution was equated to the sample mean.

Although the unimodal distributions were sufficient to describe the variables of the long-holding-time systems investigated earlier, several variables could not be described by a single, unimodal distribution for the short-holding-time systems. Our initial analyses of these data indicated that in some cases a mixture of the same common distributions was appropriate. Consequently Pack developed a new procedure for fitting mixtures of distributions to empirical data [4]. Using Pack's procedure we first estimated the mixture of distributions which most closely fit the data under the criterion of minimum mean squared error and then tested goodness of fit using the Kolmogorov-Smirnov test.

Table 2 summarizes the average values of each of the variables of the traffic models for each of the four systems. Table 3 summarizes the results of fitting the data for each of the variables to standard unimodal and sums of unimodal distributions. It must be emphasized that the objective of the distribution fitting exercise is not to find the best fit or the fit which may be hypothesized with the highest confidence to be a model of the source process. Rather, a model is desired that describes the statistical data at least at the five percent level of significance, that has properties that reasonably well fit the physical process modelled, and that best lends itself to traffic analyses and systems studies.

Examining table 2, we find that the holding times range from 20 sec to 43 sec with a grand mean of 33 sec and a standard deviation about that mean of 9.5 sec.* Two components of the holding time that only serve to obscure the interpretation of data flow tim-

* It should be noted that the estimated mean holding time does not necessarily equate to the sum of the estimated means of the holding time components. The difference occurs because the test used for removing outlier data points from the data set for each variable is specific to the characteristics of that data set, and each data set was measured independently.

Table 3
Results of goodness of fit tests
acceptable * distributions **

Random Variable	Systems			
	A	B	C	D
H - Holding Time	Γ	Γ	$\Sigma\Gamma$	Γ
T - Think Time	$\Sigma\Gamma$	Γ	Γ	Γ
W - Character Width	Γ	Γ	Γ	Γ
G - Intercharacter Time	$\Sigma\Gamma$	$\Sigma\Gamma$	Γ	Γ
I - Idle Time	$\Sigma\Gamma$	$\Sigma\Gamma$	Γ	Γ
N^w - No. Characters/User Segment	NR	NR	NR	G
N^u - No. User Segments/Call	G	G	G	G
N^c - No. Computer Segments/Call	E	E	B	E

* Acceptable at the five percent level of significance.

** Γ - gamma distribution,
$\Sigma\Gamma$ - sum of two gamma distributions,
E - exponential distribution,
B - Binomial distribution,
G - geometric distribution,
NR - nonrandom process such as a fixed response time.

ing are the Dropoff Time, the time from the end of the last transaction to disconnect, and the referral time. For example, System C allows only one transaction per call; the computer therefore disconnects immediately at the termination of its response, resulting in a dropoff time which is identically zero for all calls. For the other systems, more than one transaction per call is allowed. Therefore, the computer initiates a time-out interval (which differs from system to system) after each response, waiting for either an indication of terminal disconnect (carrier-off) or additional input. At the end of the time-out interval, the computer disconnects. The dropoff time is therefore a race between near-end and far-end disconnect and is peculiar to the selected time-out interval for each system and the communication configuration in which it is imbedded. We therefore find it useful to eliminate the dropoff time from our model by subtracting its average value from the average holding time to arrive at a modified holding time, and by removing it from our set of random variables. Although its magnitude and causal factors are of interest to the telephone companies, it is not a relevant component of our systems or traffic studies.

Similarly, the referral time represents a nondata use of the communications channel and is not relevant to the flow of information from the data terminal to the computer. In addition, the fraction of systems employing referrals in their operations is declining as the number of fully automated short holding time data systems increases.

Our examination of the data and our understanding of the processes underlying the audio response time variable have led to the conclusion that it should not be characterized as a random variable. Neglecting for a moment calls aborted during an audio response, we find that the several systems have one or two - at most three- standard length response types, the difference between responses of constant length being solely in the choice of words at various operative positions in the phrases of the response. Thus, the observed data on response length is distributed as one or two or three impulses, modified only by aborted calls and measurement noise.

Indeed the audio response time given for System C is not even meaningful. It results from an overlap of transmission of the last TOUCH-TONE digit of an inquiry and the computer-generated audio response. Our measurement equipment was designed to be faithful to our half-duplex model. Hence, it suppressed recording the beginning of the audio response until the end of the TOUCH-TONE digit transmission.

Fig. 2 is a graphic characterization of the data shown in table 2. The macroscopic variables are displayed as a percentage of the modified holding time. We focus our attention first on the average values of

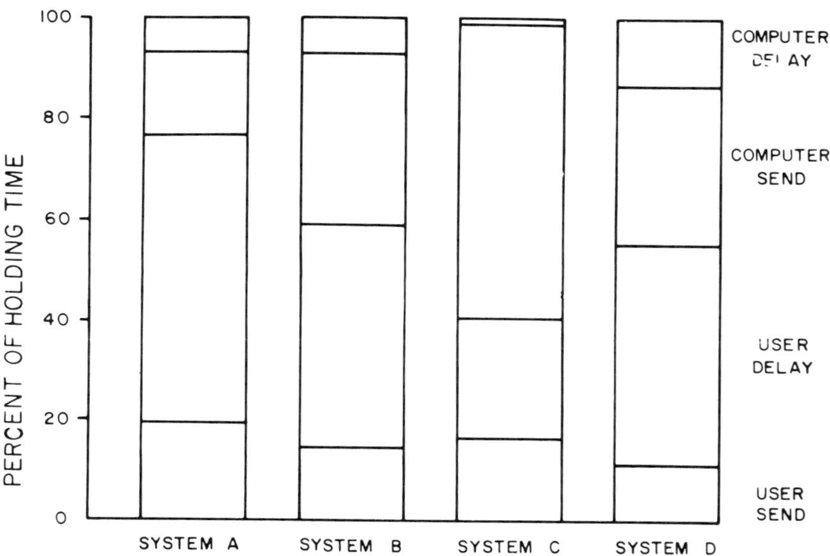

Fig. 2. Holding time of components as percent of adjusted holding time.

the model variables and make the following observations.

The human-factor–determined averages (think time, character width and intercharacter time) for the two systems with the same applications are virtually identical. Further, the interarrival times of characters (a derived variable in the model, being the sum of character width and intercharacter time) exhibits a marked and important robustness between all systems. The grand mean character interarrival time for characters within user segments is 0.553 sec with a standard deviation of 0.042 sec. This variable is an important one; it is employed in statistical multiplexing analyses that are directed at harnessing efficiently the statistical properties of multiaccess communications.

The length of each user segment varies from a low of 5.2 characters for the moderately interactive System D to a high of 28 characters for system A. Systems A, B, and C were noninteractive as each normal transaction had only one user segment and one computer segment. System C allowed only one transaction per call while Systems A and B allowed multiple transactions. Notice, however, that the average number of transactions per call was close to one for these systems. In contrast, the long holding time systems had a mean of 41 user segments per call (called "Burst Segments" by Jackson and Stubbs [1]).

In contrast to the extensive generalizations that were made for long holding time systems based upon or derived from the average values of the data stream model variables, there is little more of general significance that one can draw from the data on the mean values of the parameters of short holding time systems. The short duration of each transaction preserves the tailor-made properties of the individual systems in most of the observed communication characteristics. For example, the average total delay per call (sum of user delay and computer delay) as a percent of adjusted holding time varied from a low of 25% of System C to a high of 64% for System A and was greater than 50% for three of the systems. In addition, as each of the computers was lightly loaded, the idle times were all short and conclusions about system loading cannot be made similar to those for the long holding time systems.

To some lesser extent, this property of individuality of system characteristics is also carried over to the more important characterization of the distributional form of the model variables.

The continuous random variables in the model can all be described by either the gamma distribution or by a sum of gamma distributions. So, while the model retains much of the robustness of the model for long holding time systems, here we found it necessary to fall back on a mixture of distributions (the sum of two gamma distributions). Thus the simplicity of the long holding time model is somewhat diminished and the comments by Fuchs and Jackson [2] on approximating certain gamma distributions by the exponential distribution must be re-evaluated. For many types of analyses, though, the sum of gamma distributions is tractable for analysis and it certainly is useful for studies of large-scale networks using simulation techniques.

The discrete variables exhibited considerably more variability in the form of the acceptable distributions. The number of characters per user segment was non-random in three of the systems as the data given to the computer consisted of a fixed-length character string. Only in System D could N^w be described as a random variable, where it could be described by a geometric distribution.

Both the discrete exponential distribution and the geometric distribution have exponential tails, but the discrete exponential distribution has mass at the origin (a nonzero probability of the random variable having the value zero) while the geometric distribution has no mass at the origin. The geometric distribution could be used to characterize the number of user segments per call, while the number of computer segments per call is described by the discrete exponential distribution for every system but one. These results are consistent with the long-holding time system results.

SUMMARY

The results presented in this paper provide to those engaged in research and design of inquiry-response computer communication systems estimates of significant system random variables. It has been shown that for most cases, assumptions ordinarily made in system studies about the behavior of input processes are supportable within tolerable error bounds.

REFERENCES

[1] P.E. Jackson and C.D. Stubbs, A study of multiaccess computer communications, AFIPS Conference Proceedings, Volume 34.

[2] E. Fuchs and P.E. Jackson, Estimates of distributions of random variables for certain computer communications traffic models, Commun. ACM, (December, 1970).

[3] W. Feller, An Introduction to Probability Theory and its Applications, Vol. II, (Wiley, New York, 1966) 53–54.

[4] C.D. Pack, A constrained curve-fitting procedure based on Prony's method, unpublished paper.

APPENDIX

The "Constrained Prony Procedure" is a curve-fitting procedure based on the classical Prony method.* Given, the sampled data and a hypothesized distribution family (e.g., exponential) the problem is to determine the value of the parameters associated with the distribution (at least) two alternatives are available for determining the parameters:

(1) estimation by such means as maximum likelihood, moment matching (as used by Jackson's "Fourier Series Tests"), etc.,

(2) attempting to find the member of the given family of distributions (say exponential) which is the best fit, in some sense, to the empirical histogram formed from the sampled data.

Either method determines estimates of the parameters associated with the given distributional form. It is the method (2) which is used by the Constrained Prony (Pack's) Procedure. Constraints must be imposed in order to ensure that the parameters are real** and are within allowed ranges (e.g., the exponent of the exponential must be negative). The procedure allows for fitting mixtures of distribution from a large selection of classical distributions of the form

$$f_x \approx \sum_{i=1}^{K} C_i \mu_i^x , \qquad x = 0, 1, ..., N-1$$

where ‡

$$C_i = P_i D(\lambda_i)$$

$$\mu_i = B(\lambda_i)$$

λ_i = parameter of distribution i of a given family

P_i = mixing proportion of distribution i.

Included in the distributions of this form are the binominal, negative binominal, Poisson, geometric, Erlangian, gamma, normal, and exponential.

The problem is then to

$$\min_{\{C_i\},\{\mu_i\}} \quad \| f_x - \sum_{i=1}^{K} C_i \mu_i^x \| \qquad \text{(in some sense)}$$

such that,

* See F. Hildebrand, Introduction to Numerical Analysis (McGraw-Hill, 1956).

** Because the Prony procedure involves transformation extraneous, nonreal roots are often created.

‡ For the exponential distribution

$F_i(x) = 1 - \exp(-\lambda_i x)$, $D(\lambda_i) = \lambda_i$, $B(\lambda_i) = \exp(-\lambda_i)$.

$$P_i = C_i/D(\lambda_i) \geqslant 0$$

$$\underline{\lambda} \leqslant \lambda_i = D^{-1}(C_i/P_i) \leqslant \bar{\lambda}$$

$$\sum_{i=1}^{K} P_i = 1$$

$$P_i, \lambda_i \in R'$$

Reprinted by permission from C.V. Freiman (ed.),
Information Processing 71
(North-Holland, Amsterdam, 1972)

This nonlinear programming problem is solved by applying the Prony transformation and some theorems from numerical analysis to obtain a sequential (and suboptimal) solution to the problem in either a sum of least squares or sum of absolute values sense.

Having obtained estimates of the parameters, classical (Kolmogorov–Smironov) goodness of fit tests are applied in the standard manner.

Error Control Techniques

The nature of the errors that occur on telephone data communications channels, and the basic techniques for dealing with these errors, are discussed in this chapter.

To determine telephone channel error performance and data speed capabilities, a survey measurement program of the telephone network is necessary. A series of studies started by the Bell System in 1958 was directed toward this goal.

For recent survey results (1969-1970) on high speed voice band data transmission performance on a switched telecommunications network, see [BAL 71]; and for results on low speed data transmission performance on a switched telecommunications network, see [FLE 71]. In these two papers, the distributions or error per call are given on a bit, burst and block basis. Information is also presented on the distribution of intervals between errors, the structure of burst errors and the number of errors in blocks of various sizes. Such statistics provide information on channel reliability and are also useful in the design of efficient error control procedures.

Errors and Error Control

H. O. BURTON, MEMBER, IEEE, AND D. D. SULLIVAN, MEMBER, IEEE

Invited Paper

***Abstract*—In this paper the nature of errors on telephone data communications channels and the basic techniques for dealing with these errors are discussed. Results of measurements recently taken on dialed connections are reviewed, and it is observed that conventional random-error- or burst-error-correcting codes cannot assure reliable communication on these channels. More generally, it is shown qualitatively that automatic-repeat-request (ARQ) systems are inherently better suited to the task than forward-error-control (FEC) systems. The throughput, or effective data rate, of ARQ systems is discussed, and two basic types of ARQ systems, stop-and-wait and continuous, are compared. It is concluded that with the more common stop-and-wait system, the throughput is unsatisfactory in applications involving high transmission rates and/or long propagation delays.**

A brief summary of error-correcting codes suitable for use on telephone channels (when a return channel is not available for ARQ) is included. Finally, hybrid schemes where FEC systems are embedded within ARQ systems are briefly discussed.

I. Introduction

THE MOST PRECISE statement that can be made about errors in data transmission is that they will occur; hence no realistic system can be designed without at least giving some thought to the effect of errors on the information being transmitted. In some applications, such as facsimile, the message itself may be so redundant that the errors that do occur can be tolerated and nothing need be done about them. In this paper we will assume that this is not the case and that some provision must be made for dealing with the errors.

For the purpose of simplicity, we will restrict our discussion to point-to-point binary data communication systems. There are fundamentally two categories of techniques for improving reliability in such systems. The first of these, commonly called ARQ (automatic-repeat-request), is represented diagrammatically in Fig. 1. In an ARQ system, data are delivered from a source to a sending terminal. The sending terminal can be thought of as an all-purpose box that arranges data in blocks, buffers the blocks, attaches control and synchronization bits, and generally controls the network. (See Gray, this issue.) The data blocks are then delivered to an encoder that attaches a number of parity bits, each of which is determined from a subset of the data (and possibly control) bits. Usually, the encoder is physically part of the sending terminal, but this is not necessarily the case. If each encoded block contains k information bits and $n-k$ parity bits, the code is said to be an (n, k) *block code*, with rate $R=k/n$.

The encoded block is then delivered to the modulator and transmitted over the channel. At the receiving end, the block is demodulated and delivered to the receiving terminal through the decoder, which recomputes the parity bits from the received data and compares them with the received parity

Manuscript received July 19, 1972.
The authors are with Bell Telephone Laboratories, Holmdel, N. J. 07733.

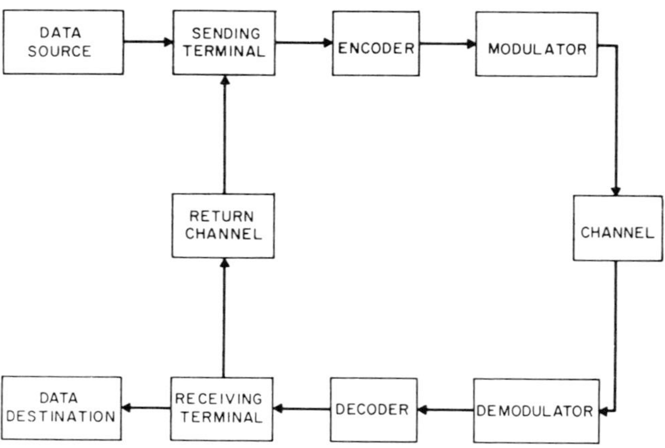

Fig. 1. ARQ system.

bits. If there are no discrepancies, the block is delivered to the data destination and the receiving terminal notifies the sending terminal, through a suitable return channel, that the block has been correctly received. If discrepancies exist, the sending terminal is so notified and the block is retransmitted (it has been assumed that the block is stored at the sending terminal until the acknowledgent or retransmission request is received). With this system, erroneous data are delivered to the destination only if the decoder fails to detect the presence of errors.

The second general technique for dealing with transmission errors can be depicted by removing from Fig. 1 the reverse channel. The decoder is then a more complicated device that attempts to determine the location of the errors from the *pattern* of discrepancies between the received and recalculated parity bits. With this system, called *forward error control* (FEC), erroneous data are delivered to the data destination whenever the decoder cannot determine the exact location of the errors.

Depending on the nature of the error patterns expected on the channel, codes for FEC systems may be designed to correct a maximum number, say, t of *random* errors (i.e., errors which may occur anywhere in the block) or a *burst* error which does not exceed a maximum span of B bits, subject to an error-free *guard space* of G bits. By this we mean spans of B bits or less, beginning and ending with an error, such that any two successive spans are separated by at least G error-free bits. Each of the $B-2$ or fewer bits in the interior of a burst may or may not be in error, but, in any case, there is no span of G or more consecutive error-free bits within any burst (if there were, we would interpret the pattern as consisting of two bursts). Codes have also been designed to correct combinations of random and burst patterns, usually called "compound" errors. An exact definition of a compound error pattern is difficult and we will not attempt it here, but intuitively we have in mind a block in which errors in a certain segment are quite dense (the "burst") and the rest of the block contains more widely scattered ("random") errors.

It should be noted that in the design of codes for ARQ systems, some consideration is also given to the nature of the errors on the channel. However, as we shall see, this is a far less critical problem than it is with FEC systems.

Lying midway between these two techniques is a hybrid scheme consisting of an FEC system contained within an ARQ system. The function of the FEC portion is then to *reduce* the frequency of retransmission requests by correcting ing as many of the erroneous blocks as possible. The receiving terminal then requests a retransmission only for those blocks where the decoder determines that errors exist but cannot tell where they are.

In later sections we will discuss the relative performance of these systems. In the next section, however, we will direct our attention to the channel which, in our idealized version of the system, contributes all the errors and makes some form of error control necessary.

II. Errors and Error Statistics

When one attempts to describe and quantify errors on telecommunications channels, significant complications are encountered. These complications are often simply ignored, as evidenced by descriptions of data modems (*modem* means *mod*ulator–*dem*odulator) which typically characterize the performance of the modem in terms of probability of error. What is meant is that in the laboratory, under controlled test conditions with only white Gaussian noise introduced into a perhaps linearly distorted signal with a "typical" signal-to-noise ratio, a certain error rate is achieved. Unfortunately (or fortunately for those who make error-control systems), conditions in the real world differ significantly from those in the aforementioned laboratory setup. Errors are caused by a variety of causes in addition to Gaussian noise—including, but not limited to, fades on microwave facilities and associated switching of the facility to a guard channel; impulses caused, for example, by lightning or by central-office switching equipment; noise-induced turnaround of echo suppressors; misaligned transmission equipment; and maintenance "hits."

The result is that error data are widely varied. Surveys conducted by the Bell System over the last decade attest to this [1]–[4]. The most recent such survey, the 1969–1970 Connection Survey [4], contains results consistent in form and diversity with earlier surveys. In that survey, tests were conducted with several modems using a nationwide sampling plan for selecting a large number of connections. For example, at 1200 bits/s there were 568 (30-min) test calls, and at 3600 bits/s there were 277 (20-min) calls. There were 110 test sites throughout the continental United States. The mean error rate for all calls for both 1200- and 3600-bit/s transmission was slightly better than 10^{-4} errors per bit transmitted. However, this average error rate is misleading because for both cases more than 80 percent of the connections had better than average error rates, as can be seen from Figs. 2 and 3.[1] In fact, as can be seen from the figures, average error rates per connection varied over almost five decades from between 10^{-7} and 10^{-6} to 10^{-2}. It is clear that errors are not independent randomly distributed events. In fact, it is concluded

[1] Figs. 2–7 have been drawn from [4].

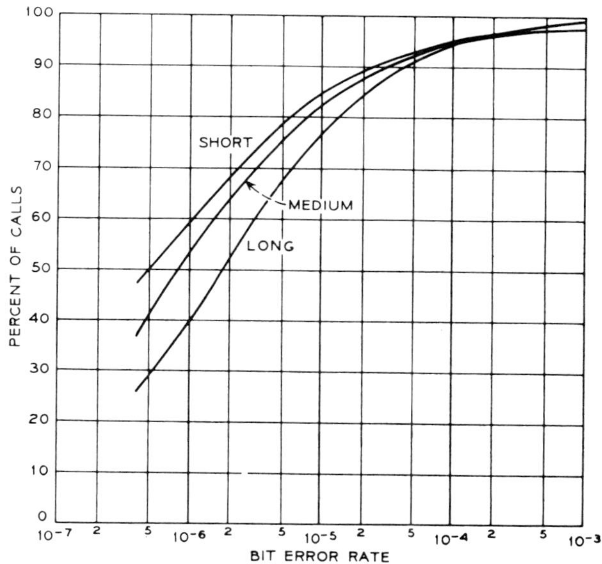

Fig. 2. Bit error rate distributions by mileage strata at 1200 bits/s. Copyright, 1971, American Telephone and Telegraph Company, reprinted by permission.

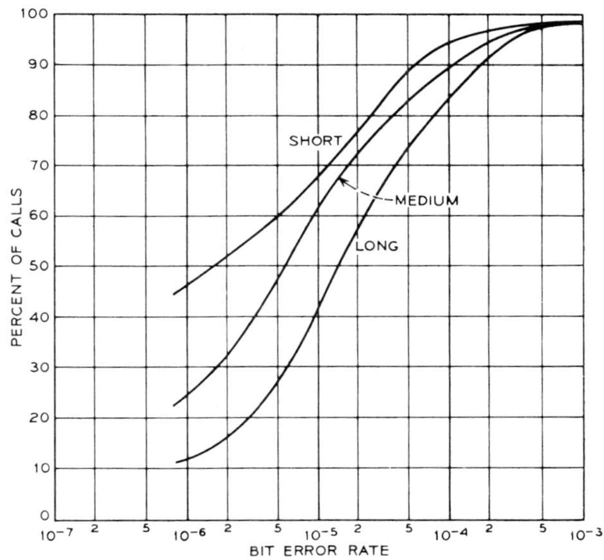

Fig. 3. Bit error rate distributions by mileage strata at 3600 bits/s. Copyright, 1971, American Telephone and Telegraph Company, reprinted by permission.

that impulse noise is the principal source of errors. Other conclusions that may be drawn from the various surveys are that error rates are not mileage or speed related in a way that would significantly influence error-control procedures for those speeds generally used on switched voice-band facilities. To some extent the surveys also indicate that different modulation methods are equally sensitive (or insensitive) to the error phenomena of switched voice-band connections and that the facilities are improving with respect to their capabilities of data transmission.

In the past few years the design of error-control systems has become much more sophisticated. A concurrent need therefore arose for more detailed information about channel

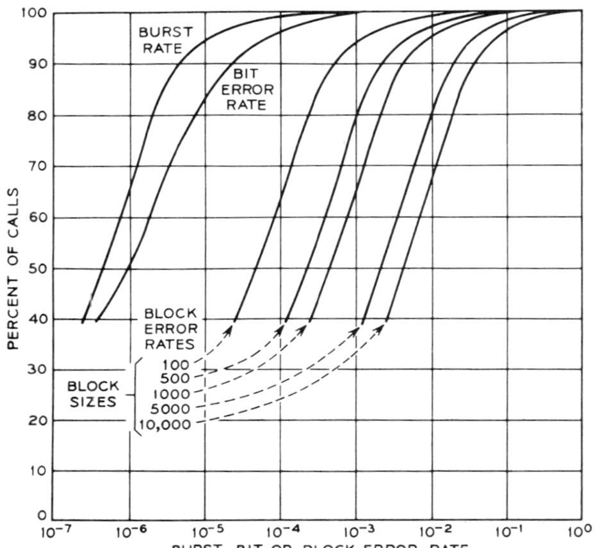

Fig. 4. Total burst, bit, and block error rate distributions at 2000 bits/s (each mileage band weighted equally). Copyright, 1971, American Telephone and Telegraph Company, reprinted by permission.

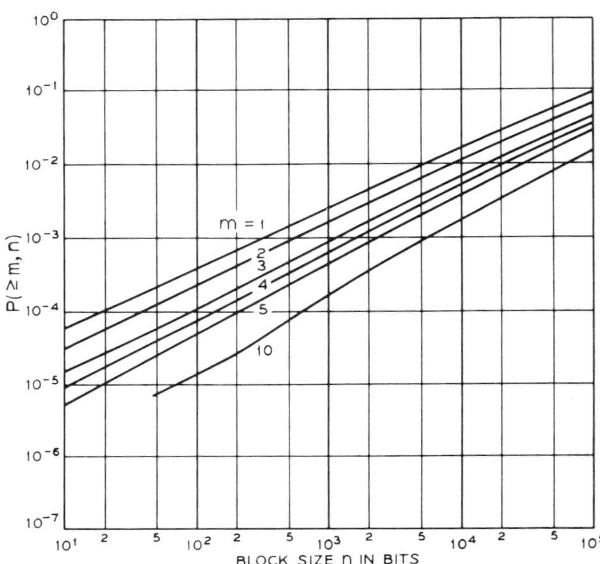

Fig. 6. Probability of m or more errors in a block of size $n[P(\geq m, n)]^1$ at 2000 bits/s. Copyright, 1971, American Telephone and Telegraph Company, reprinted by permission.

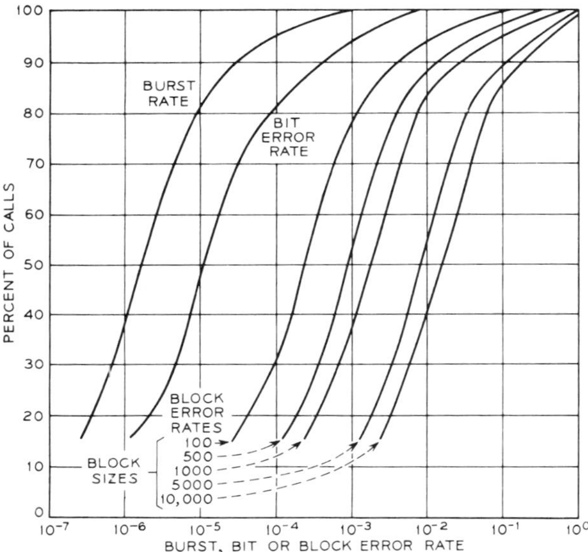

Fig. 5. Total burst, bit, and block error rate distributions at 4800 bits/s (each mileage band weighted equally). Copyright, 1971, American Telephone and Telegraph Company, reprinted by permission.

errors for evaluating these systems. The remainder of this section will describe the types of error statistics the authors have found useful in evaluating error-control systems and comment on some of the attempts to model these error statistics.

The key figure of merit in the evaluation of ARQ systems is the transmission efficiency or throughput T, which is defined as the ratio of the average number of information bits accepted by the receiving terminal per unit time to the bit rate of the channel. We will see in our discussion of ARQ systems that once such a system has been specified, the only uncertain variable affecting T is the block error probability. Block error probabilities for voice-band telephone data transmission are presented in Figs. 4 and 5 for various data transmission modems. These data and data from other earlier field tests of voice-band modems have an approximate form

$$P(n) = P(\geq 1, n) = an^x, \qquad \text{for } n \geq N_0$$

where N_0 is perhaps 10 and x is approximately unity.[2] Thus simple comparisons of retransmission strategies for different block lengths can be obtained using $P(n) \cong an$. For example, Fig. 6 displays $P(n)$ for a 2000-bit/s system. This curve can be approximated by $P(n) = 4 \times 10^{-6} n$. For $n = 20$ the data point is 10^{-4} compared to an estimate of 8×10^{-5}, and for $n = 5000$ the data point is 10^{-2} compared to an estimate of 2×10^{-2}.

Derivations of useful error statistics and approximations for FEC systems can become more complicated. Some simple observations can be made, however. It is easy to observe that average bit error probability is not going to be reduced much for data transmission, such as described in the 1969–1970 Connection Survey, with random-error-correcting codes. Referring to Fig. 6 again, the curves exhibit $P(\geq m, n)$ for various values of m. For a random-error-correcting code which corrects errors for moderate values of t, it is clear that of the blocks of length n which contain errors, those which contain more than t errors, and hence cannot be corrected by the code, constitute a significant fraction of all error blocks. For example, if $n = 100$, the probability of a block error is about 4×10^{-4}, but the probability of a block with more than four errors is just slightly less than 10^{-4}. Thus a code for which $t = 4$ would correct only about one fourth of the blocks in error. It is interesting to note that this same code would be effective on a channel with errors that are independent randomly distributed events. In that case, if bit errors occur with probability 10^{-4}, $P(\geq 5, 100)$ is approximately 10^{-12}.

It is clear that errors are correlated and that any effective error-control techniques must take account of this

[2] $P(\geq m, n)$ means the probability of m or more errors in a block of n bits.

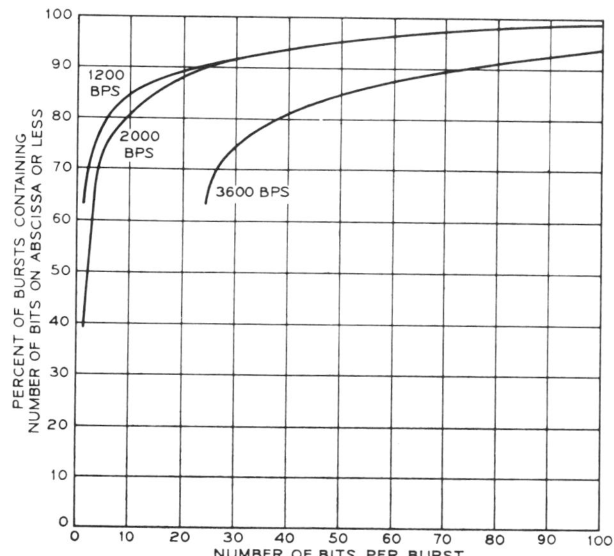

Fig. 7. Burst length distributions. Copyright, 1971, American Telephone and Telegraph Company, reprinted by permission.

property. For this reason, burst-error-correcting codes have been studied in this application. For such codes to be effective, the length of the burst must not exceed (or exceed with low probability) B bits, subject to an error-free guard space of G bits. Unfortunately, telecommunications channels do not conform to such a burst model any better than to the random error model. For example, Fig. 7 shows burst length distributions for a guard-space length of 50 bits. It is well known that an optimum burst-correcting code with rate $\frac{1}{2}$ (i.e., an equal number of redundant or check bits and information bits) and a guard space of 50 bits can correct error bursts of length up to 16 bits. From the figure and the 2000-bit/s curve, it can be seen that about 14 percent of the bursts have lengths in excess of 16 bits. This example is not atypical.

Having seen from experimental data that random-error- or burst-error-correcting codes are not suited to telephone data applications, we will return in Section VI to a discussion of what kinds of FEC systems are effective. In concluding this section, a few remarks on the various attempts at modeling telecommunications error statistics are in order. Several authors [5]–[10] deal with this subject. Although some success has been realized at fitting models to various observed error statistics, there have been few cases when predictions have been made using the various models where actual recorded error statistics could not have been used instead. Furthermore, for FEC schemes especially, one is interested in the less frequent or atypical error events because these are the ones that lead to undetected or uncorrected errors, and it is just such events that the models are likely to estimate poorly.

III. ARQ versus FEC

In this section we will consider the relative merits of ARQ and FEC systems and show, in a heuristic way, which of these techniques is better suited to the problem of error control on telecommunications channels.

ARQ systems have been extensively compared with FEC systems, both on real telephone channels [11] and with theoretical models [12]–[17]. In every instance the results have demonstrated the superiority of the former technique. The most striking characteristics of an ARQ scheme are its inherent reliability and the relative insensitivity of this reliability to conditions on the channel. This results from the fact that if the number of parity bits is r, the fraction of undetectable error patterns is only $1/2^r$, regardless of the length of the code [11]. It follows that since a code can be easily chosen to detect the vast majority of all error patterns, it does not matter very much how errors occur on the channel. Furthermore, by judicious selection of a code, it is possible to guarantee the detection of certain of the more likely error patterns. For example, a code used by IBM in many of their computer-communications systems [18]–[19] has 16 parity bits and is capable of detecting all blocks with three or fewer errors or with burst patterns spanning 16 or fewer bits, provided the block length is less than $2^{15}-1$ (about 32 000) bits. With a block length of 800 bits, the probability of having an undetected block error with this code has been pessimistically estimated at 10^{-8} [20]. Therefore, for systems which employ parity check codes for error detection, the problem of undetected errors is, for all practical purposes, nonexistent.

Unfortunately, the robustness of ARQ systems is not shared by FEC systems; for although the majority of error patterns are detectable with a parity check code, only a very small fraction are correctable (at most $1/2^k$, where k is the number of information bits in a block [21]), regardless of the algorithm used. Error-correcting codes are therefore most effective on channels where the vast majority of error events are contributed by a very small fraction of the possible error patterns.[3] Unfortunately, as we have seen, the telephone channel cannot be relied upon to be so well behaved.

Even in applications where error-correcting codes have some merit, they generally require many more check bits than do codes which are intended only for error detection. Furthermore, while the hardware required for carrying out error detection is almost trivial, that required for error correction can become extremely complicated and costly. The problem of obtaining simple algorithms for error correction has been a very active research area for several years, and significant strides have been made in this direction [21], [23], [24]. Fundamentally, however, it is one thing to recognize that there are parity check failures and quite another to associate, in a simple manner, such failures with specific error patterns.

There have, nevertheless, been recent developments in error-correcting codes for telephone channels which indicate that significant improvements in reliability can be obtained with FEC systems and that such codes may yet be useful in applications where, for one reason or another, retransmission is impractical. In Section VI we will return to a discussion of these developments.

Thus far, however, we have neglected the most important aspect of an ARQ system, namely, the effective rate at which information is transferred from source to destination. In the next two sections we will discuss the dependence of this rate on the channel error statistics, on the system parameters, and on the specific technique used to carry out the retransmission.

IV. Stop-and-Wait ARQ

The simplest and by far most widely used detection–retransmission scheme is the so-called stop-and-wait ARQ system [13], [14], [18]. With this system, after sending a block, the sending terminal waits for a positive or negative acknowledgment from the receiving terminal before sending

[3] This is the case, for example, in deep-space satellite communications [21], which is fortunate since retransmission is impractical in such applications.

another block or retransmitting the same block. (More details of this procedure are given in this issue in the paper by Gray.) The throughput T of such a system is given by [25]

$$T = \frac{n(1 - P(n))}{n + c \cdot \nu} \tag{1}$$

where, as previously defined, n is the block length, $P(n)$ is the block error probability, c is the time delay from the end of transmission of one block to the beginning of transmission of the next, and ν is the signaling rate of the modem. Here we are ignoring such factors as rate loss due to parity bits or to control and synchronization bits, since the effect of these factors in reducing the throughput is slight and does not depend on the other system parameters.[4] The effective information rate is then given by

$$R_e = T\nu. \tag{2}$$

From (1) it can be seen that T (and hence R_e) is degraded whenever $P(n)$ becomes appreciable, or when $c \cdot \nu$ is a significant fraction of the block length. From Figs. 4 and 5 it can be seen that for standard data modems and most direct-distance-dialing (DDD) connections, $P(n) \ll 1$ for $n \leq 10\,000$ bits, and hence errors usually do not seriously degrade the performance of a stop-and-wait ARQ system for block lengths in this range.

However, for short block lengths, certain applications may result in very inefficient operation even when there are no errors in the received data. For example, consider a DDD coast-to-coast connection. The propagation delay for such a link has been estimated at 60 ms [25]. In addition, since the facility is two-wire (half duplex), the return channel is normally obtained by reversing the direction of transmission, a process that may typically require 150 ms.[5] Since two reversals per block are required, i.e., one to establish the return channel and one to reestablish the forward channel, $c = 60 + 2(150) = 360$ ms. Hence, for example, on an error-free channel with $\nu = 4800$ bits/s and a clock length of 1000 bits, $R_e = 1760$ bits/s, which is only about 37 percent of the modem rate. Therefore, in this application a longer block length should be used. For example, if $n = 10\,000$ bits and the channel is error free, $R_e = 4100$ bits/s.

With the advent of higher speed modems (e.g., 7200 and 9600 bits/s), the product $c \cdot \nu$ becomes even more significant and it becomes increasingly important to use long blocks; otherwise, such a modem may increase R_e very little.

Unfortunately, there are two problems associated with longer blocks. The first is that, for a given connection, $P(n)$ increases with n; hence the percentage of connections with excessively large values of $P(n)$ will increase. Secondly, in many applications it may be impractical to use long block lengths because of restrictions imposed by the data. It is likely, however, that such higher speed modems will be used primarily on private lines. Since full duplex operation is then possible, there is no delay associated with channel turnaround and c is greatly reduced.

[4] We are also ignoring the effect of additional retransmissions due to garbled return messages. This is reasonable since the probability of error in the return message is generally much lower than in the much longer forward message.

[5] This delay is primarily due to the presence of echo suppressors on switched circuits [25] which are intended to improve the quality of voice calls on these facilities, but which make it impossible to reverse the direction of energy flow instantaneously. If the transmitter and receiver themselves require additional time to start up following this reversal, the total "turnaround time" could be larger than assumed here.

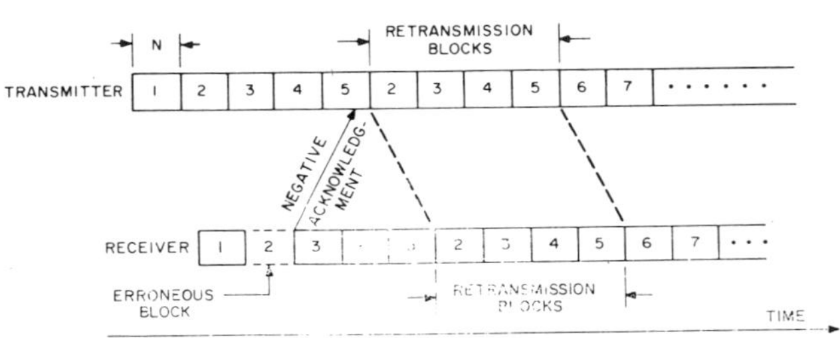

Fig. 8. Continuous retransmission.

Should domestic satellites be incorporated into the DDD network, or should intercontinental satellite data communications become prevalent, stop-and-wait ARQ systems are likely to prove highly unsatisfactory. For example, round-trip propagation delays for satellite links have been estimated at 540 ms [25]. Thus, if we again allow 150 ms to reverse the transmission direction on a DDD facility, $c = 540 + 300 = 840$ ms. On an error-free channel, if $n = 10\,000$ bits and $\nu = 4800$ bits/s, $R_e = 3410$ bits/s. If $n = 500$ bits, $R_e = 2650$ bits/s. On private-line full duplex facilities, there is no turnaround delay and $c = 540$ ms. If we let $\nu = 9600$ bits/s, then for $n = 10\,000$ bits, $R_e = 6300$ bits/s, while for $n = 5000$ bits, R_e is only 4700 bits/s. It may be argued that since satellite channels can be made quite reliable, the user can, without worrying about errors, simply increase n until he obtains a satisfactory value for R_e. However, error rates on such connections can be no better than the error rates of the terrestrial facilities leading to and from the satellite ground station and that these rates will probably not be significantly different from those of present facilities.

Thus, although stop-and-wait ARQ systems are very simple, they are inherently inefficient due to the idle time spent waiting for acknowledgments for each transmitted block. This inefficiency, while not serious on most present systems, may become unacceptable on systems which employ higher modem speeds and/or satellite channels. In the next section, we will discuss one relatively simple method of circumventing this difficulty.

V. Continuous ARQ

In this type of ARQ system [13], [14], [27], [28], the sending terminal does not wait for an acknowledgment after sending a block; as soon as it finishes one block, it begins the next one. When a negative acknowledgment for a given block is received, the sending terminal effectively "pulls back" and retransmits that block and all blocks transmitted in the intervening time between the original transmission and the receipt of the negative acknowledgment. It is assumed here that buffering is provided at the sending terminal for these blocks.[6] Fig. 8 shows an example of transmitted and received sequences for a typical continuous system. In this example, block 2 is received in error. However, by the time the negative acknowledgment is received at the sending terminal, block 5 is being transmitted. Thus the sending terminal retransmits blocks 2–5 (to maintain block synchronization, when a negative acknowledgment is received, transmission of the current block is completed before commencing the retransmission).

[6] It is possible to operate more efficiently by retransmitting only the block that was detected in error. However, if it is necessary to preserve the block sequence, extensive logic and buffering may be required [12]. Thus we will consider only the simpler, but slightly less efficient, "pull-back" scheme in this paper.

The reader may verify that the minimum number of blocks which must be retransmitted is given by $x+1$, where $x = \lfloor (c \cdot \nu)/N \rfloor (\lfloor y \rfloor$ signifies the least integer greater than or equal to y). In the example, if the sending terminal, while retransmitting blocks 2, 3, 4, and 5, receives a negative acknowledgment associated with the first transmission of blocks 3, 4, or 5, no additional loss of time is incurred since the retransmission of these blocks is effectively "free" as a result of the retransmission of block 2. In this paper we make the simplifying assumption that such overlapping negative acknowledgments do not occur. Under this assumption, a lower bound for the throughput T can be written as[7]

$$T \geq \frac{1 - P(n)}{1 + xP(n)}. \tag{3}$$

As an example of the performance of a continuous ARQ system, consider a four-wire satellite channel. Recalling that $c = 540$ ms, let $n = 5000$ bits and $\nu = 9600$ bits/s; then $x = 2$. If we assume a poor channel for which $P(n) = 10^{-1}$, $R_e = T \cdot \nu \geq 7200$ bits/s. For a better channel with $P(n) = 2 \times 10^{-2}$, $R_e \geq 9050$ bits. Now let $n = 1000$ bits; then $x = 6$. If we assume that the block error rate is proportional to n, then, for the poor channel, $P(n) = 2 \times 10^{-2}$ and $R_e \geq 8400$ bits/s. For the better channel, $P(n) = 4 \times 10^{-3}$ and $R_e \geq 9350$ bits/s. The values chosen for $P(n)$ are conjectural. However, unless they are extremely optimistic, which is unlikely, it appears that, at this rate, a continuous ARQ system is much more efficient than a stop-and-wait system.

On DDD channels, a problem arises from the fact that such channels are inherently two-wire. One way to operate in the full duplex mode required by the continuous ARQ system is to frequency-multiplex a narrow-band reverse channel with the forward channel.[8] If we assume that such a channel operates at 150 bits/s and that the return message is 32 bits long,[9] then the time required to transmit the acknowledgment message is 32/150 s = 213 ms and is significant enough that it must be included in the calculation of c. Therefore, on a DDD satellite connection, $c = 540 + 213 = 753$ ms. Suppose $\nu = 4800$ bits/s and $n = 5000$ bits; then $x = 1$. At the 90-percent point on the appropriate curve of Fig. 5 (a poor connection), $P(n) = 10^{-1}$ and $R_e \geq 3930$ bits/s.[10] At the 50-percent point (a "median" connection), $P(n) = 9 \times 10^{-3}$ and $R_e \geq 4710$ bits/s. If we let $n = 1000$, then $x = 4$. Thus for the 90-percent case, $P(n) = 3 \times 10^{-2}$ and $R_e \geq 4150$ bits/s, while for the 50-percent case $P_b = 2 \times 10^{-3}$ and $R_e \geq 4750$ bits/s. Again, this time using actual data, the continuous ARQ system is much more efficient than the stop-and-wait system. It is also interesting to note that, in contrast to the stop-and-wait ARQ system, the efficiency of the continuous ARQ system generally increases as the block length is decreased. However, system considerations may require that a small value of x be chosen, thus placing a lower bound on the block length which can be used.

Before concluding this section, it should be noted, however, that almost all commercial computer-communication systems today operate in a half-duplex mode (i.e., they cannot send and receive simultaneously, even though the transmission facility may be inherently capable of simultaneous two-way operation). Thus, despite their superiority in terms of efficiency, it is unlikely that we will see widespread use of continuous ARQ schemes in the near future.

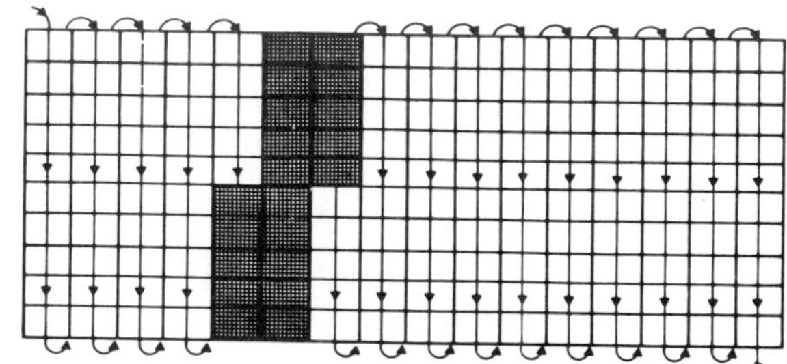

Fig. 9. Burst correction with interleaved codes, $n = 16$, $m = 10$, $t = 2$.

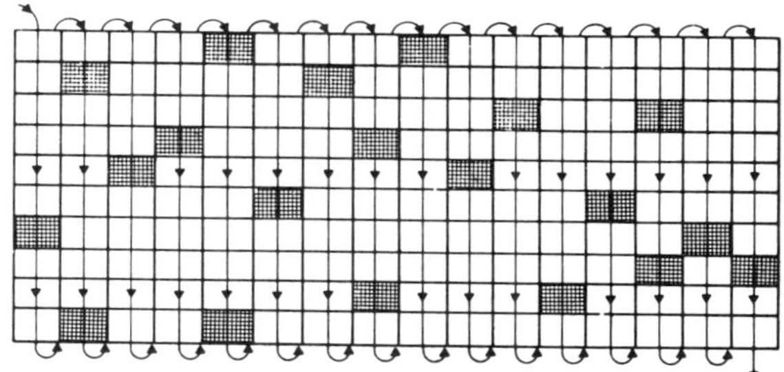

Fig. 10. Random-error correction with interleaved codes, $n = 16$, $m = 10$, $t = 2$.

VI. Forward Error Control (FEC)

It was seen in Section II that error occurrences on telecommunications channels do not conform to the constraints imposed by purely random-error-correcting codes or purely burst-error-correcting codes. Therefore, if FEC systems are to be effective, they must do more than correct only bursts or only random errors. We will therefore very briefly cite a few examples of codes which are capable of correcting both kinds of errors.

The easiest way to achieve protection against both random and burst errors is by interleaving the code. The matrix of Fig. 9 gives a simple example of interleaving where each row represents a code word and the arrows indicate the order in which the bits in the array are sent over the chanel. With interleaving we have effectively constructed an mn-bit block code consisting of m codewords from an n-bit code. If t random errors can be corrected in each n-bit code word, then the interleaved code can correct a burst of mt errors, as indicated in Fig. 9. Alternatively, scattered random errors, as illustrated in Fig. 10, can also be corrected. The only restriction is that the errors fall in such a way that no row contains more than t errors. Unfortunately, this same restriction also implies that, to guarantee the correction of any burst of mt errors, there must be no additional errors in the remainder of the mn-bit word. The ratio between the required length of this error-free guard space and the length of the burst to be corrected is unduly large, particularly in the light of what we now know about codes for random and burst errors, and, as a result, interleaved codes appear to be limited to applications where only modest improvements are desired for a low price.

Somewhat related to the interleaved codes are the diffuse

[7] We will omit the proof of this inequality. It can be easily obtained from Section B of [25] under the assumption that the sending terminal always completes the present block before initiating a retransmission.

[8] Such a channel is available, for example, on the Bell System Data Set 203.

[9] This is the minimum required in many current systems [18], [19], i.e., 16 bits for synchronization and 16 bits for the actual acknowledgment message.

[10] We again assume that error rates on satellite connections are dominated by the associated terrestrial facilities.

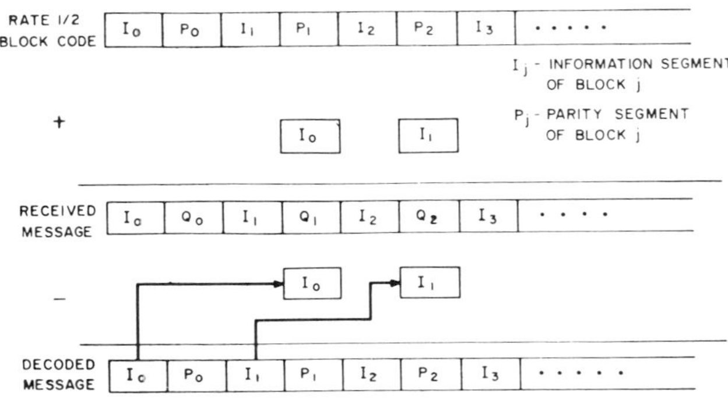

Fig. 11. Encoding and random-error decoding for a rate $\frac{1}{2}$ BT code.

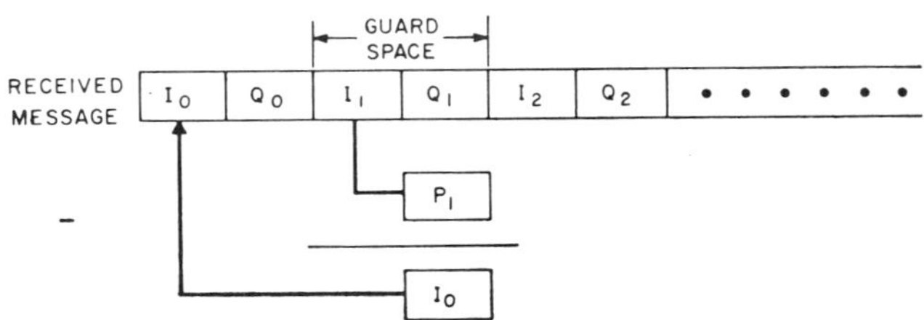

Fig. 12. Burst decoding of a rate $\frac{1}{2}$ BT code.

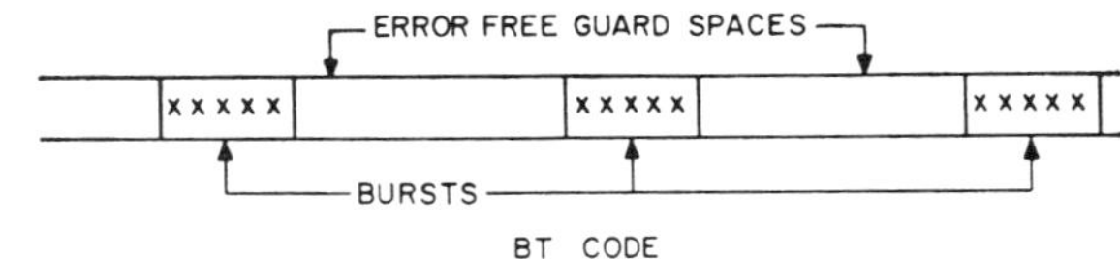

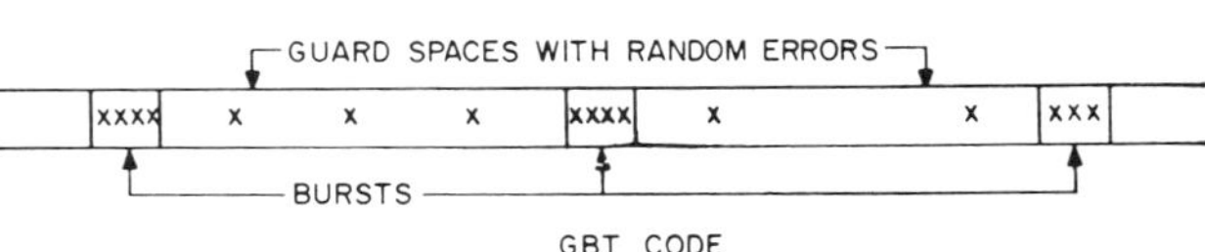

Fig. 13. Comparison of error-correcting capability of BT code and GBT code.

codes [29] which have the capability of correcting random errors as well as (but not necessarily simultaneously with) bursts. The principal advantage of diffuse codes is that the guard-space-to-burst ratio is usually much lower than for interleaved codes and, since they are threshold decodable [30], they are extremely simple to implement. Since its inception, this class of codes has been considerably augmented [31], [32]. Unfortunately, practically nothing is known about the performance of these codes on telephone channels.

Further improvement, in terms of the guard-space-to-burst ratio, can be obtained with the burst trapping (BT) codes invented by Tong [33]. With these codes, the information segment of a given block is added to the parity segment of a later block (or blocks) before transmission. This is illustrated in Fig. 11 for the case of a block code with rate equaling $\frac{1}{2}$. A given block can be decoded in the usual manner for the correction of randomly occurring errors, after which its information segment must be subtracted from the parity segment of the next block before decoding that block, thus cancelling the information bits added at the encoder. Alternatively, as illustrated in Fig. 12, if the number of errors in a block, say, block 0, is excessive (possibly due to a burst) and the errors cannot be corrected with the random-error-correcting algorithm, then if the errors can be detected and if the next block (block 1) has no errors, the information portion of this block (I_1) can be used to recalculate the corresponding parity bits (P_1). If these bits are subtracted from the actual received parity segment (Q_1), the information bits of the uncorrectable block (I_0) can be recovered. In general, if the code rate is given by $b/b+1$, where b is an integer, the information bits of a given block are distributed among the parity segments of b later blocks. To be corrected, each block which is affected by a burst must then be followed by an error-free guard space of b blocks. This condition is a significant improvement over that required when interleaving a random-error-correcting code[11] and is, in fact, optimal in a sense described recently by Forney [34]. Unlike an interleaved code, however, an error-free guard space of the requisite length does not, by itself, guarantee the correction of the burst since, with a BT code, the presence of the burst must first be detected. However, this is only a minor problem since it is very easy to choose the code parameters such that the vast majority of uncorrectable block error patterns are detectable. We note further that by properly interleaving the blocks, the burst-correcting capability of the code can be increased to any desired length while maintaining the same guard-space-to-burst ratio. Results of simulations of BT systems, using actual data from telephone channels [35], [36], have been very encouraging.

Conceptually similar to the BT codes is the adaptive coding scheme invented by Gallager [29]. This scheme predates the BT codes and differs from them in that it incorporates convolutional codes[12] in its structure rather than block codes. However, it is essentially the same in error-correcting capability.

On many channels, the requirement that a burst be followed by an error-free guard space may limit the effectiveness of the BT codes. Generalized burst-trapping (GBT) codes [37] are designed to deal with this problem. The capabilities of a BT code and a GBT code of identical rate are contrasted qualitatively in Fig. 13. Basically, a GBT code can correct a certain number of errors in the guard space following a burst at the expense of a longer guard-space-to-burst ratio than would be required for a BT code. A discussion of how these codes are derived and decoded is beyond the scope of this paper, but is presented in [37] and [38]. GBT codes have been evaluated both on real channels [38]–[39] and on channel models derived from empirical data [40], with favorable results in both cases.

An analogous scheme using convolutional codes has also been developed using a generalization of Gallager's adaptive scheme [41]. However, it appears at this time to be limited in its usefulness, due to the absence of good convolutional codes from which it can be built up.

Finally, Forney has recently shown [34] that, by using a more sophisticated type of interleaving (proposed earlier and independently by Cowell and Burton [17] and Ramsey [42]), it is possible to derive codes which are similar in performance

[11] For example, when interleaving a three-error-correcting 24-bit Golay code having 12 information bits, we arrive at a guard-space-to-burst ratio of 7:1. By contrast, a rate equal to $\frac{1}{2}$ BT code has a guard-space-to-burst ratio of only 1:1.

[12] Convolutional codes are parity check codes for which each parity bit in a given block depends not only on the information bits in that block but also on information bits in previous blocks. The aforementioned diffuse codes are convolutional codes, and closer inspection of Fig. 11 reveals that the BT codes are also convolutional codes, albeit constructed from block codes.

to the BT codes and the GBT codes (see Fig. 13). An interesting aspect of Forney's scheme is that the *same* encoded sequence of blocks can be decoded either in a BT type of mode or in a GBT type of mode, depending on the decoding algorithm employed.

VII. Hybrid Schemes

In our discussion of ARQ systems, we have seen experimental evidence that, at least for speeds up to 4800 bits/s, errors generally do not occur frequently enough to seriously reduce the effective transmission rate. In the minority of cases where the error rates are relatively high, the customer can, of course, hang up and redial if he is using the switched network. Alternatively, if he has a private line, he can request that the source of the problem be isolated and corrected. In contrast to these remedies, a more symptomatic treatment of the problem would be to imbed a forward-error-correcting code within the ARQ system. Hopefully, the decrease in R_e due to the additional redundancy required for forward-error correction would be more than offset by the increase due to the reduced number of retransmission requests. Theoretical results [43] have shown that if the channel is affected by independent errors, then there is indeed something to be gained with a relatively simple high-rate random-error-correcting code if the bit error rate is greater than 10^{-4}. The situation for real telephone channels is not quite as clear, since most channels have bit error rates less than 10^{-4} and, in any case, the errors are generally not independent. Nevertheless, experimental evidence indicates that R_e will occasionally be improved by this strategy [44]. It should be noted, however, that it matters a great deal where the FEC function is carried out. If we assume a decoding algorithm which operates essentially instantaneously upon receipt of a block, then no delay is encountered if the decoder is placed in the receiving terminal and if the FEC code is a *block* code whose length is the same as, or an integer fraction of, the ARQ block length. Unfortunately, the BT and GBT codes, as well as the diffuse codes, are convolutional codes (although the BT and GBT codes are built up from block codes) and so cannot be conveniently utilized in this manner. If the FEC system is instead part of the modem, then the entire FEC code block must be demodulated and decoded before the modem can *begin* to deliver it to the receiving terminal. Thus the FEC code will effectively introduce a delay in the forward transmission path (as seen by receiving terminal) which is equal to its block length.[13] This delay will be significant relative to the propagation delay and hence will noticeably reduce R_e unless the code is relatively short (of the order of 100 bits). Since the FEC systems discussed in the previous section generally involve long codes (usually of the order of 1000 bits or more), they would not be suitable for this application. One way to avoid this problem when a long block code is used in the modem is to have an interface which transfers the decoded block from the modem to the receiving terminal at a rate which is much higher than the channel bit rate. Unfortunately, most standard arrangements do not operate in this fashion.

Therefore, it is likely that the more elegant FEC techniques discussed in this paper will be limited to applications where the customer cannot, or prefers not to, use retransmission. Where ARQ systems are used, the role of FEC will most likely be a minor one, involving relatively simple short high-rate codes, designed for a limited amount of error correction.

[13] If a convolutional code is used, the data are subject to a fixed delay in passing through the decoder, corresponding to what is called the *constraint* length of the code.

VIII. Conclusion

A significant portion of this paper has been spent justifying what is essentially a *fait accompli*, namely, the widespread use of ARQ techniques in computer communications. While we have seen that ARQ systems currently in use may not be satisfactory in future applications, the solution lies not in FEC systems, but rather in a better ARQ technique. The conclusion drawn in this paper may leave coding theorists somewhat upset, and indeed the authors have been frequently confronted with arguments which have the following general tone: Shannon's capacity theorem states that for any channel there is a quantity called the channel capacity. As long as the information rate through the channel does not exceed this capacity, it is theoretically possible, with the use of forward error-correcting codes alone, to achieve an error probability as low as one desires. Therefore, there should, in principle, be no need for ARQ systems.

Our answer lies in the difference between principle and practice. For certain idealized models of telephone channels, the channel capacity has indeed been calculated. To our knowledge, however, no one knows how to determine the capacity of a real telephone channel, warts and all. Furthermore, while the FEC techniques discussed in this paper appear promising, there is a very *ad hoc* tone about them; they are based more on coarse intuitive notions of what the channel is like than on any fundamental understanding. In short, then, to a coding theorist, the telephone channel is a very formidable problem, and there is little hope that forward-error-correcting codes capable of performing to the satisfaction of most computer-communications users can be developed in the near future. In the meantime, ARQ systems are likely to continue filling the need simply and efficiently.

References

[1] A. A. Alexander, R. M. Gryb, and D. W. Nast, “Capabilities of the telephone network for data transmission,” *Bell Syst. Tech. J.*, vol. 39, no. 3, pp. 431–476, May 1960.

[2] R. L. Townsend and R. N. Watts, “Effectiveness of error control in data communications over the switched telephone network,” *Bell Syst. Tech. J.*, vol. 43, no. 6, pp. 2611–2638, Nov. 1964.

[3] C. W. Farrow and L. N. Holzman, “Nationwide field trial performance of a multilevel vestigial sideband data terminal for switched network voice channels,” in *Conf. Rec., 1968 IEEE Conf. Communications* (Philadelphia, Pa.), June 12–14, pp. 782–787.

[4] M. D. Balkovic, H. W. Klancer, S. W. Klare, and W. G. McGruther, “High-speed voiceband data transmission performance on the switched telecommunications network,” *Bell Syst. Tech. J.*, vol. 50, no. 4, pp. 1349–1384, Apr. 1971.

[5] E. N. Gilbert, “Capacity of a burst-noise channel,” *Bell Syst. Tech. J.*, vol. 39, no. 5, pp. 1253–1265, Sept. 1960.

[6] E. O. Elliott, “Estimates of error rates for codes on burst-noise channels,” *Bell Syst. Tech. J.*, vol. 42, no. 5, pp. 1977–1997, Sept. 1963.

[7] ——, “A model of the switched telephone network for data communications,” *Bell Syst. Tech. J.*, vol. 44, no. 1, pp. 89–109, Jan. 1965.

[8] P. Mertz, “A model of impulsive noise for data transmission,” *IRE Trans. Commun. Syst.*, vol. CS-9, pp. 130–137, June 1961.

[9] M. Muntner and J. K. Wolf, “Predicted performance of error-control techniques over real channels,” *IEEE Trans. Inform. Theory*, vol. IT-14, pp. 640–650, Sept. 1968.

[10] J. M. Berger and B. Mandelbrot, “A new model for error clustering in telephone circuits,” *IBM J. Res. Develop.*, vol. 7, no. 3, pp. 224–235, July 1963.

[11] A. B. Fontaine and R. G. Gallager, “Error statistics and coding for binary transmission over telephone circuits,” *Proc. IRE*, vol. 49, pp. 1059–1065, June 1961.

26

[12] J. J. Metzner and K. C. Morgan, "Coded binary decision-feedback communication systems," *IRE Trans. Commun. Syst.*, vol. CS-8, pp. 101–113, June 1960.

[13] R. J. Benice and A. H. Frey, Jr., "An analysis of retransmission systems," *IEEE Trans. Commun. Technol.*, vol. COM-12, pp. 135–145, Dec. 1964.

[14] ——, "Comparisons of error control techniques," *IEEE Trans. Commun. Technol.*, vol. COM-12, pp. 146–154, Dec. 1964.

[15] J. J. Metzner and K. C. Morgan, "Coded feedback communication systems," *Proc. Nat. Electron. Conf.*, pp. 250–255, Oct. 1960.

[16] ——, "Reliable fail-safe binary communication," in *Proc. IRE WESCON Conv.*, Aug. 1960, pp. 192–206.

[17] W. R. Cowell and H. O. Burton, "Computer simulation of the use of a group code with retransmission on a Gilbert burst channel," *AIEE Trans.*, Jan. 1962, pt. 1, no. 58, pp. 577–580.

[18] J. L. Eisenbies, "Conventions for digital communication link design," *IBM Syst. J.*, vol. 6, no. 4, pp. 267–302, 1966.

[19] *General Information—Binary Synchronous Communications*, 2nd ed., *IBM Syst. Ref. Library*, File TP-09, Order GA27-3004-1, Dec. 1969.

[20] James Martin, *Teleprocessing Network Organization*. Englewood Cliffs, N. J.: Prentice-Hall, 1970.

[21] W. W. Peterson, *Error Correcting Codes*. Cambridge, Mass.: M.I.T. Press, 1961.

[22] G. D. Forney, Jr., "Coding and its application in space communications," *IEEE Spectrum*, vol. 7, pp. 47–62, June 1970.

[23] E. R. Berlekamp, *Algebraic Coding Theory*. New York: McGraw-Hill, 1968.

[24] S. Lin, *An Introduction to Error Correcting Codes*. Englewood Cliffs, N. J.: Prentice-Hall, 1970.

[25] M. D. Balkovic and P. E. Muench, "Effect of propagation delay, caused by satellite circuits, on data communications systems that use block retransmission for error correction," in *ICC Conf. Rec.*, June 1969, pp. 29-31–29-36.

[26] Members of Technical Staff of Bell Laboratories, *Transmission Systems for Communications*. Winston-Salem, N. C.: Western Electric, 1970.

[27] B. Reiffen, W. G. Schmidt, and H. L. Yudkin, "The design of an error-free data transmission system for telephone circuits," *AIEE Trans. Commun. Electron.*, vol. 80, pt. 1, July 1961, pp. 224–231.

[28] F. E. Froehlich and R. R. Anderson, "Data transmission over a self-contained error detection and retransmission channel," *Bell Syst. Tech. J.*, vol. 43.

[29] A. Kohlenberg and G. D. Forney, Jr., "Convolutional coding for channels with memory," *IEEE Trans. Inform. Theory*, vol. IT-14, pp. 618–626, Sept. 1968.

[30] J. L. Massey, *Threshold Decoding*. Cambridge, Mass.: M.I.T. Press, 1963.

[31] M. J. Ferguson, "Diffuse threshold decodable rate ½ convolutional codes," *IEEE Trans. Inform. Theory*, vol. IT-17, pp. 171–180, Mar. 1971.

[32] S. Y. Tong, "Systematic construction of self-orthogonal diffuse codes," *IEEE Trans. Inform. Theory*, vol. IT-16, pp. 594–604, Sept. 1970.

[33] ——, "Burst-trapping techniques for a compound channel," *IEEE Trans. Inform. Theory*, vol. IT-15, pp. 710–715, Nov. 1969.

[34] G. D. Forney, Jr., "Burst correcting codes for the classic bursty channel," *IEEE Trans. Commun. Technol.*, vol. COM-19, pp. 772–781, Oct. 1971.

[35] S. Y. Tong, "Performance of burst-trapping codes," *Bell Syst. Tech. J.*, vol. 49, no. 4, pp. 477–492, Apr. 1970.

[36] W. K. Pehlert, Jr., "Analysis of a burst-trapping error control procedure," *Bell Syst. Tech. J.*, vol. 49, no. 4, pp. 493–520, Apr. 1970.

[37] H. O. Burton, D. D. Sullivan, and S. Y. Tong, "Generalized burst-trapping codes," *IEEE Trans. Inform. Theory*, vol. IT-17, pp. 736–742, Nov. 1971.

[38] W. K. Pehlert, Jr., "Design and evaluation of a generalized burst-trapping error control system," *IEEE Trans. Commun. Technol.*, vol. COM-19, pp. 863–868, Oct. 1971.

[39] P. J. Trafton, "Comparative performance results for three rate ½ burst-trapping codes," *IEEE Trans. Commun.* (Corresp.), vol. COM-20, pp. 485–487, June 1972.

[40] P. J. Trafton, H. A. Blank, and N. F. McAllister, "Data transmission network computer-to-computer study," in *Proc. 2nd Symp. Problems in the Optimization of Data Communications Systems* (Palo Alto, Calif.), pp. 183–191, Oct. 1971.

[41] D. D. Sullivan, "A generalization of Gallager's adaptive error control scheme," *IEEE Trans. Inform. Theory*, vol. IT-17, pp. 727–735, Nov. 1971.

[42] J. L. Ramsey, "Realization of optimum interleavers," *IEEE Trans. Inform. Theory*, vol. IT-16, pp. 338–345, May 1970.

[43] E. Y. Rocher and R. L. Pickholtz, "An analysis of the effectiveness of hybrid transmission schemes," *IBM J. Res. Develop.*, pp. 426–433, July 1970.

[44] W. G. McGruther, Bell Labs. Intern. Memo.

Reprinted from the PROCEEDINGS OF THE IEEE
VOL. 60, NO. 11, NOVEMBER, 1972
pp. 1293-1301

Modems

To transmit digital signals over analog channels (e.g., telephone channels), it is necessary for a data transmitter to MODulate the digital signal and for a data receiver to DEModulate this signal. This data transceiver is commonly known as Modem. The paper by Davey describes the characteristics of various types of modulations, intersymbol interference, automatic equalization, methods of synchronization and related problems. For a flavor of real modems in a hardware and feature sense, we have included a paper by Kretzmer describing the Bell System Modems. Many of the features and techniques described by Kretzmer are common in modems manufactured by independent suppliers.

For selection and evaluation of Modem, the interested reader should consult the book by Vilips [VIL 72].

Modems

J. R. DAVEY, FELLOW, IEEE

Invited Paper

Abstract—The rapidly rising need for computer communications has been met for the most part by utilization of the ever expanding network of voice-bandwidth channels. Transmission of digital signals over these analog channels involves a modem for modulation and demodulation of a voice-frequency carrier. The usual forms of amplitude, frequency, and phase modulations are described together with their basic characteristics, such as efficiency of bandwidth utilization. The principles of signal shaping and filtering for optimum signal-to-noise performance and minimization of intersymbol interference are discussed. Also covered are methods of synchronization, carrier recovery, effects of channel impairments, and the application of automatic equalization. The choice among modem designs is shown to be influenced by bit speed requirement, permissible error rate, type of channel, receiver startup characteristic, and tradeoff between modem and line costs.

The functions of the usual transmission and control leads between a data modem and a data terminal are described, and examples are given of leased private-line and switched telecommunications network applications. A current look at the physical aspects of voice-band modems is given and future trends are considered.

Introduction

DURING THE PAST two decades there has been a rapidly rising need for higher speed data transmission to furnish computer communications. The initial demand was in connection with national defense systems but was immediately followed by commercial applications. This need has been met for the most part by utilizing the widespread network of voice-bandwidth channels developed for voice communications. To transmit digital signals over these analog channels, which pass frequencies in the range 300–3000 Hz, it is necessary for a data transmitter to MOdulate a voice-frequency carrier signal and for a data receiver to DEModulate this signal. A data transceiver is consequently known as a MODEM. Such a modem serves to interconnect data terminal equipment with communication circuits. In addition to its basic function of translating between the binary digital signals of the data terminal equipment and the modulated voice-frequency signals of the communication channel, it also performs a number of control functions which coordinate the flow of data between the data terminal equipments.

Manuscript received June 16, 1972; revised July 17, 1972.
The author is with Bell Telephone Laboratories, Holmdel, N. J. 07733.

At the present time there are over 60 manufacturers of modems in the United States, together offering some 400 different models. At the beginning of 1972 there were over 300 000 modems in use in the United, States. About half of these were in the low-speed category of up to 300 bits/s. Approximately 70 percent of the total are leased by the common carriers, and the remainder is sold or leased by independent suppliers. The modems are roughly equally divided between private-line and switched telecommunications network applications. The lower speed modems are more often used on the switched network, while the higher speed modems are more often used on private lines. The non-common-carrier suppliers of modems have been active in the private-line applications for the past 15 years, but only since the Carterfone decision have they been able to participate in switched telecommunications network applications. At the beginning of 1972 about 11 000 data-access couplers had been installed to permit customers to use non-common-carrier modems.

The majority of modems are designed to accept and deliver a serial stream of binary data at the data terminal interface. There are, however, some types of modems which

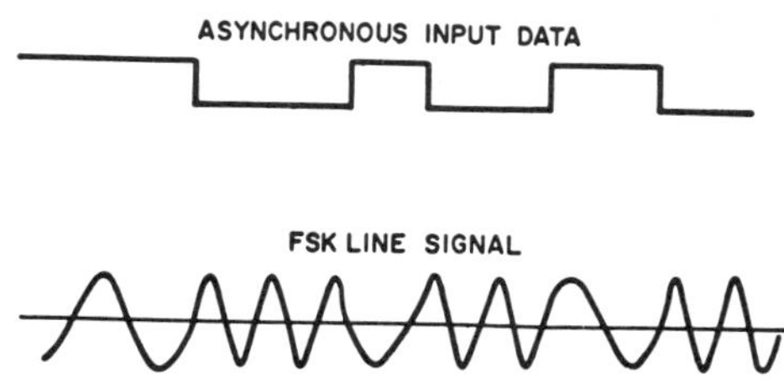

Fig. 1. Asynchronous FSK signal.

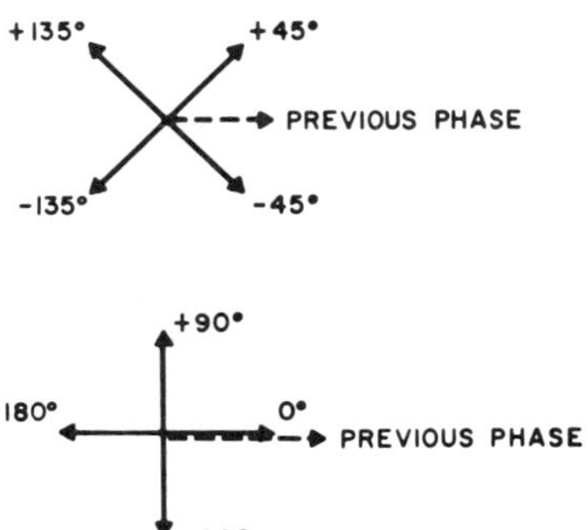

Fig. 2. Choices of phase shift for a four-phase signal.

31

handle a character at a time by accepting and delivering binary signals on several parallel interface leads and which modulate multiple voice-frequency carriers for parallel transmission over the voice channel. In this paper we will limit attention to modems handling a single serial data stream. Also modems using acoustic coupling to telephone handsets will not be discussed.

Types of Modulation

The voice-frequency signal transmitted between modems is modulated into intervals which vary in amplitude, frequency, phase, or some combination of these. These variations are used to represent the binary digital information to be transmitted. For asynchronous binary transmission two signal states are used, and the lengths of the intervals are prescribed by the transitions of the input binary data wave. For synchronous transmission the intervals are uniform in duration, and the choice of signal states may be more than two. The number of choices is usually made an integer power of two to simplify the relationship to the binary data being handled. The successive modulated intervals are called symbols.

The type of modulation used depends on the specific application. Binary frequency modulation in the form of frequency-shift keying (FSK) is the usual choice where simplicity and economy are more important than bandwidth efficiency. Typically the frequency shift in hertz is from one half to three quarters of the maximum bit rate, and the bandwidth in hertz is nearly equal to twice the maximum bit rate. This permits recovery of the baseband wave without excessive perturbation of the transitions, and the system can be operated asynchronously using start–stop codes at any speed up to the maximum capability. Speeds up to 1800 bits/s have been found to be feasible on conditioned private lines. An example of an FSK signal is shown in Fig. 1.

One form of FSK detection is based on the rate of occurrence of zero crossings of the carrier. Another involves a phase comparison between two versions of the received signal, one of which is passed through a network having a linear phase slope versus frequency over the band of interest.

Phase modulation in the form of differential phase-shift keying (DPSK) is a good choice for medium bandwidth efficiency. The term differential implies that the symbol meaning is based on the change in phase from the previous symbol and not on an absolute phase reference. For example, with four choices of phase shift, two bits per symbol are transmitted and the required bandwidth is somewhat less than the bit rate. A speed of 2400 bits/s has been found to be satisfactory over basic 3002-type channels. Most four-phase modems in the United States have used phase shift choices of ±45° and ±135°. Another set of choices which has been used is 0°, ±90°, and 180°. The first arrangement has the advantage of continuous phase changes, which aids in maintaining symbol synchronism. These two sets of phase shifts are illustrated in the vector diagrams of Fig. 2. Increasing the number of phase-shift choices to eight, giving three bits per symbol, permits a speed of 4800 bits/s to be achieved over most channels.

One method of detection for DPSK signals is to obtain a measure of the phases of each received symbol with respect to a local noise-free reference carrier which is maintained in phase lock with the pattern of received phase changes. A decision is made for each symbol as to the nominal phase which was transmitted. The difference between successive values of nominal phase is then used to determine which phase shift was transmitted. This is termed coherent detection. The decisions on received phase are sometimes based on the amplitude of in-phase and quadrature components of the received signal with respect to the reference carrier. In digital implementations, the decisions are usually based on time measurements between zero crossings of the received signal and the reference. To assure zero crossings near the center of the symbols the phase measurement is made after translating the voice-band signal to a higher intermediate frequency.

An alternative method of detection of DPSK signals is to make a direct comparison between the phases of adjacent symbols. One way of doing this is to delay the signal one-symbol interval and use this as a reference to measure the phase of the succeeding symbol. For a digital implementation the phase change can be obtained directly by time measurements of zero crossings in adjacent symbols. This is termed comparative phase detection. Since the signal itself is the reference and is disturbed by noise and other channel impairments, this method suffers a loss in signal-to-noise ratio, which for a four-phase system amounts to 2.3 dB [1].

Double-sideband AM was used in the earliest binary data channels but has since been replaced by FSK. Today AM is mainly of interest in transmitting multilevel symbols, particularly where one sideband or most of one sideband is eliminated. Typical of this class are modems transmitting four- or eight-level vestigial sideband signals and using coherent detection. Such modems achieve rates up to the 10 000-bit/s range over a conditioned voice channel. Signal power restraints and channel impairments make higher rates impractical at the present time.

An alternative to eliminating one sideband is to transmit two double-sideband signals in quadrature phase which can be separately coherently demodulated. This is possible because double-sideband signals have no quadrature component, and

32

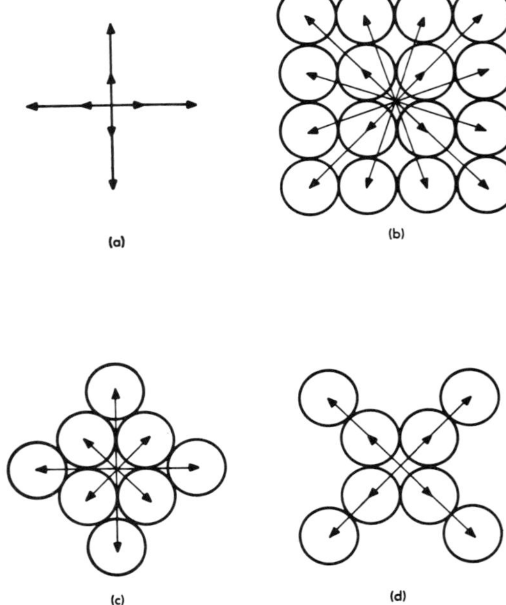

Fig. 3. Combined phase and amplitude modulated signals. (a) and (b) Two four-level AM signals in quadrature and resulting 16-symbol states. (c) and (d) Possible configurations for 8-symbol states.

thus there is no interference between the two channels. In fact, a quadrature AM system can be described as a combination phase and amplitude system. Two similar four-level quadrature AM signals combine to form 16-symbol states which have a total of 12 values of phase and 3 values of amplitude. Likewise any combination of phase and amplitude can be resolved into an equivalent pair of quadrature AM components. Examples of quadrature AM and of combinations of phase and amplitude signals are shown in the vector diagrams of Fig. 3. Centered on each symbol state is a circle with a diameter equal to the minimum distance between symbol states. This gives an indication of the amplitude of interference that can be tolerated before onset of symbol error. An efficient signal design results when these circular areas are closely packed into a roughly circular pattern about the origin, thus minimizing the average signal power for a given minimum separation of states. The patterns of Fig. 3(b) and (c) are more efficient than that of Fig. 3(d).

Where an intermediate speed is desired between those obtained with two and four levels, three-level symbols are sometimes used. For example two three-level symbols provide nine states. Three binary bits can be encoded into eight of the nine states with the ninth state being either ignored or utilized to provide auxiliary information. The use of three-level symbols thus effectively gives a means of achieving $1\frac{1}{2}$ bits per symbol.

Signal Shaping and Filtering

Signal shaping and filtering are used in modems to confine the signal to a specific frequency band, to minimize influence of noise, and to control intersymbol interference. The long-haul portion of a typical voice-channel facility has a well defined frequency band determined by the channel bank filters. However, in the local area where transmission is over metallic multipair cables, the band is not restricted, broad-band noise may exist, and crosstalk between pairs can occur over a very wide frequency range.

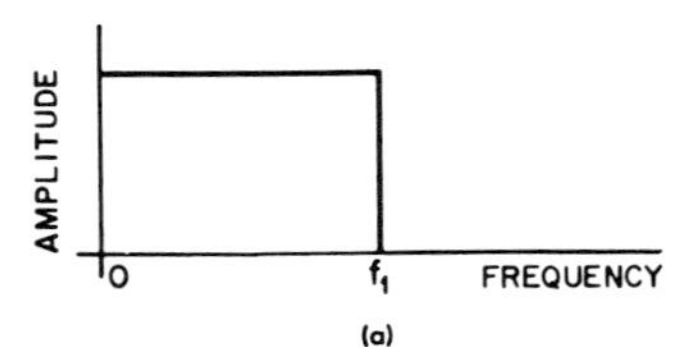

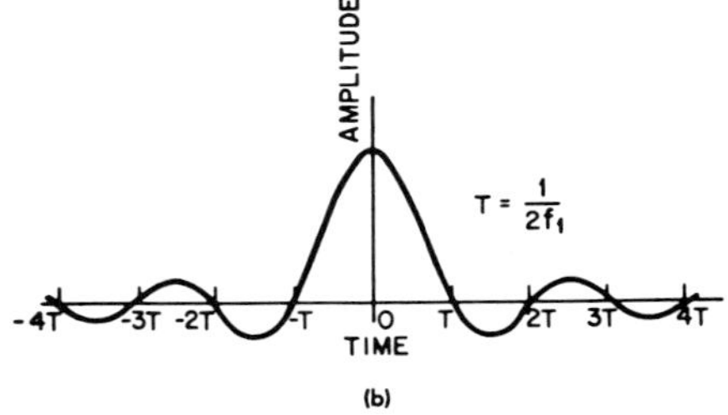

Fig. 4. (a) Baseband signal with rectangular spectrum. (b) Time response.

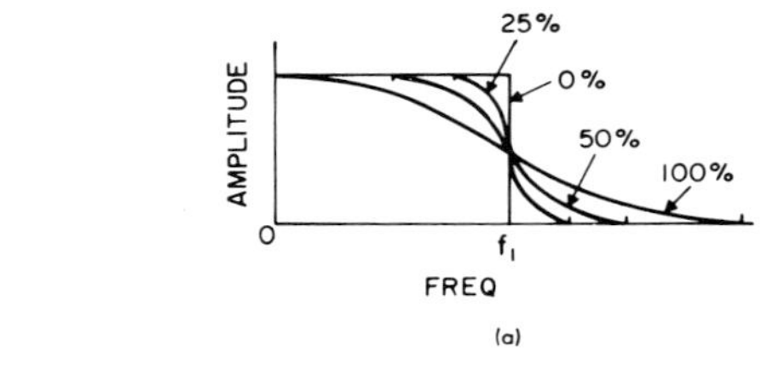

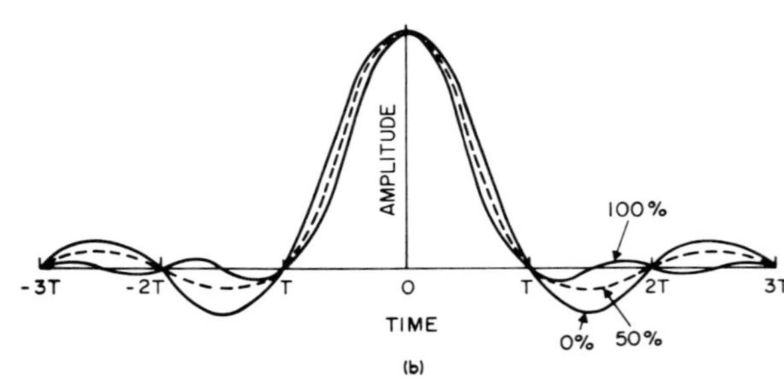

Fig. 5. (a) Modified baseband spectra. (b) Corresponding time responses.

A general class of spectral amplitude shaping which avoids intersymbol interference was described by Nyquist [2], [3]. A baseband signal having a rectangular spectral shape and a linear phase characteristic has the sin x/x type of time response shown in Fig. 4, which passes through zero at intervals of $1/2f_1$, where f_1 is the low-pass cutoff frequency. It is thus possible to signal at the rate $2f_1$ without interference between the peaks of the received pulses. Nyquist's theorem on vestigial symmetry showed that the rectangular spectrum could be modified by an amplitude characteristic having odd symmetry about the cutoff without disturbing the original zero points although others are added. Possible modifications using sinusoidal shapes are shown in Fig. 5. These modified shapes are of interest because they are more representative of practical filter designs. The amount of additional bandwidth devoted to this more gradual "rolloff" can be expressed as a percentage of the basic bandwidth. Fig. 5 indicates both a 50-percent and a 100-percent rolloff together with the associated time responses. The 100-percent or full-$\cos^2$ rolloff has the added property that there is no interference at the half-

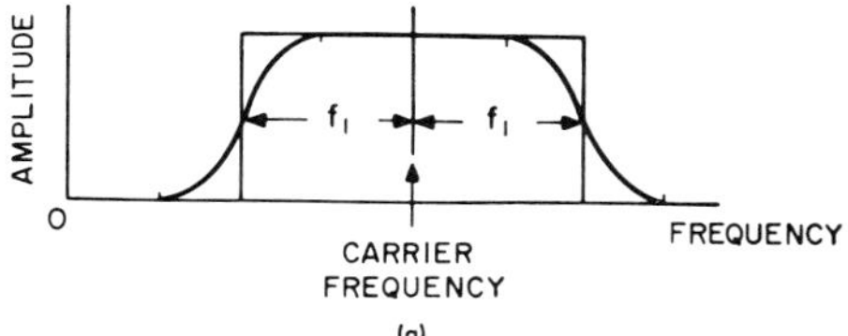

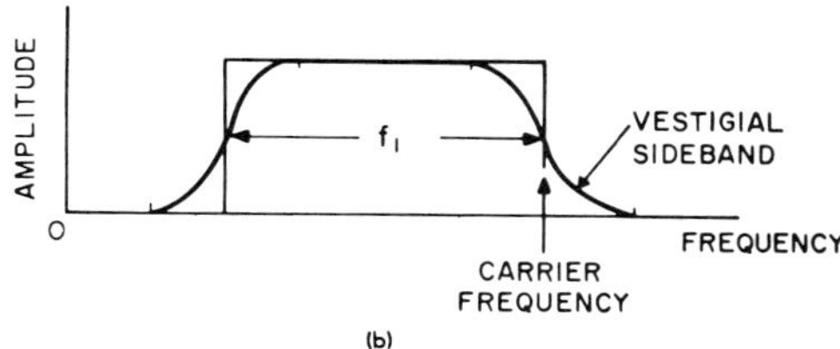

Fig. 6. Passband spectral shapes. (a) Double-sideband spectrum. (b) Vestigial sideband spectrum.

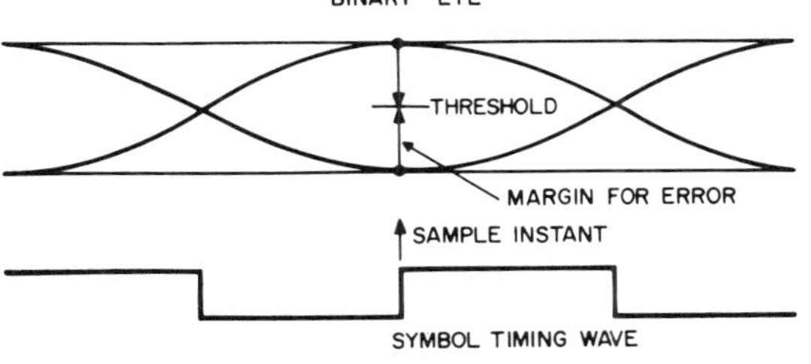

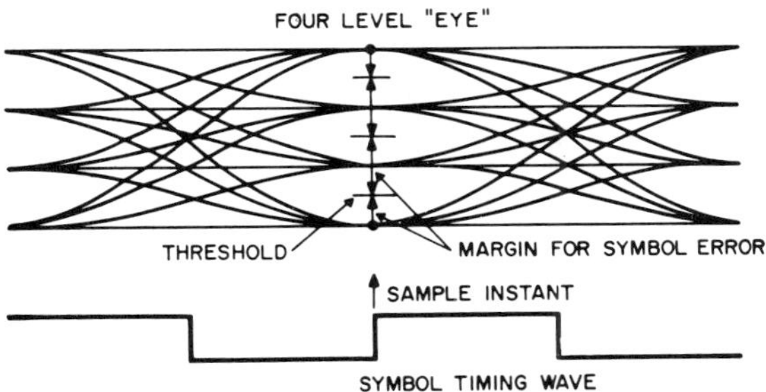

Fig. 7. Binary and four-level "eye" patterns.

amplitude points and the response dies away rapidly. This permits asynchronous signaling over a range of pulsewidths with little time distortion.

Another type of spectral shaping which has been used in data transmission has as an objective a pulse response having controlled intersymbol interference over a specific number of intervals. This can be arranged to produce a signal exhibiting more levels than the original input symbols but which can be interpreted as a multilevel signal free from intersymbol interference. This has been termed partial response signaling [4]. An example of this is the duobinary system, in which a binary input becomes a three-level signal at the receiver [5].

When a baseband signal with the shaping indicated in Fig. 5 is used to amplitude-modulate a carrier, both sidebands of the resulting double-sideband signal retain the same rolloff characteristic. Control of the spectral shaping can be accomplished either at baseband before modulation or at passband after modulation, or by a combination of both. The envelope of an isolated symbol has the shape of the equivalent baseband wave. The envelope resulting from a sequence of overlapping symbols depends on the amplitudes and carrier phases of the individual symbols. For vestigial sideband systems most of one sideband is eliminated after modulation by a filter having a rolloff about the carrier such that the sum of the sidebands in the cutoff regions adds up to full response of one sideband. The cutoff is typically $\cos^2$ in shape and again can be expressed in percent of the basic band. Sample passband shapes are shown in Fig. 6.

Having selected the overall transmission characteristic to minimize intersymbol interference, there remains the problem of the best division of the characteristic between the transmitting and receiving filters. A common type of optimization for this problem is to maximize the signal-to-noise ratio at the demodulator, assuming white Gaussian noise and a fixed limit on transmitted power. If most of the spectral shaping is done at the receiver, the maximum amount of noise is excluded, but the demodulated signal amplitude is also reduced because an appreciable part of the allowable transmitted power is out of band. On the other hand, if the spectral shaping is mainly at the transmitter, the maximum useful signal is placed on the line, but the receiver accepts more out-of-band noise. The signal-to-noise ratio is maximized when the shaping at the receiver is the square root of the overall desired shaping [6], [7]. For example, if the overall shaping is to have the $\cos^2$ cutoff of Fig. 6, then the receiver filtering should have a cos cutoff shape. With a cos rolloff for the transmitted symbol spectrum and with a cos rolloff for the receiver filter, the signal-to-noise ratio at the output of the receiver filter is independent of the percent rolloff used.

The quality of a demodulated data signal is illustrated by a so-called "eye pattern." The eye pattern is a superposition of the various baseband waveforms over a symbol interval. Two examples of eye patterns are given in Fig. 7. Where intersymbol interference is small, the signal assumes well defined levels at the center of the symbol interval. It is at this point of maximum differentiation that the symbol is sampled to determine its state. This is done by setting thresholds halfway between adjacent levels. This half distance between adjacent states is a measure of the margin against noise and other disturbing influences. When the signal is disturbed beyond a threshold into the region of another symbol state, an error results. For a binary wave this results in a single binary digit error. For multilevel systems, where a single symbol represents two or more binary digits, more than one error may result. It is of advantage to assign binary values to the symbol states which differ only in one digit position between adjacent states. Since the most probable symbol error results when the signal is perturbed into an adjacent state, this keeps the number of binary digits in error per symbol in error near to one. Such a code sequence which progresses by a change in only one digit position at a time is known as a Gray code [8].

One convenient measure of modem performance is that of error rate in the presence of random noise. The theoretical error performance of a given type of system can usually be calculated, and noise sources are readily available which are close to being both white and Gaussian. The difference between the theoretical and measured error rates indicates how well the system is implemented.

In comparing the performance of modems using different modulation schemes two measures are commonly used. One is the ratio of average transmitted power to the noise power in the Nyquist band required to achieve a given probability of

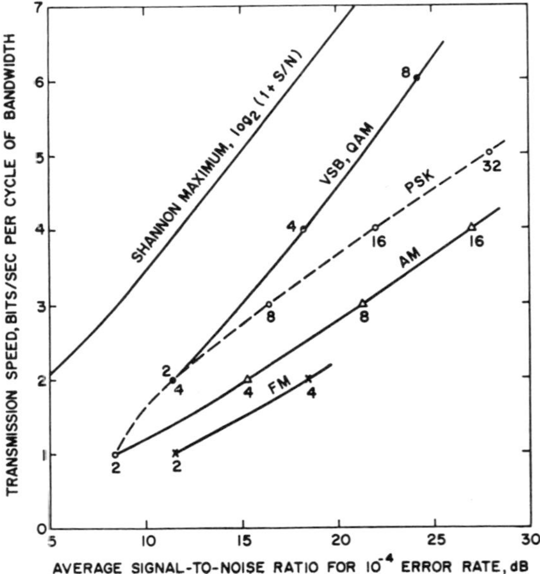

Fig. 8. Comparison of modulation methods.

error, such as 10^{-4}. The other is the nominal speed of transmission in bits per second per cycle of this band. Using these two measures the theoretical performance of the various modulation methods can be plotted as points, as in Fig. 8. The horizontal coordinate gives the signal-to-noise ratio for an error rate of 10^{-4}, and the vertical coordinate gives the transmission speed in bits per second per cycle of bandwidth. The number of symbol states is indicated at each point. This type of presentation indicates how well the various modulation methods are able to exchange signal-to-noise ratio for rate of information flow. Once the available bandwidth is fully utilized, higher rates are obtained only at the cost of decreased margin against noise and other uncontrolled variables. The upper solid line indicates the theoretical bound for rate of information transfer over a channel limited by white Gaussian noise, as formulated by Shannon [9].

The vestigial sideband and quadrature AM methods are seen to be the most efficient, and they fall along a line having the same slope as the Shannon limit. Other efficient combinations of PM and AM also fall near this line. The most rugged binary signal is one using two-phase or suppressed carrier binary AM. Binary vestigial sideband, two binary AM channels in quadrature, and quarternary PM have equal rating. For more than four phases the PM systems fall along a line that diverges considerably from vestigial sideband and quadrature AM. The AM and FM systems also fall along lines having this lesser slope. Where coherent detection is involved, some transmitted power may be required to maintain a reference carrier at the receiver; no allowance for this has been made in Fig. 8.

In addition to performance in the presence of noise, the ability to combat other forms of impairments is often of as great if not greater importance. These other impairments are amplitude–frequency distortion, phase–frequency distortion, nonlinear distortion, frequency offset, spurious amplitude and phase variations, and echo in 2-wire circuits [10], [11]. Of these impairments the modem can be designed to compensate for the channel amplitude and phase characteristic, frequency offset, and amplitude and phase variations that are slow relative to the signaling speed. Fortunately these are also the impairments which cause the major amount of data signal distortion. Once they are effectively dealt with, nonlinear distortion and noise become the main remaining obstacles to maximum channel utilization. These impairments are normally small on well maintained voice channels. Typical performances of modems in the presence of these impairments are exemplified by the error-rate measurements reproduced in the companion paper "Errors and Error Control" in this issue.

Symbol and Bit Timing Recovery

At the receiving end of a synchronous data link, it is necessary to recover symbol and bit timing both for use within the modem and for the use of the data terminal equipment. In the modem the symbol timing is used to sample the demodulated signal at the centers of the symbols to determine their state. For a binary system, the symbol and bit timing are the same. For a multilevel system, the required multiple of the symbol timing must be generated for use in generating the serial bit stream output of the modem. A bit-timing wave must also be furnished to the connecting data terminal equipment so it can properly interpret the non-return-to-zero received data wave.

In current modems the bit and symbol timing is usually generated by a digital countdown chain driven by a crystal oscillator. By adding or deleting count pulses at a higher frequency point in the chain, the phase of the timing can be adjusted in steps of a small fraction of the symbol interval. The symbol timing can thus be phase-locked to some property of the received symbols. If the demodulated symbols occur as a baseband wave, the instants of transition through the decision thresholds can be used for the phase lock. AM and PSK signals may have sufficient AM at the symbol rate to use the detected envelope for symbol-timing information. The symbol-timing wave enables the symbol to be sampled at the center of the "eye," where maximum margin exists against error. This is illustrated in Fig. 7.

Since recovery of symbol timing is based on variations in symbol state, it is often desirable to use a scrambler to assure continual variation for any normal data input pattern. The scrambling is usually accomplished by multiplying the binary input data to the transmitter by a pseudorandom binary sequence generated by a shift register with feedback. At the receiver the data are unscrambled by multiplying by the same sequence in proper synchronism. One way to avoid the necessity of startup procedures to establish scrambler synchronization is to use self-synchronizing scrambler–descrambler configurations [12]. One disadvantage of such an arrangement is the multiplication of errors. A single isolated bit in error may cause two or three errors in the output in typical designs.

Coherent Carrier Recovery

Modems designed to achieve a high ratio of bits per second per cycle of bandwidth often use coherent detection. This requires the generation of a reference carrier in the receiving modem that is accurately phased with respect to the received signal which may have undergone a frequency offset. In an AM system a straightforward method is to transmit some of the carrier used in modulation at the transmitter and detect it at the receiver by a narrow filter or phase-locked loop. If the data wave being transmitted has a dc component, the amplitude and phase of the received carrier component will be variable. It is, therefore, advisable to scramble the data before modulation so that the dc component will be minimized. In a vestigial sideband (VSB) system it is also of benefit to have the low-level carrier inserted in a quadrature relationship with the signal so that it will not contribute to the demodulated signal. An alternative method of avoiding interaction between the carrier signal and the data signal is to remove the very low frequencies of the data signals that would fall in the band used to detect the carrier. The missing low frequencies of the data wave can then be restored by quantized feedback.

For coherent detection of a PSK signal, a local reference of near the correct frequency can be phase-locked to the expected pattern of received phase shifts. This also applies to two binary signals in quadrature phase. Another method for AM systems with suppressed carrier is to select a narrow band of double-sideband energy near the carrier position and subject it to a nonlinear process in which the upper and lower sideband components modulate each other to form a twice-carrier-frequency component. This can then be filtered out and divided by two to obtain a reference carrier. The resulting 180° ambiguity will cause no difficulty if the polarity of the data wave is derived from differential encoding.

Still another method of transmitting carrier information is by use of two pilot tones. The frequencies of the two pilots are selected so that the frequency difference between the carrier and one of the pilots is in some simple ratio to the frequency difference between the two pilots. The required reference carrier can then be constructed at the receiver from the detected pilots. The recovered carrier, although of the correct frequency, must be phase adjusted to match that of the actual carrier when transmitted. This is usually done in a startup procedure at the beginning of transmission.

The effects of low-frequency phase jitter can be greatly reduced if the coherent reference has a phase jitter matching that of the received signal. This requires that the filter bandwidths used in deriving the reference be wide enough to include the sidebands associated with the phase jitter. This, however, results in unwanted noise being accepted and some decrease in signal-to-noise ratio.

Equalization

Filter characteristics which optimize the signal-to-noise ratio and minimize intersymbol interference have been described. However, because of the wide variations encountered in voice-band channels, these ideal conditions cannot be maintained without adjustments to fit the specific channel. The signal-to-noise ratio is not significantly degraded, but the intersymbol interference rapidly increases with envelope delay distortion. The typical type of pulse distortion caused by delay distortion is illustrated in Fig. 9. It will be seen that such a pulse centered at $t=0$ will contribute errors in amplitude of pulses centered at other positions, such as $t=-1, +1$, and $+2$. These contributions can be viewed as positive or negative echoes occurring both before and after the original pulse [13]. Likewise a delay-equalizing network can be considered to generate a set of canceling echoes.

For modems operating up to 2400 bits/s, it is usually adequate to use a fixed compromise equalizer chosen to match the mean of the range of expected delay distortion. For higher speeds and especially where more than two levels are used, it is usually necessary to provide an equalizer that can be adjusted to fit the specific channel being used. One approach is to use variable all-pass network sections which can be adjusted in midfrequency and Q. Such sections give an offsetting "bump" of envelope delay that can be adjusted in amplitude and frequency position to build out the channel characteristic to have a flatter envelope delay. The adjustment procedure can be simplified by use of multiposition switches to choose among a range of judiciously selected expected channel characteristics. It is necessary to have some measure of signal quality in order to tell which choice is best. Typically a meter is utilized to indicate some measure of margin against error.

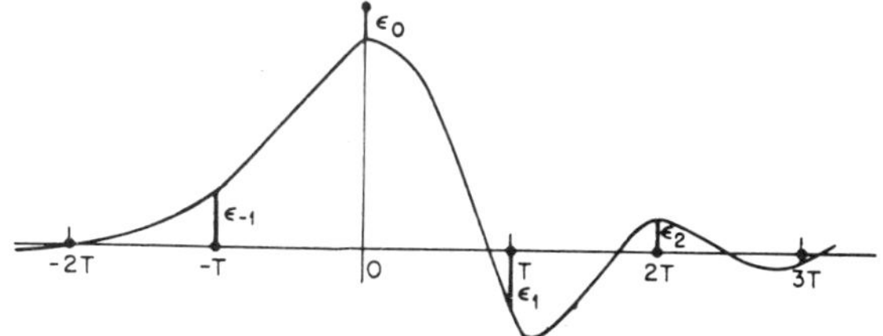

Fig. 9. Intersymbol interference as a result of delay distortion.

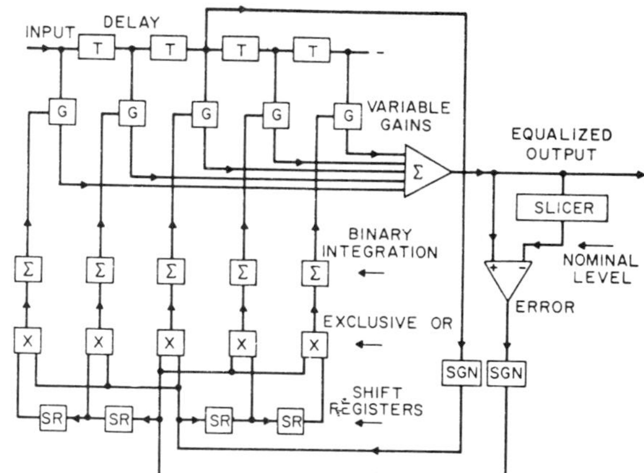

Fig. 10. Example of an automatic adaptive equalizer.

To achieve the maximum capability of the channel, more precise control of intersymbol interference is required. This is accomplished in current high-speed modems by automatically adjusted equalizers of the transversal filter type [14]. In one form of this type of equalizer, the demodulated signal is passed through a delay line having taps at symbol intervals. Each tap is provided with variable gain which can be positive or negative, and the various tap outputs are summed to provide the equalizer output. The main contribution is from a central tap, with the other taps contributing echoes of the main signal at symbol intervals both preceding and following the main signal. Fig. 10 shows one configuration of an automatic adaptive equalizer [15], [16]. The equalizer output is compared at the center of each symbol interval with the normally expected symbol levels to determine the closest level and also the sign of the error from that level. The direction of adjustment of each tap gain is determined by correlating the sign of the unequalized symbol value with the sign of the corresponding error in the equalized output. The correlation is accomplished by binary multiplication in exclusive OR circuits, and the results are averaged in an up–down counter so that corrective

TABLE I

EIA Standard Interface Leads

Connector Pin No.	Lead Designation	Lead Description
1	*AA*	protective ground
2	*BA*	transmit data
3	*BB*	receive data
4	*CA*	request to send
5	*CB*	clear to send
6	*CC*	data set ready
7	*AB*	signal ground-common return
8	*CF*	received signal detector
12	*SCF*	secondary received signal detector
13	*SGB*	secondary clear to send
14	*SBA*	secondary transmit data
15	*DB*	transmit signal element timing (DCE source)[a]
16	*SSB*	secondary receive data
17	*DD*	receive signal element timing
19	*SCA*	secondary request to send
20	*CD*	data terminal ready
21	*CG*	signal quality detector
22	*CE*	ring indicator
23	*CH/CI*	data signal rate selector (DTE/DCE source)[a,b]
24	*DA*	transmit signal element timing (DTE source)[b]

[a] DCE Data Communication Equipment
[b] DTE Data Terminal Equipment

steps are taken only for persistent trends. In order to match the symbol sign information with its contribution to the error sign at a position either earlier or later in time, both types of signs are delayed by shift registers, as indicated in Fig. 10. For initial startups it may be desirable to use a binary signal to obtain more accurate error sign information and then shift to normal multilevel operation after partial equalization has occurred. The great advantage of such an adaptive equalizer is that it continually adjusts itself to any channel variations and controls intersymbol interference to a degree that is impossible to achieve with manual adjustments.

Interface with Data Terminal Equipment

The interface between a modem and the associated data terminal equipment has been standardized by EIA Standard RS232. For voice-band modems the interface leads are single leads with a common ground return. Polar-type signals are specified with a minimum amplitude of ± 3 V at the terminating end. The maximum allowable voltage is ± 25 V. A ground potential difference between equipment of up to 2 V is allowed for by specifying that the driver source must provide a ± 5-V signal. The terminating impedance is required to be in the 3000–7000-Ω range. The drivers typically provide voltages in the range ± 6–10 V with a source impedance of a few hundred ohms. A negative polarity indicates the binary state "1," marking, or an OFF control state. The positive polarity indicates the binary state "0," spacing, or an ON control state.

The interface leads commonly used are listed in Table I together with the standard designations. The transmitting and receiving data circuits *BA* and *BB* hold the marking or spacing condition for the total nominal duration of each signal element The data-set-ready circuit *CC* turns ON to indicate that the local modem is connected to the channel and is ready to receive data or to accept a request to transmit. This circuit is OFF at all other times and is an indication that the data terminal equipment is to disregard signals on any other interface lead. The data-terminal-ready circuit *CD* is turned ON to indicate a readiness to accept data from the modem and in switched service to accept an automatically answered call. The OFF condition causes the modem to disconnect in switched service and to require manual answer of an incoming call.

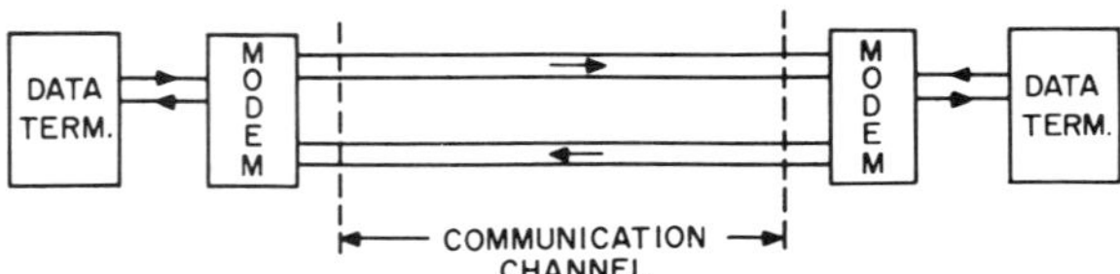

Fig. 11. Point-to-point 4-wire data circuit.

The request-to-send circuit *CA* is used to condition the local modem for transmitting data and in half-duplex operation to control the direction of transmission. The clear-to-send circuit *CB* indicates whether or not the modem is ready to transmit data. The interval between the request on *CA* and the *CB* response varies with the type of modem and is used to transmit preparatory signals to establish the communication path, including preparation of the distant modem to receive data.

The receive-line-signal-detector circuit *CF* is turned ON when the modem is receiving a signal suitable for demodulation. The OFF condition indicates that no suitable signal is being received, and the received-data circuit *BB* is held clamped in the idle marking condition. The signal-element timing circuits *DA*, *DB*, and *DD* carry equal ON and OFF timing waves for proper interpretation of the send and receive data circuits *BA* and *BB*. The ON to OFF transition of the timing wave indicates the nominal center of each signal element, and the OFF to ON indicates the nominal position for signal-element transitions.

The ring-indicator circuit *CE* turns ON to indicate the presence of a ringing signal on the communication channel. It turns OFF between rings and at all other times when ringing is not being received.

Leased Line Applications

Modem applications on leased private lines are usually 4-wire and may be either point to point or multipoint. Fig. 11 shows a point-to-point 4-wire circuit. In such a configuration both modems are usually provided with a continuous request-to-send signal resulting in continuous carrier on the line and a readiness for data flow in each direction. Although data can flow in both directions simultaneously, it is currently common practice to operate in a half-duplex mode in which data flow proceeds in one direction and is broken up into blocks of a few thousand bits including some type of error-detection encoding [17]. During the pause between blocks the receiving terminal either acknowledges receipt of valid data or requests a repeat of the block. (See the papers on "Errors and Error Control" and "Line Control Procedures" in this issue.)

Fig. 12 shows a multipoint 4-wire circuit. Since only one modem can transmit at a time on each side of the circuit, a control procedure is required. A typical method of working assigns one point as the control, and the other points transmit only on request. This configuration is used where a number of remote stations exchange data with a central processing station. In Fig. 12 station *A* is the control. It transmits continuously on the outgoing line to all the remote receivers which are bridged on the line. The remote stations transmit one at a time and only upon a polling request from the control station. An airline reservation system is a typical example of this type of configuration. The modem at the central station is required

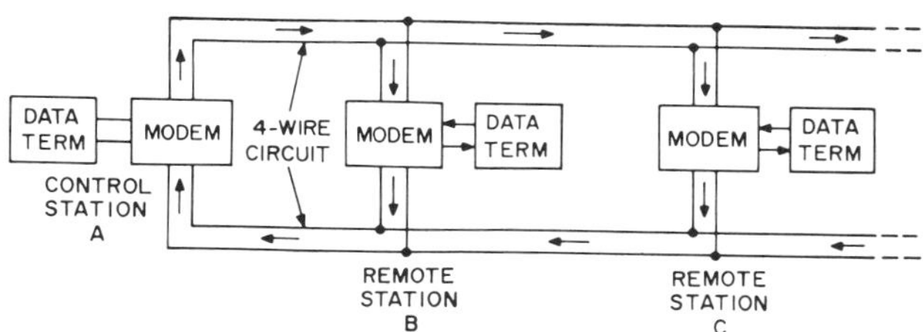

Fig. 12. Multipoint 4-wire data circuit.

to receive data from the remote stations in succession and must rapidly accommodate to each transmission. Modems designed for these multipoint polling applications typically have a request-to-send/clear-to-send interval of 10–50 ms.

Switched Telecommunications Network Applications

Where the volume of data flow between two points can be handled in a few hours per day, a full-time leased line cannot usually be justified. Use of the switched telephone network for such cases is often attractive [18]. This is particularly true where data are to be exchanged with a number of locations but in relatively low volume averaged over a month. Connections over the switched telecommunications network utilize 2-wire circuits and often include echo-suppressing arrangements which normally restrict the transmission to one direction at a time. The echo suppressors can be disabled by initially transmitting a single frequency in the 2010–2240-Hz range. The voice spectrum can then be divided between two directions of transmission by band-separation filters.

One example is the provision of two narrow-band channels, one near 1000 Hz and one near 2000 Hz, for full-duplex transmission of low-speed asynchronous data. The FSK modems used with teletypewriter terminals in TWX service are of this type, as are the "100 series" of modems which are used in many time-shared computer services. Another example is the provision of a low-speed secondary channel at the low end of the spectrum in addition to a high-speed primary channel occupying the main portion of the band. Such a secondary channel may be used for control purposes in an error detection and retransmission system. In both examples it is necessary to initiate data transmission with control signals which insure the disabling of any echo suppressors. Where the full capacity of the voice channel is required, half-duplex operation is necessary unless two separate connections are set up, one for each direction of full-duplex data flow. Half-duplex operation usually requires a clear-to-send interval of 150–200 ms to insure reversal of echo suppressors. For short connections not involving echo suppressors, the turnaround time can be shortened to only that required for echoes to subside, usually about 50 ms. Some types of modems require a period of time to establish a coherent reference and achieve symbol synchronization which exceeds the 200 ms associated with turnaround of the switched network trunks. In such case the modem becomes the limiting factor in efficient half-duplex operation. For example, a modem requiring several seconds to start up is not attractive for use in stop-and-wait-for-acknowledgment type of data transmission.

Call origination on the switched network can proceed in a manual mode as for an ordinary telephone voice call. The distant station is alerted by the usual bell signal and manually answered by voice followed by a manual switch to the data mode at each end of the circuit. Alternatively, the distant station can be provided with automatic answering capability in which detection of the 20-Hz ringing current causes the modem to go off hook and generate an answering tone to indicate to the calling end that it has answered and is about to enter the data mode. The call origination can also be automated by use of an automatic calling unit which can be directed by the originating data terminal to dial any desired number. Upon detection of the answering tone from the distant station, the local modem is switched to the data mode. (More about modern applications in typical Bell System offerings is contained in the companion paper "AT&T Facilities and Services" in this issue.)

TABLE II

Types of Modulation and Bandwidth Requirements for 4800, 7200, and 9600 bits/s

Type of Modulation	Bits/ Cycle	Basic Nyquist Band Required for 4800 bits/s	7200 bits/s	9600 bits/s
2-level VSB or QAM	2	2400		
4 ϕ PSK	2	2400		
3-level VSB or QAM	3	1600	2400	
4 ϕ+2 AM levels	3	1600	2400	
8 ϕ PSK	3	1600	2400	
4-level VSB or QAM	4		1800	2400
8 ϕ+2 AM levels	4		1800	2400
6-level VSB or QAM	5			1920
8-level VSB or QAM	6			1600

Choice of Modem Designs

For data speeds up to 2400 bits/s, the choice has become clear by past experience. Both for narrow-band FDM systems for low-speed data up to 300 bits/s and for full voice-band systems up to the 1200–1800-bit/s range, FSK is the clear choice. For 2400 bits/s, DPSK has become the worldwide standard. For the 4800–9600-bit/s range, the choice is wider and depends on the specific objective much more than at the lower speeds. The range of variation in voice-band channels accounts for this, mainly with respect to bandwidth and nonlinear distortion. The maximum symbol rate is limited by the available bandwidth, while the number of symbol states that can be used and still attain satisfactory error rates depends to a great extent on nonlinear distortion and phase jitter.

The standard high-speed rates for voice-band modems are 4800, 7200, and 9600 bits/s. Table II indicates the common forms of modulation which may be utilized to accomplish these rates with a basic Nyquist bandwidth of 1600–2400 Hz. Ordinary voice channels cannot be relied upon to have usable transmission outside the 400–3000-Hz range. This means that if a basic 2400-Hz band is to be used, there is no room for more than an 8-percent rolloff. Unless the modem is designed to operate with this sharp rolloff, it is likely not to operate over some percentage of available channels. A conservative approach to operating over almost all channels would require the basic band to be lowered to about 2000 Hz, where room for a 25-percent rolloff is available. However, since increasing the bandwidth causes much less loss in operating margin than does an increase in the number of symbol states, there is incentive to design for the larger bandwidth even if occasional channels are unusable.

Current Look at Modem Designs

As previously mentioned, modems for speeds up to 1800 bits/s uniformly use FSK and at 2400 bits/s use PSK. At 4800–9600 bits/s, current modems use PSK, VSB, quadrature amplitude modulation (QAM), or a combination of PSK and AM.

The typical modem is constructed using plastic encapsulated dual-in-line integrated circuits and digital techniques wherever practical. Carrier signals, clocking signals, and control timing are all derived by counting down from a crystal oscillator operating in the megahertz range. Analog filtering is often done by active filters utilizing integrated-circuit operational amplifiers.

Often the shaping of the transmitted signal can be done more easily and precisely by digital methods by which the desired shaping is done directly in the time domain rather than by control of the spectrum by analog filters. Where automatic equalizers are used, these are typically digital, in which the signal to be equalized is encoded and then delayed by shift registers. The tap gains are varied by digital multiplication.

Self-testing arrangements are usually provided to aid in isolating causes of faulty operation. These include means for connecting the transmitter to the receiver for a local back-to-back test, a digital loop back of the received data to the transmitter so that a complete check of the modem plus line can be made from the distant end, the incorporation of a random bit sequence to simulate typical data, and some indication of signal quality or occurrence of errors.

The majority of current modems are individually packaged in small stand-alone cabinets suitable for desk or shelf mounting. One exception to this occurs at computers having access to a number of communication channels. Here it is preferable to mount the multiple modems in a single cabinet with a common power supply. Another exception occurs where it is desirable to integrate closely the modem and the data terminal. In such a case, the modem may be packaged as one or several printed circuit boards which are inserted into the data terminal equipment and powered from it. Wide use of integrated circuits has greatly reduced the size of modems. The most sophisticated high-speed modems occupy only 1–2 ft^3 and weigh no more than 50 lb.

Some manufacturers have started to introduce large-scale integrated circuits of the MOS type into their designs. As the cost of logic and memory circuits continues to fall, it becomes feasible to implement more and more of modem circuitry digitally. This can be expected to be the future trend with the overall size and weight being drastically reduced.

References

[1] C. R. Cahn, "Combined digital phase and amplitude modulation communications systems," *IRE Trans. Commun. Syst.*, vol. CS-8, pp. 150–155, Sept. 1960.

[2] H. Nyquist, "Certain topics in telegraph transmission theory," *AIEE Trans.*, vol. 47, pp. 617–644, Apr. 1928.

[3] E. D. Sunde, "Theoretical fundamentals of pulse transmission," *Bell Syst. Tech. J.*, vol. 33, pp. 721–788, May 1954; vol. 33, pp. 987–1010, July 1954.

[4] E. R. Kretzmer, "Generalization of a technique for binary data communication," *IEEE Trans. Commun. Technol.*, vol. COM-14, pp. 67–68, Feb. 1966.

[5] A. Lender, "The duobinary technique for high speed data transmission," presented at the IEEE Winter General Meeting, 1963, Conf. Paper CP63-283.

[6] W. R. Bennett and J. R. Davey, *Data Transmission*. New York: McGraw-Hill, 1965.

[7] R. W. Lucky, J. Salz, and E. J. Weldon, Jr., *Principles of Data Communications*. New York: McGraw-Hill, 1968.

[8] W. M. Goodall, "Television by pulse code modulation," *Bell Syst. Tech. J.*, vol. 30, pp. 33–49, Jan. 1951.

[9] C. E. Shannon, "Probability of error for optimal codes in a Gaussian channel," *Bell Syst. Tech. J.*, vol. 38, pp. 611–655, 1959.

[10] A. A. Alexander, R. M. Gryb, and D. W. Nast, "Capabilities of the telephone network for data transmission," *Bell Syst. Tech. J.*, vol. 45, pp. 255–286, Feb. 1966.

[11] E. P. Duffy and T. W. Thatcher, Jr., "Analog transmission performance on the switched telecommunications network," *Bell Syst. Tech. J.*, vol. 50, pp. 1311–1347, Apr. 1971.

[12] J. E. Savage, "Some simple self-synchronizing digital data scramblers," *Bell Syst. Tech. J.*, vol. 46, pp. 449–487, Feb. 1967.

[13] H. A. Wheeler, "The interpretation of amplitude and phase distortion in terms of paired echoes," *Proc. IRE*, vol. 27, pp. 359–385, June 1939.

[14] H. E. Kallmann, "Transversal filters," *Proc. IRE*, vol. 28, pp. 302–310, July 1940.

[15] R. W. Lucky, "Techniques for adaptive equalization of digital communication," *Bell Syst. Tech. J.*, vol. 45, pp. 255–286, Feb. 1966.

[16] D. Hirsch and W. J. Wolf, "A simple adaptive equalizer for efficient data transmission," *IEE Trans. Commun. Technol.*, vol. COM-18, pp. 5–12, Feb. 1970.

[17] R. W. Hamming, "Error detecting and error correcting codes," *Bell Syst. Tech. J.*, vol. 26, pp. 147–160, Apr. 1950.

[18] M. D. Balkovic, H. W. Klancer, S. W. Klare, and W. G. McGruther, "High-speed voiceband data transmission performance on the switched telecommunications network," *Bell Syst. Tech. J.*, vol. 50, pp. 1349–1384, Apr. 1971.

Reprinted by permission from *Proceedings of the IEEE* Vol. 60, No. 11, November 1972, pp. 1284-1292

Bell Labs' new family of data sets—featuring compactness, attractive styling, and diagnostic testing features—will help the Bell System sharpen its competitive thrust into the data communications market. The new family concentrates on the major needs of users.

The New Look in Data Communications

E. R. Kretzmer

WITH THE FCC'S CARTERFONE DECISION in 1968, Bell System data communications entered a new phase. Before the decision, which opened the switched network to the interconnection of non-Bell data sets, the Bell System had provided whatever services were needed by a wide range of users. This emphasis resulted in a proliferation of diverse types of Bell data sets (or "modems"—modulator-demodulators). Now, with a great variety of data communications apparatus available for sale or lease from many outside manufacturers, Bell Laboratories and AT&T engineers are focusing new developments in areas where the greatest needs are foreseen. The result is a new family of Bell System data sets (for a basic discussion, see "Why Data Sets?" page 261).

Bell System data communications over the analog voice network started in the 1950's, when the government needed means of transmitting aircraft radar data to central locations. Commercial DATAPHONE® service began around 1960, initially concentrating on speeds ranging from about 100 bits per second to 2400 bits per second. The Bell System then developed a large family of modems and auxiliary sets that not only spanned an even wider range of speeds, but also handled many different data formats—such as digital and analog, serial and parallel, and voiceband and wideband. This family, however, began to show its age as well as its size—many of its members are selling at rates of less than a thousand per year. Thus the old family is being replaced, even as a new chapter in data communication is about to begin—the Dataphone Digital Service (DDS), a new service based primarily on the use of digital transmission facilities. For many years to come, however, the established analog voice network will still serve its share of the growing data communications market through the new family of data sets.

The new family was designed to keep pace with many changing market factors:

• There has been a great growth in the need for sets operating at 4800 bits per second—2400 bit-per-second systems are running out of capacity.

• Users can reduce their costs if they use data sets that do not require special line conditioning—extra delay and amplitude equalizers inserted to compensate for distortion. A basic voiceband data transmission (3002-type) channel should be sufficient.

• Small size is important—space is at a premium on the customer's premises and multiple arrangements of data sets in one cabinet are common.

• Diagnostic features should allow the user to do much of his own testing, either locally or remotely with the aid of an Operating Company test center.

• Users who have large volumes of data to transmit require data sets of the highest speed currently attainable over private-line voiceband channels—9600 bits per second.

• Efficient handling of short messages requires data sets with fast startup. Thus, automatic equalizers used in high-speed sets must be fast in adapting to a particular channel, and the time needed to synchronize transmitter and receiver should be small compared with message length.

• For the potentially numerous applications of digital inquiry by TOUCH-TONE® keying, a com-

The Bell System's old family of data sets had many members—some of which served only specialized applications. Other members of the family did not allow convenient multiple-set installations on a customer's premises. The new family of data sets zeros in on the major applications with fewer, more compact members.

pact Touch-Tone receiver should be available—primarily for multiple mounting near a computer.

- New, uniform, attractive styling is desirable to blend with modern computer-room environments.

The new family of data sets has the following members to meet the above requirements:

- 208A, which operates at 4800 bits per second on private lines and requires only 50 milliseconds for equalizer adaptation and synchronization.
- 208B, which is similar to the 208A, but is designed for use on the switched, or DDD (Direct Distance Dialing), network.
- 201C, which operates at 2400 bits per second over either DDD or unconditioned private lines.
- 202S, which operates asynchronously at speeds up to 1200 bits per second on the DDD network (in asynchronous operation, bits of data are sent at irregular intervals, rather than at the precisely timed intervals of synchronous operation; asynchronous operation generally results in lower hardware costs).
- 202T, which operates asynchronously at speeds up to 1800 bits per second on private lines.
- 209A, which operates at speeds up to 9600 bits per second on private lines.
- 407A, which receives and decodes Touch-Tone signals—primarily for use in DIVA (Digital-Inquiry, Voice Answerback) systems.

The first member of the new family, the 208A Data Set, celebrated its first birthday in April, 1973. The 208A—designed with painstaking attention to hold down its cost—grew out of the redesign of the 201-type data sets. The 201 sets for the past decade have provided synchronous-mode service at 2400 bits per second on private lines and 2000 bits per second on the DDD network. These sets use a four-phase signal format in which successive pairs or bits, or "dibits," are encoded as one of four possible phase shifts of the carrier signal. Thus, with a basic signaling, or "baud," rate of 1200 per second (the signal can assume 1200 different states per second), and with two bits associated with each state, the bit rate is 2400 bits per second. However, Bell Labs designers have found that by encoding three bits, or "tribits," as one of eight possible phase shifts and by pushing the baud rate from 1200 up to 1600 per second, 4800 bit-per-second performance could be achieved on basic voiceband data channels if the data set automatically equalized out most of the delay and amplitude distortion of the transmission line.

The 208A uses digital integrated logic and memory circuits to perform eight-phase processing. Analog networks perform filtering and delay functions, using the latest thin-film technology and integrated-circuit operational amplifiers. Such networks occupy much less space than their discrete-component, inductor-capacitor predecessors. And they offer far greater precision in setting cutoff frequencies and delay times, a vital requisite to good data-set performance.

Light-emitting diodes indicate the status of the 208A's vital signs. If, for example, a line disturbance or other problem causes the automatic equalizer to readjust itself to the new line conditions, or "retrain," an indicator light marked ER (equalizer retrain) indicates this to the user.

Earlier automatic equalizers required up to 10 seconds to adapt to a particular channel. For example, the older Data Set 203 has a minimum delay of approximately six seconds before it is ready to send data. This delay (from the time a sending customer indicates "request to send" to the time he obtains "clear to send") is needed by the receiver to achieve synchronization as well as equalizer adaptation; it limits the rate at which data sets can exchange data in certain applications that involve messages of short duration. In contrast, the 208A requires only 50 milliseconds for initial startup—short enough to allow the rapid exchanges of data typical of so-called multipoint polling networks. In such networks, a central computer location interrogates many outlying stations in rapid succession, asking them to transmit any messages they may be holding. Short messages then flow back and forth in rapid succession, and the centralized receiver must rapidly adapt itself to receive data from each outlying location. Longer startup delays can be tolerated with point-to-point four-wire lines, where a path is continuously available for each direction of transmission.

A typical application for the 208A is in the motor vehicle department of a large eastern state. A computer at the state capital serves offices spread around the state, where clerks can query the computer using private lines and the 208A. The high speed of the 208A—4800 bits per second—reduces the waiting time for customers at the local offices.

The second member of the new family, a close cousin of the 208A, is the 208B data set, which was designed expressly for use on the DDD network. Shipments for trial by Bell System Operating Companies began in mid-1973, to be followed by full introduction in the fall. Although this set shares most of the features in circuitry of the 208A, it provides several additional functions. First, compared with private-line transmission, the DDD network presents greater variations in end-to-end signal level, and thus the 208B's receiver section needs substantially larger dynamic range. To accommodate the control functions associated with the DDD network, the 208B also requires a more complex line interface. This interface provides such functions as automatic answer, disabling of echo suppressors (an echo suppressor makes the channel unidirectional and takes time to reverse, thus cutting the data-transfer efficiency in rapid data exchanges), line holding, disconnect, and alternate voice communication. For voice communication, there is another significant departure from past practice: now a standard six-button 500-type key telephone set is used (instead of a special handset built into the data set or a special auxiliary set). In fact, the key set is used with this and all other new DDD data sets; it can be shared among up to five data sets on five individual telephone lines.

A major challenge in designing modems for DDD use is to provide remote or local testing and fault diagnosis. Such features allow localizing faults to, say, the telephone line, the modem, or the associated computer terminal. Private lines are gener-

A closeup photo of the edge of the one of the printed wiring boards used in the 201C data set shows the convenient two-pronged plugs used to change circuit configurations and thus the service options.

42

ally four-wire and thus allow simultaneous transmission in both directions; this makes it possible to test the set by simply connecting the received signal directly to the input of the transmitter. This signal loop-around is a handy method of quickly checking both directions of a line as well as both the transmitter and receiver of a data set such as the 208A. DDD circuits, on the other hand (except for certain government networks), terminate at the customer's location as two-wire lines and so cannot be looped back. Data sets such as the 208B thus require more sophisticated tests, involving several steps in proper sequence. The 208B has such diagnostics, and also a self-test feature, which is completely internal. Depressing a button causes the transmitter section to send a digital test pattern through a simulated transmission line to the receiver section, where it is demodulated and matched against the original. Failure to match is indicated on one of the light-emitting diodes that make up the monitor lamp display.

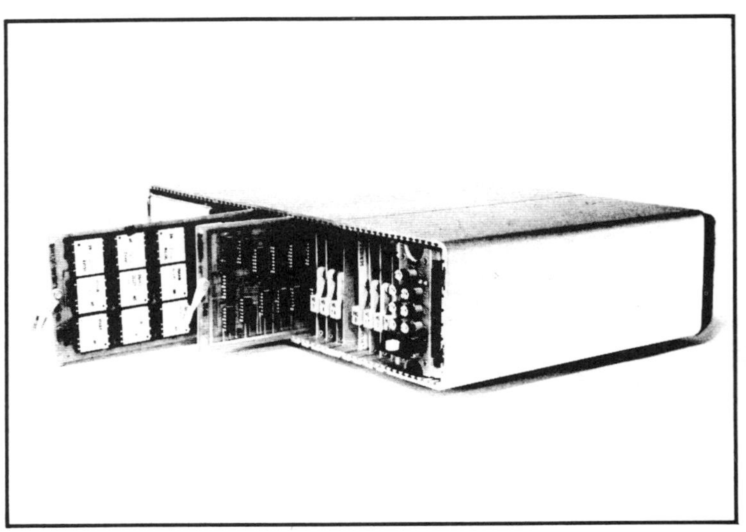

The 208A data set's modular construction allows easy maintenance. Here, two circuit packs have been pulled out of the case with the face plate removed. One pack holds several active filters (left), which are built with thin-film technology and integrated-circuit amplifiers, and the other holds digital integrated circuits. Status lamps—light-emitting diodes—are mounted at the right.

Performance of the 208B will reflect the fact that the DDD network is somewhat more subject to impulse noise, such as switching transients, than are private lines. However, error control procedures (see "Controlling Errors in Data Transmission" on page 265) now in common use will help the 208B to perform well within the requirements for highly efficient operation of present-day computer-communication systems. The initial startup is, of course, subject to whatever delays are involved in setting up the switched connection. However, once the connection is established, the set has the same 50-millisecond training time as the 208A. And the 208B's built-in means for disabling echo suppressors permits 50-millisecond "turnaround"—a valuable feature for two-wire (half-duplex) service.

A typical application for the 208B is in an automobile manufacturer's headquarters. Every day, a computer in Detroit calls each of the 21 sales offices across the country using an Automatic Calling Unit (ACU) and WATS (Wide Area Telephone Service) lines. After making the connection, the ACU puts the 208B on the line, and ordering information is automatically transmitted to Detroit. The information is loaded onto disk memory, the computer processes it, and then, using another 208B link, auto assembly plants are given instructions for filling the orders. The 208B, operating at 4800 bits per second, reduces the time for a typical call from 21 minutes using the older 201A (which operates at 2000 bits per second) to about nine minutes.

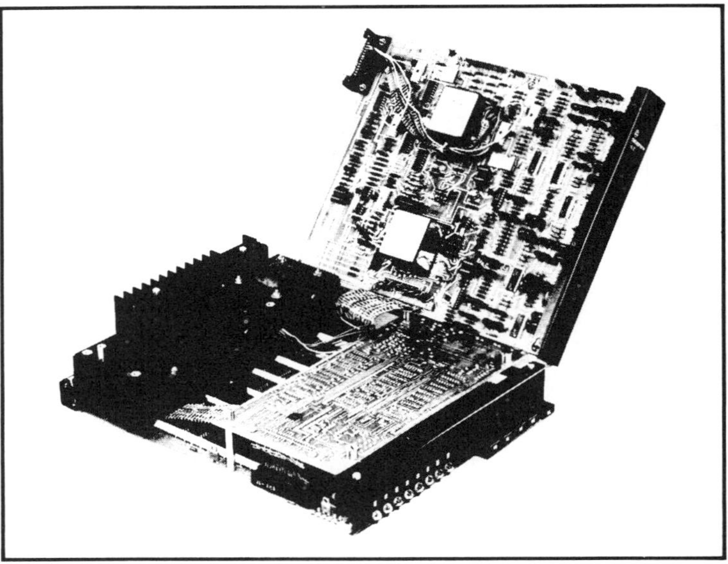

The 201C data set is constructed as a sandwich of two large printed wiring boards. Visible on the unit's face (right) are the light-emitting-diode status lamps and the pushbutton controls. For multiple-set mounting, the set is uncased, as shown. For individual use, the set is placed in its housing, which has a smoked-glass face plate, through which the status lamps are visible. The white strips running across the bottom board distribute power and ground to the components, offering very low impedance as well as simplifying wiring layout on the board.

The 201C, which made its debut in the spring of

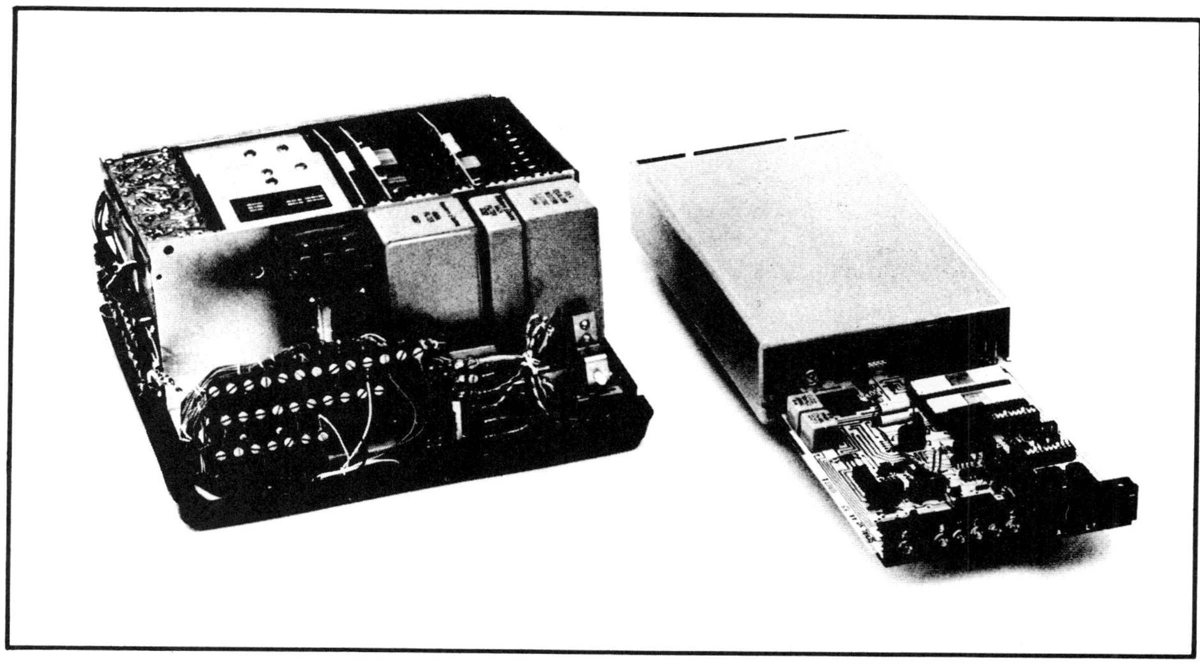

43

The new 202T data set, right, is much simpler and smaller than the older 202D, which it replaces. For example, the 202D uses large filters (the tall cans at the right front) and a wire-spring relay (next to the filters). The 202T has a single printed wiring board and uses integrated circuits. The two rectangular white packages are large-scale integrated circuits. In front of these circuits is a set of small rocker switches, which are used by the installer to set up the customer's service options.

1973, is intended to replace both the 201A and B, long the workhorses of the data communication industry. It operates at 2400 bits per second over either DDD or unconditioned private-line facilities. At 2400 bits per second, it needs no automatic equalization and thus features a startup time of only seven milliseconds (on private lines). Because of the many 201B-type modems presently in the field—both Bell and non-Bell—the same four-phase signal format was chosen for the 201C. All the same digital processing techniques, diagnostic functions, and indicator lights described for the 208A and 208B modems are also incorporated. In addition, the set was designed for easy mounting in multiple arrangements of, say, 24 in one cabinet. A typical application for the 201C is in a large utility company, where it helps answer customer inquiries on billing, similar to the motor vehicle application of the 208A.

Still other workhorses are the lower-speed, lower-cost sets in the 202 series, which use frequency modulation. They operate asynchronously at speeds up to 1200 bits per second on DDD and, with appropriate line conditioning, up to 1800 bits per second on private lines. As this series evolved, a considerable number of design variations sprang up both within and outside the Bell System. Now, almost all the diverse designs have been combined in a single miniaturized housing. There will be two new versions—the 202S for DDD and the 202T for private lines—and both largely share the same circuitry.

In spite of their small size, the 202S and 202T incorporate essentially the same line-control, diagnostic, and light-display features as their larger "cousins." The combination of small size and many features was accomplished with large-scale integrated circuitry.

Since large-scale integration technology is primarily applicable to digital functions, the designers had to convert the analog-type circuitry commonly used for frequency modulation and demodulation to digital-type circuitry. Even though the new circuits require 1500 logic gates using 3100 devices, the result is a more compact unit with fewer internal interconnections. Furthermore, functions such as generating and comparing digital test patterns can be included at little additional cost.

To round out the family of voiceband data sets in what has traditionally been called the 200 series, there is what might be called a maximum-capability design—one that gives the greatest possible speed currently achievable on a voiceband private-line channel. The older 203A data set, introduced in the late 1960's, was intended to approach such speeds and is today serving in substantial numbers. It is modular in concept, offering numerous options, with principal speeds of 4800, 7200, 9600 and 10,800 bits per second. It must be noted, though, that the 203A's 9600 and 10,800 bit-per-second options do not generally provide the same insensitivity to line disturbances as the lower-speed options. However, there is now improved knowledge of the transmission problems and of effective high-speed signaling formats.

To meet the growing need for 9600 bit-per-second operation, the 209A, which looks like a somewhat larger 208A-type, is scheduled to appear in the spring of 1974. One of its added features will be a built-in multiplexing capability, so the set can simultaneously transmit two independent 4800 bit-per-second streams or four 2400 bit-per-second streams—all on a single private line. With the help of a "dial backup" arrangement, it will also be able to provide 4800 bit-per-second DDD operation. One potential application of the 209A is for transmitting the extremely large volumes of inventory-control information and similar data between a corporate computation center and widely separated subsidiary locations.

The new data set family includes one member which might at first seem somewhat out of place. It is the 407A, intended for receiving and decoding the ever-increasing number of Touch-Tone signals used in digital-inquiry, voice-answerback systems. The 407A replaces the higher-cost 403D, in a housing one-eighth the size. Conventional analog tone-filtering circuitry has been replaced by integrated circuits. It is easy to imagine that applications of this type receiver will increase with the growing number of Touch-Tone telephones and also with the rapid decline in the cost of automatic voice-answer units. The 407A can be used, for example, for credit checking—a clerk in a store could gain access to computer records with a Touch-Tone phone, before completing a transaction. The central computer could give a voice signal or other indication of the customer's credit.

Bell Laboratories involvement has not ended with the design of the new family of data sets. To assure the 208A's success in the field, a team of Bell Labs engineers supported AT&T and local Operating Company personnel in solving installation problems while simultaneously getting valuable feedback from the field. The same quick-response field support is being provided for other members of the new family.

We are complementing these practical developments with continued work on the theory of data transmission. We are still learning things about various high-speed signal formats—particularly their capabilities of approaching the upper bound, known as the channel capacity, defined by C. E. Shannon a quarter-century ago. This improved understanding and innovation should continue to help us achieve still better utilization of the widespread analog network.

Controlling Errors in Data Transmission

Error control, despite some clever inventions in the last decade, is in fact handled by the computer industry almost uniformly in a most simple, pragmatic way. The data stream is subdivided into blocks and the blocks are augmented with enough redundant bits to afford reliable error detection. Whether it finds an error or not, the receiving terminal automatically stops after every block and briefly becomes the transmitter, sending back a message either to acknowledge receipt or to ask for a repeat of the block ("ACK" or "NACK"). Regardless of whether the line is four-wire or two-wire, transmission is thus always half-duplex—only in one direction at a time.

Such a detection-retransmission scheme clearly obviates the need for a reverse channel—a low-speed link operating simultaneously with, but in the direction opposite to, the main channel. The reverse channel was originally intended (for example, in the older 202 series sets) as a fail-safe channel by which senders of data could be assured that the receiving end was satisfied with the message. In fact, later data sets such as the 203 incorporated full-fledged 150 bit-per-second modems for simultaneous use in either the forward or reverse direction on the DDD network. In the mid-'60's, designers envisioned that high-speed transmission could be taking place in one direction (for example, to a cathode-ray tube display) while a teletypewriter message was being printed simultaneously in the other direction. Or, high-speed transmission could be proceeding in one direction while the lower-speed reverse channel was conveying information about the accuracy of the received data, and telling the transmitting terminal to stop and repeat one or more blocks of data when errors were detected. However, such uses of reverse channels have turned out to be far fewer than envisioned and half-duplex operation is the more common mode.

But the simplicity of half-duplex operation comes at the cost of efficiency—the data transmission is continually interrupted. The efficiency will especially decline in cases of long propagation delays—for example, with earth-satellite channels. In such cases, it may, in the future, be preferable to transmit data continuously, interrupting and retransmitting only when an error has actually been detected.

Forward-acting error correction with sophisticated codes (which have been perfected in recent years) would be practiced only if reverse communication is not feasible. But forward-acting error correction cannot give as much protection as detection-retransmission, especially during extreme channel disturbances. Thus, although forward-acting error control has been seriously considered for inclusion, it has never found significant usage in data communications over the telephone network.

Why Data Sets?

Digital data, as it is manipulated by a computer, is represented by pulses, or square waves. However, such waveforms cannot be applied directly to the telephone network because their frequency spectrum would not be faithfully preserved. The pulse signal must first be converted to a modulated-wave format which has no d-c component and fits well into the voice transmission band; the new format must also be rugged enough to survive transmission impairments, such as frequency shift, while still permitting accurate recovery of the original "baseband" signal. This signal conversion and reconversion is the job of the data set or, as it is sometimes called, the modem (modulator-demodulator).

Digital data has been represented on telephone lines by waves that are amplitude modulated, frequency modulated, or phase modulated. Many modern data sets use phase modulation because it is relatively insensitive to transmission impairments. A common modulation scheme for medium-speed data sets is four-phase modulation (see *Four-Phase Data Transmission*, RECORD, *May 1965*), in which the internally generated carrier signal (with a frequency of about 1800 kilohertz) can be shifted in phase by four increments: 45°, 135°, 225°, and 315° (the shift in phase—not the absolute phase of the signal—carries the digital information). With four possible phase increments, the set can encode two bits—01, 00, 10, and 11, each pair of bits corresponding to a particular phase shift. If eight phase shifts were used, then three bits could be represented and the bit rate could be doubled—see polar-coordinate signal displays at right.

The major problem in transmitting phase-encoded information over a telephone line at speeds greater than about 2400 bits per second is that the line has delay distortion—the signals tend to "smear" out in time and overlap each other, producing errors. Private lines can be conditioned to compensate for such effects, but DDD lines are not normally given such treatment. Automatic equalizers, first demonstrated at Bell Labs in 1965 and introduced in commercial data sets in 1968, automatically adjust themselves to compensate for the delay distortion, even tracking possible line changes. These early versions, however, required about 10 seconds to fully adjust the circuit (the "training period"). Newer equalizers are much faster; those used for 4800 bit-per-second service require less than 50 milliseconds for "training" and thus permit fast turnaround.

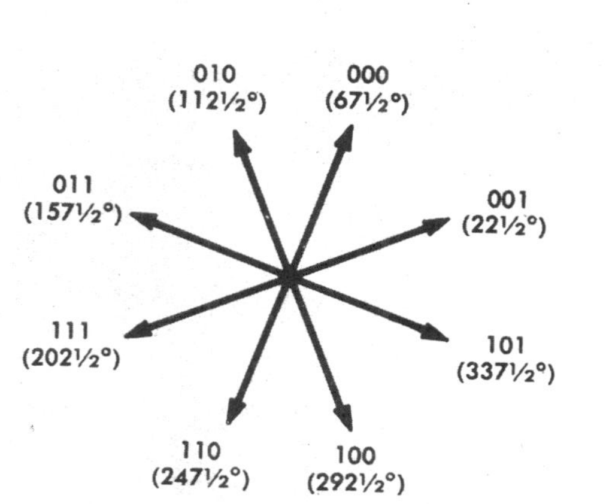

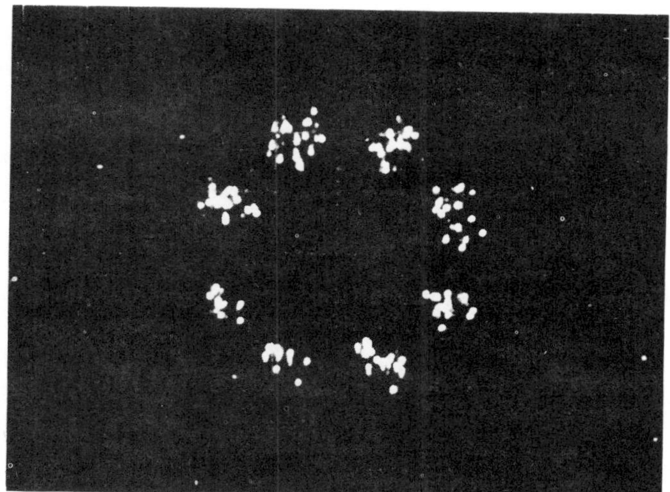

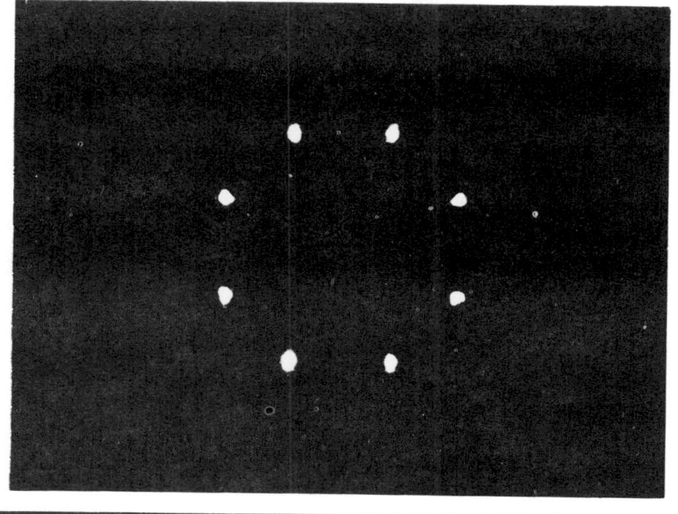

In eight-phase modulation, each phase shift represents three bits. For example, to transmit the three-bit combination 000, the data set shifts the phase of the signal 67½° from whatever the previous phase was. If the next three-bit combination also happens to be 000, the carrier would again be shifted by 67½°. The upper oscilloscope photo shows how noise and distortion create a scattered pattern of the tips of the phase vectors, while the lower photo shows how the pattern might appear after being "cleaned up" by the equalizers in the receiving data set.

Statistical Multiplexing

Multiplexing is commonly used to share and to efficiently utilize a communication channel. Currently, data multiplexing has taken two forms: frequency division multiplexing (FDM) and synchronous time division multiplexing (STDM), commonly known as time division multiplexing. Frequency division multiplexing divides the channel bandwidth into several subchannels such that the bandwidth of each subchannel is greater than that required for a message channel. Because of the need to employ guard bands to prevent data signals from each of the data channels from feeding into adjacent channels, and because of the relatively poor data transmission characteristics of the voiceband channel near the edges of its bandwidth, FDM does not make as efficient use of the voiceband as does STDM.

In STDM, each user (terminal) is assigned a fixed time duration or time slot on the communication channel for the transmission of messages from terminals to computer. The multiplexing apparatus scans the set of users in a round-robin fashion. After one user's time duration has lapsed, the channel is switched to another user. The STDM technique, however, also has certain disadvantages. It is inefficient in channel utilization to permanently assign a segment of bandwidth that it utilized only a portion of the time. Computer traffic statistics (Ch. 1) reveal that during a call (connect to disconnect), the user-to-computer traffic in the long holding time case is active only 5 percent of the time. Thus STDM would be very inefficient for channel utilization in such an environment since it allocates a time slot to each user independent of his activity. In order to increase channel utilization, statistical multiplexing or asynchronous time division multiplexing (ATDM) could be used for computer communications. The basic idea is to switch from one user to another user whenever the former is idle and the latter is ready to transmit data. Thus the data is asynchronously or statistically multiplexed with respect to the users. With such an arrangement, each user would be granted access to the channel only when he has a message to transmit. This chapter deals mainly with this new multiplexing technique.

The first paper in this chapter (p. 48) studies the feasibility of such a multiplexing technique. The second paper (p. 58) reports the buffer behavior for mixed input traffic. The third paper (p. 64) describes the simulation result of the demultiplexor buffer behavior, and the last paper (p. 71) develops an implementation of a dynamic buffer management for computer communications which provides an efficient method for managing a shared buffer.

put statistics, interested readers should refer to [CHU 69], [CHU 70], [PAC 72], and [RUD 72]. For general reading on multiplexing and concentration, see [DOL 72]. For an implementation example on statistical multiplexing, interested readers should refer to the paper by Schwartz et. al. in Chapter VIII of this book and [TEN 74].

Reprinted from –
AFIPS – Conference Proceedings, Volume 35

48

A study of asynchronous time division multiplexing for time-sharing computer systems

by W. W. CHU*

Bell Telephone Laboratories, Incorporated
Holmdel, New Jersey

INTRODUCTION

In order to reduce the communications costs in time-sharing systems and multicomputer communication systems, multiplexing techniques have been introduced to increase channel utilization. A commonly used technique is Synchronous Time Division Multiplexing (STDM). In Synchronous Time Division Multiplexing, for example, consider the transmission of messages from terminals to computer, each terminal is assigned a fixed time duration. After one user's time duration has elapsed, the channel is switched to another user. With synchronous operation, buffering is limited to one character per user line, and addressing is usually not required. The STDM technique, however, has certain disadvantages. As shown in Figure 1, it is inefficient in capacity and cost to permanently assign a segment of bandwidth that is utilized only for a portion of the time. A more flexible system that efficiently uses the transmission facility on an "instantaneous time-shared" basis could be used instead. The objective would be to switch from one user to another user whenever the one user is idle, and to asynchronously time multiplex the data. With such an arrangement, each user would be granted access to the channel only when he has a message to transmit. This is known as an Asynchronous Time Division Multiplexing System (ATDM). A segment of a typical ATDM data stream is shown in Figure 2. The crucial attributes of such a multiplexing technique are:

1. An address is required for each transmitted message, and
2. Buffering is required to handle the random message arrivals.**

If the buffer is empty during a transmission interval, the channel will be idle for this interval.

An operating example of an ATDM system for analog speech is the "Time Assignment Speech Interpolation" (TASI) system used by the Bell System on the Atlantic Ocean Cable.[1] Using TASI, the effective transmission capacity has been doubled and the system operates with a negligible (with respect to voice transmission) overflow probability of about 0.5 percent, even without buffering.

The feasibility of the ATDM system depends on: (1) An acceptably low overflow probability—of the same or lower order of magnitude as the line error rate—that can be achieved by a reasonable buffer size, and (2) an acceptable expected message queuing delay due to buffering. To estimate these parameters, analyses of the statistical behavior of the buffer are presented below. The user-to-computer traffic is in

* Present address: Computer Science Dept., UCLA, Los Angeles California, 90024.

** There may be other reasons for providing buffering such as: tolerating momentary loss of signals (e.g., fading), momentary interruptions of data flow, permitting error control on the line, etc. Under these conditions, the buffer should be designed to satisfy also the above specific requirements.

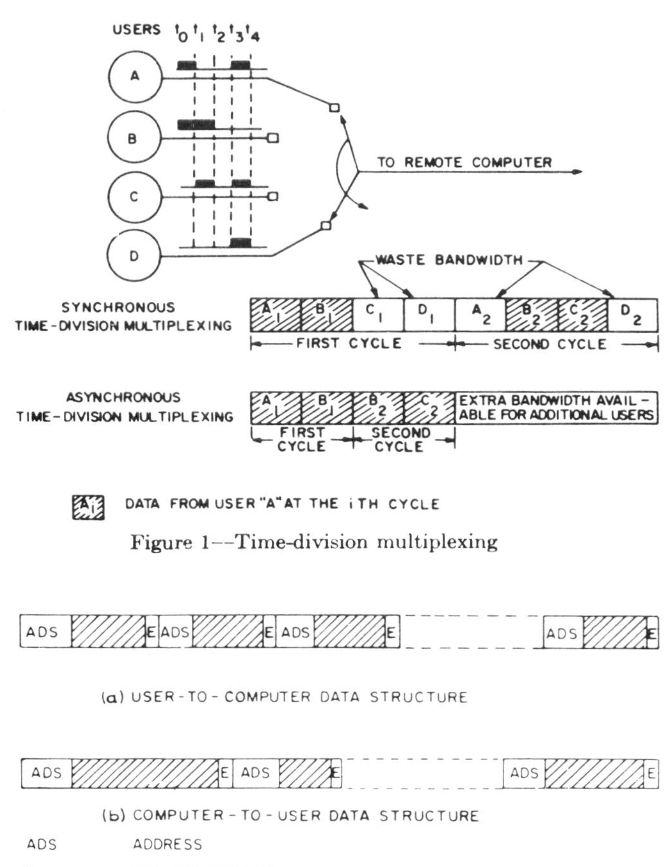

Figure 1—Time-division multiplexing

Figure 2—Asynchronous time division multiplexing data stream

units characters, while the computer-to-user traffic is in units strings of characters which we shall call bursts. The length of the bursts are different from one to another and are treated as random variables. Because of the asymmetrical nature of the traffic characteristics, the statistical behavior of the buffer in the user-to-computer multiplexer and the computer-to-user multiplexer are quite different and, therefore, are treated separately. An example is given to illustrate the multiplexer design in a time-shared computer-communications system that employs ATDM technique.

Analysis of buffer behavior

User-to-computer buffer

An ATDM system consists of a buffer, encoding/decoding circuit, and a switching circuit (in the case of multiple multiplexed lines) as shown in Figure 3. For the analysis of the statistical behavior of user-to-computer buffer, the character (fixed length) arrivals

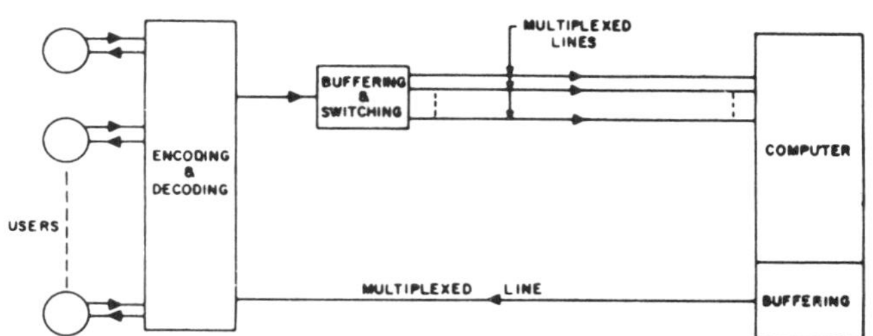

Figure 3—Asynchronous time division multiplexing system for time-sharing computer communications

from the sources to the buffer are assumed to be generated from a renewal counting process; that is, the character interarrival times are independent and identically distributed. Since the line transmits with constant speed, the time it takes to transmit each fixed length character (service time), $1/\mu$, is assumed to be constant. For reliability and simplicity in data transmission, synchronous transmission is assumed. The data are taken out synchronously from the buffer for transmission at each discrete clock time. The data arriving at the buffer during the periods between clock times have to wait to begin transmission at the beginning of the next clock time, even if the transmission facility is idle at the time of arrival. In queuing theory terminology, the above system implies there is a gate between the server and waiting room which is opened at fixed intervals. Thus we shall analyze the queuing model† with finite buffer size (waiting line) and synchronous multiple transmission channels (servers). Powell and Avi-Itzhak[2] analyzed a similar queuing model with an unlimited waiting line. Birdsall,[3] and later Dor[4] analyzed a queuing model with limited waiting room but with a single server. In here, the model is generalized to accommodate multiple servers with limited waiting room.

To establish the set of state equations for analysis of a buffer with a size of N characters and c servers, we assume that the system has reached its equilibrium. Let p_n be the probability that there are exactly n characters in the system (in the buffer and in service) at the end of a service time, and a_c be the probability

† The results derived from this study can also be used as a conservative estimate (upper bound) for the case in which the lines are permitted to transmit the characters arrived during the service interval. The estimate yields better approximation for the heavy than light traffic intensity case. Because under heavy traffic case, the lines are usually all busy and the characters that arrive during the service interval have to wait and cannot be serviced during the service interval. The maximum over design in a buffer system with c transmission lines that permits to transmit the characters arrived during service interval is c characters.

there are no more than c characters in the system at that time, i.e.,

$$a_c = \sum_{i=0}^{c} p_i \tag{1}$$

Without loss of generality, we can let the service interval equal to unity. We shall express the probability of number of characters present in the buffer at
50 the end of the unit service time interval (left side of equation (2)) in terms of the probability of the number present in the system at the beginning of the interval (right side of equation (2)), multiplied by the probability of a given number of characters arriving during the service interval. As this can occur in different combinations, we add the probabilities. With synchronous transmission, all characters in service would finish their service and leave this system at the end of a service interval.

Thus in a unit service interval of time, we have

$$\left.\begin{aligned}
p_0 &= a_c\pi_0 \\
p_1 &= a_c\pi_1 + p_{c+1}\pi_0 \\
p_2 &= a_c\pi_2 + p_{c+1}\pi_1 + p_{c+2}\pi_0 \\
&\;\;\vdots \\
p_n &= a_c\pi_n + p_{c+1}\pi_{n-1} + \cdots + p_{c+n-1}\pi_1 \\
&\qquad + p_{c+n}\pi_0, \text{ for } n \le N - c \\
&\;\;\vdots \\
p_n &= a_c\pi_n + p_{c+1}\pi_{n-1} + \cdots \\
&\qquad + p_{N-1}\pi_{n+1-(N-c)} + p_N\pi_{n-(N-c)} \\
&\qquad \text{for } N - 1 \ge n > N - c \\
\sum_{i=0}^{N} p_i &= 1
\end{aligned}\right\} \tag{2}$$

Due to limited buffer size,

$$p_{i>N} = 0 \tag{3}$$

Where

π_n = probability of n characters originating from a renewal counting process during a service interval

N = buffer length in characters

c = number of transmission lines

The first equation describes the case in which the buffer is vacant, if no more than c characters are in transmission at the beginning of the interval, and no arrivals occur during the interval. The second equation describes the case in which one character is in the buffer if no more than c characters are in transmission at the beginning and one arrives during the service time interval; or there are c + 1 in the buffer at the beginning and no character arrives during the service interval, etc. In the numerical computation carried out in this paper, we assume the character arrivals are generated from a Poisson process; that is, $\pi_n = \exp(-\lambda_u)\lambda_u^n/n!$, where λ_u is the average character arrival rate to the user-to-computer buffer (offered load) from the m independent users. Since the buffer has a finite size of N, $p_{i>N} = 0$. Thus, when a character arrives and finds the buffer is full, an overflow will result. Therefore, the average character departure rate from the user-to-computer buffer (carried load), α_u is less than the offered load from the users λ_u. The carried load can be computed from the buffer busy period

$$\alpha_u = \sum_{i=0}^{c-1} i \cdot p_i + c \sum_{i=c}^{N} p_i \tag{4}$$

The overflow probability of the user-to-computer buffer, the expected fraction of total number of characters rejected by the buffer, is then equal to

$$P_{of} = \frac{\text{offered load—carried load}}{\text{offered load}} = 1 - \alpha_u/\lambda_u \tag{5}$$

The traffic intensity from user-to-computer, ρ_u, measures the degree of congestion and indicates the impact of a traffic stream upon the service streams. It is defined as

$$\rho_u = \lambda_u/c\mu \tag{6}$$

Channel (server) utilization, η, measures the fraction of time that the lines are busy. It can be expressed as

$$\eta = (1 - P_{of})\lambda_u/c\mu = \alpha_u/c\mu \le \rho_u \tag{7}$$

Since physically it is impossible for the transmission lines to be more than 100 percent busy, the utilization is limited to a numerical value less than unity. In the no-loss case (unlimited buffer size), $P_{of} = 0$, then $\eta \equiv \rho$.

The time average queuing length in the user-to-computer buffer, L_u, is equal to

$$L_u = \sum_{i=c}^{N} (i - c)p_i + \lambda_u/2 \text{ characters} \quad \text{for } N > c. \quad (8)$$

The first term in Equation (8) is the expected number of characters in the system at the beginning of a service interval. Since the characters could not leave the system during the service interval, we add the time average number of character arrival (for Poisson arrivals) during the service interval which is $\lambda_u/2$. The expected (time average) queuing delay of each character at the user-to-computer buffer due to buffering, D_u, can be evaluated by using Little's[5] result. We have

$$D_u = L_u/(\lambda_u(1 - P_{of})) \text{ service times} \quad (9)$$

For the single server case, that is, $c = 1$, the set of state equations (2) becomes an imbedded Markov Chain, and can be solved iteratively to obtain the state probabilities as shown in References 3 and 4. For the multiple server case, however, the multiple dependence on the various states prevents us from using the iterative techniques for solution. Thus, the set of state probabilities, p_i's, must be solved from the set of linear matrix equations (2). The overflow probability, queuing delay, and queue length are then computed from the p_i's via Equations 4, 5, 8 and 9.

The size of the matrix (Equation 2) corresponds to the buffer length. The matrix equation was solved by the Gauss elimination method.[6] For purposes of accuracy, double precision was used in all phases of the computation. From the character arrival rate, λ_u, the coefficient values can be computed from (2) and they are stored in the computer program. Due to the limitation of the computer word size, double precision on IBM 360/65 provides 15-digit accuracy. Therefore, when the coefficient value is less than 10^{-15}, it is set equal to zero. The computation time required to solve this type of system equation is largely dependent on its size. For a 10×10 matrix the computation time is about 0.8 seconds, while a 50×50 matrix equation takes about 1.67 minutes.

Numerical results are presented in Figures 4, 5 and 6. These results reveal the relationships among the overflow probabilities, number of transmission lines used, traffic intensities, and buffer sizes.

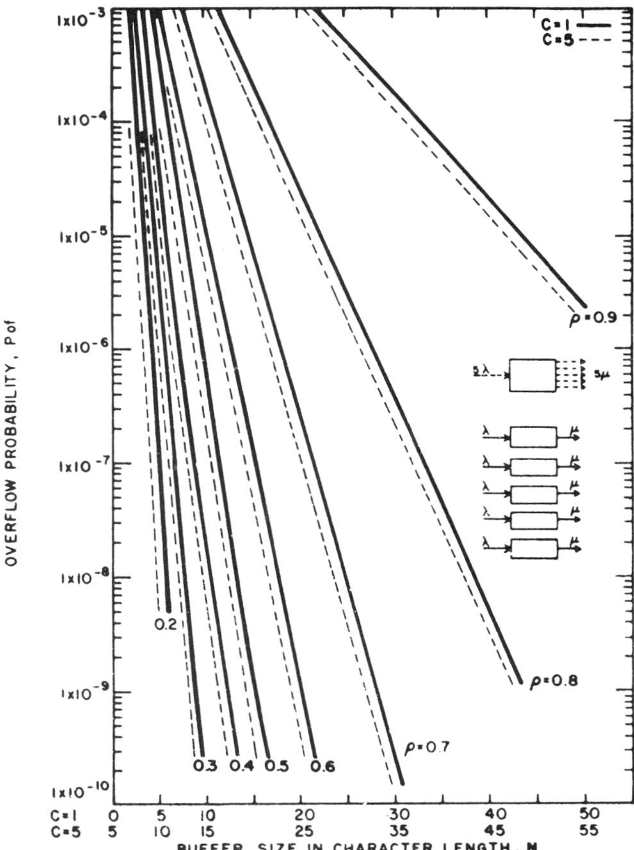

Figure 4—Overflow probability vs buffer size

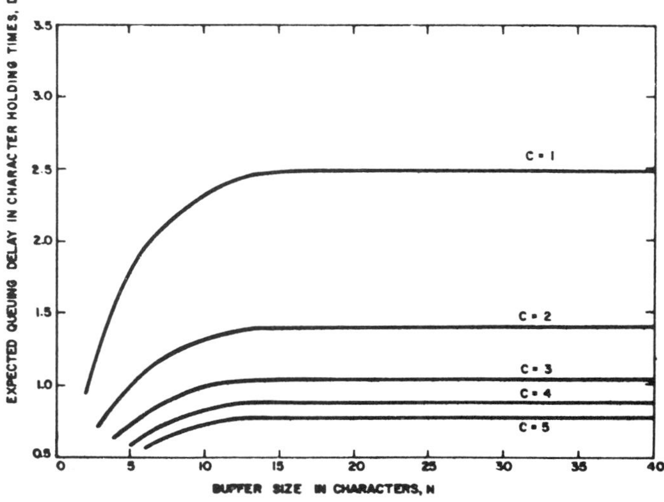

Figure 5—Expected queuing delay vs buffer size

Computer-to-user buffer

In a previous section, the buffer behavior has been analyzed for a finite queue with multiple server, Poisson arrivals, and constant service time, which corresponds to the users-to-computer traffic. The

$$f_L(\ell) = \theta(1 - \theta)^{\ell - 1} \qquad \ell = 1, 2, \cdots \tag{10}$$

$$f_N(n) = \exp(-\lambda_c)\lambda_c^n/n! \qquad n = 0, 1, 2, \cdots \tag{11}$$

52

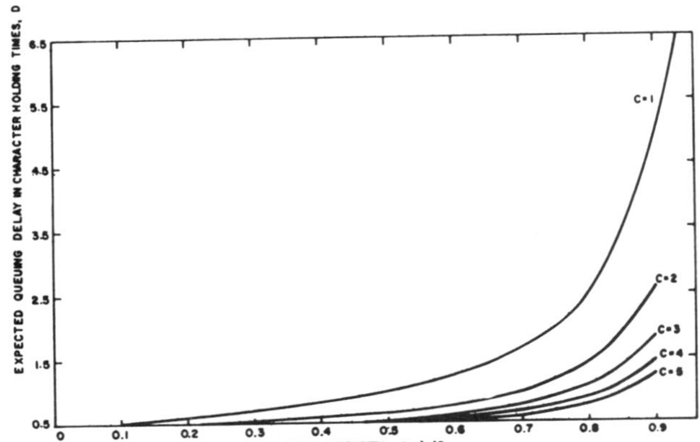

Figure 6—Expected queuing delay vs traffic intensity

computer-to-user traffic, however, is quite different from the users-to-computer traffic. The central processor of a time-sharing computer sequentially performs fractions of each user's job and the output traffic to the users are strings of characters which we shall call bursts. The length of the bursts are different from one to another and are treated as random variables. It is assumed that the internal processing speed of the computer is very fast as compared to the line transmission speed. Further, it is assumed that the various processing tasks generated by the user-computer interactions are independent from one user to another and have exponential interarrival times for a given user. In ATDM operation with these assumptions, the arrivals of bursts at the common output transmission buffer for the group of users are approximated as random. In this section, we shall analyze this buffer behavior under the assumptions of a finite queue, single server with batch (burst) arrivals, and constant service time.

Using the burst length and traffic intensity as parameters, we would like to find the relationships among the overflow probabilities, expected burst delays due to buffering, and buffer sizes.

Let us consider the case that the burst length, L is geometrically distributed with mean, $\bar{\ell} = 1/\theta$; and the number of bursts arrived during a unit service interval (time to transmit a character from the multiplexed line), N, is Poisson distributed with mean, λ_c bursts/service time. The distributions of L and N are as follows:

The total number of characters that arrived during the time to transmit a character on the multiplexed line is a random sum, S_N, and is equal to

$$S_N = \sum_{i=0}^{N} L_i \tag{12}$$

where L_i, a random variable distributed as (10), is the number of characters contained in the ith arriving burst. N, a random variable distributed as (11), is the total number of bursts arriving during the unit service interval. For simplicity in notation, we let $S = S_N$

The characteristic function of S, $\phi_S(u)$, can be expressed in terms of the characteristic function of L, $\phi_\ell(u)$, and λ_c.

$$\phi_S(u) = \exp[-\lambda_c + \lambda_c\phi_L(u)] \tag{13}$$

Since the burst lengths are geometrically distributed the characteristic function of L is

$$\phi_L(u) = \theta\cdot\exp(iu)/\Big(1 - (1 - \theta)\exp(iu)\Big) \tag{14}$$

where $i = \sqrt{-1}$. Substituting (14) into (13), then

$$\phi_S(u) = \exp[-\lambda_c + \lambda_c\cdot\theta\cdot\exp(iu)/ (1 - (1 - \theta)\exp(iu))] \tag{15}$$

From (15), it can be shown that the probability density of j characters arriving during a unit service interval, $f(S = j) = f_j$, is a compound Poisson distribution as shown in (16)

$$f_j = f(S = j) = \begin{cases} \sum_{k=1}^{j} \binom{j-1}{k-1} (\lambda_c\theta)^k (1-\theta)^{j-k}\exp(-\lambda_c)/k! & j = 1, 2, \cdots \\ \exp(-\lambda_c) & j = 0 \end{cases} \tag{16}$$

The expected value of S is given by $E[S] = E[L]E[N] = \lambda/\theta$, and the variance of S is given by

$$\mathrm{Var}[S] = \lambda(2 - \theta)/\theta^2 \tag{17}$$

The time required to compute the probability density function of S, f_j, from (16) is dependent on the size of j. For large j (e.g., j > 1000), the computation time could be very large and prohibitive. A convenient and less time consuming way to compute f_j is from $\phi_S(u)$ by using the Fast Fourier Transform[7] inversion method as follows:

$$f_j = \sum_{r=1}^{M} \phi_S(r)\exp[-2\pi irj/M]$$

$$j = 0, 1, 2, \cdots, M - 1 \qquad (18)$$

where

$r = 2\pi u/M$

M = total number of input points to represent $\phi_S(r)$ = total number of output values of f_j.

In order to accurately determine $\phi_S(r)$, it is computed with double precision on the IBM 360/65. Further, we would like to use as many points as possible to represent $\phi_S(r)$; that is, we would like to make M as large as possible. Because of the word length limitation of the computer, double precision provides 15–digit accuracy. Therefore, when $f_j < 10^{-15}$, it is set equal to zero. M is selected such that $f_{j \geq M} < 10^{-15}$. The M's are different for different values of λ_c and $\bar{l}$.

The following is the set of state equations for a buffer size of N characters with batch renewal arrivals, single server, and constant output rate.

$$p_n = \pi_0 p_{n+1} + \sum_{i=1}^{n} \pi_{n-i+1} p_i + \pi_n p_0$$

or

$$p_{n+1} = \frac{1}{\pi_0}\left[p_n - \sum_{i=1}^{n} \pi_{n-i+1} p_i - \pi_n p_0\right] \qquad (19)$$

$$n = 0, 1, 2, \cdots, N - 1$$

$$\sum_{i=0}^{N} p_i = 1 \qquad (20)$$

and

$$p_{i>N} = 0 \qquad (21)$$

The above equations are reduced from Equation (2) by letting c = 1.

The average character departure rate from the buffer (carried load), α_c, is less than the average character arrival rate to the buffer (offered load), $\beta = \lambda_c/\theta$, from the computer. The carried load can be computed from the probability that the buffer is idle,

$$\alpha_c = 1 - p_0 \qquad (22)$$

The overflow probability of the buffer with burst input, the expected fraction of total number of characters rejected by the buffer, is equal to 53

$$P'_{of} = \frac{\text{offered load-carried load}}{\text{offered load}} = 1 - \alpha_c/\beta \qquad (23)$$

The traffic intensity from computer-to-user is

$$\rho_c = \beta/\mu = \lambda_c/(\theta\mu) = \lambda_c\bar{l}/\mu \qquad (24)$$

The set of state Equations (19) is an imbedded Markov Chain. In the following numerical computations, we shall assume that the character arrivals are generated from a compound Poisson process, i.e., $\pi_i = f_i$. The state probabilities can be solved iteratively and expressed in terms of p_o. From (20), we can find the value of p_o. Thus we find all the state probabilities. The overflow probabilities for various burst lengths can then be computed from (23). These results are presented in Figure 7 which provides the relationships (at $P'_{of} = 10^{-6}$) between burst lengths and buffer sizes for selected traffic intensities.

In the above analysis, we have treated each character as a unit. However, in computing the expected burst delay, D_c, due to buffering, we should treat each burst as a unit. The service time is now the time required to transmit the entire burst. For a line with

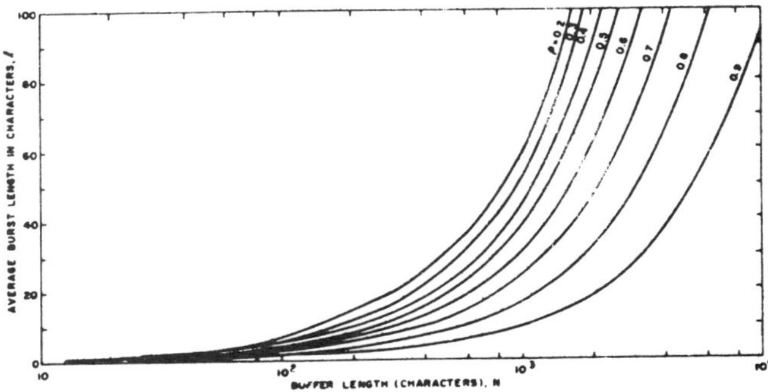

Figure 7—Buffer length vs average burst length, $P'_{of} = 10^{-6}$

constant transmission rate, the service time distribution is the same as the burst length distribution except by a constant transmission rate factor. When overflow probability is very small, for example, $P'_{of} = 10^{-6}$, then D_c can be approximated by the expected burst delay of the infinite waiting room with Poisson Arrivals and single server with geometric service time, M/G/1, model.[8,9] Hence

54

$$D_c = \frac{\lambda E(L^2)}{2(1 - \rho)} = \frac{\lambda_c(2 - \theta)}{2(\theta - \lambda_c)} \quad \text{character-holding times} \quad (25)$$

where $E(L^2)$ = second moment of burst length, L. The delays are computed from (25) for selected traffic intensities and burst lengths. Their results are portrayed in Figure 8.

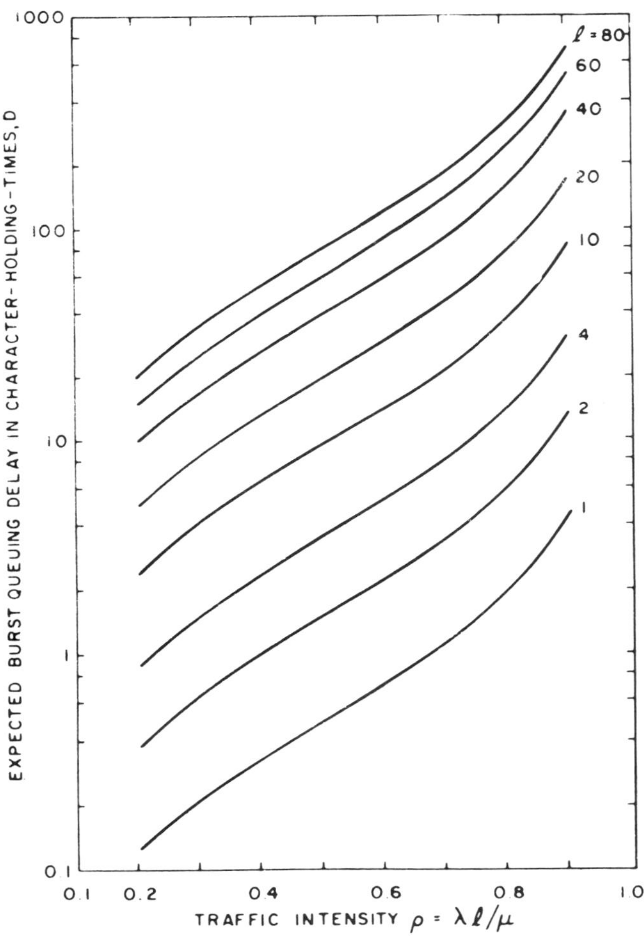

Figure 8—Traffic intensity vs expected burst queuing delay

Discussion of results

We shall first discuss the user-to-computer buffer behavior. Figure 4 portrays the relationships between overflow probabilities and buffer size for selected traffic intensities and selected numbers of servers. The curves for two-, three-, and four-servers lie in the region between the single and the five-server curves. For a given traffic intensity, the overflow probability decreases exponentially with buffer size. For a typical traffic intensity of 0.8 ,a buffer of twenty-eight character length will achieve an overflow probability in the order of 10^{-6}. A larger buffer size is needed for $\rho_u > 0.8$ in order to achieve the same degree of buffer performance. For a given ρ, the queuing delay increases as the overflow probability decreases (or the buffer size increases). When the overflow probability is less than 10^{-4} (for $\rho_u = 0.8$, this overflow probability corresponds to a buffer size of about eighteen characters), the delay increment with buffer length becomes negligible and the delay can be approximated as independent of buffer size as shown in Figure 5.

For the data transmissions in time-sharing systems, the buffer overflow probability should be somewhat less than the line error rate. For currently available lines, the error rate is about 10^{-5}. Therefore from Figure 5, we know that the queuing delay range of interest is almost independent of the buffer length. Figure 6 describes the queuing delays (at overflow probability = 10^{-6}) for various traffic intensities. The queuing delay increases exponentially with ρ. For a given ρ, the queuing delay decreases with the increase of number of servers. Figures 4 and 6 agree with our intuition that whenever multiple servers are needed, it is always advantageous to use a common buffer rather than using several single lines with separate buffers.

Next we shall discuss the computer-to-user buffer behavior. The overflow probability depends upon the buffer size, the traffic intensity, and expected burst length. For a given average buffer length, the overflow probability increases as the traffic intensity increases. For a given traffic intensity, and a desired buffer overflow probability, the required buffer size increases as the average burst length increases. Figure 7 provides the relationships between the average burst length and required buffer size to achieve an overflow probability of 10^{-6} for selected traffic intensities.

When the average burst length equals unity, then the result reduces to the case of Poisson arrivals, single server and constant service time as had been analyzed.[3,4] For a given traffic intensity, required buffer size for average burst lengths $\bar{\ell}(\bar{\ell} > 1)$, N_{ℓ}, to achieve the same degree of overflow probability is much greater than that for unity burst length, N_1. In general, $N_\ell > \bar{\ell} \times N_1$. As $\bar{\ell}$ increases, the difference between N_ℓ and $\bar{\ell} \times N_1$ increases. For example, for $\rho_c = .8$, $\bar{\ell} = 1$, the required buffer size to achieve $P'_{of} = 10^{-6}$ is $N_1 = 28$ characters. When $\bar{\ell} = 4$, then from Figure 7, $N_4 = 212 > 4 \times 28 = 112$ characters. In the same manner, if $\ell = 20$, $N_{20} = 1200 > 20 \times 28 = 580$ characters. This is due to the fact that the variance of S is proportional to $\bar{\ell}$ as shown in (17). Figure 8 portrays the relationship between expected burst queuing delay and traffic intensity for selected expected burst lengths. For a given expected burst length, the expected queuing delay increases as traffic intensity increases; for a given traffic intensity, the expected queuing delay increases with burst length. These are important factors that affect the delay.

Optimal design of multiplexing system

Let us first consider the design of the user-to-computer multiplexer. Based on the user-to-computer traffic characteristics, the number of user terminals, maximum allowable queuing delay, and overflow probability, several different buffer system configurations might satisfy the desired requirements. Hence there are trade-offs among the number of transmission lines we might use, the transmission rates of the lines, and the buffer sizes. We would like to design the multiplexing system whose total cost (transmission cost and buffer storage cost) is minimum. One way to proceed with this is first to select the set of possible multiplexing system configurations based on the queuing delay requirements from Figure 6. Based on the maximum allowable overflow probability, we can obtain the required buffer length for this set of possible multiplexing system configurations. The optimal user-to-computer part of the multiplexing system can then be selected as that which minimizes the cost of the system.

Next, we shall consider the optimizations of the computer-to-user multiplexer. Data collected from several operating time-sharing systems[10] revealed that the average number of characters sent by the computer to the group of users is an order of magnitude greater than the number of characters sent by the group of users to the computer. Thus, using high transmission rate line for computer output data would significantly reduce in buffer size and the queuing delay due to buffering. Further, the change in the computer system such as changes in the scheduling algorithm[11–17] in the central processor can strongly influence the computer output traffic statistics, which will directly affect the buffer performance, and the design of the decoding system.

In practice, we would like to design a system that has minimum total cost yet satisfies all the requirements such as the inquiry-response delay, average holding time of each user, etc. Since the multiplexing system and the central processor intimately interact with each other, the multiplexing system should be treated as a subsystem of the time-shared computer system. The economical and performance optimization should be carried out jointly between the central processor and available communication facilities.

Example

Consider the design of a time-sharing system that consists of many remote terminals and that employs the ATDM technique with full duplex operation between the terminals and the central processor. Measurements of the traffic characteristics from several operating systems have revealed that the character interarrival time per user line can be approximated as exponentially distributed with mean about 0.5 seconds.[10] Thus, the character arrivals can be treated as Poisson arrivals with a rate of 2 char/sec. A reasonable conservative guess is that 50 percent of the transmitted information is sufficient for addressing and framing. Voice-grade private lines can easily transmit 240 char/sec from users. Suppose this operating system consists of $m = 48$ terminals, all the terminals are assumed to be independent and have the same traffic characteristics. The buffer is designed such that the overflow probability is less than about 10^{-6}. We shall use our model to determine the buffer size and the average queuing delay incurred by each character.

The traffic intensity is $\rho_u = 1.5 \times m\lambda_u / c\mu_u = 1.5 \times 48 \times 2/240 = 0.6$. To achieve the desired overflow probability, from Figure 4, the required buffer length is 14 characters. From Figure 6, the normalized queuing delay due to buffering is equal to 1.25 holding times. Since each holding time is equal to $1/\mu_u = 1/240 = 4.16$ millisecond, the waiting time of each character is 5.06 milliseconds. Now suppose the number of terminals is increased from 48 to 96. In order that traffic intensity be less than unity, two transmission lines are required and the traffic intensity is still equal to 0.6. From Figure 5, the buffer length corresponding to the desired overflow probability for two transmission lines is about 14 characters. The waiting time is about 0.8 holding times which is equal to 3.33 milliseconds. Although the difference between 5.06 milliseconds and 3.33 milliseconds may not be detected by a user at a terminal, a common buffer of the same size operating with two output lines can handle twice the number of input lines as with one output line. Thus, the common buffer approach permits handling a wide range of traffic without substantial variation in buffer size.

Next, we shall consider the buffer design problem that employs the ATDM technique to transmit data from central processor to remote terminals. The traffic statistics as well as the message length are different from that of the users. The burst interarrival time[10] can be approximated as exponentially distributed with a mean of 2.84 seconds. Thus, the bursts can be approximated as Poisson arrivals with a rate of λ_c = 0.35 bursts/sec. Further, data collected in the same study indicate that the burst length can be approximated as geometrically distributed with a mean of ℓ = 20 characters. Suppose we use a wideband transmission line that transmits 480 char/sec to provide communications from the central processor to 48 terminals. Assuming 20 percent of the transmitted information is used for addressing and framing, then the traffic intensity, $\rho_c = 1.2\lambda_c\bar{\ell}/\mu_c \approx 0.84$. To achieve an overflow probability of 10^{-6}, from Figure 7, we find that the required buffer size is 1,400 characters. From Figure 8, the expected queuing delay for each burst is 85 character-holding times, or 85/480 = 0.176 seconds.

Suppose now we changed our transmission rate from 480 to 960 char/sec; then the traffic intensity $\rho_c \approx 0.42$. The corresponding required buffer size in order to achieve an overflow probability of 10^{-6} is 480 characters, and the delay is 15 character-holding times or 16 milliseconds. Thus, these results also provide insight regarding the trade-off between transmission costs and storage costs.

The above example is based on the output traffic characteristics of a specfic computer scheduling algorithm. As the output traffic statistics changes with different scheduling algorithms, the buffer performance in the multiplexing system is affected. To design an optimal system, we should jointly optimize the scheduling algorithm and the multiplexing system such that yield minimum total cost and also meet the required system performance such as maximum allowable inquiry-response delay, desired overflow probability, etc.

CONCLUSIONS

Queuing analyses indicate that for an allowable overflow probability and queuing delay, moderate buffer sizes can be achieved for asynchronous time division multiplexing for time-sharing computer systems. Further, when multiple transmission lines are required, better buffer performance will be achieved by using a common buffer rather than by using separate ones.

Because of the asymmetric nature of the traffic characteristics of user-to-computer transmission versus computer-to-user transmission, a much larger buffer is required for the computer-to-user multiplexer to handle the larger volume of data generated by the central processor.

The multiplexing system and the central processor in a time-shared environment directly interact with each other. To design an optimal operating system, we should jointly optimize the central processor and the multiplexing system (for example, the interaction between scheduling algorithm and buffer performance) to obtain a minimum cost system that meets the system performance requirements. It is apparent that closer coordination between the computer and communication system designs would be fruitful in terms of economics and technological improvements to the overall system design.

ACKNOWLEDGMENTS

The author wishes to thank E. Fuchs and D. Heyman of Bell Telephone Laboratories for their helpful discussions.

REFERENCES

1 K BULLINGTON J M FRASER
Engineering aspects of TASI
B S T J March 1959 353-364

2 B A POWELL B AVI-ITZHAK
Queuing system with enforced idle time
Operations Research Vol 15 No 6 Nov 1967 1145-1156

3 T G BIRDSALL et al
Analysis of asynchronous time multiplexing of speech sources
IRE Trans on Communications Systems Dec 1962 390-397

4 N M DOR
Guide to the length of buffer storage required for random (Poisson) input and constant output rates
IEEE Trans on E C Oct 1967 683-684

5 J D C LITTLE
A proof of the queuing formula $L = \lambda W$
Operations Research Vol 9 1961 383-387

6 R W HAMMING
Numerical methods for scientists and engineers
McGraw-Hill Book Co Inc N Y 1962 363-364

7 W M GENTLEMAN G SANDE
Fast fourier transforms—for fun and profit
Proc FJCC Vol 29 563-578

8 N U PRABHU
Queues and inventories
John Wiley and Sons Inc N Y 1965 42

9 P M MORSE
Queues Inventories and Maintenance

John Wiley and Sons Inc 1958 15-18

10 P E JACKSON C D STUBBS
A study of multiaccess computer communications
Proc SJCC Vol 34 1969 491-504

11 A L SCHERR
An analysis of Time-Shared Computer Systems
MIT Research Monograph No 36 MIT Press Cambridge Mass 1967

12 P E DENNING
Effect of scheduling on file memory operations
Proc SJCC Vol 30 1967 9-21

13 J E SHEMER
Some mathematical considerations of time-sharing scheduling algorithms
J ACM Vol 14 No 2 April 1967 262-272

14 E G COFFMAN JR
Analysis of two time-sharing algorithms designed for limiting swapping
J ACM July 1968

15 E G COFFMAN L KLEINROCK
Feedback queuing models for time-shared system
J ACM Vol 15 No 4 Oct 1968 549-576

16 L KLEINROCK
Certain analytic results for time-shared processors
Proc IFIP Congress 1968 Edinburgh Scotland Aug 5-10 1968 D119-D125

17 W W CHU
Optimal file allocation in a multicomputer information system
Proc IFIP Congress 1968 Edinburgh Scotland Aug 5-10 F80-85

57

ERRATA

P. 671 Column 2 Line 39, replace ρ by ρ_u

P. 672 Eq. 8 and Column 1 Line 8, replace λ_u by α_u

Figure 4 (P. 672) and Figure 6 (P. 673), replace λ by λ_u and ρ by ρ_u

P. 673 Column 2 Line 33 and Eq. 17, replace λ by λ_c

Figure 7 (P. 674) and Figure 8 (P. 675), replace ρ by ρ_c, ℓ by $\bar{\ell}$, and λ by λ_c

P. 675 Eq. 25, replace λ by λ_c and ρ by ρ_c; replace $\frac{\lambda_c(2-\theta)}{2(\theta-\lambda_c)}$ by $\frac{\lambda_c(2-\theta)}{2\theta(\theta-\lambda_c)}$

P. 675 Column 2 Lines 14, 30, and 31, replace ρ by ρ_c

58

Reprinted by permission from
IEEE TRANSACTIONS ON COMMUNICATIONS
Vol. COM-20, No. 2, April 1972

Buffer Behavior for Mixed Input Traffic and Single Constant Output Rate

WESLEY W. CHU, MEMBER, IEEE, AND LEO C. LIANG

***Abstract*—A queueing model with limited waiting room (buffer), mixed input traffic (Poisson and compound Poisson arrivals), and constant service rate is studied. Using average burst length, traffic intensity, and input-traffic mixture rate as parameters, we obtain relationships among buffer size, overflow probabilities, and expected message-queueing delay due to buffering. These relationships are portrayed on graphs that can be used as a guide in buffer design. Although this study arose in the design of statistical multiplexors, the queueing model developed is quite general and may be useful for other industrial applications.**

Paper approved by the Data Communications Committee of the IEEE Communications Society for publication without oral presentation. This research was supported by the U. S. Office of Naval Research, Research Program Office, Contract N00014-69-A-0200-4027, NR 048-129. Manuscript received July 26, 1971; revised October 19, 1971.
The authors are with the University of California, Los Angeles, Calif. 90024.

I. Introduction

In many engineering problems such as computer-storage allocation, data compression, and data communication [1], buffer design is one of the important considerations. Birdsall *et al.* [2], and later Dor [3] have analyzed buffer behavior with Poisson input arrivals and constant output rate. Chu [4] has studied the buffer behavior of a similar model with multiple synchronous constant output rates. He has further studied buffer behavior for batch Poisson arrivals and a single constant output rate [5]. In many data communication systems, input traffic is a mixture of bursts (string of characters) and single characters. For example, in a computer communication system, the cathode-ray-tube terminal outputs are in bursts and the teletypewriter outputs are in characters. Buffer behavior with such mixed input traffic is studied in this paper.

For a given mixed input traffic and a constant output rate, we are interested in 1) the relationship between overflow probability (the average fraction of the total number of arriving characters rejected by the buffer) and buffer size at various traffic intensities, and 2) the expected queueing delay due to buffering. These relationships are obtained by a technique similar to Chu [5]. The results in this paper represent a generalization of his work.

II. Analysis of Buffer Behavior

Let us define the time to transmit a character on the multiplexed line as a unit service interval. The input traffic arriving at the buffer is assumed to be a mixture of single-character inputs and burst (string of characters) inputs. The single-character input X is assumed to be Poisson distributed, with a rate λ_p characters per unit service interval as shown in (1).

$$f_X(k) = \frac{\lambda_p^k}{k!} \exp(-\lambda_p), \qquad k = 0, 1, 2, \cdots . \tag{1}$$

The characteristic function for $f_X(k)$ is

$$\phi_X(u) = \exp[-\lambda_p + \lambda_p \exp(iu)]. \tag{2}$$

For burst input traffic, we assume the length l of the burst Y is geometrically distributed with mean $\bar{l} = 1/\theta$, and the number of bursts Z arriving during a unit service interval is Poisson distributed with a rate λ_c bursts/unit service interval. The distribution of l is

$$f_Y(l) = \theta(1-\theta)^{l-1}, \qquad l = 1, 2, \cdots \tag{3}$$

and the distribution of the number of bursts arriving during a unit service interval is

$$f_Z(n) = \frac{\lambda_c^n}{n!} \exp(-\lambda_c), \qquad n = 0, 1, 2, \cdots . \tag{4}$$

The total number of characters due to burst inputs that arrive during the time to transmit a character on the multiplexed line is a random sum and equals

$$S = \sum_{i=0}^{Z} Y_i \tag{5}$$

where Y_i, a random variable distributed as (3), is the number of characters contained in the ith arriving burst and Z, a random variable distributed as (4), is the total number of bursts arriving during the unit service interval. All of these random variables are assumed to be statistically independent of each other. It can be shown that $\phi_S(u)$, the characteristic function of S [5], is

$$\phi_S(u) = \exp\{-\lambda_c + \lambda_c\theta \exp(iu)/[1-(1-\theta)\exp(iu)]\}. \quad (6)$$

and $f_S(j)$ (the probability that exactly j characters will arrive due to burst arrivals during a unit service interval) has a compound Poisson distribution

$$f_S(j) = \begin{cases} \sum_{k=1}^{j} \binom{j-1}{k-1} (\lambda_c\theta)^k (1-\theta)^{j-k} \frac{\exp(-\lambda_c)}{k!}, & j = 1, 2, \cdots \\ \exp(-\lambda_c), & j = 0. \end{cases} \quad (7)$$

For mixed traffic of single-character inputs (Poisson) and burst inputs (compound Poisson), the probability that exactly n characters arrive during a unit service interval Π_n is the convolution of $f_X(k)$ and $f_S(j)$; that is,

$$\Pi_n = f_S(n) \circledast f_X(n)$$

$$\Pi_n = \sum_{j=1}^{n} \frac{\lambda_p^{\,n-j}\exp(-\lambda_p)}{(n-j)!} \sum_{k=1}^{j} \binom{j-1}{k-1} \cdot \frac{(\lambda_c\theta)^k(1-\theta)^{j-k}\exp(-\lambda_c)}{k!} + \frac{\lambda_p^{\,n}}{n!}\exp[-(\lambda_p+\lambda_c)], \quad n = 1, 2, \cdots$$

$$\Pi_0 = \exp[-(\lambda_p + \lambda_c)]. \quad (8)$$

The characteristic function for Π_n is

$$\phi_{SX}(u) = \phi_S(u)\phi_X(u) = \exp\{-(\lambda_p+\lambda_c) + \lambda_p \exp(iu) + \lambda_c\theta\exp(iu)/[1-(1-\theta)\exp(iu)]\}. \quad (9)$$

The time required to compute Π_n from (8) is dependent on n. For large n (e.g., $n > 1000$), the computation time is prohibitive. Using the same technique as [5], we compute Π_n via the fast Fourier transform (FFT) inversion method as follows:

$$\Pi_n = \frac{1}{M}\sum_{r=0}^{M-1} \phi_{SX}(r)\exp(-2\pi irn/M), \quad n = 0, 1, 2, \cdots, M-1 \quad (10)$$

where

- r $2\Pi u/M$;
- i $(-1)^{1/2}$;
- M total number of points used to represent $\phi_{SX}(r)$ = total number of Π_n.

In order to determine Π_n accurately, they are computed with double precision on the IBM 360/91 at the University of California, Los Angeles. Furthermore, we want to use as many points as possible to represent $\phi_{SX}(r)$; that is, we want to make M as large as possible. Because of the word-length limitation of the computer, double precision provides 15-digit accuracy. Therefore, when $\Pi_n < 10^{-15}$, it is set equal to zero. M is selected such that $\Pi_{n>M} < 10^{-15}$. The M is different for different values of λ_p, λ_c, and $\bar{l}$.

Since the buffer has a finite size of N, an overflow will result when a character arrives at the buffer and finds the buffer is full. Thus, the average-character departure rate from the buffer (carried load) β is less than the average-character arrival rate at the buffer (offered load) $\gamma = \lambda_p + \lambda_c\bar{l}$. The carried load can be computed from the probability that the buffer is busy; that is, $\beta = 1 - p_0$, where p_0 is the probability that the buffer is empty, which can be obtained in the exact manner as in [5].

The traffic intensity ρ measures the degree of congestion and indicates the impact of an input traffic stream upon the departure stream. Since the offered load is represented in a unit service interval, $\rho = \gamma = \lambda_p + \lambda_c\bar{l}$.

The overflow probability of the buffer (the average fraction of the total number of arriving characters rejected by the buffer) is

$$P_{of} = \frac{\text{offered load} - \text{carried load}}{\text{offered load}} = 1 - \beta/\gamma. \quad (11)$$

59

Let α be the input-traffic mixture rate that describes the percentage of the traffic contributed by compound Poisson arrivals. Clearly, $1 - \alpha$ is the percentage of the traffic contributed by Poisson arrivals. Thus,

$$\alpha = \lambda_c\bar{l}/\rho$$

and

$$1 - \alpha = \lambda_p/\rho.$$

In the preceding analysis, we have treated each character as a unit. However, in computing the expected message delay D due to buffering, we should treat each message as a unit. The service time is the time required to transmit the entire message. When the buffer size N is large, for a line with a constant transmission rate, the service-time distribution is the same as the message-length distribution except scaled by a constant transmission rate factor. The message-length distribution for the mixed input traffic of length m is

$$f_M(m) = \frac{\lambda_p}{\lambda_p+\lambda_c}\delta(m) + \frac{\lambda_c}{\lambda_p+\lambda_c}\theta(1-\theta)^{m-1}, \quad m = 1, 2, 3, \cdots \quad (12)$$

where

$$\delta(m) = \begin{cases} 1, & m = 1 \\ 0, & m > 1. \end{cases}$$

When the overflow probability is very small, a good approximation for the expected message delay can be computed from a queueing system with infinite waiting room [4]. The expected queueing delay for an M/G/1 (Poisson arrivals /general service/single output) queueing system is

$$D = \frac{\lambda E[m^2]}{2(1-\rho)} \quad (13)$$

where

$$\lambda = \lambda_p + \lambda_c$$

$$E[m^2] = \text{second moment of } f_M(m).$$

It can be shown that

$$E[m^2] = \frac{1}{\lambda}[\lambda_p + \lambda_c(2-\theta)/\theta^2]. \quad (14)$$

Substituting (14) into (13), we have

$$D = \frac{\rho}{2(1-\rho)} + \frac{\alpha(\bar{l}-1)\rho}{1-\rho}, \quad \text{character-service-times.} \quad (15)$$

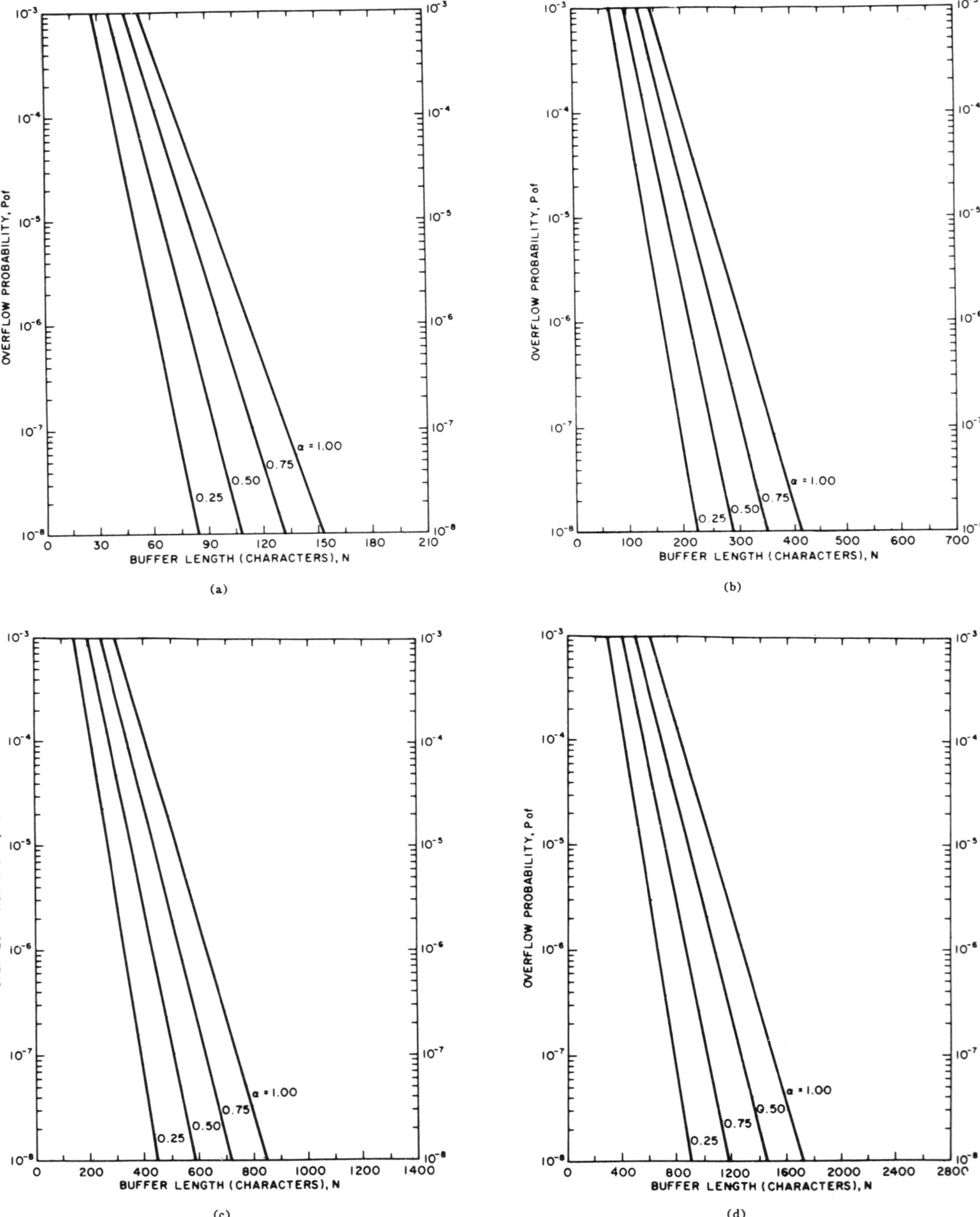

Fig. 1. Buffer length N versus overflow probability P_{of} for traffic intensity $\rho = 0.60$. (a) $\bar{l} = 4$ characters. (b) $\bar{l} = 10$ characters. (c) $\bar{l} = 20$ characters. (d) $\bar{l} = 40$ characters.

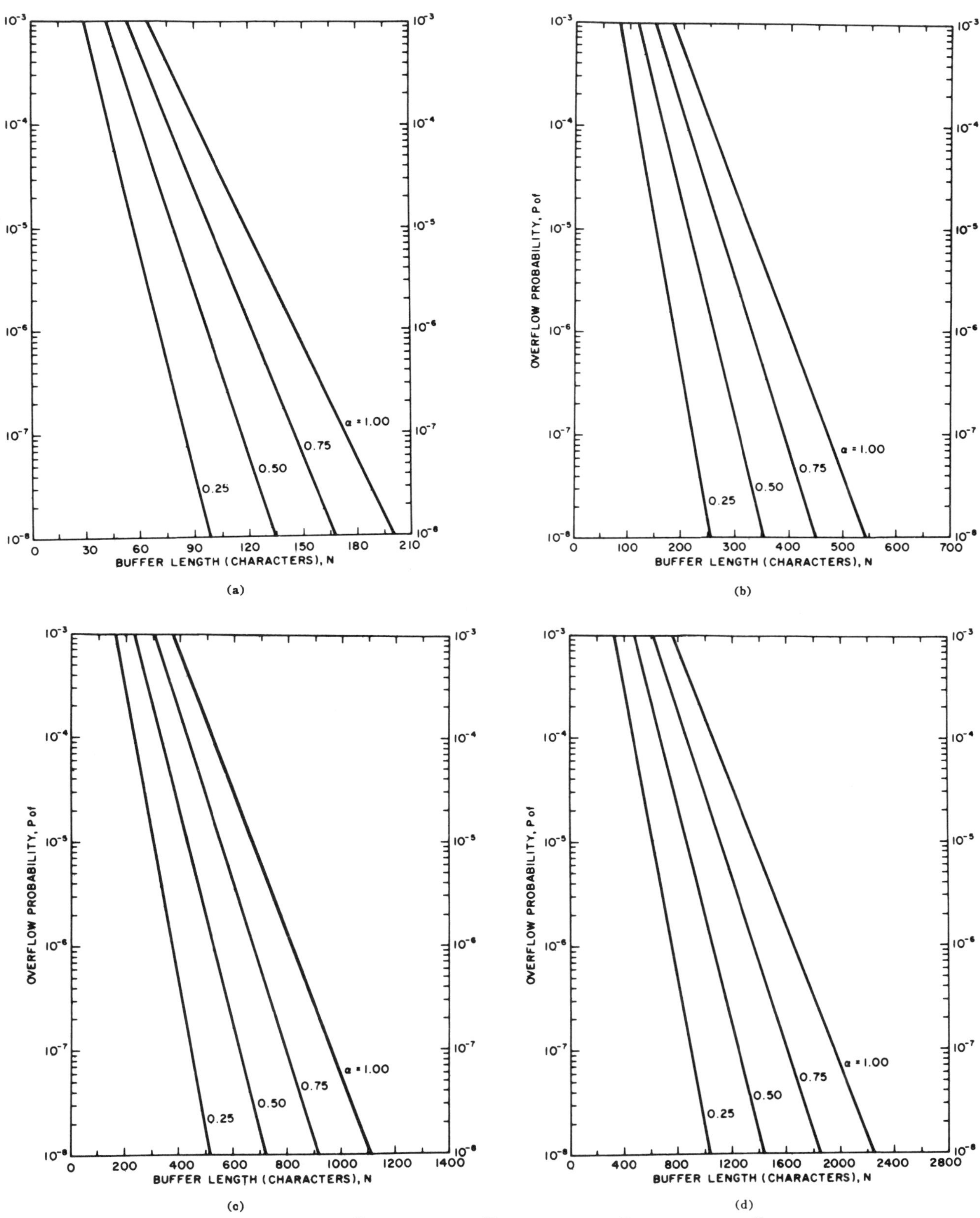

Fig. 2. N versus P_{of} for ρ = 0.70. (a) $\bar{l}$ = 4 characters. (b) $\bar{l}$ = 10 characters. (c) $\bar{l}$ = 20 characters. (d) $\bar{l}$ = 40 characters.

61

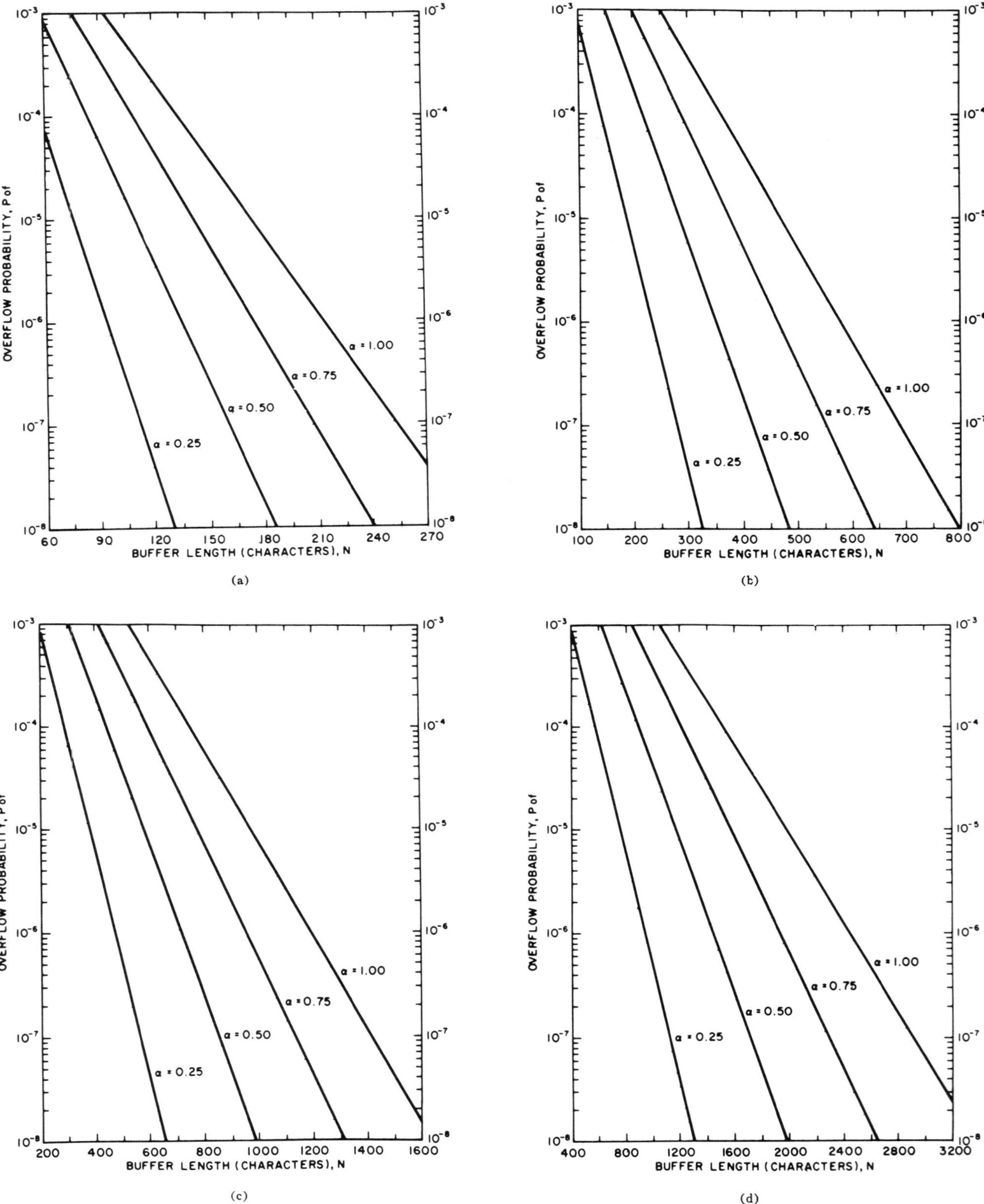

Fig. 3. N versus P_{of} for $\rho = 0.80$. (a) $\bar{l} = 4$ characters. (b) $\bar{l} = 10$ characters. (c) $\bar{l} = 20$ characters. (d) $\bar{l} = 40$ characters.

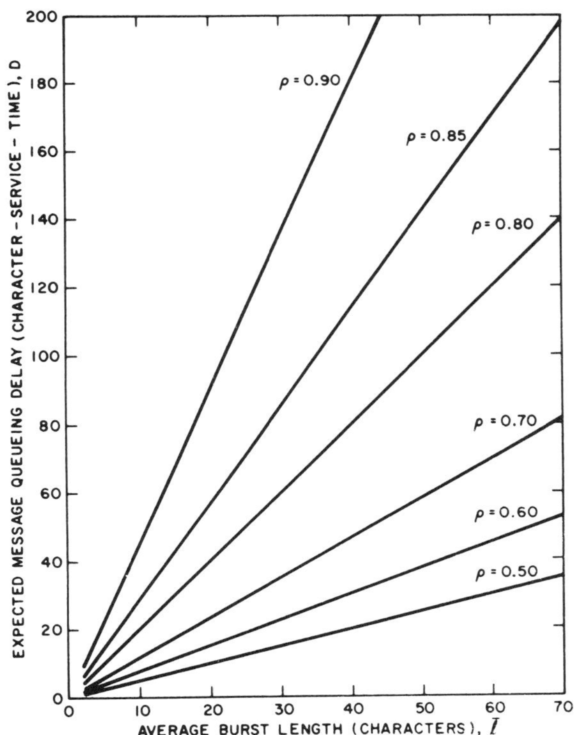

Fig. 4. Average burst length $\bar{l}$ versus expected message delay D for traffic mixture rate $\alpha = 0.5$.

III. Discussion of Results

The relationship of buffer length to overflow probability has been computed for selected traffic intensities ρ, the expected burst length $\bar{l}$, and input-traffic mixture rate α as shown in Figs. 1–3.

The overflow probability depends upon the N, ρ, $\bar{l}$, and α. For a given buffer size N, the overflow probability increases as ρ, $\bar{l}$, and α increase. For a given overflow probability, the required buffer size increases as ρ, $\bar{l}$, and α increase.

In our analysis, we have assumed that the burst length is geometrically distributed and takes values from one to infinity. In practice, however, the maximum burst length is limited to a finite number of characters. Because of the long-tail effect of the geometric distribution, the result obtained here will be more conservative than that of a truncated geometric distribution.

When the average burst length $\bar{l}$ equals unity or when the input-traffic mixture rate α equals zero, the model reduces to the Poisson arrivals with constant output rate, which has been obtained by Birdsall *et al.* [2], Dor [3], and Chu [4]. When α equals unity, then the model reduces to batch Poisson arrivals with a constant output rate, which has been analyzed by Chu [5]. For given ρ and $\bar{l}$, the buffer size required to achieve a desired level of P_{of} is not simply proportional to α. For a desired level of P_{of}, $N\bar{l}$ (the required buffer size for average burst length $\bar{l}$) is much greater than $\bar{l} \cdot N_1$, where N_1 is the required buffer size for burst length of one (Poisson input arrivals).

The expected message delay D due to buffering (calculated from an M/G/1 system with an infinite waiting room) depends upon α, ρ, and $\bar{l}$. For a given ρ and a given $\bar{l}$ (or α), from (15) we note that D is linearly proportional to α (or $\bar{l}$). This agrees with our intuition that for a given traffic intensity, the message delay increases as the message length increases and as the amount of burst input traffic increases. The relationships between $\bar{l}$ and D for $\alpha = 0.5$ and selected ρ are portrayed in Fig. 4.

IV. Conclusion

A finite waiting-room queueing model with mixed input traffic and constant output rate has been studied. For a given traffic intensity and a given input-traffic mixture rate, buffer behavior (in terms of buffer overflow probability and average queueing delay) lies between that for Poisson input arrivals and that for compound Poisson input arrivals. When the traffic mixture rate α approaches zero, the buffer behavior reduces to the Poisson input case. When α equals one, the buffer behavior corresponds to the compound Poisson input case. The numerical results for buffer behavior are portrayed in graphs that are useful in buffer designs.

References

[1] W. W. Chu, "Design considerations of statistical multiplexors," in *Proc. ACM Symp. Problems in the Optimization of Data Communication Systems*, 1969, Pine Mountain City, Ga., pp. 36–60.

[2] T. G. Birdsall, M. P. Ristenbatt, and S. B. Weinstein, "Analysis of asynchronous time multiplexing of speech sources," *IRE Trans. Commun. Syst.*, vol. CS-10, pp. 390–397, Dec. 1962.

[3] N. M. Dor, "Guide to the length of buffer storage required for random (Poisson) input and constant output rates," *IEEE Trans. Electron. Comput.* (Short Notes), vol. EC-16, pp. 683–684, Oct. 1967.

[4] W. W. Chu, "Buffer behavior for Poisson arrival and multiple synchronous constant outputs," *IEEE Trans. Comput.*, vol. C-19, pp. 530–534, June 1970.

[5] ——, "Buffer behavior for batch Poisson arrivals and single constant output," *IEEE Trans. Commun. Technol.*, vol. COM-18, pp. 613–618, Oct. 1970.

[6] E. Fuchs and P. E. Jackson, "Estimates of distributions of random variables for certain computer communication traffic models," *Commun. Ass. Comput. Mach.*, vol. 13, pp. 752–757, Dec. 1970.

Demultiplexing Considerations for Statistical Multiplexors

WESLEY W. CHU, MEMBER, IEEE

64

Abstract—**Demultiplexing serves as an important function for statistical multiplexors. Its purpose is to reassemble the received message and distribute it to the appropriate destination. An important cost consideration for this function is the size of the buffer necessary to meet a specified overflow service requirement. The demultiplexing buffer can be modeled as a finite waiting room queueing model with batch Poisson arrivals and multiple distinct constant servers. Stimulation is used to study buffer behavior for traffic arriving at the buffer according to the uniform, linear, step, and geometric destination functions. The relationships among buffer overflow probability, buffer size, traffic intensity, average message length, and message destination are presented in graphs to provide a guide in the design of demultiplexing buffers. Simulation results reveal that buffer input messages that have short average message lengths and uniform traffic destinations yield the best buffer behavior. Thus, in planning the CPU scheduling algorithm and in selecting the demultiplexing output rates, the designing of a computer communications system that uses the statistical multiplexing technique should also consider the output statistics needed to achieve optimal demultiplexing performance.**

I. INTRODUCTION

TO INCREASE information processing capability and to share computer resources, remotely located computers and/or terminals are connected together by communication links. Many of these computer communication systems, such as time-sharing systems and distributed computer systems, are already in existence and in operation. In many cases, the communication cost of such systems is a significant portion of the total operating cost. To increase channel utilization and reduce communication cost, asynchronous time-division multiplexing has been proposed for data communications [1]. The design considerations of such a multiplexing (statistical multiplexing) system have been reported in recent literature [2]–[6]. In this paper, we study design considerations of an asynchronous time-division demultiplexing system, which is an integral part of the design of a statistical multiplexor. In a multiplexing system, outputs from the system go to a single destination, e.g., to a computer, while outputs from a demultiplexing system go to many destinations, e.g., to different users and/or computers as shown in Fig. 1.

The demultiplexor may consist of a buffer, a buffer control unit, and a switching circuit. Input messages to the buffer consist of strings of characters (bursts). The switching circuit distributes the output from the buffer to the appropriate destinations according to the designation in the message address. Thus demultiplexor performance is strongly influenced by buffer behavior that depends on buffer input traffic and its destination characteristics. A queueing model with a finite waiting room, batch Poisson arrivals, and multiple distinct constant outputs (Fig. 2) is used to study buffer behavior. The complexity of the demultiplexing buffer makes exact mathematical analysis of such a model very difficult. Therefore, computer simulation has been used to study the relationships among message destination function, average traffic level, message burst length, overflow probability (the fraction of the total number of messages rejected by the buffer), and buffer size. These relationships, in graphs, are important in designing demultiplexing systems and store-and-forward computer networks.

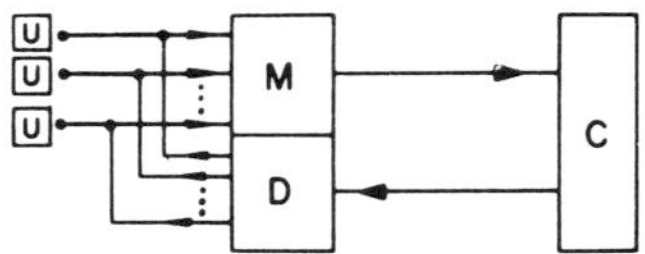

(a) for a time sharing system

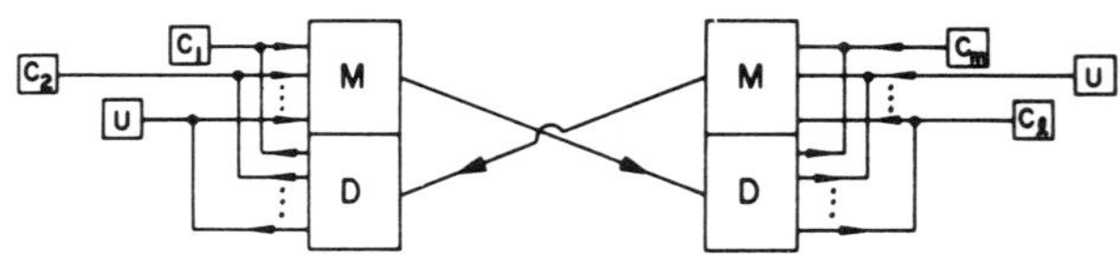

(b) for a distributed computer system

U : user terminal
D : statistical demultiplexor
M : statistical multiplexor
C : computer
C_i : i^{th} computer

Fig. 1. Statistical multiplexing systems.

II. ANALYSIS OF DEMULTIPLEXING BUFFER

Input messages to the buffer can be represented by three parameters: message arrivals, message lengths, and message destinations. These parameters are intimately

Manuscript received June 15, 1971; revised January 31, 1972. This research was supported by the U. S. Office of Naval Research, Mathematical and Information Sciences Division, under Contract N00014-69-A-0200-4027, NR 048-129 and the Advanced Research Projects Agency of the Department of Defense, under Contract DAHC 15-69-C-0285. This paper was presented at the 2nd Symposium on Problems in the Optimization of Data Communications Systems, Palo Alto, Calif., October 20–22, 1971.

The author is with the Department of Computer Science, University of California, Los Angeles, Calif. 90024.

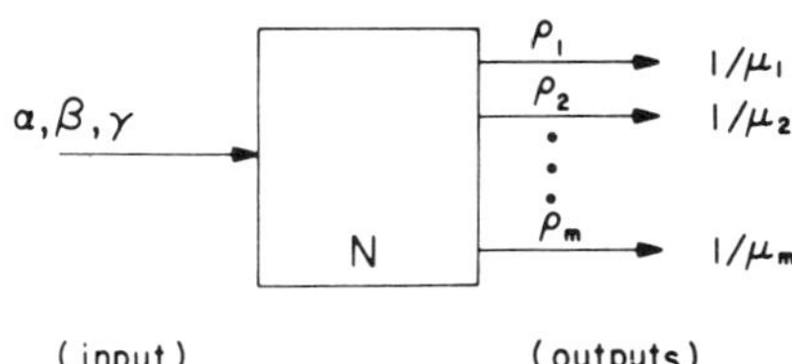

α	message inter-arrival time
β	message length
γ	destination function
μ_i	transmission rate for the ith destination
ρ_i	traffic intensity for the ith destination
N	buffer size
m	total number of message destinations

Fig. 2. Model for demultiplexing buffer.

related to buffer behavior. In order to describe the input messages arriving at the buffer, three random number generators are used: α is the message interarrival time, β the number of characters in the message, and γ the destination of the message. In the simulation model, the message interarrival times α are assumed to be exponentially distributed,[1] and the message lengths β are assumed to be geometrically distributed. The destination distribution is transformed from the destination function as discussed in the following.

The destination function describes traffic intensities for the set of m destinations, that is,

$$f_d(i) = \rho_i, \qquad i = 1, 2, \cdots, m \tag{1}$$

where ρ_i is the traffic intensity for the ith destination.

The message destination function for a given set of users depends on their applications and should be derived from measured statistics.

In order to perform random sampling on traffic destination for simulation, we need to transform $f_d(i)$ into a message destination distribution $f_\gamma(i)$. This transformation can be carried out by normalizing (1) to a probability function, that is,

$$f_\gamma(i) = f_d(i) \Big/ \sum_{i=1}^{m} \rho_i, \qquad i = 1, 2, \cdots, m. \tag{2}$$

Thus,

$$\sum_{i=1}^{m} f_\gamma(i) = 1.$$

A set of random numbers $\{\xi_\alpha, \xi_\beta, \xi_\gamma\}$ corresponding to random variables α, β, and γ, is generated to represent a message arriving at the demultiplexing system. When a message arrives at the buffer, two operations take place. First, the status of the designated facility is interrogated. If the facility is busy and the buffer is not full, the burst enters the buffer and is concatenated with the queue of characters. If the facility is idle and if the buffer is not full, the first character of the burst is sent to the facility while the remaining characters enter into the buffer and output at each subsequent clock time. Second, the content of the register that keeps track of the total length of the buffer is updated. Because of distinct destinations, the total volume of output from the buffer varies with α, β, and γ. The output from the demultiplexing buffer depends on both the number of characters in the buffer and their destinations. The simulation program keeps a record of the number of characters in the buffer at the beginning of each message service interval. When the length of an arriving message exceeds the unoccupied storage space of the buffer, a buffer overflow event has occurred. The frequency of occurrence of such an overflow event gives the estimate of buffer overflow probability P_{of}. Using the above finite buffer size model for estimating buffer overflow probability requires simulating buffer behavior at various buffer sizes. As a result, the computation time required for such a model, especially for estimating small overflow probabilities, could be prohibitive. Therefore, we introduce an infinite-buffer-size model, as shown in the flow chart in Fig. 3, to estimate buffer overflow probabilities. In this case, we say that an overflow event has occurred if the buffer queue length from simulation exceeds the fictitious buffer size. Thus, this provides us with a way to estimate buffer overflow events for various buffer sizes via buffer queue-length statistics that can be obtained from a single simulation pass. This represents a significant reduction in computation time. In the case of small overflow probabilities (e.g., $P_{of} < 10^{-4}$), this model provides a good approximation of the finite-buffer-size model.

Traffic intensity is one of the most important parameters that describes the traffic congestion of the demultiplexing system. Since the output messages from the buffer are sent to various destinations, the traffic intensity of each destination would be different and would equal

$$\rho_i = \lambda_i \bar{l}_i / \mu_i \tag{3}$$

where

λ_i message arrival rate for the ith destinations,
$\bar{l}_i$ average message length for the ith destination,
μ_i transmission rate for the ith destination.

The average traffic level $\bar{\rho}$ for the demultiplexing system is the average of the traffic intensities of the m destinations, that is,

$$\bar{\rho} = \frac{1}{m} \sum_{i=1}^{m} \rho_i. \tag{4}$$

[1] In the distributed computer network shown in Fig. 1(b), the traffic input to the demultiplexor is the output from the multiplexor. In some cases the traffic output from the multiplexor can be approximated as Poisson distributed. Should the multiplexor output become very different from Poisson [7], then the actual message interarrival-time statistics should by used in the simulation.

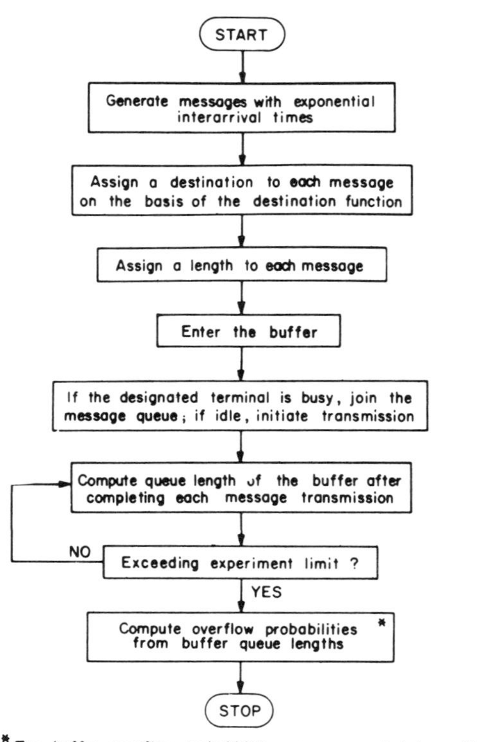

Fig. 3. Logic flow chart for buffer simulation model.

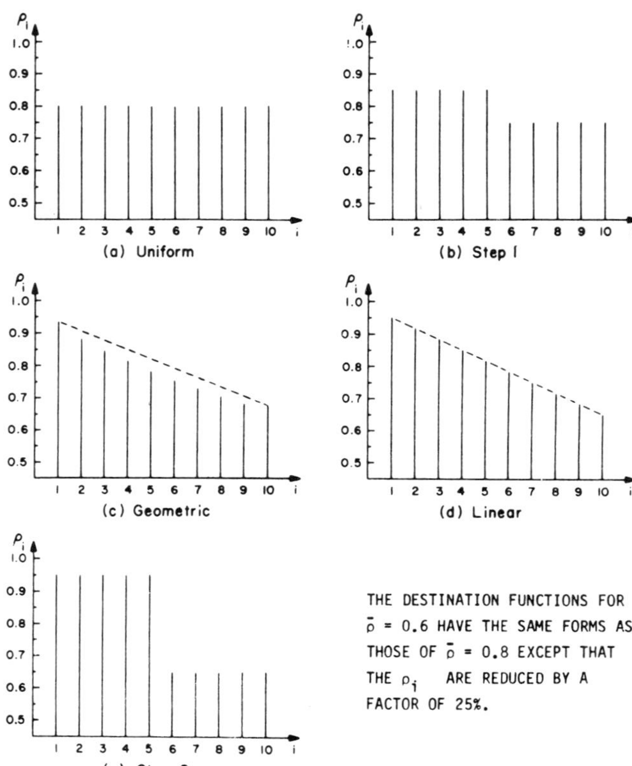

Fig. 4. Various types of destination functions for $\bar{\rho} = 0.8$.

To study the effect of destination distributions on buffer behavior, five types of destination functions are used in the simulation model as shown in Fig. 4. Further, to isolate the effect of message length of various destinations on buffer behavior, we assumed the average message length for various destinations are equal, that is, $\bar{l} = \bar{l}_i$. The relationships among p_{of}, buffer sizes, and destination distributions for selected $\bar{l}$ and $\bar{\rho}$ are obtained from simulation and are portrayed in Figs. 5 and 6.

The expected queuing delay because of buffering during demultiplexing is another important parameter in considering the design of statistical multiplexors. Since most systems allow a very low overflow probability, the expected waiting time because of buffering can be approximated by that of an infinite waiting room queuing model with Poisson arrivals and geometric service time. The expected waiting time W_i for sending messages to the ith destination is

$$W_i = \frac{\lambda_i E(X_i^2)}{2(1-\rho_i)} = \frac{\rho_i(2\bar{l}_i - 1)}{2(1-\rho_i)} \quad \text{character-service times} \tag{5}$$

where $E(X_i^2)$ is the second moment of the message length X_i for the ith destination.

Since the traffic intensity and the average message length for each destination are different, the expected queuing delay due to demultiplexing for each destination is also different and should be computed from its associated traffic intensity and average message length.

III. Discussion of Results

The relationships between buffer size and buffer overflow probability for selected average traffic levels, average burst lengths, and traffic destination functions are shown in Figs. 5 and 6. For a given average message length and desired level of overflow probability, the required buffer size increases as the average traffic level increases. Further, the required buffer size varies drastically with message destination functions. Comparing the five types of traffic destination functions used in our simulation, for a given average traffic level the uniform destination function required the smallest buffer size, and the Step 2 destination function required the largest buffer size. This is because both buffer size and queuing delay increase exponentially with ρ_i. Thus for a given average traffic level, different types of destination functions yield different buffer behavior. For example, if one of the destinations is heavily loaded, the average traffic level of the system could be very low but an extremely large buffer is needed. Further, the expected queuing delay for sending messages to that heavily loaded destination would be very long. We notice that the effect of destination function on buffer behavior increases as average traffic level increases.

Results of buffer behavior simulation shed light on the relationships between demultiplexor traffic inputs and demultiplexing system performance. The results show that to minimize the size of the demultiplexing

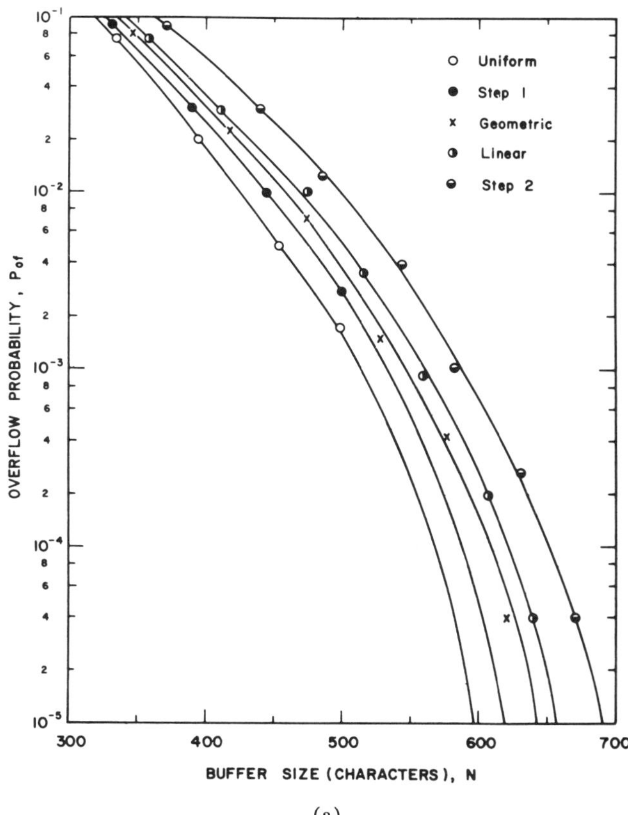

(a)

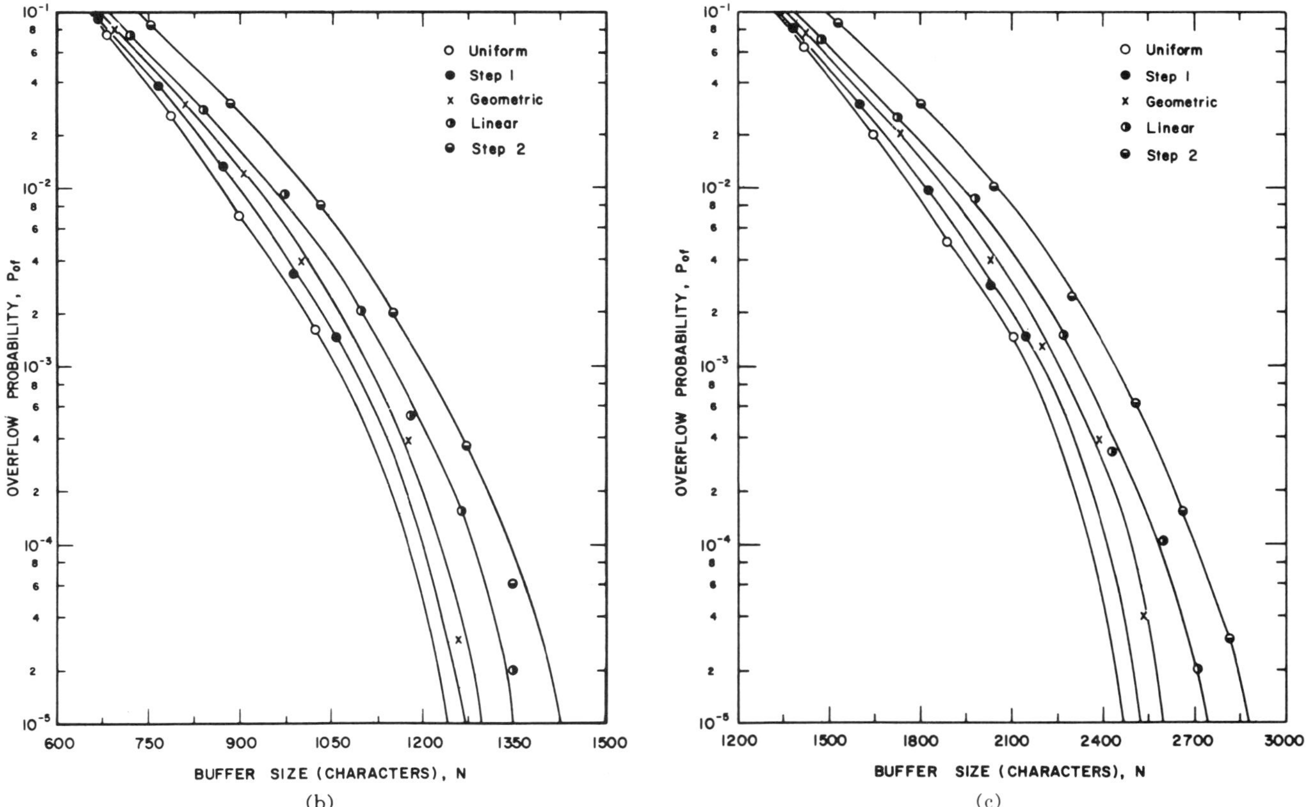

(b) (c)

Fig. 5. Buffer overflow probabilities versus buffer size for average traffic level $\bar{\rho} = 0.6$. (a) $\bar{l} = 10$ characters. (b) $\bar{l} = 20$ characters. (c) $\bar{l} = 40$ characters.

67

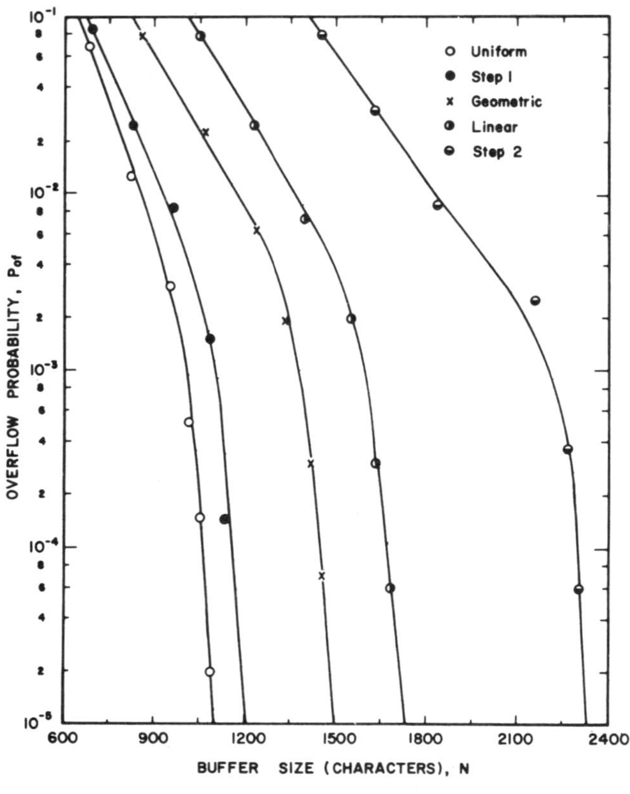

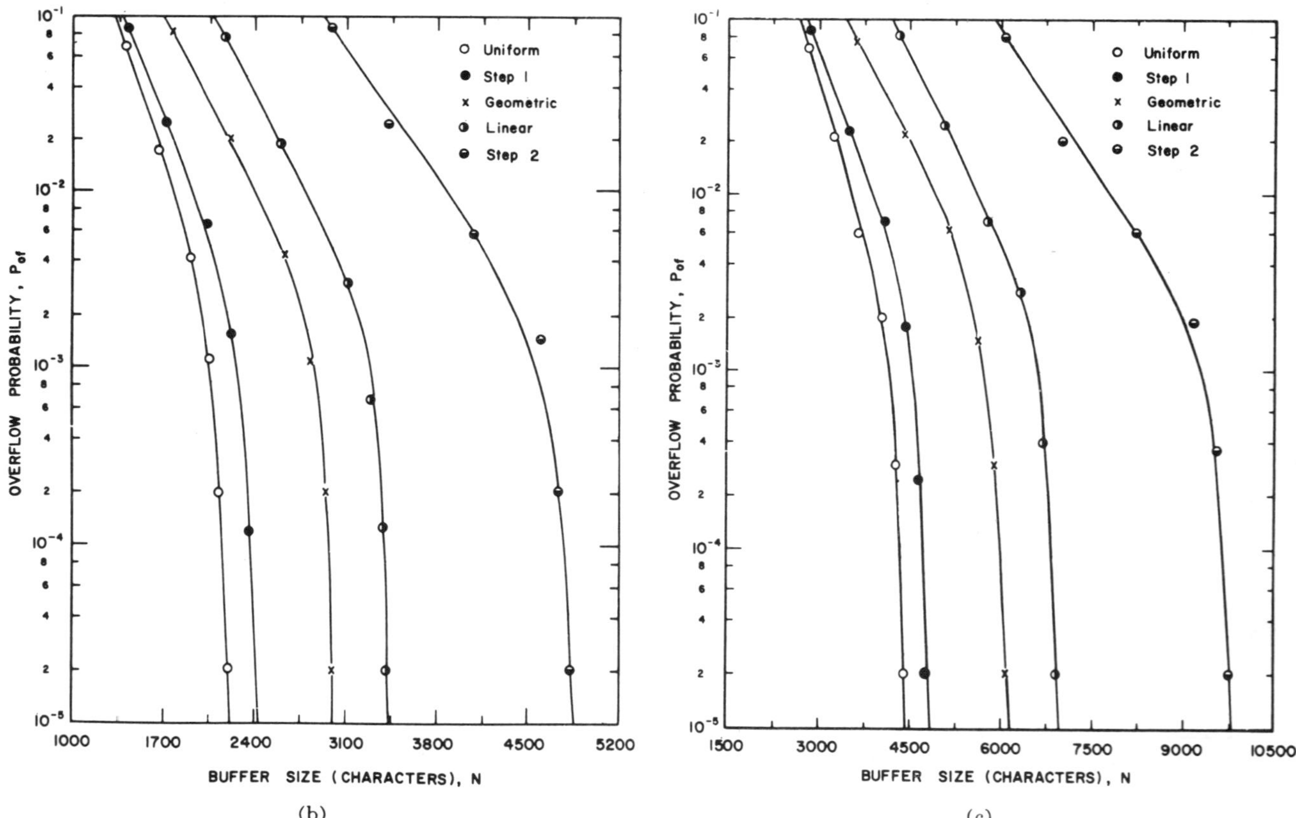

Fig. 6. Buffer overflow probabilities versus buffer size for average traffic level $\bar{\rho} = 0.8$. (a) $\bar{l} = 10$ characters. (b) $\bar{l} = 20$ characters. (c) $\bar{l} = 40$ characters.

buffer and the queuing delay due to buffering, we should schedule the inputs to the demultiplexor buffer approximately equally. This can be achieved by controlling the volume of input traffic to the buffer for various destinations, selecting the output transmission rate of the buffer, or both. In a time-sharing system, input traffic to the demultiplexor buffer is governed by the computer scheduling algorithm, such as the process scheduling and the size of central processing unit (CPU) quantum time. If we know the relationship[2] between the CPU quantum time and the volume of the CPU outputs, then a variable quantum time scheduling algorithm would be effective to schedule an equal amount of output traffic to various destinations. The process scheduling as well as the buffer output rate can also be changed to adjust the traffic intensity. To achieve a uniform traffic destination distribution, we should assign high transmission rate lines to those destinations that have high volumes of traffic.

In our simulation model, ten buffer output destinations are used. Since the input traffic to the buffer is random, the ten output destinations can also be viewed as ten groups of outputs, provided that the outputs in each group have approximately the same value of traffic intensity.[3] When a demultiplexing buffer has more than ten outputs, we could group them into ten groups according to their traffic intensities and then select the appropriate graph to estimate buffer behavior.

The simulation was performed by using the general purpose system simulation (GPSS) program on the IBM 360/91 at the University of California, Los Angeles. The computing time required for the simulation depends largely on the sample size and the number of destinations used. For a given α,β, and a destination distribution, the computing time required for an experiment (which represents a curve on the graph) of 10^5 samples and ten destinations is about 5 min. As is common in many stochastic experiments, the results are sensitive to sample size. A larger sample size yields a more accurate estimation. For a compromise between accuracy and the computing time required, a sample size of 10^5 was selected for each experiment.

IV. Example

Consider the design of a demultiplexing system for a time-sharing system that employs the statistical multiplexing technique shown in Fig. 1(a). Input traffic to the demultiplexor is generated from the computer and is approximated as Poisson arrivals. Message length is approximated as geometrically distributed with a mean of 20 characters. Further, message destinations are partitioned into ten groups and the destination function is a step-like function as shown in Fig. 4(e). The average traffic level is about 0.8. From Fig. 6(b), to achieve an overflow probability of 10^{-5}, the required buffer size is 4850 characters. From (5), the expected queuing delay because of buffering for the higher traffic destination group is 271 character-service times and the lower traffic destination group is 35 character-service times. Therefore, the average service time is $(271 + 35)/2 = 153$ character-service times. Now suppose we change the CPU scheduling to a variable quantum time scheduling algorithm. By assigning larger quantum times to those lower traffic intensity destinations, the destination function changes from a step-like function to an approximately uniform function. From Fig. 6(b), the required buffer size to achieve $P_{of} = 10^{-5}$ is 2200 characters, and from (5) the queuing delay is 78 character-service times. We note that both the required buffer size and the queuing delay because of buffering have been improved after changing the CPU scheduling algorithm. In a practical system design we should further consider the inquiry-response-time constraints, the overhead cost of various scheduling algorithms, and the CPU throughput.

V. Conclusions

The statistical demultiplexor consists of a buffer, a buffer control unit, and a switching circuit. Due to the complex output structure of demultiplexing buffer, its behavior is studied via computer simulation. Simulation results reveal that the traffic destination function has a drastic effect on the behavior of the demultiplexing buffer. Optimal buffer behavior is achieved by the uniform destination function, that is, when equal amounts of traffic are sent to the various destinations. Since the CPU scheduling algorithm in a time-sharing system and the message-routing algorithm in a distributed computer system strongly affect the traffic destination function, computer operating systems and/or message-routing algorithms greatly influence demultiplexor performance. For example, a variable CPU quantum time scheduling algorithm may be effective in producing a uniform destination function and may yield better demultiplexing performance. Thus the simulation model and the results in this paper should serve as a guide in designing a demultiplexing system and in planning an optimal computer communications system.

Acknowledgment

The author wishes to thank L. Liang of the University of California, Los Angeles, for his assistance in the GPSS simulation and E. Fuchs and R. J. Roddy of Bell Telephone Laboratories, Holmdel, N. J., for their critical comments on this paper.

[2] This relationship depends on the computer system and program behavior in question and could be obtained via measurement or simulation.

[3] Simulation results verified this conjecture for two or three outputs in a group.

References

[1] W. W. Chu, "A study of asynchronous time division multiplexing for time-sharing computer system," in *1969 Spring Joint Computer Conf., AFIPS Conf. Proc.*, vol. 35. Montvale, N. J.: AFIPS Press, 1969, pp. 669–678.

[2] ——, "Design considerations of statistical multiplexors," in

Proc. ACM Symp. Problems in the Optimization of Data Communication Systems, Pine Mountain, Ga., 1969, pp. 36–60.
[3] ——, "Selection of optimal transmission rate for statistical multiplexors," in *Proc. 1970 Int. Conf. Communications,* San Francisco, Calif., pp. 28-22–28-25.
[4] T. G. Gordon *et al.,* "Design of performance of a statistical multiplexor," in *Proc. 1970 Int. Conf. Communications,* San Francisco, Calif., pp. 28-7–28-21.
[5] H. Rudin, Jr., "Performance of a simple multiplexor–concentrator for data communication," *IEEE Trans. Commun. Technol.,* vol. COM-19, pp. 178–187, Apr. 1971.
[6] J. H. Chang, "Comparison of synchronous and asynchronous time division multiplexing techniques," in *Proc. 1970 Int. Conf. Communications,* San Francisco, Calif., pp. 16-10–16-17.
[7] C. D. Pack, "The effect of multiplexing on a computer communication system," submitted to *Commun. Ass. Comput. Mach.*

DYNAMIC BUFFER MANAGEMENT FOR COMPUTER COMMUNICATIONS*

by

WESLEY W. CHU
University of California
Los Angeles, California

ABSTRACT

Buffer management plays an important role in store-and-forward computer communication systems. The management policy will influence the cost as well as the performance of the system. In this paper we present an implementation of a dynamic buffer management strategy for a shared buffer computer communication system. Such a management policy provides flexibility as well as efficiency in utilization of buffer space. An estimation of required buffer size and strategies for handling buffer overflow are described. Finally, methods for allocating buffer resources among the set of buffer outputs (destinations) are discussed.

I. INTRODUCTION

As asynchronous time division multiplexing[1] (or statistical multiplexing) and packet switching[2,3,4] grow in their usage in computer communications, the problem of buffer management is of increasing interest. The basic problem is: How can we optimally manage (allocate and distribute) a stream of addressed messages designated to various locations?

ADS: DESTINATION ADDRESS

MESSAGE

Figure 1. A Stream of Addressed Messages.

A simple way to manage these message streams is to assign to each destination a fixed amount of buffer space. However, such assignments result in waste of storage space, a result which is supported by studies of buffer behavior which reveal that shared buffers yield much more efficient buffer utilization.[1] This motivated us to use an address translation technique to implement a shared buffer memory. The basic element in this technique is an address translation table that translates logical addresses of the buffer outputs (destinations) into physical addresses of the buffer memory. Such address translation permits us to dynamically assign buffer space for each buffer output, which greatly improves buffer utilization and flexibility.

We shall first describe the shared buffer organization and its operation under dynamic buffer management; next we will discuss the required buffer size for a given operating environment; and lastly we will consider the fixed size partitioning and variable size partitioning of buffer allocation for a shared buffer memory.

II. A SHARED BUFFER ORGANIZATION

A communication processor commonly consists of two major parts: a controller and a buffer, as shown in Figure 2. The controller consists of three parts:

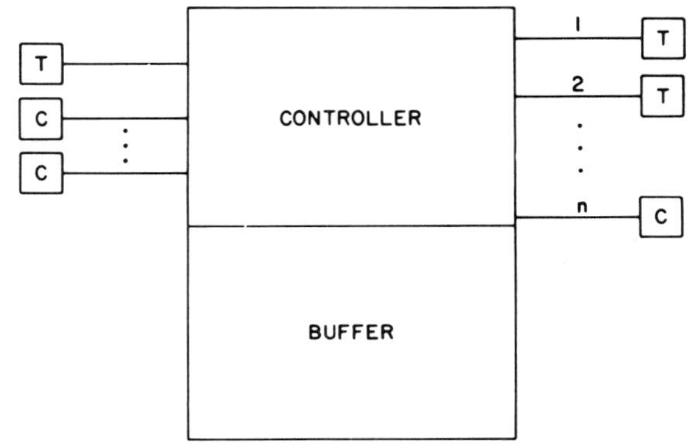

T TERMINAL

C COMPUTER

Figure 2. A Communication Processor.

network controller, message queuing controller, and message editor. The network controller performs functions such as transmission control, device control, and message routing. The message queuing controller performs queuing, scheduling, and optimizing overall system performance. The message editor performs text coding and resegmentation, message header interpretation, and line editing. All three parts of the controller are involved with buffer management, which is the main subject of this paper. Let us first present a shared buffer organization.

The organization of the shared buffer consists of an Address Translation Table (ATT), a Buffer Memory (BM), a Block Available List (BAL), and a Waiting Queue (WQ). The ATT (Figure 3A) translates the message destination addresses into the physical addresses of the buffer memory. Therefore, each entry of the ATT corresponds to a buffer output or message destination. The total number of entries in the ATT equals the total number of destinations. Each entry of the ATT consists of: first block address, last block address, and a buffer status bit. The first

*This work was supported by the Advanced Research Projects Agency of the Department of Defense under Contract No. DAHC 15-73-C0368 and the U. S. Office of Naval Research, Mathematical and Information Science Division, Contract Number N00014-69-A-0200-4027, NR048-129.

i	$A(B_{i1})$	$A(B_{i\ell})$	b_i
1	3000	6000	1
2	9000	1000	1
3	2000	2000	0
.	-	-	-
.	-	-	-
.	-	-	-
n	-	-	-

Figure 3A. The Address Translation Table (ATT).

B_{i1} = First block of the message for the ith buffer output (destination), i = 1,2,...,n

$B_{i\ell}$ = Last block of the message for the ith buffer output (destination), i = 1,2,...,n

n = Total number of buffer outputs or message destinations

$A(B_{i1})$ = Physical address of B_{i1}

$A(B_{i\ell})$ = Physical address of $B_{i\ell}$

b_i = Buffer status bit for the ith buffer output (destination)

= { 0 No message in the buffer for the ith output; 1 Otherwise

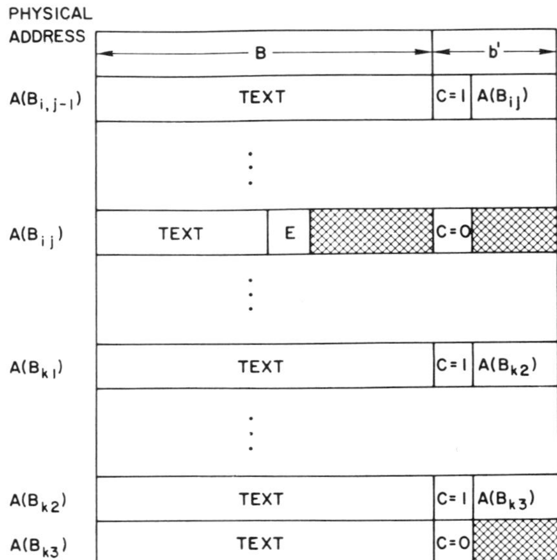

Figure 3B. Buffer Memory (BM)

C = Block continuation bit

= { 0 last block; 1 otherwise

$A(B_{ij})$ = Physical address of the jth block for the ith buffer output = linkage pointer

E = End of message character

 Dummy information

block address is a pointer which points to the physical address of the beginning of a message; the last block address serves as a pointer which points to the last block of a message and as a pointer for linking a newly arrived message with those messages in the buffer that have the same destination addresses. The buffer status bit, b, for a specific entry indicates if there is any message in the buffer for that destination.

The Buffer Memory is partitioned into fixed size blocks with contiguous addresses. This is similar to the definition of pages used in the virtual memory systems. The structure of a block consists of: the text, a block continuation bit C, and a linkage pointer (Figure 3B). The block continuation bit indicates whether the block is the last block. If the block is not the last block, the information following the block status bit is a linkage pointer which is the physical address of the next message block. If the block is the last block, then the linkage pointer is ignored. The optimal block size depends on many parameters such as overhead of the linage pointers, wasted space in the last unfilled block,[5] buffer control techniques, and channel error statistics.[6]

The Block Available List (BAL) is the list of available blocks of the buffer memory. This list is updated as soon as a block of buffer memory becomes available.

The Waiting Queue (WQ) stores those requests for buffer space when the buffer memory is full or those buffer allocation has been used up. The requests, designated by their addresses, are recorded in the Waiting Queue. The message queuing controller processes these requests when buffer memory space becomes available.

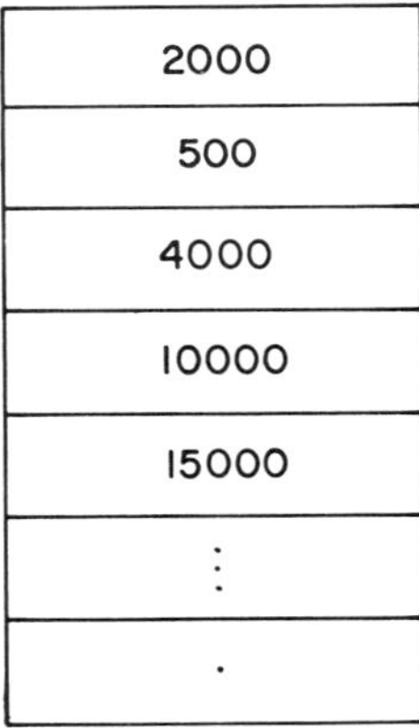

PHYSICAL ADDRESS
A(Bij)
2000
500
4000
10000
15000

Figure 3C. Block Available List (BAL).

Figure 3. A Shared Buffer Organization.

III. OPERATION OF THE SHARED BUFFER ORGANIZATION

Let us now describe the operation of a shared buffer memory as shown in Figure 3. The buffer organization consists of two processes: input process and output process. These two processes do not operate concurrently. The function of the input process is to collect the addressed input messages and efficiently allocate them into the buffer memory. The output process schedules according to preassigned priorities and efficiently distributes the data in the buffer to various destinations.

The input process is initiated when a request for a buffer has arrived at the Buffer Memory. We then examine the Block Available List to determine if there is any available space. The input process is "unlocked"* if there is buffer space available. According to the message address, the input process examines the corresponding entry of the ATT. The buffer status bit indicates whether there is any message block for the destination remaining in the buffer waiting for processing. Therefore, we have the following two cases:

1) If the buffer does not contain any message blocks for that destination--that is, the buffer status bit for that destination is "0"--then we let the selected available memory address from BAL be the first block address of the ATT for that destination. We proceed to store the data into the buffer memory and set the block status bit according to whether we need another block of buffer memory for that message. The next block address or linkage pointer is obtained from the BAL. We continue this process until we reach the end of the message. We then mark the end of the message by an end of message character, set the block continuation bit to "0", and record the last message block address in the ATT.

2) If there are already messages for a destination stored in the buffer--that is, if the buffer status bit for that destination is "1"--then we shall first connect the newly arrived message with the messages in the buffer that have the same destination address. Since the last block address in the ATT provides us with the physical address of the last message block in the buffer, this connect operation is performed by the following two operations:

   a) Changing the block continuation bit from "0" to "1", which implies that there are now one or more blocks following this block;

   b) Updating the linkage pointer (located next to the continuation bit) to point to the physical address of the first block of the newly arrived message. This address is taken from the BAL. Thus we have linked together the newly arrived addressed message with all those messages which are already in the buffer and have the same destination.

   After the above linking operation, we then store data into the buffer in the same manner as described in 1). The last block address in the ATT is finally updated to point to the last block address of the newly arrived message.

Let us now describe the output process. The output process is initiated by the terminal devices and is "unlocked" if there is a message in the buffer to be sent to that destination. This can easily be tested by examining the buffer status bit for that destination in the ATT. After the output process is "unlocked", based on the first block address of that destination in the ATT, the output process sends the message from the buffer memory to the destination. As soon as a block of data has been transmitted to the terminal, the Block Available List (BAL) is updated. Furthermore, the first block address in the ATT is also updated by the linkage pointer and points to the updated first block address. We continue this process until we reach the last message block; then we set the buffer status bit b_i in the ATT for that destination to "0", which means there is now no more data for that destination stored in the buffer memory. Because of the updating of the ATT and the BAL after outputting each block of data, the first block address should be equal when $b_i = 0$. If not, a fault interrupt should be generated.

IV. BUFFER SIZE CONSIDERATIONS

For a given required buffer performance, the required buffer size depends on many parameters such as message arrival statistics, message length, traffic intensity for various buffer outputs (destination function) and the number of buffer outputs. Usually, to reduce delay due to buffering, we would like to keep the frequency of occurrence of buffer overflow relatively low. We would like to know how large the buffer should be to assure us a given level of performance. The quantative relationship of buffer behavior obtained from the study of a finite waiting room buffer with multiple distinct outputs can be used for such estimation.[7]

Since the study in [7] is character-oriented while the system we describe here is block-oriented, some modification is needed to account for the last unfilled block as well as for the increases in traffic intensity due to addressing of each block and the last unfilled block. Thus for a given message traffic source, the buffer memory for the block oriented system is larger than that of the character-oriented buffer system.

We shall now consider such modifications. Let λ_i be the message arrival rate for the ith buffer output in messages/second; $\bar{\ell}$ be the average message length in characters; μ_i be the ith buffer output rate in characters/second; $\bar{n}(B,\ell)$ be the average number of blocks for a message** with block size B; and b' be the sum of the linkage pointer and the block continuation bit in characters. Then the traffic intensity for the ith buffer output is

$$\rho_i = \frac{\lambda_i \cdot \bar{n}(B,\ell) \cdot (B+b')}{\mu_i} \qquad i = 1,2,\ldots n \tag{1}$$

The average traffic level, $\bar{\rho}$, for the buffer system is the average traffic intensity of the n buffer outputs; that is,

$$\bar{\rho} = \sum_{i=1}^{n} \rho_i / n \tag{2}$$

Based on a given buffer overflow probability P_{of}, $\bar{\ell}$, and $\bar{\rho}$, we can find the buffer size, $N_c(P_{of}, \bar{\rho}, \bar{\ell})$, for a character-oriented buffer system from [7].

Let us now consider the extra storage due to the last unfilled block, the linkage pointer, and block continuation bit. The buffer block size is equal to $B' = B + b'$ (See Figure 3B). The expected extra

---

*For efficiency in buffer utilization, the shared buffer operates as a single bucket (series) queue rather than as the conventional two bucket queues, of which one is used for input traffic to fill the buffer while the other is used for outputting the buffer. In operating the single bucket buffer, deadlock problems may arise when the buffer is full and the output process arrived after the input process, or when the buffer is empty and the input process arrived after the output process. The "lock" and "unlock" operations are used for avoiding such deadlock problems.

**When the message length is geometrically distributed with parameter $p = 1/\bar{\ell}$ and $q = 1 - p$, then it can be shown [6] that the average number of blocks per message for a block size B is $\overline{n}(B,\ell) = (1 - q^B)^{-1}$.

buffer space for storing a message in blocks rather than in characters is

$$\Delta = \bar{n}(B,\ell)\cdot(B+b') - (\bar{\ell} + b'') \quad (3)$$

where b" is the address overhead for storing the message in characters. The effective average message length for storing in a block-oriented buffer system is then equal to

$$\bar{\ell}' = \bar{\ell} + \Delta = \bar{n}(B,\ell)\cdot(B+b') - b'' \quad (4)$$

Thus the buffer size for the block-oriented buffer system for a specified P_{of}, $\bar{\rho}$ and $\bar{\ell}$ can be approximated by

$$N_b(P_{of}, \bar{\rho}, \bar{\ell}) \doteq N_c(P_{of}, \bar{\rho}, \bar{\ell}') \quad (5)$$

74

If the destination function ρ_i, $i = 1,2...,n$ for a particular buffer system has not been considered in [7], then a simulation is needed to estimate the buffer behavior for the block-oriented system.

V. MEMORY ALLOCATION IN A SHARED BUFFER

The advantage of using the above described shared memory organization is the efficient utilization of buffer memory among the set of buffer outputs. For convenience in discussion, we shall designate those terminal devices that are signed on with the communication processor as active buffer outputs and those that are not signed on as inactive buffer outputs. Further, we shall define those active buffer outputs that have no messages in the buffer memory as virtually inactive buffer outputs which are idling and waiting for output. The buffer status bit for these virtually inactive outputs is "0". With these definitions, we shall now describe two methods for allocating the shared buffer, and strategies for handling buffer overflow.

1) Fixed Size Partitioning

In the fixed size partitioning method, each active buffer output is allocated a fixed amount of buffer space. For a buffer memory of M blocks with n buffer outputs in which m of them are active ($m < n$), we assign a maximum buffer space for the ith output equal to S_i. Since the total buffer space is M, we have $\sum_{i=1}^{m} S_i = M$. A special case is to assign an equal amount of allowable buffer size for all the outputs--that is, $S_i = M/m$ for all i.* To implement such a policy, the Network Controller examines the set of buffer outputs at regular intervals. Any change of buffer output status (inactive to active, or active to inactive) can only be accomplished at these time instances. The maximum amount of buffer space for each buffer output is revised whenever there is a change in buffer output status. The requests for buffer space that cannot be accomplished by the revised allocation are stored in the Waiting Queue (WQ), as shown in Figure 4. The Message Queuing Controller then schedules the input to the memory buffer to meet the fixed size allocation. The advantage of such partitioning is that no buffer space is allocated for inactive buffer outputs. The disadvantage, however, is the inability to dynamically share buffer spaces that are assigned to each active buffer output. As a result, some active buffer outputs may need more space

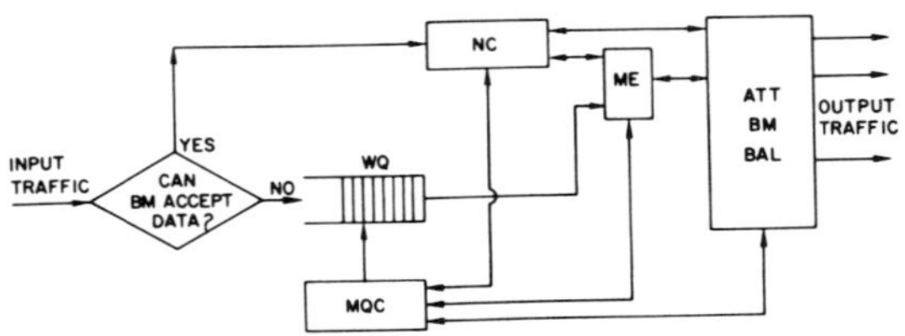

BM = BUFFER MEMORY
WQ = WAITING QUEUE
MQC = MESSAGE QUEUING CONTROLLER
NC = NETWORK CONTROLLER
ME = MESSAGE EDITOR

Figure 4. Implementation of Buffer Allocation for a Shared Buffer Memory.

than they have been allocated. This causes extra delay due to buffering. To remedy this situation, we shall discuss the variable size partitioning method which allocates buffer space for each buffer output according to input traffic demand and priority.

2) Variable Size Partitioning

This method allocates to each active buffer output a variable amount of buffer space. The maximum allowable amount of buffer space for each buffer output varies according to buffer occupancy as well as to the number of active buffer outputs at the particular moment. If the buffer is not full--that is, the Block Available List is not empty--the amount of buffer space for the ith active buffer output is

$$S_i = \frac{M}{m} + k_i \qquad \text{for } i = 1, 2, \ldots, m. \quad (6)$$

where

$$-\frac{M}{m} + 1 \le k_i \le M - \frac{M}{m} - m + 1.$$

The above equation states that for a buffer space with M blocks and m active buffer outputs, the maximum buffer space allocation for a buffer output is $\frac{M}{m} + k_i = \frac{M}{m} + M - \frac{M}{m} - m + 1$ which is $M - m + 1$ blocks, and the minimum buffer space allocation for an active buffer output is $\frac{M}{m} + k_i = \frac{M}{m} - \frac{M}{m} + 1$ which is 1 block. Clearly $k_i = 0$ for all i reduces to the fixed buffer partition. From experimental measurement, we know that the computer output messages are in burst form and are arriving at the buffer randomly. This motivates us to propose a buffer management policy according to buffer input demand. One possible strategy is to let the buffer accept data for various buffer outputs according to the buffer input demand until the buffer becomes full; then the buffer stops accepting any more data. All subsequent requests for buffer space will be entered into the WQ, waiting for available buffer space (See Figure 4). When a block becomes available, we assign the buffer to those requests in the WQ in accordance with the following queuing service discipline. We always first assign buffer space (a block at a time) to those requests in the WQ whose outputs are inactive or virtually inactive. These outputs can be easily determined by examining the corresponding buffer status bit, b_i, if it is 0. We then allocate the buffer (a block at a time) to those buffer outputs ($b_i = 1$) according to a pre-selected

---

*Due to physical constraints, S_i must be of integer value. Should S_i be non-integer value, then we have to adjust the S_i to integer value such that all S_i are approximately equal and $\sum_{i=1}^{m} S_i = M$.

priority discipline. From [7] we know that in order to optimize buffer performance we should schedule the traffic intensity to various buffer outputs approximately equally. Since the expected buffer length is a function of traffic intensity, we can implement this policy according to the number of buffer blocks occupied (queue length) by each active buffer output. The relative traffic intensity among these buffer outputs is directly proportional to the number of occupied buffer blocks. Therefore, we schedule the incoming traffic such that the amount of buffer occupancy for each of the active buffer outputs is approximately equal. This can be implemented by a round-robin system that favors terminals with a smaller number of occupied blocks. Thus far we have not considered job priority such as urgency, interaction, batch, etc. In an actual design we should also consider job priority to assure a certain grade of service for each buffer output (destination). When the WQ becomes empty and the buffer is not full, we then repeat the above process by accepting input data according to input traffic demand. The queuing service discipline clearly will influence the performance of the system, and should be determined by the traffic characteristics to each destination, such as message length, arrival rate, the type of devices used at that destination, i.e., CRT or TTY, and job characteristics of a destination, i.e., urgency of the job, interactive, or batch.

Let us now summarize the variable buffer partitioning algorithm. When the buffer is not full and the WQ is empty, we accept data into the buffer according to buffer input demand. When the buffer is full and the WQ is not empty, we always first assign buffer space a block at a time to those requests in the WQ whose buffer outputs are inactive or virtually inactive ($b_i = 0$), and then assign those active outputs ($b_i = 1$) according to a preselected priority service discipline. Thus the variable buffer partition provides an adaptive method of buffer space allocation.

To implement this policy, when a request for buffer space arrives at the controller, we examine the BAL to determine what actions are to be taken: 1) If the BAL is not empty, the input process is "unlocked" and we proceed to the buffer operations as described in III; 2) If the BAL is empty, then we store the request--designated by its address-- in the WQ, and the Message Queuing Controller is notified that there are requests waiting in the WQ for processing. When the output process release a buffer block, the Message Queuing Controller is notified, and it performs scheduling (notifying terminal or CPU to send message) of input messages from the WQ according to the preassigned priority discipline. When a buffer output is down (dead) and the buffer memory is not full, acceptance of excess messages for that buffer output (destination) could cause buffer overflow. To remedy this, the Network Controller monitors all buffer outputs and notifies the input process as soon as a dead buffer output is detected. All of the messages stored in the buffer for this dead output should now be released from the buffer.

VI. CONCLUSION

A dynamic buffer management system for computer communications that utilizes virtual address concepts has been proposed in this paper. This buffer management system provides an implementation of the shared buffer that efficiently utilizes buffer memory. Further, the ATT provides a convenient method of process restructuring in case of buffer fault. The problem of allocation of a shared buffer space among a set of active buffer output destinations is discussed. The fixed size partitioning method is simple to implement but less efficient in memory utilization. The variable size partitioning method assigns buffer space according to traffic demand when the buffer is not full and according to a preassigned priority when the buffer becomes full. Such a variable buffer partitioning method yields more efficient buffer utilization than the fixed buffer partitioning method. The dynamic buffer management described in this paper has been sucessfully implemented in the statistical demultiplexor which was constructed at UCLA and should have high potential for use in other types of communication processors as well.

ACKNOWLEDGMENT

The author wishes to thank H. Opderbeck at UCLA for his stimulating discussions during the writing of this paper.

75

REFERENCES

[1] Chu, W. W., "Design Considerations of Statistical Multiplexors" Proceedings of the ACM Symposium on Problems in the Optimization of Data Communication Systems, October 13-16, 1969, pp. 36-60.

[2] Davies, D. W., "The Principles of a Data Communication Network for Computers and Remote Peripherals," Proceedings of IFIP, Hardware, Edinburgh, 1968, D11.

[3] Roberts, L. G. and B. Wessler, "Computer Network Development to Achieve Resource Sharing," AFIPS Proceedings, SJCC, 1970, pp. 543-549.

[4] Farmer, W. D. and E. E. Newhall, "An Experimental Distributed Switching System to Handle High Speed Aperiodic Computer Traffic," Proceedings of the ACM Symposium on Problems in the Optimization of Data Communications Systems, October 13-16, 1969.

[5] Wolman, E., "A Fixed Optimum Cell Size for Records of Various Length," JACM, Vol. 12, No. 1, January 1965, pp. 53-70.

[6] Chu, W. W., "Optimal Fixed Message Block Size for Computer Communications," Proceedings IFIP, Hardware, Ljubljana, Yugoslavia, August 1971.

[7] Chu, W. W., "Demultiplexing Considerations for Statistical Multiplexors," IEEE Transactions on Communications, Vol. COM-20, June 1972, pp. 603-609.

ERRATA

1. Page 70 Column 1 Line 17 should read:
   set the block continuation bit according
2. Page 70 Column 2 Line 15 should read:
   should be equal to the last block address when $b_i = 0$. If not, . . .

Reprinted by permission from *Proceedings of the Third Data Communications Symposium*
November 1973, pp. 68-72

Packet Switching via Satellites

Satellites provide quite effective and economically competitive transoceanic and domestic communication channel capacity. Further, because of their inherent property of multi-access broadcast, satellites can be a very attractive media for distributed multi-station data interaction with each station which has different traffic characteristics. Abramson (p. 78) describes the properties of packet switching with satellites. Kleinrock and Lam (p. 86) provide analytical results on the performance of packet switching in a slotted satellite channel, and Roberts (p. 95) presents a packet reservation system that dynamically allocates channel capacity. For further information on this subject, the interested reader should refer to [SCH 73].

Packet radio systems represent another interesting branch of multi-access broadcasting. For further readings on this subject, the reader should refer to a series of papers from the session entitled "Packet Radio — Future Impact" in *AFIPS Proceedings,* Vol. 44, 1975, pp. 217-262.

Packet switching with satellites*

by NORMAN ABRAMSON

University of Hawaii
Honolulu, Hawaii

INTRODUCTION

History

The first computer-communication networks put into operation were designed around the communications provided by the existing worldwide telephone network. Lucky has given a convincing rationale for that decision.[1]

> "The voice telephone network is perhaps the most remarkable information processing system yet constructed by man. In 1970 it served 100,000,000 telephones in the United States. The number of possible interconnections is clearly enormous. The worth of this plant is approximately 50 billion dollars. Over one million people are employed by AT&T alone in the care and feeding of this huge network. Virtually every statistic associated with the telephone network can be phrased in some extraordinary manner. Its ready accessibility and virtual ubiquity make it the obvious first contender for handling data traffic."

As the limitations of this system for data communications became apparent, a number of methods were introduced to overcome the limitations of dial-up telephone and leased line systems. Data concentrators are used to increase the utilization of expensive long distance lines. High speed, wideband facilities are used to handle those situations where the burst data rate requirement of the network is larger than can be transmitted in a single voice channel. A few large systems use leased line data channels in a network with multiple paths between nodes for increased reliability. All of the systems built before 1970 however based the organization of their data communication channels on the circuit switching methods developed for voice signals during the latter part of the 19th century.

As the need for more powerful and more flexible computer-communication networks, distributed over large geographical areas, increased the basic limitations imposed by the organization of circuit switched systems was questioned.[2,3,4] By 1970 the ARPA Network,[5] the first computer-communication system to employ packet switching techniques suited to the peculiar statistics of digital data had gone into operation. The network is described in Reference 6:

> "The ARPA Network is a new kind of digital communication system employing wideband leased lines and message switching, wherein a path is not established in advance and instead each message carries an address. Messages normally traverse several nodes in going from source to destination, and the network is a store-and-forward system wherein, at each node, a copy of the message is stored until it is safely received at the following node. At each node a small processor (an *Interface Message Processor*, or *IMP*) acts as a nodal switching unit and also interconnects the research computer centers, or *Hosts*, with the high bandwidth leased lines."

By January 1973 the use of packet switching techniques in the ARPA Network had made possible a resource sharing computer network among more than 30 large machines; these machines represent an investment of more than $80,000,000, span a geographical region from Hawaii to Massachusetts and the network is still expanding at a rapid rate. At this time packet switched techniques are under consideration for other computer-communication networks in the USA, Canada, Japan and Western Europe.[7,8] But no common carrier has yet announced plans for a packet switched data service for the general user of data communications.

Although the basic packet switched method of organizing communication channels in the ARPA Network represents a significant step forward from the circuit switched methods of the voice oriented common carriers the communications medium of the ARPA Network (with the exception of a special satellite link to the University of Hawaii) is still the point-to-point wire (or microwave) channel.

---

* THE ALOHA SYSTEM is a research project at the University of Hawaii, supported by the Advanced Research Projects Agency under NASA Contract No. NAS2-6700 and by the U.S. Air Force Office of Aerospace Research under Contract No. F44620-69-C-0030. Part of the work reported in this paper was supported by Systems Research Corporation, Honolulu, under ONR Contract N00014-70-C-0414.

The medium is the multiplexor

In June 1971 the first remote terminal in THE ALOHA SYSTEM, an experimental UHF radio, packet switched network was put into operation at the University of Hawaii.[9] THE ALOHA SYSTEM is a packet switched computer communication network using many of the design concepts of the ARPA Network. The design of THE ALOHA SYSTEM departs from that of the ARPA Network in two major respects however. The first is in the use of a new form of burst random access method of employing a data communication channel. That method is particularly attractive for use with a broadcast radio channel such as in THE ALOHA SYSTEM; the characteristics of the ALOHA burst random access communication method are described in the next section.

The other respect in which the design of THE ALOHA SYSTEM departs from that of the ARPA Network, and indeed from the design of all other computer networks, is in the form of multiplexing which occurs in THE ALOHA SYSTEM. The network uses two 24,000 bits/second channels for all remote units—one of these channels is used by all remote units for data into a central machine (an IBM 360/65) and the other channel is used for data out of the central machine. Since data packets from all remote users access the same 24,000 bits/second radio channel in 30 millisecond bursts, each user automatically multiplexes their data onto that single channel at the time it transmits its packet. Thus the multiplexing is accomplished between the transmitting antenna at each user station and the receiving antenna at the central station. Steven Crocker of ARPA has characterized this effect by noting that in THE ALOHA SYSTEM, "the medium is the multiplexor".

A final point should be brought out about the lack of need for multiplexing equipment in THE ALOHA SYSTEM. The cost of communications for a network of terminals connected to a central time sharing system is often thought of as being composed of the line charges (lease cost or dial-up charges), the modem charges at either end of the link plus perhaps some portion of the cost of the communications processor. For long distance connections to a machine the line charges will usually dominate the cost of communications. Even for local connections however the real costs of simply connecting a terminal to a machine by common carrier communication facilities are hard to come by. A good portion of these costs can often be attributed to the front end communications processor and multiplexor. The need to sample telephone input lines on a frequent basis and to assemble characters, limits the number of input lines which can be handled by a single processor and the data rates at which these lines can operate. Some indication of the magnitude of the cost of performing these functions can be obtained from a survey of national time sharing services published in November, 1971.[10] The typical charge for connect time to one of these services (that is, the cost necessary for simply tying up communications resources, not CPU time) was about $10/hour.

Since multiplexing in THE ALOHA SYSTEM is accomplished automatically the channel now used in the system is capable of handling over 500 active terminals[9] each transmitting packets at a *burst* data rate of 24,000 bits/second. (Of course the *average* data rate of each user must be well below 24,000 bits/second.)

The ALOHA channel

Consider a number of widely separated users each wanting to transmit data packets over a single high speed communication channel. Assume that the rate at which the users generate packets is such that the average time between packets from a single user is much greater than the time needed to transmit a single packet. (In THE ALOHA SYSTEM the ratio of these times is about 2,000 to 1.)

Conventional time or frequency multiplexing methods or some kind of polling scheme could be employed to share the channel among the users. Some of the disadvantages of these methods are discussed by Roberts in a related paper in this session.[14] The method used by THE ALOHA SYSTEM is suggested by the statistical characteristics of the packets generated by remote users. Since each user will generate packets infrequently[11] and each packet can be transmitted in a time interval much less than the average time between packets the following scheme seems natural.

Each user station has a buffer which it uses to store one line of text. When the line is complete a header containing address, control and parity information for a cyclic error detecting code is appended to the text to form a packet and the packet is transmitted to the central station. Each user at a console transmits packets to the central station over the same high data rate channel in a completely unsynchronized (from one user to another) manner. If and only if a packet is received without error it is acknowledged by the central station. After transmitting a packet the transmitting station waits a given amount of time for an acknowledgment; if none is received the packet is automatically retransmitted. This process is repeated until a successful transmission and acknowledgment occurs or until some fixed number of unsuccessful transmissions has been attempted.

A transmitted packet can be received incorrectly because of two different types of errors; (1) random noise errors and (2) errors caused by interference with a packet transmitted by another console. The first type of error has not been a serious problem on the UHF channels employed. The second type of error, that caused by interference, will be of importance only when a large number of users are trying to use the channel at the same time. Interference errors will limit the number of users and the amount of data which can be transmitted over this ALOHA random access channel as more remote stations are added to THE ALOHA SYSTEM.

Capacity of ALOHA channels

In order to describe these limits we assume that the start times of message packets in our channel comprise a Poisson point process with parameter λ packets/second. If each packet lasts τ seconds we can define $S=\lambda\tau$, where

$$S = \text{normalized channel message rate} \quad (1)$$

S is called the normalized channel message rate since a value of S equal to one would correspond to a channel with packets synchronized perfectly so that the start of one packet always coincided with the end of the previous packet. (Of course this will not occur because of our Poisson assumption.) Note that S takes into account only message packets, not retransmission packets.

In addition we assume that the start times of the message packets plus packet retransmissions comprise another Poisson point process. (This assumption will hold only if the packet retransmission delays are large. See Reference 9.) Then we can define a quantity G, analogous to the normalized channel message rate, which takes into account the message packets plus the retransmission packets.

$$G = \text{normalized channel traffic rate} \tag{2}$$

In general we know that

$$G \geq S \tag{3}$$

In Reference 9 we showed that

$$S = Ge^{-2G} \tag{4}$$

and this relationship is plotted in Figure 1.

Note from Figure 1 that the message rate reaches a maximum value of $1/2e = 0.184$. For this value of S the channel traffic is equal to 0.5. The traffic on the channel becomes unstable at $S = 1/2e$ and the average number of retransmissions becomes unbounded. Thus we may speak of this value of the message rate as the *capacity* of this random access data channel. Because of the random access feature the channel capacity is reduced to roughly one sixth of its value if we were able to fill the channel with a continuous stream of uninterrupted data.

The form of channel analyzed above corresponds to THE ALOHA SYSTEM channel now in operation.

It is possible to modify the completely unsynchronized use of the ALOHA channel described in order to increase the capacity of the channel. In the pure ALOHA channel each user simply transmits a packet when ready without any attempt to coordinate his transmission with those of other users. While this strategy has a certain elegance it does lead to somewhat inefficient channel utilization. If we can establish a time base and require each user to start his packets only at certain fixed instants it is possible to increase the channel capacity. In this kind of channel, called a *slotted ALOHA channel*, a central clock establishes a time base for a sequence of "slots" of the same duration as a packet transmission. Then when a user has a packet to transmit he synchronizes the start of his transmission to the start of a slot. In this fashion, if two messages conflict they will overlap completely, rather than partially.

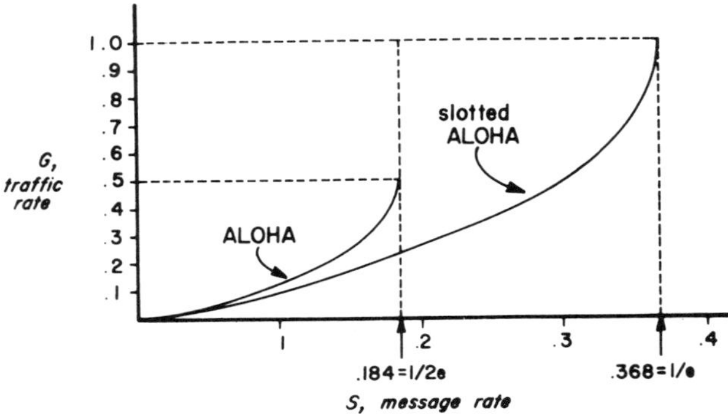

Figure 1—Traffic rate vs. message rate for a pure ALOHA channel and a slotted ALOHA channel

To analyze the slotted ALOHA channel define S_i as the probability that the i'th user will send a packet in some slot. Assume that each user operates independently of all other users and that whether a user sends a message in a given slot does not depend upon the state of any previous slot. If we have n users we can define $S = \sum_{i=1}^{n} S_i$, where

$$S = \text{normalized channel message rate} \tag{5}$$

As before we can also consider the rate at which a user sends message packets plus packet retransmissions. Define the probability that the i'th user will send a message packet or a packet retransmission as G_i. Then, for n identical users we define $G = \sum_{i=1}^{n} G_i$ where

$$G = \text{normalized channel traffic rate} \tag{6}$$

and, as in the pure ALOHA channel

$$G \geq S \tag{7}$$

We note here that although S, the sum of the S_i, is the probability that some user will send a message packet in a given slot, the analogous statement is not true for G. The sum of the G_i is not the probability that some user will send a message or repetition packet in a given slot. In fact even though G is the sum of the probabilities G_i, G is not itself a probability and G may be greater than 1.

For the slotted ALOHA channel with n independent users, the probability that a packet from the i'th user will not experience an interference from one of the other users is

$$\prod_{j=1,\, j\neq i}^{n} (1-G_j)$$

Therefore we may write the following relationship between the message rate and the traffic rate of the i'th user.

$$S_i = G_i \prod_{j=1,\, j\neq i}^{n} (1-G_j) \tag{8}$$

If all users are identical we have

$$S_i = \frac{S}{n} \tag{9}$$

and

$$G_i = \frac{G}{n} \tag{10}$$

so that (8) can be written

$$S = G\left(1-\frac{G}{n}\right)^{n-1} \tag{11}$$

and in the limit as $n \rightarrow \infty$, we have

$$S = Ge^{-G} \tag{12}$$

Equation (12) is plotted in Figure 1 (curve labeled Slotted ALOHA). Note that the message rate of the Slotted ALOHA channel reaches a maximum value of $1/e = 0.37$, twice the capacity of the pure ALOHA channel.

This result for Slotted ALOHA channels was first derived by Roberts[12] using a different method.

PROPERTIES OF SATELLITE CHANNELS

The cable in the sky

In the worldwide telephone system satellites are used more or less interchangeably with cables for transmission of voice signals. Because of this desirable feature, it is not surprising that the common carriers and even satellite designers have tended not to emphasize the differences between cable and satellite channels.

A communications satellite however is not just a big cable in the sky. There are several significant differences between the communication channel properties of a cable or microwave link and the communication channel properties of a satellite transponder.

In the next three sections we shall explain some of these differences and how they can affect the operation of a packet switched system using a satellite. But first we should mention one property of a satellite channel which the common carriers have emphasized. A satellite transponder in geosynchronous orbit is stationed 36,000 kilometers above the equator. A signal transmitted using the satellite will therefore experience a delay of about a quarter second, corresponding to the round trip propagation time up to the satellite and down again. This delay can decrease the effective data rate of certain error control schemes requiring positive acknowledgments sent from the receiver back to the transmitter. Such schemes should not ordinarily be used over satellite channels.

There are three properties of communication satellites which we want to discuss here, in terms of their significance to packet switched communications. These are:

(a) data rates
(b) bilateral broadcasting
(c) perfect information feedback

Data rates

The first property of satellite channels is not a fundamental property of the satellite itself, but rather a property of how the satellite is used. A single voice channel on INTELSAT IV uses a bandwidth of 45 Khz. and provides the capability of transmitting data at 56 kilobits on a single voice channel. This mode of operation is in fact employed in the SPADE demand assignment system now used in the Atlantic satellite; it is employed in the single-channel-per-carrier digital voice link installed in the Paumalu earth station in Hawaii and the Jamesburg earth station in California. Since December 1972, THE ALOHA SYSTEM has been linked to the ARPANET using a single leased satellite voice channel to transmit data at 50 kilobits to NASA Ames Research Center in California.

Bilateral broadcasting

In the conventional use of communication channels the term "broadcasting" refers to the fact that many receivers may obtain the transmission from a single transmitter. Perhaps the most striking feature of a satellite channel is its broadcast nature as opposed to the point-to-point nature of wire channels. The reception of broadcast signals for satellite communication channels used with conventional circuit switched methods is a natural idea. But when a satellite channel is used in a packet switched mode it is possible to consider broadcasting use of the channel by transmitters as well as receivers. This capability we have called *bilateral broadcasting.*

Since a number of transmitting ground stations operating in a packet switched mode may all access the same channel in an unsynchronized (from ground station to ground station) fashion the analysis of an earlier section applies to bilateral broadcasting without any change. Each of the twenty or more ground stations accessing a given INTELSAT IV channel can transmit packets at will up to the ALOHA random access capacity of that single channel.

There is no technological reason why such a system could not be employed now to extend the capabilities of the existing worldwide satellite communication network in data communications. There is an existing regulatory restriction on such an unconventional use of INTELSAT IV however and discussions are under way with several agencies to remove these regulatory barriers in either the INTELSAT system or one of the several domestic satellite systems to be installed (or already installed in two countries).

Except for the not inconsiderable constraints imposed by regulatory considerations the same 50 kilobit leased satellite channel linking THE ALOHA SYSTEM to the ARPANET could be used to link machines in Alaska, Japan, Australia and any of the other sixteen earth stations which access the Pacific satellite. While these regulatory problems are being worked out however THE ALOHA SYSTEM has established a limited burst random access satellite network using the packet switching techniques described. In a joint experiment with NASA Ames Research Center in California and the University of Alaska we are operating such a link by means of the NASA ATS-1 satellite. The satellite transponder is operated as an unslotted ALOHA channel between earth stations in Hawaii, Alaska and California, and although usage of that channel is now restricted to two hours per day or less and the data rate of the channel is only 20,000 bits/second, the experiment is providing valuable information on this new communications technique.

Perfect information feedback

In the use of satellites for packet switching yet another property of little value in circuit switching assumes importance. In a packet switched system each ground station has the capability of transmitting packets up to the satellite addressed to any other ground station (or to all other ground stations). Each packet is then received by all ground stations, *including the ground station which transmitted the packet*, approximately one quarter second later. Therefore each ground station can initiate transmission of a packet at will as in THE ALOHA SYSTEM. However, whereas in THE ALOHA SYSTEM, it is necessary to provide information on packet interference to the sender in the form of positive ac-
32 knowledgments, such information is not necessary in the system we are describing. Since each sender can listen to his own packet retransmitted from the satellite each sender can be considered to have the same information on packet interference available to the receiver earth station. (In information theory terms, these channels are modeled as channels with perfect information feedback.)

Unfortunately in the real world, nothing is perfect and there will undoubtedly be circumstances when the transmitter and the receiver do not detect the same bit string from the satellite. The fact remains however that positive acknowledgments to combat packet interference are not required, and the more efficient use of a negative acknowledgment scheme in conjunction with packet numbering is feasible for this system.

EXCESS CAPACITY OF AN ALOHA CHANNEL

The idea

The type of packet switched satellite data channel we have described so far (either pure ALOHA or slotted ALOHA) has a certain elegant simplicity to it. The user of the channel simply transmits a burst of data when he wants at a data rate equal to that of the entire channel. Nevertheless there is a price to be paid for this simplicity in terms of channel capacity and in terms of delay. The question of delay is dealt with by Kleinrock[13] and Roberts[14] in the other two papers of this session. Roberts also discusses an effective method of employing the channel at rates significantly higher than the 37 percent capacity indicated by Figure 1. In the next section we provide some results which show that a slotted ALOHA channel can be used at rates well above 37 percent of capacity, if all users of the channel do not have identical message rates.

The idea of excess capacity in an ALOHA channel was first suggested by Roberts who derived a result for the case of several small users and a single large user of a slotted ALOHA channel. Roberts' proof was published along with a number of other interesting analytic results by Kleinrock and Lam.[15] The approach we shall take was suggested by Rettberg,[16] who also treated the case of a single large user and was able to obtain numerical results for that case. In the next section we provide a complete analytic and numerical solution to the use of slotted ALOHA channels by any number of users, each operating at an arbitrary rate.

The theory

From equation (8) we have a set of n equations relating the message rates and traffic rates of the n users

$$S_i = G_i \prod_{j=1,\, j\neq i}^{n} (1-G_j) \qquad i=1, 2, \ldots, n \tag{13}$$

Define

$$\alpha = \prod_{j=1}^{n} (1-G_j) \tag{14}$$

then (13) can be written

$$S_i = \frac{G_i}{1-G_i}\,\alpha \qquad i=1, 2, \ldots, n \tag{15}$$

For any set of n acceptable traffic rates $G_1, G_2, \ldots, G_n$ these n equations define a set of message rates $S_1, S_2, \ldots, S_n$, or a region in an n-dimensional space whose coordinates are the S_i. In order to find the boundary of this region we calculate the Jacobian,

$$J\left(\frac{S_1, S_2, \ldots, S_n}{G_1, G_2, \ldots, G_n}\right).$$

Since

$$\frac{\partial S_j}{\partial G_k} = \begin{cases} \prod_{i\neq j} (1-G_i) & j=k \\ -G_j \prod_{i\neq j,k} (1-G_i) & j\neq k \end{cases} \tag{16}$$

after some algebra we may write the Jacobian as

$$J\left(\frac{S_1, S_2, \ldots, S_n}{G_1, G_2, \ldots, G_n}\right) = \alpha^{n-2} \begin{vmatrix} (1-G_1) & -G_1 & -G_1 & \\ -G_2 & (1-G_2) & -G_2 & \cdots \\ -G_3 & -G_3 & (1-G_3) & \\ & \vdots & & \end{vmatrix}$$

$$= \alpha^{n-2}[1-G_1-G_2-\ldots-G_n] \tag{17}$$

Thus the condition for maximum message rates is

$$\sum_i G_i = 1 \tag{18}$$

This condition can then be used to define a boundary to the n dimensional region of allowable message rates, $S_1, S_2, \ldots, S_n$.

The results

Consider the special case of two classes of users with n_1 users in class 1 and n_2 users in class 2.

$$n_1 + n_2 = n \tag{19}$$

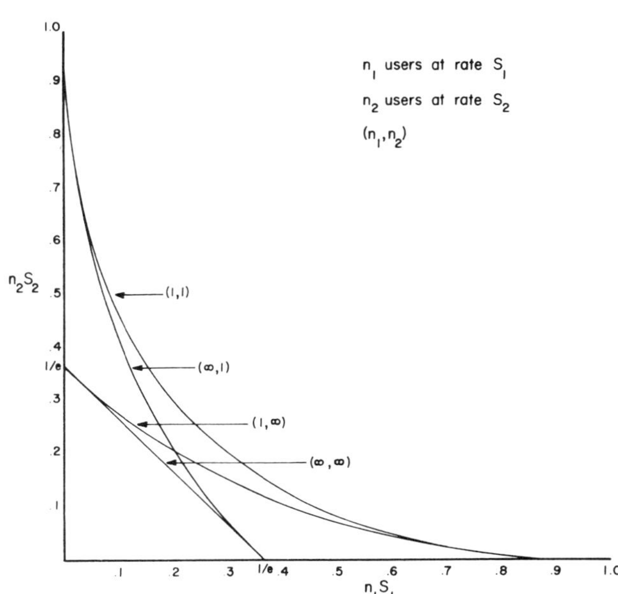

Figure 2—Allowable message rates

Let S_1 and G_1 be the message and traffic rates for users in class one, and S_2 and G_2 be the message and traffic rates for users in class 2. Then the n equations (13) can be written as the two equations

$$S_1 = G_1(1-G_1)^{n_1-1}(1-G_2)^{n_2} \tag{20a}$$

$$S_2 = G_2(1-G_2)^{n_2-1}(1-G_1)^{n_1} \tag{20b}$$

For any pair of acceptable traffic rates G_1 and G_2 these two equations define a pair of message rates, S_1 and S_2, or a region in the S_1, S_2 plane.

From (18) we know that the boundary of this region is defined by the condition

$$n_1G_1 + n_2G_2 = 1 \tag{21}$$

We can use (21) to substitute for G_1 in equation (20) and obtain two equations for S_1 and S_2 in terms of a single parameter G_2. Then as G_2 varies from 0 to 1 the resulting S_1, S_2 pairs define the boundary of the region we seek. A FORTRAN program to calculate the boundary was written and used to calculate several curves of the allowable region for different values of (n_1, n_2) (Figures 2, 3).

The important point to notice from Figures 2 and 3 is that in a lightly loaded Slotted ALOHA channel, a single large user can transmit data at a significant percentage of the total channel data rate, thus allowing use of the channel at rates well above the limit of 37 percent obtained when all users have the same message rate. This capability is important for a computer network consisting of many interactive terminal users and a small number of users who send large but infrequent files over the channel. Operation of the channel in a lightly loaded condition of course may not be desirable in a bandwidth limited channel. For a communications satellite where the average power in the satellite transponder limits the channel however[19] operation is a lightly loaded condition in a packet switched mode is an attractive alternative. Since the satellite will transmit power only when it is relaying a packet, the duty cycle in the transponder will be small and the average power used will be low.

Finally we note it is possible to deal with certain limiting cases in more detail, to obtain equations for the boundary of the allowable S_1, S_2 region.

(a) for $n_1 = n_2 = 1$
Upon using (21) in (20) we obtain

$$S_1 = G_1^2 \tag{22a}$$

$$S_2 = (1-G_1)^2 \tag{22b}$$

(b) for $n_2 \rightarrow \infty$

$$S_1 = G_1(1-G_1)^{n_1-1} \cdot \exp[-(1-n_1G_1)] \tag{23a}$$

$$S_2 = (1-n_1G_1)(1-G_1)^{n_1-1} \cdot \exp[-(1-n_1G_1)] \tag{23b}$$

(c) for $n_1 = n_2 \rightarrow \infty$

$$S_1 = \frac{G_1}{e}$$

$$S_2 = \frac{1-G_1}{e}$$

Additional details dealing with excess capacity and the delay experienced with this kind of use of a slotted ALOHA channel may be found in References 17 and 18.

PACKET SWITCHING IN DOMSAT

Background

The 50 kilobit INTELSAT channel now being used to link THE ALOHA SYSTEM to the ARPA Network could em-

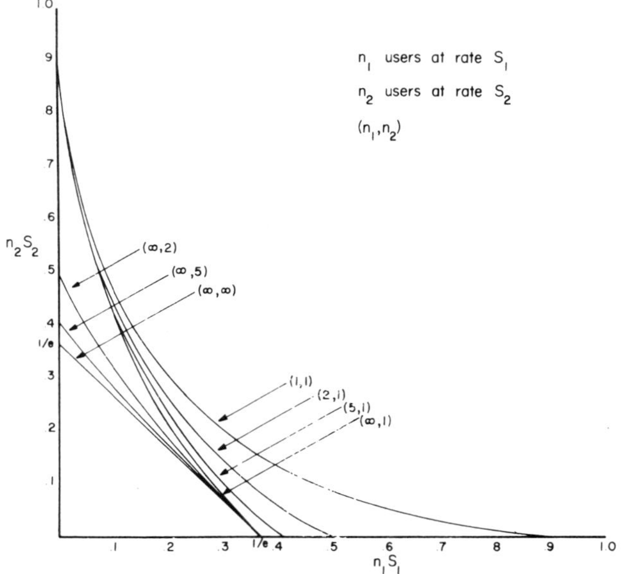

Figure 3—Allowable message rates

ploy the techniques we have described to link additional nodes in the ARPANET at each of the 16 earth stations with access to the Pacific satellite. These same techniques could also be employed by a common carrier to offer packet switched data communications of a quality to which we would all like to become accustomed.

As this is being written, there are in operation two domestic satellite systems (Molniya in the USSR and Anik in Canada) in addition to the worldwide INTELSAT system. Seven US domestic systems (DOMSAT) are under consideration and one has entered the construction phase with a first launch planned for 1974. Japan has announced plans for its domestic communications satellite and several other national systems are expected in the late 1970's. Most of the DOM-
84 SAT proposals plan a system of less expensive and therefore more numerous earth stations than the standard 97 foot earth station antennas now used in the INTELSAT system. Thus the advantage of using a lightly loaded packet switched channel in a power limited situation[19] assumes added importance.

A proposal

Consider the use of a single transponder in a US domestic satellite system to provide a public packet switched data communication service. INTELSAT IV employs 12 transponders each with 36 Mhz. bandwidth. Only one of these transponders devoted completely to a public packet switched service in a US domestic satellite system could easily provide data at a rate of 10 million bits/second into a small earth station. The public packet switched service in the US could provide burst data rates between small communication controllers at each earth station of 10 megabits. Assuming 100 earth stations over the US, and assuming the system is operated at a message rate $S = 0.15$, the average data rate into and out of each station would be about 15 kilobits although the variance about this average (both from earth station to earth station and at different times at the same earth station) would be large. A packet switched system would function without difficulty in the face of large variations of this type.

The capacity of such a system measured in terms of interactive users of alphanumeric terminals would be about 100,000 such active users at any one time on the system. Of course the system would be used by other devices generating larger amounts of traffic than a single terminal and the number of active users would have to be decreased accordingly. The point is that in a public packet switched service using a US domestic satellite the user of data communications could be charged by the packet, since the user would consume resources in the system proportional to the number of packets sent and received.

The preceding three sections and the accompanying papers by Kleinrock and Roberts explain many of the technological advantages of such a system. We need only add some short observations concerning the operational advantages of a public packet switched service. The system would possess a flexibility of operation simply not attainable with circuit switched systems. Although the *average* data rate into each of 100 earth stations would be 15 kilobits, the *burst* data rate into any given terminal could be close to 10 megabits. This capability for remote job entry and file transfer leads to the same potential for resource sharing shown to be so valuable in the ARPANET.

Another kind of flexibility is the flexibility in being able to start such a system with a small number of communication controllers at a few earth stations. The system would become operational with only two stations and would yield data on packet interference patterns and delay with only three stations. Since the computer-communication network brought into being by such a service is completely connected (topologically) there is no need for routing algorithms at each earth station (such as used in the ARPANET IMPS and TIPS) and to add a new earth station into the network it is only necessary to activate the identification number of that station. Peak load averaging of such a system would operate to increase its total capacity since the system is peak load limited only at the satellite and not at the separate ground stations. (This particular advantage could be especially important for a Pacific packet switched service where the international dateline would serve to average peak loads over different days as well as different hours.)

Finally we note that the economics of such a system are consistent with the economics of existing computer communication systems. The ARPANET in its present configuration provides a factor of ten or more in cost advantage over conventional circuit switched systems.[5] During the month of January 1973, approximately 45,000,000 packets were transmitted by the ARPANET. The capacity of the ARPANET based on an eight hour day was about 300 million packets per month at that time. A public packet switching service using a single transponder of a domestic satellite system, operating at a normalized message rate of 0.15 would have a capacity of about 1,500 million packets per month, again based on an eight hour day. Furthermore, at such a low message rate the system would easily accommodate intermittent users with large files at a megabit data rate and still draw average power from the satellite corresponding to a transponder duty cycle of less than 16 percent. The 50 kilobit lines now used in the ARPANET cost about $1,200,000 per year in January 1973 and this figure was growing rapidly. The ARPANET is but one possible customer of a public packet switched service. The projected average annual revenue of a single transponder in the several proposed US domestic satellite systems ranges from less than $1,000,000 to about $3,000,000 per year.[20]

REFERENCES

1. Lucky, Robert W., "Common Carrier Data Communication," *Computer-Communication Networks*, edited by Norman Abramson and Franklin F. Kuo, Prentice-Hall, 1973.
2. Baran, Paul "On Distributed Communications: V. History, Alter- *Document No. 13044*, Stanford Research Institute, December 6, *PR, The Rand Corporation*, August 1964.

3. Baran, Paul., "On Distributed Communications: XI. Summary Overview," *Memorandum RM-3767-PR, The Rand Corporation*, August 1964.
4. Davies, D. W., Bartlett, K. A., Scantlebury, R. A., Wilkinson, P. T., "A Digital Communication Network for Computers Giving Rapid Response at Remote Terminals," *ACM Symposium on Operating System Principles*, Gatlinburg, Tennessee, October 1-4, 1967.
5. Roberts, Lawrence G., "The ARPA Network," *Computer-Communication Networks*, edited by Norman Abramson and Franklin F. Kuo, Prentice-Hall, 1973.
6. Ornstein, S. M., Heart, F. E., Crowther, W. R., Rising, H. K., Russell, S. B., Michel, A., "The Terminal IMP for the ARPA Computer Network," *AFIPS Conference Proceedings, Spring Joint Computer Conference*, 1972, pp. 243-254.
7. deMercado, J., Guindon, R., DaSilva, J., Kadoch, M., "The Canadian Universities Computer Network Topological Considerations," *Computer Communication: Impacts and Implications, Proceedings of the First International Conference on Computer Communication*, Washington, D.C., October 24-26, 1972, pp. 220-225.
8. Barber, D. L. A., "The European Computer Network Project," *Computer Communication: Impacts and Implications, Proceedings of the First International Conference on Computer Communication*, Washington, D.C., October 24-26, 1972, pp. 192-200.
9. Abramson, Norman, "THE ALOHA SYSTEM," *Computer-Communication Networks*, edited by Norman Abramson and Franklin F. Kuo, Prentice-Hall, 1973.
10. Trifari, J. C., "Rating National Timesharing Services," *Computer Decisions*, November 1971, pp. 28-32.
11. Jackson, P. E., Stubbs, C. D., "A Study of Multi-access Computer Communications," *AFIPS Conference Proceedings, Spring Joint Computer Conference*, 1969, pp. 491-504.
12. Roberts, Lawrence G., "ALOHA Packet System With and Without Slots and Capture," *ARPANET Satellite System Note 8, NIC Document No. 11290*, Stanford Research Institute, June 26, 1972.
13. Kleinrock, L., Lam, S. S., "Packet Switching in a Slotted Satellite Channel," *Proceedings of the National Computer Conference*, June 1973.
14. Roberts, Lawrence G., "Dynamic Allocation of Satellite Capacity Through Packet Reservation," *Proceedings of the National Computer Conference*, June 1973.
15. Kleinrock, L., Lam S. S., "Analytic Results with the Addition of One Large User," *ARPANET Satellite System Note 27, NIC Document No. 12736*, Stanford Research Institute, October 30, 1972.
16. Rettberg R., "Random ALOHA with Slots-Excess Capacity," *ARPANET Satellite System Note 18, NIC Document No. 11865*, Stanford Research Institute, October 11, 1972.
17. Abramson, Norman, "Excess Capacity of a Slotted ALOHA Channel," *ARPANET Satellite System Note 26, NIC Document No. 12735*, Stanford Research Institute, November 15, 1972.
18. Abramson, Norman, "Excess Capacity of a Slotted ALOHA Channel (continued)," *ARPANET Satellite System Note 30, NIC Document No. 13044*, Stanford Research Institute, December 6, 1972.
19. Cacciamani, E. R., Jr., "The Spade System as Applied to Data Communications and Small Earth Station Operation," *COMSAT Technical Review*, Vol. 1, No. 1, Fall 1971.
20. McDonald, J., "Getting Our Communication Satellite Off the Ground," *Fortune*, July 1972.

Packet-switching in a slotted satellite channel*

by LEONARD KLEINROCK and SIMON S. LAM

University of California
Los Angeles, California

INTRODUCTION

86

Imagine that two users require the use of a communication channel. The classical approach to satisfying this requirement is to provide a channel for their use so long as that need continues (and to charge them for the full cost of this channel). It has long been recognized that such allocation of scarce communication resources is extremely wasteful as witnessed by their low utilization (see for example the measurements of Jackson & Stubbs).[1] Rather than provide channels on a user-pair basis, we much prefer to provide a single high-speed channel to a large number of users which can be shared in some fashion; this then allows us to take advantage of the powerful "large number laws" which state that with very high probability, the demand at any instant will be approximately equal to the sum of the average demands of that population. In this way the required channel capacity to support the user traffic may be considerably less than in the unshared case of dedicated channels. This approach has been used to great effect for many years now in a number of different contexts: for example, the use of graded channels in the telephone industry,[2] the introduction of asynchronous time division multiplexing,[3] and the packet-switching concepts introduced by Baran et al.,[4] Davies,[5] and finally implemented in the ARPA network.[6] The essential observation is that the full-time allocation of a fraction of the channel to each user is highly inefficient compared to the part-time use of the full capacity of the channel (this is precisely the notion of time-sharing). We gain this efficient sharing when the traffic consists of rapid, but short bursts of data. The classical schemes of synchronous time division multiplexing and frequency division multiplexing are examples of the inefficient partitioning of channels.

As soon as we introduce the notion of a shared channel in a packet-switching mode then we must be prepared to resolve conflicts which arise when more than one demand is simultaneously placed upon the channel. There are two obvious solutions to this problem: the first is to "throw out" or "lose" any demands which are made while the channel is in use; and the second is to form a queue of conflicting demands and serve them in some order as the channel becomes free. The latter approach is that taken in the ARPA network since storage may be provided economically at the point of conflict. The former approach is taken in the ALOHA system[7] which uses packet-switching with radio channels; in this system, in fact, *all* simultaneous demands made on the channel are lost.

Of interest to this paper is the consideration of satellite channels for packet-switching. The definition of a packet is merely a package of data which has been prepared by a user for transmission to some other user in the system. The satellite is characterized as a high capacity channel with a fixed propagation delay which is large compared to the packet transmission time (see the next section). The (stationary) satellite acts as a pure transponder repeating whatever it receives and beaming this transmission back down to earth; this broadcasted transmission can be heard by every user of the system and in particular a user can listen to his own transmission on its way back down. Since the satellite is merely transponding, then whenever a portion of one user's transmission reaches the satellite while another user's transmission is being transponded, the two collide and "destroy" each other. The problem we are then faced with is how to control the allocation of time at the satellite in a fashion which produces an acceptable level of performance.

The ideal situation would be for the users to agree collectively when each could transmit. The difficulty is that the means for communication available to these geographically distributed users is the satellite channel itself and we are faced with attempting to control a channel which must carry its own control information. There are essentially three approaches to the solution of this problem. The first has come to be known as a pure "ALOHA" system[7] in which users transmit any time they desire. If, after one propagation delay, they hear their successful transmission then they assume that no conflict occurred at the satellite; otherwise they know a collision occurred and they must retransmit. If users retransmit immediately upon hearing a conflict, then they are likely to conflict again, and so some scheme must be devised for introducing a random retransmission delay to spread these conflicting packets over time.

The second method for using the satellite channel is to "slot" time into segments whose duration is exactly equal to the transmission time of a single packet (we assume constant length packets). If we now require all packets to begin their transmission only at the beginning of a slot, then we

* This research was supported by the Advanced Research Projects Agency of the Department of Defense under Contract No. DAHC-15-69-C-0285.

enjoy a gain in efficiency since collisions are now restricted to a single slot duration; such a scheme is referred to as a "slotted ALOHA" system and is the principal subject of this paper. We consider two models: the first is that of a large population of users, each of which makes a small demand on the channel; the second model consists of this background of users with the addition of one large user acting in a special way to provide an increased utilization of the channel. We concern ourselves with retransmission strategies, delays, and throughput. Abramson[8] also considers slotted systems and is concerned mainly with the ultimate capacity of these channels with various user mixes. Our results and his have a common meeting point at some limits which will be described below.

The third method for using these channels is to attempt to schedule their use in some direct fashion; this introduces the notion of a reservation system in which time slots are reserved for specific users' transmissions and the manner in which these reservations are made is discussed in the paper by Roberts.[9] He gives an analysis for the delay and throughput, comparing the performance of slotted and reservation systems.

Thus we are faced with a finite-capacity communication channel subject to unpredictable and conflicting demands. When these demands collide, we "lose" some of the effective capacity of the channel and in this paper we characterize the effect of that conflict. Note that it is possible to use the channel up to its full rated capacity when only a single user is demanding service; this is true since a user will never conflict with himself (he has the capability to schedule his own use). This effect is important in studying the non-uniform traffic case as we show below.

SLOTTED ALOHA CHANNEL MODELS

Model I. Traffic from many small users

In this model we assume:

(A1) an infinite number of users* who collectively form an independent source

This source generates M packets per slot from the distribution $v_i = \text{Prob}[M=i]$ with a mean of S_0 packets/slot.

We assume that each packet is of constant length requiring T seconds for transmission; in the numerical studies presented below we assume that the capacity of the channel is 50 kilobits per second and that the packets are each 1125 bits in length yielding $T = 22.5$ msec. Note that $S_0' = S_0/T$ is the average number of packets arriving per second from the source. Let d be the maximum roundtrip propagation delay which we assume each user experiences and let $R = d/T$ be the number of slots which can fit into one roundtrip propagation time; for our numerical results we assume $d = 270$ msec. and so $R = 12$ slots. R slots after a transmission, a user will either hear that it was successful or know that it was destroyed. In the latter case if he now retransmits during the next slot interval and if all other users behave likewise, then for sure they will collide again; consequently we shall assume that each user transmits a previously collided packet at random during one of the next K slots, (each such slot being chosen with probability $1/K$). Thus, retransmission will take place either $R+1$, $R+2$, ... or $R+K$ slots after the initial transmission. As a result traffic introduced to the channel from our collection of users will now consist of new packets and previously blocked packets, the total number adding up to N packets transmitted per slot where $p_i = \text{Prob}[N=i]$ with a mean traffic of G packets per slot. We assume that each user in the infinite population will have at most one packet requiring transmission at any time (including any previously blocked packets). Of interest to us is a description of the maximum throughput* rate S as a function of the channel traffic G. It is clear that S/G is merely the probability of a successful transmission and G/S is the average number of times a packet must be transmitted until success; assuming

(A2) the traffic entering the channel is an independent process

We then have,

$$S = Gp_0 \tag{1}$$

If in addition we assume,

(A3) the channel traffic is Poisson

then $p_0 = e^{-G}$, and so,

$$S = Ge^{-G} \tag{2}$$

Eq. (2) was first obtained by Roberts[11] who extended a similar result due to Abramson[7] in studying the radio ALOHA system. It represents the ultimate throughput in a Model I slotted ALOHA channel without regard to the delay packets experience; we deal extensively with the delay in the next section.

For Model I we adopt assumption A1. We shall also accept a less restrictive form of assumption A2 (namely assumption A4 below) which, as we show, lends validity to assumption A3 which we also require in this model. Assume,

(A4) the channel traffic is independent over any K consecutive slots

We have conducted simulation experiments which show that this is an excellent assumption so long as $K < R$.

Let,

$$P(z) = \sum_{i=0}^{\infty} p_i z^i \tag{3}$$

$$V(z) = \sum_{i=0}^{\infty} v_i z^i \tag{4}$$

* These will be referred to as the "small" users.

* Note that $S = S_0$ under stable system operation which we assume unless stated otherwise (see below).

Using only assumption A4 and the assumption that M is independent of $N-M$, we find [10] that $P(z)$ may be expressed as

$$\left[\frac{p_1}{K}(1-z)+P\left(1-\frac{1-z}{K}\right)\right]^K V(z)$$

If, further, the source is an independent process (i.e., assumption A1) and is Poisson distributed then $V(z)=e^{-S(1-z)}$, and then we see immediately that,

$$\lim_{K\uparrow\infty} P(z)=e^{-G(1-z)}.$$

This shows that assumption A3 follows from assumptions A1 and A4 in the limit of large K, under the reasonable condition that the source is Poisson distributed.

We have so far defined the following critical system parameters: S_0, S, G, K and R. In the ensuing analysis we shall distinguish packets transmitting in a given slot as being either newly generated or ones which have in the past collided with other packets. This leads to an approximation since we do not distinguish how many times a packet has met with a collision. We have examined the validity of this approximation by simulation, and have found that the correlation of traffic in different slots is negligible, except at shifts of $R+1$, $R+2$, . . . , $R+K$; this exactly supports our approximation since we concern ourselves with the most recent collision. We require the following two additional definitions:

q = Prob[newly generated packet is successfully transmitted]

q_t = Prob[previously blocked packet is successfully transmitted]

We also introduce the expected packet delay D:

D = average time (in slots) until a packet is successfully received

Our principal concern in this paper is to investigate the trade-off between the average delay D and the throughput S.

Model II. Background traffic with one large user

In this second model, we refer to the source described above as the "background" source but we also assume that there is an additional single user who constitutes a second independent source and we refer to this source as the "large" user. The background source is the same as that in Model I and for the second source, we assume that the packet arrivals to the large user transmitter are Poisson and independent of other packets over $R+K$ consecutive slots. In order to distinguish variables for these two sources, we let S_1 and G_1 refer to the S and G parameters for the background source and let S_2 and G_2 refer to the S and G parameters for the single large user. We point out that the identity of this large user may change as time progresses but insist that there be only one such at any given time. We introduce the new variables

$$S=S_1+S_2 \tag{5}$$

$$G=G_1+G_2 \tag{6}$$

S represents the total throughput of the system and G represents the traffic which the channel must support (including retransmissions). We have assumed that the small users may have at most one packet outstanding for transmission in the channel; however the single large user may have many packets awaiting transmission. We assume that this large user has storage for queueing his requests and of course it is his responsibility to see that he does not attempt the simultaneous transmission of two packets. We may interpret G_2 as the probability that the single large user is transmitting a packet in a channel slot and so we require $G_2\leq 1$; no such restriction is placed on G_1 (or on G in Model I).

We now introduce a means by which the large user can control his channel usage enabling him to absorb some of the slack channel capacity; this permits an increase in the total throughput S. The set of packets awaiting transmission by the large user compete among each other for the attention of his local transmitter as follows. Each waiting packet will be scheduled for transmission in some future slot. When a newly generated packet arrives, it immediately attempts transmission in the current slot and will succeed in capturing the transmitter unless some other packet has also been scheduled for this slot; in the case of such a scheduling conflict, the new packet is randomly rescheduled in one of the next L slots, each such slot being chosen equally likely with probability $1/L$. Due to the background traffic, a large user packet may meet with a transmission conflict at the satellite (which is discovered R slots after transmission) in which case, as in Model I, it incurs a random delay (uniformly distributed over K slots) plus the fixed delay of R slots. More than one packet may be scheduled for a future slot and we assume that these scheduling conflicts are resolved by admitting that packet with the longest delay since its previous blocking (due to conflict in transmission or conflict in scheduling) and uniformly rescheduling the others over the next L slots; ties are broken by random selection. We see, therefore, that new packets have the lowest priority in case of a scheduling conflict; however, they seize the channel if it is free upon their arrival. The variable L permits us a certain control of channel use by the large user but does not limit his throughput. We also assume $K, L<R$. Corresponding to q and q_t in Model I, we introduce the success probabilities q_i and q_{it} $(i=1, 2)$ for new and previously blocked packets respectively and where $i=1$ denotes the background source and $i=2$ denotes the single large source. Finally, we choose to distinguish between D_1 and D_2 which are the average number of slots until a packet is successfully transmitted from the background and large user sources respectively.

RESULTS OF ANALYSIS

In this section we present the results of our analysis without proof. The details of proof may be found in Reference 10.

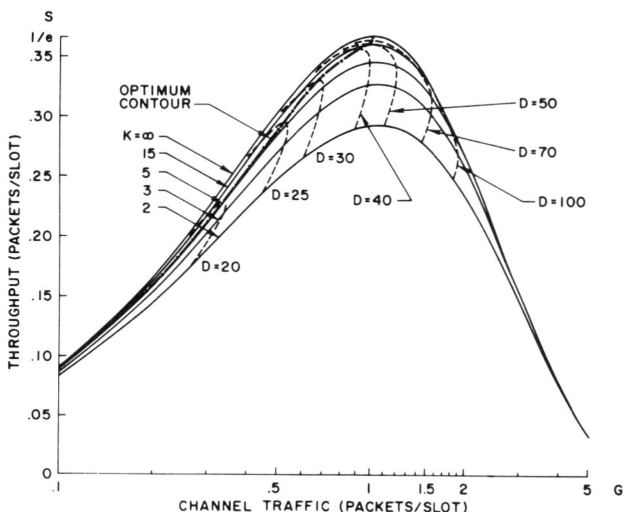

Figure 1—Throughput as a function of channel traffic

Model I. Traffic from many small users

We wish to refine Eq. (2) by accounting for the effect of the random retransmission delay parameter K. Our principal result in this case is

$$S=G\frac{q_t}{q_t+1-q} \tag{7}$$

where

$$q=\left[e^{-G/K}+\frac{G}{K}e^{-G}\right]^K e^{-S} \tag{8}$$

and

$$q_t=\left[\frac{1}{1-e^{-G}}\right]\left[e^{-G/K}-e^{-G}\right]\left[e^{-G/K}+\frac{G}{K}e^{-G}\right]^{K-1} e^{-S} \tag{9}$$

The considerations which led to Eq. (7) were inspired by Roberts[11] in which he developed an approximation for Eq. (9) of the form

$$q_t \cong \frac{K-1}{K}e^{-G} \tag{10}$$

We shall see below that this is a reasonably good approximation. Equations (7–9) form a set of non-linear simultaneous equations for S, q and q_t which must be solved to obtain an explicit expression for S in terms of the system parameters G and K. In general, this cannot be accomplished. However, we note that as K approaches infinity these three equations reduce simply to

$$\lim_{K\uparrow\infty}\frac{S}{G}=\lim_{K\uparrow\infty} q=\lim_{K\uparrow\infty} q_t=e^{-G} \tag{11}$$

Thus, we see that Eq. (2) is the correct expression for the throughput S only when K approaches infinity which corresponds to the case of infinite average delay; Abramson[8] gives this result and numerous others all of which correspond to this limiting case. Note that the large K case avoids the large delay problem if T is small (very high speed channels).

The numerical solution to Eqs. (7–9) is given in Figure 1 where we plot the throughput S as a function of the channel traffic G for various values of K. We note that the maximum throughput at a given K occurs when $G=1$. The throughput improves as K increases, finally yielding a maximum value of $S=1/e=.368$ for $G=1$, $K=$infinity. Thus we have the unfortunate situation that the ultimate capacity of this channel supporting a large number of small users is less than 37 percent of its theoretical maximum (of 1). We note that the efficiency rapidly approaches this limiting value (of $1/e$) as K increases and that for $K=15$ we are almost there. The figure also shows some delay contours which we discuss below. In Figure 2, we show the variation of q and q_t with K 89
for various values of G. We note how rapidly these functions approach their limiting values as given in Eq. (11). Also on this curve, we have shown Roberts' approximation in Eq. (10) which converges to the exact value very rapidly as K increases and also as G decreases.

Our next significant result is for packet delay as given by

$$D=R+1+\frac{1-q}{q_t}\left[R+1+\frac{K-1}{2}\right] \tag{12}$$

We note from this equation that for large K, the average delay grows linearly with K at a slope

$$\lim_{K\uparrow\infty}\frac{\partial D}{\partial K}=\frac{1-e^{-G}}{2e^{-G}}$$

Using Eq. (11), we see that this slope may be expressed as $G-S/2S$ which is merely the ratio of that portion of transmitted traffic which meets with a conflict to twice the throughput of the channel; since $G-S/2S=\frac{1}{2}(G/S-1)$, we see that the limiting slope is equal to $\frac{1}{2}$ times the average number of times a packet is retransmitted. Little's well-known result[12] expresses the average number ($\bar{n}$) of units (packets in our case) in a queueing system as the product of the average arrival rate ($S_0=S$ in our case) and the average time in system (D). If we use this along with Eqs. (7) and (12), we get

$$\bar{n}=SD=G\left[R+1+\frac{K-1}{2}\right]-S\left[\frac{K-1}{2}\right] \tag{13}$$

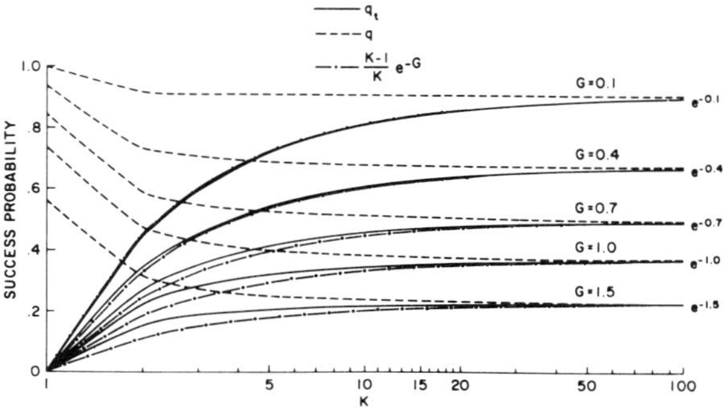

Figure 2—Success probabilities as a function of retransmission delay

In Figure 1 we plot the loci of constant delay in the S, G plane. Note the way these loci bend over sharply as K increases defining a maximum throughput $S_{max}(D)$ for any given value of D; we note the cost in throughput if we wish to limit the average delay. This effect is clearly seen in Figure 3 which is the fundamental display of the tradeoff between delay and throughput for Model I; this figure shows the delay-throughput contours for constant values of K. We also give the minimum envelope of these contours which defines the optimum performance curve for this system (a similar optimum curve is also shown in Figure 1). Note how sharply the delay increases near the maximum throughput $S=0.368$; it is clear that an extreme price in delay must be paid if one wishes to push the channel throughput much above 0.360 and the incremental gain in throughput here is infinitesimal. On the other hand, as S approaches zero, D approaches $R+1$. Also shown here are the constant G contours. Thus this figure and Figure 1 are two alternate ways of displaying the relationship among the four critical system quantities S,G,K, and D.

From Figure 3 we observe the following effect. Consider any given value of S (say at $S=0.20$), and some given value of K (say $K=2$). We note that there are two possible values of D which satisfy these conditions ($D=21.8$, $D=161$). How do we explain this?* It is clear that the lower value is a stable

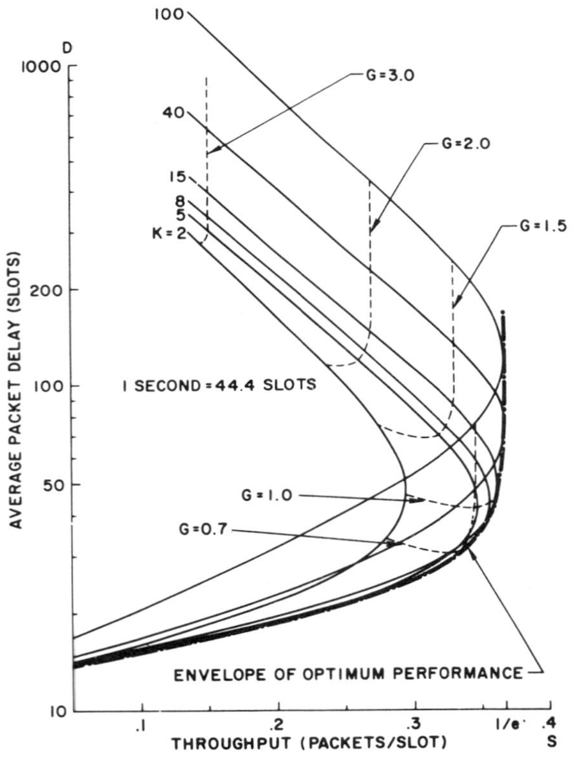

Figure 3—Delay-throughput tradeoff

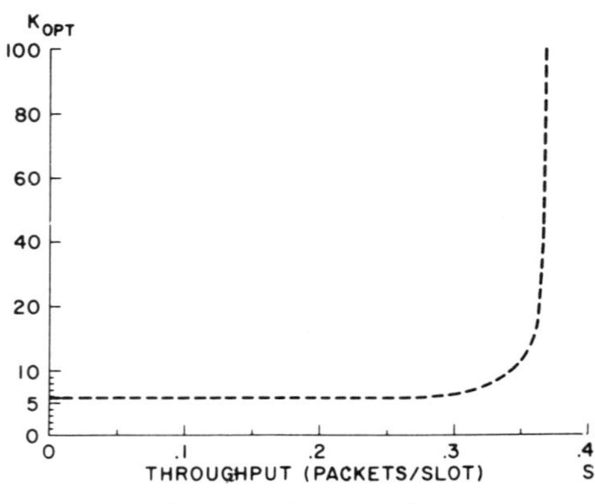

Figure 4—Optimum K

operating point since the system has sufficient capacity to absorb any fluctuation in the rate S_0. Suppose that we now slowly increase S_0 (the source rate); so long as we do not exceed the maximum value of the system throughput rate for this K (say, $S_{max}(K)$), then we see that $S=S_0$ and the system will follow the input. Note that $S_{max}(K)$ always occurs at the intersection of the $G=1$ curve as noted earlier. However, if we attempt to set $S_0>S_{max}(K)$, then the system will go unstable! In fact, the throughput S will drop from $S_{max}(K)$ toward zero as the system accelerates up the constant K contour toward infinite delay! The system will remain in that unfortunate circumstance so long as $S_0>S$ (where now S is approaching zero). All during its demise, the rate at which new packets are being trapped by the system is S_0-S. To recover from this situation, one can set $S_0=0$; then the delay will proceed down the K contour, round the bend at $S_{max}(K)$ and race down to $S=0$. All this while, the backlogged packets are being flushed out of the system. The warning is clear: one must avoid the knee of the K contour. Fortunately, the optimum performance curve does avoid the knee everywhere except when one attempts to squeeze out the last few percent of throughput. In Figure 4, we show the optimum values of K as a function of S. Thus, we have characterized the tradeoff between throughput and delay for Model I.

Model II. Background traffic with one large user

In this model the throughput equation is similar to that given in Eq. (7), namely,

$$S_i=G_i\frac{q_{it}}{q_{it}+1-q_i} \qquad i=1,2 \tag{14}$$

the quantities q_{it} and q_i are given in the appendix. Similarly the average delays for the two classes of user are given by

$$D_1=R+1+\frac{1-q_1}{q_{1t}}\left[R+1+\frac{K-1}{2}\right] \tag{15}$$

$$D_2=R+1+\frac{1-q_2}{q_{2t}}\left[R+1+\frac{K-1}{2}\right]+\frac{L+1}{2}\left[E_n+\frac{1-q_2}{q_{2t}}E_t\right] \tag{16}$$

* This question was raised in a private conversation with Martin Graham (University of California, Berkeley). A simulation of this situation is reported upon in Reference 13.

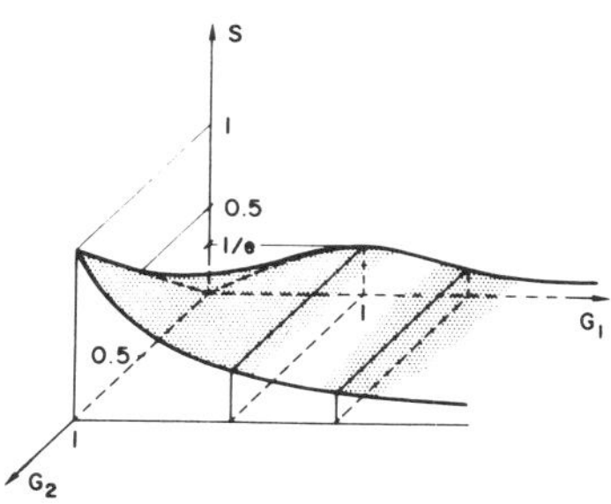

Figure 5—Throughput surface

where E_n and E_t are given in the appendix. It is easy to show that as K, L approach infinity,

$$q_1 = q_{1t} = e^{-G_1}(1-G_2) \tag{17}$$

$$S_1 = G_1 e^{-G_1}(1-G_2) \tag{18}$$

$$q_2 = q_{2t} = e^{-G_1} \tag{19}$$

$$S_2 = G_2 e^{-G_1} \tag{20}$$

$$S = (G - G_1 G_2) e^{-G_1} \tag{21}$$

where we recall $G = G_1 + G_2$ and $S = S_1 + S_2$. From these last equations or as given by direct arguments in an unpublished note by Roberts, one may easily show that at a constant background user throughput S_1, the large user throughput S_2 will be maximized when

$$G = G_1 + G_2 = 1 \tag{22}$$

This last is a special case of results obtained by Abramson in Reference 8 and he discusses these limiting cases at length for various mixes of users. We note that,

$$\frac{\partial S}{\partial G_2} = e^{-G_1}(1-G_1) \tag{23}$$

$$\frac{\partial S}{\partial G_1} = -e^{-G_1}(G - G_1 G_2 - 1 + G_2) \tag{24}$$

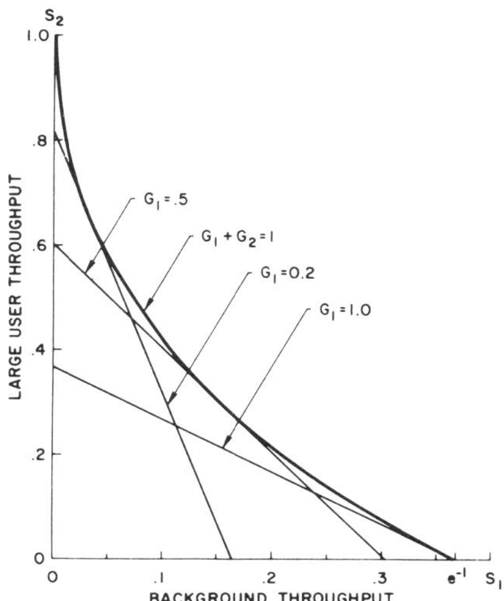

Figure 6—Throughput tradeoff

In Figure 5 we give a qualitative diagram of the 3-dimensional contour for S as a function of G_1 and G_2. We remind the reader that this function is shown for the limiting case K, L approaching infinity only. From our results we see that for constant $G_1<1$, S increases linearly with G_2 $(G_2<1)$. For constant $G_1>1$, S decreases linearly as G_2 increases. In addition, for constant $G_2<\frac{1}{2}$, S has a maximum value at $G_1 = 1-2G_2/1-G_2$. Furthermore, for constant $G_2>\frac{1}{2}$, S decreases as G_1 increases and therefore the maximum throughput S must occur at $S=G_2$ in the $G_1=0$ plane.

The optimum curve given in Eq. (22) is shown in the S_1,S_2 plane in Figure 6 along with the performance loci at constant G_1. We note in these last two figures that a channel throughput equal to 1 is achievable whenever the background traffic drops to zero thereby enabling $S=S_2=G_2=1$; this corresponds to the case of a single user utilizing the satellite channel at its maximum throughput of 1. Abramson [8] dis- 91

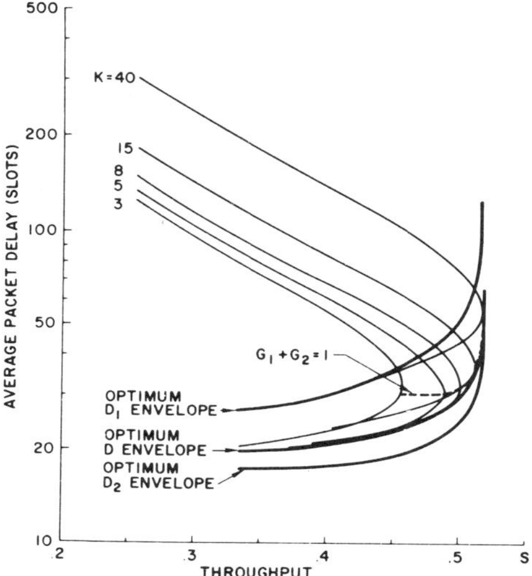

Figure 7—Delay-throughput tradeoff at $S_1=0.1$

cusses a variety of curves such as those in Figure 6; he considers the generalization where there may be an arbitrary number of background and large users.

In the next three figures, we give numerical results for the finite K case; in all of these computations, we consider only the simplified situation in which $K=L$ thereby eliminating one parameter. In Figure 7 we show the tradeoff between delay and throughput similar to Figure 3. (Note that Figure 5 is similar to Figure 1.) Here we show the optimum performance of the average delay $D=S_1D_1+S_2D_2/S$ along with the behavior of D at constant values of K and $S_1=0.1$ (note the instability once again for overloaded conditions). Also shown are minimum curves for D_1 and D_2, which are obtained by using the optimum K as a function of S. If we are willing to reduce the background throughput from its maximum at $S_1=0.368$, then we can drive the total throughput up to approximately $S=0.52$ by introducing additional traffic from the large user. Note that the minimum D_1 curve is much higher than the minimum D_2 curve. Thus our net gain in channel throughput is also at the expense of longer packet delays for the small users. Once again, we see the sharp rise near saturation.

In Figure 8, we display a family of optimum D curves for various choices of S_1 as a function of the total throughput S. We also show the behavior of Model I as given in Figure 3. Note as we reduce the background traffic, the system capacity increases slowly; however, when S_1 falls below 0.1, we begin to pick up significant gains for S_2. Also observe that each of the constant curves "peels off" from the Model I curve at a value of $S=S_1$. At $S_1=0$, we have only the large user operating with no collisions and at this point, the optimal value of L is 1. This reduces to the classical queueing system with Poisson input and constant service time (denoted $M/D/1$) and represents the *absolute optimum performance* contour for any method of using the satellite channel when the input is Poisson; for other input distributions we may use the $G/D/1$ queueing results to calculate this absolute optimum performance contour.

In Figure 9, we finally show the throughput tradeoffs between the background and large users. The upper curve shows the absolute maximum S at each value of S_1; this is a clear display of the significant gain in S_2 which we can achieve if we are willing to reduce the background throughput. The middle curve (also shown in Figure 6 and in Reference 8) shows the absolute maximum value for S_2 at each value of S_1. The lowest curve shows the net gain in system capacity as S_1 is reduced from its maximum possible value of $1/e$.

CONCLUSIONS

In this paper we have analyzed the performance of a slotted satellite system for packet-switching. In our first model, we have displayed the trade-off between average delay and average throughput and have shown that in the case of traffic consisting of a large number of small users, the limiting

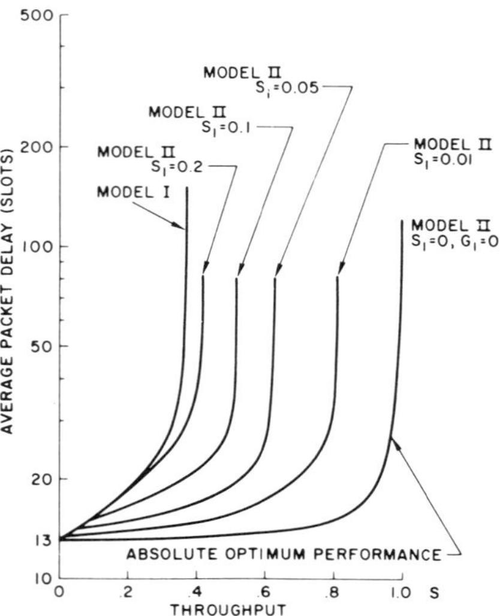

Figure 8—Optimum delay-throughput tradeoffs

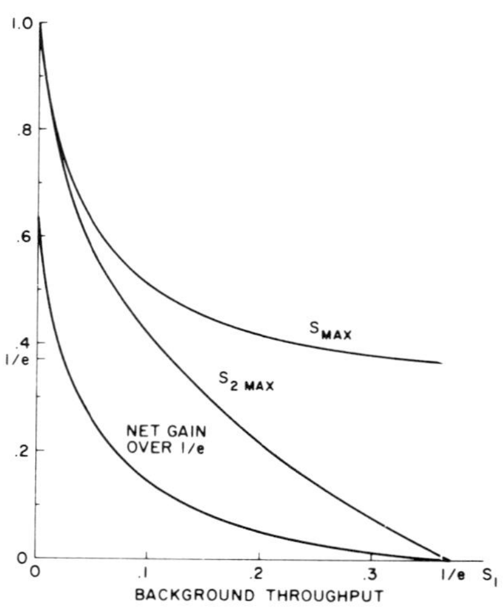

Figure 9—Throughput countours

throughput of the channel ($1/e$) can be approached fairly closely without an excessive delay. This performance can be achieved at relatively small values of K which is the random retransmission delay parameter. However, if one attempts to approach this limiting capacity, not only does one encounter large delays, but one also flirts with the hazards of unstable behavior.

In the case of a single large user mixed with the background traffic, we have shown that it is possible to increase the throughput rather significantly. The qualitative behavior for this multidimensional trade-off was shown and the numerical calculations for a given set of parameters were also displayed. The optimum mix of channel traffic was given in Eq. (22) and is commented on at length in Abramson's paper.[8] We have been able to show in this paper the relationship between delay and throughput which is an essential trade-off in these slotted packet-switching systems.

In Roberts' paper[9] he discusses an effective way to reserve slots in a satellite system so as to predict and prevent conflicts. It is worthwhile noting that another scheme is currently being investigated for packet-switching systems in which the propagation delay is small compared to the slot time, that is, $R=d/T\ll 1$. In such systems it may be advantageous for a user to "listen before transmitting" in order to determine if the channel is in use by some other user; such systems are referred to as "carrier sense" systems and seem to offer some interesting possibilities regarding their control. For satellite communications this case may be found when the capacity of the channel is rather small (for example, with a stationary satellite, the capacity should be in the range of 1200 bps for the packet sizes we have discussed in this paper). On the other hand, a 50 kilobit channel operating in a ground radio environment with packets on the order of 100 or 1000 bits lend themselves nicely to carrier sense techniques.

In all of these schemes one must trade off complexity of implementation with suitable performance. This performance must be effective at all ranges of traffic intensity in that no unnecessary delays or loss of throughput should occur due to complicated operational procedures. We feel that the slotted satellite packet-switching methods described in this paper and the reservation systems for these channels described in the paper by Roberts do in fact meet these criteria.

REFERENCES

1. Jackson, P. E., Stubbs, C. D., "A Study of Multi-access Computer Communications," Spring Joint Computer Conf., *AFIPS Conf. Proc.*, Vol. 34, 1969, pp. 491-504.
2. Syski, R., *Introduction to Congestion in Telephone Systems*, Oliver & Boyd, Edinburgh and London, 1960.
3. Chu, W. W., "A Study of Asynchronous Time Division Multiplexing for Time-Sharing Computer Systems," Spring Joint Computer Conf., *AFIPS Conf. Proc.*, Vol. 35, 1969, pp. 669-678.
4. Baran, P., Boehm, S., and Smith, P., "On Distributed Communications," series of 11 reports by Rand Corp., Santa Monica, Calif., 1964.
5. Davies, D. W., "The Principles of a Data Communication Network for Computers and Remote Peripherals," *Proc. IFIP Hardware*, Edinburgh, 1968, D11.
6. Roberts, L. G., "Multiple Computer Networks and Inter-Computer Communications," *ACM Symposium on Operating Systems*, Gatlinburg, Tenn., 1967.
7. Abramson, N., "The ALOHA System—Another Alternative for Computer Communications," Fall Joint Computer Conf., *AFIPS Conf. Proc.*, Vol. 37, 1970, pp. 281-285.
8. Abramson, N., "Packet Switching with Satellites," these proceedings.
9. Roberts, L. G., "Dynamic Allocation of Satellite Capacity through Packet Reservation," these proceedings.
10. Kleinrock, L., Lam, S. S., Arpanet Satellite System Notes 12 (NIC Document #11294); 17 (NIC Document #11862); 25 (NIC Document #12734); and 27 (NIC Document #12756), available from the ARPA Network Information Center, Stanford Research Institute, Menlo Park, California.
11. Roberts, L., Arpanet Satellite System Notes 8 (NIC Document #11290) and 9 (NIC Document #11291), available from the ARPA Network Information Center, Stanford Research Institute, Menlo Park, California.
12. Kleinrock, L., *Queueing Systems: Theory and Applications*, to be published by Wiley Interscience, New York, 1973.
13. Rettberg, R., Arpanet Satellite System Note 11 (NIC Document #11293), available from the ARPA Network Information Center, Stanford Research Institute, Menlo Park, California.

APPENDIX

Define $G_S \triangleq$ Poisson arrival rate of packets to the transmitter of the large user

$$= S_2[1+E_n+E_2(1+E_t)] \tag{A.1}$$

The variables q_i, q_{it} $(i=1, 2)$ in Eqs. (14–16) are then given as follows (see Reference 10 for details of the derivations):

$$q_1 = (q_0)^K (q_h)^L e^{-S} \tag{A.2}$$

$$q_{1t} = (q_0)^{K-1} q_{1c} (q_h)^L e^{-S} \tag{A.3}$$

where

$$q_0 = e^{-G_1/K} + \frac{1}{K}\left[(1-e^{-G_s})(e^{-G_1}-e^{-G_1/K}) + G_1 e^{-(G_1+G_s)}\right] \tag{A.4}$$

$$q_h = \begin{cases} (G_s+1)e^{-G_s} & L=1 \\ \dfrac{1}{L-1}(Le^{-G_s/L}-e^{-G_s}) & L\geq 2 \end{cases} \tag{A.5}$$

$$q_{1c} = \frac{1}{1-e^{-(G_1+G_s)}}\left[e^{-G_1/K}\left(1-\frac{1-e^{-G_s}}{K}\right) - e^{-(G_1+G_s)}\right] \tag{A.6}$$

Let us introduce the following notation for events at the large user:

SS = scheduling success (capture of the transmitter)
SC = scheduling conflict (failure to capture transmitter)
TS = transmission success (capture of a satellite slot) 93
TC = transmission conflict (conflict at the satellite)
NP = newly generated packet

Then,

$$q_2 = \frac{r_n + r_s E_n}{1+E_n} \tag{A.7}$$

$$q_{2t} = \frac{r_t + r_s E_t}{1+E_t} \tag{A.8}$$

where

$E_n \triangleq$ average number of SC events before an SS event conditioning on NP $= \dfrac{1-a_n}{a_s}$ (A.9)

$E_t \triangleq$ average number of SC events before an SS event conditioning on TC $= \dfrac{1-a_t}{a_s}$ (A.10)

The variables a_i, r_i $(i=n, t, s)$ are defined and given below:

$$a_n \triangleq \text{Prob}\ [SS/NP] = \left(\frac{q_0}{q}\right)^K (q_h)^L \left(\frac{1-e^{-S_2}}{S_2}\right) \tag{A.11}$$

$$r_n \triangleq \text{Prob}\ [TS/SS,\ NP] = q^K e^{-S_1} \tag{A.12}$$

$$a_t \triangleq \text{Prob}\ [SS/TC] = \frac{1}{K}\,\frac{1-(q_0/q)^K}{1-q_0/q} \tag{A.13}$$

$$r_t \triangleq \text{Prob}\ [TS/SS,\ TC] = q^{K-1} q_{2c} e^{-S_1} \tag{A.14}$$

$$a_s \triangleq \text{Prob}\ [SS/SC] = \left(\frac{q_0}{q}\right)^K \frac{q_{sc}}{L}\,\frac{1-(q_h)^L}{1-q_h} \tag{A.15}$$

$$r_s \triangleq \text{Prob}\ [TS/SS,\ SC] = q^K e^{-S_1} \tag{A.16}$$

where

$$q = e^{-G_1/K} + \frac{G_1}{K} e^{-(G_1+G_s)} \tag{A.17}$$

$$q_{2c} = \frac{e^{-G_1/K} - e^{-G_1}}{1-e^{-G_1}} \tag{A.18}$$

$$q_{sc} = \frac{1}{G_s - 1 + e^{-G_s}}\left(\frac{L}{L-1}\right)^2 \left[G_s\left(1-\frac{1}{L}\right)e^{-G_s/L} - e^{-G_s/L} + e^{-G_s}\right] \tag{A.19}$$

PACKET-SWITCHING IN A SLOTTED SATELLITE CHANNEL

by Leonard Kleinrock and Simon S. Lam

ERRATA:

1. Page 704, column 2, line 13. Change "pl" to "p_i"

2. Page 706, column 2, paragraph preceding Eq. (13). Replace "G - S/2S" by "(G - S)/(2S)"

3. Page 708, column 2, line 8. Replace "$1 - 2G_2/1 - G_2$" by "$(1 - 2G_2)/(1 - G_2)$"

4. Page 708, column 2, 10th line from the bottom. Replace "$S_1D_1 + S_2D_2/S$" by "$(S_1D_1 + S_2D_2)/S$"

5. Page 709, Fig. 9. Caption should read: "Throughput contours"

6. Page 710, Eq. (A.1). Replace "E_2" by "$(1 - q_2)/q_{2t}$"

95

Dynamic allocation of satellite capacity through packet reservation

by LAWRENCE G. ROBERTS

Department of Defense
Arlington, Virginia

INTRODUCTION

If one projects the growth of computer communication networks like the ARPANET[1,2,3,4] to a worldwide situation, satellite communication is attractive for intercommunicating between the widespread geographic areas. For this variable demand, multi-station, data traffic situation, satellites are uniquely qualified in that they are theoretically capable of statistically averaging the load in total at the satellite rather than requiring each station or station-pair to average the traffic independently. However, very little research has been done on techniques which permit direct multi-station demand access to a satellite for data traffic. For voice traffic statistics, COMSAT Laboratories has developed highly efficient techniques; the SPADE[5] system currently installed in the Atlantic permitting the pooled use of 64KB PCM voice channels on a demand basis, and the MAT-1[6] TDMA (Time Division Multiple-Access) experimental system. Both systems permit flexible demand assignment of the satellite capacity, but on a circuit-switched basis designed to interconnect a full duplex 64KB channel between two stations for minutes rather than deliver small blocks of data here and there. This work forms the technical base for advanced digital satellite communication, and provides a very effective means for moving large quantities of data between two points. However, for short interactive data traffic between many stations, new allocation techniques are desirable.

TRAFFIC MODEL

In order to evaluate the performance of any new technique for dynamic assignment of satellite capacity and compare it with other techniques, a complete model of the data traffic must be postulated. Given the model, each technique can be analyzed and its performance computed for any traffic load or distribution. Although it is difficult to fully represent the complete variation in traffic rates normal in data traffic, the following model describes the basic nature of data traffic which might arrive at each satellite station from a local packet network.

There are Poisson arrivals of both single packets (1270 bits including the header) and multi-packet blocks (8 packets) at each station. The overall Poisson arrival rate for both is L with a fraction F of single packets and the remainder multi-packets. For simplicity, the arrival rates at all stations are stationary and equal. This is not completely representative of normal data traffic but for the assignment techniques of interest, non-stationary and unequal arrival rates will produce nearly identical performance to the stationary case. Techniques which subdivide the satellite capacity in a preassigned manner would be seriously hurt by non-stationary traffic rates but the poor performance of these systems will be demonstrated, at least in part, by their inability to handle Poisson packet arrivals effectively. The average station traffic in packets per second is:

$$T = L(F + 8(1 - F)) \qquad (1)$$

The destination of this traffic is equally divided between all of the other stations.

For a truly reliable data communications network, each packet or block should be acknowledged as having been correctly received. Positive error control using acknowledgments and retransmissions is very important for data traffic. Thus, acknowledgment traffic must be added to the station traffic. To achieve rapid recovery from errors there must be one small packet (144 bits) sent for each packet or block sent. This traffic is administrative overhead and will not be counted when computing the channel utilization.

The analytic results presented later in the paper are all for equal arrival rates for single packets and multi-packets (F = .5). Other values of F have been examined as well as cases where the input traffic contains small (144 bit) data packets as well. The detailed effect of these variations is not sufficiently pronounced to consider here, however. For comparing techniques the equal arrival distribution is quite representative.

ARPANET experience indicates that the data traffic one can expect is proportional to the total dollar value of computer services being bought or sold through the network. The total traffic generated by one dollar of computer activity is about 315 packets, half going each way.[3] Thus, $200K/year of computer activity within a region produces 2KB of traffic, of which IKB is leaving the region. Within the next few years it is probable that the computer services exchanged internationally will be between $50K/country and $2M/country which suggests that the traffic levels, T,

Reprinted from AFIPS Conference Proceedings, Vol 42

to consider are from .25KB to 10KB. For domestic satellite usage the dollar flow would be far greater than this if the regions are ones like the east and west coast. However, if small stations become economically attractive, the individual user complexes or computer sites will have traffic levels well within this range. Therefore, several of the analytic results presented are for a station traffic of T=1KB. This corresponds to one packet or multi-packet arriving every 4.5 seconds, on the average. It is extremely important to note the infrequency of this, considering that the block must be delivered within less than a second. Even at 10KB, with arrivals every .45 seconds, each arrival must be treated independently, not waiting for a queue to build up if rapid response is to be maintained. Only after the individual traffic exceeds 50KB is there significant smoothing and uniformity to the station's traffic flow. Thus, it is quite important to devise techniques which do not depend on this smoothing at each station if stations with under $10M of remote computer activity are to be served economically.

96

CHANNELIZED SATELLITE TRANSMISSION TECHNIQUES

FDM—FULL interconnection

The most common technique in use today is for each pair of stations which have traffic to lease a small full duplex data channel directly. If this technique were used for a large net of N stations, it would require N (N−1) half duplex channels, each large enough to provide the desired delay response. The total satellite bandwidth required is the sum of the N(N−1) individual requirements plus 2KHz* per channel (minimum) for guardbands. However, since the channels are dedicated, variable packet sizes can be handled and the small acknowledgments fit in efficiently.

FDM—Store and forward star

Since it is clearly very costly for full interconnection, store and forward is an obvious alternative. With short, leased ground lines, the ARPANET very effectively uses this technique, but since each hop adds at least .27 sec due to the propagation delay, it is important to minimize the number of hops. Thus a star design is probably as good an example of this technique as any. The total number of channels for a star is N−1. The delay is the two hop total plus any switch delay (herein presumed zero and of infinite capacity).

TDMA

Since all stations could theoretically hear all the transmissions, a store and forward process is really unnecessary if each packet has an address and its destination can receive it. Further, the guardbands required for FDM can be eliminated if Time Division Multiple Access techniques are used. Instead, an 80 bit start up synchronization leader is required. This increases the small acknowledgment packets to 225 bits and the normal packets to 1350 bits, a 7.6 percent overhead. For this type of data traffic a strict alternation of time slot ownership between the stations was evaluated. All slots are the same size, 1350 bits, except for small acknowledgment packets which are packed in at the necessary intervals. Thus, each station has one Nth of the channel capacity and can use it freely to send to any station. Each station must examine all packets for those addressed to itself. To adapt to unequal or non-stationary traffic levels, there are many techniques[6] for slowly varying the channel split.

ALOHA

Instead of preassigning time slots to stations and often having them be unused, in the ALOHA system they are all freely utilized by any station with traffic. When there are many stations this reduces the delay caused in waiting for your own slot, but introduces a channel utilization limit of 36 percent to insure that conflicts are not too frequent. When conflicts do occur the sum check clearly indicates it and both stations retransmit. A very complete treatment of this technique is presented in the papers by Abramson[7] and Kleinrock and Lam.[8] For the comparison curves presented here, an approximation to the precise delay calculation was used and the possibilities of improved performance due to excess capacity were ignored. Thus, the ALOHA results are slightly conservative.

RESERVATION SYSTEM

In order to further improve the efficiency of data traffic distribution via satellite, the following reservation system is proposed. As with TDMA and ALOHA the satellite channel is divided into time slots of 1350 bits each. However, after every M slots one slot is subdivided into V small slots. The small slots are for reservations and acknowledgments, to be used on a contention basis with the ALOHA technique. The remaining M large slots are for RESERVED data packets. When a data packet or multi-packet block arrives at a station it transmits a reservation in a randomly selected one of the V small slots in the next ALOHA group. The reservation is a request for from one to eight RESERVED slots. Upon seeing such a reservation each station adds the number of slots requested to a count, J, the number of slots currently reserved. The originating station has now blocked out a sequence of RESERVED slots to transmit his packets in. Thus, there is one common queue for all stations and by broadcasting reservations they can claim space on the queue. It is not necessary for any station but the originating station to remember which space belongs to whom, since the only requirement is that no one else uses the slots.

* Two KHz is the minimal possible channel separation determined by oscillator stability for current INTELSAT IV equipment based on a private communication with *E*. Cacciamani, COMSAT Laboratories. Actual guardbands in use are wider.

Referring to Figure 1, a reservation for three slots is transmitted at t = 0 so as to fall in an ALOHA slot at t = 5. If a conflict occurs, the originating station will determine the sum check is bad at t = 10 and retransmit the reservation. However, if it is received correctly at t = 10 and assuming the current queue length is thirteen, the station computes that it can use the slots at t = 21, 22 and 24. It does this by transmitting at t = 16, 17 and 19. By t = 30 the entire block of three packets has been delivered to their destination. If no other reservations have been received by t = 19 the queue goes to zero at this point and the channel reverts to a pure ALOHA state until the next valid reservation is received.

Reservations

To maintain coordination between all the stations, it is necessary and sufficient that each reservation which is received correctly by any station is received correctly by all the stations. This can be assured even if the channel error rate is high by properly encoding the reservation. The simplest strategy is to use the standard packet sum check hardware, and send three independently sumchecked copies of the reservation data. A reservation requires 24 bits of information and with the sum check is 48 bits. Three of these together with the 80 bit sync sequence made a 224 bit packet. Given this size for the small slot and 1350 bits for the large slot, we can pack six reservations in the large slot space; therefore, V = 6. If the channel error rate is 10^{-5} and there are 1000 stations, the probability that one or more of the stations will have errors in all three sections is approximately 1000 $(48 \times 10^{-5})^3$ or 10^{-7}. With a 1.5MB channel this is one error every three days, a very tolerable rate considering the only impact is to delay some data momentarily. If the reservation were not triplicated, however, the probability of an error is .48, sufficient to totally confuse all the stations.

Channel states

There are two states, ALOHA and RESERVED. On start up and every time thereafter when the reservation queue goes to zero, the channel is in the ALOHA state. In this state, all slots small and the ALOHA mode of transmission is used. Reservations, acknowledgments and even small data packets can be sent using the 224 bit slots. However, the first successful reservation causes the RESERVED state to begin. Let us define Z to be the channel rate in large slots per second and R to be the number of large slots per round trip (R = .27Z). Then, considering time as viewed from the satellite, the data packets associated with the first reservation should be transmitted so as to start R + 1 large slots after the reservation. To avoid confusion, M is kept constant for the entirety of each RESERVED state but it is allowed to change each time the state is entered. The initial reservation which starts the state contains a suggested new value for M. This value is used until the state terminates. The determination of M will be considered later.

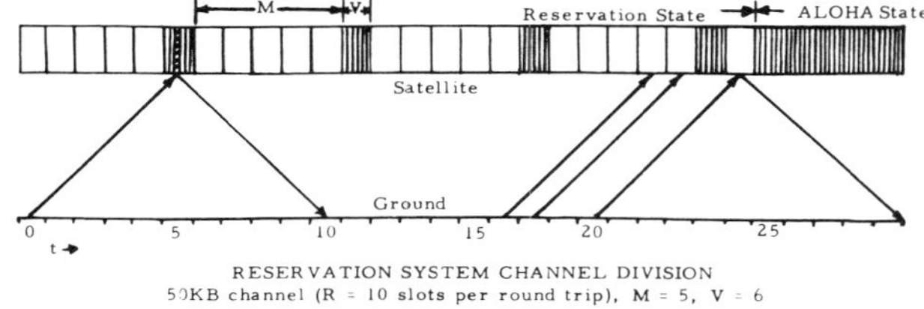

RESERVATION SYSTEM CHANNEL DIVISION
50KB channel (R = 10 slots per round trip), M = 5, V = 6

Figure 1

Channel utilization

The traffic of small packets (reservations, acknowledgments) is twice the overall arrival rate (NL) since every data block requires a reservation and an acknowledgment. If we assume that the arrival rate of these small packets is independent of the state (a good approximation since they are fully independent at both low and high traffic levels where the average duration of one of the states is short compared to R), then:

Small Slot Channel Utilization in ALOHA State:

$$S_1 = 2NL/ZV \quad (2)$$

Small Slot Channel Utilization in RESERVED State:

$$S_2 = 2NL(M+1)/ZV \quad (3)$$

The channel utilization for large slots must be computed as if the channel were always in the RESERVED state since the ALOHA state is a *result* of the non-utilization of the reserved slots, not the cause. Thus:

Large Slot Channel Utilization: $S_3 = BNL(M+1)/MZ$

Where, average block size: $B = F + 8(1-F)$

$$B = 4.5 \quad (4)$$

For the ALOHA transmissions, the channel utilization is related to the actual transmission rate (G) by the relation (see references 7 and 8):

ALOHA State: $S_1 = AG_1e^{-G_1}$

RESERVED State: $S_2 = AG_2e^{-G_2}$

These relations must be solved for G by iteration since S is the known quantity. The correction constant, A, depends on the retransmission randomization technique and R, but is always between .8 and 1.0. As a result of these relations the maximum useful ALOHA throughput is S = A/e. An empirically derived approximation* to A used for this analysis was (K = retransmission randomization period in slots):

$$A = \frac{K-1}{K} \quad \text{where } K = 2.3\sqrt{R}$$

* For an accurate and more detailed solution to the effect of a fixed retransmission delay, refer to Reference 8.

Small packet delay

The average fraction of time the system is in the RESERVED state is equal to the large slot channel utilization, S_3, since that is the fraction of time the reserved packets are being sent. Thus, if we compute the delay for the small packets in both states a weighted average can be taken, using S_3, to obtain the average delay.

ALOHA State:

Initial queueing delay: $$W_1=\frac{G_1/N}{2V(1-G_1/N)}$$

98

Retransmissions: $$H_1=\frac{1-Ae^{-G_1}}{Ae^{-G_1}}$$

Small Packet Delay: $$D_1=\frac{R+1.5/V+W_1+H_1}{Z}\times\frac{(R+W_1+1/V+K/2V)}{Z}$$

RESERVED State:

Initial queueing delay: $$W_2=\frac{(M+1)G_2/N}{2V(1-G_2/N)}$$

Retransmissions: $$H_2=\frac{1-Ae^{-G_2}}{Ae^{-G_2}}$$

Small Packet Delay: $$D_2=\frac{R+1.5V+M/2+W_2}{Z}$$

$$\frac{+H_2\left(R+W_2+1/V+\dfrac{K(M+1)}{2V}\right.}{Z}$$

Now, the overall average small packet delay can be determined:

Overall Small Packet Delay: $$D^2=D_1(1-S_3)+D_2S_3 \qquad (5)$$

Large packet and block delay

For the reserved packets, the delay has three components; the reservation delay (D_S), the central queueing delay and the transmission-propagation delay of the packet or block. For a block of B packets where the general load is the defined traffic distribution the delay is:

Average Delay for reserved: $$D_r=\frac{ZD_S+R+B\dfrac{(M+1)}{M}+\dfrac{YS_3(M+1)}{2M(1-S_3)}}{Z} \qquad (6)$$

Where: $Y=7.2$ packets (second moment of block size/avg. block size)

and: $B=4.5$ packets (average block size)

Determination of M

An optimal value for M can now be determined numerically for any given channel and traffic load. However, this value is not very critical at low channel loading factors. It is only when the channel is operating near peak capacity that M affects the delay more than a few percent. Since M cannot be changed rapidly it is desirable to set M to the value which optimizes the channel capacity and thereby minimizes the delay at peak load. For peak capacity, both the small and large slot portions of the channel in the RESERVED state should be fully loaded. This occurs when $S_2=A/e$ and $S_3=1$. Doing this and solving equations (3) and (4) for the arrival rate, L, gives us:

$$L=\frac{ZVA}{2eN(M+1)}=\frac{ZM}{BN(M+1)}$$

Solving for M:

$$M=\frac{AV}{2e}B \text{ rounded up to nearest integer}$$

for $B=4.5$, $V=6$: $M=5$

If this peak capacity value for M is always used the delay is within 10 percent of optimal and the system is quite stable. As can be seen, the only traffic parameter M depends on is B, the average block size. M can be adjusted by the stations if the channel is monitored and the fractions of each type of packet sent are measured. From these fractions it is easy to determine M.

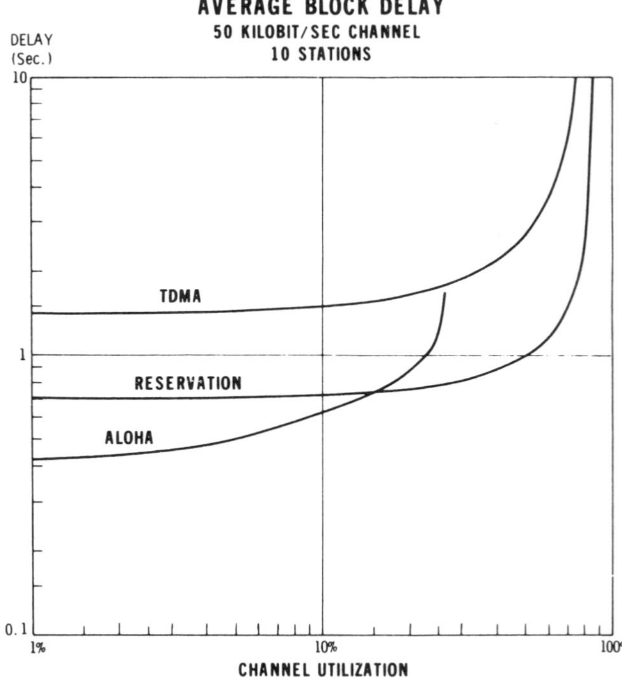

Figure 2

99

Performance

Now it is possible to determine the delay given the traffic distribution (F,B), number of stations (N), and input arrival rate (L). One common way to examine performance is by plotting delay versus the channel utilization for a fixed channel. The channel utilization, C, is the ratio of the good data delivered to the new channel speed:

Channel Utilization: $C = NLB/Z$

Figure 2 shows the delay vs. C for the TDMA, ALOHA, and Reservation techniques. The traffic distribution is as

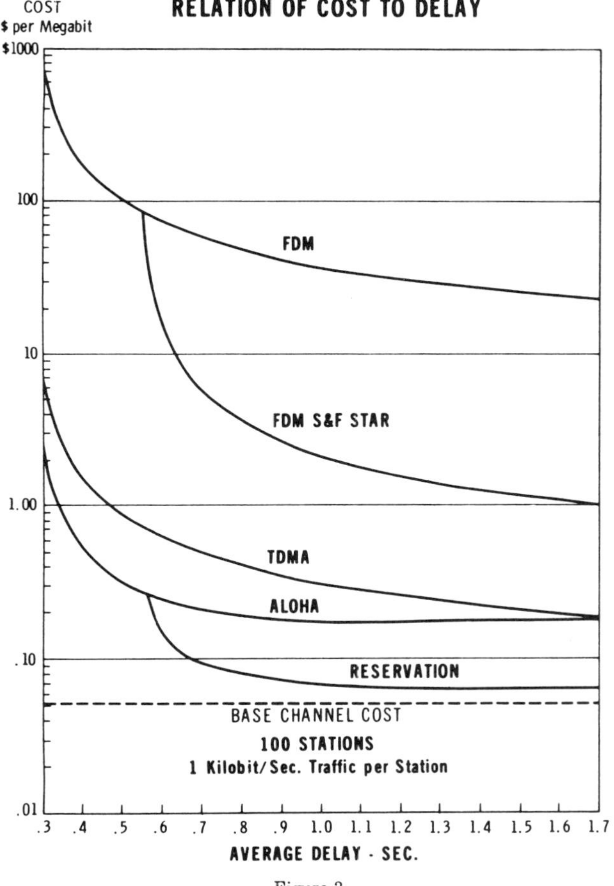

Figure 3

previously defined; half single packets and half blocks of eight.

This type of presentation is not the best for deciding what technique to use for a specific job, but it does show the general behavior of the systems for a fixed channel size, as the traffic load varies.

In order to really compare the cost of the various techniques to do a certain job, it is necessary to set the traffic level, number of stations, and the delay permissible. Then, for each technique, the channel size required to achieve the delay constraint can be searched for. To make the presentation more meaningful the cost of this channel per

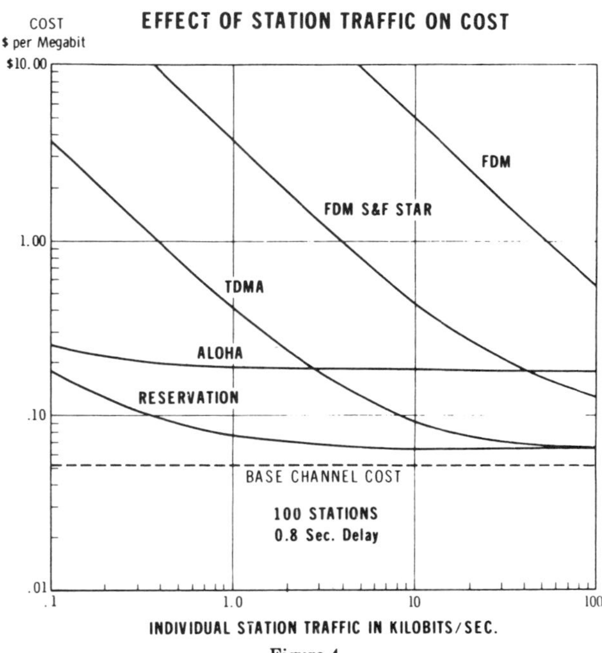

Figure 4

megabit of traffic can then be determined using as a price basis the current tariffed price of the 50KB INTELSAT IV channel (45 KHz) used in the ARPANET between California and Hawaii. It is presumed that any bandwidth could be purchased for the same price per KHz. Converting the cost to dollars per megabit permits easy comparison with the cost in the current ARPANET where distributed leased line capacity can be achieved for $.10 per megabit.

Figures 3, 4 and 5 show communications cost as a function of the three variables; delay, traffic and number of

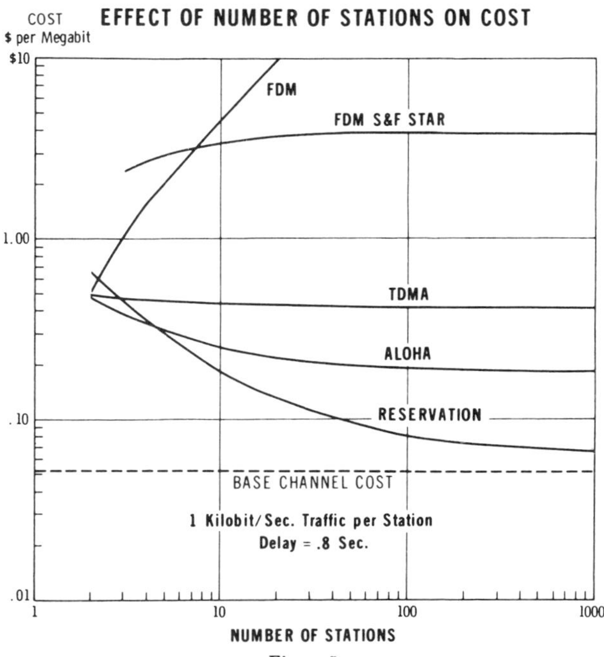

Figure 5

stations. Examining Figure 3 it is clear that if a delay of less than two round trips (.54 sec) is required, the ALOHA system is superior. However, the cost for .4 sec service is over 6 times that of .8 sec service (using the reservation technique). It is also clear that delays of more than .8 sec are not necessary and save very little money. Figure 4 shows that as the individual station traffic is increased to 50KB or higher, TDMA becomes almost as good as the reservation system since there is sufficient local averaging of traffic. Similarly, at this same traffic level FDM—Store and Forward achieves its maximum efficiency but due to sending each packet twice its asymptotic cost is twice that of TDMA or Reservation. These traffic levels for each station are un-
100 realistically high, however, and the flat performance of ALOHA and the Reservation System is vastly preferable since the cost of data communications to small stations is the same as for large stations. Finally, Figure 5 shows the effect of adding stations to the net. With FDM the cost grows out of bounds quickly whereas the reservation technique improves its efficiency until the total traffic from all stations exceeds 100KB. Below 5KB total traffic ALOHA is superior, but this is not a very important case. For large numbers of stations at 1KB traffic per station and .8 seconds delay the reservation system is 3 times cheaper than ALOHA, 6 times cheaper than TDMA, and 56 times cheaper than FDM Store and Forward.

CONCLUSIONS

The reservation technique presented here is one of several techniques which have been developed recently to take full advantage of the multi-access capabilities of satellites for data traffic.[9,10] Both the ALOHA technique and the reservation system depend for their efficiency on the total multi-station traffic rather than the individual station traffic as does TDMA and FDM Store and Forward. The performance improvement reflects this with the reservation system being up to 10 times as efficient as TDMA for small station traffic levels. The worst possible technique for data traffic is pure FDM links between each station pair since this is only efficient if all *pairs* of stations have 50KB of traffic, driving the cost out of bounds for normal usage. The reservation system is also a factor of 3 more efficient than the ALOHA system and for large (100KB) traffic levels achieves almost perfect utilization of the channels.

REFERENCE

1. Roberts, L. G., Wessler, B., "Computer Network Development to Achieve Resource Sharing," *AFIPS Spring Joint Computer Conference Proceedings*, pp. 543-549, 1970.
2. Heart, F., Kahn, R. E., Ornstein, S., Crowther, W., Walden, D., "The Interface Message Processor for the ARPA Computer Network," *AFIPS Spring Joint Computer Conference Proceedings*, pp. 551-567, 1970.
3. Roberts, L. G., "Network Rationale: A 5-Year Reevaluation," *Proceedings of COMPCON 73*, February 1973.
4. Kahn, R. E., "Resource-Sharing Computer Communications Networks," *Proceedings of IEEE*, pp. 1397-1407, November 1972.
5. Cacciamani, E. R., "The Spade System as Applied to Data Communications and Small Earth Station Operation," *COMSAT Technical Review*, Vol. 1, No. 1, Fall 1971.
6. Schmidt, W. G., Gabbard, O. G., Cacciamani, E. R., Maillet, W. G., Wu, W. W., "MAT-1: INTELSAT's Experimental 700-Channel TDMA/DA System," *INTELSAT/IEE International Conference on Digital Satellite Communications Proceedings*, London, November 25-27, 1969.
7. Abramson, Norman, "Packet Switching With Satellites," *These proceedings*.
8. Kleinrock, Leonard, Lam, Simon S., "Packet-Switching in a Slotted Satellite Channel," *These proceedings*.
9. Crowther, W., Rettberg, R., Walden, B., Ornstein, S., Heart, F., "A System for Broadcast Communication: Reservation—ALOHA," *Proceedings of the Sixth Hawaii International Conference on System Sciences*, 1973.
10. Binder, Richard, *Another ALOHA Satellite Protocol*, ARPA Satellite System Note 32, NIC 13147.

Loop Systems

A special distributed computer system architecture of considerable recent interest is the loop (ring) system. This type of system connects all terminals and/or computers by a common bus or loop. The major advantages are the simple routing algorithm and ease in control of information.

The first three papers (p. 104), (p. 122), and (p. 126) describe the architecture of the three loop systems, their operation and characteristics. The last paper (p. 130) provides an analysis of the performance of a loop system.

For more information on the analysis of loop systems, the reader is referred to [CHU 72], [KON 72], [SPR 72], [KON 72a], and [KAY 72].

TRAFFIC FLOW IN A DISTRIBUTED LOOP SWITCHING SYSTEM

**M. L. T. Yuen, B. A. Black, E. E. Newhall,
and A. N. Venetsanopoulos**

*Department of Electrical Engineering, University of Toronto,
Toronto, CANADA*

104

This paper presents some approximate results on the traffic behavior of a distributed loop switching system, first introduced by Farmer and Newhall [1]. The system consists of buffered input/output terminals connected by unidirectional digital transmission links. Each terminal has a multiple rank buffer. The input data fill the innermost rank of the buffer first, then are shifted, in series or in parallel, to the outermost rank and at the same time a *flag* is raised to request service. When control is passed down to that terminal, it will seize control until it has transmitted the message in the outermost rank of the buffer. Control is then passed down to the next terminal *downriver*. If a terminal requires no service, control will pass down to the next with only a one-bit delay. If it requires service, it will require a delay equivalent to the size of the message in bits plus the one bit delay. The time taken for the control to pass around the loop once completely, is defined as the scan time. Overflow occurs when the incoming data exceed the size of the buffer storage. The mean and the variance of the scan time are of interest.

An approximate analytical technique is outlined, which provides a simple and efficient method for calculating these statistics, under *light traffic* conditions. This technique is applied to a single loop with identical terminals as well as a loop consisting of terminals with different arrival rates. Approximate expressions for the mean and variance of the scan time are obtained and the range of validity of these approximations is discussed.

Simulation was carried out in an IBM 370/165 machine. Though the primary interest was to check the statistics of the analytical model, it also provided insight into the transient state of the system. Two models were constructed, one dealing with terminals with different word arrival rates and buffer sizes and the other with identical terminals and single rank buffers. A 40.8 kbit line and the 3.2 Mbit lines were used as examples. The mean and the variance of the steady state scan time were obtained for different numbers of terminals. The results agreed quite closely to those computed analytically. The blocking probability was also investigated.

I. INTRODUCTION

An experimental distributed switching system which shared a common transmission facility among a number of users was introduced by Farmer and Newhall and constructed at Bell Telephone Laboratories [1]. This is a study of the traffic flow in such a system.

Other systems have been recently investigated using a similar loop topology. Pierce [2] introduced a slightly different system and its traffic analysis was done by Hayes and Sherman [3]. A synchronous nonbuffered system was investigated by IBM [4]. Mack,

---

Presented at the Symposium on Computer-Communications Networks and Teletraffic
Polytechnic Institute of Brooklyn, April 4-6, 1972.

Murphy and Webb [5] have looked into the statistical analysis of a similar system whose mathematical model is described by a loop consisting of identical terminals with one-word buffer storage. Kaye [6] recently applied this model to a distributed switching loop.

The characteristics of data sources and the requirement of users make the technique of message switching suitable to data communications. With the advent of new technology, time division switching systems are receiving renewed attention for switching voice traffic. But unlike voice traffic, computer-computer traffic tends to be very bursty in nature, requiring very high bit rates for short periods of time with intervening intervals where the channel is idle. For computers separated even by short distances the cost of this high bit rate short duty factor transmission channel can be prohibitively high.

Message switching provides a way of efficiently using the channel. Several sources are asynchronously multiplexed onto the same line. The basic configuration shown in Fig. 1

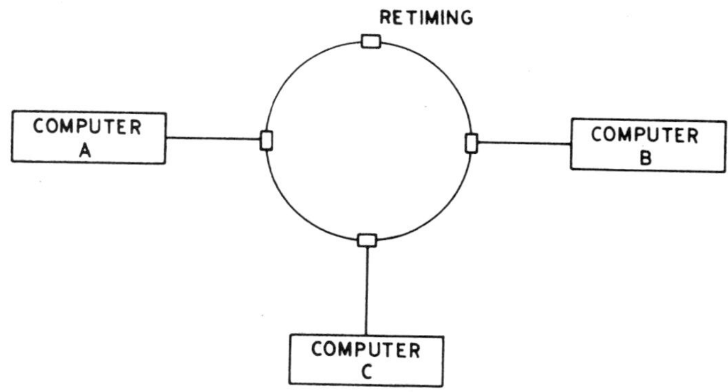

105

Fig. 1. Shared high capacity channel.

shows three computers talking to one another over a high bit rate low duty cycle channel which is shared amongst a number of users. Such a loop can be either short (hundreds of feet) or long (transcontinental). At the position where the loop is closed on itself it is necessary to retime the signals so that the transmission time around the loop is an integral number of bit times. Each computer in turn uses the loop on a message with address basis. At message end control is passed to the next computer on the loop with words to transmit; which in turn seizes control, multiplexes its message and passes control. A typical message format from the original experimental system using a set of 16 opcodes is shown in Figure 2. The system was organized to handle variable length messages, so message blocking codes were constructed that they could never occur in the normal data bit stream.

Such a system can be built starting with two terminals and allowed to grow gracefully. It has some very obvious drawbacks, the most important being the series nature of the loop causing failure of the entire loop if one of the stations fails. When the loop is operating normally it is unnecessary to have a loop supervisor, as initiation and termination of a conversation is carried out by the terminal logic. In case of loop failure, the loop supervisor seizes control for restarting purposes, otherwise it only maintains normal traffic flow through a scan-for-service routine. Scanning for service periodically allows terminals to request access to the loop and request will be granted if the loop supervisor observes no danger of traffic overflow. In a sophisticated system, dynamic traffic adjustment could be performed.

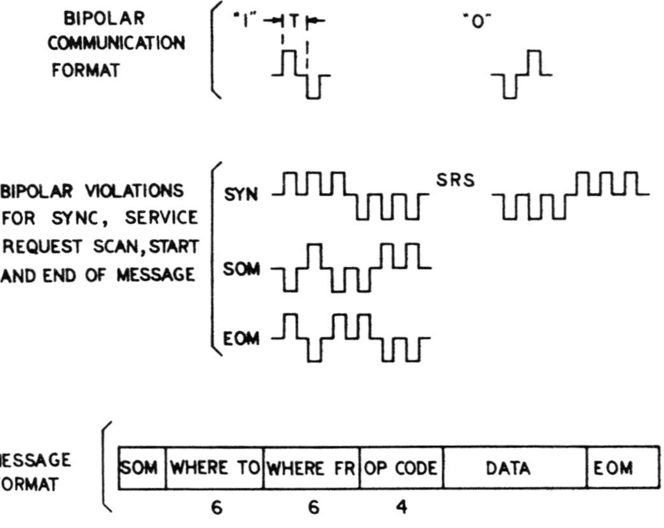

Fig. 2. Message format.

106

In interconnected loops as shown in Fig. 3, the loop supervisor can also serve as a storage and gateway point. This terminal can be addressed, as other terminals on the loop can be addressed, but it also serves as an input point to a major loop. The major loop operates in exactly the same way as the minor loop. The gateways pass control around the major loop. As long as the system is operating without fault, it is assumed that the gateway point will perform only a storage function, holding the data in storage until control is passed to the gateway at which time it will multiplex the data onto the major loop. Similarly when control is passed to the gateway point from the major loop data will be multiplexed onto the minor loop.

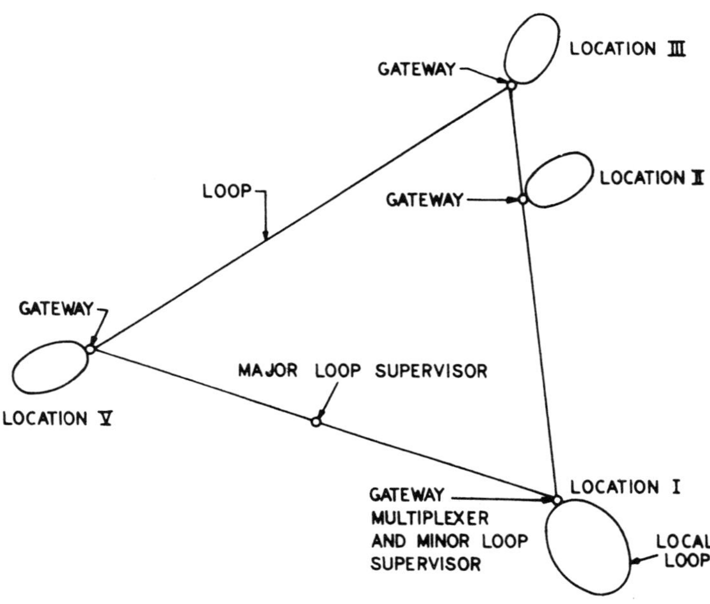

Fig. 3. Interconnected loops.

II. SYSTEM OPERATION

A sketch of the system under consideration is shown in Figure 4. After synchronization, the loop supervisor initiates and starts the communications among the terminals by passing the control to the loop. The transmission of the messages is then carried on among the terminals without the intervention of the supervisor. The loop is interrupted only when there is a loop failure or traffic overflow, etc.

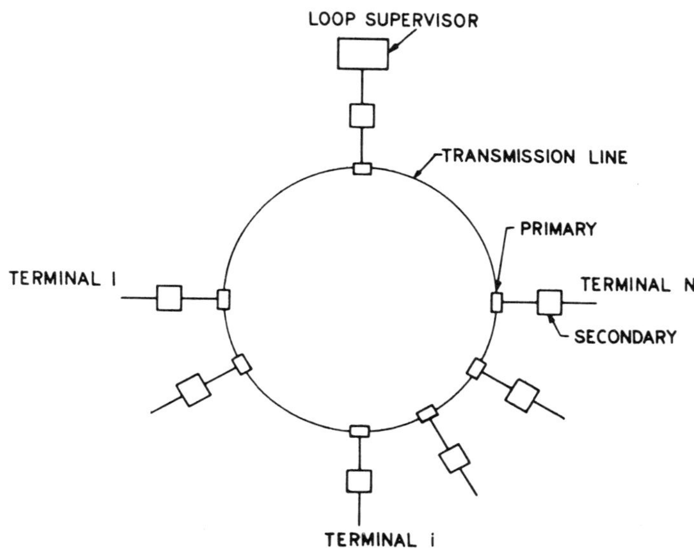

107

Fig. 4. System under consideration.

The sequential machine at each station is physically divided into two sections: primary and secondary. The primaries are line powered and are as simple as possible for maintenance reasons. They either repeat the signals on the line or multiplex signals from the secondary on to the line. Secondaries interface data sending the receiving devices with the transmission facility. Incoming signals from the transmission line are reshaped in the primary, passed to the secondary, and also outputted onto the transmission line with a one-bit delay. Each station has a multiple rank buffer. The input data fill the innermost rank of the buffer first, then the data are shifted, in series or in parallel, to the outermost rank and at the same time a *flag is raised* to request service. Buffer loading is assumed to be instantaneous. When control is passed to a station, it will seize control until it has transmitted the message in the outermost rank of the buffer. Control is then passed to the next station *downriver*. If a station requires no service, control will pass to the next with only a one-bit delay. If it requires service, it will require a delay equal to the size of the message in bits plus the one-bit delay. The service time is defined as the time taken to transmit the headers and the data, the amount of data in a message being equal to the size of one rank of the buffer. The time taken for the control to pass around the loop once completely is defined as the scan time. In general, this value should be small so that the maximum delay a message suffers will be small. Overflow occurs when the incoming data waiting to be serviced exceed the size of the buffer storage. The blocking probability is defined as the probability that a buffer overflows during a scan and in cases of light traffic can be estimated on the basis of mean scan time alone.

For example purposes the terminals chosen for a loop with identical terminals were teletype machines. The incoming words were assumed to be Poisson distributed with an average word arrival rate of 10 words per second. The arrival rate was varied when considering the general case of terminals with different arrival rates. Each word consisted of eight bits, which was also the size of the buffer. Thus the system transmitted a word at a time. For the 40.8 kbit transmission line, the message format (including data) consisted of 30 bits. For the 3.2 Mbit line, which is capable of accommodating a larger number of terminals, the message format consisted of 42 bits. In the subsequent analysis, the case of a single rank buffer is studied in detail. In Section IV the behavior of higher-rank buffers on blocking probabilities is discussed. A list of the terms used is given in Table I.

TABLE I. Definition of terms.

N	: number of terminals in the system
S	: line transmission
T_S	: time required to service a terminal
T_B	: one bit delay in passing any terminal
τ	: time to scan around the loop once
$\overline{\tau}$	: mean scan time of one term approximation
$\overline{\tau^2}$	: expected value of square of scan time
Var (τ)	: variance of the scan time
p	: probability of any terminal requiring service of one term approximation
$q = 1 - p$	: probability of any terminal not requiring service
A	: a random variable taking on values of 1 or 0 with probabilities p and q
λ	: average word arrival rate
p'	: probability of any terminal requiring service conditioned on any other terminal that does require service
PMB_S	: percentage of message blocked in a single rank buffer
PMB_D	: percentage of message blocked in a double rank buffer
LUF	: Line Utilization Factor.

III. APPROXIMATE ANALYSIS

A. Single Loop with N Identical Terminals

Assuming that the incoming data is Poisson distributed the probability of r words arriving in time t is given by

$$P\,[r, t] = \frac{(\lambda t)^r}{r!} e^{-\lambda t} \qquad (r = 0, 1, 2, \cdots) \; . \tag{1}$$

Since each word forms one message, a terminal will request service if there are one or more arrivals in time t, i.e.

$$P\,\{\text{requiring service in time } t\} = 1 - e^{-\lambda t} \; . \tag{2}$$

Assume that the system is in the steady state, and denote the probability density function of the scan time by $f_T(t)$. Let p be the probability of an arbitrary terminal requiring service during one scan. Summing over all possible scan times, we obtain

$$p = \int_{\infty}^{\infty} (1 - e^{-\lambda t}) f_\tau(t)\, dt \ . \qquad (3)$$

There is no explicit solution to Eq. (3), but since the term $1 - e^{-\lambda t}$ can be expanded into an infinite series, we may arrive at various approximations. The system may be said to block if more than one arrival occurs to any terminal in any scan.

$$\begin{aligned} P\,\{\text{blocking}\} &= P\,\{\text{more than one arrival in the scan time}\} \\ &= 1 - [e^{-\lambda t} + \lambda t e^{-\lambda t}] \\ &= 1 - e^{-\lambda t}(1 + \lambda t) \ . \end{aligned} \qquad (4)$$

We are concerned here with the low blocking probability. For this probability to be small, λt is small and

$$e^{-\lambda t} \approx 1 - \lambda t \ . \qquad (5)$$

From Eq. (3) we obtain

$$p \approx \int_{-\infty}^{\infty} \lambda t f_\tau(t)\, dt = \lambda \bar{\tau} \ . \qquad (6)$$

Let us consider a loop system consisting of N terminals. Define A_i as a random variable that takes on the value 1 if the ith terminal requires service and 0 otherwise. Denote by T_s the time required to service a terminal and T_B the one bit delay introduced in passing through any terminal. The time required for the scan to pass from the ith terminal to the $(i + 1)^{\text{th}}$ terminal is

$$\Delta\tau_i = A_i T_s + T_B \ . \qquad (7)$$

The scan time τ is given by

$$\tau = \sum_i \Delta\tau_i = \sum_{i=1}^{N} (A_i T_s + T_B) \ . \qquad (8)$$

Taking the expectation of both sides of Eq. (8)

$$\bar{\tau} = T_s \sum_{i=1}^{N} \bar{A}_i + N\, T_B \ . \qquad (9)$$

As all the terminals are assumed to have the same average word arrival rate

$$\bar{A}_i = 1 \cdot p + 0 \cdot (1 - p) \approx \lambda \bar{\tau} \ . \qquad (10)$$

Combining Eqs. (9) and (10) we obtain Eq. (11)

$$\begin{aligned} \bar{\tau} &= T_s N \lambda \bar{\tau} + N T_B \ , \\ \tau &= \frac{N T_B}{1 - \lambda N T_s} \ . \end{aligned} \qquad (11)$$

It should be noticed that since this approximation has been obtained under Eq. (5), the resulting expression for $\bar{\tau}$ is valid only for $\lambda N T_s << 1$.

Taking the expectation of the square of Eq. (8)

$$\overline{\tau^2} = T_s^2 \sum_{i=1}^{N} \overline{A_i^2} + T_s^2 \sum_{i=1}^{N} \sum_{\substack{j=1 \\ j \neq i}}^{N} A_i A_j + 2 T_s T_B \sum_{i=1}^{N} \overline{A_i} + N^2 T_B^2 . \qquad (12)$$

Now

$$\overline{A_i^2} = 1^2 \cdot p + 0^2 \cdot (1 - p) \approx \lambda \bar{\tau} , \qquad (13)$$

$$\begin{aligned} A_i A_j &= 1 \cdot 1 \cdot P\,[A_i = 1, A_j = 1] + 1 \cdot 0 \cdot P\,[A_i = 1, A_j = 0] \\ &\quad + 0 \cdot 1 \cdot P\,[A_i = 0, S_j = 1] + 0 \cdot 0 \cdot P\,[A_i = 0, A_j = 0] \\ &= P\,[A_i = 1, A_j = 1] . \end{aligned} \qquad (14)$$

110 Writing it in the conditional probability form

$$P\,[A_i = 1, A_j = 1] = P\,[A_j = 1/A_i = 1]\; P\,[A_i = 1] = p \cdot P\,[A_j = 1/A_i = 1] , \qquad (15)$$

where $P\,[A_j = 1/A_i = 1]$ can be interpreted as the probability that the jth terminal requires service given that i^{th} terminal does, with j not equal to i.

It has been previously assumed [5, p. 169] and can be shown that

$$P\,[A_j = 1/A_i = 1] = p' \qquad (i = 1, 2, 3, \cdots, N; j = 1, 2, 3, \cdots, N \quad (j \neq i)) . \qquad (16)$$

Under this conditioning, the average time for scanning the loop once can be given by

$$t' = T_s + (N - 1)\, T_s p' + N T_B , \qquad (17)$$

implying that

$$\begin{aligned} p' &= 1 - e^{-\lambda t'} \approx \lambda t' = \lambda\,[T_s + (N - 1)\, T_s p' + N T_B] , \\ p' &= \frac{\lambda\,(T_s + N T_B)}{1 - \lambda\,(N - 1)\, T_s} . \end{aligned} \qquad (18)$$

Combining Eqs. (14) and (15) we obtain

$$\sum_{i=1}^{N} \sum_{\substack{j=1 \\ j \neq i}}^{N} \overline{A_i A_j} = N\,(N - 1)\, p p' . \qquad (19)$$

Now we can rewrite Eq. (12) in the form

$$\overline{\tau^2} = T_s^2 N p + T_s^2 N\,(N - 1)\, p p' + 2 T_s T_B N p + N^2 T_B^2 , \qquad (20)$$

$$\begin{aligned} \text{Var}\,[\tau] &= \overline{\tau^2} - (\bar{\tau})^2 = T_s^2 N p\,[1 + (N - 1)\, p' - N p] \\ &\approx T_s^2 N \lambda \tau \left[1 + (N - 1) \frac{\lambda\,(T_s + N T_B)}{1 - (N - 1)\,\lambda T_s} - N \lambda \bar{\tau} \right] . \end{aligned} \qquad (21)$$

B. Single Loop With Mixed Terminals

Again assuming that there are N terminals in the loop system we can get the expectation of the scan time as in A

$$\overline{\tau} = \sum_{i=1}^{N} \overline{A_i T_{is}} + NT_B \; . \tag{22}$$

As different terminals have different arrival rates

$$p_i = P\,\{i^{\text{th}} \text{ terminal to require service}\} \approx \lambda_i \overline{\tau} \; , \tag{23}$$

and

$$\overline{A_i} = 1 \cdot p_i + 0 \cdot (1 - p_i) \approx \lambda_i \overline{\tau} \; . \tag{24}$$

Combining Eqs. (22) and (23) we obtain

$$\overline{\tau} = \frac{NT_B}{1 - \sum_{i=1}^{N} \lambda_i T_{is}} \; , \tag{25}$$

111

where we have assumed different service times for different terminals. For a loop system with fixed service time and different arrival rates

$$\overline{\tau} = \frac{NT_B}{1 - T_s \sum_{i=1}^{N} \lambda_i} = \frac{NT_B}{1 - NT_s \overline{\lambda}} \; , \tag{26}$$

where

$$\overline{\lambda} = \frac{1}{N} \sum_{i=1}^{N} \lambda_i \; ,$$

and $\overline{\lambda}$ is the average mean work arrival rate of the terminals in the loop system.

The expectation of the scan time for fixed service time can be written as

$$\overline{\tau^2} = T_s^2 \sum_{i=1}^{N} \overline{A_i^2} + T_s^2 \sum_{i=1}^{N} \sum_{\substack{j=1 \\ j \neq i}}^{N} \overline{A_i A_j} + 2 T_s T_B \sum_{i=1}^{N} \overline{A_i} + N^2 T_B^2 \; , \tag{27}$$

$$\sum_{i=1}^{N} \overline{A_i^2} = \sum_{i=1}^{N} \overline{A_i} = \sum_{i=1}^{N} \lambda_i \tau = N \overline{\lambda \tau} \; . \tag{28}$$

As the conditional probabilities are not the same for terminals with different word arrival rates, the computation of the second term in Eq. (27) becomes tedious. However, if we replace the system with a system of N identical terminals with mean word arrival rate of $\overline{\lambda}$

$$\sum_{i=1}^{N} \sum_{\substack{j=1 \\ j \neq 1}}^{N} \overline{A_i A_j} \approx N(N-1)\,\overline{\lambda\tau}\; \frac{(T_s + NT_B)}{1 - (N-1)\,\bar{\lambda}\, T_s}\,, \tag{29}$$

$$\text{Var}\,[\tau] = \overline{\tau^2} - (\bar{\tau})^2 \approx T_s^2\, N\overline{\lambda\tau} \left[1 + (N-1)\frac{\bar{\lambda}\,(T_s + NT_B)}{1 - (N-1)\bar{\lambda} T_s}\right] - N\overline{\lambda\tau}\,. \tag{30}$$

IV. SIMULATION AND RESULTS

Simulation was carried out on an IBM 370/165 machine, using FORTRAN. Though the primary interest was to check the statistics of the analytical models, it also provided insight into the transient behavior of the system. The simulation attempted to mirror as
112 closely as possible the actual operation of the real system. At each terminal, a sequence of arrivals was generated randomly with a Poisson distribution [7].

Simulation G (General) was so constructed that the system in question could consist of different kinds of terminals with different buffer sizes and arrival rates. The terminals could be switched on at or before the scanning starts, implying that the buffers would be empty or full. During each scan and for each terminal the amount of data waiting for service was noted. If the outermost rank of the buffer was full, it was emptied when the service scan passed that particular terminal. Overflow occurred if the amount of data waiting exceeded the storage in the buffer. The scan time, the number of terminals serviced and the number of terminals with buffer-overflow were recorded. The number of scans taken was also noted.

Simulation S (Special) was written for the particular case of N identical terminals with single-rank-buffers. The program was less complicated and it resembled closely the analytical model. Only the scan time was measured in this model. Steady state was assumed to be reached after a reasonable number of scans, and the mean and variance were computed only after steady state was reached. As both models gave remarkably close answers, only the results of Simulation G are listed here when comparing with analytical results.

For the 40.8 kbit line with identical terminals, the mean scan time of Model G and the Analytic Model is plotted in Figure 5. The variance from the two models is plotted in Figure 6. For the 3.2 Mbit line with identical terminals, the graphs for the mean and variance are sketched in Figs. 7 and 8, respectively.

For a single rank buffer, one can determine the fraction of messages being blocked by assuming that the scan time is constant and equal to the mean scan time as calculated by the approximate analytical technique. Thus the fraction of message being blocked would be given by

$$\text{PMB}_s = \frac{P\,[\text{buffer overflow}]}{P\,[\text{terminal requires service}]} = \frac{1 - e^{-\alpha\bar{\tau}}\,(1 + \alpha\bar{\tau})}{1 - e^{-\alpha\tau}}\,. \tag{31}$$

The results are compared with Simulation Model G for both the 40.8 kbit line and 3.2 Mbit line and are plotted in Figures 9 and 10.

It was shown by simulation results that in the case of light traffic, the mean scan time

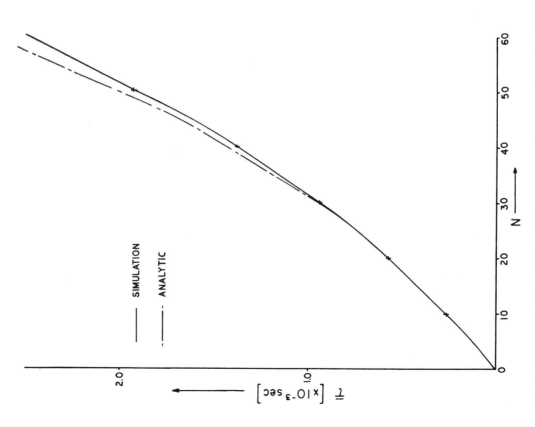

Fig. 5. 40.8 kbit line identical terminals mean scan time vs number of terminals.

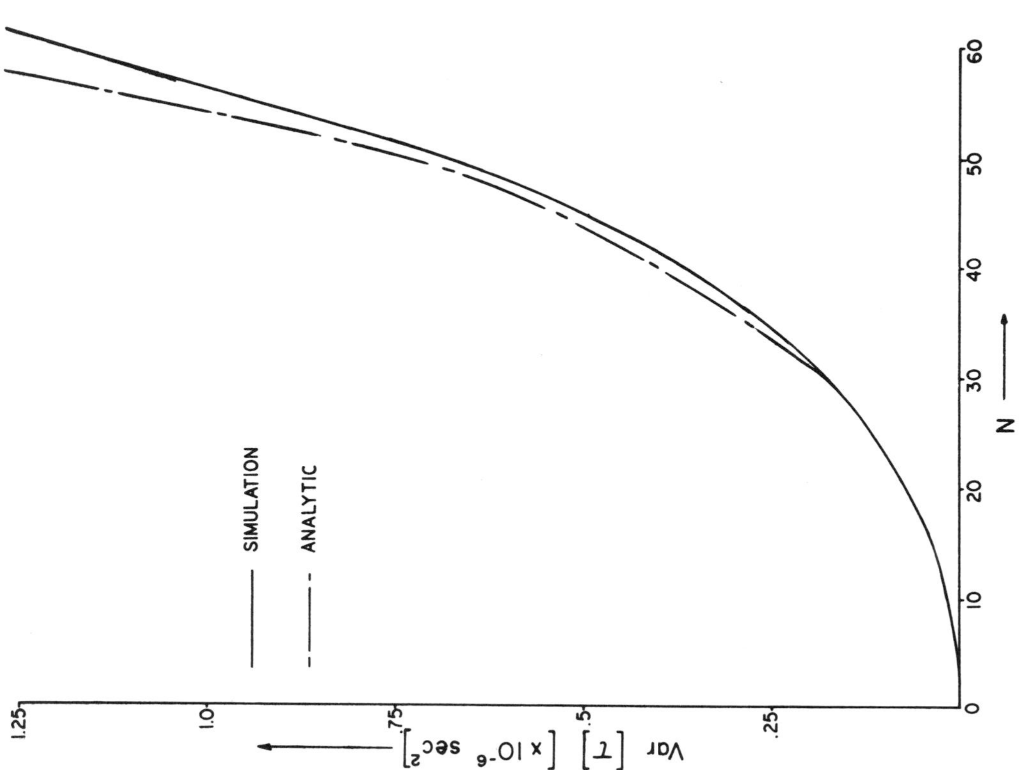

Fig. 6. 40.8 kbit line identical terminals variance vs number of terminals.

113

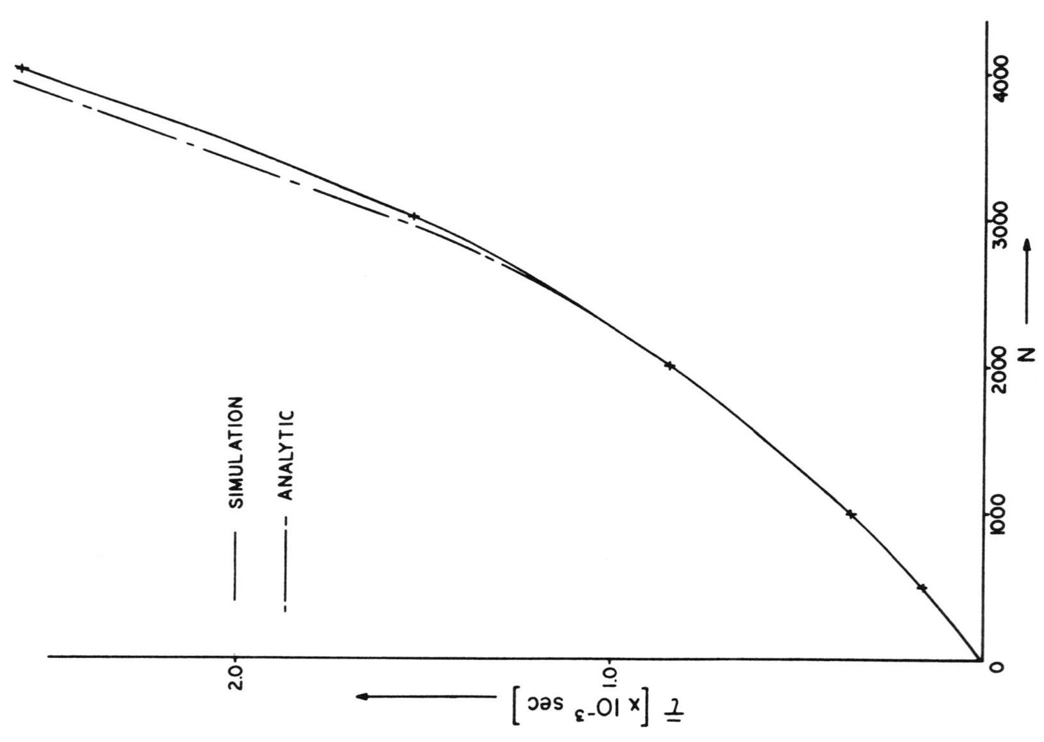

Fig. 7. 3.2 Mbit line mean scan time vs N.

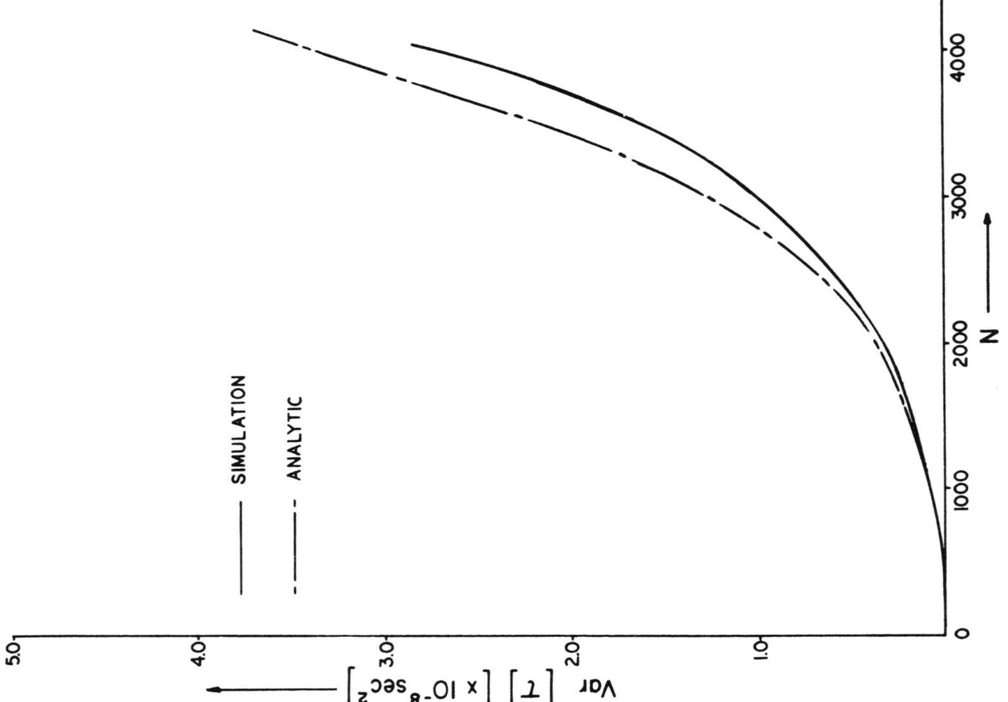

Fig. 8. 3.2 Mbit line variance vs number of terminals.

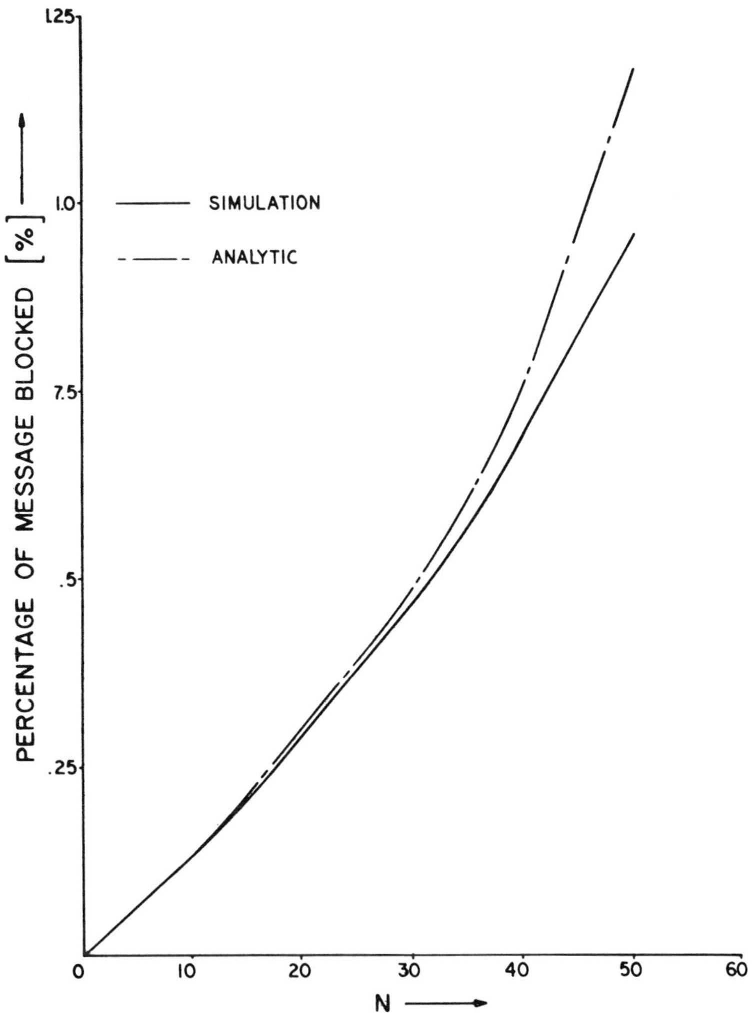

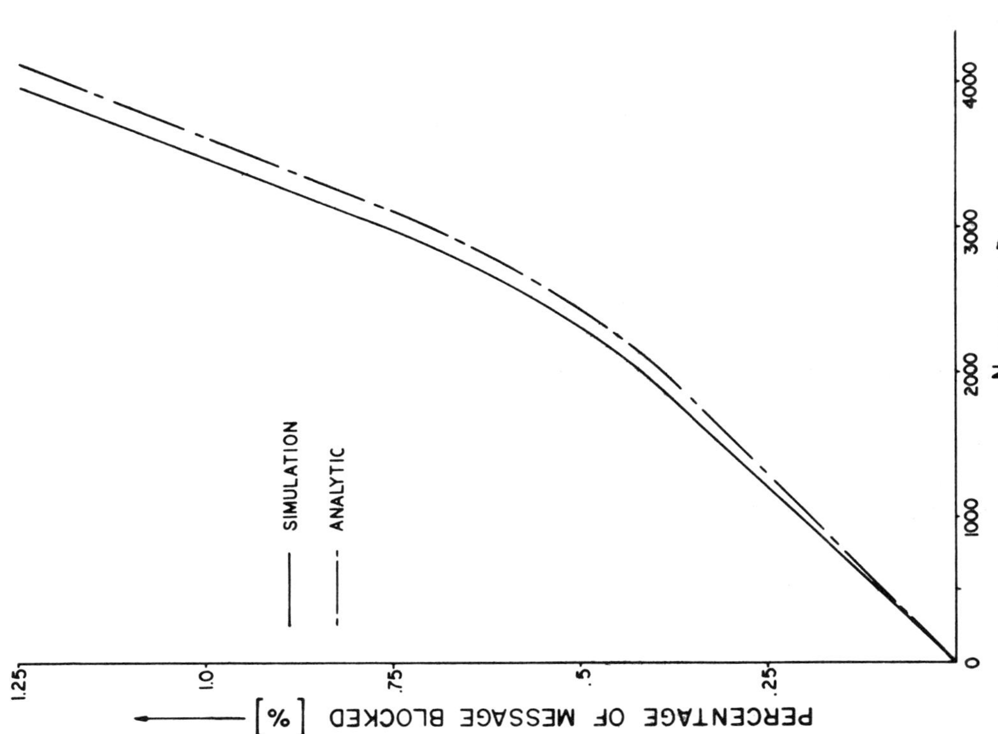

Fig. 10. 3.2 Mbit line identical terminal percentages of message blocked vs N.

Fig. 9. 40.8 kbit line identical terminals percentages of message blocked vs N.

did not change significantly even if the buffers were double ranked. Thus one can use this mean scan time to estimate the percentage of message being blocked for a double-rank buffer. To calculate the probability of a buffer overflowing, one has to consider different combinations of arrival patterns that would produce more than two messages in the buffer in any one scan. Taking only the most significant term.

$$\text{PMB}_D = \frac{P\text{ [three or more arrivals in }\bar{\tau}]}{P\text{ [one or more arrivals in }\bar{\tau}]} = \frac{1 - e^{-\alpha\bar{\tau}}\left(1 + \alpha\bar{\tau} + \dfrac{(\alpha\bar{\tau})^2}{2}\right)}{1 - e^{-\alpha\bar{\tau}}} \quad . \tag{32}$$

For comparison purposes, one example from each transmission line is shown. N = 30 is chosen for the 40.8 kbit line and N = 2000 for the 3.2 Mbit line. The results are given in Tables II and III. It should be obvious that the higher ranks of the buffers, the smaller is the probability of buffer overflow.

For the system to reach steady state the initial buffer storage as well as the transient
response of the system are important factors. The most adverse condition would be the
116 buffers being all full before scan initiation. The larger the buffer rank, the longer it
would take the system to settle down, if a light-traffic steady state can be reached. For
the same two examples, transient responses of the system are plotted in Figs. 11 and 12,

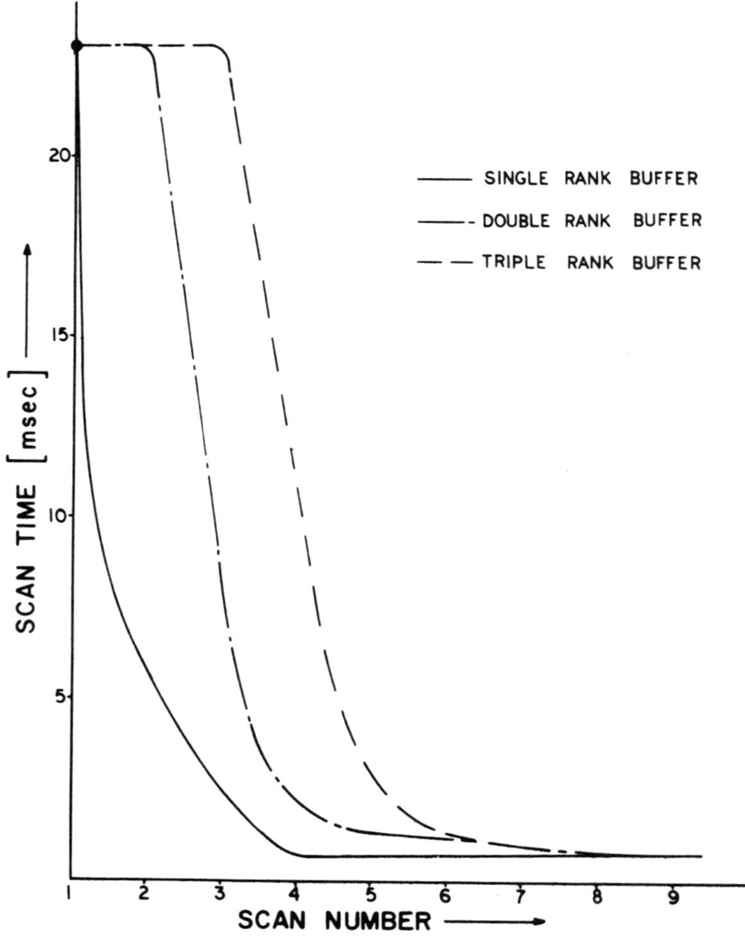

Fig. 11. 40.8 kbit line transient stage with buffer filled.

TABLE II. 40.8 kbit line. N = 30. Percentage of message blocked of single and double rank buffer.

NO. OF BUFFER RANK	SIMULATION G	ANALYTIC
SINGLE	0.4707%	0.4815%
DOUBLE	0.5173×10^{-1}%	0.1516×10^{-1}%

TABLE III. 3.2 Mbit line. N = 2000. Percentage of message blocked of single and double rank buffer.

NO. OF BUFFER RANK	SIMULATION	ANALYTIC
SINGLE	0.4031%	0.3653%
DOUBLE	0.7163×10^{-1}%	0.1214×10^{-2}%

117

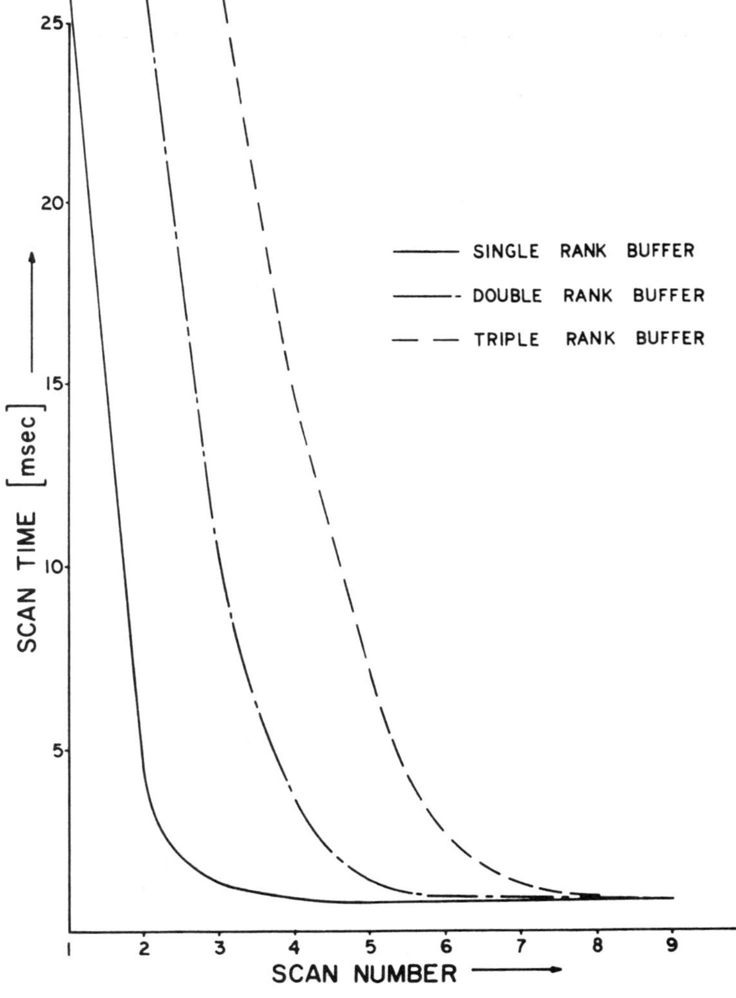

Fig. 12. 3.2 Mbit line transient stage with buffer filled.

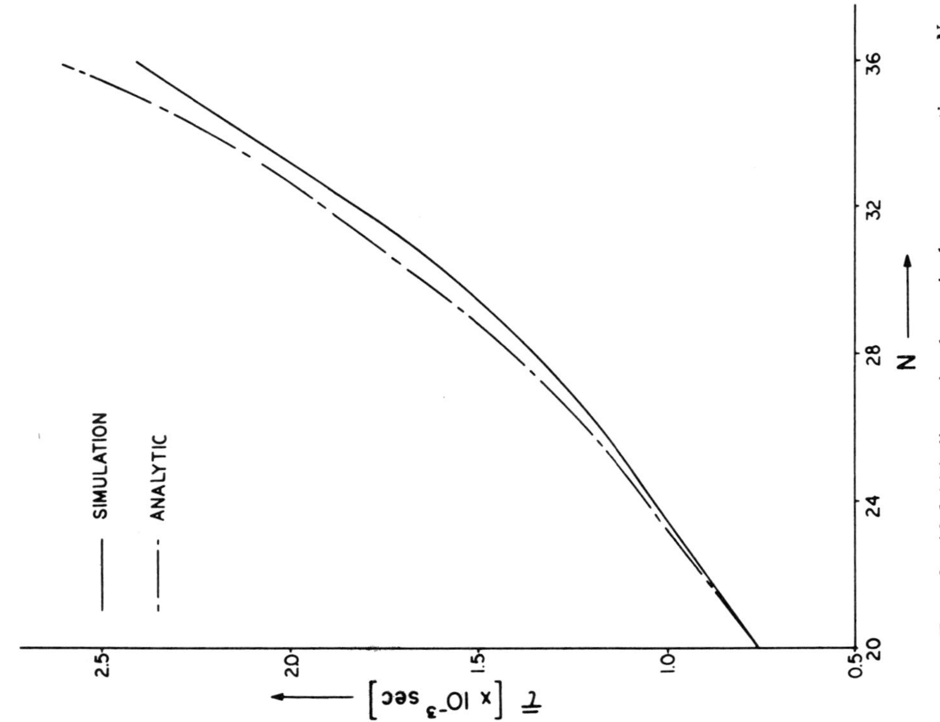

Fig. 13. 40.8 kbit line mixed terminals mean scan time vs *N*.

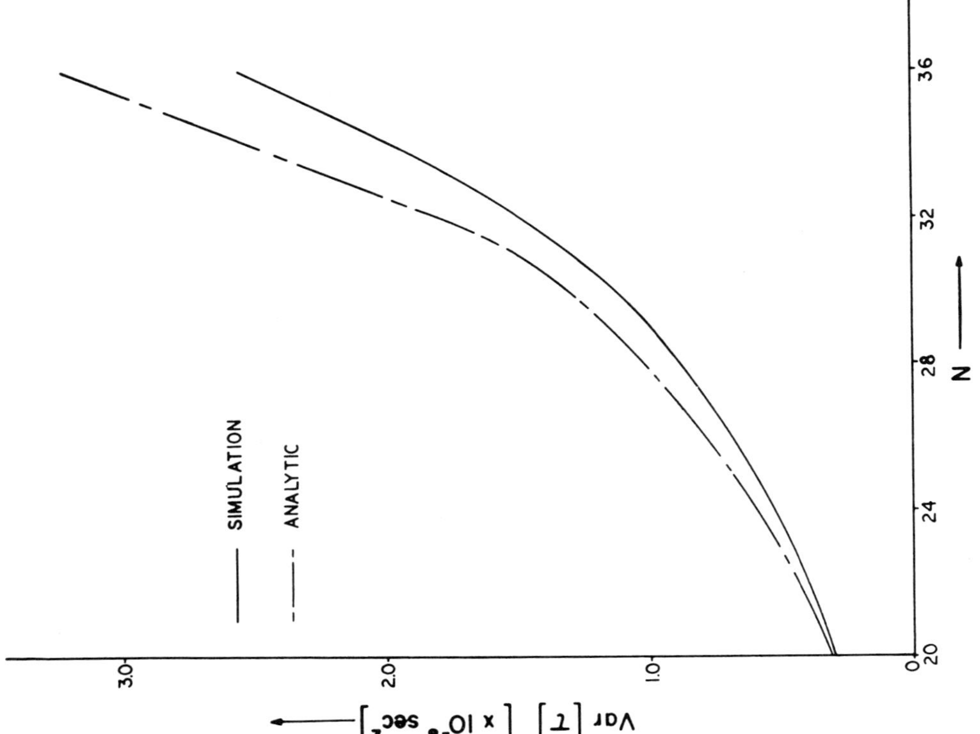

Fig. 14. 40.8 kbit line mixed terminals variance vs *N*.

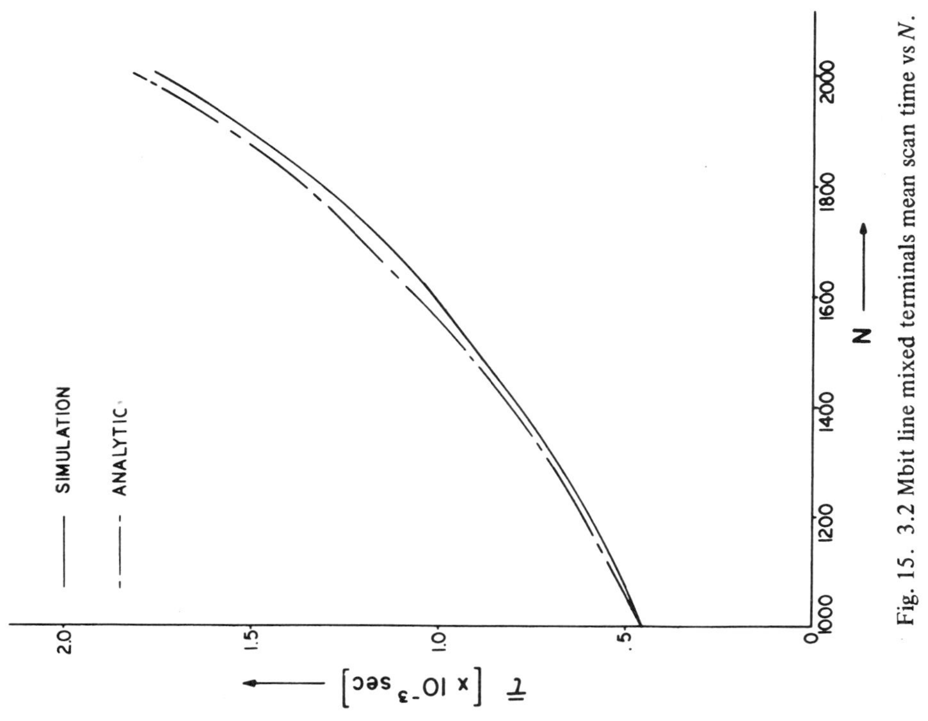

Fig. 15. 3.2 Mbit line mixed terminals mean scan time vs N.

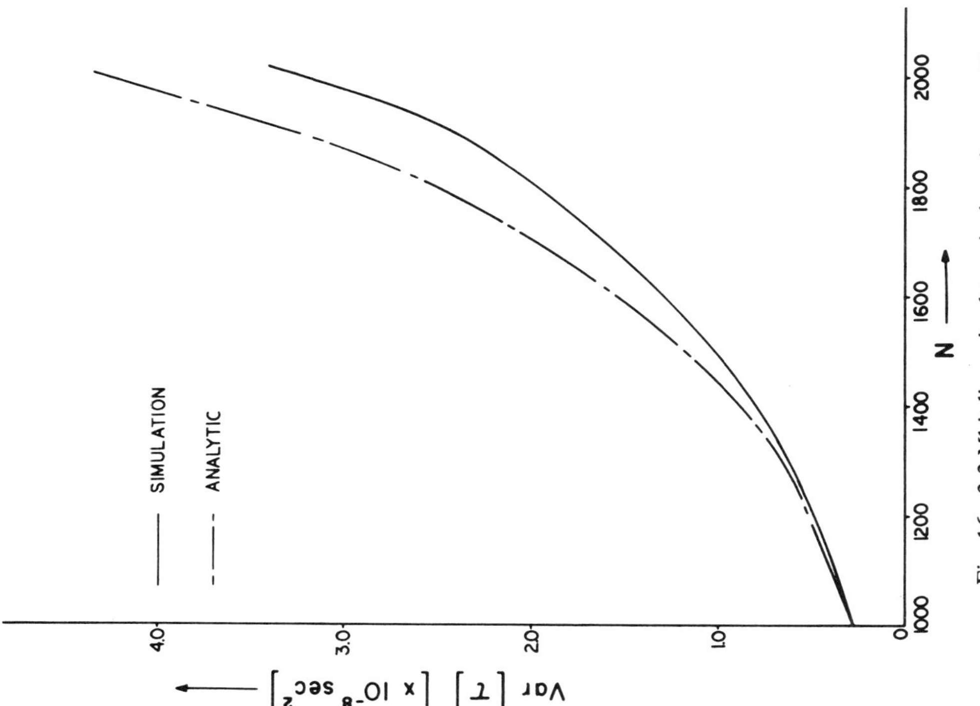

Fig. 16. 3.2 Mbit line mixed terminals variance vs N.

where the single, double, and triple rank buffers were assumed to be full at the beginning of the scan. Since the system settles down to its steady state, it can be considered to be 'absolutely' stable, pending on loop failure and buffer overflow.

For the case of mixed terminals, the loop system was assumed to consist of four different kinds of terminals with average arrival rates of 10, 20, 30, and 40 words per second, placed at random around the loop. For the 40.8 kbit line, the means and the variances determined from Model G and the Analytic Model are plotted in Figs. 13 and 14, respectively. For the 3.2 Mbit line, the means and the variances are sketched in Figures 15 and 16.

V. DISCUSSION AND CONCLUSIONS

As can be observed from Figs. 5 and 7, the analytic mean agrees with that obtained
120 by simulation in the case of light traffic, for both the 40.8 kbit line and the 3.2 Mbit line. The variance is also closely approximated, as depicted in Figures 6 and 8. It is observed that the variance of the 3.2 Mbit line is an order of magnitude less than that of the 40.8 kbit line, implying that the scan time fluctuates to a lesser extent in the 3.2 Mbit line due to the accommodation of more terminals. In the case of a single rank buffer, the percentage of messages blocked as computed analytically is similar to that obtained by direct simulation. As the mean scan time is assumed constant when performing the computation, one would expect the result to be different, and agreement to be worse for large scan time variances. In the case of a double rank buffer, the result obtained analytically is smaller than that obtained by simulation, though it provides indication that the blocking probability would be reduced by using a higher rank buffer.

The transient response of the system, shown in Figs. 11 and 12 shows that the system can settle down to steady state even in the most adverse situations. This could provide a bound on the rank of buffer to be employed. This consideration and the probability of blocking requirement determines the size of the buffer.

In the mixed traffic cases, the mean as calculated analytically agrees with that found by simulation in both the 40.8 kbit line and the 3.2 Mbit line as shown in Figures 13 and 15. The simplified method of calculating the variance analytically approximates that by direct simulation as depicted in Figures 14 and 16.

Notice that the approximate analytic technique only holds in the case of light traffic when $\alpha t \ll 1$. In all cases it is observed that the result diverges as the scan time increases, and the assumption of $\alpha t \ll 1$ is not valid. One can, however, determine the line utilization factor, defined as the useful time over the running time of the system from the mean scan time as follows

$$\mathrm{LUF} = \frac{\bar{\tau} - NT_B}{\bar{\tau}} \ . \tag{33}$$

Thus knowing the LUF and the required percentage of message blocked one can design such a system for practical usage.

It will be useful to analytically study the transient response of the system as a function of buffer size and settling time. Eventually, the results can be extended to the multiloop system.

REFERENCES

[1] W. D. Farmer, and E. E. Newhall, "An Experimental Distributed Switching System to Handle Bursty Computer Traffic," *Proc. ACM Conf.*, Pine Mountain, Georgia (October 1969).

[2] Pierce, J. R., "Network for Block Switching of Data," *Bell Sys. Tech. J.* (to be published).

[3] J. F. Hayes, and D. N. Sherman, "Traffic Analysis of a Ring Switched Data Transmission System," *Bell Sys. Tech. J.*, **50**, 2947–2978.

[4] A. Fraser, "The Coordination of Communication Processes" (unpublished work).

[5] C. Mack, T. Murphy, and N. L. Webb, "The Efficiency of *N* Machines Unidirectionally Patrolled By One Operative when Walking Time and Repair Times are Constants," *J. Roy. Stat. Soc., Ser. B.*, **19**, 173–178 (1957).

[6] R. A. Kaye, "Analysis of a Distributed Control Loop for Data Transmission," *Proc. Symp. Computer-Communications Network and Teletraffic* (New York: Polytechnic Press, 1972).

[7] D. E. Knuth, *The Art of Computer Programming* (Addison-Wesley, 1968).

Reprinted by permission from *Polytechnic Press of the Polytechnical Institute of Brooklyn.*

THE DISTRIBUTED COMPUTING SYSTEM

David J. Farber, Julian Feldman, Frank R. Heinrich,
Marsha D. Hopwood, Kenneth C. Larson, Donald C. Loomis, and Lawrence A. Rowe
Department of Information and Computer Science
University of California
Irvine, California 92664

ABSTRACT

The Distributed Computing System* is an information utility designed to provide reliable, fail-soft service at relatively low cost to a large class of users with modest requirements. The salient feature of this system is the distribution of hardware, software, and system control. Hardware distribution is achieved using a network architecture. Software and control distribution is facilitated through the use of communication by name, rather than address, among the network components. The combined effect of distribution, which provides both redundancy and isolation, and of controlled access, makes total failure of the computing system unlikely. Reliability is achieved by minimizing the probability of total failure, using isolation to keep local failures from spreading and causing global failure, and using redundancy to negate the effects of local failures.

INTRODUCTION

The Distributed Computing System (DCS) is a local network designed to provide reliable, fail-soft service at relatively low cost. The distributed organization of this system incorporates redundancy and isolation in both the hardware and software. The implementation of the DCS organization, with emphasis on how interactions are carried out, is briefly described in this paper.

ORGANIZATION AND COMMUNICATION

The DCS hardware system is a collection of computing system components connected to a digital communication ring by ring interfaces. The communication ring serves as a unidirectional information path and the ring interfaces assist in information routing. Figure 1 shows a DCS configuration with six processors.

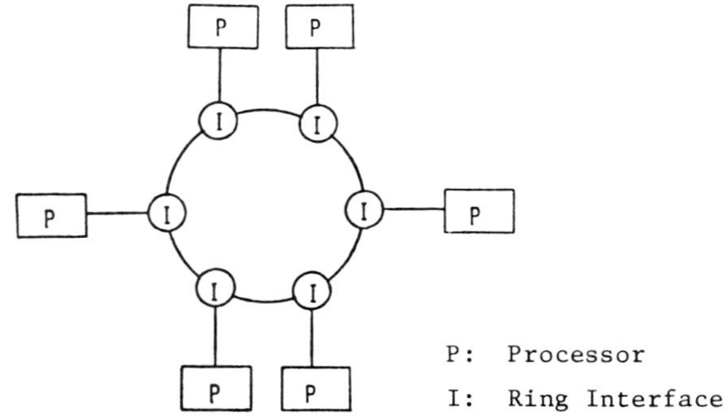

Figure 1: A DCS with Six Processors.

The DCS software system is process-oriented, that is, all activities are carried out by processes. Processes interact by sending and receiving messages. Messages are addressed to processes by name, rather than by physical hardware address. A message from one process addressed to another process is placed onto the ring. As the message arrives at each ring interface, the interface compares the destination process name with its list of all processes active in the attached processor. If the destination process name is present, the interface attempts to copy the message into the processor memory. Whether the destination process name is present or not, the interface allows the message to travel on to the next interface on the ring. The message continues around the ring until it arrives at the interface for the processor in which the sending process resides. This interface removes the message from the ring.

Two status bit, MSB1 and MSB2, are set by each ring interface as a message passes. MSB1 is set if the ring interface matches the destination process name to a name in its list of active processes and attempts to copy the message into its attached processor but is unable to do so. MSB2 is set if the message is successfully copied. Figure 2 describes the possible values and meanings associated with the message status bits. Since the ring

*This work has been supported by the National Science Foundation under Grant GJ - 1045.

interface which places the message on the ring is the one which removes the message, the sending process can tell if the message was received by examining the message status bits.

A process normally sends a message to another specific process. However, there are occasions when a process wishes to send a message to a set of processes. This is called message broadcasting. An example of message broadcasting is given below in the discussion of resource allocation.

MSB1	MSB2	Meaning
0	0	The destination process name was not matched by any ring interface.
0	1	The message has been matched and copied by at least one ring interface.
1	0	The destination process name was matched by at least one ring interface, but not copied by any of them.
1	1	The destination process name was matched by at least two ring interfaces. At least one ring interface copied the message and at least one did not.

Figure 2: Possible Values of Message Status Bits.

RESIDENT SYSTEM SERVICES

Each processor on the ring has a resident software system called the nucleus. The nucleus schedules processes running in the processor and provides message transmission facilities.

The nucleus schedules user processes in a first-come, first-serve round-robin order. Each processor has a time-out mechanism which prevents a user process from holding the processor indefinitely. Within each nucleus there are some system processes which have priority over all user processes. These system processes, such as the output message routine described below, are scheduled when their services are needed.

When a process wants to send a message, it issues a system call with two arguments: the destination process name and the message. A routine for servicing system calls in the nucleus copies the message and other message protocol information into a system buffer. This routine is also responsible for placing the originating process name into the message.

The formatted message is placed on a queue for the output message routine. The output message routine takes messages from the queue and places them on the ring. When the message has been copied into the receiving processor, that processor is interrupted signaling that a message has been received. The interrupt routine places the message on the general input message queue and reinitializes the ring interface to receive the next message.

The message is moved from the general input message queue to the input message queue for the particular process to which the message is addressed. The next time the addressed process is scheduled, a special message receiving routine copies the message into a circular buffer within the process data space. It is the responsibility of the process to check its message buffer periodically for an incoming message.

Because the majority of activities carried out between processes require sending a message and then waiting for a reply, a process may block itself waiting for a reply. This block is usually requested along with a time limit so that a process is not suspended indefinitely.

Before placing the formatted message on the output message routine queue, the routine for servicing system calls looks to see if the addressed process resides in the same processor. If it does, the message is placed on the general input message queue rather than the queue for the output message routine. In this way, a message is not needlessly transmitted around the ring.

In summary, the nucleus provides facilities for scheduling processes and transmitting and receiving messages. Other system functions, such as resource allocation, device input-output, and file system services[4], are provided by processes executing in the DCS. Because the nucleus is the only software unit bound to a particular machine, these other system services may be executing in any machine in the ring and are accessed from user processes by sending and receiving messages. A process requesting service does not need to know where in the DCS the service process resides, because messages are addressed to processes rather than processors.

PROTECTION

The functions one needs to protect a system, isolation and controlled access[1,2], are explicitly included in the DCS design. In addition to the standard machine-level protection mechanisms, the DCS must also employ network-level protection. Because the DCS is process-oriented and process access is done by sending and receiving messages, protection is achieved by insuring the integrity of messages. In particular, protection is achieved by insuring that the sending process name placed in a message by the resident
124 nucleus is actually the name of the process sending the message. If forgery of the sending process name has been prevented, a receiving process can discriminate in the services it provides depending on the source of the request.

RESOURCE ALLOCATION

Resources in the DCS are treated as processes. Each resource is associated with a process and all use of that resource is through the associated process. Resource allocation can then be achieved through the process management mechanism. The mechanism by which processes are initiated is called request-bid or request for quotation. Each processor in the network has a resource allocator, which does not necessarily reside on that processor, controlling resources, e.g., memory and peripheral devices, connected to that processor. To initiate a process, a user sends a broadcast message to all resource allocators requesting a bid on the services desired. The resource allocators reply with bids to perform the requested service. The requestor receives these bids and selects the best according to its own criteria. A message accepting the bid is then returned to the offering resource allocator, but this does not yet complete the agreement. Bids are not binding and the resource allocator may have accepted other work between the time the allocator sent the bid and the requestor sent the acceptance. Thus the allocator may not be able to satisfy the request, in which case the requestor is notified and must renegotiate a contract. If, on the other hand, the resource allocator can still honor the bid, it returns a message to the requestor acknowledging the contract. At this point the agreement is complete and the requestor can assume that the resource has been assigned to him.

There are three points to notice about this scheme: control is distributed, load balancing is carried out implicitly by the relationships between the different bids, and expansion or contraction of available resources requires little or no programming effort. In this resource allocation scheme, control is distributed throughout the system. No central authority controls the relationship of the bids which determines which processor will provide the service. Load balancing, dynamically distributing the load so that each processor receives some portion of the total work, is being effected every time a new process is created. The processor with the most unused capacity, or best able to provide the requested service, will return a low bid, while processors that are relatively full will bid high. This insures the distribution of work. A change of configuration, thereby altering available resources, is achieved with little programming effort, since all that is required is the addition, deletion, or change of the appropriate resource allocators.

CONCLUSION

The Distributed Computing System is a reliable, fail-soft information utility with a network architecture. Reliability is achieved through redundancy, isolation, and controlled access. Redundancy allows the DCS to continue to function with no loss of capability but some loss of capacity if a component fails. Isolation and controlled access prevent the failure of one component from causing the failure of other components and thus precipitating a total system failure.

Several other papers give greater detail about certain aspects of the DCS, in particular, the communication system[6], the communications protocols[7], the file system[4], and the fail-soft behavior of the software system[5]. For purposes of comparing the DCS to other networks, [3,8] may be helpful.

REFERENCES

1. Brinch Hansen, P. "The Nucleus of a Multiprogramming System." Comm. ACM 13, (April 1970), 238-241, 250.

2. Denning, P. J. "Third Generation Computer Systems." Computing Surveys 3, (Dec. 1971), 175-216.

3. Farber, D. J. "A Survey of Computer Networks." Datamation 18, 4 (April 1972), 36-39.

4. Farber, D. J. and F. R. Heinrich. "The Structure of a Distributed Computer System--The Distributed File System." Proc. International Conference on Computer Communications, (Oct. 1972), 364-370.

5. Farber, D. J., M. D. Hopwood, and L. A. Rowe. "Fail-Soft Behavior of the Distributed Computer System." Technical Report #24, Department of Information and Computer Science, University of California, Irvine, California, (November 1972).

6. Farber, D. J. and K. Larson. "The Structure of a Distributed Computer System--The Communications System." Proc. Symposium on Computer-Communications Networks and Teletraffic, Microwave Research Institute of Polytechnic Institute of Brooklyn, (April 1972).

7. Loomis, D. C. "Ring Communication Protocols." UC Irvine Distributed Computer Project, Memo 46-A, (May 1972).

8. Roberts, L. G. and B. D. Wessler. "Computer Network Development to Achieve Resource Sharing." Proc. AFIPS 1970 SJCC, Vol. 36, AFIPS Press, Montvale, N. J., 543-549.

How Far Can Data Loops Go?

JOHN R. PIERCE, FELLOW, IEEE

***Abstract*—The switching of addressed blocks of data through a network (message switching) is particularly suited to the sort of inquiry–response communication characteristic of many business transactions. In a system of interconnected loops, efficient message switching can be attained with distributed control rather than common control. The initial capital investment in such a system would be low and the investment would grow only as the system grew.**

126

DATA transmission can be local transmission in a building or a complex of buildings; it can be transmission within a geographically extensive but highly integrated complex of machines (an airline reservation service, for example), or it can be communication among a variety of separately owned machines, as in the ARPA network [1] and in some banking applications. In this last case, the compatibility required for communication is attained partly by agreement among those who desire to communicate with one another and partly by acceptance of certain operating characteristics of the network over which the communication is carried out, as, the switched telephone network or the ARPA network.

Communication among separately owned computers and terminals is bound to grow, especially in such widespread commercial applications as verification of credit cards. Thus, widespread multiuser networks will come into being. These may be either common-carrier networks, or networks operated to serve a consortium of users such as banks (which can operate in a single state only but carry out a variety of transactions with other banks and with various businesses). Such multiuser networks will necessarily involve switching, whether this is explicitly built into their operation or is somehow supplied as a part of the users' hardware and software.

The switching may be line switching. That is, a circuit may be assigned exclusively to a pair of users for the time needed to complete a transaction. Line switching is well suited to lengthy transactions, as, the transmission of a day's accumulated data. Or, switching may be message switching. That is, a block of data addressed by one user to another finds its way through circuits that are not assigned exclusively to a pair of terminals, but on which other addressed blocks of data may be interspersed between those sent between a particular pair of terminals.

Manuscript received September 22, 1971; revised December 30, 1971.

The author is with the Department of Electrical Engineering, California Institute of Technology, Pasadena, Calif. 91109.

Message switching avoids the time wasted in setting up a particular circuit for exclusive use. Message switching is particularly suited to short inquiry–response transactions, such as credit-card verifications and various other financial or information transactions.

Message-switching networks can be organized in what might be thought of as series or parallel configurations. Fig. 1 illustrates a parallel configuration. Customers are connected by individual circuits to nodes, which in turn are interconnected by trunks. Fig. 2 illustrates a series or loop system. In such a system the customers are connected in a local loop or ring. Local loops can be connected to a trunk loop by means of nodes. These nodes can involve buffering, so that the rate on a trunk loop need not be the same as the rate on a local loop that is connected to it.

In the operation of a parallel system such as that of Fig. 1, each customer might simply direct a message at a node and take his chance that his message would not overlap a message from another customer. With such operation, the efficiency of a parallel system would be very low, for traffic would have to be very light in order to avoid serious overlap. Rather, in parallel systems it seems essential that the nodes provide a fairly sophisticated form of common control; that they interrogate customers concerning demand for service according to a plan, provide service to customers, and assign messages to trunks in a way that assures both small delay and efficient use of trunks.

A series or loop system such as that shown in Fig. 2 can operate in a variety of ways. In the Collins C-8500 direct digital control system a separate time slot is allocated to each multiplex channel unit.[1] This is simple but it would be unsatisfactory in long-haul communication because of the inefficient use of the circuit.

At least one system has used a geographically extensive loop [2]. In this loop, all messages go to or from a central processor, so it does not exemplify a multiuser network.

IBM has used the serial or loop configuration for transmission within a restricted geographical area [3], [4]. This system allows a more efficient use of the channel by allowing an "area station" to write into any blank frame which is generated by a system controller.

All the loop systems previously referred to interface with other nonloop transmission systems by means of complex common control devices. Thus, none is the sort of interconnection among loops that is shown in Fig. 2.

[1] See company brochures.

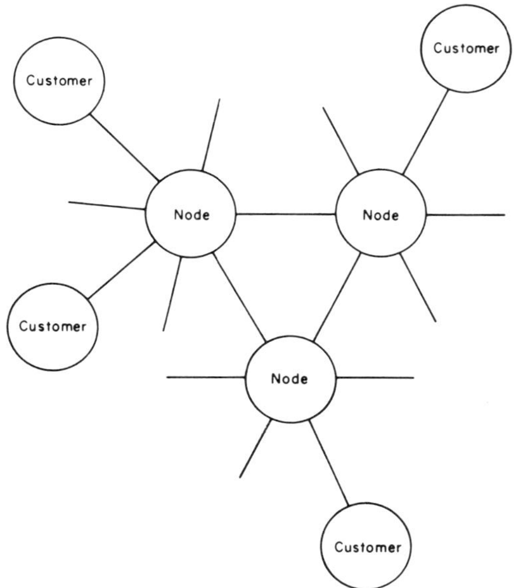

Fig. 1. Parallel system.

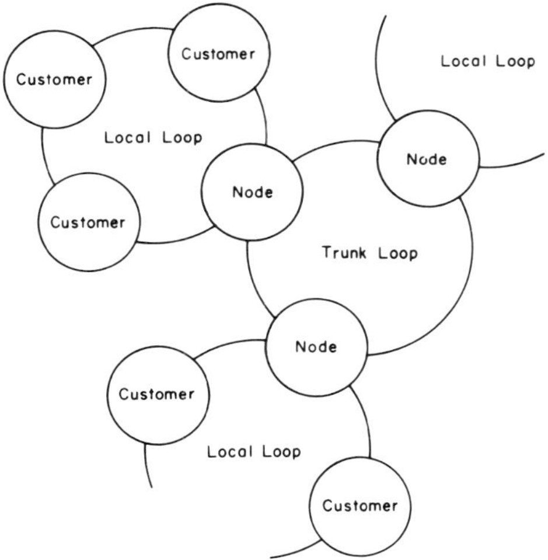

Fig. 2. Series (loop) system.

Another experimental loop system also made use of common control [5].

Pierce *et al.* [6] have shown that a loop system can be so designed that the nodes can be very simple and merely provide clock for the loop, generate formatted message blocks, provide buffering, determine whether a message address is the same as a wired-in address, and perform a few simple wired-in logical functions.

Efficient operation is attained, not by sophistication at the nodes, but because a customer must wait for access until a message block that is marked empty passes his terminal. In transferring a message to a trunk loop a node must hold a message block in buffer until a blocked marked as empty passes the buffer on the trunk loop. Analyses show that the average waiting time is moderate [7], [8].

By using this technique, a very extensive system such as that indicated in Fig. 3 could be built up. The *A* boxes in the figure provide clock, generate empty data blocks, and perform simple supervisory functions. The *B* boxes are customer terminals. Regional and national loops are interconnected by means of *C* boxes. Addresses would be made up of a number on the local loop, a number of the local loop, and a number of the regional loop. The *C* boxes that interconnect loops are not common control devices. In transferring messages from one loop to another they merely compare a part of the address of a block (or frame) with a wired-in address.

Thus, a loop switching system can differ from other line or message switching systems in one important way. An efficient loop systems can be designed without any sophisticated common control. The cost of switching is distributed among the customers' terminals and equipment at the nodes.

Such a system can be designed for a large ultimate capacity by establishing at the start an adequate numbering plan, by ascertaining the nature and availability 127
of common-carrier circuits, and by planning an ultimate topology of the network. However, the system could be brought into being as service is needed. In a local loop, presumably two circuits would run from a wire center to each customer and would be interconnected within or among wire centers to form the loop, somewhat as illustrated in Fig. 4. In this way it would be very easy to add customers to a loop without altering the circuits used for existing customers. Further, simple equipment could monitor the output of each incoming circuit and bridge across the circuit to and from a customer if it ceased to operate.

In Fig. 4, two wire centers are involved in a single local loop; one houses the *A* box. The loop serves a number of customers, one of whom has two *B* boxes. The *C* box interconnecting the local loop with a regional loop would be located in one or the other of the wide centers. Similarly, regional and national loops would be made up of existing circuits between existing wire centers, and *B* and *C* boxes would be located at wire centers. Switching cost, and transmission cost, for that matter, would grow roughly in proportion to the number of customers. Because the customer's terminals and the equipment at the nodes are both simple, the capital investment required for start-up would be small, and the investment would grow slowly as customers were added and as low-speed trunks were replaced with high-speed trunks.

In contrast, in order to offer widespread service with a line-switching or message-switching system, which requires common control, a considerable capital investment must be made initially before service can be offered at all. This could prove financially embarrassing if the demand for and growth of service proved to be small.

Loop systems have another advantage over other message-switched and over line-switched systems. A large organization may require service at several points within

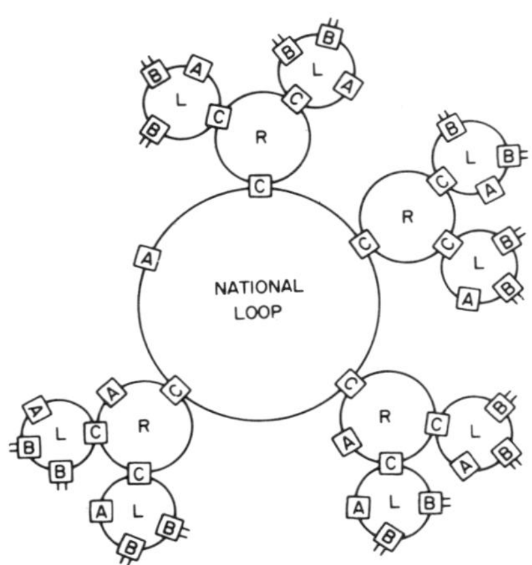

Fig. 3. Loop system with local, regional, and national loops.

one building. If service is provided by means of a loop system with a high bit rate, one circuit to and an another
128 circuit from the premises are sufficient; users on the premises can be connected in series to form part of the loop. Other systems would require as many pairs of circuits as there are users. Although these circuits could conceivably be of lower speed than the loop circuits, it seems likely that the total cost would be greater.

The advantages cited are of a general nature, but digital communication systems must thrive in a real world and their performance must be related to the nature of real data traffic.

If customers transmitted data continuously over a fixed route, private line service, synchronous or asynchronous, would clearly be optimal, and any consideration of switched data systems would be academic.

If data messages were long compared with the setup time for line switching (2–10 s for present telephone switching; perhaps a tenth of this is feasible), line switching would be suitable and economical for customers who needed intermittent service.

It appears, however, that much future data traffic will be of an intermittent inquiry–response nature and that many messages may be quite short. This would certainly be true for credit-card verification and for many messages involving transfer of funds, ordering goods, or information retrieval. Private lines seem ill suited to such traffic, and line switching is ill suited if the data rate is so high that message length is very short compared with setup time.

Message switching seems ideally suited for inquiry–response traffic; loop systems appear to allow the initiation and growth of message switching with a small capital outlay.

However, it would be wrong to assume that message switching and loop systems would be advantageous for short messages only. It is possible that some customers who use private lines do not transmit continously, but rather, use private lines so as to have a circuit instantly available. A high-capacity loop system with addresses

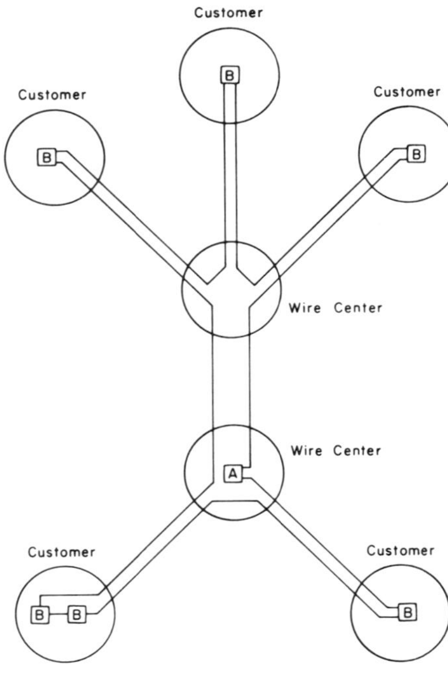

Fig. 4. Circuit paths in a local loop involving two wire centers and several customers.

wired in at the customer's terminals could provide almost instantaneous transmission. If it was engineered so as not to overload, it would give a customer essentially the same service as a private line. If the customer used the service for a reasonable small fraction of the time, the loop system could be as satisfactory as and cheaper than a private line.

Several general objections have been raised to loop systems.

1) Reliability. A break in a loop denies service to all customers on the loop.

2) Privacy. One customer's messages pass through another customer's premises.

It seems to the writer that a satisfactory degree of privacy and reliability can be attained. As to reliability, simple circuits can automatically bridge across an inactive *B* box. If the topology is as shown in Fig. 4, simple circuits at a wire center can bridge defective portions of a loop. The error rate of T_1 circuits is presumably very low. The reasonable approach would seem to be to attempt to attain adequate privacy and reliability rather than to forgo possible advantages of loop systems on the basis of reliability or privacy.

There are what seem to the writer to be more compelling practical objections to the loop system.

3) The cheapest and most widely available digital transmission system suitable for local loops is the T_1 carrier whose 1.5-Mbit rate is uncomfortably high even for computers.

4) The T_1 carrier is widely available but it is not available everywhere and requires repeaters every mile. It may be too expensive to install.

5) The customers' terminals in a loop system, though fairly simple, may be too expensive for very small users; i.e., for the verification of credit cards in a small store.

6) When traffic becomes very large, some more complicated systems might be more economical.

The objection to T_1 [3) and 4) above] may not be as serious as it seems. Buffering at terminals could take care of the speed problem. For customers within a mile of a central office, no T_1 repeaters would be needed between the customer's premises and the central office. Further, data transmission needs might ultimately bring into being a digital transmission system somewhat slower than T_1, which could tolerate less perfect cables and larger repeater spacings.

Objection 5) might be overcome by means of a simple multiplexer in a central office, which would enable one loop customer terminal at the central office to serve a number of small slow intermittant users over low-speed unrepeatered lines.

In regard to objection 6), it may be that the most immediate problem of economics is that of getting started, not that of providing service many years from now.

In conclusion, loop switching systems offer several possible advantages.

1) Low initial capital investment, the investment growing with the number of customers.

2) One high-speed data circuit to a location and one high-speed data circuit from the location can serve many independent users at the location.

3) If addresses are wired in at the customer's equipment, the service becomes equivalent to a private line, that is, instantly available, but the cost will be lower if the customer's traffic is sufficiently intermittent.

The question concerning loop switching systems is not whether or not they can be built and used; that has been demonstrated. The questions are rather: can a widespread multiuser system be built economically? Are certain objections as serious as some maintain, and if they are, can they be overcome? If loop switching systems are sound will someone have the enterprise to offer a widespread multiuser service?

References

[1] L. Roberts, "A computer network designed to achieve resource sharing," in *1970 Spring Joint Computer Conf., AFIPS Conf. Proc.*, vol. 36. Montvale, N. J.: AFIPS Press, 1970.

[2] H. K. M. Grosser and F. J. Schramel, "Data transmission and switching equipment for the seat reservation system of United Airlines (1)," *Philips Telecommun. Rev.*, vol. 24, pp. 13–24, Feb. 1963.

[3] J. Martin, *Teleprocessing Network Organization*. Englewood Cliffs, N. J.: Prentice Hall, 1970, pp. 122–125.

[4] E. H. Steward, "A loop transmission system," in *Proc. 1970 Int. Conf. Communications,* San Francisco, Calif., June 8–10.

[5] W. D. Farmer and E. E. Newhall, "An experimental distributed switching system to handle high-speed aperiodic computer traffic," in *Proc. HCM Symp. Problems on the Optimization of Data Communication Systems,* Oct. 13–16, 1969.

[6] J. R. Pierce, C. H. Coker, and W. J. Kropfl, "An experiment in addressed block data transmission around a loop," in *IEEE Int. Conv. Rec.*, Mar., 1971, pp. 222–223.

[7] J. F. Hayes and D. N. Sherman, "Traffic analysis of a ring switched data transmission system," *Bell Syst. Tech. J.*, vol. 50, pp. 2947–2978, Nov. 1971.

[8] B. Avi-Itzhak, "Heavy traffic characteristics of a circular data network," *Bell Syst. Tech. J.*, vol. 50, pp. 2521–2549, Oct. 1971.

129

John R. Pierce (S'35–A'38–SM'46–F'48) received the B.S., M.S., and Ph.D. degrees from the California Institute of Technology, Pasadena, in 1933, 1934, and 1936, respectively.

From 1936 to 1971 he was employed by the Bell Telephone Laboratories, Inc., where he became Executive Director of Research, Communication Sciences Division. He has worked in the fields of microwave tubes and communication, communication satellites, and acoustics. He is now Professor of Engineering at the California Institute of Technology.

Dr. Pierce has received various awards including the Morris Liebman Memorial Award, the Edison Medal, the Poulsen Medal, and the Cedegren Medal. He has received seven honorary degrees.

Reprinted by permission from
IEEE TRANSACTIONS ON COMMUNICATIONS
Vol. COM-20, No. 3, June 1972

THE BELL SYSTEM TECHNICAL JOURNAL
Vol. 50, No. 9, November, 1971
Printed in U.S.A.

Traffic Analysis of a Ring Switched Data Transmission System

By J. F. HAYES and D. N. SHERMAN

(Manuscript received April 12, 1971)

130

This paper is concerned with a study of traffic and message delay in a ring switched data transmission system. The system, by asynchronous multiplexing and data storage, shares transmission facilities among many users. It is the random component of message delay due to buffering that is the focal point of our study.

The basic configuration of the system is a ring connecting stations where traffic enters or leaves the system. A mathematical model of the ring is developed which accommodates an arbitrary number of stations and any given pattern of traffic between stations. Studied in detail is the uniform traffic pattern in which each user is identical and communicates equally to all others. Intrinsic to the model is a recognition of the bursty nature of data sources. Other factors that are taken into account are line and source rates as well as the blocking of data into fixed size packets. Formulas are derived from which average message delay induced by traffic in the ring can be calculated.

The results of the study are presented in a set of curves where normalized delay due to traffic within specific system configurations is plotted as a function of the number of stations and source activity. The delay here is normalized to average message lengths. An important parameter of these curves is the ratio of source rate to line rate. The results show that, in certain quite reasonable circumstances, the delay is less than two average message lengths.

Rings of 10, 50, and 100 users have been simulated on a digital computer. Data obtained from these investigations are presented and compared to the theoretical estimates for line busy and idle periods and message delay. The results of simulated average message delay show that, for inter-station link utilizations of about 60 percent, the difference between the theoretical estimates and experimental observations is small.

I. INTRODUCTION AND BACKGROUND

In a recent paper[1] J. R. Pierce has proposed a data communication network in which users are connected in a ring or loop topology. In this paper we study the behavior of this network. We examine the relationship between source and line utilizations and the message delay within the system. We propose mathematical models of station behavior and, by making use of reasonable input data traffic models, predict the average delay as a function of network parameters. A principal result of our study shows that, in many cases of interest, average delay in storage is less than two message lengths.

The network is *buffered*, operates on a *distributed control* philosophy, and user entry is gained by *asynchronous* multiplexing into the line bit stream. Other systems have used the ring topology. For example, IBM offers a synchronous, nonbuffered system[2] in which a central
controller monitors the loop and allows access by the users. Buffered, 131
centrally controlled systems have been proposed by W. D. Farmer and E. E. Newhall[3] and A. G. Fraser.[4] In the first a computer controls several peripheral devices, while in the second, several computers are interconnected.

The characteristics of data sources and the requirements of users make the technique of message switching applicable to data communications. One important characteristic is that data sources are often bursty; i.e., relatively short sequences of bits followed by long pauses. A basic need of many data customers is rapid response to data bursts. One way to meet this need is by devoting a line to a source for a long period of time. However, because of the long pauses between data bursts the line will be underutilized. On the other hand, dropping the line between data bursts may be inefficient because of long setup times. For the line switching techniques that are currently used, the setup time will often be longer than the holding time.

Message switching provides a way of efficiently using the line and obtaining rapid response. The idea is to asynchronously multiplex several sources onto the same line. For example, in the present system, data from each source are formed into fixed size packets and supplied with a header. The header contains source and destination addresses as well as bookkeeping information. Packets from all sources are buffered and fed onto the line according to some scheduling algorithm. (One such algorithm will be seen presently when the detailed operation of the ring is described.) Clearly as more packets seek access to the same line, more storage is required. The storage requirements and the attendant buffering delay are important characteristics of system operation. It is precisely these characteristics that are the focal point of our study.

A sketch of the basic ring system is shown in Fig. 1. As indicated, traffic flows in one direction around the ring from station to station. The stations are indicated as B-boxes in Fig. 1. For purposes of explanation let us begin with the operation of the B-box before considering the other components of the loop (A-box and C-box). The data source is connected to the B-box where its output is formed into fixed size blocks or packets and supplied with header. A message from a source may consist of several packets. If the line is free a packet is multiplexed on the line immediately. The packet is then passed from B-box to B-box to its destination. At each B-box on its itinerary the address of a packet is examined to determine whether the packet's
132 destination is at that particular B-box. This examination entails a fixed delay for each B-box which can be calculated given the source and destination. It is, however, the random delay encountered by the last bit of a message before it gets on the loop that commands our

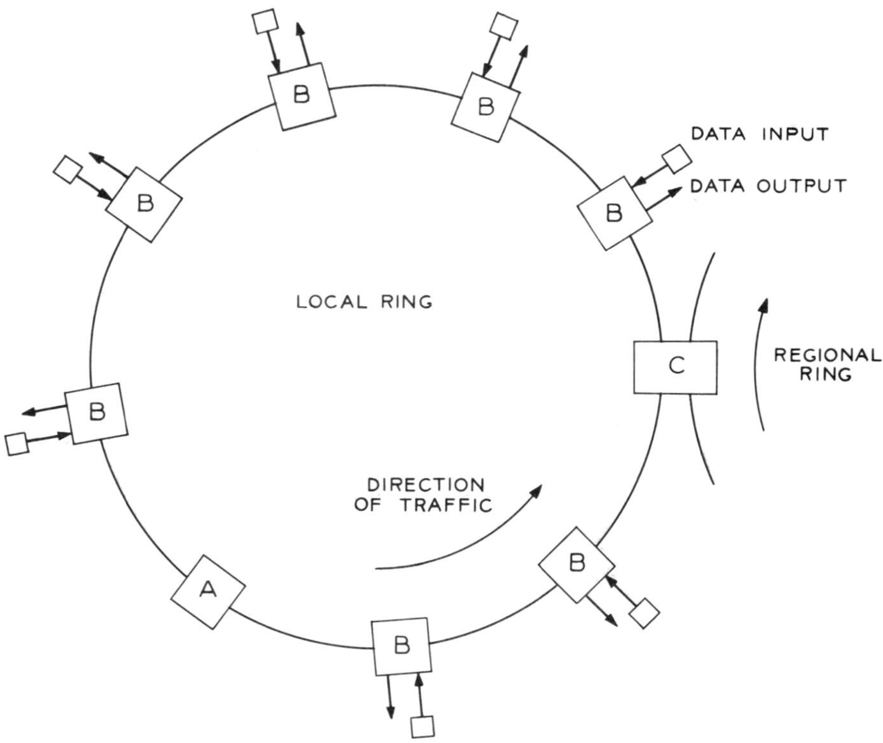

Fig. 1—Pierce ring.

attention. A fundamental property of the system is that traffic presently in transmission has priority over traffic seeking entrance to the ring. If the line at a B-station is busy with information packets passing through it, the packets produced at that station are buffered until the line is free. The reading onto the line of a message consisting of more than one packet will be interrupted when packets from another station pass through. The reading of the message is resumed from the point of interruption when the line is free again.

In order to explain the mechanism of multiplexing packets on and off the line, it is helpful to draw an analogy between the ring and a conveyer belt (see Fig. 2 for an illustration). Time slots into which packets may be placed circulate around the loop. The A-box insures that synchronism is maintained (see below). At the beginning of each time slot is a marker indicating whether the ensuring packet slot is empty or full. The B-box senses this marker and acts accordingly. 133
In a full packet, address bits follow the occupancy marker. If a B-box senses its own address the packet is removed from the line and sent to its destination. This same B-box may take advantage of the empty slot to feed its own packet on the line. Of course if a packet slot is full and destined for a source beyond a particular B-box, then the line is momentarily blocked for that B-box.

While there are many B-boxes in a ring, there is only one A-box. The A-box has two basic functions. The first, as mentioned earlier,

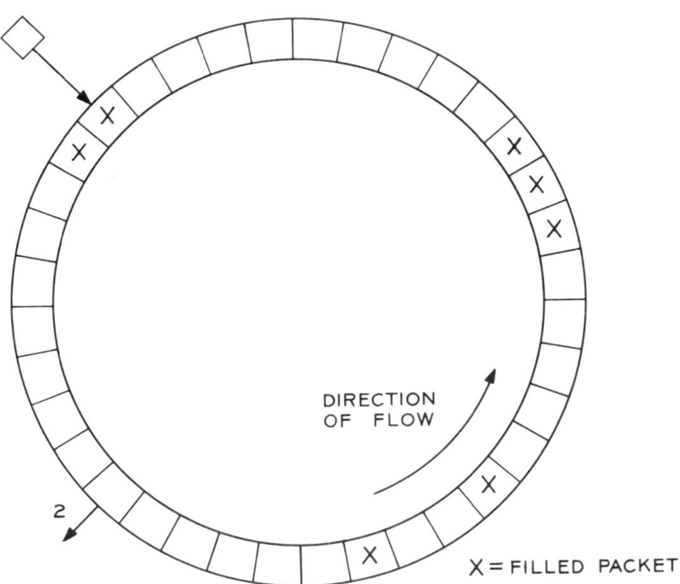

Fig. 2—Conveyor belt. Packets enter at 1 and leave at 2.

is synchronization of the ring. The second function is that of preventing the buildup of traffic in the ring due to undeliverable packets. The header of each packet passing through an A-box is marked. If a packet tries to pass through an A-box a second time it is either destroyed, creating an empty packet slot, or sent back to its destination. Sending a packet back to its destination is done simply by interchanging source and destination addresses. In this way a busy signal is provided.

The C-box shown in Fig. 1 provides interconnection of rings (see Fig. 3). Packets destined for a station outside a particular ring have addresses indicating this and are picked off by the C-box in exactly the same way that intraring traffic is picked off by B-boxes. This traffic is buffered and multiplexed onto the next ring in the same way that traffic from a local station is multiplexed on a ring. Since traffic already on a loop has priority, inter-ring traffic will suffer some delay. A likely realization of the C-box suggested by W. J. Kropfl[5] is the tandem connection of buffer and B-boxes shown in Fig. 4.

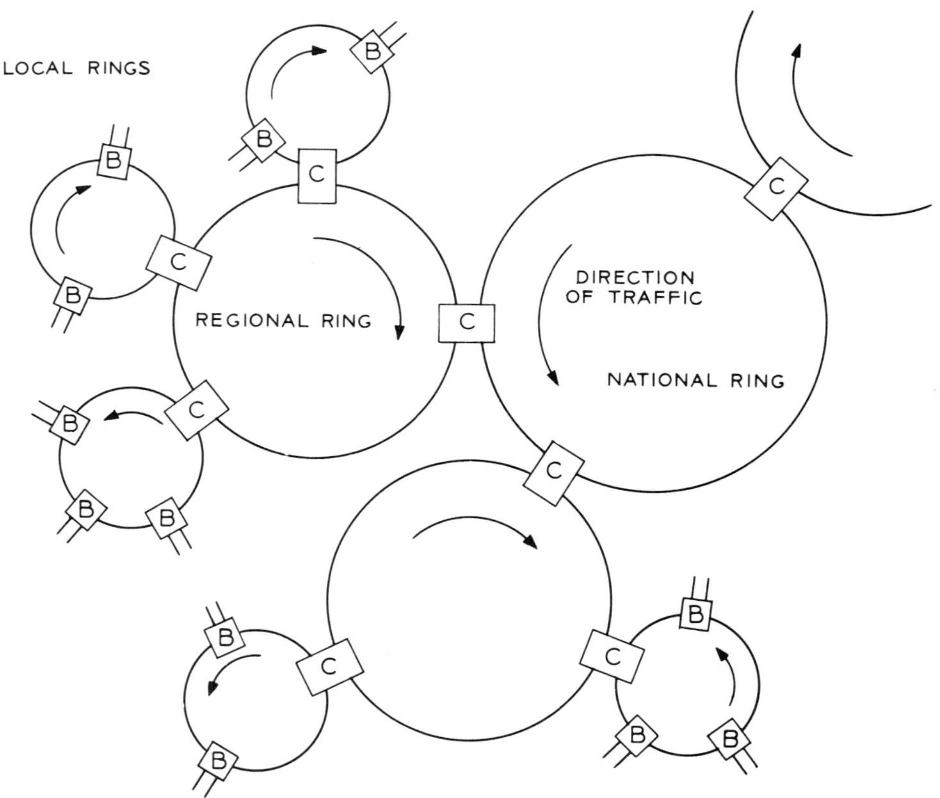

Fig. 3—Three-stage hierarchy of Pierce ring.

In the remainder of this paper a mathematical model of the ring will be developed and analyzed. The results of this study will be presented in the form of sets of curves which illustrate the behavior of normalized delay as a function of either the number of stations in the ring or the utilization of the source.

In order to carry this analysis forward it was necessary to make several assumptions and approximations. Thus in order to verify our results and to refine our model, a simulation program was developed. Simulation results have been obtained for rings ranging from 10 stations to 100 stations. These results are compared to the results of analysis.

II. GLOSSARY OF TERMS

C_b—Line rate in bits per second.
C_p—Line rate in packets per second.
b_i—Bit rate during the activity period of the ith source. 135
B_p—Number of information bits per packet.
H—Number of header bits per packet.
$1/\lambda_i$—Average duration of idle period of ith source in seconds.
$1/\mu_i$—Average duration of active period of ith source in seconds.
Q_i—Average number of packets per message at ith source.
γ_i—Ratio of source packet rate to the line packet rate.
u_i—Utilization of source i [see equation (3)].
θ_i—Intensity of source i [see equation (4)].
r_i—Average number of packets per second from source i.
N—Number of stations in ring.
P_{ij}—Portion of traffic from station i to station j.
R_k^*—Traffic passing through station k in packets per second.
R_k—Traffic out of station k in packets per second.
U_k^*—Line utilization as seen by station k [see equation (9a)].
Θ_k^*—Line intensity as seen by station k [see equation (10)].
U_k—Line utilization after station k [see equation (9b)].
Θ_k—Line intensity after station k [see equation (10b)].
$1/\Lambda_k^*$—Average duration of line idle period in seconds as seen by station k.
$1/M_k^*$—Average duration of line busy period in seconds as seen by station k.

III. SYSTEM MODEL

3.1 *Source Input Model*

In this section a mathematical model for a ring is presented thereby

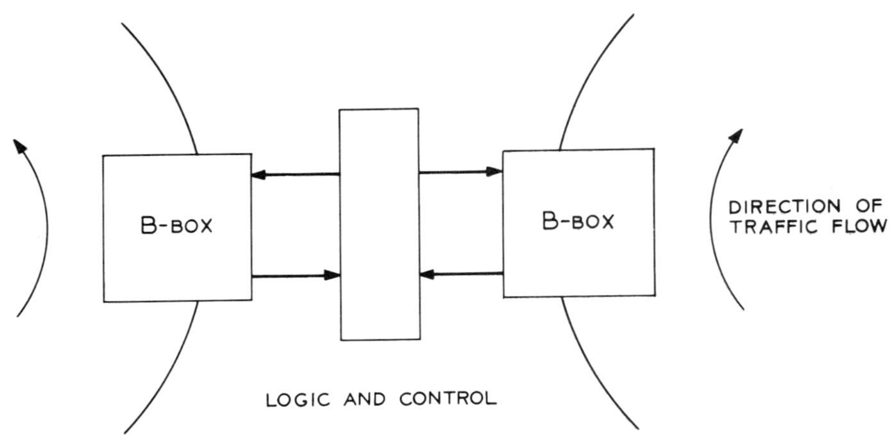

Fig. 4—Tandem connection of B-boxes for ring switching.

136 laying a foundation for succeeding sections where the model is analyzed. We are primarily interested in the traffic characteristics of the ring and the attendant delay. In order to focus on this aspect of ring operation, we assume that there are no equipment failures or transmission errors so that, once on the ring, a packet is ultimately delivered to its destination. Thus the action of the A-box in destroying packets or providing a busy signal is not part of the model. At present the study is confined to an analysis of a single ring. Finally the study was predicated on light to moderate loading of the system. In a heavily loaded system long queues of messages form and the response time of the system may be excessive for data applications.

Throughout the analysis the parameter N designates the number of B-boxes or stations that are on the ring. The capacity of the line connecting the stations to one another is designated as C_b bits/second.

To each B-box is connected a source, which as we have noted above, is bursty in nature. The output of the ith data source is modeled as consisting of alternate idle and active periods. During the latter, transmission is at a constant rate of b_i bits/second. The durations of the source activity and idle periods are assumed to be exponentially distributed and statistically independent of one another. Successive idle and busy periods are also independent of one another. The average durations in seconds of the active and idle periods of the source connected to the ith station in the loop are denoted as $1/\mu_i$ and $1/\lambda_i$ respectively. Studies of computer user statistics[6,7] indicate that the foregoing is a reasonable, if somewhat simplified, model of a data source.†

† An initial study of this model of the data stream is due to R. J. Pilc.[8]

Each message (bits generated in a source activity period) is bundled into an integral number of fixed size packets. The maximum number of information bits in each packet is B_p . The number of header bits that accompany each packet is denoted by the parameter H. In Appendix A it is shown that the number of packets in a message is geometrically distributed with mean

$$Q_i = \frac{1}{1 - \exp(-B_p \mu_i / b_i)}, \qquad i = 1, 2, \cdots, N. \tag{1}$$

During an active period of a source, the rate at which packets are produced is $\mu_i Q_i$. The rate at which packets can be transmitted on the line is $C_b/(B_p + H)$. An important quantity in our consideration is the ratio of source packet rate to line packet rate,

$$\gamma_i = \frac{\mu_i Q_i}{C_p}, \qquad i = 1, 2, \cdots, N. \tag{2a}$$

It may well be that in some applications a typical message consists of many packets, i.e., $b_i/\mu_i \gg B_p$. In this case we have

$$\gamma_i \cong \frac{b_i/B_p}{C_p}. \tag{2b}$$

Other source parameters that are important in our study can be derived. The utilization of source i or the fraction of time that source i is active is

$$u_i = \frac{\lambda_i}{\lambda_i + \mu_i}, \qquad i = 1, 2, \cdots, N. \tag{3}$$

The intensity of source i is defined as

$$\theta_i = \frac{\lambda_i}{\mu_i}, \qquad i = 1, 2, \cdots, N. \tag{4}$$

The average number of packets/second transmitted from source i is

$$r_i = \frac{Q_i}{1/\lambda_i + 1/\mu_i} = \mu_i Q_i u_i . \tag{5}$$

IV. LINE TRAFFIC

4.1 *Line Utilization*

From the way in which traffic is multiplexed onto the line it is clear that message delay is dependent upon the line traffic. As a prelude to the calculation of delay, the relevant characteristics of line traffic are considered in this section. A precise mathematical characterization of line traffic is extremely difficult. In fact, for reasons that will be explained presently, we encounter the most difficulty in this phase of the analysis.

We begin by calculating the average line utilization at each point in the ring. The basic assumption in this calculation is that a conservation law holds so that, over a sufficiently long time period, the average packet rate into a station is equal to the average packet rate out of a station. The traffic into and out of a station includes data to and from a customer connected to the station as well as line traffic. The implication is that there is no continuous buildup of packets in storage at a station, which is as it should be for normal ring operation.

Let the number of packets/second emanating from the source connected to station i $(i = 1, 2, \cdots, N)$ be designated as r_i. In terms of
138 parameters defined earlier $r_i = Q_i[1/\lambda_i + 1/\mu_i]^{-1}$. P_{ij} is defined as the portion of traffic originating at station i that is destined for station j with $P_{ii} = 0$. The average number of packets per second going from station i to station j is $P_{ij}r_i$. All of these packets pass through each station on the ring between stations i and j. The average number of packets per second from station i passing through station k is given by

$$R^*_{ik} = \begin{cases} r_i \sum_{1}^{i-1} P_{ij} + r_i \sum_{k+1}^{N} P_{ij} & \text{if } 1 < i < k,\ k \neq N \\ r_i \sum_{1}^{i-1} P_{ij} & \text{if } 1 < i < k,\ k = N \\ r_i \sum_{k+1}^{N} P_{ij} & \text{if } i = 1,\ k \neq N \\ r_i \sum_{k+1}^{i-1} P_{ij} & \text{if } k + 1 < i \leqq N \\ 0 & \text{otherwise.} \end{cases} \tag{6}$$

The total volume of traffic passing through station k is given by

$$R^*_k = \sum_{i=1}^{N} R^*_{ik}. \tag{7}$$

The total volume of traffic out of station k, including traffic from the local source, is

$$R_k = R^*_k + r_k, \quad k = 1, 2, \cdots, N. \tag{8}$$

Perhaps the distinction between R_k and R^*_k here can be emphasized by referring to Fig. 5. Here a B-box is shown as being split into its two functions, viz., taking data off the line and reading data onto the line. At point Z the line carries all of the traffic out of station k at an average rate of R_k packets/second. At point Y the average traffic rate seen by the local source as it attempts to multiplex data on the line is R_k^* packets/second. (Throughout the remainder of the analysis an asterisk on a line traffic parameter denotes a quantity as seen by the location station after message deletion.) Since the packet capacity of the line is C_p, the line utilization as seen by the source at station k is

$$U_k^* = R_k^*/C_p . \tag{9a}$$

The line intensity at this point is

$$\Theta_k^* = R_k^*/(C_p - R_k^*). \tag{10a}$$

The utilization and intensity on the line after station k are given by

$$U_k = R_k/C_p \tag{9b}$$

139

$$\Theta_k = R_k/(C_p - R_k). \tag{10b}$$

In the case where ring traffic is symmetric, i.e.,

$$P_{ij} = \begin{cases} 0 & i = j \\ 1/(N-1) & i \neq j \end{cases} \tag{11}$$

and $r_i = r, i = 1, 2, \cdots, N$, these expressions simplify greatly. We have

$$R_k^* = r\left(\frac{N}{2} - 1\right). \tag{12}$$

4.2 *Busy Period*

We turn now to the calculation of the average duration of idle and busy periods on the line. An exact calculation of either quantity is

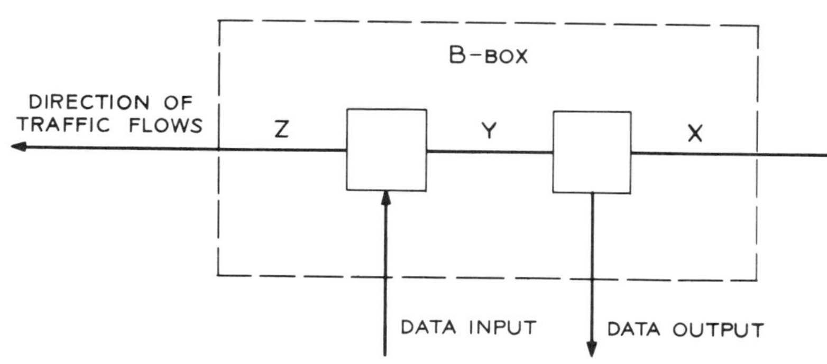

Fig. 5—Station decomposition.

difficult for all but very specific cases. The reason for this difficulty can be seen by examining the mechanism for multiplexing traffic on and off the line. Packets destined for a particular station may be interspersed in a sequence of contiguous packets. This sequence is broken up at random when the packets are delivered. On the other hand, the packets with the same destination may be concentrated at the beginning of a long sequence. In this case the long sequence will be scarcely affected when the packets in question are taken off the line.

In the remainder of this section are presented two approaches to the problem of calculating the average duration of the line busy period. While neither calculation is exact, both take into account the various factors involved, and, in those special cases where the answer is known, the same correct result is obtained. The basic difference between the two methods lies in the kind of line traffic that they are designed to
140 model. As we proceed in the calculation this will be pointed out.

Both of these approaches draw on a result from storage theory concerning the data sequence out of a buffer. Suppose that n sources feed into a common buffer. The sources turn on and off at random transmitting at a constant rate during the active period, and data are read out of the buffer at a constant rate. The output will consist of successive idle and busy periods. Suppose that the durations of input idle periods are exponentially distributed with mean $1/\alpha_i$, $i = 1, 2, \cdots, n$. By definition, the probability of an input idle period terminating in any incremental interval dt is $\alpha_i\, dt$. An output idle period terminates when any one of the input idle periods terminate. Thus the probability of an output idle period terminating in any incremental interval dt is $\sum_{i=1}^{n} \alpha_i\, dt$; consequently the duration of the output idle period is exponentially distributed with mean $1/\sum_{i=1}^{n} \alpha_i$.

In both calculations the line traffic intensity [see equations (10a) and (10b)] is assumed to be equal to the ratio of the average durations of the line busy period to the line period. It is implicit in this assumption that the active and idle periods on the line are independent of one another and that they are stationary in the mean.

The first method that calculates the average duration of the busy period looks at each station individually. In equation (6) an expression for R_{ik}^*, the number of packets per second from station i passing through station k, is given. If this were the only source active, the line intensity at station k would be

$$\Theta_{ik}^* = \frac{R_{ik}^*}{C_p - R_{ik}^*}.$$

The average length of a message from source i is Q_i packets. We take the average duration of the idle period of the packet stream in seconds from the ith source as

$$1/\Lambda_{ik}^* = Q_i/C_p\Theta_{ik}^* = \frac{Q_i(C_p - R_{ik}^*)}{C_pR_{ik}^*}. \tag{13}$$

Now the assumption is made that the durations of the idle periods in the packet streams are exponentially distributed. To find the average duration of the idle period of the packet stream as seen by the source connected to station k, we call upon the result from storage theory quoted earlier. The duration of the idle period is exponentially distributed with mean

$$1/\Lambda_k^* = 1\Bigg/\sum_{\substack{i=1\\ i\neq k}}^{N} \Lambda_{ik}^* . \tag{14}$$

The average duration of the busy period of the line in seconds as seen 141
by the source at station k is given by

$$\frac{1}{M_k^*} = \frac{\Theta_k^*}{\Lambda_k^*}. \tag{15}$$

Combining (13), (14), and (15) we obtain

$$\frac{1}{M_k^*} = \frac{\Theta_k^*}{\displaystyle\sum_{\substack{i=1\\ i\neq k}}^{N} \frac{C_pR_{ik}^*}{Q_i(C_p - R_{ik}^*)}}. \tag{16}$$

When the ring traffic is symmetric [see equation (11)], these results simplify. We have

$$\Lambda_k^* = \sum_{j=2}^{N-1} \frac{\lambda u((j-1)/(N-1))}{1 - \gamma u((j-1)/(N-1))}, \tag{17}$$

where $\mu = \mu_i$, $\Theta = \Theta_i$, and $u = u_i$, $i = 1, 2, \cdots , N$. In many cases of interest γ is small so that the term $\gamma u((j-1)/(N-1))$ in the denominator of (17) contributes little and may be ignored. In this case we may make a convenient approximation:

$$\Lambda_k^* \cong \mu u\left(\frac{N}{2} - 1\right), \qquad k = 1, 2, \cdots , N \tag{18}$$

and

$$\frac{1}{M_k^*} = \frac{\gamma}{\left[1 - \gamma u\left(\frac{N}{2} - 1\right)\right]}. \tag{19a}$$

This expression may be put in the alternate form

$$1/M_k^* = \gamma(1 + \Theta^*)/\mu. \tag{19b}$$

The key assumption in this calculation suggests the region of application of this model. In the packet stream from station i passing through station k, at average rate R_{ik}^*, it is assumed that the messages stay together. Thus the average busy period of this stream is Q_i packets long. The model is not valid when the messages from individual sources are broken up in the act of multiplexing. Thus the model should hold best when the sources emit short messages or when line utilization is low.

The foregoing method of calculating the duration (length) of the average busy period on the line essentially ignores the ring and treats each station as a separate entity. In contrast the second method makes explicit use of the ring structure. The algorithm begins with the as-
142 sumption that the length of the line busy period at the input to a station is known. Based on this assumption the length of the busy period on the line out of the station is calculated. The process continues all the way around the ring until one returns to the starting point. The ring is closed by setting the duration of the final busy period equal to that of the initial busy period.

The algorithm for calculating the change in the busy period is best explained by referring to Fig. 5. The line intensities at points X and Y are Θ_{k-1} and Θ_k^* respectively. The assumption, fundamental to this approach, is that whole busy periods are deleted from the data stream. While there may be fewer busy periods at point Y, the average length of a busy period is the same from X to Y. The average durations of the idle periods are related by

$$\frac{1}{\Lambda_k^*} = \frac{\Theta_{k-1}}{\Theta_k^*} \frac{1}{\Lambda_{k-1}}. \tag{20}$$

The durations of the idle periods between Y and Z can be related by calling upon the previously quoted result from storage theory. If the length of the idle period at point Y is assumed to be exponentially distributed with mean $1/\Lambda_k^*$, and the length of the source idle period is exponentially distributed with mean $1/\lambda_k$, then the duration of the idle period at point Z is exponentially distributed with parameter

$$\Lambda_k = \Lambda_k^* + \lambda_k . \tag{21}$$

The average duration of the busy period at point X is given by

$$\frac{1}{M_k} = \frac{\Theta_k}{\Lambda_k}. \tag{22}$$

One can continue in this fashion until the starting point is reached.

In the case of a ring with a symmetric distribution of traffic the solution simplifies considerably since, by assumption, we have

$$\frac{1}{M_{k-1}} = \frac{1}{M_k}.$$

Substituting into equations (20), (21), and (22) we have that

$$\frac{1}{M_k} = \frac{\Theta - \Theta^*}{\lambda} = \frac{\Theta - \Theta^*}{\mu\theta}, \tag{23a}$$

where $\lambda = \lambda_i$, and $\theta = \theta_i$, $i = 1, 2, \cdots, N$. This result can be put into the form

$$\frac{1}{M_k} = \frac{\gamma}{(\lambda + \mu)[1 - \gamma u(N/2)][1 - \gamma u(N/2 - 1)]}. \tag{23b}$$

The key assumption in this calculation is that entire busy periods are destined for a single station. As the line traffic begins to build up, messages from different stations will tend to cluster in the same sequence and the validity of the model is weakened. The model should hold well when messages are multiplexed into light to moderate traffic.

V. DELAY CALCULATIONS

In this section we shall consider models for calculating message delay. As mentioned earlier we are primarily interested in calculation of message delay that is induced by traffic in the ring. Other delays such as propagation and processing delays are invariant with traffic intensity and are fixed for a given implementation of the ring.

Two separate approaches to the calculation of message delay have been considered. These approaches are complementary in the sense that they apply to different kinds of source traffic while neither approach is applicable to the whole range of source traffic. The exponential on-off model of the source as presented in the foregoing is difficult to handle analytically. The difference in the two approaches lies in the way this exponential on-off model is approximated.

The first approach that we shall consider uses a classical queueing theory model for the source.† Messages arriving at a terminal are viewed as customers arriving for service. An analogy is drawn between the length of the message (in bits or packets) and the service time of

† The queueing theory model of a source in message switched networks is widely used, e.g., Refs. 9 and 10.

a customer in queueing theory. Thus the exponential on-off source is approximated by messages with exponential length which arrive at a Poisson rate.

The queueing theory model is well suited to sources that are not very active. (However the line into which these sources are multiplexed may be very active if many sources are connected to the ring.) When the source is more active the queueing model has some inherent inaccuracies. The queueing model implies that the distribution of time between messages is an exponentially distributed random variable and there is a nonzero probability of successive messages overlapping. In contrast for the exponential on-off model, the distribution between beginnings of successive messages is the convolution of two exponential distributions and the probability of message overlap is zero.

The second approach to delay calculation uses a smoothed version of the traffic out of a source. Thus if the *average* number of bits per second out of a source is X bits/second, the calculation assumes that bits emanate from the source at a *constant* rate of X bits/second. This model of the source is meant to take up where the previous model leaves off, i.e., active sources. The effect of smoothing the bit flow will be less deleterious for more active sources.

The analysis of message delay based on a modified $M/G/1$ queue† is based on work by B. Avi-Itzhak and P. Naor.[11] The line into which a message is multiplexed is viewed as a server that is subject to random breakdown. As the line is either idle or busy the server is operating or under repair. Four assumptions on probability distributions are necessary in order to carry out the analysis: messages arrive at a Poisson rate, the interval between message arrivals is independent of the message size, the duration of the line idle period is exponentially distributed, and the lengths of line idle and busy periods are statistically independent. The distributions of the size of a message and of the duration of a line busy period are arbitrary.

We take the arrival rate of messages from source i as λ_i. The amount of time required to multiplex a message onto a completely free line at station i is denoted by the random variable S_i. It is assumed that the duration of the idle period on the line is exponentially distributed with parameter Λ_i^* [see equations (17) and (21)]. The random variable L_i denotes the duration of the line busy period as seen by the source at station i. In Appendix B it is shown that the Laplace-Stieltjes

† According to standard queueing theory notation an $M/G/1$ queue is one where a single server accommodates customers that arrive at a Poisson rate with an arbitrarily distributed service time per customer.

transform of T_i, the delay suffered by a message at station i, is given by

$$\mathcal{L}_{T_i}(v) = (1 - U_i^* - \gamma\theta_i) \frac{[\Lambda_i^*\mathcal{L}_{L_i}(v) - \Lambda_i^* - v]\mathcal{L}_{S_i}(\Lambda_i^* - \Lambda_i^*\mathcal{L}_{L_i}(v))}{\lambda_i - v - \lambda_i\mathcal{L}_{S_i}(v + \Lambda_i^* - \Lambda_i^*\mathcal{L}_{L_i}(v))}, \tag{24}$$

where $\mathcal{L}_{L_i}(v)$ and $\mathcal{L}_{S_i}(v)$ denote the $L - S$ transforms of L_i and S_i respectively. By differentiating $\mathcal{L}_{T_i}(v)$ with respect to v and allowing v to approach zero, one obtains the following expression for the expected value of T_i,

$$\begin{aligned} E[T_i] &= E[S_i]\,\Theta_i^* \\ &+ E[S_i^2]\frac{\lambda_i(1 + \Theta_i^*)^2}{2[1 - \gamma_i\theta_i(1 + \Theta_i)]} \\ &+ E[L_i^2]\frac{\Lambda_i^*}{2(1 + \Theta_i^*)[1 - \gamma_i\theta_i(1 + \Theta_i^*)]}. \end{aligned} \tag{25}$$

145

Now the mean number of packets per message is Q_i. Since the line packet rate is C_p packets per second, the average time that it takes to multiplex a message onto a clear line is

$$E[S_i] = Q_i/C_p = \frac{\gamma_i}{\mu_i}.$$

In the previous section we have made estimates of the line busy period which we have designated as $1/M_i^*$. These quantities can be substituted into (25) yielding

$$\begin{aligned} E[T_i] = \frac{\gamma_i\Theta_i^*}{\mu_i} &+ \frac{\gamma_i^2}{\mu_i}\frac{\theta_i(1 + \Theta_i^*)^2(1 + \beta_{S_i})}{2[1 - \gamma_i\theta_i(1 + \Theta_i^*)]} \\ &+ \frac{1}{M_i^*}\frac{U_i^*(1 + \beta_{L_i})}{2[1 - \gamma_i\theta_i(1 + \Theta_i^*)]}, \end{aligned} \tag{26}$$

where

$$\beta_{S_i} = \frac{\mathrm{Var}\,(S_i)}{E^2(S_i)}$$

and

$$\beta_{L_i} = \frac{\mathrm{Var}\,(L_i)}{E^2(L_i)}.$$

The quantities β_{S_i} and β_{L_i} indicate the sensitivity of the calculation of delay to assumptions about probability distributions. In the next section sample calculations are presented in which we assume that

$\beta_{L_i} = \beta_{S_i} = 1$ as would be the case if S_i and L_i were exponentially distributed.

By taking a second derivative of equation (24) and letting v approach zero, the second moment of delay can be found. For brevity we have omitted this expression; however, calculations based on it will be presented in Section VII.

$\mathcal{L}_{T_i}(v)$ can also be used to calculate the probability that a message has zero delay. Let us assume that $\lim_{u\to\infty} \mathcal{L}_{L_i}(v) = 0$ and that S is exponentially distributed. Then

$$\Pr[\text{zero message delay}] = \lim_{v\to\infty} \mathcal{L}_{T_i}(v)$$

$$= (1 - U_i^* - \gamma\theta_i)\left[\frac{\gamma\mu_i}{\gamma\mu_i + \Lambda_i^*}\right]. \tag{27}$$

As mentioned previously, the second calculation of delay is predicated on the assumption that the data flow from the source is at a *constant* rate equal to the average rate from a source. Thus we assume that the source associated with station i generates data at a constant rate of r packets per second. Because the line is not continuously available to receive these packets buffering is required. It is the content of the buffer that is the key element in the calculation of delay.

As stated earlier, the line traffic consists of alternate busy and idle periods. In the following it is assumed that the durations of the busy and idle periods are independent and exponentially distributed. The mean values of these quantities are known from the calculations in the previous section. Under these assumptions, constant input rate and exponentially distributed durations of line idle and busy periods, it can be shown[12†] that the probability density of the content of the buffer in packets of the ith station is given by

$$f(B_i) = K_i\delta(B_i) + (1 - K_i)\alpha_i \exp(-\alpha_i B_i), \tag{28}$$

where $\delta(\cdot)$ is the Dirac delta function and K_i and α_i are related to the parameters of the system by

$$K_i = \frac{C_p - r_i(1 + \Theta_i^*)}{(C_p - r_i)(1 + \Theta_i^*)} \tag{29a}$$

and

$$\alpha_i = \frac{M_i^*}{r_i} - \frac{\Lambda_i^*}{C_p - r_i}. \tag{29b}$$

† In the reference, the solution was obtained for a hyper-exponential density. In the present work the density is exponential, which can be obtained from the hyper-exponential density.

Notice that K_i is the probability that buffer i is empty. The average content of buffer i in packets is

$$E[B_i] = \frac{1 - K_i}{\alpha_i}. \tag{30}$$

The delay suffered by a packet is the amount of time that it spends in the buffer while waiting to be put on the line. From Little's Theorem[13] the average delay of a packet is the average content of the buffer divided by the arrival rate:

$$E[T_i] = E[B_i]/r_i , \quad i = 1, 2, \cdots , N. \tag{31}$$

Substituting (29) and (30) into (31) yields

$$E[T_i] = \frac{1}{M_i^*}\left[\frac{U_i^*}{1 - \gamma_i u_i(1 + \Theta_i^*)}\right]. \tag{32}$$

147

VI. RESULTS—AVERAGE DELAY

This section is devoted to numerical examples of the foregoing results. We shall look at two contrasting modes of system operation, complete symmetry and complete asymmetry. In the symmetric case all stations transmit equally to all other stations and the destination matrix is given by equation (11). All stations in this case are precisely alike in their traffic characteristics. This symmetric traffic pattern may be encountered on a national ring which connects regional rings. The presumption here is that each of the regional rings to which it is connected receives and transmits the same volume of traffic.

The asymmetric case models the situation where one station on the ring receives all of the output of the other stations. This singular station, in turn, distributes its traffic equally among the remaining stations. The asymmetric traffic pattern will be encountered in a ring which is composed of inquiry response users connected to a computer through a C-box.

Let us begin with the symmetric ring. Calculations were made for two separate models of delay. Model 1 is based on the queueing model of delay that resulted in equation (26). The model of line busy period here is that which led to equations (16)–(19). The combination of these two models is best suited to the situation where there are many lightly loaded sources on the line which send short messages. Model 2 is a combination of the smoothed approximation to the source that led to equation (32) and the calculation of line busy period lengths that resulted in equation (23).

The estimates of average delay yielded by Models 1 and 2 are given in terms of average message lengths. Presumably, in a particular application, the duration of an average message is known and the delay in seconds due to line traffic can be evaluated.

The results of the calculation for the symmetric ring are shown in Figs. 6–10. On Figs. 6 and 7 delay normalized to the average message duration is shown as a function of the number of stations for two different values of source utilization. The difference between these curves lies in the factor γ which is equal to 1 on Fig. 6 and 1/30 on Fig. 7. The value of 1/30 for γ corresponds roughly to sources with 50×10^3-bit-per-second active rate feeding into a 1.5×10^6-bit-per-second line. The results predict that, for $\gamma = 1/30$, the ring can accommodate many stations with delay less than one average message length.

148 Another view of system performance is shown on Figs. 8–10, where delay is shown as a function of source utilization for 10-, 50-, and 100-station rings when $\gamma = 1$. We see from these curves that, for moderate line loading, delays are not large. For example, when the line utilization on a 50-station ring (see Fig. 9) is 0.5, the delay is less than two average message lengths. Also shown on Figs. 8–10 are the results of simulations which will be discussed presently.

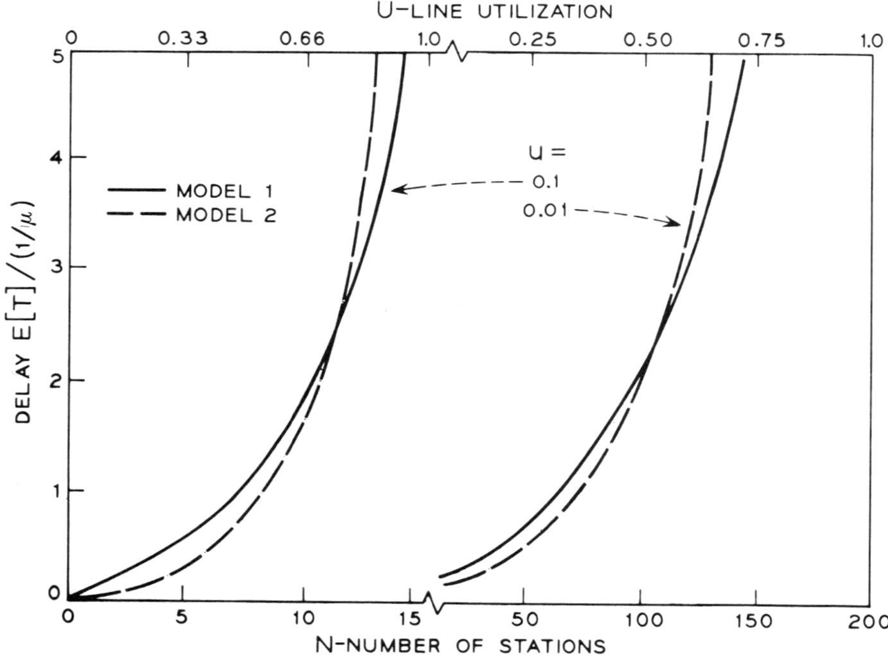

Fig. 6—Normalized delay for $u = 0.1$ and 0.01 (uniform inputs), $\gamma = 1$.

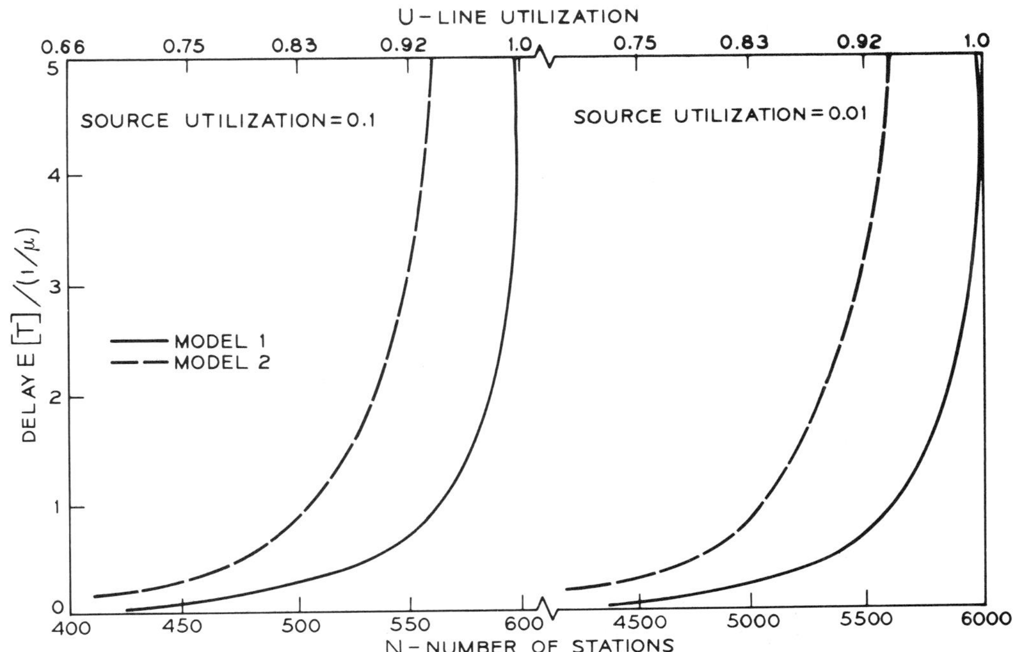

Fig. 7—Normalized delay for $u = 0.1$ and 0.01 (uniform inputs), $\gamma = 1/30$.

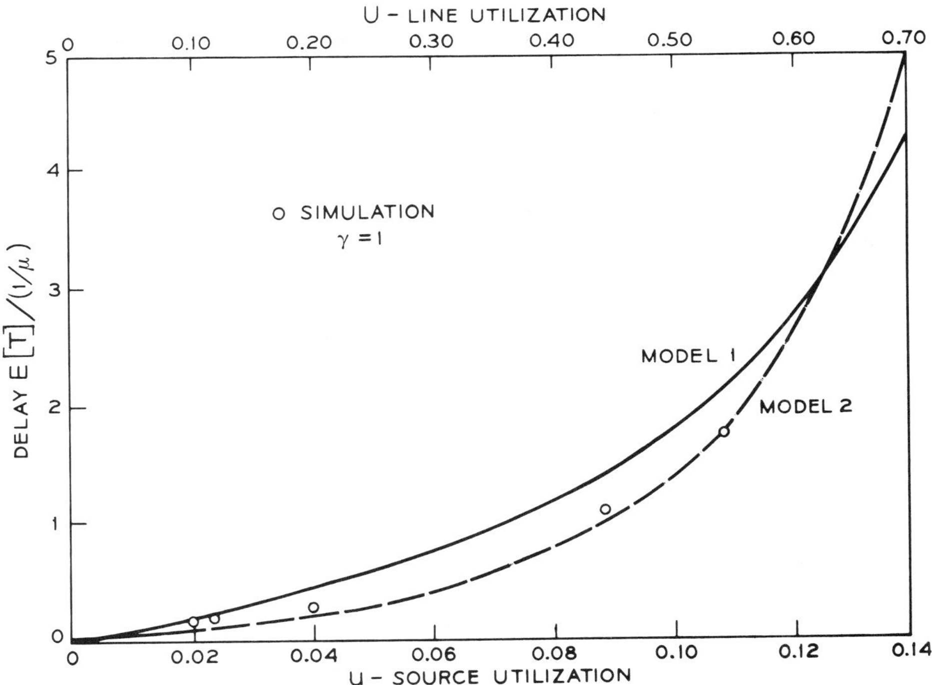

Fig. 8—Normalized delay for 10-station ring (uniform inputs).

149

150

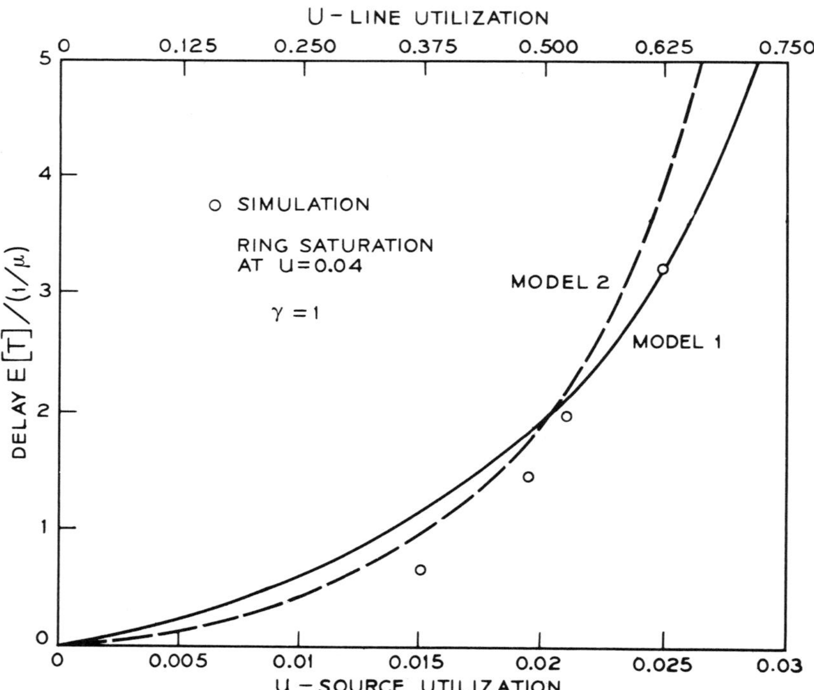

Fig. 9—Normalized delay for 50-station ring (uniform inputs).

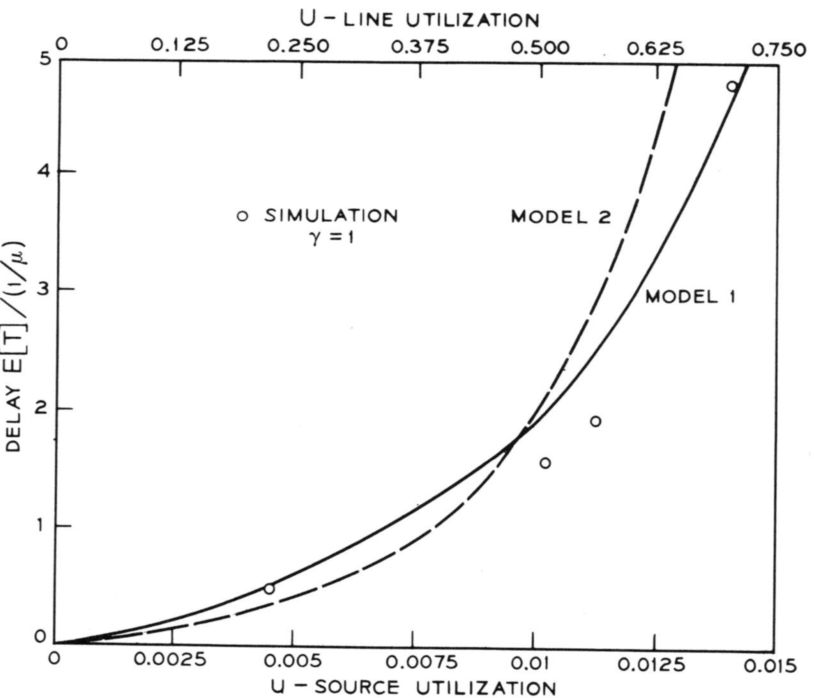

Fig. 10—Normalized delay for 100-station ring (uniform inputs).

A comparison of Figs. 10 and 11 shows the impact of different values of γ. On both figures delay is shown as a function of line utilization for 100-station rings. The difference between them is that $\gamma = 1$ on Fig. 10 and $\gamma = 1/30$ on Fig. 11. For $U = 0.5$ and $\gamma = 1$ (Fig. 10), we find that the delay is two message units. In contrast, for $\gamma = 1/30$ and the same line loading (Fig. 11), the delay is near zero. When $\gamma = 1/30$, the line has very large capacity compared to the source data rates, even when the line is moderately loaded.

It is convenient to use Model 2 to examine the asymmetric case of many users communicating with a single computer on the ring. Let u_c denote the utilization of the computer and u_s denote the utilization of the customer in each of the N stations connected to the computer. We assume that the computer distributes its traffic equally among all the other stations. Applying equations (7) and (9) the line utilization as seen by the ith station after the computer is

$$U_i^* = \gamma_c u_c \frac{(N-i)}{N} + \gamma_s u_s (i-1), \qquad i = 1, 2, \cdots, N, \tag{33}$$

where γ_c and γ_s are the ratios of source packet rate to line packet rate for the computer and the user, respectively [see equation (2)].

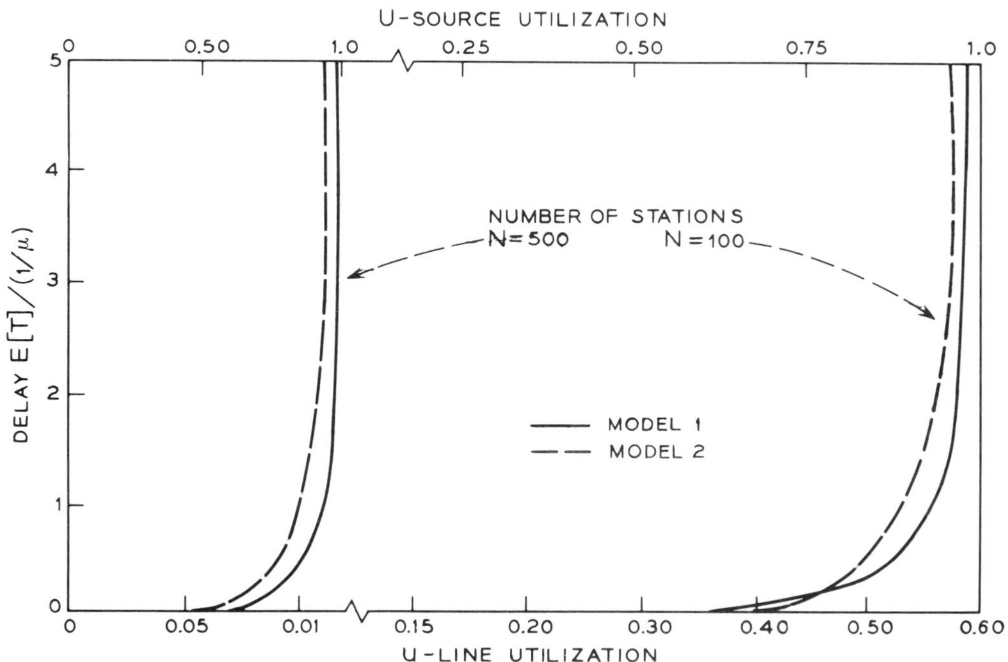

Fig. 11—Normalized delay for 100 and 500 stations (uniform inputs), $\gamma = 1/30$.

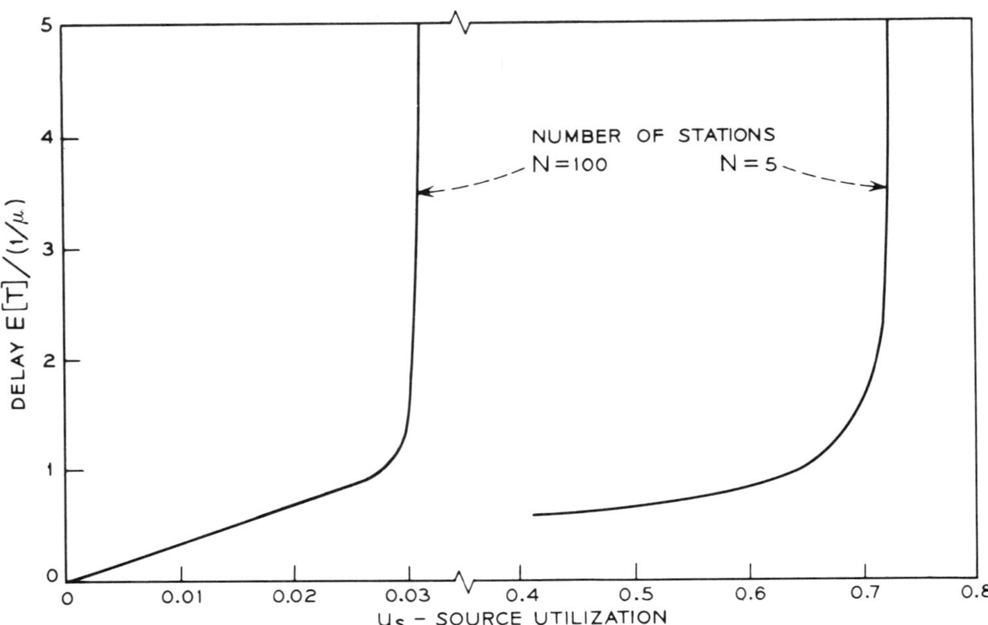

Fig. 12—Normalized delay at most critical station for $N = 5$ and 100 stations, $\gamma = 1/30$ (asymmetric case).

In our computations we assume that the computer-to-user traffic is ten times the user-to-computer traffic ($u_c\gamma_c = 10\ \gamma_s N u_s$).† Equation (33) leads us to conclude that under this assumption the most critical station in the ring is the one right after the computer ($i = 1$) since the line traffic at this point is heaviest.

Equation (33) may be used in conjunction with equation (32) to find the delay normalized to the line busy period at the most critical station. Because of the way the line busy period is calculated in Model 2, we may in turn normalize the line busy period to the activity time of the computer. The results are shown in Fig. 12 where delay, normalized to the computer busy period, is shown as a function of u_s and u_c and the number of stations as parameters. In Fig. 12 we have taken $\gamma_s = 1/30$ and $\gamma_c = 1$.

VII. SIMULATION RESULTS AND COMPARISON WITH THEORY

An investigation of the system was carried out by means of simulation as well as analysis. Single rings comprising the one A-box and from 10 to 100 B-boxes were simulated. All of the simulation results were for symmetric rings in which each station has identical traffic

† Studies of computer traffic support this assumption.[6]

characteristics and transmits equal portions of its traffic to the other stations.

In the simulation, as in the analysis, our attention was focused on average delay. Nevertheless, as we shall see, the simulation yielded information on other characteristics of delay which can be compared to analytical results.

The simulations attempted to mirror as closely as possible the actual operation of the ring. At each station a sequence of message and idle period lengths are chosen randomly from exponential distributions. As the messages are generated they are assembled into an integral number of packets. Bit stuffing is used to round out the last packet in a message. The destination of each message is found by a random selection from $N - 1$ equally probable choices.

After packets are generated they are given an initial time tag and sent to a buffer. The packets are stored in the buffer until they are multiplexed on the line. When a packet is multiplexed on the line, 153
the time is noted and a difference in multiples of packets is taken with the initial time for each packet. It may happen, especially in a lightly loaded system, that a packet is multiplexed on the line immediately. In this case the time difference is zero.

These time differences indicate the delay suffered by a packet due to line traffic. By noting the time difference for the last packet in a message, we have a measurement of message delay. Histograms of message delay were compiled and results drawn from these histograms will be presented in the sequel.

A key step in the theoretical calculation was the estimation of line busy and idle period durations. Accordingly, in order to check the consistency of the models, measurements were made of line busy and idle period durations. These measurements will also be presented in the sequel.

In order to keep the simulation effort within reasonable bounds, it was necessary to fix some of the parameters of the system. Thus for most of the data that follow the average message length was fixed at 100 bits. The messages were quantized into 125-bit packets (B_p = 125). Header information was neglected ($H = 0$). Source utilization was varied by choosing appropriate idle durations. In this case 70 percent of the messages are of one packet duration. As a check, selected simulations were run with different ratios of message length to packet size.

As seen in the previous section, the theoretical models estimated average delays of one or two average message lengths for light to moderate line loadings. For $\gamma = 1/30$, estimates of average delay were small even for reasonably heavy line loadings. In Figs. 8, 9, and 10 average delays yielded by simulation are shown in comparison with theoretical results. These averages were taken over all stations for each of the line loadings shown. In Fig. 8 we see that for the 10-station ring the theoretical estimates given by Model 2 are quite close to simulation results, differing by substantially less than a message duration. The estimates produced by Model 1 for moderate line loads are also fairly good, overestimating delay by about 0.3 message duration. Theoretical estimates compare well with simulation results for the 50- and 100-station ring as well. In general both models overestimate the simulation delays somewhat. For line loadings below 0.5, Model 1's estimates are within 0.5 message duration above simulation values, while Model 2's estimates are somewhat closer. For line loadings above 0.5, Model 1's estimates are closer to simulation results.

It is significant that delay estimates obtained for line loadings below the knee of the curve ($U \cong 0.5$ for the 10-station ring) are well within an average message duration. Since the system would probably be operated in this region, delay estimates for these line loadings are important.

Each of the simulation points presented above is an average of between 7000 and 14,000 data points obtained through simulation. Along with average delay the standard deviation of delay was estimated. Estimates of the standard deviation of average delay were obtained by assuming that the standard deviation obtained from simulation was equal to the standard deviation of the underlying distribution of delay. The results showed that standard deviations of the averages are reasonably low. For example, for a 10-station ring at a line loading of 0.43, 10,000 data points were taken and the standard deviation was estimated to be 1.61 average message durations. The standard deviation of the mean is estimated to be 0.016 average message duration which is less than 2 percent of the average delay. The situation is the same on the 100-station ring. At a line loading of 0.52 where 7000 data points were taken, the standard deviation of the mean was estimated to be approximately 2 percent of the average delay.

Average delay is clearly not the only characteristic of delay that is important in judging the performance of a system. Both the simulation and the analysis provided results on characteristics of delay beyond averages. As mentioned earlier, histograms of message delay were compiled by the simulation program. On Fig. 13 the cumulative probability graph of message delay is shown. Also shown on Fig. 13 is the

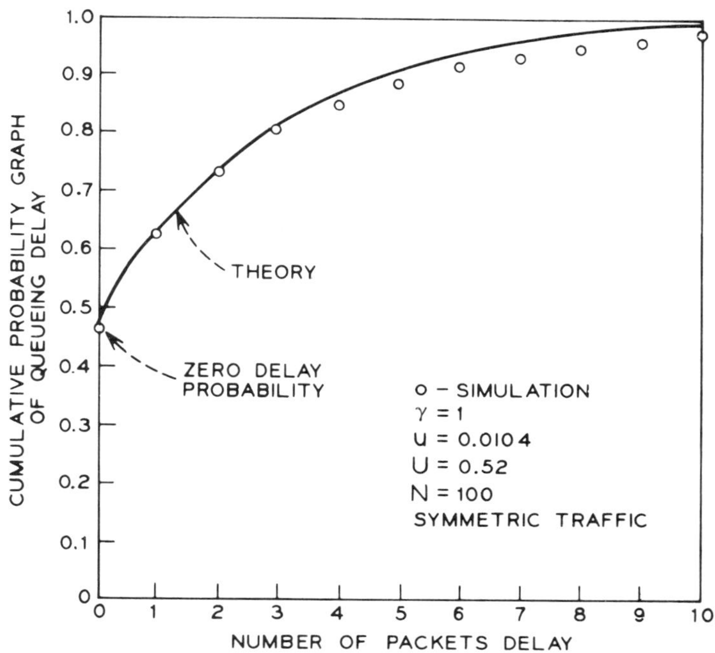

Fig. 13—Cumulative probability graph of queueing delay in a 100-station ring. Data compared with estimates from Model 2.

probability distribution predicted by Model 2 from the same line loading and system configuration [see equation (28)]. The probability distribution for Model 1 was not readily obtainable. The cumulative probability graph shown here is typical of other system configurations and line loadings. It shows a nonzero component at zero delay with diminishing probabilities of larger packet delays.

In order to summarize simulation results along these lines, three sets of numbers will be presented. They are probability of zero delay and a conditional mean and standard deviation of delay. The mean and standard deviation of message delay here are conditioned on the message having nonzero delay.

In Table I are shown the probability of zero delay given by simulation and by Model 1 [equation (27)] and Model 2 [equation (29a)]. For the smallest utilization in the 10-station ring the error between simulation and theory is within 15 percent. For the other line loadings the estimate obtained from Model 2 is within 10 percent of simulation values while Model 1 considerably underestimates zero message delay probability. For the highest loading considered, $U = 0.7$ on the 100-station ring, neither model predicts the simulation value very well.

Estimates of means and standard deviations of delay conditioned

TABLE I—PROBABILITY OF ZERO MESSAGE DELAY

N–Number of Stations	U–Line Utilization	Simulation	Theory	
			Model 1	Model 2
10	0.10	0.906	0.833	0.918
10	0.20	0.80	0.688	0.833
10	0.43	0.565	0.418	0.624
10	0.54	0.464	0.311	0.514
100	0.235	0.773	0.622	0.769
100	0.52	0.454	0.318	0.485
100	0.54	0.418	0.264	0.420
100	0.70	0.252	0.178	0.304

on nonzero delay for both simulation and theory are presented in Table II. Comparison of the theoretical estimates of the mean shows
156 that for the lightest loading in both the 10- and the 100-station rings the analysis estimates the delay within 3 percent. For the heavier loadings, excluding the $U = 0.7$ loading on the 100-station ring, the error is about 20 percent of the simulated results for Model 1 and about 25 percent for Model 2.

In summary, the data presented in Tables I and II indicate that a substantial portion of the messages (i.e., those that have no delay) are accounted for, and that the remaining messages have an average delay that is predictable, in the lighter loads, within 3 percent. For example, in the 10-station ring with a line loading of 0.1, 90.6 percent

TABLE II—MEAN AND STANDARD DEVIATION FOR DELAYED MESSAGES (IN AVERAGE MESSAGE LENGTHS)

N–Number of Stations	U–Line Utilization	Simulation		Theory		
		Mean, $E[T \mid T > 0]$	Standard Deviation $\sigma[T \mid T > 0]$	Model 1 Mean	Model 1 Std Dev	Model 2† Mean
10	0.10	1.18	0.79	1.19	1.22	1.18
10	0.20	1.34	0.99	1.44	1.46	1.44
10	0.43	2.06	1.89	2.33	2.48	2.58
10	0.54	2.66	2.75	3.12	3.34	3.78
100	0.235	1.57	1.59	1.61	1.61	1.69
100	0.52	2.95	3.20	3.13	3.16	4.26
100	0.54	3.29	3.55	3.78	3.81	4.83
100	0.70	6.48	7.89	5.60	5.65	10.72

† The density in this case is exponential, and thus the mean and standard deviation are equal.

of the messages have no delay and the remaining 9.4 percent have an average delay of 1.18 average message durations.

One observed difference between theory and simulation lies in the prediction of zero message delay by Model 1, which, for moderate line loadings, noticeably underestimates this quantity. There is evidence that the difficulty here may lie in the way that Model 1 treats quantization effects. For example, message lengths were taken to be exponentially distributed when, in fact, they are geometrically distributed. As pointed out in the beginning of this section, most of the simulation results are carried out for an average message length of 100 bits and a packet length of 125 bits. Investigations of the effect of quantizing messages into packets are continuing.

As mentioned earlier in this section, data were gathered on line busy and idle periods in order to check the consistency of our models. In Table III are shown the average durations of line busy periods for different loadings measured at one station in the ring. For comparison the average line busy periods predicted by Models 1 and 2 are also shown. Model 1 underestimates the length of the busy period by approximately 10 percent. The estimates given by Model 2 consistently overestimate the duration of the line busy period. For line loadings greater than 0.5, the estimate is poor.

The average durations of line idle periods as found in simulation are shown in Table IV. Again Model 1 underestimates while Model 2 overestimates. The error for Model 1 is higher than for the corresponding line busy periods. For line loadings greater than 0.5, Model 2 yields high estimates.

If the data on the durations of line busy periods obtained from

Table III—Line Busy Periods[†] (Packets)

No. of Stations	U–Line Utilization	Simulation		Theory	
		Mean	Standard Deviation	Mean (Model 1)	Mean (Model 2)
10	0.10	1.58	1.02	1.53	1.65
10	0.20	1.81	1.41	1.70	1.98
10	0.43	2.66	2.74	2.24	3.36
10	0.54	3.20	3.64	2.80	4.76
100	0.235	1.94	1.52	1.78	2.36
100	0.52	2.96	3.07	2.80	5.87
100	0.54	3.32	3.87	3.24	7.9
100	0.70	5.08	7.32	4.49	14.5

[†] The results shown here are averages for a single station. The line utilization is averaged over the entire ring.

TABLE IV—LINE IDLE PERIODS† (PACKETS)

No. of Stations	U–Line Utilization	Simulation		Theory	
		Mean	Standard Deviation	Mean (Model 1)	Mean (Model 2)
10	0.10	14.07	13.30	17.60	18.90
10	0.20	7.22	6.80	6.80	7.93
10	0.43	3.40	2.97	2.84	4.48
10	0.54	2.74	2.24	2.34	3.95
100	0.235	6.34	5.71	5.95	7.70
100	0.52	2.96	2.75	2.54	5.85
100	0.54	2.78	2.39	2.3	5.65
100	0.70	2.05	1.58	1.95	6.20

† The results shown here are averages for a single station. The line utilization is averaged over the entire ring.

158 simulation are used in the calculation of average delay the conclusions do not change substantially. Except for the $U = 0.7$ load point in the 100-station ring, the average delays predicted by Model 1 increase by less than 10 percent. Below line loadings of $U = 0.5$, the predictions of Model 2 decrease but are still fairly close to simulation points. Regions where the line loading is light to moderate are of greatest interest since it is most likely that systems would be operated in this region. For higher line loadings, delay in terms of average message lengths is large and small changes in loading lead to large changes in delay.

VIII. CONCLUSION

We conclude with a summary of our results. The analysis and the simulation of 10-, 50-, and 100-station rings show that for $\gamma = 1$, i.e., source rate and line rate equal, message delay is less than 2 average message durations for line loading up to 0.5 of capacity. For line loadings greater than 0.5, delay increases substantially. For $\gamma = 1/30$, i.e., a low-speed source feeding into a high-speed line, average delay in terms of average message durations is low for line loadings up to 0.8. Analytical and simulation results indicate that there is a nonzero probability of zero message delay at all line loadings. The probability of zero message delay is greater than 0.5 for line loadings less than 0.5. Analysis and simulation indicate that the probability of a specific message delay decreases monotonically with the value of delay. The rate of decrease is similar to that of an exponential distribution (see Fig. 13).

For light to moderate line loads the theoretical models of average message delay show good agreement with the simulation results. For high line loads some of the approximations used in the theoretical models are weakened and agreement is not as good. However, even for heavy loading, there is meaningful agreement between analysis and simulation since both predict large delay and large shifts in delay with small shifts in line loading.

Some of the discrepancy between analysis and simulation may be due to the fact that the analysis did not take into account quantizing effects. For example, line busy periods must be an integral number of packets in duration, whereas the analysis treated line busy periods as a continuous random variable. Investigation of these effects on message delay will be carried out in the future.

The simulation program is capable of simulating systems where the traffic pattern is not symmetric and work will continue in this direction. 159

IX. ACKNOWLEDGMENTS

The authors wish to thank M. J. Ferguson for many fruitful discussions. Acknowledged also is the assistance of B. Avi-Itzhak and M. Segal in deriving results on the server with breakdown queueing model.

The simulation programming was done by R. R. Anderson, who is also responsible for coaxing from the computer all of the simulation points that are shown here. The authors are deeply appreciative of his efforts.

APPENDIX A

Effect of Quantization

In the text we have assumed that the duration of a source active period is exponentially distributed with parameter μ_i (for source i). During the active period the source emits bits at a constant rate of b_i bits/second. The data is bundled into packets with B_p bits/packet. The probability that there are j packets in a message is given by

$$D_j = \int_{(j-1)B_p/b_i}^{jB_p/b_i} \mu_i \exp(-\mu_i t)\,dt, \qquad i = 1, 2, \cdots, N$$
$$= \exp(-(j-1)B_p\mu_i/b_i)[1 - \exp(-B_p\mu_i/b_i)].$$

Let

$$A \triangleq \exp[-B_p\mu_i/b_i];$$

then

$$D_j = A^{j-1}(1 - A).$$

The mean number of packets per message is

$$1/M_i = \sum_{j=1}^{\infty} jD_j = \frac{1}{1 - \exp(-B_p\mu_i/b_i)}.$$

APPENDIX B

In an earlier paper Avi-Itzhak and Naor[11] found the average delay of a customer arriving at a server that is subject to random breakdown. Recently, using a similar line of reasoning, Avi-Itzhak[14] found the Laplace–Stieltjes transform of the density of this delay T_i' to be:

160

$$\mathcal{L}_{T_i'}(v) = (1 - U_i^* - \gamma\theta_i) \cdot \frac{[\Lambda_i^*\mathcal{L}_{L_i}(v) - \Lambda_i^* - v]\mathcal{L}_{S_i}(v + \Lambda_i^* - \Lambda_i^*\mathcal{L}_{L_i}(v))}{\lambda_i - v - \lambda_i\mathcal{L}_{S_i}(v + \Lambda_i^* - \Lambda_i^*\mathcal{L}_{L_i}(v))}, \qquad (34)$$

where $\mathcal{L}_{L_i}(v)$ and $\mathcal{L}_{S_i}(v)$ are the Laplace–Stieltjes transforms of L_i and S_i respectively. (Recall that in the main body of the text L_i is defined as the duration of the line busy period at station i and S_i is defined as the time required to multiplex a message on a free line.) In this derivation it is assumed that the line idle periods are exponentially distributed with parameter Λ_i^*. It is also assumed that messages arrive at a Poisson rate λ_i.

In order for this result to be applicable to our problem, some modification of equation (34) is necessary. The expected value of T_i' yielded by (34) when the line is entirely free for a long period of time is $E[S_i]$. But this is a delay that is due to multiplexing alone and is not a function of line traffic. Since we are interested in delay that is dependent on line congestion we remove this multiplexing delay.

The delay described by equation (34) is the sum of two independent components, the waiting time and the residence time. The waiting time is the interval from when the message first arrives until it is first multiplexed on the line. The residence time is the interval in which the message is multiplexed on the line, including line busy periods during which the message is blocked. The L − S transform of the density of the residence time is given by

$$\mathcal{L}_{S_i}(v + \Lambda_i^* - \Lambda_i^*\mathcal{L}_{L_i}(v)) = \int_0^\infty dt\, e^{-vt} \sum_{k=0}^{\infty} \int_0^t dx\, \frac{(\Lambda_i^* x)^k e^{-x\Lambda_i^*}}{k!} f_{L_i}^{*k}(t - x) f_{S_i}(x), \qquad (35)$$

where $f_{S_i}(x)$ is the density of the message multiplexing time and $f_{L_i}^{*k}(x)$ is the k-fold convolution of the line busy period. This expression is obtained by adding the message multiplexing times and all of the intervening line busy periods. Now if we simply add together only the line busy periods, removing the line multiplexing time, we have

$$\mathcal{L}_{S_i}(\Lambda_i^* - \Lambda_i^*\mathcal{L}_{L_i}(v)) = \int_0^\infty dt\, e^{-vt} \sum_{k=0}^\infty \int_0^\infty dx\, \frac{(\Lambda_i^* x)^k}{k!}\, e^{-x\Lambda_i^*} f_{L_i}^{*k}(t) f_{S_i}(x). \tag{36}$$

Equation (34) becomes

$$\mathcal{L}_{T_i}(v) = (1 - U_i^* - \gamma\theta_i) \cdot \frac{[\Lambda_i^*\mathcal{L}_{L_i}(v) - \Lambda_i^* - v] S_i(\Lambda_i^* - \Lambda_i^*\mathcal{L}_{L_i}(v))}{\lambda_i - v - \lambda_i \mathcal{L}_{S_i}(v + \Lambda_i^* - \Lambda_i\mathcal{L}_{L_i}(v))}. \tag{37}$$

REFERENCES

1. Pierce, J. R., Coker, C. H., and Kropfl, W. J., "Network for Block Switching of Data," IEEE Conv. Rec., New York, March 1971.
2. Steward, E. H., "A Loop Transmission System," 1970 ICC, vol. 2, pp. 36–1, 36–9.
3. Farmer, W. D., and Newhall, E. E., "An Experimental Distributed Switching System to Handle Bursty Computer Traffic," Proc. ACM Conf., Pine Mountain, Georgia, October 1969.
4. Fraser, A. G., "The Coordination of Communicating Processes," unpublished work.
5. Kropfl, W. J., "An Experimental Data Block Switching System," unpublished work.
6. Jackson, P. E., and Stubbs, C. D., "A Study of Multi-access Computer Communications," AFIPS, Conf. Proc., vol. 34, p. 491.
7. Jackson, P. E., and Fuchs, E., "Estimates of Distributions of Random Variables for Certain Computer Communications Traffic Models," Proc. ACM Conf., Pine Mountain, Georgia, October 1969.
8. Pilc, R. J., unpublished work.
9. Chu, W. W., "An Analysis of Buffer Behavior for Batch Poisson Arrivals and Single Server with Constant Output Rate," IEEE Trans. Commun. Tech., *COM-18*, No. 5 (October 1970), pp. 613–619.
10. Kleinrock, L., *Communications Nets–Stochastic Message Flow and Delay*, New York: McGraw-Hill, 1964.
11. Avi-Itzhak, B., and Naor, P., "Some Queueing Problems with the Service Station Subject to Breakdown," Oper. Res., *11*, No. 3, 1963, pp. 303–320.
12. Sherman, D. N., "Data Buffer Occupancy Statistics for Asynchronous Multiplexing of Data in Speech," Proc. ICC, San Francisco, California, June 1970.
13. Little, J. D. C., "A Proof of the Queueing Formula L = λW," Oper. Res., *9*, 1961, pp. 383–387.
14. Avi-Itzhak, B., unpublished work.

Examples of Computer Communications Networks

There are many experimental computer communication networks already in existence. As we achieve a better understanding of network characteristics and related problems, more and more networks will be constructed. Due to the limited space available in this volume, we can only present a few currently operating computer networks as examples.

Roberts and Wessler (p. 170) describe the ARPA Network, its properties and comparison with alternative communication designs. Davies (p. 164) and Scantlebury and Wilkinson (p. 177) describe the characteristics and design considerations of the experimental computer network at the National Physical Laboratory, U.K.

Schwartz, Boorstyn and Pickholtz (p. 185) describe the properties of terminal-based systems, using as illustrations four commercial systems: TYMNET, INFONET, the General Electric Network, and the NASDAQ securities quotation system. De Mercado et. al. (p. 209) describe the Canadian Universities Computer Network. The paper by Kuo and Abramson (p. 215) describes the ALOHA system which is a UHF-radio computer communication network. The ALOHA system represents an alternative to the use of conventional wire communications for computer-computer and console-computer link. Pouzin (p. 219) describes the Cyclades Computer Network which is a general purpose network being installed in France.

For additional reading on the ALOHA system, the reader should refer to Chapter V of this book and Chapter 14 of "Computer Communication Networks," edited by N. Abramson and F. Kuo, Prentice-Hall, 1973. For information on the new data network in Europe, see [BAR 72] and [AND 72].

INFORMATION PROCESSING 68 - NORTH-HOLLAND PUBLISHING COMPANY - AMSTERDAM (1969)

THE PRINCIPLES OF A DATA COMMUNICATION NETWORK FOR COMPUTERS AND REMOTE PERIPHERALS

D. W. DAVIES
National Physical Laboratory, Teddington, Middlesex, UK

Many computer systems are coming into operation in which a central computer gives rapid response to requests from a widely distributed collection of remote terminals. Use of the telephone network for such systems has many limitations because the telephone network was designed for a different purpose entirely and these limitations will become more troublesome as new terminal devices come into use.

In the paper, the design of a data network for computers and terminals is outlined. Further details of parts of the system are given in companion papers. The new design seems, on the evidence available, to be economic and adaptable to future changes both in users' requirements and in the technologies of transmission, logic and storage.

1. INTRODUCTION

164

Many computer systems are coming into operation in which a central computer gives rapid response to requests from a widely distributed collection of remote terminals. Where the speed and error rate are acceptable, connections through the switched telephone networks are often used. An alternative is a network of 'private' speech-grade circuits. These methods have many disadvantages, one of which is the cost of the special equipment, both at the terminals and the computer, which is required to buffer, concentrate, control transmission and assemble messages for the computer.

It is clear that a common-carrier data network could give great economies, since many of the communication functions would, in such a system, be handled by common equipment. The difficulty in such an approach is to develop a system design general enough to deal with the wide range of users' requirements, including those that may arise in the future. This paper proposes a design for a common-carrier data network.

The network proposed has similarities to many existing systems. Thus the SITA high-level network for air-line seat bookings and the proposed CCITT No. 6 signalling system show some resemblance, while there is a superficial resemblance to telegraph message switching systems. The reader acquainted with these systems will find that the proposal differs significantly from each of those mentioned.

The most closely related previous work was by Paul Baran and is reported in a paper "On Distributed Communications" [1]. Our proposal is like Baran's in its high-level network but the similarity does not extend to the manner of using the network.

The development of a new network has technical, economic, organizational and commercial aspects. This paper is concerned with the technical features of the network and the communication requirements which it is designed to meet. Further details of the design are contained in refs. [2-4].

The present proposal does not depend essentially on the installation of digital transmission channels, but these will be needed for its full, economic development. The ideas have developed around the use of 1.5 Mbit/sec as minimum capacity in the high level part of the network. As will be seen later, a minimum data rate in the high-level network is established mainly to achieve good response time.

It would, of course, be unreasonable on economic grounds to propose a network which was entirely separate from the existing telephone system. The system proposed would share digital communication links with the telephone system.

2. THE USERS OF THE NETWORK

The digital communication network will be attached to a wide variety of subscribers' equipment at its terminals having different characteristics as sources and acceptors of data. Keyboard consoles, enquiry stations, graphic display consoles, bank proof-machines, line printers, document readers, file storage systems, multi-access computers, remote actuators and sensors for transport systems and pipelines, meteorological and hydrological instruments, and a steadily increasing variety of new equipments will be attached to it.

The design of the network would allow any of these equipments to send information to any other but in practice many corporate users of the network will have designed their various equipments to operate as a sub-network. On the other hand, there will be standard terminals (such as enquiry stations) that can make use of a wide variety of computer-based services through the network. The provision of such services will develop into a major field of business.

Use of the network can be divided into three categories, man-computer, computer-computer and computer-machine.

Man-computer interaction is able to provide highly efficient and effective systems. The use of this interaction in industry and commerce is in its infancy. An important early use of such interaction is the validation of input data, and there are many systems in operation today for this purpose alone. An interactive system with many remote terminals is often necessary for the sharing of a collection of data. Access to remote computing power, as in scientific systems, will become less important than the, apparently simpler, data base for business systems.

Computer-computer applications include the development of business systems involving direct transfers of information, analogous to human correspondence by letter. Such developments will increase the pace of business activity. Services can be offered by one computer to another, often with very favourable economics. For example, small local computers can call on a remote service for backing storage, for the compilation of programs, for phototypesetting or elaborate graphic work - any service which is cheaper if it can be purchased in bulk and retailed.

An example of computer-machine interaction could be the telemetry and control of an electrical distribution system. The use of the data network to carry control and signalling data for the telephone network is another example arising from recent developments in the concepts of telephone switching systems.

3. OUTLINE OF THE PROPOSAL

The requirement of versatility to handle a wide variety of bit rates almost rules out circuit switching methods in conjunction with multiplexers of the usual kind. Since one end of nearly all 'conversations' is a computer holding data in stored form, the natural unit of transmission to consider is not bandwidth or data rate but a message unit. Reluctance to consider so-called 'message switching' or store-and-forward techniques is due to the cost and performance characteristics of telegraph speed systems. Designed for the present purpose, it transpires that store-and-forward methods can be very efficient.

The network carries short messages in the "store-and-forward" manner. These messages are handled by a *high level network* consisting of *nodes* connected by digital links. Each message enters the high-level network in a well-defined format which includes a note of its source and destination. The responsibility for putting messages into this format belongs to the network, not the user; a vital principle of the design. Between the high-level network and the users there are *interface computers* each handling a mixed collection of subscribers within a geographical region. Fig. 1 illustrates the form of the network. To the user, the store-and-forward nature of the network might in some instances be hidden. It will become obvious, when the design of the node is described, that storing each message before retransmission simplifies the design and

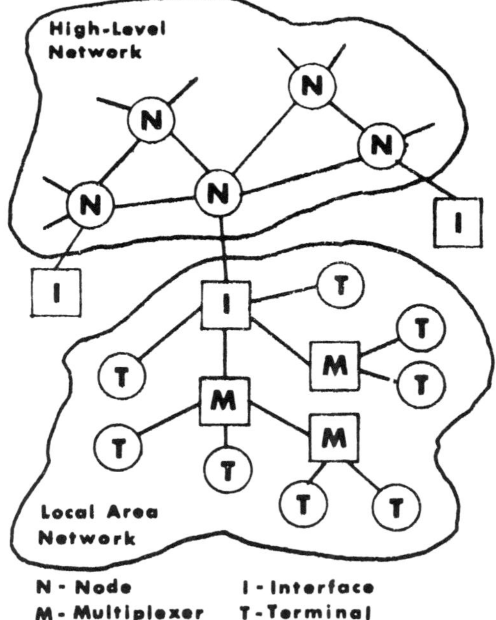

Fig. 1.

makes it adaptable to technical improvements. The short messages in fixed format that are carried by the high-level network are called *packets*. These must be distinguished from the *messages* as understood by the user of the network which can, if necessary, be sent in a number of packets. The term 'packet' in addition to its technical meaning introduced here, underlines a useful analogy with a postal system. The contents of the packet are, indeed, enclosed in a communication envelope, which carries an address of the destination (as well as an address of the sender), among other things.

The choice of packet size is a compromise between efficient use of the transmission paths and rapid response. Packet size must be restricted because response time is roughly proportional to packet size. The size limit must not be too small, because of the finite size of the envelope, which must not be allowed to form a large part of the total material transmitted. The size distribution of messages in 'real-time' computer systems can only be guessed, and it will be influenced by the communication facili-
166 ties available, but a maximum packet size equal to a full line of printing appears to be a reasonable choice, say about 100 characters.

In the design as proposed, there is no multiplexing of channels over the links between nodes. In general, the high rate of transmission, chosen as 1.5 Mbit/sec for the study, is used to transmit each packet as quickly as possible. There need be no standard transmission speed for the links of the network but the packet format must be standardised, because efficiency of packet handling depends on having no unnecessary operations on the packet.

Subscribers to the network are of many kinds and two subscribers engaged in conversation will in general differ in their interfaces with the network, having different bit-rates. Consider, for example, a computer and a slow terminal. The use they make of the high-level network with its capacity for handling short messages is organised by their respective interface computers.

Because the network employs 'store-and-forward' methods there is a delay to the passage of data in addition to the unavoidable transmission delay. The time elapsing between the receipt by the network of the last character of a packet and the beginning of output at the far end is called the *response time* of the network. The aim was a response time less than 100 milliseconds and calculations [2] indicate that this will easily be achieved.

Some consideration must be given to the way in which the network can be prevented from a major breakdown in the event of equipment failure. In the high-level network the method adopted is to arrange that the network is over-connected and uses adaptive routing to maintain service. A computer failure in a node would only destroy the few packets that are stored there. It is thought that all users of the network will use the rapid response to provide themselves with an immediate acknowledgement which would show up a missing packet. Loss of a few packets due to a failure, if it is sufficiently rare, can be tolerated.

4. THE HIGH-LEVEL NETWORK

There is some economy in having packets of variable size. The unit for allocation of store in a node is a segment of 16 bytes or 128 bits. A packet is made of a number of segments following one another without a break. The first segment contains all the special information of the envelope, so that the following segments contain mainly the message. The range of packet size chosen was 1 to 8 segments, therefore 128 characters is the maximum size of packet for the design that has been studied.

The method proposed for communication over the links employs a synchronizing pattern transmitted between packets which is extended for an arbitrary time if the output queue feeding the link is empty. While the queue is full, packets are sent with a certain interval between them determined by software considerations. There is no acknowledgement, but at a detected error or in case of congestion a short message over the return link initiates the necessary retransmission or halt in the stream.

The hardware of a node consists of a general purpose computer and special units dealing with the input and output of each link. An outline design has been made and some optimization of design carried out for a node serving five links. A small, 16-bit computer of modern design was assumed and the logic design for the special units was carried out. Programmes for the main functions were written. The design has not yet been tested experimentally. The cost of the link hardware for five links equalled that of the computer.

A fuller description of the design of the node and its performance is contained in [2].

5. PERFORMANCE OF THE NODE

Approximate estimates have been made of the peak traffic that the node can handle as well as the queue lengths and delays as a function of traffic. Only simple queue theory was employed because at the present stage computer simulation would be an unnecessary refinement.

With a store cycle time of 0.6 microseconds and a mean packet length of 7 segments it was found that the node could handle 2600 packets per second.

The performance of the node compared with that of telegraph message switching systems is very high. This is mainly due to the use of a packet format which is designed for computer handling, obviating any treatment of the packet's message content by the node computer. A proper division of the work between the central processor and the link hardware is also necessary to obtain this performance. It is believed that development of the design could increase further the performance obtainable from a single computer but this is not an urgent matter to determine at the present time.

6. THE INTERFACE COMPUTER

Interface functions could be carried out by the same computer system that performs the function of a node. It is however simpler to consider these aspects separately. The organisation of the interface computer represents the most critical part of the network design.

The two primary functions are to control the communication between different peripherals and to reconcile the fixed format of the high-level network with the widely varying requirements of the users. A secondary function is to collect the information necessary for logging and accounting.

The peripheral logic associated with the interface computer is closely related to the local network, one form of which has been studied in detail, but the software is dependent on the protocol employed for interaction between users via the network. Th extent of the software depends on the variety of control procedures allowed.

The development of new control procedures for different and complex applications of the network will require experience that we do not have at this time. The information carried in status packets (that is, control packets not carrying user's data) can be increased, and there is little impediment to devising new control procedures except the need to avoid an unnecessary load on the interface computer. Ref. [4] gives more information on this subject.

The ability of the network to take part in the control procedures contrasts with 'data transmission' as it is usually understood where the network is transparent to control information as well as data. Centralisation of some of the tasks of controlling data transfer is one of the factors that makes the network economically attractive.

It is difficult to determine how many subscribers an interface computer can handle but a rough estimate is that, if data rate is the only limitation, 1500 simple consoles could be simultaneously active.

The design of an interface computer, particularly the software, is highly dependent on the facilities the subscriber needs and the variety of peripheral devices. In order to work with a real example of user's needs, a communication network for the NPL laboratory site is being developed. This includes, in effect, the interface functions and the local network. The descriptions in refs. [3] and [4] refer in part to the design of the NPL network. The ideas and principles involved can, it is believed, be applied to the design of a national common-carrier data network.

167

7. THE LOCAL NETWORK

Subscribing devices were divided into two main categories. Firstly there are those such as computers having sufficient intelligence and possibly a high enough data rate to assemble their messages into packet-like blocks. These subscribers could be connected directly to the interface computer by methods like those used between nodes in the high-level network. Secondly, there are less complicated devices with various data rates which would require concentration in various groups and at various levels to make economic use of transmission paths and which rely on the interface computer for message assembly.

The prime considerations governing the design of the network to service the latter group were:

a) Short response time between peripheral subscribers and the interface computer.

b) Simplicity of out-lying equipment, that is, subscribers' terminals and multiplexers.

c) The ability of the network to handle all data codes and procedures.

To satisfy the response time requirement, high data rate connections have been assumed and a system of on-demand byte multiplexing has been devised. This method of concentration also covers the requirements for equipment simplicity and transparency to subscriber code. The requirement for equipment simplicity necessitates there being only one point in the network with the intelligence for message assembly and manipulation - the interface computer. All subscribing terminals are connected to this point through concentrators.

Ref. [3] contains fuller information on this local network design.

It must be emphasized that this is only one of many possible local network schemes and it developed in the direction it did because of the circumstances for which it was devised - a compact region, namely a large laboratory site, provided with cables for the purpose. There is, however, some evidence to suggest that a similar system could operate over a local network made of lines from the telephone system. Speeds of up to 500 characters/sec should be achievable.

8. NETWORK ECONOMICS

Any conclusions about network economics are necessarily tentative in the absence of a planned project. We nevertheless consider it worthwhile to give some rough estimates of the cost of the network services.

Two rough estimates were made, the cost of using the high-level network and the cost of local line equipment. The first of these is of interest to the user with a high data rate. The second indicates the problem of cost reduction for the low-rate terminal.

The cost of using the node computer depends on the extent to which it is used. Its computing facilities can be idle for many reasons: the need to keep a margin of capacity in the busy hour, the random arrivals of packets and poor distribution of traffic among the lines it serves. With extremely adverse assumptions for these factors a node would handle 2 million packets per day, giving a cost per packet for transit through the network of about 1/20 penny, derived from the cost of the nodes. The cost of the links between nodes depends on the average distance between nodes. For lengths of links appropriate to the geography of the United Kingdom, link cost will be roughly the same as the cost of nodes. The total cost per packet is therefore 1/10 penny for the use of the high-level network.

The cost of local line equipment can, no doubt, be greatly reduced by development of an integrated local network and the application of the emerging techniques of large-scale integration, but we have assumed current I.C. techniques and the use of telephone pairs. The largest item of cost is the pair of wires to the nearest concentrator and the logic required at the ends. This cost is estimated at £1,000 per terminal, which is larger than we would like it to be. The subscriber must also bear part of the cost of the interface computer, estimated at approximately £100-£200 per subscriber. These capital costs which are independent of traffic generated might be met by a rental paid by the subscriber.

The capital cost of the network, it seems, will lie mainly in the local distribution system, and attention should be directed to the problem of cost reduction in this area.

In considering network economics, the cost of the network must be compared with the full cost of the alternatives, including the control equipment and modems at the ends of data links and the multiplexers and communication terminals attached to computers engaging in conversation with remote peripherals. When these things are taken into account there seems no doubt that a data network of the proposed design would be economic, even at a low initial loading of traffic. The estimates on which this conclusion was based were made with 20 nodes and 10,000 terminals for the United Kingdom.

9. CONCLUSIONS AND RECOMMENDATIONS

The possibility of a common-carrier communication network for digital data has been explored and a particular design has been outlined in this paper. The system has a number of features which are obtainable, if at all, only at greatly increased cost from systems based on adaption of the switched telephone network. These features are:

1) Control procedures to suit the terminals are provided by the network. This can reduce the cost of control equipment at the subscriber's terminal and concentrate many of the control tasks at central (interface) computers.

2) Bit rates to suit the terminal are provided by the network, with no restriction to standard rates. Data transfer can be sporadic or irregular over short time intervals. The use made of long distance facilities depends on the quantity of information sent, rather than time occupied at the terminal.

3) The network can provide transparency for data with no extra cost.

4) The routing of data is handled by the network which can provide the equivalent of a 'private' wire without tying up equipment.

5) The network design can be adapted to take account of technological advances without making older equipment obsolete or requiring newer equipment to bear extra costs.

The development history of the telephone network shows the importance of this last point. In the design proposed, the maximum packet size for the whole network can be increased, and the speeds of links and nodes can be increased piecemeal. Local networks can be modified and improved and control procedure over the local network can be chosen to suit special conditions. A certain number of overall control procedures must be standardised, but development of new procedures or variants is possible.

The rate of growth of computer-based systems depending on rapid response at remote locations, and the number of new schemes of this kind now being developed, indicates the urgency of decisions about digital communication networks.

We hope to have shown the way in which the system design will develop for a digital network to meet economically the full range of users requirements and allow full advantage to be taken of future developments in computer and transmission technology.

ACKNOWLEDGEMENT

The work described above forms part of the research programme of the National Physical Laboratory.

REFERENCES

[1] P. Baran, On Distributed Communication, Rand Corporation Memorandum, RM-3420-PR, Aug. 1964.

[2] R. A. Scantlebury, P. T. Wilkinson and K. A. Bartlett, The Design of a Message Switching Centre for a Digital Communication Network*.

[3] K. A. Bartlett, Transmission Control in a Local Data Network*.

[4] P. T. Wilkinson and R. A. Scantlebury, The Control Functions of a Local Data Network*.

* Presented at the IFIP Congress 68, at Edinburgh, Scotland, 1968.

Reprinted by permission from A.J.H. Morrell (ed.), *Information Processing 68* (North-Holland, Amsterdam, 1969)

170

Computer network development to achieve resource sharing

by LAWRENCE G. ROBERTS and BARRY D. WESSLER

Advanced Research Projects Agency
Washington, D.C.

INTRODUCTION

In this paper a computer network is defined to be a set of autonomous, independent computer systems, interconnected so as to permit interactive resource sharing between any pair of systems. An overview of the need for a computer network, the requirements of a computer communication system, a description of the properties of the communication system chosen, and the potential uses of such a network are described in this paper.

The goal of the computer network is for each computer to make every local resource available to any computer in the net in such a way that any program available to local users can be used remotely without degradation. That is, any program should be able to call on the resources of other computers much as it would call a subroutine. The resources which can be shared in this way include software and data, as well as hardware. Within a local community, time-sharing systems already permit the sharing of software resources. An effective network would eliminate the size and distance limitations on such communities. Currently, each computer center in the country is forced to recreate all of the software and data files it wishes to utilize. In many cases this involves complete reprogramming of software or reformatting the data files. This duplication is extremely costly and has led to considerable pressure for both very restrictive language standards and the use of identical hardware systems. With a successful network, the core problem of sharing resources would be severely reduced, thus eliminating the need for stifling language standards. The basic technology necessary to construct a resource sharing computer network has been available since the advent of time-sharing. For example, a time-sharing system makes all its resources available to a number of users at remote consoles. By splicing two systems together as remote users of each other and permitting user programs to interact with two consoles (the human user and the remote computer), the basic characteristics of a network connection are obtained. Such an experiment was made between the TX–2 computer at Lincoln Lab and the Q–32 computer at SDC in 1966 in order to test the philosophy.[1] Logically, such an interconnection is quite powerful and one can tap all the resources of the other system. Practically, however, the interconnection of pairs of computers with console grade communication service is virtually useless. First, the value of a network to a user is directly proportional to the number of other workers on the net who are creating potentially useful resources. A net involving only two systems is therefore far less valuable than one incorporating twenty systems. Second, the degradation in response caused by using telegraph or voice grade communication lines for network connections is significant enough to discourage most users. Third, the cost to fully interconnect computers nation-wide either with direct leased lines or dial-up facilities is prohibitive. All three problems are a direct result of the inadequacy of the available communication services.

DESIGN OF A NETWORK COMMUNICATIONS SERVICE

After the Lincoln-SDC network experiments, it was clear that a completely new communications service was required in order to make an effective, useful resource-sharing computer network. The communication pipelines offered by the carriers would probably have to be a component of that service but were clearly inadequate by themselves. What was needed was a message service where any computer could submit a message destined for another computer and be sure it would be delivered promptly and correctly. Each interactive conversation or link between two computers would have messages flowing back and forth similar to the type of traffic between a user console and a computer. Message sizes of from one character to 1000 characters are characteristic of man-machine interactions and this should also be true for that network traffic where a man is the end consumer of the information being exchanged. Besides having a heavy bias toward short messages, network traffic will also be diverse. With twenty computers, each with dozens of time-shared users, there might be, at peak times, one or more conversations between all 190 pairs of computers.

Reliability

Communications systems, being designed to carry very redundant information for direct human consumption, have, for computers, unacceptably high downtime and an excessively high error rate. The line errors can easily be fixed through error detection and retransmission; however, this does require the use of some computation and storage at both ends of each communication line. To protect against total line failures, there should be at least two physically separate paths to route each message. Otherwise the service will appear to be far too unreliable to count on and users will continue to duplicate remote resources rather than access them through the net.

Responsiveness

In those cases where a user is making more or less direct use of a complete remote software system, the network must not cause the total round-trip delay to exceed the human short-term memory span of one to two seconds. Since the time-sharing systems probably introduce at least a one-second delay, the network's end-to-end delay should be less than ½ second. The network response should also be comparable, if possible, to using a remote display console over a private voice grade line where a 50 character line of text (400 bits) can be sent in 200 ms. Further, if interactive graphics are to be available, the network should be able to send a complete new display page requiring about 20 kilobits of information within a second and permit interrupts (10–100) to get through very quickly, hopefully within 30–90 ms. Where two programs are interacting without a human user being directly involved, the job will obviously get through sooner, the shorter the message delay. There is no clear critical point here, but if the communications system substantially slows up the job, the user will probably choose to duplicate the remote process or data at his site. For such cases, a reasonable measure by which to compare communications systems is the "effective bandwidth" (data block length for the job/end-to-end transmission delay).

Capacity

The capacity required is proportional to the number and variety of services available from the network. As the number of nodes increase, the traffic is expected to increase more than linearly, until new nodes merely duplicate available network resources. The number of nodes in the experimental network was chosen to: (1) involve as many computer researchers as possible to develop network protocol and operating procedures, (2) involve special facilities, such as the ILLIAC, to distribute its resources to a wider community, (3) involve as many disciplines of science as possible to measure the effect of the network on those disciplines, and (4) involve many different kinds of computers and systems to prove the generality of the techniques developed. The nodes of the network were generally limited to: (1) those centers for which the network would truly provide a cost benefit, (2) government-funded projects because of the use of special rate government-furnished communications, and (3) ARPA-funded projects where the problems of intercomputer accounting could be deferred until the network was in stable operation. The size of the experimental network was chosen to be approximately 20 nodes nation-wide. It was felt that this would be large and diverse enough to be a useful utility and to provide enough traffic to adequately test the network communication system.

For a 20 node network, the total traffic by mid-1971 at peak hours is estimated to be 200-800 KB (kilobits per second). This corresponds to an average outgoing traffic per node of 10–40 KB or an average of 0.5–2 KB traffic both ways between each pair of nodes. Traffic between individual node-pairs, however, will vary considerably, from zero to 10 KB. The total traffic per node will also vary widely, perhaps from 5–50 KB. Variations of these magnitudes will occur in both space and time and, unless the connumications system can reallocate capacity rapidly (seconds), the users will find either the delay or cost excessive. However, it is expected that the total capacity required for all 20 nodes will be fairly stable, smoothed out by having hundreds of active network users spread out across four time zones.

Cost

To be a useful utility, it was felt that communications costs for the network should be less than 25% of the computing costs of the systems connected through the network. This is in contrast to the rising costs of remote access communications which often cost as much as the computing equipment.

If we examine why communications usually cost so much we find that it is not the communications channel per se, but our inefficient use of them, the switching costs, or the operations cost. To obtain a perspective on the price we commonly pay for communications let us evaluate a few methods. As an example, let us use a distance of 1400 miles since that is the average distance between pairs of nodes in the projected ARPA Network. A useful measure of communications cost is the cost to move one million bits of information, cents/megabit. In the table below this is computed for each media. It is assumed for leased equipment and data set rental that the usage is eight hours per working day.

TABLE 1—Cost per Megabit for Various Communication Media 1400 Mile Distance

Media		
Telegram	$3300.00	For 100 words at 30 bits/wd, daytime
Night Letter	565.00	For 100 words at 30 bits/wd, overnight delivery
Computer Console	374.00	18 baud avg. use[2], 300 baud DDD service line & data sets only
TELEX	204.00	50 baud teletype service
DDD (103A)	22.50	300 baud data sets, DDD daytime service
AUTODIN	8.20	2400 baud message service, full use during working hours
DDD (202)	3.45	2000 baud data sets
Letter	3.30	Airmail, 4 pages, 250 wds/pg, 30 bits/wd
W. U. Broadband	2.03	2400 baud service, full duplex
WATS	1.54	2000 baud, used 8 hrs/working day
Leased Line (201)	.57	2000 baud, commercial, full duplex
Data 50	.47	50 KB dial service, utilized full duplex
Leased Line (303)	.23	50 KB, commercial, full duplex
Mail DEC Tape	.20	2.5 megabit tape, airmail
Mail IBM Tape	.034	100 megabit tape, airmail

Special care has also been taken to minimize the cost of the multiplexor or switch. Previous store and forward systems like DoD's AUTODIN system, have had such complex, expensive switches that over 95% of the total communications service cost was for the switches. Other switch services adding to the system's cost, deemed superfluous in a computer network, were: long term message storage, multi-address messages and individual message accounting.

The final cost criteria was to minimize the communications software development cost required at each node site. If the network software could be generated centrally, not only would the cost be significantly reduced, but also the reliability would be significantly enhanced.

THE ARPA NETWORK

Three classes of communications systems were investigated as candidates for the ARPA Network: fully interconnected point to point leased lines, line switched (dial-up) service, and message switched (store and forward) service. For the kind of service required, it was decided and later verified that the message switched service provided the greater flexibility, higher effective bandwidth, and lower cost than the other two systems.

The standard message switched service uses a large central switch with all the nodes connected to the switch via communication lines; this configuration is generally referred to as a Star. Star systems perform satisfactorily for large blocks of traffic (greater than 100 kilobits per message), but the central switch saturates very quickly for small message sizes. This phenomenon adds significant delay to the delivery of the message. Also, a Star design has inherently poor reliability since a single line failure can isolate a node and the failure of the central switch is catastrophic.

An alternative to the Star, suggested by the Rand study "On Distributed Communications"[3], is a fully distributed message switched system. Such a system has a switch or store and forward center at every node in the network. Each node has a few transmission lines to other nodes; messages are therefore routed from node to node until reaching their destination. Each transmission line thereby multiplexes messages from a large number of source-destination pairs of nodes. The distributed store and forward system was chosen, after careful study, as the ARPA Network communications system. The properties of such a communication system are described below and compared with other systems.

A more complete description of the implementation, optimization, and initial use of the network can be found in a series of five papers, of which this is the first. The second paper by Heart, et al[4] describes the design, implementation and performance characteristics of the message switch. The third paper by Kleinrock[5] derives procedures for optimizing the capacity of the transmission facility in order to minimize cost and average message delay. The fourth paper by Frank, et al[6] describes the procedure for finding optimized network topologies under various constraints. The last paper by Carr, et al[7] is concerned with the system software required to allow the network computers to talk to one another. This final paper describes a first attempt at intercomputer protocol, which is expected to grow and mature as we gain experience in computer networking.

Network properties

The switching centers use small general purpose computers called Interface Message Processors (IMPs) to route messages, to error check the transmission lines and to provide asynchronous digital interface to the main (HOST) computer. The IMPs are connected together via 50 Kbps data transmission facilities using common carrier (ATT) point to point leased lines. The topology of the network transmission lines was selected to minimize cost, maximize growth potential, and yet satisfy all the design criteria.

Reliability

The network specification requires that the delivered message error rates be matched with computer characteristics, and that the down-time of the communications system be extrememly small. Three steps have been taken to insure these reliability characteristics: (1) at least two transmission paths exist between any two modes, (2) a 24 bit cyclic check sum is provided for each 1000 bit block of data, and (3) the IMP is ruggedized against external environmental conditions and its operation is independent of any electromechanical devices (except fans). The down-time of the transmission facility is estimated at 10–12 hours per year (no figures are currently available from ATT). The duplication of paths should result in average down-time between any pair of nodes, due to transmission failure, of approximately 30 seconds per year. The cyclic check sum was chosen based on the performance characteristics of the transmission facility; it is designed to detect long burst errors. The code is used for error detection only, with retransmission on an error. This check reduces the undetected bit error rate to one in 10^{12} or about one undetected error per year in the entire network.

The ruggedized IMP is expected to have a mean time to failure of 10,000 hours; less than one failure per year. The elimination of mass storage devices from the IMP results in lower cost, less down-time, and greater throughput performance of the IMP, but implies no long term message storage and no message accounting by the IMP. If these functions are later needed they can be added by establishing a special node in the network. This node would accept accounting information from all the IMPs and also could be routed all the traffic destined for HOSTs which are down. We do not believe these functions are necessary, but the network design is capable of providing them.

Responsiveness

The target goal for responsiveness was .5 seconds transit time from any node to any other, for a 1000 bit (or less) block of information. The simulations of the network show the transit time of a 1 kilobit block of .1 seconds until the network begins to saturate. After saturation the transit time rises quickly because of excessive queuing delays. However, saturation will hopefully be avoided by the net acting to choke off the inputs for short periods of time, reducing the buffer 173
queues while not significantly increasing the delay.

Capacity

The capacity of the network is the throughput rate at which saturation occurs. The saturation level is a function of the topology and capacity of the transmission lines, the traffic distribution between pairs of nodes (traffic matrix) and the average size of the blocks sent over the transmission lines. The analysis of capacity was performed by Network Analysis Corporation during the optimization of the network topology. As the analysis shows, the network has the ability to flexibly increase its capacity by adding additional transmission lines. The use of 108 and 230.4 KB communication services, where appropriate, considerably improves the cost-performance of the network.

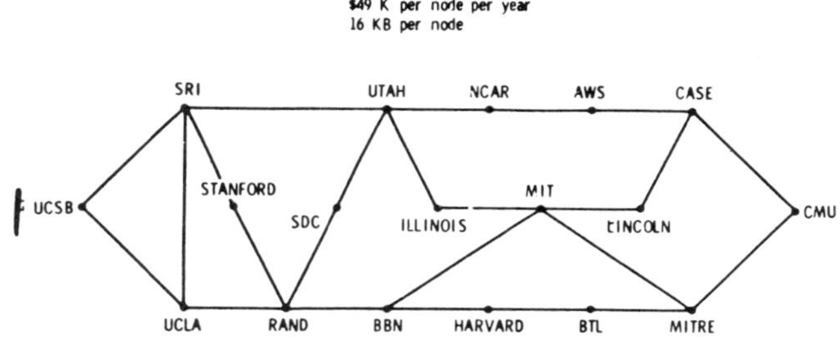

Figure 1—ARPA network initial topology

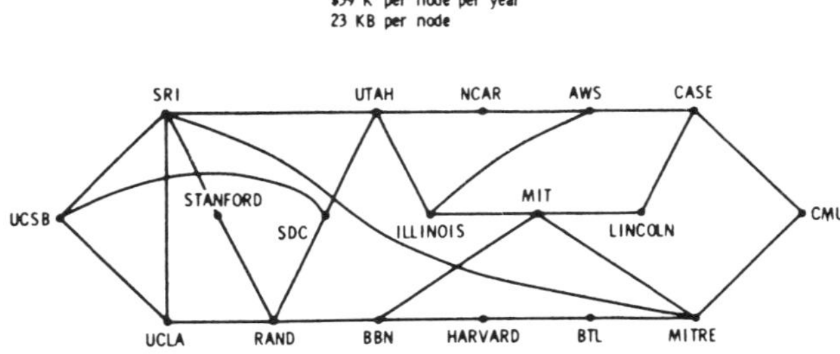

Figure 2—ARPA network expanded topology

Configuration

Initial configuration of the ARPA Network is currently planned as shown in Figure 1. The communications circuits for this network will cost $49K per node per year and the network can support an average traffic of 16 KB per node. If the traffic builds up, additional communication lines can be added to expand the capacity as required. For example, if 23 KB per node is desired, the network can be expanded to the configuration shown in Figure 2 for an increase of only $10K per node per year. Expansion can be continued on this basis until a capacity of about 60 KB per node is achieved, at which point the IMPs would tend to saturate.

COMPARISON WITH ALTERNATIVE NETWORK COMMUNICATIONS SYSTEMS DESIGNS

For the purpose of this comparison the capacity required was set at 500 baud to 1 KB per node-pair. A minimal buffer for error checking and retransmission at every node is included in the cost of the systems.

Two comparisons are made between the systems: the cost per megabit as a function of the delay and the effective bandwidth as a function of the block size of the data. Several other functions were plotted and compared; the two chosen were deemed the most informative. The latter graph is particularly informative in showing the effect of using the network for short, interactive message traffic.

The systems chosen for the comparison were fully interconnected 2.4 KB and 19 KB leased line systems, Data-50 the dial-up 50 KB service, DDD the standard 2 KB voice grade dial-up system, Star networks using 19 KB and 50 KB leased lines into a central switch, and the ARPA Network using 50 KB leased lines.

The graph in Figure 3 shows the cost per megabit versus delay. The rectangle outlines the variation caused by a block size variation of 1 to 10 Kilobits and

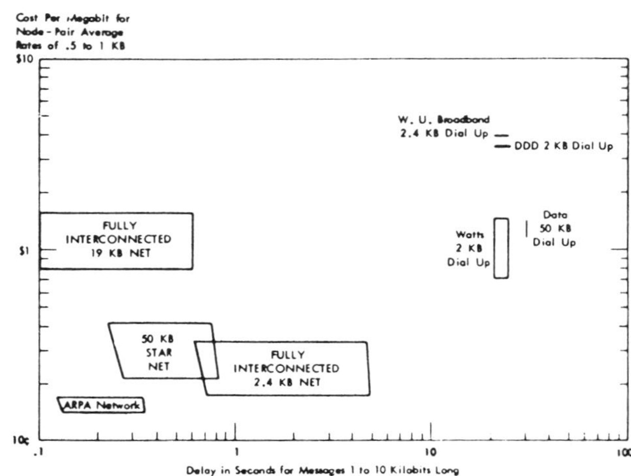

Figure 3—Cost vs delay for potential 20 node network designs

capacity requirement variation of 500 to 1000 baud. The dial-up systems were used in a way to minimize the line charges while keeping the delay as low as possible. The technique is to dial a system, then transmit the data accumulated during the dial-up (20 seconds for DDD, 30 seconds for Data-50). The dial-up systems are still very expensive and slow as compared with other alternatives. The costs of the ARPA Network are for optimally designed topologies. The 19 KB Star was eliminated because the system saturated just below 1 KB per node-pair which did not provide adequate growth potential though the cost was comparable to the ARPA Network. For the 50 KB Star network, the switch is assumed to be an average distance of 1300 miles from every node.

The graph in Figure 4 shows the effective bandwidth

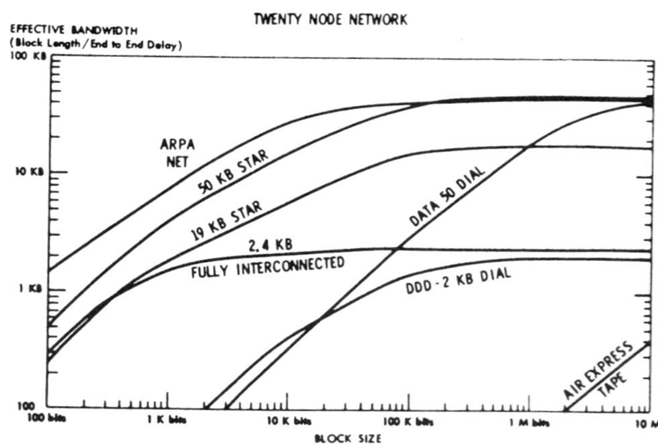

Figure 4—Effective Bandwidth vs block size

versus the block size of the data input to the network. The curves for the various systems are estimated for traffic rates of 500 to 1000 baud. The comparison shows the ARPA Net does very well at small block size where most of the traffic is expected.

NETWORK PLANS

Use of the Network is broken into two successive phases: (1) Initial Research and Experimental Use, and (2) External Research Community Use. These phases are closely related to our plans for Network implementation. The first phase, started in September 1969, involves the connection of 14 sites involved principally in computer research. These sites are current ARPA contractors who are working in the areas of Computer System Architecture, Information System Design, Information Handling, Computer Augmented Problem Solving, Intelligent Systems, as well as Computer Networks. This phase should be fully implemented by November 1970. The second phase involves the extension of the number of sites to about 20 to include ARPA-supported research disciplines.

Initial research and experimental use

During Phase One, the community of users will number approximately 2000 people. This community is involved primarily in computer science research and all have ARPA-funded on-going research. The major use they will make of the network is the sharing of software resources and the educational experience of using a wider variety of systems than previously possible. The software resources available to the Network include: advanced user programs such as MATHLAB at MIT, Theorem Provers at SRI, Natural Language Processors at BBN, etc., and new system software and languages such as LEAP, a graphic language at Lincoln Lab, LC^2, an interactive ALGOL system at Carnegie, etc.

Another major use of the Network will be for accessing the Network Information Center (NIC). The NIC is being established at SRI as the repository of information about all systems connected into the Network. The NIC will maintain, update and distribute hard copy information to all users. It will also provide file space and a system for accessing and updating (through the net) dynamic information about the systems, such as system modifications, new resources available, etc.

The final major use of the Net during Phase One is for measurement and experimentation on the Network itself. The primary sites involved in this are BBN, who has responsibility for system development and system maintenance, and UCLA, who has responsibility for the Net measurement and modeling. All the sites will also be involved in the generation of intercomputer protocol, the language the systems use to talk to one another.

External research community use

During the time period after November 1970, additional nodes will be installed to take advantage of the Network in three other ARPA-funded research disciplines: Behavioral Science, Climate Dynamics and Seismology. The use of the Network at these nodes will be oriented more toward the distribution and sharing of stored data, and in the latter two fields the use of the ILLIAC IV at the University of Illinois.

The data sharing between data management systems or data retrieval systems will begin an important phase in the use of the Network. The concept of distributed data bases and distributed access to the data is one of the most powerful and useful applications of the network for the general data processing community. As described above, if the Network is responsive in the human time frame, data bases can be stored and maintained at a remote location rather than duplicating them at each site the data is needed. Not only can the data be accessed as if the user were local, but also as a Network user he can write programs on his own machine to collect data from a number of locations for comparison, merging or further analysis.

175

Because of widespread use of the ILLIAC IV, it will undoubtably be the single most demanding node in the Network. Users will not only be sending requests for service but will also send very large quantities of input and output data, e.g., a 10^6 bit weather map, over the Net. Projected uses of the ILLIAC include weather and climate modeling, picture processing, linear programming, matrix manipulations, and extensive work in other areas of simulation and modeling.

In addition to the ILLIAC, the University of Illinois will also have a trillion bit mass store. An experiment is being planned to use 10% of the storage (100 billion bits) as archival storage for all the nodes on the Net. This kind of capability may help reduce the number of tape drives and/or data cells in the Network.

FUTURE

There are many applications of computers for which current communications technology is not adequate. One such application is the specialized customer service computer systems in existence or envisioned for the future; these services provide the customer with information or computational capability. If no commercial computer network service is developed, the future may be as follows:

One can envision a corporate officer in the future having many different consoles in his office: one to the stock exchange to monitor his own company's and competitor's activities, one to the commodities market to monitor the demand for his product or raw materials, one to his own company's data management system to monitor inventory, sales, payroll, cash flow, etc., and one to a scientific computer used for modeling and simulation to help plan for the future. There are probably many people within that same organization who need some of the same services and potentially many other services. Also, though the data exists in digital form on other computers, it will probably have to be keypunched into the company's modeling and simulation system in order to perform analyses. The picture presented seems rather bleak, but is just a projection of the service systems which have been
176 developed to date.

The organization providing the service has a hard time, too. In addition to collecting and maintaining the data, the service must have field offices to maintain the consoles and the communications multiplexors adding significantly to their cost. A large fraction of that cost is for communications and consoles, rather than the service itself. Thus, the services which can be justified are very limited.

Let us now paint another picture given a nationwide network for computer-to-computer communication. The service organization need only connect its computer into the net. It probably would not have any consoles other than for data input, maintenance, and system development. In fact, some of the service's data input may come from another service over the Net. Users could choose the service they desired based on reliability, cleanliness of data, and ease of use, rather than proximity or sole source.

Large companies would connect their computers into the net and contract with service organizations for the use of those services they desired. The executive would then have one console, connected to his company's machine. He would have one standard way of requesting the service he desires with a far greater number of services available to him.

For the small company, a master service organization might develop, similar to today's time-sharing service, to offer console service to people who cannot afford their own computer. The master service organization would be wholesalers of the services and might even be used by the large companies in order to avoid contracting with all the individual service organizations.

The kinds of services that will be available and the cost and ultimate capacity required for such service is difficult to predict. It is clear, however, that if the network philosophy is adopted and if it is made widely available through a common carrier, that the communications system will not be the limiting factor in the development of these services as it is now.

REFERENCES

1 T MARILL L ROBERTS
Toward a cooperative network of time-shared computers
AFIPS Conference Proceedings Nov 1966

2 P E JACKSON C D STUBBS
A study of multi-access computer communications
AFIPS Conference Proceedings Vol 34 p 491 1969

3 PAUL BARAN et al
On distributed communications
RAND Series Reports Aug 1964

4 F E HEART R E KAHN S M ORNSTEIN W R CROWTHER D C WALDEN
The interface Message Processor for the ARPA network
AFIPS Conference Proceedings May 1970

5 L KLEINROCK
Analytic and simulation methods in Computer network design
AFIPS Conference Proceedings May 1970

6 H FRANK IT FRISCH W CHOU
Topological considerations in the design of the ARPA computer network
AFIPS Conference Proceedings May 1970

7 S CARR S CROCKER V CERF
HOST–HOST Communication protocol in the ARPA network
AFIPS Conference Proceedings May 1970

THE DESIGN OF A SWITCHING SYSTEM TO ALLOW REMOTE ACCESS TO COMPUTER SERVICES BY OTHER COMPUTERS AND TERMINAL DEVICES

R A Scantlebury and P T Wilkinson
National Physical Laboratory, Teddington, Middlesex, U.K.

Summary

An experimental store-and-forward data communication network has been set up within the National Physical Laboratory (NPL) site. The system represents one element of a national data network scheme proposed by NPL.

The network is currently offering a data communication service on a trial basis and is operating successfully.

Work on an enhanced communication system is in hand. This new system has been organised along strictly hierarchical lines and is intended to meet the requirements of computer to computer communications in a general manner, permitting resource-sharing applications and remote-access computer services to be developed in the Laboratory.

1. Introduction

An experimental data communication network has been set up within the National Physical Laboratory site[1,2]. The system uses the store-and-forward principle and carries out some of the functions of the local data exchange or 'Interface Computer' element of a proposed national data communication network scheme developed in outline by the Computer Science Division of NPL[3,4].

The existing system is essentially a terminal handling network allowing the connection of a large variety of peripheral devices, which may exchange data with each other. From a user's point of view, the network is rather similar to the voice telephone networks in that one terminal may dial up another, interchange data with it, and then disconnect. Computers are not treated in any special way, thus if a machine offers multiple-access services, it must be connected to the network as several "terminals"; i.e. each computer port has a separate line, like present time-sharing services on the public telephone network.

The NPL network is currently offering a service to users within the Laboratory and a number of internal computer services are being made available through it. However, one of the principal aims of the research programme is to develop a network which meets the communications requirements of computers in a general manner so that advanced resource-sharing applications and multiple-access computer services can later be established. To achieve this aim a hierarchical communication system architecture has been devised. This architecture will be described in general terms in the following section. Sections 3 and 4 enlarge upon the three principal layers of of the hierarchy and Section 5 describes the way in which this architecture will be realised in the enhanced NPL network.

2. Communication Hierarchies

The problem of communication between computers has been broken down into a number of hierarchical layers with a well defined interface between each layer. The application of this principle to the problem of designing computer communication networks permits both a clearer understanding of the functions involved, and a proper separation so that each "layer" may be implemented independently and may subsequently be resolved, extended or otherwise modified without affecting other layers so long as the interface definitions are adhered to. The type of system which we are considering may be regarded not as one composite network, but a hierarchy of networks each with well defined properties.

The proposed hierarchical network scheme is illustrated in Figure 1 (note that throughout the text the various levels are described as inner (or lower) and outer (or higher) in relation to this diagram). We assume the existence of a Communications Network to which subscribers' computers (referred to as User Machines or UMs) are attached by means of a single duplex communication link. A UM in this context may be some complex system, not necessarily one single computer. The link will in general have a hardware realisation, but it may be just a software interface. The Communications Network represents the innermost level in the hierarchy. It may be a complex or a simple system, whose internal operating details need not concern other levels. Its business is to permit the UMs to intercommunicate in some convenient way, thus its properties must be such as to suit the general requirements placed upon it by the UMs, for example, in terms of effective bandwidth, response time, error rate and reliability. However, all the UM needs to know is how to utilise its single duplex link in order to interchange information with remote UMs. We propose that this interchange takes place in the form of discrete messages of up to some maximum number of bits, including a "heading" which contains an identification of the source or destination UM. The flow of these messages on the duplex link to the UM is controlled by a standard procedure known as the link control procedure, which represents the Communication Network interface. The operation of this procedure and control of any special hardware needed to attach the link to the UM, is vested in a UM-resident program module which we will call the Link Control Module (LCM). The LCMs will in general differ internally for different types of

177

UM, but will present the same functional interface to other program modules in all UMs.

Here, then, we have the next level in the hierarchy, the Message Handling Network. This network allows UMs to communicate by means of messages, via standard modules (the LCMs) resident in each UM. The body of each message (i.e. excluding the heading) is of no concern to the Message Handling Network, which is "transparent" to message data. It therefore follows that the organisation and operation of this network level and any inner levels *is in no way dependent upon* any agreement between UMs as to the meaning of messages, and *is in no way dependent* upon the facilities offered by UMs.

Having established a Message Handling Network allowing UMs to exchange messages according to simple rules, the question arises of a communications protocol between UMs. It is clearly necessary for each UM to be able to exercise some control over the type, volume, etc. of traffic which it receives. Each UM is some collection of hardware and software which executes programs on behalf of users; we will refer to running programs as "processes". Any intercommunication between UMs will in fact be taking place between processes in the UMs. We thus require a means of organising communication between processes via the Message Handling Network.

We therefore state the need for further standards which are necessary for the widespread and general use of a communication facility by computers. These standards form a yet higher network level which may be called the "Inter Process Communication Network". The functions of this "network" will be embodied in an "Inter Process Communication Module" (IPCM) resident in each UM, which provides the same functional interface (the Process Interface of Figure 1) to processes in every UM. The body of each message passed from the IPCM to the LCM (to which the latter attaches a routing and control header) will itself be made up of a header containing appropriate interprocess control information, and a body. The IPCM level is again transparent to the data contained in the message body and is therefore still independent of the particular services provided by UMs insofar as the standards which it imposes are general purpose.

The choice of standards to embody in the IPCM is a difficult one. Far-reaching standards which imply a very precise definition of the term "process", its identification, states and so-on could prove very restricting. The concept, if it is to be useful, must be capable of being implemented in UMs with widely differing types of operating system; large overheads of store space and processor time must be avoided as it is desirable that relatively small UMs which perform simple, perhaps dedicated, tasks should be able to be connected. The solution proposed is defined more fully in Section 4; briefly, the IPCM will offer a number of logical *channels* which processes may use to establish *calls* to remote processes. During the course of a call, messages may be exchanged and rules are imposed which permit processes to control the flow of messages according to the availability of buffer space. The IPCM effectively acts as a "multiplexer" mapping the many logical channels onto the single interleaved stream of messages passing into and out of each UM.

We now have a framework which provides for communication between processes in subscribers' computers. If and when such networks come into widespread use, other protocols of a more specialised nature will become established, governing the identification of users and services, the control of terminals or whatever. Some of these requirements may prove sufficiently general to warrant the definition of another "layer" or modification of the IPCM standards. Clearly there is no substitute for experience in this area; a balance between all the factors governing effective use of data communication systems by computers must be determined by a process of evolution. It is, however, necessary to have a good starting point.

3. *The Communications Network and the Link Control Module*

The concepts developed in the preceding section ensure that UM modules higher than the LCM are insulated from the detailed operation of the Communications Network; it is the function of the LCM to take care of the details of communication and to present a simple internal message interface to higher levels in the UM. However, it is necessary that the network used shall have the desired characteristics for intercomputer communication. It is argued[3,4,5] that store-and-forward networks are most appropriate, and this is the method of operation that has been adopted for the NPL system.

Each UM is connected by means of a single full-duplex high speed link to a store-and-forward switch referred to as the Communications Processor (CP). Each CP will serve a small area (say 10 miles in radius), each UM in this area being connected to the one CP. A "packet switching" nodal network will be used to interconnect CPs, as shown in Figure 2. Since the characteristics of this network have been described in earlier work[3,4], this section will concern itself mainly with the outer level of the Communication Network.

One important element of the Communications Network Interface is the unit for information transmission between UMs and the CP. This is chosen to be a message having a maximum total length of 1024 bytes (8192 bits). Too short a unit leads to high overheads when large volumes of data are transmitted (since overheads, e.g. headers, occur mainly on a per message basis), while too large a maximum can lead to store management problems.

The Communication Network itself consists of two levels, an inner packet handling and an outer message handling network. The packet proposed for the nodal network has a maximum total length of 128 bytes. The internal message/packet interface will be implemented in the CP, which has the task of disassembling messages into packets for transmission to a remote CP, reassembling packets into messages in the reverse direction.

The messages exchanged between UM and CP, and their formats, are shown in Figure 3. The transmission hardware joining the UM to the CP is byte organised, hence all messages must consist of an integral number of 8-bit bytes. Control messages consist of a single byte while DATA messages (which carry the "through traffic") have a 3 byte header followed by from 1 to 1021 bytes of information. The header contains a count of the number of bytes in the data field, and a UM address. In the case of messages from UM to CP, this address specifies the destination UM; for the reverse direction it specifies the originating UM, the address field alteration being performed by the CP. When messages are divided into packets for transmission through the nodal network, each packet will carry both source and destination UM addresses.

The D-bit on each message distinguishes between control and DATA; for the former, the type field indicates the function of the message. Every message also carries an A-bit, which is used as a modulo 2 message count (in fact the A-bit is only of significance for the DATA, ACK and IUM messages).

The basic link control procedure allows the transmission of one DATA message at a time; once DATA has been sent an ACK response message must be received, acknowledging its correct receipt and acceptance, before the next DATA may be transmitted. After a timeout period, an unacknowledged DATA message is retransmitted, this cycle repeating until a response is obtained (up to some limit, after which it will be assumed that the link has gone down). The function of the A-bit, essentially, is to allow the recipient of a DATA message to determine whether that message is a new one or a repetition of the previously accepted one. Each acknowledgement must carry the same value of the A-bit as the DATA message to which it is the response. The flow of DATA messages into and out of each UM is controlled by two independent half-duplex procedures, as described, sharing the same full-duplex link.

This handshake method of operation means that backlog queues of unacknowledged messages are avoided. The procedure also offers a simple method of controlling the rate of flow of DATA messages. If either the UM or the CP becomes congested, the influx of new messages is prevented by withholding the acknowledgement. To prevent unnecessarily frequent retransmission of messages a long timeout period will be used, coupled with a "please repeat" request which is issued when conditions are again favourable for the receipt of messages. This request takes the form of an ACK with the *wrong* A-bit value. One implication of the hierarchy principle is illustrated by this problem of congestion and the way in which it must be handled. Any internal property of some level in a hierarchical system can only be taken into account by higher levels if this property is made *explicit* at the interface between the levels.

The IUM control message is used in place of the ACK response to a DATA message received by the CP when the specified destination UM is unavailable. This "number unobtainable" response will arise when the addressed UM is offline from the network. The immediate response implies that each CP must keep a table of current UM availabilities.

Each end of a link must keep a check on the continued availability and correct operation of the other party. The CP does this partly by issuing periodic IDLE messages, to which the UM must respond with an IDLE message within a set time. If a link failure is detected, then a restart procedure is initiated by the CP, as soon as possible, using the CLS message which it outputs regularly until it receives a CLS response from the UM. This sequence is also used on initial start-up; it causes the link control procedure to be resynchronised by resetting the A-bit counters. The DOWN message may be issued by either the UM or the CP if one wishes to become unavailable to the other.

The main functions of the Message Interface which each LCM presents to its IPCM will be "send message" and "accept message" commands, which may be given by the IPCM. Thus if an "accept message" command is current, the LCM will accept another DATA message from the CP, otherwise it will hold off. The LCM must also make available "startup" and "shutdown" commands which allow the IPCM to control the online/offline state of the UM to the network. The LCM must signal the IUM error response to DATA output back to the IPCM, as well as informing it when the network becomes unavailable. The parameters passed to the LCM in a "send message" command must include the address of the destination UM.

179

4. Interprocess Communication

In order to provide a simple yet general method of organising communication between processes in remote UMs, the concepts of *channels* and *calls* are used. Each UM is assigned 256 logical channels, all equivalent, using which calls may be set up between processes via channels in other UMs. A channel may only be involved in one call at a time. A pair of channels linked together in this way provide a full-duplex logical communication path, along which control messages pass between IPCMs and data between processes via the IPCMs.

These logical channels are resources offered by the Inter Process Communication Network. The channel numbers are regarded not as having a unique association with processes in general, but rather as intermediate addresses. When one process wishes to communicate with another, it must first obtain a free channel which it then uses to set up a call to a channel in the destination UM. There remains the problem of knowing which of these channels to address in order to access the desired process. If a UM does in fact have a convention whereby it uniquely assigns processes to channels, then this convention must be known to other UMs. A more likely eventuality is that one channel is assigned, by convention, to a "login process". A calling process communicates initially with a login process, passing it information to identify the target process. An association is then set up between a free channel and the desired process and this channel number returned to the calling process, enabling it to set up a new call.

The UM to UM messages and their formats are shown in Figure 4. Control messages consist of 3 or 4 bytes, while messages carrying inter-process data have a 3 byte header. It must be stressed that all these messages are DATA messages as far as the LCM is concerned; they may be up to 1021 bytes long and will have an "outer" 3 byte header added by the LCM. Thus processes communicate, via the Process Interface, in terms of messages variable in length from 1 to 1018 bytes, to which a total of 6 bytes of control information is added before the message leaves the UM.

All UM-UM messages carry a type code to distinguish the various message functions, and a modulo 16 cyclic message number. In addition, each message carries the origin and destination channel numbers specifying the logical path.

To initiate a call, the IPCM sends a CALL message to the required remote channel. If the remote IPCM cannot accept the connection, an END message is returned, otherwise the reply is another CALL message. The successful completion of this dialogue means that a connection is set up between the channels and a call established between the associated processes. Once established, a call may be terminated by either IPCM sending an END message. Cleardown is not effective until an END has been received in reply.

The "reset" field in the CALL message allows the called IPCM to switch the connection onto a new channel at its end, which will be used during the subsequent call. The channel addressed initially is left free to accept new calls. This facility is intended for use by multiple-access services which can create processes to provide the services to each user. The calls will initially be addressed to a "login" channel, by which the service is externally known; a process will then be created and allocated a free channel to which the incoming call is switched. No additional information need be sent to the login channel, and the calling process will not be aware that switching has occurred. When channel switching is not required, the "reset" field is simply made equal to the "from" address in the CALL response.

Once a call is established, full duplex data exchange may take place between processes in the form of discrete messages which are tagged as DATA messages by the IPCM. Although data transfer at the Process Interface level could be organised differently, it is simpler to retain the message framework offered at the Message Interface level.

Before a process can send a DATA message, a NEXT message must have been received from its correspondent. The sending of this message implies that the latter is prepared to accept one maximum length message (unless, by convention, shorter messages are used). This procedure allows each process to control the inward flow of DATA according to the availability of buffers, or any other criteria. More than one NEXT message may be sent before a DATA message is received in reply, allowing processes to minimise the effect of delays in the Communication Network. The usefulness of this "multiple buffering" technique will be limited by the possibility of congestion, and it has been decided that the IPCM itself will restrict the maximum number of NEXT requests that may be outstanding on any channel to a small number, probably two. For the sake of simplicity, this flow control scheme operates strictly on a message basis, that is, no information on permitted length of each DATA message is carried in the NEXT request.

When full-duplex data exchange is taking place between processes, interleaved streams of DATA and NEXT messages will flow between the connected channels. Processes may use a simplex or half-duplex method of data interchange; the latter is considered to be a sufficiently frequent requirement to warrant the provision of a combined DATA and NEXT (D/NEXT of Figure 4) message, thus saving on overhead. Where a process is controlling the operation of a terminal, for example, the receipt of the D/NEXT message may be regarded as a command from the remote process to output the given data to the terminal and then to permit the user to respond.

The cyclic numbers on each message are used by the IPCM to detect the loss or duplication of messages. When message loss is detected, a recovery sequence involving the REQ STATUS and STATUS messages is initiated, each channel informing the other of the number (modulo 4) of DATA and NEXT messages sent and received. By checking these numbers each IPCM can discover the nature of the error; lost NEXT requests can be recovered but the loss of DATA (or D/NEXT) can only be signalled to the appropriate processes.

As implied above, processes are not themselves expected to output or interpret control messages; all detailed "housekeeping" is performed by the IPCM, which has the task of ensuring that the UM-UM protocol rules are obeyed. The Process Interface will take the form of commands issued by processes to the IPCM and responses by the latter when the command has been executed. The following brief account is intended to cover some of the more important features of the Process Interface.

An association between a process and a channel is set up when a process gives a "make call" or a "wait for call" command. When no "wait for call" is issued to a channel, the IPCM will reject any incoming CALL request for that channel. Otherwise, the associated process is informed and may "accept call" (specifying channel switching if desired) or "reject call". The response by the IPCM to "make call" will inform the process whether or not the attempt succeeded. When a call is established, the processes may exchange data by means of "send data", "request next" and "send/request" commands which give rise to the messages already described. Finally, either process may give an "end call" command to terminate the call and the association between process and channel.

When a "make call" command is issued, the destination channel and UM numbers must be passed as parameters to the IPCM; thereafter, these numbers cannot be changed. Similarly, the source channel number to be used must be specified in the "make call" and "wait for call" commands.

One of the problems arising with the IPCM is the amount of detail with which a specification of the Process Interface should be given. The IPCM will usually be a part of the operating system of the UM; operating systems differ widely in the way in which they make resources available to user programs, so that a specification of the interface complete in every detail is not possible. Hence this interface must be specified in fairly broad terms, as above, leaving the implementor to complete the definition for each UM. The main requirement is that all the features of the IPCM, which are fully defined, should be made available to users. This point also arises with the LCM and the Message Interface, and must be dealt with in the same way.

5. The NPL Network

In this section we shall examine some of the implications of the above general scheme in a little more detail, and discuss briefly the proposed realisation of these ideas for the NPL network.

No consideration has yet been given to terminal devices through which users gain access to the resources provided by User Machines. Since the Communications Network only interconnects UMs, clearly terminals must be controlled by UMs. Each terminal connected to a UM may be regarded as having a process in the UM to control its operation. Communication between terminals, or between terminals and service processes may then use the facilities of the Inter Process Communication Network in the normal way. Terminals remote from UMs must be joined to them by means of some communications system separate from that interconnecting UMs, and standards established to permit the meaningful use of terminals by remote processes. Although in principle any UM may handle terminals, it is considered preferable to employ special UMs which are dedicated to this task, and this is the intention in the case of the NPL network, these UMs being known as "Terminal Processors" (TPs).

An attempt has been made here to isolate and define a number of distinct elements in the total communications system, namely the packet handling Node, the Communications Processor, Link Control Module, Inter Process Communication Module, User Machine and Terminal Processor. The generalised scheme does not specify the way in which these elements may be realised in a practical system. Thus, particular elements may be implemented in hardware or by program, and in a number of possible combinations. The Node and CP functions could be placed in separate computers which must then be physically linked together. Alternatively, these two functions might be realised in the same computer, with an internal interface between them. The LCM and IPCM both reside in the UM, and may be incorporated into its operating system. However, if the UM consists of two computers, say, a main machine and a communications front-end, then the LCM and a part of the IPCM could be placed in the front-end and the remainder of the IPCM in the main machine.

The way in which the present scheme maps onto the earlier NPL proposals[3,4] for a national data network is illustrated in Figure 2. Both schemes employ a packet switching nodal network for trunk routing. In the earlier proposal this network interconnected a number of "Interface Computers" which were responsible for the handling of all subscribers' devices, be they simple peripherals or computers. In the present scheme, these tasks of the Interface Computer are split between the CP and the TP. Furthermore, since the TP has the status of a UM there is no reason why several TPs should not be attached to a CP if conditions require it, so that this scheme can be seen to be more flexible.

The type of network under consideration has many similarities with that being developed in the USA by the Advanced Research Projects Agency (ARPA)[5,6]. In that system, User Machines (referred to as HOSTs) are connected to standard communications computers (known as IMPs) which are themselves linked together to form a store-and-forward communication network. Each IMP can be connected to a small number of HOSTs, which must be physically close to it. The IMP combines the Node and CP functions as they are defined here. The ARPA equivalents of the Communications Network Interface and LCM (the HOST-IMP Protocol[6]) and the Process Interface and IPCM (the HOST-HOST Protocol[7]) differ in some respects from their NPL counterparts. A few functions here ascribed to the IPCM are incorporated into the IMP which therefore has a "UM front-end" aspect (for example, the "Request for Next Message" feature, which is similar to the NEXT message in the UM-UM protocol).

Returning to the experimental network under development in NPL, since this system will initially provide a service within a limited geographical area, all UMs will be attached to one CP and the inner packet switching part of the Communications Network will consequently not be implemented. Terminals will be connected to a single TP and both the CP and TP will be implemented as two independent program partitions within one DDP516 computer, sharing the resources of the DDP516 and the existing communications hardware[1]. A new standard hardware control unit is being developed to interface UMs to the communications links. The design of the system will allow a separation of the CP and TP functions into two computers, eventually, if the traffic load justifies it.

The existing version of the NPL network is, as was implied in the introduction, essentially a stand-alone TP. The type of service offered by the new TP will be essentially the same as that given at present[2]. However, as well as allowing communication between terminals, the new TP will permit terminals to interact with processes in other UMs. In order to make this possible, the new TP must of course incorporate an IPCM and an LCM. The LCM will in fact be much simpler than that required for other UMs, since it has only to cater for communication across the internal interface between the CP and TP partitions.

The programs for the stand-alone TP are written in a conventional assembly language for the DDP516 (DAP16) but using fairly general and modular programming techniques. However, the extent of the change in system architecture has led us to the decision that the program for the new combined CP/TP must be written from scratch. The programs will be written in PL516[8], which is an ALGOL-structured assembly language recently developed for the DDP516.

6. Conclusion

The task of understanding the communication requirements of computers, data terminals and their users has only just been started. It is only by obtaining and analysing experience with a realistic communication system carrying meaningful traffic that progress can be made. One consequence of this is that a considerable effort must be made to attract users, understand their needs and provide services accessible through the network which are really useful to them.

If these problems can be understood then we shall be in a position to state clearly to the public communications authorities the characteristics required of national and international networks satisfying the needs of data communication. Furthermore, we shall be able to set standards which will allow computers to make proper use of such networks and which will make resource-sharing on a large scale feasible. Clearly, it will take time to attain these objectives, but they are surely worth striving for.

Acknowledgment

The authors would like to thank Alan Gardener of the British Post Office, and Derek Baker of the N.P.L. Network Group for their invaluable help in the design of the above system.

References

1. SCANTLEBURY, R.A. - A model for the local area of a data communication network - objectives and hardware organization. A.C.M. Symposium on Data Communications. (Pine Mountain 1969).

2. WILKINSON, P.T. - A model for the local area of a data communication network - software organization. A.C.M. Symposium on Data Communications. (Pine Mountain 1969).

3. DAVIES, D.W., BARTLETT, K.A., SCANTLEBURY, R.A. and WILKINSON, P.T. - A digital communication network for computers giving rapid response at remote terminals. A.C.M. Symposium on Operating System Principles (Gatlinburg) 1967.

4. DAVIES, D.W. - The principles of a data communication network for computers and remote peripherals. PROC IFIP 1968 (Edinburgh) Hardware D11.

5. ROBERTS, L.G. and WESSLER, B.D. - Computer network development to achieve resource sharing. Proc AFIPS 1970 SJCC pp 543-549.

6. HEART, F.E., <u>et al</u> - The Interface Message Processor for the A.R.P.A. Computer Network. Proc AFIPS 1970 SJCC pp 551-567.

7. CARR, C.S., CROCKER, S.D. and CERF, V.G. - HOST-HOST communication protocol in the ARPA network. Proc. AFIPS 1970 SJCC pp 589-597.

8. BELL, D.A. and WICHMANN, B.A. - An ALGOL-like assembly language for a small computer. Software-Practice and Experience 1, pp 61-72, 1971.

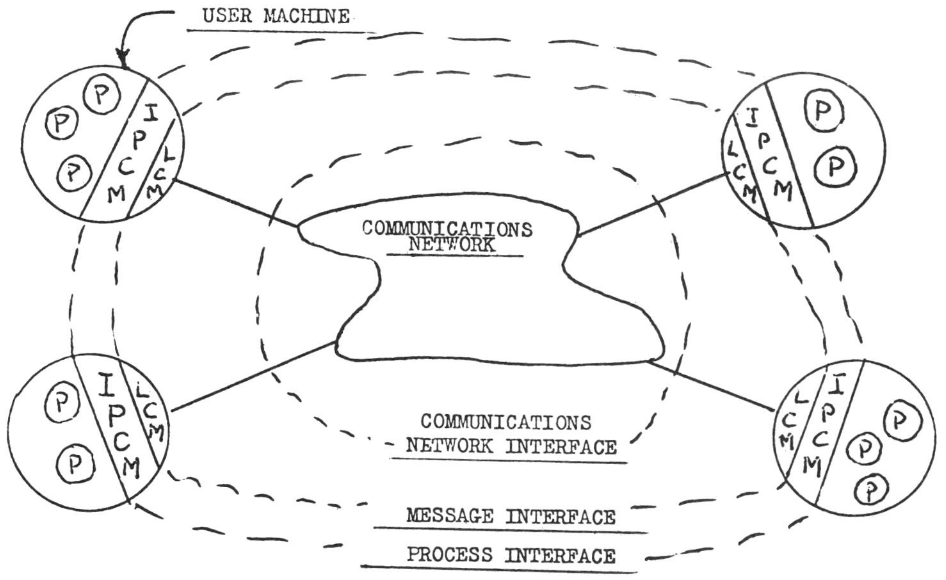
USER MACHINE
COMMUNICATIONS NETWORK
COMMUNICATIONS NETWORK INTERFACE
MESSAGE INTERFACE
PROCESS INTERFACE

FIGURE 1

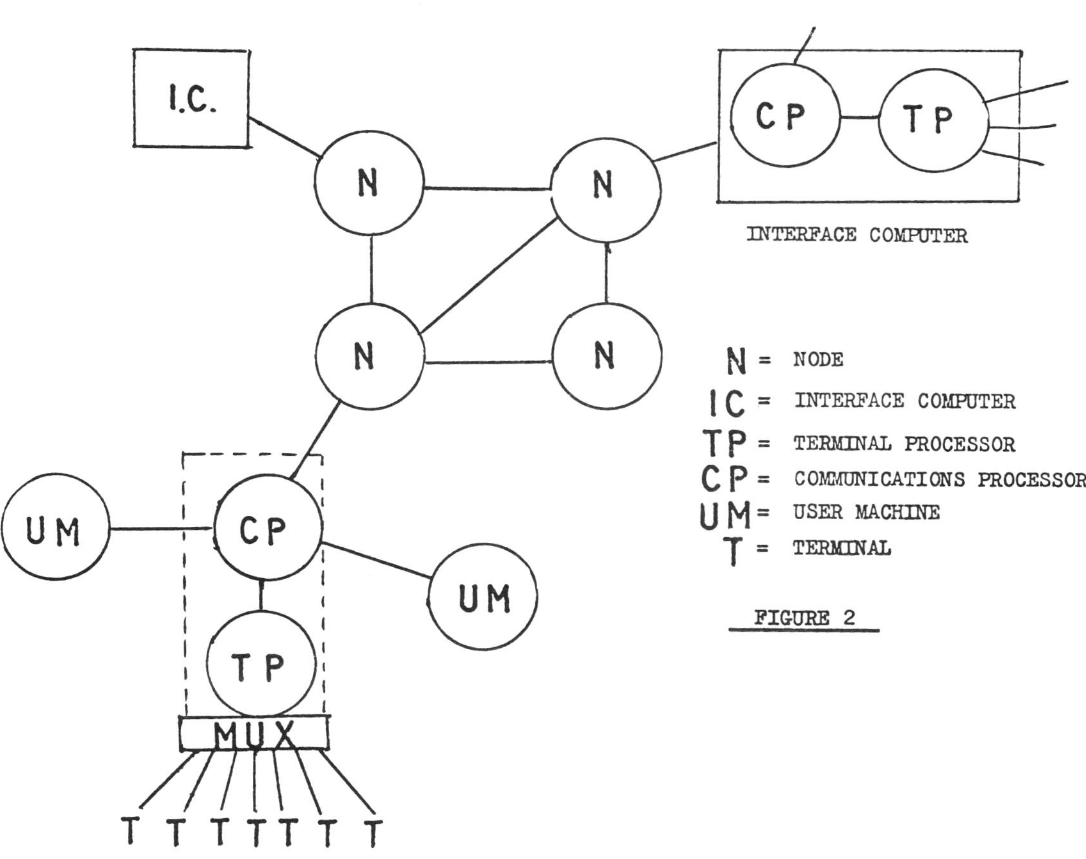
I.C.
CP
TP
INTERFACE COMPUTER
N
UM
MUX
T T T T T T T
N = NODE
IC = INTERFACE COMPUTER
TP = TERMINAL PROCESSOR
CP = COMMUNICATIONS PROCESSOR
UM = USER MACHINE
T = TERMINAL

FIGURE 2

183

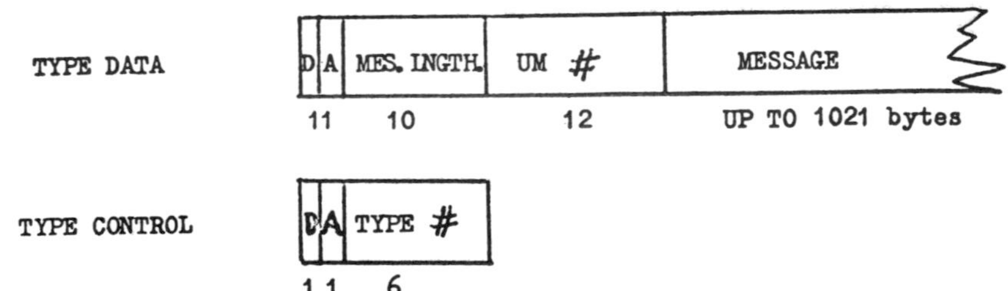

TYPE	MEANING	RESPONSE
DOWN	UM ABOUT TO GO OFF-LINE (OR CP!)	—
CLS	CLEAR LINK TO SEND (RESYNCHRONISE A BIT)	CLS
IDLE	DUMMY TRANSFER FOR TIMING AND CHECKING	IDLE
(DATA)	(MESSAGE)	ACK/ IUM
ACK	POSITIVE RESPONSE TO DATA	—
IUM	ILLEGAL USER MACHINE (NU) (FROM CP ONLY)	—

FIGURE 3 LINK CONTROL MESSAGE FORMAT

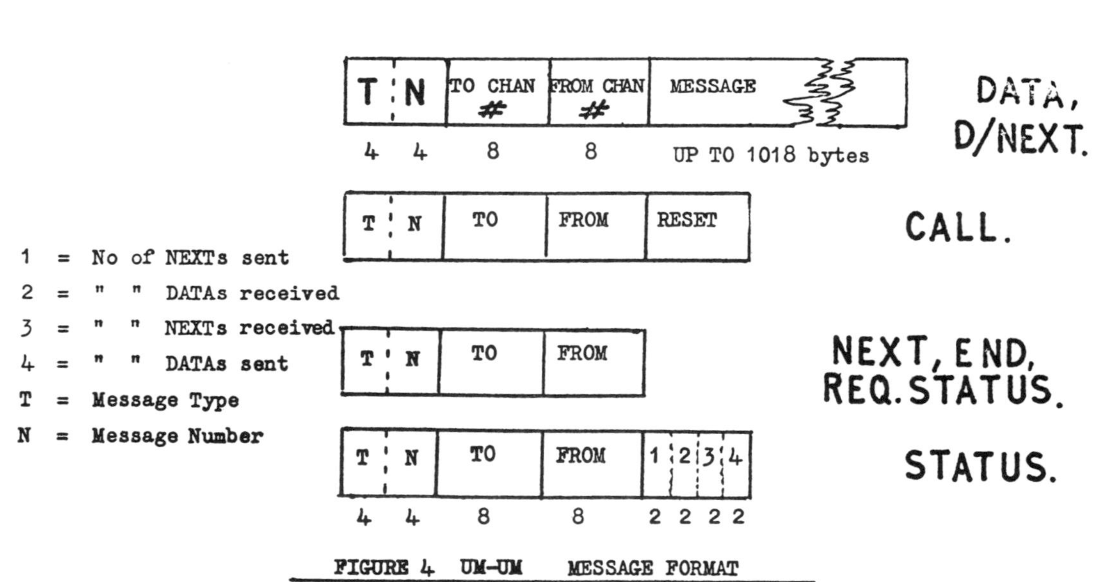

FIGURE 4 UM-UM MESSAGE FORMAT

PROCEEDINGS OF THE IEEE, VOL. 60, NO. 11, NOVEMBER 1972

Terminal-Oriented Computer-Communication Networks

MISCHA SCHWARTZ, FELLOW, IEEE, ROBERT R. BOORSTYN, MEMBER, IEEE, AND RAYMOND L. PICKHOLTZ, MEMBER, IEEE

Invited Paper

***Abstract*—Four examples of currently operating computer-communication networks are described in this tutorial paper. They include the TYMNET network, the GE Information Services network, the NASDAQ over-the-counter stock-quotation system, and the Computer Sciences Infonet. These networks all use programmable concentrators for combining a multiplicity of terminals. Included in the discussion for each network is a description of the overall network structure, the handling and transmission of messages, communication requirements, routing and reliability consideration where applicable, operating data and design specifications where available, and unique design features in the area of computer communications.**

Introduction

DATA NETWORKS of various kinds are currently in operation, are in the process of being set up, or have been proposed for future development and construction. They include large-scale computer networks (e.g., the Advanced Research Projects Agency (ARPA) network and similar networks under development in Europe and elsewhere), multipurpose data networks (e.g., AT&T, Western Union, and the system proposed by Datran), airline reservation systems, bank transaction systems, retail chain data-flow systems, stock information and securities exchange networks, medical data networks, geographically dispersed time-shared computer systems operated by various computer service organizations, public service networks (combining fire, police, health, and other vital functions) under development in various urban areas, educational data networks, etc. The list is seemingly endless and growing larger literally day by day.

Although the applications and uses for which they are intended cover a broad spectrum of sometimes overlapping data-flow functions, and although the designs entailed may cover a seemingly bewildering variety of approaches, all these networks are similar in their symbiotic mix of computers and communications. It is for this reason that we find them labeled computer-communication networks. It is also no accident that the traditional common-carrier companies, the computer manufacturers, and computer-communication companies are all vitally interested in this burgeoning field.

Although the variety of networks in existence or under development is large, and their design philosophies are often complex—often based as much on questions of history and original applications for which they are intended as on up-to-date technical and cost considerations—a detailed overview may bring out similarities in structure and design (as well as differences), and inject some order into the seeming chaos. It is for this purpose that this tutorial paper has been written. It is geared to the nonspecialist in the field of computer-communication networks, interested in obtaining an overall view of how the interaction of computer and communication facilities is used to manage the data flow in rather complex networks.

We focus here by way of example on terminal-oriented networks, those designed to accommodate input–output devices, such as Teletypewriters, push-button control units, and their associated display devices, where they exist. The network design and design philosophy is then predicated on providing the appropriate services to these terminal-type users. Four existing networks will be described in some detail so that comparisons can be made in the overall system design, in message formatting and processing, in data-handling capability, etc. These particular networks (the NASDAQ over-the-counter stock quotation network, the Computer Sciences Infonet, the Tymshare TYMNET, and the GE Information Services Network) are typical of many of the other networks in existence and were chosen because information concerning their design and operation was available or could be obtained readily. (Acknowledgment is given at the end of this paper to individuals consulted in the gathering of the necessary information.)

Except for TYMNET, the pattern of data flow in these networks is generally inbound from a particular terminal to a large computer (or group of computers) that carry out the data processing and/or data retrieval that may be called for, and then outbound back from the computer to the same terminal. This contrasts with a more general network in which data could be switched or routed from one terminal to one or more others, geographically distant, either going through a computer or sets of computers first, or directly to the other terminals. TYMNET provides an example here. The Western Union Telex and TWX systems, among other networks, the AT&T public switched network, and the proposed Datran system provide other examples of this more general type of message routing. The basic concepts of network design and data handling, derived from a comparative study of these four network examples, are thus appropriate to a large class of networks, including those with more complex routing strategies.

Overall View

Before undertaking a summary of the four networks mentioned, it is appropriate to attempt an overall view of the terminal-oriented computer-communications network. This will serve to put the networks described in focus and to enable some sort of comparison of network designs and operations to be made.

Two distinct tasks may be distinguished in the design of any network: 1) the problem of putting a terminal on line, when it desires service, combining its messages with those of

Manuscript received July 21, 1972. This work was supported by the National Science Foundation under Grants GK 31469 and GK 33352, and by NASA under Grant NGR 33-006-020.

M. Schwartz and R. R. Boorstyn are with the Polytechnic Institute of Brooklyn, Brooklyn, N. Y. 11201.

R. L. Pickholtz is with George Washington University, Washington, D. C.

185

other, geographically contiguous terminals; and 2) the problem of then directing the resultant message stream to the appropriate destination for further processing. We can call these tasks, respectively, message combining, concentration, or multiplexing, and message distribution or routing.

In the message-combining phase the individual message characters, once in the system, may be recoded to a standardized message character format (generally the United States of America Standard Code for Information Interchange (USASCII) 8-bit character code) for use throughout the network, if different types of input devices may be used in the network. Additional bits or characters may be added for error control, addressing, synchronization, and other necessary control purposes. The combining function itself may be carried out in a variety of ways: a polling technique may be used in which terminals associated with the particular concentration point are regularly (or irregularly) asked to transmit any data ready to enter the system. The combiner may have a fixed number of input ports to which the terminals are either always connected, or to which they may be connected, if not already occupied. Messages may be fed directly into a buffer in the combiner, after address bits are added, and then the buffered messages taken out, either sequentially or following some priority scheme.

Note that the combining procedures [13] vary from rather simple multiplexing schemes to sophisticated concentration schemes requiring a small computer [14] to carry them out. The incoming messages may be directly multiplexed onto outgoing trunks, using either frequency-division modulation (FDM) or time-division modulation (TDM) trunks, or multiplexed onto the outgoing trunks after buffering and some preliminary processing of the type noted previously. Corresponding to these two alternatives, two types of networks are currently in use or under development—the line- or circuit-switched type and the message-switched or store-and-forward type.[1] (Some planned networks call for a combination of the two.) In the line-switched system multiplexers are used throughout the network to allow entry of messages and their continuous transmission throughout the network. Here, as in the analogous public switched-voice telephone network, a terminal desirous of entering the network calls in its destination. A complete path is set up, from end to end, and then, once the complete connection is established, messages may be multiplexed into the system. In the message-switched case a message may enter the system at a message concentrator, queuing up or being stored in a buffer until the outgoing trunk is ready to accept it, and then work its way through the network, from concentration point ("node") to concentration point, queuing up at various points if necessary, until the destination is reached.

The line-switching system, requiring only multiplexers for the combining function, may be considerably less costly, equipment-wise, than the equivalent message-swtiching system. The latter requires as its combiner a small computer (minicomputers are often used). These latter devices have been variously labeled *communications processor*, *programmable concentrator*, *message concentrator*, and the like [14], [15]. Because of their computational capability these devices can, however, carry out some processing normally associated with larger computers in a system, and they may do the routing and switching associated with switching computers in the line-switched system. They are of course quite flexible and can be programmed to accept various types of terminals at their inputs; they may carry out some control functions, etc. Because of their buffering capability they can smooth out statistical variations in the incoming data—number of terminals vying for service, lengths of messages and frequency of message transmission of a particular terminal, etc.

For example, a terminal that transmits short messages spaced at relatively long time intervals apart, once connected into the system, might find a programmable concentrator type of combiner and message switching throughout the network more economical for its purposes. For the terminal then *shares* the network facility with the other terminals connected in: it is charged only for the time that messages are actually transmitted, and messages from other terminals fill in the empty time gaps. The same terminal connected to the line-switched network must pay for the *entire* time it is connected, just as in telephone transmission, for it has a channel *dedicated* to its use throughout the connection time. Conversely, a data terminal with relatively long messages, spaced close together, may find the line-switched network more economical for its purposes. But this is not a clear-cut situation—it depends on trunk line costs, type of service available from the common carrier if leased lines are used, etc. (For example, the same terminal transmitting short messages may receive long messages back from the computer. Full duplex lines—those capable of handling two-way traffic simultaneously—are commonly used, and the line capacity would then be dictated by the outbound computer–user message stream. The inbound lines are then very inefficiently used, but current communication line costs do not warrant any change in this procedure.) The systems to be described in the sections following provide message switching in the sense previously described. (TYMNET system personnel prefer to use the words *virtual line switching* to describe the function of their network, however, because of the use of dedicated paths or routes once a connection is set up. This will be discussed in more detail in the next section.)

The message distribution or routing task, once the messages from geographically contiguous terminals are combined and formatted for transmittal, consists, of course, of directing the messages to their appropriate destination. Various design questions immediately arise here. In mentioning message concentration or multiplexing we did not at all indicate the placement or location of the combining point. This is part of the rather broad or global question of overall network design [16]—where shall the network nodal points be placed? (These are the points where terminals are concentrated or multiplexed, where messages may be dropped, where they may be further mutiplexed with other message streams in a hierarchy of multiplexing procedures, where they may be rerouted, etc.) Involved here are questions of cost, reliability, network response or delay time, trunk or link capacities, etc. These are all interrelated and much of the network design, as will be noted in the examples following, involves a mixture of some analysis, simulation, and engineering "feel" for the problem.

Specifically, what are the tradeoffs, cost-wise, in adding more concentrators to cover widely dispersed terminals and decreasing cable costs correspondingly, or vice versa? What capacity (in bits per second) trunks are needed to cover the anticipated traffic between nodes (these are called the *links* of

[1] The term "packet switching" is sometimes used in place of "message switching."

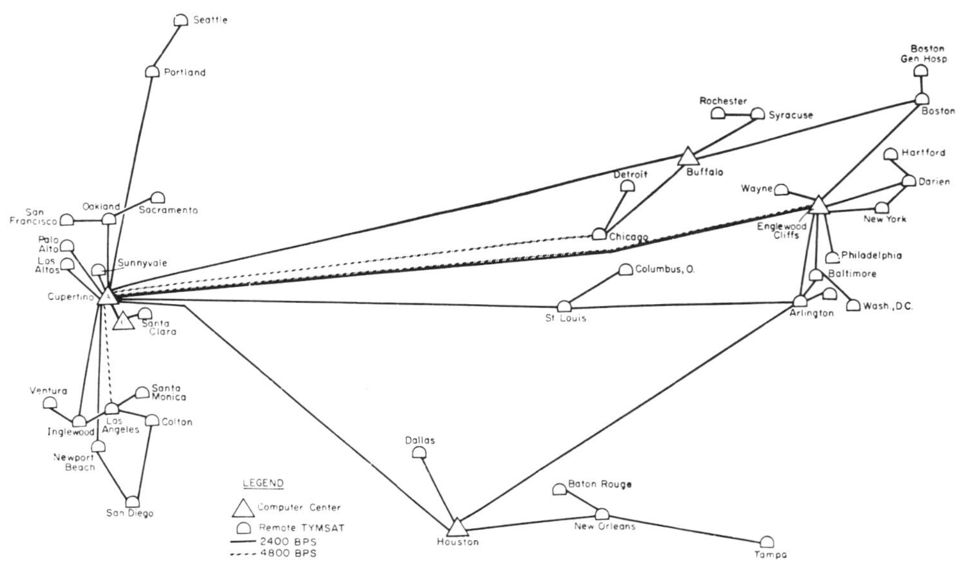

Fig. 1. TYMNET map.

the network)? How many terminals can a given combiner handle? Both of these latter two questions are related to the network delay or response time, a typically important constraint in network design. In the case of a message-switched network, increasing trunk capacity decreases the queuing (buffer) time of messages as they traverse the network and hence reduces the overall response or delay time. In the case of a line-switched network, the chance of a busy signal is obviously reduced as capacity is increased. In addition, as provision is made for more terminals to be handled at any concentrator, the outgoing trunk capacity must be increased correspondingly to handle the additional traffic and keep the response time acceptable. The network performance criterion is sometimes given as an average or median response time, or some related measure. Alternatively, it may be given in terms of a tolerable busy-signal probability.

Reliability also plays an extremely important role in network design [16]. Systems are often designed to ensure at least *two* alternate paths between any two nodes in the network. In some cases this is accomplished by using two geographically separate trunk connections, in others by designing the network topology to ensure an alternate route between any two nodes if any link in a given route is interrupted.

Finally, once the network design is established, routing strategies must be established in those networks in which messages may traverse several modes before arriving at a destination. Examples will be given in the systems to be considered of strategies adopted in practice. It is apparent that the routing procedures are related to the reliability constraint. For should a link in the network fail, an alternate route must be used. Routing is also an attempt to equalize the traffic and response time throughout the network—messages should be sent via routes that carry relatively less traffic and that are relatively less error prone than other routes. The route set up for a given user–destination pair may be globally determined by a centralized computer that monitors the state of the entire network, or, locally, by each node making estimates of least time to any other node in the network and corresponding paths to follow. In the message-switched networks the nodal processors are often used to carry out the processing needed to determine the message routing or to direct messages following the directions from the centralized source. The routing strategy in the line-switched network case is generally determined beforehand and used to search out a complete route or circuit before allowing messages to enter the system. In the message-switched network case, the routing can be adaptive and updated periodically, or on demand, as traffic conditions change.

TYMNET

Overall Network

A recent article has stressed the fact that time-sharing companies have in the past two years moved dramatically beyond their initial phase of providing service for the "one-time problem solver" [1]. The networks they have set up have begun to emerge as national computer-communications networks, in the fullest sense of the words: they are used to provide computer power and access to data bases for various businesses, often replacing or augmenting expensive in-house computer operations, as well as providing a data-communications facility for connecting user computers and remote terminals.

Tymshare, Inc.'s TYMNET computer-communication network exemplifies this change in function and approach. The network, as shown in the accompanying map (see Fig. 1), is a sophisticated data-communications network employing 80 communications processors deployed all over the country to access 26 large host computers located at computer centers in Cupertino, Calif.; Englewood Cliffs, N. J.; Houston, Tex.; and Buffalo, N. Y. (The European network CETNET has been operational for two years with one XDS 940 computer located in Paris. The two networks were scheduled to be connected in September, 1972.) The communications processors, called TYSMATS, use modified Varian 620 computers. Twenty-three of them serve as so-called base computers (base TYMSATS), each associated directly with its own central processing unit (CPU); the other 57 form remote nodes (remote TYMSATS), through which individual terminals gain entry to the system. The 26 large computers include 23 XDS 940's and 3 PDP 10's.

The network topology, as shown in the map (see Fig. 1),

has not been laid out following any specific design strategy. It has essentially just "grown" in response to customer's needs or to the business expected in various areas. Unlike some of the other time-shared networks (see, e.g., the section on the GE network following), the network configuration is basically that of a multiple ring rather than a star, although, depending on the traffic expected at any node, some of the nodes are connected daisy-chained or in a star fashion, in addition to the ring configuration [2].

Most of the 48 links connecting the various nodes are made up of leased 2400-bit/s full duplex trunks. Any one nodal concentrator may have as many as 200–300 terminals associated with it. But no more than 31 terminals at any one time can have full duplex access to the concentrator. A terminal joining the network gets a local number to call, connecting to the closest node. The network may be extended with the addition of a new concentrator if business in any one nodal region approaches or exceeds 31 simultaneous users during the busy hour.

Since the network is of the store-and-forward type with computers used to carry out processing and routing at each node, it would normally be called a message-switched system in the sense indicated in the Introduction to this paper. TYMNET personnel and publications [3] prefer to consider the network a *line*-switched network in a *virtual* sense, however: a user calling into a particular node is assigned a route or "virtual channel" (circuit) through the network to the appropriate CPU. The user keeps that virtual channel throughout transmission. The route is assigned by a supervisory program maintained at one of the CPU's. The routing algorithm, in selecting the set of links between user remote TYMSAT and the appropriate CPU that comprises the virtual channel, chooses an unused virtual channel and avoids links that are heavily loaded or that have a high error rate. A heavily loaded link is one that is carrying 57 users over that link in the same direction. A high error rate means at least 10 detected errors in transmission per minute.

Because of the ring configuration, traffic over any one link, in a given direction, may be either outbound (computer to user) or inbound (user to computer). There is no distinction made as to direction, unlike the star configuration. Tymshare personnel indicate that the "virtual-channel" or line-switched approach used provides more efficient message transmission: the overhead (nondata characters transmitted) is reduced since message addressing is much smaller than in the usual message-switched case. (As will be seen later in discussing the message format, a one-character virtual-channel number is used for addressing.) Message transmission in the computer-to-user direction (the bulk of the traffic carried, as in most time-shared systems) can approach 80-percent efficiency, rather than the 60-percent figure that might be associated with message switching.

Message Transmission

Although TYMNET is often used for computer-to-computer communication and for driving high-speed peripherals, it was primarily designed for the 10–30 character/s terminal. The system allows any 10–30-character/s terminal device to access the network. An identifying character is first typed in. A software program at the incoming TYMSAT uses the character to identify the type of terminal, code used, and speed of character transmission [4]. All characters following are then converted to American Standard Code for Information Interchange (ASCII) (8-bit) code [5] for internal network transmission.

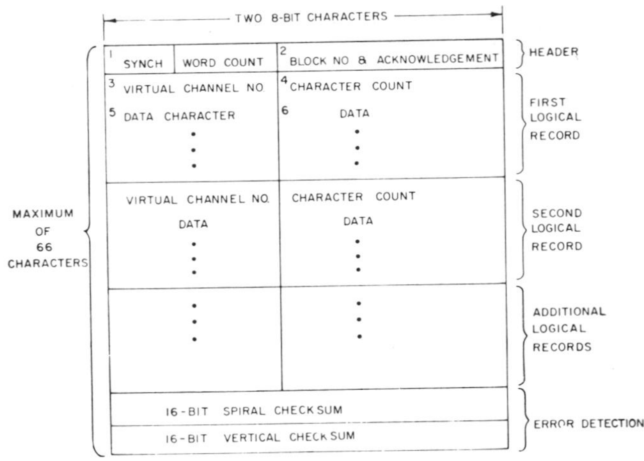

Fig. 2. TYMNET message format.

A user calling the TYMSAT with which he is associated is connected in through one of the 31 ports of the TYMSAT. The identifying character he types in, in addition to allowing code conversion at the TYMSAT, sets up a special duplex path to the network supervisor. The supervisor asks for the user name and password, and then uses these to determine at which CPU the user file is located. (Alternatively the user may ask for a particular one of several computers in which he has files.) The supervisor then proceeds to determine and set up the virtual channel mentioned. (This takes of the order of milliseconds.) It sets up the channel by sending control information to each TYMSAT along this route, causing the appropriate entries to be made in each TYMSAT's switching tables. These tables essentially associate a particular channel number with one of the outgoing links from the TYMSAT in question.

Any given TYMSAT handles traffic from its 31 ports as well as traffic coming through from the adjacent nodes to which it is connected. Messages from all these sources are stored (in ASCII code) in character buffers as they arrive. The character buffers as a group occupy 1200 words of core (2400 characters) in the concentrator. This space is dynamically allocated as needed. Each character—whether locally inputted from one of the 31 ports or passing through—has a virtual channel number associated with it.

Message transmission to adjacent nodes is accomplished by assembling a block of characters, from those stored in the buffers, for each outgoing link. A block is assembled by searching through the character buffers, on a first-come-first-served basis, for those characters with virtual channel numbers associated with that particular link (i.e., those virtual channels associated with that link in the TYMSAT switching table). The search continues in round robin fashion (returning to the first buffer queried for additional characters that might have been entered in the interim) until a maximum of 66 characters, including control and error detection characters to be discussed below, have been assembled. If fewer than 66 characters are assembled, whatever is available is transmitted. If there are no data to be sent, control characters only are transmitted.

The format of the block as finally assembled is shown in Fig. 2. A 16-bit header is first transmitted. This consists, in order as shown, of a 4-bit synchronization pattern, a 4-bit word count, and 8 bits for block number and acknowledgment. (These are discussed later.) Each message associated with a particular user then follows. The user message, called a logical record, consists first of a one-character virtual channel number, then of a one-character count, telling how many data characters are to follow, followed by the 8-bit data characters themselves. Additional logical records, for different users, follow. The final 32 bits or 4 characters of the block are used for error detection. They consist first of a 16-bit spiral check sum and then a 16-bit vertical check sum.

No more than one such 66-character block is transmitted every 0.25 s. This corresponds to 264 characters/s or 2112 bits/s to be transmitted over the 2400-bit/s trunks. There will always be at least one block sent every half second because the data rate control logic executes every half second. Experience has shown that this format will accommodate up to 50 users over a 2400-bit/s link and up to 100 on a 4800-bit/s link. This is based on an average user transmission rate of up to 4 characters/s [2]. As noted earlier, this information is used in the routing strategy for the system.

The block as transmitted is disassembled at the next node, at the end of the link, the message characters are stored in the appropriate buffers at that node, and the block assembly process is then again repeated, as before.

Error correction is carried out by retransmission of the entire block if necessary: as soon as a block is received, the number of that block is returned to the sending TYMSAT as part of the next outgoing block on the reverse path of the link in question. If a block is *not* acknowledged for any reason, it is automatically retransmitted by the sending TYMSAT. If an error in the block is detected at the receiving TYMSAT, the block is disregarded and not acknowledged. Retransmission then automatically takes place. In addition, notification of the error is sent to the supervisor which keeps track of error counts on all links. As noted earlier, this information is then used in establishing a user–computer route. (Links with more than 10 block errors/min are avoided.) The check-sum technique used for error detection (see Fig. 2) provides a very low error rate, theoretically of the order of 1 bit in 2^{32} or the order of 1 in 10^9 bit transmitted.

Errors occurring between the user terminal and the connected TYMSAT are detected visually by remote echoing: the TYMSAT itself retransmits each character as received over the full duplex local loop, causing the terminal keyboard to print. (Originally characters were echoed by the CPU, but this caused an unacceptable time lapse between the time of the user depressing his key and the printing of the character.) The TYMSAT does the echoing only if no other characters are waiting to be printed, if no characters are known to be coming down the channel from the CPU, or if it has not been signaled by the CPU not to echo. If the remote TYMSAT does not echo the character, the CPU is so notified. The CPU itself then echoes the character at an appropriate place in the character stream [2].

Traffic-Handling Capability

As noted earlier, each remote TYMSAT is capable of accommodating up to 31 simultaneous users. This provides some indication of the possible number of simultaneous users on the network. In addition, each CPU has 60 input ports, each corresponding to a different user. This corresponds to the order of 1600 simultaneous users. In practice the traffic carried peaks at about 1000 users. Typically a peak figure of 24–30 users may be accessing one of the XDS computers while 40–50 may be accessing the PDP-10's.

In addition to this use by customers accessing the network's own computers, the TYMNET system has begun to take on a network service function. This is precisely one of the areas of applicability mentioned at the beginning of this section on TYMNET. In this service the system provides routing and connection facilities while the customer provides his own computing facilities. This service is provided under FCC Tariff 260 "Joint User" section. As an example, the National Library of Medicine uses TYMNET to provide access by remote terminals located anywhere in the United States to its own computer facilities (several 370/155's and a PDP-9) distributed at several locations. Such a service presumably provides higher efficiency at less cost than would be possible if the customer were to set up his own network using leased lines, for the network in this case is shared with the other TYMNET customers. The customer in this case also shares in the increased dependability and reliability made available through the network rerouting and error-detection capabilities.

The reader may have wondered how 2400-bit/s trunks could possibly handle all the traffic that might be encountered, particularly on links close to the CPU's. The routing strategy, avoiding heavily loaded links, serves to distribute the traffic more smoothly over the network and thus helps to avoid traffic pileups. In addition, there is a computer-to-user direction shutoff feature that prevents traffic from building up. This is particularly necessary in buffering the output flow from the CPU. For the computer output rate may run as high as 1000 characters/s, yet the terminal to which it is directed may only be able to print 10 characters/s. Intermediate node buffers are limited in size and so cannot handle too large a data input. To prevent data from piling up on any one channel, a given sending node subtracts the number of characters sent out over that channel from a counter associated with the channel. When the counter reaches zero, no more characters are sent over that channel. Twice a second the receiving node sends 1 bit back to the sending node, indicating whether it has less than or more than 32 characters in the receiving buffer for the channel. If it has less the sending node resets its counter to 32 and starts transmitting again [3]. (For high-speed channels that accommodate 120 characters/s, a count of 128 is used.)

Final Comments

Some features utilized in the TYMNET system bear expansion and further discussion. First, note that minicomputers are used throughout the network in a manner similar to the IMP's and/or TIP's in the ARPA network: they serve as interfaces to the larger computers; they connect computer centers for intercomputer communications; they serve as intermediate nodes in the routing of messages; and finally they serve as terminal multiplexers and drivers. Since most of the functions are carried out under software control, there is built-in flexibility. New types of terminals coming on the market can be readily accommodated by simple changes in a program.

The cost of minicomputers has been decreasing rapidly

189

with a concomitant increase in speed. Since each node is essentially an independent module, new hardware and software can be phased in one unit at a time. (The software used at present at each node is of the order of 4000 instructions. The special hardware used is also very primitive. It is therefore relatively easy to convert to another minicomputer if necessary.)

Some words on the supervisory concept are in order [3]. As noted earlier, a supervisor handles channel assignment and routing. This is actually a program run under time sharing in one of the XDS 940's. In addition to establishing an initial route or virtual channel, the supervisor will reroute all circuits affected by node or link failures, if an alternate route can be found. (Node failures have in practice been infrequent, averaging 1.4 failures/year/TYMSAT.)

To guard against supervisor failure, three other host computers have supervisory programs running as well, arranged in a predetermined pecking order. (The CPU in Paris will contain a supervisor as well when the two networks are joined in September.) These dormant supervisors receive messages from the active supervisor about once a minute, confirming its activity. If a confirmation is not received, the next supervisor in order takes over. The dormant supervisors have no prior knowledge of the state of the network, so that the new supervisor must learn the network. It does this by probing the network systematically node by node and link by link until an up-to-date representation of the network (including, for example, all virtual channels and the contents of the nodal switching tables) is constructed in its memory.

This centralized supervisory control provides the following features [3].

1) The individual nodes have no global knowledge of the network. They may thus be handled independently. The software in one does not affect the software in another, simplifying any debugging necessary.

2) A newly activated supervisor has no prior knowledge of the network. It simply accepts the network configuration as it exists. Changes in the network are thus easily made.

3) The fact that the supervisory programs are run under time sharing provides debugging advantages.

4) All global information about the network is available at one place: this facilitates diagnostics, record keeping, and debugging.

GE Information Services

Overall Network

The GE Information Services Network is also an example of a computer-communication network that has in the past few years evolved from an initial phase of providing time-shared computer service for the problem solver to the current one of providing facilities as an information network. For example, it now offers a service called *Interprocessing,* in which files may be transferred from a customer's own computer to the GE System computers for accessing by the customer's own terminals that may be geographically dispersed throughout North America and Europe. Pontiac Division of General Motors, as an example, uses this service to provide up-to-date information to several thousand car dealers [1].

The network, as shown in the accompanying map (see Fig. 3), covers the United States, portions of Canada and Mexico, plus Europe. The configuration follows a hierarchical

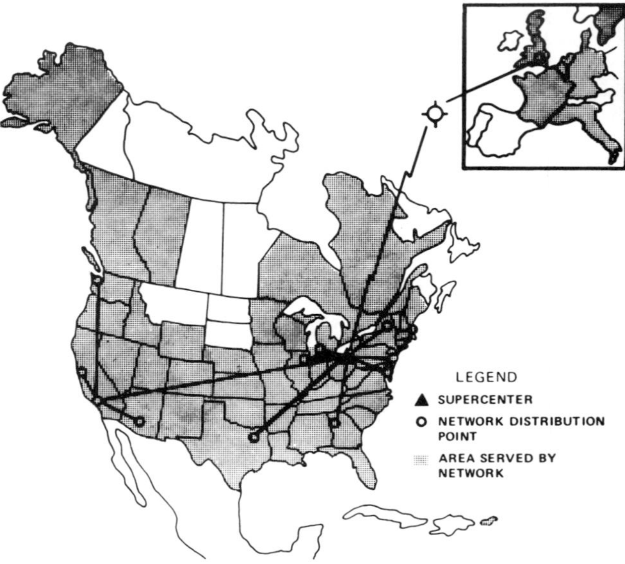

Fig. 3. GE network map.

or a tree-like structure: individual terminals are connected into remote concentrators located in 13 U. S. and 3 European cities. (These are indicated as distribution points in the map.) The remote concentrators are in turn connected to central concentrators located at the main computer center in Cleveland, Ohio. The central concentrators then access the computer systems that are at the heart of the network.

The approximately 50 remote concentrators consist of modified Honeywell 416's with 16K word (16-bit) memory. The concentrators have 48 ports connected to the public switched telephone network, via local loops, foreign exchange lines, or multiplexed lines. A customer wanting to access the network dials a number that connects him to an available port. At the periphery of the network there are some FDM multiplexers used that combine up to three ports before coming in, on a local loop, to the remote concentrator. Local telephone numbers are available in more than 250 cities.

Most of the communications cost of the network is in the local loops, and the remote concentrators are generally placed to reduce these costs. There may be several remote concentrators located in heavy load regions.

The remote concentrators are connected via full duplex 4800- or 9600-bit/s lines to the central concentrators in Cleveland. Two alternate paths or circuits are available to maintain reliability. The central concentrators consist of GEPAC 4020 computers. Each central concentrator may have a maximum of eight remote concentrators connected to it. A central concentrator in London, England, fed by three remote concentrators for European traffic, is also connected to the central concentrators in Cleveland. Satellite and underwater cable are used to provide the alternate-path reliability in this case.

Each central concentrator in turn is connected to a number of large computer systems. The number connected ranges from one to six and depends on the type of computer system. (Fewer Mark II systems will be served by the concentrator than Mark I systems. These terms are briefly explained in the following paragraphs.) Each central concentrator is also con-

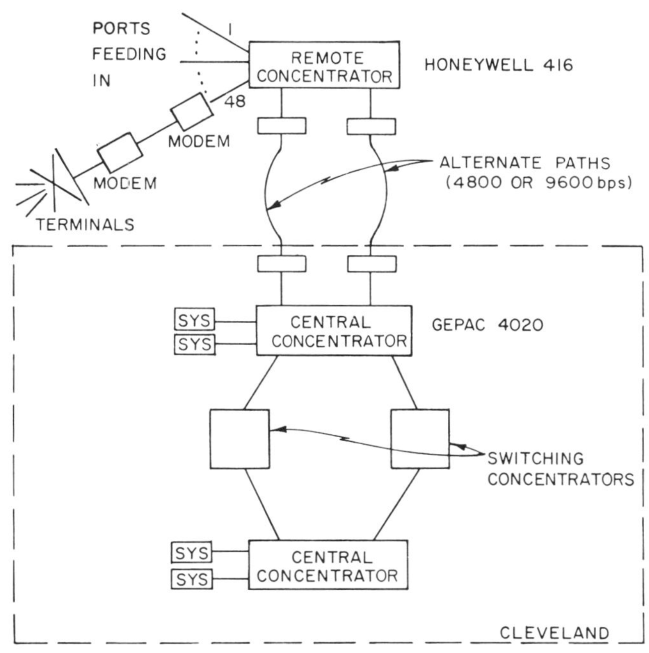

Fig. 4. GE network hierarchy.

nected to two switching concentrators located within the same building that connect users coming in on a particular central concentrator to the one associated with the computer system holding their files. The process is explained schematically in Fig. 4.

Four types of computational service are available from the system, each corresponding to a particular one of the computer systems previously noted.

1) Mark I time-shared services. This is essentially a problem-solving service. It handles the Basic language, some Algol, and a simple version of Fortran. This service is an outgrowth of the original Dartmouth-designed system. It is currently handled by Honeywell G-265 computers.

2) Mark II time-shared service. This is provided by a number of Honeywell G-635 computers. It is the largest and most used system in the network. The system is the outgrowth of a joint Dartmouth–GE project and was commercially introduced in 1968.

3) Mark Delta service. Provided by Honeywell G-605's, this is the most demanding system in terms of the customer's ability to program.

4) Resource service. This service provides remote batch processing plus some time-shared service and is handled by a Honeywell 6070 system.

In addition, a Mark III system is due to go on the air by the third quarter of 1972. In this system multiple Mark II's will be coupled to a Honeywell 6080 (a much larger machine) for batch processing.

Although the fundamental design of the current network grew out of the original Mark II time-sharing system developed at Dartmouth, the network, as it exists at present, is very different. As in the case of TYMNET discussed earlier, the network has essentially evolved in response to market demand and customer needs, with incremental changes made as required. It is a store-and-forward *message-switched* network, as will become apparent in the following section. The use of remote concentrators provides flexibility in accepting various types of user terminals and in adjusting to market demands.

Message Transmission

Any terminal transmitting up to 30 characters/s (300 bits/s) may be used to access this system. The remote concentrator will convert non-ASCII code inputs to ASCII, used throughout the system. Identification of the machine, speed, and code used is accomplished by typing in the letter **H**. The sign-on procedure consists of typing in this identifying character, followed by the user number. This number is forwarded by the remote concentrator to the central concentrator to which it is connected. Each central concentrator has a user table showing the central concentrator associated with the computer system responsible for each user, thus indicating the appropriate computer or central concentrator to which a particular user message should be forwarded. Following the user number a password is typed in. This is checked against the password stored in the user system to see if it is valid. The user is then ready for transmission.

User inputs are of two types generally. These consist of system-command and file-building-mode messages. The file-building mode begins with a line number. The characters following, up to 150 in number, and comprising a line, are stored in the remote concentrator message buffer. (Recent characters or the entire line may be deleted if the user desires.) 191
The line is concluded by depressing the carriage-return key, causing one or more messages of up to 36 characters to be transmitted, with appropriate overhead characters added to the appropriate computer system. (Note that this differs from the TYMNET format, in which messages from various users may be combined to form one block.) System-command messages with no line number at the beginning are handled as priority messages and sent right out as received. (There is no echoing in this system. Characters are printed by the *terminal* as soon as the key is depressed.)

The message buffer at the remote concentrator is dynamically managed, with space allocated to terminals that need it, on demand. Buffer allocation to any one terminal is based on terminal speed and mode. Messages flowing in either direction (user–computer or computer–user) use the same set of buffers and are provided the same buffer allocation. GE personnel indicate that the buffer sizes are quite sufficient with very little message queuing taking place at this point.

The message format, in block form, uses a modified version of the ASCII format [5]. It consists of 9 characters of overhead and from zero to 36 characters of text. The same format is used in both directions of data transmission. As shown in Fig. 5, the first 7 characters constituting the header consist, in order, of 1) an ASCII start-of-header (SOH) character, 2) the port number of the remote concentrator, 3) the number of the remote concentrator (R/C), 4) the length of text following, 5) type of message character, 6) a control character for setting up a function, and 7) the ASCII start-of-text (STX) character. The text then follows, and the block is concluded with an ASCII end-of-text (ETX) character and an error-detection character. (This final character is the EXCLUSIVE-ORed value of everything but itself.)

Messages are sent, a block at a time, from the remote concentrator to the central concentrator to which it is connected. The path used (of the two available) is the one which is free or the one not used for the last transmission. Each

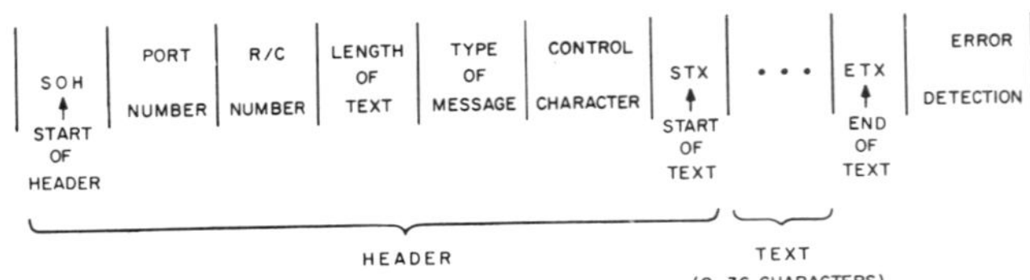

Fig. 5. GE network message format.

block is acknowledged as received by the transmission over the return path of a six-character acknowledgment block. This consists of six of the overhead characters in the standard message block (see Fig. 5)—the first three characters and the STX character of the header, plus the last two characters in the block. If an acknowledgment is not received, the remote concentrator retransmits the message. This automatically provides alternate path selection in the event of a noisy path or circuit. Since the remote concentrator selects the path of the two available that has been most recently vacant, a noisy circuit with a correspondingly increased number of retransmissions is vacant less often and is hence not used.

A second acknowledgment step is similarly carried out if the message must further be switched through the switching concentrators to a second central concentrator interfacing with the user's computer system. The switching concentrator remains transparent to this additional acknowledgment step. Each remote and central concentrator counts the number of retransmissions over each circuit, and every 30 min the central concentrator prints out on its own console a report on the condition of each circuit.

The process of transmitting a user message to a second central concentrator if necessary is first begun with the transmission of the user number, as indicated earlier. The central concentrator to which the user message is first transmitted (corresponding to the remote concentrator to which the user is connected) associates the user port and remote concentrator number with the first character of the user number. This character in the user table, available at each central concentrator, determines the central concentrator to which the user message should be switched. Once log-on is complete and the remote concentrator port-processor association has been established, further messages originating from the same port on the same remote concentrator are accorded the same routing. The message format in going through the switches is essentially the same as that of the transmission format between remote and central concentrators, with the addition of two delete characters added after the SOH character plus one character indicating the central concentrator for which it is destined. The switching concentrator ports are numbered to represent the destination central concentrators.

Traffic-Handling Capability

The maximum port capacity of the network as deployed in June 1972 was of the order of 2000 simultaneous users. This is of course the current maximum capacity. The message and routing disciplines used make it possible to expand the network indefinitely and to serve computers of many kinds which may be located at any major node.

To make sure the network can accommodate the traffic, there is a daily review of the network, in which the following four items are assessed: 1) the assignment of user numbers (and hence number of users) to each computer system, 2) the assignment of remote concentrators to central concentrators, 3) the assignment of ports to the remote concentrators, and 4) the deployment of ports.

Based on this assessment, the network topology may actually be changed daily. Thus a computer algorithm reassigns user numbers and remote concentrators daily in an attempt to balance the peak load of the machines. User file catalogs may thus be moved from machine to machine. The reassignments are also facilitated since all programs in the remote concentrators are loaded from the center. The last two items above are changed once a month, or more often if necessary.

The performance criterion used for the network provides a 95-percent probability of port availability on a Poisson basis at the local peak load, generally 2–3 P.M. local time. On this basis roughly 5–6 users can be accommodated per remote concentrator port, for a total of 10 000 individual users for the entire system. There are currently about 3000 firms with varying numbers of individual users validated for use of the network.

GE personnel indicate that response time throughout the network is negligible and is hence not used as a criterion of performance. The only significant queuing occurs within the computer systems themselves. Several queues may exist there, depending on the user's needs. (For example, there may be a queue of programs waiting to be processed.)

Some additional traffic statistics may be of interest. As in most such systems, the outbound traffic (computer–user) dominates. It runs typically 3–5 times the input speed. The average length of messages, outbound, runs 30 characters per line. Although most terminals currently used are 10-character/s units, a growing number are 30-character/s units. Terminal duty factors based primarily on outbound statistics run 70 percent—i.e., 7 character/s on 10-character/s terminals and 21 character/s on 30-character/s terminals.

The NASDAQ System [7], [8], [9]

How the System Is Used

The National Association of Securities Dealers Automated Quotations (NASDAQ) System is a computerized communications system, designed by Bunker–Ramo Corp., which makes available to its users a means of rapidly obtaining quotations on the bid and asked prices of over-the-counter securities. In addition, changes in these quotations, by specially designated users, are rapidly entered into the system.

Each security[2] in the over-the-counter market, which is regulated by the National Association of Securities Dealers, has assigned at least two but not more than 64 traders, specially approved as market makers. These market makers are responsible for individually establishing their own bid (buy) and ask (sell) prices for their security. They are committed to trade at least 100 shares of the security at their price. Previously, a trader receiving a request about a certain security would have to contact, by telephone, a number of the market makers in that security to determine their current prices and, after deciding the "best deal," recontact that market maker and complete the transaction. Often the trader would shorten this lengthy procedure by calling only several of the market makers. Frequently the prices would change before the trader could return to the market maker. Thus it was difficult and time consuming to determine all current prices in a security. Even representative bid and ask prices (median prices of all market makers in a security) were some-

[2] As of this writing there are 3000 securities in the NASDAQ system.

times several days old. As a consequence, there were often large differences between the prices of different market makers. The NASDAQ system, which began operation on February 8, 1971, was set up to automate this process.

Now a broker can type in the code name for a security on a special terminal and receive in seconds on a cathode-ray tube (CRT) display the current representative bid and ask prices. Terminals which are restricted to only this response are called Level I terminals and are not essentially part of the network. This, and other information, is also supplied periodically to the news media. Level II and III terminals receive, in addition to the representative bid and ask prices, the current bid and ask prices of each market maker in that security. If a bid price is requested, the market makers are listed in order of descending bid price. If an ask price is requested, they are listed in order of ascending ask prices.

For example, suppose a customer wants information on a particular security. He contacts his broker and immediately receives the current representative bid and ask price. If the customer wants to buy the stock, the broker contacts his trader, who, using a Level II or III terminal, types in the code name of the security and an "ask" symbol to denote that he wants the market makers listed in order of ascending ask price, i.e., the price at which the market maker will sell. The market makers' prices are displayed in frames of up to five market makers each. If there are more than five market makers in that security, the characters MOR are printed in the lower right half corner of the CRT, and the trader, by pressing a MOR key, can receive the prices of the next five market makers. This continues until all market makers are listed. If the trader wants to buy the stock from one of the market makers, he calls him on a telephone and arranges the transaction.

The Level III terminal, used by the market maker, has all the capabilities of a Level II terminal. In addition, the market maker can change the bid and ask prices in his securities. These changes are processed by the system in seconds.

Overall Network (Fig. 6)

The terminals (Levels II or III) are connected directly to over-the-counter control units (OCU's). There is one OCU in each brokerage office. Although the system is designed so that up to 24 terminals may be connected to each OCU, most offices have only a few terminals. The national average of terminals per OCU is 1.45 (1.75 in the Northeast, only 1.2 elsewhere). The terminals are relatively simple, consisting mainly of a specially designed keyboard and a CRT display. Most of the work is done in the OCU—buffering, message formatting, addressing, etc.

The OCU's are connected by leased full duplex 1600-bit/s multidrop lines to a concentrator. Each of these lines, called regional circuits, can accommodate up to 32 OCU's. Each concentrator can handle up to 48 regional lines. These design limitations, and the maximum number of terminals per OCU, are due to the addressing structure, the amount of storage, etc. If the entire capability were used, inordinate delays would result. Thus, to achieve adequate performance, the actual numbers are far below these maxima (see Table I).

The concentrators are located at four sites—New York, N. Y.; Chicago, Ill.; San Francisco, Calif; and Atlanta, Ga. These sites were chosen on the basis of expected customer density and were located at existing Bunker–Ramo locations to save on the cost of installation. Originally a concentrator at Dallas, Tex., was also planned, but after a network study it

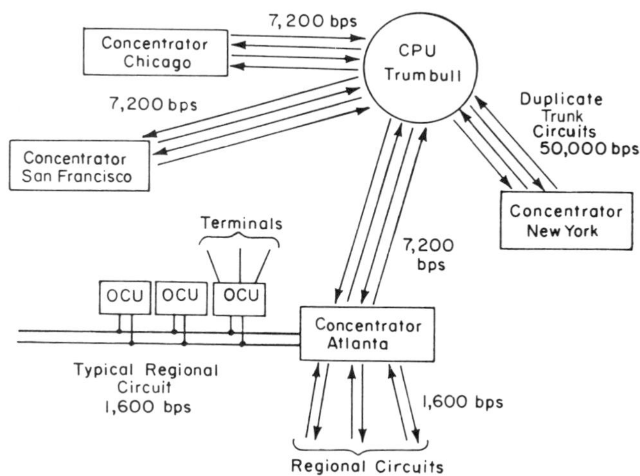

Fig. 6. The NASDAQ network.

TABLE I
NASDAQ SYSTEM CONFIGURATION

Concentrator Location	No. of Regional Circuits	No. of OCU's	No. of Terminals
New York	75	595	1045
Chicago	20	195	232
San Francisco	17	178	226
Atlanta	9	124	141
	121	1092	1644

193

was found that considerable savings resulted from merging this with the Atlanta facility. The concentrator sites in Chicago, San Francisco, and Atlanta consist of a pair of concentrators, each using a Honeywell DDP-516 computer, and other equipment. Both concentrators are always on line and share the traffic. For reliability the system is designed so that if any unit fails, the entire traffic can be handled by the remaining unit. The switchover can be accomplished in several minutes. The New York site contains four such concentrators and has the same redundancy capability. The concentrators poll the OCU's on each regional circuit, store the messages, control traffic to the CPU, and perform multiplexing and other communications tasks.

Each concentrator site is connected to the CPU by a pair of leased full duplex high-speed lines called trunk circuits. Again for redundancy either one of a pair of lines can handle the entire traffic if necessary. Furthermore, each of a pair of lines is diversely routed—connected over separate geographic paths. The trunks connecting New York to the CPU each have a capacity of 50 000 bits/s; the other trunks each have a capacity of 7200 bits/s. The CPU is located in Trumbull, Conn., and contains two UNIVAC 1108 multiprocessing computers, again operating redundantly so if necessary either one can handle the combined traffic. The CPU receives requests, searches its files, responds, updates quotations, and performs other operations of the system. The network is shown in Fig. 6.

Terminals and OCU's (Query Message)

The terminals consist mainly of a specially designed keyboard and a CRT display. A typical query (quote request) message (Level II or III) would be a bid or ask character and the four- or five-character code for a security. (A quote-change message by a market maker would require a slightly longer message. The ratio of quote requests to quote changes is approximately 20:1.) Since the connection between the terminals and the OCU's is asynchronous, the five characters are each 10 bits long—8 for the ASCII code, including 1 for parity, and 2 for start and stop. The OCU's have provisions for up to 24 buffers, one for each terminal, arranged in six delay lines of four buffers each. Thus each terminal has a specific fixed address in the OCU. Each delay line can store approximately 10 000 bits. (Since the reply (return) message is very much longer than the query message, and they always occur in pairs, the network is designed on the basis of the reply messages. The CRT has a maximum of six lines with 37 characters each and thus requires 2220 bits.) The OCU rapidly receives these characters from the keyboard and stores them in the appropriate buffer. This operation can be considered instantaneous. Once a query message is finished, indicated by an appropriate key on the terminal, the message at the OCU is ready to be transmitted to the appropriate concentrator.

The OCU appends to each query message of five characters one SOH character, two characters permanently identifying the brokerage office,[3] two characters identifying the OCU address and the terminal address, one more for control, the query message, one "end-of-transmission" (EOT) character, and a horizontal parity character—13 characters in all.

Concentrators (Query Message)

The OCU's are connected to their concentrators by full duplex asynchronous 1600-bit/s multidrop lines arrayed in several regional circuits. The concentrators have a single buffer for each regional circuit to be used for the query message only. The concentrators poll the OCU's on a regional line cyclically. The poll messages are two characters long—one character to initiate the polling request and a second used for addressing each OCU in turn. If a message is present, that message is transmitted to the concentrator; if not, then a one-character reply is sent to the concentrator. If more than one message is waiting at an OCU, only one of these is transmitted on a single poll. Once a query message is received by the concentrator, the polling stops on that regional circuit until that message is transmitted to the CPU. Furthermore, to prevent any OCU from dominating the traffic, an OCU will not be repolled until a response to an earlier query or an error message has been received. Additional features of the polling and multiplexing will be discussed when the reply message is considered. The concentrator inserts two characters into the message for concentrator and line address. Since the high-speed lines connecting the concentrators to the CPU are synchronous, each character is only 8 bits long—the start and stop bits are no longer needed. But three synchronication characters precede the message. Thus the message is a total of 18 characters.

CPU

The CPU is connected to each concentrator by a pair of full duplex synchronous high-speed 7200- (50 000- in New York) bit/s trunk lines. The CPU has a pair of separate input buffers (three input buffers for the lines from New York) for each trunk line. These buffers, each capable of storing 225 characters, are filled cyclically. Messages are routed over each pair of lines so as to equalize traffic. The CPU consists of two UNIVAC 1108 processors operating duplexed so that, again for reliability, if any one unit fails, the other can handle the entire load. Similarly, the drums for storing data are duplicated. In addition to its other functions—reporting of prices and indices to the media, supervision of trading, system control, etc.—the CPU receives quote requests, searches its memory for the appropriate security, formats the message comprising the prices for the particular frame of five market makers in appropriate order, and transmits the reply message. If a quote change message is received from a market maker, the files must be updated in that security, including a recomputation of the median bid and asked prices.

The first frame (first five market makers) in any security is more frequently requested than subsequent frames. Thus the first frame is always kept ready for transmission; subsequent frames must be formatted when requested. Furthermore, data for frequently requested securities are stored on readily accessible drums. Data for less active securities require additional time for retrieval. Typical times required for the CPU to respond to the various request messages are 4 ms to process the first frame of a quote request and 8 ms to process a quote request for subsequent frames or a quote change. In addition the average time required to retrieve the data from the files is 4 ms for a quote request and 8 ms for a quote change for active securities, and four or five times this for inactive securities. Thus the total time required by the CPU is, on the average, 8–50 ms.

The reply message is similar in form to the query message, except that the two permanent identification characters for the brokerage firm are not transmitted. The reply message is typically about 115 characters long. The CPU has a pool of 70 buffers, each 225 characters long, to store reply messages. If more than five messages are waiting to be transmitted to any one concentrator on any one trunk, then a message is sent to that concentrator to stop polling for a specified period of time. Typically, during a busy period, 20–30 of the buffers are occupied.

Reply Message

Each concentrator has a pool of 31 reply buffers. (The concentrators will transmit a query message to the CPU only if there is a reply buffer available.) The reply message is then transmitted to the appropriate OCU. An excessive delay would result if polling were to be suspended during the time a reply message is being transmitted from the concentrator to the OCU along the multidrop regional line. To alleviate this, a system of nested polling is used. Two-character polling messages are inserted into the reply message. A result of this entire procedure is that messages are made to wait at the OCU rather than the concentrator.

System Design and Performance

The network design (assignment of OCU's to regional circuits and regional circuits to concentrators) was based upon location of existing Bunker–Ramo facilities (for location of concentrators and CPU), estimates of numbers and locations of customers and frequency of use, and line tariffs for the trunk lines and the multidrop regional lines, taking into account differences between interstate and intrastate rates. Response times called for in the design were a response to a quote request or a quote change within 5 s 50 percent of the time and within 7 s 90 percent of the time. The quote files were to be updated within 5 s at least 95 percent of the time. The system design encompassed the indicated response time assuming a busy-time load of 28 calls/s system-wide.

The following peak statistics have been obtained: 1 262 000 calls on a very busy day, 240 000 calls during a busy hour, and

[3] The assignments of OCU's to regional circuits are infrequently changed to equalize traffic flow. These two characters provide permanent identification of the brokerage office for bookkeeping purposes. The next two characters identify the current physical address of the terminal and the OCU for message routing.

100 calls/s during a peak minute—67 from New York, 14 from Chicago, 12 from San Francisco, and 7 from Atlanta. On the average $1\frac{1}{2}$ calls/min are to be expected per terminal. Twice this number has been observed during peak periods, and even an extreme of 12 calls/min has been observed on a single very active terminal. A design rule of thumb that has been developed is that a limitation of 20 terminals per regional circuit will guarantee meeting of response time specifications. Even during observed peak activity the system is still performing satisfactorily. During such peak activity, however, trunk line redundancy may be lost in certain areas for a certain time period if one of a pair fails, but in this event there is a dial-up capability which is used as a second-level backup. In sum, the system seems to be well designed and can even handle traffic well in excess of what it was designed for.

INFONET

Introduction

INFONET is a remote computing system conceived and designed by Computer Sciences Corporation in response to the requirement for a versatile remote computing environment which would fulfill the needs of a wide spectrum of user-oriented requirements. The INFONET system architecture and communication network are based upon the objective of providing service to both conversational (10–30 characters/s) and remote job entry (2000–8000 bits/s) terminals in a single integrated system and the ability of the network to evolve to the next generation of hardware, software, and communications.

INFONET has been in full commercial operation in the United States since January, 1970, and also has networks installed in Canada, Australia, and South Africa. Since the initial operation, the network has expanded geographically, and a second-generation oprating system and enhanced communication network have been installed. INFONET was recently selected by the General Services Administration to be a unified supplier of nationwide teleprocessing services for Federal agencies.

The operating system for INFONET is known as the Computer Sciences Teleprocessing System. This system was specifically designed to avoid partitioning of resources to support multiple operating modes, but to allow all hardware capabilities, operating-system features, language processors, application programs, and data files to be available for both interactive and batch processing without special user action. To support the single integrated-system concept, the communication network for both low-speed conversational access and high-speed batch was designed and implemented as a single common network.

Two principal programming subsystems are used—the BASIC subsystem and the General Programming Subsystem (GPS). Both systems have access to the full computing resource and the same files. BASIC is an enhanced version of the Dartmouth College BASIC. GPS includes several language processors: Fortran IV, Fortran V, Cobol, Data Management Language, Program Checkout Facility, and an Assembler.

INFONET currently uses six UNIVAC 1108 computers in the network. The 1108 has a main storage capacity of 10^6 characters, which is augmented by a magnetic drum subsystem. Immediate-access storage is provided by a Multiple Disk Drive subsystem. Dual access and multiple drives provide improved reliability. Additional storage is provided by eight magnetic tape drives per 1108 with support for both seven- and nine-track recording formats.

Communications Network

The computer centers are in Washington, D. C., Chicago, and Los Angeles. Each location contains from one to three 1108's and associated peripherals. Each functions as a regional center serving several major metropolitan cities via communications concentrators and multiplexers. In addition, the Los Angeles center serves as the national center, providing access on a nationwide basis to customers with requirements for access to common data bases and files from geographically dispersed locations throughout the country. By designing a nationwide system with only three centers and multiple computers per center, INFONET is more dependent upon a reliable communictions network than it would be had it elected to place a single main frame in each of numerous centers. Principal motivations for the small number of centers were the higher reliabilities and longer operating hours achievable with such a configuration, greater flexibility, and user access to common files from diverse locations. Efficient utilization of existing common-carrier facilities also renders this a more economical choice. Recall that both the TYMNET and GE Information Service Networks used a small number of centers as well (see Figs. 1 and 3).

A map of the INFONET communication network is shown in Fig. 7. Only the major cities and the backbone network are shown. The number of circuits connecting each remote branch to a computer center is not indicated; a minimum of two diversely routed circuits are provided. INFONET utilizes one network with common hardware for all comunications—both low-speed asynchronous requirements and high-speed remote batch terminal needs. In order to provide highly versatile communications, a special concentrator was necessary. This led to the design and development of the Remote Communications Concentrator (RCC). The RCC serves as the communications interface for the network and functions as a combination of statistical multiplexer, incremental front end, and error-control device.

A functional diagram showing the essential elements of the INFONET network and their relation to the RCC is shown in Fig. 8. In Fig. 8, City *A* represents a typical major branch location. Users with low-speed terminal devices in the metropolitan area of City *A* would place a local (toll-free) call to the low-speed access rotary. As in the GE and TYMNET systems described previously, a variety of low-speed data terminals will be handled by this system. Upon hearing the tone from the low-speed data set at the RCC (Bell 103E5 or 113B), the user types a single character. The RCC will use this character to determine the terminal speed and code type. Currently, INFONET supports ASCII code at 110, 150, and 300 bits/s (10, 15, and 30 characters/s), and IBM Correspondence and EBCD codes at 134.2 bits/s (14.8 characters/s). All terminal devices compatible with these code descriptions may be used with the INFONET system.

Once the RCC has identified the code and terminal type, the user may sign on the system and perform his desired tasks. RCC software converts all terminal codes to ASCII; This relieves the central computer of performing any code translation tasks.

In addition to providing access for low-speed terminals, the RCC accommodates high-speed (2000 bits/s), remote job entry (RJE) dual access (2000 bits/s), high-speed RJE with dedicated lines (up to 4800 bits/s), and multiplexer ports. Currently, the network supports all remote terminals (card-reader, card-punch, and line-printer) which are compatible with the 2780 Binary Synchronous Communication discipline.

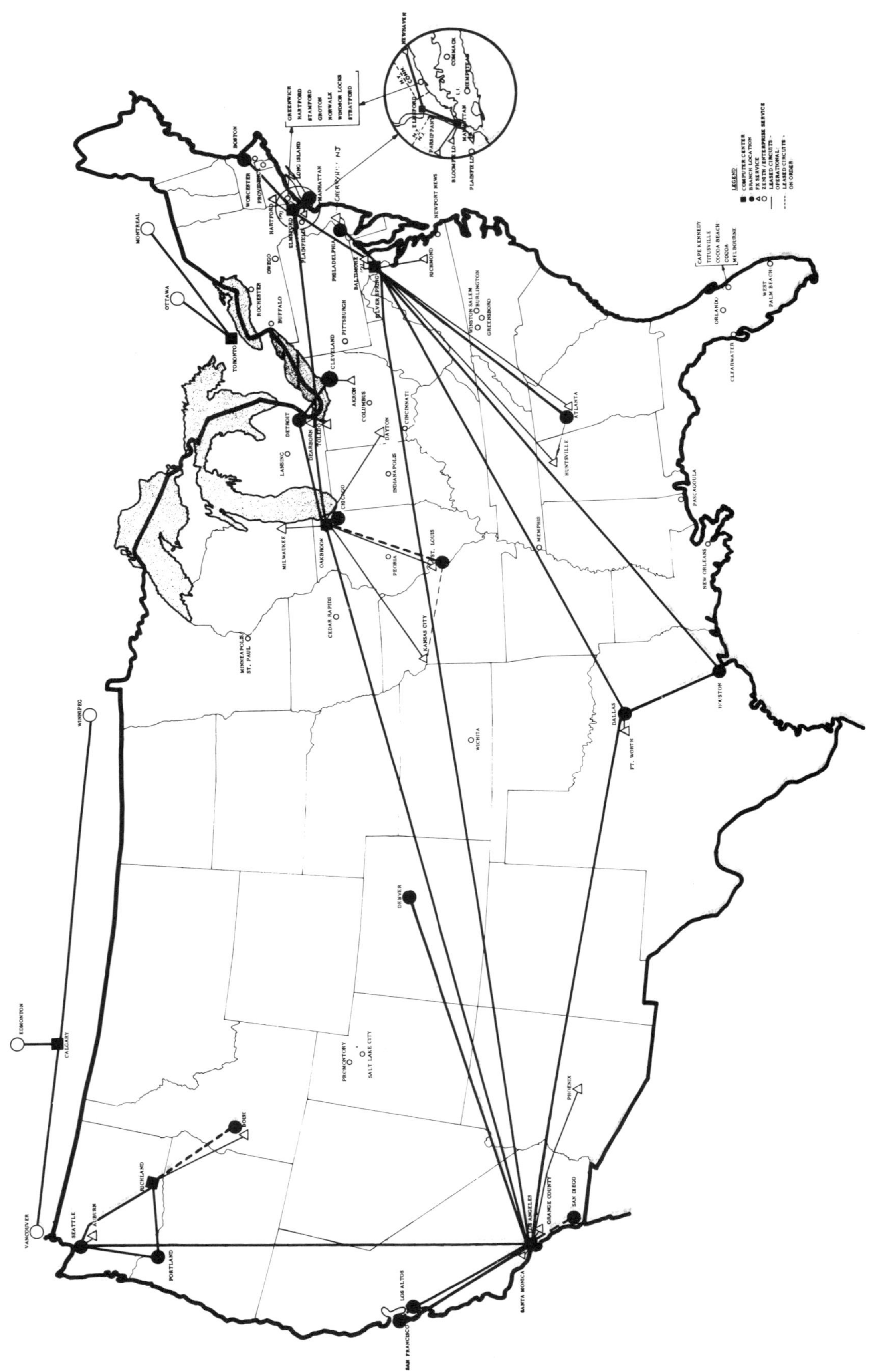

Fig. 7. INFONET communications networks.

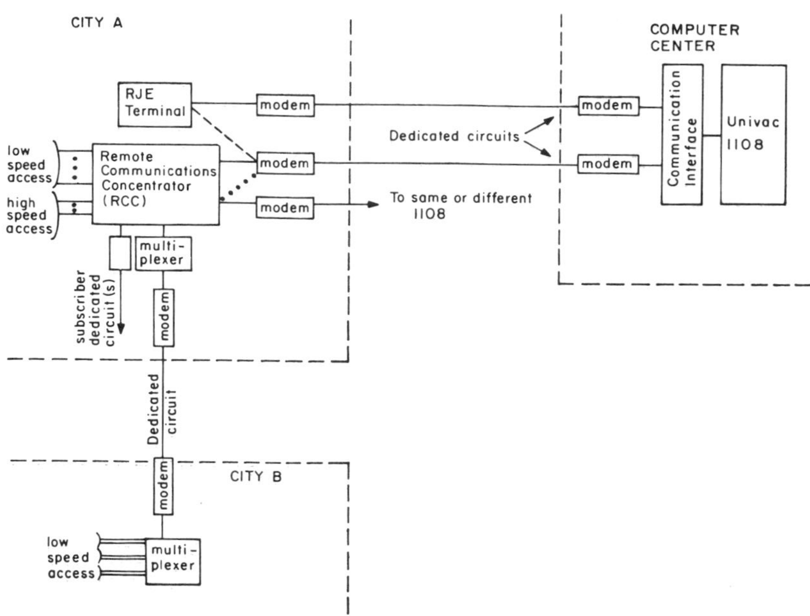

Fig. 8. Functional schematic of INFONET.

Other disciplines may be accommodated by adding a new high-speed terminal handler (software) in the RCC.

High-speed dial access permits users with their own RJE terminals to access INFONET via a local call and a standard Bell System 201A data set (or equivalent). Users with a requirement for a dedicated RJE circuit may interface the RCC via standard Bell leased circuits and either Bell or non-Bell modems.

As depicted in Fig. 8, the RCC may also be used as an interface for multiplexer links. Typically, cities with smaller traffic requirements will be served by a multiplexer with evolution to an RCC as usage demands. INFONET uses time-division multiplexers in conjunction with high-speed synchronous modems for these applications. The multiplexers are synchronous character-oriented devices with frame division such that 10-, 15-, and 30-character/s inputs are accommodated. Since the multiplexers do not have provision for automatic speed and code detection, separate telephone rotary groups are provided for each of the various terminal classes served.

The multiplexers are connected to the nearest RCC via a dedicated circuit and synchronous modems. Forward error correction is used on certain multiplexer links to overcome transmission errors. The code is a rate-$\frac{3}{4}$ convolutional burst correcting code. The transmission rate is 4800 bits/s with an information rate of 3600 bits/s. The burst correction interval (i.e., the span over which all errors are guaranteed to be corrected) is selectable at 32, 64, 128, 256, 512, or 1024 bits; this choice is dependent upon channel characteristics. The longer correction intervals introduce greater delays into the system; a correction interval of 256 bits is normally used.

The primary communication link from the RCC to the 1108 is a Bell System C2 dedicated full duplex circuit. The transmission rate (modem speed) is selected according to anticipated input load. Currently, transmission rates of 4800, 7200, and 9600 bits/s are used. The software and hardware has been designed to accommodate higher rates; however, these have not been utilized to date because of adverse performance and economies of remote transmission above 9600 bits/s. RCC's which are located together with an 1108 may operate at 19 200 bits/s since there is no complex modem/transmission path to be considered.

As indicated in Fig. 8, each INFONET branch office has a high-speed RJE terminal. This terminal may communicate with the central computer either via dedicated circuits or directly interfaced with the RCC. Typically, a separate diversely routed circuit is used, with this circuit serving as a backup for the RCC. (In this case, the RJE terminal would use the dial-up backup which has been provided.) In all cases, an INFONET branch has at least two dedicated diversely routed circuits (to increase overall reliability) connecting the branch location to the central computer site.

Further flexibility is achieved by the multiple trunk capability of the RCC. As shown in Fig. 8, the RCC can serve two distinct high-speed trunks. This facilitates access to two distinct 1108's from the same RCC. For example, users in city A could access either the regional center or the national center depending upon their specific requirements. Similarly, the dual high-speed trunks may be connected to the same 1108 if required by capacity considerations. This same functional capability may be achieved in cities served by multiplexers. This is obviously less efficient than the RCC implementation but is used if that functional capability is required for a particular city.

This network has been designed to facilitate load balancing in a way similar to that previously described in the GE system. If one central processor becomes heavily loaded, one or more RCC's serving that processor may be shifted to another 1108. User files are transferred on an overnight basis, the communications are realigned, and the shift is accomplished unknown to the user.

The network was designed to facilitate a logical evolution of hardware in each city. The most economical means of servicing a given load is a complex function of statistics of the user population, distance from the central computer site, and other RCC's and intra- and interstate tariffs. A general

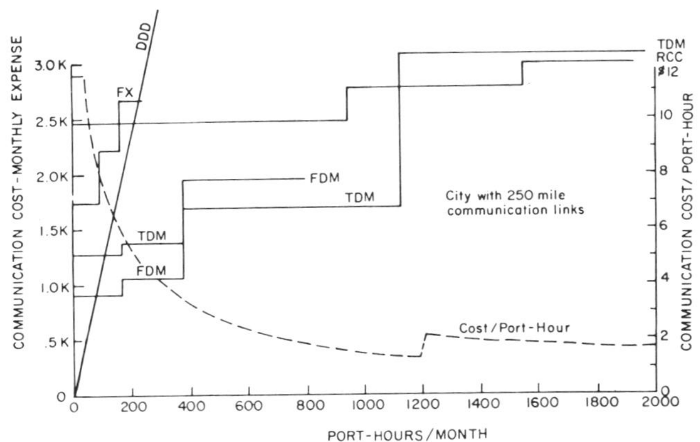

Fig. 9. Economics of data communications—Summary.

evolution within a city may be from Direct Distance Dialing (DDD) to Foreign Exchange (FX), to time-division multiplexing (TDM) and/or frequency-division multiplexing (FDM), and finally to an RCC. Calculations as to the economics of network growth, characteristic of all the networks described in this paper, may be carried out on the basis of curves such as those given in Fig. 9.

Fig. 9 illustrates an example of the basic economic trade-offs for a city which requires 250-mi communication links. The abscissa is a measure of incoming load and is expressed in port-hours per month. Loading and rotary capacities are based upon Erlang B statistics with a daily peak-to-average ratio of 1.8 and a design busy probability of 0.05 during the peak hour. The step functions are points at which new hardware is assumed to be added to meet capacity requirements. The ordinate shows monthly expense for this example; interstate tariffs, hardware amortization, and local data service are included.

The dashed line in Fig. 9 is referenced to the right-hand ordinate. This line shows the locus of minima and is normalized to cost per port hour. This curve shows the high "startup" cost for providing service in a new location. Similar relationships may be obtained for different distances; the relationships become more complex as adjacent RCC's and multipoint networks are considered. Hence the above should be viewed as illustrative of the considerations involved but not construed as a "design chart."

As is true of other networks, operational reliability is of paramount importance in the network operation. Incorporated as an integral part of the network design were such aspects as extensive fault isolation, on-line performance monitoring, instrumentation, and redundancy. On-line performance monitoring includes both hardware and software means. The objective is to sense circuit degradation before it becomes sufficiently adverse and affects user terminal performance. Communication hardware used in the network contains complete loopback facilities to facilitate fault isolation. For example, high-speed modems have both analog and digital transmit and receive loopback.

Remote Communications Concentrator (RCC)

The RCC was built for INFONET by Comten Corp. and is designated the Comten-20. The Comten-20 has a maximum core memory size of 65K bytes, which may be incrementally increased in 16K-byte modules. Typical INFONET configurations use 48K words with variations determined by such factors as total load and conversational bulk-terminal mix. Cycle time of the Comten-20 is 900 ns.

The Comten-20 communication interfaces are designated Modem Interface Modules. A combination of asynchronous and synchronous modules are used to interface with the range of terminals and speeds supported by INFONET. The modules provide the necessary timing, data-set interfacing, automatic answering, and error checking (either cyclic redundancy check or longitudinal/vertical parity checking) required to interface the communications network with the RCC software.

One of the more important and interesting functional characteristics of the software is the combined ability to allocate buffers dynamically and provide a temporary choke mechanism. This choke mechanism permits operation at high trunk utilizations without the inherent risk of buffer overflow which is characteristic of statistical multiplexing. As a function of buffer filling and trunk utilization, the RCC will automatically slow down the terminals by appropriate action. As either input or output to the RCC approaches capacity, RCC buffers will "choke down" and reduce terminal transmission rate. For example, the apparent print rate of an RJE terminal may be temporarily slowed down by a small percentage in order that conversational terminals may not be affected.

As evidenced by the description of the network, the RCC is the key element of the INFONET communication system; there are currently about 25 RCC's in the network. They are the major "building blocks" which provide both the flexibility and the capacity for network expansion.

A major aspect of the flexibility of the RCC arises from its ability to interface with low-speed, high-speed, and multiplexer inputs. For example, in Fig. 8, routing the lower traffic density of city *B* via the RCC in city *A* is substantially more economical than routing that traffic directly to the computer center if city *B* is considerably closer to city *A* than to the computer center.

The statistical (asynchronous) multiplexing function of the RCC permits a much more efficient dedicated circuit utilization than synchronous TDM, which is, in itself, more efficient than FDM. The RCC realizes this efficiency by taking advantage of the statistical nature of both inbound (toward the computer) and outbound (toward the terminal) data. For a representative discussion of statistics of time-sharing systems inbound and outbound traffic, the reader is referred to [11]. Experience at INFONET has shown that inbound traffic statistics are evolving from those presented in [11] to a higher utilization per input terminal; this is attributed to the increased use of higher speed asynchronous devices (e.g., 30-character/s CRT devices) and increased use of magnetic tape cassettes. The net effect is a requirement for increased buffer space in the RCC.

The RCC provides sufficient high-speed trunk buffer space to permit a complete full duplex error-control system. Data in both inbound and outbound directions are formatted in variable length blocks which may contain up to 2048 information bits. Positive and negative acknowledgments (ACK/NAK) are embedded in data blocks to reduce message-acknowledgment time. All blocks are verified as correct by either the 1108 communications interface (see Fig. 8) or the RCC, depending upon the direction. This positive error detection and retransmission facilitates the use of higher speed data transmission between RCC and 1108. That is, while bit error probabilities increase at the higher data rates (7200 and 9600 bits/s), the block throughput remains on the order of 99 percent and the net effect is transparent to the user. In addition, the use of the higher data rates is a more efficient use of a standard voice grade leased circuit.

A very significant system feature made possible by the RCC is the shielding of the user from temporary communication or system problems. During such problem periods, the user will observe a "STANDBY" message but will not be "dropped off" the system. Upon correction of the trouble condition, the user may resume his session (The system will even inform him of the last valid transmission.)

The RCC is designed so that the software can be remote-loaded from the central computer site. This capability is important since many remote sites are INFONET sales offices which are not staffed on a 24-h basis. Operations personnel may remote-load (bootstrap) the remote RCC and restore it to operation after a major communications outage, computer failure, or normal shutdown. Similarly, RCC software changes may be made without visiting the RCC physical location to perform the change. This remote loading is a special mode of operation in which the 1108 commands the RCC to consider a block of information as an executable program rather than as data to be sent on to a terminal.

The capacity of the RCC, expressed in terms of number of simultaneous users, is a complex function of user input and output statistics; a mix of low-speed, asynchronous, and high-speed RJE terminals; buffer size; and high-speed trunk capacity. Typically, INFONET RCC's are configured for a maximum of eight RJE ports and 64 low-speed ports. High-speed trunks range from 4800–9600 bit/s. The precise configuration for any specific location depends upon the customer mix and projected growth.

The RCC capacity is essntially limited only by the high-speed trunk capacity and not by any number of physical input ports. Because of this, it is difficult to discuss the number of "terminals" supported by a single RCC. Experience has shown that the 48 low-speed/4 high-speed configuration results in an inbound and outbound statistical distribution of the composite information rate which is at or below the trunk maximum data rates and thereby provides the design performance.

Since the state of the art of statistical or asynchronous multiplexing is quite new, the RCC was heavily instrumented to maintain continually good performance. The work of Chu [12] was used as a guide during the design. However, the multiple tandem buffers used in the RCC software lead to unsolved problems of queuing theory. Hence the approach was to parameterize the design so that optimization could occur as buffer interaction became known, based upon observed behavior. The RCC collects statistics on buffer usage and error rates and reports these statistics to the 1108 for subsequent analysis.

Diagnostics have been provided in the RCC to assist in problem analysis. There is a remote dump program which the central computer can load into the RCC, in case of a software error; the content of the core is then communicated back to the central computer. It is also possible to diagnose certain RCC hardware faults by a remote diagnostic program. The RCC was designed so that it can be used either remotely or as described above or located together with the 1108; location is transparent to the operating system. Because of this design concept, it was not necessary to provide a local "front-end" computer for the 1108—the RCC provides all required functions; hence a user's transmission is always routed via only one RCC. This concept provides fewer queues than there would be if the concentrators were concatenated, and therefore tends to provide shorter response times.

Conclusions

This paper has presented descriptions of four representative terminal-oriented computer-communication networks. All four have been operational for some time now and are continually in a state of growth and modification. The GE and TYMNET systems evolved from remote conversational-mode computing systems; INFONET was designed from the beginning to handle remote job entry and batch processing along with conversational general computing, while NASDAQ had the narrower objective of remote automatic quotation and updating of files. Nevertheless, the communication-network features of all four show a great similarity in structure and function. A key component in all the networks is a programmable concentrator which not only permits more economical use of the communication lines, but affords the opportunity to do the vital communication tasks such as buffering, line control, message assembly and formatting, error control, and traffic control. The concentrators, whether remote or located at the central computer site, handle virtually all the communications functions of the network, leaving both the user and the computer free to perform their primary tasks. In addition, since the concentrators (which are essentially minicomputers) are programmable, they can
be modified to accommodate any new needs that arise in the 199
network. All of the networks contain considerable sophisticated software for network control, which was only lightly touched upon in the paper.

The evolution of computer-communication networks such as those described in this paper and others is progressing at a very rapid rate, and the pressure is constant to expand the network and add new features. For example, because of the adaptability of software as contrasted with hardware, there will likely be a tendency to replace hardware devices with programmable ones. The trend has been established, and the movement toward more "intelligent" terminals and concentrators will be inexorable.

There is already pressure to introduce network features such as higher speed dialup, positive error control complete from terminal to computer, higher speed asynchronous terminals (120 characters/s), and even provisions for computer-to-computer communications with all the potential for file and load sharing. Virtually all the existing networks today rely on leased lines from the common carriers such as AT&T. The evolution of the special service carriers such as DATRAN and MCI may have a significant impact not only on the growth of the networks, but on the design philosophy. This would be especially true if the tariffs were based on the number of bits transferred rather than monthly cost of a voice grade line. The economic factors (principally communications costs) play a dominant role in the design of these networks. Finally, the introduction of domestic communication satellites within the next five years is certain to play a part in shaping data networks.

Acknowledgment

The authors wish to thank the following individuals for help in the preparation of this article: M. P. Beere, Tymshare, Inc.; N. C. Sullivan, Tymshare, Inc.; Dr. R. C. Raymond, General Electric Co.; M. Sumner, Bunker–Ramo Corp.; Dr. G. Harrison, Bunker–Ramo Corp.; Dr. H. Frank, Network Analysis Corp.; and Dr. P. Tenkhoff, Computer Sciences Corp.

References

[1] E. C. Gaines, Jr., and J. M. Taplin, "The emergence of national networks: Remote computing—Year VI," *Telecommunications*, p. 27, Dec. 1971.

[2] M. P. Beere and N. C. Sullivan, "TYMNET—A serendipitous evolution," *IEEE Trans. Commun.*, vol. COM-20, pp. 511–515, June 1972.

[3] L. Tymes, "TYMNET—A terminal oriented communications network," Tymshare, Inc., Internal Memo.; also in *AFIPS Conf. Proc.*, vol. 38, 1971.

[4] J. F. Ossanna, "Identifying terminals in terminal-oriented systems," *IEEE Trans. Commun.*, vol. COM-20, pp. 565–568, June 1972.

[5] S. R. Rosenblum, "Progress in control procedure standardization," in *Proc. ACM/IEEE 2nd Symp. Problems in the Optimization of Data Communications Systems* (Palo Alto, Calif.), pp. 153–159, Oct. 1971.

[6] "The long arm of teleprocessing networks," *ADP Newslett.*, vol. 15, June 14, 1971.

[7] M. Sumner, "What is NASDAQ?" *Bus. Commun. Rev.*, vol. 1, pp. 23–28, Nov.-Dec. 1971.

[8] N. Mills, "NASDAQ—A user-driven, real time transaction system," in *Spring Joint Computer Conf., AFIPS Conf. Proc.* Washington, D. C.: Spartan, 1972, pp. 1197–1206.

[9] H. Frank, I. T. Frisch, and R. Van Slyke, "Testing the NASD automated quotation system," in *Proc. Symp. Computer-Communications Networks and Teletraffic* (Polytech. Inst. of Brooklyn, Brooklyn, N. Y.), Apr. 1972.

[10] "Switching networks and traffic concepts," in *Reference Data for Radio Engineers*, 5th ed. Indianapolis: Howard W. Sams and Co., 1968, Ch. 31, pp. 31-11–31-16.

[11] P. E. Jackson and C. D. Stubbs, "A study of multiaccess computer communications," in *1969 Spring Joint Computer Conf., AFIPS Conf. Proc.*, vol. 34. Washington, D. C.: Spartan, 1969, pp. 491–504.

[12] W. W. Chu, "A study of asynchronous time division multiplexing for time-sharing computer systems," in *1969 Fall Joint Computer Conf., AFIPS Conf. Proc.*, vol. 35. Washington, D. C.: Spartan, 1969, pp. 669–678.

[13] D. R. Doll, "Multiplexing and concentration," this issue, pp. 1313-1321.

[14] C. B. Newport and J. Ryzlak, "Communication processors," this issue, pp. 1321–1332.

[15] D. L. Mills, "Communications software," this issue, pp. 1333–1341.

[16] H. Frank and W. Chou, "Topological optimization of computer networks," this issue, pp. 1385–1397.

Reprinted by permission from *Proceedings of the IEEE* Vol. 60, No. 11, November 1972, pp. 1408-1423

Extensions of packet communication technology to a hand held personal terminal

by LAWRENCE G. ROBERTS

Advanced Research Projects Agency
Arlington, Virginia

INTRODUCTION

Electronic communications technology has developed historically almost completely within what might be called the circuit switching domain. Not until the last decade has the other basic mode of communication, packet switching, become competitive. Thus, as a technology, packet communication has only begun to be explored. Circuit switching can be defined in the broad sense as the technique of establishing a complete path between two parties for as long as they wish to communicate, whereas packet switching is where the communication is broken up into small messages or packets, attaching to each packet of information its source and destination and sending each of these packets off independently and asynchronously to find its way to the destination. In circuit switching all conflicts and allocations of resources must be made before the circuit can be established thereby permitting the traffic to flow with no conflicts. In packet switching there is no dedication of resources and conflict resolution occurs during the actual flow perhaps resulting in somewhat uneven delays being encountered by the traffic. Clearly, without the speed and capability of modern computers, circuit switching represented a cheaper and more effective way to handle communications. For radio frequency assignment and telephone exchanges the resource allocation decisions could be made infrequently enough that manual techniques were originally sufficient. Also, since voice was the main information being communicated, the traffic statistics were sufficiently compatible with this approach to make it quite economic for the period. Packet switching of a kind, the telegram, persisted throughout this period but due to the high cost of switching and the limited demand for fast message traffic never attracted much attention.

For almost a century circuit switching dominated the communications field and thus dominated the development of communications theory and technology. Now, within the last decade or less, the advances in digital computers and electronics have, in many cases, reversed the economic balance between circuit and packet communication technology. Perhaps the best proof of this is the economy of the ARPA Network[1–6] for country-wide computer to computer communication, but many other examples are beginning to appear such as the University of Hawaii's ALOHA System[7] utilizing packet radio transmission for console communications and the experiments with digital loops for local distribution. However, most of the experiments with packet communications have been undertaken by computer scientists, and it is not even generally recognized yet in the communications field that a revolution is taking place. Even where the knowledge of one of these experiments has penetrated the communications field, it is generally written off as a possibly useful new twist in communications utilization, and not recognized as a very different technology requiring a whole new body of theory. Throughout the development of the ARPA Network, communication engineers compared it with conventional circuit switched systems but, perhaps unconsciously, used rules of thumb, statistics and experience applicable only to circuit switched systems as a basis for comparison. A century of experience and tradition is not easy to ignore and in fact should not be ignored, only it should be properly classified and segregated as resulting from a different technology.

Packet communication technology is only beginning to be explored but already it is clear that the design of all forms of communications channels and systems should be rethought. As an example of the kind of difference packet communications can make in a perhaps unexpected area, the design of a personal terminal will be explored in some detail. Although such a terminal has never been built, it is most likely completely feasible to build and would provide many unique advantages.

201

Reprinted from AFIPS Conference Proceedings, SJCC

HAND HELD PERSONAL TERMINAL

Let us start with the goal of providing each individual with a pocket-sized, highly reliable and secure communications device which would permit him to send and receive messages to other individuals or to coputers. Leaving the consideration of design alternatives muntil the end, a device fulfilling these objectives is as follows:

Output

Text or graphics displayed on a 2.8″×1″ plasma panel with 80 dots per inch resolution. The screen, divided into 7×10 dot rectangles, using 5×7 characters would hold 8 lines of 32 characters each for a total of 256 characters. Text this size is almost the same size as typewriter print, except that the lines are closer together. The plasma panel has internal storage and is digitally addressed to write or erase a point.

Input

Five capacity or stress sensitive buttons used by the five fingers of one hand simultaneously to indicate one of 31 characters. This five finger keyboard technique was developed by Doug Englebart at SRI[8] to permit users to type with only one hand while working on a display console. Recently the keyboard has become fairly widely used at SRI due to its great convenience. Training time for a new user is evidently less than a day and speeds of 30 words per minute can be achieved.[9] Although somewhat slower than a good typist (½ speed) the speed is clearly sufficient for a terminal device even at 10 words/minute.

Transmission

Each input character will be transmitted to a central controller station using the random access radio transmission techniques developed at the University of Hawaii.[7] The 5 bit character is embodied in a 64 bit packet containing:

30 bits—Terminal Identification Number
8 bits—Character plus alternation bit, or Count
2 bits—Type of packet (CHAR, ACK, CNT, ERR, ST ERR)
24 bits—Cyclic Sum Check
64 bits

All terminals transmit their packets independently and asynchronously on a single frequency and the receiver at the central controller merely listens for a complete packet which has a correct sum check. If two terminals' transmissions overlap the sum check will be wrong, and the terminals will retransmit when they find they don't receive an acknowledgment. Retransmission time-out intervals are randomized between the terminals to avoid recurrence of the problem. Upon receipt of a good packet, the central station transmits a display-acknowledgment packet back to the terminal on a second frequency. This 144 bit packet contains a 70 bit display raster field and an 8 bit position on the screen. The display raster is a 7×10 dot array for the character sent in and the position includes 3 bits for vertical by 5 bits for horizontal. Current position information for each active user is kept by the central station by user ID in a hash table. Thus, the individual terminal needs no character generation logic, position advancement logic, or any other local verification of the input since the response from the central station both acknowledges the character and displays it in an input text line at the top of the display. If a character display-acknowledgment is somehow lost in transmission the terminal will continue to time-out and retransmit the character. The central station must somehow differentiate this from a new character. This is achieved by an alternation bit[10,11] in the terminal's packet which is complemented for each *new* character. On a repeat the bit is the same as previously and the central station just retransmits the same character and position again. When a prearranged terminating character is sent the central station examines the message and takes an appropriate action. Considerable flexibility exists here, and operational modes could be established. However, the first message of a sequence should contain a destination as the first item. This might be the ID of another terminal in the same area, it might be the address of a service computer or it might be the ID of another terminal halfway around the world. In the latter two cases, a more global network such as the ARPA Network comes into play. It would be perfectly feasible for a message to another terminal to be sent to a central or area-coded directory computer to locate the particular control station the other terminal was near. Note that the location of neither man was given to the other, only the message and the ID of the sender. (Based on ARPA Network cost estimates and international satellite tariff trends, such a message exchange should cost less than 0.1 cents, independent of distance.)

Reception

At any time when a message destined for a terminal arrives at the central control station, a transmission to the terminal may begin, character by character, each in its own 144 bit packet as follows:

30 bits—Terminal Identification Number
70 bits—7×10 dot pattern, character display
8 bits—position of character
1 bit —alternation bit
1 bit —broadcast mode
3 bits—Message Type (Response, initial, normal)
8 bits—Characters Left in message
24 bits—Cyclic Sum Check
144 bits

The terminal must always be checking all transmission to detect those with its ID and a correct sum check. When one occurs which is not a "response" to an input character, a message is being sent. The first character of a message is marked type "initial," and has the count of the remaining characters. Each character is displayed where the central station placed it. Following the "initial" character "normal" characters are checked to make sure the count only decreases by one each time. After the character with count zero, an acknowledgment type packet is sent by the terminal. If this is lost (as it may be due to conflicts) the central control will retransmit the final character over again without complementing the alternation bit until it is acknowledged (or it determines the station is dead). If a count is skipped the terminal sends a CNT ERR message with the count of the character expected. The transmitter then starts over at that count. If a "normal" type character is received before an "initial" type a ST ERR message is sent and the message is restarted. A broadcase bit is included which overrides the ID check for general messages.

Security

Since all transmissions are digital, encryption is possible and would be important no matter what the application, military or civilian. Most private uses such as personal name files, income-expense records, family conversations, etc., would be far more sensitive than current computer console use.

Bandwidth

Personal terminals for occasional use for message exchange, maintaining personal files, querying computer data bases for reference data, etc., would not lead to very heavy use, probably no more than two query-responses per hour. The query we might estimate at 64 characters in length and the response at 256. (Clearly 256 character response could also consist of an 80× 224 point graphic display since each character is sent as a full 7×10 raster.) The average bandwidth consumed by each terminal is therefore 2.3 bits/second transmitted and 25.6 bits/second received. The random access technique used for transmission requires the channel bandwidth to be six times the average bandwidth actually utilized in order to resolve all conflicts properly. Thus, the terminal transmission bandwidth consumption is 14 bits/second, still less than the receiver bandwidth needed. Thus, the central control station's transmitter bandwidth is the limiting factor assuming equal bandwidths on both transmitter and receiver. If a 50KHz bandwidth is used for each and modulated at 50K bits/sec, then a total of 2000 terminals can be accommodated. Of course this number depends on the activity factor. At one interaction every two minutes a data rate equal to average time shared console use is obtained and even at this activity 130 terminals can be supported, more than most time-sharing systems can support. With 50 KB channels, the time required to
write 256 characters is about one second. Lower band- 203
widths require increased time, thus, 10KB (5 sec write time) would be the lowest bandwidth reasonable. Even at this bandwidth, with the estimated 2 interactions per hour, 400 terminals could be supported.

COMPARISON

Comparing the effect of the packet technology with the same terminal operating with preassigned Frequency or Time Division Multiplexed channels (ignoring the losses due to TDM sync bits or FDM guard bands) the circuit oriented terminal would require a 40 bit/sec transmit channel and a 4KB receive channel if a 5 sec write time is to be achieved. For 400 terminals with a 5 sec write time, the circuit method would require a total of 1.6 Megabits/sec bandwidth whereas the packet method only requires 20 Kilobits/sec bandwidth. Thus, the circuit technology requires a factor of 80 more bandwidth than the packet technique. Of course, the circuit mode terminals could interact more often within the same bandwidth right up to continual rewrite of the display every five sec, but you would have to massively reshape the user statistics to suit the technology.

Another possibility, to design the terminal so that it performed more effectively in a circuit oriented mode, would be to put character generation logic and position logic in the terminal. This would considerably increase the cost of the terminal, which originally had very little logic except shift registers. The result of adding this logic, however, is to reduce the bandwidth by a factor of 10 to .16MB or still 8 times the packet technique. The same logic would help reduce the packet size but, in order to maintain the graphic output capability and gross simplicity, it does not seem to pay.

CONCLUSION

As can be seen from the example, packet technology is far superior to circuit technology, even on the simplest radio transmission level, so long as the ratio of peak bandwidth to average bandwidth is large. Most likely, the only feasible way to design a useful and economically attractive personal terminal is through some type of packet communication technology. Otherwise one is restricted to uselessly small numbers of terminals on one channel. This result may also apply to many other important developments, only to be discovered as the technology of packet communication is further developed.

204

REFERENCES

1 L G ROBERTS B D WESSLER
Computer network development to achieve resource sharing
SJCC 1970

2 F E HEART R E KAHN S M ORNSTEIN W R CROWTHER D C WALDEN
The interface message processor for the ARPA network
SJCC 1970

3 L KLEINROCK
Analytic and simulation methods in computer network design
SJCC 1970

4 H FRANK I T FRISCH W CHOU
Topological considerations in the design of the ARPA computer network
SJCC 1970

5 S CARR S CROCKER V CERF
HOST-HOST communication protocol in the ARPA network
SJCC 1970

6 L G ROBERTS
A forward look
Signal Vol XXV No 12 pp 77-81 August 1971

7 N ABRAMSON
THE ALOHA System—Another alternative for computer communications
AFIPS Conference Proceedings Vol 37 pp 281-285 November 1970

8 D C ENGELBART W K ENGLISH
A research center for augmenting human intellect
AFIPS Conference Proceedings Vol 33 p 397 1968

9 D C ENGELBART
Stanford Research Institute Menlo Park Calif (Personal communication)

10 W C LYNCH
Reliable full-duplex file transmission over half-duplex telephone lines
Communications of the ACM Vol 11 No 6 pp 407-410 June 1968

11 K A BARTLETT R A SCANTLEBURY P T WILKINSON
A note on reliable full-duplex transmission over half-duplex links
Communications of the ACM Vol 12 No 5 pp 260-261 May 1969

COMMUNICATIONS TECHNOLOGY

CHANNELS

- END-TO-END CIRCUIT
- INFREQUENT DECISIONS

  - TELEPHONE (1876)
  - RADIO (1901)
  - FACSIMILE (1924)

PACKETS

- ADDRESSED MESSAGE
- DYNAMIC RESOURCE ALLOCATION

  - TELEGRAPH (1844) AND DESCENDANTS (1960's)
  - ARPANET (1969)
  - ALOHA NET (1969)

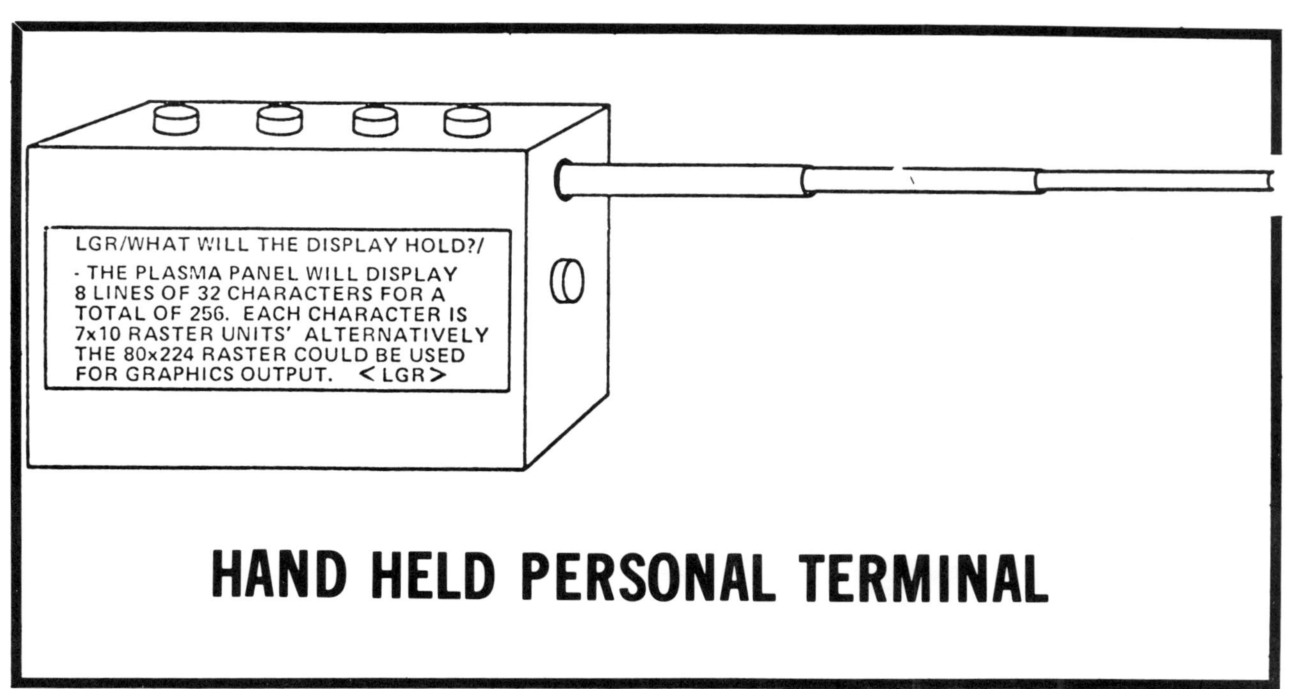

LGR/WHAT WILL THE DISPLAY HOLD?/
- THE PLASMA PANEL WILL DISPLAY
8 LINES OF 32 CHARACTERS FOR A
TOTAL OF 256. EACH CHARACTER IS
7x10 RASTER UNITS' ALTERNATIVELY
THE 80x224 RASTER COULD BE USED
FOR GRAPHICS OUTPUT. <LGR>

HAND HELD PERSONAL TERMINAL

TERMINAL PACKET FORMAT

ID	*	C	SC

BITS		
30	—	TERMINAL IDENTIFICATION
2	—	PACKET TYPE
8	—	CHARACTER +ALT. BIT OR LAST GOOD COUNT
24	—	CYCLIC SUM CHECK
64		BITS TOTAL

CENTRAL CONTROL PACKET FORMAT

ID	*	#	XY	7×10 DISPLAY	SC

BITS		
30	—	TERMINAL IDENTIFICATION
5	—	PACKET TYPE
8	—	NO. CHARACTERS LEFT
8	—	XY POSITION
70	—	CHAR. DISPLAY DOT MATRIX
24	—	CYCLIC SUM CHECK
144		BITS TOTAL

PERFORMANCE WITH 80 KB BANDWIDTH

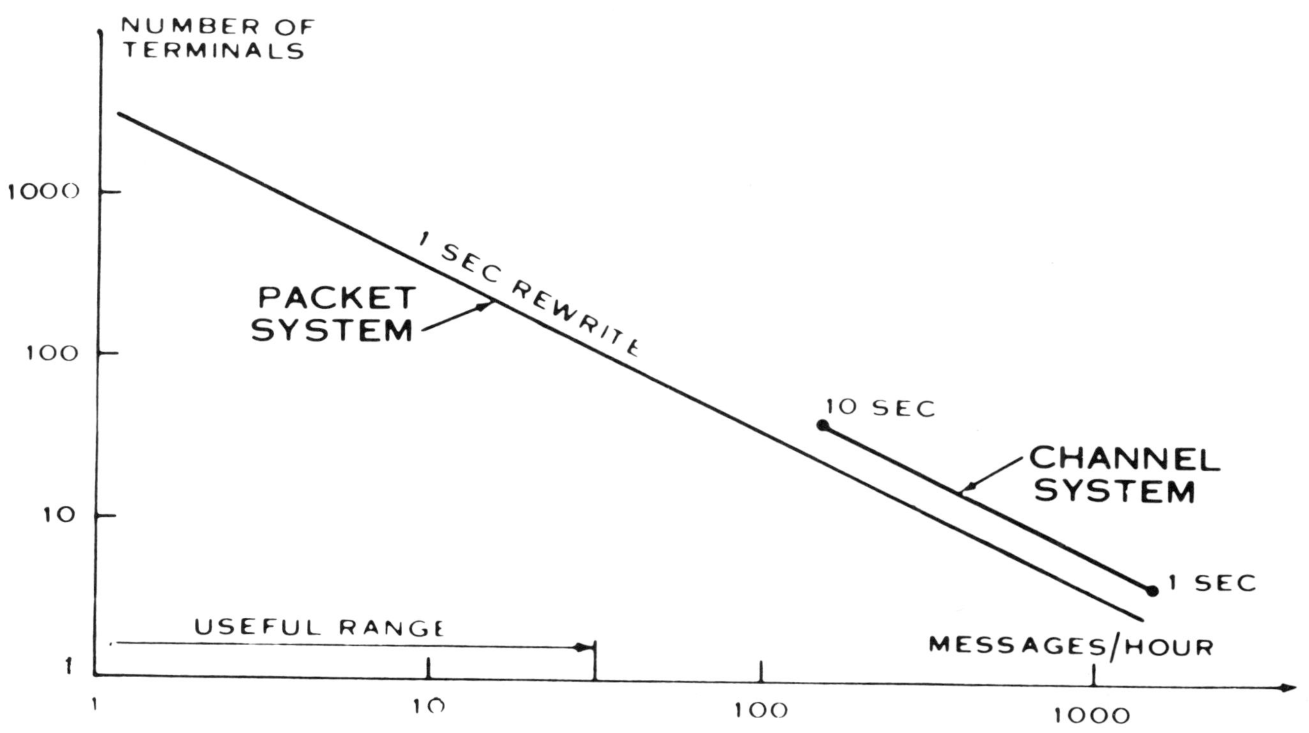

BANDWIDTH REQUIREMENTS FOR 1000 TERMINALS

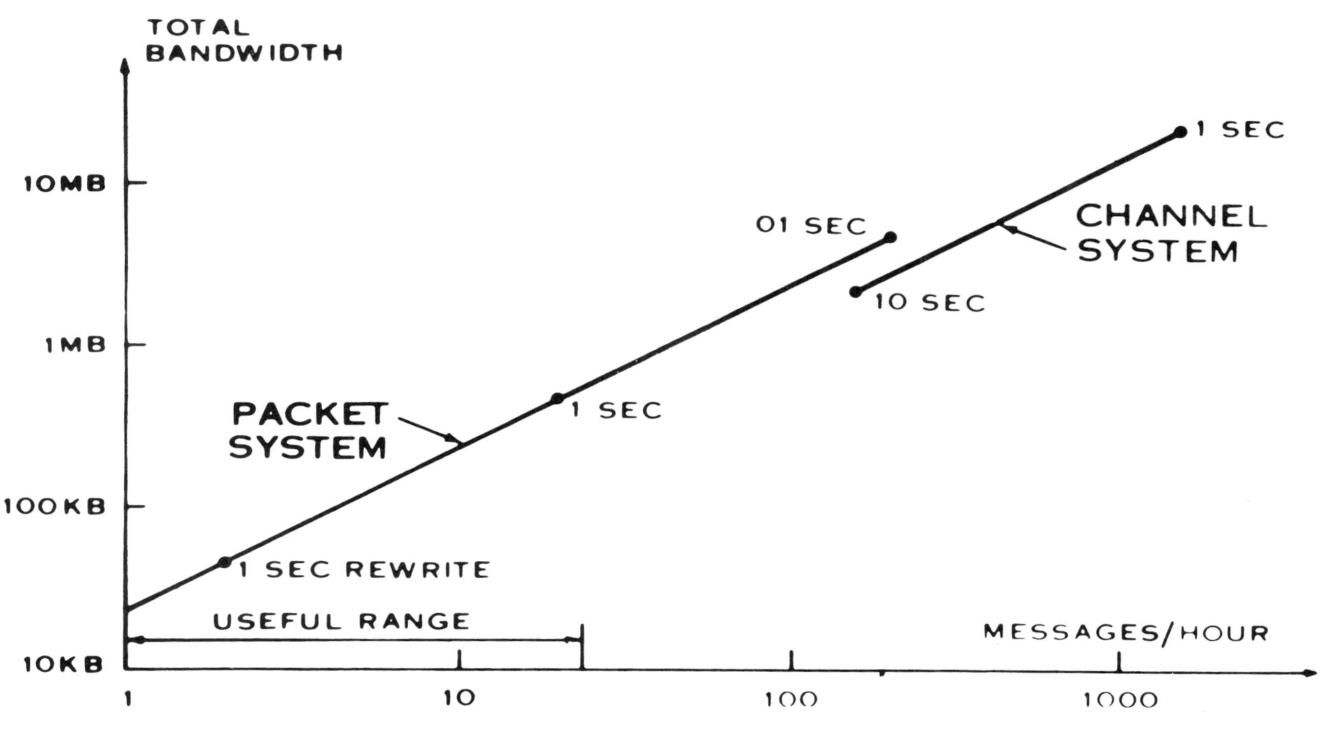

PERFORMANCE WITH ≤ 5 SEC DISPLAY REWRITE FOR A RATE OF 2 MESSAGES/HOUR

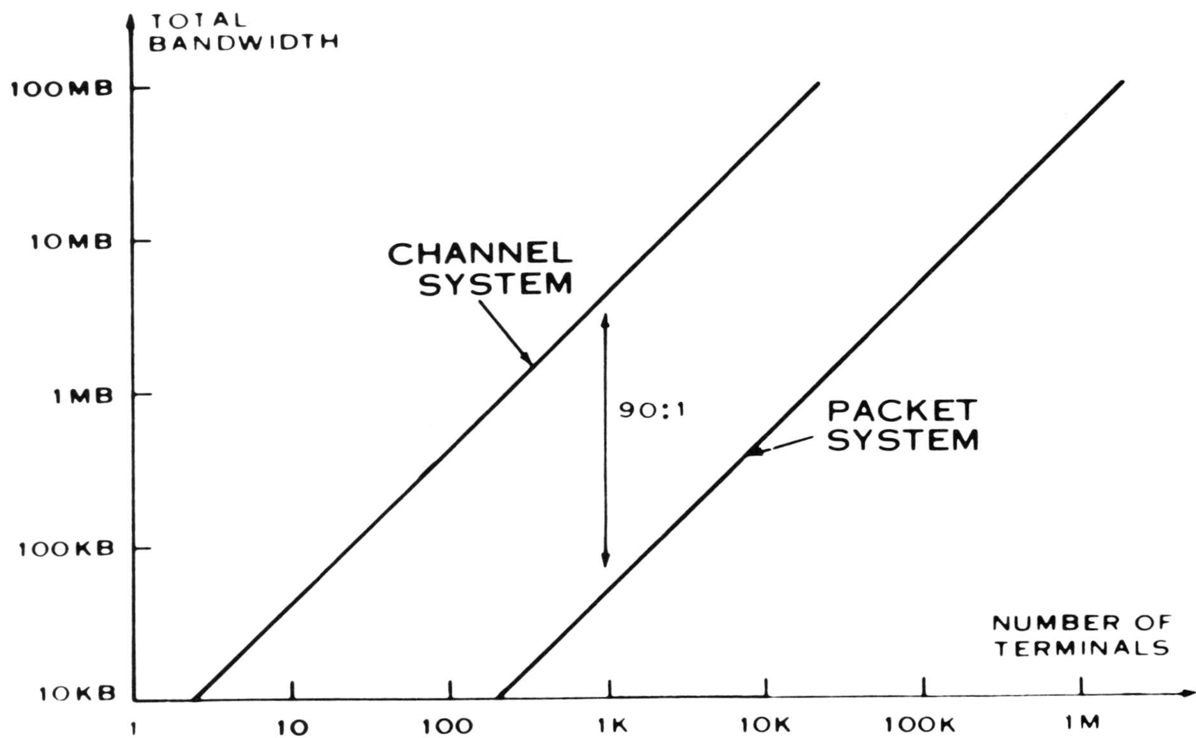

THE CANADIAN UNIVERSITIES COMPUTER NETWORK TOPOLOGICAL CONSIDERATIONS

John deMercado, Rene Guindon, John DaSilva and Michel Kadoch
Ministry of Communications, Ottawa, Canada

SUMMARY

In Canada plans are being developed[1] for a Canadian Universities Computer Network (CANUNET). This activity is co-ordinated by the Canadian Government's Ministry of Communications in Ottawa which is also participating directly in the study programs.

This paper reviews the results of the study prepared within the Ministry of Communications on the topological analysis of various possible networks for CANUNET[2]. In particular, simulation results for two possible 18 node topologies for CANUNET are presented. One of these topologies is based on the use of purely terrestrial communication facilities, and the other, a hybrid realization, is based on a combination of terrestrial and ANIK satellite facilities. Further details can be found in the report[2] which is part of the study program.

INTRODUCTION

The Canadian Universities Computer Network (CANUNET) program is a joint undertaking of the Canadian Government's Ministry of Communications and some twenty universities that lie across the 4000 miles of territory joining the east and west coasts on which some 20,000,000 Canadians live.

The present objectives and expectations of this project are to develop a plan for providing effective resource sharing of University computing power and serve as a facility for educating Canadians in all aspects of the design, implementation and operation of computer-communication networks.

The master plan for CANUNET is being developed with the following general constraints. Namely the plan

- must be for a truly national network with a minimum of one campus in each province invited to participate in some aspect of its development;
- should accommodate regional diversity and technological alternatives within a framework of objectives, standards and conventions;
- should permit the network to accept various types of computers and to operate over a variety of lines and be transparent to its computers and terminals;
- should permit the network to be compatible with future general computer networks in so far as the outlines of the latter can be discerned, and preferably it should be a subnetwork of such networks;
- should permit decisions to be made in terms of the ultimate network, rather than in terms of the easiest or cheapest communication between a few computers.

This paper summarizes the analysis of two possible 18 node configurations for CANUNET. One of these configurations is based on the use of only terrestrial communication network facilities and the other on the use of a hybrid combination of terrestrial and ANIK satellite facilities. For both of these topologies curves of total input message traffic versus total average message delay for given message lengths are presented. In addition, as discussed, these simulations have been performed for topologies that use either 4.8, 9.6 or 50 kb/s communication links. The theoretical considerations are given in the appendix.

NETWORK TOPOLOGIES

At the present time it is not possible to settle on a topology for CANUNET and various ten, fourteen and eighteen node topologies have been studied[2]. Three speeds of lines, namely 4.8 kb/sec, 9.6 kb/sec and 50 kb/sec were assumed for each of these networks. Table I summarizes the results obtained for these various topologies. These studies have shown that the performance of a given network from the point of view of message delay will depend more on line speed than on the particular topology, however, the topological configuration directly influences the reliability of the network.

Line Speed kbit/s	100% Network Capacity (kbit/s)	Cost $/Mbit
4.8	1 to 45	.23 to 8.78
9.6	47 to 108	.12 to .26
50	302 to 591	.11 to .20

TABLE I

* John deMercado is also an adjunct professor of engineering at Carleton University in Ottawa

209

In Table I, 100% Network Capacity represents the total input data for which the total average delay per message does not exceed 0.5 sec. Also the cost in $/Megabit transmitted is for a network operating with this average delay of 0.5 seconds, 24 hours per day, 7 days a week. This cost does not include the cost of the local lines and the NCU's (node control units).

An 18 Node Terrestrial Network for CANUNET

A possible 18 node topology for CANUNET based on the use of terrestrial communication links is shown in Figure 1. Curves of the total average message delay versus total input data rate for 9.6 and 50 kb/sec communication line realizations of this network are shown in Figure 2. Further results for routing schemes etc. can be found in the study report[2]. The preliminary common carrier quotations are that the communication lines costs for the network (50 kb/s option) including the cost of the modems and lines from local exchange are of the order of $250,000 per month or $13,900 per node per month. Further cost details for this topology are shown in Tables II and III.

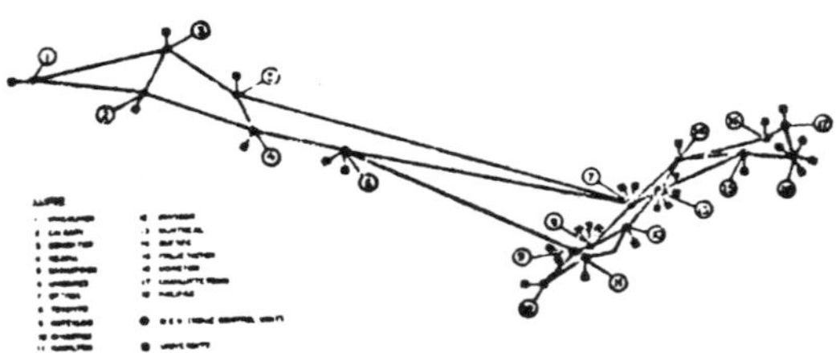

Figure 1

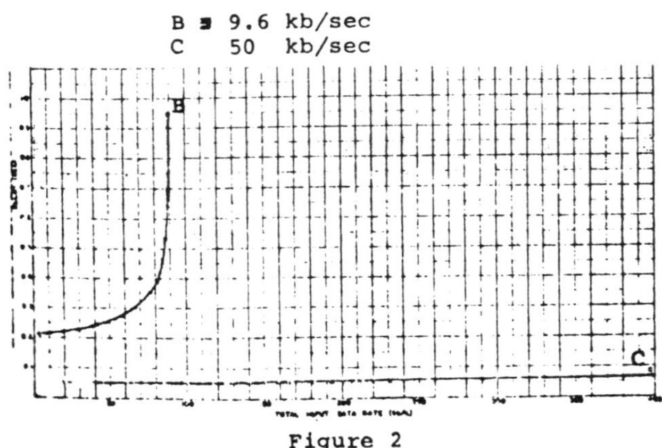

Figure 2

An 18 Node Terrestrial-Satellite (Hybrid Network for CANUNET

A possible 18 node topology for CANUNET based on the use of the ANIK satellite and terrestrial communication facilities is shown in Figure (3). Curves of the total average message delay versus total input data rate for 4.8, 9.6 and 50 kb/s lines are shown in Figure (4). Further results for routing etc. can be found in the study report[2].

A single ANIK radio frequency channel rents for $3,000,000 per year and can support many such 9.6 or 50 kb/sec eighteen node networks. Thus the total communications cost of the single 18 node network using all 50 kb/sec lines and having the topology shown in Figure (3) would be of the order of $310,000 monthly, of which $250,000 per month would go for the rental of the ANIK channel. On the other hand, if four such 50 kb/sec networks with the same earth stations as shown in Figure (3), were being supported by an ANIK channel, then the total monthly communications cost per network would be of the order of $140,000. This compares with the $250,000 monthly cost of the purely terrestrial network. It should be emphasized however that the message/delay performances of both network realizations are different (see Figures 2 and 4).

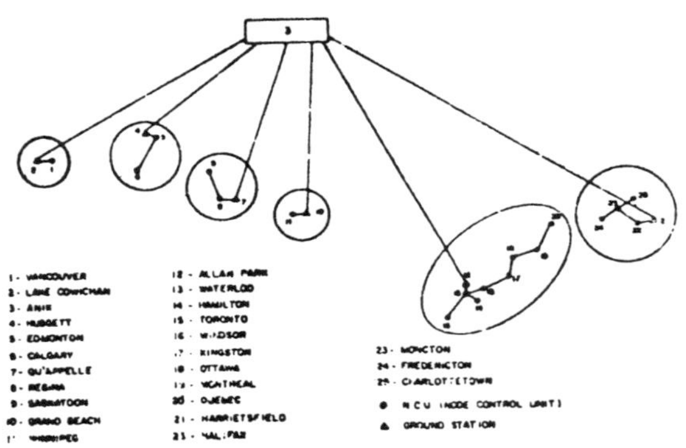

Figure 3

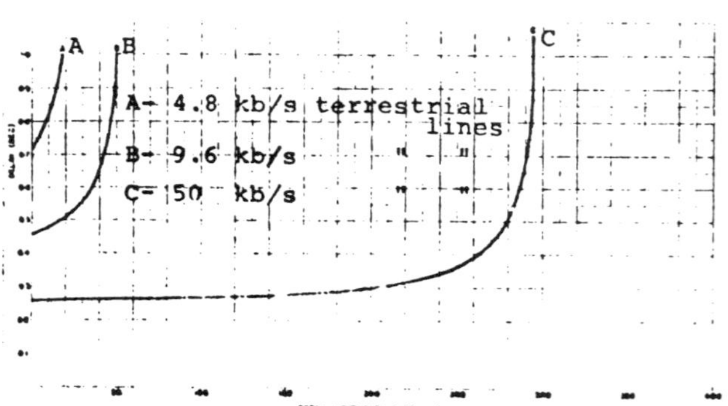

Figure 4

Communication Cost Comparisons

Table II shows the yearly communications cost comparisons for the networks of Figures 1 and 3. Table III shows the costs per megabit transmitted for each of these networks. These costs are for networks operating with a total average message delay of 0.5 sec, 24 hours per day, 7 days a week, and do not include local communications costs. Local communication costs can be expected to increase these monthly figures by between 5% and 10%.

For example, from these two tables it is seen that an 18 node purely terrestrial network with all 9.6 kb/sec communication lines, would cost about $659,000 per year and the cost per megabit of traffic under the operating assumptions listed above would be of the order of $.25.

Network	Yearly Rental Costs		
Line speed	4.8 kb/s	9.6 kb/s	.50 kb/s
Figure 1 costs	$472,164	$659,364	$2,914,200
Figure 3 (single network)			
Terrestrial costs	$198,800	$306,800	$711,300
Satellite costs	$3,000,000	$3,000,000	$3,000,000
Total costs	$3,198,800	$3,306,800	$3,711,300
Figure 3 (4 networks)			
Terrestrial costs	$198,800	$306,800	$711,300
Satellite costs	$960,000	$960,000	$960,000
Total costs	$1,158,800	$1,266,800	$1,671,300

Table II

It is emphasized that no commitment has been sought to date from any common carrier or from Telesat Canada, the owners of the ANIK satellite, to provide facilities for CANUNET. These organizations however, have been most cooperative and helpful in providing their first estimates and other technical assistance.

Network	Cost per Megabit ($/Mbit)		
Line speed	4.8 kb/s	9.6 kb/s	50 kb/s
Figure 1	.607	.246	.196
Figure 3 (single network)	*	*	.553
Figure 3 (four networks)	*	*	.249

Table III

* No cost is computed because the total average message delay of 0.5 seconds is exceeded.

APPENDIX: THEORETICAL CONSIDERATIONS

Network Configuration

There is no single best topology for a network like CANUNET. Only those topologies were considered that are flexible and adaptable to new demands without incurring too high additional costs. In all cases, the topologies are predicated on the use of existing common carriers or other communication facilities. No attempt was made to optimize the cost of any particular topology at this stage.

Node Selection

The node locations shown in this study do not necessarily represent the actual final form of the proposed network. The flexibility of the model is such that, as the need arises, modifications to the node locations can easily be accommodated by it.

There are two possible choices that govern the selection of nodes in a Province, and these which dictate the basic network configuration as far as the required numbers of node control units (IMP's in the ARPANET) are

- assign one node control unit per host computer

- assign one node control unit to several host computers. This has the advantage that new hosts could be added to the network, at least up to a point, without changing the topology.

Traffic Simulation

There are no known methods that allow precise estimates of traffic levels to be given apriori; there is however, an empirical formula used by Frank and Chou[6] that allows the simulation of various levels of traffic. A variation of this formula has been used in the CANUNET Model Computer program[3] to generate various levels of traffic (in bits per second) at each node. This has allowed a given networks message-delay performance to be examined under these traffic loads. The formula is quite a simple one, it simulates the traffic from node i to node j, as

$$K \frac{p_i p_j \, d_{ij}^{\alpha}}{\sum_k p_k \, d_{ik}^{\alpha}}$$

where

- p_i and p_j are the populations, in university students at node i and j respectively;

- d_{ij} is the distance in miles, between nodes i and j (for $i \neq j$);

- α is a non negative constant ($\alpha = 0$ was used in CANUNET studies; that is the traffic was independent of distances between nodes);

- k is a numerical constant which determines the traffic level. The value of k used in the simulation varied from .1 to a maximum of 2 for the case where 50 kb lines were being used.

Routing Procedures

Route selection was one of the most important design parameters for CANUNET. The selection of routing schemes in a computer network is of prime importance because they affect the average time that a message spends in the network. In order to minimize this average time delay the route selection should be adaptive[8], that is a function of the traffic level. The ARPA network has in a sense optimal routing in that it provides a minimum of two physically separate routes for each message. The ARPA network is also capable of adaptive routing, that is routes can be chosen according to the traffic level and availability of the lines.

In the CANUNET network simulations fixed routing schemes were adopted. Under these schemes messages are routed between two given points along the shortest path that has the fewest number of nodes that joins these points.

Queuing Theory Considerations

The queuing theory model used in the simulation of CANUNET's topological performance is based on Leonard Kleinrock's work[9]. It has been shown that the average time a message spends using and waiting for a given channel i, is given by the standard M/M/1 queue model

$$T_i = \frac{\rho_i/\lambda_i}{1 - \rho_i} \qquad \ldots (1)$$

where

- λ_i = average number of messages per second on the ith channel

- ρ_i = utilization factor of the ith channel $= \lambda_i/\mu C_i$

- C_i = capacity of the ith channel in bits/sec

- $\frac{1}{\mu}$ = mean of the exponentially distributed message lengths

using these coefficients equation (1) can be written as

$$T_i = \frac{1}{\mu C_i - \lambda_i} \qquad \ldots (2)$$

and the average message delay T for an M channel network is therefore

$$T = \frac{1}{\gamma} \sum_{i=1}^{M} \lambda_i T_i \qquad \ldots (3)$$

where γ is the total input data rate. That is γ is the traffic offered to the network in mess/sec. In order to take into account the fact that nodal delays are not negligible, a constant 10^{-3} is added to the average delay on the ith channel, and the total average message delay averaged over all the channels in the network becomes from (3)

$$T = \frac{1}{\gamma} \sum_{i=1}^{M} \lambda_i (T_i + 10^{-3}) \qquad \ldots (4)$$

The time that a message spends waiting for a channel is dependent upon the total traffic (including acknowledgements) whereas the time spent in transmission over a channel is proportional to the message length of the real message traffic flow. Equation (2) is therefore not correct, and the correct expression for T_i, derived[9] from the POLLACZEK-KHINCHIN formula is

$$T_i = \frac{\rho_i}{\lambda_i} + \frac{(\rho_i)^2}{\lambda_i(1-\rho_i)} \qquad \ldots (5)$$

where

$$\rho_i = \frac{\lambda_i}{\mu C_i}$$

The first term on the right side of (5) is the average service time per message on the ith channel, and the second term is the average waiting time per message on the ith channel. Since this service time depends on the average message length $1/\mu^1$, and the waiting time of the average of the message plus acknowledgement $1/\mu$, equation (5) can be rewritten as

$$T_i = \frac{1}{\mu^1 C_i} + \frac{\lambda_i/\mu C_i}{\mu C_i - \lambda_i} + PL_i \qquad \ldots (6)$$

where the term PL_i has been added to take into account the propagation delay associated with the ith channel. Thus the total average delay T for a message in the network obtained by substituting (6) into (3) is,

$$T = \frac{1}{\gamma} \sum_{i=1}^{M} \lambda_i \left(\frac{1}{\mu^1 C_i} + \frac{\lambda_i/\mu C_i}{\mu C_i - \lambda_i} + PL_i + 10^{-3}\right) + 10^{-3} \qquad \ldots (7)$$

The last term in equation (7) accounts for the delay introduced by the final destination node control unit in delivering the message to its host. This figure of 10^{-3} was used in the case of ARPA network where each host is located only a short distance away from its IMP. In the CANUNET studies, equation (7) was used. It should be emphasized however, that should a host be located far from its network control unit, then the delay of 10^{-3} sec. could be increased. Furthermore the total average delay as given by equation (7) takes into account only short message (packet) traffic.

Message Lengths*

In the model for CANUNET, the fact that acknowledgement traffic affects message throughput was taken into account. Therefore for the CANUNET simulations the following packet lengths were used:

- average message length = $\frac{1}{\mu^1}$ = 640 bits
- average of (message length plus acknowledgements) = $\frac{1}{\mu}$ = 400 bits.

It has been shown[4] that by giving priority to the acknowledgement traffic over the message traffic in particular for line loadings exceeding 50%, that the overall average message delay is decreased. It is worthwhile pointing out that further improvement in the message/delay performance could be achieved if more than two priority classes are introduced. However software and storage costs associated with routing would increase.

Program Description

The input/output for the CANUNET model Computer program[3] is

Input

- N → Number of nodes
- {P} → Vector of the Population at each node
- {D} → Distance matrix
- {C} → Branch capacity matrix
- $1/\mu$ → Overall average message length
- $1/\mu^1$ → Average message (packet) length

Output

- {T} → Traffic matrix
- γ → Total input data rate
- {S} → Shortest distance matrix
- {ρ} → Network utilization matrix
- {R} → Routing matrix
- {A} → Average delay matrix
- T → Total average message delay

Reliability Considerations

Preliminary reliability analysis using some new techniques [5,7] of the two 18 node topologies considered in this paper, indicate that the probability is less than 5% that any two nodes will not be able to communicate with each other within 2000 hours. Furthermore for this worse case situation the mean time at which no communication would be possible between a given pair of nodes for a period exceeding 10 hours is of the order of 12000 hours. The probability that this event

---

* These lengths are variable in the simulation program and the studies could have been done using the corresponding ARPA lengths which are 560 bits, and 350 bits, respectively.

will occur within this time is 98%.

ACKNOWLEDGEMENTS

The authors wish to acknowledge many stimulating discussions with Dr. D. Parkhill, of the Department of Communications, Prof. J. Reid of the University of Quebec, Dr. D. Cowan of Waterloo University, Dr. B. Holmlund of the University of Saskatchewan, Dr. J. Kennedy of the University of British Columbia and Mrs. E. Payne of Dalhousie University. Many other people, too numerous to mention individually, are participating in the CANUNET program. The authors would like to thank Miss Gail Widdicombe for expertly typing the manuscript in record time.

REFERENCES

1 University of Quebec — A Proposal for a Canadian University Computer Network (CANUNET), prepared by the CANUNET advisory committee for the Department of Communications. Available from the library of the Department of Communications, 100 Metcalfe Street, Ottawa. March 72.

2 J. deMercado, R. Guindon, J. DaSilva, M. Kadoch — Topological Analysis of CANUNET. Peport of the Communications Planning Branch. Available from the library of the Department of Communications, 100 Metcalfe Street, Ottawa. April 1972.

1

3 J. deMercado, R. Guindon, J. Da Silva, M. Kadoch — The CANUNET Model Computer Program.

4 J. DaSilva, J. deMercado — Priority Assignment in a Network of Computers. Internal Report of the Communications Planning Branch. Available from the library, Department of Communications, 100 Metcalfe Street, Ottawa. April 1972.

5 J. deMercado — Reliability Prediction Studies of Complex Systems Having Many Failed States. IEEE Transactions on Reliability Theory, Vol R-20, No. 4, November 1971, pp. 223-230.

6 H. Frank, W. Chou — Cost and Throughput in Computer Communication Networks. Network Analysis Corporation, Beechwood, Old Tappan Road, Glen Cove, N.Y. 11542. 1971.

7 J. deMercado — Minimum Cost-Reliable Computer Communication Networks. To appear in the Proceedings of the 1972 Fall Joint Computer Conference, Anaheim, California.

8 H. Frank — Research in Store and Forward Computer Networks. Fourth semi-annual Technical Report, Network Analysis Corporation, Beechwood, Old Tappan Road, Glen Cove, N.Y. 11542. 1971.

9 L. Kleinrock — Analytic and Simulation Methods in Computer Network Design. AFIPS Conference Proceedings, Vol. 36, pp 569-579. May 1970.

10 Science Council of Canada — A Trans-Canada Computer Communication Network. Report No. 13, August 71.

Reprinted by permission from *International Conference of Computer Communications*

SOME ADVANCES IN RADIO COMMUNICATIONS FOR COMPUTERS

Franklin F. Kuo and Norman Abramson
Department of Electrical Engineering
University of Hawaii
Honolulu, Hawaii

INTRODUCTION

In this paper we describe an experimental UHF radio computer communication network - THE ALOHA SYSTEM - under development for the past five years at the University of Hawaii [1]. Presently in operation on an experimental basis, the existing ALOHA SYSTEM computer-communication network uses two 24,000 baud channels at 407.350 MHz and at 413.475 MHz in the upper UHF band. The system uses packet switching techniques similar to that employed by the ARPANET [2], in conjunction with a novel form of random-access radio channel multiplexing. Recently THE ALOHA SYSTEM has become the first satellite node on the ARPANET, in which a TIP (Terminal Interface Processor) [3] located at the University of Hawaii campus communicates through a 50 kilobit data channel using INTELSAT IV with the NASA/AMES TIP and into the ARPANET. The 50 kilobit satellite channel occupies a single PCM voice channel on INTELSAT IV. We will describe some of our current activities in this paper and present a look into the future of our project.

THE ALOHA SYSTEM

In Figure 1 we show the present configuration of THE ALOHA SYSTEM. The central computer of the University, an IBM 360/65 with 2.5 MBytes of core memory presently runs under OS MVT and in addition to background batch, runs two timesharing systems, APL and TSO. THE ALOHA SYSTEM is one of the TSO users and is connected to the 360 computer via the HP 2115A computer which serves as a data-concentrator and multiplexor. Since the functions of the 2115A machine is much like that of the Interface Message Processor (IMP) [4] used in the ARPANET, we have dubbed the 2115A the MENEHUNE, a legendary Hawaiian elf. The modem operates at 24,000 baud and uses differential phase shift keyed modulation. The demodulator has been specially designed for our application so as to optimally operate on the coherent signal by using a phase-locked-loop to recover bit timing and a matched filter to recover the signal in the presence of noise. The transmitter-receivers are primarily standard commercial transceivers, modified to accommodate the system specifications. On the terminal end, the central piece of equipment is the communications module developed by THE ALOHA SYSTEM called the Terminal Control Unit (TCU). The TCU consists of a UHF antenna, transceiver, modem and buffer control unit, and is shown in Figure 2. Thus the TCU duplicates on the terminal end, all of the separate pieces of equipment on the HOST side. A TCU can interface a wide variety of terminals operating at speeds up to 24,000 baud. At present, we have connected teletype terminals, alphanumeric displays, graphics processors and minicomputers to the TCU's with equal ease.

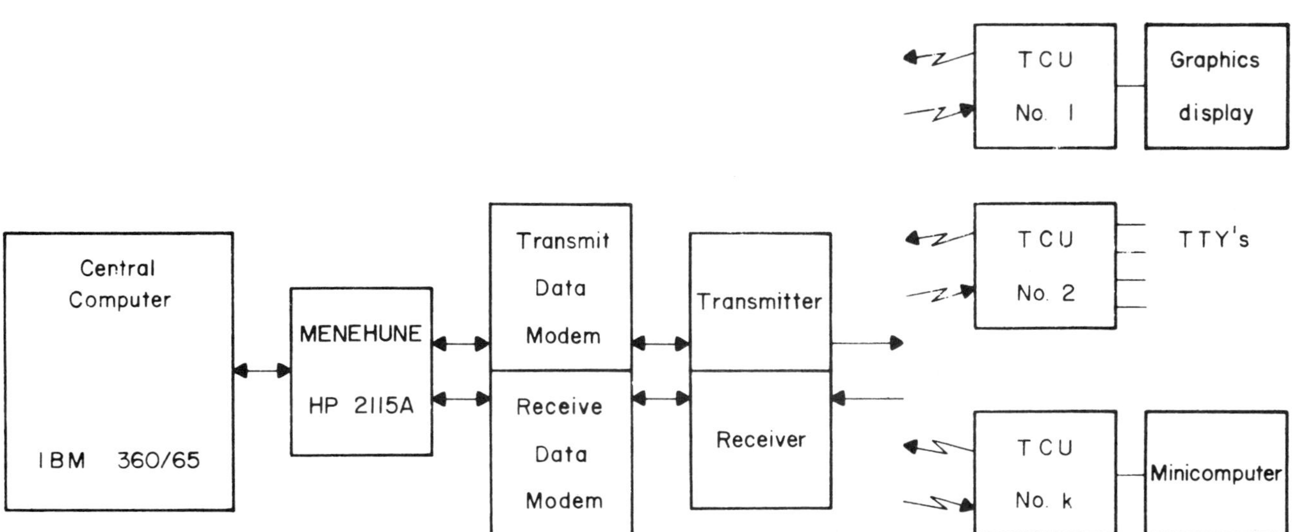

Figure 1. · THE ALOHA SYSTEM

Figure 2. Terminal Control Unit (TCU)

ALOHA INTERFACE *

In order to connect a remote station into the ALOHA channel it is necessary to provide buffering up to a full packet of data together with automatic generation of certain identification, control and parity information. This information is generated in a hardware buffer/control interface unit from each user console to a modem. The buffer/control unit also provides for reception of messages and acknowledgements into its remote station, rejection of unwanted packets and automatic retransmission of packets not receiving an acknowledgement [5]. In the case of buffered terminals, intelligent terminals and minicomputers some of the buffer/control functions may be handled by software packages in the remote station.

216

To transmit a packet using the radio link, the MENEHUNE places each word of the message in an output buffer register located in the MENEHUNE and sends a flag signal to a hardware device connecting it to the radio transmit modem. The hardware device stores the word in a second buffer and converts it to a serial bit-stream which is then passed to the modem. Whenever a word is read from the MENEHUNE output buffer, an interrupt signal is sent to the MENEHUNE which causes the program to output the next word of the packet.

In addition to the message words, control words are transferred between the MENEHUNE and the radio link and between the MENEHUNE and the 360. Each packet in the radio link is preceeded by two control words (the packet "header") and a header parity word, and each packet's text is followed by a text parity word (Figure 3). At this time the hardware circuits between the radio modems and the MENEHUNE perform the tasks of both parity and syndrome generation. The parity words are inserted into the packet by the hardware prior to entering the transmit modem, and the syndrome words are inserted in place of the received parity words of the packet prior to being placed in the MENEHUNE input buffer register. Consideration is being given to incorporating parity and syndrome generation in the MENEHUNE multiplexor program. A word with all bits set to 'one' is also sent to the MENEHUNE by the hardware units preceeding the start of each packet, providing synchronization for the MENEHUNE program.

A control word is sent between the MENEHUNE and the 360 prior to a packet transfer in either direction. This word contains the terminal ID number and a packet length indicator (now restricted to 20 or 40 words). The length information allows the block size to be specified so that direct-memory-access transfers can be made by both the 360 and the MENEHUNE.

The program is modular in design, allowing the processing functions for a particular user channel to be easily changed. Editing functions are localized within each user channel module, allowing the editing characters used by a particular terminal to be changed without affecting the other modules in the program. Fixed buffer areas are assigned for each system user in the program. Because of the relative data transmission rates of the user MENEHUNE and MENEHUNE-360 links, it is necessary to store only one packet for each user within the MENEHUNE at any particular time (although the most recent packet sent to a remote station will be kept in storage for user retransmission requests). This fact and the small number of users anticipated for the initial system led to the choice of fixed storage allocation in the current implementation, allowing a later implementation of dynamic storage allocation to be made on the basis of a more detailed study which can include actual operating characteristics of the system.

To facilitate coding, debugging and future modifications, the MENEHUNE program was written in a high-level language XPL. A compiler was written for this purpose which produced HP machine code from an XPL source program. The compiler runs on the IBM 360, providing that system's I/O facilities as an aid in debugging syntax errors and in producing program documentation.

	header	parity	text	parity
bits	32	16	640	16

Figure 3. ALOHA SYSTEM Message Format

* Portions of this section were obtained from [5].

The MENEHUNE compiler (HPCOM) was written for use on an IBM 360 to take in a program written in a subset of XPL (called HPL) and emit the proper machine language for a Hewlett-Packard 2115 computer. The compiler had two main design considerations, efficiency of the machine language, and versatility, so that most operations could be done in the higher level language.

Since the programs written in HPCOM are to be loaded into the HP 2115 via the IBM 360, the compiler has no input-output in the higher level language. However, many features and conventions have been implemented in the compiler such that it is easy for the programmer to write his own I/O routines exactly as he wants them, and to utilize the interrupt system of the Hewlett-Packard. To do this, the programmer needs a basic knowledge of the HP input-output system, and how to use some of the built-in functions of the compiler.

The output of the compiler is the raw machine code for the Hewlett-Packard ready to be loaded into the machine, a printed output of the source program, the machine code resulting from each statement with explanation in assembly code for readability, and error statements.

PRESENT STATE OF THE ALOHA SYSTEM

At present THE ALOHA SYSTEM has seven TCU's in operation which service a number of teletypes, Hazeltine terminals, and a graphics terminal. In addition we have interfaced an IMLAC display computer and a HP 2114 minicomputer into the ALOHA channels. In these two latter cases the buffer control function of the TCU is handled by a software package in the IMLAC and in the HP 2114. Because of the efficient use of channel capacity by the ALOHA burst random access communication method the present channel is only lightly loaded. We have calculated that well over 500 active alphanumeric terminals could use the present communication channels of THE ALOHA SYSTEM.

At present we are performing system studies to investigate properties of the random-access channel used in different modes (unsynchronized, synchronized, contention, file scheduling, multiple frequency, etc.) by both analytical and computer simulation studies. We are also investigating the effects of different channel protocols upon system performance. We have also purchased an INTEL CPU on a single integrated circuit chip for the purpose of developing a TCU with considerably more flexibility than the present hardwired versions. The TCU-on-a-chip will enable the system to respond to a variety of different transmission protocols, including variable length packets and character-by-character transmission. Various error control procedures can also be studied and implemented with this new TCU.

Our main emphasis, however, is in the area of satellite data communications, which we describe in the following section.

SATELLITE COMMUNICATIONS

Because of the geographic isolation of Hawaii, one of the original objectives of THE ALOHA SYSTEM project was to study the feasibility of computer communications by means of satellite. With the development of digital communication systems by COMSAT in which data at the rate of 50 baud can be transmitted through a single voice channel [7], data transmission by satellite has become both technologically and economically feasible.

There is a basic and important difference between the use of a satellite channel and a wire channel for data communications. The satellite channel is a broadcast channel as opposed to a point-to-point wire channel, so that a single voice channel, say between ground stations A and B can be used in broadcast mode among any set of ground stations, providing a full broadcast capability of two 50 baud channels. Thus a single commercial satellite voice channel could be employed with the following characteristics: (1) The single voice channel could provide two up-link and two down link 50 baud data channels. (2) Each of these four channels could be simultaneously available to any COMSAT ground station in sight of the satellite.

During the past year we have initiated two specific research projects for satellite extension of THE ALOHA SYSTEM and several theoretical studies involving the unique properties of satellite channels. The first of the projects involves the use of large commercial ground stations and the establishment of an ARPANET SATELLITE SYSTEM; the second involves the use of small inexpensive ground stations in a joint research effort with NASA/AMES. In regard to the ARPANET SATELLITE SYSTEM, we have been involved in a joint study with ARPA, Bolt Beranek and Newman, Xerox Data Systems and UCLA to design a suitable protocol for packet communications via satellite. These studies are of a tentative nature at present and will not be reported on in this paper. In December 1972, a digital communication subsystem was installed between the COMSAT ground stations at Paumalu, Hawaii, and Jamesburg, California. The first subscriber of this service was THE ALOHA SYSTEM, which, with its newly installed TIP, became the first operational satellite node on the ARPANET. As of this moment (December 1972) the BCC 500 computer is connected as a HOST computer of the Hawaii TIP. Shortly we expect to connect the MENEHUNE to the TIP as a second HOST. With the TIP in operation, we plan to experiment with system protocols and sharing of remote data bases.

The second satellite project involves the use of the NASA satellite ATS-1 using small, inexpensive ground stations, which cost less than $5,000 each. Thus far we have progressed to the point where a random access burst mode data channel is in operation between the University of Hawaii and NASA/AMES Research Center in California. Early in 1973 this network will be joined by the University of Alaska. During the following year we plan to interface this channel into computers near each of these ground stations, extend the number of ground stations to other sites, including possibly universities in Japan and Taiwan and establish a small ground station satellite network on an experimental basis.

It is now quite apparent that satellite communications will become the main emphasis of THE ALOHA SYSTEM. In addition to the two hardware projects described above THE ALOHA SYSTEM has begun a two year feasibility study of a Pacific Educational Computer Network using advanced data communication techniques to link computers in developed countries and developing countries in the Pacific. This study is a cooperative effort of THE ALOHA SYSTEM and Tohoku University in Japan and is supported by the U.S. National Science Foundation and the Japan Society for the Promotion of Science.

REFERENCES

[1] N. Abramson, "THE ALOHA SYSTEM - Another Alternative for Computer Communications," FJCC 1970, pp. 281-285.

[2] L.G. Roberts and B. Wessler, "Computer Network Development to Achieve Resource Sharing," SJCC 1970, pp. 543-549.

[3] S.M. Ornstein, F.E. Heart, W.R. Crowther, H.K. Rising, S.B. Russell, and A. Michel, "The Terminal IMP for the ARPA Computer Network," SJCC 1972, pp. 243-254.

[4] F.E. Heart, R.E. Kahn, S.M. Ornstein, W.R. Crowther, and D.C. Walden, "The Interface Message Processor for the ARPA Computer Network," SJCC 1970, pp. 551-567.

[5] R. Binder, Multiplexing in THE ALOHA SYSTEM: MENEHUNE-KEIKI Design Considerations, ALOHA SYSTEM Technical Report B69-3, November 1969.

[6] R. Binder, ALOHA SYSTEM Multiplexor Program Description, ALOHA SYSTEM Technical Report B71-3, June 1971.

[7] E.R. Cacciamani, Jr., "The SPADE System as Applied to Data Communications and Small Earth Station Operation," COMSAT Technical Review, Vol. 1, No. 1, Fall 1971, pp. 171-182.

INFORMATION PROCESSING 74 – NORTH-HOLLAND PUBLISHING COMPANY (1974)

CIGALE, THE PACKET SWITCHING MACHINE OF THE CYCLADES COMPUTER NETWORK

Louis POUZIN

Institut de Recherche d'Informatique et d'Automatique (IRIA)
78150, Rocquencourt, France

CIGALE is designed to handle message transfer between computers at the best possible speed. Messages are handled independently, as letters in the mail. There are no end-to-end functions, but any higher level protocol may be used to control message flows. Hosts may be connected through several lines, and there can be several hosts on a line. The host address space is independent from the topology. Regions make up a 2nd level addressing and routing. They can be viewed as local networks. Also, hosts can be networks. A network name is a 3rd level intended for inter-network traffic. Various services may be added for some classes of users and terminals may be connected through concentrators, or a packet interface. Congestion control and routing are associated to control the message flow. A simple message interface is all that is needed to interconnect networks. Complicated interfaces make networks incompatible. The best value is transparency.

1. INTRODUCTION

CYCLADES [1] is a general purpose computer network being installed in France under government sponsorship (Fig. 1). Its goals are to foster experiment and develop know-how in computer-to-computer communications, data transmission techniques, and distributed data bases. CYCLADES is also to be an operational tool for the French Administration. The project started on the beginning of 1972. Various demonstrations of distributed activities have been presented in November 1973, including 4 host computers and a packet switch. The complete network of 16 computers, linked by a 5-node packet switching network, is to be on the air by mid-1974. Additional hosts and nodes may be connected later on.

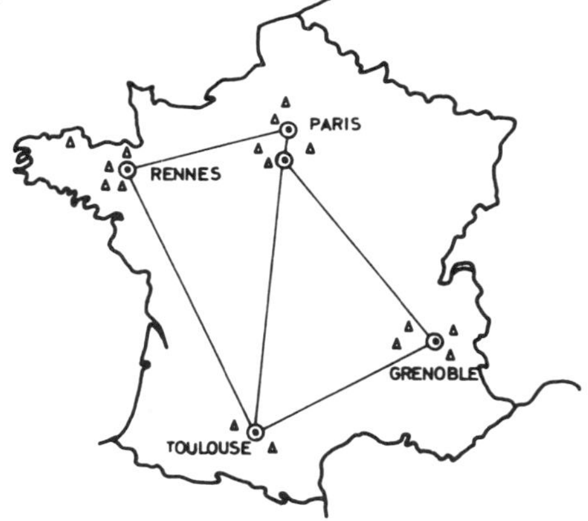

Fig. 1 - CYCLADES topology

The communications network within CYCLADES is called CIGALE [2, 3]. It is a store-and-forward packet switching network similar to the one included in Arpanet [4]. A brief summary of the CIGALE description will be given here. More details may be found in the referenced papers.

2. THE CIGALE NETWORK

Nodes are MITRA-15 minicomputers, with 16 K words (16 bits). Except for a teletype, no other peripheral is necessary. Communication lines are point-to-point PTT leased lines ranging from 4.8 Kbs to 48 Kbs. All host computers are connected via telephone lines and V24 interfaces, typically using 19.2 Kbs base-band modulation on voice grade circuits (Fig. 2). Transmission procedures between hosts and nodes are those of the various computer manufacturers, in transparent binary synchronous mode.

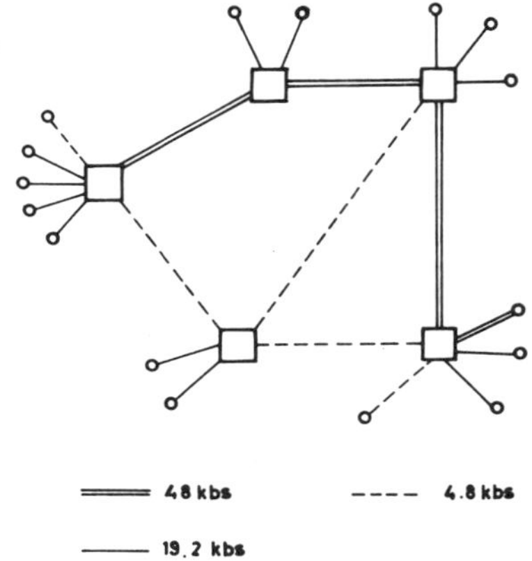

Fig. 2 - CIGALE topology

Specific components within CIGALE provide for some basic services, such as : echoing, statistics recording, debugging aids, node configuration, artificial traffic, clock. Other services may be requested with regard to a particular packet : priority, tracing, routing. Switching is implemented on a very simple manner by asynchronous processes feeding each other through queues.

A control center receives various reports and helps in locating failing components. Every node can be reloaded individually from this center by sending its program in packets.

3. DESIGN OPTIONS

The remainder of this paper will concentrate on the choices made at the design stage, and discuss the rationale behind. Indeed, a distinctive character of CIGALE is not its gadgetry, but its basic simplicity. The result is an unusual flexibility in handling all sorts of protocols and connections. It will be a trivial task to connect CIGALE with other packet switching networks, as long as they do just that.

3.1. Computer-to-computer traffic :

No statistics are yet available. Consequently, only prospective assumptions can be made. A set of frequently mentionned characteristics are following :

a) Bursty traffic, ranging from sparse short messages to a file transfer steady flow.

b) Very short delay, ideally nil. Actually, a few milliseconds or seconds may be acceptable, depending on the environment.

c) Error rate less than 10^{-10} bit.

219

d) If an initial set up time is required, it should be small as compared to transmission time.

e) Transmission availability at least 98 % of the time.

f) Throughput as high as suitable for an I-O channel (several Mbs).

g) Traffic between host and network multiplexed on a small number of I-O ports, typically 2 for reliability.

h) Standard communication interface where applicable.

i) Host computers are heterogeneous.

j) Data to be carried unaltered, in a transparent mode.

3.2. Packet switching :

Direct circuits between computers would not meet conditions e and g. If circuits are switched, conditions d and f would not be met. Other media could be considered [5, 6, 7] (radio, satellite, coaxial cables), but equipment and infrastructures are not available. Packet switching on mini-computers has been introduced recently, but its validity is now well established. It can be implemented with existing hardware at a small cost. All constraints above can be reasonably met, within the speed limits of presently available transmission lines, (typically 48 Kbs). When PCM links are installed, they will provide for higher throughput and shorter delay.

3.3. Transit delay :

Conventional message switching systems, using secondary storage,
220 take a few seconds, or a few hours, to carry a message through, depending on priority[8]. On the other hand, in the range of 100 ms, Arpanet is the only known network of large geographical extension. CIGALE is aiming at this domain of performance.

Very distinct architectures result from these two different ranges of objectives. CIGALE is not designed to cater for traffic with deferred delivery and long term storage. However nothing prevents a conventional message switching system from using CIGALE as a communication tool between centers. As CIGALE basic service is fast transit delay, this objective carries a major weight in the choice of other characteristics of the network.

3.4. Added services :

This objective of fast transit delay suggests eliminating some mechanisms, which certain kinds of users might find desirable in a data communications system, e.g. for terminal handling[9]. But various services may be added on, as custom-tailored devices, for certain classes of users. E. g. asynchronous character terminals, data conversion, hot circuits, restricted traffic, multiple addresses, etc... This can be implemented as pluggable pieces of hardware/software. It may also entail some additional delay or restricted throughput in carrying messages.

This approach, which is classical in properly designed systems, insulates basic functions from market oriented services [10]. Indeed, the former must be kept very stable and customer independent if it has to be reliable, while the latter may be introduced on demand for changing needs. Customers who rely on an interface providing only basic facilities are guaranteed to protect their investment against modifications likely to occur in more specialized services. Furthermore, they are not penalised in being forced to use functions that they do not need.

Computer-to-computer traffic is predictably going to be the most demanding data transmission consumer in terms of throughput and transit delay. Furthermore, computers do not require any help in managing their own data transfer. Therefore, the communications system they need should offer the simplest possible functions and the highest possible throughput.

Along these lines, CIGALE offers a basic service, message transfer, and allows grafting additional functions through more specialized interfaces. The development of micro-components with a parallel decrease in cost will gradually make these devices appear as trivial hardware integrated in user equipment. For example, character oriented devices will soon be equipped with a message interface, so that they be linked directly to a network. They will look like simple computers. This is one of the reasons not to consider terminal handling in a packet switching network, since present terminal interfaces will fade out.

3.5. Packet size :

The term *packet* refers here to bit strings exchanged between CIGALE nodes. Various studies might be made to evaluate an optimum size depending on a number of parameters. Practically, as long as efficiency and delay stay within an acceptable range, it seems that its main virtue is to be stable. This allows an adequate optimization of customer software and hardware.

Furthermore, it will be necessary to interconnect different packet switching networks. A generally agreed maximum size for a packet would be highly desirable in order to simplify interface mechanisms. A proposal has been made to set 255 octets as the maximum text size [11]. This is long enough to accept packets from existing networks, and it suits nicely present computer hardware. This choice has been made for the British Post-Office network presently being implemented[12]. So it is for CIGALE.

3.6. Packet header :

It contains the following items :

- Header format	4 bits
- Header length	4 bits
- Text length	8 bits
- Packet identification	16 bits
- Facilities, accounting	16 bits
- Destination network	8 bits
- Source network	8 bits
- Destination host	16 bits
- Source host	16 bits

The *header* length is 96 bits, a multiple of 6, 8, 12, 16, 24, 32. This facilitates formatting on most types of computers. The *format* field anticipates future adjustments in connection with other networks. CIGALE may have to handle various packet formats in a mixed traffic. They will be segregated easily.

The *identification* field is left for the user to identify his packets. It is not processed nor altered by CIGALE, but it is used to report about anomalies, or when special services are invoked. An obvious use is to contain all or part of a tag for multiplexing internal users within a host along with some serial number. But this belongs to host level protocols, and CIGALE does not require any specific scheme, since it is transparent to any outer protocol.

A 3-bit *time-out* field will be introduced in a future version, so that older packets be exterminated rather than roam about the network for any reason. It will not appear at the host interface.

3.7. Host interface :

The term *host* refers here to any computer connected to CIGALE. A host is assumed to be located at some distance away from a CIGALE node, and must use PTT lines. Indeed, putting a node on host premises carries several drawbacks :

- it increases the network cost and places an additional transit delay.
- it reduces reliability, since the node is under user's control.
- it is a security risk, as it can be tapped and tampered with.

A single line between a host and CIGALE would be somewhat unreliable. Two lines in parallel would not help in case of node failure. Therefore, it is possible to run several lines between a host and several CIGALE nodes. The traffic can be dispatched arbitrarily over all lines, according to speed and load. It is also a way to increase the maximum throughput when lines cannot be speeded up.

In order to avoid any predicament usually associated with special hardware, the electrical interface is typically CCITT V24 up to 19.2 Kbs. At higher speeds, V35 is required.

Also, it was found undesirable to introduce a special transmission procedure between a host and CIGALE. Current manufacturer procedures are accepted, even though they are generally not very efficient. Hence no modifications to operating systems are necessary, as long as a transparent binary synchronous procedure is available, which happens in most cases. A consequence is that host-to-host protocols may be implemented at user level without modification to operating systems. This is of course immaterial in CIGALE, but it makes quite a difference for users who want to keep their system under manufacturer's responsibility.

A 16-bit cyclical checksum is a common feature of synchronous transmission. Any polynomial is acceptable, but the ISO standard $X^{16} + X^{12} + X^{5} + 1$ is recommended to maintain the error rate below 10^{-10} per bit.

3.8. Message size

In some networks the quantum of information exchanged between nodes is different from the one exchanged between host and node [13, 14]. It is called a *message*, in order to prevent confusion. This need arises when message sizes adapted to user traffic are too different from an adequate packet size. But computers can exchange messages of many different sizes :

- a few characters for control messages
- a few dozens of characters for transactions
- a few hundreds of characters for file records
- millions of characters for complete files.

Since we lack statistics it would not make sense to pick an ideal size. Furthermore, packetizing costs overhead. Since a host is to fragment his data anyway, the advantages of putting an additional level of fragmentation do not appear to compensate for its inconvenience [15]. Consequently, a host message is simply a packet.

A possible objection is that too short host messages increase I-O overhead. Let us remark that this is mainly traceable to a clumsy design of communications software in some operating systems. I-O would be better handled by direct memory access. On the other hand, if this turns out to be a critical factor, some blocking scheme might be installed, to wrap several unrelated packets into a single I-O burst.

3.9. Name space :

Existing networks consider message addresses as meaning some physical component : a node, a line. As a result, there is a solid coupling between host addresses and network topology. CIGALE implements an abstract name space independent from the physical components. Consequently there is no constraint in naming hosts.

Furthermore, messages may be delivered to a single host address from several distinct nodes. Also, several host addresses may be reached over the same line. The first case is intended for reliability, as said before-hand. The second case allows several *logical* hosts to be connected on the same line. This is particularly convenient for having several distinct host protocols within the same host (as in CYCLADES), or to have several virtual hosts (as in IBM-CP 67), or to reach several hosts through a front end computer, or to have a set of hosts making up a private network. Actually, the exact nature of a host is immaterial in CIGALE ; it is a name capable of sending and receiving messages over one or several lines.

Part of the CIGALE name space is reserved for its internal components, such as software modules providing special services for network control and diagnostics aids. This saves the overhead and complexity associated with specially formatted packets. As far as switching is concerned, CIGALE handles only one packet format. But an internal component may be a real host, considered as part of CIGALE. This is a handy way to plug in any desirable function without making any technical modification to the CIGALE software, except putting a name in tables. This would be quite of a hang-up if network services were designated with special bits in special fields of special packets. Some variations in the address format allow to locate an internal component within a particular node, some nodes, or all the nodes. On this way network services may be distributed according to traffic patterns, and even relocated dynamically, should the need arise.

A brute application of the previous principles would result in every node containing the list of all possible addresses (internal components and external hosts). This is perfectly acceptable for small networks, but not large ones, as lists would be too bulky. Therefore, the CIGALE name space is divided up into *regions*, and host names are prefixed with a region name, like telephone numbers. Thus, only local hosts and other regions need be listed in any node. Addressing and routing is based on host name within a region, and on region name across regions. In this respect, CIGALE is an aggregate of local CIGALE's (Fig. 3).

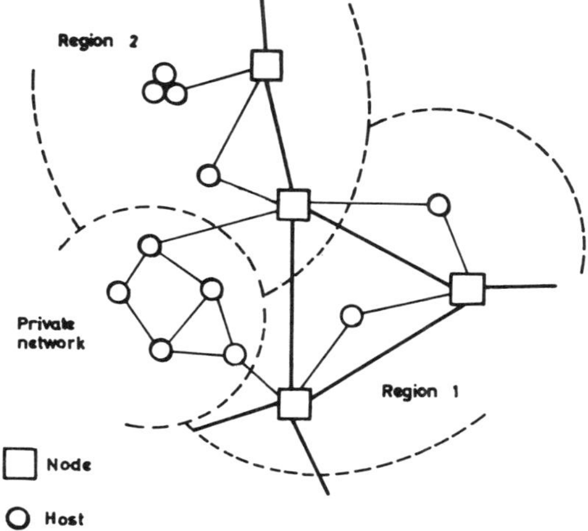

Fig. 3 - Address space

A region can contain one or several nodes, or not at all. This allows implementing an addressing plan without necessarily putting immediately as many nodes as regions. In addition, a host can be linked to nodes of different regions, even though its name belongs to one. This is intendedly restricted to hosts which cannot avoid straddling regions due to their geographical location. Or else address tables could become too large.

This name space is only a first step towards a general network interconnection scheme. In a multi-network context, the total name space is to be tree-structured at several levels [16]. Local networks (or regions) are to carry local traffic using shorter addresses, and long distance traffic using longer addresses. A common addressing plan is a prerequisite to network interconnection.

3.10. Circuits :

This term means a point-to-point logical connection established between two network users, be they hosts, or some entities within hosts. This can be simulated on both ends within the network [17], or even implemented physically as a fixed path through specific resources allocated within intermediate nodes (buffers, names, slots) [14]. Another common terminology is *call set up* [12].

Circuits can be predefined, and their use requires some allocation scheme [4]. Or they must be established on demand [12, 14]. In both cases a initial phase is mandatory before message transfer can take place.

Circuits may be useful for simple terminals which carry on a conversation with a single correspondent for a certain period of time. This is typical of time-sharing and remote batch users. On the other hand terminals may switch rapidly between various correspondents, when they participate in distributed activities, such as data base inquiries, monitoring. They may even have to handle several conversations in parallel, i.e. several circuits.

The host software is necessarily designed to manage a variety of parallel and independent activities, including logical connections with other hosts over a network. This is precisely the core of host-host protocols, which should be completely insulated from packet network characteristics [10]. Setting up network circuits is an additional constraint without any useful counterpart. Presumably, it is also an additional trouble-maker, since circuits will have jinxes of their own requiring special recovery procedures. Moreover circuit shortage or overhead can create congestion without any real traffic. One also looses the reliability of multiple links between host and network.

Since circuits present far more undesirable aspects than useful ones, they do not exist in CIGALE. However, they may be implemented on various ways as added services, as long as some users request it.

Fixed or switched circuits may be custom-tailored through private interfaces [17].

Actually packet switching networks with virtual circuits are a completely different approach to data communications. Instead of offering a message transfer service, like a mail system, they simulate a circuit switch. But the nature of the circuits do not allow transmitting bits at any time, like on a couple of wires. That sort of circuits can only transmit packets of bits, in some predefined manner, which is imposed by the network. In other words, a specific transmission procedure is required. Packet switching is carried out inside the network, but this is no longer a service. As far as the user is concerned, he only gets a circuit with a transmission procedure, which is not too unfamiliar.

3.11. Sequencing :

This is a usual corollary of circuits, i.e. the property of delivering packets in the same order as they have been sent over a particular circuit.

Bit transmission should be independent from applications, but data transmission is not. Indeed, data are bits plus structure plus semantics. So far semantics is transferred through human channels. Structure is application dependent and is taken care of by specific user protocols. Some of them are sequential, some are not. Transactions, labeled records, statistics, are usually independent pieces of data and can be delivered in any order.

Since there are no circuits in CIGALE, there is no sequencing.

222

3.12. Error control :

In CIGALE packets are checked and acknowledged between nodes. However node and line failures coupled with adaptive routing may result in packets being lost or duplicated. Consequently, some control mechanism is necessary to catch this type of error. It can only be done as part of a transmission procedure between a pair of correspondents. There is none in CIGALE, for several reasons :
- due to multiple links between host and CIGALE, there is no correspondent pair at network level,
- user protocols require end-to-end error control, since host mechanisms and host-node lines may also fail.

Consequently, end-to-end error control within CIGALE would not be sufficient, would not easily fit multiple links, and would introduce additional overhead [15].

As a general rule, protocols using CIGALE should include message error control. This is done in CYCLADES [18, 19]. Actually these mechanisms are an intrinsic part of host-to-host protocols.

3.13. Flow control :

This term covers usually mechanisms intended to keep a sender process from overrunning a receiver. Again this implies end-to-end control between a pair of correspondents. Only transmission lines are controlled in CIGALE. On the other hand, error and flow controls can be identical mechanisms, as they are no more than producer-consumer relationships [10]. They should normally be part of host-to-host protocols. This is done in CYCLADES.

End-to-end flow control has sometimes been considered as a mechanism for controlling traffic congestion within a network. E.g. this idea was behind the *link* mechanism in Arpanet, which is a variety of circuit [4]. Since then, it has been shown that congestion could still develop, while throughput on links is restricted [20, 27]. Actually they are two different classes of problems.

3.14. Congestion :

This term means a state within which network throughput drops to nil, or almost, due to saturation of network resources, such as buffers, line bandwidth, processor time, etc... It is a ubiquitous problem in resource sharing systems, where supply is constant, while demand is at random. [21].

Congestion may be local if it is only limited to a few nodes, e.g. when a receiver stops working, but not senders. Total congestion may also develop if the network gets so crammed with packets that they can hardly move. This phenomenon is somewhat elusive on real networks, as most of them are too small to allow for significant experiments. Actually most investigations are based on models and simulation [21, 22, 23].

Research pursued in Arpanet and NPL indicates that global network control should be obtained by using simple queue disciplines and storage allocation [24, 27]. Although CIGALE is small enough to dispense with sophisticated control techniques, it appeared worthwhile to experiment some variation of congestion control. Modelling studies have been undertaken, but no results were available at the time of the preparation of this paper. The basic idea is to couple routing and buffer allocation as two related facets of a global resource sharing exercise over the network [25].

Similarly to Arpanet [26], routing information propagates continuously throughout CIGALE. In addition to an estimation of transit delay, an estimation of available buffers is given per destination. Due to the hierarchical name space of CIGALE, a destination is actually a region, or a local host in a region. Again, this 2-level structure saves considerable overhead in handling routing tables. When solicited for entering packets, a node allows in only a limited number, based on buffer availability towards the requested direction.

At this point, it is clear that various traffic classes might be accomodated, e.g. a shortest delay class, within the limits of a few packets per destination, and a highest throughput class using most of the buffer supply on alternate routes towards the same destination. This scheme is expected to prevent local congestion instead of curing it once an increase in delay shows that it is developing.

Furthermore, each node may evaluate the total available capacity in the network, by adding up the supply for each destination. By convention, each node may be allowed to accept no more than a certain fraction of this total supply, until it gets fresh reports. Assuming that all nodes are solicited for an upsurge of entering traffic, the network might fill up to its maximum allowed capacity, but no more, so that traffic keep flowing. On the other hand, it is statistically predictable that only a few nodes will have to choke excess traffic at any given time. In this case, the propagation of the available network capacity results in a gradual absorption of the transient, following roughly a logarithmic law.

Thus, both local and total congestion are expected to be in control. Actually, this scheme is akin to the isarithmic technique [21], at least for controlling total congestion. A significant difference is that buffer supply is reevaluated constantly, instead of being assumed fixed. Indeed, a weakness of the isarithmic technique is that no error is supposed to occur. If a node smuggles permits in or out, the whole network gets out of hand. Also, network partitionning may throw traffic off balance. Such accidents should be corrected automatically in CIGALE.

As a safeguard, old packets will be destroyed, so that solid hang-up be excluded. But this is only a way to recover from a pathological condition, not a normal management policy. Actually, eliminating old packets is mainly intended to reduce the deviation of transit delays, so that host protocols be tuned for quick reaction on lost packets.

3.15. Routing :

Routing has already been discussed previously in connection with congestion control. A slight difference with Arpanet is that packets never flow backwards. In case no other way can be found, they are just dropped.

3.16. Accounting :

There is no specific mechanism in CIGALE for traffic accounting. On the other hand, various statistics are collected within nodes, and shipped to a network control center, for further analysis and reduction. The research environment presiding over most network development is admittedly not too obsessed with accounting problems. Some exposure to a more commercial approach would certainly be beneficial.

4. NETWORK INTER-CONNECTION

CIGALE has been thought out keeping in mind inter-connection problems. So far its design has been discussed mainly with regard to its function within CYCLADES, i.e. a communication tool between computers. Occasionally, it has been mentionned that a host could be a private network, and that regions in CIGALE could be viewed as local networks.

These are just examples of a more general capability (Fig. 4).

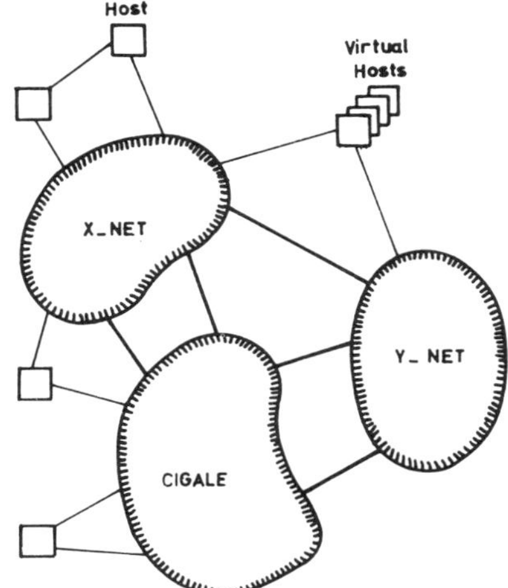

Fig. 4 - Network inter-connection

As long as a network carries messages as in a mail system, putting several networks together does not alter the picture, so that :

<network> : : = <network> <network> ... <network>

Passing a message between networks reduces to a local border problem, i.e. a mutually agreed transmission procedure.

Routing a message is a distributed activity. A common naming scheme is necessary at network level, so that each network know on which direction it should send a message to the network containing the final destination. Routing to the local user is only taken care of within the end network. As far as addressing and routing are concerned, inter-connected networks behave like nodes of a super-network.

This means that one might apply recursively the same approach to design a network, or a network of networks. Actually, there are real life differences which put some restrictions. Nodes of a network are homogeneous, and abide by the same rules. Networks tend to belong to different organizations, which do not necessarily wish to be homogeneous. However, they may agree that they are willing to carry one another's messages under minimum constraints.

In that context a network interface like CIGALE is likely to be the least constraining. A few common agreements would be required among all networks[16]:

- an addressing plan to designate networks
- a basic header format
- a maximum packet size
- a plain packet delivery service, without additional function
- a set of accounting practices.

Other necessary agreements are just neighbour problems.

In view of inter-connection experiments with other networks, e.g. NPL, the CIGALE header contains source and destination network names, according to the CATENET proposal [16]. Linking with Arpanet would not raise any particular difficulty, as long as message length is restricted to one packet. On the other hand, experience now acquired tends to support the desirability of redesigning Arpanet protocols along simpler principles, such as in CYCLADES-CIGALE [28]. But there remain unsolved issues with EPSS-like systems [12].

It is clear that the CIGALE transparency is its major trump to provide a communication service between existing systems. Any additional well-wishing function tied with the external world is likely to be incompatible and detrimental to a good service. In particular, communications networks studded with all sorts of bells and chimes will end up as one of a kind networks, unable to communicate, unless an ad hoc kludge be interposed so that they at last exchange packets.

5. CONCLUSIONS

CIGALE has been developped as the communications tool of a computer network. However, it is designed so that it can be inserted as a component of larger systems to carry any data traffic in a transparent mode. Except for timing parameters, CIGALE does not impose any particular protocol. Furthermore, it may include custom-tailored components to implement specific services.

ACKNOWLEDGEMENTS

The CIGALE development has been a joint effort by the Délégation à l'Informatique, the French PTT, and IRIA. Many dedicated people have put some contribution at various stages of the construction. Among individuals who created major parts of the software are A. DANET, J.L. GRANGE, D.PREVOST and S. SEDILLOT. Packets would not have traveled very far without F. DENJEAN's interfacing skill. D. WALDEN (BBN) suggested many good ideas.

REFERENCES

[1] L. Pouzin, Presentation and major design aspects of the Cyclades computer network. 3rd Data Comm. Symp. Tampa (Nov. 73), 80-87.

[2] J.L. Grangé, L. Pouzin, Cigale, la machine de commutation de paquets du réseau Cyclades, Congrès AFCET, Rennes (Nov. 73), 249-263.

[3] L. Pouzin, Les choix de Cigale, Congrès AFCET, Rennes (Nov. 73), 265-274.

[4] F.E. Heart et al, The interface message processor for the ARPA computer network. SJCC (1970), 551-567.

[5] L. Roberts, Extensions of packet communication technology to a hand-held personal terminal. SJCC (1972), 295-298.

[6] L. Roberts, Dynamic allocation of satellite capacity through packet reservation, Nat. comp. conf. (June 1973), 711-716.

[7] I. Switzer, The cable television system as a computer communication network. Symp. on computer communication network and teletraffic, New York (Apr. 1972), 339-346.

[8] G.J. Brandt, G.J. Chretien, Methods to control and operate a message switching network, Symp. on computer communication network and teletraffic, New York (Apr. 1972), 263-276.

[9] S.M. Ornstein et al, The terminal IMP for the ARPA computer network. SJCC 1972, 243-254.

[10] L. Pouzin, Network Architectures and Components, 1st European workshop on computer networks, Arles (Apr. 1973), 227-265. IRIA édit.

[11] D.L.A. Barber, Hierarchical control of a communications channel, Nat. Phys. Lab. (Nov. 1972), 10 p.

[12] Experimental packet switched service, British Post Office Telecommunications (Nov. 1972), 50 p.

[13] BBN report n° 1822, Specifications for the interconnection of a host and an IMP (1973), 120 p.

[14] L. Tymes, Tymnet, a terminal oriented communications network. SJCC 1971, 211-216.

[15] L. Pouzin, Network protocols, NATO Advanced Study Institute on computer communication networks, Brighton (Sept. 1973), 25 p.

[16] L. Pouzin, A proposal for interconnecting packet switching networks, EUROCOMP, (May 1974), 13 p.

[17] L. Pouzin, Use of a packet switching network as circuit switching, Réseau CYCLADES, TRA 507 (April 1973), 5 p. Also IFIP-TC6.1, doc. 31, NIC 16735.

[18] M. Elie, H. Zimmermann et al, Spécifications fonctionnelles des stations de transport du réseau CYCLADES, SCH 502 (Nov. 1972), 105 p.

[19] M. Elie, H. Zimmermann, Vers une approche systématique des protocoles sur un réseau d'ordinateurs, Congrès AFCET, Rennes (Nov. 1973), 277-291.

[20] L. Kleinrock, Performance models and measurements of the ARPA computer network. Sémin. AFCET, Paris (May 1972), 37 p.

[21] D.W. Davies, The control of congestion in packet switching networks, 2nd Symp. on problems in the optim. of data comm. Sys. (Oct. 1971), 46-49.

[22] H. Frank, R.E. Kahn, L. Kleinrock, Computer communication network design. Experience with theory and practice. SJCC 1972, 255-270.

[23] W.L. Price, Survey of NPL simulation studies of data networks, 1968-72, NPL report Com. 60 (Nov. 1972), 27 p.

[24] W.L. Price, Simulation of packet switching networks controlled on isarithmic principles. 3rd Data Comm. Symp. Tampa (Nov. 1973), 44-49.

[25] L. Pouzin, Another idea for congestion control in packet switching networks, Réseau CYCLADES, SCH 504 (Jan. 1973), 6 p. Also IFIP-TC6.1, doc. 21, NIC 14498.

[26] G.L. Fultz, L. Kleinrock, Adaptative routing techniques for store-and-forward computer-communication networks. Internat. Conf. on communications, Montréal (1971), 39-1 à 39-8.

[27] R.E. Kahn, Flow control in a resource sharing computer network, 2nd Symp. on problems in the optim. of data comm. sys. (Oct. 1971), 108-116.

[28] V. Cerf, An assessment of ARPANET protocols (To be published), 20 p.

Reprinted by permission of J.L. Rosenfeld (ed.), *Information Processing 74* (North-Holland, Amsterdam, 1975)

Computer Network Design Considerations

There are many parameters that need to be considered in the planning and designing of a computer network which will achieve resource sharing. Examples of such parameters are as follows: network cost, throughput, response time, reliability, channel capacity, system topology, etc. The interrelationship of these parameters is often nonlinear and very complex. Thus both analytical and simulation techniques are used in designing a computer network. Further, the "optimal solution" is often not obtainable.

Kahn (p. 226) provides an overview of resource sharing network design considerations. Gray (p. 237) describes basic principles underlying data communication line control procedures. Tymann (p. 249) presents high level data link control procedures for data communication. For further information on data link control procedures, the reader should refer to [DON 74].

Kleinrock (p. 255) discusses analytical and simulation models for studying the performance of a computer network. Kahn and Crowther (p. 266) discuss traffic flow control in a resource sharing network. Price (p. 275) presents simulation studies which indicate that the isarithmic flow control is able to reduce network end-to-end transmission times. However, we feel the actual implementation of such flow control schemes is rather difficult. Chu (p. 279) derives optimal fixed block size for the class of computer communications using error detection and retransmission for error control systems. Fraser (p. 290) specifies problems on interfaces between computers and data communication systems and provides detailed specifications for a particular computer-communications system interface. Frank, Kahn and Kleinrock (p. 298) present some theory and practical design experience in designing the ARPA network. Kleinrock and Naylor (p. 315) present measurement results of input traffic, line traffic and message delay of the ARPA network and provide insight regarding the performance of computer networks. Roberts (p. 329) reports the computer cost, the communication cost and the composite costs for packet switching trends. Frank and Chou (p. 336) and Chou and Kershenbaum (p. 349) deal with topological optimization of a computer network. Whitney and Doll (p. 358) propose to use a data base as an aid in the design and management of voice and data networks. The data base is comprised of sets of data describing the network terminals, communication channels, traffics, maps, charts, and cost tables.

For further reading about computer network design considerations, the reader is referred to [BAR 64], [DAV 67], [WHI 72], [PAN 72], [VAN 73], [PRI 73], [GER 73], [FRAS 73], [WOO 73], [McG 75], [LAV 75], [ALE 75], [KLEa 75], and [KLE 75].

Resource-Sharing Computer Communications Networks

ROBERT E. KAHN, MEMBER, IEEE

Invited Paper

Abstract—The development of resource-sharing networks can facilitate the provision of a wide range of economic and reliable computer services. Computer-communication networks allow the sharing of specialized computer resources such as data bases, programs, and hardware. Such a network consists of both the computer resources and a communications system interconnecting them and allowing their full utilization to be achieved. In addition, a resource-sharing network provides the means whereby increased cooperation and interaction can be achieved between individuals. An introduction to computer-to-computer networks and resource sharing is provided and some aspects of distributed computation are discussed.

I. Introduction

THE INTERACTION between computers and communications has steadily developed over the last two decades. While many universities, government agenies, and business firms prefer to make use of thier own computers, an increasing number of people are using communication facilities to access commercial computer services [1]. Time-sharing and batch processing services are offered in most major United States cities or are accessible via telephone circuits, and communication charges for local telephone access to these services are, in general, substantially lower than the computer charges. As the use of computer services increases, the demand for reliable and low-cost means of communicating over wide geographic areas also increases.

For many years, networks of interconnected computers have been planned or under study, and more recently several have been under development [16], [18], [24]. A common objective underlying the interest in these networks has been to demonstrate that economic savings or increased capabilities are possible by sharing computer or communication resources. Program access to specialized data bases is an important example of resource sharing in a computer-to-computer network.

The growing usage of these data-processing services and the objective of sharing resources raise communication issues far more extensive than those of achieving increased capability and lower costs in the telephone network, or developing improved communication services [2]. They involve a num-

Manuscript received June 7, 1972; revised August 1, 1972. This work was supported by the Advanced Research Projects Agency of the Department of Defense under Contract DAHC-71-C-0088.

The author is with Bolt Beranek and Newman Inc., Cambridge, Mass. 02138.

ber of complex regulatory issues, the need for common methods of access to and interchange between data-processing systems, the pooling of computer resources for increased utilization and reliability, the provision of specialized services, data conferencing, and so forth. A set of associated regulatory issues involving telecommunications policy has been raised and is under intensive study. Are separate common-carrier data networks desireable or not? What is the most effective way to plan for interconnection of data networks and how should their usage be tariffed? (Some of these questions are discussed in the paper by S. L. Mathison and P. M. Walker, this issue.)

It is too early to accurately predict in what way this interaction of computers and communications is likely to evolve. The technology is changing rapidly, and regulatory policies are in flux. If communication costs are not to dominate the overall cost of using remote data-processing services, technological advances must allow communications at substantially lower per bit costs than are possible with the current switched telephone plant.

In this paper, we present one view of computer communications network development and explore a number of the important issues in distributed computation which have arisen. This paper is neither a completely general treatment of computer networks, nor a full case study, but rather it contains selected aspects of the two. The reader will no doubt be able to identify where general considerations give way to specific ones derived primarily from the author's experience with the development of the Advanced Research Projects Agency Computer Network (ARPANET) [7], [8]. It is impossible for this to be an exhaustive treatise, or even a comprehensive one, and no such attempt is made.

II. Distributed or Concentrated Resources

Many economic factors support the conclusion that geographic "clustering" of computers is a desirable strategy for computer service organizations [9]. One possible advantage is better equipment utilization due to the pooling of resources. Clustering implies that a single maintenance staff (which is often underutilized) and scarce system personnel can support more equipment, more reliably, and that space, auxiliary equipment, and overhead can be consolidated. In fact, several commercial time sharing firms have already chosen to concentrate their computer resources in a small number of geographic areas. In contrast, however, many individual research or development machines under private or government ownership are distributed throughout the United States. The valuable resources on many of these machines provide a strong incentive for them to be made available to users and computers at many other locations [10], [11], [33].

The location of computers at a few geographic locations requires that both local and remote users be provided with an economic and reliable way to access the service. The switched telephone network currently appears to be a poor candidate to provide the long-distance communications service. In addition to being considerably more costly than local service, the error performance of long-distance circuits is degraded from shorter circuits and is insufficient for many computer applications. In addition, frequent disconnections, busy signals, etc., during peak traffic hours often make its usage inconvenient. These factors, coupled with user desires for increased bandwidth, lower setup times, and more suitable tariffs, have encouraged several vendors to competitively enter the common-carrier market [28].

The tariffs and the technical characteristics of the circuit-switched telephone network reflect the nature of voice communication requirements that are quite different from those of computer communications. Due to the "bursty" nature of computer traffic and the extremely low utilization of a typical voice-grade circuit by a terminal, a substantial portion of the data-communications capacity in a circuit-switched system is simply not used. This results in inefficient utilization of telephone company resources from the users' point of view. Frequency- or time-division multiplexing techniques have been usefully applied for deriving individual channels, but the statistical nature of computer traffic makes fixed allocation strategies such as these inefficient or unacceptable.

On the other hand, statistical multiplexing techniques allow these circuit resources to be more widely shared, at the possible expense of occasional delays in transmission. Message switching employs a generalized form of multiplexing for a network environment that allows all circuits to be shared among all users in a statistical fashion without being allocated in advance. (Multiplexing is the subject of a separate paper in this issue by D. R. Doll.)

This has been the motivation for the development of new communication systems as well as combined computer communication networks. The construction of both common-carrier data-communication systems and "private" networks (using leased common-carrier facilities) is a natural outcome of the need for economic and reliable communication between users and geographically distributed computers. In addition to potential cost savings, many of these networks provide error control, as well as asynchronous operation, local echoing, speed, and code conversion, which are better suited to data communication with computers than use of the telephone network alone. A reevaluation of the tariff structures for data communication has recently been undertaken by the FCC, and efforts are being made to provide the public with data-communications service having lower error rates, smaller service charging intervals, and faster setup times than the switched voice network currently provides.

III. Computer-to-Computer Communications

A computer network is a complex collection of many types of resources, including data bases, programs, operating systems, and special-purpose hardware, all of which are capable of being accessed from any other resource in the net. Computer-to-computer communication is necessary to achieve effective resource sharing, but the ability to transfer information between machines does not automatically result in useful machine-to-machine interactions. Aroused by the exciting possibilities in using multiple machines, system designers have recently begun to provide the major technical effort required to achieve effective computer-to-computer communication. The existence of the ARPANET is having precisely this effect, and as a result the extent of computer-to-computer interactions is certain to grow substantially in the next few years [6].

The ARPANET is one of the most advanced examples of a computer communication network [8], [16], [18]. It consists of a geographically distributed set of different computers, interconnected by a communication system based upon very fast response (interactive) message switching. This network was developed to ultimately allow economic and reliable sharing of specialized computer resources. The ARPANET has demonstrated the feasibility of message-switching technology, illustrated its advantages, and fostered the development of techniques for computer-to-computer communication. It is interesting to note that the ARPANET was originally designed with the notion of computer-to-computer communication in mind. It has subsequently been extended in capability to allow users with terminal equipment but no computer to connect to the net and communicate with computers and other users. In this sense, the ARPANET has taken the opposite approach from every other network designed with user access originally in mind.

For many years, the National Physical Laboratory (NPL) in England has experimented with the use of "single packet" messages for switching in the "local area of a data communication network" [31]. A number of terminal devices were successfully interconnected into a local network at NPL, and recently they have been concerned with extending the local network into a distributed network [30]. A computer-to-computer network is also under development in France to allow data sharing without costly duplication of files and its attendant problems of control, updating, security, etc. Central files, each accessible via a local computer, will be made accessible to other computers and hence to an extended user community. This network is expected to use a message-switching technique similar to that used by the ARPANET in the United States. In addition, networks are under design or development in other countries (e.g., Canada and Japan). Some of the European networks are described in other papers in this issue.

In general, the properties and structure of a computer communications network must reflect the overall requirements for which it was designed. This may consist of high-speed (megabit/second) circuits for rapid computer-to-computer communication, or low-speed (voice and telegraph grade) circuits for terminal access or slow-speed communications; it may be circuit switched or message switched, etc. Whatever its detailed structure, the network contains a communication system (private or common carrier) and a set of computer-system resources and users that interact via the communications system. This system is also called a communication subnet or simply a subnet for short. This organization not only characterizes the organization of geographically distributed networks, but can also serve as a model for the local structure of a single computer complex [3]. Its structure is therefore quite fundamental.

In operating a computer communications network as a "marketplace" for computer-related services, a number of important issues arise [34]. We allude to a few of them here. What criteria are appropriate to determine whether a service may be removed from the system? When and where should additional services be incorporated and what procedures are needed to maintain effective competition? What subnet changes are appropriate for changes in the distribution of resources? The total operational procedure should also include a strategy for utilization of the resources consistent with its intended functions (e.g., load sharing, data sharing, etc.).

An overriding concern of the network design is the overall reliability of the communications and computer resources. For a user to entrust his computing to a network, he must develop confidence in its availability when he needs it. It must be convenient to use and it must provide a believable guarantee to maintain standard and expected grades of service. An investment in time and energy to use a network resource can be negated by the failure to maintain a consistent service offering. Insuring that proper concern exists for the remote user of a computer resource is an important administrative problem that affects almost every phase of computer network development.

IV. Message-Switched Communications

Since the message-switching technology is not as well established as the circuit-switched technology, the fundamentals of its operation are reviewed in this section. Considerable discussion on the nature of these two switching doctrines is taking place. Are they merely different ends of a common spectrum (with a key variable such as packet size), or are they fundamentally different communication techniques? An argument in favor of their similarity is that both types rely on store and forwarding of data, whether a single bit is transiently stored, a byte-sized envelope, or a larger sized packet. The most significant external characteristics that "appear" to distinguish the two systems are that 1) circuit-switching systems are better equipped to maintain a time frame for users that require continuity in transmission, as in speech, while 2) message-switching systems allow speed and code conversion, thus permitting direct connection of and communication between devices of widely varying type. But it is possible to mask even these "seemingly" essential differences by the provision of a small amount of buffering and "byte manipulation" capability at the periphery of either system. It is actually the manner in which internal system resources are managed and utilized that provides a useful measure of comparison between them.

Briefly, in a circuit-switched network, the source and destination are connected by a dedicated communication path that is established at the beginning of the connection and broken at the end. This type of connection was specifically selected for use in switched telephony, where subscribers require a continuity in voice transmission and reception. Since the communication path remains fixed for the duration of a conversation, the output speech signal appears to be a time translate of the input speech signal as far as the ear can tell. In addition, for most voice conversations, the allocated analog voice channel is used in a fashion that seems reasonably efficient to the average user.

To establish a connection, the subscriber provides the local central office with an address which is used in setting up a path. Central office equipment detects off-hook, provides a dial tone, retains dialed digits, generates ringing, busy signals, etc. In the current telephone plant, long-haul circuits are primarily multiplexed analog channels. Routing selection is performed using a set of prespecified paths and usually based on the first few dialed digits. Call setup times generally take between 5 and 25 s, depending upon the number and type of central offices in the link and the amount of traffic. Recent experience has also indicated that reliability and overload problems are becoming increasingly prevalent in certain high-density population areas.

A message-switching system accepts, transmits, and delivers discrete entities called messages. In such a system, no physical path is set up between the source and the destination and no resources (e.g., capacity, buffer storage, etc.) are allocated to its transmission in advance. Rather, the source includes a destination address at the beginning of each message. The message-switching system then uses this address to guide the message through the network to its destination, provides error control, and notifies the sender of its receipt [17], [18].

A simple form of message-switching system employing a single central switching computer is commonly referred to as a "star" configuration and has all its lines connected to the central message switch. For many local applications this configuration can be quite practical. Three of its main disadvantages are 1) the central switch may be an unreliable link which will disrupt all communications if it fails, 2) the total circuit mileage for geographically distributed users to connect to the switch may be substantially larger than necessary, resulting in excessive communications cost, and 3) every circuit failure can result in some loss of user communications.

A distributed message-switching system is one in which many distributed switching computers are employed and the network control is decentralized in such a way that the failure of any switching computer disrupts communications only for its local customer. The distributed system is usually more economic and reliable than a star configuration for handling geographically distributed users.

The components of a message-switching system are dedicated point-to-point communication circuits and switching nodes which interconnect the circuits in such a way that a message arriving on one circuit may be transmitted out another. Communication over a message-switched system occurs via a sequence of transmitted messages, each consisting of its address followed by text. The address is inspected by each node in routing the message to the next node on the way to its destination. In the ARPANET, one or more computers may be directly connected to a node and are known as Host Computers, or Hosts for short. The nodes are called Interface Message Processors or IMP's for short.

A distributed message-switched network, such as the ARPANET, contains no mass storage, and as little buffering in the nodes as necessary to utilize the full capacity of the communication circuits.[1] The network design allows a message to remain in the net only as long as necessary to transport it from source to destination; no long-term storage is provided in the communication system. Messages that cannot be delivered to the destination are simply not accepted into the net and must be retransmitted at a later time. Clearly, one or more Hosts on the net with low cost per bit bulk storage could provide or even be dedicated to providing long-term storage of messages with subsequent automatic retransmission.

The combinatorial aspect of the interconnection of large numbers of computers is an important consideration in network design. Each computer in a message-switching system is connected to the net via a single full-duplex channel to its IMP over which messages are multiplexed. This single connection to the network makes the computing service accessible to all computers and all users on the net. Furthermore, all users and all computers on other digital networks can access this computer by the simple expedient of a single interconnection between nets. Thus not only is complete digital access possible, it is achieved in a strikingly economic way for each installation. This technique solves a massive combinatorial access problem with a single economic stroke.

In Fig. 1, we show the communications portion of the ARPANET as of April 1972 when it consisted of twenty-four nodes and 28 circuits. Since that time it has grown to over thirty nodes. Each node is a possible source and destination of

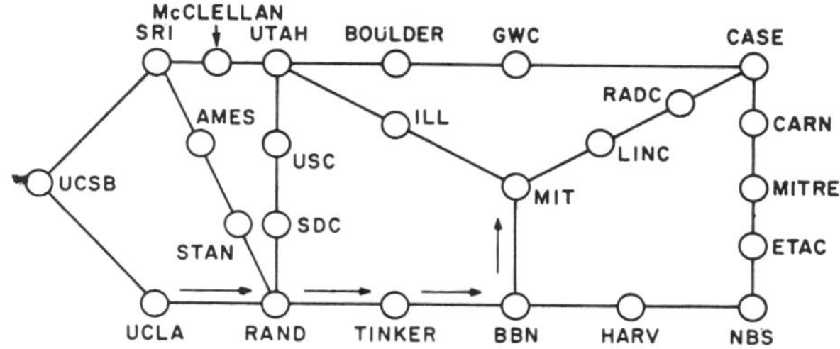

Fig. 1. Routing a message through the ARPANET.

messages. We assume (for the moment) that messages may be of variable length up to a maximum of 1000 bits,[2] and are known as packets while in the network. The path taken by a packet traversing the net from node 1 (UCLA) to node 6 (M.I.T.) is indicated by arrows in the figure. The circles indicate the nodal processors and the lines indicate synchronous point-to-point circuits. The message enters the net at node 1, which examines its address and decides to transmit it out its circuit to node 7 (RAND). Upon receipt, node 7 examines the address and decides to send it to node 21 (TINKER), which in turn sends it to node 5 (BBN) which sends it to node 6 (M.I.T.). Node 6, discovering the message is for itself, replaces the destination address by the source address (which is carried along by the message-switching system) and "delivers" the message. The text of the message thus appears at the destination exactly as it was transmitted and the address portion identifies the sender. After delivery, the sender is notified of its receipt by a small message that goes back across the network.

An important part of a computer network design is the specification of the location and capacity of all circuits in the net. Fifty kilobit/second circuits are currently used in the ARPANET to achieve an average delay of 0.2 s or less. Programs have been developed that iteratively analyze various possible network configurations and select reliable high-throughput low-cost designs through the use of circuit-exchange heuristics [20], [22]. Analytical techniques have been developed for estimating the average transit-time delay under assumed traffic loads. These techniques show that the delay remains almost that of an unloaded net until the capacity of one or more "cutsets" begins to saturate [7]. (Network optimization is the topic of a paper by H. Frank and W. Chou in this issue.)

An important design consideration is the method for dynamically selecting routes. (We assume that routes are not allocated in advance.) A central controller could provide the routing information and distribute it to all the processors, or the processors could collaborate in computing the routing information directly. This is but one of many instances of a design choice between distributed and centralized control. In the initial ARPANET design, the route selection is performed independently by each IMP according to a distributed routing algorithm. Routing information is stored in a table and individually maintained by each IMP for rapid look-up. It identifies the output line to select for each destination and is updated according to a rule evaluated periodically (e.g., every half second). It could also be evaluated asynchronously (whenever status changes occur) or a combination of both. In the

[1] The Defense Departments Autodin network, however, employs mass storage in the communication network for deferred retrieval and delivery of messages.

[2] In the ARPANET, messages may actually vary up to 8095 bits in length.

simple algorithm used in Fig. 1, each IMP sends the message on its choice of a path with the fewest intermediate IMP's and, using the update procedure, each IMP adapts its routing to other IMP and circuit failures.

A simple method for implementing this algorithm is for each IMP to keep a table with the count of the number of IMP's on the shortest path to each destination, which it frequently transmits to its immediate neighbors. Each IMP also announces to its neighbors that it is 0 IMP's away from itself. Upon receipt of the routing information from its neighbors, the IMP increments the neighbors' counts and keeps the lowest value for each destination.

Each IMP buffers a packet until receipt is acknowledged by the adjacent IMP. A cyclic checksum, generated in hardware by each IMP, is appended to the transmitted packet for error control. If an error is detected by the hardware at the adjacent IMP, or no buffer space exists, the packet is simply discarded and will shortly be retransmitted by the neighboring IMP when a condition (such as a time-out) occurs and no acknowledgement is received.

The design of an efficient network without mass storage requires that the number of buffers be kept to a minimum, and that they be used so that each IMP is able to use its circuits efficiently and to their maximum capacity. This means that the minimum number of buffers must be at least as large as the number of full-sized packets which must be stored from the time one full-size packet is transmitted until its acknowledgment returns. This number is determined by the circuit propagation delay, the packet size, and the circuit data rates, as well as the total number of circuits. To utilize these buffers efficiently, stored packets must be quickly released upon receipt of their acknowledgement or activated for retransmission, as appropriate, in a timely way.

Each IMP contains only a small amount of buffering for messages in transit and no mass storage, and a flow control strategy is needed to insure that the IMP's do not become "congested" thus preventing useful data from being communicated. This situation is particularly apparent if the network design allows the source or the destination to temporarily stop the transmission or reception of data and then continue without a loss of messages. This is appropriate to time-sharing computers, and is used in the ARPANET, because it allows occasional delays to occur, for example, while a word is stored in memory or a procedure is activated by the processor. In practice, a Host can neither guarantee to accept all messages at their instantaneous arrival rate, guarantee not to crash while receiving heavy traffic, or expect the transmitting Host to buffer messages should he prefer to discard them upon receipt. In particular, flow control is necessary to protect the network against the sudden dispatch of a larger number of messages to a single destination than it is prepared to accept [13].

An often overlooked but important consideration in the network design is whether or not to keep the circuits fully loaded even in the absence of maximum traffic. For instance, should "test messages" be continuously transmitted or only periodically transmitted to check circuits? Under light traffic loads, is it desireable to transmit duplicate packets and accept the first one with a valid checksum, in order to reduce occasional retransmission delays or to improve the response time on a very noisy circuit? For land-based circuits, the extra traffic during otherwise light loads appears to be acceptable and desireable to reduce delays on noisy circuits. The extra processor capacity is ordinarily available for heavy traffic in any event. For multiaccess satellite circuits, however, the extra traffic during light loads may interfere with other processors sharing the same channel.

In an unloaded net, the transit time is determined primarily by the number of IMP's encountered in the routing and the time for the packet to pass from one IMP to the next. This, in turn, is determined directly from the packet length, the circuit data rate, and the speed of light propagation delay. Under increasing traffic loads, the transit time also begins to increase due to occasional delays in the IMP's. However, if the network is designed to begin rejecting the further input of traffic as the capacity limitation of the network is approached, these delays can be kept to a few times that of an unloaded net. Traffic is thus queued outside the net (rather than allowed to enter and be queued inside the net) so the nominal transit time during peak traffic is not very different from that experienced in an unloaded net. In these cases, an attempt must be made to insure that the effective bandwidth is shared "fairly" among all the competing sites.

Network usage generally requires a combination of short transit times for interactive usage and high bandwidth for file transmission. These two objectives may be attained with single-packet messages. To achieve interactive transit times, no setup delay must be incurred. A simple way to achieve this is for the source IMP to retain a copy of each packet which is nominally discarded after the delivery is made, but retransmitted when, for lack of buffer space, the original is discarded at the destination IMP. To achieve high bandwidth, enough messages must be allowed to enter the net between source and destination so as to fill the "pipeline," but this flow must be able to be readily quenched at the source when the buffer space at the destination IMP begins to fill.

The current ARPANET design actually allows variable length messages with a maximum size just over 8000 bits. The message is partitioned by the source IMP into separate 1000-bit packets to speed its transmission through the network. Each packet makes its way to the destination independently where it may conceivably arrive out of order. These packets could be reassembled into the proper order by the destination Host (using sequence numbers), but when the assumption is made that the communications net should preserve sequencing at least at the level of a single process-to-process conversation, the IMP's are obliged to reassemble the packets. The destination Host thus receives the text of each message exactly as it was transmitted in a single-block transfer.

When these larger messages are used and the IMP's undertake the responsibility for reassembly, yet another type of congestion phenomenon called reassembly lockup is introduced [13]. The flow-control mechanism, which is used to prevent the backup of messages in the net, is also powerful enough to prevent the lockup problem. But in its application, it can subject long messages to setup delays and thus delay succeeding short messages from its Host.

If "sufficient" buffer space were available for reassembly at the destination IMP, there would be no *a priori* compelling reason for the subnet to preclude a Host from sending full 8000-bit messages (or even somewhat larger ones). However, the presence of 8000-bit messages may noticeably delay shorter messages from other Hosts 1) while it is being delivered to the destination, and 2) by tying up 8 buffers rather than 1 during reassembly. This provides one valid reason to restrict the Hosts to single-packet messages, if these delays become significant. However, as we indicate in Section V, there may be other factors which favor retention of the larger size.

If there is a fundamental distinction between circuit switching and message switching, it is undoubtedly in the way internal resources are managed. For example, circuit switching requires that network bandwidth as well as local control equipment and storage be allocated to a given transmission circuit in advance, whereas a message-switching system does not. Secondly, the presence of circuit-switched routes means that user messages are identified by their circuit and no user control signalling need accompany the transfer of information. In message switching, however, all record of activity (except accounting) associated with a message is contained in the message, which vanishes when the message leaves the system. This signaling information, in the form of an address, must accompany each message and the message must be examined and processed at each stage of the transmission process.

Two practical consequences of the difference are that the circuit-switched system usually requires a nontrivial setup time to allocate resources. Message-switched systems can avoid setup delays, but may introduce occasional variations in transit time. These delays can generally be maintained to within a few times the delay of an unloaded net, but wider variations may result from queueing delays outside the net, particularly under heavy traffic load. Under similar conditions, though, a circuit-switched user might fail to obtain a circuit and would incur this probabilistic situation on subsequent tries. Any allocated but idle channels are simply unavailable at this time to handle these overload conditions.

V. Network Use of Individual Computer Systems

The term network has been used and misused in a variety of ways. Some people have referred to the use of dial-up facilities to access a single computer as a network. Others have referred to any interaction between computers and a communication system as a network capability. Several distributed networks were developed to allow simple forms of communication between identical machines using standard dial-up or leased voice circuits, thus providing a convenient way to transfer jobs and files and to maintain and update the systems in the net. This latter application exemplifies a true networking activity, even though it only concentrates on selected aspects of computer resource sharing [19], [21].

In general, only a subset of the network sites possess computing power, and certain of them will offer regular service to users via the network. Other sites may choose to offer service only on a limited basis, or to cooperatively interact via the net with selected co-workers, but not offer general service. This latter situation is more likely to occur for many specialized research facilities. In addition, large private computer centers as well as commercial firms may welcome the opportunity to connect their systems, since it offers a large potential market for usage of unused capacity.

Host service on the network ought to be as reliable as the communications, although this objective is often difficult to achieve. For example, in the ARPANET, total uptime of the IMP at any site is currently on the order of 98 or 99 percent, while Host availability is generally no higher than 90 percent. It is certainly possible to improve on this score; some commercial firms claim to provide over 99-percent availability of service, and certain private and government systems must obviously be operated with near-perfect reliability. The airline systems and the computers in the space program provide two key examples.

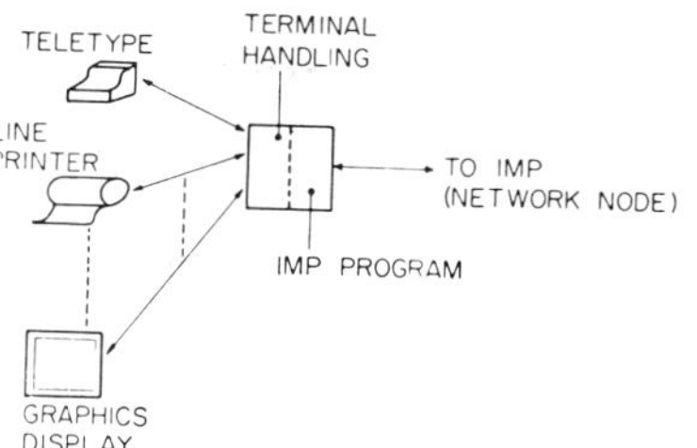

Fig. 2. Terminal IMP.

A. Network Access

In a network that supports computer-to-computer communication, user groups with a local computer can access another computer in the net by first logging into their home computer and then into the other computer, using the home computer in a transparent mode as a switch. However, this is an expensive way to access another computer since it incurs charges in two computers and ties up jobs in both. Furthermore, since Hosts may be unreliable, the connection is more vulnerable than a direct connection into the other machine.

Sites with expensive computer installations might deem it economic to depart from their machine if "equivalent" service can be economically obtained via the net. In general, such a site requires the ability to service local users with a full complement of terminals and peripheral devices, such as Teletypes, graphics displays, line printers, magnetic tapes, and possibly other mass storage. In addition, many sites with no computer will derive maximum benefit in connecting to a net if the full range of peripherals can be provided locally. Other users, however, may be satisfied with a simpler approach that provides terminal access to remote computers but does not handle peripheral devices other than line printers.

For this latter class of users, an addition may be made to the IMP which allows a set of terminals to be directly connected. This addition consists of multiplexing equipment that collects characters from the terminals and packages them in the form suitable for delivery to the IMP. Likewise, it receives messages from the IMP and sorts the characters out to the various terminals. This addition requires hardware and software designed to make the set of terminals interface to the network as a "mini-Host," and this IMP is referred to as a Terminal IMP. (See Fig. 2.)

A more elaborate approach is appropriate for user sites that wish to support many different types of peripheral equipment. Since their characteristics and operation can vary widely, device-dependent programming is mandatory, and substantial buffering may be required for the higher speed devices. Furthermore, sites with mass storage will generally wish it to be accessible from other computers in the net, which generally requires the implementation of a full set of standard and specialized network protocols. These considerations make it appropriate to provide a separate processor devoted to the handling of peripherals.

This latter approach is particularly desirable for a site which is both a user site and a server site. The architecture of such a site should be organized so that if the serving site central processing unit (CPU) is down, local users can access other network computers and local mass storage can be accessed by them over the net. Similarly, if the local storage should fail, others across the net can temporarily replace them. If the net fails, local users can still obtain full access to the local system. Only if both the local CPU and the network fail will the users be unable to obtain computation.

Modularity and logical reconfiguration are conveniently achievable in this way. Substantial progress in the design of modular communication-oriented architectures can be expected from innovative usage of interconnection ideas [3]–[5].

B. User Requirements

Let us now turn our attention to the use of these facilities by the user. We note three potential locations where user computation can be performed—in the terminal itself, in the peripheral processor (or Terminal IMP), or in the Host computer(s). Although the bulk of the "pure computation" will undoubtedly take place in the Host computers, some aspects of the processing must, in general, be distributed. For example, local echoing is required to obviate the otherwise noticeable effects of speed of light propagation delay, as on satellite links. This raises the important question of location of functions in a distributed network. In other words, what intelligence is needed to allow distributed system usage and where should it be placed?

Let us concentrate on the echoing problem for the moment. As a general rule, a remote user should see the same output and otherwise obtain service from a remote Host as if he were a local user. To achieve this objective, the user's local system (programmable terminal, "mini-Host," etc.) must have considerable information available to it about each subsystem in use at the remote Host. For example, a simple local echo/remote echo strategy is generally insufficient to handle echoing for users on half-duplex terminals, or users on full-duplex terminals that prefer to type ahead. A remote user editing the character string ABCDEFG can delete the last three characters by typing successive delete characters (echoed as\) and he sees the output ABCDEFG\G\F\E. Using the system from a remote site with local echoing and typeahead he would see ABCDEFG\\\GFE.

More striking, perhaps, is the remote use of a debugging program DDT. To examine successive registers 120–123, a local user would first type 120/ to print the contents of the first register and then strike successive line feed characters to examine the successive registers. The system would respond with (say the contents are all zeroes):

```
120/ 0
121/ 0
122/ 0
123/ 0
```

and leave the cursor following the last 0. A remote user with typeahead and local echo would see one of several possible responses (depending on the remote systems response to a received line feed). Assuming the remote system echoes only the formatted data and the local system echoes linefeed as linefeed (no carriage return), the output would look as follows:

```
120/



                    0121/ 0122/ 0123/ 0.
```

In general, the local echoing system should have full knowledge of the time-varying syntactical operation of the subsystem in use. This requires feedback of information about subsystem break and separator characters, control signalling, special conventions, etc.

Each terminal has characteristics peculiar to it and a convention is required for a computer system to initially recognize a terminal. Although the remote computer could then convert to the characteristics of the terminal, it is far more manageable if each terminal could appear to the network as a standard terminal employing an agreed upon set of characters and signalling conventions. One such standard (developed for the ARPANET) is 7-bit United States of America Standard Code for Information Interchange (USASCII) with the eighth bit set to 0. In that scheme, the other 128 possible characters are reserved for special control characters. In addition, most terminals need attention to details, such as carriage return, keyboard locking and unlocking, interrupt signalling, and other peripherals indicate out of paper, buffer full, and may require complete two-way channel control, etc.

Local computation is therefore needed for the user's terminal to interact properly with other remote systems and their subsystems. At a minimum, his local computation must allow the user to 1) identify his terminal to the network, 2) select a destination Host, 3) select a transmission mode, 4) perform echoing and code conversion, and 5) allow the remote Host to be interrupted.

It seems probable that, in the long run, many terminals will contain mini-processors and thus user programming in a separate "mini-Host" will be unnecessary. (This is amplified in the paper on terminals by L. C. Hobbs in this issue.) However, until this possibility is a widespread reality rather than an expectation, users may be hindered if they are unable to provide local user code in one place or the other.

C. Message Processing

Before considering various examples of usage of a computer network, let us briefly indicate how messages are processed within the Host computers [15], [32]. Messages travel through several layers of protocol in the Host system. The first layer of protocol handles the IMP, activating I/O buffers, fielding control messages, etc. The second layer interacts with the local processes and remote Hosts monitor, allocating buffer storage, providing process identification, formatting control information, etc. Subsequent layers correspond to specific user-oriented functions, such as the standard network terminal, file transmission, etc.

The ARPANET Host protocol utilizes the notion of connections over which messages are transmitted. A connection must first be established before communication over it may occur. The Hosts at either end of the connection must keep full information about the use of the connection (which is obtained during its establishment) to handle flow control. This strategy appears to be close in spirit to telephone circuit switching.

A few limitations to this strategy are apparent [14]. An important concern is that it requires each Host to maintain resources in the form of connection tables that can become filled, thus preventing any further communication with that Host. In particular, a single process can attempt to establish its maximum limit of connections, although it cannot, in general, make full use of them at one time. Entries in this connection table are permanently allocated, and thus only a fixed number of connections can be established at any time.

A second limitation with the use of a connection table is that it can be vulnerable to error conditions and Host status, particularly since both Hosts must generally agree on its contents for flow control. Finally, the strategy requires the connection information to be used for termination, which means that information which otherwise would be nominally discarded by Hosts with limited space, must be retained merely to close the connection. These limitations, as well as others, may be obviated with a message-switched Host protocol [14].

The desired size of Host messages may have an important impact on the operating system as well as on the communication system. The original ARPANET design specification allowed individual messages to be as large as 8192 bits, a design choice based largely on intuition.

As the design specification originally stated [29]:

> . . . a packet is defined as the inter-IMP unit and Message as the inter-Host unit. A packet will not exceed 1024 bits in length. The IMPs must break all longer messages into multiple packets. Messages will be limited to 8192 bits so as not to require excessive buffer space.

Undoubtedly, this latter reference is interpretted as referring to buffer space in the IMP's, but it could equally well apply to buffer space in the Hosts. In particular, the argument defends why the size is not larger, but does not entertain the possibility that it ought to be kept smaller for any specific reason.

If there is a convenient maximum Host message size, it is probably a maximum-sized page, which corresponds to 1 K of 36-bit (or possibly 48-bit) words. However, transmission of such large messages (say 50 000 bits) to the IMP and from the IMP to the Host produces excessive delays for short messages queued up behind them, and provides a prime reason for Hosts to prefer that these long messages be subdivided into shorter messages. Since no experience with network software was available during the initial design, it was intuitively concluded that a shorter 8192-bit message was short enough. Interestingly, we note that two hardware paths between each Host and its IMP, one for short messages and one for long messages, could remedy this problem at some extra cost in hardware and buffer storage.

Since efficient transmission is possible with 1024-bit packets, it appears in retrospect that the selection of the larger message size may be unnecessary. The Host overhead in network communication increases with the number of messages, so there is some incentive for making all Host messages sufficiently large that a typical short transaction can occur in a single message. No evidence yet obtained by us indicates that 1024-bit Host messages would impose a limitation that is significant, but an increased demand for page transfers or the presence of higher bandwidth circuits could tip the balance more strongly in favor of a larger size. The jury seems to be still out on this issue.

VI. Applications of Multicomputer Interaction

Network utilization involving the combined use of two or more computers in a productive way began during the initial experimentation with the ARPANET. It has provided experience in the development of techniques for performing distributed computation and allowed some simple application areas to be identified. Some applications involving multiple computers have been discussed for many years, partly as a result of their inherent interest and ease of conceptualization. One important example is the access to specialized data bases that are only available from a remote source. Several information banks have already been developed or are under development, and their expected usage is being projected upward. Another example is in the use of "future" computer communication networks for handling the distribution and delivery of mail and other transient information. However, these applications are only beginning to develop in any significant way. Much effort has already been devoted to the study of topics such as concurrency and parallel processing, which may result in faster program execution and otherwise make efficient usage of available resources. We expect that computer networking will enhance these efforts. For other applications, the sensation of dealing with one system rather than two (or more) is overwhelmingly evident to the user and this pleasant feeling often generalizes to other multicomputer interactions as well.

Three areas in which applications have already occurred are briefly identified below.

A. File Transfer

The first application for combining two computer systems in the ARPANET in a nontrivial way involved the use of an XDS-940 computer at Stanford Research Institute (SRI) and a PDP-10 computer at Utah. SRI, anticipating the delivery of a PDP-10, began to use the Utah machine in the development of PDP-10 software.

At first a higher level language was developed. Source code was generated on the 940, converted to object code, and executed on the 10. Patches were made on the Utah machine during debugging and, periodically, an updated source and binary version would be generated at SRI and sent over the net. Subsequently, other higher level languages were similarly developed.

A simple protocol to handle file transfers was developed for the TENEX operating system [10] and has proven useful for transferring new subsystems and system revisions between TENEX sites. In addition, it has been a useful initial step to allow cooperating processes in two TENEX systems to share a single file.

In this protocol, the network appears as a device to which a file may be output or from which a file may be input. The two ends of the transfer must coordinate by having one end execute the input and the other end execute the output. This simple file transfer protocol requires the intervention of the user to log into both ends, assign a file name for the destination, invoke the proper format, etc. Other experience in the transfer of files has been recorded by the University of California at Santa Barbara, as well as by IBM, by Control Data and others [19], [21].

B. Remote Job Service

A simple example of a computer-to-computer interaction is provided by users who write, debug, edit, and store programs on an interactive time-sharing facility and run them on a separate batch processing system. While time sharing has created an interactive environment for programming and the development of programming techniques, batch processing systems, and small dedicated computers have maintained a predominance for performing extensive computations. The availability of both kinds of service in a computer-communications network provides a single user with convenient access to the best features of both. (See Fig. 3.)

While a user can become accustomed to using both services independently, he need not be required to physically collect

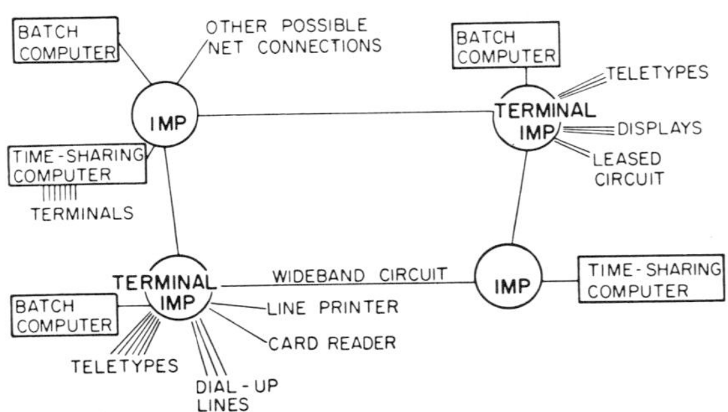

Fig. 3. A simple IMP network.

time-sharing output on tape or punched cards for submission to the batch system. The most convenient user option is for the interactive machine to submit his job to the batch processing machine under user initiated control. He can then specify the location for output to be stored or printed, revise the program in the time-sharing system, and resubmit it under fully interactive procedures from a single location, with no need to keep physical copies of files, program, etc.

For over a year the RAND Corporation had been using the ARPANET for remote job service from an IBM 360/65 at RAND to a 360/91 at UCLA [26], [27]. This facility was only accessible to internal RAND users until recently when it was replaced by a PDP-10, which allowed network users to create and submit jobs for remote service elsewhere.

Both the program and its relevant files must be transferred to the 360/91 before a job can be run. They are typically shipped together as successive "card images." The remote job service program will allow the users to start or stop the execution of his program, cause the system output to be stored on a designated file, or be output on a device such as a local printer. The user is also provided with options to check the status of the execution, receive confirmation and error messages that indicate its progress, and allow certain actions to be taken.

These facilities are used by RAND researchers in the generation and processing of simulated weather data. Weather modeling programs can be activated from a remote site, output from these programs can be temporarily stored, or shipped to a remote site for preparation and display. This separation of the computation into components is particularly appropriate when one part may be devoted almost exclusively to extensive numerical or symbolic computation and another part to user-related manipulation or preparation of the output data.

A "complex" weather simulation program requires many hours of computation on the 360/91, and thus is not well suited to rapid on-line activities such as the updating of a display. Rather, precomputed weather data (from the models) are retrieved from 360/91 disk packs (with operator assistance) and used by the PDP-10 for further processing and display. The availability of a high-speed parallel processing system such as the Illiac IV [33] may eventually allow real-time weather experimentation without operator intervention.

C. *Multiprocess Operation in Many Machines*

The combined use of two or more computers allows additional processing capability over the use of a single system. One such example is provided by the McRoss system [12] that coordinates the operation of two or more cooperating air-traffic-control simulation programs running in one or more TENEX systems. Each simulation program, called Route Oriented Simulation System (ROSS) [23], models the airspace of one air-traffic-control center in detail. To simulate the airspace of a Boston to New York flight, four simulation programs would be activated; one for the Boston terminal area, one for the Boston enroute area, one for the New York enroute area, and one for the New York terminal area. The four ROSS programs may be run simultaneously in as many as four TENEX systems in the ARPANET.

When a single machine is used to house all the components of a programming system, it has the disadvantage that computing will stop if that machine crashes. When one piece of a multicomputer programming system becomes unavailable, the other parts can learn to adjust to the change in configuration. A desirable objective is to provide enough backup information to enable the multicomputer programming system to be restarted in the event of a single Host failure and to proceed from a recent point in simulated time as if nothing had happened.

Other applications involving multiple computers are certain to arise for which simple examples are more difficult to construct. For example, as special areas of expertise develop, it is natural to expect that individual efforts by specialists also trained in the use of computers will produce new and useful resources on different machines. These resources may represent state of the art or proprietary developments that cannot be conveniently transferred to other machines, and must therefore be used at the site of their creation or where they currently exist. An important application for distributed computation is thus likely to involve the coordination of separate research projects into combined efforts that utilize these specialized or proprietary and hence nontransferable resources.

A second major application of distributed computation is likely to be the facilitation of interactive cooperation between people at different locations. Interactive cooperation may be regarded as an extension of normal voice communication to include the ability for several persons at different locations to "simultaneously" observe, communicate about, and manipulate both common data structures and programs. Since the people are assumed not to be colocated, the programs which support the interactive cooperation (such as display protocol routines) must also be distributed.

A third major application for distributed computation is in providing for conveniently feasible demonstrations of prototype systems to be performed from different locations. This technique can allow new capabilities to be readily conveyed without the inconvenience of moving the observer to a home site for the demonstration.

VII. A Distributed Operating System

A network in which basic differences exist between the computers at each installation is said to be inhomogeneous. It is possible to develop a standard network protocol for an inhomogeneous system that allows usage of various pieces of the system to be coordinated in a uniform manner. However, this task is one of substantial complexity that will probably require changes in system architecture and program design techniques before it can be fully realized. Even if it were a straightforward matter, it would not be generally useful to transfer portions of any one system to another, and standard operations that involve systems at a remote site must typically be performed at that remote site.

A collection of similar operating systems may also be organized into a virtual subnetwork of homogeneous computers that interact with each other in a uniform way. These systems are more easily organized into a single distributed operating system with common file systems, address space, naming conventions, etc. In general, every type of interaction between two systems in a homogeneous network must be evaluated to determine what is to be transmitted and what is to be remotely evaluated. No single answer will suffice for all applications. As we noted above, it is not generally possible to apply both alternatives in an inhomogeneous network. We consider some of the properties a system like this ought to possess.

The user accesses the distributed homogeneous network by logging into a distributed system rather than into a specific computer in the net. An appropriate machine is selected for him and he logs in with the standard log-in sequence for his home computer, including password, account number, and other information as required. Upon completion of the log-in sequence, the computer initiates a brief exchange with the users home computer to notify it of the impending job which it then proceeds to service. The home computer may then request that the job be transferred, alter credit or accounting information, or merely note the event.

Under conventional design constraints, the combined operation of several Host computers will require a separate job to be established in each machine. In a distributed system, though, it is important to allow access to each system without the user logging into each system individually. Furthermore, it is also desireable to permit certain transient activities to occur which do not tie up valuable resources or otherwise interfere with users on the system. The system merely performs the transient activity and logs the transaction into a suitable file for accounting purposes. Once logged into one of the Hosts, the user is able to access and utilize any programs, files, and most other facilities on other computers in the system as if they were all on one virtual machine.

The availability of many resources in this system makes it possible to achieve reliable operation when one or more resources are disabled. The user can be affected by failure in several ways. For example, his program or a piece of it may be aborted by machine failure or he may lose part or all of his files. The user may also find the local file storage to be unusable while running his job. If local storage is not initially available, he can specifically designate another system to store his files. Alternatively, he can allow the local system to store files in other Hosts and expect them to be returned without his knowing the identity of the temporary storage location. Obviously, a small amount of local storage is needed for this application. The distributed system thus not only makes resources more widely available; it can use them to provide increased reliability to a user.

A system designed to operate stand-alone may not be as efficient in serving its network users as in serving its local users. Certain performance improvements are obtainable by streamlining critical portions of the system code, attention to organizational details and to carefully engineered improvements to scheduling, the file system, etc. However, a major improvement in speed and efficiency may require structural overhaul of the system organization to allow for efficient process-to-process communication at high bandwidths and for efficient overall utilization of resources. In particular, the portion of the system devoted to protocol and message handling (byte manipulation) can consume a considerable amount of CPU time at high bandwidth. In a time-sharing system, particularly, these functions, which appear to be communication functions, can be usefully separated from the "computation" functions. This decomposition also allows more human engineered network interfacing, since a local CPU failure can usually be reported by the communications portion of the system if it remains up. The delegation of all protocol functions to a separate processor that can directly deposit into and retrieve from process buffers makes it possible for the operating system to communicate over the network at speeds at least an order of magnitude faster than before. This increase in capability is achieved by performing the protocol operations on the fly in a separate processor and by avoiding the unnecessary overhead in moving real-time data around in memory.

Techniques for computer-to-computer communication are still in their infancy and a great deal of exploration and experimentation is occurring in this area. How should programs be written to run in a network environment and what debugging and control techniques are suitable for distributed computation? What operating system architectures are appropriate to computer communication? The efficient utilization of a distributed operating system involves the sensible decomposition of a task into components. This requires timely access to status information and the ability to use this information wisely in the allocation of tasks to resources and in their scheduling. Just as the management of communication resources was central to the operation of a communication subnet, so will the management of computer resources be to the overall utilization of a computer network.

VIII. Conclusions

A principal motive underlying computer network development is to provide a convenient and economic method for a wide variety of resources to be made available and to be shared. Such a network provides more than an increased collection of hardware and software resources; it affords the capability for computers as well as individuals to interact in the exchange and processing of information.

It is not usually the case that a program written for one computer can be shipped to another computer and run there to completion, correctly. It may be possible in a number of cases where the machines are nominally identical, but it is usually the case that a program must be run on the machine for which it was written. It is thus desireable to strive for compatibility between at least a subset of the system resources, including the use of machine-independent higher level languages, the use of network wide standard protocols, or the use of nominally identical systems.

The development of communication subnets has been strongly influenced by the regulatory climate and the need for reliable and economic ways to achieve both remote terminal access and high bandwidth switched computer-to-computer communication. Message switching has emerged as a strong contender for computer-to-computer communications. It has been demonstrated to provide a highly reliable, error-free method of achieving interactive switched communications. Although its technical feasibility has been firmly established, its practical utility is under evaluation, and under close scrutiny it may prove to be a viable economic alternative to conventional circuit switching.

It is important that a communication system not preclude the possibility that separate or private data networks may be accessed through it in a standard and convenient way. A digital message-switched network has this property, while an analog frequency-based system may not. Incompatible data networks are clearly undesirable if all resources are to be mutually accessible. If separate data networks are jointly planned before development, at least at the interconnection level, they may be connected at a later date and viewed together as a single network that evolved by way of separate networks.

The great diversity of resources in a computer network may initially hinder its growth. Users must familiarize themselves with many different systems often without the aid of substantive interaction with systems personnel or clear and complete documentation. But the potential benefits of computer networks are sufficiently great that, over time, this obstacle will surely be surmounted, and in the process may lead to superior standards for system operation and documentation.

Computer networks provide a unique mechanism for increased participation between individuals. Participation in research and development using the distributed resources of a computer network can lead to the close cooperation between individuals who might otherwise have little incentive to work together. This interaction can further cross-fertilize the network community and encourage even higher levels of achievement through technical cooperation.

References

[1] "Pinched budgets promote growth of university computer networks," *Commun. Ass. Comput. Mach.*, vol. 15, no. 3, pp. 206–207.

[2] P. M. Walker and S. L. Mathison, "Regulatory policy and future data transmission services," *Computer Communication Networks*. Abramson and Kuo Eds. Englewood Cliffs, N. J.: Prentice-Hall, 1973, ch. 9.

[3] D. Farber and K. Larson, "The architecture of a distributed computer system—An informal description," Dept. Informat. Comput. Sci., Univ. of California, Irvine, Tech. Rep. 11. 1970.

[4] H. Baskin, B. Borgerson, and R. Roberts, "PRIME—An architecture for terminal oriented systems," presented at the AFIPS Spring Joint Comput. Conf., pp. 431–437, 1972.

[5] R. Davis, S. Zucker, and C. Campbell, "A building block approach to multiprocessing," presented at the AFIPS Spring Joint Comput. Conf., pp. 685–703, 1972.

[6] S. Crocker *et al.*, "Function oriented protocols for the ARPA network," presented at the AFIPS, Spring Joint Comput. Conf. pp. 271–279, 1972.

[7] H. Frank, R. E. Kahn, and L. Kleinrock, "Computer communication network design—experience with theory and practice," presented at the AFIPS Spring Joint Comput. Conf., pp. 255–270, 1972.

[8] L. G. Roberts and B. Wessler, "The ARPA network," in *Computer Communication Networks*, Abramson and Kuo, Eds. Englewood Cliffs, N. J.: Prentice-Hall, 1973.

[9] M. Beere and N. Sullivan, "Tymnet—A serendipitous evolution," presented at the 2nd Ass. Comput. Mach. IEEE Conf. Problems in the optimization of Data Communication Systems, Palo Alto, Calif., 1971.

[10] D. G. Bobrow, J. Burchfiel, D. Murphy, and R. Tomlinson, "TENEX—A paged time-sharing system for the PDP-10," *Commun. Ass. Comput. Mach.*, vol. 15, no. 3, pp. 135–143, Mar. 1972.

[11] F. J. Corbato *et al.*, "An introduction and overview of the multics system," presented at the AFIPS Fall Joint Comput. Conf., pp. 185–196, 1965.

[12] R. Thomas and D. Henderson, "McRoss—A multi-computer programming system," presented at the AFIPS Spring Joint Comput. Conf., pp. 281–293, May 1972.

[13] R. E. Kahn, and W. R. Crowther, "Flow control in a resource-sharing computer network," *IEEE Trans. Commun. Technol.* (*Special Issue on Computer Communications*, pt. II), vol. COM-20, pp. 539–546, June 1972.

[14] D. C. Walden, "A system for interprocess communication in a resource sharing computer network," *Commun. Ass. Comput. Mach.*, vol. 15, no. 4, pp. 221–230, Apr. 1972.

[15] *The Host/Host Protocol for the ARPA Network*, Network Informat. Center, Stanford Research Institute, Menlo Park, Calif., Document No. 7147.

[16] L. G. Roberts and B. Wessler, "Computer network development to achieve resource sharing," presented at the AFIPS Spring Joint Comput. Conf., pp. 543–549, 1970.

[17] P. Baran, S. Boehm, and P. Smith, "On distributed communications," RAND Corporation, Santa Monica, Calif., Series of RAND Reps., 1964.

[18] F. Heart, R. E. Kahn, S. Ornstein, W. Crowther, and D. Waldenk. "The interface message processor for the ARPA computer network," presented at the AFIPS Spring Joint Comput. Conf., pp. 551–567, 1970.

[19] A. H. Weis, "Distributed network activity at IBM," IBM Res. Rep. RC3392, June 1971.

[20] H. Frank, I. Frisch, and W. Chou, "Topological considerations in the design of the ARPA computer network," presented at the AFIPS Spring Joint Comput. Conf., pp. 581–587, 1970.

[21] W. J. Luther, "Conceptual bases of CYBERNET," Courant Symp. 3, 1970, in *Computer Networks*. Englewood Cliffs N. J.: Prentice Hall, pp. 111–116.

[22] R. Van Slyke and H. Frank, "Reliability of computer communication networks," in *Proc. 5th Conf. Applications of Simulation*, New York, Dec. 1971.

[23] W. Sutherland, T. Myer, D. Henderson, and E. Thomas, "Ross, A route oriented simulation system," in *Proc. 5th Conf. Applications of Simulation*, New York, Dec. 1971.

[24] T. Marill and L. G. Roberts, "Toward a cooperative network of time-shared computers," presented at the Fall Joint Computer Conf., 1966.

[25] Project MAC Conf. on Concurrent Systems and Parallel Computation, Woods Hole, Mass., June 1970.

[26] E. Harslem. RAND Corporation, Unpublished Memo, 1972.

[27] R. Braden, Univ. of California at Los Angeles, Unpublished Memo, 1972.

[28] C. R. Fisher, "Introduction to the DATRAN switched digital network," in *Proc. Int. Conf. Communication*, pp, 23-1–23-3, June 1971.

[29] Request for Quotation (Interface Message Processors for the ARPA Computer Network), Defense Supply Service, Washington, D. C., July 1968.

[30] R. A. Scantlebury and P. T. Wilkinson, "The design of a switching system to allow remote access to computer services by other computers," presented at the 2nd Ass. Comput. Mach. IEEE Symp. Problems in the Optimization of Data Communication Systems, Palo Alto, Calif., Oct. 1971.

[31] D. W. Davies, K. A. Bartlett, R. A. Scantlebury, and P. T. Wilkinson, "A digital communication network for computers giving rapid response at remote terminals," presented at the Ass. Comput. Mach. Symp. Operating System Principles, Gatlinburg, 1967.

[32] "Specifications for the interconnection of a Host and an IMP," Bolt Beranek and Newman Inc., Cambridge, Mass. 02138, Rep. 1822, Oct. 1971.

[33] W. J. Bouknight *et al.*, "The Illiac IV system," *Proc. IEEE*, vol. 60, pp. 369–388, Apr. 1972.

[34] *Datamation*, pp. 36–46, Apr. 1972.

Reprinted by permission from *Proceedings of the IEEE* Vol. 60, No. 11, November 1972, pp. 1397-1407

Line Control Procedures

JAMES P. GRAY, MEMBER, IEEE

Invited Paper

***Abstract*—An exposition of the basic principles underlying data communication line control procedures is presented. Two specific line controls are then described, with special attention given to their embodiments of these principles.**

I. Introduction

A. An Overview

LINE CONTROL procedures, or data link controls (DLC's) are hardware and software protocols used to transfer data and control information between separated computing devices. In order to do this, a connection must be established, synchronization of the parties to the exchange obtained, messages passed, and the inevitable errors recog nized and corrected.

Manuscript received May 11, 1972; revised July 20, 1972.

The author is with IBM Research Division, Research Triangle Park, N. C. 27709.

From another perspective, data link controls convert a wide variety of transmission facilities, capable of sending signals over distances, into data communication facilities, capable of sending information over distances. The transmission environment for this conversion ranges from short local lines to long-distance links via satellite, transatlantic cable, microwave, and laser beams. In another dimension, connections can be operated as simplex (unidirectional), half-duplex (one way at a time, but alternating directions), or full duplex (both ways at once) over 2-wire and 4-wire connections. Also, links are available on a leased basis, or over the direct dialing telephone network, the latter tariffed on a per call or WATS basis in the United States and Canada. Similar facilities are available throughout the world. Finally, leased lines can be point to point or multipoint, and private lines can duplicate these variations. These facilities encompass wide variations in error rates (10 000 to 10 000 000 bits/error), bit rate (50 to 230 000 bits/s), and propagation delays (0.001 to 0.5 s).

The conversion of transmission into communication is accomplished by synchronization, a process which is discussed in Section II assuming that the transmission channel is error-free. Since the transmission facilities do introduce errors, Section III discusses the recovery of synchronization after it has been lost due to errors.

Other sections of the paper are devoted to extensions of the concepts contained in Sections II and III. In Section IV, the influence of line topology is examined, while in Section V some of the performance related aspects of line controls are mentioned. Also in Section V, the contamination of line controls with functions from other areas of a data communication system is explored and then in Section VI two specific line controls are presented briefly and evaluated as embodiments of the principles developed in the previous sections.

B. The Language Analogy

There is an obvious analogy between half-duplex data communication with line controls and the use of natural language for communication between two people: data messages (sentences) are exchanged alternately between the machines (people) which (who) are communicating (talking). The messages (sentences) are composed of strings of characters (words) arranged according to definite rules (grammatical rules). The characters, in turn, are constructed from bit strings (as words are constructed from letters). Since artificial constrained languages have been widely studied [1], [2], it has seemed natural to exploit this language/DLC analogy by applying language theory to DLC's [3]. Certain (finite-state) artificial languages are closely related to finite-state sequential machines, and this relationship has been explored by Bjørner [4] in application to line controls. While the work based on language theory has not had much practical impact, some practical applications of finite-state models to line controls have been published [5]–[7], and the finite-state sequential machine model seems to be the most natural one for designers to use in developing DLC's.

II. Line Controls for Error-Free Transmission Channels

In Section II-A, we develop a sequential machine model of simplex data communication in order to elucidate the fundamental sense in which communication is a form of synchronization. The subsequent sections discuss practical methods for converting transmission into communication through the acquisition of synchronization on error-free channels.

A. Synchronization as the Meaning of Communication

In technology, the narrow sense of the verb synchronize is "to cause to have the same period or, to cause to have the same period and phase." This definition applies directly to clocks and to oscillators; by simple extension it applies to machinery such as electric generators. It is this sense of the verb which applies in the phrases "synchronous detection" (demodulation) or "synchronous sequential machine" (digital logic) [8]. The broader sense is "to cause to happen at the same time, or, to cause to happen at a known time." It is this sense which is of particular interest for communication: the receiver's operations must occur at a known time relative to the transmitter's operations in order for communication to take place. This thought will be developed more fully within the framework of the following model.

Definition of Sequential Machines: Define a sequential machine [9] as a quadruple (I, S, O, p) where

- I Input, a vector of i binary signal components.
- S State transition matrix, mapping the pair (current input, current state) into the next sequential state:

$$s(t + 1) = S(I(t), s(t)).$$

  Sometimes the state number will be expressed in radix 2. The resulting binary digits form the state vector.
- O Output, a vector of j binary functions of the current state.
- p The clock period. The state matrix is evaluated at intervals of p seconds.

If the clock period p is taken as zero, the machine is called an asynchronous sequential machine since state transitions do not occur at known intervals. Conversely, if p is greater than zero, the machine is said to be synchronous, since all state transitions occur in synchronism with the basic clock period. We will assume that p is greater than zero in this section since most digital circuits and computers can be better modeled by synchronous sequential machines.

Input, output, and state vectors of a sequential machine are continuous functions of time. Changes in the input can occur at any time, but will have no effect on the state or the output until the next clock pulse at time $t(n) = np$, when the values $I(np)$ and $s(np)$ determine the next state by

$$s(np + p) = S(I(np), s(np)).$$

State transitions are assumed to occur instantaneously in accordance with this equation. As a result, the machine samples the input at the clock rate.

In Fig. 1, an example of a simple sequential machine is given to illustrate these definitions. The machine looks for a single input pulse, and when one is found, emits an output pulse. The output is held up until two input pulses spaced a unit time apart are found at the input. When this reset signal is found, the machine returns to its initial state and begins to scan for a single input pulse again. In Fig. 1(a) this verbal description has been represented as a state diagram or state graph, in which the states of the sequential machine are nodes, and the paths between states are represented by the links or edges of the graph. The edges are labeled with the input values which drive the machine along that state transition. In Fig. 1(b) this same information is presented in the form of a state matrix, and the state vectors corresponding to the state numbers are shown. The output function is also defined.

The stars next to three of the state numbers in the state matrix mark stable states, that is, states which can only be left by a change in the input vector. The stability of a state is shown in the state graph by a link beginning and ending on the same node.

In Fig. 1(c), a sample operation of the machine is diagrammed. The vertical lines represent the sampling instants: the instants in time at which the input values have meaning to the sequential machine, and the times at which the instantaneous evaluations of the state matrix result in a state transition. This means, among other things, that if the input changes value twice between two clock sample instants, then

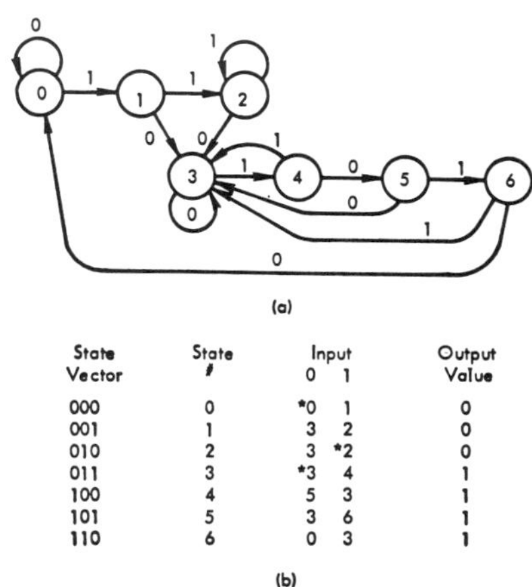

(a)

State Vector	State #	Input 0	Input 1	Output Value
000	0	*0	1	0
001	1	3	2	0
010	2	3	*2	0
011	3	*3	4	1
100	4	5	3	1
101	5	3	6	1
110	6	0	3	1

(b)

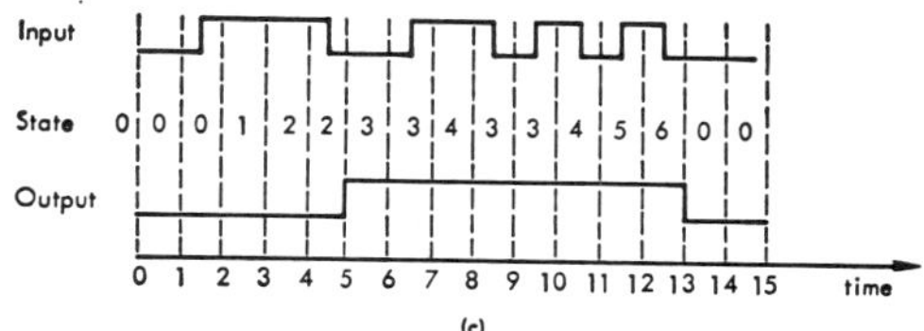

(c)

Fig. 1. A sequential machine. (a) The state diagram. (b) The next state matrix and output function. (c) Sample operation sequence.

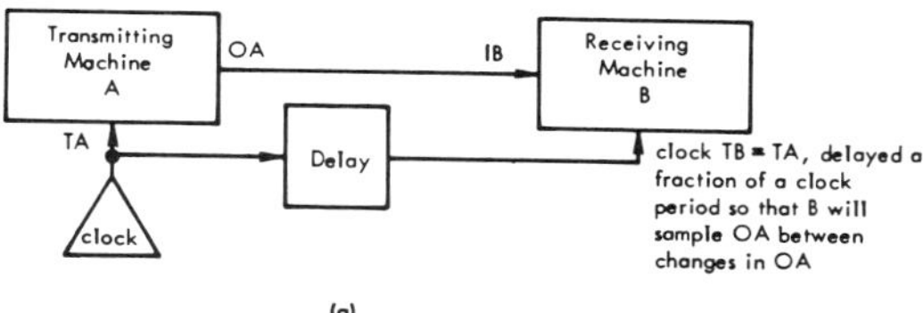

(a)

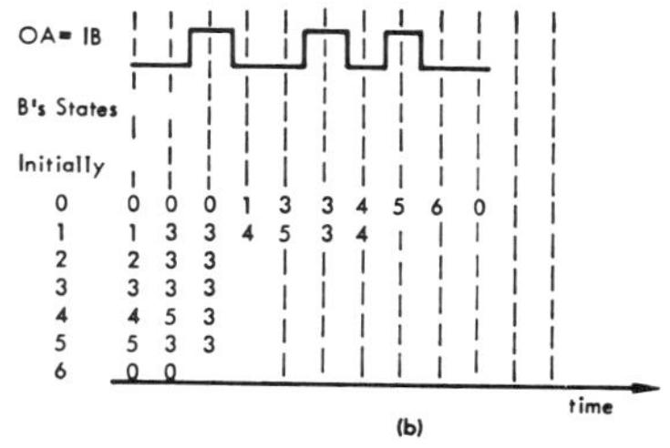

(b)

Fig. 2. A simplex communication system. (a) Basic system with data transmission and shared clock. (b) Signals sent by A in order to synchronize B at state zero.

the sequential machine will not detect the change. This is a version of aliasing: the change has been aliased onto no change (zero frequency), by the sampling process.

A Simplex Communication System: In Fig. 2(a), two sequential machines are connected in a simplex communication system. Machine A is the originator and transmitter of the information, while machine B is the receiver. The output of A connects to the input of B, and, for the present example, they share a common clock TA (see Section II-B for more discussion of the clock used to drive machine B). Since A and B already share the same clock, their clocks are synchronized, but machine A may not know what state machine B is in at a given instant, even assuming error-free transmission. If, however, B is the machine diagrammed in Fig. 1, then A can drive B into a known state as shown in Fig. 2(b). At the end of nine clock pulses, B is in state zero regardless of B's initial state. After B has entered a known state, any further transmission by A will have the effect of writing over part or all of B's state vector in a known way. In fact, we can say that the basic goal of a simplex communication system is to allow one finite-state machine, the transmitter, to write over part or all of the state vector of another finite-state machine, the receiver. This rewriting changes the state number of the receiver, and does it in a known way, a process which we call synchronization of the remote machine. In this simplex communication situation, synchronization amounts to control: the goal of the system is to allow A to establish and maintain control over B's state.

While the purpose of a data link control within a communication system is to convert transmission into communication by acquiring and maintaining synchronism between separated machines, there is usually another level of processing, a higher order user of the communication facility. In this perspective, the DLC does not so much convert transmission into communication as it acquires and maintains synchronism for the benefit of the higher level user. The user ultimately performs the transformation of the message transmitted into communication through itself being synchronized by the information contained in the message. In this view, a DLC must act as a conduit for some of the transmitted data the content of which should not affect, or be affected by, the DLC.

Sequential machines are often built to have just the property described above, and an example is shown in Fig. 3. In Fig. 3(a), a sequential machine is shown that has been separated into a control logic portion and a storage or buffer portion. The state of the whole machine is the concatenation of the state vector for the control with the state vector for the storage. Appended state vector components are identified as storage when their values do not affect the state transitions within the logic portion of the machine. A very simple single bit buffer machine is shown in Fig. 3(b) to further illustrate this point.

Synchronization as Communication: In summary, we view DLC's as paired finite-state machines (alternatively, as paired algorithms) which acquire and maintain synchronization in order to pass messages between higher level users. Synchronization is established and maintained by the transmission of signals which establish and maintain a known state in the remote machine, i.e., by initially writing all of the remote machine's (logic) state vector. The higher level users, programs or human, are themselves synchronized (driven into a known state) by the message contents, and in this sense communication means synchronization.

B. Serialization

Conceptually, the message is the indivisible unit of communication, and if messages were fixed length they could be transmitted as 500 or 1000 bits in parallel. Of course, that many parallel transmission channels would be very expensive, and messages are usually variable length anyway, so, for practical reasons, messages are serialized into character streams

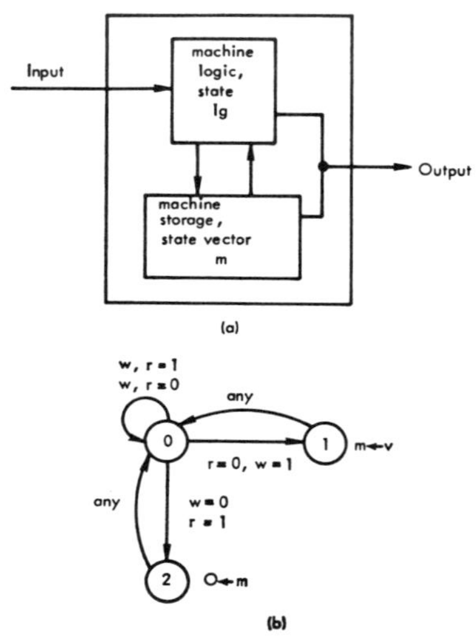

Fig. 3. Sequential machines with storage in their state vectors. (a) Separation, or factorization, of storage from logic. Whole state vector is $s=(lg, m)$, output is $O(s)=O(lg, m)$. (b) State diagram showing factorization of logic and storage expressed as logic state not being a function of storage value. Inputs: value v, write w, read r. Output: O. Storage: m, 1 bit. This machine saves v when w is pulsed, and outputs the saved value when r is pulsed. Note that the state transitions do not depend on the value of m. Only the logic states are shown and numbered.

even for communication via local I/O facilities. These character serial cables include a separate clock line, often called a sample line or deskewing line, which is used by the receiver to tell precisely when, and just how often, to sample the receive data lines. The separate clock and data lines in Fig. 2 illustrate the usefulness of an explicit clock.

Remote transmission links are more expensive than local ones, so a single channel is provided and character streams are serialized into bit streams. This bit level serialization creates problems of clock recovery at the receiver: if a data independent bit clock is not recovered by the modem (so called "modem clock," see [10]), then the transmitter clock has to be recovered from the single serial bit stream, which implies that there must be transitions in the received raw data. That in turn implies that certain characters will not be allowed, or, that additional bits will be embedded in the transmission in order to ensure an adequate number of transitions for reliable clock recovery. An additional requirement created by the serialization is for an agreed upon speed of transmission, since the clock recovery algorithm and the bit embedding or code sensitivity problems are greatly simplified by knowing the approximate bit rate *a priori* [11]. Except for this additional bit clock recovery complexity and the high error rate environment, DLC's are completely analogous to communication conventions used between locally attached I/O and the host [20] or between independent programming processes in a multiprogramming system.

C. Practical Simplex Synchronization

For simplex communication, synchronization is the receiver's problem in a practical sense: it does not have, but needs, clocks at the bit, character, and message levels of transmission. Table I summarizes the methods of bit and character

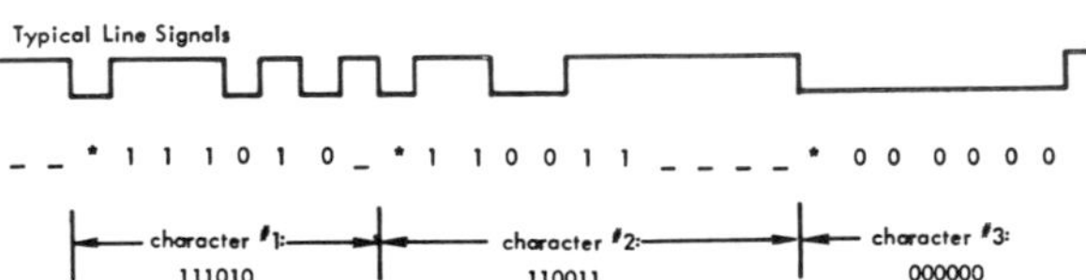

Fig. 4. Start–stop bit and character clock recovery. Start bits: *. These have the line value 0, also called space. Stop bits: __. These have the line value 1, also called mark.

Note: Timing: The timing shown indicates that the stop bits are an integral number of bit times in duration. This is typical of many electronically timed start–stop line controls, where the bit clock is derived from an oscillator that is not actually turned on and off, but is corrected very much as the data-derived bit clocks used in synchronous data link controls. Nomenclature: Start and stop bits are not really bits since they carry no information content for the ultimate user of the characters being transmitted. For this reason they are sometimes called start and stop elements.

TABLE I
RELATIONSHIP BETWEEN DLC'S AND MODEMS

	Start–Stop DLC	Synchronous DLC
Asynchronous modems: (e.g., FSK and baseband) B.M. clock[a]	natural design point	useful, but a terminal with a synch. DLC can often justify a higher speed modem; code sensitivity may occur[c]
Synchronous modems: modem clock derived from the data	possible only under unnatural constraints on length of stop bit, or, with NRZI or similar coding.[b]	natural design point; code sensitivity may occur.[c]
Synchronous modems: modem clock independent of the data	possible but wasteful of transmission capacity	natural design point

[a] B.M. (business machine) clock means that the bit clock is generated (on transmission) and recovered (on reception) by the DLC. Modem clock means that the bit clock is generated and recovered by the modem. A modem clock channel looks like Fig. 2.

[b] NRZI Non-Return to Zero, Invert, coding is explained in the text under the synchronous clock recovery section.

[c] Code sensitivity is also explained in the synchronous clock recovery section (Section II-C).

clock recovery that have been used in DLC's, and shows their relationship to the modem methods that can be employed for transmission (see also [10]).

Start–Stop Methods of Bit and Character Clock Recovery: In start–stop methods (Fig. 4), introduced with the first teletypewriters, characters are transmitted as separate entities with variable amounts of time between characters. At the beginning of each character a start bit is inserted to mark the beginning of the character. To ensure a transition at the start bit, a stop bit is appended to each character. To permit sync acquisition and recovery on a character-by-character basis, the stop bit is variable length.

When the receiver detects the stop-to-start bit transition, the local bit sync clock is started and the line is sampled once each local receive clock time. Before the local and transmitter clocks drift apart enough to cause an error, which in this case would be a dropped (slow local clock) or inserted (fast local clock) bit, the end of character arrives and the receiver turns off its bit-sync clock and goes back to hunting for a start bit. Notice that start–stop bit synchronization requires that char-

```
ANSI SYN Character = 0110001

Left shifted:     1 = 110001x ≠ SYN
                  2 = 10001xx ≠ SYN
                  3 = 0001xxx ≠ SYN
                  4 = 001xxxx ≠ SYN
                  5 = 01xxxxx ≠ SYN except when the next character
                                    begins with 1000lyy, which
                                    means H,X,h,x, none of which
                                    can be used to start a message

Right shifted:    1 = x011000 ≠ SYN
                  2 = xx01100 ≠ SYN
                  3 = xxx0110 ≠ SYN
                  4 = xxxx011 ≠ SYN
                  5 = xxxxx01 ≠ SYN except if the preceeding
                                    character ends with yy01100
                                    which means A,E,I,M, none of
                                    which can be used to start a
                                    message.
```

Fig. 5. Synchronous character framing in ANSI line control [13] using the SYN character Method. SYN SYN is sufficient, as a prefix to every transmission, to establish character framing. To allow for reliable bit clock recovery 3 or 4 SYN's are often used at the beginning of a transmission.

acters be fixed-length bit strings, hence the character clock is available directly from the bit clock.

Synchronous Methods of Bit and Character Clock Recovery: The extra start and stop bits of start–stop clock recovery methods lower the transmission efficiency of the line. Therefore, when higher speed transmission is desired, a synchronous method is employed. There are two methods of interest. In the first, the bit clock is derived by the modem from data-independent signals on the line; this case is equivalent to a separate clock channel. In the other case, the bit clock is derived from the serial data stream itself, either within the modem or within the business machine, depending upon the form of detection that the modem uses (see Table I). In either case, once the bit clock has been started it is not stopped until the transmission is complete and all signals disappear from the line. In the case of data derived clock, the clock is corrected periodically, usually after every transition on the line [10], [12]. Clearly, there must be enough line transitions to keep the local clock in sync with the transmitter's bit clock or else a dropped or inserted bit will result (which is a form of code sensitivity). For this purpose, special characters (often called SYN's) may be inserted periodically within the message text. Alternatively, or in addition, a restriction on the length of one transmission block may be imposed, so that long messages have to be transmitted as several blocks.

Once bit clock has been recovered, character clock must still be obtained. This can be done, as is shown in Fig. 5, by prefixing the transmission with a unique bit pattern which does not replicate itself under left or right translations. In some line controls, multiple SYN's also serve this purpose [13].

Alternatively, a unique bit pattern can be generated by bit insertion on transmission and bit deletion on reception. For instance, in the advanced data communication control procedure (ADCCP) (discussed in Section VI-B, also in [14]), a "0" is added after five consecutive "1's", making six consecutive "1's" a unique control character (called a frame) at the receiver. Every transmission block sent in ADCCP starts with one of these frames, which serve to establish character synchronism. The receiver, of course, must delete every zero that follows five consecutive "1's" in order to recover the proper message text.

Message Synchronism: The recognition of start of message is relatively easy: either the first character received marks the start of message (most start–stop DLC's), or the reception of a reserved start of message character signals the beginning of the message. The start of message character can be just the frame of ADCCP.

Once the transmission of a message has been started, and the receiver has sync at the bit, character, and start of message levels, the termination of the message must be synchronized too. This can be done by an implicit count, i.e., all messages will be the same length, which is analogous to the way in which characters are recovered from the bit stream, and to the way unit record equipment operates; or, an explicit count field can be embedded in the transmission right after the start of message or lead frame, which is analogous to the operation of I/O channels operating under count controlled channel commands; or, a terminal frame can be recognized, similar to end-of-record recognition for channel commands on local tapes and disks.

Code Sensitivity: Start-of-message synchronization and (possibly) end-of-message marking require that special characters be recognized. This means that certain characters must not appear in the message text itself, i.e., the line control is code sensitive at the character level.

This code sensitivity may not cause any trouble if the message text is not allowed to contain special characters. Alternatively, trouble can be avoided by two kinds of marker insertion techniques which then allow "transparent text transmission" (no special restrictions on which characters can be contained in the text). At the character level, the DLC algorithm can scan the message text for reserved characters and insert an escape character (e.g., DLE's are doubled within the text in IBM's BSC [15]), followed by the text character. The receiver strips these markers out of the text. Instead of character insertion, bit insertion may be used as in ADCCP. These insertion tricks are similar to quote insertion in programming language representations of character string literals, e.g., in PL/1 or APL.

Code sensitivity at the bit level is also possible with data dependent synchronous bit clock recovery. Just which bit patterns are disallowed depends on the modem design, and modern modems often include a scrambler circuit to make the sensitive pattern a highly unlikely one in normal data streams. Some older modems were sensitive to patterns (e.g., 0101010101) that can easily occur in data streams, so that a restricted text transmission format sometimes had to be used just in order to obtain correct modem operation.

Synchronous operation with asynchronous modems usually means that the clock is sensitive to long strings of zeros or long strings of ones. In ADCCP, long strings of ones cannot occur due to the bit stuffing, and long strings of zeros are prevented by encoding the line signal in a Non-Return to Zero, Invert to transmit a zero format (NRZI encoding). This just means that transmission of a one is accomplished by not changing the line signal, while transmission of a zero is accomplished by inverting the line signal. Basically, the width of the zero intervals is sent as a series of transitions in the line signal. At the receiver, a differentiation extracts impulses which are used to repeatedly trigger a timing circuit which emits a zero bit for one bit time when triggered. This restores the data to true data form.

Another modem-related sensitivity of line controls is the need to pad a transmission with one extra character at the end of transmission. This is needed because some modems turn off abruptly when told to stop sending and start listening, so abruptly that a portion of the last character may be lost if a pad is not added at the end of the message [16], [17].

D. Duplex Synchronization

Duplex transmission consists of transmission in both directions at once (full duplex or FDX) or alternatingly (half duplex or HDX), but in either case it is more than just two simplex links. The something more lies in the sequential coordination between the transmission and reception operations on both ends of the link. We will concentrate on HDX since it is easier to understand, yet contains all the essential elements of duplex operation.

At the initiation of transmission, two HDX stations may be "equals," meaning, their respective finite state machines are identical so far as the DLC behavior is concerned. If this is the case, and both wish to transmit, a race condition can develop. Thus when A sends its initiation sequence, since it is HDX, it will not see B's initiation sequence and will try again. In practice, this try-again effort is done after a time-out, so that when A and B try again, with the same time-out (they are identical, remember), a race or contention will again exist on the line. Sooner or later, of course, the asynchronous nature of their local clocks will get them out of the race, but, it can be a long time (experiments have demonstrated races lasting over an hour), so, a master–slave mode of communication is desirable. That is, one of the stations is designated the master, and, in case of a race, only the master tries again. FDX operation could solve this start of transmission condition, at least in theory. However, other aspects of FDX operation, such as error recovery and system cost, have motivated master–slave architecture in modern line controls (e.g., ADCCP).

Once the master–slave concept is adopted, there are fixed master, and rotating master options. In the fixed master system, one station is "bigger" or more equal than the others, and when in doubt about races or other error induced asynchronisms, the master reestablishes the connection and the synchronism. In a rotating master system, the station that initiated the transmission is responsible for the health of the link until that transmission has been acknowledged. This increases the cost of the slave stations and complicates the error recovery procedures, but was a natural outgrowth of experience with terminal to terminal networks.

In HDX systems, during the course of connection, both ends may have occasion to wait for a transmission by the other. If this occurs at the same time, each waiting for the other, a deadlock occurs, which can only be broken by time-outs or by some outside intervention. With a properly designed line control, such deadlocks can only occur at higher levels of the system, and not from processes arising within the line control itself [18], [19].

E. Reverse Interrupt Facilities

HDX operation with reverse interrupt (RVI) is an extension of the HDX mode to allow interruption of transmission by the receiving station, or to allow a slave to signal "attention" to the master station. It is added to HDX protocols and engineered into the communications equipment primarily for human-factor reasons since the interrupt or control functions are freely available when the line is turned around at the end of a transmission. On Teletypewriters this function is called "break," while on IBM 2741 terminals it is called "attention." The exact meaning of the interrupt must be assigned by application logic (hardware and software). One kind of reverse interrupt that is used internally to a DLC is the WAK, or wait-acknowledge type of response. This is issued to a transmitter when the receiver is temporarily unable to receive any additional messages due to a buffer full condition or some other condition that requires a delay. RVI has been used in locally attached equipment [20] to signal error or emergency situations, but this is not done for attachment via communications facilities because errors have to be handled locally anyway when the link fails.

III. Errors

One of the biggest differences between line control procedures as we are discussing them here and their philosophical brothers in such areas as local I/O channel connection is the expected error rate and the types of errors experienced [21]. Error rates on common carrier channels generally range from one error in 10 000 to one in 10 000 000 bits transmitted, while in specialized applications such as mobile radio channels, the rates may be as high as one error in 10 bits. Errors include bit insertion and deletion due to faulty synchronization, single bit errors, and burst errors. Short-term outages may occur, and if short enough, these will appear to be burst errors; if the outage is on the order of a message length, an entire message can be lost. Line quality can change abruptly for a few characters, or messages, or longer periods as the carrier's equipment fails, degrades, and is manually or automatically reconfigured. The complexity and variability of the carrier channels available to the data user make prediction of data channel error rates and error behavior impossible, and survey data [22] very expensive to obtain and of limited value once obtained. Error considerations have also made it necessary for limits to be placed on the number of drops engineered for some multipoint leased lines [23].

A. Detection of Errors

Although we cannot predict ahead of time how many errors a particular communications channel will introduce into a data stream, we can detect such a large fraction of the ones that do occur that, with retransmission, as few as one block in 10 billion will contain an undetected error for blocks of about 80 characters [21], [24]. If the raw error rate is so high that the probability of transmitting a message correctly is appreciably less than 1, 0.9, or 0.95, say, then some forward error correcting codes (FEC) may have to be employed to obtain satisfactory throughput on channels using error detection and retransmission. These codes do not have to be nearly as elaborate, or as expensive to implement as some FEC codes that, theoretically speaking, would allow transmission with arbitrarily low error rates without retransmission.

Error detection is based on some kind of redundancy built into the transmitted information, and the transmission of a duplicate copy of the data is the simplest. The next simplest kind of checking is based on a parity check across some group of bits. This kind of checking provides excellent protection against single-bit errors, but it is inadequate in many applications utilizing communications facilities. Nonetheless, single-bit parity checking on characters is employed in many line controls in use today [25], [26]. It is usually called VRC, for vertical redundancy checking. An improvement in single-character error detection can be obtained by sparse use of the characters, as is done in 4 out of 8 codings [27], but this is done at the expense of transmission efficiency and size of character set.

In order to obtain better checking while still maintaining transmission efficiency, checking must be done across the whole message. If the added redundancy across the message is just a parity bit for each bit position of all the characters in the message, then the message has been protected with LRC, or longitudinal redundancy checking. When both VRC and LRC are employed together [13], [28], all double bit errors and many patterns of multiple bit errors can be detected. LRC check characters consist of 8 bits if a 7-bit transmission code such as ASCII is used, and LRC checking is sometimes called CRC8, where CRC stands for cyclic redundancy checking. CRC-n check codes are the most powerful and efficient error detection methods in general use today, where n can be 8 for short messages (say up to 16 characters or so) and should be longer, often 16 bits, for longer messages (the length of the CRC code is fixed for a given terminal, however). The general theory of the behavior of these check codes is well known [21], but somewhat involved, so it will not be repeated here, except to note that the best CRC checking is so good that VRC is not needed.

B. *Half-Duplex Error Recovery Algorithms*

Once an error has been detected by a check code of some kind, a retransmission of the erroneous character or message must be agreed upon by the communicating stations. The coordination of this retransmission is the basic element of error recovery algorithms for use with line control procedures. The transmitter and receiver finite state machines must be properly designed to avoid message duplication or loss occasioned by cascaded errors, but this is not difficult once the principle is grasped. The basic principle, as illustrated in Fig. 6, is based on two ideas: first, number the messages so that the receiver can tell if a correctly received message has been previously received, and, second, have the receiver acknowledge every message received, replying ACK (acknowledge) when the message was received correctly, and NAK (negative acknowledge) when the message was received incorrectly. If the line control procedures allow more than one message to be outstanding before acknowledgment, then ACK's and NAK's must be numbered to correspond to the messages. For HDX operation we assume that only one message is outstanding at any given instant, so that unnumbered replies suffice.

Whenever a message is received, it is checked for errors. If in error, a request for retransmission is made, by replying NAK. If no error is detected by the error detection methods used, then the message number is checked. If it is $n+1$, where n was the last message accepted, it is accepted via ACK. If it is n, it is accepted via an ACK, but is thrown away by the receiving station since it must have been a duplicate transmission caused by an error in one of the acknowledgments. If it is anything else, such as $n+2$, it is negatively acknowledged.

At the transmitter, each acknowledgment is also checked for errors. If an erroneous reply is received, the most recent message sent is retransmitted (this would be message number n). If the reply received is free of errors, it is either an ACK or a NAK, and if it is an ACK, then message $n+1$ is transmitted, while if it is a NAK, then message n is retransmitted.

This set of linked algorithms can be seen to provide perfect transmission under all conditions of detected errors. Undetected errors can still cause trouble, however. For instance, if a NAK is changed, without being detected, into an ACK, then a message will be dropped, and the reverse undetected error will cause no problem.

Line controls that have unchecked control characters are more susceptible to undetected errors, including transmutation of addresses (a simple protection is repeated addresses), hits of start-of-message or end-of-message markers, and the like. The possible effects of undetected errors must be examined in detail for each line control, including both the transmission formats and the algorithms at each end of the line.

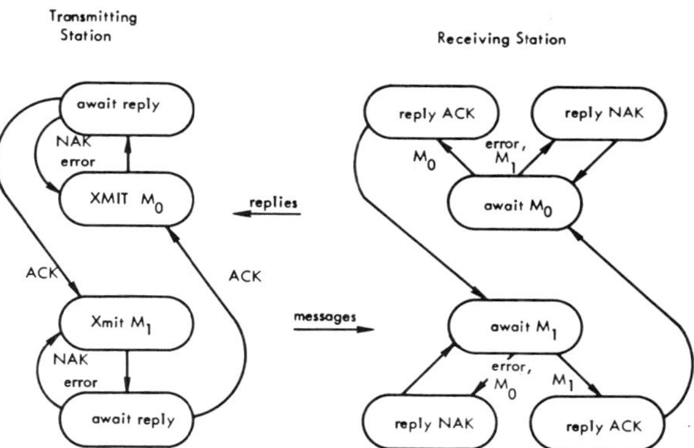

Fig. 6. Reliable simplex message transfer with HDX operation of the communication line.

Note: This diagram has been simplified by adoption of message numbering modulo 2, which still allows unique identification of all messages that have not yet been positively acknowledged.

If the ACK–NAK concept is retained, but the messages are not numbered, then lost and duplicated messages can easily occur. If an ACK reply is changed to a NAK without detection of the change, then a duplicated message is created by the retransmission. The reverse change causes a message to be lost. On the other hand, if a reply is hit by an error, and the error is detected, either a duplicate message must be risked, a dropped message must be risked, or the master station must send a special message asking for retransmission of the reply! This is the second stage in a recursion, and is hence undesirable.

Implicit in this discussion has been the assumption that no messages are totally lost in the channels, but this can happen due to a short-term outage of some portion of the communications channel. If a message is lost without detection of this fact, then the whole system may become deadlocked, with the receiver waiting for the next message, say, and the transmitter waiting for the reply to the previous message, the reply having been lost.

This and other possible forms of deadlock (for instance, the operator of the terminal goes out on a coffee break, but does not sign off the system) at higher levels in the system can be broken by time-outs in the data link control. The length of the time-outs should be, strictly speaking, system dependent, but, the vast majority of users of a particular DLC can be served well with a compromise value. The time-out is typically operative in the master station on the link, and when it times out, transmission of various interrogation and control messages to the slave stations is usually attempted in an attempt to get the link operating again.

The basic retransmission protocols previously described can be modified in a number of ways to take advantage of special circumstances. For instance, in the case of HDX operation, n can be expressed modulo 2 without harm, while links operated in an FDX mode must express n as modulo p where p is one more than the number of messages that can be in the round-trip transmission channel at one time. If the line is multipoint (see Section IV-A for a discussion of multipoint),

```
no errors:  time delay to ACK B1 must be inserted
 A sends:    A1   .A2   .A3   .A4   .A'1+.A'2.
 A receives:            B1+ .B2+ .
 B sends:             B1+ .B2+ .
 B receives:  A1   .A2   .A3   .
                         (a)

detected error with loss of three good messages
 A sends:    A1   .A2   .A3   .A4   .A'1+.A2+ .A3+ .
 A receives:            B1+ .B2- .
 B sends:             B1+ .B2- .
 B receives:  A1   .(A2).
                         (b)

dropped message with loss of three good messages and 'bubble'
creation.
 A sends:    A1   .A2   .A3   .A4   .A'1+.(   )A2- .
 A receives:            B1+ .     B3+ .
 B sends:             B1+ .B2+ .B3+ .
 B receives:  A1   .A2   .A3   .
                         (c)
```

Fig. 7. Behavior of single sequence numbered FDX protocols (+ is ACK, — is NAK, period is end of message separator).

Note: It has been assumed here that all messages are the same length. If messages are broken up into transmission blocks, then the length of the transmission blocks can be varied, and the problem depicted in (a) and (c) can be avoided or solved by dynamically adjusting the transmission block length. Of course, blocking of messages is only possible in noninteractive transmission, so this solution to some of the single sequence number problems is not applicable in general.

and an HDX polling discipline is used, then ACK's to inbound messages can be elided (possibly with some loss in error immunity) since the polling of the next terminal is an implicit acceptance of the message just received. Many other specific special conditions of operation have been capitalized on in one or another line control discipline. (See [30] for example.)

C. Full Duplex Error Recovery

If an FDX channel is operated in the FDX mode, then line control protocols sufficient for an HDX operation will no longer work, or will not work efficiently. The central issue in extending HDX protocols to FDX usage is sequence numbering: are there two sequence numbers, one for transmission A to B and another independent number for transmission B to A, or is there only one sequence number used for both directions of transmission? If there are two independent sequences, then the error recovery actions in the two directions can be independent too. Further, the sequence number modulus p can be independent of the delay in the channel without affecting throughput, so long as p messages overfill the channel round trip delay (this is also a function of message length).

The behavior of single sequence number FDX line controls is complicated by the synchronization between inbound and outbound message streams enforced by the single sequence number. In Fig. 7(a) for instance the ACK to message $B1$ must be delayed one full message time since the modulus of sequence numbers must be an invariant if sequencing from $p-1$ to 0 is to be unambiguous at both ends of the line. This additional delay increases the response time of the communications portion of the system, and, at fixed response time, decreases the loading possible on multidropped lines. In Fig. 7(b), message $A2$ is received with a detected error, as shown by the parentheses. When the negative acknowledgment, $B2-$ is received by terminal A, $A2+$ must be retransmitted. Since there is but a single sequence number, $A3$ must follow (since $A2$ has not yet been transmitted), not $A'3$, so that error recovery on message $A2$ forces the loss of three good messages. In Fig. 7(c), a message is lost between B and A. A stops transmitting until the lost message situation is revealed by the receipt of $B3+$ some time later. Again three messages are lost, and further, that bubble of delay will stay in the message stream indefinitely unless special fixes (such as controlled variable length transmission blocks) are added to the protocols.

All of the difficulties with single sequence numbering stem from attempting to tie two asynchronous processes together with a time inelastic connection. The conclusion is inescapable: FDX line controls for general use should employ double sequence numbering.

IV. Line Topology

A. Multipoint Systems

Simplex operation of a link can be point-to-point as we have already discussed or it can be multipoint-tandem, commonly called just multipoint. This means that there are more than two stations on the link and that the connections are engineered so that when one of the stations transmits, all other stations receive the transmission. In order to operate such a link in a simplex mode, one station would be the transmitter and the others the receivers. The DLC would need to include selection by address for the receiving (tributary) stations if messages were to be directed to individual stations, and this addressing might allow for a maximum number of attached stations or it might be extendable (fixed or variable length address: the tradeoff is between addressing overhead and breadth of application). Notice that multipoint lines provide a form of multiplexing and concentration [29].

Multipoint FDX operation is similar to simplex in that selection or addressing is required. But, since the tributary stations can also transmit inbound, some method of babel control is required. If traffic is light, so that the probability that two tributary stations will want to transmit at the same time is small, then pure contention can be used. When a contention (race) situation does develop, the master can calm the line by issuing quiesce orders and then asking each station in turn if it has something to send. This latter procedure is called polling, or serial selection with enable. Mixtures of contention (group enable) and polling (serial enable) are also possible.

The use of serial enable or polling involves a considerable amount of transmission that transfers no useful data, that is, it involves inefficiencies in the use of the transmission capacity of the line and in the master station's CPU cycles. In order to avoid this, hardware with autopolling capability can be installed on the line, or additional distributed polling facilities can be added in hardware or DLC or both. For instance, so-called hub polling can be used in the IBM Programmed Airlines Reservation System (PARS) line control [30]. This requires an extra line which connects the terminals in a chain, thereby establishing through a physical means the relative priority of the terminals. The master issues a poll command which enables the first terminal, which when done, signals the next terminal on the chain that a poll is outstanding, and so on. The same effect can be achieved without the extra wire by defining an address register within each tributary station which is loadable from the master, and which points to the next terminal in the polling list. Each station, when it has nothing to send, signifies this by sending a message addressed to the next terminal on the polling list. This process relieves the master station of a significant amount of the line housekeeping, which saves a significant amount of CPU time. Redundant messages are also eliminated from the line, thereby increasing effective line capacity.

B. Loop Systems

So far we have discussed line controls for point-to-point and multipoint communications facilities. Another topology has been used, that of loops [31], [32]. We shall not try to give an exhaustive description of data handling in loop topologies, but shall point out several of the more interesting line-control questions that come up.

In loop systems, each link is simplex (although dual-simplex loops have been used for increased availability [33]), and this fact makes possible efficient character level multiplexing. When character multiplexing is used in loop DLC's, the transmission on the loop consist of a periodic synchronizing or framing sequence followed by a fixed-length or variable-length sequence of slots which contain one or a few characters intended for specific terminals. The slots can be addressed to their destination either by position or by an address carried in the slots. For message multiplexed operation, the lengths of the slots become the message length.

Another benefit of loop operation is that the loop structure, in effect, wires in a priority among the terminals (the terminals upstream nearest the controller receive control messages first), so that loop systems can utilize hub poll operation. While the links are simplex, the central station both sends and receives, so that the operation is full duplex at the central and either full or half duplex at the tributary stations.

Tributary stations on a loop facility can be connected to the loop in a variety of ways, but the method used depends not only on the DLC performance, but on the cost of the connection and on the amount of delay introduced into the loop. If the loop bit rate is low, then even one bit of delay per connected terminal may make the loop delay too long for the application under consideration. If that is the case, a DLC structure must be used that involves zero insertion delay. Addressed or position assigned slots allow this, but for slot contention operations, a free slot marker bit at the beginning of a free slot on the loop must be used to achieve zero insertion delay. A terminal wishing to capture and use this slot for a transmission into the central simultaneously reads and writes into this bit. It always writes a one, marking the slot full, and if it also reads a one, it looks for the next slot to try and capture. If, however, it reads a zero, it has captured a slot and can insert its data. The problem with zero delay loop connection is that it does not allow for regeneration and retiming of the bits as they are repeated around the loop. Therefore, either the length of the loop must be limited, or regeneration equipment with its attendant bit delays must be inserted periodically.

C. Message Multiplexed Loops

So far we have emphasized fixed-length slots, but one of the more attractive loop DLC's is based on message multiplexing with an elastic connection to the loop. In this scheme, inactive terminals introduce zero or one bit time delay into the loop, but active terminals cut the loop and transmit into one end at the same time that they buffer the outpouring bits from the other end. When the terminal has finished transmitting its own message, the loop is reconnected with the partially full buffer in series with the data flow. The buffer, which must operate in a trickle down fashion (that is, as a first in, first out queue), is gradually purged by the arrival of free slots in between messages, or by the arrival of a message addressed to the terminal.

This method does introduce a long delay into the loop under heavy load situations, but it is also very efficient in terms of throughput. The response time is good under light to moderate loads, but if the master station is not operated carefully, some terminals can actually be locked out of operation during heavy load periods. This happens when the master is sending messages to terminals one after the other without any free slots. If the first terminal on the loop, say, gradually fills its elastic buffer by sending longer messages into the central than the central sends back, a point will be reached when the elastic buffer does not have enough space left to allow the next terminal-to-central message to be inserted into the loop. At that point terminal number one is locked out of operation, and will remain locked out until the central starts to send free slots or until it directs an inquiry, perhaps prompted by a time-out, to it.

The loop line controls that we have been discussing have been operated in a centralized fashion similar to most multipoint lines. However, just as multipoint lines can be operated in a contention mode and used for terminal-to-terminal communication, loops can be operated with decentralized allocation of the loop transmission capacity. This mode of operation has not achieved common use to date.

Aside from the increased throughput made possible by the elimination of line turn around delays, loops may be attractive in some systems because of the reduced length of line required, depending on the terminal locations. On the other hand, loops are more susceptible than point-to-point or multipoint lines to errors and availability problems, this just because of the serial links. Whether this is a serious drawback depends on the application under consideration and on the communication facilities, but in general, as the communications facilities become of poorer quality, either with higher error rates or lower availability, loops become less attractive as a system solution.

V. Additional Considerations

The performance properties of a data link control are a major additional consideration. Broadly speaking, desirable operation at a fixed cost is obtained by maximizing throughput while maintaining a bounded response time. The practical impediments to the achievement of this goal consist of DLC control character overhead, transmission wasted because of errors and error recovery retransmissions, unproductive polling in polling based systems, transmission delay in the channel used, and turn-around delays in modems used on HDX links. An accurate prediction of the performance of a DLC requires the use of simulation techniques, and may involve modeling not only the DLC itself, but other portions of the system, such as operator behavior. Further information on the details of performance modeling is available in [34].

Many useful line controls were developed to be used in a specific application context, as for instance the PARS line control [30] for the airline reservations systems developed by IBM. Many others, not developed for specific application environments, were nonetheless developed for specific terminals and devices at the terminals, such as teletypewriter line controls. As a result, their line control functions of synchronization and data transfer are mixed in with miscellaneous terminal and device controls and status signals such as figures/letters shift, line feed, carriage return, jammed card reader, and the like.

Line controls intended for use on dial-up lines usually make provision for an additional stage of control concerned with connection and disconnection from the line. For instance, IBM BSC [15] contains a disconnect control message that is issued by the master station at the end of the conversation to indicate that the master is going "on hook." Dialing, however, is usually left outside of the line control protocols.

Some line controls include routing information beyond the local link, as for instance the Western Union Plan 115A for Teletypewriters. It is even possible to designate multiple destinations in some message switching systems. In message switching systems other elaborations of line control are not uncommon, such as time stamping of the messages at the switch, logging of the message in a central file if requested (or, sometimes, logging is performed automatically), and, in some cases, editing functions including message conversions for interconnection of terminals that are incompatible as to line transmission codes or speeds.

Another function closely related to line controls, but not yet contained in any of the commercial ones, is cryptographic security for protection of the communication link. Of course, for most applications, such cryptographic encoding would be best performed on the message text before it was passed through the line control procedures at each end of the link.

Finally, the important concept of data compaction is relevant to line controls. Compaction may be applied at the bit stream level (modem–DLC interface) or at the message level (DLC–user interface), the latter being by far more common. Widespread use has been made of deletion of trailing blanks, and more sophisticated encoding methods have also been used in specialized application areas.

246

VI. Example

In the following subsections, two examples of line control disciplines will be given in order to illustrate the principles already discussed. The presentation will be brief, and is not intended to be authoritative. The first example is ANSI Subcategory 2.4 as described in [13]. A contemporary of IBM's BSC, it shares many of the same design philosophies.

A. ANSI Subcategory 2.4

The ANSI DLC is defined on a base character set which uses 7 bits/character for a total of 128 characters. For DLC use, an eighth parity bit is added (odd for synchronous transmission, even for asynchronous). Some 10 of the 128 characters are reserved for line control uses:

- SOH Start of heading, used to mark the beginning of a sequence of characters used as a station address or for message routing purposes. The heading so marked is terminated by an STX character.
- STX Start of text, used to terminate the heading and mark the beginning of the text or message.
- ETX End of text, used to mark the end of text.
- EOT End of transmission, used to mark the end of a transmission which may have contained any number of texts and associated headings. EOT is sent as a separate transmission.
- ETB End of transmission block, used to mark the end of a transmission block when a text or message has been split into several pieces or blocks for transmission purposes (to allow interleaved messages from other sources, or, to provide better throughput in the presence of errors, or to decrease the probability of an undetected error). ETB only marks intermediate blocks, ETX is used to end the last block of a text.
- ENQ Enquiry, used to solicit a response from a station. Uses include a who are you function, the requesting of station status information, or part of a polling or selection sequence. ENQ can be preceded by a prefix which includes addressing and control information.
- ACK Acknowledgment, used to affirm the reception of a message without detected errors.
- NAK Negative acknowledgment, used to request retransmission of the last block due to detected error or because the receiving station is momentarily unable to receive.
- SYN Synchronous idle, used on synchronous channels only, transmitted in the absence of any other characters for the purpose of obtaining or maintaining synchronism. It is not to be used for time fill or media fill applications connected with the application, but only transmission synchronism and transmission fill on the local channel. Some implementations do hardware insertion/deletion of SYN's in order to ensure continued transmission synchronism. This, of course, makes SYN a reserved character in the sense of Section II-C.
- DLE Data link escape, used to construct multicharacter data link control sequences. It provides a way to extend the command set defined by the previous 9 characters. DLE allows the definition of additional control functions, including (the commas signify concatenation and are not transmitted):
  - DEOT Mandatory disconnect, used to force the disconnection of a switched connection. It is the sequence DLE, EOT.
  - ACK-N Acknowledgment N, used to provide numbered ACK's. ACK0 is DLE, 0 and ACK1 is DLE, 1.
  - BCC Block check character, used to provide LRC checking. BCC follows ETB or ETX and sums over the entire message exclusive of the starting SOH or STX, but including the ETX. Automatically inserted/deleted SYN's are not included in the BCC.

In ANSI DLC there are many categories of operation; we will discuss Subcategory 2.4, two-way alternate nonswitched multipoint with centralized operation. Central to this form of operation is the designation of one control station for the line, with all others becoming tributary stations. In practice, the control station would be a computer and the tributary stations would be terminals.

When the line is first activated or is reactivated, the control station has master status and none of the tributary stations have slave status, although they are monitoring the line. The first thing that the control station has to do, then, is to confer slave status on one of the tributary stations, that is, it has to select one of them. There are two subcategories here: 1) selection, in which the selected tributary station assumes slave status and the message transfer that follows will be from master to slave which in this case means control station to tributary; 2) polling, in which the selected tributary station assumes master status and the control station relinquishes master status in order to assume slave status. The message transfer will still be master to slave, but in this case it is tributary to control station. At the end of the message transfer the master station sends EOT and the line becomes inactive again, that is, all tributary stations monitor the line and the control station resumes master status. In both cases, the master station is responsible for error recovery action, meaning retransmission either upon receipt of an invalid reply, a NAK, or upon a no reply time out. An abort action in the event of too many retransmissions is also necessary. The tributary stations in master status can abort with an EOT, while the control station in master status can move on to poll or select another tributary station, after sending EOT to cancel the slave status of the previously selected tributary station. Of course, if the selected slave is not operating correctly and does not become inactive, further operation of the line will not be possible, so the control station will have to signal error to higher levels of the application system. If the control station has assumed slave status, then it, too, must time-out on no transmission from the current master station in order to guard against tributary station failure.

One ambiguity in this category of operation is that both polling and selection begin with the transmission of "prefix ENQ" by the control station. The prefix, which needs to carry the station address as well as specification of polling, selection or other command information, must be further defined by the DLC user.

ANSI DLC suffers from multiple dialects as a result of the many categories of operation that are defined and as a result of the many details, such as the previously mentioned prefix, within each category that are not defined. This multiplicity of versions has limited its usefulness as a standard interface specification. Another weakness is the lack of defined and standardized definitions of the algorithms in the control and tributary stations, especially as regards the error recovery actions to be taken. To further complicate the situation, most of the control characters are not subject to block checking; the "prefix ENQ" sequence mentioned above is an example of this. Burst errors are thus able to introduce undetected errors in control sequences, thereby greatly complicating the required error recovery procedures. The weak protection of control sequences means that the undetected error rate experienced in most application environments will be somewhat greater than that achievable with the best available line controls.

B. *Advances Data Communication Control Procedure (ADCCP)*

ADCCP is currently in the process of being defined, standardized, and introduced to data communication use [14]. It is also known as synchronous data link control (SDLC). Whereas ANSI DLC starts with a character set, and adds line control, ADCCP starts with the premise that a line control should be code insensitive and transparent to the characters in the text to be transmitted.

In order to achieve the transparency, a special control character called a "frame" is defined to be the bit sequence "0111 1110," that is a zero, six ones, and a trailing zero. All transmissions are then constructed so that they begin and end with frames:

F A C text BC F.

This is the only transmission format allowed, where F is frame, A is an 8-bit address field, C is an 8-bit control field, text is an information field of arbitrary length, restricted only by the buffering constraints of the stations involved and by the error characteristics of the channels used, BC is a 16-bit block check field using the International Telegraph and Telephone Consultative Committee (CCITT) V41 CRC polynomial [35], and F is the terminal frame, which may also be the lead frame of the next message block. The transparency is achieved during transmission by scanning the "A C text BC" bits for five ones in a row and inserting a zero, thereby preserving the uniqueness of the frame on the line. Since frames are unique at the receiving station, "A C text BC" can be isolated and one zero deleted after every string of five ones. "A C" and "BC" are then positionally identified as the first 16 and last 16 bits of the resulting string of bits and "text" is everything else. In order to allow efficient implementation, "text" is forced to be an integral multiple of the character width native to the stations on the line.

Zero insertion allows transparency, but code sensitivity of asynchronous modems remains a problem. To eliminate this, NRZI–Zero encoding of the data stream is employed: the transmitter complements the state of the Send Data interchange circuit in the modem's EIA232C [10], [16] interface to transmit a zero bit, and the Send Data lead is left unchanged to transmit a one bit. If a long string of ones should occur in a transmission, then the zero insertion will create transitions for use in clock recovery at the receiver.

The block check accumulation operates on "A C text BC" before zero insertion, so that all address and control data are checked. To further improve reliability, long-term mode switching (such as ANSI subcategory 2.4 employs when it specifies that the master station will always be the station originating the message regardless of the control station/tributary station definition) is avoided. Instead, a single primary station for each line is designated, and all other stations on the line are secondary stations. The primary station is responsible for the operation of the line at all times, and it alone initiates error recovery action in the event of an error.

Three message formats are defined. The first, shown above, provides for normal HDX and FDX message transfer between the primary and a single secondary station by defining a transmit sequence number and a receive sequence number, each of three bits, and a response bit for the primary station, which is a final bit for the secondary station. As each station transmits a block, it includes the block's sequence number in the transmit sequence number field, and the number of the last received block which was accepted. If a received block is not accepted, the next transmission will contain the sequence number of the last block that was accepted, and since out of sequence blocks are rejected, an error causes all of the blocks in the communication channel to be temporarily lost, very much like the blocks that were lost in Fig. 3(b). The response bit is set to one by a primary station whenever it wants to enable a secondary station. Once enabled, the secondary transmits blocks until it runs out of traffic, or must delay since seven blocks are outstanding without acknowledgment, or is told to stop by the primary station (on FDX lines only). The last transmission block from a secondary station must set the final bit to one.

The second message format is "F A C BC F" and is used by the primary to acknowledge secondary transmissions, to request additional transmissions, to request the retransmission of the indicated blocks, and to inhibit the secondary from transmitting. It is used by the secondary to acknowledge or reject primary transmissions and to inform the primary that it cannot accept additional transmissions until some condition has cleared (this is a WAK function). The control field contains only one sequence number.

The third format is used for nonsequenced transmissions and contains no sequence number at all. It may or may not contain a text field. In addition to broadcast messages, the primary uses this format to:

1) Group or single station enable when the secondary station(s) have been in a quiesce state. This allows the secondary station(s) to initiate an asynchronous interrupt, i.e., to contend for the line.

2) Disconnect switched connections or to enter the quiesce state on nonswitched links.

3) Transfer channels to backup facilities or to switch channels of an asymmetrical duplex channel.

4) Reset one or all of the secondary stations.

5) Hub poll on both multipoint and loop facilities.

6) Transmit control messages to permit the primary to configure, reconfigure, test, and diagnose the data link control portion, only, of the secondary stations.

The secondary stations use this format to:

1) propagate an address linked hub poll;

2) request an asynchronous interrupt;

3) respond to control messages from the primary (see 6 of preceding list);

4) report exception conditions such as intervention required;

5) reject a command.

A variety of categories of operation have been defined for ADCCP, with detailed error recovery procedures included. These categories include HDX and FDX operation, full conversational operation, hub poll operation, and operation on point-to-point, multipoint, and loop facilities. The architectural advantages of this line control, including some already mentioned are: code independence, full transparency, unique synchronization, full checking of data and commands, high efficiency in FDX mode on channels with long propagation delays, no long-term mode switching, and finally, open endedness of the definition so that additional controls and responses can be added at a later date without impacting already built equipment.

248

Acknowledgment

The author would like to thank G. Schultz and J. Spragins of IBM Research for valuable discussions concerning the synchronization function of line controls, B. Steen of IBM Systems Development Division (SDD) for discussion of FDX operation, and J. R. Kersey of IBM SDD for providing drafts of several of his tutorial memoranda on line controls.

References

[1] S. Ginsburg, *The Mathematical Theory of Context Free Languages.* New York: McGraw-Hill, 1966.
[2] F. R. A. Hopgood, *Compiling Techniques.* New York: American Elsevier, 1969.
[3] H. J. Hoffman, "On linguistic aspects of communication line control procedures," IBM Res., Zurich, Switzerland, Rep. RZ345, 1970.
[4] D. Bjørner, "Finite state automaton definition of data communication line control procedures," IBM Res., San Jose, Calif., Rep. RJ668, 1970.
[5] W. C. Lynch, "Reliable full-duplex file transmission over half-duplex telephone lines," *Commun. Ass. Comput. Mach.*, vol. 11, pp. 407–410, June 1968.
[6] K. A. Bartlett, R. A. Scantlebury, and P. T. Wilkinson, "A note on reliable full-duplex transmission over half-duplex links," *Commun. Ass. Comput. Mach.*, vol. 12, pp. 260–261, May 1969.
[7] W. C. Lynch, "Commentary on the foregoing note," *Commun. Ass. Comput. Mach.*, vol. 12, p. 261, May 1969.
[8] *Proc. IEEE (Special Issue on Time and Frequency)*, vol. 60, pp. 476–648, May 1972.
[9] E. F. Moore, ed., *Sequential Machines, Selected Papers.* Reading, Mass.: Addison-Wesley, 1964.
[10] J. R. Davey, "Modems," this issue, pp. 1284–1292.
[11] "Synchronous signaling rates for data transmission," EIA RS-269-A, Electronic Industries Association, Engineering Department, Washington, D. C. 20006, Feb. 1969.
[12] W. R. Bennet and J. R. Davey, *Data Transmission.* New York: McGraw-Hill, 1965, p. 260.
[13] "Proposed USA standard, data communication control procedures for the USA standard code for information interchange," *Commun. Ass. Comput. Mach.*, vol. 12, 3, Mar. 1969. (This is a reprint of USASI Doc. X3.3.4/212, Sept. 1968. USA Standards Institute has since changed its name to American National Standards Institute, of ANSI.) ANSI Doc. X3S3.4/#437, the latest version, is available from X.3 Secretary, Business Equipment Manufacturers Association, Washington, D. C.
[14] "SDLC: Synchronous data link control," ANSI Doc. X3S3.4/#349 was the original submission by IBM of its improved synchronous buffered line control, now called ADCCP.
[15] "General information—Binary synchronous communications," IBM Tech. Rep. SRL GA27-3004.
[16] "Interface between data processing terminal equipment and data communication equipment," Electron. Indust. Ass., Tech. Rep. EIA-RS-232C, Aug. 1969.
[17] "Data sets 202C and 202D interface specifications," Bell Syst. Tech. Ref. PUB 41202, May 1964. (For a copy write to Western Electric Co., Commercial Relations, P.O. Box 1579, Newark, N. J. 07102.)
[18] J. F. Havender, "Avoiding deadlocks in multitasking systems," *IBM Sys. J.*, vol. 7, 1968.
[19] A. N. Haberman, "Prevention of system deadlocks," *Commun. Ass. Comput. Mach.*, vol. 7, pp. 373–377, 385, July 1969.
[20] "System/360 and system/370 I/O interface channel to control unit original equipment manufacturer's information," IBM Tech. Rep. SRL GA22-6974.
[21] H. Burton and D. Sullivan, "Errors and error control," this issue, pp. 1293–1301.
[22] "1969–1970 connection survey: Analog and data transmission performance on the switched telecommunications network—Results of nationwide field measurements," *Bell Syst. Tech. J.*, pp. 1311–1405, Apr. 1971.
[23] "Transmission specifications for voice grade private line data channels," Bell Syst. Tech. Ref., July 1972. (For a copy write to Western Electric Co., Commercial Relations, P.O. Box 1579, Newark, N. J. 01702.)
[24] ANSI Doc. X3S3.4/482, Feb. 1972.
[25] "IBM 2740/2741 communication terminal OEM information," IBM Tech. Rep. SRL GA27-3002.
[26] "Models 33, 35 and 37 stations for point-to-point private line service," Bell Syst. Tech. Ref. PUB 41713, Aug. 1971.
[27] "General Information Manual: The IBM Tele-Processing 1009, 1013 and 7702 Transmission Units," IBM Tech. Rep. SRL E20-8080.
[28] "IBM 2260 Display Station and 2848 Display Control Component Description." IBM Tech. Rep. SRL A27-2700.
[29] D. Doll, "Multiplexing and concentrating," this issue, pp. 1313–1321.
[30] *IBM 2946 Terminal Control Subsystem.* IBM Tech. Rep. SRL GL24-3570.
[31] J. D. Spragins, "Analysis of loop transmission systems," in *Proc. ACM/IEEE 2nd Symp. Problems in the Optimization of Data Communication Systems*, pp. 175–182.
[32] L. P. West, "Loop-transmission control structures," *IEEE Trans. Commun.*, vol. COM-20, pp. 531–539, June 1972.
[33] J. M. Unk, "Communication networks for digital information," *IRE Trans. Commun. Syst.*, vol. CS-8, pp. 207–214, Dec. 1960.
[34] J. Martin, *Systems Analysis for Data Transmission.* Englewood Cliffs, N. J.: Prentice Hall, 1972.
[35] "Code independent error control system," recommendation V.41, Rep. of IV Plenary Assembly, Mar del Plata, Int. Telecommun. Union, 1969.

Bibliography

[36] J. L. Eisenbies, "Conventions for digital data communication link design," *IBM Syst. J.*, vol. 6, pp. 267–302, 1967.
[37] "Proposed American standard: Character structure and character parity sense for serial-by-bit data communication in the American Standard Code for information interchange," *Commun. Ass. Comput. Mach.*, vol. 8, Sept. 1965. (ASA Doc. X3.3/23.)
[38] "Heading format for data transmission (a USASI tutorial)," *Commun. Ass. Comput. Mach.*, vol. 11, June 1968. (USASI Doc. X3.3.3/44, Oct. 4, 1967.)
[39] "Proposed USA standard: Procedures for the standardization process," *Commun. Ass. Comput. Mach.*, vol. 11, Dec. 1968. (USASI Doc. X3.4/68-1, X3/SAC/93 July 10, 1968.)
[40] "Description of systems used for data transmission (an ASA tutorial)," *Commun. Ass. Comput. Mach.*, vol. 9, Oct. 1966. (ASA Doc. X3.3.5/51, Mar. 1966.)
[41] J. Martin, *Teleprocessing Network Organization.* Englewood Cliffs, N. J.: Prentice-Hall, 1970.

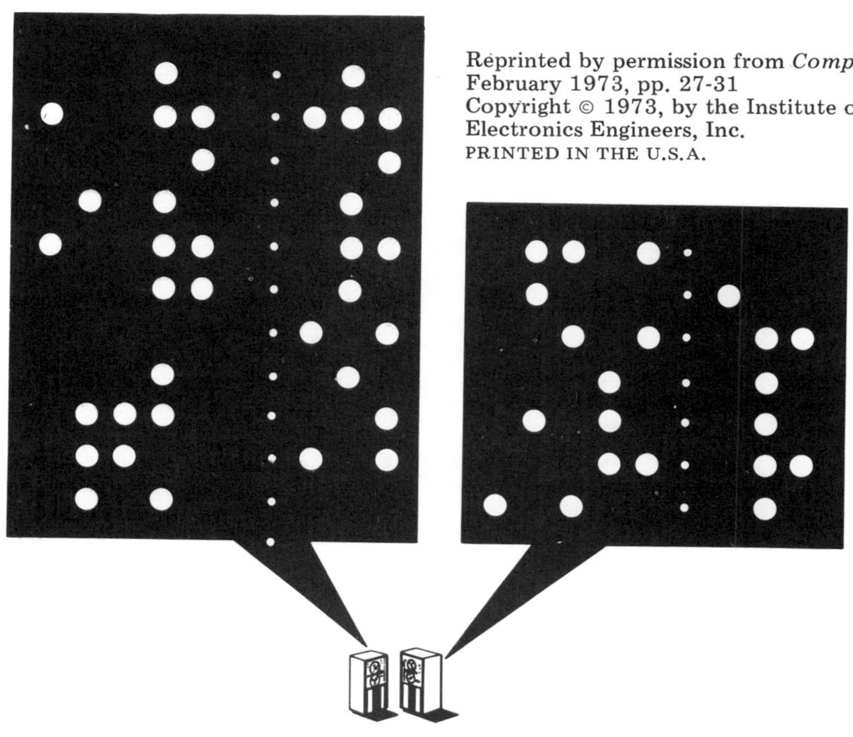

Reprinted by permission from *Computer*
February 1973, pp. 27-31

BIT— ORIENTED CONTROL PROCEDURES FOR COMPUTER-TO-COMPUTER COMMUNICATIONS SYSTEMS

Brian Tymann

BIT-ORIENTED CONTROL PROCEDURES ARE A NEW GENERATION OF COMMUNICATION LINK CONTROL PROCEDURES WHICH HAVE EVOLVED DURING THE PAST SEVERAL YEARS. THESE NEW PROCEDURES OFFER MANY ADVANTAGES OVER CHARACTER-ORIENTED OR BASIC MODE CONTROL PROCEDURES WHICH ARE COMMONLY USED TODAY. BECAUSE OF THIS, IT IS EXPECTED THAT BIT-ORIENTED CONTROL PROCEDURES WILL EVENTUALLY REPLACE CHARACTER-ORIENTED PROCEDURES FOR MOST SYNCHRONOUS DIGITAL COMMUNICATIONS APPLICATIONS.

This paper introduces basic concepts and terminology associated with bit-oriented control procedures and describes the use of these procedures for computer data interchange applications, in point-to-point configurations, and computer networks.

Why Do We Need New Control Procedures?

Most, if not all of today's communication systems use some form of character-oriented control procedures. The most commonly used procedures are:

- ANSI: Communication Control Procedures/ASCII Code
- ISO: Basic Mode Control Procedures
- IBM: Binary Synchronous Communication Procedures

These procedures were initially developed during the early 1960's to serve the batch-oriented communication needs of that period. The growth of communications during the last decade was characterized not only by an increase in communication volume, but, more significantly, by a growing diversity of applications: time-sharing, inquiry/response, transaction-oriented data collection, and computer-based information networks. As it became apparent that the basic character-oriented procedures were not suited to these new applications, the procedures were expanded to incorporate new functions and operating modes. This expansion of the basic procedures involved the definition of new communication control sequences, the introduction of transparency features, and the expansion of the number of establishment/termination and message transfer operational subcategories. The resultant procedures are a collection of distinct procedural categories for specific operating modes, with no true compatibility among the various modes.

The effectiveness of character-oriented control procedures is limited by the following factors:

- Character-oriented procedures impose a common character structure (typically 8 bits) on all link control information and text data. This is inefficient for applications which use some other data structure.
- The procedures use a "select-hold" mode of operation. This involves an establishment or "handshaking" phase prior to message transfer, and a termination phase following message transfer. Select-hold operation is suitable for batch applications, but can reduce system performance in other real-time applications.
- Different error checking procedures are used for asynchronous/synchronous transmission and for transparent/nontransparent modes. Message data are protected by transmission block check sequences (LRC, CRC), but link control sequences (polling sequences, acknowledgements) use character parity checking only.
- Distinct establishment/termination and message transfer procedures are used for specific operating modes. This can
250 lead to unique hardware/software implementations for
different applications.
- The procedures are message dependent; that is, a common control character or sequence (e.g. ETX) is used to delimit both end of message text and end of transmission block. This constrains the ways in which data can be segmented for transmission.

Development of Bit-Oriented Control Procedures

The concept of bit-oriented control procedures was introduced by IBM in 1969 in the form of Synchronous Data Link Control Procedures (SDLC). Following this, both ANSI and ISO standards organization adopted bit-oriented control procedures in the work programs of their respective task groups responsible for the development of data communication control procedure standards (ANSI X3S3.4 and ISO TC97/SC6). SDLC became the starting point for the development of ANSI Advanced Data Communication Control Procedures (ADCCP), and ISO High Level Data Link Control Procedures (HDLC). To date, ANSI has prepared a draft standard for ADCCP, and ISO has issued several proposed standards for HDLC. Currently, ANSI and ISO procedures are quite similar in definition, and it is expected that they will continue to evolve towards compatible standards for ADCCP and HDLC bit-oriented control procedures.

Objectives. Bit-oriented control procedures are intended to provide a communication discipline which covers a wide range of applications involving data communication between computers, concentrators, and terminals. The procedures can be used for switched or private, point-to-point or multipoint, half duplex or full duplex data communication links.

These new procedures are expected to provide a number of advantages over character-oriented procedures, including the following:

- Improved Reliability: all link control information and text data are protected by a CRC error checking sequence.
- Improved Performance: the elimination of select-hold operation, and the provision of transparency and code independence features will result in improved performance for many applications.
- Improved Compatibility: common formats and basic procedures will apply to all operating modes; terminals with widely varying characteristics may cohabit a common data link.
- Code Independence: the procedures do not impose any constraint on the data structure; data can be byte-oriented with any byte size, or can be bit stream data of any length.

General Properties. General properties of bit-oriented control procedures are described below:

Link Configurations: these procedures can be used for any link configuration: switched/private; point-to-point/multipoint; half duplex/full duplex.

- Synchronous: synchronous data transmission must be used.
- Buffered: all stations must have at least single frame buffering.
- Non-Select Hold: station establishment/termination procedures are not used; each frame is individually addressed.
- Transparent: no restrictions on data bit patterns; procedures include a bit-oriented transparency mechanism.
- Code Independent: no restriction on data byte structure; procedures will accommodate byte-oriented data (any byte size) or bit stream data.
- Message Independent: procedures are completely independent of data message structure and message delimiters.
- Security: all data and control information is protected by an error checking sequence.
- Operating Modes: common formats, control functions and procedures can be used to implement a variety of operating modes for a wide range of applications.

Concepts

Bit-oriented control procedures have introduced a number of new concepts which differ from character-oriented procedures. Basic concepts are described below, together with associated terminology.

Primary and Secondary Stations

Bit-oriented control procedures are based on the concept of data interchange between a Primary station and one or more Secondary stations on a common communication link. The Primary is responsible for control of the link, including initialization, organization of data transfer, and link error recovery. Secondary stations are responsible only for performing operations, as instructed by the Primary. Primary and Secondary station assignments are fixed; they do not change dynamically (as do basic mode Master/Slave status).

Commands and Responses. Link operation is controlled by the exchange of Commands and Responses between Primary and Secondary stations. Commands are sent from Primary to Secondary, requesting the Secondary to perform a specific operation (e.g. initialize, accept data, return data). Responses are sent from Secondary to Primary only when requested to acknowledge (accept/reject) prior commands. Certain types of commands and responses may include data; others are used for link control functions only (see Figure 1).

Figure 1. Commands and Responses

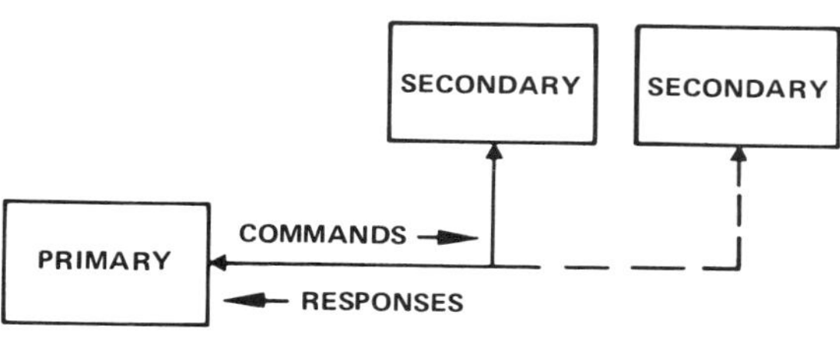

The complete set of commands and responses is not defined in this paper; the subset required for the Primary/ Primary class of procedures is defined later.

Frame Structure. A frame is an integral block of information transferred between Primary and Secondary stations via the link. A frame is somewhat analogous to a transmission block in basic mode terminology.

A standard frame format (Figure 2) is used for all frames. Each frame contains standard link control information and may also include data for certain command and response types. The standard link control information includes opening and closing flag sequences, Address and Control fields, and a Frame Check Sequence (FCS).

Figure 2 Standard Frame Format

FLAG	ADDRESS	CONTROL	INFORMATION	FCS	FLAG

Field	Length	Contents/Function
FLAG	8 bits	Delimits start/end of frame(3)
ADDRESS	8 bits(1)	Secondary station link address
CONTROL	8 bits(1)	Link control information: a) Command or Response code b) Sequence number (Ø-15), or modifier
INFORMATION(2)	any length	Transparent, code independent data (any code level, or bit stream)
FCS	16-bits	CRC error checking sequence

NOTES
(1) The Address and Control fields can be extended in 8-bit multiples.
(2) The information field is omitted from supervisory commands and responses.
(3) Flag Sequence is (01111110).

Flag is an 8-bit sequence which delimits the start and end of each frame. A single flag can be used as both the closing flag of one frame and the opening flag of the next frame, or any number of flags can be used between adjacent frames.

The Address field contains the address of the associated Secondary station. For command frames, this address indicates the intended Secondary recipient. Since all response frames are implicitly directed to the Primary, the address in a response frame serves to identify the Secondary source. The basic Address field is one octet (8 bits) in length, and can represent one of 128 unique addresses (one bit is reserved for Address field extension). The Address field can be extended in octet multiples, if required.

The Control field contains a command or response code, and may also include a frame sequence number which is used with numbered commands and responses for frame sequence checking, acknowledgements and error recovery procedures. The basic control field is one octet in length, and can accommodate a 4-bit command or response code, and a 4-bit sequence number (sequence number range of 16). The Control field can be extended in octet multiples to provide additional control information or sequence number extension.

The FCS is a 16-bit error checking sequence which protects the contents of the Address, Control and Information fields. The FCS is calculated using the CRC generator polynomial ($X^{16} \pm X^{12} + X^5 + 1$). The procedures provide for using a higher degree polynomial and increasing the FCS field length in octet multiples, if required.

Information field contents are completely unrestricted; it may contain either byte-oriented data of any code level, 251
or bit stream data. The procedures do not limit the Information field length; however the practical limits will be determined by station buffering capacities and link error characteristics.

The procedures also include an Abort feature which can be used to terminate a frame such that it will be ignored by the receiving station. This is accomplished by using an abort sequence of 7 or more contiguous 'one' bits.

Transparency. The control procedures allow the use of any bit pattern in the Address, Control and Information fields. A bit-oriented transparency algorithm is used to modify frame contents so that link control or text information will not be falsely interpreted as either a flag sequency or abort sequence.

Frame contents are tested before transmission on the link, and a 'zero' bit is inserted following each sequence of five contiguous 'one' bits. The receiving station will use the same algorithm to delete the inserted 'zeros' as the first step in processing the incoming bit stream. The transparency algorithm is applied to all frame contents except flag or abort sequences.

Balanced System Concept

The Primary/Secondary station relationship imposes a link hierarchy in which a single Primary station is responsible for initiating and controlling all data interchange on the link. The balanced system is an extension of the basic concept which allows two Primary stations to share control of a common link. This dual Primary concept allows each station to independently originate data transfer to the other station, using two-way simultaneous operation.

The balanced system configuration (Figure 3) has two stations on a single point-to-point full duplex link, with each station having both a Primary and a Secondary component. Each station acts as Primary with respect to the data which it transmits, and as Secondary with respect to the data which it receives. As illustrated, Primary 1, (P1), sends commands to Secondary 2, (S2), and receives responses from S2; while Primary 2, (P2), sends Commands to Secondary 1 (S1), and receives responses from S1. The balanced system is therefore analogous to two independent Primary/Secondary systems (P1/S2 and P2/S1) integrated on a common full duplex link.

Figure 3. Balanced System Concept

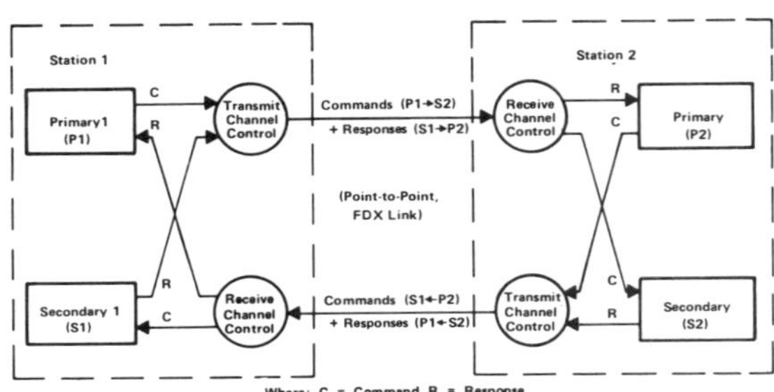

The Primary and Secondary components of each station function according to standard procedures. The Channel Control functions provide the logical interface between the independent Primary and Secondary components and the station's transmit and receive channels. Channel Control is responsible for interleaving commands and responses for transmission to the other station according to a priority scheme; and for interpreting each received frame as either command or response, and steering each frame to the appropriate Primary or Secondary component.

252

Since each station can originate data independently, all data is transferred in command frames, while response frames contain only supervisory information (positive or negative acknowledgment). The balanced system concept serves as the basis for developing Primary/Primary control procedures, which are described below.

Control Procedures For Computer-To-Computer Applications

In general, bit-oriented control procedures can be developed for two distinct categories of link configuration, Primary/Secondary and Primary/Primary. In Primary/Secondary configurations, one Primary station is responsible for link management, and all Secondaries function as terminals or satellites to the Primary. In Primary/Primary configurations, two Primaries share responsibility for link management, and each Primary can independently originate and transmit data to the other station. Although Primary/Secondary procedures can be used for certain applications, Primary/Primary procedures cover a wider range of computer-to-computer applications, including:

- Bulk File Transfer
- Remote Job Entry (multiple job stream)
- General Purpose Batch
- Remote Concentrator
- Computer Networks

This paper deals only with Primary/Primary procedures for computer-to-computer applications, using point-to-point, full duplex links. The balanced system concept described above serves as the basis for developing Primary/Primary procedures, using a minimal set of commands and responses as defined below:

1. **Reset Command.** The Reset Command instructs the receiving Secondary to intialize (reset sequence count, discard previously stored responses), and send an Accept Response. Reset is normally used only at system startup.

2. **Select and Respond Command (SR).** Select and Respond is the only data transfer command used. This Command instructs the receiving Secondary to accept the accompanying data, and to respond as soon as possible. The SR command frame includes a sequence number which is used for frame sequence checking and error recovery.

3. **Enquire Command.** The Enquire Command instructs the receiving Secondary to send a response which identifies the last command accepted or rejected by the Secondary. Enquire is used only for abnormal error recovery situations.

4. **Accept Response.** The Accept Response indicates that the Secondary has accepted the command frame which is identified by the sequence number included with the response, and also implies acceptance of all prior command frames.

5. **Not Accept Responses.** Not Accept Responses are a set of negative responses which indicate that the Secondary has rejected a received command frame and is waiting for retransmission. The response code will indicate either a link error condition (frame check error, sequence number error, invalid command), or a Secondary exception condition (device fault, no receive buffer available). The sequence number included with the response will identify the next command frame number expected by the Secondary.

At this point, we can proceed to define the Primary/Primary control procedures, in terms of the Primary and Secondary functions implemented in each station. The following is certainly not a rigorous definition of the control procedures, but does describe the general procedures used for initialization, data transfer, and error recovery.

Prior to initiating data transfer, each Primary must first initialize the other station by sending a Reset command, and then wait for the Accept Response indicating that the other Secondary is ready to start receiving data. All data is transferred using a sequence of Select & Respond (SR) frames which are transmitted and received in continuous numeric sequence. The Primary must store all SR frame contents for possible retransmission until corresponding Accept responses are received.

For each SR frame accepted the Secondary will send an Accept response having a sequence number corresponding to the received command frame. When a queue of responses exists, the Secondary will send the single highest numbered response, indicating acceptance of all SR frames up to that point. When a received command is rejected due to a detected link error or Secondary error, the Secondary will send the appropriate Not Accept response, and will reject all subsequent commands until the rejected command is successfully retransmitted.

The Primary may send SR frames continuously without wating for responses, as long as the corresponding Accept responses are received before the sequence number range is exhausted. When a Not Accept response is received, the Primary will begin retransmission, starting with the SR frame indicated by the negative response's sequence number. When no valid response is received within a response timeout period, the Primary can send an Enquire command to solicit a response from the Secondary. After receiving that response, the Primary will either resume normal transmission sequence, or initiate retransmission, as indicated by the response.

The Abort feature is not essential for these procedures, but can be useful in certain applications. For error recovery, after receiving a Not Accept response, the Primary can abort the SR frame in process and begin retransmission immediately. For those applications which assign message priority the Primary can abort a low priority message in order to immediately begin transmission of a high priority message.

The above description outlines the control procedure functions which must be implemented for Primary and Secondary components of each station. In addition, the Channel Control function is required to integrate Primary and Secondary functions on common transmit and receive channels. Commands and responses must be interleaved on the transmit channel, with Secondary responses having higher priority. Each frame arriving on the receive channel must be interpreted as either command or response, with commands steered to the Secondary function and responses steered to the Primary function.

Network Applications

The Primary/Primary procedures described above are directly applicable to computer communication applications using point-to-point link configurations. These procedures can also be used for computer network applications which use a network configuration comprising an array of switching centers interconnected by point-to-point links between adjacent nodes.

In general, network applications require two levels of communication control procedures – link control procedures and network control procedures. Link control procedures are used to control data interchange and error recovery on each link between adjacent network nodes. Network control procedures provide end-to-end network functions such as network routing, message priority, message assembly, and network error recovery.

For network applications, Primary/Primary procedures can be used as the link control procedures and can also accommodate the required network control information. This is accomplished by imbedding network control information within the Information field, using the standard format:

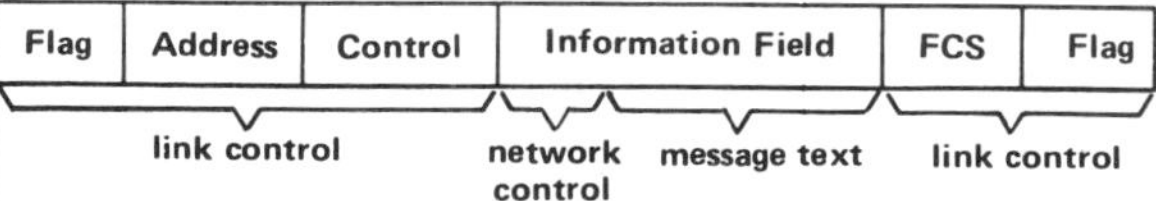

Since the information field contents are completely transparent to the link control procedures, the Information field can be used to transfer both network control information and message data through the network. The separation and interpretation of network control information is a higher level function which is not visible to the link control procedures.

Summary

Bit-oriented control procedures offer a number of advantages over character-oriented procedures and can provide a compatible set of procedures for a wide range of communication system applications.

The Primary/Primary class of procedures is particularly suited to computer-to-computer applications using both point-to-point link configurations and network configurations. These procedures are relatively straightforward, yet provide all of the functionality required for initialization, data transfer and error recovery. The concept of separate Primary and Secondary functions in each station is used as a basis for describing the control procedures. Although system implementation is not necessarily constrained to follow this Primary/Secondary organization, it does provide a good logical basis for system design. Another potential advantage of this approach is that the separate Primary and Secondary components can be used as the basis for implementing Primary/Secondary control procedures for other applications, that is, applications in which the computer is configured as either a Primary or a Secondary station.

References

[1] ANSI X3.4-1968, U.S.A. Standard Code for Information Interchange (ASCII).

[2] ANSI X3.28-1971, American National Standard: Procedures for the Use of the Communication Control Characters of the ASCII Code in Specified Data Communication Links.

[3] ANSI X3S34/437, Proposed USA Standard: Procedures for the Use of the Communication Control Characters of the ASCII Code in Specified Data Communication Links, May 12, 1971.

[4] ISO Recommendation No. 1745, Basic Mode Control Procedures for Data Communication Systems, 1971.

[5] IBM SRL Document, From GA27-3004-1. General Information – Binary Synchronous Communications, December, 1969.

[6] ANSI X3S3.4/475, Fifth Draft USA Standard for Advanced Data Communication Control Procedures (ADCCP), January, 1973.

[7] ISO/TC 97/SC 6/651, HDLC Procedures, Proposed Draft International Standard on Frame Structure, June, 1972.

[8] ISO/TC 97/SC 6/659, HDLC Procedures, Proposed Draft International Standard on Point to Point Type 1, June 1972.

[9] ISO/TC 97/SC 6/660, HDLC Procedures, Proposed Draft International Standard on Commands and Responses, June, 1972.

BRIAN TYMANN is a Principal Engineer at Honeywell Information Systems. He received a B.S. degree in electrical engineering from Manhattan College in 1960, and the M.S. degree in electrical engineering from New York University in 1962. From 1960 to 1966 he was with Bell Telephone Laboratories as a Member of Technical Staff primarily involved in the development of the 101 ESS-Electronic PBX Switching System. In 1966 he joined Honeywell Information Systems where he has been involved in system design of data communication products. He has also worked on development of communication control procedures for terminal products and network applications. Presently, Mr. Tymann is the Honeywell Alternate representative to ANSI Task Groups: x353.4 – Data Communication Control Procedures, and x353.5 – Data Communications System Performance.

Analytic and simulation methods in computer network design*

by LEONARD KLEINROCK

University of California
Los Angeles, California

INTRODUCTION

The Seventies are here and so are computer networks! The time sharing industry dominated the Sixties and it appears that computer networks will play a similar role in the Seventies. The need has now arisen for many of these time-shared systems to share each others' resources by coupling them together over a communication network thereby creating a computer network. The mini-computer will serve an important role here as the sophisticated terminal as well as, perhaps, the message switching computer in our networks.

It is fair to say that the computer industry (as is true of most other large industries in their early development) has been guilty of "leaping before looking"; on the other hand "losses due to hesitation" are not especially prevalent in this industry. In any case, it is clear that much is to be gained by an appropriate *mathematical analysis* of performance and cost measures for these large systems, and that these analyses should most profitably be undertaken before major design commitments are made. This paper attempts to move in the direction of providing some tools for and insight into the design of computer networks through mathematical modeling, analysis and simulation. Frank et al.,[4] describe tools for obtaining low cost networks by choosing among topologies using computationally efficient methods from network flow theory; our approach complements theirs in that we look for closed analytic expressions where possible. Our intent is to provide understanding of the behavior and trade-offs available in some computer network situations thus creating a qualitative tool for choosing design options and not a numerical tool for choosing precise design parameters.

* This work was supported by the Advanced Research Projects Agency of the Department of Defense (DAHC15-69-C-0285).

THE ARPA EXPERIMENTAL COMPUTER NETWORK—AN EXAMPLE

The particular network which we shall use for purposes of example (and with which we are most familiar) is the Defense Department's Advanced Research Projects Agency (ARPA) experimental computer network.[2] The concepts basic to this network were clearly stated in Reference 11 by L. Roberts of the Advanced Research Projects Agency, who originally conceived this system. Reference 6, which appears in these proceedings, provides a description of the historical development as well as the structural organization and implementation of the ARPA network. We choose to review some of that description below in order to provide the reader with the motivation and understanding necessary for maintaining a certain degree of self containment in this paper.

As might be expected, the design specifications and configuration of the ARPA network have changed many times since its inception in 1967. In June, 1969, this author published a paper[8] in which a particular network configuration was described and for which certain analytical models were constructed and studied. That network consisted of nineteen nodes in the continental United States. Since then this number has changed and the identity of the nodes has changed and the topology has changed, and so on. The paper by Frank et al.,[4] published in these proceedings, describes the behavior and topological design of one of these newer versions. However, in order to be consistent with our earlier results, and since the ARPA example is intended as an illustration of an approach rather than a precise design computation, we choose to continue to study and therefore to describe the original nineteen node network in this paper.

The network provides store-and-forward communication paths between the set of nineteen computer re-

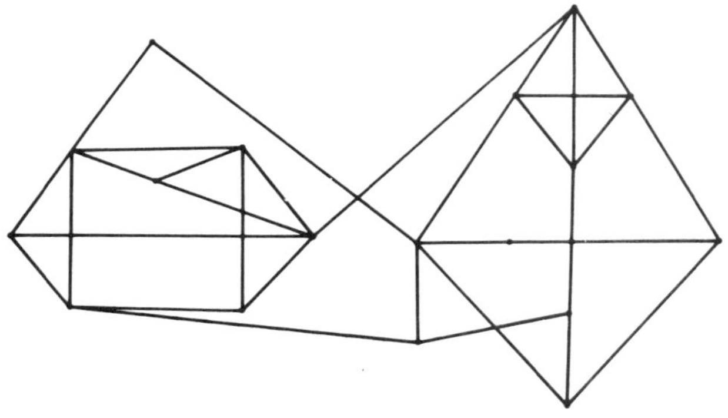

Figure 1—Configuration of the ARPA network in Spring 1969

search centers. The computers located at the various nodes are drawn from a variety of manufacturers and are highly incompatible both in hardware and software; this in fact presents the challenge of the network experiment, namely, to provide effective communication among and utilization of this collection of incompatible machines. The purpose is fundamentally for resource sharing where the resources themselves are highly specialized and take the form of unique hardware, programs, data bases, and human talent. For example, Stanford Research Institute will serve the function of network librarian as well as provide an efficient text editing system; the University of Utah provides efficient algorithms for the manipulation of figures and for picture processing; the University of Illinois will provide through its ILLIAC IV the power of its fantastic parallel processing capability; UCLA will serve as network measurement center and also provide mathematical models and simulation capability for network and time-shared system studies.

The example set of nineteen nodes is shown in Figure 1. The traffic matrix which describes the message flow required between various pairs of nodes is given in Reference 8 and will not be repeated here. An underlying constraint placed upon the construction of this network was that network operating procedures would not interfere in any significant way with the operation of the already existing facilities which were to be connected together through this network. Consequently, the message handling tasks (relay, acknowledgment, routing, buffering, etc.) are carried out in a special purpose Interface Message Processor (IMP) co-located with the principal computer (denoted HOST computer) at each of the computer research centers. The communication channels are (in most cases) 50 kilobit per second full duplex telephone lines and only the IMPs are connected to these lines through data sets. Thus the communication net consists of the lines, the IMPs and the data sets and serves as the store-and-forward system for the HOST computer network. Messages which flow between HOSTs are broken up into small entities referred to as packets (each of maximum size of approximately 1000 bits). The IMP accepts up to eight of these packets to create a maximum size message from the HOST. The packets make their way individually through the IMP network where the appropriate routing procedure directs the traffic flow. A positive acknowledgment is expected within a given time period for each inter-IMP packet transmission; the absence of an acknowledgment forces the transmitting IMP to repeat the transmission (perhaps over the same channel or some other alternate channel). An acknowledgment may not be returned for example, in the case of detected errors or for lack of buffer space in the receiving IMP. We estimate the average packet size to be 560 bits; the acknowledgment length is assumed to be 140 bits. Thus, if we assume that each packet transmitted over a channel causes the generation of a positive acknowledgment packet (the usual case, hopefully), then the average packet transmission over a line is of size 350 bits. Much of the short interactive traffic is of this nature. We also anticipate message traffic of much longer duration and we refer to this as multi-packet traffic. The average input data rate to the entire net is assumed to be 225 kilobits per second and again the reader is referred to Reference 8 for further details of this traffic distribution.

So much for the description of the ARPA network. Protocol and operating procedures for the ARPA computer network are described in References 1 and 6 in these proceedings in much greater detail. The history, development, motivation and cost of this network is described by its originator in Reference 12. Let us now proceed to the mathematical modeling, analysis and simulation of such networks.

ANALYTIC AND SIMULATION METHODS

The mathematical tools for computer network design are currently in the early stages of development. In many ways we are still at the stage of attempting to create computer network models which contain enough salient features of the network so that behavior of such networks may be predicted from the model behavior.

In this section we begin with the problem of *analysis* for a given network structure. First we review the author's earlier analytic model of communication networks and then proceed to identify those features which distinguish computer networks from strict communication networks. Some previously published results on computer networks are reviewed and then new improvements on these results are presented.

We then consider the *synthesis* and *optimization* question for networks. We proceed by first discussing the nature of the channel cost function as available under present tariff and charging structures. We consider a number of different cost functions which attempt to approximate the true data and derive relationships for optimizing the selection of channel capacities under these various cost functions. Comparisons among the optimal solutions are then made for the ARPA network.

Finally in this section we consider the *operating rules* for computer networks. We present the results of simulation for the ARPA network regarding certain aspects of the routing procedure which provide improvements in performance.

A model from queueing theory—Analysis

In a recent work[8] this author presented some computer network models which were derived from his earlier research on communication networks.[7] An attempt was made at that time to incorporate many of the salient features of the ARPA network described above into this computer network model. It was pointed out that computer networks differ from communication networks as studied in Reference 7 in at least the following features: (a) nodal storage capacity is finite and may be expected to fill occasionally; (b) channel and modem errors occur and cause retransmission; (c) acknowledgment messages increase the message traffic rates; (d) messages from HOST A to HOST B typically create return traffic (after some delay) from B to A; (e) nodal delays become important and comparable to channel transmission delays; (f) channel cost functions are more complex. We intend to include some of these features in our model below.

The model proposed for computer networks is drawn from our communication network experience and includes the following assumptions. We assume that the message arrivals form a Poisson process with average rates taken from a given traffic matrix (such as in Reference 8), where the message lengths are exponentially distributed with a mean $1/\mu$ of 350 bits (note that we are only accounting for short messages and neglecting the multi-packet traffic in this model). As discussed at length in Reference 7, we also make the independence assumption which allows a very simple node by node analysis. We further assume that a fixed routing procedure exists (that is, a unique allowable path exists from origin to destination for each origin–destination pair).

From the above assumptions one may calculate the average delay T_i due to waiting for and transmitting over the ith channel from Equation (1),

$$T_i = \frac{1}{\mu C_i - \lambda_i} \tag{1}$$

where λ_i is the average number of messages per second flowing over channel i (whose capacity is C_i bits per second). This was the appropriate expression for the average channel delay in the study of communication nets[7] and in that study we chose as our major performance measure the message delay T averaged over the entire network as calculated from

$$T = \sum_i \frac{\lambda_i}{\gamma} T_i \tag{2}$$

where γ equals the total input data rate. Note that the average on T_i is formed by weighting the delay on channel C_i with the traffic, λ_i, carried on that channel. In the study of communication nets[7] this last equation provided an excellent means for calculating the average message delay. That study went on to optimize the selection of channel capacity throughout the network under the constraint of a fixed cost which was assumed 257
to be linear with capacity; we elaborate upon this cost function later in this section.

The computer network models studied in Reference 8 also made use of Equation (1) for the calculation of the channel delays (including queueing) where parameter choices were $1/\mu = 350$ bits, $C_i = 50$ kilobits and λ_i = average message rate on channel i (as determined from the traffic matrix, the routing procedure, and accounting for the effect of acknowledgment traffic as mentioned in feature (c) above). In order to account for feature (e) above, the performance measure (taken as the average message delay T) was calculated from

$$T = \sum_i \frac{\lambda_i}{\gamma} (T_i + 10^{-3}) \tag{3}$$

where again γ = total input data rate and the term 10^{-3} = 1 millisecond (nominal) is included to account for the assumed (fixed) nodal processing time. The result of this calculation for the ARPA network shown in Figure 1 may be found in Reference 8.

The computer network model described above is essentially the one used for calculating delays in the topological studies reported upon by Frank, et al., in these proceedings.[4]

A number of simulation experiments have been carried out using a rather detailed description of the ARPA network and its operating procedure. Some of

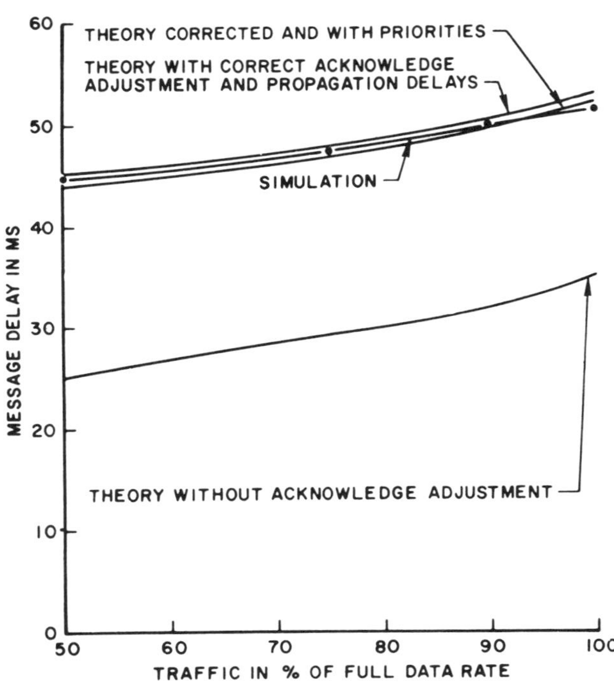

Figure 2—Comparison between theory and simulation for the ARPA network

258

these results were reported upon in Reference 8 and a comparison was made there between the theoretical results obtained from Equation (3) and the simulation results. This comparison is reproduced in Figure 2 where the lowest curve corresponds to the results of Equation (3). Clearly the comparison between simulation and theory is only mildly satisfactory. As pointed out in Reference 8, the discrepancy is due to the fact that the acknowledgment traffic has been improperly included in Equation (3). An attempt was made in Reference 8 to properly account for the acknowledgment traffic; however, this adjustment was unsatisfactory. The problem is that the average message length has been taken to be 350 bits and this length has averaged the traffic due to acknowledgment messages along with traffic due to real messages. These acknowledgments should not be included among those messages whose average system delay is being calculated and yet acknowledgment traffic must be included to properly account for the true loading effect in the network. In fact, the appropriate way to include this effect is to recognize that the time spent waiting for a channel is dependent upon the total traffic (including acknowledgments) whereas the time spent in transmission over a channel should be proportional to the message length of the real message traffic. Moreover, our theoretical equations have accounted only for transmission delays which come about due to the finite rate at which bits may be fed into the channel (i.e., 50 kilobits per second); we are required however to include also the propagation time for a bit to travel down the length of the channel. Lastly, an additional one millisecond delay is included in the final destination node in order to deliver the message to the destination HOST. These additional effects give rise to the following expression for the average message delay T.

$$T = \sum_i \frac{\lambda_i}{\gamma}\left(\frac{1}{\mu' C_i} + \frac{\lambda_i/\mu C_i}{\mu C_i - \lambda_i} + PL_i + 10^{-3}\right) + 10^{-3} \tag{4}$$

where $1/\mu' = 560$ bits (a real message's average length) and PL_i is the propagation delay (dependent on the channel length, L_i) for the ith channel. The first term in parentheses is the average transmission time and the second term is the average waiting time. The result of this calculation for the ARPA network gives us the curve in Figure 2 labeled "theory with correct acknowledge adjustment and propagation delays." The correspondence now between simulation and theory is unbelievably good and we are encouraged that this approach appears to be a suitable one for the prediction of computer network performance for the assumptions made here. In fact, one can go further and include the effect on message delay of the priority given to acknowledgment traffic in the ARPA network; if one includes this effect, one obtains another excellent fit to the simulation data labeled in Figure 2 as "theory corrected and with priorities."

As discussed in Reference 8 one may generalize the model considered herein to account for more general message length distributions by making use of the Pollaczek-Khinchin formula for the delay T_i of a

TABLE 1—Publicly Available Leased Transmission Line Costs from Reference 3

Speed	*Cost/mile/month (normalized to 1000 mile distance)*
45 bps	$ .70
56 bps	.70
75 bps	.77
2400 bps	1.79
41 KB	15.00
82 KB	20.00
230 KB	28.00
1 MB	60.00
12 MB	287.50

channel with capacity C_i, where the message lengths have mean $1/\mu$ bits with variance σ^2, where λ_i is the average message traffic rate and $\rho_i = \lambda_i/\mu C_i$ which states

$$T_i = \frac{1}{\mu' C_i} + \frac{\rho_i(1 + \mu^2\sigma^2)}{2(\mu C_i - \lambda_i)} \quad (5)$$

This expression would replace the first two terms in the parenthetical expression of Equation (4); of course by relaxing the assumption of an exponential distribution we remove the simplicity provided by the Markovian property of the traffic flow. This approach, however, should provide a better approximation to the true behavior when required.

Having briefly considered the problem of analyzing computer networks with regard to a single performance measure (average message delay), we now move on to the consideration of synthesis questions. This investigation immediately leads into optimal synthesis procedures.

Optimization for various channel cost functions—Synthesis

We are concerned here with the optimization of the channel capacity assignment under various assumptions regarding the cost of these channels. This optimization must be made under the constraint of fixed cost. Our problem statement then becomes:*

$$\text{Select the } \{C_i\} \text{ so as to minimize } T$$

$$\text{subject to a fixed cost constraint} \quad (6)$$

where, for simplicity, we use the expression in Equation (2) to define T.

We are now faced with choosing an appropriate cost function for the system of channels. We assume that the total cost of the network is contained in these channel costs where we certainly permit fixed termination charges, for example, to be included. In order to get a feeling for the correct form for the cost function let us examine some available data. From Reference 3 we have available the costing data which we present in Table 1. From a schedule of costs for leased communication lines available at Telpak rates we have the data presented in Table 2.

We have plotted these functions in Figure 3. We

TABLE 2—Estimated Leased Transmission Line Costs Based on Telpak Rates.*

Speed		*Cost (termination + mileage) /month*	*Cost/mile/month (normalized to 1000 mile distance)*
150	bps	\$ 77.50 + \$ .12/mile	\$ .20
2400	bps	232 + .35/mile	.58
7200	bps	810 + .35/mile	1.16
19.2	KB	850 + 2.10/mile	2.95
50	KB	850 + 4.20/mile	5.05
108	KB	2400 + 4.20/mile	6.60
230.4	KB	1300 + 21.00/mile	22.30
460.8	KB	1300 + 60.00/mile	61.30
1.344	MB	500 + 75.00/mile	80.00

*These costs are, in some cases, first estimates and are not to be considered as quoted rates.

must now attempt to find an analytic function which fits cost functions of this sort. Clearly that analytic function will depend upon the rate schedule available to the computer network designer and user. Many analytic fits to this function have been proposed and in particular in Reference 3 a fit is proposed of the form:

$$\text{Cost of line} = 0.1 C_i^{0.44} \quad \$/\text{mile/month} \quad (7)$$

259

Based upon rates available for private line channels, Mastromonaco[10] arrives at the following fit for line costs where he has normalized to a distance of 50 miles (rather than 1000 miles in Equation (7))

$$\text{Cost of line} = 1\ 08 C_i^{0.316} \quad \$/\text{mile/month} \quad (8)$$

Referring now to Figure 3 we see that the mileage

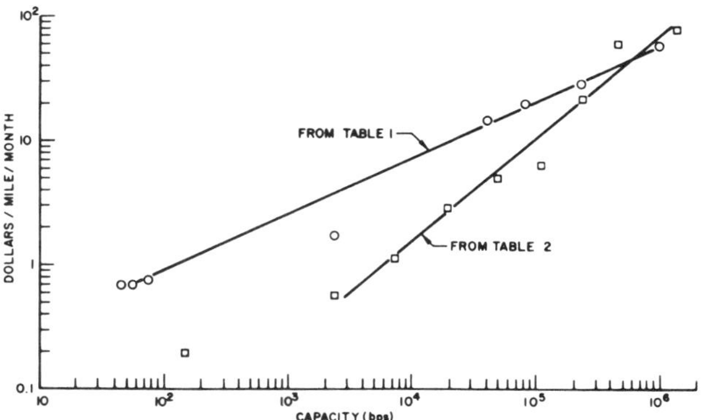

Figure 3—Scanty data on transmission line costs: \$/mile/month normalized to 1000 mile distance

* The dual to this optimization problem may also be considered: "Select the $\{C_i\}$ so as to minimize cost, subject to a fixed message delay constraint." The solution to this dual problem gives the optimum C_i with the same functional dependence on λ_i as one obtains for the original optimization problem.

costs from Table 2 rise as a fractional exponent of capacity (in fact with an exponent of .815) suggesting the cost function shown in Equation (9) below

$$\text{Cost of line} = AC_i^{0.815} \quad \$/\text{mile}/\text{month} \tag{9}$$

These last three equations give the dollar cost per mile per month where the capacity C_i is given in bits per second. It is interesting to note that all three functions are of the form

$$\text{Cost of line} = AC_i^{\alpha} \quad \$/\text{mile}/\text{month} \tag{10}$$

It is clear from these simple considerations that the cost function appropriate for a particular application depends upon that application and therefore it is difficult to establish a unique cost function for all situations. Consequently, we satisfy ourselves below by considering a number of *possible* cost functions and study optimization conditions and results which follow from those cost functions. The designer may then choose from among these to match his given tariff schedule. These cost functions will form the fixed cost constraint in Equation (6). Let us now consider the collection of cost functions, and the related optimization questions.

260

1. *Linear cost function.* We begin with this case since the analysis already exists in the author's Reference 7, where the assumed cost constraint took the form

$$D = \sum_i d_i C_i \tag{11}$$

where D = total number of dollars available to spend on channels, d_i = the dollar cost per unit of capacity on the ith channel, and C_i once again is the capacity of the ith channel. Clearly Equation (11) is of the same form as Equation (10) with $\alpha = 1$ where we now consider the cost of all channels in the system as having a linear form. This cost function assumes that cost is strictly linear with respect to capacity; of course this same cost function allows the assumption of a constant (for example, termination charges) plus a linear cost function of capacity. This constant (termination charge) for each channel may be subtracted out of total cost, D, to create an equivalent problem of the form given in Equation (11). The constant, d_i, allows one to account for the length of the channel since d_i may clearly be proportional to the length of the channel as well as anything else regarding the particular channel involved such as, for example, the terrain over which the channel must be placed. As was done in Reference 7, one may carry out the minimization given by Equation (6) using, for example, the method of Lagrangian undetermined multipliers.[5] This procedure yields the following equation for the capacity

$$C_i = \frac{\lambda_i}{\mu} + \left(\frac{D_e}{d_i}\right) \frac{\sqrt{\lambda_i d_i}}{\sum_j \sqrt{\lambda_j d_j}} \tag{12}$$

where

$$D_e = D - \sum_i \frac{\lambda_i d_i}{\mu} > 0 \tag{13}$$

When we substitute this result back into Equation (2) we obtain that the performance measure for such a channel capacity assignment is

$$T = \frac{\bar{n}\left(\sum_i \sqrt{\lambda_i d_i/\lambda}\right)^2}{\mu D_e} \tag{14}$$

where

$$\bar{n} = \frac{\sum_i \lambda_i}{\gamma} \equiv \frac{\lambda}{\gamma} = \text{average path length} \tag{15}$$

The resulting Equation (12) is referred to as the square root channel capacity assignment; this particular assignment first provides to each channel a capacity equal to λ_i/μ which is merely the average bit rate which must pass over that channel and which it must obviously be provided if the channel is to carry such traffic. In addition, surplus capacity (due to excess dollars, D_e) is assigned to this channel in proportion to the square root of the traffic carried, hence the name. In Reference 7 the author studied in great detail the particular case for which $d_i = 1$ (the case for which all channels cost the same regardless of length) and considerable information regarding topological design and routing procedures was thereby obtained. However, in the case of the ARPA network a more reasonable choice for d_i is that it should be proportional to the length L_i of the ith channel as indicated in Equation (10) (for $\alpha = 1$) which gives the per mileage cost; thus we may take $d_i = AL_i$. This second case was considered in Reference 8 and also in Reference 9. The interpretation for these two cases regarding the desirability of concentrating traffic into a few large and short channels as well as minimizing the average length of lines traversed by a message was well discussed and will not be repeated here.

We observe in the ARPA network example since the channel capacities are fixed at 50 kilobits that there is no freedom left to optimize the choice of channel capacities; however it was shown in Reference 8 that one could take advantage of the optimization procedure in the following way: The total cost of the network using 50 kilobit channels may be calculated. One may then optimize the network (in the sense of minimizing T) by allowing the channel capacities to vary while maintaining the cost fixed at this figure. The result of such optimization will provide a set of channel capacities which vary considerably from the fixed capacity network. It was shown in Reference 8 that one could improve the performance of the network in an efficient way by allowing that channel which required the largest capacity as a result of optimization to be increased from 50 kilobits in the fixed net to 250 kilobits. This of course increases the cost of the system. One may then provide a 250 kilobit channel for the second "most needy" channel from the optimization, increasing the cost further. One may then continue this procedure of increasing the needy channels to 250 kilobits while increasing the cost of the network and observe the way in which message delay decreases as system cost increases. It was found that natural stopping points for this procedure existed at which the cost increased rapidly without a similar sharp decrease in message delay thereby providing some handle on the cost-performance trade-off.

Since we are more interested in the difference between results obtained when one varies the cost function in more significant ways, we now study additional cost functions.

2. *Logarithmic cost functions.* The next case of interest assumes a cost function of the form

$$D = \sum_i d_i \log_e \alpha C_i \tag{16}$$

where D again is the total dollar cost provided for constructing the network, d_i is a coefficient of cost which may depend upon length of channel, α is an appropriate multiplier and C_i is the capacity of the ith channel. We consider this cost function for two reasons: first, because it has the property that the incremental cost per bit decreases as the channel size increases; and secondly, because it leads to simple theoretical results. We now solve the minimization problem expressed in Equation (6) where the fixed cost constraint is now given through Equation (16). We obtain the following equation for the capacity of the ith channel

$$C_i = \frac{\lambda_i}{\mu}\left[1 + \frac{1}{2\gamma\beta\, d_i} + \left(\frac{1}{\gamma\beta\, d_i} + \left(\frac{1}{2\gamma\beta\, d_i}\right)^2\right)^{1/2}\right] \tag{17}$$

In this solution the Lagrangian multiplier β must be adjusted so that Equation (16) is satisfied when C_i is substituted in from Equation (17). Note the unusual simplicity for the solution of C_i, namely that the channel capacity for the ith channel is *directly proportional to the traffic* carried by that channel, λ_i/μ. Contrast this result with the result in Equation (12) where we had a square root channel capacity assignment. If we now take the simple result given in Equation (17) and use it in Equation (2) to find the performance measure T we obtain

$$T = \sum_i \left\{\frac{1}{2\, d_i\beta} + \left[\frac{\gamma}{d_i\beta} + \left(\frac{1}{2\, d_i\beta}\right)^2\right]^{1/2}\right\}^{-1} \tag{18}$$

In this last result the performance measure depends upon the particular distribution of the internal traffic $\{\lambda_i/\mu\}$ through the constant β which is adjusted as described above.

3. *The power law cost function.* As we saw in Equations (7), (8), and (9) it appears that many of the existing tariffs may be approximated by a cost function of the form given in Equation (19) below.

$$D = \sum_i d_i C_i^{\alpha} \tag{19}$$

where α is some appropriate exponent of the capacity and d_i is an arbitrary multiplier which may of course depend upon the length of the channel and other pertinent channel parameters. Applying the Lagrangian again with an undetermined multiplier β we obtain as our condition for an optimal channel capacity the following non-linear equation:

$$C_i - \frac{\lambda_i}{\mu} - C_i^{(1-\alpha)/2} g_i = 0 \tag{20}$$

where

$$g_i = \left(\frac{\lambda_i}{\mu\gamma\beta\alpha\, d_i}\right)^{1/2} \tag{21}$$

Once again, β must be adjusted so as to satisfy the constraint Equation (19).

It can be shown that the left hand side of Equation (20) represents a convex function and that it has a unique solution for some positive value C_i. We assume that α is in the range

$$0 \leq \alpha \leq 1$$

as suggested from the data in Figure 3. We may also show that the location of the solution to Equation (20) is not especially sensitive to the parameter settings. Therefore, it is possible to use any efficient iterative technique for solving Equation (20) and we have found that such techniques converge quite rapidly to the optimal solution.

4. *Comparison of solutions for various cost functions.* In the last three subsections we have considered three different cost functions: the linear cost function; the logarithmic cost function; and the power law cost function. Of course we see immediately that the linear

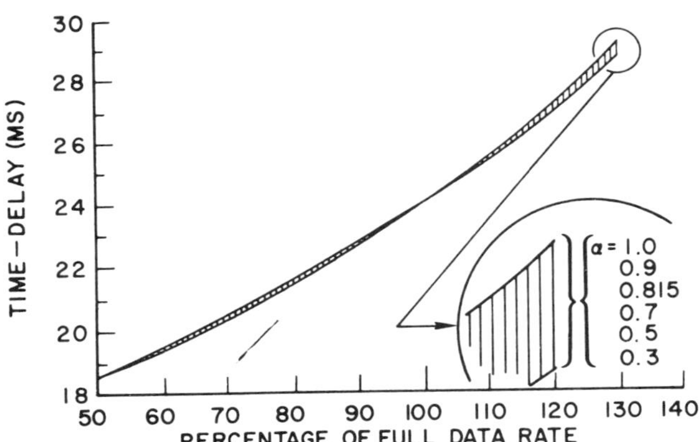

Figure 4—Average message delay at fixed cost as a function of data rate for the power law and linear cost functions

cost function is a special case $\alpha = 1$ of the power law cost function. We wish now to compare the performance and cost of computer networks under these various cost functions. We use for our example the ARPA computer network as described above.

262

It is not obvious how one should proceed in making this comparison. However, we adopt the following approach in an attempt to make some meaningful comparisons. We consider the ARPA network at a traffic load of 100% of the full data rate, namely 225 kilobits per second (denoted by γ_0). For the 50 kilobit net shown in Figure 1 we may calculate the line costs from Table 2 (eliminating the termination charges since we recognize this causes no essential change in our optimization procedures, as mentioned above); the resultant network cost is approximately \$579,000 per year (which we denote by D_0). Using this γ_0 and D_0 (as well as the other given input parameters) we may then carry out the optimization indicated in Equation (6) for the case of a linear cost function where $d_i = AL_i$ and A is immediately found from the mileage cost in Table 2. This calculation results in an average message delay T_0 (calculated from Equation (14)) whose value is approximately 24 milliseconds. We have now established an "operating point" for the three quantities γ_0, D_0, and T_0, whose values are 100% of full data rate, \$579,000, and 24 milliseconds, respectively.

We may now examine all of our other cost functions by forcing them to pass through this operating point. We assume $d_i = AL_i$ throughout for these calculations. Also we choose $\alpha = 1$ for the logarithmic case in Equation (16). (Note for the logarithmic and power law cases that two unknown constants, β and A, must be determined; this is now easily done if we set $T = T_0$ and $D = D_0$ for $\gamma = \gamma_0$ in each of these two cases independently.) In particular now we wish to examine the behavior of the network under these various cost functions. We do this first by fixing the cost of the network at $D = D_0$ and plotting T, the average time delay, as we vary the percentage of full data rate applied to the network; this performance is given in Figure 4 where we show the system behavior for the power law cost function and the linear cost function. The result is striking! We see that the variation in average message delay is almost insignificant as α passes through the range from 0.3 to 1.0. It appears then that the very important power law cost function may be analyzed using a linear cost function when one is interested in evaluating the average time delay at fixed cost.*

We also consider the variation of the network cost D as a function of data rate at fixed average message delay, namely $T = T_0 = 24$ milliseconds. This performance is shown in Figure 5 for all three cost functions. We note here that the linear cost function is only a fair approximation to the power law cost function over the range of α shown; the logarithmic cost function is also shown and behaves very much like the linear cost function for data rates above γ_0 but departs from that behavior for data rates below γ_0. It can be shown that the network cost, D, at fixed $T = T_0$ for the case $\alpha = 1$ (linear cost function) varies as a constant plus a linear dependence on γ. It is also of interest to cross plot the average time delay T with the network cost

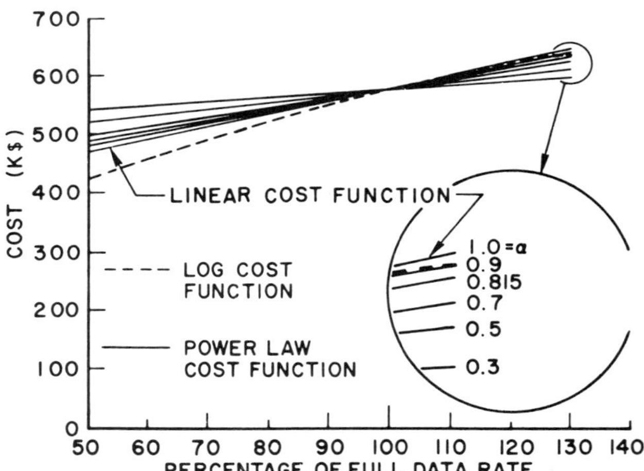

Figure 5—Network cost at fixed average message delay as a function of data rate

* The logarithm cost function is not shown in Figure 4 since the time delay is extremely sensitive to the data rate and bears little resemblance to the power law case.

D. This we do in Figure 6 for the class of power law cost functions. In Figures 6a and 6b we obtain points along the vertical and horizontal axes corresponding to fixed delay and fixed cost, respectively. These loci are obtained by varying γ and we connect the points for equal γ with straight lines as shown in the figure (however, we in no way imply that the system passes along these straight lines as both T and D are allowed to vary simultaneously). We note the increased range of D as α varies from 0.3 to 1.0, but very little change in the range of T. In Figure 6c we collect together the behavior in this plane for many values of α where the lines labeled with a particular value of α correspond to the 50% data rate case in the lower left-hand portion of the figure and to the 130% data rate case in the upper right-hand portion of the figure. From Figure 6c we clearly observe that for fixed cost the time delay range varies insignificantly as α changes (as we emphasized in discussing Figure 4). Similarly, we observe the moderate variation at fixed time delay of network cost as α ranges through its values (this we saw clearly in Figure 5).

These studies of network optimization for various cost functions need further investigation. Our aim in this section has been to exhibit some of the performance characteristics under these cost functions and to compare them in some meaningful way.

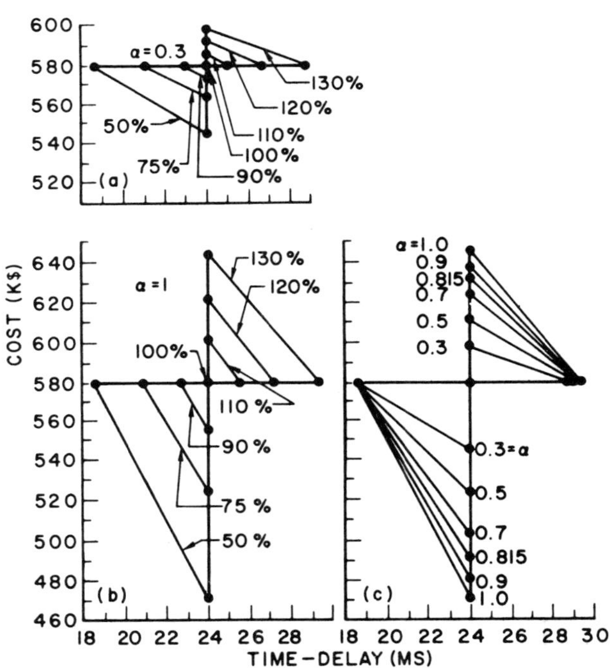

Figure 6—Locus of system performance for the power law cost function

263

Simulated routing in the ARPA network—Operating procedure

We have examined analysis and synthesis procedures for computer networks above. We now proceed to exhibit some properties of the network operating procedure, in particular, the message routing procedure.

The ARPA network uses a routing procedure which is local in nature as opposed to global. Some details of this procedure are available in Reference 6 in these proceedings and we wish to comment on the method used for updating the routing tables. For purposes of routing, each node maintains a list which contains for each destination an estimate of the delay a message would encounter in attempting to reach that destination node were it to be sent out over a particular channel emanating from that node; the list contains an entry for each destination and each line leaving the node in which this list is contained. Every half second (approximately) each node sends to all of its immediate neighbors a list which contains its estimate of the shortest delay time to pass to each destination; this list therefore contains a number of entries which is one less than the number of nodes in the network. Upon receiving this information from one of its neighbors, the IMP adds to this list of estimated delays a measure of the current delays in passing from itself to the neighbor from whom it is receiving this list; this then provides that IMP an estimate of the minimum delay required to reach all destinations if one traveled out over the line connected to that neighbor. The routing table for the IMP is then constructed by combining the lists of all of its neighbors into a set of columns and choosing as the output line for messages going to a particular destination that line for which the estimated delay over that line to that destination is minimum. What we have here described is essentially a periodic or *synchronous* updating method for the routing tables as currently used in the ARPA network. It has the clear advantages of providing reasonably accurate data regarding path delays as well as the important advantage of being a rather simple procedure both from an operational point of view and from an overhead point of view in terms of software costs inside the IMP program.

We suggest that a more efficient procedure in terms of routing delays is to allow *asynchronous updating*; by this we mean that routing information is passed from a node to its nearest neighbors only when significant enough changes occurr in its own routing table to warrant such an information exchange. The definition of "significant enough" must be studied carefully

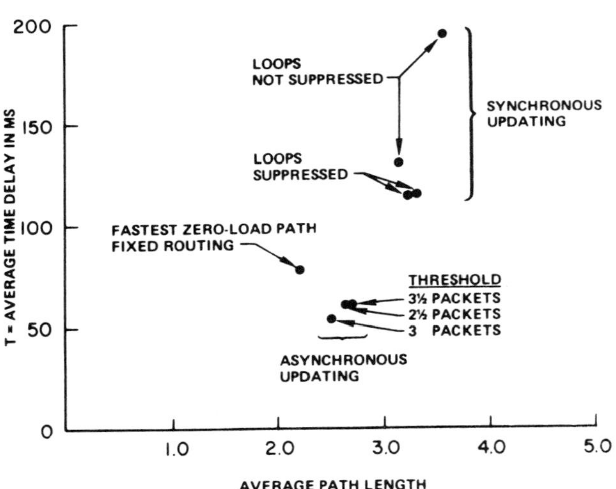

Figure 7—Comparison of synchronous and asynchronous updating for routing algorithms

but certainly implies the use of thresholds on the percentage change of estimated delays. When these thresholds are crossed in an IMP then routing informa-
264 tion is transferred to that IMP's nearest neighbors. This asynchronous mode of updating implies a large overhead for updating and it remains to be seen whether the advantages gained through this more elaborate updating method overcome the disadvantages due to software costs and cycle-stealing costs for updating. We may observe the difference in performance between synchronous and asynchronous updating through the use of simulation as shown in Figure 7. In this figure we plot the average time delay T versus the average path length for messages under various routing disciplines. We observe immediately that the three points shown for asynchronous updating are significantly superior to those shown for synchronous updating. For a comparison we also show the result of a fixed routing algorithm which was computed by solving for the shortest delay path in an unloaded network; the asynchronous updating shows superior performance to the fixed routing procedure. Moreover, the synchronous updating shows inferior performance compared to this very simple fixed routing procedure if we take as our performance measure the average message delay.

It was observed that with synchronous updating it was possible for a message to get trapped temporarily in loops (i.e., traveling back and forth between the same pair of nodes). We suppressed this looping behavior for two synchronous updating procedures with different parameter settings and achieved significant improvement; nevertheless, this improved version remains inferior to those simulated systems with asynchronous updating. As mentioned above, asynchronous updating contains many virtues, but one must consider the overhead incurred for such a sophisticated updating procedure before it can be incorporated and expected to yield a net improvement in performance.

CONCLUSIONS

Our goal in this paper has been to demonstrate the importance of analytical and simulation techniques in evaluating computer networks in the early design stages. We have addressed ourselves to three areas of interest, namely the analysis of computer network performance using methods from queueing theory, the optimal synthesis problem for a variety of cost functions, and the choice of routing procedure for these networks. Our results show that it is possible to obtain exceptionally good results in the analysis phase when one considers the "small" packet traffic only. As yet, we have not undertaken the study of the multi-packet traffic behavior. In examining available data we found that the power law cost function appears to be the appropriate one for high-speed data lines. We obtained optimal channel capacity assignment procedures for this cost function as well as the logarithmic cost function and the linear cost function. A significant result issued from this study through the observation that the average message delay for the power law cost function could very closely be approximated by the average message delay through the system constrained by a linear cost function; this holds true in the case when the system cost is held fixed. For the fixed delay case we found that the variation of the system cost under a power law constraint could be represented by the cost variation for a linear cost constraint only to a limited extent.

In conjunction with pure analytical results it is extremely useful to take advantage of system simulation. This is the approach we described in studying the effect of routing procedures and comparing methods for updating these procedures. We indicated that asynchronous updating was clearly superior to synchronous updating except in the case where the overhead for asynchronous updating might be severe.

The results referred to above serve to describe the behavior of computer network systems and are useful in the early stages of system design. If one is desirous of obtaining numerical tools for choosing the precise design parameters of a system, then it is necessary to go to much more elaborate analytic models or else to resort to efficient search procedures (such as that described in Reference 4) in order to locate optimal designs.

ACKNOWLEDGMENTS

The author is pleased to acknowledge Gary L. Fultz for his assistance in simulation studies as well as his contributions to loop suppression in the routing procedures; acknowledgment is also due to Ken Chen for his assistance in the numerical solution for the performance under different cost function constraints.

REFERENCES

1 S CARR S CROCKER V CERF
Host to host communication protocol in the ARPA network
These proceedings

2 P A DICKSON
ARPA network will represent integration on a large scale
Electronics pp 131–134 September 30 1968

3 R G GOULD
Comments on generalized cost expressions for private-line communications channels
IEEE Transactions on Communication Technology V Com-13 No 3 pp 374–377 September 1965
also
R P ECKHERT P M KELLY
A program for the development of a computer resource sharing network
Internal Report for Kelly Scientific Corp Washington D C February 1969

4 H FRANK I T FRISCH W CHOU
Topological considerations in the design of the ARPA computer network
These proceedings

5 F B HILDEBRAND
Methods of applied mathematics
Prentice-Hall Inc Englewood Cliffs N J 1958

6 F E HEART R E KAHN S M ORNSTEIN W R CROWTHER D C WALDEN
The interface message processor for the ARPA network
These proceedings

7 L KLEINROCK
Communication nets; stochastic message flow and delay
McGraw-Hill New York 1964

8 L KLEINROCK
Models for computer networks
Proc of the International Communications Conference pp 21-9 to 21-16 University of Colorado Boulder June 1969

9 L KLEINROCK
Comparison of solutions methods for computer network models
Proc of the Computers and Communications Conference Rome New York September 30–October 2 1969

10 F R MASTROMONACO
Optimum speed of service in the design of customer data communications systems
Proc of the ACM Symposium on the Optimization of Data Communications Systems pp 127–151 Pine Mountain Georgia October 13–16 1969

11 L G ROBERTS
Multiple computer networks and intercomputer communications
ACM Symposium on Operating Systems Principles Gatlinburg Tennessee October 1967

12 L G ROBERTS B D WESSLER
Computer network developments to achieve resource sharing
These proceedings

265

Flow Control in a Resource-Sharing Computer Network

ROBERT E. KAHN, MEMBER, IEEE, AND WILLIAM R. CROWTHER

Abstract—**In this paper, we discuss flow control in a resource-sharing computer network. The resources consist of a set of inhomogeneous computers called hosts that are geographically distributed and are interconnected by a store-and-forward communications subnet. In the communication process, messages pass between hosts via the subnet. A protocol is used to control the flow of messages in such a way as to efficiently utilize the subnet and the host resources. In this paper, we examine in some detail the nature of the flow control required in the subnet and its relation to the host flow control and subnet performance.**

Manuscript received August 2, 1971. This paper was presented at the 2nd Symposium on Problems in the Optimization of Data Communications Systems, Palo Alto, Calif., October 20–22, 1971. This research was supported by the Advanced Research Projects Agency, Department of Defense, under Contract DAHC15-69-C-0179.

The authors are with Bolt Beranek and Newman, Inc., Cambridge, Mass.

I. Introduction

IN THIS PAPER we discuss flow control in a resource-sharing computer network [1]. The network resources consist of a set of inhomogeneous computers called hosts that are geographically distributed and are interconnected by a store-and-forward communications subnet. Each host is connected to a store-and-forward switching node called an interface message processor (IMP), which is located on or nearby its premises [2]. IMP's are then interconnected by leased synchronous communication circuits to form the subnet.

In such a network, the combined resources of all the host computers are available to each host as if the network were a single distributed computer system. A process in one host communicates with a process in another by sending it a sequence of one or more messages, each of which is a finite stream of bits, preceded by an address. For economy of implementation, each message leaves or enters a host via a multiplexed asynchronous channel to its IMP.

Within each host computer, several levels (or layers) of protocol are needed to escort each message from its originating process to the IMP and similarly to escort each message from the destination IMP to its eventual destination process. The first two levels of protocol are known as the host/IMP protocol [3] and the host-to-host protocol [4], respectively. The host/IMP protocol handles the transfer of data between a host and its IMP. The host-to-host protocol, in general, acts as a software multiplexor (or demultiplexor) between one or more active host processes and the single asynchronous channel to the IMP. In this role, it typically handles process wakeup and dispatching, message flow control, and validity checking and provides testing and error recovery features. Additional levels of protocol are needed, for example, to 1) achieve standardized characteristics for teletype-like terminal devices, 2) handle the transfer of graphics information, and 3) provide standard conventions for the transfer of data or the manipulation of files.

In the host computers, flow control involves coordinating the dispatch and arrival of messages with the availability of buffer space and/or process accessibility, as well as establishing and closing process-to-process connections and allowing for the transfer of control as, for example, using breaks or interrupts. Many alternatives are possible for establishing and closing connections and for transferring control, including, at one extreme, dispensing with the notion of connections entirely. However, these issues are nominally host specific and therefore we make no attempt to elaborate on them in this paper. The allocation of buffer space is an important aspect of flow control not only in the hosts but in the IMP's as well.

Within the IMP's flow control is a distributed computational task requiring coordination between the source and destination IMP as to sequencing of messages, subnet connectivity, host responsiveness, IMP buffer allocation, etc. Messages from one process to another are normally to be delivered to the destination host in the order they were dispatched (this requirement may be relaxed in some cases) and without error or duplication. If a message cannot be delivered, for example, because no path currently exists to the destination host or because the host is not accepting messages, the message may be discarded by the subnet, but the source host must be notified of that event. The allocation of buffers at the destination IMP is required to prevent network congestion. Although the availability of mass storage in the IMP's would greatly increase the mean time to congestion, more storage alone cannot, in general, prevent its occurrence. Without mass storage, of course, the flow control must be even more diligent to prevent network congestion from occurring.

A partition of flow control responsibility between the IMP's and the hosts may increase the overall reliability of network operation. In general, however, the inherent operation of the interface between the host and the IMP need not be considered to be partitioned. A combined structure for the interface, which suggests a truly software interface, was pointed out by Licklider [5].

One method of handling host flow control has each host initially allocate some number of buffers and notify the other host of that amount. As successive messages are transmitted, the allocation is decremented accordingly by both hosts. The receiving host may then allocate additional buffers as the supply dwindles. This system is described in [4].

Another method of handling host flow control [6] introduces the notion of crates for transporting the contents of a buffer. A pair of processes that wish to communicate would each have provided some number of buffers for flow control and have the other host informed of that number. In an efficient implementation only a few buffers would typically be provided at each end and each host might provide the same number. Let us assume the crates to be in buffers at one end initially. When a crate arrives at the other end, it may then be used to send a message in the reverse direction. Crates may be removed from operation or transmitted to the other host. When no more crates are available at a host, it is not allowed to send additional messages. With a single crate in use, the communication flow alternates between the two directions. With a very large number of crates in use, the flow is essentially full duplex.

A third method of handling flow control [7] couples the flow control more directly to actions taken by the user processes at either end. A process must always either expect to receive a message or specifically ask to receive one from the sender. In the latter case, after a buffer has been set up, a RECEIVE message is dispatched to the sending host, which issues a SEND message when it in turn has the message to dispatch. When the SEND and RECEIVE have rendezvoused, typically at the sending host, the message is transmitted.

If a host faithfully executes any one of the above schemes and accepts messages from its IMP at a rate at least equal to the arrival rate, no congestion should occur at the destination IMP. However, if a host should err (for example, by losing count of its current allocation) or should fail to be prompt in accepting messages from its IMP, the IMP subnet can become congested. Consequently, for reliability, a portion of the flow control mechanism must reside in the IMP so that a malfunction in one host does not adversely affect the service obtained by other hosts using the net. A recent discussion of congestion is also given in [8].

In this paper we examine in some detail the nature of the flow control required in the IMP and its relation to the host flow control and subnet performance.

II. Subnet Flow Control

It is important to distinguish between the dual objectives of introducing small transmission delays to speed the delivery of short interactive messages and obtaining high-bandwidth transmission for the transfer of long files of data. The flow-control mechanism must allow for both these objectives to be simultaneously satisfied. It appears to be more the rule than the exception that a modification to the flow control mechanism that favors high-bandwidth traffic does so at the expense of short interactive traffic and vice versa. As a result, the process of algorithm definition and adjustment is often a delicate matter involving at least two iterations per change to account for both objectives.

Flow control within the subnet must provide a smooth message flow, without the introduction of undue delay, from the time of each message entry into the net until it is delivered to the destination. With a finite number of buffers in each IMP, this task requires that the flow of traffic be directly regulated by the availability of buffers at the destination IMP for holding messages for its host, and affected by (but not necessarily regulated by) the availability of buffers at the intermediate IMP's for storing messages while in transit. The former kind are referred to as reassembly buffers and the latter as store-and-forward buffers.

The management of reassembly buffers to regulate the flow between a pair of hosts involves a signaling strategy between the IMP at the two ends of the connection, i.e., the source and the destination. This aspect of flow control is discussed in Section II-A. The use of store-and-forward buffers in controlling the flow from IMP to IMP is discussed in Section II-B.

A. Source/Destination Flow Control

An early form of subnet flow control developed for use in the Advanced Research Projects Agency network (ARPANET) [2] involved the concepts of "link" and "request for next message" (RFNM). A link is defined to be a unidirectional logical connection between a pair of hosts. The host may make further use of links as an addressing mechanism to specify particular process-to-process connections. Each end of a connection is called a socket. A process typically communicates with another process by sending it a sequence of messages over a given link. The two processes agree upon a link for use in connecting a pair of sockets in advance, by means of the host-to-host protocol. The link identification is included by the sending host in the address of each message. Two links (and therefore four sockets) must be used for transmitting messages in both directions.

Only one message at a time is allowed to be present in the subnet on a link. After each message is delivered, an RFNM on that link is returned to the source IMP, which passes the RFNM along to the host. The source host must refrain from sending the next message on that link until it has received the RFNM. The source IMP will discard any message that is sent from the host on that link before the RFNM has been received. While waiting for a RFNM to arrive, the host may use any links that have no outstanding RFNM.

This strategy assures proper sequencing of message delivery, allows duplicates on a link to be easily detected (by use of a sequence number) and discarded, and ensures that a single link cannot cause network congestion. If a source host stops getting RFNM's, it is thus prevented by its IMP from sending additional messages into the net on that particular link.

The IMP's further subdivide each message into one or more "packets" to speed its transmission through the network. The packets of a message are independently transmitted through the subnet to the destination. Each packet thus contains a piece or segment of a message and all packets of a message must be present at the destination IMP for the original message to be pieced back together. A message that is subdivided into two or more packets is called a multipacket message. The destination IMP then reassembles the message from the individual packets and sends the message to the destination host as a single stream of bits preceded by the addressing information. This subdivision is completely invisible to the host computers.

This flow control technique is reliable when the destination IMP has a sufficiently large amount of reassembly buffer storage to hold arriving packets on all the links in use. However, when a limited amount of reassembly space is available, the subnet buffer storage can become filled if messages are sent into the net on a sufficient amount of links destined for a given host. Equivalently, the subnet buffers will become filled with backed-up messages if a sufficient number of messages arrive for a host (or hosts) at a faster rate than the host is accepting them.

Deadlock conditions are known to be possible in systems that involve competition for limited resources, and precautions must be taken to prevent their occurrence [9], [10]. A type of deadlock called "reassembly lockup" can occur in the subnet when reassembly space is unavailable to store incoming multipacket messages. Let us assume that IMP A is the source of multipacket messages destined for IMP A' and that all the reassembly buffers at IMP A' are either occupied or reserved for awaited packets of partially reassembled messages. Reassembly lockup exists when the neighbors of A' are filled with store-and-forward packets also headed to A' which IMP A' cannot accept, thereby preventing packets at other IMP's from reaching the destination A' and completing the partially reassembled messages.

A simulation program that models an early version of the ARPANET was used to obtain some quantitative measures of this aspect of system performance. The simulation showed the occurrence of reassembly lockup for the simple case of eight-packet traffic on many links between a pair of hosts, as well as for other traffic patterns involving multipacket traffic among more than two hosts. It is characteristic of the simulation that the resulting throughput values (measured in kilobits/second) are often quite different from one run to the next, indicating a throughput statistic with sizeable variance. Several values of throughput versus number of links obtained by simulation are shown in Fig. 1. Traffic consisting of eight-packet messages is sent from A to A'. The circuits are assumed to be 50 kbits/s, two paths are available for use, and in this case, reassembly lockup occurs after ten links are in use. The length of each run was limited to be on the order of tens of thousands of messages. Only a few representative points are shown on the figure. The simulation is basically straightforward and is not otherwise described in this paper.

A simple solution to the reassembly lockup problem is to allow the destination IMP to discard the packets of any message that it cannot accept into reassembly and to notify the sending host of the disposal. The sending host can make provision to retransmit the message if it desires. The destination IMP must still perform the reassembly bookkeeping, but it need not provide the buffer storage for discarded packets. The main difficulty with this approach is that it introduces transmission failures that may be avoided with the use of other strategies.

A more elaborate solution to this problem is to have the source IMP ask the destination IMP if reassembly space is available for each message prior to sending it into the net and then to transmit the message only after buffer space has been reserved at the destination IMP. This approach introduces occasional delays in transmission rather than failures and is similar to the protocol suggested in [7]. In essence, the destination IMP executes a RECEIVE to the sending IMP only after reassembly buffer space is available. However, a space-request message must first be sent from the source IMP to the destination IMP to ask for space. If reassembly space is not available, the space request is queued at the destination IMP until space becomes free.

In order to minimize delay, single-packet messages serve as their own requests for space. A copy of each single-packet message is held at the source IMP. If no space is available when the packet arrives at the destination, it is discarded and a message to send the copy is returned to the source IMP when space is finally reserved. This strategy ensures that no setup delay is incurred whenever space is immediately available at the destination. Conversely, a setup delay is incurred only when reassembly space is unavailable. From another point of view, single-packet messages that cannot be accepted at the destination are discarded from the subnet and retransmission is provided by the source IMP.

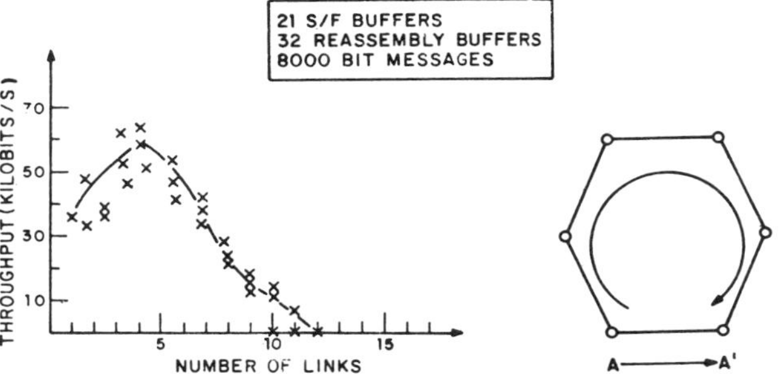

Fig. 1. Reassembly lockup.

For the first of a sequence of multipacket messages, a short space request message is sent by the source IMP ahead of the regular message, if space has not yet been reserved but a full copy is not kept at the source IMP. Instead the source IMP halts the host/IMP line until either space is known to be available, or a short duration timeout occurs. This typically introduces a setup delay on the order of tens of milliseconds for the first such multipacket message. However, it does ensure that multipacket messages that could congest the net are not permitted to enter.

The technique of subnet flow control should allow high-bandwidth traffic between any two hosts in an otherwise empty net. However, high bandwidth cannot be obtained unless a setup delay per multipacket message is avoided. As described above, the first multipacket messages to a given destination will encounter a setup delay. However, each succeeding multipacket message to that destination can avoid encountering the delay if each is sent promptly upon receipt of the RFNM. For the subnet to achieve this objective, an additional set of reassembly buffers is reserved as soon as possible after the first packet of a multipacket message is sent to the destination host, after which the RFNM is returned to the source IMP. The host's next multipacket message to that destination will be sent by the source IMP without first asking the destination IMP if buffer space exists, provided it is received by the source IMP within a short period (e.g., 125 ms) after the host received the RFNM. If several RFNM's for multipacket messages have been sent to the host, they will be timed out one at a time in sequence. If such a timeout occurs, a message is sent to the destination IMP to free the reserved buffers. Thus, in essence, for multipacket messages, the destination IMP issues a RECEIVE to the source IMP for each arriving multipacket message. A host attempting to achieve high bandwidth can ensure that RECEIVE's will continue to be returned by promptly sending its next message. There is no possibility for a host to achieve high bandwidth on a given link unless it is prepared to send its next message on that link promptly.

In a subnet without mass storage, reserving space at the destination is a more powerful method for flow control than the link-handling scheme described earlier (which blocks and unblocks links) since it completely frees the net from congestion and lockup due to insufficient reassembly space. As these two schemes strongly overlap in function and the link-handling scheme is costly in both program time and space, it may be deleted with the following small attendant loss. In the link-handling scheme, if a message is lost on any link due to subnet failure, that link experiences an incomplete transmission but no other links are affected. As a result of removing the link-handling scheme, an incomplete transmission between two IMP's may introduce short delays on other active transmissions between the pair of IMP's. However, this event is assumed to be acceptable since the penalty is not severe and the event is expected to be quite infrequent.

The space-allocation scheme must explicitly attend to sequence control and discarding duplicate messages, which it accomplishes by using sequential message numbers. If each IMP used a single message number for each other IMP and delivered all messages in the order of insertion, priority messages could occasionally experience unnecessary delays in transit, as for example, whenever one or more multipacket messages are sent immediately preceding the priority message (and must also be delivered before the priority message). This delay points to the need to distinguish between 1) priority messages that should precede other messages into the destination host whenever possible and 2) short messages that must retain their original position in the sequence, as for example, the last message of a file transfer. Therefore, the host must specifically mark a priority message as such if the subnet is to be able to deliver it with priority. Of the several methods of implementing a priority-handling mechanism, a simple way is for each IMP to keep two message numbers for each other IMP. The second message number is provided to handle priority messages as marked by the host. These two message numbers correspond to two pipes between the IMP's and within each pipe messages are delivered in order. However, the two pipes may "slide" relative to each other so that a message in the priority pipe can be delivered before a message on the regular pipe, even though it was transmitted later in time.

The question arises as to the function of delivering RFNM's past the source IMP to the host. Since links are no longer blocked and unblocked, the RFNM may appear to serve no useful function in designating a request for the next message, since the host need not wait for an RFNM. Conveniently, the RFNM still indicates that the message arrived at the destination and the host can use links and RFNM's in the old way as always.

RFNM's are useful, however, for a host that wishes to obtain good system response when the net is heavily loaded. For example, when a host tries to communicate with a destination that is receiving high-bandwidth traffic, it may encounter delays for messages headed to other destinations unless it dispatches messages sequenced to the return of RFNM's. If a given host tries to obtain high bandwidth to several destinations at once, the returning RFNM's tell how to order its incoming traffic to the IMP. Furthermore, the use of RFNM's by the host's interfacing software can regulate a single user from causing interference with other users' communication.

When space is unavailable to queue requests for reassembly buffers at the destination IMP, a busy signal will be returned to the sending host and the message will be discarded. Although this condition may be circumvented (e.g., by having the source IMP continually ask for reassembly buffer space, hold onto the message and experience a short delay) the whole consideration appears to be nonessential. However, discarding of the message in this infrequent case does have some obvious advantages.

B. *IMP/IMP Flow Control*

We begin by describing a simple form of flow control between two adjacent IMP's. Each IMP contains N buffers, each of which may be placed on any output queue. Each IMP also keeps a copy of each transmitted packet until either an acknowledgment is returned by the neighbor, in which case the copy is discarded, or a timeout occurs, in which case the packet is retransmitted. When a packet arrives without error and a buffer is available, the packet is accepted and an acknowledgment is returned. If the packet is in error or no space is available, the packet is discarded and no acknowledgment is returned. This extremely simple technique allows maximum autonomy between the two IMP's.

Unfortunately, such a simple strategy can result in deadlock situations that are called store-and-forward lockups. Two types of store-and-forward lockups are described below. For simplicity, we assume that only single packet messages are in transit and that the destination IMP discards each arriving packet so that no subnet congestion can occur due to reassembly lockup or backup from the destination IMP.

1) Direct Store-and-Forward Lockup: This type of lockup is illustrated by the network in Fig. 2. When IMP's A and B each send packets to IMP's A' and B' respectively, on at least N links and vice versa, IMP C can become filled with packets on the queue to IMP D and IMP D can become filled with packets on the queue to IMP C. Due to the lack of free buffer space, neither IMP can accept packets from the other and the flow of traffic is halted.

The simulation program was used to obtain a quantitative measure of this phenomenon. Several values of throughput versus number of links for 1000-bit packet traffic that were obtained are shown in Fig. 2. The number of links is per IMP and the throughput is total throughput for all messages. Store-and-forward lockup is shown to occur when more than 11 links per IMP are in use.

2) Indirect Store-and-Forward Lockup: This type of lockup is illustrated by the loop network in Fig. 3. Each IMP in the loop can become filled with packets headed

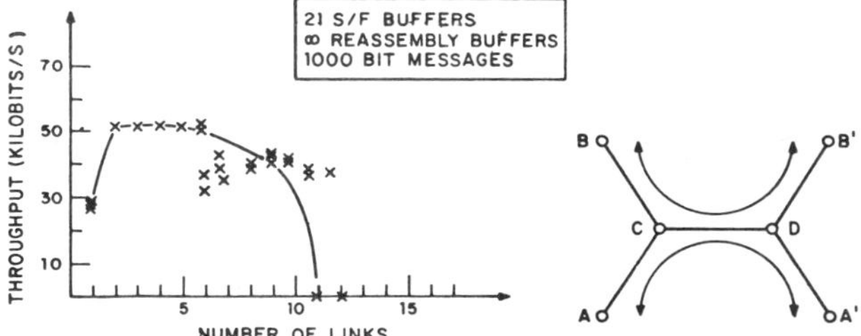

Fig. 2. Direct store-and-forward lockup.

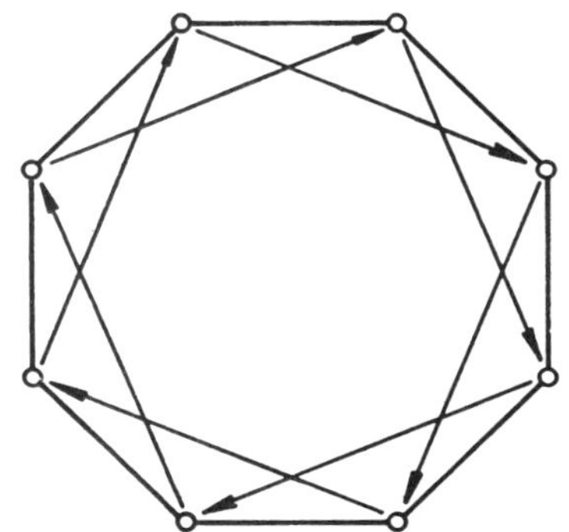

Fig. 3. Indirect store-and-forward lockup.

to one of its neighbors and no two IMP's have packets headed to each other. In general, however, it appears to be difficult to induce an indirect store-and-forward lockup without carefully arranging the network topology, the offered traffic, and the details of the routing algorithm. In fact, the details of the selected routing algorithm can permit the net in Fig. 3 to experience a combined direct and indirect store-and-forward lockup. However, it is one of the few cases in which an indirect lockup is known to be possible and is presented here for concreteness.

A simulation of this network with 21 store-and-forward buffers per IMP and 1000-bit packets shows that for 1, 4, and 16 links in operation per IMP, no lockup occurs; however, lockup occurs for 32 links. The net is obviously primed for lockup when a number of links per IMP in excess of the number of store-and-forward buffers are in use. For 1, 4, and 16 links per IMP and 50 kbit/s circuits, the total throughput was found to be 91.33, 145.68, and 44.43 kbits/s.

Since no analytical procedures appear to be available for use in the selection of a buffer allocation scheme, heuristics are used to improve the efficiency of a system operation. The following heuristics seem appropriate to a good system design.

1) Not all the IMP buffers should be allowed to reside on a single output queue. Each input and output line must always be able to get some nonzero share of the buffers. One technique is to dedicate at least one buffer to each output line. Double buffering of the input lines allows all incoming messages to be examined although not necessarily stored. This heuristic ensures that a direct store-and-forward lockup will not occur. Another technique, slightly more difficult to implement, is to dedicate at least one buffer for storing data to each input line. Indirect store-and-forward lockup may be prevented by an overflow network as described in Section II-C.

2) Enough buffers should be provided so that all lines may operate at full capacity. A communication circuit requires enough store-and-forward buffering to keep the line occupied during the round-trip propagation time and to handle occasional surges and line errors. As the propagation time and the communication bit rate increase, the required number of buffers increases. A short line undoubtedly needs at least double buffering. For simplicity of implementation a fixed or equal number of buffers may be allocated to each output line or a statistically sufficient pool of buffers may be provided.

3) Negative acknowledgments are useful in activating dormant buffers more quickly, but add complexity. Although not required for system operation, they are useful in achieving a more efficient buffer utilization and are useful in routing.

4) Fifty percent of all packets in the network are acknowledgments. It is possible to save both line capacity and program time by using an IMP/IMP serialized transmission strategy. A serial number (e.g., 8 bits) is attached by the IMP to each transmitted packet out a given line and the receiving IMP expects to receive packets on that line with numbers in sequence. Each arriving packet is acknowledged by the receiving IMP by returning its sequence number (to the transmitting IMP) at the front of a standard packet rather than as a separate acknowledgment packet. In the absence of regular traffic, empty messages are used to house acknowledgments. This technique produces a perpetual flow of packets back and forth between each pair of IMP's. Missing sequence numbers are negatively acknowledged as are packets that are correctly received by the receiving IMP but are discarded. Schemes using a single phase bit (coupled with a half-duplex circuit and/or the precise timing of a hardware rather than a software implementation) were described by Wozencraft and Horstein [11], Scantlebury [12], and Bartlett *et al.* [13].

Several acknowledgments can be delivered as a few bits at the beginning of a normal message, thus reducing the amount of acknowledgment traffic by a factor of 5 or 10 and increasing the overall capacity by upwards of 10 percent. Furthermore, this scheme assures that no duplicates will be generated, except when a circuit breaks.

This serialization scheme is similar to the crate scheme of [6] except that a fixed number of buffers per line are not provided at each end. With sufficient buffering available at each IMP, a crate scheme is possible but, in general, it makes less efficient use of IMP buffers. If no buffer space exists for a packet, it is discarded.

5) To ensure that several lines competing for a given output line are handled fairly and efficiently, a receiving

IMP can designate the kind of traffic it wishes to receive from its neighbors, (for example, by supplying and dynamically updating a list of acceptable destinations). This type of indication is similar in intent to RFNM's in a heavily loaded net, but it only passes between adjacent IMP's to allow efficient ordering of packets on the IMP queues. At the current time, however, little is known about the properties of IMP/IMP control messages that order the flow of traffic. Thus, this heuristic is viewed merely as an interesting idea.

C. Overflow

In this section, we describe the use of two overflow buffers per IMP in thwarting indirect store-and-forward lockup. Whenever traffic appears to have stalled in the regular net, the IMP will occasionally mark a packet (henceforth known as overflow packet) for delivery via special buffers that comprise an overflow net. An overflow packet is handled by the IMP in such a way as to guarantee that, at any time, at least one such packet will reach its destination. Packets are delivered according to a randomized priority.

One buffer is provided in each IMP to store an overflow packet for eventual transmission. A second buffer is used in each IMP to hold an overflow packet that is being transmitted, if any, and is thus unavailable for use by the algorithm. The provision of two buffers, rather than only one, ensures that an IMP will never reject an arriving overflow packet with a higher priority than the one currently stored. Indeed, in half the cases when both buffers are occupied, the arriving overflow packet will replace the stored copy that will simply be discarded.

When an IMP has received no acknowledgments for its packets in several seconds, it periodically selects one packet (e.g., every 125 ms) and marks it for delivery via the overflow net. Let us call this IMP an overflow source IMP. The overflow packet will pass from IMP to IMP using only the overflow buffers until it reaches the destination. The destination IMP will return an overflow acknowledgment to the overflow source IMP, if the packet is accepted by the destination IMP. Otherwise, the packet will simply be discarded by the destination IMP and no overflow acknowledgment will be returned. At some later time, the packet will again be transmitted via the overflow net, unless it has already begun to move through the net in the normal fashion.

To minimize storage, the overflow ACK also uses the IMP overflow buffers in returning to the overflow source IMP. The overflow source IMP will discard the designated packet when the overflow ACK returns. If the packet is no longer in that IMP, the overflow ACK is simply discarded and the packet will eventually arrive at the destination as a duplicate packet and be discarded.

A packet is stamped with a unique random number by the IMP when it first delivers it into the overflow net. When an overflow packet is received at an IMP that already has both its overflow buffers filled, the arriving overflow packet will vie for the overflow buffer with its current occupant and one with the lowest number will emerge victorious. The other packet will be simply discarded. Furthermore, a returning overflow ACK will always emerge victorious over an overflow packet if they compete for the same overflow buffer. Packets from the host can also be inserted into the overflow net since the host line can also be hung for a lack of buffer space.

The overflow network will always deliver the packet that has highest priority, barring phone-line errors, and will also deliver any other overflow packets which do not encounter a higher priority packet. In this way, a small fraction of the circuit capacity and buffer space is thus devoted to guaranteeing that a small fraction of the host traffic will always be able to reach its destination.

The discussion of overflow has been included here primarily for completeness. It is expected that indirect store-and-forward lockup will not occur very often, indeed if at all, in the actual operation of the net. In the rare instance that it does occur, however, recovery can occur within a short time (e.g., a minute) with a reset. The overflow net merely provides a more sophisticated solution to this lockup problem without the loss of messages if such a recourse is eventually required.

Acknowledgment

The network simulation was performed with a program that models the IMP program in detail. The network simulation runs slightly slower than real time on a Honeywell DDP-516 computer. The simulation program was constructed by W. Crowther and B. Cosell and the experiments were run by R. Satterfield.

We would like to acknowledge the participation of B. Cosell of Bolt Beranek and Newman and Dr. R. Sittler of ARCON Corporation in many helpful discussions about flow control.

References

[1] L. G. Roberts and B. Wessler, "Computer network development to achieve resource sharing," in *1970 Spring Joint Computer Conf., AFIPS Conf. Proc.*, vol. 36. Montvale, N. J.: AFIPS Press, 1970, pp. 543–549.

[2] F. Heart *et al.*, "The interface message processor for the ARPA computer network," in *1970 Spring Joint Computer Conf., AFIPS Conf. Proc.*, vol. 36. Montvale, N. J.: AFIPS Press, 1970, pp. 551–567.

[3] "Specifications for the interconnection of a host and an IMP," Bolt Beranek and Newman Inc., Cambridge, Mass. BBN Rep. 1822, Feb. 1971; also available from Network Information Ctr., Stanford Res. Inst., Menlo Park, Calif., NIC 5735.

[4] S. Crocker, "Host-to-host protocol," Doc. 1. Unpublished memo., 1970. (A more comprehensive description and version of this protocol is also available in "Host/host protocol for the ARPA network," Network Information Ctr., Stanford Res. Inst., Menlo Park, Calif., NIC 7147.)

[5] J. C. R. Licklider, private communication, 1970.

[6] R. Kalin, "A simplified NCP protocol," unpublished memo., available from Network Information Ctr., Stanford Res. Inst., Menlo Park, Calif., NIC 4762, 1970.

[7] D. Walden, "A system for interprocess communication in a resource sharing computer network," unpublished memo.,

available from Network Information Ctr., Stanford Res. Inst., Menlo Park, Calif., NIC 4692, 1970.

[8] D. W. Davies, "The control of congestion in packet switching networks," presented at the 2nd ACM Symp. Problems in the Optimization of Data Communications Systems, Palo Alto, Calif., 1971; also this issue, pp. 546–550.

[9] A. N. Haberman, "Prevention of system deadlocks," *Commun. Ass. Comput. Mach.*, July 1969, pp. 373–378.

[10] E. Dijkstra, "Cooperating sequential processes," Math. Dep., Technol. Univ., Eindhoven, the Netherlands, 1965, EWD123; also in F. Genuys, Ed., *Programming Languages*. New York: Academic Press, 1968.

[11] J. Wozencraft and M. Horstein, "Coding for two-way channels," in *Proc. 4th London Symp. Information Theory*, C. Cherry, Ed. Washington, D. C.: Butterworth, 1961, pp. 11–23.

[12] R. A. Scantlebury, "A model for the local area of a data communication network—Objectives and hardware organization," *ACM Symp. Problems in the Optimization of Data Communication Systems*, 1969, pp. 179–201.

[13] K. Bartlett, R. Scantlebury, and P. Wilkinson, "A note on reliable full-duplex transmission over half-duplex links," *Commun. Ass. Comput. Mach.*, May 1969, pp. 260–261.

Robert E. Kahn (M'65) was born in Brooklyn, N. Y., on December 23, 1938. He received the B.E.E. degree from the City College of New York, New York, in 1960 and the M.A. and Ph.D. degrees from Princeton University, Princeton, N. J., in 1962 and 1964, respectively.

During 1960–1962, he was a Member of the Technical Staff of the Bell Telephone Laboratories, Murray Hill, N. J., engaged in traffic and communication studies. From 1964 to 1966 he was a Ford Postdoctoral Fellow and an Assistant Professor of Electrical Engineering at the Massachusetts Institute of Technology, Cambridge, where he worked on communications and information theory. Since 1966, he has been a Senior Scientist at Bolt Beranek and Newman, Inc., Cambridge, Mass., where he has worked on computer communications network design and techniques for distributed computation.

Dr. Kahn is a member of Tau Beta Pi, Sigma Xi, Eta Kappa Nu, the Institute of Mathematical Statistics, and the Mathematical Association of America. He was selected to serve as a Lecturer for the Association for Computing Machinery in 1972.

William R. Crowther was born in Schenectady, N. Y., on June 29, 1936. He received the B.S. degree in physics from the Massachusetts Institute of Technology, Cambridge, in 1958.

From 1958 to 1968, he was a Staff member at the M.I.T. Lincoln Laboratory where he worked on real-time programming of small computers. In particular, he had the full responsibility for the design and implementation of the computer program for the Univac 1218 for the Lincoln Experimental Terminal (LET). He also designed and implemented a scheme for automatic speech recognition and speech compression logic. Since 1968, he has been a Computer Scientist at Bolt Beranek and Newman Inc., Cambridge, Mass., where he has had responsibility for IMP software development and has been involved in the design of other real-time computer systems.

Reprinted by permission from *IEEE Transactions on Communications*
Vol. COM-20, No. 3, June 1972, pp. 539-46

INFORMATION PROCESSING 74 – NORTH-HOLLAND PUBLISHING COMPANY (1974)

SIMULATION STUDIES OF AN ISARITHMICALLY CONTROLLED STORE AND FORWARD DATA COMMUNICATION NETWORK

Wyn L. PRICE

National Physical Laboratory, Teddington, Middlesex, UK

The principle of isarithmic flow control of data traffic in store and forward networks is described in outline. A series of simulation experiments has been carried out which indicate that isarithmic flow control is able to reduce network end-to-end transmission times substantially. However, it is shown that this gain is in certain cases at the expense of additional time spent in waiting for admission to the network. The value of the isarithmic system lies in its ability to keep the network running satisfactorily at a time when a potential overload of traffic is offered to it for transmission.

1. INTRODUCTION

The program of work at NPL on data communication networks has included simulation in the theoretical study of the behaviour of "transit" or "high-level" packet-switched networks (as distinct from "local" or "low-level" networks). Various topologies and node and link protocols have been postulated and then tested with artificially generated traffic [1-4].

In some of the early work it was noted that the network as then simulated performed best, in terms of maximum throughput and minimum delay, if the number of data packets in transit at any time was relatively small, of the order of three packets per network node. From this observation there developed the concept of "isarithmic" (meaning constant number) flow control [5], which was designed deliberately to restrict admission of new traffic to the high-level network in such a way that an absolute limit was placed on the number of data packets in transit at any time.

The mechanism of achieving this form of control passed through several stages of development until the idea of "permits" was conceived. Under this concept the network is initially provided with a number of permits, several held in store at each node; as traffic is offered by a local network to its high-level node, each packet must secure a permit before admission to the high-level node is allowed. Each accepted packet causes a reduction of one in the store of permits available at the accepting node. The accepted data packet is able to traverse the network, under the control of node and link protocols, until its destination high-level node is reached. When the packet is handed over to the destination low-level network for delivery to the destination subscriber, the permit which has accompanied it during its journey becomes free and an attempt is made to add it to the permit store of the high-level node in which it now finds itself.

In order to achieve a viable system in which permits do not accumulate in certain parts of the network at the expense of other parts, it is necessary to place a limit on the number of permits that may be held in store by each high-level node. If then, because of this limit, a newly freed permit can not be accommodated at a node, it must be sent elsewhere. The normal method of carrying the permit in these circumstances is to "piggy-back" it in other traffic, be this data or control. Only in the absence of other traffic need a special permit-carrying packet be generated.

The network model first investigated at NPL [1] was rather unsophisticated and was prone to fail due to congestion when an excess of traffic was offered to it. Various refinements improved its performance until it was able to withstand an offered overload and still carry traffic moderately efficiently. However, even without these refinements, the addition of isarithmic control was able to achieve at least as great an improvement. It was felt that isarithmic control, being a very simple concept, easily added to an existing network, was a valuable means of introducing a measure of flow control into a network where this feature was deficient.

A program of work to investigate more fully the properties of isarithmic flow control was then undertaken, using a more sophisticated node and link protocol for the network simulated. This later work forms the subject of the present paper.

2. THE SIMULATION MODEL

The hypothetical network simulated consisted of ten nodes joined by thirteen links arranged as an unsymmetrical ladder (fig. 1). The link lengths

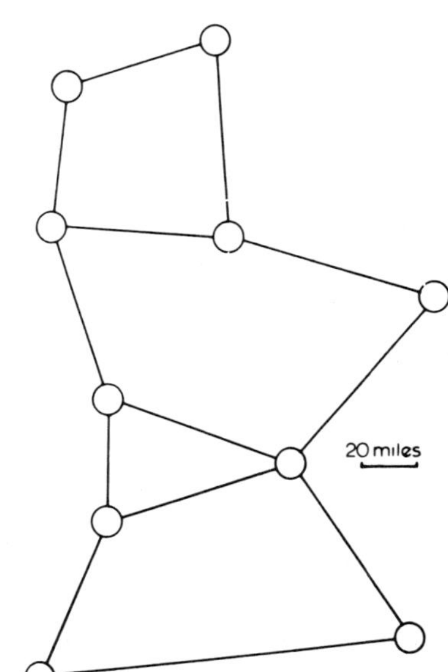

Fig. 1 The network simulated

ranged from 45 to 135 miles, but all links were deemed to have the same bandwidth of 1.5 Mbits/sec, full duplex. In determining the pattern of traffic offered to the high-level by the low-level networks a relative incoming traffic level was set for each node; the time intervals between successive packets offered at each node were assumed to be distributed according to a negative exponential function. An overall traffic level parameter determined the mean interval between packets offered for acceptance at the node receiving most traffic. By varying this overall parameter the general level of traffic was variable, whilst maintaining a constant proportionality of traffic being offered at the various nodes.

The node and link protocol includes acknowledgement of each separate data packet and the retransmission of any data packets not acknowledged after a predetermined time interval. Input and output processes are specified for each link at a node. The node central processor gives attention to these processes on demand and a queue of calls for the central processor is established to handle this requirement. A set of Dijkstra semaphores is used to indicate the state (busy or free) of the node resources, notably storage buffers and peripheral devices.

Flow control of traffic from the local network to its node is determined by the state of the input buffer. A single input buffer, accommodating one packet, is provided for each incoming link at a node, including that from the local network. The latter link is subject to the special control provision that no further packet may be accepted by it whilst the input buffer is occupied. The input buffer is emptied when its contents can be transferred, as an action of the input process, to the appropriate
276 output queue. Traffic that cannot be accepted by the input buffer as soon as it is offered by the local network is deemed to have to wait on an admission queue; in practice this queue may be the responsibility of the subscriber or of the low-level network or of the high-level node (in some backing store). It is perhaps best left to the subscriber, because it is not possible to predict what storage capacity should be allocated for this purpose either in the low-level network or in the node.

A fixed routing doctrine was used in all the simulation experiments described in the present paper. Two sets of routing matrices were used in different experiments, the one giving shortest path routes (routing matrix 1) and the other (routing matrix 2), derived from the first, a more even distribution of traffic.

The node-to-node protocol is described in fuller detail in [2].

3. THE SIMULATION EXPERIMENTS

3.1 The Non-isarithmic System

The network operating according to the protocol which has just been outlined was first modelled without isarithmic control in order to verify its functioning.

One of the first observations made was that there was serious conflict between originating traffic and through traffic at the nodes. As originally specified in the node-to-node protocol, any packet arriving from a distant node that could not be accommodated in a buffer attached to the required output queue to await onward transmission was not acknowledged and would eventually be retransmitted by the distant node following the expiry of a timeout. A packet from the local network for which there was no room on an output queue would simply wait in the input buffer until room became available and was not subject to the retransmission delay before resubmission (a short fixed time interval was inserted between successive submissions). The effect of this arrangement was that local originating traffic had an "unfair advantage" and the network rapidly became congested with packets and soon collapsed, with traffic at a standstill. A solution to this problem was found by reserving one or two storage buffers on each output queue for through traffic. This point is discussed at greater length in [2].

Having made this adjustment to the protocol it was found that the high-level network was able to continue satisfactory operation even when the overall traffic level offered from the local networks was raised to over 50% more than the load the network could actually carry. Measurements were made at various offered loads of the average network throughput rate, the average end-to-end delay encountered by delivered traffic and the average time spent by packet waiting for admission at the entrances to the high-level network.

The results of these experiments expressed as averages are summarised in fig. 2. Here we see the

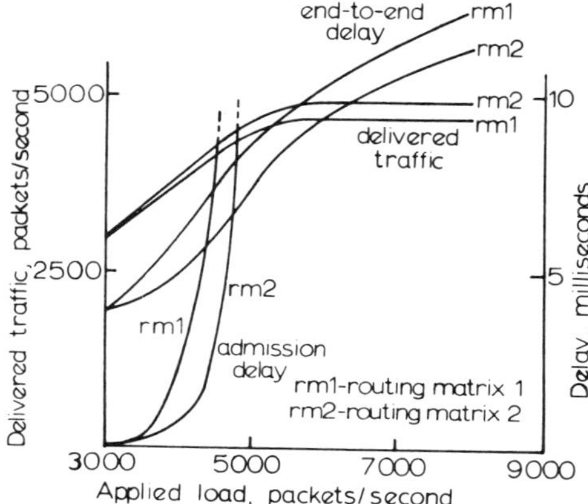

Fig. 2 Performance of non-isarithmic network

effect of the flow control on the network being modelled. Delivered traffic is seen to increase linearly with increasing applied load until the latter reaches about 5 000 packets/sec (about 3.1 Mbits/sec); thereafter, with a further increase of applied load, the delivered traffic reaches a maximum and the network reaches saturation level, whilst still continuing to deliver traffic satisfactorily.

The end-to-end delay increases from the low-load value with increasing load; the rate of increase falls as the throughput rate reaches saturation, but the delay shows no sign of reaching a maximum up to the highest level of applied load.

Admission delay starts at very low values, but as might be expected, increases dramatically with increasing applied load, as the delivered traffic nears its maximum. As the saturation point is reached, so the admission queues begin to increase in length indefinitely with increasing time and the average admission delay must soon tend towards infinity. This effect is first observed at the nodes to which the heaviest applied loads are directed.

The network thus simulated is well-behaved in that it does not collapse through congestion even in the face of an applied overload. This feature is valuable since, if the overload is temporary, the network may be able later to clear its admission queues and again reduce the admission delay to an acceptable level.

A comparison of the effect of changing the routing matrix on the behaviour of the network may be seen in fig. 2. The routing matrix with more evenly distributed traffic can be seen, as might be expected, to behave better on all counts than the shortest path matrix.

Having established the validity of the non-isarithmic model, experiments were next undertaken to determine whether the addition of isarithmic flow control would produce any further improvement in the network behaviour.

3.2 The Isarithmic System

Perhaps the most important parameter in the setting up of an isarithmic control system is the number of permits provided in the network; this number places an absolute maximum on the number of packets that may be in transit at one time. Another parameter is the number of permits that may be allowed to wait at each node for incoming traffic from the interface (maximum length of permit queue).

To investigate the first of these parameters a series of experiments was carried out in which a single level of load (6 200 packets/sec.) was offered to the network (more than the network could actually carry), and a range of permit provision was made extending from one per node to ten per node. For this set of experiments the maximum length of permit queue was made equal to the number of permits provided per node. The results are summarised in fig. 3. Here we see that for one permit provided

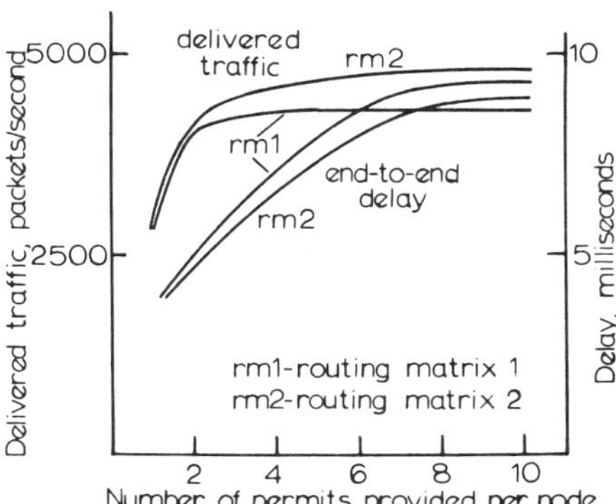

Fig. 3 Network performance vs number of permits (through traffic has priority; applied load 6 200 packets/sec.)

per node (and the more efficient routing matrix) the rate of delivered traffic was as low as 3 000 packets/sec.; two permits per node gave about 4 000 packets/sec. delivered and three permits about 4 400 packets/sec. The rate of delivered traffic then increased slowly as the permit content was increased. End-to-end delay, on the other hand, appears to have been much more dependent on permit content, increasing from a value of about 3.5 milliseconds more or less linearly between permit contents of one and six per node, and then tapering off towards a maximum in the region of 9 milliseconds with ten permits per node.

It is suggested that as the number of permits is increased towards ten per node, the degree of isarithmic flow control becomes less and the network relies more on its other means of flow control, touched on in sections 2 and 3.1. The region in which the throughput is fairly constant, whilst the delay increases more or less linearly with increasing number of permits, illustrates Little's result as quoted by Kleinrock [6]. This result states that the product of the throughput and the average end-to-end delay for a network of queues is equal to the number of packets in transit at the same time.

The present result contrasts interestingly with the result [1] of applying isarithmic control to an earlier network with a less efficient in-built flow control system. In the earlier case the traffic flow reached a maximum for three permits provided per node and then decreased to zero as the number of permits was increased to six per node. In such a case it is obviously very important to choose very carefully the number of permits provided. Where the basic flow control is already fairly effective, as in the present series of experiments, the exact choice of permit content is less important.

Before undertaking the main range of isarithmic experiments a short series of tests was made to investigate at fairly light loads the effect of changing the maximum length of the permit queue. In particular the effect on admission delay was studied and it was again shown (as in the earlier work [1,4]) that the variation of admission delay with maximum length of permit queue had the U-shaped characteristic illustrated in fig. 4. In this case

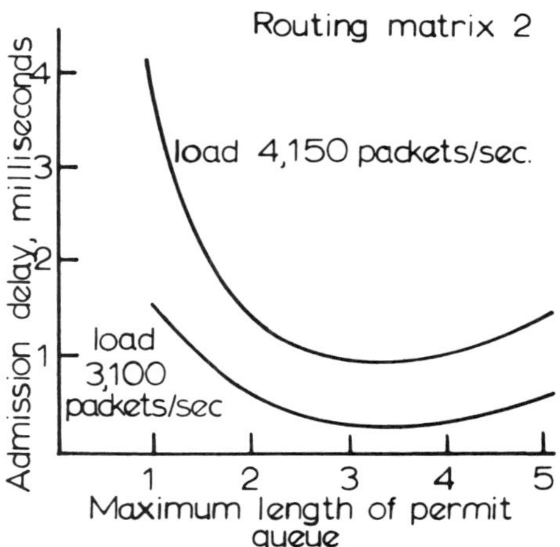

Fig. 4 Admission delay vs length of permit queue (5 permits provided per node)

five permits were provided per node and a fairly definite minimum admission delay was seen for a maximum length of permit queue of about three. This result seems logically correct, since, if the permit queue is made too short, then permits are not readily available for new traffic and spend much of their time wandering round the network "looking" for traffic; if the permit queue is allowed to be too long, then permits will congregate in certain nodes to the disadvantage of others and some nodes may be starved of permits.

The U-shaped characteristic is only observable at light applied loads, there being a great deal of scatter in the admission delays for different traffic sequences at greater applied loads.

Since, in the present work, especially at higher loads, fractions of milliseconds are not really significant when comparing delays, any value of maximum permit queue length between two and five would seem to be acceptable. Therefore for the main isarithmic experiments, with five permits per node provided in the network, the maximum length of permit queue was set at five.

Having now chosen the values of these parameters, a series of experiments was carried out with applied loads ranging from about 3 000 packets/sec. to just over 7 500 packets/sec. The results obtained are summarised in fig. 5 and are broadly similar to

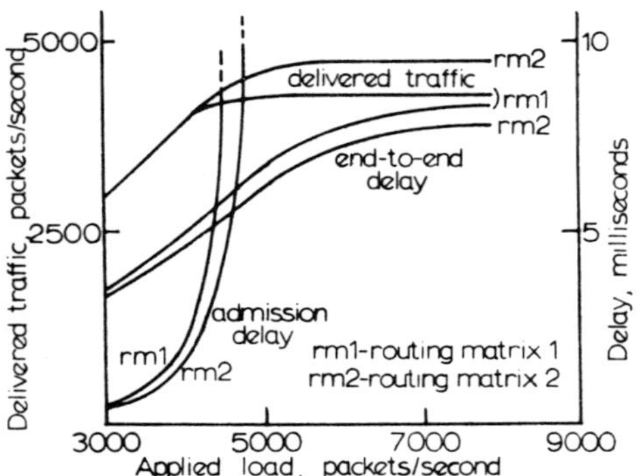

Fig. 5 Performance of isarithmic network (5 permits provided per node)

those for the non-isarithmic network which were illustrated in fig. 2. However, there are a number of significant differences.

Below the throughput cut-off point the isarithmic network has a marginally higher throughput than the non-isarithmic, but the cut-off point is reached at an applied load of about 4 500 packets/sec. instead of 5 000 packets/sec. and the delivered traffic saturation level is about 5% less in the isarithmic case. The end-to-end delay is for all loads greater in the non-isarithmic case, ranging from slightly greater at low applied loads to nearly twice as great for the greatest applied loads. In the isarithmic case a maximum end-to-end delay in the region of 8 milliseconds appears to be attained at the highest load.

On the other hand, when we consider the admission delay, we see that in the isarithmic case it commences at a slightly higher value (albeit low in absolute terms) than at the same load in the non-isarithmic case. As the load is increased, so the admission delay increases, becoming unstable at the throughput cut-off point. At all loads below the cut-off point the admission delay is somewhat greater in the isarithmic case than in the non-isarithmic. This is contrary to the behaviour of the end-to-end delay.

Now, in considering the performance of any network, be it isarithmic or no, if the flow control is such that traffic is made to wait for admission to the network, then the time spent in awaiting admission should be added to the end-to-end delay. If this is done in the present case, then it will be seen that there is very little difference in overall delay between the network operating with and without isarithmic flow control. On this criterion, therefore, there is no benefit to be gained by adding isarithmic control to a network whose flow control is already fairly efficient. Neither is there, below the throughput cut-off point, a sufficient difference in the traffic delivered to justify the addition of isarithmic control.

Above the throughput cut-off point the isarithmic network carries marginally less traffic than the non-isarithmic, but takes significantly less time to transport traffic across the network. Thus, if short term overloads are likely to occur, the isarithmic network may be considered to be rather more satisfactory during the period of the overload. This effect is believed to be due to the stronger flow control afforded by the isarithmic system. In the non-isarithmic case traffic will continue to be admitted at the lightly-loaded nodes even when the heavily-loaded nodes are refusing new traffic; this will happen to a much lesser extent in the isarithmic case because of the upper limit placed on the total amount of traffic allowed in the network at any time.

4. DISCUSSION AND CONCLUSIONS

The isarithmic studies at NPL have covered the effect of this novel control system on networks having both weak (the early NPL model) and strong flow control. It has been shown that considerable benefit accrues from the imposition of the isarithmic principle on a network having weak flow control. On the other hand, where the flow control is already fairly strong, the addition of isarithmic control has little effect on overall delay and throughput.

Its chief virtue lies in its simplicity and the salutary effect that it has in improving the performance of a weakly controlled network without the introduction of sophisticated control methods. However, isarithmic control has also been shown to improve the end-to-end delay performance of a strongly controlled network when a traffic overload is offered to it.

It is recognised that certain safeguards must be introduced into a practical isarithmic system. These must guard against faulty operation leading to a node acting as a permit sink, to permits being lost from the network by some other means, or to additional permits being created by some malfunction.

Future work on network simulation is planned to include the effects of sudden changes of applied load at individual nodes and the design of protocols to cope with link or node failure.

REFERENCES

[1] W.L. Price, Survey of NPL simulation studies of data networks, 1968-72. NPL Report COM 60, November 1972.

[2] W.L. Price, Simulation of a packet-switched data network operating with a revised link and node protocol. NPL Report COM 68, April 1973.

[3] W.L. Price, Simulation of a packet-switched data network operating under isarithmic control with a revised link and node protocol. NPL Report COM 71, September 1973.

[4] W.L. Price, Simulation of packet-switching networks controlled on isarithmic principles. Proceedings of 3rd ACM/IEEE Data Communications Symposium, St Petersburg, Florida, November 1973, 44-49.

[5] D.W. Davies, The control of congestion in packet-switching networks. Transactions of the IEEE, vol. COM-20, no. 3, June 1972, 546-550.

[6] L. Kleinrock, Queuing Systems: Theory and Applications, Wiley Interscience, New York, 1974.

Reprinted by permission of J.L. Rosenfeld (ed.), *Information Processing 74* (North-Holland, Amsterdam, 1975)

Optimal Message Block Size for Computer Communications with Error Detection and Retransmission Strategies

WESLEY W. CHU, SENIOR MEMBER, IEEE

***Abstract*—Error detection and retransmission are used as error control in many computer communication systems. In these systems, random length messages are partitioned into fixed size blocks for ease in data handling and memory management. A mathematical model is developed in this paper to determine the optimal message block size that minimizes the expected waiting time in retransmission and acknowledgment delay and thus maximizes channel efficiency. The model considers two classes of error detection and retransmission strategies: 1) stop-and-wait and 2) continuous transmissions. Using the relationships among acknowledgment time, channel transmission rate, channel error characteristics (random error or burst error), average message length, optimal block size are computed from the model and presented in graphs. The model and the graphs should be useful as a guide in the selection of the optimal fixed message block size for computer communication systems.**

I. INTRODUCTION

TO INCREASE utilization of computer capability and to share computer resources, remotely located computers and/or terminals may be connected with communication links. Such integrated computer communication systems allow many users to economically share data bases and computer software systems. These shared computing facilities can greatly increase our computing capacity. In the design and planning of such systems, communication problems between computers and terminals greatly influence system performance (e.g., inquiry-response delay) and overall system costs. Hence, computer communications become an integral part of the overall system design consideration. In this paper we address the problem of determining the optimal message block size to improve efficiency in data communication systems. Kucera [2], Balkovic and Muench [3], and Kirlin [4] have studied the optimal message block size for the error detection and retransmission system that maximizes transmission efficiency. In this paper, we consider an additional important parameter—the average message (file) length—in determining the optimal message block size, which significantly affects the selection of the optimal message block size.

For economic and reliability reasons [5], [6], the error detection and retransmission scheme is used by many data communication systems. Using this error control technique, encoding circuits are required to operate on the message information to generate redundant data. There are two classes of error detection and retransmission strategies: 1) stop-and-wait and 2) continuous transmission. In the stop-and-wait strategy, the receiver checks the received message (together with the check bits) and generates acknowledgment signal for the sender to indicate whether the message is correctly received. If the message is correctly received, (positive acknowledgment), then the sender is permitted to send a new message. If the message is incorrectly received (negative acknowledgment), then the sender retransmits the same message, until a positive acknowledgment of that message is received by the sender.

In the stop-and-wait strategy, for each transmission of a block of message, the transmitter is idling and waiting for the acknowledgment signal from the receiver. In order to reduce this idling period, continuous transmission strategies can be used. There are two types of continuous error detection and retransmission systems: 1) transmit message blocks continuously without waiting for its acknowledgment and retransmit each unconfirmed message block[1] and 2) transmit message blocks continuously without waiting for its acknowledgment and retransmit each unconfirmed message block[1] together with the message blocks which follow it. In both these strategies, a message block is transmitted and stored at the transmitter while subsequent message blocks are being transmitted. In the meantime, the receiver examines the incoming message blocks and appropriate acknowlegment signals are sent to the transmitter. When an erroneous message block is received, the transmitter either repeats the error message block or repeats the error message block and the message blocks that follow that error message block. For the first type of continuous transmission system, message blocks at the receiver will be out of sequence order. Additional hardware is required at the receiver to restore the proper order.

The message outputs from a computer are usually in strings of characters or bursts. The message length may be different from one to another and can best be described by a probability distribution. For case in data handling and memory management, the random message length is usually partitioned into several fixed size blocks. Due to the random length of the message, the last partitioned block usually cannot be entirely filled by the message and

[1] In some systems, when a message block is incorrectly received, no acknowledgment is sent and that message block is discarded. The sender used a time-out mechanism to detect the unconfirmed message block.

Paper approved by the Associate Editor for Computer Communications of the IEEE Communications Society for publication after presentation at the 1971 International Federation of Information Processing Societies Congress, Ljubljana, Yugoslavia. Manuscript received November 5, 1973; revised January 19, 1974. This research was supported in part by the U. S. Office of Naval Research, Research Program Office under Contract No. N0014-69-A-4027 and NR 048-129 and in part by the National Science Foundation under Grant No. GJ33007X.

The author is with the Department of Computer Science, University of California, Los Angeles, Calif.

is either terminated by an end-of-message character or is filled with dummy information. From the acknowledgment point of view, it is desirable to select the largest possible block size. On the other hand, since the larger message block has a higher probability of error and also has a higher channel wastage due to the last unfilled partitioned block (for the case of not using the end-of-message character), it is desirable to select the smallest possible block size. Thus there is a tradeoff in selecting the optimal block size. The basic problem is: suppose the average message length, the message length distribution, the channel error characteristics, block overhead, and the acknowledgment overhead are known. What is the optimal message block size for a given transmission strategy that minimizes the time wasted in acknowledgments, retransmissions, and block overhead?

A mathematical model is developed in this paper to treat this problem. The model considers two types of transmission strategies: 1) stop-and-wait and 2) continuous transmission. Further, the model treats two types of error channels: 1) random error channel; that is, the errors are generated in a statistically independent fashion and the error rate can be approximated as a linear function of the block size, and 2) burst error channel; that is, the errors are generated in a statistically dependent fashion such as the noise produced by radio static or switching transients, and the error rate is a nonlinear function of the block size. In general, error characteristics can be obtained only from actual measurements [7]. For a given average channel error rate, the performance of the burst error channels is, in general, better than that of the random error channel [8]. Using our mathematical model, the relationships among message length (assuming the messages are geometrically distributed), transmission rate, acknowledgment overhead, block overhead, and optimal block size are obtained and portrayed in graphs.

II. ANALYSIS

The message length, l, is a random variable and can be described by a probability distribution $P_L(l)$ with average length $\bar{l}$ bits per message. When the message is partitioned into a fixed size block of B bits per block, the expected number of blocks per message is equal to

$$\bar{N}(B) = \sum_{n=1}^{\infty} n \cdot P_L\{(n-1)B < l \leq nB\}, \qquad l = 1,2,\cdots. \tag{1}$$

The structure of a fixed message block consists of an address b_1 in the front of the message block and a checking code b_2 after the message block as shown in Fig. 1. The overhead of such a block is then equal to $b = b_1 + b_2$ bits. Thus for a message block size of B bits, the whole block length is equal to $B + b$ bits. Let $E(B + b)$ be the probability that a block of $B + b$ bits (a message block of B bits with a block overhead of b bits) transmitted over a channel will have at least one detected error. We know that $E(B + b)$ is dependent on both the error characteristics of the channel and the whole block size $B + b$. Clearly, a large value of $B + b$ and/or a noisier transmission channel yields a higher value of $E(B + b)$. We shall now consider the following two error detection and retransmission strategies.

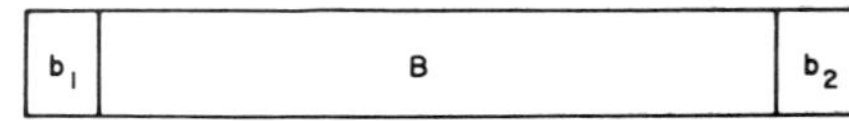

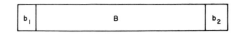

B = FIXED SIZE MESSAGE BLOCK

b_1 = ADDRESS

b_2 = CHECK BITS

$b = b_1 + b_2$ = BLOCK OVERHEAD

Fig. 1. Data structure of a fixed size message block.

A. *Stop-and-Wait Transmission Strategies*

We shall first consider the stop-and-wait transmission strategy for the case that the last unfilled message block is filled with dummy information. When error detection and retransmission are used for error control, there is a certain amount of acknowledgment delay, A, associated with each message block. In half duplex transmission mode, the acknowledgment delay should also include the modem turn-around times if modems are used in the channel. Thus the expected acknowledgment overhead for a message block transmitted over a channel is equal to the first acknowledgment time plus the expected retransmission time and reacknowledgment time. Assuming that the probability of error of each message block during transmission is independent of transmission or retransmission, then mathematically the expected acknowledgment overhead for a message block of size B (or whole block size $B + b$) on a channel with a transmission rate R bits/s is

$$\bar{A}(B+b) = A + \sum_{i=1}^{\infty} [E(B+b)]^i \cdot \left(A + \frac{B+b}{R}\right). \tag{2}$$

The expected wasted time due to acknowledgment and retransmission in transmitting a message in fixed sized blocks, $\bar{W}_1(B)$, is equal to the expected number of blocks (of size $B + b$) per message multiplied by the expected acknowledgment overhead of each block. Thus,

$$\bar{W}_1(B) = \bar{N}(B) \cdot \bar{A}(B+b)$$
$$= \bar{N}(B) \cdot \left\{A + \sum_{i=1}^{\infty} [E(B+b)]^i \cdot \left(A + \frac{B+b}{R}\right)\right\}. \tag{3}$$

Since $0 \leq E(B + b) \leq 1$, $B > 0$, and $b > 0$,

$$\sum_{i=1}^{\infty} [E(B+b)]^i = \frac{E(B+b)}{1 - E(B+b)}. \tag{4}$$

Substituting (4) into (3) yields

$$\bar{W}_1(B) = \bar{N}(B) \cdot \left\{A + \frac{E(B+b)}{1-E(B+b)} \cdot \left(A + \frac{B+b}{R}\right)\right\}. \tag{5}$$

The expected wasted time due to block overhead and the last unfilled partitioned block in transmitting a message in fixed sized blocks $W_2(B)$ is equal to the difference between the time to transmit the blocked message and the unblocked message.

Thus,

$$\bar{W}_2(B) = \bar{N}(B)\cdot\frac{B+b}{R} - \frac{\bar{l}+b'}{R} \tag{6}$$

where b' is the overhead for the unblocked message.

The total expected wasted time to transmit a message in blocks, $\bar{W}(B)$, is equal to the sum of (5) and (6). Thus

$$\bar{W}(B) = \bar{N}(B)\cdot\left\{A + \frac{E(B+b)}{1-E(B+b)}\cdot\left(A+\frac{B+b}{R}\right) + \frac{B+b}{R}\right\} - \frac{\bar{l}+b'}{R}. \tag{7}$$

We wish to find the optimal block size B^0 that minimizes (7).

Let us assume that the message length is geometrically distributed[2]; that is, $P_L(l) = pq^{l-1}$, $l = 1,2,3,\cdots$, with average message length $\bar{l} = p^{-1}$ and where $p + q = 1$. The average number of blocks per message in this case can be computed from (1) and is equal to

$$\begin{aligned}\bar{N}(B) &= \sum_{n=1}^{\infty} n\cdot \sum_{l=(n-1)B+1}^{nB} pq^{l-1}\\ &= \sum_{n=1}^{\infty} n\cdot(1-q^B)(q^B)^{n-1}\\ &= (1-q^B)^{-1}.\end{aligned} \tag{8}$$

Substituting (8) into (7), we have

$$\bar{W}(B) \Rightarrow (1-q^B)^{-1}\left[A + \frac{E(B+b)}{1-E(B+b)}\cdot\left(A+\frac{B+b}{R}\right) + \frac{B+b}{R}\right] - \frac{1}{pR} - \frac{b'}{R}. \tag{9}$$

To minimize $\bar{W}(B)$, we pretend B is a continuous variable and set

$$\frac{\partial \bar{W}(B)}{\partial B} = 0,$$

or

$$(q^{-B}-1)\left[\frac{1}{AR} + \left(1+\frac{B+b}{AR}\right)\frac{E'(B+b)}{1-E(B+b)}\right] + \left[1+\frac{B+b}{AR}\right]\ln q = 0. \tag{10}$$

where $E'(B+b)$ is the first derivative of $E(B+b)$.

Let us study the behavior of (10) and denote

$$X(B) = (q^{-B}-1)\left[\frac{1}{AR} + \left(1+\frac{B+b}{AR}\right)\frac{E'(B+b)}{1-E(B+b)}\right]$$

and

$$Y(B) = -\left[1+\frac{B+b}{AR}\right]\cdot\ln q.$$

Thus,

$$X(B) - Y(B) = 0. \tag{11}$$

First let us evaluate $X(B)$ and $Y(B)$ at $B = 0$,

$$X(B)\,|_{B=0} = 0$$

$$Y(B)\,|_{B=0} = \left[1+\frac{b}{AR}\right]|\ln q|, \qquad 0 \le q \le 1. \tag{12}$$

From (12), we know $Y(0) \ge X(0)$. Further, if the slope of $X(B)$ is greater than the slope of $Y(B)$ for all $B \ge 0$, then $X(B)$ intersects $Y(B)$ at some B, $0 < B < \infty$, as shown in Fig. 2. This implies that $\bar{W}(B)$ exists as a single minimum for some B. Hence, the optimal block size B^0 located by the numerical technique attains a global optimum.

Next, differentiating $X(B)$ and $Y(B)$ with respect to B, we have

$$\begin{aligned}\frac{dX(B)}{dB} = (q^{-B}-1)&\left\{\frac{1}{AR}\cdot\frac{E'(B+b)}{1-E(B+b)} + \left(1+\frac{B+b}{AB}\right)\cdot\frac{[1-E(B+b)]E''(B+b)+[E'(B+b)]^2}{[1-E(B+b)]^2}\right\}\\ &+ \frac{1}{AR}\left[1+(AR+B+b)\frac{E'(B+b)}{1-E(B+b)}\right]\cdot q^{-B}\cdot|\ln q|\end{aligned} \tag{13}$$

$$\frac{dY(B)}{dB} = \frac{1}{AR}\cdot|\ln q|, \tag{14}$$

where $E''(B+b)$ is the second derivative of $E(B+b)$.

Since the error probability increases as B increases, $E'(B+b) \ge 0$. Also, since $0 < E(B+b) \le 1$, the second term of (13) is greater than $dY(B)/dB$. Further, if $E''(B+b) \ge -[E'(B+b)]^2$, then the first term of (13) is positive. Thus $dX(B)/dB \ge dY(B)/dB$ for all $B \ge 0$. Therefore, $E''(B+b) \ge -[E'(B+b)]^2$ is a *sufficient* condition to assure the convexity of $\bar{W}(B)$. The physical meaning of $E''(B+b) \ge 0$ $(> -[E'(B+b)]^2)$ implies that $E(B+b)$ is a convex function of $B+b$. Comparing (13) and (14), we know that even if $E''(B+b) < -[E'(B+b)]^2$ for some B, $[dX(B)/dB] \ge [dY(B)/dB]$ might still be satisfied. Therefore, $E''(B+b) \ge -[E'(B+b)]^2$ is not a necessary condition for convexity of $\bar{W}(B)$.

[2] Measurements collected from several time sharing systems revealed that the message length output from these computers can be approximated by a geometric distribution [8].

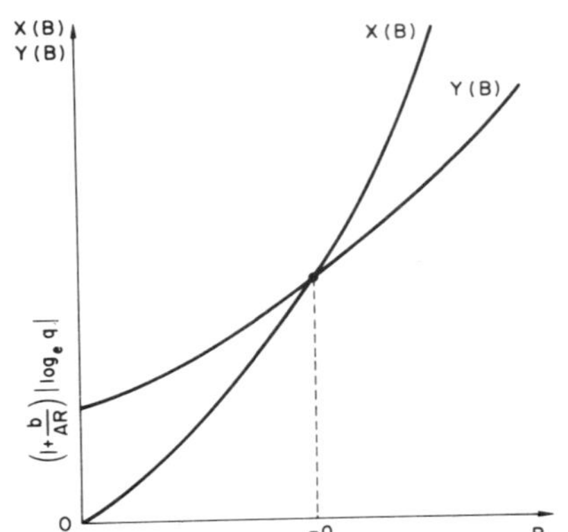

Fig. 2. $dX(B)/dB \geq dY(B)/dB$ and $Y(0) > X(0)$.

We shall next consider the stop-and-wait transmission strategy using end-of-message character in the last unfilled message block.

To increase channel efficiency, we can use an end-of-message character to designate the end of the last unfilled message block rather than fill the rest of the block with dummy information.[3] Thus the last block takes on variable sizes from one character to the maximum block size. This reduces the expected wasted time in transmitting the last block of the message. The $\bar{W}_2(B)$ function is now reduced from (6) to

$$\bar{W}_2(B) = \bar{N}(B) \cdot \frac{b}{R} - \frac{b'}{R}. \tag{6a}$$

The total expected wasted time to transmit a message using the end-of-character strategy is equal to the sum of (5) and (6a). Thus $W(B)$ is reduced from (7) to

$$\bar{W}(B) = \bar{N}(B) \left\{ A + \frac{E(B+b)}{1 - E(B+b)} \left(A + \frac{B+b}{R} \right) + \frac{b}{R} \right\} - \frac{b'}{R}. \tag{7a}$$

Substitute (9) into (7a), differentiating (7a) with respect to B and set to zero; (10) reduces to

$$(q^{-B} - 1) \left[\frac{E(B+b)}{AR} + \left(1 + \frac{B+b}{AR} \right) \frac{E'(B+b)}{1 - E(B+b)} \right] + \left[1 + \frac{b}{AR} + \frac{B \cdot E(B+b)}{AR} \right] \ln q = 0. \tag{10a}$$

In the same manner as shown in the previous section, it can be shown that $E''(B+b) \geq -[E'(B+b)]^2$ is a sufficient condition for $\bar{W}(B)$ to be convex. Optimal block size B^0 that minimizes the expected wasted time can be obtained by solving (10a) numerically.

[3] Another way to implement this scheme is to use a bit- or byte-count character right after the address bits to indicate the number of bits or bytes in that block.

B. Continuous Transmission Strategies

Let us now consider the continuous transmission strategies. We shall first treat the case in which message blocks are transmitted continuously without waiting for acknowledgment and each unconfirmed message block is retransmitted. In case a reverse acknowledgment channel is used, the acknowledgment time $A = 0$, and the overhead is the fixed cost of the reversed channel which is independent of block size. If a reverse channel is not used, the acknowledgment overhead will be the time required to transmit those acknowledgment signals. Since the acknowledgment signal is very short compared to the length of the message block; that is,

$$A \ll \frac{B+b}{R},$$

we can assume $A \doteq 0$. For the case of using an end-of-message character in terminating the last unfilled block then (7a) and (10a) reduce to

$$\bar{W}(B) = \bar{N}(B) \left\{ \frac{E(B+b)}{1 - E(B+b)} \frac{(B+b)}{R} + \frac{b}{R} \right\} - \frac{b'}{R} \tag{7b}$$

and

$$(q^{-B} - 1) \left[E(B+b) + (B+b) \frac{E'(B+b)}{1 - E(B+b)} \right] + [b + B \cdot E(B+b)] \ln q = 0. \tag{10b}$$

In the same manner as shown in the previous section, it can be shown that $E''(B+b) \geq -[E'(B+b)]^2$ is a sufficient condition for $\bar{W}(B)$ to be convex. Optimal block size B^0 that minimizes the expected wasted time can be obtained by solving (10b) numerically.

Let us consider the acknowledgment overhead for the system that transmits message blocks continuously without waiting for acknowledgment and the transmitter retransmits the unconfirmed message block together with those message blocks that follow it. In this type of transmission strategy the whole duration of acknowlegment time is wasted when an error block is detected. The acknowledgment time A_1 is the sum of the time required to detect an error message block t_1, and the time required to send the acknowledgment signal to the transmitter[4] t_2. Since all the message blocks transmitted during this period need to be retransmitted when an error message block is detected, the expected acknowledgment overhead (2) becomes

$$\bar{A}(B+b) = \sum_{i=1}^{\infty} \left(A_1 + \frac{B+b}{R} \right) E(B+b)^i \tag{2a}$$

where

$$A_1 = t_1 + t_2.$$

Consider the case of using the end-of-message character

[4] For those systems using time-out mechanisms, t_2 = time-out limit.

in terminating the last unfilled block. We substitute (2a) into (7a); we have

$$\bar{W}(B) = \bar{N}(B)\left\{\frac{E(B+b)}{1-E(B+b)}\left(A_1+\frac{B+b}{R}\right)+\frac{b}{R}\right\}-\frac{b'}{R}. \tag{7c}$$

Differentiating (7c) with respect to B and setting it to zero, we have

$$(q^{-B}-1)\left[\left(1+\frac{B+b}{A_1R}\right)\frac{E'(B+b)}{1-E(B+b)}+\frac{E(B+b)}{A_1R}\right]$$

$$+\ln q\left[E(B+b)\left(1+\frac{B}{A_1R}\right)+\frac{b}{A_1R}\right]=0 \tag{10c}$$

In the same manner, it can be shown that $E''(B+b) \geq -[E'(B+b)]^2$ is a sufficient condition for (10c) to be convex. The optimal block size B^0 can be obtained by solving (10c) numerically.

In the following we shall analyze the optimal message block size for two types of error channels: random error channel and burst error channel.

C. Random Error Channel

For a random error channel, the probability that a block of $B + b$ bits transmitted over a channel will have at least one error is

$$E(B+b) = 1-(1-K)^{B+b}$$

$$= 1-\left[1-(B+b)K+\frac{(B+b)(B+b-1)K^2}{2!}-\cdots\right] \tag{15}$$

where K equals average channel bit error rate. For most practical systems, $(B + b)\cdot K \ll 1$ (e.g., $(B + b)K = 1000 \times 10^{-4} = 0.1$). Hence, (15) can be approximated as

$$E(B+b) = (B+b)K \tag{16}$$

which is linearly proportional to the total block size $B + b$. Physically, (16) implies that $E(B + b)$ is approximately equal to the expected number of error bits in the block during transmission. The first and second derivatives of $E(B + b)$ equal to $E'(B + b) = K$ and $E''(B + b) = 0$.

To determine the optimal message block size for the stop-and-wait strategies, we substitute $E(B + b) = K(B + b)$ and $E'(B + b) = K$ into (10) and (10a), respectively. We have

$$(q^{-B}-1)\left[\frac{1}{AR}+\left(1+\frac{B+b}{AR}\right)\frac{K}{1-K(B+b)}\right]$$

$$+\left[1+\frac{B+b}{AR}\right]\ln q = 0. \tag{17}$$

$$(q^{-B}-1)\left[\frac{K(B+b)}{AR}+\left(1+\frac{B+b}{AR}\right)\frac{K}{1-K(B+b)}\right]$$

$$+\left[1+\frac{b}{AR}+\frac{K(B+b)B}{AR}\right]\ln q = 0. \tag{17a}$$

Since $E''(B + b) = 0$, $W(B)$ is a convex function of B. Based on the values of the product of acknowledgment delay and transmission rate AR, K, and $\bar{l} = (1 - q)^{-1}$, the Newton–Raphson's Iterative Method [9] can be used to solve (17) and (17a) for the optimal average block size B^0. The iteration is terminated when the improvement on $W(B)$ from each new B is less than 10^{-4} s and the difference between the value of new B and its previous B is less than 1 bit. The optimal message block sizes for selected ranges of AR, K, $\bar{l}$, and b are portrayed in Figs. 3 and 4.

For the optimal message block size for the continuous transmission strategies, we substitute $E(B + b) = K(B + b)$, and $E'(B + b) = K$ into (10b) and (10c), respectively; we have

$$(q^{-B}-1)\left[K(B+b)+(B+b)\frac{K}{1-K(B+b)}\right]$$

$$+[b+BK(B+b)]\ln q = 0 \tag{17b}$$

and

$$(q^{-B}-1)\left[\left(1+\frac{B+b}{A_1R}\right)\frac{K}{1-K(B+b)}+\frac{K(B+b)}{A_1R}\right]$$

$$+\left[K(B+b)\left(1+\frac{B}{A_1R}\right)+\frac{b}{A_1R}\right]\ln q = 0. \tag{17c}$$

283

In the same manner, the optimal block size B^0 can be obtained numerically. Note that (17c) reduces to (17b) when $A_1 = 0$. Thus the results from (17b) ($AR = 0$) and (17c) ($AR > 0$) are portrayed in one single graph as shown in Fig. 5. The B^0 for $A_1 = 0$ corresponds to the case of only retransmitting the unconfirmed block.

D. Burst Error Channel

In a burst error channel, errors tend to cluster rather than be evenly distributed throughout the messages. For example, the noise produced by radio interference or switching transients may cause such burst errors. Two burst error channel characteristics of switched telecommunication networks [7] for 2000 and 4800 bits/s are shown in Fig. 6. These curves represent the error characteristics of 90 percent of the test calls. The error characteristics for the 1200 and 3600 bits/s channels lie between these curves.

In order to express these curves analytically, a curve fitting technique [9] is used to represent $E(B + b)$ as a polynomial. A good fit[5] with a mean of the square errors =

[5] Because of the large variance in ranges of B and $E(B)$, a scale transformation of $\log_{10} B$ is used for the B's and a scale transformation of 10^{-3} is used for the corresponding $E(B)$'s. Such transformation is necessary for reducing errors in curve fittings.

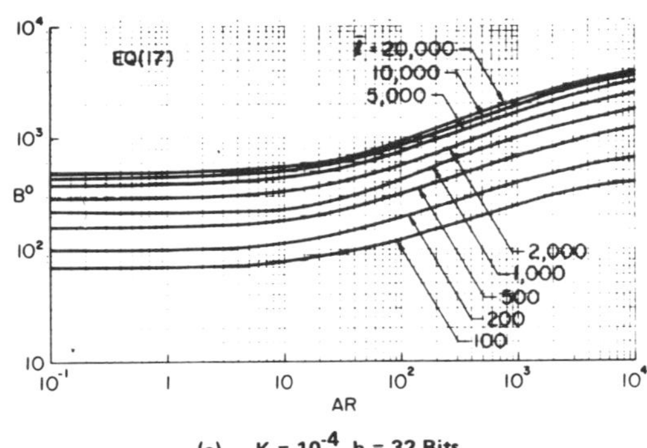

(a) K = 10^{-4}, b = 32 Bits

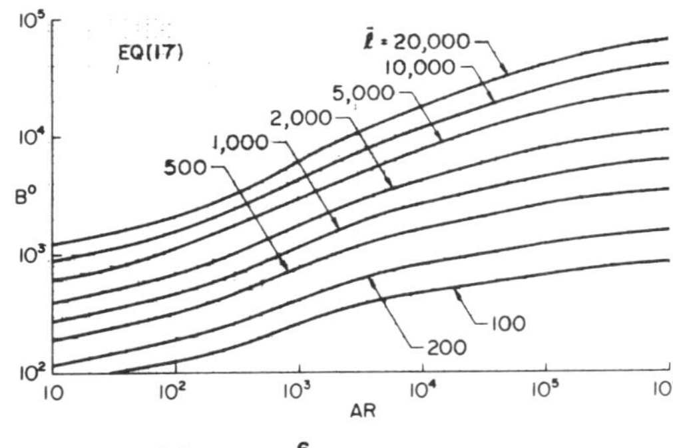

(b) K = 10^{-6}, b = 32 Bits

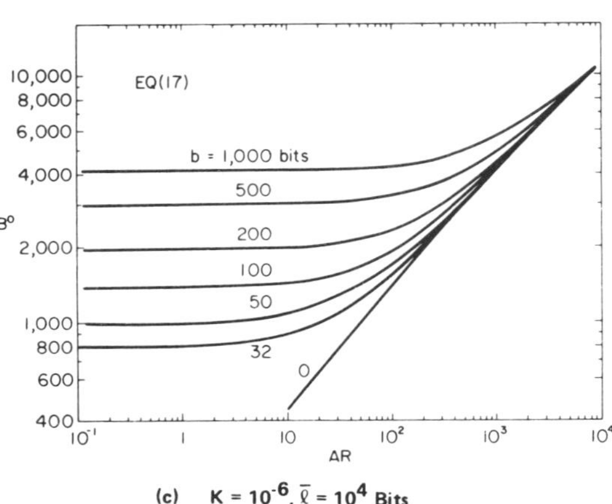

(c) K = 10^{-6}, $\bar{l}$ = 10^4 Bits

Fig. 3. Optimal message block size for random error channel with stop-and-wait transmission strategies (all units in bits).

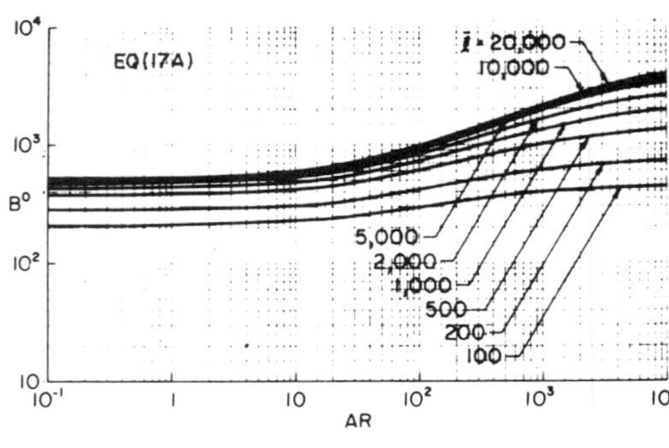

(a) K = 10^{-4}, b = 32 Bits

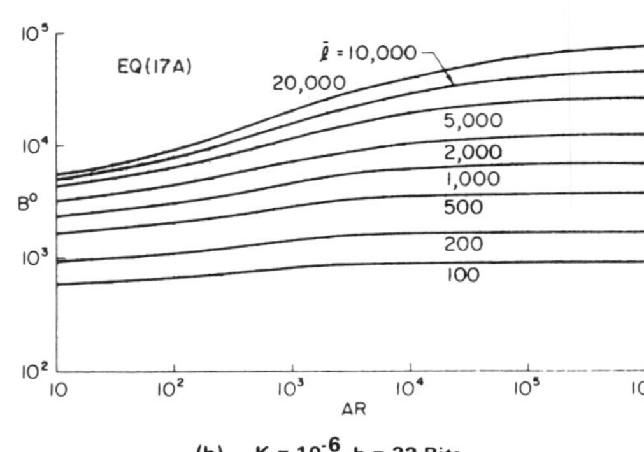

(b) K = 10^{-6}, b = 32 Bits

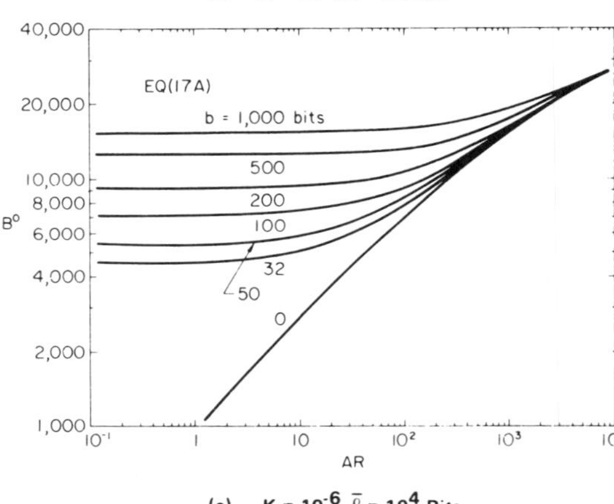

(c) K = 10^{-6}, $\bar{l}$ = 10^4 Bits

Fig. 4. Optimal message block size for random error channel with stop-and-wait transmission strategies and using end-of-message characters to terminate the last unfilled block (all units in bits).

0.879×10^{-9} for the 2000 bits/s channel is

$$\begin{aligned} E_1(B+b) = 10^{-3}[&0.181 \times 10^{-1} + 0.138 (\log_{10} B + b) \\ &- 0.429(\log_{10} B + b)^2 + 0.678(\log_{10} B + b)^3 \\ &- 0.397 (\log_{10} B + b)^4 \\ &+ 0.788 \times 10^{-1}(\log_{10} B + b)^5 \\ &+ 0.310 \times 10^{-2}(\log_{10} B + b)^6 \\ &+ 0.407 \times 10^{-2}(\log_{10} B + b)^7 \\ &- 0.139 \times 10^{-2}(\log_{10} B + b)^8 \\ &- 0.343 \times 10^{-3}(\log_{10} B + b)^9 \\ &+ 0.118 \times 10^{-3}(\log_{10} B + b)^{10}] \end{aligned} \quad (18)$$

for $100 \leq B + b \leq 30\,000$ bits. In the same manner, a good fit[5] with a mean of the square errors = 0.410×10^{-7} for the 4800 bits/s channel is

$$\begin{aligned} E_2(B+b) = 10^{-3}[&0.380 + 0.320(\log_{10} B + b) \\ &+ 1.74(\log_{10} B + b)^2 + 2.25(\log_{10} B + b)^3 \\ &+ 1.19(\log_{10} B + b)^4 + 0.142(\log_{10} B + b)^5 \\ &- 0.137(\log_{10} B + b)^6 \\ &+ 0.784 \times 10^{-2}(\log_{10} B + b)^7 \\ &+ 0.486 \times 10^{-2}(\log_{10} B + b)^8] \end{aligned} \quad (19)$$

for $100 < B + b < 30\,000$ bits.

From (18) and (19) we know that both $E_1''(B + b)$ and $E_2''(B + b)$ are negative. Hence, we need to compute and compare $dX(B)/dB$ and $dY(B)/dB$. We find that for the range of B of interest; that is, $100 \leq B \leq 30\,000$ bits, $dX(B)/dB \geq d(Y)/dB$. Therefore, $\bar{W}(B)$'s for $E_1(B + b)$ and $E_2(B + b)$ are convex functions of B.

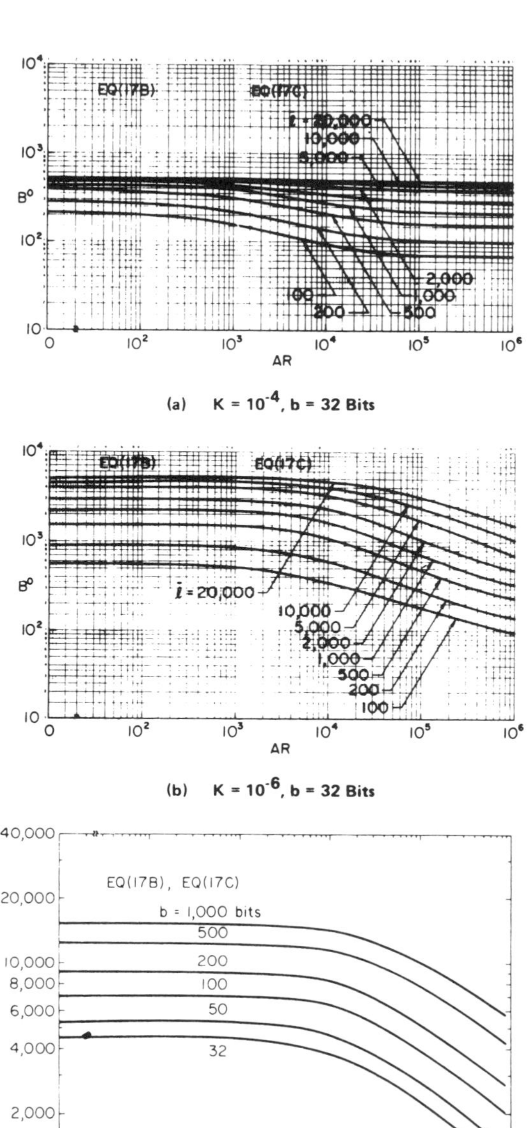

Fig. 5. Optimal message block size for random error channel with continuous transmission strategies (all units in bits).

As is done in the random error case, we substitute (18) into (10), (10a), (10b), and (10c), respectively, and then (19) into (10), (10a), (10b), and (10c), respectively, and use numerical techniques to solve for B^0. The relationships among the optimal block size, average message length $\bar{l}$ and AR for $E_1(B+b)$ and $E_2(B+b)$ are shown in Figs. 7–9, respectively.

When $dX(B)/dB \geq dY(B)/dB$ are not satisfied for some regions of B, numerical results might lead to a local optimal. In this case, a numerical search should be performed in these regions to locate the local optimals of each regions. The global optimal block size B^0 should then be selected from these local optimals.

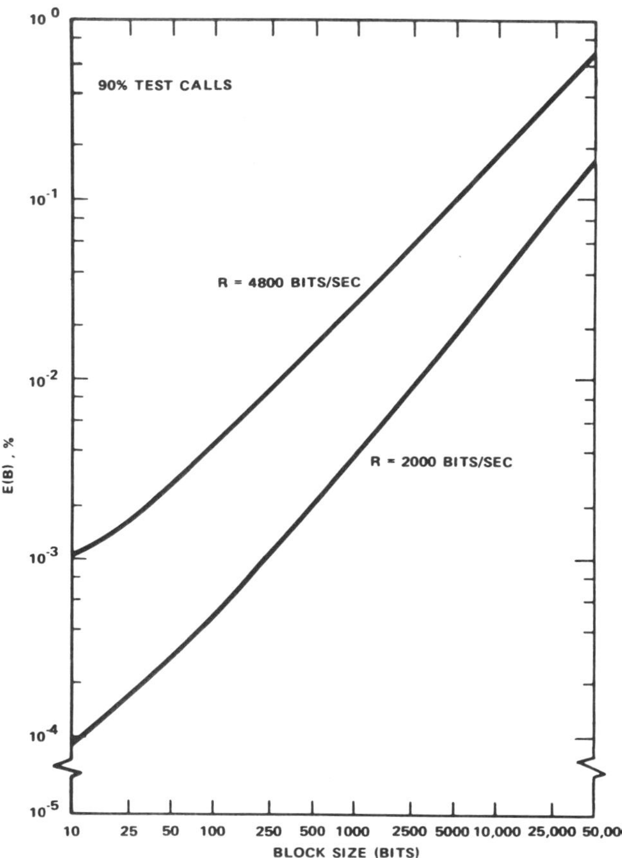

Fig. 6. Burst error channel characteristic of 90 percent test call cases.

III. DISCUSSION OF RESULTS

For stop-and-wait transmission strategies, as A and R increase (A is independent of R), larger block size reduces the number of blocks per message and thus yields better channel utilization. Therefore B^0 increases as AR increases (see Figs. 3 and 4). For continuous transmission strategies, the expected acknowledgment time is rather small, and when channel error probability is relatively low, using smaller size blocks yields better channel utilization. Thus B^0 decreases as AR increases (see Fig. 5). We also note that for a given AR and $\bar{l}$, the optimal block size for a smaller error rate channel is larger than that for a larger error rate channel.

For the system that uses an end-of-message character to terminate the last unfilled message block, the wasted space of the last unfilled block is eliminated; hence, the optimal block size is always larger than when not using the end-of-message characters. Further, for small AR values (e.g., $AR < 10$) and low channel error rate (e.g., $K < 10^{-4}$), the acknowledgment delay is so small that the message block size has very little effect on $\bar{W}(B)$; therefore the optimal message block size for the stop-and-wait strategy is approximately equal to that of the continuous transmission strategy. On the other hand, for large AR values (e.g., $AR > 10^3$), the expected ac-

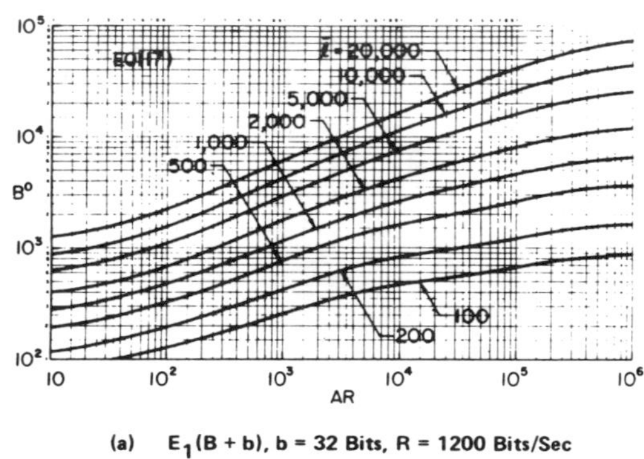

(a) $E_1(B + b)$, b = 32 Bits, R = 1200 Bits/Sec

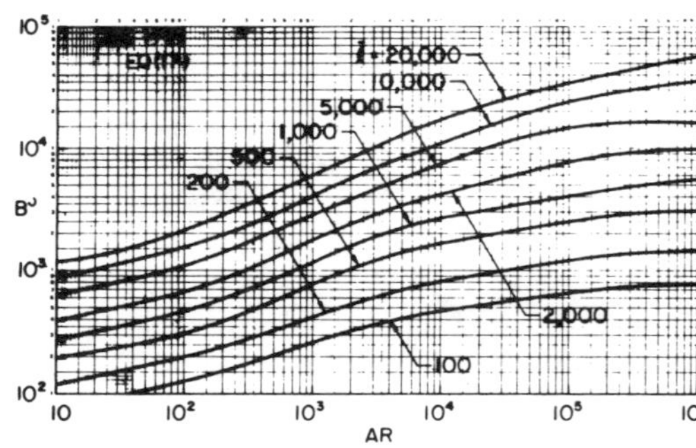

(b) $E_2(B + b)$, b = 32 Bits, R = 4800 Bits/Sec

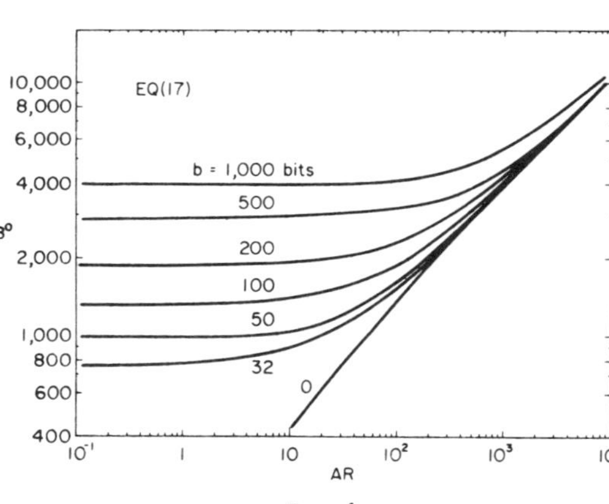

(c) $E_2(B + b)$, $\bar{l} = 10^4$ Bits, R = 4800 Bits/Sec

Fig. 7. Optimal message block size for burst error channel with stop-and-wait transmission strategy.

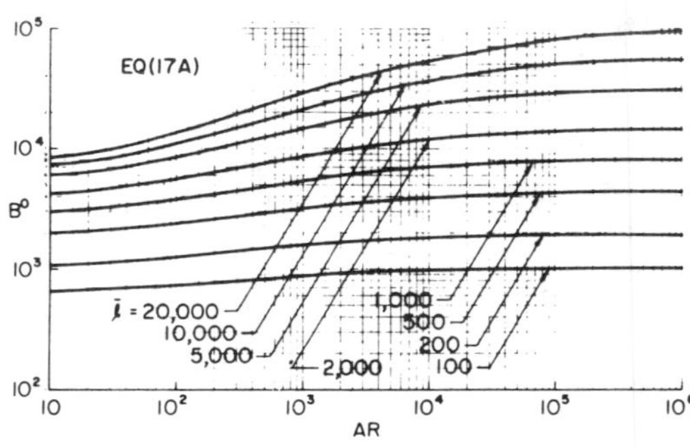

(a) $E_1(B + b)$, b = 32 Bits, R = 1200 Bits/Sec

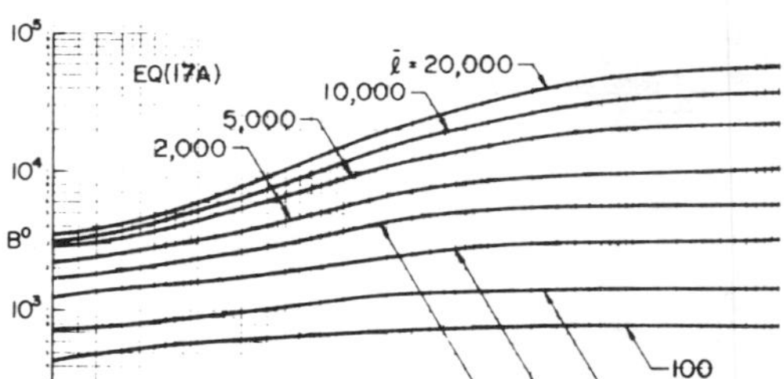

(b) $E_2(B + b)$, b = 32 Bits, R = 4800 Bits/Sec

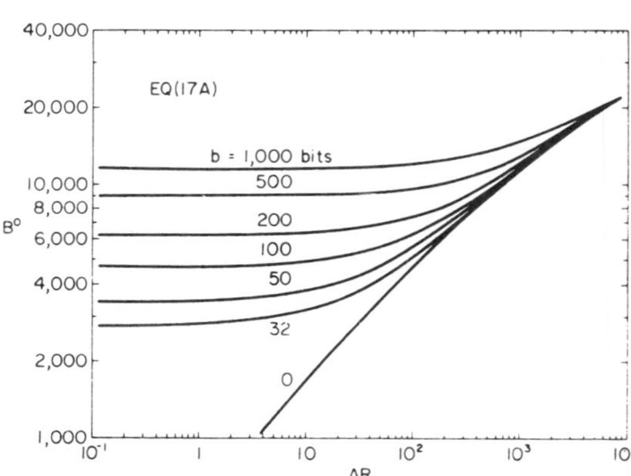

(c) $E_2(B + b)$, $\bar{l} = 10^4$ Bits, R = 4800 Bits/ Sec

Fig. 8. Optimal message block size for burst error channel with stop-and-wait transmission strategy and using end-of-message character to terminate the last unfilled block.

knowledgment delay for the continuous transmission strategy is much smaller than that of the stop-and-wait strategies. As a result, using shorter message blocks yields better reliability and thus less wasted channel time. Therefore, the optimal block size for the continuous transmission strategy is smaller than that of the stop-and-wait system. By the same reasoning, in the continuous transmission systems, the strategy that retransmits only the unconfirmed block yields larger block size than is yielded by the strategy that transmits the unconfirmed block and the subsequent blocks that follow it.

For a given burst error channel, the error characteristics for 70 percent and 80 percent of the test calls yield a better error performance than that of the 90 percent test calls [6] (since more error calls are included in the later case). Thus the B^0 for 70 percent and 80 percent of the test calls are larger than the B^0 for the 90 percent test calls. We have evaluated the B^0 based on the error characteristics of 70 percent and 80 percent of test calls for a larger number of cases. The results reveal that the difference in optimal block size varies from 1 percent to 30 percent. This variation depends on $\bar{l}$ and AR, and such variation decreases as $\bar{l}$ and/or AR decreases.

The $\bar{W}(B)$ for a random error channel is always a convex function. The $\bar{W}(B)$'s for a burst error channel with error characteristics $E_1(B + b)$ and $E_2(B + b)$ are also convex

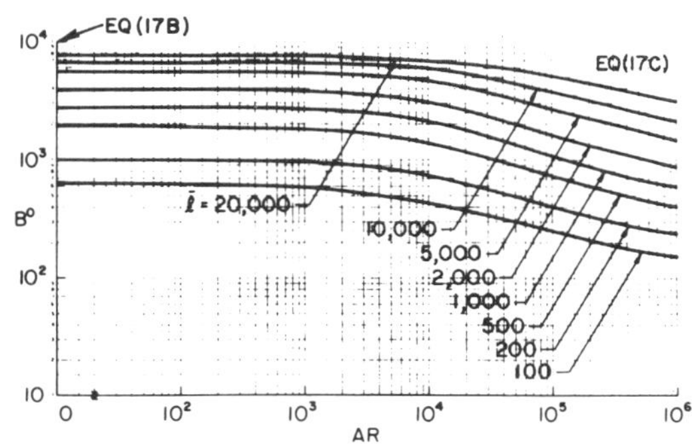

(a) $E_1(B + b)$, b = 32 Bits, R = 1200 Bits/Sec

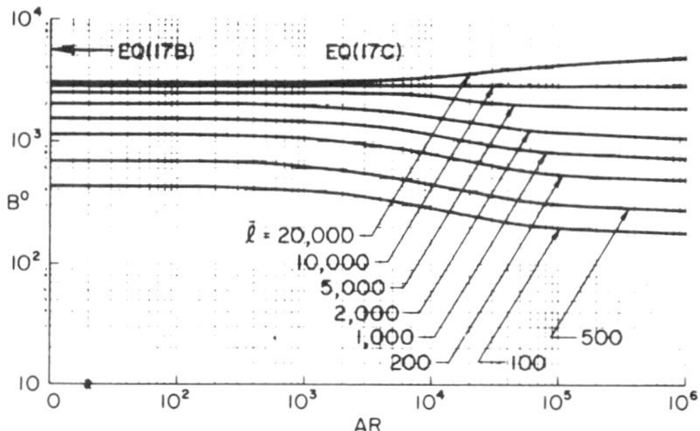

(b) $E_2(B + b)$, b = 32 Bits, R = 4800 Bits/Sec

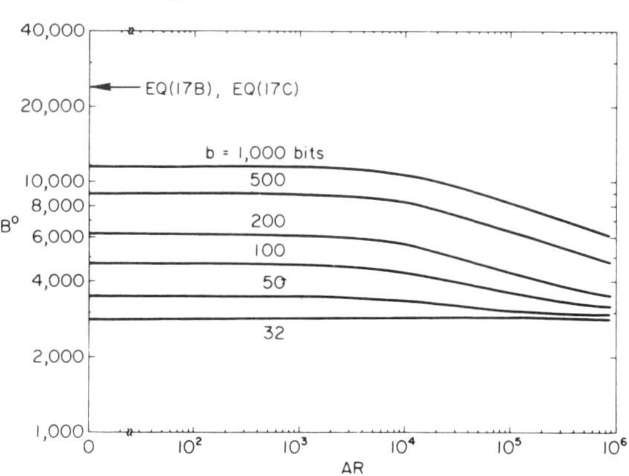

(c) $E_2(B + b)$, $\bar{l}$ = 10^4 Bits, R = 4800 Bits/Sec

Fig. 9. Optimal message block size for burst error channel with continuous transmission strategies.

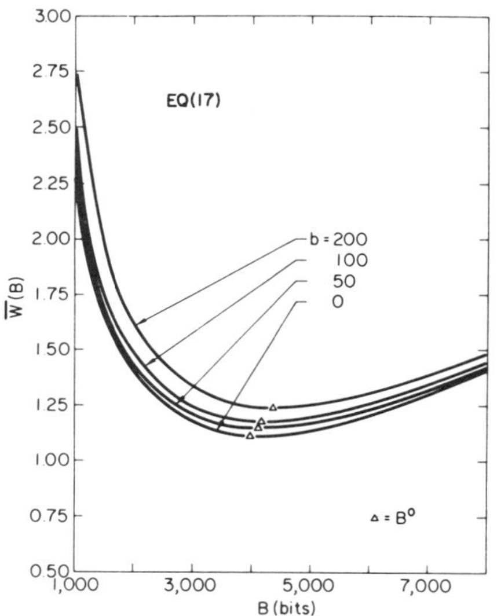

$E_2(B + b)$, AR = 10^3 Bits, $\bar{l}$ = 10^4 Bits, R = 4800 Bits/Sec

Fig. 10. Several typical $\bar{W}(B)$ versus B and b, $b = b'$.

nctions. In general, however, the $\bar{W}(B)$ for a burst ror channel is not necessarily a convex function. A few pical $\bar{W}(B)$'s are shown in Fig. 10. We noted that the (B)'s are rather insensitive around B^0. For a given $\bar{l}$, R, and channel error characteristic, the $\bar{W}(B)$ increases the block overhead b increases. We also note that B^0 creases as b increases and the amount of difference etween $B^0(b_1)$ and $B^0(b_2)$ for $b_2 > b_1$, decreases as AR creases. Thus $B^0(b = 32)$ can be used as a good approxiation for estimating optimal block size for $64 \geq b \geq 16$. lthough the numerical computation was carried out ainly for the message length that is geometrically disibuted, the formulas (7), 7(a), 7(b), and (7c) are quite general and can be applied to any message length distribution. For example, if the message length has a multimode distribution, we can compute $\bar{W}(B)$ by substituting $\bar{N}(B)$ for each B, A, b, and $\bar{l}$ into (7) [or (7a) or (7b) or (7c)] for the range of B of interest. The optimal block size can thus be obtained.

The total amount of time required for transmission of the message from the transmitter to a receiver consists of the time required for transmission of the actual message T and the total expected wasted time $\bar{W}(B)$ [(7) or (7a) or (7b) or (7c)]. The expected channel efficiency for using fixed size message blocks with error detection and retransmission strategy can be defined as $T/[T + \bar{W}(B)]$. Thus minimizing $\bar{W}(B)$ also maximizes channel efficiency. Hence, B^0 maximizes expected channel efficiency.

ACKNOWLEDGMENT

The author wishes to thank M. Shen of the University of California, Los Angeles, for his programming assistance in the numerical solution for the optimal message block size.

REFERENCES

[1] J. J. Kucera, "Transfer rate of information bits," *Comput. Design*, pp. 56–59, June 1968.
[2] M. D. Balkovic and P. E. Muench, "Effect of propagation delay, caused by satellite circuits, on data communication systems that use block retransmission for error correction," in *Conf. Rec., 1969 IEEE Conf. Communications*, Boulder, Colo., pp. 29-31–29-36.
[3] R. L. Kirlin, "Variable block length and transmission efficiency," *IEEE Trans. Commun. Technol.*, vol. COM-17, pp. 350–355, June 1969.
[4] R. L. Townsent and R. N. Watts, "Effectiveness of error control in data communication over the switched telephone network," *Bell Syst. Tech. J.*, vol. 43, pp. 2611–2638, Nov. 1964.
[5] S. Y. Tong, "A survey of error control techniques on telephone channels," in *Proc. Nat. Electronics Conf.*, vol. 26, 1970, pp. 462–467.
[6] M. D. Balkovic *et al.*, "High speed voiceband data transmission performance on the switched telecommunication network," *Bell Syst. Tech. J.*, vol. 50, pp. 1349–1384, Apr. 1971.

[7] E. N. Gilbert, "Capacity of a burst-noise channel," *Bell Syst. Tech. J.*, vol. 39, pp. 1253–1265, Sept. 1960.
[8] E. Fuchs and P. E. Jackson, "Estimates of distributions of random variables for certain computer communications traffic model," *Commun. Ass. Comput. Mach.*, vol. 13, pp. 752–757, Dec. 1970.
[9] R. W. Hamming, *Numerical Methods for Scientists and Engineers.* New York: McGraw-Hill, 1962.

Reprinted by permission from
IEEE TRANSACTIONS ON COMMUNICATIONS
Vol. COM-22, No. 10, October 1974

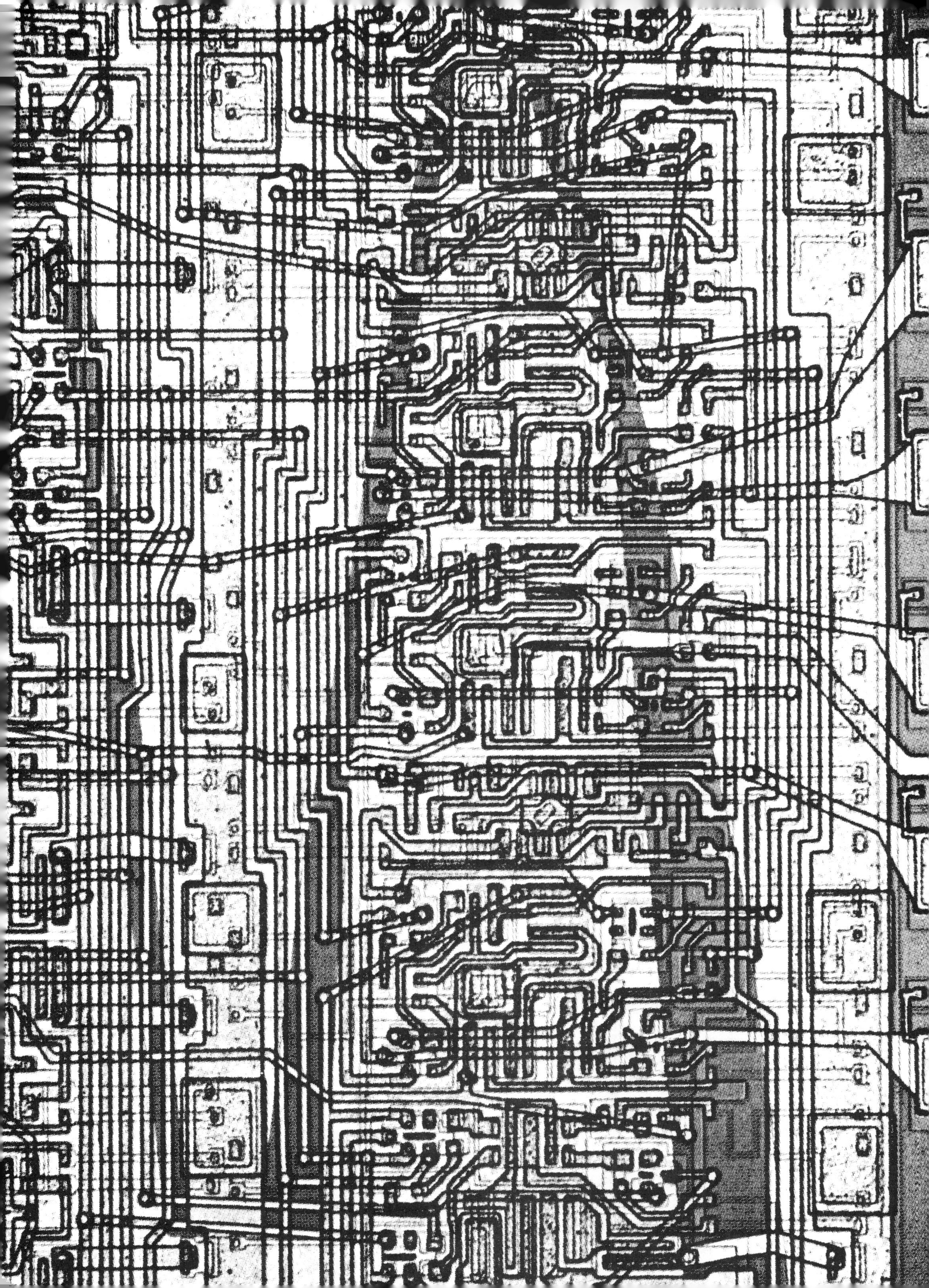

On the Interface Between Computers and Data Communications Systems

A.G. Fraser
Bell Telephone Laboratories

Future systems that combine computers, digital terminals, and communications equipment present design optimization problems that require reconsideration of the traditional functional responsibilities of the respective subsystems. Several "standard" interfaces, by means of which computers and digital terminals connect to the communications systems will be required. When specifying these interfaces, consideration must be given to problems of coordination, synchronization, error control, signaling, stream multiplexing, and switch control, in addition to minimizing the technological interdependence of specific subsystem designs. A focus on some of the problems is obtained in a discussion of a detailed specification for a particular computer-communications system interface.

Key Words and Phrases: communications, standard interface communications protocol, virtual channel, multiplexed input/output, coordination of input/output

CR Categories: 3.81, 6.0, 6.35

Author's address: Bell Telephone Laboratories, Inc., Murray Hill, NJ 07974.

1. Introduction

There must surely come a time when computers, digital terminals, and other devices will be connected by a communication system that provides for an arbitrary and complex pattern of data flow between them. Ideally we shall see a "Compatible Communications System," by which is implied not only a set of mutually compatible hardware interfaces but a universal protocol governing the basic elements of information exchange. Some form of common protocol, if not a common language for information exchange, is essential if such an assembly of machines is to be meaningful. Within this ideal system it would be possible to construct a digital device or write a computer program largely independently of the machines with which they will ultimately communicate.

What form might such a system take, and what are those basic elements of information exchange that of necessity we will have to standardize? No widespread system of communication is erected by a single act; even less easily is it reconstructed once put into regular use. We should therefore consider these questions not with respect to the present temporary state of computing technology but with respect to those aspects which will still apply when the ideal system finally exists.

One look at existing voice communication systems will teach us that there may be many implementations of a communications system that conform to a single functional specification. Indeed such is desirable for then there is freedom, within the constraints of the specification, to employ new inventions when they offer performance or economic advantage. The functional specification of the communications system is what we require to have longevity. The functional specification at the interface between digital device and communications system should first command our attention. But this is just the area of greatest difficulty since it is the interface between two very complex, and substantially independent, industries.

I shall speculate about the form that a Compatible Communications System may take, and I will concentrate on the functional specification at the interface. These speculations, which arise out of research performed at Bell Laboratories, in no way imply plans or proposals for the Bell System, but merely describe a set of signals that *could* form the basis for such an interface. This description implies a division of responsibility between the communications system and attached devices, which I believe, demonstrates a satisfactory level of functional independence. Mutual independence promises longevity for the functional specification of the interface; without it, changes in the internal operation of the communication system might necessitate changes to the attached devices.

2. Some Design Problems

Five major problem areas that have immediate impact on the communications interface specification are: coordination of input/output, multiplexed input/output, device-to-device signaling, error handling, and data format translation.

Coordination of Input/Output

A data source must be so regulated that the rate at which it outputs data is compatible with the rate at which the corresponding sink is absorbing data, and data input actions by the sink must be compatible with the rate at which data can be made available at the source.

The maximum rate at which a device is able, or prepared, to absorb data is a characteristic of that device. Maximum data rates currently range from about 100 bits per second to well over one million bits per second. In spite of this disparity in performance, devices with different capabilities commonly need to communicate with one another. Procedures must be established which allow each device to coordinate with the other. In a fully interconnected network these procedures will become a network standard.

The most appropriate procedures to be used to effect "end-to-end" coordination in a communications system are determined by some detailed characteristics of the transmission and signaling systems used. For example, an end-to-end handshake is appropriate when the transmission delay for end-to-end signaling is short compared to the acceptable delay for packet transfer in a packet switched system. For higher data transfer rates, larger buffers and a separate handshake on each link in a multistage transmission path may be required. In any case the handshake frequency should be related to the data storage capacity of the transmission path.

When an adaptively multiplexed network [1] is designed to avoid a loss of transmitted data as the result of buffer overflow, the network will employ coordination procedures that limit the intake of data. The network will not admit more data traffic than it can properly handle. Procedures that obtain this effect are similar to those needed for end-to-end coordination. It may be the case that the two problems can be solved by one mechanism. Since each is determined by network characteristics, we conclude that minimum interdependence will be achieved when the coordination procedures are contained within the network function.

The coordination problem exists whenever two asynchronous devices are connected even though the devices may not be far apart. The Peripheral Bus of a computer must provide a solution to this problem although its detailed design will typically be optimized for a specific range of machines. A generally applicable, if not the most efficient, peripheral interface design has been described and is the British Standard Digital Input/Output Interface [2]. The communications interface that we shall describe is developed from that British Standard but is made broader in scope by taking into account the switching and multiplexing functions that may be found in a communications system. An experimental communications system [3] in operation at the National Physical Laboratory, England, has already shown that, for simple terminals at least, the British Standard Interface can be resonably effective.

Multiplexed Input/Output

The problem is to provide one interface through which a single device can maintain many simultaneous conversations. It is commonly observed that one computational process, such as a filing system, may simultaneously handle data from many sources and may generate data that are directed toward several destinations. A separate network interface for each conversation in progress is an extravagance that should not be necessary, particularly when all data transfers relating to these conversations are actually handled by one port on a computer.

A multiplexed interface must include a means of specifying which channel the transmitted data refers to. The communications system and a digital device will each undoubtedly be operating under internal constraints that determine when any particular conversation can, in fact, be processed. The interface must therefore transmit signals that allow these mechanisms to coordinate their activities without one dominating and assuming performance characteristics for the other.

When the communications mechanism is packet-switched, an obvious, but not very satisfactory, way of handling the multiplexed interface is to pass addressed packets across the interface. Each packet would consist of data and an identifier for the conversation to which that data relates [4]. The problem with this technique is that it does not recognize that there must be mutual control of the multiplexing arrangement. The mechanism that transfers a packet across an interface does not give the recipient any option but to accept or discard it. Additionally, the packet layout usually reveals some unnecessary detail of the technology of the communications network. For example, there is typically a constraint on packet length and that contradicts the criterion of minimum interdependence between the interfaced mechanisms.

Device-to-Device Signaling

The problem is to provide the basic command and status signaling upon which a universal protocol for information exchange can be built. At every level of communication, whether between equipment at either end of a transmission line or between programs conversing through a network, there is a need to mix signals with data. The signals will typically denote commands, report status changes, and add structure to the conversation. It is desirable that the means whereby signals are distinguished from data should be uniform across all devices connected to one network even if a standard set of signal codes cannot be agreed upon. Furthermore, it makes sense to reveal the difference between signal and data at the interface since these two information types can be expected to receive substantially different treatment both in the network and in the attached device. For example, the transmission facility may sensibly provide a narrowband signaling path and a path with substantially greater bandwidth for data, thereby reducing the cost of transmitting signals.

Error Handling

The problem is to obtain, with some assurance, a prespecified level of reliability when parts of the communication system fail at different rates. It is not really a problem that can have a universal solution. Although error detection and control is a matter of concern for all involved with data communications, the economic pressure for correct transmission depends upon individual circumstance. Furthermore, the detailed design of the error detection and correction system will depend upon the type of error most commonly encountered on a particular transmission path and on the signaling facilities available over that path. For example, on short transmission paths with a burst error characteristic, a retransmission scheme may be most effective, whereas for satellite transmission, forward error correcting codes might be more appropriate [5]. If the error handling procedures were not internal to the communications system, the user would require substantial knowledge of the transmission techniques employed, and this contradicts the criterion of minimum interdependence.

It therefore seems that the communications network will include whatever internal mechanisms are necessary to maintain a specified level (or levels) of reliability. It may even be possible to specify the level of required reliability when establishing a new conversation. Of course a data processing system will invariably contain overall checks on its operation and may have procedures that compensate for loss of proper control. Such systems are complex. From a total systems viewpoint it is desirable to build "shells" around the lower level subsystems making each such subsystem in some sense reliable. The communications network should be one such subsystem.

Format Translation

In contrast to error handling, data format translation is probably not an appropriate task for a Compatible Communications System. The problem emerges when communicating devices use different character codes or have different internal "word" lengths. Unfortunately the diversity of codes and control functions is such that any simple translation scheme is unlikely to achieve wide acceptance so that it is probably unrealistic to try to solve that problem by translation within the communications system. Code translation and word length adjustment can be handled by the digital devices in-involved, or they will communicate by means of some translator machine connected to the network. Probably we should work toward an effective industry standard as the most effective solution to the problem. The communications system should transmit all data patterns without either decoding or altering them.

3. A Possible Interface Design

In this section we describe a communications interface that might serve for a Compatible Communications System. The ideas described here are closely related to an experimental research tool which is in operation at Bell Laboratories, Murray Hill, New Jersey. The description addresses only the question of which signal lines should make up the interface. Any discussion of electrical standards for these signal lines is omitted because our present interest is in the functional specification for a Compatible Communications System rather than a specific implementation.

Virtual Channels

Two essential elements of a Compatible Communications System are a general purpose interface that provides, for all digital devices, one way of expressing all equivalent input/output operations and a traffic control system that provides strategic control of communications between arbitrary pairs of these interfaces. In practice there will be a small number of mutually compatible variants of the general interface designed to yield economic advantages in certain special situations, but they will all be consistent with the same universal protocol for information exchange.

For the purposes of multiplexing several conversations through one interface, a digital device works in

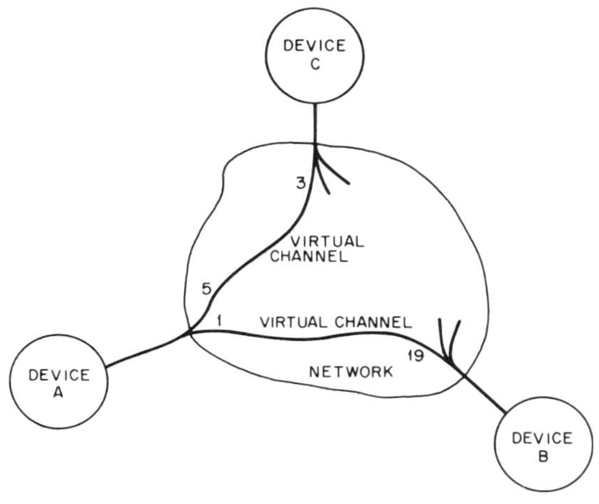

Fig. 1. Virtual channels.

terms of "virtual channels" which are really little more than route maps for data output from one device and input to another. For example, device A might perform input/output operations in terms of channel numbers 1 and 5 when conversing with devices B and C respectively (see Figure 1). Device B might use its own channel number 19 for its part of this conversation, and C might use its channel number 3. The single conversation between B and A defines one virtual channel wherein channel number 1 for A is mapped into channel number 19 for B. A second virtual channel maps channel number 5 for A into channel number 3 for C. The input/output operations performed by A on each of the two virtual channels will be interleaved in time and the communications system could share one physical transmission path between them.

Coordination of Input/Output

There is just one way of performing input/output operations on a virtual channel, and the mechanism for this takes into account the disparity in speed, if any, between a data source and the corresponding data sink. If device A is a data source and B is the corresponding sink, then the method by which A outputs data into the communications system is independent of the frequency with which B inputs data from that system. The communications system itself acts as traffic coordinator (speed regulator). If A works faster than B, then A will be restrained; if B is ready for data before A has produced it, then B must wait.

Controls which are designed to coordinate data transfer between asynchronous devices should pose no particular problem to computers and related devices. Controls of this type are an integral part of such machines. But the role of coordinator is not one that rests easily on a distributed communications system even though experiments show it to be possible [3, 4]. The requirement essential for economical and practical solutions to this problem is allowing flexibility in the detailed design of the communications system. The functional specification for the communications interface must not restrict unnecessarily the design options available to the communications engineer. For example data are transmitted in bursts, but it should not be necessary to specify the burst size or to specify whether bursts relating to different virtual channels should be transmitted on one or many actual communication lines. Data input operations should be subject to the availability of actual data, but there is no limit to the amount of data that a communications system may choose to accept providing only that all accepted data can be delivered when the appropriate data input operation is executed.

Table I. List of Control Lines for One Simplex Path.

Signal Name	Abbreviation	Direction
Acceptor Control	AC	Acceptor to Source
Source Control	SC	Source to Acceptor
Acceptor Error	AE	Acceptor to Source
Parity Valid	PV	Source to Acceptor

The interface provides a full duplex data path which handles the transmission and reception of data and signals. The duplex path consists of two simplex paths: one handles data input to the digital device; the other handles data output. In each case the simplex data path consists of ten information lines and four control lines. The direction of information transfer on a simplex path is from a "Source" to an "Acceptor." (The device is Source for its data output path and Acceptor for its data input path.)

The four control lines of each simplex interface (Table I) are as defined for the British Standard Interface [2]. They are as follows.

a. Acceptor Control (AC) indicates when the Acceptor is ready to accept more information and also serves to indicate when it has accepted the previously offered information.

b. Source Control (SC) indicates when valid information is present on the information lines.

c. Parity Valid (PV) indicates when the parity digit, which is part of the transferred information, is correctly set. Some acceptors may choose not to check parity. A source that does not compute parity would indicate that parity was not valid.

d. Acceptor Error (AE) indicates when the information accepted by the acceptor contained a detected error.

A handshake method of controlling data transfer is used (Figure 2). Control signals on the lines AC and SC complete one handshake cycle for each transfer of information between Source and Acceptor. To start the cycle the Acceptor sets logic 1 on AC indicating readiness to accept information. Until this occurs the Source must keep the control line SC at logic 0. When AC is at logic 1 and the Source has set information on the information lines, the Source sets SC to logic 1. SC

293

must then be held at logic 1 until the Acceptor has taken the information from the information lines and has then set AC to logic 0. Only when the Source has set logic 0 on SC can the Acceptor start the cycle again.

Since each transition of SC is followed by a transition of AC, and vice versa, there are no timing requirements placed upon either of the interfaced mechanisms. A fast device can be interfaced to a slow device and operate satisfactorily.

The transfer of data is in 8 bit bytes and any data pattern can be transmitted without danger of interference by the communications system. To *write* one byte of data into the communications system, a digital device must perform a single handshake on the data output path. That is, the device must wait for AC to rise to logic 1 and then it must raise SC after putting data on the data lines. To *read* one byte of data, the device uses the data input path. It first sets AC to logic 1, then waits for SC to rise to logic 1, then takes data from the data lines before completing the handshake.

Signals and Data

In addition to sending ordinary data the digital device can transmit "signal bytes," which pass through the communications system unaltered. Signal bytes are intended for use by software systems in reporting change in status and discontinuities in the structure of the data being transmitted.

A device can send or receive any number of bytes of data in sequence, and signal bytes can be interspersed amongst them. Eight data lines are used to send signal or data bytes and another eight data lines receive signal or data bytes (see Table II). In each case a separate signal line determines whether the byte is a signal or data. The data and signal bytes arrive at the receiving terminal in the same sequence in which they were sent.

When a buffered communications system is used, there may be no certain way for a user to determine when the data that he has transmitted will be properly delivered. The system may only deliver data in buffer loads and a partially filled buffer will wait to be filled before it is sent on to its final destination. For this reason a separate control line could be provided so that the sender can force delivery of all data previously transmitted. However, we have assumed that it is sufficient to associate this function with the transmission of a signal byte. When a digital device sends a signal byte the communications system is required to deliver, without further delay, that signal and all previously transmitted data.

Channel Controls

When a user of the telephone system desires to make a call, he must first use the dial on his handset to request that a connection be made. The procedures required to make the connection are complex; they involve accounting, route selection, allocation of physical equipment, and verification that the recipient can take the call. Once the connection has been made, switching office and transmission line resources are dedicated to the call. For voice transmission that is usually appropriate because the exchange of information is an almost continuous process. But data transmission is different; data are commonly transmitted in bursts, and the inter-burst gaps can be very long. For this reason it is desirable to make the communications interface such that resource allocation and call set-up can be handled separately. The function of *establishing* a channel involves accounting, route selection, and verification that the recipient can take the call. However, resources need not be allocated until the channel is *selected* prior to data being *written* by the sending device.

In order for one device to send data to another, three steps must be taken.

a. A virtual channel linking the two devices must be *established.*

b. The virtual channel must then be *selected.*

c. Data to be sent must be *written* into the communication system.

Fig. 2. Handshake method of controlling data transfer.

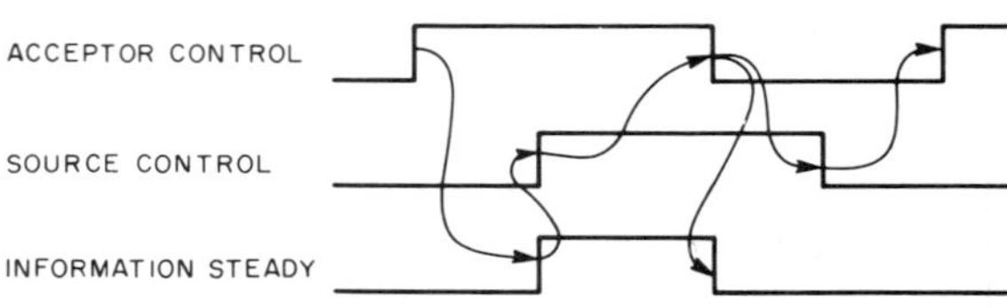

Table II. Interface Lines.

For data transfer from Device to Network
- 4 control (see Table I)
- 8 data output
- 1 signal byte indication
- 1 parity

For data transfer from Network to Device
- 4 control (see Table I)
- 8 data input
- 1 signal byte indication
- 1 parity

For channel select from Device to Network
- 4 control (see Table I)
- 6 channel number
- 1 ready to read
- 1 ready to write
- 1 parity

For channel request from Network to Device
- 4 control (see Table I)
- 6 channel number
- 1 ready to read
- 1 ready to write
- 1 parity

For machine status
- 1 Device operable (from device to network)
- 1 Network operable (from network to device)

When data are to be read from an established channel, the following steps are necessary.

d. The virtual channel must be *selected.*
e. The data must be *read* from the communications system.

In the previous section we indicated how *read* and *write* operations are effected. In this section we deal with the matter of channel *selection* and leave the question of *establishing* a channel until later.

When a digital device has conversations in progress on several virtual channels at the same time, it is necessary that each input/output operation should specify both the data and the channel involved. The channel number and data could be two arguments in a *write* operation, but there are two reasons to believe that separate *select* and *write* operations are appropriate. First, there will usually be a succession of write operations on any one virtual channel before another channel is serviced; the communications system should be encouraged to take advantage of this. Second, the settings of the *read* and *write* controls are determined separately for each virtual channel. To avoid having separate control wires in the interface for every virtual channel that may exist, we suggest that a single set of controls be used and that these apply to the virtual channel currently selected. The *read/write* controls can be expected to change when a *select* operation is executed.

A device that supports many concurrent conversations must schedule its input/output operations so that each virtual channel is serviced at an appropriate time. For this purpose the device will need to keep abreast of the current control status for all virtual channels including the one currently selected. The control status for each channel consists of two bits: one bit indicates when the communications system is prepared to allow more *write* operations; the other bit indicates when *read* operations are possible. (The control status for the selected channel is always immediately available to the device since control lines that indicate which operations can take place form an integral part of of the handshake referred to earlier.) Unfortunately, the control status for a nonselected channel is not continuously available to the device and would normally become available only when that channel is *selected.*

Fig. 3. The four simplex paths of one interface.

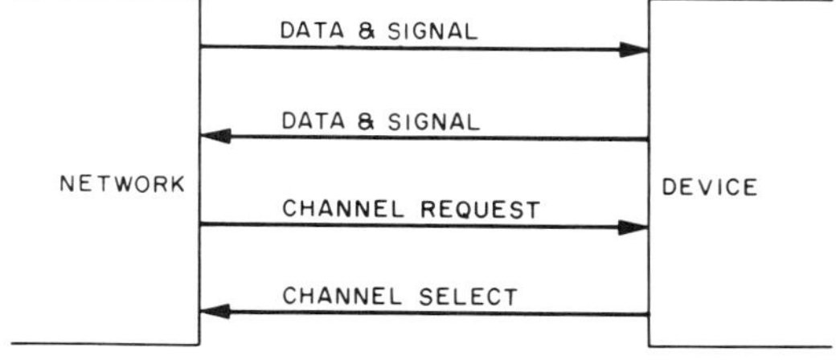

To overcome this difficulty, we provide a means whereby the communications system can tell a digital device when there is a change in control status for a nonselected channel. It operates as follows. When the control status of a nonselected channel changes, the communications system initiates a *request* operation and, in doing so, tells the device the number of the channel and its new control status. Suppose, for example, that a virtual channel maps channel number 1 for A into channel number 19 for B. When B starts to output data on this channel, A will get a *request* for channel 1 if A does not already have that channel selected. It is up to A to decide when to schedule service on the channel. Meanwhile the communications system will retain all data that it permits B to transmit and will restrain B when all available storage space is used.

Channel *select* and *request* operations are complementary operations. *Request* specifies when the communications system would like to have input/output operations performed on a specific virtual channel; *select* specifies which channel will in fact be used. Whereas a digital device may use the status information provided by *request* to schedule its future activities, the communications system should be offered status information during a *select* operation so that it too can optimize its own activities. *Select* therefore specifies not only the virtual channel number but also which input/output operations the device anticipates that it will perform. One bit each for *read* and *write* is sufficient.

Channel *select* and *request* are handled by a full duplex channel control path that is avialable in addition to the full duplex data path already described (Figure 3). As with the data path, the full duplex channel control path is made up from two simplex paths. *Select* is handled by a simplex path in which the device is Source and the communications system is Acceptor. *Request* is handled by a path in which the device is Acceptor. Both simplex paths have four control lines and nine information lines. There are six lines for the channel number, two lines for channel status, and one line for parity (see Table II). The handshake procedure described for the data paths applies for these paths also.

A *select* operation is performed by the digital device when AC of the *select* path is at logic 1. The number and status for the channel to be selected are set on the information lines and the handshake proceeds by the

295

device setting SC to logic 1 (Figure 4). If the status of a nonselected channel changes the communications system will raise SC on the channel *request* when the device next sets AC to logic 1. The device reads the channel number and new status from the information lines and then drops AC to logic 0.

Establishing a Virtual Channel

The most obvious role of a communications system is as a machine for relaying information from one place to another. But a practical system usually offers more than this. For example, the telephone system provides a directory enquiry service, a maintenance service, and an accurate clock. To make use of any one of these services, one must give the system commands and obtain responses from it. Commands and responses also play a part in the basic matter of relaying information since they are required when new connections are made and when conversations are completed.

The language of commands and responses for a Compatible Communications System should be consistent with the normal mode of operation for its users; in this case the users are digital devices. Since the machines that control the communications system are most likely to resemble computers, it seems reasonable to assume that a mechanism designed for communication between digital devices should be appropriate to carry the commands and responses between a digital device and the system central common control.

We give the name "Control Channel" to that special type of virtual channel which joins a digital device to the controller of a communications system. Typically there will be one control channel for each digital device (see Figure 5). The mechanics of *select, read, write*, and *request* apply to control channels as they do to all virtual channels. The only special characteristic of a control channel is that it is routed to the system central common control.

Commands are sent as data from a device to the system controller; responses are returned as data from the system controller to a device. The variety of commands and responses can be expected to be a function of time with new commands added when appropriate.

The basic service is establishing virtual channels for the digital devices which wish to communicate. The procedure is as follows. When device A wishes to communicate with device B, A chooses an unused channel number, 1 say. A sends an ATTACH command over a control channel and that command specifies the full identity of B and the channel number 1. The controller sends an ATTACH response to B indicating that A wishes to communicate. B chooses an unused channel number, 15 say, and sends an ACCEPT command over a control channel. The virtual channel mapping A-1 into B-15 is established and the sequence ends with an ACCEPT response from the controller to A.

In practice the details can be more elaborate than indicated here. The communications system might

Fig. 4. Channel selection timing.

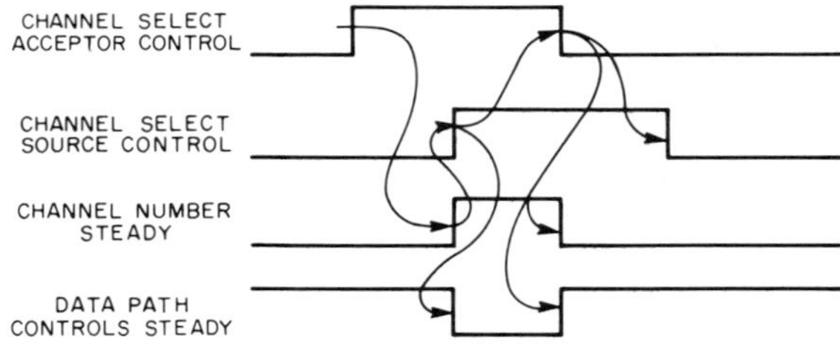

Fig. 5. Control channels.

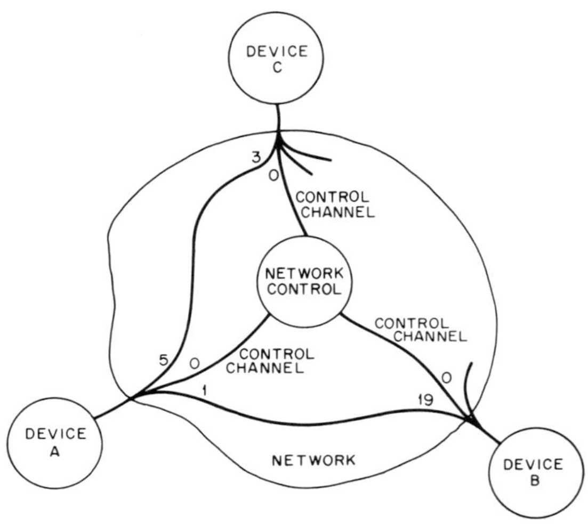

offer several grades of service, and these would be selected by means of appropriate commands. For example, the communications system might assign cheap transmission facilities to a virtual channel if it knew that A and B would accept a low transmission speed; the ATTACH command would then include a measure of the required transmission speed. Alternatively, the buffer allocation used by a packet switching system to service one virtual channel might be specified as an option when establishing a virtual channel.

4. Summary of Interface Details

The device interface for a Compatible Communications System will have two main parts: one part will handle data transfers; the other part will control the selection of virtual channels. Each part of the interface will be asynchronous and full-duplex (see Figure 3).

The duplex paths will each consist of two simplex paths. The data input path transfers data from the communications system to the digital device. The data output path transfers information from the device to the communications system. The channel select path provides the communication system with the number and status of a channel to which subsequent data transfers will relate. The channel request path provides the digital device with the number and status of a virtual channel when the status of that channel changes.

A simplex path provides a means of asynchronously transferring information from a Source to an Acceptor. The digital device is Source for the data output path and for the channel select path. The communications system is Source for the data input path and for the channel request path.

Each simplex path consists of four control lines and a number of information lines. The four control lines are used to effect a simple handshake during which one unit (byte) of information crosses the interface from Source to Acceptor (Figure 2). The Acceptor Control (AC) indicates, to the Source, when information can be transferred; the Source Control (SC) indicates, to the Acceptor, when the transfer is actually to take place.

Ten information bits are transferred over a data path. One bit is a parity bit and another is used to indicate whether the remaining eight are to be treated as a signal byte or as a data byte. Signal bytes and data bytes can be interleaved in arbitrary sequence and are transmitted through the communications system without alteration.

Nine information bits are transferred over a channel control path. One bit is a parity bit, six bits specify a channel number, and two bits indicate "Ready to Read" and "Ready to Write" status for the channel when it is selected.

Finally, an additional pair of lines join the digital device to the communications system so that each can indicate to the other when it is turned on and fully operational.

References

1.
Chu, W.W. Design considerations of statistical multiplexors. Proc. ACM Symposium on the Optimization of Data Communications Systems, Pine Mountain, Georgia, Oct. 1969.

2.
A digital input/output interface for data collection systems. Rep. B.S. 4421 (1969), British Standards Institution, 101 Pentonville Road, London N1.

3.
Davies, D.W. Communication networks to serve rapid-response computers [and papers by Scantlebury, Barlett and Wilkinson]. Proc. IFIP Congress. 1968, Vol. 2, North Holland Pub. Co., Amsterdam, pp. 650–658.

4.
Roberts, L.G., and Wessler, B.D. Computer network development to achieve resource sharing. Proc. AFIPS 1970 SJCC, Vol. 36, AFIPS Press, Montvale, N.J., pp. 543–549.

5.
Trafton, P.J., et al. Data transmission network computer-to-computer study. Proc. ACM Symposium on the Optimization of Data Communications Systems, Palo Alto, Calif., Oct. 1971.

Reprinted from —
AFIPS — Conference Proceedings
Volume 40

Montvale, N. J. 07645

Computer communication network design—Experience with theory and practice*

by HOWARD FRANK
Network Analysis Corporation
Glen Cove, New York

ROBERT E. KAHN
Bolt Beranek and Newman Inc.
Cambridge, Massachusetts

and

LEONARD KLEINROCK
University of California
Los Angeles, California

INTRODUCTION

298

The ARPA Network (ARPANET) project brought together many individuals with diverse backgrounds, philosophies, and technical approaches from the fields of computer science, communication theory, operations research and others. The project was aimed at providing an efficient and reliable computer communications system (using message switching techniques) in which computer resources such as programs, data, storage, special purpose hardware etc., could be shared among computers and among many users.[38] The variety of design methods, ranging from theoretical modeling to hardware development, were primarily employed independently, although cooperative efforts among designers occurred on occasion. As of November, 1971, the network has been an operational facility for many months, with about 20 participating sites, a network information center accessible via the net, and well over a hundred researchers, system programmers, computer center directors and other technical and administrative personnel involved in its operation.

In this paper, we review and evaluate the methods used in the ARPANET design from the vantage of over two years' experience in the development of the network. In writing this paper, the authors have each made equal contributions during a series of intensive discussions and debates. Rather than present merely a summary of the procedures that were used in the network design, we have attempted to evaluate each other's methods to determine their advantages and drawbacks. Our approaches and philosophies have often differed radically and, as a result, this has not been an easy or undisturbing process. On the other hand, we have found our collaboration to be extremely rewarding and, notably, we have arrived at many similar conclusions about the network's behavior that seem to be generally applicable to message switched networks.

The essence of a network is its design philosophy, its performance characteristics, and its cost of implementation and operation. Unfortunately, there is no generally accepted definition of an "optimal" network or even of a "good" network. For example, a network designed to transmit large amounts of data only during late evening hours might call for structural and performance characteristics far different from one servicing large numbers of users who are rapidly exchanging short messages during business hours. We expect this topic, and others such as the merits of message switching vs. circuit switching or distributed vs. centralized control to be a subject of discussion for many years.[1,14,24,32,34,37]

A cost analysis performed in 1967-1968 for the ARPA Network indicated that the use of message switching would lead to more economical communications and better overall availability and utilization of resources than other methods.[36,38] In addition to its impact on the availability of computer resources, this decision has generated widespread interest in store-and-forward communications. In many instances, the use of store-and-forward communication techniques can result in

* This work was supported by the Advanced Research Projects Agency of the Department of Defense under Contract No. DAHC 15-70-C-0120 at the Network Analysis Corporation, Contract Nos. DAHC 15-69-C-0179 and DAHC-71-C-0088 at Bolt Beranek and Newman Inc., and Contract No. DAHC 15-69-C-0285 at the University of California at Los Angeles.

greater flexibility, higher reliability, significant technical advantage, and substantial economic savings over the use of conventional common carrier offerings. An obvious trend toward increased computer and communication interaction has begun. In addition to the ARPANET, research in several laboratories is under way, small experimental networks are being built, and a few examples of other government and commercial networks are already apparent.[6,7,31,40,41,47,48,52]

In the ARPANET, each time-sharing or batch processing computer, called a Host, is connected to a small computer called an Interface Message Processor (IMP). The IMPs, which are interconnected by leased 50 kilobit/second circuits, handle all network communication for their Hosts. To send a message to another Host, a Host precedes the text of its message with an address and simply delivers it to its IMP. The IMPs then determine the route, provide error control, and notify the sender of its receipt. The collection of Hosts, IMPs, and circuits forms the message switched resource sharing network. A good description of the ARPANET, and some early results on protocol development and modeling are given in References 3, 12, 15, 23 and 38. Some experimental utilization of the ARPANET is described in Reference 42. A more recent evaluation of such networks and a forward look is given in References 35 and 39.

The development of the Network involved four principal activities:

(1) The design of the IMPs to act as nodal store-and-forward switches,
(2) The topological design to specify the capacity and location of each communication circuit within the network,
(3) The design of higher level protocols for the use of the network by time-sharing, batch processing and other data processing systems, and
(4) System modeling and measurement of network performance.

Each of the first three activities were essentially performed independently of each other, whereas the modeling effort partly affected the IMP design effort, and closely interacted with the topological design project.

The IMPs were designed by Bolt Beranek and Newman Inc. (BBN) and were built to operate independent of the exact network connectivity; the topological structure was specified by Network Analysis Corporation (NAC) using models of network performance developed by NAC and by the University of California at Los Angeles (UCLA). The major efforts in the area of system modeling were performed at UCLA using theoretical and simulation techniques. Network performance measurements have been conducted during the development of the network by BBN and by the Network Measurement Center at UCLA. To facilitate effective use of the net, higher level (user) protocols are under development by a group of representatives of universities and research centers. This group, known as the Network Working Group, has already specified a Host to Host protocol and a Telnet protocol, and is in the process of completing other function oriented protocols.[4,29] We make no attempt to elaborate on the Host to Host protocol design problems in this paper.

THE NETWORK DESIGN PROBLEM

A variety of performance requirements and system constraints were considered in the design of the net. Unfortunately, many of the key design objectives had to be specified long before the actual user requirements could be known. Once the decision to employ message switching was made, and fifty kilobit/second circuits were chosen, the critical design variables were the network operating procedure and the network topology; the desired values of throughput, delay, reliability and cost were system performance and constraint variables. Other constraints affected the structure of the network, but not its overall properties, such as those arising from decisions about the length of time a message could remain within the network, the location of IMPs relative to location of Hosts, and the number of Hosts to be handled by a single IMP.

In this section, we identify the central issues related to IMP design, topological design, and network modeling. In the remainder of the paper, we describe the major design techniques which have evolved.

IMP properties

The key issue in the design of the IMPs was the definition of a relationship between the IMP subnet and the Hosts to partition responsibilities so that reliable and efficient operation would be achieved. The decision was made to build an autonomous subnet, independent (as much as possible) of the operation of any Host. The subnet was designed to function as a "communications system"; issues concerning the use of the subnet by the Hosts (such as protocol development) were initially left to the Hosts. For reliability, the IMPs were designed to be robust against all line failures and the vast majority of IMP and Host failures. This decision required routing strategies that dynamically adapt to changes in the states of IMPs and circuits, and an elaborate flow control strategy to protect the subnet against Host malfunction and congestion due to IMP buffer limitations. In addition, a statistics and status reporting mechanism was needed to monitor the behavior of the network.

The number of circuits that an IMP must handle is a design constraint directly affecting both the structure of the IMP and the topological design. The speed of the IMP and the required storage for program and buffers depend directly upon the total required processing capacity, which must be high enough to switch traffic from one line to another when all are fully occupied. Of great importance is the property that all IMPs operate with identical programs. This technique greatly simplifies the problem of network planning and maintenance and makes network modifications easy to perform.

The detailed physical structure of the IMP is not discussed in this paper.[2,15] However, the operating procedure, which guides packets through the net, is very much of interest here. The flow control, routing, and error control techniques are integral parts of the operating procedure and can be studied apart from the hardware by which they are implemented. Most hardware modifications require changes to many IMPs already installed in the field, while a change in the operating procedure can often be made more conveniently by a change to the single operating program common to all IMPs, which can then be propagated from a single location via the net.

Topological properties

The topological design resulted in the specification of the location and capacity of all circuits in the network. Projected Host—Host traffic estimates were known at the start to be either unreliable or wrong. Therefore, the network was designed under the assumption of equal traffic between all pairs of nodes. (Additional superimposed traffic was sometimes included for those nodes with expectation of higher traffic requirements.) The topological structure was determined with the aid of specially developed heuristic programs to achieve a low cost, reliable network with a high throughput and a general insensitivity to the exact traffic distribution. Currently, only 50 kilobit/second circuits are being used in the ARPANET. This speed line was chosen to allow rapid transmission of short messages for interactive processing (e.g., less than 0.2 seconds average packet delay) as well as to achieve high throughput (e.g., at least 50 kilobits/second) for transmission of long messages. For reliability, the network was constrained to have at least two independent paths between each pair of IMPs.

The topological design problem requires consideration of the following two questions:

(1) Starting with a given state of the network topology, what circuit modifications are required to add or delete a set of IMPs?

(2) Starting with a given state of network topology, when and where should circuits be added or deleted to account for long term changes in network traffic?

If the locations of all network nodes are known in advance, it is clearly most efficient to design the topological structure as a single global effort. However, in the ARPANET, as in most actual networks, the initial designation of node locations is modified on numerous occasions. On each such occasion, the topology can be completely reoptimized to determine a new set of circuit locations.

In practice, there is a long lead time between the ordering and the delivery of a circuit, and major topological modifications cannot be made without substantial difficulty. It is therefore prudent to add or delete nodes with as little disturbance as possible to the basic network structure consistent with overall economical operation. Figure 1 shows the evolution of the ARPANET from the basic four IMP design in 1969 to the presently planned 27 IMP version. Inspection of the 24 and 27 IMP network designs reveals a few substantial changes in topology that take advantage of the new nodes being added. Surprisingly enough, a complete "reoptimization" of the 27 IMP topology yields a network only slightly less expensive (about 1 percent) than the present network design.[28]

Network models

The development of an accurate mathematical model for the evaluation of time delay in computer networks is among the more difficult of the topics discussed in this paper. On the one hand, the model must properly reflect the relevant features of the network structure and operation, including practical constraints. On the other hand, the model must result in a mathematical formulation which is tractable and from which meaningful results can be extracted. However, the two requirements are often incompatible and we search for an acceptable compromise between these two extremes.

The major modeling effort thus far has been the study of the behavior of networks of queues.[21] This emphasis is logical since in message switched systems, messages experience queueing delays as they pass from node to node and thus a significant performance measure is the

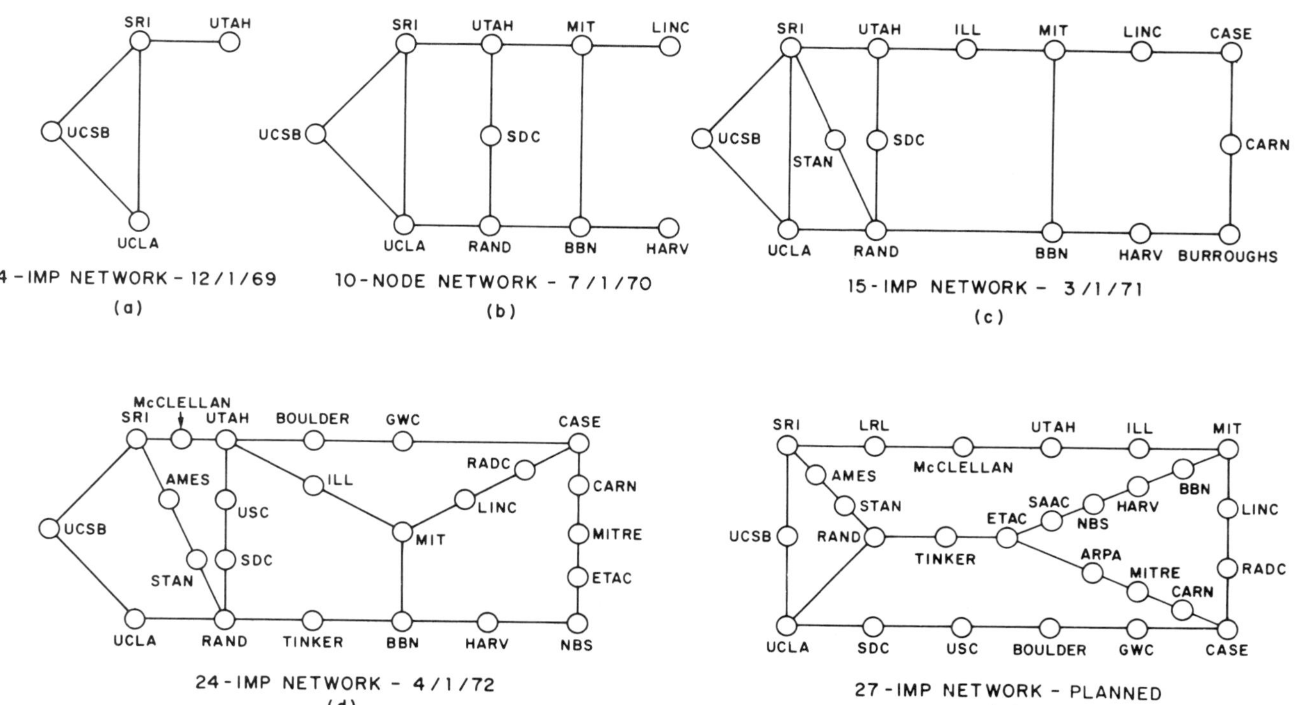

Figure 1—The evolution of the ARPANET

speed at which messages can be delivered. The queueing models were developed at a time when there were no operational networks available for experimentation and model validation, and simulation was the only tool capable of testing their validity. The models, which at all times were recognized to be idealized statements about the real network, were nonetheless crucial to the ARPANET topological design effort since they afforded the only known way to quantitatively predict the properties of different routing schemes and topological structures. The models have been subsequently demonstrated to be very accurate predictors of network throughput and indispensable in providing analytical insight into the network's behavior.

The key to the successful development of tractable models has been to factor the problem into a set of simpler queueing problems. There are also heuristic design procedures that one can use in this case. These procedures seem to work quite well and are described later in the paper. However, if one specializes the problem and removes some of the real constraints, theory and analysis become useful to provide understanding, intuition and design guidelines for the original constrained problem. This approach uncovers global properties of network behavior, which provide keys to good heuristic design procedures and ideal performance bounds.

DESIGN TECHNIQUES

In this section we describe the approaches taken to the design problems introduced in the previous section. We first summarize the important properties of the ARPANET design:

(1) A communications cost of less than 30 cents per thousand packets (approximately a megabit).
(2) Average packet delays under 0.2 seconds through the net.
(3) Capacity for expansion to 64 IMPs without major hardware or software redesign.
(4) Average total throughput capability of 10-15 kilobits/second for all Hosts at an IMP.
(5) Peak throughput capability of 85 kilobits/second per pair of IMPs in an otherwise unloaded network.
(6) Transparent communications with maximum message size of approximately 8000 bits and error rates of one bit in 10^{12} or less.

(7) Approximately 98 percent availability of any IMP and close to 100 percent availability of all operating IMPs from any operable IMP.

The relationships between the various design efforts are illustrated by these properties. The topological design provides for both a desired average throughput and for two or more paths to be fully used for communication between any pair of Hosts. The operating procedure should allow any pair of Hosts to achieve those objectives. The availability of IMPs to communicate reflects both the fact that IMPs are down about 2 percent of the time and that the topology is selected so that circuit failures contribute little additional to the total system downtime.

IMP design

The IMP design consists of two closely coupled but nonetheless separable pieces—the physical hardware specification (based on timing and reliability considerations and the operating procedure) and the design and implementation of the operating procedure using the specified IMP hardware. The IMP originally developed 302 for the ARPANET contains a 16-bit one microsecond computer that can handle a total of about ¾ megabits/second of "useful" information on a total of approximately one megabit/second of circuit capacity (e.g., twenty 50 kilobit/second circuits). Hardware is likely to change as a function of the required IMP capacity but an operating procedure that operates well at one IMP capacity is likely to be transferable to machines that provide different capacity. However, as a network grows in size and utilization, a more comprehensive operating procedure that takes account of known structural properties, such as a hierarchical topology, is appropriate.

Four primary areas of IMP design, namely message handling and buffering, error control, flow control, and routing are discussed in this section. The IMP provides buffering to handle messages for its Host and packets for other IMPs. Error control is required to provide reliable communication of Host messages in the presence of noisy communication circuits. The design of the operating procedure should allow high throughput in the net under heavy traffic loads. Two potential obstacles to achieving this objective are: (1) The net can become congested and cause the throughput to *decrease* with increasing load, and (2) The routing procedure may be unable to always adapt sufficiently fast to the rapid movement of packets to insure efficient routing. A flow control and routing procedure is needed that can efficiently meet this requirement.

Message handling and buffering

In the ARPANET, the maximum message size was constrained to be approximately 8000 bits. A pair of Hosts will typically communicate over the net via a sequence of transmitted messages. To obtain delays of a few tenths of a second for such messages and to lower the required IMP buffer storage, the IMP program partitions each message into one or more packets each containing at most approximately 1000 bits. Each packet of a message is transmitted independently to the destination where the message is reassembled by the IMP before shipment to that destination Host. Alternately, the Hosts could assume the responsibility for reassembling messages. For an asynchronous IMP-Host channel, this marginally simplifies the IMP's task. However, if *every* IMP-Host channel were synchronous, and the Host provided the reassembly, the IMP task can be further simplified. In this latter case, "IMP-like" software would have to be provided in each Host.

The method of handling buffers should be simple to allow for fast processing and a small amount of program. The number of buffers should be sufficient to store enough packets for the circuits to be used to capacity; the size of the buffers may be intuitively selected with the aid of simple analytical techniques. For example, fixed buffer sizes are useful in the IMP for simplicity of design and speed of operation, but inefficient utilization can arise because of variable length packets. If each buffer contains A words of overhead and provides space for M words of text, and if message sizes are uniformly distributed between 1 and L, it can be shown[45] that the choice of M that minimizes the expected storage is approximately $\sqrt{AL}$. In practice, M is chosen to be somewhat smaller on the assumption that most traffic will be short and that the amount of overhead can be as much as, say, 25 percent of buffer storage.

Error control

The IMPs must assume the responsibility for providing error control. There are four possibilities to consider:

(1) Messages are delivered to their destination out of order.

(2) Duplicate messages are delivered to the destination.

(3) Messages are delivered with errors.

(4) Messages are not delivered.

The task of proper sequencing of messages for delivery to the destination Host actually falls in the province of both error control and flow control. If at most one message at a time is allowed in the net between a pair of Hosts, proper sequencing occurs naturally. A duplicate packet will arrive at the destination IMP after an acknowledgment has been missed, thus causing a successfully received packet to be retransmitted. The IMPs can handle the first two conditions by assigning a sequence number to each packet as it enters the network and processing the sequence number at the destination IMP. A Host that performs reassembly can also assign and process sequence numbers and check for duplicate packets. For many applications, the order of delivery to the destination is immaterial. For priority messages, however, it is typically the case that fast delivery requires a perturbation to the sequence.

Errors are primarily caused by noise on the communication circuits and are handled most simply by error detection and retransmission between each pair of IMPs along the transmission path. This technique requires extra storage in the IMP if either circuit speeds or circuit lengths substantially increase. Failures in detecting errors can be made to occur on the order of years to centuries apart with little extra overhead (20-30 parity bits per packet with the 50 kilobit/second circuits in the ARPANET). Standard cyclic error detection codes have been usefully applied here.

A reliable system design insures that each transmitted message is accurately delivered to its intended destination. The occasional time when an IMP fails and destroys a useful in-transit message is likely to occur far less often than a similar failure in the Hosts and has proven to be unimportant in practice, as are errors due to IMP memory failures. A simple end to end retransmission strategy will protect against these situations, if the practical need should arise. However, the IMPs are designed so that they can be removed from the network without destroying their internally stored packets.

Flow control

A network in which packets may freely enter and leave can become congested or logically deadlocked and cause the movement of traffic to halt.[5,17] Flow control techniques are required to prevent these conditions from occurring. The provision of extra buffer storage will mitigate against congestion and deadlocks, but cannot in general prevent them.

The sustained failure of a destination Host to accept packets from its IMP at the rate of arrival will cause the net to fill up and become congested. Two kinds of logical deadlocks, known as reassembly lockup and store-and-forward lockup may also occur. In reassembly lockup, the remaining packets of partially reassembled messages are blocked from reaching the destination IMP (thus preventing the message from being completed and the reassembly space freed) by other packets in the net that are waiting for reassembly space at that destination to become free. In a store-and-forward lockup, the destination has room to accept arriving packets, but the packets interfere with each other by tying up buffers in transit in such a way that none of the packets are able to reach the destination.[17] These phenomena have only been made to occur during very carefully arranged testing of the ARPANET and by simulation.[49]

In the original ARPANET design, the use of software links and RFNMS protected against congestion by a single link or a small set of links. However, the combined traffic on a large number of links could still produce congestion. Although this strategy did not protect against lockup, the method has provided ample protection for the levels of traffic encountered by the net to date.

A particularly simple flow control algorithm that augments the original IMP design to prevent congestion and lockup is also described in Reference 17. This scheme includes a mechanism whereby packets may be discarded from the net at the destination IMP when congestion is about to occur, with a copy of each discarded packet to be retransmitted a short time later by the originating Host's IMP. Rather than experience excessive delays within the net as traffic levels are increased, the traffic is queued outside the net so that the transit time delays internal to the net continue to remain small. This strategy prevents the insertion of more traffic into the net than it can handle.

It is important to note the dual requirement for small delays for interactive traffic and high bandwidth for the fast transfer of files. To allow high bandwidth between a pair of Hosts, the net must be able to accept a steady flow of packets from one Host and at the same time be able to rapidly quench the flow at the entrance to the source IMP in the event of imminent congestion at the destination. This usually requires that a separate provision be made in the algorithm to protect short interactive messages from experiencing unnecessarily high delays.

Routing

Network routing strategies for distributed networks require routing decisions to be made with only information available to an IMP and the IMP must execute those decisions to effect the routing.[14,15] A simple example of such a strategy is to have each IMP handling a packet independently route it along its current estimate of the shortest path to the destination.

For many applications, it suffices to deal with an idealized routing strategy which may not simulate the IMP routing functions in detail or which uses information not available to the IMP. The general properties of both strategies are usually similar, differing mainly in certain implementation details such as the availability of buffers or the constraint of counters and the need for the routing to quickly adapt to changes in IMP and circuit status.

The IMPs perform the routing computations using information received from other IMPs and local information such as the alive/dead state of its circuits. In the normal case of time varying loads, local information alone, such as the length of internal queues, is insufficient to provide an efficient routing strategy without assistance from the neighboring IMPs. It is possible to obtain sufficient information from the neighbors to provide efficient routing, with a small amount of computation needed per IMP and without each IMP requiring a topological map of the network.
304 In certain applications where traffic patterns exhibit regularity, the use of a central controller might be preferable. However, for most applications which involve dynamically varying traffic flow, it appears that a central controller cannot be used more effectively than the IMPs to update routing tables if such a controller is constrained to derive its information via the net. It is also a less reliable approach to routing than to distribute the routing decisions among the IMPs.

The routing information cannot be propagated about the net in sufficient time to accurately characterize the instantaneous traffic flow. An efficient algorithm, therefore, should not focus on the movement of individual packets, but rather use topological or statistical information in the selection of routes. For example, by using an averaging procedure, the flow of traffic can be made to build up smoothly. This allows the routing algorithm ample time to adjust its tables in each IMP in advance of the build-up of traffic.

The scheme originally used in the ARPA network had each IMP select one output line per destination onto which to route packets. The line was chosen to be the one with minimum estimated time delay to the destination. The selection was updated every half second using minimum time estimates from the neighboring IMPs and internal estimates of the delay to each of the neighbors. Even though the routing algorithm only selects one line at a time per destination, two output lines will be used if a queue of packets waiting transmission on one line builds up before the routing update occurs and another line is chosen. Modifications to the scheme which allow several lines per destination to be used in an update interval (during which the routing is not changed) are possible using two or more time delay estimates to select the paths.

In practice, this approach has worked quite effectively with the moderate levels of traffic experienced in the net. For heavy traffic flow, this strategy may be inefficient, since the routing information is based on the length of queues, which we have seen can change much faster than the information about the change can be distributed. Fortunately, this information is still usable, although it can be substantially out of date and will not, in general, be helpful in making efficient routing decisions in the heavy traffic case.

A more intricate scheme, recently developed by BBN, allows multiple paths to be efficiently used even during heavy traffic.[18] Preliminary simulation studies indicate that it can be tailored to provide efficient routing in a network with a variety of heavy traffic conditions. This method separates the problem of defining routes onto which packets may be routed from the problem of selecting a route when a particular packet must be routed. By this technique, it is possible to send packets down a path with the fewest IMPs and excess capacity, or when that path is filled, the one with the next fewest IMPs and excess capacity, etc.

A similar approach to routing was independently derived by NAC using an idealized method that did not require the IMPs to participate in the routing decisions. Another approach using a flow deviation technique has recently been under study at UCLA.[13] The intricacies of the exact approach lead to a metering procedure that allows the overall network flow to be changed slowly for stability and to perturb existing flow patterns to obtain an increased flow. These approaches all possess, in common, essential ingredients of a desirable routing strategy.

Topological considerations

An efficient topological design provides a high throughput for a given cost. Although many measures of throughput are possible, a convenient one is the average amount of traffic that a single IMP can send into the network when all other IMPs are transmitting according to a specified traffic pattern. Often, it is assumed that all other IMPs are behaving identically and each IMP is sending equal amounts of traffic to each other IMP. The constraints on the topological design are the available common carrier circuits, the target cost or throughput, the desired reliability, and

TABLE I—23 Node 28 Link ARPA

Number of Circuits Failed	Number of Combinations to be Examined		Number of Cutsets
28	1		1
27	28		28
26	378		378
25	3276		3276
24	20475		20475
23	98280		98280
22	376740		376740
21	1184040		1184040
20	3108105		3108105
19	6906900		6906900
18	13123110	same	13123110
17	21474180		21474180
16	30421755		30421755
15	37442160		37442160
14	40116600		40116600
13	37442160		37442160
12	30421755		30421755
11	21474180		21474180
10	13123110		13123110
9	6906900		6906900
8	3108108		3108108
7	1184040		1184040
6	376740		349618
5	98280		≈70547
4	20475		≈9852
3	3276		827
2	378		30
1	28		0

the cost of computation required to perform the topological design.

Since, there was no clear specification of the amount of traffic that the network would have to accommodate initially, it was first constructed with enough excess capacity to accommodate any reasonable traffic requirements. Then as new IMPs were added to the system, the capacity was and is still being systematically reduced until the traffic level occupies a substantial fraction of the network's total capacity. At this point, the net's capacity will be increased to maintain the desired percentage of loading. At the initial stages of network design, the "two-connected" reliability constraint essentially determined a minimum value of maximum throughput. This constraint forces the average throughput to be in the range 10-15 kilobits per second per IMP, when 50 kilobit/sec circuits are used throughout the network, since two communication paths between every pair of IMPs are needed. Alternatively, if this level of throughput is required, then the reliability specification of "two-connectivity" can be obtained without additional cost.

Reliability computations

A simple and natural characterization of network reliability is the ability of the network to sustain communication between all operable pairs of IMPs. For design purposes, the requirement of two independent paths between nodes insures that at least two IMPs and/or circuits must fail before any pair of operable IMPs cannot communicate. This criterion is independent of the properties of the IMPs and circuits, does not take into account the "degree" of disruption that may occur and hence, does not reflect the actual availability of resources in the network. A more meaningful measure is the average fraction of IMP pairs that cannot communicate because of IMP and circuit failures. This calculation requires knowledge of the IMP and circuit failure rates, and could not be performed until enough operating data was gathered to make valid predictions.

To calculate network reliability, we must consider elementary network structures known as cutsets. A

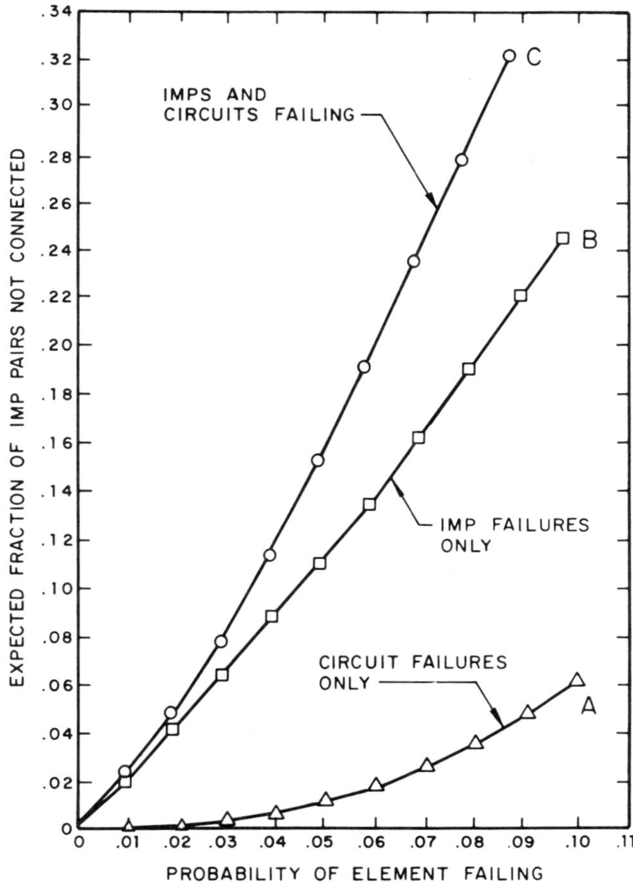

Figure 2—Network availability vs. IMP and circuit reliability

cutset is a set of circuits and/or IMPs whose removal from the network breaks all communication paths between at least two operable IMPs. To calculate reliability, it is often the case that all cutsets must be either enumerated or estimated. As an example, in a 23 IMP, 28 circuit ARPA Network design similar to the one shown in Figure 1(d), there are over twenty million ways of deleting only circuits so that the remaining network has at least one operable pair of IMPs with no intact communication paths. Table 1 indicates the numbers of cutsets in the 23 IMP network as a function of the number of circuits they contain.

A combination of analysis and simulation can be used to compute the average fraction of non-communicating IMP pairs. Detailed descriptions of the analysis methods are given in Reference 44 while their application to the analysis of the ARPANET is discussed in Reference 43. The results of an analysis of the 23 IMP version of the network are shown in Figure 2. The curve marked A shows the results under the assumption that IMPs do not fail, while the curve marked B shows the case where circuits do not fail. The curve marked C assumes that both IMPs and circuits fail with equal probability. In actual operation, the average failure probability of both IMPs and circuits is about 0.02. For this value, it can be seen that the effect of circuit failures is far less significant than the effect of IMP failures. If an IMP fails in a network with n IMPs, at least $n-1$ other IMPs cannot communicate with it. Thus, good network design cannot improve upon the effect directly due to IMP failures, which in the ARPANET is the major factor affecting the reliability of the communications. Further, more intricate reliability analyses which consider the loss of throughput capacity because of circuit failures have also been performed and these losses have been shown to be negligible.[28] Finally, unequal failure rates due to differences in line lengths have been shown to have only minor effects on the analysis and can usually be neglected.[27]

Topological optimization

During the computer optimization process, the reliability of the topology is assumed to be acceptable if the network is at least two-connected. The object of the optimization is to decrease the ratio of cost to throughput subject to an overall cost limitation. This technique employs a sophisticated network optimization program that utilizes circuit exchange heuristics, routing and flow analysis algorithms, to generate low cost designs. In addition, two time delay models were initially used to (1) calculate the throughput corresponding to an average time delay of 0.2 seconds, (2) estimate the packet rejection rate due to all buffers filling at an IMP. As experience with these models grew, the packet rejection rate was found to be negligible and the computation discontinued. The delay computation (Equation (7) in a later section) was subsequently first replaced by a heuristic calculation to speed the computation and later eliminated after it was found that time delays could be guaranteed to be acceptably low by preventing cutsets from being saturated. This "threshold" behavior is discussed further in the next section.

The basic method of optimization was described in Reference 12 while extensions to the design of large networks are discussed in Reference 9. The method operates by initially generating, either manually or by computer, a "starting network" that satisfies the overall network constraints but is not, in general, a low cost network. The computer then iteratively modifies the starting network in simple steps until a lower cost network is found that satisfies the constraints or the process is terminated. The process is repeated until no further improvements can be found. Using a different starting network can result in a different solution. However, by incorporating sensible heuristics and by using a variety of *carefully chosen* starting networks and some degree of man-machine interaction, "excellent" final networks usually result. Experience has shown that there are a wide variety of such networks with different topological structures but similar cost and performance.

The key to this design effort is the heuristic procedure by which the iterative network modifications are made. The method used in the ARPANET design involves the removal and addition of one or two circuits at a time. Many methods have been employed, at various times, to identify the appropriate circuits for potential addition or deletion. For example, to delete uneconomical circuits a straightforward procedure simply deletes single circuits in numerical order, reroutes traffic and reevaluates cost until a decrease in cost per megabit is found. At this point, the deletion is made permanent and the process begins again. A somewhat more sophisticated procedure deletes circuits in order of increasing utilization, while a more complex method attempts to evaluate the effect of the removal of any circuit before any deletion is attempted. The circuit with the greatest likelihood of an improvement is then considered for removal and so on.

There are a huge number of reasonable heuristics for circuit exchanges. After a great deal of experimentation with many of these, it appears that the choice of a particular heuristic is not critical. Instead, the speed and efficiency with which potential exchanges can be investigated appears to be the limiting factor affecting the quality of the final design. Finally, as the size of the network increases, the greater the cost becomes to perform *any* circuit exchange optimization. Decomposition of the network design into regions becomes necessary and additional heuristics are needed to determine effective decompositions. It presently appears that these methods can be used to design relatively efficient networks with a few hundred IMPs while substantially new procedures will be necessary for networks of greater size.

The topological design requires a routing algorithm to evaluate the throughput capability of any given network. Its properties must reflect those of an implementable routing algorithm, for example, within the ARPANET. Although the routing problem can be formulated as a "multicommodity flow problem"[10] and solved by linear programming for networks with 20-30 IMPs,[8] faster techniques are needed when the routing algorithm is incorporated in a design procedure. The design procedure for the ARPA Network topology iteratively analyzes thousands of networks. To satisfy the requirements for speed, an algorithm which selects the least utilized path with the minimum number of IMPs was initially used.[12] This algorithm was later replaced by one which sends as much traffic as possible along such paths until one or more circuits approach a few percent of full utilization.[28] These highly utilized circuits are then no longer allowed to carry additional flow. Instead, new paths with excess capacity and possibly more intermediate nodes are found. The procedure continues until some cutset contains only nearly fully utilized circuits. At this point no additional flow can be sent. For design purposes, this algorithm is a highly satisfactory replacement for the more complicated multi-commodity approach. Using the algorithm, it has been shown that the throughput capabilities of the ARPA Network are substantially insensitive to the distribution of traffic and depend mainly only on the total traffic flow within the network.[8]

Analytic models of network performance

The effort to determine analytic models of system performance has proceeded in two phases: (1) the prediction of average time delay encountered by a message as it passes through the network, and (2) the use of these queueing models to calculate optimum channel capacity assignments for minimum possible delay. The model used as a standard for the average message delay was first described in Reference 21 where it served to predict delays in stochastic communication networks. In Reference 22, it was modified to describe the behavior of ARPA-like computer networks while in Reference 23 it was refined further to apply directly to the ARPANET.

The single server model

Queueing theory[20] provides an effective set of analytical tools for studying packet delay. Much of this theory considers systems in which messages place demands for transmission (service) upon a single communication channel (the single server). These systems are characterized by $A(\tau)$, the distribution of interarrival times between demands and $B(t)$, the distribution of service times. When the average demand for service is less than the capacity of the channel, the system is said to be stable.

When $A(\tau)$ is exponential (i.e., Poisson arrivals), and messages are transmitted on a first-come first-served basis, the average time T in the stable system is

$$T = \frac{\lambda \overline{t^2}}{2(1-\rho)} + \bar{t} \qquad (1)$$

where λ is the average arrival rate of messages, $\bar{t}$ and $\overline{t^2}$ are the first and second moments of $B(t)$ respectively, 307
and $\rho = \lambda\bar{t} < 1$. If the service time is also exponential,

$$T = \frac{\bar{t}}{1-\rho} \qquad (2)$$

When $A(\tau)$ and $B(t)$ are arbitrary distributions, the situation becomes complex and only weak results are available. For example, no expression is available for T; however the following upper bound yields an excellent approximation[19] as $\rho \to 1$:

$$T \leq \frac{\lambda(\sigma_a^2 + \sigma_b^2)}{2(1-\rho)} + \bar{t} \qquad (3)$$

where σ_a^2 and σ_b^2 are the variance of the interarrival time and service time distributions, respectively.

Networks of queues

Multiple channels in a network environment give rise to queueing problems that are far more difficult to solve than single server systems. For example, the variability in the choice of source and destination for a message is a network phenomenon which contributes to delay. A principal analytical difficulty results from the fact that flows throughout the network are correlated. The basic approach to solving these stochastic network problems is to *decompose* them into analyzable single-server problems which reflect the original network structure and traffic flow.

Early studies of queueing networks indicated that such a decomposition was possible;[50,51] however, those results do not carry over to message switched computer networks due to the correlation of traffic flows. In Reference 21 it was shown for a wide variety of communication nets that this correlation could be removed by considering the length of a given packet to be an independent random variable as it passes from node to node. Although this "independence" assumption is not physically realistic, it results in a mathematically tractable model which does not seem to affect the accuracy of the predicted time delays. As the size and connectivity of the network increases, the assumption becomes increasingly more realistic. With this assumption, a successful decomposition which permits a channel-by-channel analysis is possible, as follows.

The packet delay is defined as the time which a packet spends in the network from its entry until it reaches its destination. The average packet delay is denoted as T. Let Z_{jk} be the average delay for those packets whose origin is IMP j and whose destination is IMP k. We assume a Poisson arrival process for such

packets with an average of γ_{jk} packets per second and an exponential distribution of packet lengths with an average of $1/\mu$ bits per packet. With these definitions, if γ is the sum of the quantities γ_{jk}, then[21]

$$T=\sum_{j,k}\frac{\gamma_{jk}}{\gamma}Z_{jk} \tag{4}$$

Let us now reformulate Equation (4) in terms of single channel delays. We first define the following quantities for the ith channel: C_i as its capacity (bits/second); λ_i as the average packet traffic it carries (packets/second); and T_i as the average time a packet spends waiting for and using the ith channel. By relating the $\{\lambda_i\}$ to the $\{\gamma_{jk}\}$ via the paths selected by the routing algorithm, it is easy to see that[21]

$$T=\sum_{i}\frac{\lambda_i}{\gamma}T_i \tag{5}$$

With the assumption of Poisson traffic and exponential service times, the quantities T_i are given by Equation (2). For an average packet length of $1/\mu$ bits, $\bar{t}=1/\mu C_i$ seconds and thus

$$T_i=\frac{1}{\mu C_i-\lambda_i} \tag{6}$$

Thus we have successfully decomposed the analysis problem into a set of simple single-channel problems.

A refinement of the decomposition permits a non-exponential packet length distribution and uses Equation (1) rather than Equation (2) to calculate T_i; as an approximation, the Markovian character of the traffic is assumed to be preserved. Furthermore, for computer networks we include the effect of propagation time and overhead traffic to obtain the following equation for average packet delay[22,23]

$$T=K+\sum_{i}\frac{\lambda_i}{\gamma}\left[\frac{1}{\mu' C_i}+\frac{\lambda_i/\mu C_i}{\mu C_i-\lambda_i}+P_i+K\right] \tag{7}$$

Here, $1/\mu'$ represents the average length of a Host packet, and $1/\mu$ represents the average length of all packets (including acknowledgments, headers, requests for next messages, parity checks, etc.) within the network. The expression $1/\mu' C_i+[(\lambda_i/\mu C_i)/(\mu C_i-\lambda_i)]+P_i$ represents the average packet delay on the ith channel. The term $(\lambda_i/\mu C_i)/(\mu C_i-\lambda_i)$ is the average time a packet spends waiting at the IMP for the ith channel to become available. Since the packet must compete with acknowledgments and other overhead traffic, the overall average packet length $1/\mu$ appears in the expression. The term $1/\mu' C_i$ is the time required to transmit a packet of average length μ'. Finally: K is the nodal processing time, assumed constant, and for the ARPA IMP approximately equal to 0.35 ms; P_i is the propagation time on the ith channel (about 20 ms for a 3000 mile channel).

Assuming a relatively homogeneous set of C_i and P_i, no individual term in the expression for delay will dominate the summation until the flow λ_i/μ in one channel (say channel i_o) approaches the capacity C_{i_o}. At that point, the term T_{i_o}, and hence T will grow rapidly. The expression for delay is then dominated by one (or more) terms and exhibits a threshold behavior. Prior to this threshold, T remains relatively constant.

The accuracy of the time delay model, as well as this threshold phenomenon was demonstrated on a 19 node network[14] and on the ten node ARPA net derived from Figure 1(c) by deleting the rightmost five IMPs. Using the routing procedure described in the last section[28] and equal traffic between all node pairs, the channel flows λ_i were found for the ten node net and the delay curves shown in Figure 3 were obtained. Curve A was obtained with fixed 1000 bit packets,* while curve B was generated for exponentially distributed variable length packets with average size of 500 bits. In both cases A and B, all overhead factors were ignored. Note that the delay remains small until a

* In case A, the application of Equation (1) allows for constant packet lengths (i.e., zero variance).

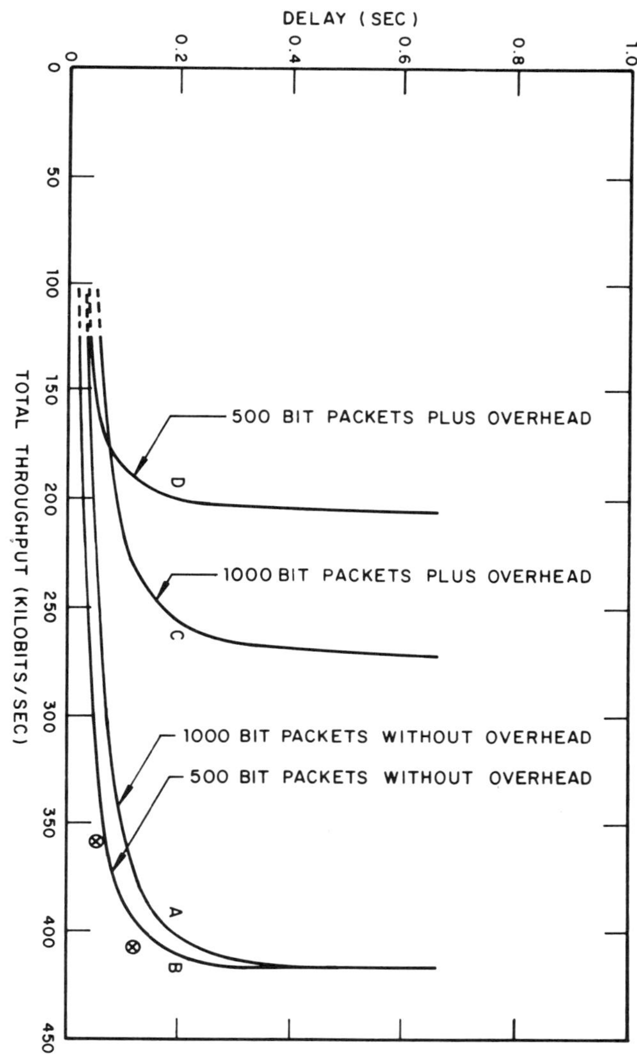

Figure 3—Delay vs. throughput

total throughput slightly greater than 400 kilobits/second is reached. The delay then increases rapidly. Curves C and D respectively represent the same situations when the overhead of 136 bits per packet and per RFNM and 152 bits per acknowledgment are included. Notice that the total throughput per IMP is reduced to 250 kilobits/second in case C and to approximately 200 kilobits/second in case D.

In the same figure, we have illustrated with x's the results of a simulation performed with a realistic routing and metering strategy. The simulation omitted all network overhead and assumed fixed lengths of 1000 bits for all packets.

It is difficult to develop a practical routing and flow control procedure that will allow each IMP to input identical amounts of traffic. To compare the delay curve A with the points obtained by simulation, the curve should actually be recomputed for the slightly skewed distribution that resulted. It is notable that the delay estimates from the simulation (which used a dynamic routing strategy) and the computation (which used a static routing strategy and the time delay formula) are in close agreement. In particular, they both accurately determined the vertical rise of the delay curve in the range just above 400 kilobits/second, the formula by predicting infinite delay and the simulation by rejecting the further input of traffic.

In practice and from the analytic and simulation studies of the ARPANET, the average queueing delay is observed to remain small (almost that of an unloaded net) and well within the design constraint of 0.2 seconds until the traffic within the network approaches the capacity of a cutset. The delay then increases rapidly. *Thus, as long as traffic is low enough and the routing adaptive enough to avoid the premature saturation of cutsets by guiding traffic along paths with excess capacity, queueing delays are not significant.*

Channel capacity optimization

309

One of the most difficult design problems is the optimal selection of capacities from a *finite* set of options. Although there are many heuristic approaches to this problem, analytic results are relatively scarce. (For the specialized case of centralized networks, an algorithm yielding optimal results is available.[11]) While it is possible to find an economical assignment of discrete capacities for, say, a 200 IMP network, very little is known about the relation between such capacity assignments, message delay, and cost.

To obtain theoretical properties of optimal capacity assignments, one may ignore the constraint that capacities are obtainable only in discrete sizes. In Reference 21 such a problem was posed where the network topology and average traffic flow were assumed to be known and fixed and an optimal match of capacities to traffic flow was found. Also, the traffic was assumed to be Markovian (Poisson arrivals and exponential packet lengths) and the independence assumption and decomposition method were applied. For each channel, the capacity C_i was found which minimized the average message delay T, at a fixed total system cost D. Since λ_i/μ is the average bit rate on the ith channel, the solution to *any* optimal assignment problem must provide more than this minimal capacity to each channel. This is clear since both Equations (6) and (7) indicate that T_i will become arbitrarily large with less than (or equal to) this amount of capacity. It is not critical exactly how the *excess* capacity is assigned, as long as $C_i > \lambda_i/\mu$. Other important parameters and insights have been identified in studying the continuous capacity optimization problem. For example, the number of excess dollars, D_e, remaining after the minimum capacity λ_i/μ is assigned to each channel is of great importance. As $D_e \rightarrow 0$, the average delay must grow arbitrarily large. In this range, the critical parameters become ρ and $\bar{n}$ where $\rho = \gamma/\mu C$ is the ratio of the rate γ/μ at which bits enter the network to the rate C at which the net can handle bits and $\bar{n} = \lambda/\gamma$, where $\lambda = \sum \lambda_i$ is the total rate at which packets flow within the net. The quantity ρ represents a dimensionless form of network "load" whereas $\bar{n}$ is easily shown to represent the average path length for a packet.

As the load ρ approaches $1/\bar{n}$, the delay T grows very quickly, and this point $\rho = 1/\bar{n}$ represents the maximum load which the network can support. If capacities are assigned optimally, all channels saturate simultaneously at this point. In this formulation $\bar{n}$ is a design parameter which depends upon the topology and the routing procedure, while ρ is a parameter which depends upon the input rate and the total capacity of the network. In studying the ARPANET[23] a closer representation of the actual tariffs for high speed telephone data
310
channels used in that network was provided by setting $D = \sum_i d_i C_i$ where $0 \leq \alpha \leq 1$.* This approach requires the solution of a non-linear equation by numerical techniques. On solving the equation, it can be shown that the packet delay T varies insignificantly with α for $.3 \leq \alpha \leq 1$. This indicates that the closed form solution discussed earlier with $\alpha = 1$ is a reasonable approximation to the more difficult non-linear problem. These continuous capacity studies have application to general network studies (e.g., satellite communications)[33] and are under continued investigation.[25,26,46]

In practice, the selection of channel capacities must be made from a small finite set. Although some theoretical work has been done in this case by approximating the discrete cost-capacity functions by continuous ones, much remains to be done.[13,25] Because of the discrete capacities and the time varying nature of network traffic, it is *not* generally possible to match channel capacities to the anticipated flows within the channels. If this were possible, all channels would saturate at the same externally applied load. Instead, capacities are assigned on the basis of reasonable estimates of average or peak traffic flows. It is the responsibility of the routing procedure to permit the traffic to adapt to the available capacity.[14] Often two IMP sites will engage in heavy communication and thus saturate one or more critical network cutsets. In such cases, the routing will not be able to send additional flow across these cuts. The network will therefore experience "premature" saturation in one or a small set of channels leading to the threshold behavior described earlier.

DISCUSSION

A major conclusion from our experience in network design is that message switched networks of the ARPA type are no longer difficult to specify. They may be implemented straightforwardly from the specifications; they can be less expensive than other currently available technical approaches; they perform remarkably well as a communication system for interconnecting time-sharing and batch processing computers and can be adapted to directly handle teletypes, displays and many other kinds of terminal devices and data processing equipment.[16,30]

The principal tools available for the design of networks are analysis, simulation, heuristic procedures, and experimentation. Analysis, simulation and heuristics have been the mainstays of the work on modeling and topological optimization while simulation, heuristic procedures and experimental techniques have been the major tools for the actual network implementation. Experience has shown that all of these methods are useful while none are all powerful. The most valuable approach has been the simultaneous use of several of these tools.

Each approach has room for considerable improvement. The analysis efforts have not yet yielded results in many important areas such as routing. However, for prediction of delay, this approach leads to a simple threshold model which is both accurate and understandable. Heuristic procedures all suffer from the problem that it is presently unclear how to select appropriate heuristics. It has been the innovative use of computers and analysis that has made the approach work well. For designing networks with no more than a few hundred IMPs, present heuristics appear adequate but a good deal of additional work is required for networks of greater size. Simulation is a well developed tool that is both expensive to apply and limited in the overall understanding that it yields. For these reasons, simulation appears to be most useful only in validating models, and in assisting in detailed design decisions such as the number of buffers that an IMP should contain. As the size of networks continues to grow, it appears that simulation will become virtually useless as a total design tool. The ultimate standard by which all models and

---

* Of course the tariffs reflect the discrete nature of available channels. The use of the exponent α provides a continuous fit to the discrete cost function. For the ARPANET, $\alpha \cong .8$.

conclusions can be tested is experimentation. Experimentation with the actual network is conceptually relatively straightforward and very useful. Although, experiments are often logistically difficult to perform, they can provide an easy means for testing models, heuristics and design parameters.

The outstanding design problems currently facing the network designer are to specify and determine the properties of the routing, flow control and topological structure for large networks. This specification must make full use of a wide variety of circuit options. Preliminary studies indicate that initially, the most fruitful approaches will be based on the partitioning of the network into regions, or equivalently, constructing a large network by connecting a number of regional networks. To send a message, a Host would specify both the destination region and the destination IMP in that region. No detailed implementation of a large network has yet been specified but early studies of their properties indicate that factors such as cost, throughput, delay and reliability are similar to those of the present ARPANET, if the ARPA technology is used.[9]

Techniques applicable to the design of large networks are presently under intensive study. These techniques appear to split into the same four categories as small network design but approaches may differ significantly. For example, large nets are likely to demand the placement of high bandwidth circuits at certain key locations in the topology to concentrate flow. These circuits will require the development of a high speed IMP to connect them into the net. It is likely that this high speed IMP will have the structure of a high speed multiplexor, and may require several cooperating processors to obtain the needed computer power for the job. Flow control strategies for large networks seem to extrapolate nicely from small network strategies if each region in the large network is viewed as a node in a smaller network. However, this area will require additional study as will the problem of specifying effective adaptive routing mechanisms. Recent efforts indicate that efficient practical schemes for small networks will soon be available. These schemes seem to be applicable for adaptive routing and flow control in networks constructed from regional subnetworks. The development of practical algorithms to handle routing and flow control is still an art rather than a science. Simulation is useful for studying the properties of a given heuristic, but intuition still plays a dominant role in the system design.

Several open questions in network design presently are: (1) what structure should a high bandwidth IMP have; (2) how can full use be made of a variety of high bandwidth circuits; (3) how should large networks be partitioned for both effective design and operation; and (4) what operational procedures should large networks follow? Much work has already been done in these areas but much more remains to be done. We expect substantial progress to be achieved in the next few years, and accordingly, the increased understanding of the properties of message switched networks of all sizes.

ACKNOWLEDGMENT

The ARPA Network is in large part the conception of Dr. L. G. Roberts of the Advanced Research Projects Agency to whom we owe a debt of gratitude for his support and encouragement. We also acknowledge the helpful contributions of S. Crocker and B. Dolan of ARPA. At BBN, NAC, and UCLA many individuals, too numerous to list, participated in the network effort and we gratefully acknowledge their contributions.

REFERENCES

1 P BARAN S BOEHM P SMITH
On distributed communications
Series of 11 reports by Rand Corporation Santa Monica California 1964

2 *"Specifications for the interconnection of a Host and an IMP*
BBN Report No 1822 1971 revision

3 S CARR S CROCKER V CERF
Host-Host communication protocol in the ARPA network
SJCC 1970 pp 589-597

4 S CROCKER et al
Function oriented protocols for the ARPA network
SJCC 1972 in this issue

5 D W DAVIES
The control of congestion in packet switching networks
Proc of the Second ACM IEEE Symposium on problems in the Optimization of Data Communications Systems Palo Alto California Oct 1971 pp 46-49

6 D FARBER K LARSON
The architecture of a distributed computer system—An informal description
University of California Irvine Information and Computer Science Technical Report #11 1970

7 W D FARMER E E NEWHALL
An experimental distribution switching system to handle bursty computer traffic
Proc of the ACM Symposium on Problems in the Optimization of Data Communication Systems 1969 pp 1-34

8 H FRANK W CHOU
Routing in computer networks
Networks John Wiley 1971 Vol 1 No 2 pp 99-112

9 H FRANK W CHOU
Cost and throughput in computer-communication networks
To appear in the Infotech Report on the State of the Art of Computer Networks 1972

10 H FRANK I T FRISCH
Communication transmission and transportation networks
Addison Wesley 1972

11 H FRANK I T FRISCH W CHOU R VAN SLYKE
Optimal design of centralized computer networks
Networks John Wiley Vol 1 No 1 pp 43-57 1971

12 H FRANK I T FRISCH W CHOU
Topological considerations in the design of the ARPA computer network
SJCC May 1970 pp 581-587

13 L FRATTA M GERLA L KLEINROCK
The flow deviation method; An approach to store-and-forward network design
To be published

14 G FULTZ L KLEINROCK
Adaptive routing techniques for store-and-forward computer-communication networks
Proc of the International Conference on communications 1971 pp 39-1 to 39-8

15 F HEART R KAHN S ORNSTEIN W CROWTHER D WALDEN
The interface message processor for the ARPA computer network
SJCC 1970 pp 551-567

16 R E KAHN
Terminal access to the ARPA computer network
Proc of Third Courant Institute Symposium Nov 1970
To be published by Prentice Hall Englewood Cliffs, NJ

17 R E KAHN W R CROWTHER
Flow control in a resource sharing computer network
Proc of the Second ACM IEEE Symposium on Problems in the Optimization of Data Communications Systems Palo Alto California October 1971 pp 108-116

18 R E KAHN W R CROWTHER
A study of the ARPA network design and performance
BBN Report No 2161 August 1971

19 J F C KINGMAN
Some inequalities for the queue GI/G/1
Biometrica 1962 pp 315-324

20 L KLEINROCK
Queueing systems; Theory and application
To be published by John Wiley 1972

21 L KLEINROCK
Communication nets: Stochastic message flow and delay
McGraw-Hill 1964

22 L KLEINROCK
Models for computer networks
Proc of the International Conference on Communications 1969 pp 21-9 to 21-16

23 L KLEINROCK
Analysis and simulation methods in computer network design
SJCC 1970 pp 569-579

24 T MARILL L G ROBERTS
Toward a cooperative network of time-shared computers
FJCC 1966

25 B MEISTER H MULLER H RUDIN JR
Optimization of a new model for message-switching networks
Proc of the International Conference on Communications 1971 pp 39-16 to 39-21

26 B MEISTER H MULLER H RUDIN
New optimization criteria for message-switching networks
IEEE Transactions on Communication Technology Com-19 June 1971 pp 256-260

27 N. A. C. Third Semiannual Technical Report for the Project Analysis and Optimization of Store-and-Forward Computer Networks
Defense Documentation Center Alexandria Va June 1971

28 N. A. C. Fourth Semiannual Technical Report for the Project Analysis and Optimication of Store-and-Forward Computer Networks
Defense Documentation Center Alexandria Va Dec 1971

29 *The Host/Host protocol for the ARPA network*
Network Working Group N I C No 7147 1971 (Available from the Network Information Center Stanford Research Institute Menlo Park California)

30 ORNSTEIN et al
The terminal IMP for the ARPA network
SJCC 1972 In this issue

31 J PIERCE
A network for block switching of data
IEEE Convention Record New York N Y March 1971

32 E PORT F CLOS
Comparisons of switched data networks on the basis of waiting times
IBM Research Report RZ 405 IBM Research Laboratories Zurich Switzerland Jan 1971 (Copies available from IBM Watson Research Center P O Box 218 Yorktown Heights New York 10598)

33 H G RAYMOND
A queueing theory approach to communication satellite network design
Proc of the International Conference on Communication pp 42-26 to 42-31 1971

34 L G ROBERTS
Multiple computer networks and inter-computer communications
ACM Symposium on Operating Systems Gatlinburg Tenn 1967

35 L G ROBERTS
A forward look
SIGNAL Vol XXV No 12 pp 77-81 August 1971

36 L G ROBERTS
Resource sharing networks
IEEE International Conference March 1969

37 L G ROBERTS
Access control and file directories in computer networks
IEEE International Convention March 1968

38 L G ROBERTS B WESSLER
Computer network development to achieve resource sharing
SJCC 1970 pp 543-549

39 L G ROBERTS B WESSLER
The ARPA computer network
In Computer Communication Networks edited by Abramson and Kuo Prentice Hall 1972

40 R A SCANTLEBURY P T WILKINSON
The design of a switching system to allow remote access to computer services by other computers
Second ACM/IEEE Symposium on Problems in the Optimization of Data Communications Systems Palo Alto California October 1971

41 R A SCANTLEBURY
A model for the local area of a data communication network—Objectives and hardware organization
ACM Symposium on Problems in the Optimization of Data Communication Systems Pine Mountain Ga 1969 pp 179-201

312

42 R H THOMAS D A HENDERSON
McRoss—A multi-computer programming system
SJCC 1972 In this issue

43 R VAN SLYKE H FRANK
Reliability of computer-communication networks
Proc of the Fifth Conference on Applications of Simulation New York December 1971

44 R VAN SLYKE H FRANK
Network reliability analysis—I
Networks Vol 1 No 3 1972

45 E WOLMAN
A fixed optimum cell size for records of various length
JACM 1965 pp 53-70

46 L KLEINROCK
Scheduling, queueing and delays in time-sharing systems and computer networks
To appear in Computer-Communication Networks edited by Abramson and Kuo Prentice Hall 1972

47 A H WEIS
Distributed network activity at IBM
IBM Research Report RC3392 June 1971

48 M BEERE N SULLIVAN
Tymnet—A serendipitous evolution
Second ACM IEEE Symposium on Problems in the Optimization of Data Communications Systems Palo Alto California 1971 pp 16-20

49 W TEITELMAN R E KAHN
A network simulation and display program
Third Princeton Conference on Information Sciences and Systems 1969 p 29

50 P BURKE
The output of a queueing system
Operations Research 1956 pp 699-704

51 J R Jackson
Networks of waiting lines
Operations Research Vol 5 1957 pp 518-521

52 D B McKAY D P KARP
Network/440—IBM Research Computer Sciences Department Computer Network
IBM Research Report RC3431 July 1971

Reprinted from —
AFIPS — Conference Proceedings
Volume 43

On measured behavior of the ARPA network*

by LEONARD KLEINROCK and WILLIAM E. NAYLOR

University of California
Los Angeles, California

INTRODUCTION

The purpose of this paper is to present and evaluate the results of recent measurements of the ARPA network. We first discuss the tools available for performing these measurements. We then describe the results of a particular experiment, which consisted of data collection over a continuous seven day period. The measured quantities included input traffic, line traffic, and message delays. This data is discussed in terms of network behavior and compared to analytic models. Lastly, we consider some implications and tradeoffs derived from these measurements which provide insight regarding the performance of computer networks.

The ARPANET is now more than four years old.[1-8] However, the network did not become generally useable until the middle of 1971 when the HOST-to-HOST protocol[5] was finally implemented at most of the sites connected to the network at that time. Currently, the network consists of approximately 40 switching computers (the IMPs and TIPs) and approximately 50 HOST machines attached to these switching computers as shown in Figure 1 (this map corresponds to the network configuration as of 1 August 1973; we use this particular map since it gives the network topology which existed at the initiation of our experiment; a 39th site had just been installed in the network by BBN for test purposes and thus does not appear in Figure 1). We notice that the ARPANET spans the United States, crossing over to Hawaii by means of a 50 KBPS (kilobit per second) satellite channel and extends to Europe by means of a trans-Atlantic 7.2 KBPS satellite channel. From October of 1971, the traffic and use of the network has been growing exponentially at a phenomenal rate, slowing down a bit toward the end of 1973; this traffic growth is shown in Figure 2 on a log-linear scale.[14] In this paper we examine the details of that traffic flow.

The ARPANET began as an *experimental* network and has since grown into a powerful tool for resource sharing. The essence of an experiment is measurement, and it is this aspect of the ARPANET which we wish to discuss herein. Can we, in fact, determine what is going on within the network? The answer is an emphatic yes, if we restrict ourselves to the behavior of the communication subnetwork which provides the message service for the user-HOST systems. Early on, during the days when the ARPANET was still a concept rather than a reality, we were careful to include in every specification of the network design the ability to monitor network behavior with the use of specific measurement tools. This paper deals with a description of those tools and how they have been used in a particular experiment designed to elucidate the behavior of traffic in the ARPANET.

Among the various centers in the network are two which are deeply concerned with measurements; the Network Control Center (NCC), at Bolt, Beranek and Newman, Inc. (BBN), and the Network Measurement Center (NMC) at the University of California, Los Angeles (UCLA). The experiment we describe below was designed, conducted and interpreted by the UCLA-NMC research staff.

At this point, it is perhaps helpful to review a few of the network parameters which affect traffic flow in the ARPANET.[9] All traffic entering the network is segmented into messages whose maximum length is 8063 bits. These, in turn, are partitioned into smaller pieces called packets which are at most 1008 bits long (a maximum length message, therefore, will be partitioned into eight packets, the last of which has a maximum length of 1007 bits). As messages enter the network from the HOSTs they carry with them a 32 bit "leader" which contains the addressing information necessary for delivery to the destination. Incoming messages also carry a small number of "padding" bits for word boundary adjustment between the IMP word size of 16 bits and various HOST word sizes. Packets are transmitted through the network with some addressing and control information which adds 168 bits to their transmitted length, while the packet overhead for storage within an IMP is 176 bits. The packets make their way through the network individually and are passed from IMP to IMP according to an adaptive routing procedure; in each IMP-to-IMP transmission an acknowledgment is returned if the packet was accepted; when possible, these acknowledgments are piggybacked on return traffic. The packets of a multipacket message are reassembled at the

* This research was supported by the Advanced Research Projects Agency of the Department of Defense under Contract No. DAHC-15-73-C-0368.

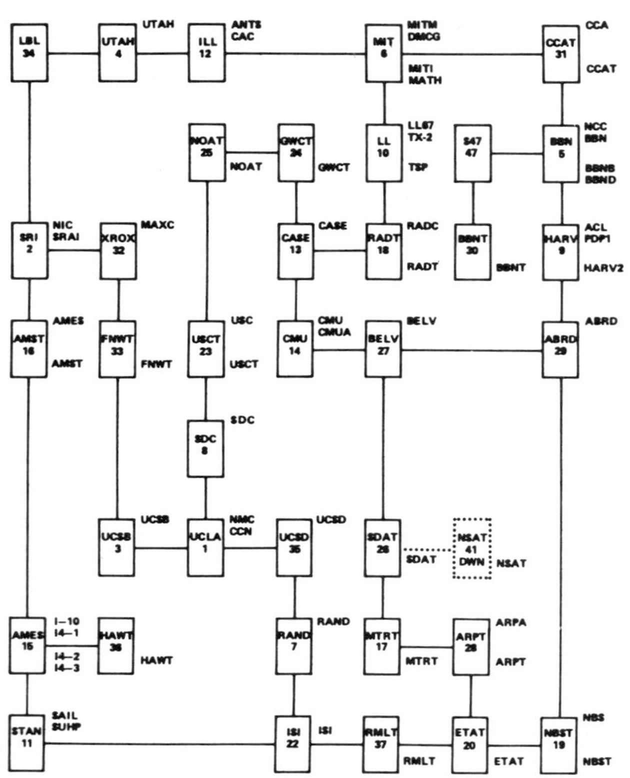

316

Figure 1—Logical map of the ARPANET (August 1, 1973 0834 PDT)

destination IMP before they are delivered to the destination HOST. When a message proceeds in its transmission to the destination HOST, a special control message (known as a Request For Next Message—RFNM) which acts as an end-to-end acknowledgment is returned from the destination IMP to the source HOST. The IMP itself buffers packets as they pass through the network and has the ability to store approximately 77 packets at most. Except for the channel connecting AMES to AMST (which is 230.4 KBPS) and the Atlantic satellite link (which is 7.2 KBPS) all lines in the network are 50 KBPS, full-duplex channels (as of August 1973).

In the following section, we describe the network measurement tools. Following that, we give details of a recently performed experiment and present its results in graphic form. We also include a section in which a mathematical model for delay is developed and the results of that model prediction are compared with measured network delays.

MEASUREMENT TOOLS

In this section, we describe the means by which this and other measurements are performed. In order to evaluate the performance of the network, several measurement tools (as originally specified by the UCLA-NMC) were implemented as part of the first IMP program (and have been slightly modified throughout the developmental stages of th ARPANET). These tools, which execute in each IMP' "background" mode, may be used selectively at the variou network nodes under program control. Upon request, the collect data regarding their node, summarize these data i special measurement messages, and then send these message to a collection HOST (normally UCLA-NMC). We have therefore, developed at UCLA-NMC the capability for con trol, collection, and analysis of the data messages. Below, w describe these network measurement tools.

Trace

Trace is a mechanism whereby messages may be "traced" as they pass through a sequence of IMPS. Those IMPs whos trace parameter has been set will generate one trace bloc for each marked packet (i.e., a packet with its trace bit set which passes through that particular IMP. (An "auto-trace" facility exists by which every *n*th message entering the net work at any node may be marked for tracing.) A trace bloc contains four time stamps which occur when: (1) the las bit of the packet arrives; (2) the packet is put on a queue (3) the packet starts transmission; and (4) the acknowledg ment is received (for store and forward packets sent to a neighboring IMP), or transmission is completed (for re assembly packets sent to a HOST). (Time (1) correspond to the time at which storage is actually allocated to the packe

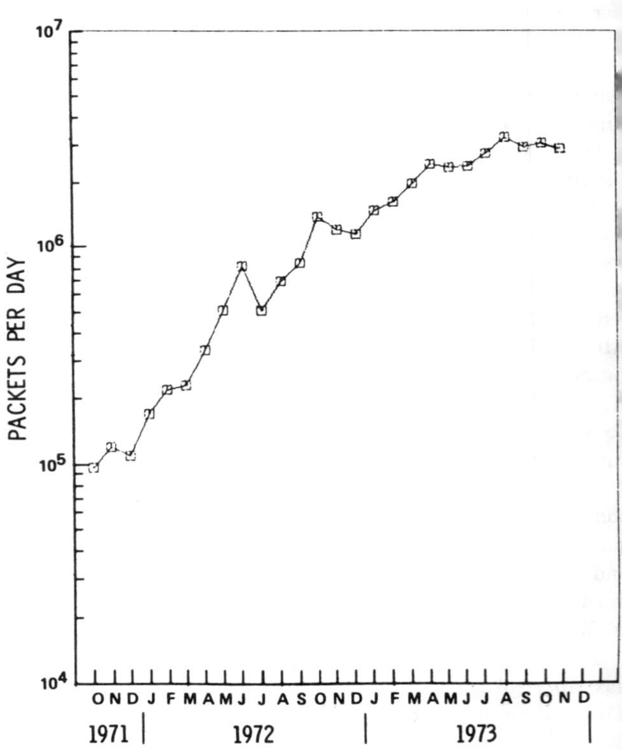

Figure 2—Long term traffic growth

rather than to the input source. Time (4) corresponds to the time at which the storage for the packet is returned to the free pool after successful transmission.) Also contained in the trace block are the length of the packet, an address indicating where the packet was sent, and the IMP header (which consists of the source and destination addresses and several other pieces of control information).

Accumulated statistics

The accumulated statistics message consists of several tables of data summarizing activity at a network node over an interval of time (ranging from 25.6 msec to some 14 minutes) which is under program control. Included in the accumulated statistics is a summary of the sizes of messages entering and exiting the network at the set of real (as opposed to fake, i.e. IMP-simulated) HOSTs connected to that IMP. The message size statistics include a histogram of message lengths (in packets) for multipacket messages and a log (base 2) histogram of packet lengths (in words) for all last packets (i.e., a count is recorded of those packets whose length, in data bits, is from 0 to 1, 2 to 3, 4 to 7, 8 to 15, 16 to 31, or 32 to 63 IMP words in length). Also included is the total number of IMP words in all the last packets, and the total number of messages from each HOST (real and fake), and the total number of control messages (RFNM, etc.) to each HOST.

A row of the global traffic matrix is contained in each IMP's round-trip statistics. These contain the number of round-trips (message sent and RFNM returned) sent from the probed site to each site, and the total time recorded for those round-trips. These statistics are listed for each possible destination from the probed site.

For those channels connected to the probed site, we have the channel statistics. These consist of: (1) the number of hellos sent per channel (channel test signals); (2) the number of data words sent per channel; (3) the number of inputs received per channel (all inputs: data packets, control packets, acknowledgments, etc.); (4) the number of errors detected per channel; (5) the number of "I-heard-you" packets received per channel (response to hello); (6) the number of times the free buffer list was empty per channel; and (7) log (2) histograms of packet length, in data words (one histogram per channel).

Snapshots

Snapshots give an instantaneous peek at an IMP. The snapshot records several queue lengths as well as the IMP's routing table. The HOST (real or fake) queue (normal and priority) lengths appear in each snapshot message. Also included is information about storage allocation: the length of the free storage list, the number of buffers in use for reassembly of messages, and the number of buffers allocated to reassembly (but not yet in use). Snapshots also include the IMP routing table and delay table. Entry i in the routing table contains the channel address indicating where to send a packet destined for site i. A delay table entry consists of the minimum number of hops to a site, and the delay estimate to reach a site.

Artificial message generation

In addition to the above instrumentation package built into each IMP, we have the capability to generate artificial messages. This message generator in any IMP can send fixed length messages to one destination at a fixed or RFNM driven interdeparture time. Together with the generation facility there exists a discard capability in each IMP. Several message generator/acceptor pairs have been implemented for a subset of the HOSTs on the network as well. These are extremely useful for experimentation, but we will not attempt to discuss them in this paper.

Control, collection, and analysis

The above-mentioned measurement and message generation facilities are controlled by sending messages to the "parameter change" background program in the IMPs. We have constructed a set of programs which, after an experiment is specified, automatically format and send the correct parameter change messages to initiate that experiment. In order to be able to send these messages, it was necessary to modify the system code in the NCP to bypass the normal HOST-to-HOST protocol.[5] The bypass was then used as the means of collecting the measurement messages as well, since these too do not adhere to HOST-to-HOST protocol. After a message is received over this mechanism, it is stored in the file system at UCLA-NMC. Reduction and analysis of the data is accomplished by supplying specific subroutines for a general driver program; the data analysis is currently done on the UCLA 360/91.

Status reports

In addition to the above tools, which are mainly for experimental use, the NCC has built into the IMPs a monitoring function called "status reports."[10] Each IMP sends a status report to the NCC HOST once a minute. Contained in the status report are the following: (1) The up/down status of the real HOSTs and channels; (2) for each channel, a count of the number of hello messages which failed to arrive (during the last minute); (3) for each channel, a count of the number of packets (transmitted in the last minute) for which acknowledgments were received; and (4) a count of the number of packets entering the IMP from each real HOST. These status reports are continually received at the NCC and are processed by a minicomputer which advises the operator of failures in the network and creates summary statistics.

Let us now address ourselves to the experiment itself.

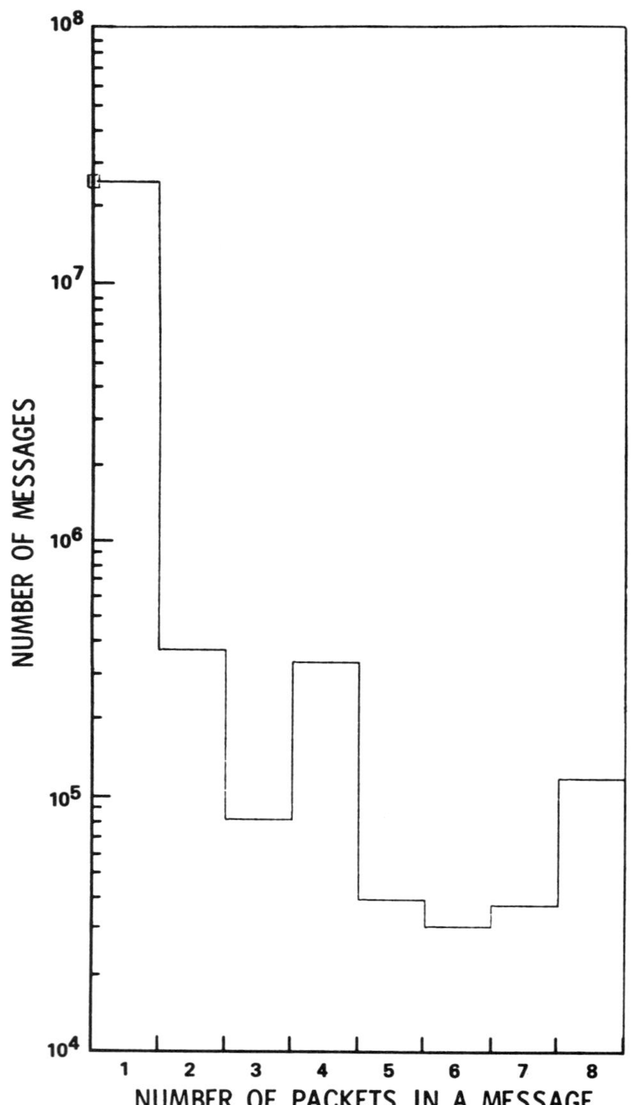

Figure 3—Histogram of HOST message length in packets

THE EXPERIMENT DESCRIPTION AND RESULTS

Experiment description

The purpose of this experiment was to observe the traffic characteristics of the operating network. These characteristics include: (1) message and packet size distributions; (2) mean round-trip delay; (3) mean traffic-weighted path length; (4) incest (the flow of traffic to and from HOSTs at the same local site); (5) most popular sites and channels; (6) favoritism (that property which a site demonstrates by sending many of its messages to one or a small number of sites); and (7) channel utilization. We consider this data to have more than just historical significance. In particular, there are several network parameters whose values were chosen prior to the actual network implementation and which deserve to be reevaluated as a result of the measurements reported here. Among these parameters are: packet (and therefore buffer) size, number of buffers, channel capacity, single/multiple packet message philosophy, etc.

To observe the traffic characteristics, we gathered data over a continuous seven-day period from 8:36 on 1 August 1973 through 17:06 on 7 August 1973. The network configuration during this period is shown in Figure 1. (A teletype-compatible network map containing similar information may be generated from an updatable NMC survey of the network.) The experiment consisted of sending accumulated statistics messages to UCLA-NMC from each site in the network at intervals of approximately seven minutes. The

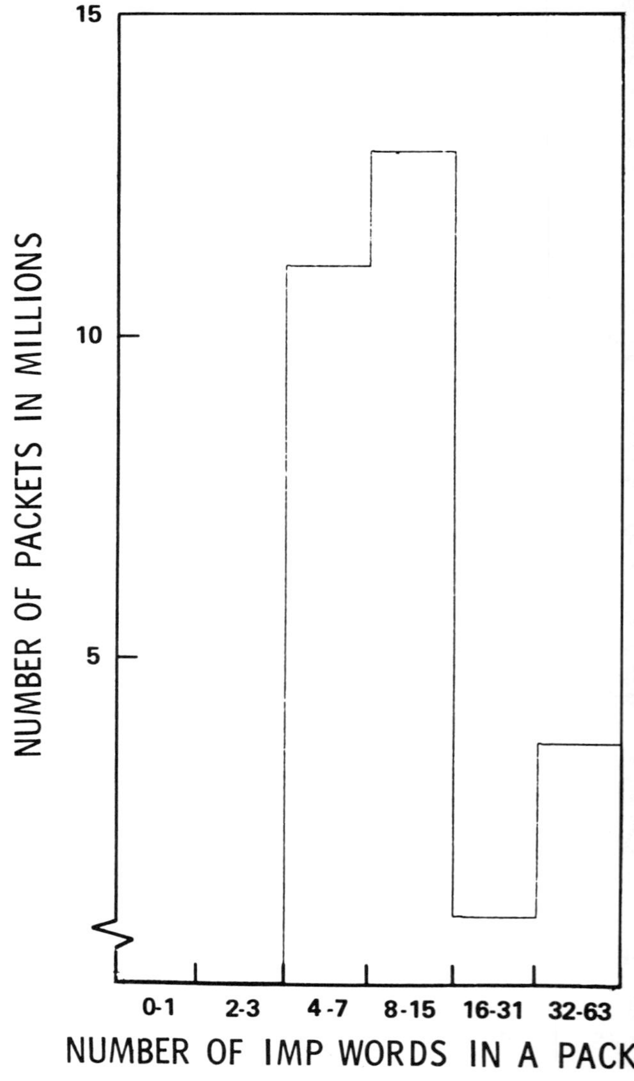

Figure 4—Histogram of packet length in words

data were subsequently processed, and the general results appear below.

Measured results

During the seven days a total of some 6.3 billion bits were carried through the network by some 26 million messages. This means that on the average the entire network was accepting some 47 messages per second and carrying roughly 11500 bits per second among HOST computers. The HOST messages were distributed in length as shown in Figure 3, and from these data, we observe a mean of 1.12 packets per message! Moreover, the mean length of a message is 243 bits of data! These facts indicate not only are there very few multipacket messages, but also that most single packet messages are quite short. This latter fact is borne out in the log (2) histogram of packet length for packets entering the network from the HOSTs as shown in Figure 4; the mean packet length is 218 bits of data.

The small message size has an impact on the efficiency of storage utilization. This may be seen by defining the buffer utilization efficiency as follows:

$$\eta = \frac{\bar{l}_p}{L+H}$$

where

$\bar{l}_p$ = the mean packet length,
L = the maximum length of data in a packet, and
H = the length of the packet storage overhead.

Using the measured value of $\bar{l}_p = 218$ bits, and the constants $L = 1008$ bits and $H = 176$ bits, we have a measured buffer utilization efficiency of .184!

There exists a buffer length which yields an optimal buffer efficiency for a given message length distribution, as shown by Cole;[11] this calculation assumes an exponential message length distribution (which we shall adopt). In the packeting of messages into L bit pieces we have truncated the exponential message length distribution at the point L, thus giving a mean packet size of

$$\bar{l}_p = \bar{l}[1 - e^{-L/\bar{l}}] \qquad (1)$$

where $\bar{l}$ = the mean message size (exponential). This gives $\bar{l}_p = 239$ bits when the value of $\bar{l} = 243$* is used in Eq. (1) and which in turn yields an efficiency of .202. (The fact that $\bar{l}_p = 239$ is greater than the measured $\bar{l}_p$ means that the actual distribution weights shorter messages more heavily than the exponential distribution.) Since $\bar{l}_p$ is significantly less than L, the truncation at L does not cause a large accumulation of packets whose length is L bits; we see this from the moderate number (12.9 percent) of maximum length packets in Figure 4.

The optimal value for buffer size L_0 is obtained by solving the following equation:

$$e^{-L_0/\bar{l}}[L_0 + H] - \bar{l}[1 - e^{-L_0/\bar{l}}] = 0$$

Using $\bar{l} = 243$, and $H = 176$ we obtain the optimal buffer size of $L_0 = 244$ bits which yields a maximum efficiency of .366 for this overhead. Thus, based upon this particular week's measured data, (which is supported by previous and later measurements), we find that the maximum efficiency can be increased significantly by reducing the packet buffer size to roughly one-quarter of its current size.

The measured mean round-trip* message delay for the seven-day period was approximately 93 milliseconds. Indeed, the network is meeting its design goal of less than 200 milliseconds for single packet messages. Thus, as desired, the communication subnet is essentially transparent to the user, so far as delay is concerned. The principal source of delay seen during a user interaction comes both from his local HOST and from the destination HOST on which he is being served. Major contributors to the small network message delay are the small message size and the fact that a significant number of messages traverse very short paths in network.

We shall return to a discussion of delay in the next section. For now, let us study the traffic distribution and the source of short paths, incest, favoritism, etc. From Reference 12 we know that the mean path length (in hops—i.e., number of channels traversed) may be calculated by forming the ratio of the total channel traffic to the externally applied traffic. This gives a value of 3.31 hops. Moreover, we may form a lower bound on the average path length by assuming all traffic flows along shortest paths; this gives a value of 3.24 hops, showing that indeed most of the traffic follows shortest paths. The (uniformly weighted) path length (average distance) between node-pairs is 5.32 as can be calculated directly from the topology shown in Figure 1. The difference between these measures of path length suggests that network users tend to communicate with sites which are nearby. This is surprising since distance in the network should be invisible to the users! This phenomenon may be explained by examining how much traffic travels over paths of a given length (in hops) as shown in Figure 5. Observe that a surprisingly large fraction (22 percent) of the traffic travels a distance of zero hops and is due to (incestuous) traffic between two HOSTs connected to the same IMP; after all, the IMP is a very convenient interface between local machines as well. Also note that 16 percent of the network traffic travels a hop distance of one; the major portion of this (13 percent of the total) is due to communication between AMST and AMES (this too is incestuous in spirit). This curve fails to account for the number of site-pairs at a given distance. For the topology

* A truncation effect occurs before messages enter the ARPA network as well. Hence the measured mean message length is actually the mean taken from the actual distribution truncated at 8063 bits (8 packets). Assuming that messages are exponentially distributed we may solve an equation similar to Eq. (1) to obtain the untruncated mean message length; this computation yields 243 bits, the same as the truncated mean message length.

* Round-trip delay is measured by the IMPS and is the time from when a message enters the network until the network's end-to-end acknowledgment in the form of a RFNM is returned.

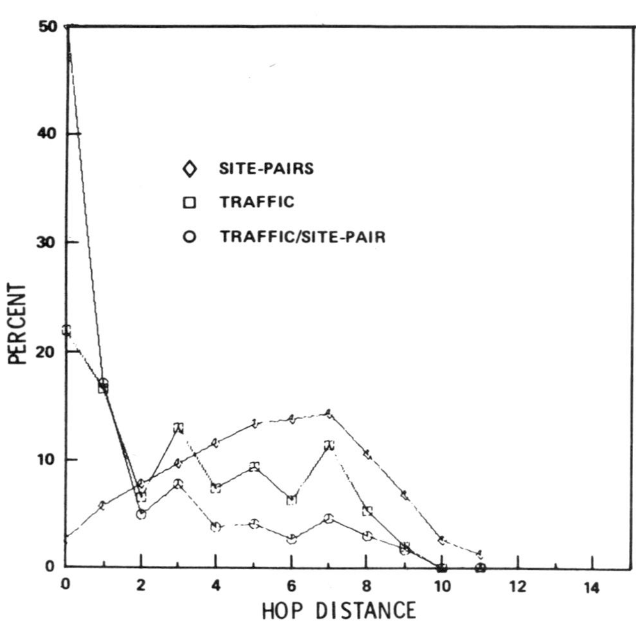

Figure 5—Distance dependence of traffic

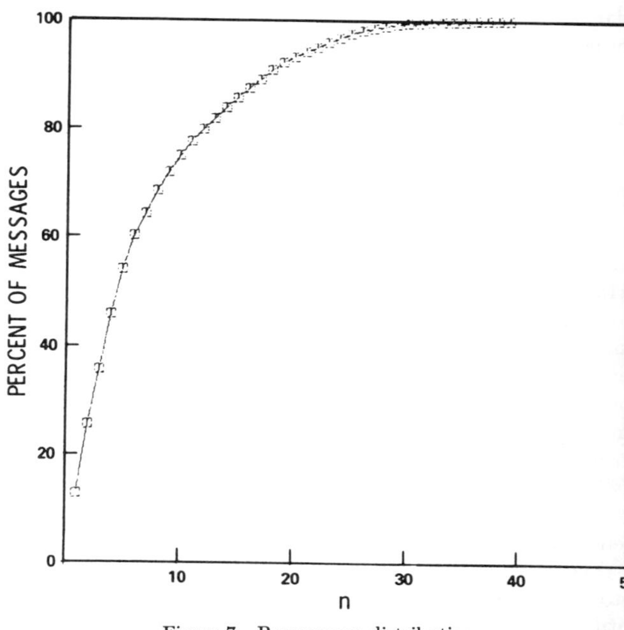

Figure 7—Busy source distribution

existing during this experiment, it can be seen that the following list of ordered pairs (x, y) provides the distribution of site-pair minimum distances (where x=hop distance and y=number* of site-pairs at this distance): (0,39), (1,86), (2,118), (3,148), (4,176), (5,204), (6,210), (7,218), (8,160), (9,102), (10,40), and (11,20). No sites are more than 11 hops apart. This data is also plotted in Figure 5. Note that more sites are at a distance of 7 than any other distance (with the average distance equal to 5.32 as mentioned above). (In a network with N nodes and M full-duplex channels, the first two entries on the list must always be $(0, N)$, $(1, 2M)$.) With this information, we may "correct" our curve by plotting the ratio of the number of messages sent between site-pairs at a given distance to the number of site-pairs at that given distance; see Figure 5 again. The ratios are normalized to sum to one. If the traffic were uniformly distributed in the network, then the resulting curve would be a horizontal line at the value 8.3 percent. We note that an even larger fraction

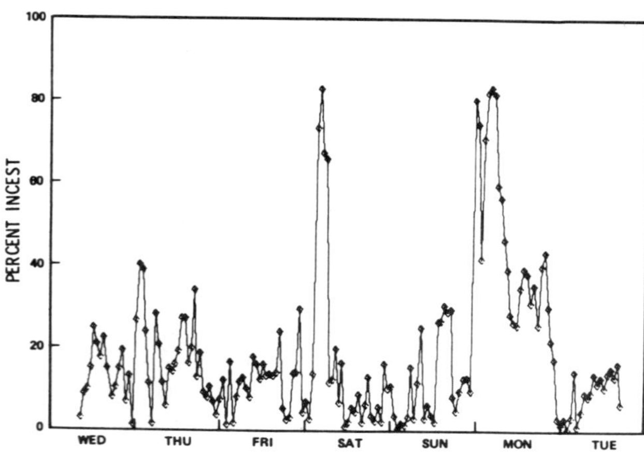

Figure 6—Incest

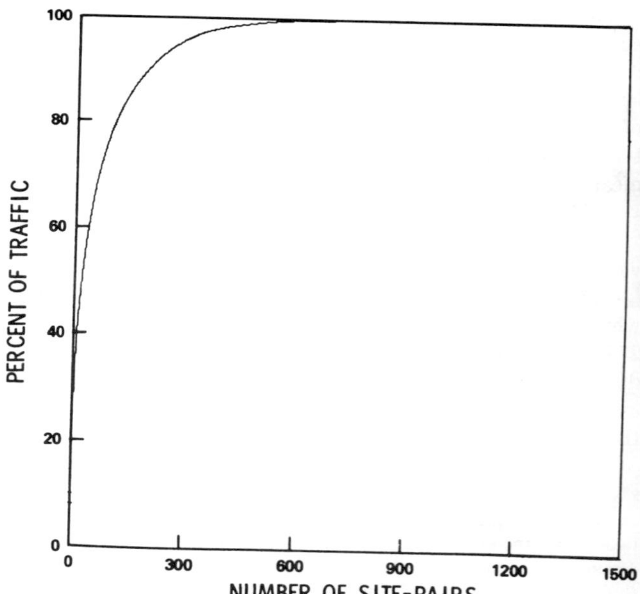

Figure 8—Busy site-pair distribution

* We consider site pairs as ordered pairs; thus, the pair (MIT, UCLA) is distinct from (UCLA, MIT). This is natural since the traffic flow is not necessarily symmetrical. The (important) special case of (SITE i, SITE i) counts as one "pair".

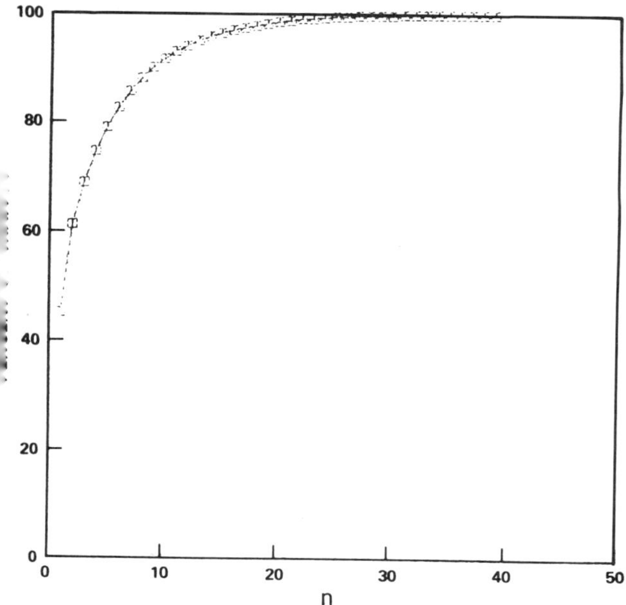

Figure 9—Distribution of traffic to favorite destinations

f the traffic is now identified with distance zero. At distances ?, 3, . . ., 9, we now see a better uniformity than earlier. The ast effect which contributes to the remaining non-uniformity s the location of the large traffic users (e.g., ILL) and large ervers (e.g., ISI). In Figure 6, we display the percent of in-est in the network during each hour* of the experiment. Note that incest accounts for over 80 percent of the traffic luring certain hours (the weekly average is 22 percent), eaking in the wee hours of the morning.

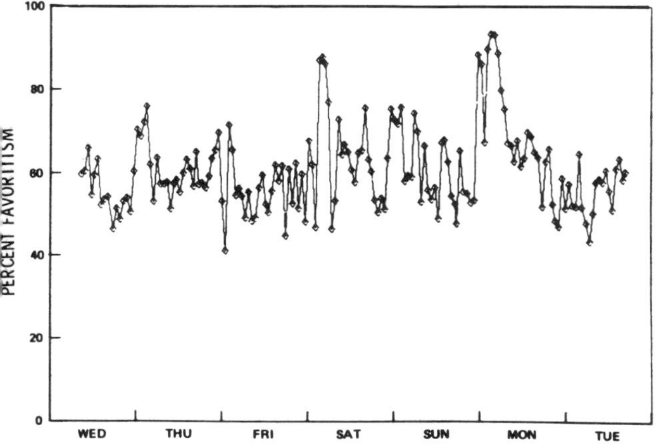

Figure 10—Percent of traffic to most favored destinations

* This, and the other "hourly" plots show points separated by approximately 56 minutes (an integral multiple of the accumulated statistics interval of roughly 7 minutes). The separation between the days on the horizontal axes occurs at midnight.

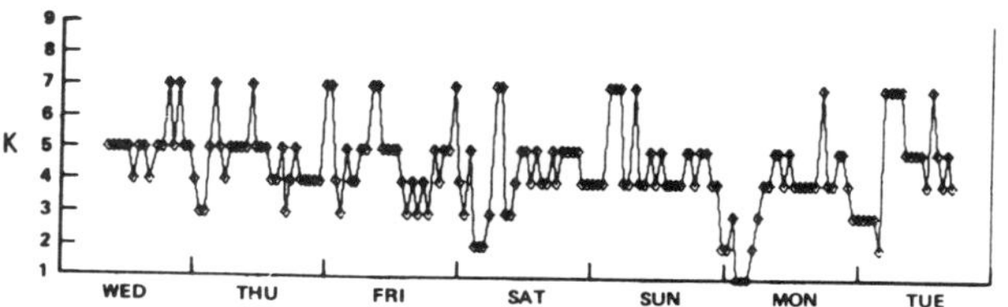

Figure 11—Number of favored destinations required to achieve 90 percent traffic

A further illustration of the non-uniformity of the traffic is seen in Figure 7. Here, we have plotted the cumulative percent of messages sent from the n busiest sources. Notice that over 80 percent of the traffic is generated by the busiest one third of the sites. A similar effect is true for the busiest (most popular) destinations. Even more striking is Figure 8, in which we have plotted the cumulative percent of traffic between site-pairs. Notice that 90 percent of the total traffic is between 192 (12.6 percent) of the site-pairs.

The interesting property of favoritism is shown in Figure 9. For each source, the destinations may be ordered by the frequency of messages to those destinations. In Figure 9, we show (summed over all sources) the percent of traffic to a source's n most favored destinations. If these orderings and percentages remained invariant over time (i.e., a stationary traffic matrix), then one could use this information in the topological design; however, it can be shown[4,13] that both the network design and performance are relatively insensitive to changes in the traffic matrix (and so, a uniform requirement is usually assumed). Note that 44 percent of the network traffic goes to the most favored sites! (A uniform traffic matrix would give a percentage of only $1/N=2.56$ percent). Also,

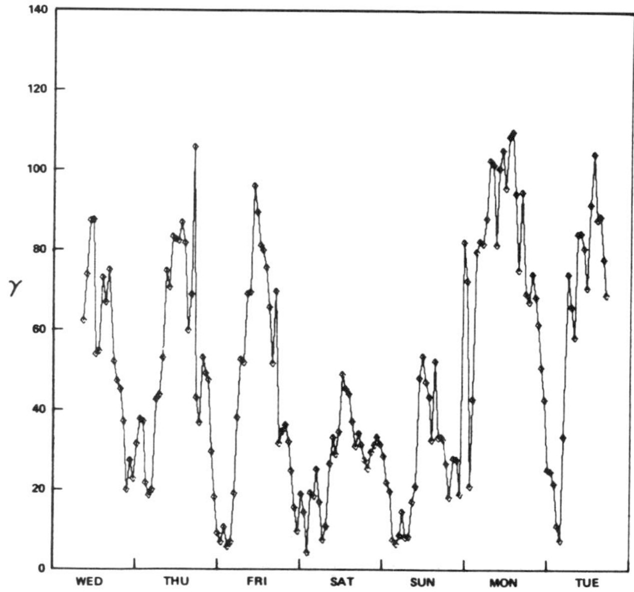

Figure 12—Arrival rate of HOST messages per second (γ)

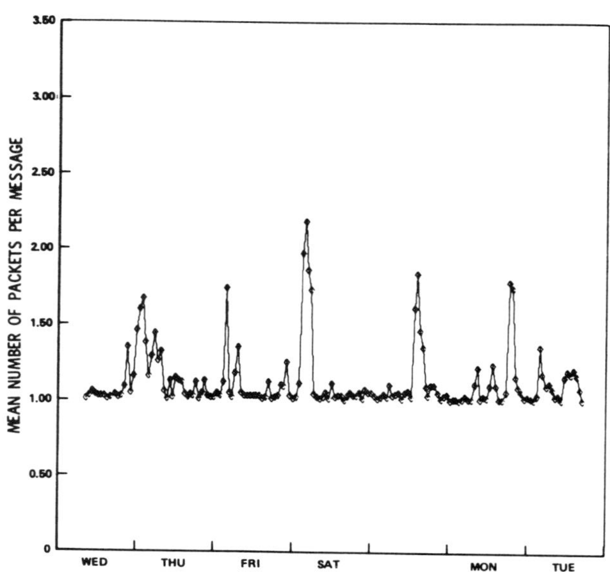

Figure 13—Mean number of packets per message

90 percent of the traffic goes to the nine most favorite sites; however, it is important to realize that this involves more than nine sites (in fact, 33 unique destinations are involved), since each source need not have the same set of nine most favorites. This favorite site effect is more dramatically displayed in Figure 10, which shows the percent of traffic to the most favored destination of all sources on an hourly basis. Most of the traffic (a minimum of 40 percent and an average of 61 percent) was caused by conversations between the N sources and their favorites. There are N^2 pairs in total; thus,

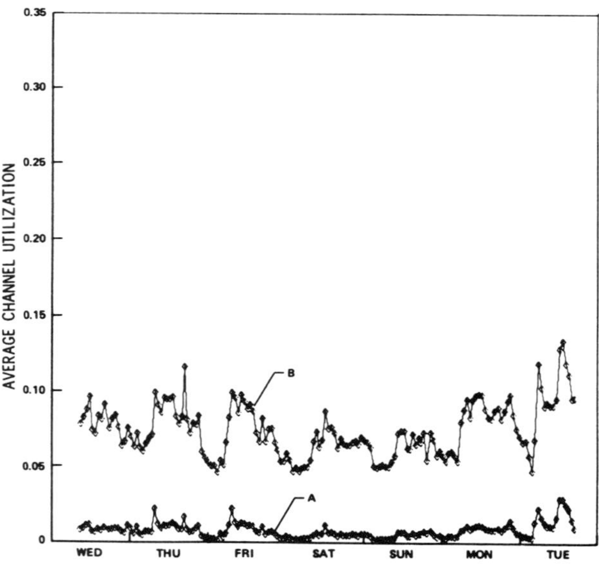

Figure 14—Network-wide mean channel utilization: (A) without overhead; (B) with overhead

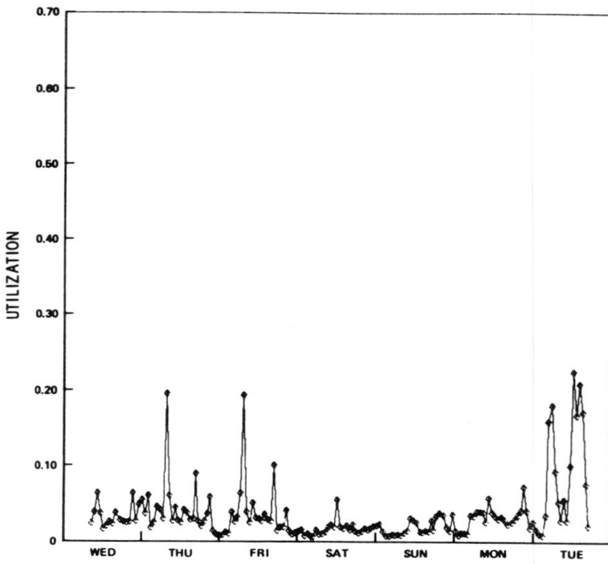

Figure 15A—Utilization of most heavily used channel in each hou
(without overhead)

on a weekly basis, the N favorites account for $.44N$ time the traffic they would have generated if the traffix matrix ha been uniform (on an hourly basis it is $.61N$). Note that th favorite site effect must increase as we shrink the time interval over which "favorite" is defined;* in fact, if we choose a interval comparable to a message transmission time, then th

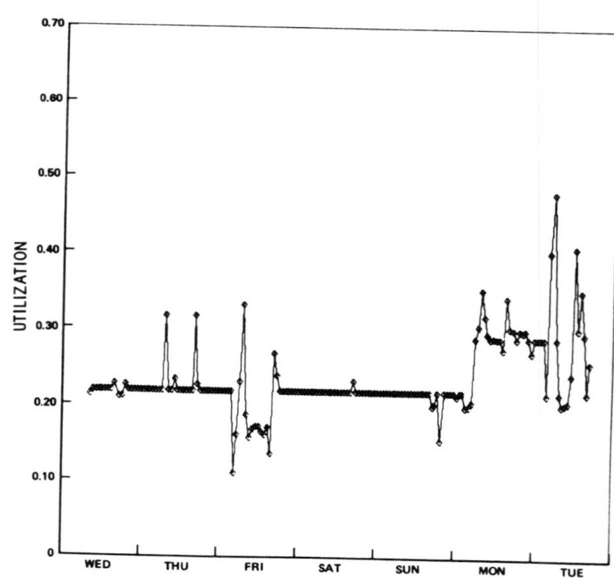

Figure 15B—Utilization of the most heavily used channel in each hour
(with overhead)

---

* We are pleased to acknowledge the assistance of Stanley Lieberson in explaining this effect.

most favorite sites will account for almost 100 percent of the traffic, since the name of each source's favorite site will change dynamically to equal the name of the destination site for this source's traffic of the moment. Thus, the amount of traffic due to favorite sites has an interpretation which changes as the time interval changes. The weekly value of 44 percent has two possible interpretations. The first is that there exists a true phenomenon of favoritism due, perhaps, to the existence of a few useful "server" systems. The second interpretation is that network users are lazy; once a user becomes familiar with some destination HOST, he continues to favor (and possibly encourages others to favor) that HOST in the future rather than experimenting with other systems, too. A further explanation for this phenomen is that it is not especially easy to use a foreign HOST at this stage of network development; this trend should diminish as network use becomes more user oriented.

Related to Figure 10 is Figure 11 in which we have plotted the number, K, of favored destinations necessary to sum to 90 percent of the overall traffic on an hourly basis. This means that in any hour, 90 percent of the messages were sent between at most NK of the total $N^2 = 1521$ pairs in the network. Notice that K has a maximum hourly value of 7 (this is less than the weekly average of $K = 9$ due to the smaller averaging interval as discussed above). Therefore, for any hour, it requires at most 18 percent of the site-pairs to send 90 percent of the messages (in the most extreme case, $K = 1$ and so for those hours at most $1/N$ or 2.56 percent of the site-pairs sent 90 percent of the messages).

Let us now discuss other global measures of the network behavior. In Figure 12, we show the average rate at which HOST messages were generated (per second) on an hourly basis; this gives us an indication as to when the work was

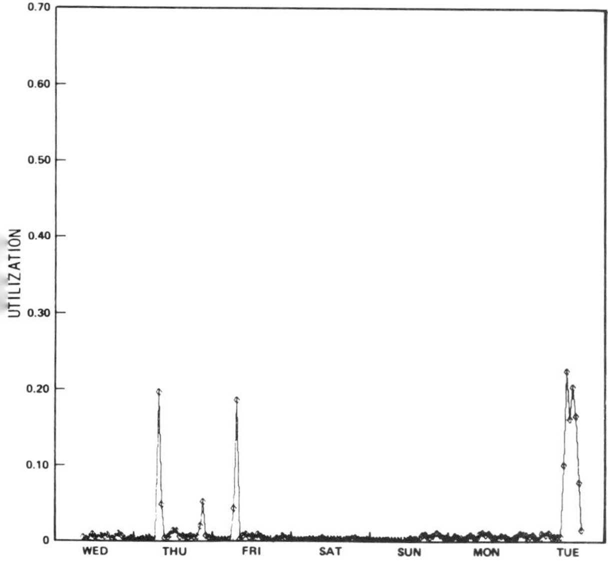

Figure 16A—Utilization of the channel (GWCT to CASE) with the highest hourly average (without overhead)

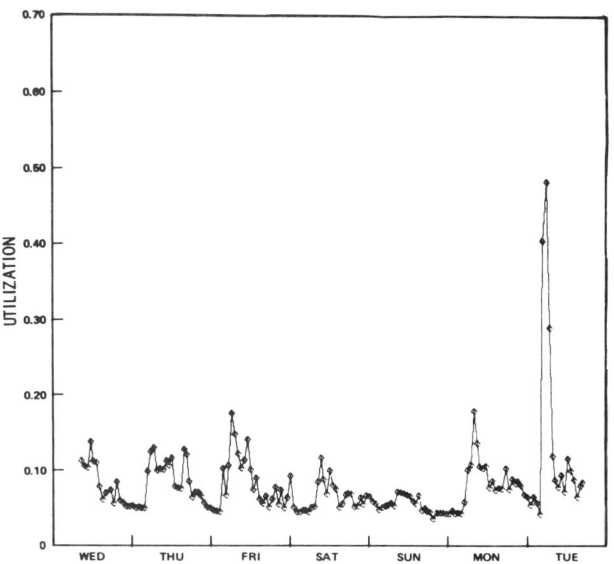

Figure 16B—Utilization of the channel (HARV to ARBD) with the highest hourly average (with overhead)

done on the network. There are no real surprises here: the curve shows a predominance of traffic during daylight hours and on weekdays. It is interesting that Monday had noticeably heavier traffic than the other weekdays (were the users manifesting feelings of guilt or anxiety for having slowed down during the weekend?). Observe that a truly worldwide network with its time zones could perhaps take advantage of these hourly and daily slow periods.

Figure 13 illustrates the change in network use as a function of time by showing the time behavior of the mean number of packets per message. The peaks are associated with those hours during which file transfers dominated the interactive traffic. These peaks in general occur during off-shift hours (as with incest). Perhaps users feel that they get better data rates, reliability, or HOST service late at night; or, perhaps the background of file transfers is continually present, but is noticed only when the interactive users are alseep.

The internal traffic on channels is one measure of the effectiveness of the network design and use. In Figure 14, we show the channel utilization averaged over the entire network on an hourly basis, both with and without overhead. The utilization (whose weekly average was .071 if overhead is included or .0077 neglecting overhead) is rather low and suggests that the lines in the network have a great deal of excess capacity on the average (this excess capacity is desirable for peak loads). The maximum hourly line load (including overhead, and averaged over all channels) was approximately 13.4 percent (occurring five hours before the end of the measurement) and corresponded to an internal network flow of roughly 600 KBPS; without overhead the maximum hourly average utilization was approximately 2.9 percent (129 KBPS internal traffic). It is interesting to obesrve the *heaviest loaded line* during each hour; this we plot in Figure 15

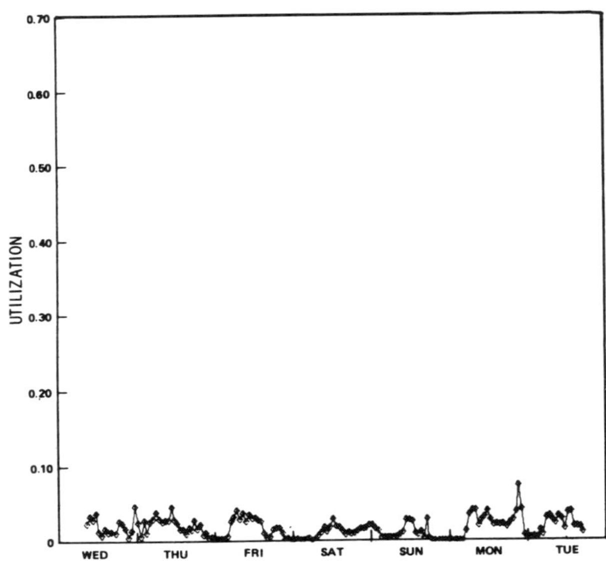

Figure 17A—Utilization of the channel (ISI to RMLT) with the highest weekly average (without overhead)

both without (part A) and with (part B) overhead. Note from part B that the *busiest line of any hour* (HARV to ABRD) had a utilization of 0.48 for that hour; without overhead the busiest line (GWCT to CASE) had a utilization of 0.225 for its busiest hour. Over the seven days, these channels had hourly load histories as shown in Figure 16. Note how bursty the traffic was on these lines (even averaged over an hour). Another interesting line is that one which had the maximum load averaged over the week. Neglecting routing

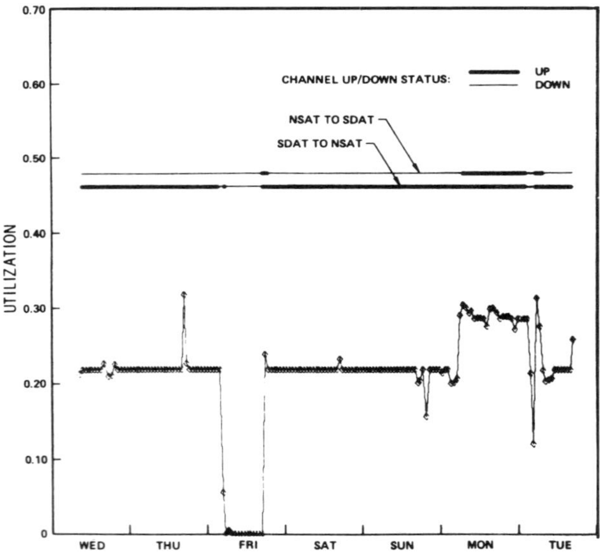

Figure 17B—Utilization of the channel (SDAT to NSAT) with the highest weekly average (with overhead)

updates and all other overhead the channel from ISI to RMLT had the largest weekly load (0.017), and its hourly behavior is shown in Figure 17A; again we see bursty behavior. If we include overhead then the satellite channel to Norway (SDAT to NSAT) had the *largest utilization averaged over the week* since it is only a 7.2 KBPS channel and therefore, all traffic placed almost seven (50/7.2) times the load on it (in this case, roughly 2KBPS, or 28 percent of the line, is used for routing updates alone). The hourly history for this channel is shown in Figure 17B. Also on this figure we have shown the UP/DOWN status of this line (in both directions).* Note that the channel was operational in both directions for a small fraction of the measurement (mainly on Monday) and only during this time was it carrying its own routing updates as well as responses to the NSAT to SDAT channel's routing updates in the form of "I heard you's"; this gives the 28 percent overhead mentioned above. This channel was down for a large part of Friday during which time it carried no traffic. For the rest (most) of the week the NSAT to SDAT channel was down and so no "I heard you" traffic was recorded on the SDAT to NSAT channel as can be seen in Figure 17B.

With few exceptions the channels in the network are fairly reliable. Over half of the channels reported packet error rates less than one in 100,000. The average packet error rate was one error in 12,880 packets transmitted. Of the 86 channels in the network 14 reported no errors during the seven days,

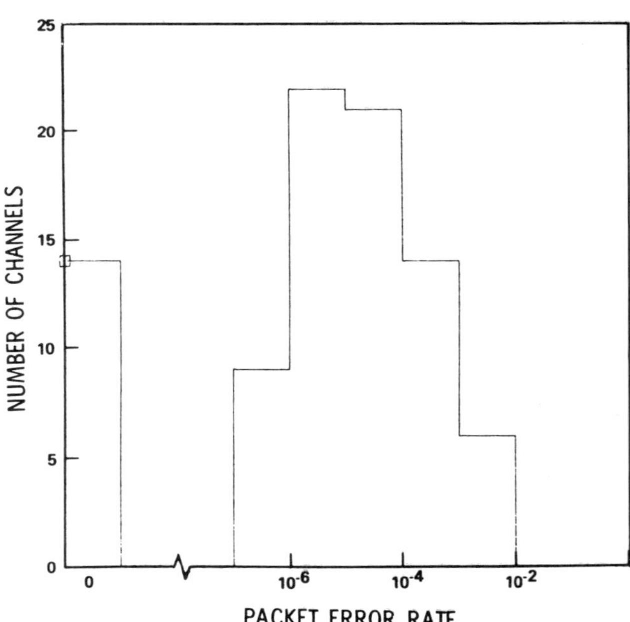

Figure 18—Channel packet error behavior

* Our measurements actually give the UP/DOWN status of the IMPs as seen by the NMC. When NSAT is declared down, we have displayed the NSAT to SDAT channel as being down in Figure 17B, and similarly, when SDAT is declared down we have shown the SDAT to NSAT (and the NSAT to SDAT) channel down.

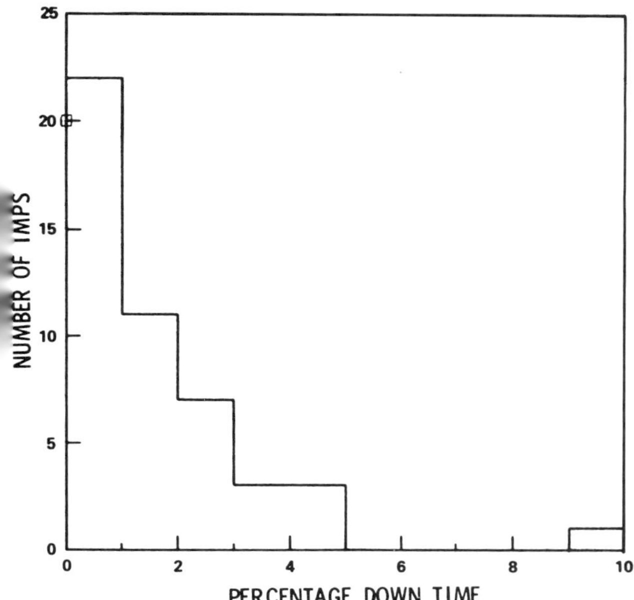

Figure 19—IMP failure behavior

while six channels had packet error rates worse than one in 1000. The worst case was one in 340 packets for the channel from RADT to LL. While these error rates are large enough to warrant the inclusion of error detection hardware and software, they are small enough so that traffic flow through the network is not impaired. In Figure 18, we show the error behavior of these lines during the seven day measurement. The failure rate of the IMPs should be included here, but clearly the seven day measurement is insufficient for this purpose. For completeness, therefore, in Figure 19 we show the performance characteristics of the IMPs over a 19 month interval (June 1972 through December 1973).[14] The average IMP down rate was 1.64 percent, with the worst case being 9.13 percent.

MODEL FOR NETWORK DELAY

In this section, we present a network delay model originally introduced by Kleinrock[12] and which was extended by Fultz[15] and Cole.[11] We then further extend this model to fit the specific implementation of the ARPA network. Following the model formulation, we present a comparison between the predicted and measured delay.

With the assumption of negligible nodal processing delays and channel propagation delays, the average message delay T (the time to traverse the network from source to destination) originally appeared as[12]

$$T=\sum_{i=1}^{M}\left[\frac{\lambda_i}{\gamma}T_i\right]$$

where

λ_i = the mean arrival rate of messages to the ith channel,
γ = the mean arrival rate of messages entering the network,
T_i = the mean time spent waiting for and using the ith channel, and
M = the number of channels in the network.

This very general result is easily extended to include nodal and propagation delays as follows:

$$T=K+\sum_{i=1}^{M}\left[\frac{\lambda_i}{\gamma}\left(\frac{1}{\mu C_i}+P_i+K+W_i\right)\right]$$

where

$1/\mu$ = mean message size,
C_i = capacity of the ith channel,
P_i = propagation delay on the ith channel,
K = nodal processing delay, and
$W_i=T_i-1/\mu C_i$ = waiting time in queue for channel i.

The delay analysis now simply requires that we solve for W_i. Perhaps the simplest (Markovian) assumption is[16]

$$W_i=\frac{\lambda_i/(\mu C_i)}{\mu C_i-\lambda_i}$$

When the queueing delay due to control traffic is also considered, we have

$$W_i'=\frac{\lambda_i'/(\mu' C_i)}{\mu' C_i-\lambda_i'}$$

where

λ_i' = arrival rate of data messages and control messages to the ith channel, and
$1/\mu'$ = mean message size including control messages.

Removing the assumption that nodal processing delay is constant and including the destination HOST transmission time we obtain the following expression for the average delay experienced by single packet messages.

$$T_{SP}=\sum_{i=1}^{M}\left[\frac{\lambda_i}{\gamma}\left(\frac{1}{\mu C_i}+P_i+K_l+\frac{\lambda_i'/(\mu' C_i)}{\mu' C_i-\lambda_i'}\right)\right]+\sum_{i=1}^{N}\left[\frac{\gamma_{\cdot j}}{\gamma}\left(K_j+\frac{1}{\mu_H C_{Hj}}\right)\right]$$

where

K_l is the packet processing time at node l (l is the origin node of channel i),
$\gamma_{\cdot j}$ = the mean departure rate of messages from the network to the HOSTs at site j,
$1/\mu_H C_{Hj}$ = the mean transmission time of messages to a HOST at site j, and
N = the number of nodes in the network.

The above formulae assume unpacketed message traffic, while in the ARPANET, messages are divided into from 1 to

8 packets. Fultz[15] and Cole,[11] therefore, extended the model to obtain the mean delay experienced by multi-packet messages

$$T_{MP}=K+\sum_{i=1}^{M}\left[\frac{\lambda_i}{\gamma}\left(\frac{1}{\mu C}+P_i+K+W_i'\right)\right]$$

$$+(\bar{m}-1)\left(\frac{1}{\mu C}+\sum_{jk}\left[\frac{\gamma_{jk}}{\gamma}\bar{\tau}_{jk}\right]\right)$$

where

C = line capacity (temporarily assumed constant)
$\bar{m}$ = mean number of packets in a multipacket message,
γ_{jk} = the arrival rate of messages from j to k, and
$\bar{\tau}_{jk}$ = mean inter-packet gap time for messages from source j to destination k.

It is difficult to measure $\bar{\tau}_{jk}$ for each j,k pair in the network. We, therefore, introduce an approximation due to Cole,[11] which yields

$$E[\tau(n \text{ hops})]=\frac{\rho(1-\rho^{(n-1)})}{1-\rho}\frac{1}{\mu C}$$

The above expression gives the expected value of τ_{jk} for nodes j and k which are n hops apart. It assumes that the channel utilizations ρ_i for the channels in the path from j to k are constant and equal to ρ. The path is assumed unique and the channel capacities are constant with value C. We will
326 use the first two assumptions to obtain an approximation to the network-wide mean interpacket gap. Note that the average path length traveled by a message is given by

$$\bar{n}=\frac{\lambda}{\gamma}$$

where

$$\lambda=\sum_{i=1}^{M}\lambda_i$$

The average line utilization is

$$\bar{\rho}=\frac{\sum_{i=1}^{M}\frac{\lambda_i'}{\mu' C_i}}{M}$$

Where once again we let C_i = capacity of the ith channel. The time it takes to transmit a full packet averaged over all channels in the network is

$$\bar{S}_F=\sum_{i=1}^{M}\left[\frac{\lambda_i}{\lambda}\frac{1}{\mu_F C_i}\right]$$

where $1/\mu_F$ = the length of a full packet.
Thus, we will use the following approximation for $\bar{\tau}$:

$$\bar{\tau}=\frac{\bar{\rho}(1-\bar{\rho}^{(\bar{n}-1)})}{1-\bar{\rho}}\bar{S}_F$$

Removing the assumptions of constant K and C, adding the HOST transmission time, and assuming that the last packets of multipacket messages have the same mean length as the single packet messages, we have the average message delay for multipacket messages:

$$T_{MP}=\sum_{i=1}^{M}\left[\frac{\lambda_i}{\gamma}\left(\frac{1}{\mu_F C_i}+P_i+K_i+\frac{\lambda_i'/(\mu' C_i)}{\mu' C_i-\lambda_i'}\right)\right]$$

$$+\sum_{i=1}^{M}\left[\frac{\lambda_i}{\lambda}\left((\bar{m}-2)\frac{1}{\mu_F C_i}+\frac{1}{\mu C_i}\right)\right]$$

$$+\sum_{j=1}^{N}\left[\frac{\gamma_{\cdot j}}{\gamma}\left(K_j+\frac{1}{\mu_{FH}C_{Hj}}\right)\right]$$

$$+(\bar{m}-1)\bar{\tau}$$

where $1/\mu_{FH}C_{Hj}$ = the transmission time of a full packet to a HOST at site j.

Let β be the fraction of the total number of messages which are single packet messages. We obtain the final expression for average message delay (from source to destination) in the network.

$$T=\beta T_{SP}+(1-\beta)T_{MP}$$

The measure of delay which is supplied by the IMPs is round-trip delay. Therefore, in order to compare the model with the measurements we need an expression for round-trip delay (i.e., we need to include the average RFNM delay T_{RFNM} in the model). A RFNM is simply another single packet message traveling from destination to source. Thus, it experiences the single packet message delay T_{SP} with an appropriate value for μ and λ without the HOST transmission term as follows:

$$T_{RFNM}=\sum_{i=1}^{M}\left[\frac{\lambda_{Ri}}{\gamma}\left(\frac{1}{\mu_R C_i}+P_i+K_i+\frac{\lambda_i'/(\mu' C_i)}{\mu' C_i-\lambda_i'}\right)\right]$$

$$+\sum_{j=1}^{N}\left[\frac{\gamma_{j\cdot}}{\gamma}K_j\right]$$

where

λ_{Ri} = the mean arrival rate of RFNMs to channel i,
$1/\mu_R$ = the length of a RFNM, and
$\gamma_{j\cdot}$ = the mean departure rate of RFNMs from the network to the HOSTs at site j (= the mean arrival rate of messages from the HOSTs at site j to the network)

The expression for mean round-trip delay T_R is therefore,

$$T_R=T+T_{RFNM}$$

For the week-long measurement we calculated the zero-load value of T_R and obtained T_R = 69 msec; the hourly variation of this quantity is shown in Figure 20. The source of the variation is the shift in the origin-destination traffic mix. This zero-load case corresponds to forcing λ_i and γ to zero, (keeping the same ratio as before for each i). The zero load value must be less than the measured value, and compares with the measurements displayed in Figure 21. This emphasizes the fact that the network is introducing very small congestion

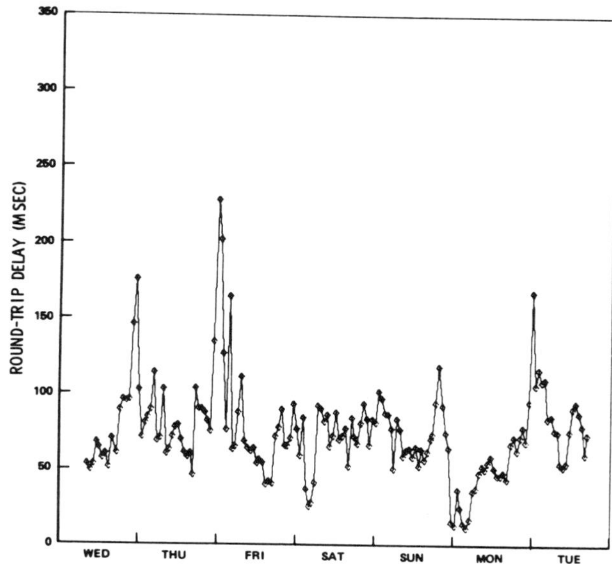

Figure 20—Computed (zero load) average message delay

effects. Furthermore, in Figure 22 we show the hourly variation of T_R (whose weekly average was $T_R=73$ msec) calculated for the actual load value as measured.

The model presented above is rather complex due mainly to the fact that not all channels (or IMPs) need have the same speed. In addition, the waiting time terms complicate the expressions as well, and represent the part of the model which is most subject to question (i.e., the Markovian assumptions). However, from Figures 20 and 22, we see that the zero-load and measured load calculations are nearly the

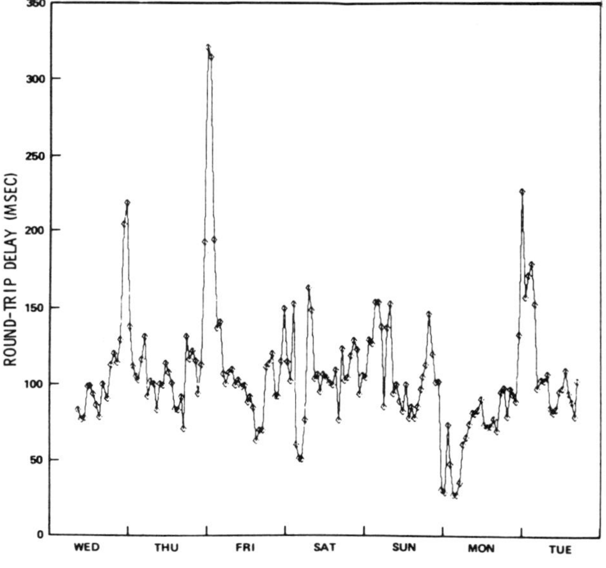

Figure 21—Measured average message delay

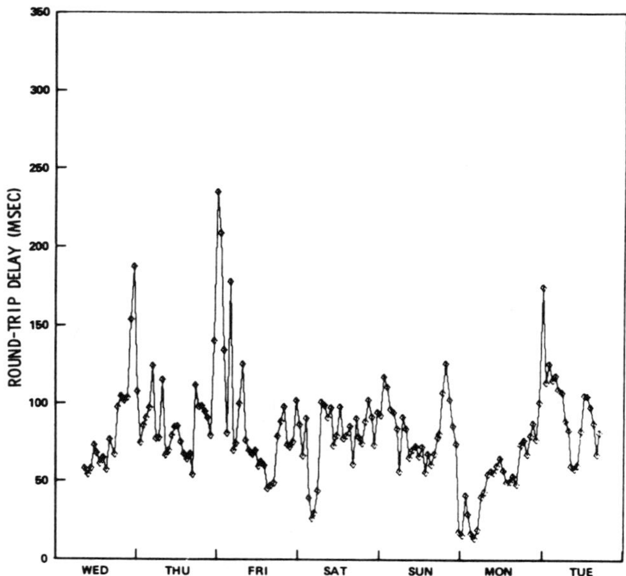

Figure 22—Computed (measured load) average message delay

same. This shows that the effect of W_i' is quite negligible and so any improvement over Markovian assumptions will yield negligible changes to T_R. This suggests a far simpler no-load model for estimating T_R as follows.[17] The expressions for 327
T_{SP} (and T_{RFNM} which is similar in form), may be simplified by dropping the W_i' terms, and setting all $K_i=K$ (a constant), all $C_i=C$ (a constant at 50 KBPS), and $C_{Hj}=C_H$ (a constant at 100 KBPS). The result is

$$\hat{T}_{SP}=\bar{n}\left(\frac{1}{\mu C}+K\right)+K+\frac{1}{\mu_H C_H}+\sum_{i=1}^{M}\left[\frac{\lambda_i}{\gamma}P_i\right]$$

(and a similar expression for $\hat{T}_{RFNM}$). Except for the last summation, these parameters are easily computed. For the sum, one must estimate (or measure) the channel traffic λ_i and the network throughput γ. The propagation delays P_i are known constants. With these simplifications (and assuming $\beta=1$, since the measured value of $\beta=0.96$ was observed), we then have the approximation

$$\hat{T}_R=\hat{T}_{SP}+\hat{T}_{RFNM}$$

Our calculation gives $\hat{T}_R=70$ msec* which is an excellent approximation to the earlier stated value of $T_R=69$ msec (at zero-load) and $T_R=73$ (at measured load)!

On the other hand, the measured value of $T_R=93$ msec is significantly larger than measured load estimate of the model of $T_R=73$ msec. This difference is due to the fact the model does not include: any delay by the destination HOST in accepting the message; any delay due to the request for storage at the destination IMP; exact data on P_i; time variations in

* The components for $\hat{T}_R$ are: $\bar{n}=3.31$, $1/\mu C=8.2$ msec, $K=.75$ msec, $1/\mu_H C_H=2.75$ msec, the propagation sum $=11.4$ msec, and $1/\mu_R C=3.36$ msec.

ρ finer than the hourly computations used; and non-Markovian assumptions. All the above omissions (except possibly the last) will increase the computed value of T_R.

CONCLUSIONS

The purpose of this paper was to present results of a week-long measurement of the ARPANET traffic behavior. In reporting upon the results of that experiment, we have observed a number of quantitative relationships which suggest that values assigned to certain of the network parameters should perhaps be reexamined. For example, we observed that the vast majority of messages are single-packet messages and one wonders at the wisdom of providing within the network the rather sophisticated mechanisms for handling multi-packet messages. Furthermore, we observed that the single-packet messages themselves are extremely small and it may be possible to improve the efficiency of the network if, in fact, the maximum packet lengths (and, therefore, the IMP buffer length) were reduced; one source of these small packet lengths is the preponderance of interactive traffic which typically creates packets containing one or a few characters. The mode of communication perhaps itself needs to be re-examined in an attempt to improve the network efficiency while maintaining a comfortable interactive feeling and response time. Incest is rampant in the network and it might be worthwhile to investigate other means for handling such traffic. Favoritism is (and perhaps will remain) even more dominant and how one would take advantage of this effect is not at this point clear. The non-uniformity of the traffic is striking and future network designs should attempt to capitalize upon this feature. The time variation of network use was discussed above and we see a fairly cyclic behavior both in traffic intensity and type of use. The lines themselves are not heavily utilized, and at the same time the network delays are so small as to render the network invisible to the typical user. We have described, in addition, a fairly extensive model for network delay and comparing it to our measured results it seems to be a fairly valid model both for single-packet and multi-packet messages. We also give a simplified model which appears adequate.

In this paper, our major purpose has been to report the measured results from our experiment. Secondarily, we have scratched the surface in attempting to evaluate and draw conclusions regarding the chosen values for some of the design parameters. In this effort, we have avoided the depth of discussion required to make a meaningful evaluation of these parameters, but rather have discussed their values only in terms of the measured data. For example, the choice of IMP buffer size depends upon many considerations beyond those we have measured (e.g., IMP processing speed, interrupt structure, line error rates, maximum network throughput, etc.); therefore, the presentation and commentary on the measured data given herein should certainly not be used alone in the selection of network parameters. The broad class of issues which must be included in decisions of this type are discussed, for example, in Kahn.[18]

The experiment described above is repeated every two months at the Network Measurement Center, and has so far produced results similar in flavor to those reported upon here. Numerous other experiments are currently being conducted and many more are in the planning stages. It is only through such experiments and through careful evaluation of the measured data that one can gain understanding of the network behavior, which in turn impacts the design and growth of the network.

ACKNOWLEDGMENT

We gratefully acknowledge the contributions of Holger Opderbeck, Stanley Lieberson, and the remainder of the staff at UCLA-NMC.

REFERENCES

1. Roberts, L. G., and B. D. Wessler, "Computer network development to achieve resource sharing," *AFIPS Conference Proceedings* 36, pp. 543-549, SJCC, Atlantic City, N.J., 1970.
2. Heart, F. E., R. E. Kahn, S. M. Ornstein, W. R. Crowther, and D. C. Walden, "The interface message processor for the ARPA computer network," *AFIPS Conference Proceedings*, 36, pp. 551-567, SJCC, Atlantic City, N.J., 1970.
3. Kleinrock, L., "Analytic and simulation methods in computer network design," *AFIPS Conference Proceedings*, 36, pp. 569-579, SJCC, Atlantic City, N.J., 1970.
4. Frank, H., I. T. Frisch, and W. Chou, "Topological considerations in the design of the ARPA computer network," *AFIPS Conference Proceedings*, 36, pp. 581-587, SJCC, Atlantic City, N.J., 1970.
5. McKenzie, A.A., *HOST/HOST Protocol for the ARPA Network*, ARPA Network Information Center # 8246, January 1972.
6. Ornstein, S. M., F. E. Heart, W. R. Crowther, H. K. Rising, S. B. Russell, and A. Michel, "The Terminal IMP for the ARPA network," *AFIPS Conference Proceedings*, 40, pp. 243-254, SJCC, Atlantic City, N.J., 1972.
7. Frank, H., R. E. Kahn, and L. Kleinrock, "Computer communication network design—Experience with theory and practice," *AFIPS Conference Proceedings*, 40, pp. 255-270, SJCC, Atlantic City, N.J., 1972.
8. Crocker, S. D., J. F. Heafner, R. M. Metcalfe, and J. B. Postel, "Function-oriented protocols for the ARPA Computer Network," *AFIPS Conference Proceedings*, 40, pp. 271-279, SJCC, Atlantic City, N.J., 1972.
9. *Specifications for the Interconnection of a HOST and an IMP*, Bolt, Beranek and Newman, Inc., Cambridge, Mass., Report No. 1822 May 1969.
10. McKenzie, A. A., B. P. Cosell, J. M. McQuillan, and M. J. Thrope, "The Network Control Center for the ARPA Network," *Proceedings of the First International Conference on Computer Communication*, 1, pp. 185-191, Washington, D. C., October, 1972.
11. Cole, G. D., *Computer Network Measurements: Techniques and Experiments*, Engineering Report No. UCLA-ENG-7165, University of California, Los Angeles, Calif., 1971.
12. Kleinrock, L., *Communication Nets: Stochastic Message Flow and Delay*, McGraw Hill, N.Y., 1964, reprinted by Dover, N.Y., 1972.
13. Gerla, M., *The Design of Store-and-Forward (S/F) Networks for Computer Communications*, Engineering Report No. UCLA-ENG-7319, University of California, Los Angeles, Calif., 1973.
14. McKenzie, A. A., Letter to S. D. Crocker, 16 January 1974.
15. Fultz, G. L., *Adaptive Routing Techniques for Message Switching Computer-Communication Networks*, Engineering Report No. UCLA-ENG-7252, University of California, Los Angeles, Calif., 1972.
16. Kleinrock, L., *Queueing Systems, Volume I: Theory*, Wiley, N.Y., 1974.
17. Kleinrock, L., *Queueing Systems, Volume II: Computer Applications*, Wiley, N.Y., 1974.
18. Kahn, R. E., "Resource-Sharing Computer Communication Networks," *Proceedings of the IEEE*, 60, pp. 1397-1407, November 1972.

Computer report III

Data by the packet

Because computing costs are now so low, an unusual new concept of data communications is feasible

The most dominant force over the past 20 years in both computer and communications architecture has been the continuous and rapid decrease in the cost of computer hardware. Not only has this electronics revolution affected the capability and design of computer systems, but it has also made possible a radically new concept of data communications. Called *packet switching*, this concept is strongly dependent on the cost of computing since it uses computers to correct transmission errors, to provide high reliability through alternate routing, and to allocate communication bandwidth dynamically on a demand basis rather than as a preassigned bandwidth.

The impact of widespread packet-switched communications networks on the computer field should be momentous. With data communications priced on a distance-independent basis, it should become economically feasible for terminals and computers throughout the country to access efficiently—on demand—a wide variety of computer services. The economics of resource sharing will undoubtedly eliminate the need for many medium-scale data processing centers and permit a considerably higher degree of specialization for the larger service centers. Moreover, packet switching will make possible far more economic realization of a comprehensive electronic funds-transfer system, on-line credit authorization, integrated corporate data networks, as well as nationwide access to all forms of data banks and retrieval services.

All these developments hinge on the availability of low-cost computer communications. Although packet switching economizes on transmission costs by maintaining high line utilization, until recently the cost of computer hardware had continued to be too high to permit practical packet-switching networks. The price of computing has been decreasing far more rapidly than the price of communications, however, and one could have anticipated a crossover point where the cost of using computers to allocate bandwidth became cheaper than the cost of the communications themselves. According to my estimate, this crossover occurred during 1969. As a result, packet switching has now become quite an economic and viable technology, permitting the establishment of large, cost-effective networks nationwide. This development in data communications will in turn have substantial effect on the course of computer technology as preliminarily indicated by results from the United States ARPA (Advanced Research Projects Agency) network research activity.

One of the main reasons for the great interest in computer networks today is the considerable economies that can be achieved through resource sharing. With a computer network that is reliable and responsive enough to permit the full resources of a remote computer to be employed locally, it becomes possible for organizations to consider the elimination or reduction of local computing facilities and the utilization of remote service centers instead. This not only can lead to considerable cost savings, as we shall see, but also has many additional advantages, including increased reliability of a multicomputer service center, improved service from a variety of competing suppliers, and increased flexibility for expansion. The main incentive for an organization changing over, however, is the cost saving. To get a feel for the magnitude of this effect, it is useful to examine the initial experience in an environment—the ARPA Computer Network (ARPANET)—where remote use of computing has been fostered by providing adequate communications facilities.[1-3]

Cost-effective remote-access computing

Although initiated in 1969, the ARPANET was not sufficiently developed to permit useful resource sharing activity until mid-1971. As network reliability and effectiveness proved out, ARPA and its contractors found many cases where newly required computer capacity could effectively be obtained through the network rather than by adding local computing resources. By March 1973, several contractors were making substantial use of the network for a majority or all of their computing resources. Several of the computer centers on the network had grown to become substantial suppliers of computer service, providing not only time-sharing service but also remote batch service. At that time, an accounting was made of the total computer usage obtained through the network, and an estimate was made for each user of the cost of purchasing comparable time on outside computers or leasing the necessary in-house computer facilities to do the same job apparently being done through the network. Table I tabulates this information by user organization, identifying both the cost of computing with and without the network. A total of $2 million a year was being spent on computing resources accessed through the network—resources that would have cost $6 million per year if the network had not existed! This savings of $4 million per year more than offset the $3.5 million annual cost of the network.*

At this stage in its development, the network was only using 20 percent of its capacity; thus, at the

Lawrence G. Roberts
Telenet Communications Corporation

* This cost includes amortization of the system's IMP (interface message processor) minicomputer units.

329

same communication cost, the ARPANET could permit five times as much remote computing to be performed. At full traffic load, the network cost would be 35 percent of the actual computing cost, or 11 percent of the original computing cost. Clearly, for a moderate investment in communications, a computing cost reduction factor of three can be achieved through resource sharing.

Examining the ARPA data, it is useful to identify a few of the different categories of network usage and explore the sources of the cost savings. The largest individual user organization was the University of Illinois, which before the network came into full operation leased its own Burroughs 6700 computer to develop programs for the ILLIAC IV computer. After the University of California at San Diego put its large B6700 complex on the network, Illinois was able to terminate its computer lease and obtain the computing support far more economically from the larger installation through the network. Moreover, Illinois required access to the ILLIAC IV computer that it obtained from the NASA Ames Research Center through the network, remote batch service on the IBM 360/91 at U.C.L.A., and time-sharing services from U.S.C. and M.I.T. To obtain this collection of services locally, Illinois would have had to continue leasing the Burroughs computer, purchase time on a local IBM 360, and either purchase a time-sharing machine or obtain service from a commercial vendor. Therefore, not only would it cost the University three times as much to obtain equivalent computing power locally, but it would not have had a convenient way of accessing these machines and transferring data and programs between them.

This case is an excellent example of a user requiring many different types of service, each being most efficiently provided by a large specialized service center. For example, program development and debugging is extremely cost-effective on a time-sharing computer, but the execution of large numerical applications programs can often be done a factor of ten less expensively on a large batch processing machine.

Another type of saving is exemplified by Massachusetts Computer Associates, a small computer software firm. This group would use the equivalent of one third of the capacity of a PDP-10 time-sharing system, if they operated locally on a dedicated basis. The required facilities, however, were provided through the network from the University of Southern California, taking advantage of the fact that peak usage hours on the east and west coasts of the U.S. do not coincide due to the time zone difference. A large number of such users of various sizes can be accommodated by a single service center with considerably greater economy of operation than with a number of independent centers. The consolidation of maintenance, software, and operational personnel in one location considerably reduces costs, as most of the time-sharing companies have found, and nationwide operation increases the machine utilization considerably due to the time zone spread.

Although there are many other combinations of resource sharing represented within the ARPA network community, these two examples illustrate the main sources of cost savings resulting from hardware sharing. Additionally, large but less easily quantifiable

I. Computer resource usage within ARPANET*

User Organization	Activity	Remote Usage, in thousands	Projected Cost for Local Replacement, in thousands
University of Illinois	Parallel processing research	$ 360	$1100
NASA Ames Research Center	Air foil design and ILLIAC	328	570
Rand Corporation	Numerical climate modeling	210	650
Mass. Computer Associates	ILLIAC IV compiler development	151	470
Lawrence Livermore Laboratory	TENSOR code on ILLIAC	94	370
Stanford University	Artificial intelligence research	91	180
Rome Air Development Center	Text manipulation and resource evaluation	81	450
ARPA	On-line management	77	370
Seismic Array Analysis Center	Seismic data processing	76	300
Mitre Corporation	Distributed file network research	60	240
National Bureau of Standards	Network research	58	200
Bolt Beranek & Newman Inc.	TENEX system support	55	80
Xerox Palo Alto Research Center	Computer science research	47	100
University of Southern California Image Processing Lab	Picture processing research	35	70
University of California, Los Angeles	Network measurement	28	90
Systems Control, Inc.	Signal processing research	23	70
University of California, Santa Barbara	Network research	22	70
U.S. Air Force Range Measurements Lab	ARPANET management	17	60
Institute for the Future	Teleconferencing research	13	40
Miscellaneous	Computer research	192	580
	Total	$2018	$6060

*Annual remote computer usage cost is based on March 1973 data.

cost savings are anticipated to be forthcoming in the future from the sharing of data base and software resources.

Computer–communication interdependence

The large savings possible from resource sharing are dependent upon having available an economic means of switched communications to access these resources. This communication facility must be reliable, sufficiently responsive to meet all of the interactive demands of time-sharing users, have sufficient data transmission speed for high-speed printer and display output, be distributed to scattered users throughout the country, and most importantly be sufficiently economic so as not to destroy the cost savings achieved through resource sharing. In the early 1960s, this kind of communications service was not available. It is only with the extremely rapid development of computers themselves that it has been possible to reduce drastically the cost of providing such a communications service to computer data users.

Since computer input/output typically is extremely bursty in nature, requiring peak data transfer rates ten to one hundred times as great as the average data rate, it is necessary to share statistically among many users a communication channel of fixed data transmission capacity in order to achieve reasonable economy. Without doing this, the cost of data communications would be 10 to 100 times as expensive as the raw communication bandwidth, thereby making resource sharing cost-ineffective over even moderate distances.

Packet-switching technology as is used in the ARPANET has been developed to permit the statistical sharing of communication lines by many diverse users. By dividing the data traffic into small addressed packets (1000 bits or less in length), extremely efficient sharing of communication resources can be achieved even at the burst rates required by interactive computer traffic. Since resource-sharing computer usage has only become economically viable with the development of packet switching, it is instructive to look at the cost trends that made this technology possible. To do this, it is necessary to have a model of the average resources utilized in moving data through a packet-switching communications network.

The basic design of a packet-switching network, as exemplified by the ARPANET, consists of a collection of geographically dispersed minicomputers called *interface message processors* (IMPs) interconnected by many 50-kilobit/second (kb/s) leased lines. An IMP accepts traffic from a computer attached to it called a *host,* formats it into packets, and routes it toward its destination over one of the 50-kb lines tied to that IMP. Each IMP in the network receiving a packet examines the header and, making a new routing decision, passes it on towards its destination, possibly through several intermediate IMPs. Thus, a packet proceeds from IMP to IMP in making its way to its destination. The destination IMP collects the packets, reformats them into messages in the proper sequence, and submits them to the destination host computer. Throughout the process, each IMP checks the correctness of each packet by means of both hardware- and software-based error-control techniques. If the packet is received incorrectly due to a transmission error on the line, the IMP does not acknowledge receipt and the preceding IMP must retransmit the packet, perhaps over a different path. Because the network uses high-speed transmission lines and short packets, and all data is stored in high-speed primary memory in the IMPs (as opposed to disk drives and other secondary storage devices) average end-to-end transit delay for a packet is 0.1 second.

This general design of a packet-switching network has proven so successful in the ARPANET that a new component of the communications industry has been formed—"value-added" packet carriers, offering the public packet communications service on a nationwide regulated basis. Two of the four value-added carriers that have applied to the FCC—Telenet Communications Corporation and Packet Communications, Inc.—intend to offer a service patterned directly on the ARPANET. The FCC has responded extremely positively to this new development in the communications field and, indicating its intention to adopt a policy of "liberal entry" in this field, has already approved the first of the value-added carrier applicants.

In a nationwide packet-switching network, there is practically no dependence of cost on distance, and for this reason both Telenet and PCI intend to charge only for the *number* of packets moved, independent of the distance. If we assume that the traffic itself is evenly distributed geographically, the average distance traversed by a packet would be about half the cross-country mileage, or 1200 miles in a network spanning the U.S. The number of *hops* (intermediate leased lines traversed) required on the average to deliver a packet is a logarithmic function of the number of *nodes* in the network and therefore increases very slowly once the network exceeds about 40 nodes. For triply connected networks of 40 to 100 nodes, the average number of hops required is three or four. Since

II. Data communications costs since 1960

Date Introduced	Data Rate	Cost per Million Bits
1960	2.4 kb	$1.00
1963	40.8 kb	$0.42
1964	50.0 kb (Telpak A)	$0.34
1967	50.0 kb (Series 8000)	$0.33
1974–76	56.0 kb (DDS)	$0.11 (est.)

III. CPU time and cost estimates for the ARPA network

Date	Machine	Cost	Total Processing Time per Kilopacket	Cost per Kilopacket
1970	Honeywell 516 IMP	$100k	26.2 seconds	$0.168
1971	Honeywell 316 IMP	$ 45k	35.4 seconds	$0.102
1974	Lockheed SUE IMP	$ 10k*	41.2 seconds	$0.026

*Estimated per processor based on multiprocessor configuration.

commercial packet-switching networks, such as that proposed by Telenet Communications Corporation, will employ "central office" facilities serving many users in a city, it is not likely that the number of central office nodes will exceed 100 for many years to come. Therefore, taking four hops as a reasonable estimate, the average packet would traverse five IMPs and four lines on its course between two locations 1200 miles apart. The average length of these leased lines would be 300 miles, a number that clearly fits the model and also matches the ARPANET experience.

Therefore, two cost factors are involved in moving the average packet: (1) the communications cost for four 300-mile leased lines, and (2) the computation required in five IMPs.

Communications cost trends

Over the past decade, there has been very little change in the actual per-mile price of leased communications channels. However, in the more recent past there have been substantial changes in modem technology, permitting higher-speed data transmission over these lines, and in the near future the American Telephone and Telegraph Co. expects to introduce Digital Data Service (DDS), a totally digital technology at a substantially lower price.

Considering the period 1960–1980, one detects a downward trend in data communications cost. To quantify this, let us examine the cost per million bits of data moved for reasonably high-bandwidth leased lines 300 miles in length (including termination and modem costs). The actual costs tabulated in Table II have been multiplied by four so that they are truly representative of the incremental cost for moving one million bits (or a thousand packets) over a packet-switched network for a total distance of 1200 miles. The calculations are based on the lines being fully utilized in full-duplex mode for eight hours each working day (173 h/month—the same level of utilization assumed in calculating subsequent computer costs). It should be noted that a single leased line 1200 miles long would in general be 20–50 percent less expensive, but such a dedicated line would not permit the multipoint access and usage-based charging provided by a packet network.

Based on this data, if one takes the cost of service for each year between 1960 and 1980 and computes the least-mean-square exponential fit, one finds that the cost of service has been decreasing by 11 percent per year over that period, resulting in a factor-of-10 decrease in communications cost each 22 years. A similar analysis was made of the costs of dial telephone service over a distance of 1200 miles, using the highest data rate modem feasible over dial telephone lines. For the dial case, a comparable rate of decrease in service costs was found, largely due to improvements in modem performance, but with an average cost per megabit eight times greater than the wideband leased line case. Thus, at least over the last decade or so, the cost of data communications service has been decreasing fairly consistently and it is safe to assume that continued advances in digital transmission technology will continue this trend into the future. There is, however, no indication that a remarkable breakthrough is about to occur, drastically decreasing the cost rate of terrestrial transmission service from common carriers.

Computer cost trends

The cost per unit capability of electronics and computer equipment has often been studied, and in all cases the trend was found to be remarkably consistent at about a factor-of-ten decrease in cost every five years. In a 1969 study made by the author[4] analyzing the cost performance of complete computer systems vs. their date of first delivery, it was found that the cost performance was increasing exponentially at a rate of 1.56 per year. This study was based on the least-mean-square best fit for all machines introduced between 1955 and 1969 having at least 32-bit word length. In a later study by Newport and Ryzlak[5] examining the cost performance of communication processors, it was found that the cost performance was increasing at a rate of 1.61 per year. In this study, minicomputers introduced between 1960 and 1972 were also examined.

Given the remarkably consistent rate of increase found by these and other studies it is quite clear that the rate of growth of computer cost performance is well established. In order to fix such a curve absolutely, however, it is necessary to examine the actual CPU time consumed by an IMP to process 1000 packets of information. Very accurate studies have been made by Bolt Beranek and Newman Inc. (BBN)—ARPA's contractor for building and operating the ARPANET—of the CPU time required for the IMPs used within the ARPANET. The time consumed depends somewhat on the length of the packet, but for consistency (equating 1000 packets to one megabit of data) full packets of a thousand bits will be considered. In Table III, the three computers developed for ARPA by BBN to provide IMP service are considered. The date of introduction, the cost, and the total CPU time consumed to move a thousand full packets through five IMPs in the network are listed. The additional processing required to accept and deliver these packets to the host computer is also included. The cost per kilopacket of traffic was found by depreciating this equipment over 50 months and assuming operations and maintenance expense to equal equipment cost; operation was set at eight hours each working day for consistency with our earlier communications cost calculations.

These costs are quite consistent with the previously described growth rate of cost performance with time and form the basis of an actual trend curve for the computational cost of packet transmission. To be consistent with the treatment of communications trends, the dates that should be utilized in considering the IMP processing costs should be delayed a year from the date of introduction to correspond more accurately with their average usage date.

Composite costs for packet switching

The graph shown in Fig. 1 shows the trend curve for the data communications and computational cost associated with moving a million bits or a thousand packets of information over an average distance of 1200 miles within a nationwide network. As can be seen, even with an 11-percent decrease per year, the cost of communications remains relatively flat,

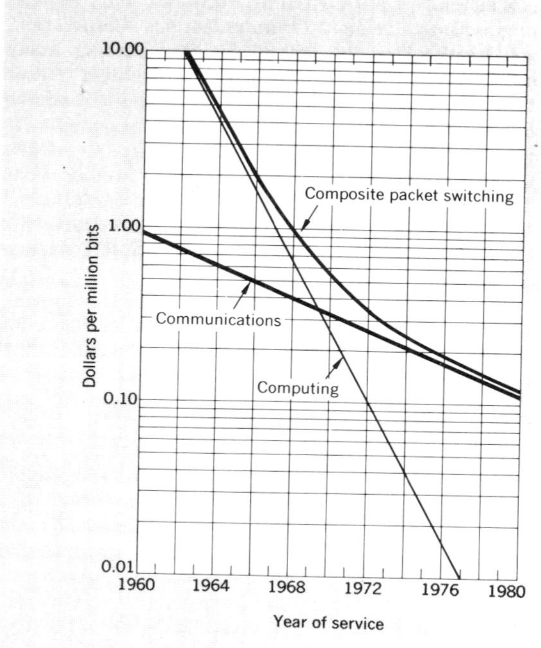

[1] A comparison of cost performance trends for computing, data communications, and packet-switching systems over a nationwide network. The impact of satellite communications on packet switching is particularly emphasized in the graph on the right, which also demonstrates the cost effectiveness of reducing the regional size of the national communications network via satellites.

whereas the cost of computing has been decreasing with extreme rapidness; these curves intersect in 1969. Before that year, the cost of the computer power required to provide dynamic allocation of communication resources would have made packet switching extremely expensive to implement and, in fact, the first packet-switched network—the ARPANET—was not initiated until 1969. The colored curve shows the overall cost of communications plus computation associated with packet switching. Since only the incremental cost of moving a kilopacket through the net have been considered here, these results should not be interpreted as indicating the entire cost of operating a communications service, but only the incremental costs associated with moving large quantities of data. Also, since the communications trend in particular has been smoothed considerably, whereas in fact the present cost of 50-kb/s communication lines is still 33 cents/Mb, the resultant cost for any particular year should not be considered as an accurate indicator of precisely what the price ought to be. For example, in Telenet Communications Corporation's publicly filed prospective tariff, incremental packet traffic is priced at 48 cents/kilopacket. This is very close to the total cost of communication (33 cents) and IMPs (10 cents) today but corresponds to 1970 on the graph.

A more general interpretation can be made of Fig. 1. Except for the numerical absolute scale numbers, it is entirely representative of the costs associated with any system that utilizes both communications and computing components in a fixed ratio! If the communications segment is only a small fraction of the overall system, the crossover will be much later in time, but the identical shape will be preserved. Thus, for any data processing system providing remote computing capability, the curve indicates that as time passes the costs will become more and more dominated by communications. This means that it is all the more important for new communications techniques such as packet switching to be introduced in order to reduce this component of the total system cost.

IV. Cost estimates for INTELSAT communication satellites

INTELSAT	Usage Year	Number of Circuits	Lifetime, years	Total Cost	Cost per Circuit per Year
I	1965–67	240	1.5	$ 8.2M	$22 800
II	1967–68	240	3	$ 8.1M	$11 300
III	1968–71	1 200	5	$10.5M	$ 1 800
IV	1971–78	6 000	7	$26.0M	$ 600
V*	1978–85	100 000	10	$28.5M	$ 30

*Estimated.

The future—satellite communications

Although terrestrial communications cost appears to limit the future price of computer-communication service, including packet-switching networks, the situation is rapidly changing with the introduction of domestic satellites. The cost trends for satellite technology are not yet sufficiently well documented for great confidence; however, a preliminary estimate can be made from the international satellite progress over the last decade. Table IV presents the space-segment cost per circuit for the INTELSAT series of satellites.

Applying the least-mean-square exponential fit to this data, the rate of technological improvement in the cost performance for satellites is found to be 40.7 percent per year, or a factor of ten every 6.7 years. This can only be treated as a crude estimate of the cost trend for satellite communication, but since it is quite in keeping with the general cost trend for electronics, it is a quite credible growth rate.

Preliminary estimates of the actual cost of wide bandwidth digital communications service on domestic satellites are in the vicinity of 5 cents/Mb for service in early 1974. As depicted in the right-hand chart of Fig. 1, if the cost trend for domestic satellites follows the initial international trend, the projection of satellite communication cost performance is very close to that of computers.

Satellites can be used extremely efficiently within a packet network when used on a broadcast basis between a large number of ground stations. A detailed study of the techniques for broadcast satellite use and

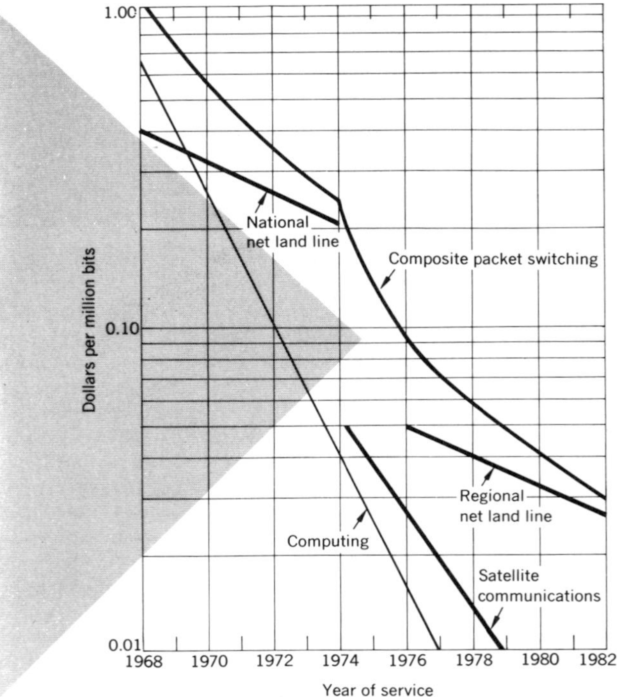

their superior performance over the use of satellites as point-to-point channels has already been described in a previous paper.[6] The cost of long-distance communications between ground stations can be reduced significantly as indicated by the satellite trend in Fig. 1. However, terrestrial leased lines are still required to interconnect the central offices of the packet network within each ground station region. By 1976–78, there should be sufficient domestic satellite stations in operation so that 12 regions can be established within the U.S., thereby reducing the size of the regional packet network to a 200-mile radius. In this case, instead of using four 300-mile leased lines, each packet would traverse four 50-mile leased lines (two in each ground station region) plus the satellite hop.

Thus, the overall cost of packet switching would be the sum of three components: computing, the satellite link, and the 50-mile terrestrial links. The trends of these three areas are plotted in Fig. 1, and the overall cost of packet switching shown to break in 1974 with the introduction of satellite service. Satellites will play an important role in reducing the future cost of packet-switching service and, for this reason, broadcast satellite service has been included as an integral part of the proposed offering by Telenet for its nationwide packet-switching system.

In the more distant future, additional technological improvements are expected to continue to occur in the packet-switching field. When they are introduced, high-frequency (15–30-GHz) satellites will most likely permit direct satellite interconnection of the central offices in a packet-switching network. This will produce an additional break in the cost trend and leave only the local distribution problem. The utilization of cable television systems and packet radio broadcast techniques[7] should permit substantial improvements in the future local distribution scene. Hence, it is entirely possible that the cost trend for packet switching will continue to decrease at almost the same rate as the cost of computation if these new packet communication techniques are vigorously pursued.

Where we stand

Experience with ARPANET has demonstrated that computing service can be obtained remotely through a computer network at one third the cost of a local dedicated system. To obtain this factor-of-three cost reduction, however, one must have available a highly responsive and reliable communications system capable of handling the peak data rate of the burst traffic normally associated with computer usage. In order to provide such an enhanced communications service, it is necessary to embed significant computational and logical capabilities within the network itself.

Until recently, the cost of computer hardware, as compared to that for the raw communication facilities, was too high to permit widespread use of computer intelligence within a data communications system. However, computer hardware costs have been falling so rapidly relative to communication facilities costs that "intelligent" and enhanced data networks have suddenly become a viable technology.

REFERENCES

1. Roberts, L. G., and Wessler, B., "Computer network development to achieve resource sharing," *Proc. AFIPS Spring Joint Computer Conf.*, pp. 543–549, 1970.
2. Heart, F., *et al.*, "The interface message processor for the ARPA computer network," *Conf. AFIPS Spring Joint Computer Conf.*, pp. 551–567, 1970.
3. Kahn, R. E., "Resource-sharing computer communications networks," *Proc. IEEE*, pp. 1397–1407, Nov. 1972.
4. Roberts, L. G., "Data processing technology forecast," internal U.S. Government paper, Apr. 23, 1969.
5. Newport, C. B., and Ryzlak, J., "Communication processors," *Proc. IEEE*, vol. 60, pp. 1321–1332, Nov. 1972.
6. Roberts, L. G., "Dynamic allocation of satellite capacity through packet reservation," *Proc. National Computer Conf.*, pp. 711–716, 1973.
7. Roberts, L. G., "Network rationale: a 5-year reevaluation," *Proc. COMPCON 73*, Feb. 1973.

Lawrence G. Roberts (M) obtained the Ph.D. degree in electrical engineering from M.I.T. in 1963. He is presently president of Telenet Communications Corporation, Washington, D.C., a firm that plans to establish and operate a nationwide packet-switching service as a common carrier under FCC regulation. Formerly director for information processing techniques with the Advanced Research Projects Agency of DOD, Dr. Roberts was principally concerned with new information processing techniques in the areas of computer systems, graphics, artificial intelligence, signal processing, weather modeling, and man–machine interaction. In addition, he was responsible for developing the ARPA computer network. Prior to his government experience, he led the computer software group at M.I.T.'s Lincoln Laboratory and was instrumental in developing a three-dimensional input device (the Lincoln Wand), the APEX time-sharing system, the CORAL list structure system, and several graphics systems. Dr. Roberts has written many professional articles and has lectured throughout the world. He was selected the 1965–66 national lecturer for ACM, of which he is a member; he is also a member of Sigma Xi.

Reprinted by permission from *IEEE Spectrum*
Vol. 11, No. 2, February 1974, pp. 46-51

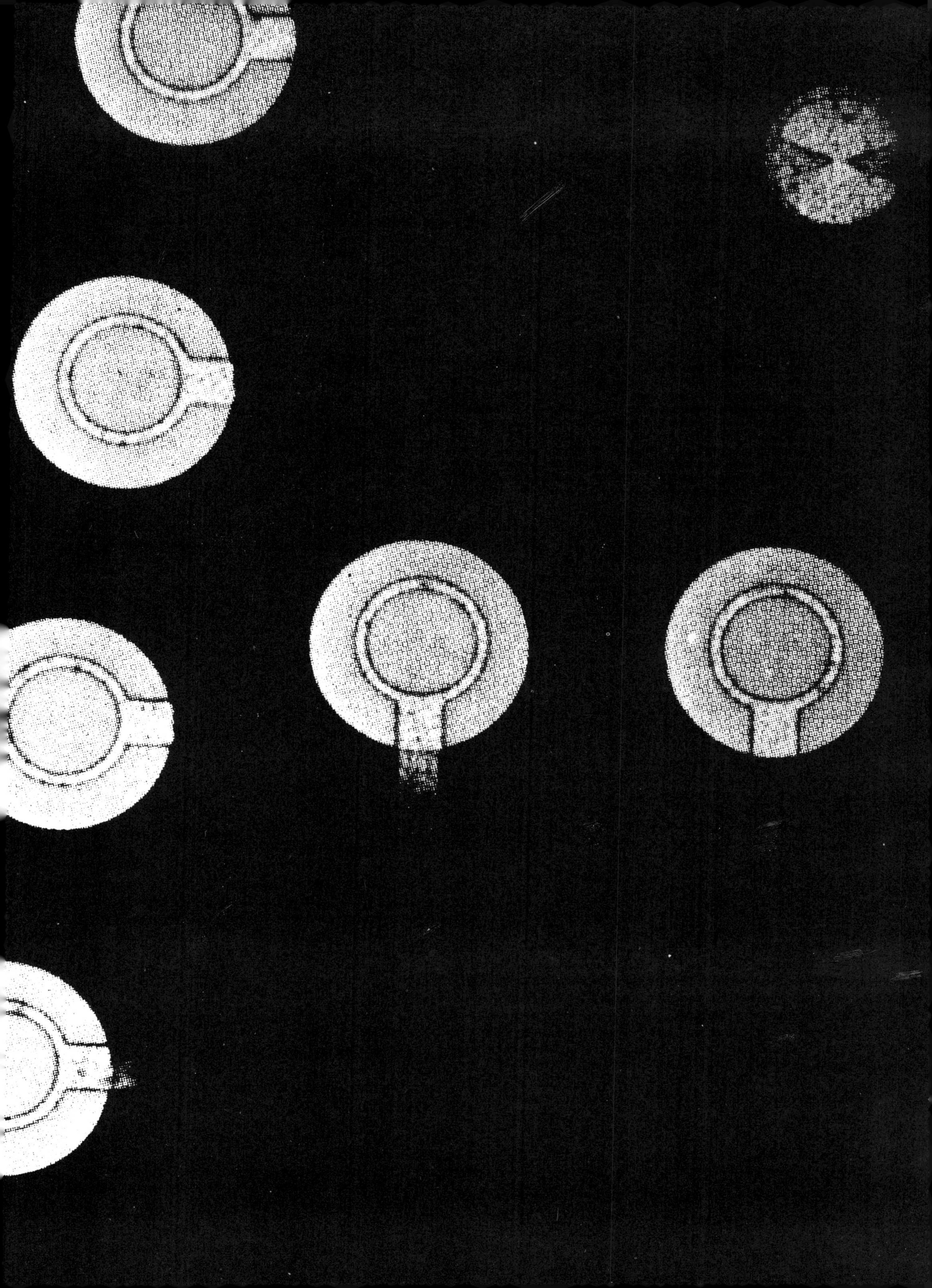

Topological Optimization of Computer Networks

HOWARD FRANK AND WUSHOW CHOU

Invited Paper

Abstract—**Modeling, analysis, and design problems and methodologies for centralized and distributed computer-communication networks are discussed. The basic problem is to specify the location and capacity of each communication link within the network. The design objective is to provide a low-cost network which satisfies constraints on response time, throughput, reliability, and other parameters. Fundamental network models for queuing and reliability analysis are described, as are basic properties of various network structures. A number of approaches to the topological design problem are presented; areas where further research is needed are indicated; possible approaches to several unsolved problems are suggested.**

I. Introduction

IN THIS PAPER we cover both centralized and distributed computer networks. For illustration, we give specific examples of two highly successful networks—the NASDAQ Over-the-Counter Quotation System (see Fig. 1) and the ARPA Computer Network (see Fig. 2).

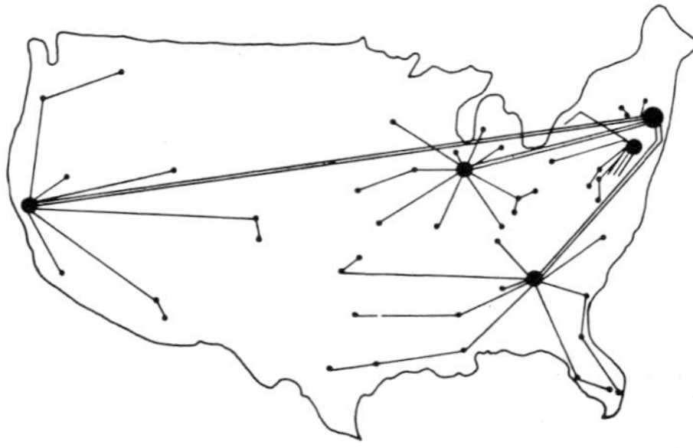

Fig. 1. The NASD automated quotation system.

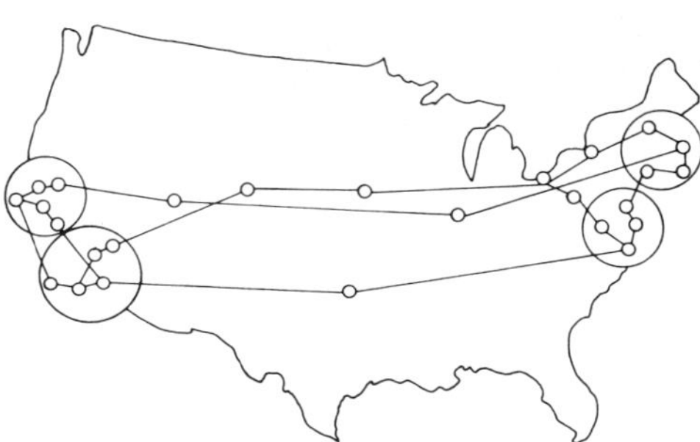

Fig. 2. The ARPA computer network (March 1972).

"NASDAQ" stands for the National Association of
336 Securities Dealers Automated Quotation System. It is a system of computers and communication and terminal devices, designed primarily for the collection and distribution of real-time quotations for the over-the-counter securities market. The NASDAQ System is composed of low-, medium-, and high-speed communication lines (from 1600–50 000 bits/s) tied to the NASDAQ Central Processing Center in Trumbull, Conn., through control units and data concentrators. Ten concentrators are utilized in the NASDAQ System–two each in Chicago, Ill., San Francisco, Calif., and Atlanta, Ga., and four in New York, N. Y. For reliability, there are two lines from the central processor to each concentrator facility. The regional circuits are dedicated leased-line multipoint data circuits. Design constraints for the system include small response times for several types of messages, extremely high reliability and availability specifications, low error rates on circuits, and the ability of the network to handle a large number of calls without loss of data.

The ARPA Network [19], [44]–[48] provides store-and-forward communications between a set of computers distributed across the United States. The message handling at each center in the network is performed by a special-purpose interface message processor (IMP). The centers are connected through the IMP's by full duplex high-speed communication lines. Messages are broken up into sets of packets each with appropriate header information. Each packet independently makes its way through the network to its destination. A goal of the system is to achieve an average delay of less than 0.2 s for single packets. The network must accommodate variations in traffic flow without degradation in performance. For reliability, the network is designed so that at least two IMP's and/or lines must fail before it can become disconnected. Control of the system is distributed throughout the network with each IMP providing routing and flow control on the basis of its current knowledge of the network status.

Although the NASDAQ and ARPA networks differ significantly in their philosophy of design and their operation, the development of networks of both types involves three similar principal activities: 1) the design of the IMP's, concentrators, and multiplexers (hereafter called *nodes*) to act as store-and-forward switches; 2) the topological modeling and design to specify the capacity and location of each communication circuit within the network; 3) the design of protocols to meet user requirements. We will concentrâte on item 2), the topological modeling and design, although this area clearly interacts with the other problems.

Many formidable theoretical problems are encountered during the topological optimization of any network. These problems include:

Network Choice: In general, there are $[N(N-1)/2)!]/\{[(N(N-1)/2-M)!]M!\}$ ways of arranging M links among N nodes. Considering all possible designs by computer is out

Manuscript received July 19, 1972. This work was supported by the Advanced Research Projects Agency of the Department of Defense under Contract DAHC15-70-C-0120.

The authors are with the Network Analysis Corporation, Glen Cove, N. Y. 11542.

of the question, and no known computationally feasible method exists for finding an optimal computer-communication layout for a system with a sufficiently large number of nodes.

Discrete Elements: Components usually are available in discrete sizes. Thus line speeds can be at 2000, 2400, 3600, $\cdots$, 9600, $\cdots$, 50 000, 240 000 bits/s, etc. This means an integer optimization problem must be solved. Except in special cases for centralized tree design, no theoretical methods now exist for problems of practical size.

Nonlinearities: Component cost structures, time-delay functions, and reliability functions are all nonlinear. Typical cost functions are neither "concave" nor "convex" and no analytical methods are available to obtain optimal solutions for networks containing such elements.

However, in spite of these difficulties, enormous progress has been made in the understanding of computer-communication networks and in the development of effective analysis and design procedures. In this paper, we will describe a number of approaches to these problems, indicate areas where additional research is needed, and suggest possible approaches to several outstanding problems.

II. Performance Criteria and System Models and Computations

To specify the topology of a computer-communication network, the following questions must be answered.

Design Constraints

What average, maximum, or distribution of time delays will be tolerated? (The ARPA Network requires average response times of less than 0.2 s, while NASDAQ requires that over 50 percent of all messages be answered by the system in less than 5 s and 90 percent in less than 7 s.)

What average and peak throughputs are required? (ARPA requirements are generally on the order of 10 kbits/s/node on the average and peak rates of 85 kbits/s/node pair in an unloaded network. NASDAQ specifies busy-hour traffic in excess of 100 000 messages (each about 900 bits long) per busy hour.)

How should reliability be defined and what degree of reliability is necessary? (Minimum ARPA Network reliability is specified by a two-connectivity constraint, while NASDAQ System requirements are specified for each component within the system.)

What types of computing and terminal equipment are available for the system? (Within the ARPA Network, there are a variety of computers and terminals while the centralized NASDAQ design contains only one main computer center and common concentrators, control devices, and I/O terminals.)

What types of communication modes, such as leased, point-to-point lines, direct-dial, multipoint polled, etc., are feasible? What are the characteristics, such as transmission rates, average downtimes, and error rates, of feasible communication lines? (NASDAQ utilizes both point-to-point and multipoint lines with transmission rates of from 1600–50 000 bits/s. The ARPA Network uses primarily 50 000-bit/s lines, although other speeds are assigned in a few selected places. In both networks, line speeds were chosen to yield required response times at minimum cost.)

Object of Network Optimization

The goal of the network optimization is to provide a "robust" network design which meets all design constraints and has the lowest possible cost. The network design must provide solutions to the following problems.

1) What are the best message formats and transmission schemes?

2) What kind of concentrator, multiplexer, and front-end configurations are needed, and where should they be located?

3) What combination of leased lines, dial-up, point-to-point, multipoint, etc., is to be used, and what are the best line speeds and locations?

4) What is the sensitivity of the design's performance to variations in traffic loads, equipment availabilities, and other parameter changes?

The two most important design constraints for both the NASDAQ System and the ARPA Network are the time-delay–throughput contraints and the network reliability constraints. These can be expected to be major considerations in the design of most significant systems. The time-delay and reliability analyses of networks are difficult problems for which only recently have adequate approaches been developed. We, therefore, summarize some of the pertinent work on these subjects.

Time Delay Models and Computations [*31*]–[*33*]

Queuing models for computer networks evolved from similar models for message-switched communication systems which are generalized from the well-established theory of single-server queues. The approach to be discussed is oriented towards the analysis of store-and-forward systems to point-to-point communication lines. Analytic approaches are also possible for multipoint lines.

Queues on a single communication link are characterized by the distribution of times between consecutive arrivals of messages and the distribution of transmission times. The *average delay time* T is most often taken as the measure of performance. The major analytical difficulty of ***network*** queuing problems is that flows throughout the network are correlated to circumvent this problem; the *length* of a given message can be considered as an independent random variable as it passes from node to node. Although this independence assumption is not physically realistic, it results in a mathematically tractable model which does not seem to affect the accuracy of the predicted time delays [31].

With the independence assumption, the network queuing analysis can be decomposed into solvable single-server problems on a link-by-link basis. Assume Poisson arrival processes for all messages with an average of $\gamma_{j,k}$ messages per second and an exponential distribution of message lengths with an average of $1/\mu$ bits per message. Then, if γ is the sum of the quantities $\gamma_{j,k}$, C_i is the capacity (bits/second) of the ith link, λ_i is its average message traffic (messages/second), and B is the number of links in the network,

$$T = \sum_{i=1}^{B} \frac{\lambda_i}{\gamma} \frac{1}{\mu C_i - \lambda_i}.$$

Moreover, the effect of propagation time and overhead traffic in the actual network can be included to obtain a more detailed equation for average delay [33]. Thus

$$T = K + \sum_{i=1}^{B} \frac{\lambda_i}{\gamma} \left[\frac{1}{\mu' C_i} + \frac{\lambda_i/\mu C_i}{\mu C_i - \lambda_i} + P_i + K \right]$$

where $1/\mu'$ represents the average number of bits in an information message, and $1/\mu$ represents the average length of all messages (including acknowledgments, headers, requests for next messages, parity checks, etc.). Finally, K is the nodal processing time, assumed constant (for the ARPA Network about 0.35 ms), and P_i is the propagation time on the ith channel (about 20 ms for a 3000-mi link).

The main difficulty in applying the above queuing approach is the calculation of the link flows $\lambda_1, \cdots, \lambda_B$. For a tree network, this is no problem since there is one unique path between any pair of points. However, for a distributed design, there may be many alternatives, and hence the queuing analysis can only be applied in conjunction with a routing strategy. We will discuss this problem later in the paper.

Reliability Models and Computations

A simple and natural characterization of network reliability is the ability of the network to sustain communication between all operable pairs of nodes. For example, for design purposes, a network may be required to have at least two independent paths between all pairs of nodes. This insures that at least two nodes and/or links must fail before any pair of operable nodes cannot communicate. This reliability criterion, while conceptually appealing, is independent of the properties of the nodes and links and does not take into account the "degree" of disruption that may occur. Hence it does not reflect the actual availability of resources in the network.

A more refined measure (among others) is the average fraction of node pairs that cannot communicate because of node and link failures. To calculate this measure, knowledge of the element failure rates must be available or estimated. If desired, the availability of specific nodes and the existence of specified communicating node pairs can also be considered using this formulation.

The most detailed level of analysis of reliability incorporates element failures, flow requirements, routing strategies, acceptable delays, and other pertinent network characteristics. At this level of analysis, an appropriate criterion is the expected throughputs of the intact portions of the overall network. Only "brute-force" procedures are presently available at this level of analysis.

A variety of approaches to the analysis problem are possible [20], [52], [53], [57]. The authors believe that purely analytical approaches are computationally intractable for large networks, and, therefore, the best presently available methods employ a combination of analysis and simulation to obtain estimates of parameters such as the probability of the network not being connected or the average fraction of noncommunicating node pairs. Computations for tree networks can be *analytically* performed [30]. Hence we outline several approaches which apply to distributed networks.

Consider the basic analysis problem given below. Suppose a network has N nodes and B links, and each element has probability p of failing. Estimate $h(p)$, the probability of the network being disconnected by the failing components. Alternatively, estimate $n(p)$, the expected number of node pairs not able to communicate, for P values of p. We discuss three approaches to this problem [52]–[54].

The first approach, which we shall call the *naive approach*, is first to generate a random number for each element. If the number is less than p, the corresponding element is considered failed and removed from the net; otherwise it is left in. Then the resulting network is checked for connectivity or the number of node pairs disconnected depending on whether $h(p)$ or $n(p)$ is desired. This computation is repeated enough times to obtain a sufficiently accurate estimate according to the usual standards of Monte Carlo simulation. This entire procedure must then be repeated for each of the P values of p of interest.

The second approach, which we will call the *functional-simulation approach*, is based on a technique used for simulation approaches to percolation problems. Here, as in the naive method, a random number is generated for each element. Now, however, we place these numbers and their corresponding nodes and links in decreasing order. Let r_i be the random number generated for the ith element, and suppose $r_{i_1}, r_{i_2}, \cdots, r_{i_{N+B}}$ are the random numbers in decreasing order. Then, in the naive method, if $r_{i_k} \geq p > r_{i_{k+1}}$, we would analyze for connectivity the subnetwork consisting of the elements $i_1, i_2, \cdots, i_k$. We can evaluate one point in the sample for each value of p for one set of random numbers using the following procedure: for $1 \geq p > r_{i_1}$ the network has no links or nodes; for $r_{i_1} \geq p > r_{i_2}$ the network consists of the element i_1 only; for $r_{i_2} \geq p > r_{i_3}$ the network consists of elements i_1 and i_2, etc. What makes this technique especially effective is that there exist connectivity algorithms which can be used to "update" the analysis of a given network when an additional element is added. Thus for example, if the network with all the components present is analyzed for connectivity, introducing the components in the order $i_1, i_2, \cdots, i_{N+B}$ using one of these techniques, we achieve the analysis for the subnetworks consisting of $i_1, i_2, \cdots, i_k$ for $k = 1, \cdots, B$. In particular, we can determine $h(p)$ or $n(p)$ for all P values of p at once using a connectivity algorithm *once* for each sample point rather than P times, as would be required in the naive method.

By a theorem due to Kruskal, each connectivity calculation is equivalent to determining a maximum total length spanning forest where the length of the ith link is r_i. This relation is discussed in detail in a paper by Kershenbaum and Van Slyke [29].

The final technique, which we call the *Moore–Shannon approach*, is based on the use of the following equation (with $q = 1 - p$):

$$h(p) = \sum_{k=0}^{N+B} C(k) p^{N+B-k} q^k$$

where $C(k)$ is the number of disconnected subnetworks with exactly k elements. This relation is similar to one due to Moore and Shannon [39] for analyzing the reliability of switching networks. A similar relation can be used for $n(p)$:

$$n(p) = \sum_{k=0}^{N+B} D(k) p^{N+B-k} q_k$$

where $D(k)$ is the average number of node pairs not communicating over all subnetworks with exactly k elements. In this approach, each $C(k)$ or $D(k)$ is estimated by simulation rather than attempting to estimate directly the sums $h(p)$ or $n(p)$. It is shown in [53] that this is especially effective for $h(p)$ because all but $B - N + 2$ of the $C(k)$ are known *a priori*. There are $\binom{B}{k}$ subnetworks with exactly k elements. If this number is reasonably small, $C(k)$ and $D(k)$ can be calculated by enumeration, and if the number is too large, they can be estimated by simulation. In either case it is useful to use a connectivity algorithm by which, after the connectivity of one subnetwork is determined, subnetworks similar to the first can be easily analyzed using the results of the first analysis. Such an algorithm is described in [54].

The Moore–Shannon approach can be made especially effective for reliability analysis by using stratified random sampling. The strata are defined by the number of links failing *and* the number of nodes failing. Proportional random sampling is then used to divide the effort devoted in the simulation according to the probability of each stratum.

Basic Design Techniques for Centralized Networks

Basic Properties and Heuristic Structures

A good "heuristic structure" may be thought of as any topology which a designer thinks is both "low" cost and feasible. Such a structure may be the result of a "back-of-the-envelope" design or the output of a sophisticated computer-design program. When a designer follows the conventional but naive approach of placing a link wherever there is enough traffic to warrant it, he is creating heuristic structure. Usually, a good designer incorporates whatever theoretical results are available from simpler network models. For example, simple structures for the design of a centralized network are often based on a shortest tree (often called a minimal spanning tree). Such a tree has the smallest total number of miles of communication lines of all possible trees. In general, the use of a tree in a centralized design may not provide the minimum cost solution. However, it can be shown that if all link costs are *convex* functions of capacity (this implies continuous functions), then some tree solution is optimal [58]. On the other hand, the use of a shortest tree connecting all communicating points even under the simplest and most ideal conditions may still not be optimal. This is because one can add a set of S additional points, called Steiner points, to an N-node system and then find the shortest tree connecting the $N+S$ points [25]. If the new points are chosen appropriately, the resulting tree is called a *Steiner minimal tree* and the total length of all lines in the Steiner tree is less than the total length of all lines in the ordinary shortest tree without Steiner points. A simple example of a shortest tree and a Steiner tree is shown in Fig. 3. Physically, a Steiner point corresponds to the location of a multiplexer or concentrator, and although some procedures are available for finding good locations, this problem is presently tractable only by using heuristic procedures. An effective heuristic approach for the problem is described in [6].

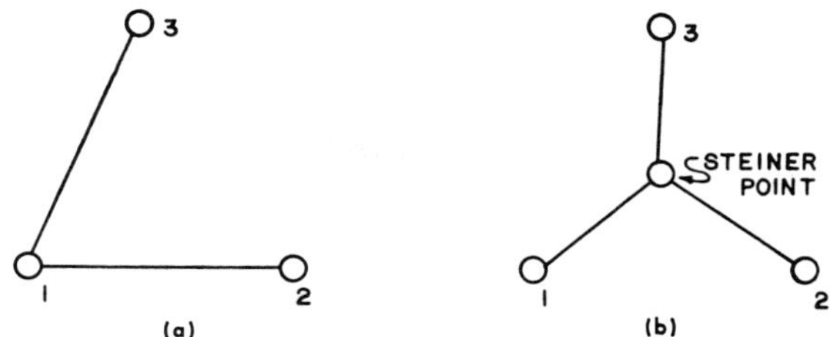

Fig. 3. (a) Shortest tree (minimal spanning tree). (b) Steiner minimal tree.

As already stated, the most economical topology, even for a centralized network, may not be a tree. In practice, there is a finite set of choices for line capacities, and thus line costs are not convex functions of capacity. In this case, a nontree topology will often be more economical than any tree topology. Fig. 4 illustrates this point with a simple example in which we must connect two points (1 and 2) to a central node 3 with either 19.2- or 50-kbit/s lines. For the flow requirements given, the most economical configuration connecting only the three points shown is not a tree. (This assumes that the facilities at nodes 1 and 2 are capable of relaying the flow.) The nontree configuration is also more reliable since, if any line should fail, the network can still transmit some traffic from both nodes 1 and 2 to the central site.

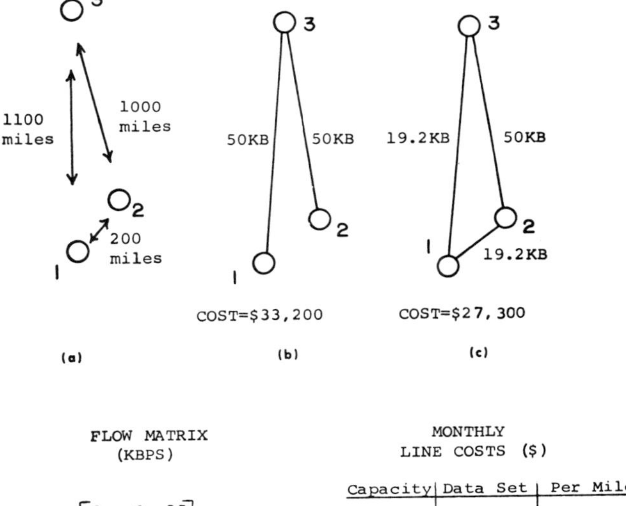

FLOW MATRIX (KBPS)

$$\begin{bmatrix} 0 & 0 & 25 \\ 0 & 0 & 40 \\ 25 & 40 & 0 \end{bmatrix}$$

MONTHLY LINE COSTS ($)

Capacity	Data Set	Per Mile
19.2	850.	7.50
50.0	850.	15.00

Fig. 4. Example of utility of nontree structure for centralized network.

An interesting and important property for centralized nontree structures is that, given any optimal topology, there exists a tree within the network such that all *unsaturated* links *are in* the tree, and, furthermore, all flows to the central node in each link are in the same direction (and vice versa). In a sense this means that the topology departs from a tree structure only when completely utilized links can be added. A complete discussion of this property is given in [49]. Several interesting design procedures could be derived from this work, but these have not yet been investigated.

A consideration in the design of a nontree structure such as the one shown in Fig. 4(c) is the use of split routing. The network shown satisfies flow requirements by sending up to 10 Kbits/s along the path from node 1 to node 2 to node 3 and the remainder of the 25-kbit/s requirement directly from node 1 to node 3 through the direct 19.2-kbit/s link. In a general network, with flow requirements between many pairs of nodes (rather than to and from only the central node), a distributed design may be best, but split routing may not be any more economical than sending all flow between any pair of nodes over a single path. If the cost of installing channel capacity is convex, this can be shown to be the case [23]. (A special case of this is when the cost of installing C units of channel capacity is linear.) Thus if $f(C)$ is the cost of installing C units of channel capacity, split routing gains nothing if

$$f(C+2) - 2f(C+1) + f(C) \leq 0.$$

An example of the *utility* of split routing is shown in Fig. 5.

There are a number of reasonable ways to generate heuristic structures for distributed networks. Some of these operate by first connecting the nodes with a tree and then "judiciously" adding links. Other methods begin with a network with a minimum number of links and specified connectivity. However, present methods of creating heuristic structures all result in networks that can be considerably improved by the use of iterative optimization techniques, and hence we will postpone our discussion of distributed network design until the next section.

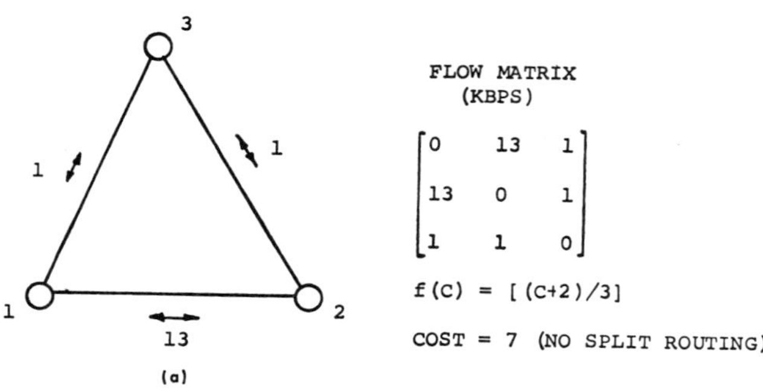

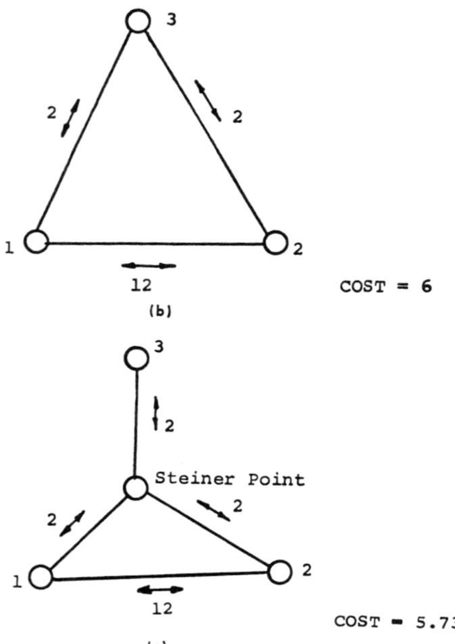

Fig. 5. (a) No split routing. (b) Split routing but no Steiner points. (c) Split routing and a Steiner point.

Design via an Interactive Terminal [3], [4], [7], [12], [42]

One of the most routine ways of enhancing human design capabilities has been the development of numerous "design" programs which enable a design to interact with a time-sharing system via a Teletype or graphics terminal. Although the computer *per se* does only a minimal amount of design, the human effort is reduced by the designer rapidly being able to test various alternatives.

A typical interactive design program accepts as input parameters such as the node locations and names, the traffic requirements and message-length statistics, and, optionally, line locations or capacities. If line locations are not input, the computer might generate a shortest tree. In application-oriented packages, the program will allow the designer to include concentrators and multiplexers in his design.

The designer would then use his terminal to modify the initial configuration. After each modification the computer would recalculate the cost for the current design. With a graphics terminal and light pen, the typical program gives the designer the following capabilities.

1) A link can be added by indicating with the light pen the two nodes to be joined.

2) A link's parameters can be changed by using the light pen to indicate a parameter set to be changed and using the keyboard to type new parameter values.

3) A link can be deleted by using the light pen.

4) The position of a node can be changed with the light pen, first indicating a new position, and then the node to be moved.

Most interactive design programs are proprietary, and, therefore, details are not available. However, nearly all presently available interactive programs known to us perform virtually no significant analysis except for cost calculation during the *design* process. A few programs allow for a network simulation either before or after a design step and some calculate simple graph theoretic properties such as the radius and average path length.

There is a useful place for interactive program packages of the type described. These programs can eliminate many of the difficult jobs of finding tariffs and costing systems and finding "reasonable" networks. However, the current interactive approach is highly inferior to iterative schemes using remote batch techniques. Some simple iterative methods are described next.

Iterative Techniques [8], [9], [16], [17], [24], [50], [56]

Iterative techniques for computer-network design involve the heuristic application of a family of optimization procedures called "node" or "link" exchanges. Exchange methods are search procedures which optimize network structure by changing small sections of a large network at a time. The methods begin with a network satisfying all constraints either selected by a human or generated by a different computer-design program. Exchange methods are then applied to the starting network until a new network which both satisfies all constraints and has lower cost is found. The process is then repeated until cost can no longer be lowered. The network resulting is then said to be "locally optimal." The process may then be repeated using either a new starting network, a different class of exchange methods, or the same methods in a different order. To illustrate the types of exchange methods that can be employed, we discuss the design of centralized networks using several different methods. We defer our discussion of distributed nets until we examine several key problems in the design of such networks. In addition to topological specification, link capacities must be selected for the network design. If time delay is the dominant constraint in capacity selection, a method for optimally choosing from an available set of options exists [16]. This procedure can be used in conjunction with any of the following methods.

Multipoint Path Creation: One of the earliest exchange methods, developed by Esau and Williams [9], forms the basis of the IBM proprietary program CNDP. This method, as initially developed, applies to a specialized class of centralized networks which has links with only one line-transmission rate. Initially, a star network of links from every terminal to the central node is chosen. At successive iterations, one of these links is removed and the terminal thus disconnected is placed on an established path to reduce costs by creating a multipoint circuit. To determine allowable link exchanges, the amount of traffic to be accommodated is checked first. The tradeoff value for performing each feasible exchange is calculated, and the one with the greatest gain is chosen.

A Simple Path Exchange [50]*:* The procedure begins with any tree, and thus each node has a unique path to the central

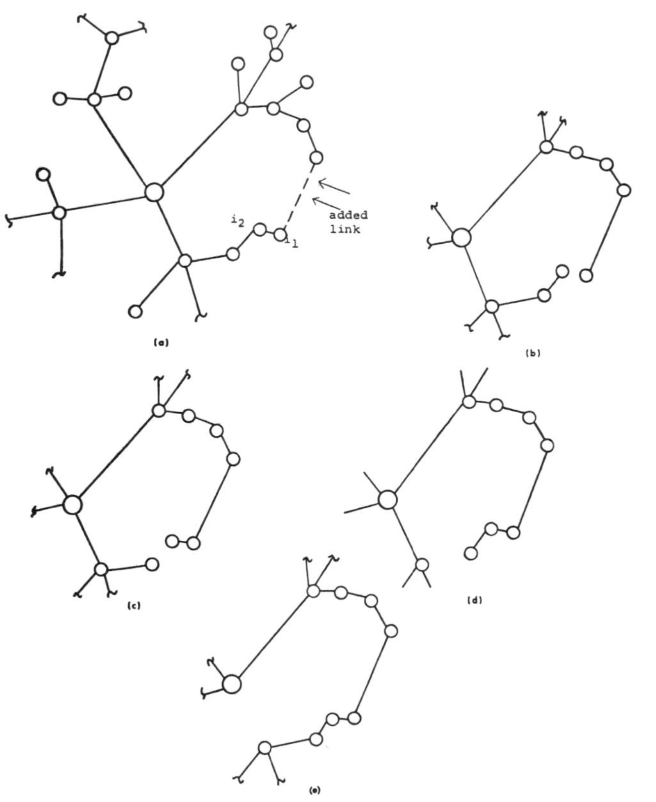

Fig. 6. Illustration of a simple branch exchange procedure.

node. Improvements are attempted by exchanging nodes on different paths. The algorithm first uniquely orders the paths as $\pi_1, \pi_2, \cdots$, and then begins by considering the farthest node, say n_1, from the central site on the first path π_1. The closest node to n_1 on a different path, say π_j, is added to the first path if the total cost is reduced and the exchange is feasible. If infeasible, then the first combination of nodes on π_1 closest to the central node whose total number of data terminals is equal to the number of data terminals of the added node is removed from π_1 and added to the path π_j. The next farthest node from the center on the first path is then considered in the same manner. When all nodes on the first path have been examined, that path is excluded from consideration. The second path π_2 is then treated, and so on.

Circuit Deletions [16]: An effective local optimization procedure operates by starting with any tree and then applying a special kind of elementary tree transformation. It can be shown that any tree can be obtained from any other tree by a sequence of such transformations. The transformation used is as follows: For a given tree, choose a node i and find the node i_1 closest to i but not already connected to i. Add link (i_1, i) to the tree and identify the circuit formed. Suppose that this circuit consists of links (i_1, i), (i, i_2), (i_2, i_3), $\cdots$, (i_j, i_1). New trees are formed by deleting in turn links (i, i_2), (i_2, i_3), $\cdots$, and finally (i_j, i_1) as illustrated in Fig. 6. Each time a link is deleted, the optimal-link-capacities algorithm is applied to determine network cost. Each node i is scanned in turn; link additions from i to its d nearest neighbors are considered. Whenever L lower cost trees have been generated, the node scan is begun again. (For most problems, $d=3$ and $L=1$ yield excellent results.) This procedure has proven to be extremely powerful in finding low-cost trees. Whenever the problem has been small enough to exhaustively find optimal trees, the method has converged to the optimum solution. In addition, tests in which link cost is set equal to link length have shown that the procedure can readily converge to the shortest tree solution.

The Capacity-Optimization Problem

One of the most difficult of all network design problems is the selection of link capacities from a *finite* set of options. Although there are many heuristic approaches to this problem, rigorous results are scarce. For most existing work, the objective is either to minimize cost subject to a fixed average time-delay constraint or minimize average time delay (or some function of the average delay) subject to fixed cost constraint.

If the object is to minimize cost subject to a specified *maximum* allowable average time delay, an *optimum* procedure exists for centralized tree networks [16]. If the object is to minimize average time delay at a fixed cost (or the sum of the kth power of average delay on each link), analytic results are available if link capacities are continuous variables [33], [38]. For distributed networks the problem is far more complex than for tree networks since the major variable affecting a link capacity choice is the link flow. A tree has only one path between any pair of points, so that link flow is known *a priori*. For a distributed design, link capacities and link flows interact since a good routing algorithm will tend to send flow around saturated portions of the network. Thus link capacity selection and the network routing should be simultaneously considered. Because of this difficulty, there are no *practical optimal* results for distributed networks, although many seemingly "good" heuristics are available. Thus to illustrate the capacity selection problem, we examine centralized nets where we can compare heuristics to known optimum solutions.

The tree in Fig. 7 has had its capacities optimally selected from a finite set of options with realistic data set and line costs. The system was designed to produce a *maximum* one-way average delay of 0.3 s from any node to the central node (node 1). The overall monthly network line cost is 21 775 dollars. The capacities resulting from the best continuous linear approximation are indicated in the same figure by encircled numbers. These correspond to the capacities chosen to minimize average delay for an expenditure of 21 775 dollars. For both sets of capacities, the average delay is 0.19 s.

The limitations of the continuous-selection method based on *average delay* can be seen by examining the decisions made for several links by each algorithm. Thus for the link (7, 15) the optimal discrete choice was 50 kbits/s, while the continuous choice was 37.8 kbits/s. (This would become 50 kbits/s if capacity were rounded up to the nearest available capacity.) Both methods recognized that this link capacity could be inexpensively made very large to make its delay contribution negligible. However, for another similar situation, link (2, 16), the optimal discrete capacity was chosen to be 4.8 kbits/s, while the continuous capacity selected was 14.7 kbits/s. (Rounded up, this becomes 19.2 kbits/s.) The optimum discrete decision recognized that this link delay contribution was not critical, even though its capacity could be inexpensively increased. The continuous choice was not able to recognize this fact. Finally, to contrast the results of optimization to the results of the application of simple heuristic, we assign discrete capacities according to the following rule: Set the capacity of a link equal to the smallest capacity that can accommodate the

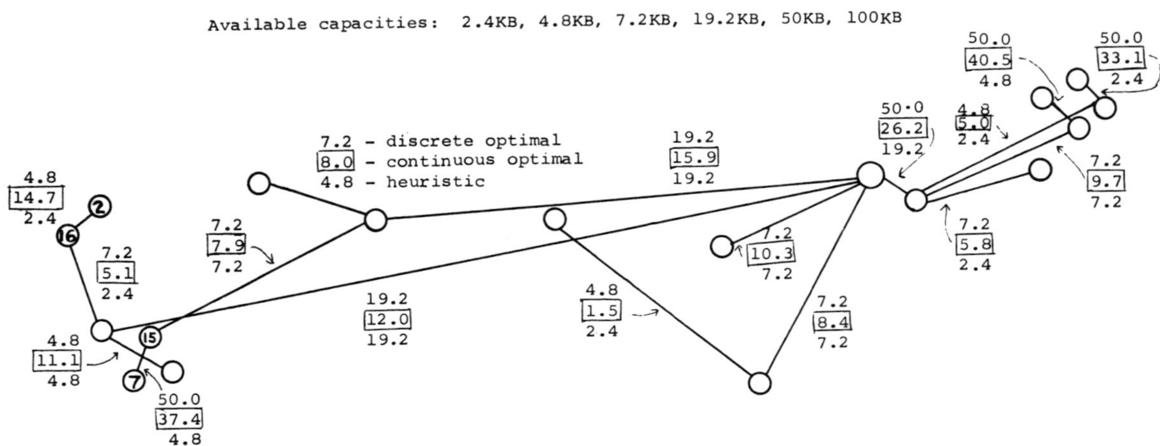

Fig. 7. Discrete optimal: Maximum average delay = 0.3 s. Discrete and continuous optimal: Average delay = 0.9 s. Cost = 21 775 dollars. Heuristic: Maximum average delay = 1.4 s. Average delay = 0.5 s. Cost = 17 692 dollars.

flow in the link. With this decision rule, the network line cost is reduced to 17 692 dollars per month. (This selection criterion produces a *stable* system whose set of capacities has the smallest possible cost.) However, the maximum average delay from any node to the central node is now 1.4 s, and the overall average delay is 0.5 s.

IV. Distributed Network Design Problems

Imbedded in the centralized network problem are a number of simplifications to the general network design problem. In a centralized network, after one specifies line speeds, transmission schemes, and traffic statistics, time-delay analyses can be performed. However, in a distributed design, these data are not sufficient since we must also specify how flow is to be routed through the net. Using current heuristic exchange techniques for minimum-cost design, the major analysis problems one encounters in feasibility analysis are routing (and delay) and reliability analysis.

The Routing Problem [1], [13], [18], [21], [22], [27], [58]

A good routing procedure must 1) make full use of available line capacities; 2) be computationally efficient for repeated use during an iterative design process; and 3) exhibit the same characteristics as the one implemented in the operating network.

If the objective is to minimize average delay, the routing problem is a nonlinear multicommodity flow problem [15]. This problem [13], [22], [58] can be formulated as a separable convex programming problem, and either minimum delay or maximum ideal throughput can be achieved if the routing procedure follows the solution of the programming problem. However, for networks with more than a few nodes, this approach is prohibitively expensive for repeated applications of the routing algorithm during the design stage.

A proven heuristic procedure is to route flow over the least utilized paths with the minimum number of intermediate nodes. This approach generally gives a result within 5–20 percent of the optimum. In addition to being fast (over three orders of magnitude faster than the programming approach) specialized procedures can be derived with this heuristics that facilitate local optimization of the network structure. However, the basic method does not take full advantage of split routing and significant variations in link capacities, and leaves room for considerable improvements especially in the case when the network contains a wide distribution of different line capacities (an apparently desirable characteristic of very large networks).

A more efficient routing procedure, called *cut saturation*, is a generalization of the above basic method which allows split routing and the utilization of paths with more than the minimum number of nodes [18]. As much flow as possible between all node pairs is first simultaneously routed over the paths with minimum numbers of nodes. (These paths are "shortest paths" using a simple unit metric for each line.) When no shortest path with excess capacity is available, the "saturated" lines are deleted from the network representation and flows are then routed over the shortest paths of the remaining subnetwork. The process is continued until the network representation has had enough lines removed to become disconnected. By this technique, a message is sent down a path with fewest intermediate nodes and excess capacity or, when that path is filled, the one with next fewest intermediate nodes and excess capacity, etc. The computational complexity of this procedure is of the same order of magnitude as the basic heuristic approach. Yet its results are extremely close to the optimal solution during heavy traffic. Furthermore, the routing strategy is very similar to physically implementable and desirable routing schemes for distributed networks such as the ARPA Network, and, both experimentally and by simulation, leads to realizable network performance.

As an example, the 23-node network shown in Fig. 8 has five saturated links. Five iterations were required to obtain these flows before a cut was saturated and the network was disconnected. The performance of the network after each iteration is illustrated by a graph of throughput versus delay in Fig. 9. Graphs illustrating computation time per iteration as a function of network size are shown in Fig. 10. The relationships shown are for specially devised algorithms described in detail in [41].

The basic limitation, and a fundamental open problem of present routing procedures, is that the performance of a particular routing strategy is critically dependent on the capacities assigned to the links. In many procedures either these capacities are assigned before the routing is performed, or a routing is first performed and capacities then assigned. The difficulty with such approaches is that *a priori* the routing-

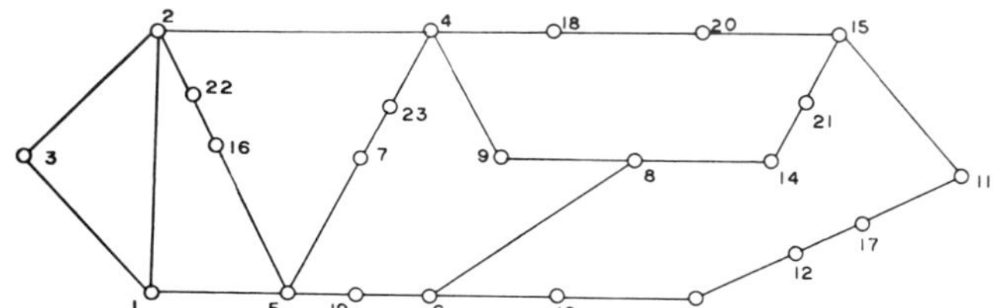

Fig. 8. Network use for example (all links have 50 000-bit/s capacity).

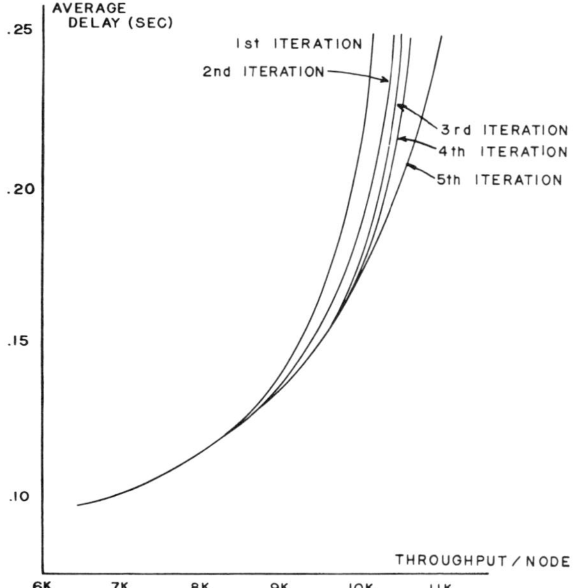

Fig. 9. Throughput versus delay using cut saturation (routing for network shown in Fig. 8).

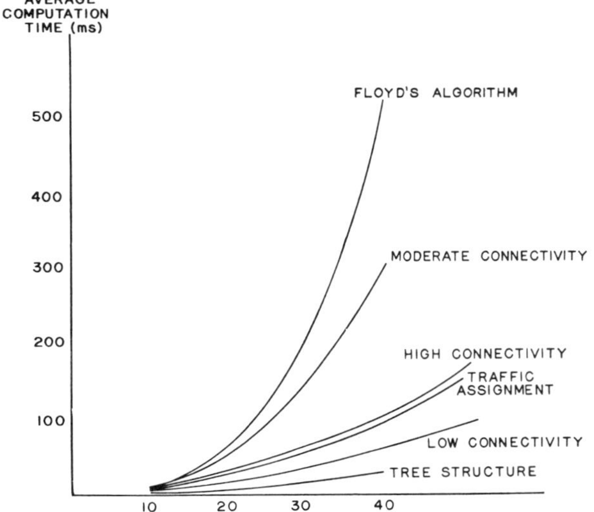

Fig. 10. Computation time versus network size and connectivity for new shortest-route algorithm and for Floyd's algorithm.

capacity assignment combination is biased, and often any chances of affecting economies are reduced. Thus a major outstanding problem is that no general procedures are yet known for assigning capacities from a wide range of options while simultaneously optimizing the routing used in the design procedure.

The Reliability Problem

An essential characteristic of any good network design is that it should not suffer significant degradation in performance if some elements fail. With the state of current technology, both nodes and communication links have nontrivial downtimes. Therefore, the network design must provide for these failures by having sufficient alternate paths to satisfy flow requirements and time-delay constraints. For example, the NASDAQ Network is made reliable by installing parallel lines and extra concentrators, while the ARPA design utilizes distributed control and at least two independent paths between each pair of nodes.

The network reliability problem has two aspects—analysis and design. Reliability analysis for centralized networks is routine. For distributed networks, it has reached the stage where large networks can be handled. Preliminary studies indicate that for large networks, reliability may be the dominant design constraint. For example, the graphs in Fig. 11 correspond to reliability analyses of 2-connected low-cost networks of 20, 40, 60, 80, 100, and 200 nodes. These networks meet all delay and throughput constraints. However, as the number of nodes increases, the probability that all nodes can simultaneously communicate continuously decreases, while the average fraction of communicating node pairs decreases for nets with more than 80 nodes.

The relationship between distributed network connectivity and availability criteria such as "average fraction of communicating node pairs" is not yet completely understood, although the problem is being studied intensively. The design problem is to identify link locations so that given reliability constraints as well as throughput and delay are satisfied. If one were to conclusively relate network connectivity to the availability constraints, then a family of proven link exchange procedures could be applied to the problem. Thus a new problem with the following formulation could be solved.

Assume we are given N geographically located nodes and a cost matrix $C=[c_{i,j}]$, where $c_{i,j}$ is the cost of constructing link $[i, j]$. We would like to construct a minimum-cost network such that there are at least $r_{i,j}$ node disjoint paths between nodes n_i and n_j, where $R=[r_{i,j}]$ is a specified redundancy matrix.

This design problem can be formulated as an integer-programming problem, but the number of constraints is astronomical even for relatively small networks. A tractable approach is to search for low-cost rather than minimum-cost networks, using link-exchange methods like the ones previously described. Initially, we generate a network satisfying all connectivity constraints using either deterministic procedures such as the ones described in [20, section IV.A.3] or randomized procedures such as those described in [51].

The optimizing routine searches for networks generated by link exchanges of two links which have lower cost and are also feasible. Feasibility analysis now requires general connectivity analysis as well as the already required throughput and time-delay analyses. A powerful local transformation for this problem is a link exchange such that if the net has two links $[i, k]$ and $[j, h]$ such that $[i, h]$ and $[j, k]$ are not in the net, a new network can be generated by removing $[i, k]$ and $[j, h]$ and adding $[i, h]$ and $[j, k]$. If

$$c_{i,h} + c_{j,k} < c_{i,k} + c_{j,h}$$

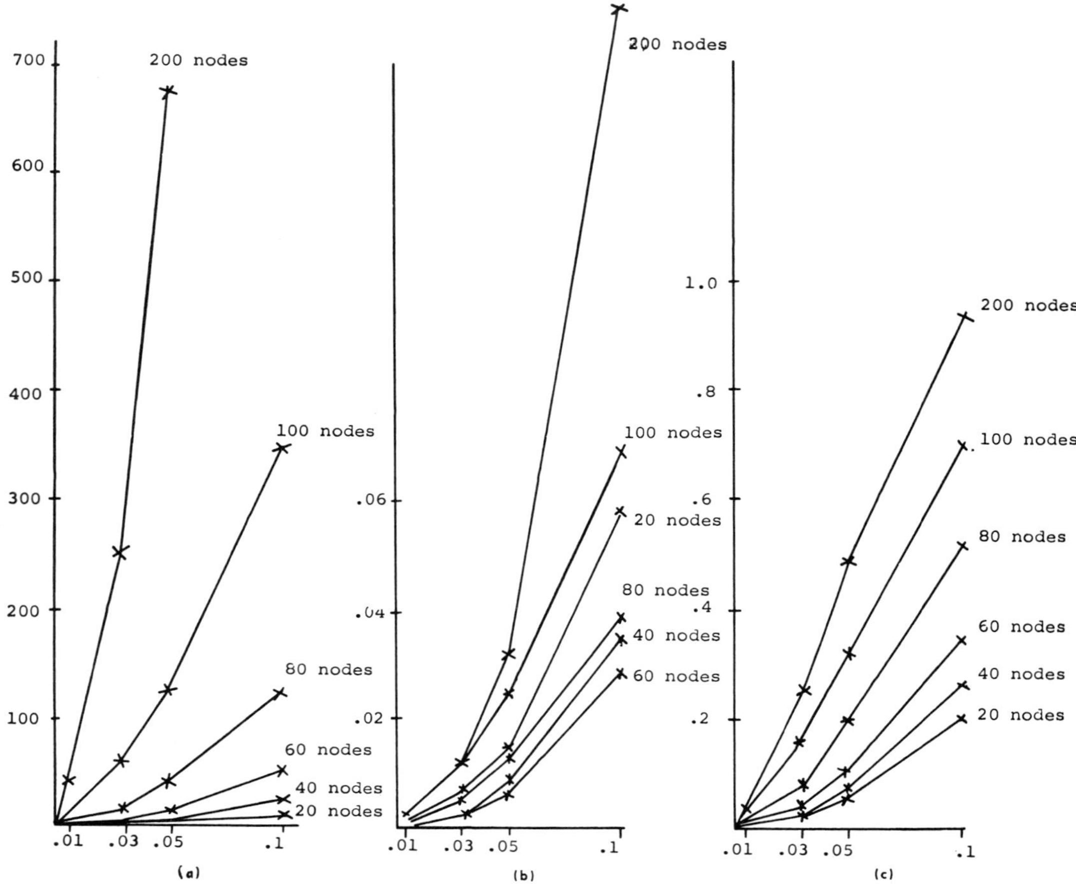

Fig. 11. Network reliability as a function of number of nodes. (a) Average number of node pairs not communicating versus probability of link failing. (b) Average fraction of node pairs not communicating versus probability of link failing. (c) Probability of net being disconnected versus probability of link failing.

the new network has lower cost than the original one and it must be analyzed for feasibility. Testing connectivity feasibility can be economically done because of the following fact: If a link exchange on a feasible network which results in a network G^* destroys feasibility by reducing the redundancy between nodes n_a and n_b below the requirement $r_{a,b}$, and if the link exchange resulted in the removal of links $[i, k]$ and $[j, h]$, then either $w_{i,k}(G^*) < r_{a,b}$ or $w_{j,h}(G^*) < r_{a,b}$. This reduces the number of computations required, and, in addition, highly efficient methods for performing this computation are available [20]. For example, if one wishes to check a network for k-connectivity, it is only necessary to make connectivity computations at k nodes in a sequence of progressively simpler network structures [34]. For example, to test a network for 4-connectivity, we would only have to perform the following operations:

Choose any node and verify that there are at least four node-disjoint paths from this node to every other node. Remove the node and all the branches connected to it. From the resulting network choose another node and verify that there are at least three node-disjoint paths connecting this node to every other node. Remove this node and its branches, choose another, and then verify that there are at least two node-disjoint paths from it to every other node. Choose a fourth node. Verify that there is at least one path from it to every other node. These are the only calculations that are required. If the number of disjoint paths between each pair of nodes had been only three, then at the last stage of analysis it would have been impossible to verify that the required number of paths existed. If the new network has lower cost and is feasible, the link exchange is adopted and the search for additional improvements continues. When no additional favorable exchanges can be found, the process terminates. After a locally optimum network is obtained, a new starting network is generated (if one can be found), and the optimization procedure is repeated.

Iterative Techniques for Distributed Network Design [*13*], [*17*], [*24*]

The basic methods for design of a distributed network follow the same patterns as the iterative centralized net-design techniques. After specifying a feasible "starting" network, the computer iteratively modifies the network in simple steps until a lower cost network satisfying all constraints is found. This network becomes a new starting network and the process is continued.

A successful set of modifications used for the ARPA Network design has been a class of link exchanges involving the removal or addition of one or two links at a time. Links may be added or deleted anywhere in the networks. However, regardless of the number of links simultaneously involved in a local modification, all transformations can be formulated in terms of the removal or addition of a *single* link at a time; that is, if a modification adds two links and removes three, an

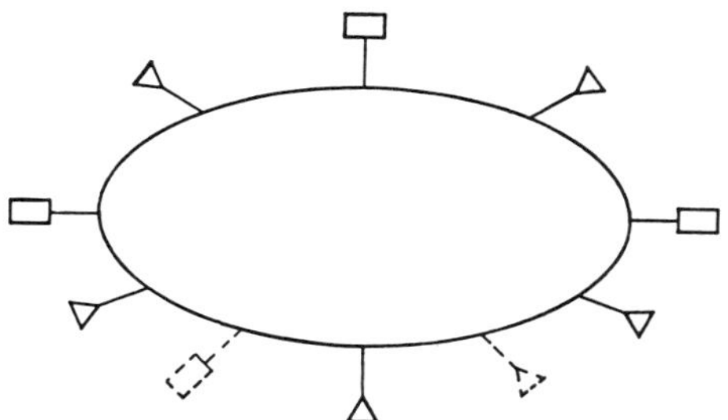

Fig. 12. A looped communication system.

equivalent set of modifications adds two links one at a time and then deletes three links, also, one at a time. Thus any set of link modifications can be considered to be composed of these two *elementary* modifications. The importance of considering such elementary transformations stems from the increased efficiency that can be obtained during each step of the optimization process. Whenever links are added or removed, traffic must be rerouted in order to reevaluate network throughput and delay. During the optimization process, it is usually adequate to route all flow over paths containing the minimum number of nodes, leaving further increases in throughput to later design stages. In this case, after a link addition or deletion, it is not necessary to reroute all traffic completely to compute the new network throughput. Note that in this case, the capacity of a link is either preassigned or set equal to the smallest capacity that will accommodate the link flow required to meet the network throughput specifications.

A simplification of the general design problem occurs in the case of *looped* networks [10], [11], [43], [55], [59]. Such a system usually consists of a set of buffered terminals and one or more computers linked by means of a single circuit, as shown in Fig. 12. The topological design problem for such a system consists in finding a minimum cost routing for the communication circuit. If the number of terminals and computers on the circuit is fixed, then design may be approached in two independent steps: 1) selection of the transmission rate of the circuit based on queuing considerations, and 2) optimization of the layout of the circuit. In this case, the layout problem is equivalent to the "traveling salesman problem" [35], [36], and can be effectively solved by using link exchanges. On the other hand, multiple loop systems in which the locations of the devices on each loop are to be selected represent "clustering" problems similar to those discussed later in this paper. Complete solutions for these problems are not yet available.

An example of distributed network optimization is shown in Fig. 13(a) and (b). The starting network is the one given in Fig. 13(a). Link additions and deletions are indicated in Fig. 13(b), and the associated throughputs and cost per megabit are listed in Table I. Note that; as described before, minimum node routing is used instead of the more optimal routing discussed in the last section. If this routing strategy had been used, for example, for the network in Fig. 13(a), a throughput of 9.9 kbits/s/node (i.e., about 15 percent higher) would result.

As the size of the network increases, the greater is the cost to perform optimization by link exchanges. Decomposition of the network design into regions becomes necessary, and additional heuristics are needed to determine effective decompositions. It presently appears that these methods can be used to

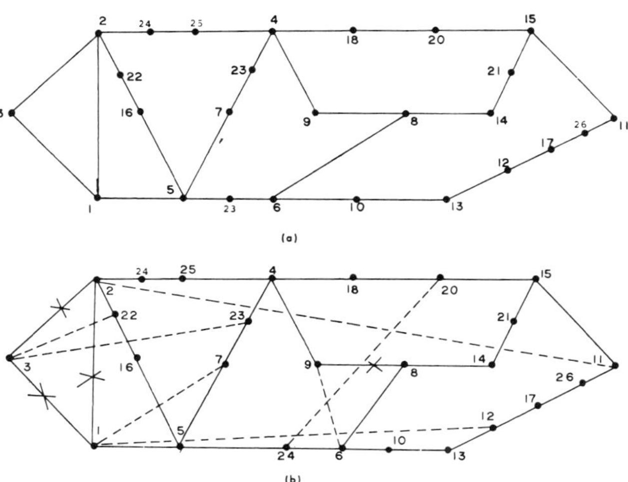

Fig. 13. Example of optimization procedure for a 26-node network. (a) Initial network. (b) Dashed lines indicate added links; "x-ed" lines indicate deleted links.

TABLE I

26-Node Optimization

Throughout (kbits/s/node) (Minimum Node Routing)	Yearly Line Cost (thousands of dollars)	Line Cost per Node	Line Cost per Megabit (cents)	Network Description Added	Removed
8.6	883	34.0	12.48	network shown in Fig. 13	
8.6	885	32.9	12.20		(1,2)
10.5	991	38.0	11.60	(1,12)	
13.0	1129	43.5	10.07	(2,11)	
14.0	1144	44.0	10.00	(3,23)	
				(1,7)	(1,3)
16.0	1173	45.1	9.00	(3,22)	(3,2)
				(9,6)	(9,8)
				(24,20)	

design relatively efficient networks with general structures containing a few hundred nodes, while substantially different procedures will be necessary for networks of greater size.

An alternative iterative approach which only uses link exchanges in a limited sense can be developed from some basic work developed for the optimization of communication networks for "Telpak" and private line tariffs. This approach is described below.

Telpak Network Design [24]

A Telpak is an AT&T tariff that allows a user to purchase either 60 or 240 service-equivalent lines at substantially reduced rates. The user must pay for all 60 or 240 lines even if he requires fewer lines to meet his needs. The Telpak design problem is then to find the most economical arrangement of Telpaks and private lines to meet a set of flow requirements. The following method was derived for optimization of Telpaks in large (3000–4000 points) networks. However, the principles are directly applicable to computer networks. The first step to achieve an economical overall design is to generate as a starting network a simple structure connecting all nodes. A subset of key points spread over the entire country is then chosen, and a series of operations involving a relatively small number of nodes at a time are then performed to improve routing for requirements including a number of key points. After this has been accomplished, sections of the structure are sequentially treated in the same way.

The starting network for each section is a tree (derived from but not identical to a shortest tree). This establishes a unique route between each node pair. Links are then added to provide alternate paths, and all requirements are then routed along the path of shortest length. Additional links, called *longlines*, are then added. For these links, flows are only allowed to be a multiple of the capacity of the highest rate line available (for Telpak, a multiple of 240 voice-equivalent circuits). The longlines are thus all fully utilized links. (For a data link, we might define "full utilization" to be, say, 95 percent of line capacity.) After adding longlines, there are many alternate paths between each pair of points, although most requirements are routed along the shortest ones. For each requirement between a pair of nodes, an attempt is made to find less expensive although possibly longer paths by 1) reducing the flow along a path by the node pair requirement, 2) calculating the additional cost for this number of lines for each link in the network, and 3) using these incremental costs, finding the least cost path and then routing the requirement along it. Finally, a triangle optimization examines every pair of links adjacent at a common node. For example, for flow on links (i, j) and (j, k), it may be less expensive to route some flow directly from i to k. A simple calculation can determine the most economical routing among these points and the local optimization can then be performed.

The principal limitations of the aforementioned approach directly stem from the computation time required to optimize a large network. During the procedure, all flow paths are always known, and throughput and time delay can be routinely calculated. For a network with several hundred points, the method can be refined to produce better results, while for a network with several thousand points, careful attention must be given to the programming aspects of the basic method to keep computation times low enough for the procedure to be practical.

Large Network Design Problems

The outstanding design problems for large distributed networks is to specify their routing and topological structures. This specification must make full use of a wide variety of circuit options. Preliminary studies indicate that, initially, the most fruitful approaches will be based on the partitioning of the network into regions or, equivalently, constructing a large network by connecting a number of regional networks. For optimization of these networks, link-exchange methods are unfeasible unless such decompositions are used, since exchange methods are search procedures, and for network designs incorporating realistic constraints on routing, throughput, delay, cost, reliability, and *physical implementation*, the complexity of the computation is on the order of N^3 to N^6, where N is the number of nodes. For networks with more than a few hundred nodes, each with its own processing capability, present link-exchange procedures fail without network decomposition because of the large amounts of computer time needed to perform the optimization. In addition to reducing the computational complexity of the topological design problem, nodes may be clustered into regions for numerous reasons, such as: a) to partition status information for use in routing, flow control, and other decision processes within the operating network [27], [28]; b) to determine regions of low-, medium-, and high-speed lines in hierarchal structures; and c) to find concentrator–multiplexer locations. For example, the NASDAQ Network connects over 2000 points and is itself a decomposed system since the concentrators create a natural partition of the nodes. However, in this case, since most nodes are unintelligent *terminals* rather than computers with local control capabilities, design problems are not grave.

In distributed networks constructed by connecting together a set of regional networks, to send a message, a node might specify both the destination region and the destination node in that region. No detailed implementation of a large network has yet been specified, but early studies of their properties indicate that factors such as cost, throughput, delay, and reliability are similar to those of the present ARPA Network, if the ARPA technology is used [14].

One of the first questions that arises in the decomposition problem is how large to make the regions and how many regions to create. (In a multilooped network, each loop would define a region.) Once the number of regions has been determined, nodes must be assigned to each and central nodes selected. This problem is extremely difficult, and little is presently known. In order to create effective partitions, we must solve a variety of "clustering" problems. The literature on clustering and partitioning is large but fragmented and spread over many domains including information retrieval, taxonomy, and networks. A potentially valuable research area is the application of known clustering techniques to computer networks. For example, Bahl and Tang have effectively used such techniques for optimization of concentrator locations in centralized networks [2].

Before any substantial progress can be made in applying clustering techniques to large computer networks, an appropriate "distance" or "nearness" measure must be selected, probably on the basis of intuition and experiment. One can see the importance and difficulty of this step by considering an analogous problem in information retrieval. Suppose book titles are stored on a disk file for reference. If, after title A is selected by a reader, there is a high probability that title B will be requested, both titles should be stored in the same record so that overall average disk-access time is minimized. The difficult part of the problem is to determine the conditional probability that B will be referenced if A is referenced. In other words, we must assign a "distance" between A and B for the clustering algorithm. If this step is done poorly, any clustering algorithm subsequently applied will not operate well.

The same basic problem applies to using clustering techniques for the design of large computer networks. Here clustering requires the assignment of distance measures to take into account cost, capacity, traffic, delay, reliability, and routing. Almost no general theoretical results are presently known for this problem.

One approach to determining the size of regions for the decomposition problem is to attempt to minimize the computation requirements for the design procedure. Suppose we have a procedure to perform on a network for which the computing time can be characterized as a polynomial function of the number of nodes. Examples are link-exchange algorithms and many connectivity and reliability analysis procedures. Suppose further that the procedure can be carried out by performing the procedure separately on each region of the decomposed network and then performing the procedure once on the global network.

For simplicity, suppose we seek a two-level hierarchal decomposition. The nodes are divided into groups called *regions*. Nodes which are end nodes of links connecting two regions are called *central* nodes. A regional subnetwork or a *local network* is the nodes of a region together with the links which connect two nodes in the region. Let N be the total number of nodes, NR the number of regions, and NG the number of central nodes per region in the global network. We assume that the number of nodes is the same for each region as is the number of central nodes and that the computing time for a subnetwork with N nodes is proportional to N^v for some $v>1$. While these assumptions are not necessary, the conclusions based on them are indicative and the techniques used can also be applied to more general cases.

Under these assumptions the total computation time is proportional to

$$T = NR\left(\frac{N}{NR}\right)^v + (NR \cdot NG)^v$$

where the first term corresponds to the regional calculation and the last term to the global calculation. Assuming that NR and (N/NR) (the number of nodes per region) can take on noninteger values, we can determine the number of regions which corresponds to minimum computer time by setting $\partial T/\partial NR$ to zero. This implies

$$NR = \left(\frac{N}{NG}\right)^{v/(2v-1)} \left(\frac{v-1}{v}\right)^{1/(2v-1)}.$$

The asymptotic result as $v \rightarrow \infty$ which is of interest is

$$\lim_{v\rightarrow\infty} \left(\frac{N}{NG}\right)^{v/(2v-1)} \left(\frac{v-1}{v}\right)^{1/(2v-1)} = \sqrt{\frac{N}{NG}}.$$

This result can also be obtained by noticing that for large v, total computer time is dominated by the subnetwork with the largest number of nodes; it is then easy to convince oneself that the minimum computation will occur when the global network has exactly as many nodes as the regions, i.e., when $NR \cdot NG = N/NR$. Solving this for NR yields $NR = \sqrt{N/NG}$.

Conclusion

The modeling, analysis, and topological design areas for computer networks have all made significant progress in recent years. General network structures with several hundred nodes can now be handled, while specialized structures (such as centralized trees) with thousands of nodes are tractable. Effective design for small networks of, say, less than about 25 nodes, is routine using the principles discussed in this paper, while design of networks with appreciably more nodes requires a high degree of both analytical and programming skill. Among the major open problems for large network design using present design philosophies are the problems of clustering and partitioning. It appears that these problems will be well in hand in the near future, but that new design philosophies will have to be developed for general network structures with significantly more than one thousand nodes.

References

[1] P. Baran, S. Boehm, and P. Smith, "On distributed communications," Series of 11 Rep. by Rand Corp., Santa Monica, Calif., 1964.

[2] L. R. Bahl and D. T. Tang, "Optimization of concentrator locations in teleprocessing networks," presented at the Symp. Computer Communications, Apr. 4–6, 1972.

[3] A. Battersby and M. L. Berners-Lee, "Communication through interactive diagrams," in *Computer Graphics in Management: Case Studies of Industrial Applications*, R. E. Green and R. D. Parslow, Eds. London: Gower, 1970.

[4] R. L. Brewster, "Designing optimum data networks," *Data Process.*, pp. 23–26, Jan. 1971.

[5] S. Carr, S. Crocker, and V. Cerf, "Host–host communication protocol in the ARPA network," in *Spring Joint Computer Conf., AFIPS Conf. Proc.* Washington, D. C.: Spartan, 1970, pp. 589–597.

[6] S. K. Chang, "The generation of a minimal tree with a Steiner topology," presented at the Symp. Computer Communications, Apr. 4–6, 1972.

[7] R. Citrenbaum, "An on-line model for computation–communication network analysis and modification," SDC, Santa Monica, Calif., Tech. Memo. 4743/003/000, May 11, 1971.

[8] D. R. Doll, "Topology and transmission rate considerations in the design of centralized computer-communication networks," *IEEE Trans. Commun. Technol.*, vol. COM-19, pp. 339–344, June 1971.

[9] L. R. Esau and K. C. Williams, "On teleprocessing system design—Part II: A method for approximating the optimal network," *IBM Syst. J.*, vol. 5, pp. 142–147, 1966.

[10] D. J. Farber and K. Larson, "The structure of a distributed communication system," presented at the Symp. Computer Communications, Apr. 4–6, 1972.

[11] W. D. Farmer and E. E. Newbell, "An experimental distributed switching system to handle bursty computer traffic," in *Proc. Ass. Comput. Mach. Symp.* (Pine Mountain, Ga.), Oct. 13–16, 1969.

[12] J. D. Foley and K. Lau, "Computer aided design of computer networks via computer graphics," presented at the Univ. of North Carolina, Chapel Hill, N. C., 1971.

[13] H. Frank and W. Chou, "Routing in computer networks," in *Networks*, vol. 1, pp. 99–112, 1971.

[14] ——, "Cost and throughput in computer–communication networks," in "Infotech Report on the State of the Art of Computer Networks," 1972.

[15] H. Frank and I. T. Frisch, *Communication, Transmission and Transportation Networks.* Reading, Mass.: Addison–Wesley, 1972.

[16] H. Frank, I. T. Frisch, W. Chou, and R. Van Slyke, "Optimal design of centralized computer networks," in *Networks*, vol. 1. New York: Wiley, 1971, pp. 43–57.

[17] H. Frank, I. T. Frisch, and W. Chou, "Topological considerations in the design of the ARPA computer network," in *Spring Joint Computer Conf., AFIPS Conf. Proc.* Washington, D. C.: Spartan, 1970, pp. 581–587.

[18] W. Chou and H. Frank, "Routing strategies for computer network design," in *Proc. Brooklyn Polytechnic Inst. on Computer Networks and Teletraffic*, Apr. 1972.

[19] H. Frank, R. Kahn, and L. Kleinrock, "Computer communication network design—Experience with theory and practice," in *Spring Joint Computer Conf., AFIPS Conf. Proc.* Washington, D. C.: Spartan, 1972.

[20] H. Frank and I. T. Frisch, "Analysis and design of survivable networks," *IEEE Trans. Commun. Technol.*, vol. COM-18, pp. 501–519, Oct. 1970.

[21] L. Fratta, M. Gerla, and L. Kleinrock, "The flow deviation method: An approach to store-and-forward network design," to be published.

[22] G. Fultz and L. Kleinrock, "Adaptive routing techniques for store-and-forward computer–communication networks," in *Proc. Int. Conf. Communications*, pp. 39-1–39-8, 1971.

[23] E. N. Gilbert, "Minimum cost communication networks," *Bell Syst. Tech. J.*, pp. 2209–2227, 1967.

[24] M. Goldstein, "Design of long distance telecommunications networks–The Telepak problem," Office of Emergency Preparedness, Rep. R4, Jan. 1971.

[25] S. L. Hakimi, "Steiner's problem in graphs and its implications," in *Networks*, vol. 1, pp. 113–134, 1971.

[26] R. E. Kahn, "Terminal access to the ARPA computer network," in *Proc. 3rd Courant Inst. Symp.* (Nov. 1970). Englewood Cliffs, N. J.: Prentice–Hall, 1970.

[27] R. E. Kahn and W. R. Crowther, "Flow control in a resource sharing computer network," in *Proc. 2nd ACM/IEEE Symp. Problems in the Optimization of Data Communication Systems* (Palo Alto, Calif.), Oct. 1971.

[28] ——, "A study of the ARPA network design and performance," Rep. 2161, Aug. 1971.

[29] A. Kershenbaum and R. Van Slyke, "Minimum spanning trees in sparse graphs," in *Proc. ACM Special Interest Group in Mathematical Programming*, Aug. 1972.

[30] ——, "Recursive analysis of network reliability," to be published.

[31] L. Kleinrock, *Communication Nets: Stochastic Message Flow and Delay.* New York: McGraw–Hill, 1964.

[32] ——, "Models for computer networks," in *Proc. Int. Conf. Communications*, pp. 21-9–21-16, 1969.

[33] ——, "Analysis and simulation methods in computer network design," in *Spring Joint Computer Conf., AFIPS Conf. Proc.* Wash-

ington, D. C.: Spartan, 1970, pp. 569–579.
[34] D. Kleitman, "Methods of investigating connectivity of large graphs," *IEEE Trans. Circuit Theory* (Corresp.), vol. CT-16, pp. 232–233, May 1969.
[35] P. Krolak, W. Felts, and G. Marble, "A man-machine approach toward solving the traveling salesman problem," *Commun. Ass. Comput. Mach.*, vol. 14, pp. 327–335, May 1971.
[36] S. Lin, "Computer solutions of the traveling salesman problem," *Bell Syst. Tech. J.*, vol. 44, pp. 2245–2269, 1965.
[37] T. Marill and L. G. Roberts, "Toward a cooperative network of time-shared computers," in *Fall Joint Computer Conf., AFIPS Conf. Proc.*. Washington, D. C.: Spartan, 1966.
[38] B. Meister, H. R. Muller, and H. R. Rudin, "New optimization criteria for message-switching networks," *IEEE Trans. Commun. Technol.*, vol. COM-19, pp. 256–260, June 1971.
[39] E. F. Moore and C. E. Shannon, "Reliable circuits using less reliable relays," *J. Franklin Inst.*, vol. 262, pp. 191–208, 1956.
[40] NAC 3rd Semiannual Tech. Rep. Project "Analysis and optimization of store-and-forward computer networks," Def. Doc. Cen., Alexandria, Va., June 1971.
[41] NAC 4th Semiannual Tech. Rep. Project "Analysis and optimization of store-and-forward computer networks," Def. Doc. Cen., Alexandria, Va., Dec. 1971.
[42] G. S. Pan, "Communications information system," *Telecommunications*, pp. 19–23, June 1970.
[43] J. Pierce, "A network for block switching of data," *Bell Syst. Tech. J.*, to be published.
[44] L. G. Roberts, "Multiple computer networks and inter-computer communications," presented at the Ass. Comput. Mach. Symp. Operating Systems, Gatlinburg, Tenn., 1967.
[45] ——, "A forward look," *Signal*, vol. 25, pp. 77–81, Aug. 1971.
[46] ——, "Resource sharing networks," presented at the IEEE Int. Conv., New York, N. Y., Mar. 1969.
[47] L. G. Roberts and B. Wessler, "The ARPA computer network development to achieve resource sharing," in *Spring Joint Computer Conf., AFIPS Conf. Proc.*, 1970, pp. 543–549.
[48] ——, "The ARPA computer network," in *Computer Communication Networks*, F. Kuo and N. Abramson, Eds. New York: Prentice-Hall, 1973, to be published.
[49] B. Rothfarb and M. Goldstein, "The one terminal Telpak problem," *Oper. Res.*, vol. 19, pp. 156–169, Jan.–Feb. 1971.
[50] R. L. Sharma and M. T. El Bardai, "Suboptimal communication network synthesis," in *Proc. Int. Conf. Communications*, vol. 7, pp. 19-11–19-16, 1970.
[51] K. Steiglitz, P. Weiner, and D. J. Kleitman, "The design of minimum cost survivable networks," *IEEE Trans. Circuit Theory*, vol. CT-16, pp. 455–460, Nov. 1969.
[52] R. Van Slyke and H. Frank, "Reliability of computer-communication networks," in *Proc. 5th Conf. Applications of Simulation* (New York, N. Y.), Dec. 1971.
[53] ——, "Network reliability analysis—I," *Networks*, vol. 1, no. 3, 1972.
[54] ——, "Network reliability analysis—II," to be published in *Networks*, 1972.
[55] L. P. West, "Loop-transmission control structures," *IEEE Trans. Commun.*, vol. COM-20, pp. 531–539, June 1972.
[56] V. K. M. Whitney, "A study of optimal file assignment and communication network configuration in remote-access computer message processing and communication systems," *Dep. Elec. Eng.* Univ. of Michigan, Ann Arbor, Rep. 02641-2-T, SEL 48, Sept. 1970.
[57] R. S. Wilkov, "Analysis and design of reliable computer networks," *IEEE Trans. Commun.*, vol. COM-20, pp. 660–678, June 1972.
[58] B. Yaged, "Minimum cost routing for static network problems," *Networks*, vol. 1, pp. 139–172, 1971.
[59] M. L. T. Yuen *et al.*, "Traffic flow in a distributed loop switching system," presented at the Symp. Computer Communications, Apr. 4–6, 1972.

A UNIFIED ALGORITHM FOR DESIGNING MULTIDROP TELEPROCESSING NETWORKS*

W. Chou and A. Kershenbaum
Network Analysis Corporation
Glen Cove, New York 11542

Summary

The problem of designing minimum cost multidrop lines which connect remote terminals to a concentrator or a central data processing computer is studied. In some cases, optimal solutions can be obtained by using either linear integer programming or a branch-bound method. These approaches are not practical since they lack flexibility and require an enormous amount of computer time for most practical problems. As a conseqence, heuristic algorithms have been developed by various authors. In this paper, we point out that all of these algorithms fall into the class of minimum spanning tree problems, constrained by traffic or response time requirements. The difference between them is mainly the sequential order with which a branch or a line is selected into the tree. Without the constraints, all algorithms converge to a minimum spanning tree. With the constraints, they form different subtrees. Most of the algorithms can be unified into a modified Kruskal's minimum spanning tree algorithm.

In the modified algorithm, a weight is associated with each terminal. Let w_i be the weight associated with terminal i, and d_{ij} be the cost for the line directed from terminal i to terminal j. When the algorithm fetches the cost for the line, it replaces it with $d_{ij} - w_i$. In some cases, w_i's need to be readjusted in the middle of the algorithm. The difference between all existing heuristic algorithms is in the way w_i's are defined. If w_i is zero for all i, the algorithm reduces to the unmodified Kruskal's algorithm; if w_i is set to zero whenever a line incident to terminal i is selected as a tree branch, the algorithm reduces to Prim's minimum spanning tree algorithm.

An extension of the algorithm to the solution of an associated problem of partitioning the terminals with respect to a predetermined set of concentrators, multiplexers, terminal interface processors, or central computers is also derived.

The efficiency of an algorithm depends greatly on how it is implemented. The computational complexity of the unified algorithm is in the order of $N^2 \log N$ for the most general case, where N is the number of terminals. By using good heuristics, it reduces to K_1 K log N + K_2 N, where K_1 and K_2 are constants, for many practical applications. The algorithm has been applied to large networks with over 1,000 terminals, yielding excellent results and using only 15 seconds of computer time on a CDC 6600 computer.

Designs obtained by using different w_i's are compared.

I. Introduction

More than a quarter of a million terminals of various types are in operation in the United States. Most of these terminals utilize transmission lines only a small fraction of the time. They send and receive messages intermittently and the messages' transmission time usually lasts no more than a few seconds. A common method to efficiently utilize transmission lines' capacity is to connect several terminals onto one line so that one line can be shared by many terminals. Lines so structured are called multidrop or multipoint lines. A typical configuration is shown in Figure 1. With rare exceptions, the multidrop lines are in tree-like structures.

Multidrop lines may terminate at central computers. In many systems they are terminated at intermediate line concentrating devices for further communication cost reduction. These line concentrating devices and the central computers are then connected together by high speed lines. These devices are multiplexers and concentrators in a centralized data communication network, and message switching computers in an ARPANET-like distributed computer communication network. (In the ARPANET, they are called TIPs, standing for Terminal Interface Processors.)

A general topological design problem of multidrop lines consists of five subproblems: (1) Determining the required number of concentrating devices, if any, (concentrator quantity problem); (2) Selecting locations for the concentrating devices and central computers (concentrator location problem); (3) Interconnecting the concentrating devices and the central computers (concentrator layout problem); (4) Associating each terminal with a concentrating device or a central computer (terminal clustering problem); (5) Interconnecting terminals to their associated concentrating devices or central computers (terminal layout problem). All of these subproblems have the same goal; to find a least cost solution under a set of traffic and performance constraints.

All the subproblems are interrelated facets of the same problem and can meaningfully be answered only within the context of the problem as a whole. However, as a practical consideration, they can be solved to a great extent sequentially if proper care is taken at each stage of the solution. The first four subproblems are theoretically much harder to solve than the last one. However, for the most practical problems, it is easier for an experienced network designer to make relatively good judgement on the first four than the last. As such, quite a few good algorithms have been developed and published for the terminal layout subproblem,[2,3,5,7,8,10,12,13,14,15,18] yet very few for the other four.[1,4,6,8,15] Due to the difficulty of the problems, the few published works on the concentrator quantity, concentrator location and terminal clustering problems are either simple exercises of repetitive trials of different choices or limited to very special cases.

For most practical problems, the concentrator quantity and location problems pose relatively little difficulty for experienced designers. While the concentrator layout problem may be non-trivial for some networks, it is essentially the same as the ARPANET topology design problem and the ARPANET design experience is readily available.[6,8] Therefore, the scope of this paper is deliberatly limited to the terminal clustering and layout subproblems.

There are three types of algorithms for constructing the multidropped lines (terminal layout): exact solutions,[2,3] constrained minimum spanning tree type solutions,[2,5,10,12,13,14,15,16] and the branch exchange type solutions.[7,15]

The class of exact solutions includes linear integer programming and branch-bound methods. Due to the lack of flexibility and the exponential growth rate of the computer running time with respect to the number of terminals, the exact solution type approaches have only limited practical usefulness. The most popular and

*This work was supported by the Advanced Research Projects Agency of the Department of Defense under Contract DAHC-15-73-C0135.

powerful ones are the constrained minimum spanning tree type solutions. They are easy to understand, simple to implement, fast in running time and give near optimal results. The branch exchange type solutions are most effective when they are used together with the constrained minimum spanning tree approaches. The solutions obtained from the minimum spanning tree approach are used as the starting networks for branch-exchanges.

A common misconception is that the only minimum spanning tree algorithms are those by Prim[14] or Kruskal.[11] In this paper we point out that many other algorithms, such as Esau-Williams' and Sharma's algorithms also fall into the class of minimum spanning tree problems, constrained by traffic or response time requirements the same as the constrained Prim's and Kruskal's algorithms do. The difference between all these is mainly the sequential order with which a branch is selected into the tree. Without the constraints, all algorithms converge to a minimum spanning tree. With the constraints, they form different subtrees. Indeed, they can all be unified into a modified Kruskal's minimum spanning tree algorithm. Furthermore, with adjustments of parameters, this unified algorithm can assume an infinite number of different forms of minimum spanning tree algorithms, and therefore is more powerful than the existing ones.

The effectiveness of a terminal clustering algorithm depends on how closely it relates to the terminal layout algorithm. Indeed, the unified algorithm can be extended to clustering and connecting terminals simultaneously.

The primary advantage of a heuristic algorithm is its efficiency in computer running time. However, the efficiency of an algorithm depends greatly on how it is implemented. When properly implemented, the computational complexity of the unified algorithm is on the order of $N^2 \log N$ for the most general case, where N is the number of terminals. By using good heuristics, it reduces to $K_1 N \log N + K_2 N$, where K_1 and K_2 are constants, for many practical applications.

II. Line Layout Optimization

The problem is to produce a low cost network connecting the terminals to a central node (a central computer, a concentrator, a multiplexer, or a message switching processor) subject to constraints on the number of terminals and total traffic in each multidrop line. Such constraints are necessary to ensure that line capacities are not exceeded and the delay time for a response along any given line is kept within desired bounds.

Many algorithms have been proposed for the solution of this problem. These algorithms can be divided into three classes which are fundamentally different in their approach and results. The first class contains all the algorithms which approach the problem from the point of view of integer programming and branch-bound methods.[2,3] There are several drawbacks to such an approach. First, it is very difficult to implement the non-linear constraints which often arise in practical communications networks using such an approach. One is usually forced to approximate such constraints by tighter linear constraints with resulting degradation of the solution. Second, it is very hard to alter the constraints during the solution. It is often desirable to do so in order to perturb the solution trading cost versus performance. Finally, such methods possess no polynomial computational bound and one usually must terminate execution before an optimal solution is found for any reasonable problem.

The second class, which is the one we will deal with here, contains certain heuristic algorithms which overcome the objections mentioned above and which for reasonable sized problems will usually produce better solutions than the algorithms in the first class do in a comparable amount of time. The basic concept underlying most of these algorithms is the same. In each case, the terminals are initially placed in separate components and pairs of components are then joined by the shortest or the least cost line separating them. (A cut of two components is defined here as the set of possible lines each of which can join the two components into one.) Rosenstiehl[17] proved that algorithms of this form will always generate tree structured networks of minimum total length or total line cost, if they are not restricted in their choice of cuts. The trees so obtained are called minimum spanning trees (MSTs). In designing teleprocessing networks each of these algorithms must consider the constraints during the course of execution and therefore their choice of cuts is restricted. Thus, unless no pair of components which these algorithms would otherwise merge violates a constraint, they do not in general generate the minimal cost tree satisfying the constraints. Experience with these algorithms has shown, however, that they do generate good solutions, within a few percent of the optimum in most cases. Furthermore, since the terminals on each multidrop line satisfy the constraints, the multidrop line is in fact an MST on these terminals and the central node.

These algorithms are powerful in their ability to treat problems with a large variety of constraints which may differ from one another in functional form. We require only that it be possible at any stage of the algorithm to connect each component directly to the central node and obtain a feasible solution. In the following discussion, each terminal (or component) is assumed to be associated with a finite state vector which contains information about the terminal (or component) relevant to the calculation of the constraints. The value of each constraint at the terminal, or the component, is then considered to be a function of this vector. A typical example of the state vector consists of the number of terminals in the component and the total traffic associated with the terminals in the component.

We now present a brief description of several of the most widely accepted heuristic constrained minimum spanning tree algorithms. In each case, before joining two components, we check to see if having the terminals in both components on the same multidrop line violates any constraints. If so, the algorithm does not join the components and proceeds to consider the next candidate pair. (In the following, "distance" and "cost" are to be used interchangeably.)

Prim's Algorithm[14]

Initially, only the central node is in the spanning tree. At each stage, the terminal whose distance or cost to any terminal already in the tree is minimal is brought into the tree.

Kruskal's Algorithm[12]

Initially, each terminal is in a separate component. At each stage, the least cost line connecting different components is found and these components are joined by that line.

Esau-Williams' Algorithm[5]

Initially, each terminal and the center are in separate components. Define a tradeoff function, t_{ij}, as the minimum cost of connecting the component containing terminal i to the center minus the cost of connecting terminals i and j. At each stage, we find $t_{i^*j^*} = \max (t_{ij})$ and bring in line (i^*,j^*), forming a new component.

Vogel's Approximation Method (VAM)[2,16]

Define $_i$ as the line cost of connecting terminal i to its nearest feasible neighbor (i.e., its nearest neighbor which can be placed on the same multidrop line as terminal i). Define b_i as the cost of the line connecting terminal i to its second nearest feasible neighbor. Define a tradeoff function, t_{ij}, as $b_i - a_i - d_{ij}$. At each stage, find the largest t_i and join terminal i to its nearest feasible neighbor and treat the resulting component as a terminal.

Sharma's Algorithm[15]

Generate polar coordinates (a_i, r_i) for each terminal relative to the center. Order the terminals by the angles, a_i, so that $a_1 \leq a_2 \leq a_3 \ldots \leq a_n$. Form the least cost tree network among terminals $t_1, t_2, \ldots, t_k$ and the center, where $t_1, t_2, \ldots, t_k$ satisfy the constraint but the addition of t_{k+1} to the same multidrop line does not. Repeat the above procedure starting with t_{k+1} until all terminals are included in the network.

Each of these algorithms starts with the terminals in separate components and subsequently joins pairs of components. They differ only in the order in which they consider joining components. If no constraints are imposed, they all yield a least cost tree structured network. Since the grouping of a given set of terminals into one component (i.e., placing them on the same multidrop line) restricts subsequent merging with other components because of the constraints, these algorithms, in general, yield different solutions. As an example, consider the application of each of the above algorithms to the graph shown in Figure 2. Prim's algorithm would consider line (A,0) first. Kruskal's algorithm would consider line (D,E) first. Easau-Williams' algorithm would consider line (B,A) first. The VAM algorithm would consider line (C,D) first. Sharma's algorithm might consider line (C,B) first. Thus each algorithm starts by forming a different component and could in general yield a different solution from any of the others. In each case, however, the line chosen links some terminal to its nearest neighbor, subject to the constraints. The reason the algorithms choose different lines is that they consider the terminals in a different order. They implicitly associate weights with the terminals and use these weights to decide the order components are to be considered for merging. Using this concept, it is possible to develop one algorithm which will implement all the above algorithms and many others of the same type. The following procedure will implement this class of algorithms given a set of rules, which we call w-rules, for initializing and updating the terminal weights.

Unified Algorithm

The unified algorithm is a modified form of Kruskal's algorithm. In this modified form, a weight is associated with each terminal. Let w_i be the weight associated with terminal i, and d_{ij} be the cost for the line directed from terminal i to terminal j. When the algorithm fetches the cost for the line, it uses $d_{ij} - w_i$. In some cases, w_i's need to be readjusted in the middle of the execution. The difference between all existing heuristic algorithms is in the way w_i's are defined. For example, if w_i is zero for all i, the algorithm reduces to the unmodified Kruskal's algorithm; if w_i is set to zero whenever a branch incident to terminal i is selected as a tree branch, the algorithm reduces to Prim's minimum spanning tree algorithm. Formally, the algorithm is stated as follows.

Definitions of Variables

w_i - weight associated with component i

C_i - component containing terminal i

(i,j) - the line connecting terminals i and j

t_{ij} - tradeoff function associated with (i,j)

d_{ij} - cost of (i,j)

Step 0: Initialize the w_i for i = 1, 2, ..., N, using the appropriate w-rule. (Examples of w-rules are shown in Table 1.) Initialize the constraints. Set $t_{ij} \leftarrow d_{ij} - w_i$ for all i,j when d_{ij} exists and $C_i \cup C_j$ does not violate any constraints.

Set $C_i \leftarrow i$ i = 1, 2, ..., N

Set $S_i \leftarrow 1$ i = 1, 2, ..., N

Go to Step 1.

Step 1: Find $t_{i^*j^*} = \min\limits_{\substack{i,j \\ C_i \neq C_j}} t_{ij}$

If $t_{i^*j^*} = \infty$, terminate, otherwise go to Step 2.

Step 2: Evaluate the constraints on $C_{i^*} \cup C_{j^*}$. If any is violated, set $t_{i^*j^*}$ to infinity and go to Step 1. Otherwise, go to Step 3.

Step 3: Add line (i^*, j^*). $C_k \leftarrow C_{i^*} \cup C_{j^*}$ for $k \in C_{i^*}$ or $k \in C_{j^*}$. (For computational efficiency, only the smaller of C_{i^*} and C_{j^*} need be changed.) Reevaluate constraints. Update w_i using the appropriate w-rule and reevaluate t_{ij}. Go to Step 1.

Table 1

Algorithm	Initialization	Update when (i,j) is brought in
Prim	$w_1 = 0$ $w_i = -\infty$ i=2,...,N	$w_j \leftarrow 0$
Kruskal	$w_i = 0$ i=1,...,N	none
Esau-Williams	$w_i = d_{i1}$ i=1,...,N	$w_i \leftarrow w_j$
VAM	$w_i = b_i - a_i$ (for definition of b_i & a_i see description of VAM Algr. above.	$w_i = b_i - a_i$ (where d_i and b_i are now defined on the newly formed component)

Note: "1" is the central node.

The third class contains heuristic algorithms which improve the network cost by exchanging lines from different sub-trees.[7,14] This type of algorithm needs a starting design and its effectiveness relys heavily on how good this starting design is. Therefore, the best way to make use of this branch-exchange type algorithm is to use the solution from the constrained MST algorithms as the starting network for improvements.

III. Efficient Implementation of the Algorithm

351

The above algorithm can be implemented in several distinct ways which vary significantly in their usage of computer time and memory. It is similar in structure to many published algorithms for computing MSTs and finding the shortest path between pairs of nodes in a graph. The techniques used are primarily those of Kershenbaum and Van Slyke[11] and Johnson[9], which take advantage of sparsity when it is present and are generally conservative of memory and running time.

Computationally, a (constrained) MST algorithm extracts a (constrained) MST from a given graph or network. Therefore, the computational complexity depends also on the complexity of the graph. In general, this graph should be a complete graph for the problem we are dealing with. (A complete graph is defined as a graph in which there is a line between every node pair in the graph.) That is, in determining the least cost teleprocessing network, considerations should be given to all possible connections. However, when the number of terminals is large, the total number of possible lines in a complete graph on these terminals may exceed the memory capacity of the computer being used. It is possible, without significantly degrading the solution obtained, to treat such problems within the context of a relatively sparse graph where each terminal can only be connected to a small number, say K, of its nearest neighbors and to the central node. Important savings in core requirements and running time can thus be obtained.

Even when K is relatively small, the solution thus obtained is not significantly worse than one obtained by consideration of a complete graph. Figure 3 shows the variation of line cost with number of neighbors considered for a 40 node network. As can be seen, there is virtually no increase in cost until the number of neighbors is reduced below 5. This is not surprising in light of the fact that it is never advantageous to connect a terminal to another terminal which is further away than the central node as the connection to the central node is always feasible and less expensive than a connection to the more remote terminal. Thus, such connections can be ignored without any danger of increasing the cost of the resulting network. For a network of terminals uniformly distributed over a region with the central node near the center, roughly 75% of the possible connections can be eliminated in this manner. This, coupled with the fact that even with constraints, it is very likely that a terminal will be connected to one of its nearest neighbors in the optimal solution explains that the consideration of only a relatively small number of neighbors will yield a very good solution.

It is possible to find the K nearest neighbors of each terminal without even evaluating all interterminal costs. In a number of operations proportional to N, the number of terminals, the area containing the terminals can be partitioned into rectangles and the terminals in each rectangle identified. The K nearest neighbors of each terminal can then be found by considering the terminals in the terminal's rectangle and rings of adjacent rectangles to whatever distance necessary. If the number of rectangles is chosen carefully, this can be done in a number of operations proportional to N × K, where K is the number of neighbors considered in the algorithm.

A potentially time consuming step in the algorithm is the recalculation of the t_{ij} every time a line is brought into the tree and the subsequent search for the minimum. We have already substantially reduced the amount of computation in this step by limiting ourselves to a solution within a sparse graph. Thus, instead of having to recalculate N × (N-1)/2 values of t_{ij}, we need only recalculate N × K values.

The effort in recalculating the t_{ij}'s can be reduced still further by noting that they are in fact defined as a difference of two quantities, w_i and d_{ij}. The d_{ij} are constants and do not need to be recalculated and the w_i need, at worst, to be recalculated once for each node when a line is brought in. Thus, the problem of recalculating N × K values of t_{ij} can be reduced to at worst recalculating N values of w_i if we are willing to have the t_{ij} represented implicitly by the values of d_{ij} and w_i. In practice, even this is usually not necessary. A w-rule such as that used by an algorithm like Esau-Williams' requires only the recalculation of the w_i for terminals in one component in the pair being merged. Prim's Algorithm requires only one w_i to be recalculated and Kruskal's Algorithm requires no recalculation at all.

If the neighbors of each terminal are kept in sorted lists and pointers maintained to the nearest neighbor of each terminal, the algorithm can be implemented with the t_{ij} represented implicitly without any increase in computation beyond the additional subtraction of w_i from d_{ij}. Furthermore, if the current values of $\min_j (t_{ij})$ are kept in a heap, the value of t_{i*j*} is always immediately obtainable from the top of the heap. (A heap is a sorted list $\{\ell_i \mid i = 1, 2, \ldots, N\}$ in which $\ell_i \leq \ell_{2i}$ and $\ell_i \leq \ell_{2i+1}$. See [11].) The only computational expense incurred by such a procedure is the updating of the heap when a line is brought into the tree. This is at worst a linear operation and is in fact proportional to $\mathrm{Log}_2 N$ when the number of w_i changed at each step is small.

Thus, the entire algorithm is bounded by

$$A \cdot N^2 + B \cdot K \cdot N + C \cdot K \cdot N \cdot \mathrm{Log}_2 K,$$

where A, B, and C are constants. This bound assumes that the computer program is implemented to allow any general w-rule. However, if w-rules requiring the update of w_i for every terminal are not allowed, the term $A \cdot N^2$ may disappear. In Table 1, only the w-rule based on the VAM Algorithm requires the updating of w_i for all terminals. Thus, for many practical applications, the algorithm can be implemented to be bounded by

$$B \cdot K \cdot N + C \cdot K \cdot N \cdot \mathrm{Log}_2 K.$$

IV. Algorithm Performance

Computer Running Time and Core Requirements

Experiments were performed using 20, 40, 60, 80, 100, 120, 140, 160, 180, and 200 terminal networks considering 5 nearest neighbors, the w-rule for the Esau-Williams Algorithm (see Table 1), and a traffic constraint of

$$T \leq N/4$$

where T is the line traffic and N is the number of terminals in the network. Traffic and locations for each terminal are generated randomly, with the traffic ranging from 0 to 1. Figure 4 summarizes the results of these experiments. The figure shows a plot of the logarithm of the number of terminals versus the logarithm of the running time. The data points fall almost perfectly onto a straight line with slope + 2, pointing out that the unified algorithm varies quadratically with problem size. (The algorithm is so implemented in the program that it allows any possible w-rule. If it is implemented to exclude general cases, the computational complexity can be less than quadratic.)

Other experiments verified that the running time

did not vary noticeably with the particular w-rule used. Also, no appreciable variation in running time was observed when constraints were varied. Neither of these observations is surprising. Generally, in the implementation of a variety of w-rules, the program assumes that all the w's are reheaped each time a line is brought in. This also accounts for the variation of running time with N^2. Constrained minimal spanning tree algorithms of this type examine roughly the same lines during their execution, stopping when they connect groups of terminals to the center. Thus, the running time remains nearly constant when the w-rules and constraints are varied.

Running time is, however, significantly altered by considering a smaller number of neighbors for each line, and thus, a smaller number of lines for possible inclusion in the tree. Table 2 shows running times for a 40 terminal network varying the number of neighbors considered. As can be seen, the running time can be reduced by a factor of 4 by considering 4 neighbors instead of 39, even in this relatively small 40 terminal case. For larger networks, the percentage of running time saved is even greater.

Table 2

Number of Neighbors	Running Time	Line Cost
1	.434	7.77
2	.491	5.26
3	.522	4.54
4	.557	4.50
5	.589	4.48
8	.691	4.45
10	.767	4.45
15	.985	4.45
20	1.240	4.45
25	1.503	4.45
30	1.767	4.45
39	2.245	4.45

Comparison of Line Costs Using Known Heuristics

Experiments were run using Prim's Algorithm, Kruskal's Algorithm, Esau-Williams' Algorithm, and the VAM Algorithm as specific subcases of the unified technique, i.e. input parameters were varied to implement the specific w-rules for these algorithms. Running times are not compared since within the context of the unified technique, they are nearly identical.

Twenty terminal networks with randomly generated traffic and coordinates were used in this comparison under a variety of constraints. Previous experience with these algorithms verified the fact that their relative performance is not affected by problem size if a large number of cases are considered. Twelve networks were run using each algorithm.

The results are summarized in Table 3. The Esau-Williams Algorithm performs better than any of the others in all cases with the VAM Algorithm producing results only slightly worse on the average. (Sharma's Algorithm is deliberately excluded from comparison. Using the same order of computational complexity, it usually yields an inferior solution. To have comparable results, it needs a N-fold increase in the complexity. Even then, it produces a less effective solution than the Esau-Williams and VAM algorithms, on the average.

These results should be interpreted in a qualitative sense rather than as an indication of actual percentage improvements obtained using one w-rule rather than another. Experience with a wide variety of problems has shown that the percentage variation between the solutions obtained using these w-rules can vary with problem size, constraints, and distribution of terminals if isolated cases are considered. Indeed, in a few cases the VAM Algorithm and even the others may actually yield a result superior to Esau-Williams. Therein lies the power of this unified approach. Not only can it easily handle a wide variety of constraints, but also, it can adapt itself to the particular problem at hand and yield results at least as good, and almost always better than any single know heuristic. Using it, one can apply several heuristics in succession or a hybrid technique using them simultaneously.

Table 3

Performance for 20 Terminal Networks with Traffic Uniformly Distributed Between 0 and 1

	Case 1	Case 2	Case 3	Case 4	Average
Kruskal	4.04	5.09	3.49	4.33	4.24
Prim	4.41	5.13	3.62	4.77	4.48
Esau-Williams	3.65	5.06	3.28	3.97	3.99
VAM	3.71	5.15	3.43	4.14	4.10

Case 1: $N + T \leq 10$
Case 2: $N + T \leq 5$
Case 3: $T \leq 5$
Case 4: $N \leq 5$

N = Number of Terminal/Line
T = Total Traffic/Line

V. Parametrization of Terminal Weights

While some w-rules will usually yield better solutions than others, no single rule has proven itself to be uniformly better than the others. Not only can examples be constructed where any w-rule mentioned above yields better results than any of the others, but practical experience with real communications networks also verifies this fact. Thus, it is meaningful to try several w-rules in the solution of the same problem. One way to do this is to parametrize the terminal weights and generate several solutions for different values of the parameters. Because of the speed of the algorithm and the relatively small number of solutions that need to be generated, extremely good results can be obtained in a small amount of time.

Karnaugh[10] proposed a parallel search algorithm which generates a family of designs using lines obtained from the largest, as well as the second largest, tradeoffs at every stage of the Esau-Williams Algorithm. He achieved an improvement of 1% in network cost at the expense of a 70-fold increase in the computation time. Sharma proposed a branch exchange algorithm to be used in conjunction with his basic algorithm. He achieved similar improvements at the expense of enormous additional computation time. By the judicious application of the parametrization approach described below, we have obtained comparable improvements with 3 to 10 different parameter values. Thus, the parametrization can be used in place of parallel searches and branch-exchanges with less computation time.

The parametrization can be achieved in many ways. We offer one method which has yielded very good results efficiently.

Define the terminal weights w_i, by:

$$w_i = a(b \times d_{i0} + (1-b)\ d_{i2}),$$

where d_{i0} is the cost of connecting terminal i to the center node, d_{i2} is the cost of connecting terminal i to its second nearest feasible neighbor. "a" and "b" are constants such that $a \geq 0$ and $0 \leq b \leq 1$. Setting "a" to zero in the above equation yields Kruskal's Algorithm. Setting "a" and "b" both to one, yields Esau-Williams' Algorithm, and setting "a" to one and "b" to zero yields the VAM Algorithm. Other intermediate values of "a" and "b" may yield algorithms with some of the properties of these known algorithms. Each of the algorithms gives preference to lines with a certain property. By setting the parameters to intermediate values, some consideration can be given to all of these properties simultaneously. In practice, the parameters are initially set to a reasonable set of values, say a = 1 and b = 1. A slightly larger value of "a" is then considered, say a = 1·1. If no improvement results, a slightly smaller value of "a" is tried. If an improvement results, "a" is varied still further. When no further improvement can be seen, "a" is fixed at the last value and "b" is varied in the same way. Experiences show that very few trials need be made. All these procedures can be coded into a program and carried out automatically.

Early experimentation with a wide variety of values of "a" and "b" revealed three important facts. First, good values of "a" and "b" are usually nearly independent of one another, allowing us to vary them separately. Second, further variation of a parameter in a direction which yielded no improvement almost never led to a better solution. Third, the cost function is relatively flat near its minimum. Thus, perturbing a good solution by smaller increments of "a" and "b" does not yield significant improvements.

Using the simple parametrization method described above, we have consistently obtained solutions between 1% and 5% better than those obtained using Esau-Williams' and the VAM algorithm separately.

VI. Terminal Clustering

A straightforward extension can be made to the parametrization approach described above to simultaneously solve the problems of terminal clustering and layout. We define w_i as above except that d_{i0} is instead the cost of connecting terminal i to the nearest central node (concentrator, multiplexer or central computer). In connecting the lines, the algorithm also associates each terminal to a central node. It is possible to alter the d_{i0} during the course of the algorithm and to set the d_{i0} to values reflecting the actual cost (line cost and contributions to hardware cost) of adding a connection at the given central node. This concept can be extended still further by generalizing the d_{i0} to include the cost of placing a concentrator or multiplexer at the given locations. We can then use the results of the algorithm in picking another set of central nodes. Such a procedure is very effective in identifying central nodes of marginal value or no value at all, as such central nodes will have few or no terminals associated with them. Likewise, central nodes with an unusually large number of associated terminals identify areas where additional central nodes may be placed.

Examples

Given:

a. Number of concentrators: 4
b. Concentrator locations: New York, Atlanta, Chicago, Los Angeles
c. Line speed: 1600 bps
d. Traffic constraints: $100 \times n + T \leq 16{,}800$, where n is the number of terminals per line and T is the traffic in messages per day on the line
e. Total number of terminals: 1673
f. Total number of distinct terminal locations (telephone exchanges): 212
g. Traffic requirements and location of each terminal (distributed across the country) total traffic: 120 million characters per day

(a,b,c,d were determined by methods not discussed in this paper.)

Tasks Performed by the Algorithm:

a. Associating each terminal to a concentrator.
b. Constructing multidrop lines

Program Requirements (CDC 6600):

a. Core: 40,000 words
b. Running time: 15 seconds

Output:

a. Topology: a simplified computer plotted output is shown in Figure 5
b. Monthly network cost: $89,000

Figure 6 is another example. This is a simplified computer plotted output for a data communication network of 500 locations.

VII. Conclusion

We have shown that all the effective heuristics currently used for designing multidrop teleprocessing networks and a whole class of extensions and combinations of these heuristics can be represented by a single algorithm. This unified algorithm is more powerful than any of the individual heuristics in that designs obtained using it are at least as good, and almost always better, than those obtained by applying other heuristics separately. Using parametrized w-rules, the solutions are competative in quality with designs obtained by extensive branch exchange and are far more effective in computer time. Furthmore, it can be extended to treat a much broader class of problems with a wide variety of constraints and also to yield good solutions to the associated problem of clustering terminals about multiplexers, concentrators, terminal interface processors, or central computers. (No other satisfactory algorithm is currently available for the solution of this clustering problem.)

The efficiency of an algorithm in both computer core and running time requirements depends on how it is implemented. By using clever sorting and searching techniques, and by employing heuristic maneuvering, both the core and running time requirements grow almost linearly proportionally to the total number of terminals for many practical problems. Even in most general cases they only grow quadratically. Thus, our program takes only about 40,000 words and 15 seconds on a CDC 6600 machine to design a network of 1673 terminals.

There is one aspect deserving further study in using the unified MST algorithm. This is the determination of a best w-rule for a given type of problem. However, it does not have any big effect on the effectiveness of the algorithm whether one knows the best w-rule or not. If the algorithm is efficiently implemented as explained in this paper, it is very inexpensive for the repetitive use of the algorithm. Therefore, one can always try several known good w-rules, or try w-rules he believes to be good, to obtain a near best w-rule with a computer time he can easily afford.

References

1. Bahl, L. R. and D. T. Tang, "Optimization of Concentrator Locations in Teleprocessing Networks," Proc. of Symp. on Comp.-Comm. Networks and Tele Traffic, Poly. Inst. of Brooklyn, April 1972.
2. Chandy, K. M. and R. A. Russell, "The Design of Multipoint Linkages in a Teleprocessing Tree Network," IEEE Trans. Comp., Vol. C-21, No. 10, October 1972, pp. 1062-1066.
3. Chandy, K. M. and Tachen Lo, "The Capacitated Minimum Spanning Tree," Networks, Vol. 3, No. 2, 1973, pp. 173-182.
4. Doll, D. R., "Topology and Transmission Rate Considerations in the Design of Centralized Computer-Communication Networks," IEEE Trans. on Comm. Tech., June 1971, pp. 339-344.

5. Esau, L. R. and K. C. Williams, "On Teleprocessing System Design," Part II, IBM Syst. Jour., Vol. 5, No. 3, 1966, pp. 142-147.

6. Frank, H., I. T. Frisch and W. Chou, "Topological Considerations in the Design of the ARPA Computer Network," Proc. SJCC, 1970, pp. 581-587.

7. Frank, H., I. T. Frisch, W. Chou and R. Van Slyke, "Optimal Design of Centralized Computer Networks," Networks, Vol. 1, No. 1, 1971, pp. 43-57.

8. Frank, H. and W. Chou, "Topological Optimization of Computer Networks," IEEE Proc., November 1972.

9. Johnson, E., "On Shortest Paths and Sorting," Proc. of ACM Annual Conf., August 1972, pp. 510-517.

10. Karnaugh, M., "Multipoint Network Layout Program," Report No. RC3723, IBM, 1972.

11. Kershenbaum, A. and R. Van Slyke, "Computing Minimum Spanning Tree Efficiently," Proc. of ACM Annual Conf., August 1972, pp. 518-527.

12. Kruskal, J. B., "On the Shortest Spanning Subtree of a Graph and the Traveling Salesman Problem," Proc. of American Math. Society, Vol. 7, 1956.

13. Martin, James, System Analysis for Data Transmission, Prentice-Hall, New Jersey, 1972.

14. Prim, R. C., "Shortest Connection Networks and Some Generalizations," Bell System Technical Journal, Vol. 36, 1957, pp. 1389-1401.

15. Sharma, R. L. and M. T. El-Bardai, "Suboptimal Communications Network Synthesis," Proc. International Conference on Communications, June 1970, pp. 19.11-19.16.

16. Reinfeld, N. V. and W. R. Vogel, Mathematical Programming, Prentice-Hall, New Jersey, 1958.

17. Rosenstiehl, P., "L' Arbre Minimum d' un Graphe," in Theory of Graphs, P. Rosenstiehl, ed., Gordon and Breach, New York, 1967.

18. Whitney, V. K. M., "Comparison of Network Topology Optimization Algorithms," Proc. of 1972 ICCC, 1972, pp. 332-337.

Reprinted by permission from *Proceedings of the Third Data Communications Symposium*
November 1973, pp. 148-156

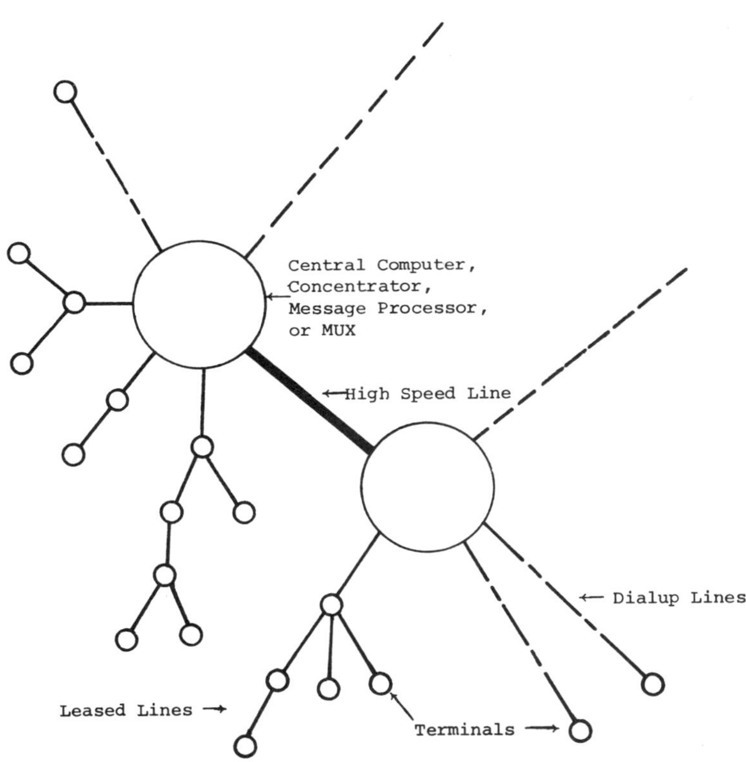

MULTIDROP TELEPROCESSING NETWORK ARCHITECTURE

FIGURE 1

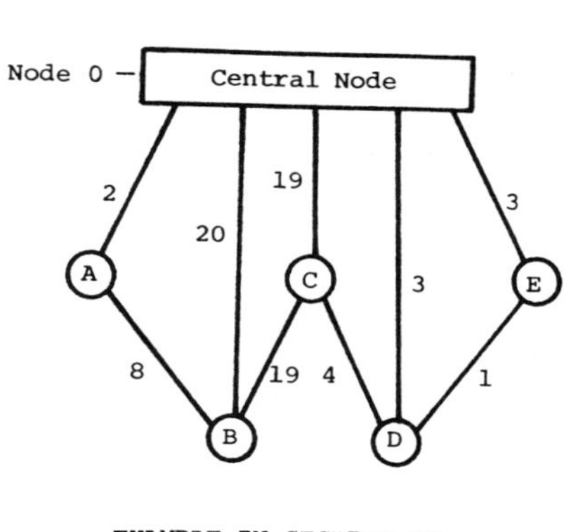

EXAMPLE IN SECTION II

FIGURE 2

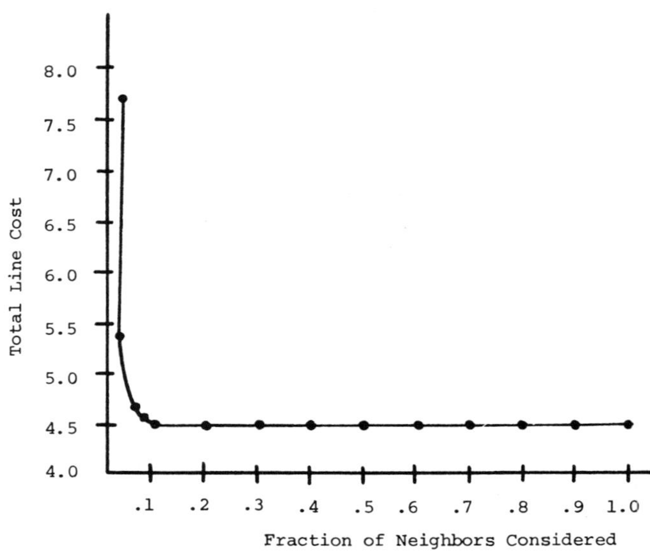

TOTAL LINE COST VS. DENSITY OF SOLUTION GRAPH

FIGURE 3

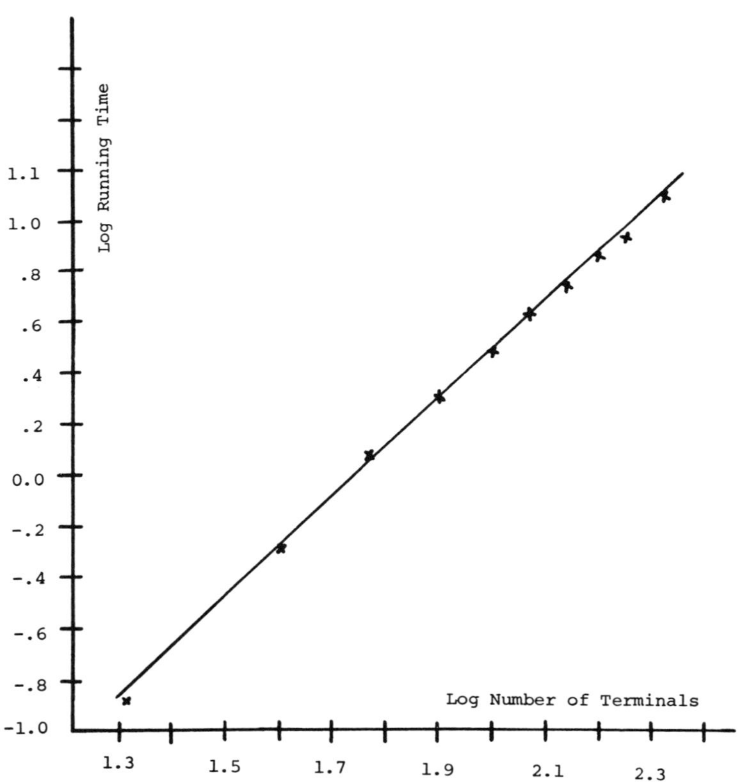

RUNNING TIME VS. NUMBER OF TERMINALS

FIGURE 4

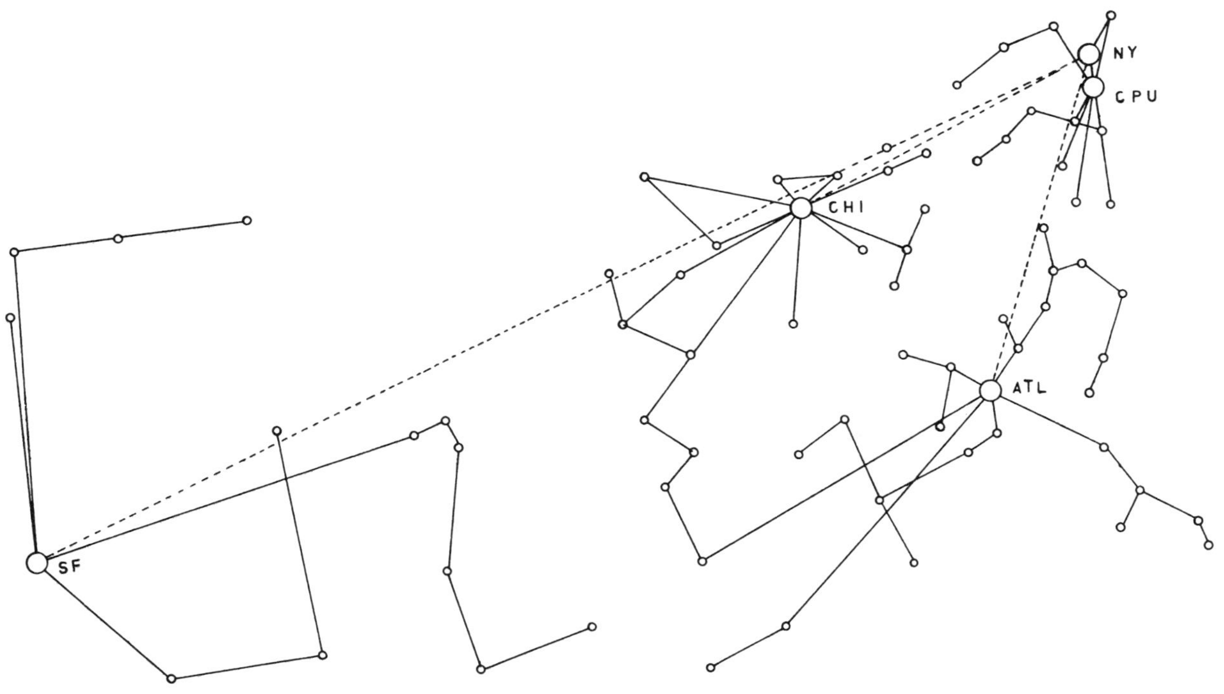

A SIMPLIFIED COMPUTER PLOTTED OUTPUT FOR THE DATA COMMUNICATION NETWORK IN THE EXAMPLE

FIGURE 5

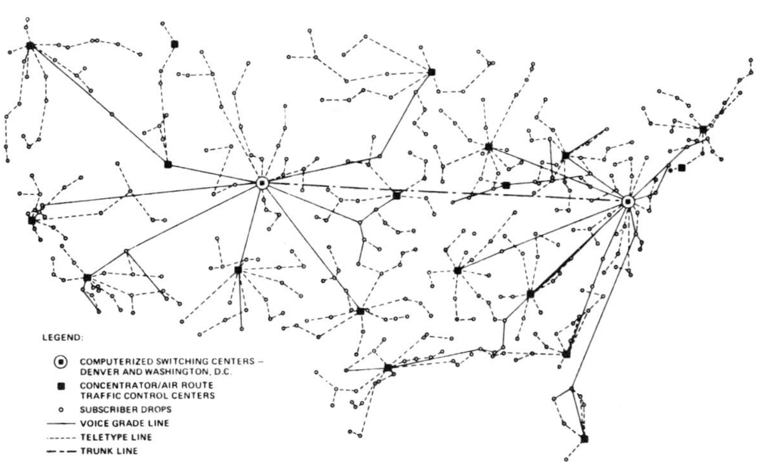

A COMPUTER PLOTTED OUTPUT FOR A DATA COMMUNICATION NETWORK OF 500 LOCATIONS

FIGURE 6

A DATABASE SYSTEM FOR THE MANAGEMENT AND DESIGN OF TELECOMMUNICATION NETWORKS

V Kevin M. WHITNEY
Detroit, Michigan

Dixon R. DOLL
Ann Arbor, Mich.

Abstract

The computer system described in this paper aids the telecommunications manager in the management and design of voice and data networks. It is built upon a relational data base comprised of sets of data describing the network terminals, communication channels, and traffics. A variety of standard reports, maps, charts, cost tables can easily be prepared from information in the data base. A hierarchy of processing programs access the data either in batch mode or interactively. At every step in the network design or management, manual interaction is possible to take full advantage of the manager's experience and intuition. The combination of computer calculation and manual guidance are illustrated with an example involving a large TELPAK network.

Introduction

358

Although many organizations have both large communication and teleprocessing networks and also data base management systems, user oriented information systems to aid the management and design of networks are uncommon. This paper describes a comprehensive and flexible information system to aid the design and management of telecommunication networks. The system consists of a hierarchy of processing programs using a relational data base manager for convenient data manipulation. All system facilities may be used either interactively or in batched mode for a wide variety of network management tasks such as the design of new networks, the modification or expansion of existing networks, and the preparation of reports on network cost and performance.

While in the past, the differences in design, usage, and management of voice communication networks and data communication networks have kept these systems separate, today the same facilities are often used for both data and voice communication. Communication channels are used alternately for voice and for data, TELPAK channels are shared by the voice and the data systems, and in most cases all the channels and modems are leased from the same common carrier. Thus it is becoming more convenient and more important to include all communication resources of the organization into a system with a single administrative responsibility.

Since the telecommunications manager is usually responsible for the design, implementation, and management of the network, a computer based system to aid him should include facilities to help with all of these tasks. Many of the tools necessary for the effective management of a network are also useful in its original design or in its modification. For example, pricing a new network configuration, pricing proposed changes to an existing network, printing lists of the terminals or lines of a network, drawing maps of a network, and keeping track of circuit requirements are important facilities for both the administration and the design of telecommunication networks. A further advantage of a single system for both design and management of networks is that a designer need not learn two different tools for two very similar tasks.

Although many communication network analysis and design programs are available from various vendors, no systems known to the authors bring the full power of comtemporary computer technology to bear on both the management and the design of communication systems. Several systems[1,2,3] provide convenient interactive network design, but do not perform significant computer network analysis. From the user's viewpoint, the best of these systems is the relational access method embedded in an APL interpreter by Lorie & Symonds.[4] Those programs which do complex and sophisticated network analysis such as IBM's Communication Network Design Program (CNDP)[5], Rothfarb & Goldstein's TELPAK design program[6], and Chandy & Russel's multipoint line design program[7], for example, are batch oriented programs which do not provide convenient means for manual interaction in the design process. One system which does an excellent job of combining powerful computer analysis with convenient human interaction has been developed by Kroletal and others[8] for the design of traveling salesman circuits.

The advantages of a single information system with facilities for both management and design of communications networks led to the specifications of a TMDS system (Telecommunications Management and Design System). Its shared data base uses a relational access method to provide flexible interchange of data about network terminals, channels, and tariffs. All system capabilities are isolated in modular sections to simplify the incorporation of new capabilities. The modular design also facilitates customization of the system to those functions needed by a particular installation. If interactive on-line operation is not needed the interactive monitor may be replaced with a batch monitor. Then the requests for system action would be punched on cards rather than typed at an interactive terminal. On-line storage of the database is unnecessary if the user is willing to maintain a card file and load it whenever necessary. Indeed, a simple system could be implemented on a mini-computer with a FORTRAN compiler. The design and use of a TMDS system are discussed in the following sections.

TMDS System Design

The major components of a TMDS are shown in the diagram of Figure 1. These components include the relational database manager, a hierarchy of communication network design and pricing programs, input/output facilities, and a command language interpreter. These are essential components, but additional facilities may be added into this structure.

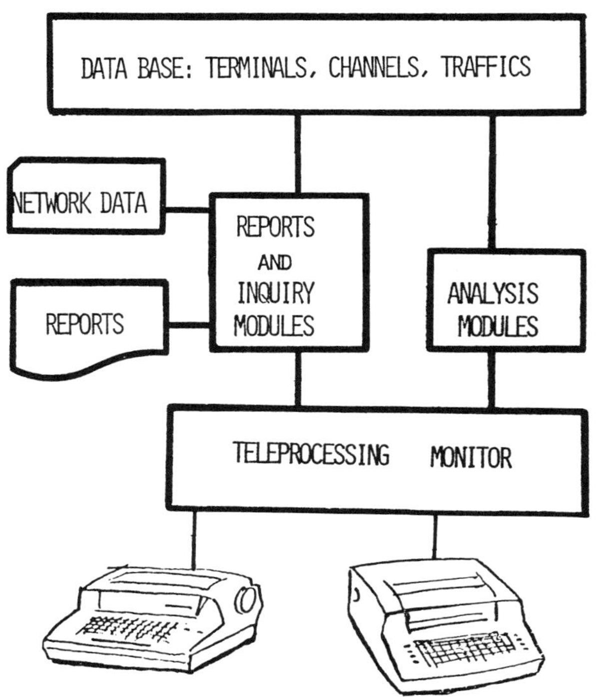

Figure 1. Essential TMDS Components

Information in the data base is organized in relation sets (unordered lists of records). Each record contains all the relevant information about a single terminal, channel, or point-to-point requirement of a network. A simple network shown in Figure 2 may be described with two relation sets shown in Figure 3. One relation describes the terminals of the network, another describes the channels. The set of terminals has four records, one corresponding to each terminal. The domains of the terminals set, defining the characteristics of the terminals, are the terminal number (#), a four character identification code (ID), the circuit requirements at that terminal (CKTS), the equipment type at that terminal (TYPE), the terminal's area code (AREA), a code indicating hi-density or low-density rate center (RATE), etc. The domains of the channels set, defining the characteristics of channels between pairs of terminals, include the channel number (#), the transmit terminal (FROM), the receive terminal (TO), the channel length (MILES), the number of circuits on that channel (TRAFFIC), the tariff on that channel (TARIFF), etc. To emphasize that these sets are unordered, neither the terminals nor the channels are listed in order of their identification numbers.

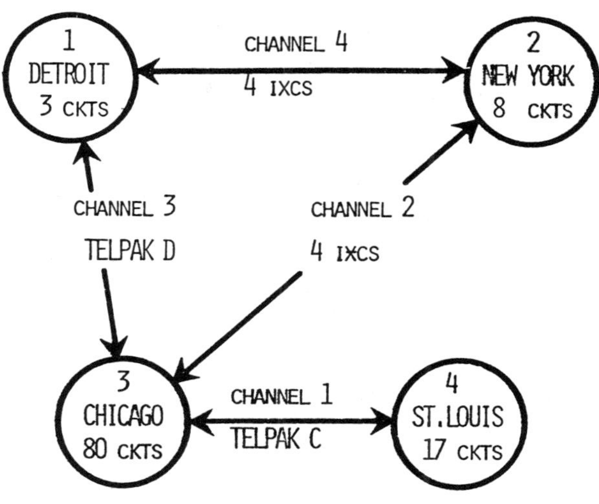

Figure 2. A 4 Terminal Network

All networks manipulated by TMDS programs are described by the relation sets in the data base. The use of standard domain types for sets of terminals and for sets of channels facilitates the interchange of network data among TMDS programs. Thus only one program to list terminals or channels, to draw a map, to punch a deck of terminal or channel cards, or to price a network is needed no matter how many different topologies are analyzed.

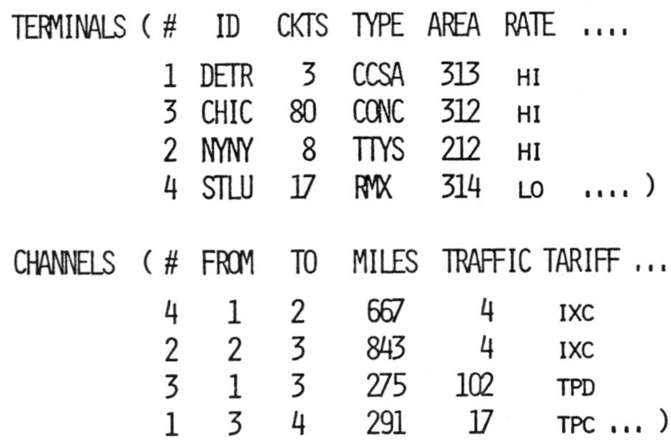

TERMINALS (

#	ID	CKTS	TYPE	AREA	RATE	....
1	DETR	3	CCSA	313	HI	
3	CHIC	80	CONC	312	HI	
2	NYNY	8	TTYS	212	HI	
4	STLU	17	RMX	314	LO	....)

CHANNELS (

#	FROM	TO	MILES	TRAFFIC	TARIFF	...
4	1	2	667	4	IXC	
2	2	3	843	4	IXC	
3	1	3	275	102	TPD	
1	3	4	291	17	TPC	...)

Figure 3. Relation Network Description

The data management facility allows data from relation sets to be retrieved either sequentially or relationally. Sequential accesses are used by programs which calculate the minimum or maximum value of a domain, by programs which list sets, and by other programs which generally require access to every record of the set. A relational (content sensitive) access finds only those records of a set which have a specific value for a particular domain. For example, a relational access may be used to locate all the channels of a network which touch a specified terminal, or which have a specified tariff, or whose length exceeds a specified value. Neither sequential access nor relational access requires a particular order for the set. Any access or program which requires the records of a set to be in a special order must sort the set into that order using the standard sort facility. Since sets describing communication networks are small, this sorting is not time consuming.

Many TMDS programs may use other TMDS programs as subroutines. Even when capabilities are cascaded, all levels of the hierarchy are made directly accessible to the user. Thus with equal facility, he may request the system to calculate the distance between two terminals, the cost of channels between those terminals, or the cost of an entire network of channels.

Communication Network Management

Managing a communications network of even a hundred terminal locations requires a considerable amount of repetitive bookkeeping such as billing network usage to different departments, keeping statistical records of network usage, updating and printing network directories, and generating a variety of other reports. These tasks are easily mechanized with a computerized information system, once the network data has been entered into the information management system.

The standard use of a network management system is the preparation of maps and reports showing the current network status. Maps of the network topology may be drawn on any graphic output device such as digital plotter or cathode ray tube terminal. In addition to scaled maps of the network, the configuration report shown in Figure 4 may be very useful. It shows the interconnections of a centralized network but does not preserve the correct terminal locations nor the distances between them. However, because the terminals do not have to be in their proper locations, much more information about each terminal and channel can be printed than would fit on a properly scaled map. The configuration report is helpful for checking line and channel loadings, for checking circuit routings, and for verifying network performance.

In addition to network maps, an integrated network management system can prepare cost reports for the current network or for proposed changes to the network. Depending on the specific needs of the organization, these reports can be made very similar to billing notices from the common carriers. In the generation of management reports, a common data base facility guarantees that all reports are made from accurate data. After a change to the network is entered in the system, all subsequent reports will reflect that change.

An information system containing up-to-date network status may also be used for answering queries relevant to network modification or expansion. Many inquiry and reporting facilities not usually included in network design programs are easily included in the TMDS. A powerful selecting and sorting capability may be used to prepare many different reports such as a list of the terminals of a network ordered by distance from a particular location (the center or a proposed new concentrator), or by V and H coordinate, or by circuit requirements at each location. Similarly, the channels of a network may be listed in order of length, cost, capacity, traffic, origin, or

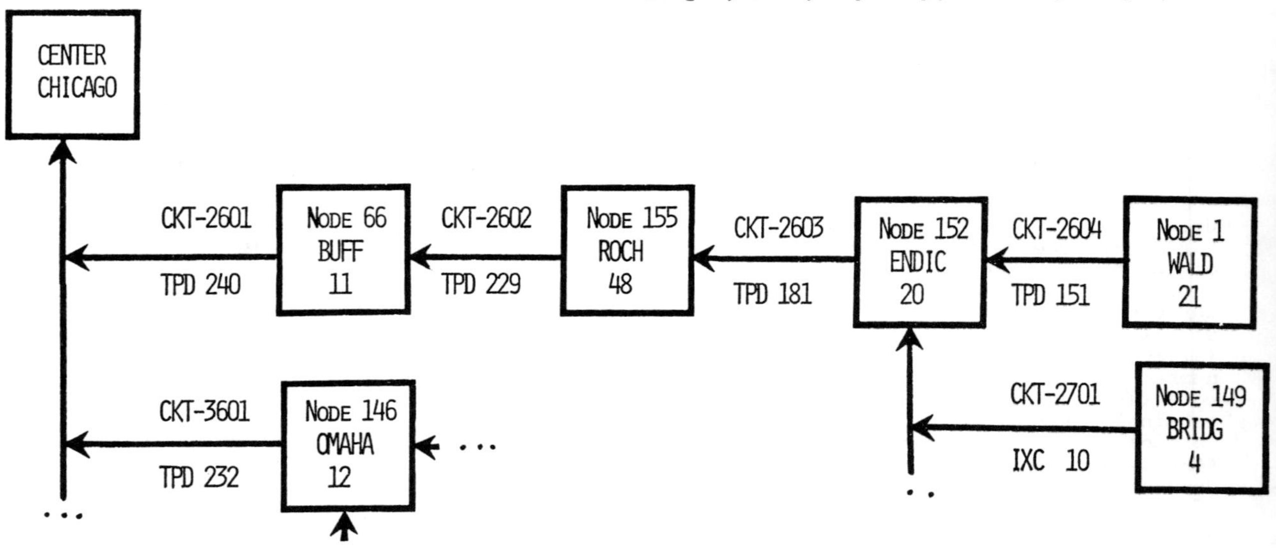

Figure 4. Network Configuration Report

destination. Other possible queries of use in network management include finding all terminals connected to a particular concentrator, finding all channels on a path between two specified terminals, and evaluating the cost of adding additional circuits.

Although the TMDS system provides little statistical or traffic analysis, such facilities could be added without changing the basic structure of the system. Indeed, the RDMS[9] system from which many of the concepts of TMDS evolved is a statistical data analysis and reporting system.

Communication Network Design

Communication network design is an excellent application of interactive computer-assisted problem solving because the problems are precisely specified, extremely complex, and thoroughly studied. Except for small and simple problems, mathematically optimal network configurations are very difficult to find. Many years of experience have led to the development of effective heuristic techniques for finding low cost networks. Powerful computer tools in the hands of an experienced network designer may provide better networks than either programs or people alone.

Most communication network design programs model the network by a graph where the nodes of the graph are the terminals of the network and the edges of the graph are the communication channels of the network. These models specify the cost of network communication components in precise detail based on the FCC tariffs used by the common carriers for billing use of their facilities. The performance of a network can be precisely specified by any of several network flow or queueing models. The usual design problem is to find the optimum (least costly) network which will satisfy the performance requirements. Hundreds of papers have been written applying the disciplines of graph theory, network flow theory, queueing theory, and simulation theory to the selection or synthesis of optimal networks. Most of this work is too complex to apply without computer assistance. An excellent introduction to current research in this area is the paper by Chou & Frank.[10]

Because optimal network configurations are not usually available even from computer programs, and to include human intuition and imprecisely specified constraints in the problem solution it is desirable to involve the communication system designer at every step in the design. In a study of the traveling salesman circuit path problem[8] it was found that while persons were better than programs for determining global strategies, the computer could do a better job of determining locally optimal portions of the circuit. This same effect is noticeable in the design of other types of networks. Although a communication system designer can do a good job of specifying the major routes of a communication network, the computer can usually suggest local improvements. Another important reason for keeping people in the design process is to include imprecise or seldom-used constraints in the a general algorithm. For example, no general design program can be expected to know that two unused circuits in a TELPAK channel were being saved by the communications manager for a new application or that certain types of lines are particularly difficult to have installed an some geographic areas. Indeed, many such constraints are discovered when a computer program or outside consultant suggests a network design which violates the constraint. Moreover, network modifications are often installed in order of convenience to the system manager or to the common carrier rather than in order of computer selection. The locations of new facilities are often constrained by non-economic considerations such plant or office locations. All of these reasons support the necessity of keeping the system managers and designers intimately involved in every step of the design process.

An integrated database oriented system provides the foundation for building an effective interactive man-computer system for management and design of telecommunication networks. Such a system has several advantages over separate design and reporting programs. A high degree of modularity simplifies the task of preparing special design facilities while giving the designer various levels of sophistication to use in his work. Thus iterative improvement techniques can be applied not only to computer generated networks, but also to existing networks which require modification or improvements. By enforcing rigid conventions on network data structure, the inputs and outputs for all system procedures are compatible facilitating the combining of different design techniques. Finally, a uniform and modular system facilitates conversion to a new tariff or the inclusion of a new tariff in the design possibilities. Thus the system is less easily made obsolete than a collection of independent special purpose programs.

Example: A TELPAK Network

Some network design and management capabilities of TMDS can be illustrated by an example, the design and modification of a TELPAK network. Before discussing the examples, a few comments on TELPAK design procedures are required.

The designer of a network may regard a TELPAK channel as a group of circuits (60 circuits in TELPAK C or 240 circuits in TELPAK D) priced at a bulk rate considerably cheaper than the rate for an equivalent number of individually priced circuits. His design problem is to configure a network of individual circuits and TELPAK channels to minimize the total system cost. Although a thorough review of network design is outside the scope of this paper, the following comments may help in understanding the examples.

Network configuration is generally done in two phases. First, a feasible network is designed. This network configuration may be uneconomical but it will satisfy the performance requirements. Then, the feasible network is modified in various ways to reduce its cost without unnecessarily degrading performance. These improvement techniques may be applied to an existing network as well as to a new design.

The TMDS system provides several different feasible network configurations, such as a minimal spanning tree, a shortest path network, a star configuration, or other common network topology. In addition to these program generated configurations, the system user may load any other configuration he believes will be useful as a feasible initial design. It is important to have a variety of different feasible networks, because no particular topology type is the best starting design for all sizes of networks. In the design of TELPAK networks, for example, a minimal spanning tree is very effective for networks of fourty or fewer terminal locations, but for larger networks other starting configurations produce lower cost final configurations with less computer time.

The modifications of the feasible network evaluated for possible cost reductions are selected by the system designer on the basis of the type of equipment available for the network, restrictions on allowable network topologies, and limitations on the computer time budgeted for the analysis. As in most other analysis and design efforts, there is a point of diminishing returns. Among the netork modifications which can be applied to a network of TELPAK channels are the following:

- Reducing the capacity of the channel between two terminals and rerouting traffic if necessary to maintain the performance requirements of the system.
- Increasing the capacity of a channel between two terminals and rerouting traffic where cost reductions are possible.
- Deleting a channel between two terminals and inserting a new channel between two other terminals, rerouting traffic where necessary.
- Moving a terminal or concentrator to its optimal (lowest cost) location without otherwise changing the network configuration.
- Adding a new terminal location to the network and routing some traffic through it. (The selection of such locations, called Steiner nodes, is discussed in reference 2.)
- Consolidating nearby terminals to reduce the cardinality of the design problem.
- Routing the traffic from a terminal by more than one route to the concentrator or to the centers.

Since some of these modifications may seek to improve the network in ways that are politically infeasible, the judgement of the system manager is necessary to guide the selections. Even when network improvements suggested by the computer programs are infeasible for non-economic reasons, they provide an indication of how much the network could be improved. If the best improvements to the existing network would only reduce its cost one percent, then probably no gross inefficiencies are being ignored.

As an example of effective computer assistance in network design and management, a set of circuit requirements located at 156 distinct locations throughout the United States totaling 2083 circuits (voice grade or equivalent) was generated. The traffic requirements of this

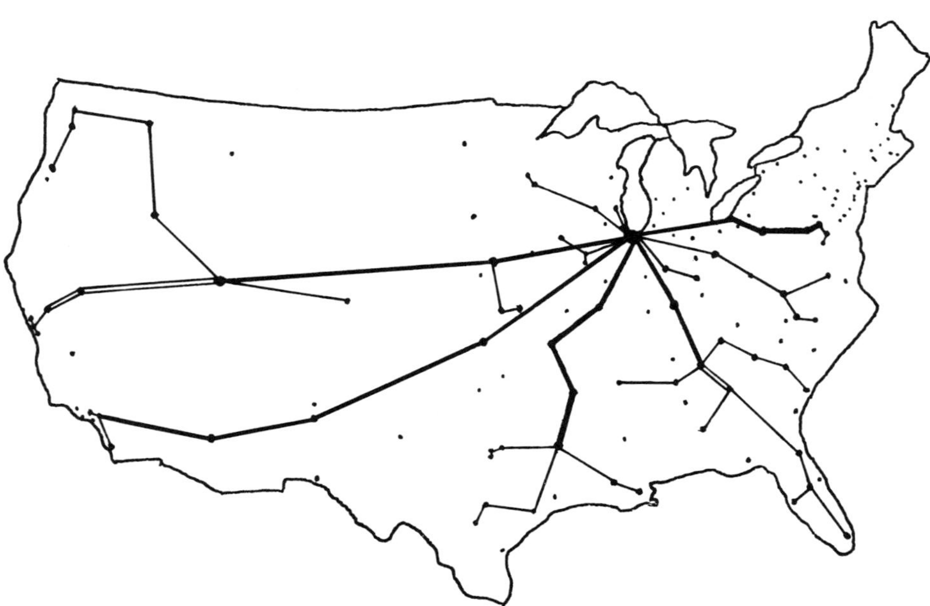

Figure 5. Network Configuration Selected without Computer Assistance.

example are similar to those of many large corporate communication networks. The terminal locations, traffics, and a network configuration generated without computer aids were loaded into the TMDS system for analysis. The manual configuration had two keypunch errors which were corrected with system editing commands. Then the network configuration was priced at a monthly rate of $920,386. The configuration is shown in Figure 5, redrawn from a large line-printer map produced by the system.

For a comparison, a computer generated network configuration was requested. An initial configuration generated by a CNDP-like algorithm was iteratively improved by deleting and adding branches to reduce the cost. This configuration, shown in Figure 6, resulted in a total monthly cost of $876,664 The computer's network was only vaguely similar to the designer's network, with 94 (60%) of the channels configured differently.

An attempt to improve the network with less drastic modifications from the manually specified configuration was made by requesting the system to generate suggested improvements. This time, twenty-six changes were suggested each of which would reduce the monthly fee by $1000 or more. Note that not all of these changes are possible, because selecting one modification may invalidate others. Twenty of the suggested changes were accepted, resulting in the network configuration shown in Figure 7. This configuration is very similar to the configuration of Figure 5, but with the much lower cost $899,664.

To illustrate the management design features, an additional circuit requirement was added to the network after the configuration studies. The system facilities permit the addition of a new terminal location to the terminal set. The new terminal may be connected into the network by adding a new channel to the set of channels representing the current configuration. Alternately, the system will calculate the best connection for the new traffic requirement. Because the configuration is represented in an on-line data base, new reports of channel traffics, costs, and configurations may be prepared quickly for the changed network.

Although this particular example discusses the design and modification of a TELPAK network, clearly the same types of analysis and reporting are applicable to other types of networks, including terminal oriented data networks, distributed networks, and networks combining both voice and data circuits.

Conclusions

Communication network analysis, design, and management seem well suited to interactive computer-assisted facilities. The combination of a relational data base and rigidly enforced program modularity form the basis for a general purpose system which may be used throughout the life of a network, for design, modification, administration, and redesign. The extra effort necessary to build a general purpose tool is repaid many times over in the extensibility, flexibility, and capability of the resulting system.

363

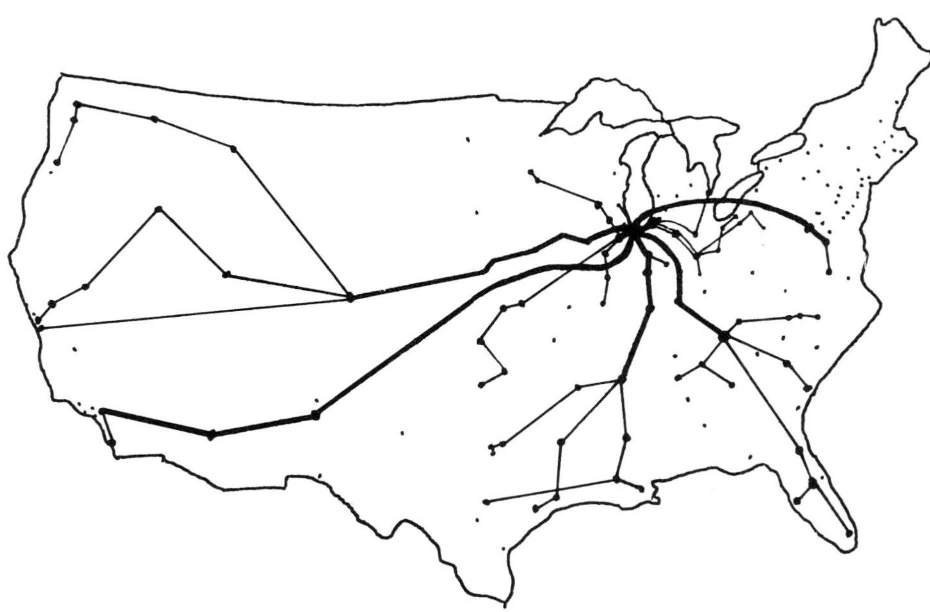

Figure 6. Network Configuration Selected by Computer System.

References

1. G.S.Pan. Communications Information System. Telecommunications, June 1970.

2. R.Citrenbaum. An On-Line Model for Computation-Communication network Analysis and Modification. SDC Technical Report 4743/003/000, May 1971.

3. D.R.Doll, M.Frazier, G.H.Runner, R.E.See. Communications Network Configurator -- Applications Manual. Raytheon Data Systems January 1972.

4. R.A.Lorie, A.J.Symonds. A Relational Access Method for Interactive Applications, Data Base Systems, Prentice-Hall, 1972.

5. J.A.Martin, Systems Analysis for Data Transmission, Prentice-Hall, 1972.

6. B.Rothfarb, M.Goldstein. The One-terminal Telpak Problem. Operations Research, Vol. 19, No. 1, January 1971.

7. K.M.Chandy, R.A.Russell. The Design of Multipoint Linkages in a Teleprocessing Tree Network. IEEE Transactions on Computers, Vol. C-21, No. 10, Jan. 1971.

8. P.Krolak, W.Felts, G.Marble. A Man-Machine Approach toward Solving the Traveling Salesman Problem. CACM, Vol. 14, No. 5, May 1971.

9. V K.M.Whitney. A Relational Data Management System (RDMS). Proc. of the IV conference on information systems, 1972.

10. H.Frank, W.Chou. Topological Optimization of computer networks. Proc. IEEE, Vol. 60, No. 11, November 1972.

11. V K.M.Whitney. Comparison of Network Topology Optimization Algorithms. Proc. of the ICCC-72, October 1972.

12. S.K.Chang. The Generation of Minimal Trees with a Steiner Topology. JACM, Vol. 19, No. 4, October 1972.

Reprinted by permission from *Proceedings of the Third Data Communications Symposium*
November 1973, pp. 141-147

364

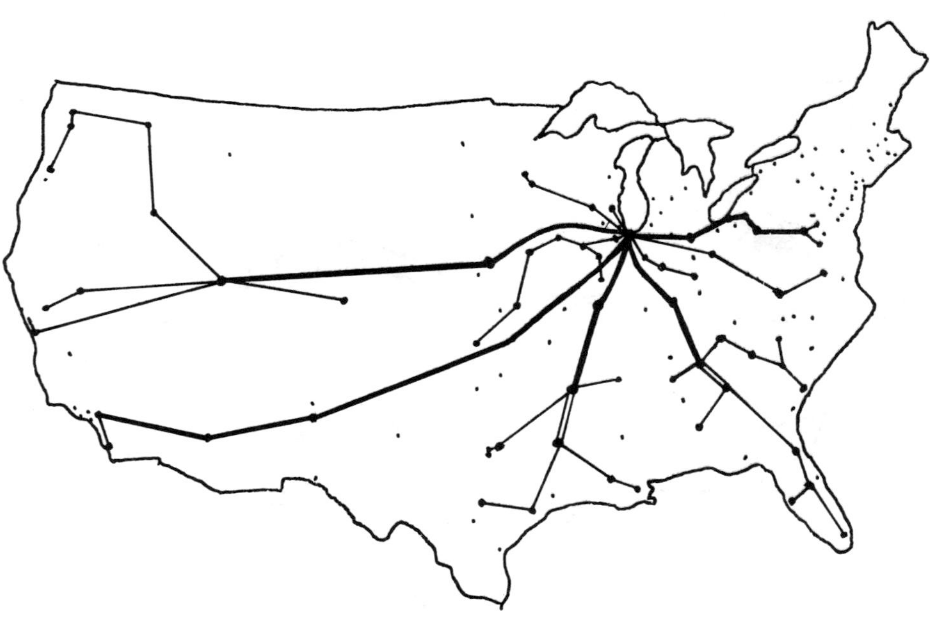

Figure 7. Network Configuration Generated by Co-operative Effort.

Communications Processors for Store-and-Forward Networks

To allow dissimilar, geographically separated computers to communicate with each other to form a computer network, one of the important problems affecting the throughput of the system is the problem of interfacing among computers and communication equipment. An effective approach is to use a small communication processor at each computer site (network node) to provide such functions as hardware interface, code conversion, message routing, synchronization, error control, reliability and other related issues. Design considerations for such processors are the main topic of this chapter.

Heart et. al. (p. 368) describe design considerations for the Interface Message Processor (IMP) for the ARPA Network. Ornstein et. al. (p. 385) discuss the Terminal IMP (TIP) which provides direct terminal access to the ARPA Network. The last paper, Heart et. al. (p. 397) presents a new mini-computer/multiprocessor communication processor which provides more expandability of I/O memory and more reliability, and is more modular than the IMP. Such systems may offer significant advantages in cost/performance. Although the communication processors described in the above papers are mainly for the ARPA Network, the concept and issues are likely to be relevant to other computer networks as well.

For further information about communication processors and related problems, the interested reader should consult [McQ 72], [McK 72], [KAR 73], and [BOU 73].

The interface message processor for the ARPA computer network*

by F. E. HEART, R. E. KAHN, S. M. ORNSTEIN, W. R. CROWTHER and D. C. WALDEN

Bolt Beranek and Newman Inc.
Cambridge, Massachusetts

INTRODUCTION

For many years, small groups of computers have been interconnected in various ways. Only recently, however, has the interaction of computers and communications become an important topic in its own right.** In 1968, after considerable preliminary investigation and discussion, the Advanced Research Projects Agency of the Department of Defense (ARPA) embarked on the implementation of a new kind of nationwide computer interconnection known as the ARPA Network. This network will initially interconnect many dissimilar computers at ten ARPA-supported research centers with 50-kilobit common-carrier circuits. The network may be extended to include many other locations and circuits of higher bandwidth.

The primary goal of the ARPA project is to permit persons and programs at one research center to access data and use interactively programs that exist and run in other computers of the network. This goal may represent a major step down the path taken by computer time-sharing, in the sense that the computer resources of the various research centers are thus pooled and directly accessible to the entire community of network participants.

Study of the technology and tariffs of available communications facilities showed that use of conventional *line switching* facilities would be economically and technically inefficient. The traditional method of routing information through the common-carrier switched network establishes a dedicated path for each conversation. With present technology, the time required for this task is on the order of seconds. For voice communication, that overhead time is negligible, but in the case of many short transmissions, such as may occur between computers, that time is excessive. Therefore, ARPA decided to build a new kind of digital communication system employing wideband leased lines and *message switching*, wherein a path is not established in advance and each message carries an address. In this domain the project portends a possible major change in the character of data communication services in the United States.

In a nationwide computer network, economic considerations also mitigate against a wideband leased line configuration that is topologically fully connected. In a non-fully connected network, messages must normally traverse several network nodes in going from source to destination. The ARPA Network is designed on this principle and, at each node, a copy of the message is stored until it is safely received at the following node. The network is thus a store and forward system and as such must deal with problems of routing, buffering, synchronization, error control, reliability, and other related issues. To insulate the computer centers from these problems, and to insulate the network from the problems of the computer centers, ARPA decided to place identical small processors at each network node, to interconnect these small processors with leased common-carrier circuits to form a *subnet*, and to connect each research computer center into the net via the local small processor. In this arrangement the research computer centers are called *Hosts* and the small processors are called *Interface Message Processors*, or *IMPs*. (See Figure 1.) This approach divides the genesis of the ARPA Network into two parts: (1) design and implementation of the IMP subnet, and (2) design and implementation of protocols and techniques for the sensible utilization of the network by the Hosts.

Implementation of the subnet involves two major

* This work was sponsored by the Advanced Research Projects Agency under Contract No. DAHC 15-69-C-0179.

** A bibliography of relevant references is included at the end of this paper; a more extensive list may be found in Cuadra, 1968.

Reprinted from AFIPS-Conference Proceedings
Volume 36 © AFIPS Press, Montvale NJ 07645

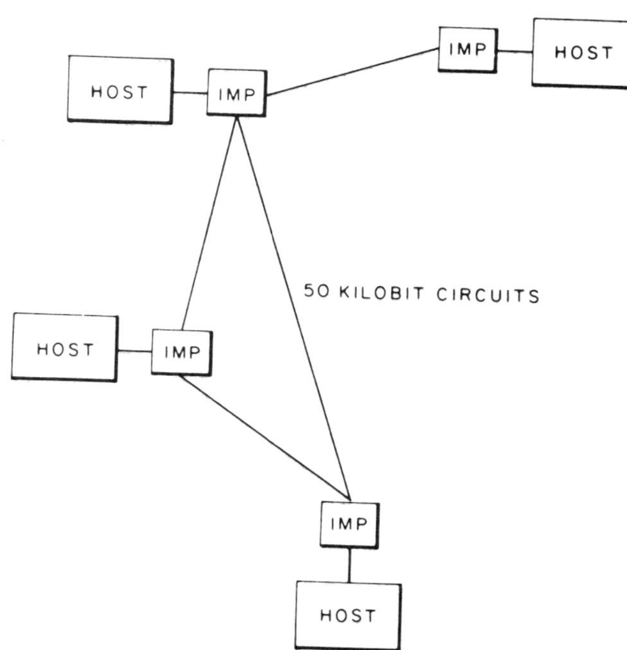

Figure 1—Hosts and IMPs

technical activities: providing 50-kilobit common-carrier circuits and the associated modems; and providing IMPs, along with software and interfaces to modems and Host computers. For reasons of economic and political convenience, ARPA obtained common-carrier circuits directly through government purchasing channels; AT&T (Long Lines) is the central coordinator, although the General Telephone Company is participating at some sites and other common carriers may eventually become involved. In January 1969, Bolt Beranek and Newman Inc. (BBN) began work on the design and implementation of IMPs; a four-node test network was scheduled for completion by the end of 1969 and plans were formulated to include a total of ten sites by mid-1970. This paper discusses the design of the subnet and describes the hardware, the software, and the predicted performance of the IMP. The issues of Host-to-Host protocol and network utilization are barely touched upon; these problems are currently being considered by the participating Hosts and may be expected to be a subject of technical interest for many years to come.

At this time, in late 1969, the test network has become an operating reality. IMPs have already been installed at four sites, and implementation of IMPs for six additional sites is proceeding. The common carriers have installed 50-kilobit leased service connecting the first four sites and are preparing to install circuits at six additional sites.

The design of the network allows for the connection of additional Host sites. A map of a projected eleven-node network is shown in Figure 2. The connections between the first four sites are indicated by solid lines. Dotted lines indicate planned connections.

NETWORK DESIGN

The design of the network is discussed in two parts. The first part concerns the relations between the Hosts and the subnet, and the second part concerns the design of the subnet itself.

Host-subnet considerations

The basic notion of a subnet leads directly to a series of questions about the relationship between the Hosts and the subnet: What tasks shall be performed by each? What constraints shall each place on the other? What dependence shall the subnet have on the Hosts? In considering these questions, we were guided by the following principles: (1) The subnet should function as a *communications system* whose essential task is to transfer bits reliably from a source location to a specified destination. Bit transmission should be sufficiently reliable and error free to obviate the need for special precautions (such as storage for retransmission) on the part of the Hosts; (2) The average 369
transit time through the subnet should be under a half second to provide for convenient interactive use of remote computers; (3) The subnet operation should be completely autonomous. Since the subnet must function as a store and forward system, an IMP must not be dependent upon its local Host. The IMP must

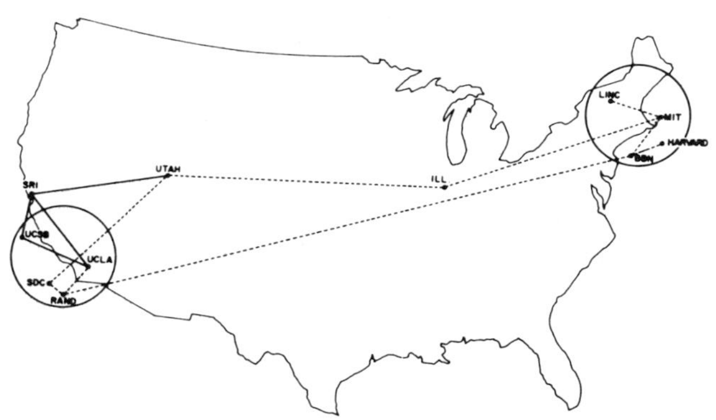

Figure 2—Network map

continue to operate whether the Host is functioning properly or not and must not depend upon a Host for buffer storage or other logical assistance such as program reloading. The Host computer must not in any way be able to change the logical characteristics of the subnet; this restriction avoids the mischievous or inadvertent modification of the communication system by an individual Host user; (4) Establishment of Host-to-Host protocol and the enormous problem of planning to communicate between different computers should be an issue separated from the subnet design.

Messages, links, and RFNMs

In principle, a single transmission from one Host to another may range from a few bits, as with a single teletype character, up to arbitrarily many bits, as in a very long file. Because of buffering limitations in the subnet, an upper limit was placed on the size of an individual Host transmission; 8095 bits was chosen for the maximum transmission size. This Host unit of transmission is called a *message*. The subnet does not impose any pattern restrictions on messages; binary text may be transmitted. Messages may be of variable length; thus, a source Host must indicate the end of a message to the subnet.

A major hazard in a message switched network is congestion, which can arise either due to system failures or to peak traffic flow. Congestion typically
370 occurs when a destination IMP becomes flooded with incoming messages for its Host. If the flow of messages to this destination is not regulated, the congestion will back up into the network, affecting other IMPs and degrading or even completely clogging the communication service. To solve this problem we developed a quenching scheme that limits the flow of messages to a given destination when congestion begins to occur or, more generally, when messages are simply not getting through.

The subnet transmits messages over unidirectional logical paths between Hosts known as *links*. (A link is a conceptual path that has no physical reality; the term merely identifies a message sequence.) The subnet accepts only one message at a time on a given link. Ensuing messages on that link will be blocked from entering the subnet until the source IMP learns that the previous message has arrived at the destination Host. When a link becomes unblocked, the subnet notifies the source Host by sending it a special control message known as *Ready for Next Message* (or RFNM), which identifies the newly unblocked link. The source Host may utilize its connection into the subnet to transmit messages over other links, while waiting to send messages on the blocked links. Up to 63 separate outgoing links may exist at any Host site. When giving the subnet a message, the Host specifies the destination Host and a link number in the first 32 bits of the message (known as the *leader*). The IMPs then attend to route selection, delivery, and notification of receipt. This use of links and RFNMs also provides for IMP-to-Host delivery of sequences of messages in proper order. Because the subnet allows only one message at a time on a given link, Hosts never receive messages out of sequence.

Host-IMP interfacing

Each IMP will initially service a single Host. However, we have made provision (both in the hardware and software) for the IMP to service up to four Hosts, with a corresponding reduction in the number of permitted phone line connections. Connecting an IMP to a wide variety of different Hosts requires a hardware interface, some part of which must be custom tailored to each Host. We decided, therefore, to partition the interface such that a standard portion would be built into the IMP, and would be identical for all Hosts, while a special portion of the interface would be unique to each Host. The interface is designed to allow messages to flow in both directions at once. A bit serial interface was designed partly because it required fewer lines for electrical interfacing and was, therefore, less expensive, and partly to accommodate conveniently the variety of word lengths in the different Host computers. The bit rate requirement on the Host line is sufficiently low that parallel transfers are not necessary.

The Host interface operates asynchronously, each data bit being passed across the interface via a *Ready For Next Bit/There's Your Bit* handshake procedure. This technique permits the bit rate to adjust to the rate of the slower member of the pair and allows necessary interruptions, when words must be stored into or retrieved from memory. The IMP introduces between bits a (manually) adjustable delay that limits the maximum data rate; at present, this delay is set to 10 μsec. Any delay introduced by the Host in the handshake procedure further slows the rate.

System failure

Considerable attention has been given to the possible effects on a Host of system failures in the subnet. Minor system failures (e.g., temporary line failures) will appear to the Hosts only in the form of reduced rate of service. Catastrophic failures may, however, result in the loss of messages or even in the loss of

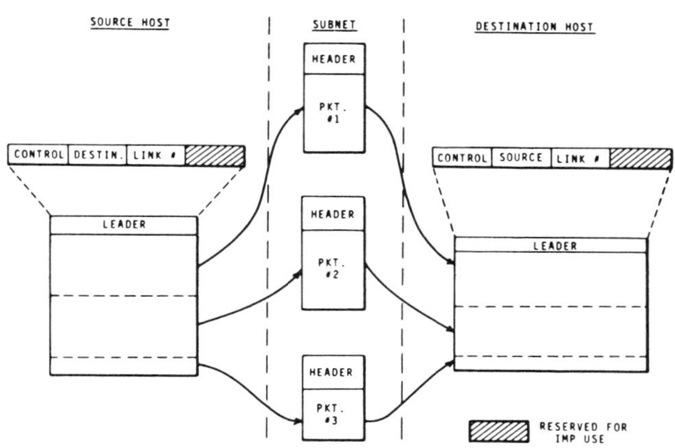

Figure 3—Messages and packets

subnet communication. IMPs inform a Host of all relevant system failures. Additionally, should a Host computer go down, the information is propagated throughout the subnet to all IMPs so they may notify their local Host if it attempts to send a message to that Host.

Specific subnet design

The overriding consideration that guided the subnet design was reliability. Each IMP must operate unattended and reliably over long periods with minimal down time for maintenance and repair. We were convinced that it was important for each IMP in the subnet to operate autonomously, not only independently of Hosts, but insofar as possible from other IMPs as well; any dependency between one IMP and another would merely broaden the area jeopardized by one IMP's failure. The need for reliability and autonomy bears directly upon the form of subnet communication. This section describes the process of message communication within the subnet.

Message handling

Hosts communicate with each other via a sequence of messages. An IMP takes in a message from its Host computer in segments, forms these segments into *packets* (whose maximum size is approximately 1000 bits), and ships the packets separately into the network. The destination IMP reassembles the packets and delivers them in sequence to the receiving Host, who obtains them as a single unit. This segmentation of a message during transmission is completely invisible to the Host computers. Figures 3, 4, and 5 illustrate aspects of message handling.

The transmitting Host attaches an identifying leader to the beginning of each message. The IMP forms a *header* by adding further information for network use and attaches this header to each packet of the message.

Each packet is individually routed from IMP-to-IMP through the network toward the destination. At each IMP along the way, the transmitting hardware generates initial and terminal framing characters and parity check digits that are shipped with the packet and are used for error detection by the receiving hardware of the next IMP.

Errors in transmission can affect a packet by destroying the framing and/or by modifying the data content. If the framing is disturbed in any way, the packet either will not be recognized or will be rejected by the receiver. In addition, the check digits provide protection against errors that affect only the data. The check digits can detect all patterns of four or fewer errors occurring within a packet, and any single error burst of a length less than twenty-four bits. An overwhelming majority of all other possible errors (all but about one in 2^{24}) are also detected. Thus, the mean time between undetected errors in the subnet should be on the order of years.

As a packet moves through the subnet, each IMP stores the packet until a positive acknowledgment is returned from the succeeding IMP. This acknowledgment indicates that the message was received without error and was accepted. Once an IMP has accepted a packet and returned a positive acknowledgment, it holds onto that packet tenaciously until it in turn receives an acknowledgment from the succeeding IMP. Under no circumstances (except for Host or IMP malfunction) will an IMP discard a packet after it has generated a positive acknowledgment. However, an IMP is always free to refuse a packet by simply not returning a positive acknowledgment. It may do this for any of several reasons: the packet may have

371

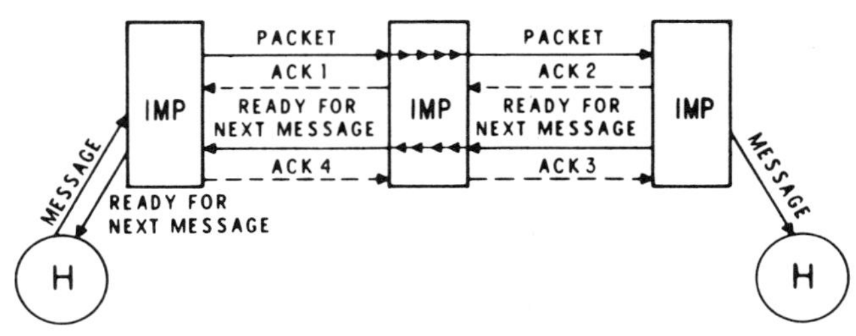

Figure 4—RFNMs and acknowledgments

been received in error, the IMP may be busy, the IMP buffer storage may be temporarily full, etc.

At the transmitting IMP, such discard of a packet is readily detected by the absence of a returned acknowledgment within a reasonable time interval (e.g., 100 msec). Such packets are retransmitted, perhaps along a different route. Acknowledgments themselves are not acknowledged, although they are error checked in the usual fashion. Loss of an acknowledgment results in the eventual retransmission of the packet; the destination IMP sorts out the resulting duplication by using a message number and a packet number in the header.

The packets of a message arrive at the destination IMP, possibly out of order, where they are reassembled. The header is then stripped off each packet and a leader, identifying the source Host and the link, followed by the reassembled message is then delivered to the destination Host as a single unit. See Figure 3.

Routing algorithm

The routing algorithm directs each packet to its destination along a path for which the total estimated transit time is smallest. This path is not determined in advance. Instead, each IMP individually decides onto which of its output lines to transmit a packet addressed to another destination. This selection is made by a fast and simple table lookup procedure. For each possible destination, an entry in the table designates the appropriate next leg. These entries reflect line or IMP trouble, traffic congestion, and current subnet connectivity. This routing table is updated every halfsecond as follows:

Each IMP estimates the delay it expects a packet to encounter in reaching every possible destination over each of its output lines. It selects the minimum delay estimate for each destination and periodically (about twice a second) passes these estimates to its immediate neighbors. Each IMP then constructs its own routing table by combining its neighbors' estimates with its own estimates of the delay to that neighbor. The estimated delay to each neighbor is based upon both queue lengths and the recent performance of the connecting communication circuit. For each destination, the table is then made to specify that selected output line for which the sum of the estimated delay to the neighbor plus the neighbor's delay to the destination is smallest.

The routing table is consistently and dynamically updated to adjust for changing conditions in the network. The system is adaptive to the ups and downs of lines, IMPs, and congestion; *it does not require the IMP to know the topology of the network.* In particular, an IMP need not even know the identity of its immediate neighbors. Thus, the leased circuits could be reconfigured to a new topology without requiring any changes to the IMPs.

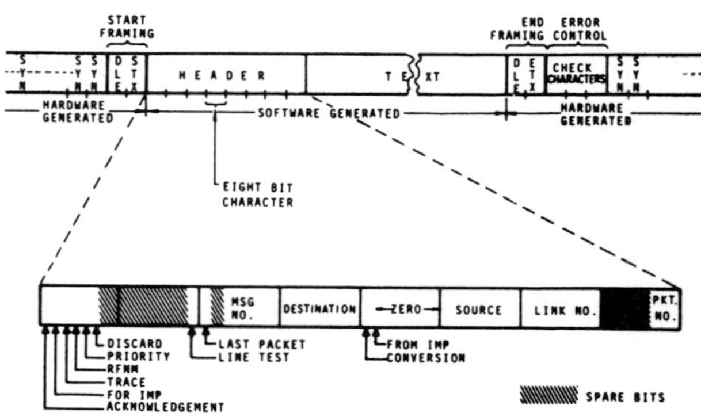

Figure 5—Format of packet on phone line

Subnet failures

The network is designed to be largely invulnerable to circuit or IMP failure as well as to outages for maintenance. Special status and test messages are employed to help cope with various failures. In the absence of regular packets for transmission over a line, the IMP program transmits special *hello* packets at half-second intervals. The acknowledgment for a hello packet is an *I heard you* packet.

A *dead line* is defined by the sustained absence (approximately 2.5 seconds) on that line of either received regular packets or acknowledgments; no regular packets will be routed onto a dead line, and any packets awaiting transmission will be rerouted. Routing tables in the network are adjusted automatically to reflect the loss. We require acknowledgment of thirty consecutive *hello* packets (an event which consumes at least 15 seconds), before a dead line is defined to be alive once again.

A dead line may reflect trouble either in the communication facilities or in the neighboring IMP itself. Normal line errors caused by dropouts, impulse noise, or other conditions should not result in a dead line, because such errors typically last only a few milliseconds, and only occasionally as long as a few tenths of a second. Therefore, we expect that a line will be defined as dead only when serious trouble conditions occur. If dead lines eliminate all routes between two IMPs, the IMPs are said to be *disconnected* and each of these IMPs will discard messages destined for the other. Disconnected IMPs cannot be rapidly detected from the delay estimates that arrive from neighboring IMPs. Consequently, additional information is transmitted between neighboring IMPs to help detect this condition. Each IMP transmits to its neighbors the length of the shortest existing path (i.e., number of IMPs) from itself to each destination. To the smallest such received number per destination, the IMP adds one. This incremented number is the length of the shortest path from that IMP to the destination. If the length ever exceeds the number of network nodes, the destination IMP is assumed to be unreachable and therefore disconnected.

Messages intended for dead Hosts (which are not the same as dead IMPs) cannot be delivered; therefore, these messages require special handling to avoid indefinite circulation in the network and spurious arrival at a later time. Such messages are purged from the network either at the source IMP or at the destination IMP. Dead Host information is regularly transmitted with the routing information. A Host computer is notified about another dead Host only when attempting to send a message to that Host.

An IMP may detect a major failure in one of three ways: (1) A packet expected for reassembly of a multiple packet message does not arrive. If a message is not fully reassembled in 15 minutes, the system presumes a failure. The message is discarded by the destination IMP and both the source IMP and the source Host are notified via a special RFNM. (2) The Host does not take a message from its IMP. If the Host has not taken a message after 15 minutes, the system presumes that it will never take the message. Therefore, as in the previous case, the message is discarded and a special RFNM is returned to the source Host. (3) A link is never unblocked. If a link remains blocked for longer than 20 minutes, the system again presumes a failure; the link is then unblocked and an error message is sent to the source Host. (This last time interval is slightly longer than the others so that the failure mechanisms for the first two situations will have a chance to operate and unblock the link.)

Reliability and recovery procedures

For higher system reliability, special attention was placed on intrinsic reliability, hardware test capabilities, hardware/software failure recovery techniques, and proper administrative mechanisms for failure management.

To improve intrinsic reliability, we decided to ruggedize the IMP hardware, thus incurring an approximately ten percent hardware cost penalty. For ease in maintenance, debugging, program revision, and analysis of performance, all IMPs are as similar as possible; the operational program and the hardware are nearly identical in all IMPs.

To improve hardware test capabilities, we built special *crosspatching* features into the IMP's interface hardware; these features allow program-controlled connection of output lines to corresponding input lines. These crosspatching features have been invaluable in testing IMPs before and during field installation, and they should continue to be very useful when troubles occur in the operating network. These hardware test features are employed by a special hardware test program and may also be employed by the operational program when a line difficulty occurs.

The IMP includes a 512-word block of protected memory that secures special recovery programs. An IMP can recover from an IMP failure in two ways: (1) In the event of power failure, a power-fail interrupt permits the IMP to reach a clean stop before the program is destroyed. When power returns, a special automatic restart feature turns the IMP back on and restarts the program. (We considered several possibilities for handling the packets found in an IMP during a power failure and concluded that no plan to salvage the packets was both practical and foolproof. For example, we cannot know whether the packet in transmission at the time of failure successfully left the machine before the power failed. Therefore, we decided simply to discard all the packets and restart the program.) (2) The second recovery mechanism is a "watchdog timer", which transfers control to protected memory whenever the program neglects this timer for about one minute. In the event of such transfer, the program in unprotected memory is presumed to be destroyed (either through a hardware transient or a software failure). The program in protected memory sends a reload request down a phone line *selected at random*. The neighboring IMP responds by sending a copy of its whole program back on the phone line. A normal IMP would discard this message because it is too long, but the recovering IMP can use it to reload its program.

Everything unique to a particular IMP must thus reside in its protected memory. Only one register (containing the IMP number) currently differs from IMP-to-IMP. The process of reloading, which requires a few seconds, can be tried repeatedly until successful; however, if after several minutes the program has not resumed operation, a later phase of the watchdog timer shuts off all power to the IMP.

In addition to providing recovery mechanisms for both network and IMP failures, we have incorporated into the subnet a *control center* that monitors network status and handles trouble reports. The control center, located at a network node, initiates and follows up any corrective actions necessary for proper subnet functioning. Furthermore, this center controls and schedules any modifications to the subnet.

Introspection

Because the network is experimental in nature, considerable effort has been allocated to developing tools whereby the network can supply measures of its own performance. The operational IMP program is capable of taking statistics on its own performance on a regular basis; this function may be turned on and off remotely. The various kinds of resulting statistics, which are sent via the network to a selected Host for analysis, include "snapshots", ten-second summaries, and packet arrival times. Snapshots are summaries of the internal status of queue lengths and routing information. A synchronization procedure allows these snapshots, which are taken every half second, to occur at roughly the same time in all network IMPs; a Host receiving such snapshot messages could presumably build up an instantaneous picture of overall network status. Ten-second summaries include such IMP-
374
generated statistics as the number of processed messages of each kind, the number of retransmissions, the traffic to and from the local Host, and so forth; this statistical data is sent to a selected Host every ten seconds. In addition, a record of actual packet arrival times on modem lines allows for the modeling of line traffic. (As part of its research activity, the group at UCLA is acting as a network measurement center; thus, statistics for analysis will normally be routed to the UCLA Host.)

Perhaps the most powerful capability for network introspection is *tracing*. Any Host message sent into the network may have a "trace bit" set in the leader. Whenever it processes a packet from such a message, the IMP keeps special records of what happens to that packet—e.g., how long the packet is on various queues, when it comes in and leaves, etc. Each IMP that handles the traced packet generates special trace report messages that are sent to a specified Host; thus, a complete analysis of what has happened to that message can be made. When used in an orderly way, this tracing facility will aid in understanding at a very detailed level the behavior of routing algorithms and the behavior of the network under changing load conditions.

Flexibility

Flexibility for modifications in IMP usage has been provided by several built-in arrangements: (1) provision within the existing cabinet for an additional 4K core bank; (2) modularity of the hardware interfaces; (3) provision for operation with data circuits of widely different rates; (4) a program organization involving many nearly self-contained subprograms; and (5) provision for Host-unique subprograms in the IMP program structure.

This last aspect of flexibility presents a somewhat controversial design choice. There are many advantages to keeping all IMP software nearly identical. Because of the experimental nature of the network, however, we do not yet know whether this luxury of identical programs will be an optimal arrangement. Several potential applications of "Host-unique" IMP software have been considered—e.g., using ASCII conversion routines in each IMP to establish a "Network ASCII" and possibly to simplify the protocol problems of each Host. As of now, the operational IMP program includes a *structure* that permits unique software plug-in packages at each Host site, but no plug-ins have yet been constructed.

THE HARDWARE

We selected a Honeywell DDP-516 for the IMP processor because we wanted a machine that could easily handle currently anticipated maximum traffic and that had already been proven in the field. We considered only economic machines with fast cycle times and good instruction sets. Furthermore, we needed a machine with a particularly good I/O capability and that was available in a ruggedized version. The geographical proximity of the supplier to BBN was also a consideration.

The basic machine has a 16-bit word length and a 0.96-μsec memory cycle. The IMP version is packaged in a single cabinet, and includes a 12K memory, a set of 16 multiplexed channels (which implement a 4-cycle data break), a set of 16 priority interrupts, a 100-μsec clock, and a set of programmable status lights. Also packaged within this cabinet are special modular interfaces for connecting the IMP to phone line modems and to Host computers; these interfaces use the same kind of 1 MHz and 5 MHz DTL packs from which the main machine is constructed. In addition, a number of features that have been incorporated make the IMP somewhat resilient to a variety of failures.

Teletypes and high-speed paper tape readers which are attached to the IMPs are used only for mainte-

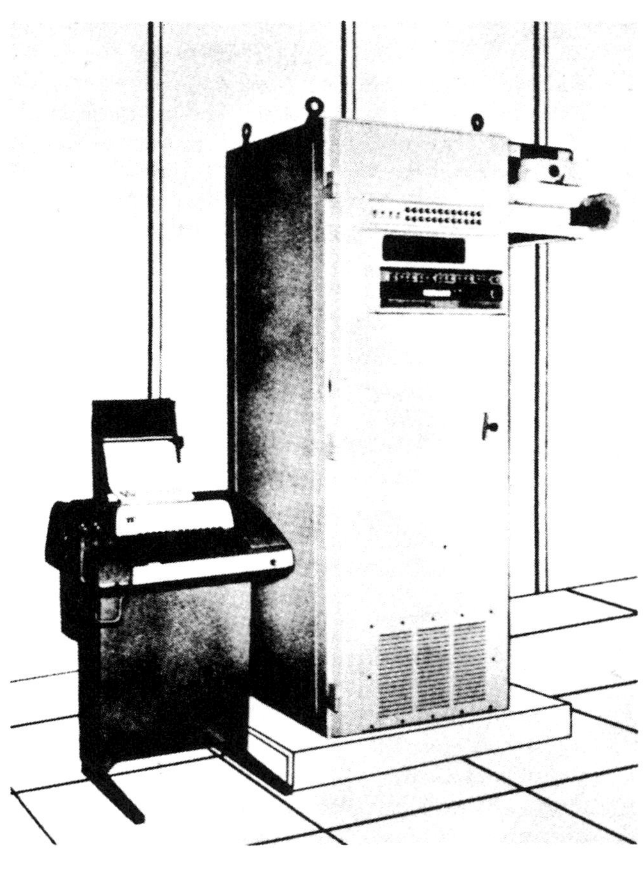

Figure 6—The IMP

nance, debugging, and system modification; in normal operation, the IMP runs without any moving parts except fans. Within the cabinet, space has been reserved for an additional 4K memory. Figure 6 is a picture of an IMP, and Figure 7 shows its configuration.

Ruggedization of computer hardware for use in friendly environments is somewhat unusual; however, we felt that the considerable difficulty that IMP failures can cause the network justified this step. Although the ruggedized unit is not fully "qualified" to MIL specs, it does have greater resistance to temperature variance, mechanical shock and vibration, radio frequency interference, and power line noise. We are confident that this ruggedization will increase the mean time to failure.

Modular Host and modem interfaces allow an IMP to be individually configured for each network node. The modularity, however, does not take the form of pluggable units and, except for the possibility of adding interfaces into reserved frame space, reconfiguration is impractical. Various configurations allow for up to two Hosts and five modems, three Hosts and four modems, etc. Each modem interface requires approximately one-fourth the amount of logic used in the C.P.U. The Host interface is somewhat smaller (about one-sixth of the C.P.U.).

Interfaces to the Host and to the modems have certain common characteristics. Both are full duplex, both may be crosspatched under program control to test their operation, and both function in the same general manner. To send a packet, the IMP program sets up memory pointers to the packet and then activates the interface via a programmable control pulse. The interface takes successive words from the memory using its assigned output data channel and transmits them bit-serially (to the Host or to the modem). When the memory buffer has thus been emptied, the interface notifies the program via an interrupt that the job has been completed. To receive information, the program first sets pointers to the allocated space in the memory into which the information is to flow. Using a control pulse it then readies the interface to receive. When information starts to arrive (here again bit-serially), it is assembled into 16-bit words and stored into the IMP memory. When either the allocated memory space is full or the end of the data train is detected, the interface notifies the program via an interrupt.

The modem interfaces deal with the phone lines in terms of 8-bit characters; the interfaces idle by sending and receiving a sync pattern that keeps them in character sync. Bit sync is maintained by the modems themselves, which provide both transmit and receive clocking signals to the interfaces. When the program initiates

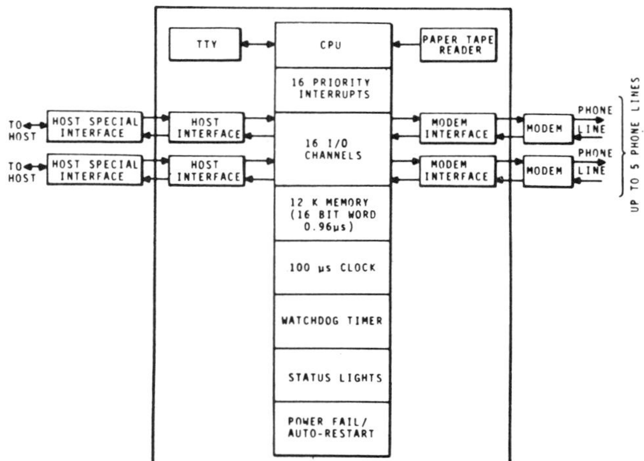

Figure 7—IMP configuration

transmission, the hardware first transmits a pair of initial framing characters (DLE, STX). Next, the text of the packet is taken word by word from the memory and shifted serially onto the phone line. At the end of the data, the hardware generates a pair of terminal framing characters (DLE, ETX) and shifts them onto the phone line. After the terminal framing characters, the hardware generates and transmits 24 check bits. Finally, the interface returns to idle (sync) mode.

The hardware doubles any DLE characters within the binary data train (that is, transmits them twice), thereby permitting the receiving interface hardware to distinguish them from the terminal framing characters and to remove the duplicate. Transmitted packets are of a known maximum size; therefore, any overflow of input buffer length is evidence of erroneous transmission. Format errors in the framing also register as errors. Check bits are computed from the received data and compared with the received check bits to detect errors in the text. Any of these errors set a flag and cause a program interrupt. Before processing a packet, the program checks the error flag to determine whether the packet was received correctly.

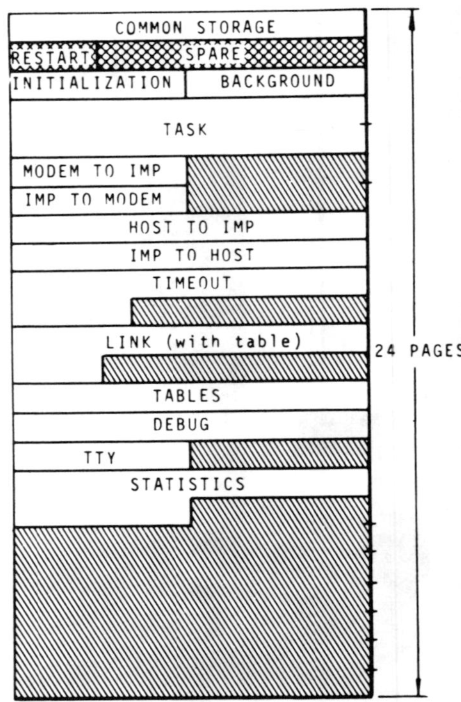

Figure 8—Map of core storage

IMP SOFTWARE

Implementation of the IMPs required the development of a sophisticated operational computer program and the development of several auxiliary programs for hardware tests, program construction, and debugging. This section discusses in detail the design of the operational program and briefly describes the auxiliary software.

Operational program

The principal function of the operational program is the processing of packets. This processing includes segmentation of Host messages into packets for routing and transmission, building of headers, receiving, routing and transmitting of store and forward packets, retransmitting of unacknowledged packets, reassembling received packets into messages for transmission to the Host, and generating of RFNMs and acknowledgments. The program also monitors network status, gathers statistics, and performs on-line testing. This real-time program is an efficient, interrupt-driven, involute machine language program that occupies about 6000 words of memory. It was designed, constructed, and debugged over a period of about a year by three programmers.

The entire program is composed of twelve functionally distinct pieces; each piece occupies no more than one or two pages of core (512 words per page). These programs communicate primarily through common registers that reside in page zero of the machine and that are directly addressable from all pages of memory. A map of core storage is shown in Figure 8. Seven of the twelve programs are directly involved in the flow of packets through the IMP: the *task* program performs the major portion of the packet processing, including the reassembly of Host messages; the *modem* programs (IMP-to-Modem and Modem-to-IMP) handle interrupts and resetting of buffers for the modem channels; the *Host* programs (IMP-to-Host and Host-to-IMP) handle interrupts and resetting of buffers for the Host channels, build packet headers during input, and construct RFNMs that are returned to the source Host during output; the *time-out* program maintains a software clock, times out unacknowledged packets for retransmission, and attends to infrequent events; the *link* program assigns and verifies message numbers and keeps track of links. A background loop

TABLE I—Program Data Structures

5000 WORDS—MESSAGE BUFFER STORAGE
120 WORDS—QUEUE POINTERS
300 WORDS—TRACE BLOCKS
100 WORDS—REASSEMBLY BLOCKS
150 WORDS—ROUTING TABLES
400 WORDS—LINK TABLES
300 WORDS—STATISTICS TABLES

contains the remaining five programs and deals with initialization, debugging, testing, statistics gathering and tracing. After a brief description of data structures, we will discuss packet processing in some detail.

Buffer allocation, queues, and tables

The major system data structures (see Table I) consist of buffers and tables. The buffer storage space is partitioned into about 70 fixed length buffers, each of which is used for storing a single packet. An unused buffer is chained onto a free buffer list and is removed from this list when it is needed to store an incoming packet. A packet, once stored in a buffer, is never moved. After a packet has been successfully passed along to its Host or to another IMP, its buffer is returned to the free list. The buffer space is partitioned in such a way that each process (store and forward, traffic, Host traffic, etc.) is always guaranteed some buffers. For the sake of program speed and simplicity, no attempt is made to retrieve the space wasted by partially filled buffers.

In handling store and forward traffic, all processing is on a per packet basis. Further, although traffic to and from Hosts is composed of *messages*, the IMP rapidly converts to dealing with packets; the Host transmits a message as a single unit but the IMP takes it one buffer at a time. As each buffer is filled, the program selects another buffer for input until the entire message has been provided for. These successive buffers will, in general, be scattered throughout the memory. An equivalent inverse process occurs on output to the Host after all packets of the message have arrived at the destination IMP. No attempt is ever made to collect the packets of a message into a contiguous portion of the memory.

Buffers currently in use are either dedicated to an incoming or an outgoing packet, chained on a queue awaiting processing by the program, or being processed. Occasionally, a buffer may be simultaneously found on two queues; this situation can occur when a packet is waiting on one queue to be forwarded and on another to be acknowledged.

There are four principal types of queues:

Task: Packets received on Host channels are placed on the Host task queue. All received acknowledgments, dead Host and routing information, *I heard you* and *hello* packets are placed on the system task queue; all other packets from the modems are placed on the modem task queue. The program services the system task queue first, then the Host task queue, and finally the modem task queue.

Output: A separate output queue is constructed for each modem channel and each Host channel. Each modem output queue is subdivided into an acknowledgment queue, a priority queue, a RFNM queue, and a regular message queue, which are serviced in that order. Each Host output queue is subdivided into a control message queue, a priority queue, and a regular message queue, which are also serviced in the indicated order.

Sent: A separate queue for each modem channel contains packets that have already been transmitted on that line but for which no acknowledgment has yet been received.

Reassembly: The reassembly queue contains those packets that are being reassembled into messages for the Host.

Tables in core are allocated for the storage of queue pointers, for trace blocks, for reassembly information, for statistics, and for links. Most noteworthy of these is the link table, which is used at the source IMP for assignment of message numbers and for blocking and unblocking links, and at the destination IMP to verify message numbers for sequence control.

377

Packet flow and program structure

Figure 9 is a schematic drawing of packet processing; the processing programs are described below.

The *Host-to-IMP* routine (H → I) handles messages being transmitted from the local site. The routine uses the leader to construct a header that is prefixed to each packet of the message. It also creates a link for the message if necessary, blocks the link, puts the packets of the message on the Host task queue for further processing by the task routine, and triggers the programmable task interrupt. The routine then acquires a free buffer and sets up a new input. The routine tests a hardware trouble indicator, verifies the message format, and checks whether or not the destination is dead, the link table is full, or the link blocked. The routine is serially reentrant and services all Hosts connected to the IMP.

The *Modem-to-IMP* routine (M → I) handles inputs from the modems. This routine consists of several identical routines, one for each modem channel. (Such duplication is useful to obtain higher speed.) This routine sets up an input buffer (normally obtained from the free list), places the received packet on the appropriate task queue, and triggers the programmable task interrupt. Should no free buffers be available for input, the buffer at the head of the modem task queue is preempted. If the modem task queue is also empty, the received packet is discarded by setting up its buffer for input. However, a sufficient number of free buffers are specifically reserved to assure that received acknowledgments, routing packets, and the like are rarely discarded.

The *task routine* uses the header information to direct packets to their proper destination. The task routine is driven by the task interrupt, which is set whenever a packet is put on a task queue. The task routine routes packets from the Host task queue onto an output queue determined from the routing algorithm.

For each packet on the modem task queue, the task routine first determines whether sufficient buffer space is available. If the IMP has a shortage of store and forward buffers, the buffers on the modem task queue are simply returned to the free list without further processing. Normally, however, an acknowledgment packet is constructed and put near the front of the appropriate modem output queue. The destination of the packet is then inspected. If the packet is not for the local site, the routing algorithm selects a modem output queue for the packet. If a packet for the local site is a RFNM, the corresponding link is unblocked and the RFNM is put on a queue to the Host. If the packet is not a RFNM, it is joined with others of the same message on the reassembly queue. Whenever a message is completely reassembled, the packets of the message are put on an output queue to the Host for processing by the IMP-to-Host routine.

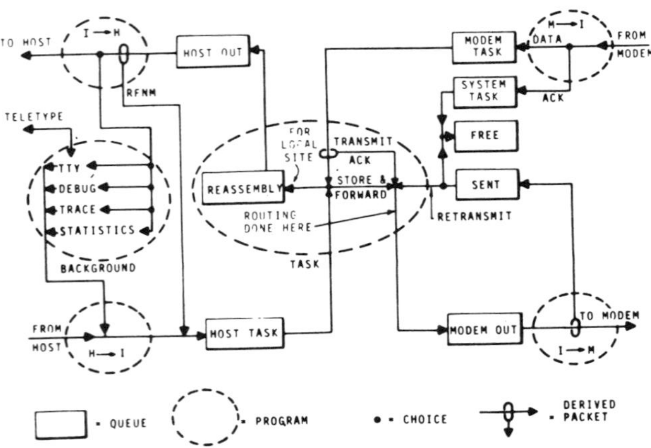

Figure 9—Internal packet flow

In processing the system task queue, the task routine returns to the free list those buffers from the sent queue that have been referenced by acknowledgments. Any packets skipped over by an acknowledgment are designated for retransmission. Routing, *I heard you*, and *hello* packets are processed in a straightforward fashion.

The *IMP-to-Modem* routine (I → M) transmits successive packets from the Modem output queue. After completing the output, this routine places any packet requiring acknowledgment on the sent queue.

The *IMP-to-Host* routine (I → H) sets up successive outputs of packets on the Host output queues and constructs a RFNM for each non-control message delivered to a Host. RFNM packets are returned to the system via the Host task queue.

The *time-out* routine is started every 25.6 msec (called the time-out period) by a clock interrupt. The routine has three sections: the fast time-out routine, which "wakes up" any Host or modem interrupt routine that has languished (for example, when the Host input routine could not immediately start a new input because of a shortage in buffer space); the middle time-out routine, which retransmits any packets that have been too long on a modem sent queue; and the slow time-out routine, which marks lines as alive or dead, updates the routing tables and does long term garbage collection of queues and other data structures. (For example, it protects the system from the cumulative effect of such failures as a lost packet of a multiple packet message, where buffers are tied up in message reassembly.) It also deletes links automatically after 15 seconds of disuse, after 20 minutes of blocking, or when an IMP goes down.

These three routines are executed in the following pattern:

```
FFFF FFFF FFFF FFFF FFFF FFFF . . .
  M    M    M    M          M
                            S
```

and, although they run off a common interrupt, are constructed to allow faster routines to interrupt slower ones should a slower routine not complete execution before the next time-out period.

The *link* routine enters, examines, and deletes entries from the link table. A table containing a separate message number entry for many links to every possible Host would be prohibitively large. Therefore, the table contains entries only for each of 63 total outgoing links at any Host site. Hashing is used to speed accessing of this table, but the link program is still quite costly; it uses about ten percent of both speed and space in a conceptually trivial task.

Initialization and background loop

The IMP program starts in an initialization section that builds the initial data structures, prepares for inputs from modem and Host channels, and resets all program switches to their nominal state. The program then falls into the background loop, which is an endlessly repeated series of low-priority subroutines that are interrupted to handle normal traffic.

The programs in the IMP background loop perform a variety of functions: TTY is used to handle the IMP Teletype traffic; DEBUG, to inspect or change IMP core memory; TRACE, to transmit collected information about traced packets; STATISTICS, to take and transmit network and IMP statistics; PARAMETER-CHANGE, to alter the values of selected IMP parameters; and DISCARD, to throw away packets. Selected Hosts and IMPs, particularly the Network Measurement Center and the Network Control Center, will find it necessary or useful to communicate with one or more of these background loop programs. So that these programs may send and receive messages from the network, they are treated as "fake Hosts". Rather than duplicating portions of the large IMP-to-Host and Host-to-IMP routines, the background loop programs are treated as if they were Hosts, and they can thereby utilize existing programs. The "For IMP" bit or the "From IMP" bit in the leader indicates that a given message is for or from a fake Host program in the IMP. Almost all of the background loop is devoted to running these programs.

The TTY program assembles characters from the Teletype into network messages and decodes network messages into characters for the Teletype; TTY's normal message destination is the DEBUG program at its own IMP; however, TTY can be made to communicate with any other IMP Teletype, any other IMP DEBUG program or any Host program with compatible format.

The DEBUG program permits the operational program to be inspected and changed. Although its normal message source is the TTY program at its own IMP, DEBUG will respond to a message of the correct format from any source. This program is normally inhibited from changing the operational IMP program; local operator intervention is required to activate the program's full power.

The STATISTICS program collects measurements about network operation and periodically transmits them to the Network Measurement Center. This program sends but does not receive messages. STATISTICS has a mechanism for collecting measurements over 10-second intervals and for taking half-second snapshots of IMP queue lengths and routing tables. It can also generate artificial traffic to load the network. When turned on, STATISTICS uses 10 to 20 percent of the machine capacity and generates a noticeable amount of phone line traffic.

Other programs in the background loop drive local status lights and operate the parameter change routine. A thirty-two word parameter table controls the operation of the TRACE and STATISTICS programs and includes spares for expansion; the PARAMETER-CHANGE program accepts messages that change these parameters.

Control organization

It is characteristic of the IMP system that many of the main programs are entered both as subroutine calls from other programs and as interrupt calls from the hardware. The resulting control structure is shown in Figure 10. The programs are arranged in a priority order; control passes upward in the chain whenever a hardware interrupt occurs or the current program decides that the time has come to run a higher priority program, and control passes downward only when the higher priority programs are finished. No program may execute either itself or a lower priority program; however, a program may freely execute a higher priority program. This rule is similar to the usual rules concerning priority interrupt routines.

In one important case, however, control must pass from a higher priority program to a lower priority program—namely, from the several input routines to the TASK routine. For this special case, the computer hardware was modified to include a low-priority hardware interrupt that *can be set by the program.* When this interrupt has been honored (i.e., when all other interrupts have been serviced), the TASK routine is executed. Thus, control is directed where needed without violating the priority rules.

Some routines must occasionally wait for long intervals of time, for example, when the Host-to-IMP routine must wait for a link to unblock. Stopping the whole system would be intolerable; therefore, should the need arise, such a routine is dismissed, and the TIMEOUT routine will later transfer control to the waiting routine.

The control structure and the partition of responsibility among various programs achieve the following timing goals:

1. No program stops or delays the system while waiting for an event.
2. The program gracefully adjusts to the situation where the machine becomes compute-bound.
3. The Modem-to-IMP routine can deliver its current packet to the TASK routine before the next packet arrives and can always prepare for successive packet inputs on each line. This timing is critical because a slight delay here might require retransmission of the entire packet. To achieve this result, separate routines (one per phone line) interrupt each other freely after new buffers have been set up.
4. The program will almost always deliver packets waiting to be sent as fast as they can be accepted by the phone line.
5. Necessary periodic processes (in the time-out routine) are always permitted to run, and do not interfere with input-output processes.

Support software

Designing a real-time program for a small computer with many high rate I/O channels is a specialized kind of software problem. The operational program requires not only unusual techniques but also extra software tools; often the importance of such extra tools is not recognized. Further, even when these issues are recognized, the effort needed to construct such tools may be seriously underestimated. The development of the IMP system required the following kinds of supporting software:

1. Programs to test the hardware.
2. Tools to help debug the system.
3. A Host simulator.
4. An efficient assembly process.

So far, three hardware test programs have been developed. The first and largest is a complete program for testing all the special hardware features in the IMP. This program permits running any or all of the modem interfaces in a crosspatched mode; it even permits operating together *several* IMPs in a test mode. The second hardware test program runs a detailed phone line test that provides statistics on phone line errors. The final program simulates the modem interface check register whose complex behavior is otherwise difficult to predict.

The software debugging tools exist in two forms. Initially we designed a simple stand-alone debugging program with the capability to do little more than examine and change individual core registers from the

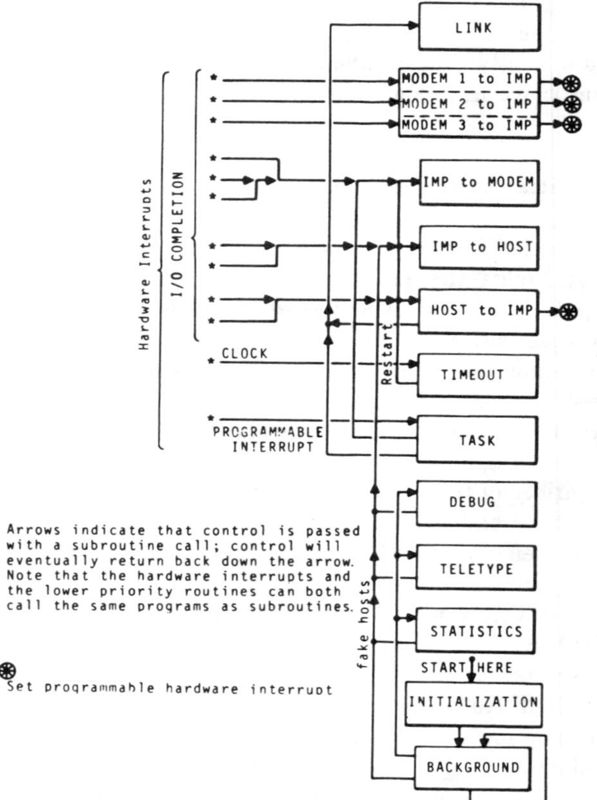

Figure 10—Program control structure

console Teletype. Subsequently, we embedded a version of the stand-alone debugging program into the operational program. This operational debugging program not only provides debugging assistance at a single location but also may be used in *network testing* and *network debugging*.

The initial implementation of the IMP software took place without connecting to a true Host. To permit checkout of the Host-related portions of the operational program, we built a "Host Simulator" that takes input from the console Teletype and feeds the Host routines exactly as though the input had originated in a real Host. Similarly, output messages for a destination Host are received by the simulator and typed out on the console Teletype.

Without recourse to expensive additional peripherals, the assembly facilities on the DDP-516 are inadequate for a large program. (For example, a listing of the IMP program would require approximately 20 hours of Teletype output.) We therefore used other locally available facilities to assist in the assembly process. Specifically, we used a PDP-1 text editor to compose and edit the programs, assembled on the

TABLE II—Transit Times And Message Rates

	Minimum	*Maximum*
SINGLE WORD MESSAGE		
Transit Time	5 msec	50 msec
Round-trip	10 msec	100 msec
Max. Message Rate/Link	100/sec	10/sec
SINGLE FULL PACKET MESSAGE		
Transit Time	45 msec	140 msec
Round-trip	50 msec	190 msec
Max. Message Rate/Link	20/sec	5/sec
8-PACKET MESSAGE		
Transit Time	265 msec	360 msec
Round-trip	195 msec	320 msec
Max. Message Rate/Link	5/sec	3/sec

DDP-516, and listed the program on the SDS 940 line printer. Use of this assembly process required minor modification of existing PDP-1 and SDS 940 support software

PROJECTED IMP PERFORMANCE

At this writing, the subnet has not yet been subjected to realistic load conditions; consequently, very little experimental data is available. However, we have made some estimates of projected performance of the IMP program and we describe these estimates below.

Host traffic and message delays

In the subnet, the Host-to-Host transit time and the round-trip time (for RFNM receipt) depend upon routing and message length. Since only one message at a time may be present on a given link, the reciprocal of the round-trip delay is the maximum message rate on a link. The primary factors affecting subnet delays are:

- Propagation delay: Electrical propagation time in the Bell system is estimated to be about 10 μsec per mile. Cross country propagation delay is therefore about 30 msec.
- Modem transmission delay: Because bits enter and leave an IMP at a predetermined modem bit rate, a packet requires a modem transmission time proportional to its length (20 μsec per bit on a 50-kilobit line).
- Queueing delay: Time spent waiting in the IMP for transmission of previous packets on a queue. Such waiting may occur either at an intermediate IMP or in connection with terminal IMP transmissions into the destination Host.
- IMP processing delay: The time required for the IMP program to process a packet is about 0.35 msec for a store-and-forward packet.

Because the queueing delay depends heavily upon the detailed traffic load in the network, an estimate of queueing delay will not be available until we gain considerable experience with network operation. In Table II, we show an estimate of the one-way and round-trip transit times and the corresponding maximum message rate per link, assuming the negligible queueing delay of a lightly loaded net. In this table, "minimum" delay represents a short hop between two nearby IMPs, and "maximum" delay represents a cross-country path involving five IMPs. In all cases the delays are well within the desired half-second goal.

In a lightly-loaded network with a mixture of nearby and distant destinations, an example of heavy Host traffic into its IMP might be that of 20 links carrying ten single-word messages per second and four more links, each carrying one eight-packet message per second.

Computational load

In general, a line fully loaded with short packets will require more computation than a line with all long packets; therefore the IMP can handle more lines in the latter case. In Figure 11, we show a curve of the computational utilization of the IMP as a function of message length for fully-loaded communication lines. For example, a 50-kilobit line fully loaded in both directions with one-word messages requires slightly over 13 percent of the available IMP time. Since a line will typically carry a variety of different length packets, and each line will be less than fully loaded, the computational load per line will actually be much less.

Throughput is defined to be the maximum number of Host data bits that may traverse an IMP each second. The actual number of bits entering the IMP per second is somewhat larger than the throughput because of such overhead as headers, RFNMs, and acknowledgments. The number of bits on the lines are still larger because of additional line overhead such as framing and error control characters. (Each packet on the phone line contains seventeen characters of overhead, nine of which are removed before the packet enters an IMP.)

The computational limit on the IMP throughput is approximately 700,000 bits per second. Figure 12 shows maximum throughput as a function of message length. The difference between the throughput curve and the line traffic curve represents overhead.

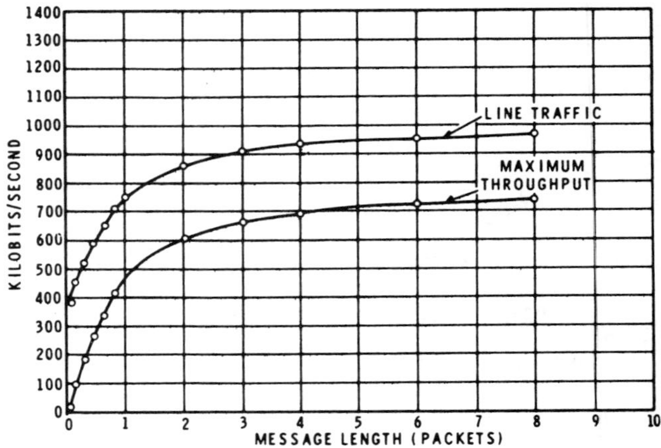

Figure 12—IMP throughput

DISCUSSION

In this section we state some of our conclusions about the design and implementation of the ARPA Network and comment on possible future directions.

We are convinced that use of an IMP-like device is a more sensible way to design networks than is use of direct Host-to-Host connection. First, for the subnet to serve a store-and-forward role, its functions must be independent of Host computers, which may often be down for extended periods. Second, the IMP program is very complex and is highly tailored to the I/O structure of the DDP-516; building such complex functions into special I/O units of each computer that might need network connection is probably economically inadvisable. Third, because of the desirability of having several Host computers at a given site connect to the network, it is both more convenient and more economic to employ IMPs than to provide all the network functions in each of the Host computers. The whole notion of a network node serving a multiplexing function for complexes of local Hosts and terminals lends further support to this conclusion. Finally, because we were led to a design having *some* inter-IMP dependence; we found it advantageous to have *identical* units at each node, rather than computers of different manufacture.

Considering the multiplexing issue directly, it now seems clear that individual network nodes will be connected to a wide variety of computer and terminal complexes. Even the initial ten-node ARPA Network includes one Host organization that has chosen to submultiplex several computers via a single Host connection to the IMP. We are now studying variants of the IMP design that address this multiplexing issue, and we also expect to cooperate with other groups (such as at the National Physical Laboratory in England) that are studying such multiplexing techniques.

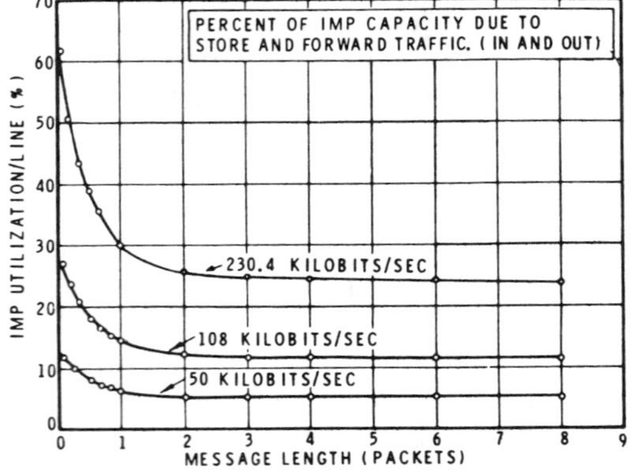

Figure 11—IMP utilization

The increasing interest in computer networks will bring with it an expanding interaction between computers and communication circuits. From the outset, we viewed the ARPA Network as a systems engineering problem, including the portion of the system supplied by the common carriers. Although we found the carriers to be properly concerned about circuit performance (the basic circuit performance to date has been quite satisfactory), we found it difficult to work with the carriers *cooperatively* on the technical details, packaging, and implementation of the communication circuit terminal equipment; as a result, the present physical installations of circuit terminal equipment are at best inelegant and inconvenient. In the longer run, for reasons of economy, performance, and reliability, circuit terminal equipment probably should be integrated more closely with computer input/output equipment. If the carriers are unable to participate conveniently in such integrations, we would expect further growth of a competing circuit terminal equipment industry, and more prevalent common carrier provision of bare circuits.

Another aspect of network growth and development is the requirement to connect different rate communication circuits to IMP-like devices as a function of the particular application. In our own IMP design, although there are limitations on total throughput, the IMP can be connected to carrier circuits of any bit rate up to about 250 kilobits; similarly, the interface to a Host computer can operate over a wide range of bit rates. We feel that this flexibility is very important because the economics of carrier offerings, as well as the user requirements, are subject to surprisingly rapid change; even within the time period of the present implementation, we have experienced such changes.

At this point, we would like to discuss certain aspects of the implementation effort. This project required the design, development, and installation of a very complex device in a rather short time scale. The difficulty in producing a complex system is highly dependent upon the number of people who are simultaneously involved. Small groups can achieve complex optimizations of timing, storage, and hardware/software interaction, whereas larger groups can seldom achieve such optimizations on a reasonable time scale. We chose to operate with a very small group of highly talented people. For example, all software, including software tools for assembly, editing, debugging, and equipment testing as well as the main operational program, involved effort by no more than four people at any time. Since so many computer system projects involve much larger groups, we feel it is worth calling attention to this approach.

Turning to the future, we plan to work with the ARPA Network project along several technical directions: (1) the experimental operation of the network and any modifications required to tune its performance; (2) experimental operation of the network with higher bandwidth circuits, e.g., 230.4 kilobits; (3) a review of IMP variants that might perform multiplexing functions; (4) consideration of techniques for designing more economical and/or more powerful IMPs; and (5) participation with the Host organizations in the very sizeable problem of developing techniques and protocols for the effective *utilization* of the network.

On a more global level, we anticipate an explosive growth of message switched computer networks, not just for the interactive pooling of resources, but for the simple conveniences and economies to be obtained for many classes of digital data communication. We believe that the capabilities inherent in the design of even the present subnet have broad application to other data communication problems of government and private industry.

ACKNOWLEDGMENTS

The ARPA Network has in large measure been the conception of one man, Dr. L. G. Roberts of the Advanced Research Projects Agency; we gratefully acknowledge his guidance and encouragement. Researchers at many other institutions deserve credit for early interactions with ARPA concerning basic network design; in particular we would like to acknowledge the insight about IMPs provided by W. A. Clark.

At BBN, many persons contributed to the IMP project. We acknowledge the contributions of H. K. Rising, who participated in the subnet design and acted as associate project manager during various phases of the project; B. P. Cosell, who participated significantly in the software implementation; W. B. Barker and M. J. Thrope, who participated significantly in the hardware implementation; and T. Thatch, J. H. Geisman, and R. C. Satterfield, who assisted with various implementation aspects of the project. We also acknowledge the helpful encouragement of J. I. Elkind and D. G. Bobrow.

Finally, we wish to acknowledge the hardware implementation contribution of the Computer Control Division of Honeywell, where many individuals worked cooperatively with us despite the sometimes abrasive pressures of a difficult schedule.

REFERENCES

1 P BARAN
On distributed communication networks
IEEE Transactions on Communication Systems Vol CS-12 March 1964

2 P BARAN S BOEHM P SMITH
On distributed communications
Series of 11 reports Rand Corporation Santa Monica California 1964

3 B W BOEHM R L MOBLEY
Adaptive routing techniques for distributed communication systems
Rand Corporation Memorandum RM-4781-PR 1966

4 *Initial design for interface message processors for the ARPA computer network*
Bolt Beranek and Newman Inc Report No 1763 1969

5 *Specifications for the interconnection of a Host and an IMP*
Bolt Beranek and Newman Inc Report No 1822 1969

6 G W BROWN J G MILLER T A KEENAN
EDUNET report of the summer study on information networks conducted by the interuniversity communications council
John Wiley and Sons New York 1967

7 S CARR S CROCKER V CERF
HOST-HOST communication protocol in the ARPA network
Proceedings of AFIPS SJCC 1970 In this issue

8 C A CUADRA
Annual review of information science and technology
Interscience Vol 3 Chapters 7 and 10 1968

9 D W DAVIES K A BARTLETT
R A SCANTLEBURY P T WILKINSON
A digital communication network for computers giving rapid response at remote terminals
ACM Symposium on Operating System Principles 1967

10 D W DAVIES
The principles of a data communication network for computers and remote peripherals
Proceedings of IFIP Hardware Paper D11 1968

11 D W DAVIES
Communications networks to serve rapid-response computers
Proceedings of IFIP Edinburgh 1968

12 *EIN software catalogue*
EDUCOM 100 Charles River Park Boston (Regularly updated)

13 R R EVERETT, C A ZRAKET H D BENINGTON
Sage–a data processing system for air defense
Proceedings of EJCC 1957

14 *Policies and regulatory procedures relating to computer and communication services*
Notice of Inquiry Docket No 16979 Washington D C 1966
Federal Communications Commission

15 L R FORD JR D R FULKERSON
Flows in networks
Princeton University Press 1962

16 H FRANK I T FRISCH W CHOU
Topological considerations in the design of the ARPA computer network
Proceedings of AFIPS SJCC 1970 In this issue

17 R T JAMES
The evolution of wideband services
IEEE International Convention Record Part I Wire and Data Communication 1966

18 S J KAPLAN
The advancing communication technology and computer communication systems
Proceedings of AFIPS SJCC Vol 32 1968

19 L KLEINROCK
Communications nets-stochastic message flow and delay
McGraw-Hill Book Co Inc New York 1964

20 L KLEINROCK
Models for computer networks
Proceedings of International Communications Conference June 1969

21 L KLEINROCK
Optimization of computer networks for various channel cost functions
Proceedings of AFIPS SJCC 1970 In this issue

22 T MARILL
Cooperative networks of time-shared computers
Computer Corporation of America Preliminary Study 1966
Also Private Report Lincoln Laboratory MIT Cambridge Massachusetts 1966

23 T MARILL L G ROBERTS
Toward a cooperative network of time-shared computers
Proceedings of AFIPS FJCC 1966

24 *Biomedical communications network-technical development Plan*
National Library of Medicine June 1968

25 *Networks of computers symposium NOC-68*
Proceedings of Invitational Workshop Ft Meade Maryland
National Security Agency September 1969

26 *Networks of computers symposium NOC-69*
Proceedings of Invitational Workshop Ft Meade Maryland (in press) National Security Agency

27 M N PERRY W R PLUGGE
American Airlines 'Sabre' electronic reservations system
Proceedings of AFIPS WJCC 1961

28 L G ROBERTS
Multiple computer networks and intercomputer communication
ACM Symposium on Operating System Principles 1967

29 L G ROBERTS
Access control and file directories in computer networks
IEEE International Convention March 1968

30 L G ROBERTS
Resource sharing computer networks
IEEE International Conference March 1969

31 L G ROBERTS B D WESSLER
Computer network development to achieve resource sharing
Proceedings of AFIPS SJCC 1970 In this issue

32 R A SCANTLEBURY P T WILKINSON K A BARTLETT
The design of a message switching centre for a digital communication network
D26 Proceedings of IFIP Hardware Edinburgh 1968

33 K STEIGLITZ P WEINER D J KLEITMAN
The design of minimum cost survivable networks
IEEE Transactions on Circuit Theory Vol CT-16 November 1969

34 R SUNG J B WOODFORD
Study of communication links for the biomedical communication network
Aerospace Report No ATR-69 (7130-06)-1 1969

35 W TEITELMAN R E KAHN
A network simulation and display program
Proceedings of 3rd Annual Princeton Conference on Information Sciences and Systems March 1969

384

Reprinted from —
AFIPS — Conference Proceedings
Volume 40
© AFIPS PRESS
Montvale, N. J. 07645

The Terminal IMP for the ARPA computer network*

by S. M. ORNSTEIN, F. E. HEART, W. R. CROWTHER, H. K. RISING, S. B. RUSSELL and A. MICHEL

Bolt Beranek and Newman Inc.
Cambridge, Massachusetts

INTRODUCTION

A little over three years ago the Advanced Research Projects Agency of the Department of Defense (ARPA) began implementation of an entirely new venture in computer communications: a network that would allow for the interconnection, via common-carrier circuits, of dissimilar computers at widely separated, ARPA-sponsored research centers. This network, which has come to be known as the ARPA Network, presently includes approximately 20 nodes and is steadily growing. Major goals of the network are (1) to permit resource sharing, whereby persons and programs at one research center may access data and interactively use programs that exist and run in other computers of the network, (2) to develop highly reliable and economic digital communications, and (3) to permit broad access to unique and powerful facilities which may be economically feasible only when widely shared.

The ARPA Network is a new kind of digital communication system employing wideband leased lines and message switching, wherein a path is not established in advance and instead each message carries an address. Messages normally traverse several nodes in going from source to destination, and the network is a store-and-forward system wherein, at each node, a copy of the message is stored until it is safely received at the following node. At each node a small processor (an *Interface Message Processor*, or *IMP*) acts as a nodal switching unit and also interconnects the research computer centers, or *Hosts*, with the high bandwidth leased lines.

A set of papers presented at the 1970 SJCC[1–5] described early work on the ARPA Network in some detail, and acquaintance with this background material (especially Reference 2) is important in understanding the current work. The present paper first discusses major developments that have taken place in the network over the last two years. We then describe the *Terminal IMP*, or *TIP*, a development which permits direct terminal access to the network. Finally we mention some general issues and discuss plans for the next stages in development of the network.

THE DEVELOPING NETWORK

The initial installation of the ARPA Network, in 1969, consisted of four nodes in the western part of the United States. A geographic map of the present ARPA Network is shown in Figure 1. Clearly, the most obvious development has been a substantial *growth*, which has transformed the initial limited experiment into a national assemblage of computer resources and user communities. The network has engendered considerable enthusiasm on the part of the participants, and it is increasingly apparent that the network represents a major new direction in both computer and communications technology.

Figure 2 is a logical map of the network, where the Host computer facilities are shown in ovals, all circuits are 50 kilobits, and dotted circuits/nodes represent planned installations. On this figure certain nodes are listed as a "316 IMP"; this machine is logically nearly identical to the original IMP, but can handle approximately two-thirds of the communication traffic bandwidth at a cost savings of approximately one-half. The original IMP includes a Honeywell 516 computer, and more recently Honeywell began to market the 316 computer as a cheaper, downward-compatible machine. As the network has grown, sites were identified which did not require the full bandwidth of the original IMP, and a decision was made to provide an IMP version built around the 316 computer. Also shown in Figure 2 are certain nodes listed as "TIP"; this new machine

* This work was sponsored by the Advanced Research Projects Agency under Contract No. DAHC15-69-C-0179.

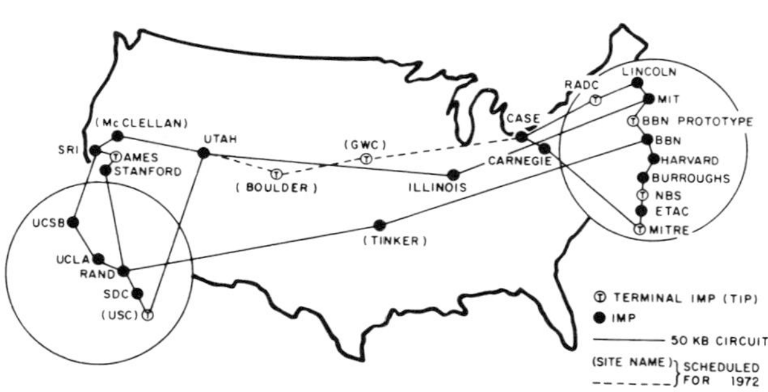

Figure 1—ARPA Network, geographic map, December 1971

is discussed in detail later in this paper. Site abbreviations shown on Figures 1 and 2 are explained in Table I.

As the network has grown, a great deal of work has been concentrated on the development of Host-to-Host protocol procedures. In order for programs within one Host computer system to communicate with programs in other Hosts, agreed-upon procedures and formats must be established throughout the network. This problem has, as predicted, turned out to be a difficult one. Nonetheless protocol procedures have evolved and are being accepted and implemented throughout the net. At the present writing, many of the Hosts have working "network control programs" which implement this protocol. Protocol development
386
is more fully reported in a companion paper,[6] but we wish to make a general observation on this subject: the growth of the network has dynamically catalyzed an area of computer science which has to do with the quite general problem of *how programs should intercommunicate*, whether in a single computer or between computers. Thus the evolution of the Host-to-Host protocol represents a side benefit of the network that reaches well beyond its utility to the network alone.

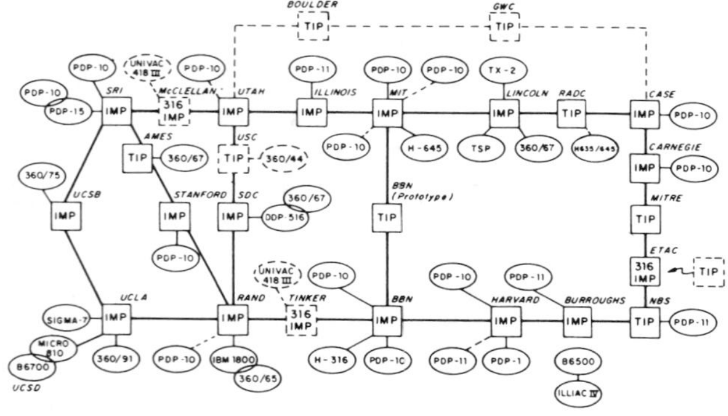

Figure 2—ARPA Network, logical map, December 1971

Since both hardware and software network connections must be implemented by each Host, it is important that the external characteristics of the IMP be relatively stable. This stability has been carefully maintained, while at the same time internal operation of the IMP program has undergone extensive revision and improvement. For example, trouble reporting, statistics gathering, and test procedures have been substantially improved. In addition to improvements that have already been incorporated into the program, there have also been extensive studies of performance and message flow control.[7] These studies have pointed up areas of vulnerability to perverse heavy traffic patterns and have suggested still other possible improvements in the routing and flow control mechanisms. Potential changes are presently being being studied in some detail and will be incorporated into one or more forthcoming major revisions of the program. They will hopefully anticipate problems which might be expected to arise as traffic flow in the network becomes heavier.

TABLE I—Site Abbreviations

NCAR	National Center for Atmospheric Research
GWC	Global Weather Central
SRI	Stanford Research Institute
MC CLELLAN	McClellan Air Force Base
UTAH	University of Utah
ILLINOIS	University of Illinois
MIT	Massachusetts Institute of Technology
LINCOLN	M.I.T. Lincoln Laboratory
RADC	Rome Air Development Center
CASE	Case Western Reserve
AMES	N.A.S.A. Ames Research Center
USC	University of Southern California
UCSB	University of California at Santa Barbara
STANFORD	Stanford University
SDC	Systems Development Corporation
BBN	Bolt Beranek and Newman
CARNEGIE	Carnegie University
MITRE	MITRE Corporation
ETAC	Environmental Technical Applications Center
UCLA	University of California at Los Angeles
RAND	Rand Corporation
TINKER	Tinker Air Force Base
HARVARD	Harvard University
BURROUGHS	Burroughs Corporation
NBS	National Bureau of Standards

Somewhat belatedly in the network design, the need to connect a single IMP to several Hosts was recognized. This required multiple Host interfaces at the IMP as well as more complex IMP software. Further, the various Host computers at a site are often physically distant from one another, thus requiring an increase in the maximum allowable physical separation between a Host and its IMP. To connect to an arbitrarily remote Host would have meant a communications interface capable of attachment to common-carrier circuits via modems. It would furthermore have required cooperative error control from the Host end. At the time, we chose not to modify the logical way in which the IMP dealt with the Host and instead we provided more sophisticated line drivers which would handle distances of up to two thousand feet. Several such "Distant Host" installations are now working in the network. Unfortunately, as the network has grown, new sites have appeared where still greater Host/IMP distances are involved. The present scheme does not include error control, and use of this scheme over greater distances is not appropriate. At the present time we are therefore considering how best to arrange IMP/Host connections over large distances and additional options will be required in this domain.

Another facility which has been tested is the ability of the IMPs to communicate over 230.4 kilobit phone lines instead of 50 kilobit lines. A short, fast link was incorporated into the network for a brief period and no problems were encountered. To date, network loading has not justified upgrading any operational network circuits to 230.4 kilobits, but this will be considered as loading rises.

Substantial effort has gone into traffic and trouble reporting. A Network Control Center (NCC) has been built at Bolt Beranek and Newman Inc. in Cambridge, where a small dedicated Host computer receives reports each minute from every IMP on the network. Traffic summaries and status and trouble reports are

```
1300     JUNE 16 197-     ARPA NETWORK LOG                 PAGE 11

1300  IMP     6:  HOST 1 UP               (Host 1 at MIT came up)
      IMP     1:  SS2 ON                  (Sense switch 2 was thrown at UCLA)
1301  IMP     1:  10 SEC STAT ON          (UCLA is using IMP statistics)
1305  IMP     1:  10 SEC STAT OFF         (UCLA has finished)
      IMP     1:  SS2 OFF                 (and turned the switch off)

1307  IMP     4:  UP ::::::               (Utah IMP was down, and has come up

      IMP     4:  RELOADED FROM NET       (A neighbor IMP sent Utah a copy of
      IMP     4:  VERSION 2614            (the IMP program over a phone line)
      IMP     4:  HOST 1 UP               (Host 1 at Utah is now up)

1310  LINE    4:  UP ::::::               (one of Utah's lines is up)

      LINE   10:  UP ::::::               (another is up)

      LINE   15:  DOWN ::::::             (but the third is making errors)

1317  LINE   15:  ERRORS MINUS 13/81      (Utah sees 20% error rate)
      LINE   15:  ERRORS PLUS 7/81        (the other end sees a 10% rate)
      IMP     6:  HOST 1 DN               (Host 1 at MIT went down)
1320  LINE   15:  ERRORS MINUS 0/81       (the line is error-free)
      LINE   15:  ERRORS PLUS 0/81        (in both directions)

1321  LINE   15:  UP ::::::               (the line is declared usable)
                   .
                   .
                   .
                   .
                   .
```

Figure 3—Typical segment of NCC log

then generated from this material. Specifically, a logger records any changes that the IMPs report to the NCC; it records line errors and IMP storage counts when they exceed certain limits, as well as unusual events, such as reloading from the net, checksum errors, etc. Figure 3 shows an example of this log. (The comments, in parentheses to the right, are not part of the log but have been added to explain the meaning of the entries.) In addition to this detailed log of interesting events, one may at any time obtain a quick summary of the status of the network. Finally, detailed and summary logs of Host and line traffic are produced. The NCC is a focal point not only for monitoring the network but also for testing and diagnosing remote troubles. Lines throughout the network can be looped from here in order to isolate difficulties. Personnel of the center coordinate all debugging, maintenance, repair and modification of equipment.

DIRECT TERMINAL ACCESS

During the early phases of network development a typical node has consisted of one or more large time-shared computer systems connected to an IMP. The IMPs at the various sites are connected together into a subnet by 50 kilobit phone lines and the large Host computers communicate with one another through this subnet. This arrangement provides a means for sharing resources between such interconnected centers,
each site potentially acting both as a user and as a provider of resources. *This total complex of facilities constitutes a nationwide resource which could be made available to users who have no special facilities of their own to contribute to the resource pool.* Such a user might be at a site either with no Host computer or where the existing computer might not be a terminal-oriented time-sharing system.

A great deal of thought went into considering how best to provide for direct terminal access to the network. One possibility, which would have essentially been a non-solution, was to require a user to dial direct to the appropriate Host. Once connected he could, of course, take advantage of the fact that that Host was tied to other Hosts in the net; however, the network lines would not have been used to facilitate his initial connection, and such an arrangement limits the terminal bandwidth to what may be available on the switched common-carrier networks.

A similar solution was to allow terminals to access the network through a Host at a nearby node. In such a case, for example, a worker in the New England area wishing to use facilities at a California site might connect into a local Boston Host and use that Host as a tap into the network to get at the facilities in California. This approach would have required Hosts to provide hardware access facilities for many terminals which would use their systems only in passing. For many Hosts, the kinds of terminals which can be connected directly are limited in speed, character set, etc. In terms of reliability, the user would have been dependent on the local Host for access; when that Host was down, his port into the network would be unavailable. Furthermore, the Hosts would have been confronted with all of the problems of composing terminal characters into network messages and vice versa as well as directing these messages to the proper terminals and remote Hosts. Time-sharing systems are generally already overburdened with processing of characters to and from terminals and many are configured with front end processors employed explicitly to off-load this burden from the main processor. Increasing the amount of such work for the Hosts therefore seemed unreasonable and would have resulted in limiting terminal access. Instead, a completely separate means for accessing the network directly seemed called for: an IMP with a flexible terminal handling capability—a *Terminal IMP*, or *TIP*.

One of the fundamental questions that arises when considering this problem is: what is the proper distribution of computational power among the remote big facility, the terminal processor, and the terminal? Shall the terminal processor be clever, have sizable

storage, be user programmable, etc., or shall it be a simpler device whose basic job is multiplexing in a flexible way? Serious work with interactive graphics seems to require the terminal to include, or be in propinquity to, a user-programmable processor and considerable storage. To date, such work has primarily been done with terminals attached directly to a Host. Some elaborate terminals, such as the Adage, include a powerful processor. Other kinds of terminals, including Teletype-like devices, alphanumeric displays, or simple graphic displays (excluding serious interactive graphics), do *not* require a user-programmable local processor or significant local storage.

We believe that the great majority of potential groups needing access to the ARPA Network will not need powerful interactive graphics facilities. Further, for the minority that will need powerful terminals, we believe that individual terminals with built-in or accompanying processors will become more common. For these reasons, we decided that the terminal processor should be simple and not programmable from the terminals. *The computational load and the storage should be in the Hosts or in the terminals and not in the terminal processor.* This simple multiplexing approach is amenable to some standardization and is philosophically close to the original IMP notion of a standard nodal device.

Another major question we faced was whether to build a separate terminal handler and then connect it to the IMP or to build an integrated unit that was housed in a common cabinet and used the IMP processor. One advantage of the two-machine approach is that it isolates the IMP functions from the terminal functions, thereby providing a barrier of safety for the net. This approach also provides the processing power of two machines and a potentially greater degree of user freedom in modifying or writing programs. Another interesting reason for considering separate machines was to reduce the large cost associated with I/O equipment (such as line controllers) by making use of the extra processing power. We discussed with several manufacturers the possibility of bringing terminal wires "into" their processors and decoding the basic line information directly in software. However, even with some of the new state-of-the-art machines, like the Meta-4, with fast 90 nsec read-only memories to handle character decoding, the I/O cost was still high, and in large part the necessary I/O equipment was yet to be designed. We therefore concluded that it was still somewhat early to proceed in this fashion, and two processors did not appear to save I/O equipment.

The principal disadvantages of the two-machine approach were the higher initial cost, the difficulties of maintaining two machines, and the software problems of dealing with two machines. In particular, the communication between two machines would require two hardware Host interfaces, and two software Host/IMP programs. This would result in a much poorer communication between the IMP program and the terminal handling program than would exist in a single machine. In either case, one machine or two, the

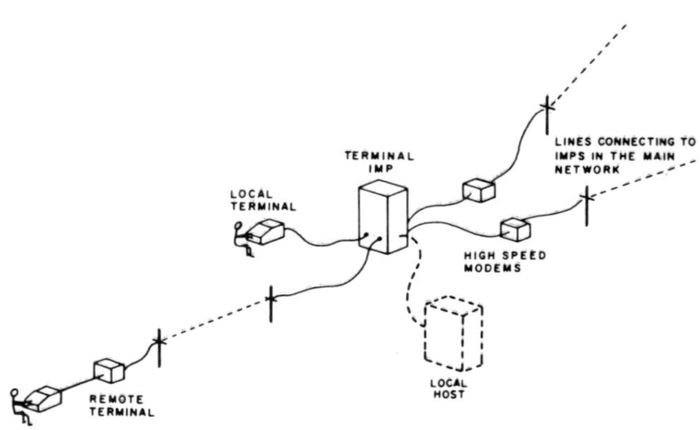

Figure 4—A TIP in the network

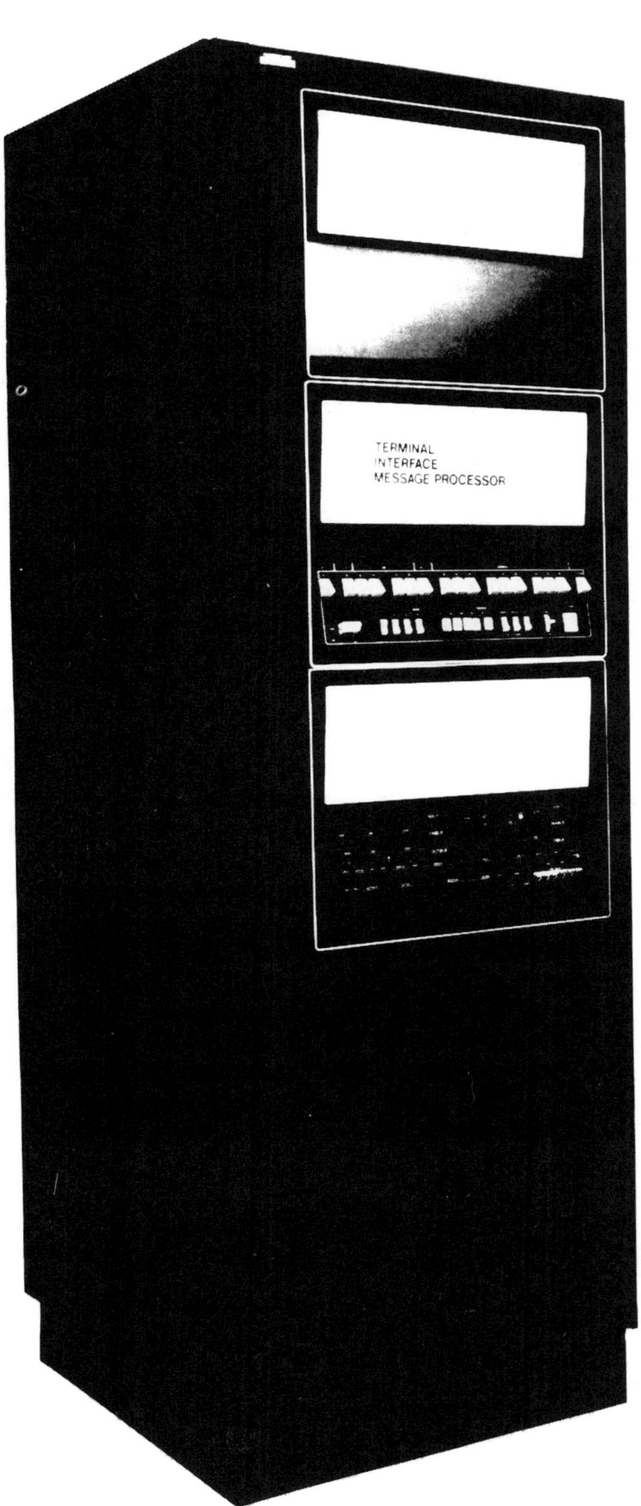

Figure 5—Photograph of TIP

terminal handling process required the implementation of a version of Host protocol.

We finally decided that the least expensive and most sensible technical alternative was to build the IMP and the terminal handler (with the necessary subset of Host protocol) together into a single machine. Then, since certain new machines appeared attractive in cost/performance relative to the Honeywell 16 series, we spent considerable time thinking about what machine to use. We decided that no alternate choice was sufficiently attractive to justify rewriting the main IMP program and redesigning the Host and modem interface hardware. This left us with a decision between the Honeywell 516 and 316 computers. We chose the 316 on the basis of size and cost, feeling that the somewhat higher bandwidth of the 516 was not essential to the job and did not justify its higher price and the second cabinet which would have been required.

TERMINAL IMP HARDWARE

Figure 4 shows how the TIP fits the user into the network. Up to 63* terminals, either remote or local, of widely diverse characteristics may be connected to a given TIP and thereby "talk" into the network. It is also possible to connect a Host to a TIP in the usual way.

The TIP is shown in Figure 5. It is built around a Honeywell H-316 computer with 20K (20,480 words) of core. It embodies a standard 16 port multiplexed memory channel with priority interrupts and includes a Teletype for debugging and program reloading. Other features of the standard IMP also present are a real-time clock, power-fail and auto-restart mechanisms, and a program-generated interrupt feature.[2] As in the standard IMP, interfaces are provided for connecting to high-speed (50 kilobit, 230.4 kilobit, etc.) modems as well as to Hosts. The single-cabinet version limits the configuration to a total of three modem and/or Host interfaces, but an expansion cabinet may be used to increase this limit. More basic limits are set by the machine's logical organization (specifically the number of available memory channels) and the program bandwidth capability as discussed below.

Aside from the additional 8K of core memory, the primary hardware feature which distinguishes the TIP from a standard IMP is a Multi-Line Controller (MLC) which allows for connection of terminals to the

* There are 64 hardware lines but line Ø is logically reserved by the program for special use.

IMP. Any of the MLC lines may go to local terminals or via modems to remote terminals. As shown in Figure 6 the MLC consists of two portions, one a piece of central logic which handles the assembly and disassembly of characters and transfers them to and from memory, and the other a set of individual Line Interface Units (all identical except for small number of option jumpers) which synchronize reporting to individual data bits between the central logic and the terminal devices and provide for control and status information to and from the modem or device. Line Interface Units may be physically incorporated one at a time as required.

The MLC connects to the high-speed multiplexed memory channel option of the H-316, and uses three of its channels as well as two priority interrupts and a small number of control instructions. The MLC is fabricated by BBN and is built from TTL integrated circuits. The MLC central controller, complete with power supply, is housed in an H-316 expansion chassis, and the entire MLC, as well as the computer itself, is mounted in a standard six-foot rack. Additional space is provided in the bottom of the rack for up to sixteen card-mounted modems of the Bell 103, 201, or 202 variety, together with their power supplies.

In order to accommodate a variety of devices, the controller handles a wide range of data rates and character sizes, in both synchronous and asynchronous modes. Data characters of length 5-, 6-, 7-, or 8-bits
390 are allowed by the controller. Since no interpretation of characters is done by the hardware, any character set, such as Baudot, Transcode ASCII or EBCDIC may be used.

The following is a list of data rates accepted by the controller:

SYNCHRONOUS	*ASYNCHRONOUS* (Nominal Rates)		
Any rate up to and including 19.2 Kb/s	75	1200	
	110	1800	
	134.5	2400	
	150	4800	output only
	300	9600	output only
	600	19200	output only
	All above in bits/second		

The data format required of all devices is bit serial and each character indicates its own beginning by means of a start bit which precedes the data and includes one or more stop bits at the end of the character. This per-character framing is quite standard for asynchronous lines but synchronous lines, generally designed for higher bandwidths, frequently adopt some form of "binary synchronous communication" where the characters are packed tightly together into messages which are then framed by special characters. Framing is thereby amortized over the entire message, thus consuming a smaller fraction of the available bandwidth than the per-character framing which uses two or more bits for every character. The difficulties with this scheme, however, are that it is more complex, requiring more sophisticated hardware at each end, and that no real standards exist which are adhered to by all or even most types of synchronous devices. We therefore decided to adopt per-character framing with start and stop bits even on synchronous lines. At a cost of some twenty percent of the bandwidth for framing, a very simple and general scheme is thus arrived at. A number of high speed terminal manufacturers, faced with the same problems, have arrived at a similar conclusion.

Given these characteristics, then, the controller will connect to the great majority of normal terminal devices such as Teletypes, alphanumeric CRT units, and modems, and also (with suitable remote interface units) to many peripheral devices such as card readers, line printers, and graphics terminals. Either full or half duplex devices can be accommodated. The standard TIP program cannot deal with a magnetic tape unit through the MLC. However, as a special option, and with the use of additional core memory, standard Honeywell tape drives can be connected to the TIP as normal peripherals.

The individual terminal line levels are consistent with EIA RS-232C convention. Data rates and character length are individually set for each line *by the the program*. For incoming asynchronous lines, the program includes the capability for detecting character length and line data rate as discussed below.

Logically, the controller consists of 64 input ports and 64 output ports. Each input/output pair is brought out to a single connector which is normally connected to a single device. However, by using a special "Y"

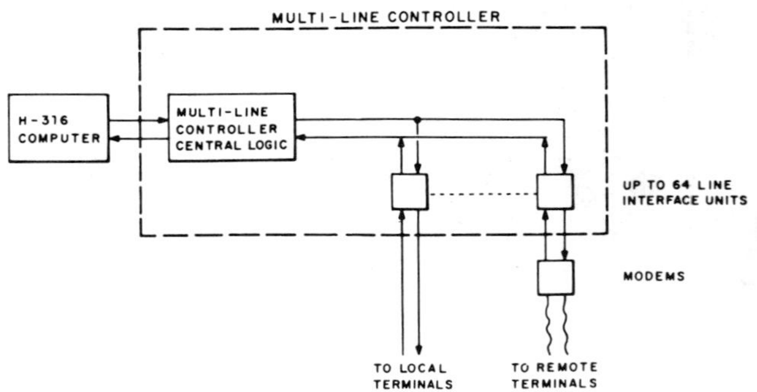

Figure 6—Block diagram of TIP hardware

cable, the ports may go to completely separate devices of entirely different properties. Thus, *input* port 16 may connect to a slow, asynchronous, 5-bit character keyboard while *output* port 16 connects to a high speed, synchronous display of some sort. In order to achieve this flexibility, the MLC stores information about each input and each output port and the program sets up this information for each half of each port in turn as it turns the ports "ON."

Several aspects of the MLC design are noteworthy. The central logic treats each of the 64 ports in succession, each port getting 800 ns of attention per cycle. The port then waits the remainder of the cycle (51.2 μs) for its next turn. For both input and output, two full characters are buffered in the central logic, the one currently being assembled or disassembled and one further character to allow for delays in memory accessing.

During input, characters from the various lines stream into a tumble table in memory on a first come, first served basis. Periodically a clock interrupt causes the program to switch tables and look for input.

Output characters are fed to all lines from a single output table. Ordering the characters in this table in such a way as to keep a set of lines of widely diverse speeds solidly occupied is a difficult task. To assist the program in this, a novel mechanism has been built into the MLC hardware whereby each line, as it uses up a character from the output table, enters a request consisting of its line number into a "request" table in memory. This table is periodically inspected by the program and the requests are used in building the next output table with the characters in proper line sequence.

The design of the terminal interface portion of the MLC is modular. Each Line Interface Unit (LIU) contains all the logic required for full duplex, bit serial communication and consists of a basic bi-directional data section and a control and status section. The data section contains transmit and receive portions each with clock and data lines. For asynchronous devices the clock line is ignored and timing is provided by the MLC itself. (For received asynchronous characters, timing is triggered by the leading edge of the start bit of each character.)

The control and status monitor functions are provided for modems as required by the RS-232C specification. Four outputs are available for control functions and six inputs are available to monitor status. The outputs are under program control and are available for non-standard functions if the data terminal is not a modem. For example, these lines could be used to operate a local line printer. RS-232C connectors are mounted directly on the LIU cards. To allow for variations in terminal and modem pin assignments, the signals are brought to connector pins via jumpers on the card.

The central MLC contains 256 ICs, many of which are MSI and some of which are LSI circuits, and it is thus about the same complexity as the basic H-316. In addition each LIU contains 31 ICs. A Terminal IMP including the MLC and with a typical interface configuration to high-speed circuits and Hosts is, order of magnitude, a $100,000 device.

THE TERMINAL USER'S VIEW

This section describes how a TIP user gains access to the network. The protocol described is of very recent origin and will undoubtedly change in response to usage which, as of this writing, is just commencing.

In general a user must have some foreknowledge of the resource which he expects to access via the network. The TIP program implements a set of commands[8] for connecting to and disconnecting from remote sites, but once a terminal is connected to a particular system, the TIP becomes transparent to the conversation unless specially signalled. This is equivalent to a time-sharing system where the executive program is essentially out of the picture during periods while the user is dealing directly with his own set of programs.

Because of the large number of different terminal types used in the network, the concept of the Network Virtual Terminal was developed. This is an imaginary but well-defined type of terminal. The TIP translates typed data to virtual terminal code before shipping it into the network, and conversely translates the remote system's response back into the local terminal's code. Thus, each Host system must deal only with this single terminal type. 391

When the user at a terminal needs to talk directly to his TIP instead of to the remote Host, he issues a command which is distinguished by the fact that it always starts with the symbol @. One or more words, perhaps followed by a single parameter, then identify the type of command.

Normally a user will go through four more or less distinct stages in typing into the net. First, he will be concerned with hardware, power, dialing in, etc. Then he will establish a dialogue with the TIP to get a comfortable set of parameters for his usage. Next, he will instruct the TIP to make a connection to a remote Host, and finally, he will mostly ignore the TIP as he talks to the remote Host.

One of the more interesting features of the TIP is that it permits great flexibility in the types of terminals which may be attached to any port. This

TABLE II—Tip Commands

CLOSE
    close all outstanding connections
HOST #
    focus attention on this host 0<#<256
LOGIN
    start the initial connection procedure to get Telnet connections
SEND BREAK
    send a Telnet break character
SEND SYNC
    send a Telnet sync character and an INTERRUPT SENDER message
ECHO ALL
    local TIP-generated echo—TIP echoes everything
ECHO NONE
    remote Host-generated echo—TIP will echo commands
ECHO HALFDUPLEX
    terminal-generated echo—TIP echoes nothing
FLUSH
    delete all characters in input buffer
TRANSMIT EVERY #
    send off input buffer at least every #th character 0<#<256
TRANSMIT ON EVERY CHARACTER
    like TRANSMIT EVERY 1
TRANSMIT ON LINEFEED
    send input buffer every time a linefeed encountered
TRANSMIT ON MESSAGE-END
    send input buffer every time an EOM encountered
TRANSMIT ON NO CHARACTER
    do not transmit on linefeed or EOM
392
TRANSMIT NOW
    send off input buffer now
DEVICE RATE #
    # is a 13 bit code specifying hardware rate and character size settings

DEVICE CODE ASCII DEVICE CODE 2741 DEVICE CODE EXECUPORT DEVICE CODE ODEC	establish code conversion
SEND TO HOST # RECEIVE FROM HOST # SEND TO SOCKET # RECEIVE FROM SOCKET #	establish parameters for manual initiation of connections
PROTOCOL TO TRANSMIT PROTOCOL TO RECEIVE PROTOCOL TO CLOSE TRANSMIT PROTOCOL TO COSE RECEIVE	initiate connection protocol manually
PROTOCOL BOTH PROTOCOL TO CLOSE BOTH	abbreviations for simultaneous transmit and receive protocols

GIVE BACK
    release control of captured device
DIVERT OUTPUT
    capture device # and divert this terminal's output to it
ABORT LOGIN
    abort the outstanding initial connection procedure

flexibility presents a problem to the program which must determine what kind of terminal (speed, character size, etc.) is attached to a given port before a sensible exchange of information is possible. To solve this problem, each terminal is assigned a special identifying character which the user types repeatedly when starting to use a terminal. When information starts to appear from a previously idle port, the TIP enters a "hunt" mode in which it interprets the arriving characters trying various combinations of terminal characteristics. All except the proper combination will cause the character to be garbled, producing something other than one of the legal terminal identifying characters. When the TIP thus identifies the correct set (which generally requires the user to repeat the identifier less than half a dozen times), it types out 'HELLO in the terminal's own language.

In the next stage, the user initializes certain conversation parameters relating to message size and when to echo. He then establishes connection to a remote site using two commands which identify the desired remote site and the fact that the user wishes to be connected to the logger at that site. These commands are:

@ HOST 15

@ LOGIN

The LOGIN command actually sets in motion an elaborate exchange of messages between the TIP and the remote Host which normally result in a connection being made to that remote system. This command will be answered by an appropriate comment to the user indicating either that a connection has been made, that the remote site is not up, that it is up but actively refusing to converse, or that it is up but not responding enough even to refuse the connection.

Once a connection is established, the user types directly to the logger. The TIP does not execute the actual login since this procedure varies from site to site.

Throughout the user-to-Host dialogue, commands remain available at any time. Prior to closing the connection, the user must log out as required by the system he is using. He then gives the command

@ CLOSE

which causes the TIP to close the connection, informing the user when the process is finished.

In addition to the above more or less standard procedures, there are a number of less usual commands which set such things as device rate, character size, code types, etc. Such commands are used by a terminal on one port in setting parameters for a non-interactive terminal, such as a printer or card reader, on some other port. Other special commands permit conversations directly between terminals on the same or different TIPs, allow for binary mode, etc. Table II is a list of the commands with a brief explanation. For details refer to Reference 8. Figure 7 gives an example of typical dialogue.

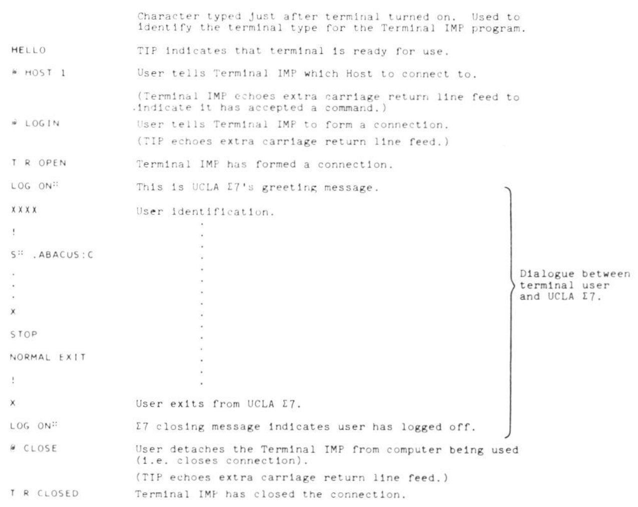

Figure 7—Typical terminal user dialogue

THE SOFTWARE

Because the terminals connected to a TIP communicate with Hosts at remote sites, the TIP, in addition to performing the IMP function, also acts as intermediary between the terminal and the distant Host. This means that network standards for format and protocol must be implemented in the TIP. One can thus think of the TIP software as containing both a very simpleminded mini-Host and a regular IMP program.

Figure 8 gives a simplified diagrammatic view of the program. The lower block marked "IMP" represents the usual IMP program. The two lines into and out of that block are logically equivalent to input and output from a Host. The code conversion blocks are in fact surprisingly complex and include all of the material for dealing with diverse (and perverse) types of terminals.

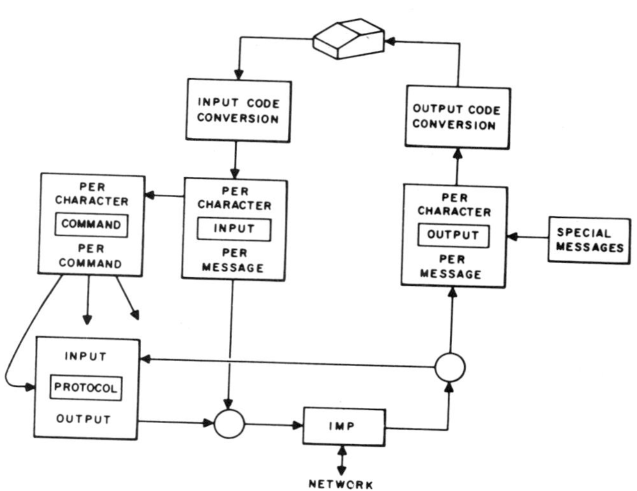

Figure 8—Block diagram of TIP program

As the user types on the keyboard, characters go, via input code conversion, to the input block. Information for remote sites is formed into regular network messages and passes through the OR switch to the IMP program for transmittal. Command characters are fed off to the side to the command block where commands are decoded. The commands are then "performed" in that they either set some appropriate parameter or a flag which calls for later action. An example of this is the LOGIN command. Such a command in fact triggers a complex network protocol procedure, the various steps of which are performed by the PROTOCOL block working in conjunction with the remote Host through the IMPs. As part of this process an appropriate special message will be sent to the terminal via the Special Messages block indicating the status (success, failure, etc.) of the procedure.

Once connection to a remote Host is established, regular messages flow directly through the Input block and on through the IMP program. Returning responses come in through the IMP, into the OUTPUT program where they are fed through the OUTPUT Code Conversion block to the terminal itself.

Storage for the TIP program, including the standard IMP program, is just over 20K. This is roughly as follows:

Standard IMP Program with buffers & tables	12,000
Special TIP code	2,650
Tables of Parameters	1,800
Buffer Storage for messages to and from terminals	1,880
Miscellaneous—I/O buffers, constants, etc.	1,880

PERFORMANCE

The program can handle approximately 100 kilobits of one-way terminal traffic provided the message size is sufficiently large that per-message processing is amortized over many characters. Overhead per message is such that if individual characters are sent one at a time there is a loss of somewhere between a factor of ten and twenty in bandwidth. A different way to look at program performance is to observe that the per-character processing time is about 75 μs.

These figures ignore the fact that the machine must devote some of its bandwidth to acting as an IMP, both for terminal traffic and for regular network traffic. About 5% of the machine is lost to acting as an IMP, even in the absence of traffic. If there is network traffic, more of the machine bandwidth is used up. Five hundred kilobits of two-way phone line and Host traffic saturates the machine without any terminal traffic*.

In addition to bandwidth which goes into the IMP part of the job, another 10 percent of the (total) machine is taken up simply in fielding clock interrupts from the Multi-Line Controller. This again is bandwidth used in idling even with no actual terminal traffic.

The following formula summarizes, approximately, the bandwidth capabilities:

$$P + H + 11T \leq 850$$

where:

394

P = total phone line traffic (in kilobits/sec) wherein, for example, a full duplex 50 Kb phone line counts as 100;

H = total Host traffic (in kilobits/sec) wherein the usual full duplex Host interface, with its usual 10 μs/bit setting, counts as 200; and

T = total terminal traffic (in kilobits/sec) wherein an ASCII terminal such as a (110-baud) full-duplex Teletype (ASR-33) counts as twice its baud rate (i.e., 0.220 Kb).

This means that it takes eleven times as much program time to service every terminal character as it does to service a character's worth of phone line or Host message.

A further factor that influences terminal traffic handling capability has to do with the terminals themselves. Certain types of terminals require more attention from the program than others, independent of their speed but based rather on their complexity. In particular, for example, while an IBM 2741 nominally runs at 134.5 bits per second, the complexity is such that it uses nearly three times the program bandwidth that would be used in servicing a half-duplex ASCII terminal of equivalent speed. Allowances for such variations must be made in computing the machine's ability to service a particular configuration. It must be borne in mind that all of these performance figures are approximations and that the actual rules are extremely complex, and will change as the program matures.

* The number 500 kilobits is for full size (8000 bit) messages. Shorter messages use up more capability per bit and thus reduce the overall bandwidth capability.

DISCUSSION

As the ARPA Network grows, a number of areas of development seem likely to require attention. Certain of these are already pressing problems whereas others will begin to appear primarily as the network continues to grow and mature.

Perhaps the most difficult aspect of a network such as this is the problem of reliability. A great deal of thought and effort has gone into trying to make the system reliable and network topology has been designed with the need for redundancy in mind. Nonetheless the problem of keeping a large number of computer systems going at widely separated sites is non-trivial. An IMP's mean-time-between-failure (MTBF) has been on the order of one month; considerably lower than expected. The problems arise from a variety of sources and the system is sufficiently complex that frequently the cause has been masked by the time the failure has been noted. Often the same failure will recur several times until the problem is identified and eliminated and this fact tends to decrease the apparent MTBF. In general a preponderance of the troubles stem from hardware failures, and we are currently modifying several noisy and/or marginal portions of the I/O and interface hardware in hopes of obtaining significant improvement.

Our strategy has generally been to spend time identifying the source of trouble, keeping the machine off the air if necessary, so that eventually the MTBF will increase. This has often meant, however, that a "down" was much longer than it would have been, had the foremost goal been to get the machine running again immediately. With this strategy the average down time has been about 9 hours, giving rise to an average per-machine down rate of about 2 percent. We hope to improve this situation in the near future by providing improved facilities for obtaining "program dumps" when a failure occurs. This will make it possible to bring machines back on the air almost immediately in many cases, without jeopardizing valuable debugging data.

A word about our experience with the phone lines appears appropriate here as well. We have apparently been an unusual, if not unique, customer for the common carriers in our degree of attention to line failures. Our ability to detect and report even brief outages has led through measured skepticism to eventual acceptance by the carriers. In general, tests have indicated that the phone line error rates are about as predicted, i.e., approximately one in 10^5. These occasional errors or error bursts do not appear to affect network performance adversely. The IMP-to-IMP error checking procedure has not, to our knowledge, admitted a single erroneous message. We have, however, had some difficulty with lines which were simply out of commission from time to time for extended periods (hours or even days). The reliability of the phone lines is roughly equivalent to the reliability of the IMPs, based on the number and duration of outages. Down times have decreased as the carriers have come to accept our complaints as generally legitimate. *Overall the performance of the telephone equipment does not appear to constitute a problem in network growth.*

From a strictly technical viewpoint we view the incorporation of higher bandwidth facilities as a natural and key part of network growth. While the present facilities are not saturated by the present loads, we view this situation as a temporary one and something of a period of grace. As the network continues to grow over the next few years traffic can be expected to increase in a very non-linear fashion. Host protocol procedures (which have presented a sizable stumbling block to usage) are settling down so that software commitments can be made, and the advent of the Terminal IMP will bring an influx of new users who do not have the alternative of local resources. As a result we expect that traffic will begin to saturate some parts of the network. Terminal IMPs may well be called upon to service a larger number of terminals of higher bandwidth than can be handled by the present version.

In anticipation of these requirements we are presently considering the design of a significantly faster and more modular version of the IMP. Its higher speed will permit it to take advantage of high speed (i.e., megabit and above) communication lines which the common carriers are currently developing. More generally it will be able to service high bandwidth requirements whenever and however they occur within the net. We are currently studying a modular design which will permit connection of a greater number of interfaces than the present IMP can handle. While this work is only in the preliminary design stage, we feel that the interest and enthusiasm which have greeted the initial network suggest that it is not too early to consider ways to cope with growing traffic requirements.

Another area of network development which has already received a great deal of attention and will require much more in the future is that of technical information interchange between the sites. To the user, the resources which are becoming available are staggering if not overwhelming. It is very difficult for an individual to discover what, if any, of the mass of programs that will be available through the network may be of interest or of use to him. To aid in this process a number of mechanisms are being implemented and we are cooperating closely with these efforts. In particular, at the Stanford Research Institute a Network Information Center (NIC) acts essentially as a library for documentation concerning the network. Here are maintained a number of pointer documents, specifically, (1) a Directory of Participants which lists critical personnel, phone numbers, etc., for each participating site, (2) a catalogue of the NIC Collection which lists the available documents indexed in a variety of ways, (3) a Resource Notebook which is a compendium that attempts to familiarize the reader with available program resources at each of the participating sites.

Finally, there is the broad and exciting issue of how to cope with success. As the ARPA Network grows, and as diverse resources and users join the net, it is clear that a technology transfer must occur; the network probably must shift from a government-supported research and development activity to an ongoing national *service* of some kind. However, the computer-communications environment in the U.S. is rather complex, and is populated with many legal, economic, and political constraints. Within this environment, it is not easy to perform the technology transfer, and many groups, including ARPA and BBN, have been considering possible alternative plans. We are optimistic that a way will be found to provide a suitable legal and political base for expansion of the present ARPA Network into a widely useful public communication system.

ACKNOWLEDGMENTS

In addition to the authors, a great many people have contributed to the work reported here. Dr. L. G. Roberts of the Advanced Research Projects Agency has continued to lend crucial support and encouragement to the project. Messrs. Blue, Dolan, and Crocker of the ARPA office have been understanding and helpful. Suggestions and helpful criticism have come from many present and prospective participants in the network community.

At BBN, W. B. Barker is responsible for much of the cleverness which appears in the MLC hardware; R. E. Kahn has contributed in many areas and has been deeply involved in studying traffic flow control; A. McKenzie has compiled the Network Resource Notebook and been concerned with Host relations and many Host protocol issues; M. Thrope has managed the Network Control Center and has kept the network on the air; J. Levin helped in implementation of the TIP software; B. P. Cosell has patiently labored with the IMP software, with help from J. McQuillan and M. Kraley; and R. Alter has offered much helpful advice and criticism.

REFERENCES

1 L G ROBERTS B D WESSLER
Computer network development to achieve resource sharing
AFIPS Conference Proceedings Spring Joint Computer Conference 1970

2 F E HEART R E KAHN S M ORNSTEIN W R CROWTHER D C WALDEN
The interface message processor for the ARPA computer network
AFIPS Conference Proceedings Spring Joint Computer Conference 1970

3 L KLEINROCK
Analytic and simulation methods in computer network design
AFIPS Conference Proceedings Spring Joint Computer Conference 1970

4 H FRANK I T FRISCH W CHOU
Topological considerations in the design of the ARPA computer network
AFIPS Conference Proceedings Spring Joint Computer Conference 1970

5 C S CARR S D CROCKER V G CERF
Host-host communication protocol in the ARPA network
AFIPS Conference Proceedings Spring Joint Computer Conference 1970

6 S CROCKER et al
Function-oriented protocols for the ARPA computer network
AFIPS Conference Proceedings Spring Joint Computer Conference 1972

7 R E KAHN W R CROWTHER
Flow control in a resource sharing computer network
Proc Second Symposium on Problems in the Optimization of Data Communications Systems October 1971

8 *User's guide to the terminal IMP*
Bolt Beranek and Newman Inc Report No 2183

9 *The BBN terminal interface message processor*
BBN Report 2184

10 L G ROBERTS B D WESSLER
The ARPA network
Computer Communication Networks Chapter 6 In preparation

11 L G ROBERTS
A forward look
Journal of Armed Forces Communications and Electronics Assoc Vol XXV No 12 August 1971 pp 77-81

12 *The MIT Lincoln Lab terminal support processor*
Graphics Semi-Annual Tech Summary Reports ESD-TR-70-151 p 355 May November 1970

13 *Progress report #1*
University of Michigan MERIT Computer Network Report #0571PR4 May 1971

14 A B COCANOWER W FISCHER W S GERSTENBERGER B S READ
The communications computer operating system—The initial design
University of Michigan MERIT Computer Network Manual #1070-TN-3 October 1970

15 R E KAHN
Terminal access to the ARPA computer network
Courant Computer Symposium 3 Computer Networks Courant Institute New York November 1970—Proceedings to be published by Prentice Hall Englewood Cliffs New Jersey In preparation

396

A new minicomputer/multiprocessor for the ARPA network*

by F. E. HEART, S. M. ORNSTEIN, W. R. CROWTHER, and W. B. BARKER

Bolt Beranek and Newman Inc.
Cambridge, Massachusetts

INTRODUCTION

Since the early years of the digital computer era, there has been a continuing attempt to gain processing power by organizing hardware processors so as to achieve some form of parallel operation.[1,2] One important thread has been the use of an array of processors to allow a single control stream to operate simultaneously on a multiplicity of data streams; the most ambitious effort in this direction has been the ILLIAC IV project.[3,4] Another important thread has been the partitioning of problems so that several control streams can operate in parallel. Often functions have been unloaded from a central processor onto various specialized processors; examples include data channels, display processors, front-end communication processors, on-line data preprocessors—in fact, I/O processors of all sorts. Similarly, dual processor systems have been used to provide load sharing and increased reliability. Still another thread has been the construction of pipeline systems in which sub-pieces of a single (generally large) processor work in parallel on successive phases of a problem.[5] In some of these pipeline approaches the parallelism is "hidden" and the user considers only a single control stream.

In recent years, as minicomputers have proliferated, groups of identical small machines have been connected together and jobs partitioned quite grossly among them. Most recently, our group and several others have been investigating this avenue further, attempting to reduce the specialization of the processors in order to employ independent processors with independent control streams in a cooperative and "equal" fashion.[6,7,8]

This paper describes a new minicomputer/multiprocessor architecture for which a fourteen-processor prototype is now (February 1973) being constructed. The hardware design and the software organization include many novel features, and the system may offer significant advantages in modularity and cost/performance. The system contains an expandable number of identical processors, each with some "private" memory; an expandable amount of "shared" memory to which all processors have equal access; and an expandable amount of I/O interface equipment, controllable by any processor. The system achieves unusual modularity and reliability by making all processors equivalent, so that any processor may perform any system task; thus systems can be easily configured to meet the throughput requirements of a particular job. The scheme for interconnecting processors, memories, and I/O is also modular, permitting interconnection cost to vary smoothly with system size. There is no "executive" and each processor determines its own task allocation.

A key issue throughout most of the attempts at parallel organization has been the difficulty of partitioning problems in such a way that the resulting computer program(s) can really take advantage of the parallel organization. This issue is raised in its most serious form when the parallel machine is expected to work well on a great diversity of problems as, for example, in a time-sharing system. Our machine design has been developed under the highly favorable circumstances that (1) the initial application, and a prior software implementation in a standard machine, was well understood; (2) the initial application lent itself to fragmentation into parallel structures; and (3) the design would be deemed successful if it handled only that one application in a meritorious fashion. However, we now believe that the design is advantageous for many other important applications as well and that it may herald a broadly useful new way to achieve increased performance and reliability.

The machine has been designed to serve initially as a modular switching node for the ARPA Network[9] and, in the following section, we briefly describe the ARPA Network application and the requirements that the network imposed upon the machine design. In subsequent sections we discuss our choice of minicomputer, describe our system design in some detail, discuss certain of the more interesting characteristics of multiprocessor behavior, and summarize our present status and plans for the near future.

* *This work was sponsored by the Advanced Research Projects Agency under Contracts DAHC15-69-C-0179 and F08606-73-6-0027.*

Reprinted from Proceedings of the NCC, 1973

CORRECTION (p. 536 of original text, first column, first new sentence):

Unless there is a careful systematic approach to interlocks, deadlocks become almost a certainty. One technique is to assign a unique number to each resource for which there is an interlock, and require that a processor never compete for a resource when it already owns a higher numbered resource.

ARPA NETWORK REQUIREMENTS

The ARPA Network, a nationwide interconnection of computers and high bandwidth (50 Kb) communication circuits, has grown during the past four years to include over 35 sites, with more than one computer at many sites. The computers at each site, called Hosts, obtain access to the net via a small communications processor known as an Interface Message Processor or IMP.[10] In order to permit groups without their own computer facility to access this powerful set of computer resources, a version of the IMP called a Terminal IMP allows, in addition, attachment of up to 63 local or remote terminals of a wide range of types.[11]

As a considerable simplification, the job to be handled by an IMP is that of a communications processor. Arriving messages must pass through an error control algorithm, be inspected to some degree (e.g., for destination), and generally be directed out onto some other line. Some incoming messages (e.g., routing control messages) must be constructed or digested directly by the IMP. The IMP must also concern itself with flow control, message assembly and sequencing, performance and flow monitoring, Host status, line and interface testing, and many other housekeeping functions. To perform these functions an IMP requires memory both for program and for message buffers, processing power for executing the program, and I/O units of various sorts for connecting to a variety of lines and devices. The original IMP, built around a Honeywell 516 processor with a 1 μs cycle time, could handle approximately three-quarters of a megabit per second of full duplex communications traffic. A later, smaller and cheaper (Honeywell 316) version handles about two-thirds as much traffic.

As the network has grown and as usage has increased, a number of demands for improvement have led to the need for a new "line" of IMP machines. Our intent is to provide a modular arrangement of flexible hardware from which it will be possible to construct both smaller and less expensive IMPs as well as far more powerful IMPs. An important specific objective is to obtain an IMP whose communications bandwidth could be at least an order of magnitude greater than the 516 IMP; such a high speed IMP would permit the direct connection of satellite circuits or land T-carrier circuits operating at approximately 1.3 megabits/second.

It is also desirable to improve the present IMP design in a number of other areas, as follows.

- Expandability of I/O: The present IMPs permit connection to a total of only seven high-speed circuits and/or Host computers. We would like to permit a much greater fanout so that an IMP might be connected to as many as 20 or more Host computers or to hundreds of terminals. This means that the number of interface units should be expandable over a wide range.
- Modularity: A number of groups have wished to make a network connection from a single Host at a considerable distance (miles) from the nearest IMP. We feel that such Hosts should be locally connected to a very small IMP in order to preserve consistency and standardization throughout the network. Therefore, a goal of this new hardware effort is the provision of a small and inexpensive but compatible IMP which could serve to connect a single, distant spur Host.
- Expandability of Memory: The new line of equipment is required for use in connection with satellite links (or longer faster links in general) and must therefore be able to expand its memory easily to provide the much greater buffer storage requirements of such links.
- Reliability: The new line of processors should be more reliable than the existing IMPs and ought to permit better self-diagnosis and simple isolation and replacement of failing units.

Of the requirements posed by the ARPA Network application, the most central was to obtain an order-of-magnitude traffic bandwidth improvement. We first considered meeting this requirement with highly specialized hardware, but the need to allow evolution of the communications algorithms, as well as the "bookkeeping" nature of much of the IMP task, militate against hardwired approaches and require the flexibility of a stored program computer. Thus we need a machine with an effective cycle time of 100 nanoseconds, a factor of ten faster than the present 1 μs IMP. Realizing that a single very fast and powerful machine would be difficult to build and would not give us compatible machines with a wide spectrum of performance, we began to consider the possibility of a minicomputer/multiprocessor in order to achieve the flexibility, reliability, and effective bandwidth required.

With the idea of a multiprocessor in mind we considered the IMP algorithm to determine which parts were inherently serial in nature and which could proceed in parallel. It seemed difficult to process a single message in a parallel fashion: the job was already relatively short and intimately coupled to I/O interfaces. However, there was much less serial coupling between the processing of separate messages from the same phone line and no coupling at all between messages from different phone lines. We thus envisage many processors, each at work on a separate message, with the number of processors carefully matched to the number of messages we expect to encounter in the time it takes one processor to deal with one message. With this simple image there seems to be no inherent limit to the parallelism we can achieve—the ultimate limit would be set by the size of the multiprocessor we can build.

CHOICE OF THE PROCESSOR

In designing a multiprocessor for the IMP application, we found ourselves iteratively exploring two related but distinct issues. First, assuming that the problem of interconnection could be solved, what minicomputer would be a sensible choice from the price/performance and physical points of view? Second, and much harder: for any specific machine, how did the CPU talk to memory, how would multiple CPUs, memories, and I/O be interconnected to form a system, and how would the program be organized?

Since the program for the existing IMPs was well understood, it was possible to identify key sections of that program which consumed the majority of the processing bandwidth. Then, for each sensible minicomputer choice, we could ask how many CPUs of this type would be needed to provide an effective 100 nanosecond cycle time; and given a price list, physical data, and a modest amount of design effort, we could define the physical structure and the price of the resulting multiprocessor. With this general approach, we examined the internal design of about a dozen machines, and actually wrote the key code in many cases. Using the fastest available minicomputers it was possible to arrive at configurations with only three or four processors; using the slowest choices, systems with 20 CPUs or more were required.

If we defer the interconnection and contention problems for a moment, it is interesting to note that "slow and cheap" may win over "fast and expensive" in this kind of multiprocessor competition to achieve a stated processing bandwidth. This is an especially happy situation if, as in our case, a spectrum of configurations is needed, including a very tiny cheap version.

In considering which minicomputer might be most easily adaptable to a multiprocessor structure, the internal communication between the processor and its memory was of primary concern. Several years ago machines were introduced which combined memory and I/O busses into a single bus. As part of this step, registers within the devices (pointers, status and control registers, and the like) were made to look like memory cells so that they and the memory could be referenced in a homogeneous manner. This structure forms a very clean and attractive architecture in which any unit can bid to become master of the bus in order to communicate with any other desired unit. One of the important features of this structure is that it made memory accessing "public"; the interface to the memory had to become asynchronous, cleanly isolable electrically and mechanically, and well documented and stable. A characteristic of this architecture is that all references between units are time multiplexed onto a single bus. Conflicts for bus usage therefore establish an ultimate upper bound on overall performance, and attempts to speed up the bus eventually run into serious problems in arbitration.[12]

In 1972 a new processor—the Lockheed SUE[13]—was introduced which follows the single bus philosophy but carries it an important step further by removing the bus arbitration logic to a module separate from the processor. This step permits one to consider configurations embodying multiple processors and multiple memories as well as I/O on a single bus. The SUE CPU is a compact, relatively inexpensive (approximately $600 in quantity), quite slow processor with a microcoded inner structure. This slowness can be compensated for by simply doubling or trebling the number of processors on the bus; performance is limited largely by the speed of the bus. With this bus architecture it becomes attractive to visualize multibus systems with a "bus coupling" mechanism to allow devices on one bus to access devices on other busses.

Similar approaches can be implemented with varying degrees of difficulty in systems with other bus structures, and we examined several approaches in some detail for those processors whose cost/performance was attractive. Rather fortuitously, the minicomputer which exhibited the most attractive bus architecture also was extremely attractive in terms of cost/performance and physical characteristics. This machine, the Lockheed SUE, would require fourteen processors to achieve the effective 100 nanosecond cycle time, and we embarked on the detailed design of our multiprocessor on that basis.

SYSTEM DESIGN

Although our design permits systems of widely varying size and performance, in the interest of clarity we will describe that design in terms of the particular prototype now under construction. Our overall design is represented in Figure 1. We require fourteen SUE processors to obtain the necessary processing bandwidth, and we estimate that 32K words of memory will be required for a complete copy of the operational program and the necessary communication buffer storage. The I/O arrangements must allow easy connection of all the communications interfaces, appropriate to the IMP job (modem interfaces, Host interfaces, terminal interfaces) as well as standard peripherals and any special devices appropriate to the multiprocessor nature of the system.

Some of the basic SUE characteristics are listed in Table I. From a physical point of view, the SUE chassis represents the basic construction unit; it incorporates a printed circuit back plane which forms the bus into which 24 cards may be plugged. From a logical point of view this bus simply provides a common connection between all

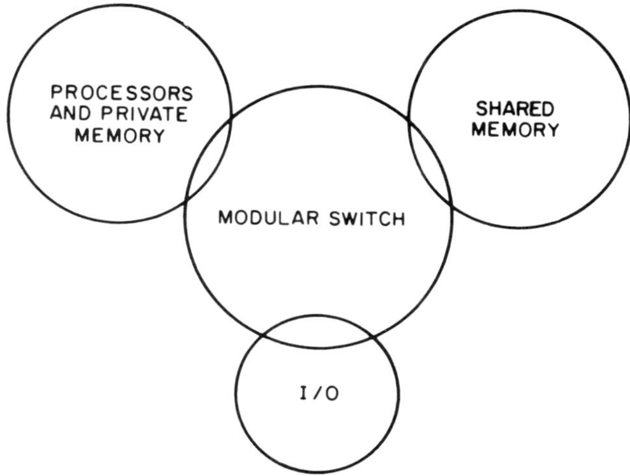

Figure 1—System structure

TABLE I—SUE Characteristics

SUE Characteristics
16-bit word
8 General Registers
△3.7 μs add or load time
Microcoded
Two words/instruction typical
8-½″×19″×18″ chassis
64K bytes addressable by a single instruction
~$3K for: 1 CPU+4K Memory+Power, Rack, etc.
200 ns minimum bus cycle time
850 ns memory cycle time
425 ns memory access time

units plugged into the chassis. We are using these chassis for the entire system: processor, memory, and I/O. All specially designed cards as well as all Lockheed-provided modules plug into these bus chassis. With this hardware, the terms "bus" and "chassis" are used somewhat interchangeably, but we will commonly call this standard building unit a "bus." Each bus requires one card which performs arbitration. A bus can be logically extended (via a bus extender unit) to a second bus if additional card space is required; in such a case, a single bus arbiter controls access to the entire extended bus.

We can build a small multiprocessor just by plugging several processors and memories (and I/O) into a single bus. For larger systems we quickly exceed the bandwidth capability of a single bus and we are forced to multi-bus architecture. Then, from a construction viewpoint, our multiprocessor design involves assigning processors, memories and I/O units to busses in a sensible manner and designing a switching arrangement to permit interconnection of all the busses. Of course, the superficial simplicity of this construction viewpoint completely hides the many difficult problems of multiprocessor system design; we will try to deal with some of those issues in the following sections.

Resources

A central notion in a parallel system is the idea of a "resource," which we define to mean a part of the system needed by more than one of the parallel users and therefore a possible source of contention. The three basic hardware resources are the memories, the I/O, and the processors. It is useful to consider the memories, furthermore, as a collection of resources of quite different character: a program, queues and variables of a global nature, local variables, and large areas of buffer storage.

The basic idea of a multiprocessor is to provide multiple copies of the vital resources in the hope that the algorithm can run faster by using them in parallel. The number of copies of the resource which are required to allow concurrent operation is determined by the speed of the resource and the frequency with which it is used. An additional advantage of multiple copies is reliability: if a system contains a few spare copies of all resources, it can continue to operate when one copy breaks.

It may seem peculiar to think of a processor as a resource, but in fact in our system the parallel parts of the algorithm compete with each other for a processor on which to run. We take the view that all processors shall be identical and equal, and we go to some trouble to insure that this is in fact so. As a consequence no single processor is of vital importance, and we can change the number of processors at will. A later section will describe how the processors coordinate to get the job done without a master of some sort.

Processor busses

A SUE bus can physically and logically support up to four processors. As more processors are added to a bus, the contention for the bus increases, and the performance increment per processor drops; but the effective cost per processor also drops, since the cost for the chassis, power supply, bus arbitration, etc., is amortized over the number of processors.

Roughly speaking, using two processors per bus loses almost nothing in processor performance, using three processors per bus loses significant efficiency, and adding a fourth processor gains less than half an "effective processor." After careful examination of the logical, economic and physical aspects of this choice, we decided to use two processors per processor bus, and we thus require seven processor busses in our initial multiprocessor system.

The next question was how the processors should access the program. In our application, some parts of the program are run very frequently and other parts are run far less frequently. This fact allows a significant advantage to be gained by the use of private memory. When a processor makes access to shared memory via the switching arrangement, that access will incur delays due to contention and delays introduced by the intervening switch. We therefore decided to use a 4K local memory with each processor on its bus to allow faster local access to the frequently run code; these local memories all typically contain the same code. With this configuration and in our application, the ratio of accesses to local versus shared memory is better than three to one. This not only reduces contention delays for access to the shared memory but also cuts the number of accesses which suffer the delays.

The final configuration of a processor bus is shown in Figure 2(a). The units marked "Bus Coupler" have to do with our multiprocessor switching arrangement, which will be discussed below.

*Shared memory busses**

The shared memory of our multiprocessor is intended to contain a copy of the program as well as considerable storage space for message buffering, global variables, etc. Application-dependent considerations led us to select a

* *The terms "I/O bus" and "memory bus" as used here and henceforth are not the same as conventional I/O and memory busses.*

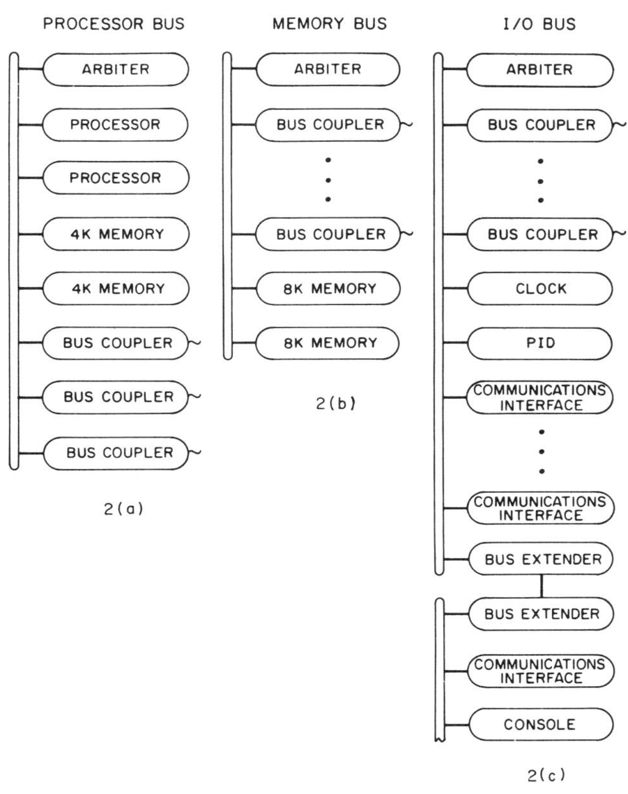

Figure 2—Bus structures

32K memory, but it is possible to configure this memory on a single bus or to divide the memory onto several busses. We first concluded that four logical memory units would be appropriate in order to reduce processor contention to an acceptable level. Then, since the bus is considerably faster than the memories, it is feasible to place two logical memory elements on a single bus with almost no interference. Thus, we are planning two memory busses in the initial multiprocessor; the configuration of a common memory bus is shown in Figure 2(b).

I/O busses

The I/O system of the multiprocessor employs standard SUE busses with standard bus arbitration units on those busses. Into the bus will be plugged cards for each of the various types of I/O interfaces that are required, including interfaces for modems, terminals, Host computers, etc., as well as interfaces for standard peripherals. Our initial system has a single I/O bus and Figure 2(c) shows its configuration; the specialized units shown (a "Clock" and "Pseudo Interrupt Device") are system-wide resources that are used to control the operation of the multiprocessor. The I/O bus will also be the access route for the multiprocessor console; we plan to use a standard alphanumeric display terminal which can be driven by code in any processor, and no conventional consoles will be used.

Interconnection system

Our prototype multiprocessor is now seen to contain seven processor busses, two shared memory busses and an I/O bus. To adhere to our requirement that all processors must be equal and able to perform any system task, these busses must be connected so that all processors can access all shared memory, so that I/O can be fed to and from shared memory, and so that any of the processors may control the operation and sense the status of any I/O unit.

A *distributed* inter-communication scheme was chosen in the interest of expandability, reliability, and design simplicity. The atom of this scheme is called a Bus Coupler, and consists of two cards and an interconnecting cable. In making connections between processors and shared memory, one card plugs into a shared memory bus, where it will request cycles of the memory; the other card plugs into a processor's bus, where it looks like memory. When the processor requests a cycle within the address range which the Bus Coupler recognizes, a request is sent down the cable to the memory end, which then starts contending for the shared memory bus. When selected, it requests the desired cycle of the shared memory. The memory returns the desired information to the Bus Coupler, which then provides it to the requesting processor, which, except for an additional delay, does not know that the memory was not on its own bus. Note that the memory access arbitration inherent in any memory switching arrangement is handled by the SUE Bus Arbiter controlling the shared memory bus, while the Bus Coupler itself is conceptually straightforward.

One additional feature of the Bus Coupler is that it does address mapping. Since a processor can address only 64K bytes (16 bit address), and since we wished to permit multiprocessor configurations with up to 1024K bytes (20 bit address) of shared memory, a mechanism for address expansion is required. The Bus Coupler provides four independent 8K byte windows into shared memory. The processor can load registers in the Bus Coupler which provide the high-order bits of the shared memory address for each of the four windows.

Given a Bus Coupler connecting each processor bus to each shared-memory bus, all processors can access all shared memory. I/O devices which do direct memory transfers must also access these shared memories. These I/O devices are plugged into as many I/O busses as are required to handle the bandwidth involved, and bus couplers then connect each I/O bus to each memory bus. Similarly, I/O devices also need to respond to processor requests for action or information; in this regard, the I/O devices act like memories and Bus Couplers are again used to connect each processor bus to each I/O bus. The path between processor busses and I/O busses is also used in a more sophisticated fashion to allow processors to examine and control other processors; this subject is described in a later section.

The resulting system is shown in Figure 3. One is struck by the number of bus couplers: P*I+I*M+P*M bus couplers are required for a system with P processor bus-

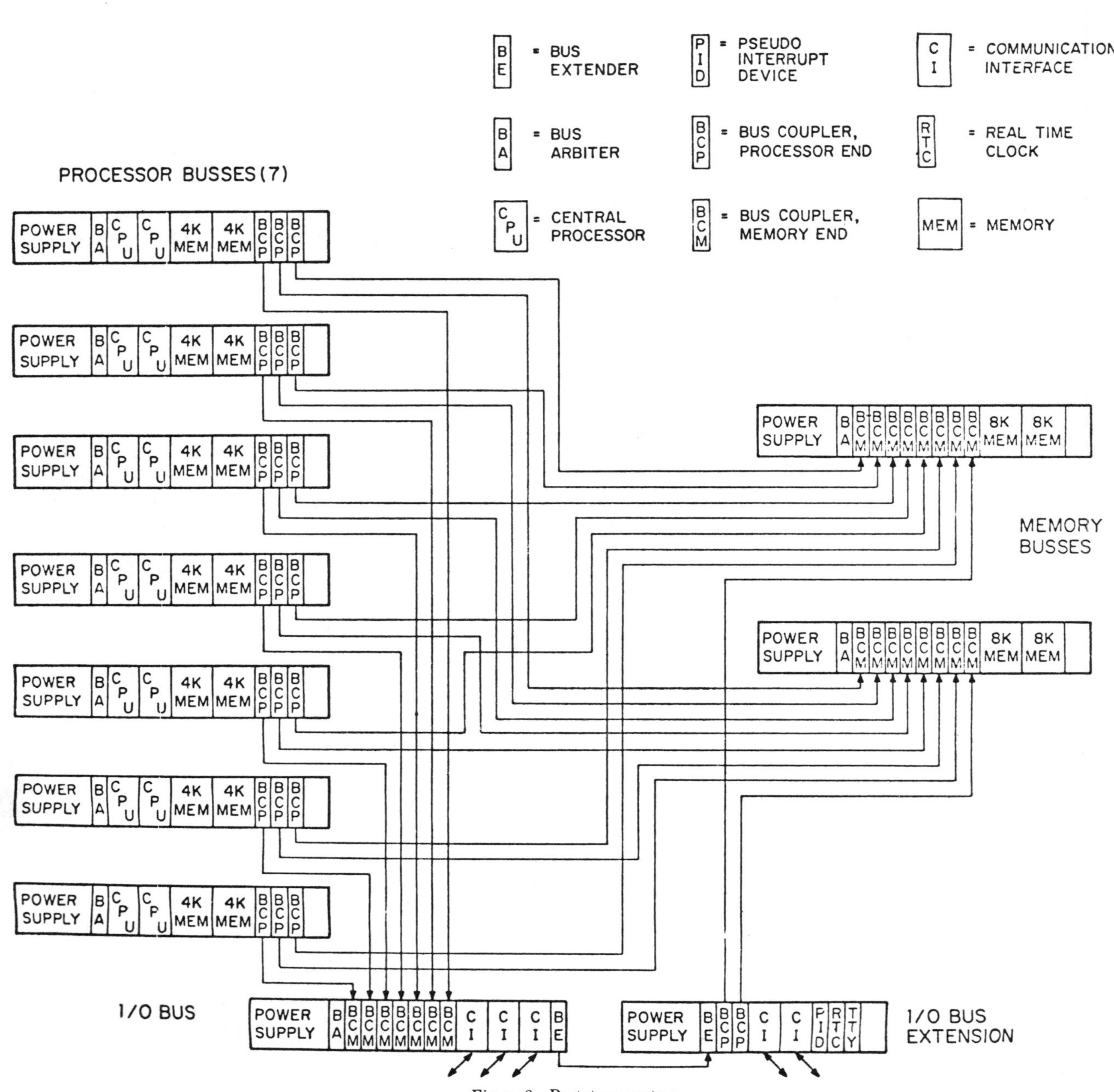

Figure 3—Prototype system

ses, I I/O busses, and M memory busses. In the case of our initial multiprocessor, 23 are needed.

This modular interconnection approach clearly permits great flexibility in the number and configuration of busses, and allows interconnection cost to vary smoothly with system size. We believe that this modular interconnection scheme also permits a complex hierarchical arrangement of busses. Actually the system exhibits a pronounced hierarchical structure already. A processor accesses the local memory when it needs instructions or local variables. Two such processor-memory combinations form a dual processor, which can be regarded as a unit and which needs access to shared resources, such as global variables, free buffers, and I/O interfaces. When one copy of a resource can only support a limited number of users, it seems sensible to provide only the corresponding limited number of connections. If a multiprocessor of this type were to grow larger, the physical number of bus couplers as well as increasing contention problems might not permit the connection of each processor to all of common memory, but might instead require a multi-level structure where groups of processors were connected to an intermediate level bus which was in turn connected to a centralized common memory. We have not explored this domain but feel it is an interesting area for future work.

MULTIPROCESSOR BEHAVIOR

Until the processors interact, a multiprocessor is a number of independent single processor systems: it is the interaction which poses the conceptual as well as the practical problems. If the various processors spend their time waiting for each other, the system degrades to a single processor equivalent; if they can usefully run concurrently, the processing power is multiplied by the number of processors. If the failure of a single processor takes the system down, the system reliability is only the probability of all processors being up; if working processors can diagnose and heal or amputate faulty processors and proceed with the job, the system reliability approaches the probability of *any* processor being up. We now consider how to keep processors running concurrently, and then how to keep the system running in the case of module failure.

The first problem in making the machines run independently is the allocation of runnable tasks to processors, so that the full requisite power can be quickly brought to bear on high priority tasks. Our scheme for doing this rests on four key ideas: (1) We break the job up into a set of tiny tasks. (2) Our processors are all identical, asynchronous, and capable of doing any task. (3) We keep a queue of pending tasks, ordered by priority, from which each processor at its convenience gets its next task. (4) For speed and efficiency, we use a hardware device to help manage the queue.

By breaking the job up into smaller and smaller tasks until each one runs in under 300 μs, we effectively determine the responsiveness of our system. Once started, a task must run to completion, but there will be a reconsideration of priorities at the beginning of each new task. We have chosen 300 microseconds as the maximum task execution time because this compromise between efficiency and responsiveness is well matched to the execution time of key IMP functions.

By making the processors identical, we can use the same program in systems of widely varying size and throughput capability. Any processor can be added to or removed from a running system with only a slight change in throughput. The power of all processors quickly shifts to that part of the algorithm where it is most needed.

By queuing pending tasks, we keep track of what must be done while focusing on the most important tasks. By using a passive queue in which the processors check for a new task when they are ready, we avoid some nasty timing problems. Tasks may be entered into the queue at any time, either by a processor or by the hardware I/O devices. This approach is an extremely important departure which avoids the use of conventional interrupts and the associated costs of saving and restoring machine state. Further, this approach neatly sidesteps the problem of routing interrupts to the proper processor.

We could not afford a software queue both because it was slow to use and because processors would have been waiting for each other to get access to the queue. Instead we use a special hardware device called a Pseudo Interrupt Device (PID), which keeps in hardware a list of what to do next. A number can be written to the PID at any time and and it will be remembered. When read, the PID returns (and deletes) the highest number it has stored. By coding the numbers to represent tasks, and keeping the parameters of the tasks in memory, a processor can access the PID at the end of each task and determine very rapidly what it should do next.

Contention

Clearly, the PID must give any task to exactly one processor. This is guaranteed because the PID is on a bus that can be accessed by only one processor at a time and because the PID completes each transaction in a single access. This is an example of the more general problem that whenever two users want access to a single resource there must be an interlock to let them take turns. This is true at many levels, from contention for a bus to processor contention for shared software resources such as a free list. When all the appropriate interlocks have been provided, the performance of the multiprocessor will depend rather critically on the time wasted waiting at these interlocks for a resource to become free. As discussed above, whenever conflicts become a serious problem one provides another copy of the resource. We studied our system behavior carefully, noting areas of conflict, in order to know how many additional copies of heavily accessed resources to provide. Table II provides examples of delays due to various conflicts. Practically speaking, the curve of delay vs. number of resources has a rather sharp knee, so that it is meaningful to make such statements as "a memory bus supports eight processors" or "a free list supports eight processors." Of course, these statements are application related and depend on the frequency and duration of accesses required.

With interlocks, deadlocks become possible (in both hardware and software). For example, a deadlock occurs

TABLE II—Expected System Slowdown Due to Contention Delays

Slowdown	Cause
5.5%	Contention for a Processor Bus.
3%	Contention for the Shared Memory Busses.
5%	Contention for the Shared Memories.
10%	Contention for a single system-wide software resource, assuming each processor wants the resource for 6 instructions out of every 120 instructions executed.
1.7%	Contention for one of two copies of a system-wide software resource, as above.
0.15%	Contention for the parameters of a single 1.3 megabit phone line, assuming the parameters will be used for 160 microseconds every 800 microseconds.

when each of two processors has claimed one of two resources needed by both. Each waits indefinitely for the other's resource to become available.[14] Unless there is a careful systematic approach to interlocks, deadlocks interlock, and require that a processor never compete for a resource when it already owns a higher numbered resource. It is not always practical or possible to do this, although we expect to be able to do so with the IMP algorithms.

An interesting example of a deadlock occurs in our bus coupling. To permit processors to access one another, for mutual turn on, turn off, testing, etc., the path connecting each processor bus with the I/O bus is made bi-directional. Thus processors access one another via the I/O bus. In a bi-directional coupler, a deadlock arises when units obtain control of their busses at each end and then request access via the coupler to the bus on the other end. Because the backward path is infrequently used, we simply detect such deadlocks, abort the backward request and try again.

Reliability

We have taken a rather ambitious stand on reliability. We plan to detect a failing module automatically, amputate it, and keep the system running without human intervention if at all possible. Critical to our approach is the fact that there are several processors each with private memory and thus each able to retreat to local operation in the face of system problems. To reduce our vulnerability further, power and cooling are provided on a modular basis so that loss of a single unit does not jeopardize system operation. We are only mildly concerned with the damage done at the time of a failure, because the IMP system includes many checks and recovery procedures throughout the network.

The first sign of a failure may be a single bit wrong somewhere in shared memory, with all units apparently functioning properly. Alternatively, the failure may strike catastrophically, with shared memory in shambles and the processors running protectively in their local memories. Against this spectrum we cannot hope for a systematic defense; instead we have chosen a few defensive strategies.

So long as a module is failing, recovery is meaningless. We must run diagnostics to identify the bad module, or see if cutting a module out at random helps things. We feel that identifying such a solid failure will be relatively easy. Since a processor without couplers is completely harmless, once we identify a malfunctioning processor, we amputate it by turning off its bus couplers. We considered the possibility of a runaway processor turning good processors off. This is unlikely to begin with but we decided to make it even less likely by requiring a particular 16-bit password to be used in turning off a coupler. A runaway processor storing throughout shared memory would need this password in its accumulator to accidentally amputate. Similarly we require a password for one processor to get at another's local memory.

Against intermittents we use a strategy of dynamic reinitialization. Every data structure is periodically checked; every waiting state is timed out; the code is periodically checksummed; memory transfers are hardware parity checked; memory is periodically tested; processors are periodically given standard tests. Whenever anything is found wrong, the offending structure is initialized. Using this scheme we may not know what caused a failure, but its effects will not persist. In the most extreme cases we will need to reload all the program in main memory. Fortunately we have a communications network handy to load from. This technique of reloading has worked remarkably well in the current ARPA Network. Each processor has a copy of the reload program in its local memory, thus making loss of reload capability unlikely.

We might seem to be vulnerable to memory or I/O failures, particularly those involving the PID and the clock. If these modules fail it does indeed hurt us more, but only because we have fewer modules of these types in our system. If we provide redundant modules, the system can reconfigure itself to substitute a spare module for a failed one. Our design allows multiple I/O busses with multiple PIDs and clocks, and we could even have separate backup interfaces to vital communication lines on separate busses.

To summarize, the mainstay of our reliability scheme is a system continually aware of the state of things and quickly responding to unpleasant changes. The second line of defense consists of drastic actions like amputation and reloading. Assuming we can make all this work, we will have quite a reliable system, perhaps even one in which maintenance consists of periodic replacement of those parts which the system itself has rejected.

STATUS AND NEAR FUTURE

In February 1973, as this paper is submitted, we are very much in the middle of our multiprocessor development. Much progress has been made and we are increasingly confident of the design, but much work remains to be done.

The broad design is complete; all Lockheed-provided units (CPUs, memories, busses, etc.) have been delivered; prototype wire-wrapped versions of the crucial special modules have been completed, including the Bus Couplers, Pseudo Interrupt Device, clock, and modem interfaces; and a multi-bus, multi-processor-per-bus assembly has been successfully tried with a test program. A substantial program design effort has been in progress and coding of the first operational program has been started. We are still doing detailed design of some hardware, and we are still learning about detailed organizational issues as the software effort proceeds. An example of such an area is: exactly how is it best for processors to watch each other for signs of failure?

We currently anticipate the parts cost of the prototype fourteen-processor system, without communication interfaces, to be under $100K.

Hopefully, by the time this paper is presented in June 1973, we will be able to report an operational prototype multiprocessor system. Beyond that, our schedule calls for the installation of a machine in the ARPA Network by about the end of 1973. We also plan to construct many variant systems out of this kit of building blocks, and to experiment with systems of varying sizes. As part of this work, we plan to concentrate on the very smallest version that may be sensible, in order to provide a minimum cost IMP for spur applications in the ARPA Network.

As the design has proceeded, our attraction to the general approach has increased (perhaps a common malady), and we now believe that the approach is applicable to many other classes of problems. We expect to explore such other applications as time permits, with initial attention to two areas: (1) certain specialized multi-user systems, and (2) high bandwidth signal processing.

With our presently planned building blocks, although we do not yet know what will limit system size, we do not now see any intrinsic problem in constructing systems with fifty or a hundred processors. As improvements in integrated circuit technology occur, and processors and memories become smaller and cheaper, organization and connection become the paramount questions in multiprocessor design. We expect to see many attempts at multiprocessors, and are hopeful that the ideas embodied in this design will help to steer that technology. Perhaps minicomputer/multiprocessors will soon represent real competition for the various brontosaurus machines that now abound.

ACKNOWLEDGMENTS

Our new machine design is a product of many minds. We gratefully acknowledge the specific design contributions of M. Kraley, A. Michel, M. Thrope, and R. Bressler. Helpful criticism and an important idea about the Pseudo Interrupt Device were contributed by D. Walden. Assistance in planning and in the choice of building blocks was contributed by H. Rising. Helpful ideas and criticism were provided by J. McQuillan, B. Cosell, and A. McKenzie. Assistance with support software was provided by J. Levin.

We also wish to express appreciation for the support and encouragement provided by Dr. L. Roberts of the Advanced Research Projects Agency.

REFERENCES

1. Lehman, M., "A Survey of Problems and Preliminary Results Concerning Parallel Processing and Parallel Processors", *Proc. IEEE*, Vol. 54, No. 12, pp. 1889-1901, December, 1966.
2. Lorin, H., *Parallelism in Hardware & Software - Real and Apparent Concurrency* Prentice-Hall, 1971.
3. Slotnick, J. L., Bork, W. C., McReynolds, R. C., "Solomon", *AFIPS Conference Proceedings*, FJCC 1962.
4. Barnes, G. H., et al, "The Illiac IV Computer", *IEEE Trans.* C-17, Vol. 8, pp. 746-757, August 1968.
5. Anderson, D. W., Sparacio, F. J., Tomasulo, R. M., "The IBM System/360 Model 91 - Machine Philosophy and Instruction Handling", *IBM Journal* No. 11, January 1967, pp. 8-24.
6. Cohen, E., "Symmetric Multi-Mini-Processors, A Better Way to Go?" *Computer Decisions*, January 1973.
7. Wulf, W. A., Bell, C. G., "C.mmp - A Multi-Mini Processor", *AFIPS Proceedings*, FJCC, Vol. 41, 1972.
8. Cosserat, D. C., "A Capability Oriented Multi-Processor System for Real-Time Applications", *Computer Communication Proc. ICCC*, pp. 282-289, October 1972.
9. Roberts, L. G., Wessler, B. D., "Computer Network Development to Achieve Resource Sharing" *AFIPS Proceedings*, SJCC, Vol. 36, 1970.
10. Heart, F. E., et al, "The Interface Message Processor for the ARPA Computer Network", *AFIPS Proceedings*, SJCC, Vol. 36, 1970.
11. Ornstein, S. M., et al., "The Terminal IMP for the ARPA Computer Network", *AFIPS Proceedings*, SJCC, Vol. 40, 1972.
12. Chaney, T., Ornstein, S., Littlefield, W., "Beware the Synchronizer", *Proc. COMPCON Conference*, 1972.
13. *SUE Computer Handbook*, Lockheed Electronics Company, Los Angeles, 1972.
14. Holt, R. C., "Some Deadlock Properties of Computer Systems", *ACM Computing Surveys*, Vol. 4, No. 3, pp. 179-196, September 1972.

SUPPLEMENTARY BIBLIOGRAPHY

Amdahl, G. M., *Engineering Aspects of Large High-Speed Computer Design - Part II Logical Organization*, IBM Tech. Report TR00.1227, December 1964.

Baskin, H. B., et al, "A Modular Computer Sharing System," *CACM*, Vol. 12, No. 10, October 1969, p. 551.

Bell and Newell, *Computer Structures*, McGraw-Hill, 1971.

Bell, G., et al, *C.mmp the CMU Multiminiprocessor Computer*, Dept. of Computer Science, Carnegie Mellon Univ., August 1971.

Burnett, G. J., et al., "A Distributed PROCESSING System for General Purpose Computing", *AFIPS Proceedings*, FJCC, Vol. 31, 1967.

Dijkstra, E. W., "Cooperating Sequential Processes", in *Programming Languages*, (Gennys, F., ed.), Academic Press, pp. 43-110, 1968.

Flynn, M. J., "Some Computer Organizations and Their Effectiveness", *IEEE Transactions on Computers*", Vol. C-21, No. 9, September 1972.

Flynn, M. J., "Very High-Speed Computing Systems", *Proc. IEEE*, Vol. 54, No. 12, pp. 1901-1909, December, 1966.

Holland, J. H., "A Universal Computer Capable of Executing an Arbitrary Number of Sub-Programs Simultaneously," *AFIPS Proceedings*, FJCC, pp. 108-113, 1959.

McQuillan, J. M., et al, "Improvements in the Design and Performance of the ARPA Network", *AFIPS Proceedings*, FJCC, Vol. 41, 1972.

Ornstein, S. M., Stucki, M. J., Clark, W. A., "A Functional Description of Macromodules" *AFIPS Proceedings*, SJCC, Vol. 30, 1967.

Pirtle, M., "Intercommunication of Processors & Memory", *AFIPS Proceedings*, FJCC, Vol. 31, 1967.

Randell, B., "Operating Systems - The Problems of Performance and Reliability", *IFIP Congress 71*, Ljubljana, North Holland Pub. Co., 1972, pp. 281-290.

A Description of the Advanced Scientific Computer System, Texas Instruments, Inc., 1972.

Thornton, J. E., "Parallel Operation in the Control Data 6600", *AFIPS Proceedings*, FJCC, Vol. 26, 1964.

Wulf, W., et al, *Hydra— A Kernel Operating System for C.mmp*, Dept. of Computer Science, Carnegie Mellon Univ., 1971.

One of the most valuable features of a computer network is the provision of facilities for resource sharing among the set of computers in the network. It is useful to view resources as being associated with processes and as being available only through communication with these processes. Thus resource sharing in a computer network is achieved via interprocess communications.

Walden (p. 408) presents a network-wide system for resource sharing which describes a set of operations enabling interprocess communications between local available remote processes. Walden states that the ideas developed in Section 3 of his paper are in no way dependent on the hypothetical application discussed

Interprocess Communications

in Section 4. Crocker et. al. (p. 418) describe the protocols (a set of agreements such as format and relative timing between communicating processes) for the ARPA Computer Network. Thomas (p. 427) describes a distributed executive-like system which provides an environment for sharing of resources among Hosts (computers) on the ARPA Computer Network. With the environment provided by such executive-like systems, a user need not concern himself directly with network detail as communication protocols nor even be aware that he is dealing with a network. Cerk and Kahn (p. 437) present a protocol design and philogophy that supports the sharing resources that exist in a different packet switching network.

For further reading on this subject, the reader should refer to [DAN 75], [BOC 75], [ZIM 75] and the *Proceedings of the ACM Interprocess Communication Workshop*, Santa Monica, California, March 1975.

Computer Systems

R.L. Ashenhurst Editor

A System for Interprocess Communication in a Resource Sharing Computer Network

David C. Walden
Bolt Beranek and Newman Inc.*

A system of communication between processes in a time-sharing system is described and the communication system is extended so that it may be used between processes distributed throughout a computer network. The hypothetical application of the system to an existing network is discussed.

Key Words and Phrases: interprocess communication, time-sharing, computer networks, resource sharing

CR Categories: 3.81, 4.39, 4.82, 4.9

408

* 50 Moulton Street, Cambridge, MA 02138. The work was primarily supported by the Advanced Research Projects Agency under Contract DAHC 15–69–C–0179.

1. Introduction

A resource sharing computer network is defined to be a set of autonomous, independent computer systems, interconnected to permit each computer system to utilize all the resources of the other computer systems much as it would normally call one of its own subroutines. This definition of a network and the desirability of such a network are expounded upon by Roberts and Wessler in [9]. Examples of resource sharing could include a program filing some data in the file system of another computer system, two programs in remote computer systems exchanging communications, or users simply utilizing programs of another computer system via their own.

The actual act of resource sharing can be performed in two ways: in an ad hoc manner between all pairs of computer systems in the network; or according to a systematic network-wide standard. This paper develops a possible network-wide system for resource sharing.

It is useful to think of resources as being associated with processes[1] and available only through communication with these processes. This is a viewpoint which has been successfully applied to time-sharing systems [1] and has more recently been suggested to be an appropriate view for computer networks [8]. Consistent with this view, the fundamental problem of resource sharing is held in this paper to be the problem of inter-

[1] Almost any of the common definitions of a process would suit the needs of this paper.

process communication. With Carr, Crocker, and Cerf [2], the view is also held that interprocess communication over a network is a subcase of general interprocess communication in a multiprogrammed environment.

These views have led to a two-part study. First, a set of operations enabling interprocess communication within a single time-sharing system is constructed. This set of operations eschews many of the interprocess communication techniques currently in use within time-sharing systems—such as communication through shared memory—and relies instead on techniques that can be easily generalized to permit communication between remote processes. The second part of the study presents such a generalization. The hypothetical application of this generalized system to the ARPA Computer Network [9] is also discussed.

This paper does not represent a Bolt Beranek and Newman position on Host protocol for the ARPA network.

2. A System for Interprocess Communication Within a Time-Sharing System

This section describes a set of operations enabling interprocess communication within a time-sharing system. Following the notation of [10], this interprocess communication facility is called an IPC. As an aid to the presentation of this IPC, a model for a time-sharing system is described; the model is then used to illustrate the use of the interprocess communication operations.

The model time-sharing system has two pieces: the monitor and the processes. The monitor performs such functions as switching control from one process to another process when a process has used "enough" time, fielding hardware interrupts, managing core and the swapping medium, controlling the passing of control from one process to another (i.e. protection mechanisms), creating processes, caring for sleeping processes, and providing to the processes a set of machine extending operations (often called "supervisor" or "monitor" calls).

The processes perform the normal user functions (user processes) as well as the functions usually thought of as being supervisor functions in a time-sharing system (system processes) but not performed by the monitor in the current model. A typical system process is the disk handler or the file system. System processes are probably allowed to execute in supervisor mode, and they actually execute I/O instructions and perform other privileged operations that user processes are not allowed to perform. In all other ways, user and system processes are identical. For reasons of efficiency, it may be useful to think of system processes as being locked in core.

Although they will be of concern later in this study, protection considerations are not our concern here; instead, all processes are assumed to be "good" processes which never make any mistakes. If the reader needs a protection structure to keep in mind while he reads this paper, the *capability* system developed in [1, 3, 6, and 7] should be satisfying.

Of the operations a process can call on the monitor to perform, the five following are of particular interest for providing a capability for interprocess communication.

RECEIVE. This operation allows a specified process to send a message to the process executing the RECEIVE. The operation has four parameters: the port (defined below) awaiting the message—the RECEIVE port; the port a message will be accepted from—the SEND port; a specification of the buffer available to receive the message; and a location to transfer to when the transmission is complete—the restart location.

SEND. This operation sends a message from the process executing the SEND to a specified process. It has four parameters: a port to send the message to—the RECEIVE port; the port the message is being sent from—the SEND port; a specification of the buffer containing the message to be sent; and the restart location.

RECEIVE ANY. This operation allows *any* process to send a message to the process executing the RECEIVE ANY. The operation has four parameters: the port awaiting the message—the RECEIVE port; a specification of the buffer available to receive the message; a restart location; and a location where the port which sent the message may be noted.

SLEEP. This operation allows the currently running process to put itself to sleep pending the completion of an event. The operation has one optional parameter—an event to be waited for. An example event is the arrival of a hardware interrupt. The monitor never unilaterally puts a process to sleep as a result of the process executing one of the above four operations; however, if a process is asleep when one of the above four operations is satisfied, the process is awakened.

UNIQUE. This operation obtains a unique number from the monitor.

A *port* is a particular data path to a process (a RECEIVE port) or from a process (a SEND port), and all ports have an associated unique *port number* which is used to identify the port. Ports are used in transmitting messages from one process to another in the following manner. Consider two processes, A and B, that wish to communicate. Process A executes a RECEIVE to port N from port M. Process B executes a SEND to port N from port M. The monitor matches up the port numbers and transfers the message from process B to process A. As soon as the buffer has been fully transmitted out of process B, process B is restarted at the location specified in the SEND operation. As soon as the message is fully received at process A, process A is restarted at the location specified in the RECEIVE operation.[2] How the processes come by the correct port numbers with which to communicate with other processes is discussed later.

Somewhere in the monitor there must be a table of port numbers associated with processes and restart locations. *The table entries are cleared after each SEND/*

RECEIVE match is made. When a SEND is executed, nothing happens until a matching RECEIVE is executed. If a proper RECEIVE is not executed for some time, the SEND is timed out after a while and the SENDing process is notified. If a RECEIVE is executed but the matching SEND does not happen for a long time, the RECEIVE is timed out and the RECEIVing process is notified. A RECEIVE ANY never times out, but may be taken back using a supervisor call.

The mechanism of timing out "unused" table entries is of little fundamental importance—it merely provides a convenient method of garbage-collecting the table. There is no problem if an entry is timed out prematurely, because the process can always reexecute the operation. However, the timeout interval should be long enough so that continual reexecution of an operation will cause little overhead. If the table where the SEND and RECEIVE are matched up ever overflows, a process originating a further SEND or RECEIVE is notified just as if the SEND or RECEIVE timed out.

The *restart location* is an interrupt entrance associated with a pseudo interrupt local to the process executing the operation specifying the restart location. If the process is running when the event causing the pseudo interrupt occurs (for example, a message arrives satisfying a pending RECEIVE), the effect is exactly as if the hardware interrupted the process and transferred control to the restart location. Enough information is saved for the process to continue execution at the point it was interrupted after the interrupt is serviced. If the process is asleep, it is readied and the pseudo interrupt is saved until the process runs again, and the interrupt is then allowed. Any RECEIVE or RECEIVE ANY message port may thus be used to provide process interrupts, event channels, process synchronization, message transfers, etc. The user programs what he wants.

Most time-sharing systems could be made to provide the five operations described above with relative ease, since these are only additional supervisor calls.

Example. Suppose that our model time-sharing system is initialized to have several processes always running. Additionally, these permanent processes have some universally known and permanently assigned ports.[3] Suppose that two of the permanently running processes are the logger-process and the teletype-scanner-process. When the teletype-scanner-process first starts running, it puts itself to sleep awaiting an interrupt from the hardware teletype scanner. The logger-process initially puts itself to sleep awaiting a message from the teletype-scanner-process via well-known permanent SEND and RECEIVE ports. The teletype-scanner-process keeps a table indexed by teletype number, containing in each entry a pair of port numbers to use to send characters from that teletype to a process and a pair of port numbers to use to receive characters for that teletype from a process. If a character arrives (waking up the teletype-scanner-process) and the process does not have any entry for that teletype, it gets a pair of unique numbers from the monitor (via UNIQUE) and sends a message containing this pair of numbers to the logger-process, using the ports for which the logger-process is known to have a RECEIVE pending. The scanner-process also enters the pair of numbers in the teletype table, and sends the character and all future characters from this teletype to the port with the first number from the port with the second number. The scanner-process must also pass a second pair of unique numbers to the logger-process for it to use for teletype output and do a RECEIVE using these port numbers. When the logger-process receives the message from the scanner-process, it may, for instance, start up a copy of what SDS 940 TSS [5] users call the executive[4] and pass the port numbers to this copy of the executive, so that this executive-process can also do its inputs and outputs to the teletype using these ports. If the logger-process wants to get a job number and password from the user, it can temporarily use the port numbers to communicate with the user before it passes them on to the executive. The scanner-process could always use the same port numbers for a particular teletype as long as the numbers were passed on to only one copy of the executive at a time.

It is important to distinguish between the act of passing a port from one process to another and the act of passing a port *number* from one process to another. In the previous example, where characters from a particular teletype are sent either to the logger-process or an executive-process by the teletype-scanner-process, the SEND port always remains in the teletype-scanner-process, while the RECEIVE port moves from the logger-process to the executive-process. On the other hand, the SEND port number is passed between the logger-process and the executive-process to enable the RECEIVE process to do a RECEIVE from the correct SEND port. It is crucial that, once a process transfers a *port* to some other process, the first process no longer uses the port. A mechanism that enforces this, such as the protected object system of [7], could be added. Using this mechanism, a process executing a SEND would need a capability for the SEND port, and only one capability for this SEND port would exist in the system at any given time. Likewise a process executing a RECEIVE would be required to have a capability for the RECEIVE port, and only one capability for this RECEIVE port would exist at a given time. Without such a protection mechanism, a port implicitly moves from one process to another by the processes merely using the port at disjoint times, even if the port's number is never explicitly passed.

[2] Interestingly, there seems no reason to prevent (and some reasons for allowing) a process concurrently having several outstanding RECEIVEs from different ports to a given port. For instance, process A might execute a RECEIVE to port N from port R concurrently with the above RECEIVE to port N from port M.

[3] Or perhaps there is only one permanently known port, which belongs to a directory-process that keeps a table of permanent-process/well-known-port associations.

[4] That program which prints file directories, tells who is on other teletypes, runs subsystems, etc.

Of course, if the protected object system is available to us, there is really no need for two port numbers to be specified before a transmission can take place. The fact that a process knows an existing RECEIVE port number could be considered *prima facie* evidence of the process's right to send to that port. The difference between RECEIVE and RECEIVE ANY ports then depends solely on the number of copies of a particular port number that have been passed out. A system based on this approach would clearly be preferable to the one described here if it was possible to assume that all autonomous time-sharing systems in a network would adopt this protection mechanism. If this assumption cannot be made, it seems more practical to require both port numbers.

Note that in the interprocess communication system (IPC) being described here, when two processes wish to communicate, they set up the connection themselves, and they are free to do it in a mutually convenient manner. For instance, they can exchange port numbers, or one process can pick all the port numbers and instruct the other process which to use, or they can just *know* the correct port numbers to use.[5] However, in a particular implementation of a time-sharing system, the builders of the system might choose to restrict the processes' execution of SENDs and RECEIVEs and might forbid arbitrary passing around of ports and port numbers, requiring instead that the monitor be called (or some other special program) to perform these functions. Generally, well-known permanently-assigned ports are used via RECEIVE ANY. The permanent ports will most often be used for starting processes, and consequently, little data will be sent via them. If a process is running (perhaps asleep) and has a RECEIVE ANY pending, then any process knowing the RECEIVE port number can talk to that process without going through loggers. This is obviously essential within a local time-sharing system and seems very useful in a more general network if the ideal of resource sharing is to be reached. For instance, in a resource sharing network, the programs in the subroutine libraries at all sites might have RECEIVE ANYS always pending over permanently assigned ports with well-known port numbers. Thus, to use a particular network resource such as a matrix inversion subroutine at a site with special matrix manipulation hardware, a process running anywhere in the network can send a message to the matrix inversion subroutine containing the matrix to be inverted and the port numbers to be used for returning the results.

Control of data flow is provided in this IPC by the simple method of never starting data transmission resultant from a SEND from one process until a RECEIVE is executed by the receiver. Of course, interprocess messages may also be sent back and forth suggesting that a process stop sending or that space be allocated.

An additional example demonstrates the use of the FORTRAN compiler. We have already explained how a user sits down at his teletype and gets connected to an executive. We go on from there. The user is typing in and out of the executive which is doing SENDs and RECEIVES. Eventually the user types RUN FORTRAN, and the executive asks the monitor to start up a copy of the FORTRAN compiler and passes to FORTRAN as start-up parameters the port numbers the executive was using to talk to the teletype. (Thus, at least conceptually, FORTRAN is passed a port at which to RECEIVE characters from the teletype and a port from which to SEND characters to the teletype.) FORTRAN is, of course, expecting these parameters and does SENDs and RECEIVES via the indicated ports to discover from the user what input and output files the user wants to use. FORTRAN types INPUT FILE? to the user, who responds F001. FORTRAN then sends a message to the file-system-process, which is asleep waiting for something to do. The message is sent via well-known ports, and it asks the file system to open F001 for input. The message also contains a pair of port numbers that the file-system-process can use to send its reply. The file-system looks up F001, opens it for input, makes some entries in its open file tables, and sends back to FORTRAN a message containing the port numbers that FORTRAN can use to read the file. The same procedure is followed for the output file. When the compilation is complete, FORTRAN returns the teletype port numbers (and the ports) back to the executive that has been asleep waiting for a message from FORTRAN and then halts itself. With nothing else to do, the file-system-process goes back to sleep.

3. A System for Interprocess Communication Between Remote Processes

The IPC described in the previous section easily generalizes to allow interprocess communication between processes at geographically different locations as, for example, within a computer network.

Consider first a simple configuration of processes distributed around the points of a star. At each point of the star there is an autonomous operating system.[6] A rather large, smart computer system, called the Network Controller, exists at the center of the star. No processes can run in this center system, but rather it should be thought of as an extension of the monitor of each of the operating systems in the network.

If the Network Controller is able to perform the operations SEND, RECEIVE, RECEIVE ANY, and UNIQUE, and if all of the monitors in all of the operating systems in the network do not perform these operations themselves but rather ask the Network Controller to perform

[5] Called ipc-setup in [10].

[6] "Operating system" rather than "time-sharing system" is used in this section to point up the fact that the autonomous systems at the network nodes may be either full-blown time-sharing systems in their own right, an individual process in a larger geographically distributed time-sharing system, or merely autonomous sites wishing to communicate.

these operations for them, then the problem of interprocess communication between remote processes is solved. No further changes are necessary since the Network Controller can keep track of which RECEIVES have been executed and which SENDS have been executed and match them up just as the monitor did in the model time-sharing system. A network-wide port numbering scheme is also possible with the Network Controller knowing where (i.e. at which site) a particular port is at a particular time.

Next, consider a more complex network in which there is no common center point, making it necessary to distribute the functions performed by the Network Controller among the network nodes. In the rest of this section it will be shown that the set of functions performed by the star Network Controller can be replicated at each of the network sites so that efficient and convenient general interprocess communication between remote processes is still possible. We call all of these network controllers taken together a *distributed Network Controller*.

Some changes must be made to each of the three SEND/RECEIVE operations described above to adapt them for use in a distributed Network Controller. To RECEIVE is added a parameter specifying a site to which the RECEIVE is to be sent. To SEND messages is added a site to which the SEND may be sent, although this is normally the local site. Both RECEIVE and RECEIVE ANY have added the provision for obtaining the source site of any received message. Thus when a RECEIVE is executed, the RECEIVE is sent to the site specified, possibly a remote site. At some (other) time a SEND appears at the same site, normally the local site of the process executing the SEND. (That is, the RECEIVE goes to the SEND site; the SEND does not go anywhere.) At this site, called the *rendezvous site*, the RECEIVE is matched with the proper SEND, and the message transmission is allowed to take place from the SEND site to the site from where the RECEIVE came.

A RECEIVE ANY never leaves its originating site; however, since it must be possible to send a message to a RECEIVE ANY port and not have the message blocked waiting for a RECEIVE at the sending site, we must introduce a new operation which will be called FORCE SEND. The FORCE SEND operation has the same parameters as SEND (a port to send the message to—the RECEIVE port; the port the message is being sent from—the SEND port; a specification of the buffer containing the message to be sent; the restart location; and the site to which to send the message). The message resultant from a FORCE SEND is always sent immediately to the rendezvous site where it is discarded if a proper RECEIVE ANY is not found. An error message is not returned, and acknowledgment, if any, is up to the processes. It is possible to construct a system so that the SEND/RECEIVE rendezvous takes place at the RECEIVE site and eliminates the FORCE SEND operation, but the ability to block a normal SEND transmission at the source site is probably worth the added complexity.

At each site a rendezvous table is kept. This table contains an entry for each unmatched SEND or RECEIVE received at that site and also an entry for all RECEIVE ANYS given at that site. A matching SEND/RECEIVE pair is cleared from the table as soon as the match takes place. As in the similar table kept in the model time-sharing system, SEND and RECEIVE entries are timed out if unmatched for too long, and the originator is notified. RECEIVE ANY entries are cleared from the table when a fulfilling message arrives.

The final change necessary is to give each site a portion of the unique numbers to distribute via its UNIQUE operation. This topic will be discussed further below.

All interprocess communication at a site, to both local and remote processes, should be done via the local portion of the distributed Network Controller. The case is less clear in a star network with a central Network Controller where there is a trade-off between efficiency if local interprocess communication does not have to go through the central Network Controller and increased versatility if it does. The correct solution might be to distribute the Network Controller even for star networks.

To make it clear to the reader how the distributed Network Controller works, an example follows. The details of what process picks port numbers, etc., are only exemplary and are not a standard specified as part of the IPC.

Suppose that, for two sites in the network, K and L, process A at site K wishes to communicate with process B at site L. Process B has a RECEIVE ANY pending at port M.

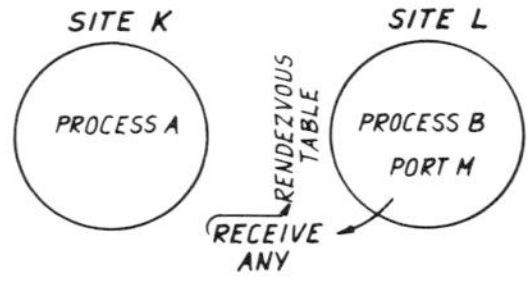

Process A, fortunately, knows of the existence of port M at site L and sends a message using the FORCE SEND operation from port N to port M. The message contains two port numbers and instructions for process B to SEND messages for process A to port P from port Q. Site K's site number is appended to this message along with the message's SEND port, N.

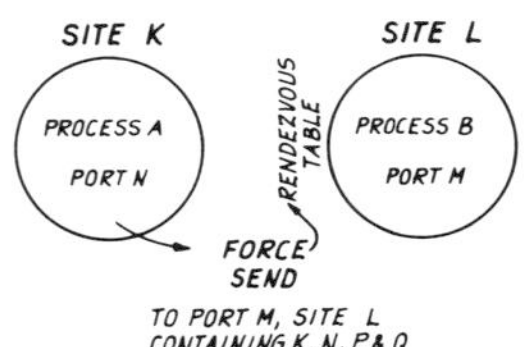

Process A now executes a RECEIVE at port P from port Q. Process A specifies the rendezvous site to be site L.

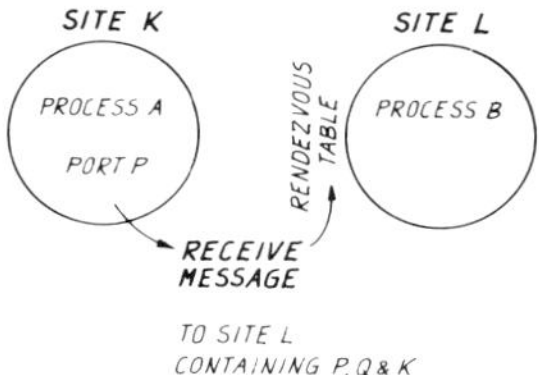

A RECEIVE message is sent from site K to site L and is entered in the rendezvous table at site L. At some other time, process B executes a SEND to port P from port Q specifying site L as the rendezvous site.

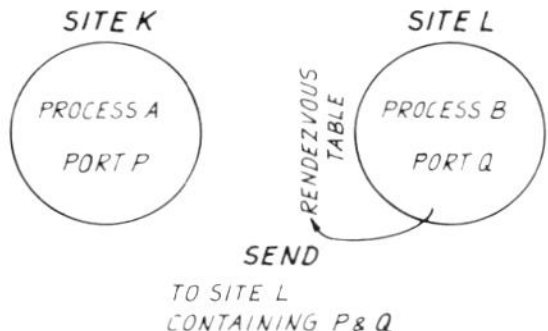

A rendezvous is made, the rendezvous table entry is cleared, and the transmission to port P at site K takes place. The SEND site number (and conceivably the SEND port number) is appended to the messages of the transmission for the edification of the receiving process.

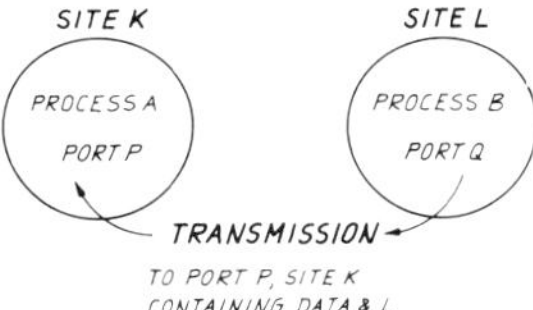

Process B may simultaneously wish to execute a RECEIVE from port N at port M.

Note that there is only one important control message in this system which moves between sites—the type of message that is called a Host/Host protocol message in [2]. This control message is the RECEIVE message. There are two other possible intersite control messages: (1) a message to the originating site when a RECEIVE or SEND is timed out, and (2) the SEND message in the rare case which we will soon see when the rendezvous site is not the SEND site. There must also be a standard format for messages between ports, for example, the following:

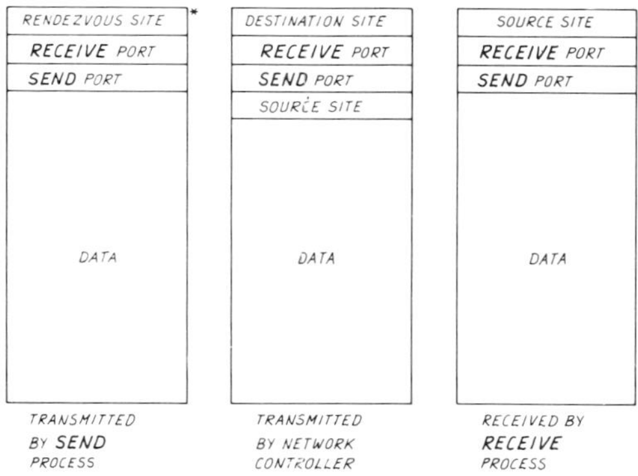

In the model time-sharing system it was possible to pass a port from process to process. This is still possible with a distributed Network Controller.

Remember, that for a message to be sent from one process to another, a SEND and a matching RECEIVE must rendezvous. Both processes keep track of where they think the rendezvous site is and supply this site as a parameter of appropriate operations. The RECEIVE process thinks it is the SEND site and the SEND process normally thinks it is the SEND site also. Since once a SEND and a RECEIVE rendezvous the transmission is sent to the source of the RECEIVE and the entry in the rendezvous table is cleared and must be set up again for each further transmission, it is easy for a RECEIVE port to be moved. If a process sends both the port numbers and the rendezvous site number to a new process at some other site which executes a RECEIVE using these same old port numbers and rendezvous site specification, the SENDer never knows the RECEIVEr has moved.

It is slightly harder for a SEND port to be moved. However, if it is, it can be done as follows: Suppose port Q from the preceding example moves from process B at site L to process C at site R. Process A will still think the rendezvous site is site L, and a RECEIVE message will still be sent there.

413

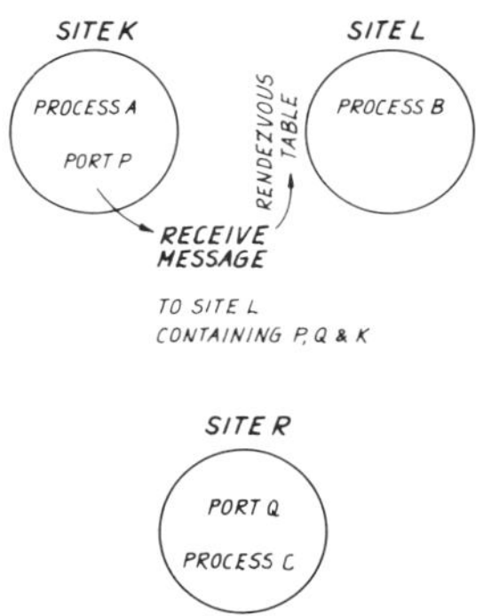

Process C specifies the old rendezvous site L, with the *first* SEND from the new site, R.

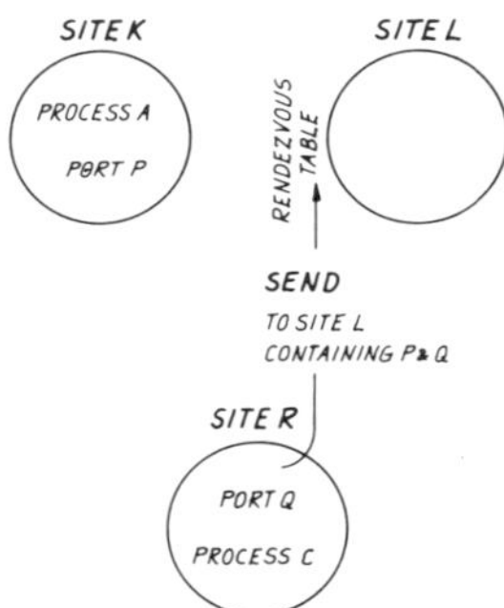

When the rendezvous is made at site L, the entry in the rendezvous table is cleared and both the SEND and RECEIVE messages are sent to the source of the SEND message, just as if they had been destined to go there all along.

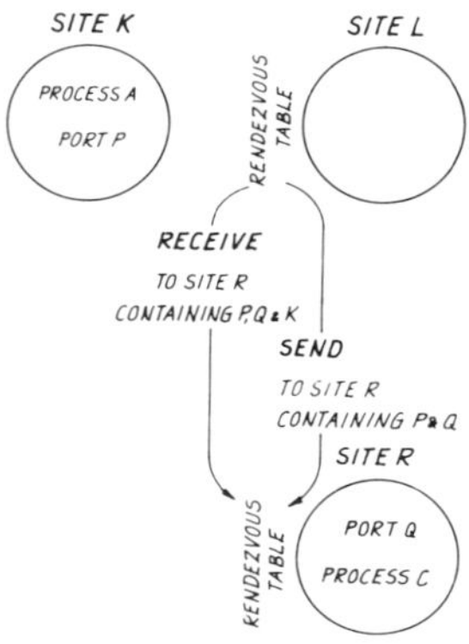

After the SEND and RECEIVE meet again at the new rendezvous site, R, transmission may continue as if the port had never moved.

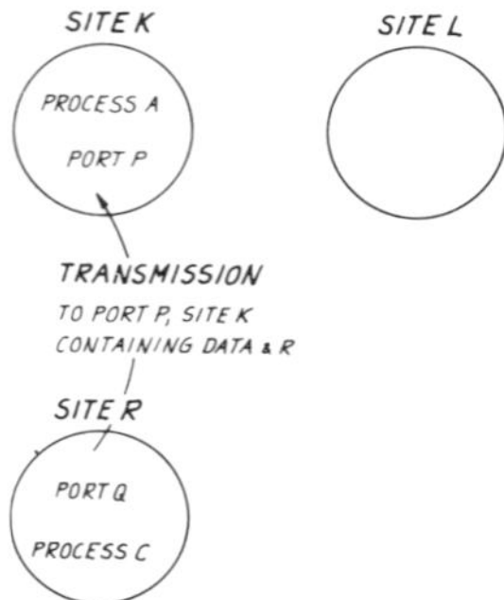

Since all transmissions contain the source site number, further RECEIVES will be sent to the new rendezvous site. It is possible to discover that this special manipulation must take place because a SEND message is received at a site that did not originate the SEND message. Note that the SEND port and the RECEIVE port can move concurrently.

Of course, all of this could also have been done if the processes had sent messages back and forth announcing any potential moves and the new site numbers.

A problem that may have occurred to the reader is how the SEND and RECEIVE buffers get matched for size. The easiest solution would be to require that all buffers have a common size, but this is unacceptable since it does not easily extend to a situation where processes in autonomous operating systems are attempting to communicate.

A second solution having great appeal due to its simplicity is for the processes to pass messages specifying buffer sizes. If this solution is adopted, excessive data sent from the SEND process and unable to fit into the RECEIVE buffer is discarded and the RECEIVE process notified.

A third solution would be for the RECEIVE buffer size to be passed to the SEND site with the RECEIVE message and to notify the SEND process when too much data is sent or even to pass the RECEIVE buffer size on to the SEND process. This last method would also permit the Network Controller at the SEND site to make two or more SENDS out of one, if that were necessary to match a small RECEIVE buffer size.

The maintenance of unique numbers is also a problem when the processes are geographically distributed. Of the three solutions to this problem presented here, the first is for the autonomous operating systems to ask the Network Controller for the unique numbers originally and then guarantee the integrity of any unique numbers currently owned by local processes and programs using whatever means are at the operating system's disposal. In this case, the Network Controller would provide a method for a unique number to be sent from one site to another and would vouch for the number's identity at the new site.

The second method is simply to give the unique numbers to the processes that are using them, depending on the nonmalicious behavior of the processes to preserve the unique numbers, or if an accident should happen, the *two* passwords (SEND and RECEIVE port numbers) that are required to initiate a transmission. If the unique numbers are given out in a nonsequential manner and are reasonably long (say 32 bits), there is little danger.

In the final method, a user identification is included in the port numbers, and the individual operating systems guarantee the integrity of these identification bits. Thus a process, while not able to be sure that the correct port is transmitting to him, can be sure that some port of the correct user is transmitting.

A third difficult problem arises when remote processes wish to communicate—the problem of maintaining high bandwidth connections between the remote processes. The solution to this problem lies in allowing the processes considerable information about the state of an ongoing transmission.

First, we examine a SEND process in detail. When a process executes a SEND, the local portion of the Network Controller passes the SEND on to the rendezvous site, normally the local site. When a RECEIVE arrives matching a pending SEND, the Network Controller notifies the SEND process by causing an interrupt to the specified restart location. Simultaneously, the Network Controller starts shipping the SEND buffer to the RECEIVE site. When transmission is complete, a flag is set which the SEND process can test. While a transmission is taking place, the process may ask the Network Controller to perform other operations, including other SENDS. A second SEND over a pair of ports already in the act of transmission is noted, and the SEND becomes active as soon as the first transmission is complete. A third identical SEND results in an error message to the SENDing process.

Next, we examine a RECEIVE process in detail. When a process executes a RECEIVE, the RECEIVE is sent to the rendezvous site. When data resultant from this RECEIVE starts to arrive at the RECEIVE site, the RECEIVE process is notified via an interrupt to the specified restart location. When the transmission is complete, a flag is set which the RECEIVE process can test. A second RECEIVE over the same port pair is allowed. A third results in an error message to the RECEIVE process. Thus there is sufficient machinery to allow a pair of processes always to have both a transmission in progress and the next one pending. Therefore, no efficiency is lost. On the other hand, each transmission must be preceded by a RECEIVE into a specified buffer, thus continuing to provide control of data flow.

4. A Hypothetical Application

Only one resource sharing computer network currently exists, the ARPA Computer Network. This section is a discussion of the hypothetical application of the system described in this paper to the ARPA Network [2, 4, 9].

The ARPA Network currently incorporates over 20 sites spread across the United States. Each site consists of one to three (potentially four) independent computer systems called Hosts and one communications computer system called an IMP. All of the Hosts at a site are directly connected to the IMP. The IMPs themselves are connected together by 50-kilobit phone lines (much higher rate lines are a potential), although each IMP is connected to only one to five other IMPs. The IMPS provide a communications subnet through which the Hosts communicate. Data is sent through the communications subnet in messages less than (about) 8,100 bits long. When a message is received by the IMP at the destination site, that IMP sends an acknowledgment, called a RFNM, (Request for Next Message), to the source site. To allow more than one "logical transmission" to be in progress at a time between a particular pair of destination and source Hosts, each message is given a *link number*, and all messages in one logical transmission are sent with the same link number.

A system for interprocess communication for the ARPA Network (let us call this IPC for ARPA) has already been designed by the ARPA Network Working Group, under the chairmanship of S. Crocker of ARPA, and this design is currently being refined and implemented.[7] In contrast to the IPC of this paper, in IPC for ARPA, before two processes can communicate, a *connection* must be set up between a send socket in one process's monitor and a receive socket in the other process's monitor (a *socket* is an element in a network-wide name space into which each monitor maps its own internal port name space). For two processes to make connection, each process makes a connection request to its own monitor. The two monitors then exchange these requests via messages over the *control link*, a special link between each pair of Hosts which is always reserved for control messages. If both monitors are in agreement, the connection is established and a link is assigned for use by the new connection. This new connection exists until it is explicitly terminated, again using intermonitor control messages over the control link. During the "life" of the connection, many messages may be sent from the port at one end to the port at the other, and all these messages are sent over the link assigned to the connection. However, since the connection exists over a series of many messages, a mechanism is provided to stop the flow of messages when the receiving process's Host is overloaded. This mechanism is a system whereby the sender is notified of the receiver's buffering capacity as part of the connection setup, and the sender stops transmitting when it has transmitted enough messages to exhaust the capacity, unless a control message carrying notification of replenishment of the buffering capacity at the receiver arrives first.

The IPC for ARPA comes in several amost distinct pieces: The Host/IMP protocol, the IMP/IMP protocol, and the Host/Host protocol. The IMPs have sole responsibility for correctly transmitting bits from one site to another; the Hosts have sole responsibility for making interprocess connections; both the Host and IMP are concerned and take a little responsibility for flow control and message sequencing.

[7] This work is documented in a series of working group notes which, with the exception of [2], have unfortunately not found their way into the open literature.

[8] This also allows messages to be completely thrown away by the IMP subnet if that should ever be useful.

[9] This is in sharp contrast to IPC for ARPA which seems to utilize software "line switching" on top of a network designed in large part to demonstrate the utility of "message switching."

Application of the IPC described in this paper to the ARPA network suggests a different allocation of responsibility: The IMP still continues to move bits from one site to another correctly, but the Network Controller also resides in the IMP (whereas in the IPC for ARPA it resides in the Host), and flow control is completely in the hands of the processes running in the Hosts, although using the mechanisms provided by the Network Controllers in the IMPS.

The SEND, RECEIVE, FORCE SEND, RECEIVE ANY, and UNIQUE operations are implemented in the IMPS and are available to each IMP's Host. The IMPS also maintain the rendezvous tables, including moving of SEND ports when necessary. Putting these operations in the IMP requires the Host/Host protocol program to be written only once, rather than many times as is currently being done in the ARPA Network—a significant saving notwithstanding the still necessary Host/IMP software interface. It is the author's belief that the existing IMPS could probably be made to include the Network Controller with the addition of 4K of core.

It is perhaps useful to step through the five operations again.

SEND. The Host gives the IMP a SEND port number, a RECEIVE port number, the rendezvous site, and a buffer specification (e.g. start and end, or beginning and length). The SEND is sent to the rendezvous site IMP, normally the local IMP. When a matching RECEIVE arrives at the local IMP, the Host is notified of the RECEIVE port of the just-arrived message. This port number is sufficient to identify the SENDing process, although a given operating system may have to keep internal tables mapping this port number into a useful internal process identifier.

Simultaneously, the IMP begins to ask the Host for specific pieces of the SEND buffer and to send these pieces as network messages to the destination site. If a RFNM is not received for too long, implying a network message has been lost in the network, the Host is asked for the same data again and it is retransmitted.[8] Except for the last piece of a buffer, the IMP requests pieces from the Host which are common multiples of the word size of the source Host, IMP, and destination Host. This avoids mid-transmission word alignment problems.

RECEIVE. The Host gives the IMP a SEND port, a RECEIVE port, a rendezvous site, and a buffer descriptor. The RECEIVE message is sent to the rendezvous site. As the network messages making up a transmission arrive for the RECEIVE port, they are passed to the Host along with the RECEIVE port number (and perhaps the SEND port number), and (using the buffer descriptor) an indication to the Host where to put this data in its input buffer. When the last network message of the SEND buffer is passed into the Host, it is marked accordingly and the Host can then detect this. (It is conceivable that the RECEIVE message could also allocate a piece of network bandwidth while making its network traverse to the rendezvous site.)

RECEIVE ANY. The Host gives the IMP a RECEIVE port and a buffer descriptor. This works the same as RECEIVE but assumes the local site to be the rendezvous site.

FORCE SEND. The Host gives the IMP RECEIVE and SEND ports, the destination site, and a buffer descriptor. The IMP requests and transmits the buffer as fast as possible. A FORCE SEND for a nonexistent port is discarded at the destination site.

In the ARPA Network, the Hosts are required by the IMPS to physically break their transmissions into messages, and successive messages of a single transmission must be delayed until the RFNM is received for the previous message. In the system described here, since RFNMS are tied to the transmission of a particular piece of buffer and since the Hosts allow the IMPS to reassemble buffers in the Hosts by the IMP telling the Host where to put each buffer piece, pieces of a single buffer can be transmitted in parallel network messages and several RFNMS can be outstanding simultaneously. This enables the Hosts to deal with transmissions of more natural sizes and higher bandwidth for a single transmission.

5. Conclusion

Since the system described in this paper has not been implemented, there are no clearly demonstrable conclusions and no performance reports that can be presented. Instead, we note what the author regards as the two significant features of the IPC system.

The first significant feature of this IPC is that connections are not maintained over a sequence of messages but instead are set up and expire on a message-by-message basis.[9] There are several advantages to this approach:

1. There is no need for a large number of intermonitor control messages to set up and break connections and consequently no need for a special "out of band" control channel.
2. The RECEIVing process has the opportunity after *each* message to stop the flow of messages. Further, since the RECEIVE process must provide a buffer, the monitor is relieved of the task of providing an indefinitely large buffering capacity.
3. Because connections exist only fleetingly, relatively complex operations such as moving a port are easy.
4. Errors have a minimal effect. For instance, if a

RECEIVE message is lost, the RECEIVing monitor will time it out and the process can do another RECEIVE just as is normally done when the SENDER refuses to SEND in response to a RECEIVE.

5. This IPC is suitable for implementation on small computers as well as large computers due to its simplicity and the nonnecessity for a large buffering capacity in the monitor.

There are also some disadvantages to this IPC; for instance:

1. There is a large amount of overhead associated with each message (e.g. port numbers).
2. To match the speed of a system based on prolonged connections, (e.g. IPC for ARPA) a significant amount of complexity had to be introduced.

The second significant feature of this IPC is the emphasis upon communication between processes and therefore the resources themselves, rather than between monitors. In the model time-sharing system described in Section 2 all possible functions (resources) were given to processes, and in Section 3 the processes (resources) control their own interprocess communication. While this seems to the author to be the proper emphasis if one's goal is flexible resource sharing, it does introduce new problems. For instance, many readers of early versions of this paper have asked, "How does a user who uses a remote process without going through the remote system's logger get billed?" There are ad hoc answers to this and probably to other infirmities in the IPC. (One answer to this particular question is that each process can send off a message to the accounting process whenever it finds itself being used.) However, we conclude with a more general *assertion* about the solutions to such questions.

Elegant solutions to many problems that will arise as computer networks are constructed and their effective utilization attempted will only be found if the computer networks are treated as single entities rather than as associations of autonomous systems. Far from allowing basically incompatible operating systems to communicate, an effective computer network will prove to require similar operating systems throughout the network, albeit running on machines of varying manufacture. General acceptance of this "fact" and its ramifications will bring closer the day when computer networks and resource sharing live up to their potential.

Acknowledgments. The author drew on many sources while developing the system suggested in this paper. Particularly influential were: (1) an early sketch of a Host protocol for the ARPA Network by S. Crocker of ARPA and W. Crowther of Bolt Beranek and Newman Inc. (BBN); (2) Ackerman and Plummer's paper [1] on the MIT PDP-1 time-sharing system; and (3) discussions with W. Crowther and R. Kahn of BBN about Host protocol, flow control, and message routing for the ARPA Network. B. Cosell of BBN and the referees made many incisive comments on the presentation of the paper.

Received August 1970; revised March 1971

References

1. Ackerman, W., and Plummer, W. An implementation of a multi-processing computer system. Proc. ACM Symp. on Operating System Principles, Gatlinsburg, Tenn., Oct. 1–4, 1967.
2. Carr, C., Crocker, S., and Cerf, V. Host/Host communication protocol in the ARPA network. Proc. AFIPS 1970 SJCC., Vol. 36, AFIPS Press, Montvale, N.J., pp. 589–597.
3. Dennis, J., and VanHorn, E. Programming semantics for multiprogrammed computations. *Comm. ACM 9*, 3 (Mar. 1966), 143–155.
4. Heart, F., Kahn, R., Ornstein, S., Crowther, W., and Walden, D. The interface message processor for the ARPA computer network. Proc., AFIPS 1970 SJCC, Vol. 36, AFIPS Press, Montvale, N.J. pp. 551–567.
5. Lampson, B. SDS 940 lectures, circulated informally.
6. Lampson, B. An overview of the CAL time-sharing system. Computer Center, U. of California, Berkeley.
7. Lampson, B. Dynamic protection structures. Proc. AFIPS 1969 FJCC, Vol. 35, AFIPS Press, Montvale, N.J., pp. 27–38.
8. Roberts, L. The ARPA Computer Network. Networks of Computers Symposium NOC-68. Proc. of Invitational Workshop, Ft. Meade, Md., National Security Agency, Sept. 1969.
9. Roberts, L., and Wessler, B. Computer network development to achieve resource sharing. Proc. AFIPS 1970 SJCC, Vol. 36, AFIPS Press, Montvale, N.J., pp. 543–549.
10. Spier, M., and Organick, E. The MULTICS interprocess communication facility. Proc. ACM Second Symp. on Operating Systems Principles, Princeton U., Oct. 20–22, 1969.

Function-oriented protocols for the ARPA Computer Network

by STEPHEN D. CROCKER

Advanced Research Projects Agency
Arlington, Virginia

JOHN F. HEAFNER

The RAND Corporation
Santa Mon ca, California

ROBERT M. METCALFE

Massachusetts Institute of Technology
Cambridge, Massachusetts

and

JONATHAN B. POSTEL

University of California
Los Angeles, California

INTRODUCTION

Much has been said about the mechanics of the ARPA Computer Network (ARPANET) and especially about the organization of its communications subnet.[1,2,3,4,5] Until recently the main effort has gone into the implementation of an ARPANET user-level communications interface. Operating just above the communications subnet in ARPANET HOST Computers, this ARPANET interface is intended to serve as a foundation for the organization of function-oriented communications.[6,7] See Figures 1 and 2 for our view of a computer system and the scheme for user-level process-to-process communications. It is now appropriate to review the development of protocols which have been constructed to promote particular substantive uses of the ARPANET, namely function-oriented protocols.

418

We should begin this brief examination by stating what we mean by the word "protocol" and how protocols fit in the plan for useful work on the ARPANET. When we have two processes facing each other across some communication link, the protocol is the set of their agreements on the format and relative timing of messages to be exchanged. When we speak of a protocol, there is usually an important goal to be fulfilled. Although any set of agreements between cooperating (i.e., communicating) processes is a protocol, the protocols of interest are those which are constructed for general application by a large population of processes in solving a large class of problems.

In the understanding and generation of protocols there are two kinds of distinctions made. Protocols in the ARPANET are *layered* and we speak of high or low level protocols. High level protocols are those most closely matched to functions and low level protocols deal with communications mechanics. The lowest level software protocols in the ARPANET involve reliable message exchange between ARPANET Interface Message Processors (IMPs).[2,5] A high level protocol is one with primitives closely related to a substantive use. At the lowest levels the contents of messages are unspecified. At higher levels, more and more is stated about the meaning of message contents and timing. The layers of protocol are shown in Figure 3.

A second way of structuring sets of protocols and their design is bound up in the word *factoring*. At any level of protocol are sets of format and timing rules associated with particular groupings of agreements. In the IMPs we find certain protocols pertaining to error handling, while others to flow control, and still others to message routing. At the ARPANET's user-level communications interface there are, among others, separable protocols associated with establishing connections and logical data blocking. These protocols do not nest, but join as modules at the same level.

Before moving on to consider the higher level function-oriented protocols, let us first make a few statements about underlying protocols. There are three lower level software protocols which nest in support of the user-level communications interface for the ARPANET. The lowest of these is the IMP-IMP protocol which provides for reliable communication among IMPs. This protocol handles transmission-error detection and correction, flow control to avoid message congestion, and routing. At the next higher level is the IMP-HOST protocol which provides for the passage of messages between HOSTs and IMPs in such a way as to create virtual communication paths between HOSTs. With IMP-HOST protocol, a HOST has operating rules which permit it to send messages to specified HOSTs on the ARPANET and to be informed of the dispensation of those messages. In particular, the IMP-HOST protocol constrains HOSTs in their transmissions so that they can make good use of available

Reprinted from AFIPS Proceedings
SJCC 1972 © AFIPS Press, Montvale NJ 07645

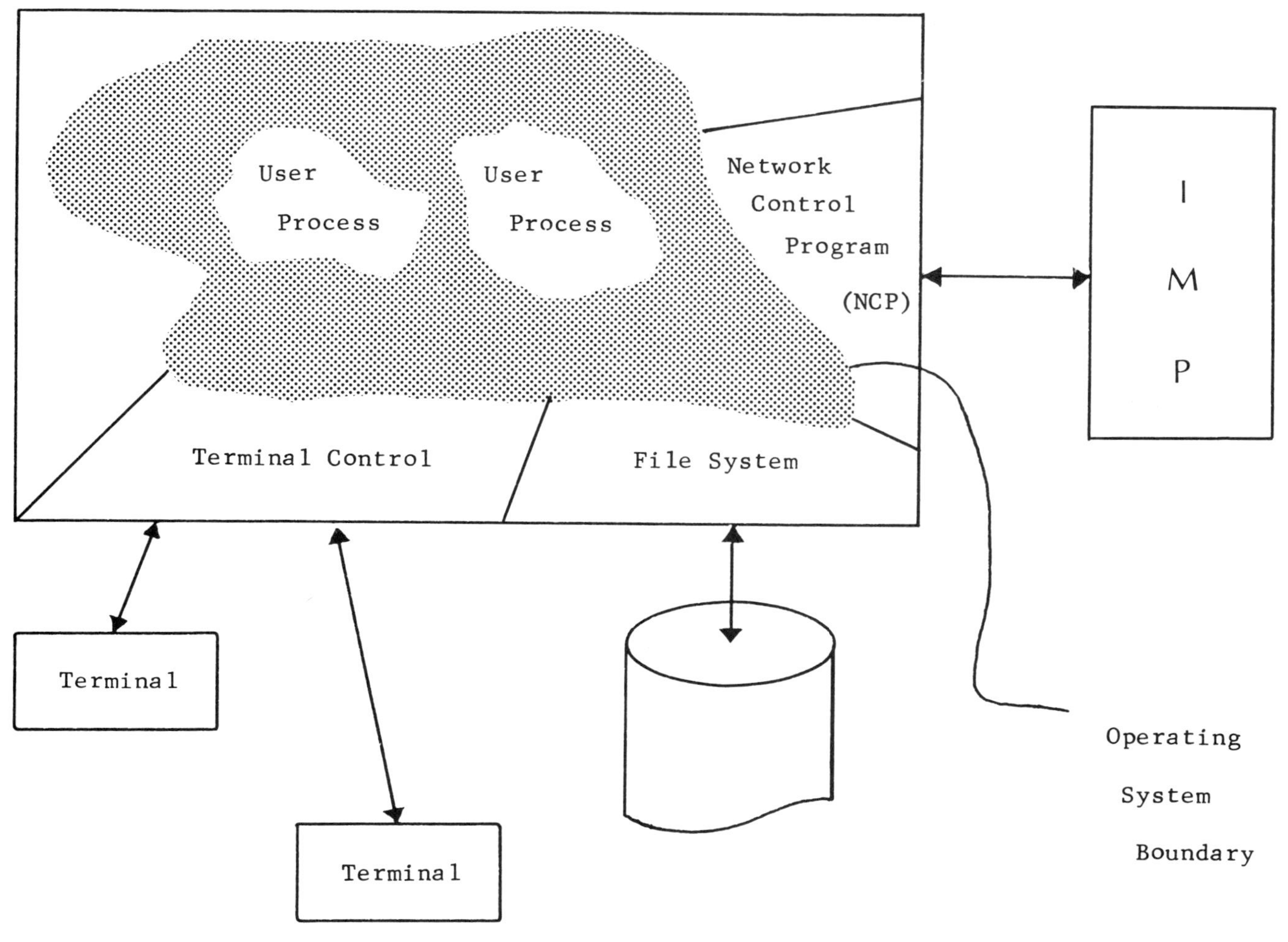

419

Figure 1—Our view of a computer system

communications capacity without denying such availability to other HOSTs.

The HOST-HOST protocol, finally, is the set of rules whereby HOSTs construct and maintain communication between processes (user jobs) running on remote computers. One process requiring communications with another on some remote computer system makes requests on its local supervisor to act on its behalf in establishing and maintaining those communications under HOST-HOST protocol.

In constructing these low levels of protocol it was the intention to provide user processes with a general set of useful communication primitives to isolate them from many of the details of operating systems and communications. At this user-level interface function-oriented protocols join as an open-ended collection of modules to make use of ARPANET capabilities.

The communications environment facing the designers of function-oriented protocols in the ARPANET is essentially that of a system of one-way byte-oriented connections. Technically speaking, a "connection" is a pair: a "send socket" at one end and a "receive socket" at the other. Primitives provided at the user-level interface include:

1. Initiate connection (local socket, foreign socket),
2. Wait for connection (local socket),
3. Send, Receive (local socket, data),
4. Close (local socket),
5. Send interrupt signal (local socket).

Processes in this virtual process network can create connections and transmit bytes. Connections are subject to HOST-HOST flow control and the vagaries of timing in a widely distributed computing environment, but care has been taken to give user processes control over their communications so as to make full use of network parallelism and redundancy. The kind of agreements which must be made in the creation of

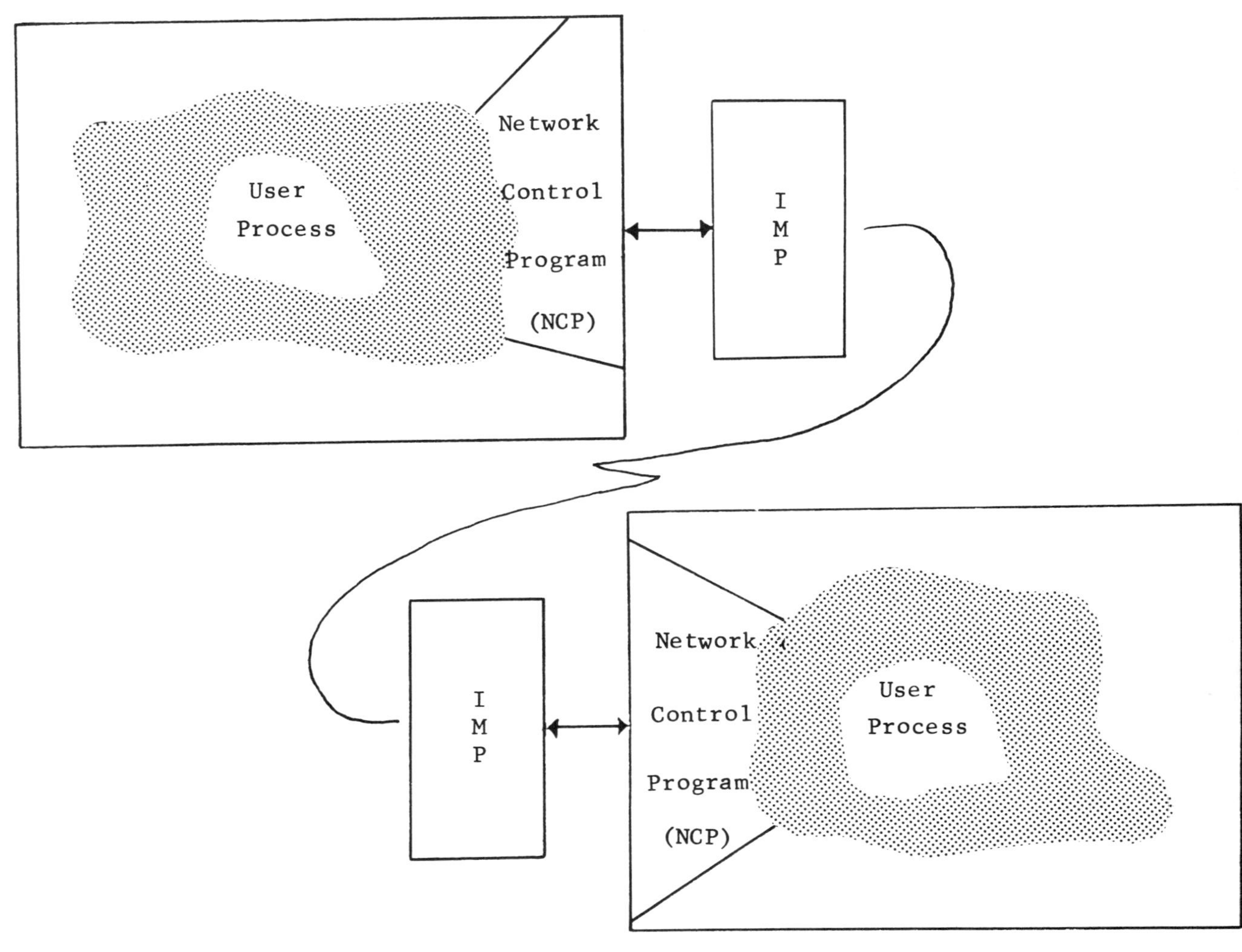

Figure 2—Two communicating processes

function-oriented protocols relate to rules for establishing connections, to the timing rules which govern transmission sequences, and to the content of the byte-streams themselves.

USE OF REMOTE INTERACTIVE SYSTEMS

The application which currently dominates ARPANET activity is the remote use of interactive systems. A Telecommunications Network (TELNET) protocol is followed by processes cooperating to support this application.[8] A user at a terminal, connected to his local HOST, controls a process in a remote HOST as if he were a local user of the remote HOST. His local HOST copies characters between his terminal and TELNET connections over the ARPANET. We refer to the HOST where the user sits as the *using HOST*, and to the remote HOST as the *serving HOST*. See Figure 4.

At the using HOST, the user must be able to perform the following functions through his TELNET user process ("user-TELNET"):

1. Initiate a pair of connections to a serving HOST,
2. Send characters to the serving HOST,
3. Receive characters from the serving HOST,
4. Send a HOST-HOST interrupt signal,
5. Terminate connections.

The user-TELNET needs to be able to distinguish between (1) commands to be acted on locally and (2) input intended for the serving HOST. An escape character is reserved to mark local commands. Conventions for the ARPANET Terminal IMP (TIP) user-TELNET are typical.[9]

In most using HOSTs, the above functions are provided by a user-TELNET which is a *user-level program*. A minimal user-TELNET need only implement the above functions, but several additional support func-

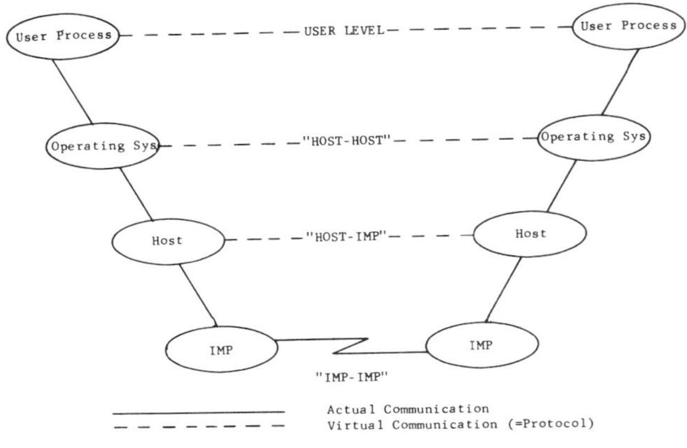

Figure 3—The layers of protocol

tions are often provided (e.g., saving a transcript of a session in a local file, sending a file in place of user-typed input, reporting whether various HOSTs are or have been up).

In the serving HOST it is desirable that a process controlled over the ARPANET behave as it would if controlled locally. The cleanest way to achieve this goal is to generalize the terminal control portion (TCP) of the operating system to accept ARPANET terminal interaction. It is unpleasant to modify any portion of a working computer system and modification could be avoided if it were possible to use a non-supervisor process (e.g., "server-TELNET" or "LOGGER") to perform the job creation, login, terminal input-output, interrupt, and logout functions in exactly the same way

USING HOST

Telnet

NCP

I M P

Terminal Control

Terminal

I M P

NCP

User Process

Terminal Control

SERVING HOST

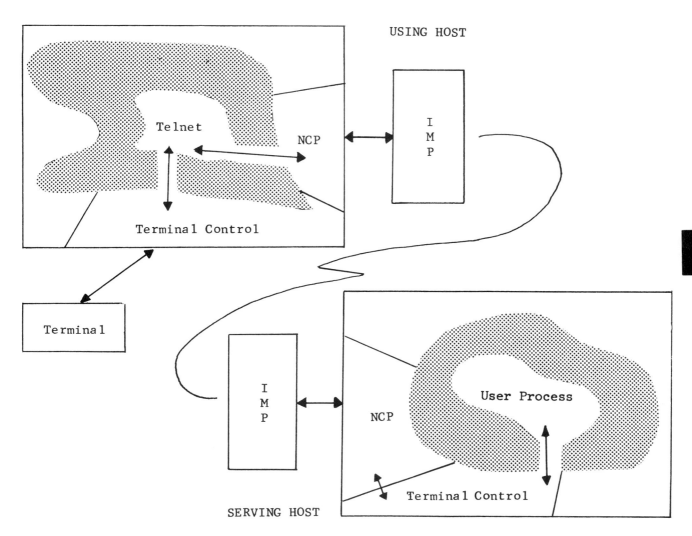

Figure 4—Data flow for remote interactive use

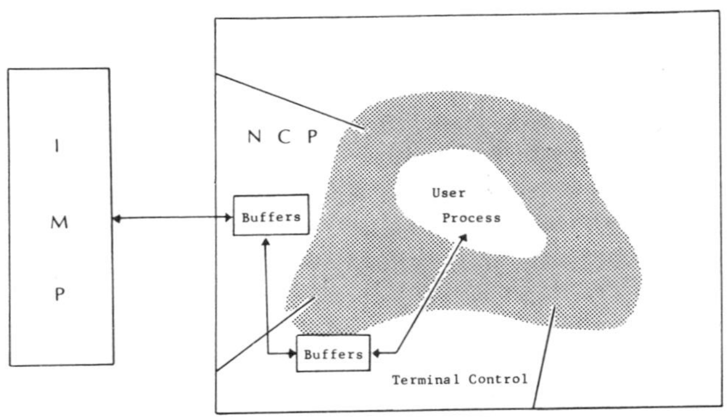

Figure 5—Data flow scheme for server

as a direct console user. Prior to the development of the ARPANET, no operating system provided these functions to non-supervisor processes in anywhere near the required completeness. Some systems have since been modified to support this generalized job control scheme. See Figures 5 and 6.

Efforts to standardize communications in the TELNET protocol focused on four issues: character set, echoing, establishing connections, and attention handling.

The chosen character set is 7-bit ASCII in 8-bit fields with the high-order bit off. Codes with the high-order bit on are reserved for TELNET control functions. Two such TELNET control function codes are the "long-space" which stands for the 200 millisecond space generated by the teletype BREAK button, and the synchronization character (SYNCH) discussed below in conjunction with the purpose of the TELNET interrupt signal.

Much controversy existed regarding echoing. The basic problem is that some systems expect to echo, while some terminals always echo locally. A set of conventions and signals was developed to control which side of a TELNET connection should echo. In practice, those systems which echo have been modified to include provision for locally echoing terminals. This is a non-trivial change affecting many parts of a serving HOST. For example, normally echoing server HOSTs do not echo passwords so as to help maintain their security. Terminals which echo locally defeat this strategy, how-

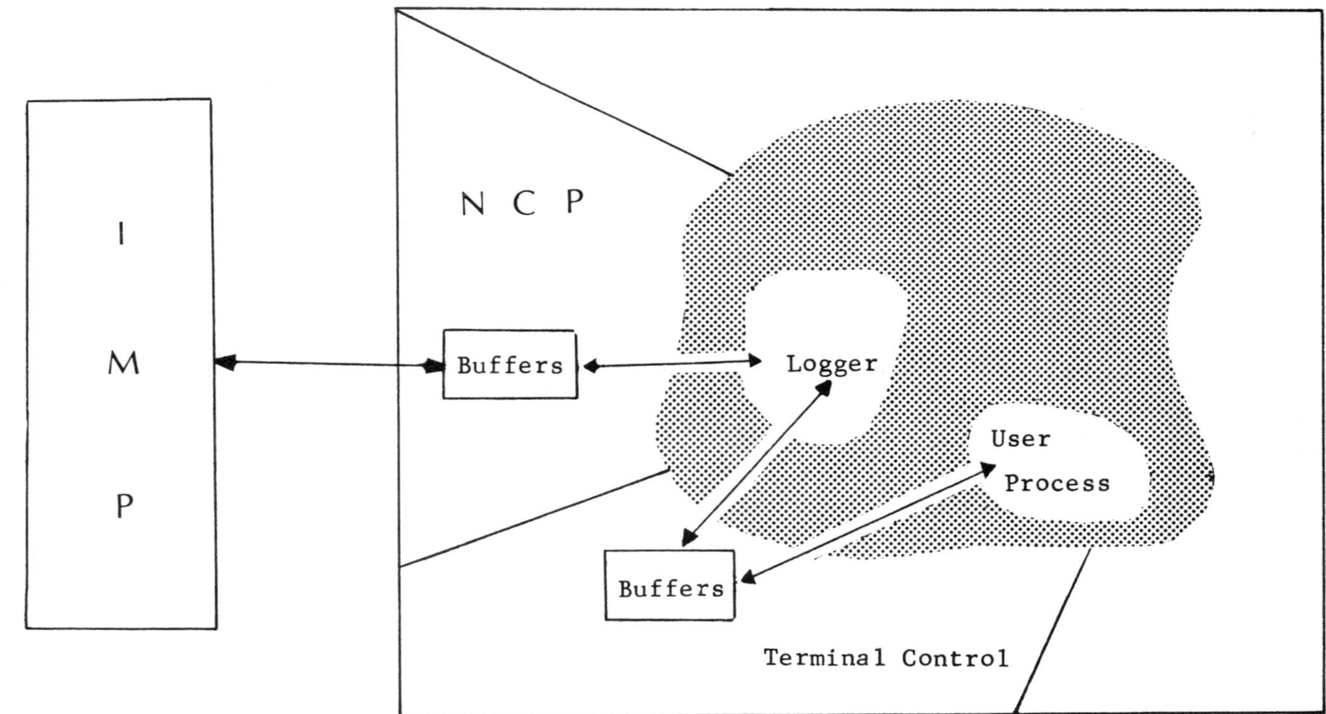

LOGGER must be a background service program capable of initiating jobs

Figure 6—Alternate data flow scheme for a server

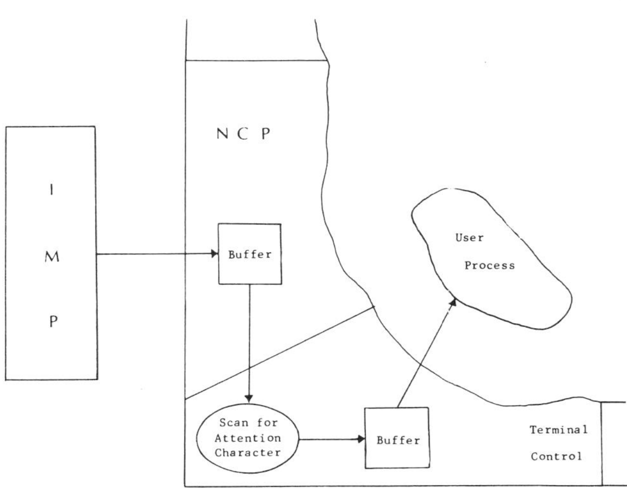

Figure 7—Data flow and processing of the character input stream

ever, and some other protection scheme is necessary. Covering the password with noise characters is the usual solution.

The HOST-HOST protocol provides a large number of sockets for each HOST, but carefully refrains from specifying which ones are to be used for what. To establish communication between a user-TELNET and a server-TELNET some convention is required. The Initial Connection Protocol (ICP)[10] is used:

1. Connection is initiated from a user-TELNET's receive socket to a serving HOST's socket 1 (a send socket).
2. When the initial connection is established, the serving HOST sends a generated socket number and closes the connection. This socket number identifies an adjacent socket pair at the serving HOST through which the user-TELNET can communicate with a server-TELNET.
3. TELNET connections are then initiated between the now specified pairs of sockets. Two connections are used to provide bi-directional communication.

Note that socket 1 at the serving HOST is in use only long enough to send another socket number with which to make the actual service connections.

One of the functions performed by a terminal control program within an operating system is the scanning of an input stream for attention characters intended to stop an errant process and to return control to the executive. Terminal control programs which buffer input sometimes run out of space. When this happens to a local terminal's input stream, a "bell" or a question mark is echoed and the overflow character discarded, *after checking to see if it is the attention character.* See Figure 7. This strategy works well in practice, but it depends rather strongly on the intelligence of the human user, the invariant time delay in the input transmission system, and a lack of buffering between type-in and attention checking. None of these conditions exists for interactive traffic over the net: The serving HOST cannot control the speed (except to slow it down) or the buffering within the using HOST, nor can it even know whether a human user is supplying the input. It is thus necessary that the terminal control program or server-TELNET not, in general, discard characters from a network input stream; instead it must suspend its acceptance of characters via the HOST-HOST flow control mechanism. Since a HOST may only send messages when there is room at the destination, the responsibility for dealing with too much input is thus transferred back to the using HOST. This scheme assures that no characters accepted by the using HOST are inadvertently lost. However, if the process in the serving HOST stops accepting input, the pipeline of buffers between the user-TELNET and remote process will fill up so that attention characters cannot get through to the serving executive. In the TELNET protocol, the solution to this problem calls for the user-TELNET to send, on request, a HOST-HOST interrupt signal forcing the server-TELNET to switch input modes to process network input for attention characters. The server-TELNET is required to scan for attention characters in its network input, even if some input must be discarded while doing so. The effect of the interrupt signal to a server-TELNET from its user is to cause the buffers between them to be emptied for the priority processing of attention characters.

To flip an attention scanning server-TELNET back into its normal mode, a special TELNET synchronization character (SYNCH) is defined. When the server-TELNET encounters this character, it returns to the strategy of accepting terminal input only as buffer space permits. There is a possible race condition if the SYNCH character arrives before the HOST-HOST interrupt signal, but the race is handled by keeping a count of SYNCHs without matching signals. Note that attention characters are HOST specific and may be any of 129 characters—128 ASCII plus "long space"—while SYNCH is a TELNET control character recognized by all server-TELNETs. It would not do to use the HOST-HOST signal alone in place of the signal-SYNCH combination in attention processing, because the position of the SYNCH character in the TELNET input stream is required to determine where attention processing ends and where normal mode input processing begins.

FILE TRANSFER

When viewing the ARPANET as a distributed computer operating system, one initial question is that of how to construct a distributed file system. Although it is constructive to entertain speculation on how the ultimate, automated distributed file system might look, one important first step is to provide for the simplest kinds of explicit file transfer to support early substantive use.

During and immediately after the construction of the ARPANET user-level process interface, several *ad hoc* file transfer mechanisms developed to provide support for initial use. These mechanisms took two forms: (1) use of the TELNET data paths for text file transfer and (2) use of raw byte-stream communication between compatible systems.

By adding two simple features to the user-TELNET, text file transfer became an immediate reality. By adding a "SCRIPT" feature to user-TELNETS whereby all text typed on the user's console can be directed to a file on the user's local file system, a user need only request of a remote HOST that a particular text file be typed on his console to get that file transferred to his local file system. By adding a "SEND-FILE" feature to a user-TELNET whereby the contents of a text file can be substituted for console type-in, a user need only start a remote system's editor as if to enter new text and then send his local file as type-in to get it transferred to the remote file system. Though crude, both of these mechanisms have been used with much success in getting real work done.

Between two identical systems it has been a simple matter to produce programs at two ends of a connection to copy raw bits from one file system to another. This mechanism has also served well in the absence of a more general and powerful file transfer system.

Ways in which these early *ad hoc* file transfer mechanisms are deficient are that (1) they require explicit and often elaborate user intervention and (2) they depend a great deal on the compatibility of the file systems involved. There is an on-going effort to construct a File Transfer Protocol (FTP)[11,12] worthy of wide implementation which will make it possible to exchange structured sequential files among widely differing file systems with a minimum (if any) explicit user intervention. In short, the file transfer protocol being developed provides for the connection of a file transfer user process ("user-FTP") and file transfer server process ("server-FTP") according to the Initial Connection Protocol discussed above. See Figure 8. A user will be able to request that specific file manipulation operations be performed on his behalf. The File Transfer Protocol will support file operations including (1) list remote directory, (2) send local file, (3) retrieve remote file, (4) rename remote file, and (5) delete remote file.

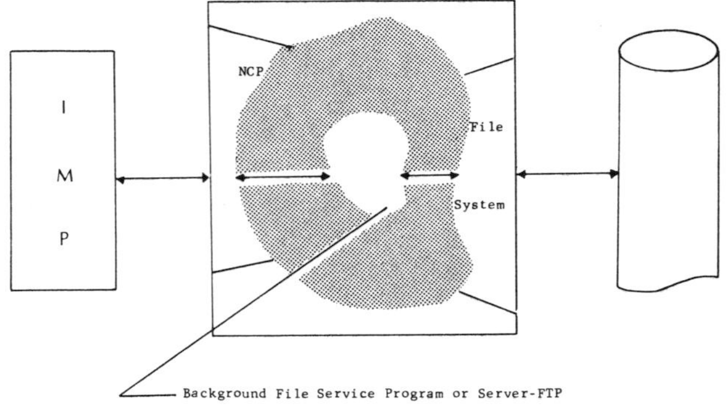

Figure 8—Data flow for file transfer

It is the intention of the protocol designers to regularize the protocol so that file transfer commands can be exchanged by consoles file transfer jobs engaged in such exotic activities as automatic back-up and dynamic file migration. The transfers envisioned will be accompanied with a Data Transfer Protocol (DTP)[11] rich enough to preserve sequential file structure and in a general enough way to permit data to flow between different file systems.

USING THE ARPANET FOR REMOTE JOB ENTRY

A very important use of the ARPANET is to give a wide community of users access to specialized facilities. One type of facility of interest is that of a very powerful number-cruncher. Users in the distributed ARPANET community need to have access to powerful machines for compute-intensive applications and the mode of operation most suited to these uses has been batch Remote Job Entry (RJE). Typically, a user will generate a "deck" for submission to a batch system. See Figure 9. He expects to wait for a period on the order of tens of minutes or hours for that "deck" to be processed, and then to receive the usually voluminous output thereby generated. See Figure 10.

As in the case of file transfer, there are a few useful *ad hoc* ARPANET RJE protocols. A standard RJE protocol is being developed to provide for job submission to a number of facilities in the ARPANET. This protocol is being constructed using the TELNET and File Transfer protocols. A scenario which sketches how the protocol provides the RJE in the simplest, most explicit way is as follows:

Via an ARPANET RJE process, a user connects his

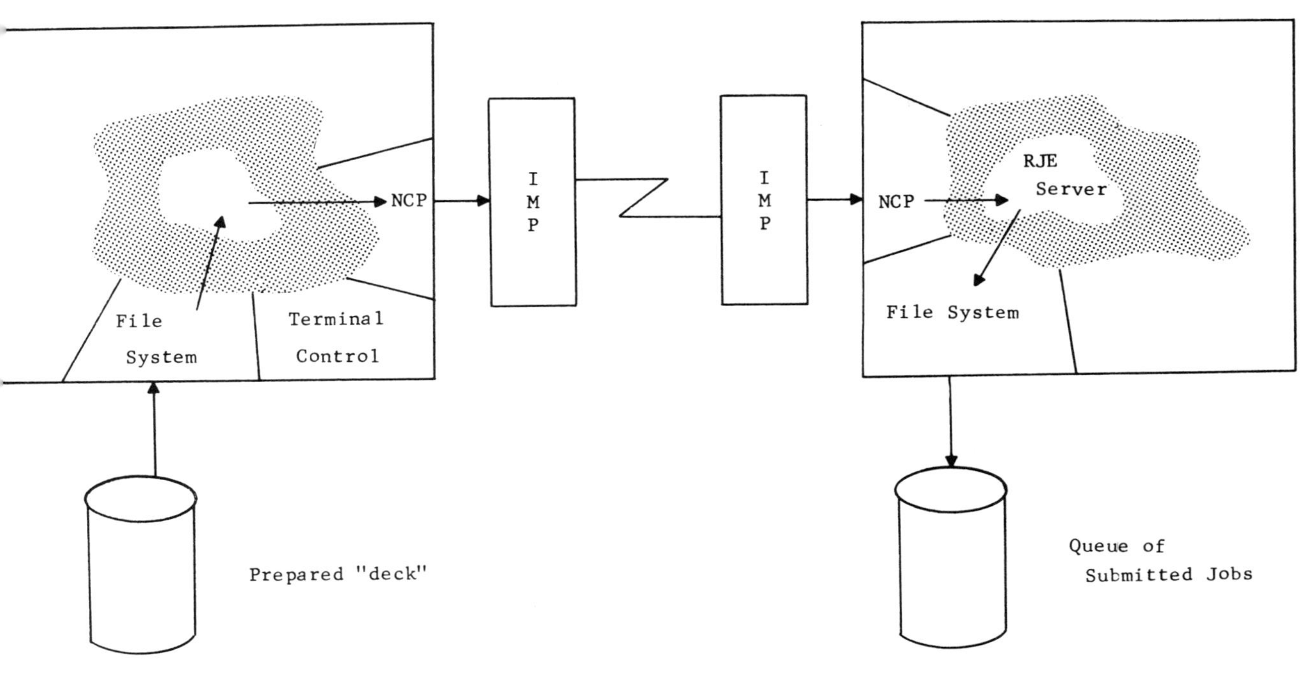

Figure 9—Submission of RJE input

erminal to an RJE server process at the HOST to vhich he intends to submit his job "deck." Through short dialogue, he establishes the source of his input and initiates its transfer using the File Transfer Protocol. At some later time, the user reconnects to the appropriate RJE server and makes an inquiry on the

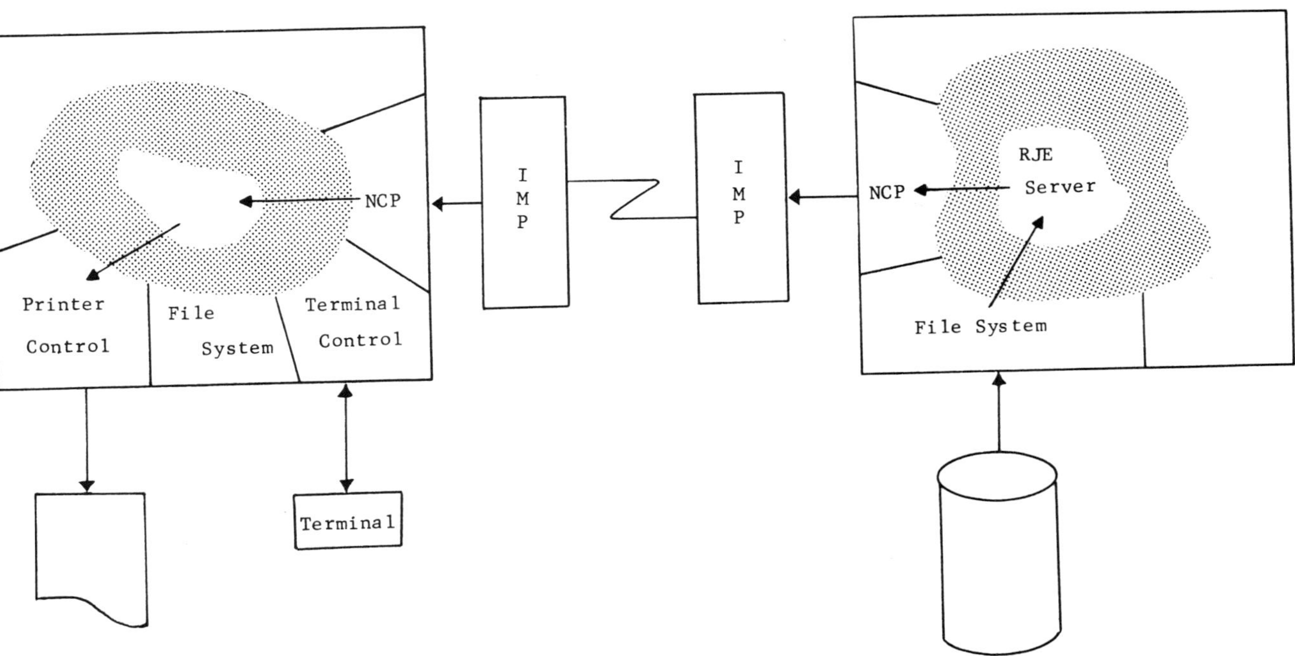

Figure 10—Retrieval of RJE output

status of his job. When notified that his input has been processed, he then issues commands to the serving HOST to transfer his output back.

We can of course imagine more automatic ways of achieving these same functions. A user might need only type a job submission command to his local system. Automatically and invisibly, then, the local system would connect and converse with the specified RJE server causing the desired output to later appear in the users file area or perhaps on a local line printer. The intention is to design the RJE protocol so that the explicit use can start immediately and the more automatic RJE systems can be built as desired.

OTHER PROTOCOLS AND CONCLUSIONS

One of the more difficult problems in utilizing a network of diverse computers and operating systems is that of dealing with incompatible data streams. Computers and their language processors have many ways of representing data. To make use of different computers it is necessary to (1) produce a mediation scheme for each incompatibility or (2) produce a standard representation. There are many strong arguments for a standard representation, but it has been hypothesized that if there were a simple way of expressing a limited set of transformations on data streams, that a large number of incompatibilities could be resolved and a great deal of computer-computer cooperation expedited.

The bulk of protocol work is being done with the invention of standard representations. The TELNET protocol, as discussed, is founded on the notion of a standard terminal called the Network Virtual Terminal

(NVT). The File Transfer Protocol is working toward a standard sequential file (a Network Virtual File?). So it is also with less advanced protocol work in graphics and data management.

There is one experiment which is taking the transformational approach to dealing with incompatibilities. The Data Reconfiguration Service (DRS) is to be generally available for mediating between incompatible stream configurations as directed by user-supplied transformations.[13]

ACKNOWLEDGMENTS

Function-oriented protocols have been the principal concern of the ARPANET Network Working Group (NWG). A list of people who have contributed to the development of the protocols discussed would include, Robert Braden, Howard Brodie, Abhay Bhushan, Steve Carr, Vint Cerf, Will Crowther, Eric Harslem, Peggy Karp, Charles Kline, Douglas McKay, Alex McKenzie, John Melvin, Ed Meyer, Jim Michener, Tom O'Sullivan, Mike Padlipsky, Arie Shoshani, Bob Sundberg, Al Vezza, Dave Walden, Jim White, and Steve Wolfe. We would like to acknowledge the contribution of these researchers and others in the ARPA Network Working Group, without assigning any responsibility for the content of this paper.

REFERENCES

1 L G ROBERTS B D WESSLER
Computer network development to achieve resource sharing
AFIPS Conference Proceedings May 1970

2 F E HEART et al
The interface message processor for the ARPA computer network
AFIPS Conference Proceedings May 1970

3 L KLEINROCK
Analytic and simulation methods in computer network design
AFIPS Conference Proceedings May 1970

4 H FRANK I T FRISCH W CHOU
Topological considerations in the design of the ARPA Computer network
AFIPS Conference Proceedings May 1970

5 *Specifications for the interconnection of a Host and an IMP*
Bolt Beranek and Newman Inc Report No 1822
February 1971

6 C S CARR S D CROCKER V G CERF
HOST-HOST communication protocol in the ARPA Network
AFIPS Conference Proceedings May 1970

7 *HOST/HOST protocol for the ARPA Network*
ARPA Network Information Center #7147

8 T O'SULLIVAN et al
TELNET protocol
ARPA Network Working Group Request For Comments (RFC) #158 ARPA Network Information Center (NIC) #6768 May 1971

9 S M ORNSTEIN et al
The Terminal IMP for the ARPA Computer Network
AFIPS Conference Proceedings May 1972

10 J B POSTEL
Official initial connection protocol
ARPA Network Working Group Document #2 NIC #7101 June 1971

11 A K BHUSHAN et al
The data transfer protocol
RFC #264 NIC #7812 November 1971

12 A K BHUSHAN et al
The file transfer protocol
RFC #265 NIC #7813 November 1971

13 R ANDERSON et al
The data reconfiguration service—An experiment in adaptable process/process communication
The ACM/IEEE Second Symposium On Problems In The Optimization Of Data Communications Systems
October 1971

A resource sharing executive for the ARPANET*

by ROBERT H. THOMAS

Bolt, Beranek and Newman, Inc.
Cambridge, Mass.

INTRODUCTION

The Resource Sharing Executive (RSEXEC) is a distributed, executive-like system that runs on TENEX Host computers in the ARPA computer network. The RSEXEC creates an environment which facilitates the sharing of resources among Hosts on the ARPANET. The large Hosts, by making a small amount of their resources available to small Hosts, can help the smaller Hosts provide services which would otherwise exceed their limited capacity. By sharing resources among themselves the large Hosts can provide a level of service better than any one of them could provide individually. Within the environment provided by the RSEXEC a user need not concern himself directly with network details such as communication protocols nor even be aware that he is dealing with a network.

A few facts about the ARPANET and the TENEX operating system should provide sufficient background for the remainder of this paper. Readers interested in learning more about the network or TENEX are referred to the literature; for the ARPANET References 1,2,3,4; for TENEX. References 5,6,7.

The ARPANET is a nationwide heterogeneous collection of Host computers at geographically separated locations. The Hosts differ from one another in manufacture, size, speed, word length and operating system. Communication between the Host computers is provided by a subnetwork of small, general purpose computers called Interface Message Processors or IMPs which are interconnected by 50 kilobit common carrier lines. The IMPs are programmed to implement a store and forward communication network. As of January 1973 there were 45 Hosts on the ARPANET and 33 IMPs in the subnet.

In terms of numbers, the two most common Hosts in the ARPANET are Terminal IMPs called TIPs[12] and TENEXs.[9] TIPs[8,9] are mini-Hosts designed to provide inexpensive terminal access to other network Hosts. The TIP is implemented as a hardware and software augmentation of the IMP.

TENEX is a time-shared operating system developed by BBN to run on a DEC PDP-10 processor augmented with paging hardware. In comparison to the TIPs, the TENEX Hosts are large. TENEX implements a virtual processor with a large (256K word), paged virtual memory for each user process. In addition, it provides a multiprocess job structure with software program interrupt capabilities, an interactive and carefully engineered command language (implemented by the TENEX EXEC) and advanced file handling capabilities.

Development of the RSEXEC was motivated initially by the desire to pool the computing and storage resources of the individual TENEX Hosts on the ARPANET. We observed that the TENEX virtual machine was becoming a popular network resource. Further, we observed that for many users, in particular those whose access to the network is through TIPs or other non-TENEX Hosts, it shouldn't really matter which Host provides the TENEX virtual machine as long as the user is able to do his computing in the manner he has become accustomed*. A number of advantages result from such resource sharing. The user would see TENEX as a much more accessible and reliable resource. Because he would no longer be dependent upon a single Host for his computing he would be able to access a TENEX virtual machine even when one or more of the TENEX Hosts were down. Of course, for him to be able to do so in a useful way, the TENEX file system would have to span across Host boundaries. The individual TENEX Hosts would see advantages also. At present, due to local storage limitations, some sites do not provide all of the TENEX subsystems to their users. For example, one site doesn't support FORTRAN for this reason. Because the subsystems available would, in effect, be the "union" of the subsystems available on all TENEX Hosts, such Hosts would be able to provide access to all TENEX subsystems.

The RSEXEC was conceived of as an experiment to investigate the feasibility of the multi-Host TENEX concept. Our experimentation with an initial version of the RSEXEC was encouraging and, as a result, we planned to develop and maintain the RSEXEC as a TENEX subsystem. The RSEXEC is, by design, an evo-

* This work was supported by the Advanced Projects Research Agency of the Department of Defense under Contract No. DAHC15-71-C-0088.

* This, of course, ignores the problem of differences in the accounting and billing practices of the various TENEX Hosts. Because all of the TENEX Hosts (with the exception of the two at BBN) belong to ARPA we felt that the administrative problems could be overcome if the technical problems preventing resource sharing were solved.

Reprinted from Proceedings of the NCC,1973

lutionary system; we planned first to implement a system with limited capabilities and then to let it evolve, expanding its capabilities, as we gained experience and came to understand the problems involved.

During the early design and implementation stages it became clear that certain of the capabilities planned for the RSEXEC would be useful to all network users, as well as users of a multi-Host TENEX. The ability of a user to inquire where in the network another user is and then to "link" his own terminal to that of the other user in order to engage in an on-line dialogue is an example of such a capability.

A large class of users with a particular need for such capabilities are those whose access to the network is through mini-Hosts such as the TIP. At present TIP users account for a significant amount of network traffic, approximately 35 percent on an average day.[10] A frequent source of complaints by TIP users is the absence of a sophisticated command language interpreter for TIPs and, as a result, their inability to obtain information about network status, the status of various Hosts, the whereabouts of other users, etc., without first logging into some Host. Furthermore, even after they log into a Host, the information readily available is generally limited to the Host they log into. A command language interpreter of the type desired would require more (core memory) resources than are available in a TIP alone. We felt that with a little help from one or more of the larger Hosts it would be feasible to provide TIP users with a good command language interpreter. (The TIPs were already using the storage resources of one TENEX Host to provide their users with a network news service.[10,11] Further, since a subset of the features already planned for the RSEXEC matched the needs of the TIP users, it was clear that with little additional effort the RSEXEC system could provide TIP users with the command language

interpreter they needed. The service TIP users can obtain through the RSEXEC by the use of a small portion of the resources of several network Hosts is superior to that they could obtain either from the TIP itself or from any single Host.

An initial release of the RSEXEC as a TENEX subsystem has been distributed to the ARPANET TENEX Hosts. In addition, the RSEXEC is available to TIP users (as well as other network users) for use as a network command language interpreter, preparatory to logging into a particular Host (of course, if the user chooses to log into TENEX he may continue using the RSEXEC after login). Several non-TENEX Hosts have expressed interest in the RSEXEC system, particularly in the capabilities it supports for inter-Host user-user interaction, and these Hosts are now participating in the RSEXEC experiment.

The current interest in computer networks and their potential for resource sharing suggests that other systems similar to the RSEXEC will be developed. At present there is relatively little in the literature describing such distributing computing systems. This paper is presented to record our experience with one such system; we hope it will be useful to others considering the implementation of such systems.

The remainder of this paper describes the RSEXEC system in more detail: first, in terms of what the RSEXEC user sees, and then, in terms of the implementation.

THE USER'S VIEW OF THE RSEXEC

The RSEXEC enlarges the range of storage and computing resources accessible to a user to include those beyond the boundaries of his local system. It does that by making resources, local and remote, available as part of a single, uniformly accessible pool. The RSEXEC system includes a command language interpreter which extends the effect of user commands to include all TENEX Hosts in the ARPANET (and for certain commands some non-TENEX Hosts), and a monitor call interpreter which, in a similar way, extends the effect of program initiated "system" calls.

To a large degree the RSEXEC relieves the user and his programs of the need to deal directly with (or even be aware that they are dealing with) the ARPANET or remote Hosts. By acting as an intermediary between its user and non-local Hosts the RSEXEC removes the logical distinction between resources that are local and those that are remote. In many contexts references to files and devices* may be made in a site independent manner. For example, although his files may be distributed among several Hosts in the network, a user need not specify where a particular file is stored in order to delete it; rather, he need only supply the file's name to the delete command.

To a first approximation, the user interacts with the RSEXEC in much the same way as he would normally interact with the standard (single Host) TENEX executive program. The RSEXEC command language is syntactically similar to that of the EXEC. The significant difference, of course, is a semantic one; the effect of commands are no longer limited to just a single Host.

Some RSEXEC commands make direct reference to the multi-Host environment. The facilities for inter-Host user-user interaction are representative of these commands. For example, the WHERE and LINK commands can be used to initiate an on-line dialogue with another user:

```
←WHERE (IS USER) JONES**
    JOB 17 TTY6 USC
    JOB 5 TTY14 CASE
←LINK (TO TTY) 14 (AT SITE) CASE
```

* Within TENEX, peripheral devices are accessible to users via the file system; the terms "file" and "device" are frequently used interchangeably in the following.

** "←" is the RSEXEC "ready" character. The words enclosed in parentheses are "noise" words which serve to make the commands more understandable to the user and may be omitted. A novice user can use the character ESC to cause the RSEXEC to prompt him by printing the noise words.

Facilities such as these play an important role in removing the distinction between "local" and "remote" by allowing users of geographically separated Hosts to interact with one another as if they were members of a single user community. The RSEXEC commands directly available to TIP users in a "pre-login state" include those for inter-Host user-user interaction together with ones that provide Host and network status information and network news.

Certain RSEXEC commands are used to define the "configuration" of the multi-Host environment seen by the user. These "meta" commands enable the user to specify the "scope" of his subsequent commands. For example, one such command (described in more detail below) allows him to enlarge or reduce the range of Hosts encompassed by file system commands that follow. Another "meta" command enables him to specify a set of peripheral devices which he may reference in a site independent manner in subsequent commands.

The usefulness of multi-Host systems such as the RSEXEC is, to a large extent, determined by the ease with which a user can manipulate his files. Because the Host used one day may be different from the one used the next, it is *necessary* that a user be able to reference any given file from all Hosts. Furthermore, it is *desirable* that he be able to reference the file in the *same* manner from all Hosts.

The file handling facilities of the RSEXEC were designated to:

1. Make it *possible* to reference any file on any Host by implementing a file name space which spans across Host boundaries.
2. Make it *convenient* to reference frequently used files by supporting "short hand" file naming conventions, such as the ability to specify certain files without site qualification.

The file system capabilities of the RSEXEC are designed to be available to the user at the command language level and to his programs at the monitor call level. An important design criterion was that existing programs be able to run under the RSEXEC without reprogramming.

File access within the RSEXEC system can be best described in terms of the commonly used model which views the files accessible from within a Host as being located at terminal nodes of a tree. Any file can be specified by a *pathname* which describes a path through the tree to the file. The *complete* pathname for a file includes every branch on the path leading from the root node to the file. While, in general, it is necessary to specify a complete pathname to uniquely identify a file, in many situations it is possible to establish contexts within which a *partial* pathname is sufficient to uniquely identify a file. Most operating systems provide such contexts, designed to allow use of partial pathnames for frequently referenced file, for their users.*

It is straightforward to extend the tree structured model for file access within a single Host to file access within the entire network. A new root node is created with branches to each of the root nodes of the access trees for the individual Hosts, and the complete pathname is enlarged to include the Host name. A file access tree for a single Host is shown in Figure 1; Figure 2 shows the file access tree for the network as a collection of single Host trees.

The RSEXEC supports use of complete pathnames that include a Host component thereby making it possible (albeit somewhat tedious) for users to reference a file on any Host. For example, the effect of the command

← APPEND (FILE) [CASE]DSK:<THOMAS>DATA.
NEW (TO FILE) [BBN]DSK:<BOBT>DATA.OLD**

is to modify the file designated ① in Figure 2 by appending to it the file designated ②.

To make it convenient to reference files, the RSEXEC allows a user to establish contexts for partial pathname interpretation. Since these contexts may span across several Hosts, the user has the ability to configure his own "virtual" TENEX which may in reality be realized by the resources of several TENEXs. Two mechanisms are available to do this.

The first of these mechanisms is the *user profile* which is a collection of user specific information and parameters

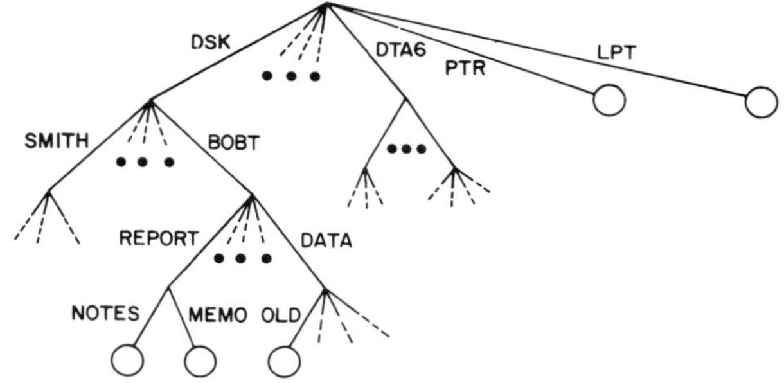

429

Figure 1—File access tree for a single Host. The circles at the terminal nodes of the tree represent files

* For example, TENEX does it by:
1. Assuming default values for certain components left unspecified in partial pathnames;
2. Providing a reference point for the user within the tree (working directory) and thereafter interpreting partial pathnames as being relative to that point. TENEX sets the reference point for each user at login time and, subject to access control restrictions, allows the user to change it (by "connecting" to another directory).

** The syntax for (single Host) TENEX pathnames includes device, directory, name and extension components. The RSEXEC extends that syntax to include a Host component. The pathname for②specifies: the CASE Host; the disk ("DSK") device; the directory THOMAS; the name DATA; and the extension NEW.

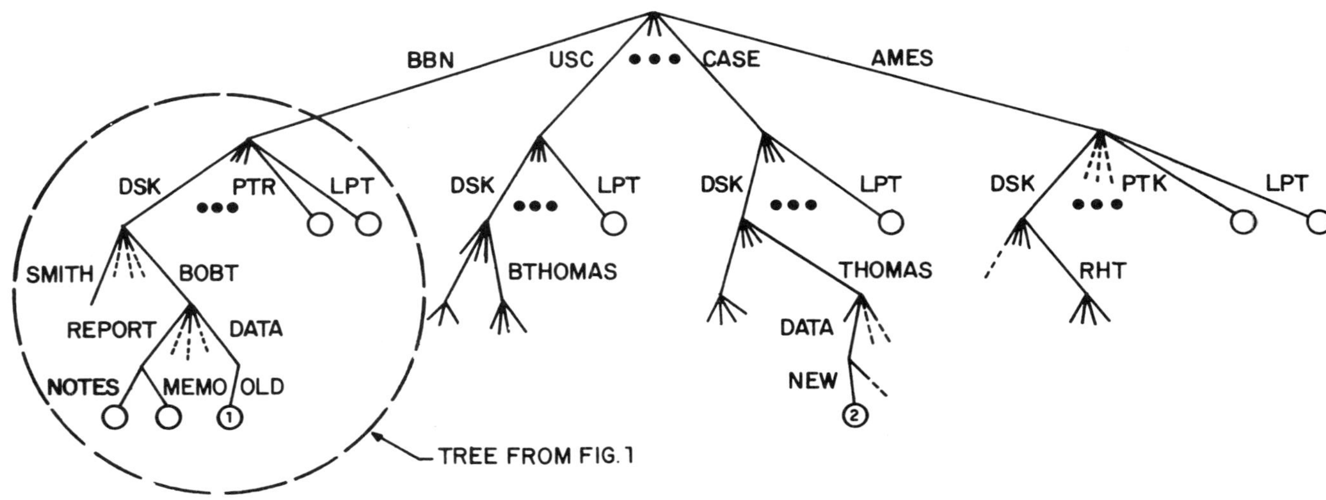

Figure 2—File access tree for a network. The single Host access tree from Figure 1 is part of this tree

maintained by the RSEXEC for each user. Among other things, a user's profile specifies a group of file directories which taken together define a *composite* directory for the user. The "contents" of the composite directory are the union of the "contents" of the file directories specified in the profile. When a pathname without site and directory qualification is used, it is interpreted relative to the user's composite directory. The composite directory serves to define a reference point within the file access tree that is used by the RSEXEC to interpret partial pathnames. That reference point is somewhat unusual in that it spans several Hosts.

One of the ways a user can reconfigure his "virtual" TENEX is by editing his profile. With one of the "meta" commands noted earlier he can add or remove components of his composite directory to control how partial
430 pathnames are interpreted.

An example may help clarify the role of the user profile, the composite directory and profile editing. Assume that the profile for user Thomas contains directories BOBT at BBN, THOMAS at CASE and BTHOMAS at USC (see Figure 2). His composite directory, the reference point for pathname interpretation, spans three Hosts. The command

←APPEND (FILE) DATA.NEW (TO FILE) DATA.OLD

achieves the same effect as the APPEND command in a previous example. To respond the RSEXEC first consults the composite directory to discover the locations of the files, and then acts to append the first file to the second; how it does so is discussed in the next section. If he wanted to change the scope of partial pathnames he uses, user Thomas could delete directory BOBT at BBN from his profile and add directory RHT at AMES to it.

The other mechanism for controlling the interpretation of partial pathnames is *device binding*. A user can instruct the RSEXEC to interpret subsequent use of a particular device name as referring to a device at the Host he specifies. After a device name has been *bound* to a Host in this manner, a partial pathname without site qualification that includes it is interpreted as meaning the named device at the specified Host. Information in the user profile specifies a set of default device bindings for the user. The binding of devices can be changed dynamically during an RSEXEC session. In the context of the previous example the sequence of commands:

←BIND (DEVICE) LPT (TO SITE) BBN
←LIST DATA.NEW
←BIND (DEVICE) LPT (TO SITE) USC
←LIST DATA.NEW

produces two listings of the file DATA.NEW: one on the line printer (device "LPT") at BBN, the other on the printer at USC. As with other RSEXEC features, device binding is available at the program level. For example, a program that reads from magnetic tape will function properly under the RSEXEC when it runs on a Host without a local mag-tape unit, provided the mag-tape device has been bound properly.

The user can take advantage of the distributed nature of the file system to increase the "accessibility" of certain files he considers important by instructing the RSEXEC to maintain *images* of them at several different Hosts. With the exception of certain special purpose files (e.g., the user's "message" file), the RSEXEC treats files with the same pathname relative to a user's composite directory as images of the same multi-image file. The user profile is implemented as a multi-image file with an image maintained at every component directory of the composite directory.*

* The profile is somewhat special in that it is accessible to the user only through the profile editing commands, and is otherwise transparent.

Implementation of the RSEXEC

The RSEXEC implementation is discussed in this section with the focus on approach rather than detail. The result is a simplified but nonetheless accurate sketch of the implementation.

The RSEXEC system is implemented by a collection of programs which run with no special privileges on TENEX Hosts. The advantage of a "user-code" (rather than "monitor-code") implementation is that ordinary user access is all that is required at the various Hosts to develop, debug and use the system. Thus experimentation with the RSEXEC can be conducted with minimal disruption to the TENEX Hosts.

The ability of the RSEXEC to respond properly to users' requests often requires cooperation from one or more remote Hosts. When such cooperation is necessary, the RSEXEC program interacts with RSEXEC "service" programs at the remote Hosts according to a pre-agreed upon set of conventions or protocol. Observing the protocol, the RSEXEC can instruct a service program to perform actions on its behalf to satisfy its user's requests.

Each Host in the RSEXEC system runs the service program as a "demon" process which is prepared to provide service to any remote process that observes protocol. The relation between RSEXEC programs and these demons is shown schematically in Figure 3.

The RSEXEC protocol

The RSEXEC protocol is a set of conventions designed to support the interprocess communication requirements of the RSEXEC system. The needs of the system required that the protocol:

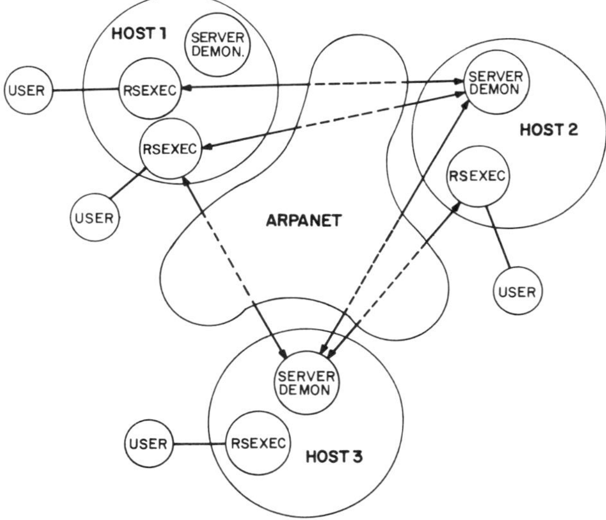

Figure 3—Schematic showing several RSEXEC programs interacting, on behalf of their users, with remote server programs

1. be extensible:
   As noted earlier, the RSEXEC is, by design, an evolutionary system.
2. support many-party as well as two-party interactions:
   Some situations are better handled by single multiparty interactions than by several two-party interactions. Response to an APPEND command when the files and the RSEXEC are all at different Hosts is an example (see below).
3. be convenient for interaction between processes running on dissimilar Hosts while supporting efficient interaction between processes on similar Hosts:
   Many capabilities of the RSEXEC are useful to users of non-TENEX as well as TENEX Hosts. It is important that the protocol not favor TENEX at the expense of other Hosts.

The RSEXEC protocol has two parts:

1. a protocol for initial connection specifies how programs desiring service (users) can connect to programs providing service (servers);
2. a command protocol specifies how the user program talks to the server program to get service after it is connected.

The protocol used for initial connection is the standard ARPANET initial connection protocol (ICP).[12] The communication paths that result from the ICP exchange are used to carry commands and responses between user and server. The protocol supports many-party interaction by providing for the use of auxiliary communication paths, in addition to the command paths. Auxiliary paths can be established at the user's request between server and user or between server and a third party. Communication between processes on dissimilar Hosts usually requires varying degrees of attention to message formatting, code conversion, byte manipulation, etc. The protocol addresses the issue of convenience in the way other standard ARPANET protocols have.[13,14,15] It specifies a default message format designed to be "fair" in the sense that it doesn't favor one type of Host over another by requiring all reformatting be done by one type of Host. It addresses the issue of efficiency by providing a mechanism with which processes on similar Hosts can negotiate a change in format from the default to one better suited for efficient use by their Hosts.

The protocol can perhaps best be explained further by examples that illustrate how the RSEXEC uses it. The following discusses its use in the WHERE, APPEND and LINK commands:

←WHERE (IS USER) JONES

The RSEXEC queries each non-local server program about user Jones. To query a server, it establishes connections with the server; transmits a "request for information about Jones" as specified by the protocol;

and reads the response which indicates whether or not Jones is a known user, and if he is, the status of his active jobs (if any).

←APPEND (FILE) DATA.NEW (TO FILE) DATA.OLD

Recall that the files DATA.NEW and DATA.OLD are at CASE and BBN, respectively; assume that the APPEND request is made to an RSEXEC running at USC. The RSEXEC connects to the servers at CASE and BBN. Next, using the appropriate protocol commands, it instructs each to establish an auxiliary path to the other (see Figure 4). Finally, it instructs the server at CASE to transmit the file DATA.NEW over the auxiliary connection and the server at BBN to append the data it reads from the auxiliary connection to the file DATA.OLD.

←LINK (TO TTY) 14 (AT SITE) CASE

Assume that the user making the request is at USC. After connecting to the CASE server, the RSEXEC uses appropriate protocol commands to establish two auxiliary connections (one "send" and one "receive") with the server. It next instructs the server to "link" its (the server's) end of the auxiliary connections to Terminal 14 at its (the server's) site. Finally, to complete the LINK command the RSEXEC "links" its end of the auxiliary connections to its user's terminal.

The RSEXEC program

A large part of what the RSEXEC program does is to locate the resources necessary to satisfy user requests. It can satisfy some requests directly whereas others may require interaction with one or more remote server programs. For example, an APPEND command may involve interaction with none, one or two server programs depending upon where the two files are stored.

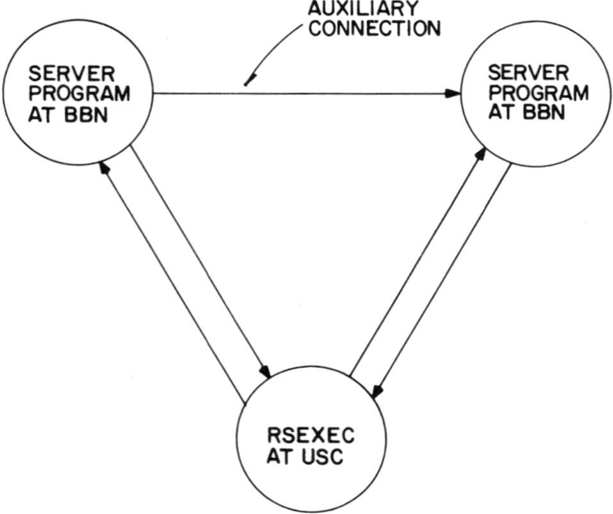

Figure 4—configuration of RSEXEC and two server programs required to satisfy and APPEND command when the two files and the RSEXEC are all on different Hosts. The auxiliary connection is used to transmit the file to be appended from one server to the other

An issue basic to the RSEXEC implementation concerns handling information necessary to access files: in particular, how much information about non-local files should be maintained locally by the RSEXEC? The advantage of maintaining the information locally is that requests requiring it can be satisfied without incurring the overhead involved in first locating the information and then accessing it through the network. Certain highly interactive activity would be precluded if it required significant interaction with remote server programs. For example, recognition and completion of file names* would be ususable if it required direct interaction with several remote server programs. Of course, it would be impractical to maintain information locally about all files at all TENEX Hosts.

The approach taken by the RSEXEC is to maintain information about the non-local files a user is most likely to reference and to acquire information about others from remote server programs as necessary. It implements this strategy by distinguishing internally four file types:

1. files in the Composite Directory;
2. files resident at the local Host which are not in the Composite Directory;
3. files accessible via a bound device, and;
4. all other files.

Information about files of type 1 and 3 is maintained locally by the RSEXEC. It can acquire information about type 2 files directly from the local TENEX monitor, as necessary. No information about type 4 files is maintained locally; whenever such information is needed it is acquired from the appropriate remote server. File name recognition and completion and the use of partial pathnames is restricted to file types 1, 2 and 3.

The composite directory contains an entry for each file in each of the component directories specified in the user's profile. At the start of each session the RSEXEC constructs the user's composite directory by gathering information from the server programs at the Hosts specified in the user profile. Throughout the session the RSEXEC modifies the composite directory, adding and deleting entries, as necessary. The composite directory contains frequently accessed information (e.g., Host location, size, date of last access, etc.) about the user's files. It represents a source of information that can be accessed without incurring the overhead of going to the remote Host each time it is needed.

* File name recognition and completion is a TENEX feature which allows a user to abbreviate fields of a file pathname. Appearance of ESC in the name causes the portion of the field before the ESC to be looked up, and, if the portion is unambiguous, the system will recognize it and supply the omitted characters and/or fields to complete the file name. If the portion is ambiguous, the system will prompt the user for more characters by ringing the terminal bell. Because of its popularity we felt it important that the RSEXEC support this feature.

The RSEXEC regards the composite directory as an approximation (which is usually accurate) to the state of the user's files. The state of a given file is understood to be maintained by the TENEX monitor at the site where the file resides. The RSEXEC is aware that the outcome of any action it initiates involving a remote file depends upon the file's state as determined by the appropriate remote TENEX monitor, and that the state information in the composite directory may be "out of phase" with the actual state. It is prepared to handle the occasional failure of actions it initiates based on inaccurate information in the composite directory by giving the user an appropriate error message and updating the composite directory. Depending upon the severity of the situation it may choose to change a single entry in the composite directory, reacquire all the information for a component directory, or rebuild the entire composite directory.

The service program for the RSEXEC

Each RSEXEC service program has two primary responsibilities:

1. to act on behalf of non-local users (typically RSEXEC programs), and;
2. to maintain information on the status of the other server programs.

The status information it maintains has an entry for each Host indicating whether the server program at the Host is up and running, the current system load at the Host, etc. Whenever an RSEXEC program needs service from some remote server program it checks the status information maintained by the local server. If the remote server is indicated as up it goes ahead and requests the service; otherwise it does not bother.

A major requirement of the server program implementation is that it be resilient to failure. The server should be able to recover gracefully from common error situations and, more important, it should be able to "localize" the effects of those from which it can't. At any given time, the server may simultaneously be acting on behalf of a number of user programs at different Hosts. A malfunctioning or malicious user program should not be able to force termination of the entire service program. Further, it should not be able to adversely effect the quality of service received by the other users.

To achieve such resiliency the RSEXEC server program is implemented as a hierarchy of loosely connected, cooperating processes (see Figure 5):

1. The RSSER process is at the root of the hierarchy. Its primary duty is to create and maintain the other processes;
2. REQSER processes are created in response to requests for service. There is one for each non-local user being served.

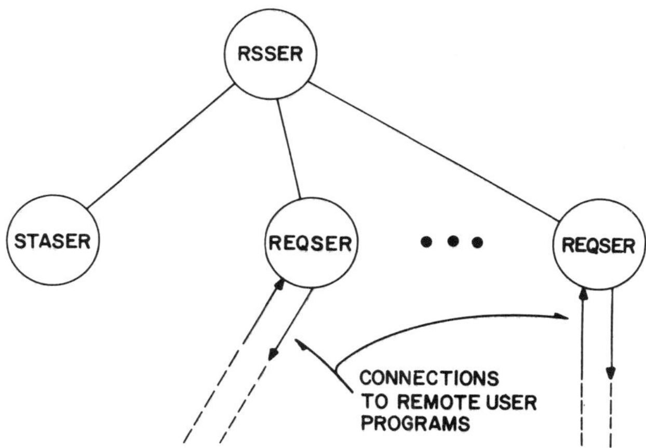

Figure 5—Hierarchical structure of the RSEXEC service program

3. A STASER process maintains status information about the server programs at other sites.

Partitioning the server in this way makes it easy to localize the effect of error situations. For example, occurrence of an unrecoverable error in a REQSER process results in service interruption only to the user being serviced by that process: all other REQSER processes can continue to provide service uninterrupted.

When service is requested by a non-local program, the RSSER process creates a REQSER process to provide it. The REQSER process responds to requests by the non-local program as governed by the protocol. When the non-local program signals that it needs no further service, the REQSER process halts and is terminated by RSSER.

The STASER process maintains an up-to-date record of the status of the server programs at other Hosts by exchanging status information with the STASER processes at the other Hosts. The most straightforward way to keep up-to-date information would be to have each STASER process periodically "broadcast" its own status to the others. Unfortunately, the current, connection-based Host-Host protocol of the ARPANET[16] forces use of a less elegant mechanism. Each STASER process performs its task by:

433

1. periodically requesting a status report from each of the other processes, and;
2. sending status information to the other processes as requested.

To request a status report from another STASER process, STASER attempts to establish a connection to a "well-known" port maintained in a "listening" state by the other process. If the other process is up and running, the connection attempt succeeds and status information is sent to the requesting process. The reporting process then returns the well-known port to the listening state so that it can respond to requests from other processes. The requesting process uses the status report to update an appropriate status table entry. If the connection attempt does not succeed within a specified time period, the requesting process records the event as a missed report in an appropriate status table entry.

When the server program at a Host first comes up, the status table is initialized by marking the server programs at the other Hosts as down. After a particular server is marked as down, STASER must collect a number of status reports from it before it can mark the program as up and useful. If, on its way up, the program misses several consecutive reports, its "report count" is zeroed. By requiring a number of status reports from a remote server before marking it as up, STASER is requiring that the remote program has functioned "properly" for a while. As a result, the likelihood that it is in a stable state capable of servicing local RSEXEC programs is increased. STASER is willing to attribute occasionally missed reports as being due to "random" fluctuations in network or Host responses. However, consistent failure of a remote server to report is taken to mean that the program is unusable and results in it being marked as down.

Because up-to-date status information is crucial to the operation of the RSEXEC system it is important that failure of the STASER process be infrequent, and that when a failure does occur it is detected and corrected quickly. STASER itself is programmed to cope with common errors. However error situations can arise from which STASER is incapable of recovering. These situations are usually the result of infrequent and unexpected "network" events such as Host-Host protocol violations and lost or garbled messages. (Error detection and control is performed on messages passed between IMPS to insure that messages are not lost or garbled within the IMP subnet; however, there is currently no error control for messages passing over the Host to IMP interface.) For all practical purposes such situations are irreproducible, making their pathology difficult to understand let alone program for. The approach we have taken is to acknowledge that we don't know how to prevent such situations and to try to minimize their effect. When functioning properly the STASER process "reports in" periodically. If it fails to report as expected, RSSER assumes that it has malfunctioned and restarts it.

Providing the RSEXEC to TIP users

The RSEXEC is available as a network executive program to users whose access to the network is by way of a TIP (or other non-TENEX Host) through a standard service program (TIPSER) that runs on TENEX Hosts.* To use the RSEXEC from a TIP a user instructs the TIP to initiate an initial connection protocol exchange with one of the TIPSER programs. TIPSER responds to the ICP by creating a new process which runs the RSEXEC for the TIP user.

* At present TIPSER is run on a regular basis at only one of the TENEX Hosts; we expect several other Hosts will start running it on a regular basis shortly.

CONCLUDING REMARKS

Experience with the RSEXEC has shown that it is capable of supporting significant resource sharing among the TENEX Hosts in the ARPANET. It does so in a way that provides users access to resources beyond the boundaries of their local system with a convenience not previously experienced within the ARPANET. As the RSEXEC system evolves, the TENEX Hosts will become more tightly coupled and will approach the goal of a multi-Host TENEX. Part of the process of evolution will be to provide direct support for many RSEXEC features at the level of the TENEX monitor.

At present the RSEXEC system is markedly deficient in supporting significant resource sharing among dissimilar Hosts. True, it provides mini-Hosts, such as TIPs, with a mechanism for accessing a small portion of the resources of the TENEX (and some non-TENEX) Hosts, enabling them to provide their users with an executive program that is well beyond their own limited capacity. Beyond that, however, the system does little more than to support inter-Host user-user interaction between Hosts that choose to implement the appropriate subset of the RSEXEC protocol. There are, of course, limitations to how tightly Hosts with fundamentally different operating systems can be coupled. However, it is clear that the RSEXEC has not yet approached those limitations and that there is room for improvement in this area.

The RSEXEC is designed to provide access to the resources within a computer network in a manner that makes the network itself transparent by removing the logical distinction between local and remote. As a result, the user can deal with the network as a single entity rather than a collection of autonomous Hosts. We feel that it will be through systems such as the RSEXEC that users will be able to most effectively exploit the resources of computer networks.

ACKNOWLEDGMENTS

Appreciation is due to W. R. Sutherland whose leadership and enthusiasm made the RSEXEC project possible. P. R. Johnson actively contributed in the implementation of the RSEXEC. The TENEX Group at BBN deserves recognition for constructing an operating system that made the task of implementing the RSEXEC a pleasant one.

REFERENCES

1. Roberts, L. G., Wessler, B. D., "Computer Network Development to Achieve Resource Sharing," *Proc. of AFIPS SJCC*, 1970, Vol. 36, pp. 543-549.
2. Heart, F. E., Kahn, R. E., Ornstein, S. M., Crowther, W. R., Walden, D. C., "The Interface Message Processor for the ARPA Computer Network," *Proc. of AFIPS SJCC*, 1970, Vol. 36.

3. McQuillan, J. M., Crowther, W. R., Cosell, B. P., Walden, D. C., Heart, F. E., "Improvements in the Design and Performance of the ARPA Network," *Proc. of AFIPS FJCC*, 1972, Vol. 41, pp. 741-754.
4. Roberts, L. G., "A Forward Look," *Signal*, Vol. XXV, No. 12, pp. 77-81, August, 1971.
5. Bobrow, D. G., Burchfiel, J. D., Murphy, D. L., Tomlinson, R. S., "TENEX, a Paged Time Sharing System for the PDP-10," *Communications of the ACM*, Vol. 15, No. 3, pp. 135-143, March, 1972.
6. *TENEX JSYS Manual—A Manual of TENEX Monitor Calls*, BBN Computer Science Division, BBN, Cambridge, Mass., November 1971.
7. Murphy, D. L., "Storage Organization and Management in TENEX," *Proc. of AFIPS FJCC*, 1972, Vol. 41, pp. 23-32.
8. Ornstein, S. M., Heart, F. E., Crowther, W. R., Rising, H. K., Russell, S. B., Michel, A., "The Terminal IMP for the ARPA Computer Network," *Proc. of AFIPS SJCC*, 1972, Vol. 40, pp. 243-254.
9. Kahn, R. E., "Terminal Access to the ARPA Computer Network," *Courant Computer Symposium 3—Computer Networks*, Courant Institute, New York, Nov. 1970.
10. Mimno, N. W., Cosell, B. P., Walden, D. C., Butterfield, S. C., Levin, J. B., "Terminal Access to the ARPA Network—Experience and Improvement," *Proc. COMPCON '73*, Seventh Annual IEEE Computer Society International Conference.
11. Walden, D.C., *TIP User's Guide*, BBN Report No. 2183, Sept. 1972. Also available from the Network Information Center at Stanford Research Institute, Menlo Park, California, as Document NIC #10916.
12. Postel, J. B., *Official Initial Connection Protocol*, Available from Network Information Center as Document NIC #7101.
13. Postel, J. B., *TELNET Protocol*, ARPA Network Working Group Request for Comments #358. Available from Network Information Center as Document NIC #9348.
14. Bhushan, A. K., *File Transfer Protocol*, ARPA Network Working Group Request for Comments #358. Available from Network Information Center as Document NIC #10596.
15. Crocker, S. D., Heafner, J. F., Metcalfe, R. M., Postel, J. B., "Function Oriented Protocols for the ARPA Computer Network," *Proc. of AFIPS SJCC*, 1972, Vol. 40, pp. 271-279.
16. McKenzie, A., *Host/Host Protocol for the ARPA Network*. Available from the Network Information Center As Document NIC #8246.

Errata:

1. P. 156, column 1, line 32 should read:

   vide their users with a network news service.[10,11]). Further,

2. P. 156, column 1, line 57 should read:

   distributed computing systems. This paper is presented

3. P. 160, Figure 4 should be:

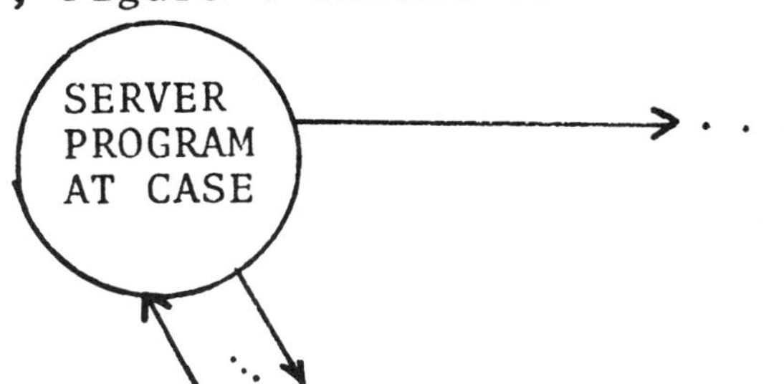

4. P. 160, Figure 4, caption line 2 should read:

   to satisfy an APPEND command when the two files and the

5. P. 160, column 2, line 14 should read:

   be unusable if it required direct interaction with several

A Protocol for Packet Network Intercommunication

VINTON G. CERF AND ROBERT E. KAHN, MEMBER, IEEE

***Abstract*—A protocol that supports the sharing of resources that exist in different packet switching networks is presented. The protocol provides for variation in individual network packet sizes, transmission failures, sequencing, flow control, end-to-end error checking, and the creation and destruction of logical process-to-process connections. Some implementation issues are considered, and problems such as internetwork routing, accounting, and timeouts are exposed.**

INTRODUCTION

IN THE LAST few years considerable effort has been expended on the design and implementation of packet switching networks [1]-[7],[14],[17]. A principle reason for developing such networks has been to facilitate the sharing of computer resources. A packet communication network includes a transportation mechanism for delivering data between computers or between computers and terminals. To make the data meaningful, computers and terminals share a common protocol (i.e., a set of agreed upon conventions). Several protocols have already been developed for this purpose [8]-[12],[16]. However, these protocols have addressed only the problem of communication on the same network. In this paper we present a protocol design and philosophy that supports the sharing of resources that exist in different packet switching networks.

After a brief introduction to internetwork protocol issues, we describe the function of a GATEWAY as an interface between networks and discuss its role in the protocol. We then consider the various details of the protocol, including addressing, formatting, buffering, sequencing, flow control, error control, and so forth. We close with a description of an interprocess communication mechanism and show how it can be supported by the internetwork protocol.

Even though many different and complex problems must be solved in the design of an individual packet switching network, these problems are manifestly compounded when dissimilar networks are interconnected. Issues arise which may have no direct counterpart in an individual network and which strongly influence the way in which internetwork communication can take place.

A typical packet switching network is composed of a set of computer resources called HOSTS, a set of one or more *packet switches*, and a collection of communication media that interconnect the packet switches. Within each HOST, we assume that there exist *processes* which must communicate with processes in their own or other HOSTS. Any current definition of a process will be adequate for our purposes [13]. These processes are generally the ultimate source and destination of data in the network. Typically, within an individual network, there exists a protocol for communication between any source and destination process. Only the source and destination processes require knowledge of this convention for communication to take place. Processes in two distinct networks would ordinarily use different protocols for this purpose. The ensemble of packet switches and communication media is called the *packet switching subnet*. Fig. 1 illustrates these ideas.

In a typical packet switching subnet, data of a fixed maximum size are accepted from a source HOST, together with a formatted destination address which is used to route the data in a store and forward fashion. The transmit time for this data is usually dependent upon internal network parameters such as communication media data rates, buffering and signaling strategies, routing, propagation delays, etc. In addition, some mechanism is generally present for error handling and determination of status of the networks components.

Individual packet switching networks may differ in their implementations as follows.

1) Each network may have distinct ways of addressing the receiver, thus requiring that a uniform addressing scheme be created which can be understood by each individual network.

2) Each network may accept data of different maximum size, thus requiring networks to deal in units of the smallest maximum size (which may be impractically small) or requiring procedures which allow data crossing a network boundary to be reformatted into smaller pieces.

3) The success or failure of a transmission and its performance in each network is governed by different time delays in accepting, delivering, and transporting the data. This requires careful development of internetwork timing procedures to insure that data can be successfully delivered through the various networks.

4) Within each network, communication may be disrupted due to unrecoverable mutation of the data or missing data. End-to-end restoration procedures are desirable to allow complete recovery from these conditions.

Paper approved by the Associate Editor for Data Communications of the IEEE Communications Society for publication without oral presentation. Manuscript received November 5, 1973. The research reported in this paper was supported in part by the Advanced Research Projects Agency of the Department of Defense under Contract DAHC 15-73-C-0370.

V. G. Cerf is with the Department of Computer Science and Electrical Engineering, Stanford University, Stanford, Calif.

R. E. Kahn is with the Information Processing Technology Office, Advanced Research Projects Agency, Department of Defense, Arlington, Va.

437

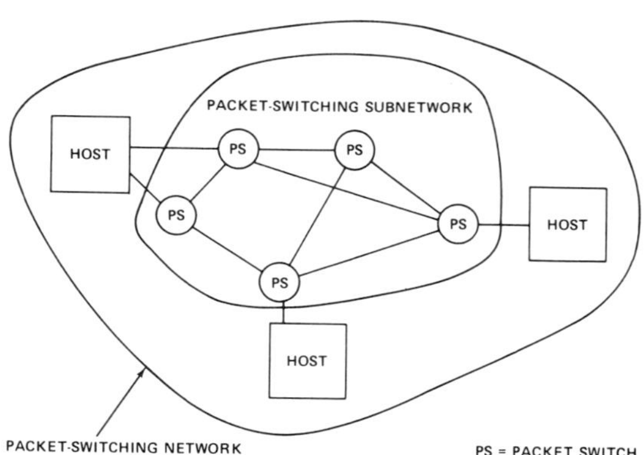

Fig. 1. Typical packet switching network.

5) Status information, routing, fault detection, and isolation are typically different in each network. Thus, to obtain verification of certain conditions, such as an inaccessible or dead destination, various kinds of coordination must be invoked between the communicating networks.

It would be extremely convenient if all the differences between networks could be economically resolved by suitable interfacing at the network boundaries. For many of the differences, this objective can be achieved. However, both economic and technical considerations lead us to prefer that the interface be as simple and reliable as possible and deal primarily with passing data between networks that use different packet switching strategies.

The question now arises as to whether the interface ought to account for differences in HOST or process level protocols by transforming the source conventions into the corresponding destination conventions. We obviously want to allow conversion between packet switching strategies at the interface, to permit interconnection of existing and planned networks. However, the complexity and dissimilarity of the HOST or process level protocols makes it desirable to avoid having to transform between them at the interface, even if this transformation were always possible. Rather, compatible HOST and process level protocols must be developed to achieve effective internetwork resource sharing. The unacceptable alternative is for every HOST or process to implement every protocol (a potentially unbounded number) that may be needed to communicate with other networks. We therefore assume that a common protocol is to be used between HOST's or processes in different networks and that the interface between networks should take as small a role as possible in this protocol.

To allow networks under different ownership to interconnect, some accounting will undoubtedly be needed for traffic that passes across the interface. In its simplest terms, this involves an accounting of packets handled by each net for which charges are passed from net to net until the buck finally stops at the user or his representative. Furthermore, the interconnection must preserve intact the internal operation of each individual network. This is easily achieved if two networks interconnect as if each were a HOST to the other network, but without utilizing or indeed incorporating any elaborate HOST protocol transformations.

It is thus apparent that the interface between networks must play a central role in the development of any network interconnection strategy. We give a special name to this interface that performs these functions and call it a GATEWAY.

THE GATEWAY NOTION

In Fig. 2 we illustrate three individual networks labeled A, B, and C which are joined by GATEWAYS M and N. GATEWAY M interfaces network A with network B, and GATEWAY N interfaces network B to network C. We assume that an individual network may have more than one GATEWAY (e.g., network B) and that there may be more than one GATEWAY path to use in going between a pair of networks. The responsibility for properly routing data resides in the GATEWAY.

In practice, a GATEWAY between two networks may be composed of two halves, each associated with its own network. It is possible to implement each half of a GATEWAY so it need only embed internetwork packets in local packet format or extract them. We propose that the GATEWAYS handle internetwork packets in a standard format, but we are not proposing any particular transmission procedure between GATEWAY halves.

Let us now trace the flow of data through the interconnected networks. We assume a packet of data from process X enters network A destined for process Y in network C. The address of Y is initially specified by process X and the address of GATEWAY M is derived from the address of process Y. We make no attempt to specify whether the choice of GATEWAY is made by process X, its HOST, or one of the packet switches in network A. The packet traverses network A until it reaches GATEWAY M. At the GATEWAY, the packet is reformatted to meet the requirements of network B, account is taken of this unit of flow between A and B, and the GATEWAY delivers the packet to network B. Again the derivation of the next GATEWAY address is accomplished based on the address of the destination Y. In this case, GATEWAY N is the next one. The packet traverses network B until it finally reaches GATEWAY N where it is formatted to meet the requirements of network C. Account is again taken of this unit of flow between networks B and C. Upon entering network C, the packet is routed to the HOST in which process Y resides and there it is delivered to its ultimate destination.

Since the GATEWAY must understand the address of the source and destination HOSTS, this information must be available in a standard format in every packet which arrives at the GATEWAY. This information is contained in an *internetwork header* prefixed to the packet by the source HOST. The packet format, including the internet-

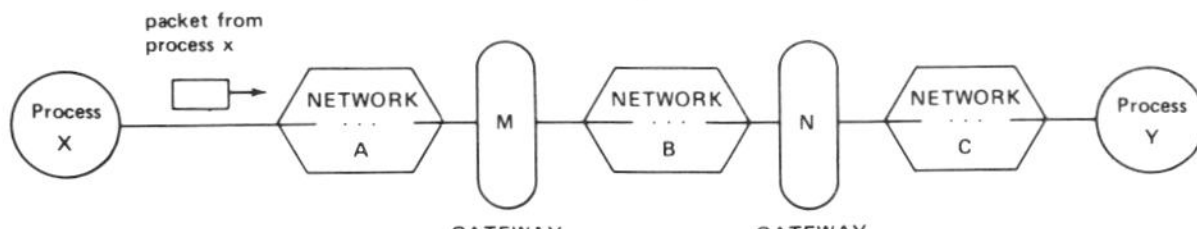

Fig. 2. Three networks interconnected by two GATEWAYS.

Fig. 3. Internetwork packet format (fields not shown to scale).

work header, is illustrated in Fig. 3. The source and destination entries uniformly and uniquely identify the address of every HOST in the composite network. Addressing is a subject of considerable complexity which is discussed in greater detail in the next section. The next two entries in the header provide a sequence number and a byte count that may be used to properly sequence the packets upon delivery to the destination and may also enable the GATEWAYS to detect fault conditions affecting the packet. The flag field is used to convey specific control information and is discussed in the section on retransmission and duplicate detection later. The remainder of the packet consists of text for delivery to the destination and a trailing check sum used for end-to-end software verification. The GATEWAY does *not* modify the text and merely forwards the check sum along without computing or recomputing it.

Each network may need to augment the packet format before it can pass through the individual network. We have indicated a *local header* in the figure which is prefixed to the beginning of the packet. This local header is introduced merely to illustrate the concept of embedding an internetwork packet in the format of the individual network through which the packet must pass. It will obviously vary in its exact form from network to network and may even be unnecessary in some cases. Although not explicitly indicated in the figure, it is also possible that a local trailer may be appended to the end of the packet.

Unless all transmitted packets are legislatively restricted to be small enough to be accepted by every individual network, the GATEWAY may be forced to split a packet into two or more smaller packets. This action is called fragmentation and must be done in such a way that the destination is able to piece together the fragmented packet. It is clear that the internetwork header format imposes a minimum packet size which all networks must carry (obviously all networks will want to carry packets larger than this minimum). We believe the long range growth and development of internetwork communication would be seriously inhibited by specifying how much larger than the minimum a packet size can be, for the following reasons.

1) If a maximum permitted packet size is specified then it becomes impossible to completely isolate the internal packet size parameters of one network from the internal packet size parameters of all other networks.

2) It would be very difficult to increase the maximum permitted packet size in response to new technology (e.g., large memory systems, higher data rate communication facilities, etc.) since this would require the agreement and then implementation by all participating networks.

3) Associative addressing and packet encryption may require the size of a particular packet to expand during transit for incorporation of new information.

Provision for fragmentation (regardless of where it is performed) permits packet size variations to be handled on an individual network basis without global administration and also permits HOSTS and processes to be insulated from changes in the packet sizes permitted in any networks through which their data must pass.

If fragmentation must be done, it appears best to do it upon entering the next network at the GATEWAY since only this GATEWAY (and not the other networks) must be aware of the internal packet size parameters which made the fragmentation necessary.

If a GATEWAY fragments an incoming packet into two or more packets, they must eventually be passed along to the destination HOST as fragments or reassembled for the HOST. It is conceivable that one might desire the GATEWAY to perform the reassembly to simplify the task of the destination HOST (or process) and/or to take advantage of a larger packet size. We take the position that GATEWAYS should not perform this function since GATEWAY reassembly can lead to serious buffering problems, potential deadlocks, the necessity for all fragments of a packet to pass through the same GATEWAY, and increased delay in transmission. Furthermore, it is not sufficient for the GATEWAYS to provide this function since the final GATEWAY may also have to fragment a packet for transmission. Thus the destination HOST must be prepared to do this task.

Let us now turn briefly to the somewhat unusual accounting effect which arises when a packet may be fragmented by one or more GATEWAYS. We assume, for simplicity, that each network initially charges a fixed rate per packet transmitted, regardless of distance, and if one network can handle a larger packet size than another, it charges a proportionally larger price per packet. We also assume that a subsequent increase in any network's packet size does not result in additional cost per packet to its users. The charge to a user thus remains basically constant through any net which must fragment a packet. The unusual effect occurs when a packet is fragmented into smaller packets which must individually pass through a subsequent network with a larger packet size than the original unfragmented packet. We expect that most networks will naturally select packet sizes close to one another, but in any case, an increase in packet size in one net, even when it causes fragmentation, will not increase the cost of transmission and may actually decrease it. In the event that any other packet charging policies (than the one we suggest) are adopted, differences in cost can be used as an economic lever toward optimization of individual network performance.

PROCESS LEVEL COMMUNICATION

We suppose that processes wish to communicate in full duplex with their correspondents using unbounded but finite length messages. A single character might constitute the text of a message from a process to a terminal or vice versa. An entire page of characters might constitute the text of a message from a file to a process. A data stream (e.g., a continuously generated bit string) can be represented as a sequence of finite length messages.

Within a HOST we assume the existence of a transmission control program (TCP) which handles the transmission and acceptance of messages on behalf of the processes it serves. The TCP is in turn served by one or more packet switches connected to the HOST in which the TCP resides. Processes that want to communicate present messages to the TCP for transmission, and TCP's deliver incoming messages to the appropriate destination processes. We allow the TCP to break up messages into segments because the destination may restrict the amount of data that may arrive, because the local network may limit the maximum transmission size, or because the TCP may need to share its resources among many processes concurrently. Furthermore, we constrain the length of a segment to an integral number of 8-bit bytes. This uniformity is most helpful in simplifying the software needed with HOST machines of different natural word lengths. Provision at the process level can be made for padding a message that is not an integral number of bytes and for identifying which of the arriving bytes of text contain information of interest to the receiving process.

Multiplexing and demultiplexing of segments among processes are fundamental tasks of the TCP. On transmission, a TCP must multiplex together segments from different source processes and produce internetwork packets for delivery to one of its serving packet switches. On reception, a TCP will accept a sequence of packets from its serving packet switch(es). From this sequence of arriving packets (generally from different HOSTS), the TCP must be able to reconstruct and deliver messages to the proper destination processes.

We assume that every segment is augmented with additional information that allows transmitting and receiving TCP's to identify destination and source processes, respectively. At this point, we must face a major issue. How should the source TCP format segments destined for the same destination TCP? We consider two cases.

Case 1): If we take the position that segment boundaries are immaterial and that a byte stream can be formed of segments destined for the same TCP, then we may gain improved transmission efficiency and resource sharing by arbitrarily parceling the stream into packets, permitting many segments to share a single internetwork packet header. However, this position results in the need to reconstruct exactly, and in order, the stream of text bytes produced by the source TCP. At the destination, this stream must first be parsed into segments and these in turn must be used to reconstruct messages for delivery to the appropriate processes.

There are fundamental problems associated with this strategy due to the possible arrival of packets out of order at the destination. The most critical problem appears to be the amount of interference that processes sharing the same TCP–TCP byte stream may cause among themselves. This is especially so at the receiving end. First, the TCP may be put to some trouble to parse the stream back into segments and then distribute them to buffers where messages are reassembled. If it is not readily apparent that all of a segment has arrived (remember, it may come as several packets), the receiving TCP may have to suspend parsing temporarily until more packets have arrived. Second, if a packet is missing, it may not be clear whether succeeding segments, even if they are identifiable, can be passed on to the receiving process, unless the TCP has knowledge of some process level sequencing scheme. Such knowledge would permit the TCP to decide whether a succeeding segment could be delivered to its waiting process. Finding the beginning of a segment when there are gaps in the byte stream may also be hard.

Case 2): Alternatively, we might take the position that the destination TCP should be able to determine, upon its arrival and without additional information, for which process or processes a received packet is intended, and if so, whether it should be delivered then.

If the TCP is to determine for which process an arriving packet is intended, every packet must contain a *process header* (distinct from the internetwork header) that completely identifies the destination process. For simplicity, we assume that each packet contains text from a single process which is destined for a single process. Thus each packet need contain only one process header. To decide whether the arriving data is deliverable to the destination process, the TCP must be able to determine whether the data is in the proper sequence (we can make provision for the destination process to instruct its TCP to ignore sequencing, but this is considered a special case). With the assumption that each arriving packet contains a process header, the necessary sequencing and destination process identification is immediately available to the destination TCP.

Both Cases 1) and 2) provide for the demultiplexing and delivery of segments to destination processes, but only Case 2) does so without the introduction of potential interprocess interference. Furthermore, Case 1) introduces extra machinery to handle flow control on a HOST-to-HOST basis, since there must also be some provision for process level control, and this machinery is little used since the probability is small that within a given HOST, two processes will be coincidentally scheduled to send messages to the same destination HOST. For this reason, we select the method of Case 2) as a part of the *internetwork transmission protocol*.

ADDRESS FORMATS

The selection of address formats is a problem between networks because the local network addresses of TCP's may vary substantially in format and size. A uniform internetwork TCP address space, understood by each GATEWAY and TCP, is essential to routing and delivery of internetwork packets.

Similar troubles are encountered when we deal with process addressing and, more generally, port addressing. We introduce the notion of *ports* in order to permit a process to distinguish between multiple message streams. The port is simply a designator of one such message stream associated with a process. The means for identifying a port are generally different in different operating systems, and therefore, to obtain uniform addressing, a standard port address format is also required. A port address designates a full duplex message stream.

TCP ADDRESSING

TCP addressing is intimately bound up in routing issues, since a HOST or GATEWAY must choose a suitable destination HOST or GATEWAY for an outgoing internetwork packet. Let us postulate the following address format for the TCP address (Fig. 4). The choice for network identification (8 bits) allows up to 256 distinct networks. This size seems sufficient for the forseeable future. Similarly, the TCP identifier field permits up to 65 536 distinct TCP's to be addressed, which seems more than sufficient for any given network.

As each packet passes through a GATEWAY, the GATEWAY observes the destination network ID to determine how to route the packet. If the destination network is connected to the GATEWAY, the lower 16 bits of the TCP address are used to produce a local TCP address in the destination network. If the destination network is not connected to the GATEWAY, the upper 8 bits are used to select a subsequent GATEWAY. We make no effort to specify how each individual network shall associate the internetwork TCP identifier with its local TCP address. We also do not rule out the possibility that the local network understands the internetwork addressing scheme and thus alleviates the GATEWAY of the routing responsibility.

PORT ADDRESSING

A receiving TCP is faced with the task of demultiplexing the stream of internetwork packets it receives and reconstructing the original messages for each destination process. Each operating system has its own internal means of identifying processes and ports. We assume that 16 bits are sufficient to serve as internetwork port identifiers. A sending process need not know how the destination port identification will be used. The destination TCP will be able to parse this number appropriately to find the proper buffer into which it will place arriving packets. We permit a large port number field to support processes which want to distinguish between many different messages streams concurrently. In reality, we do not care how the 16 bits are sliced up by the TCP's involved.

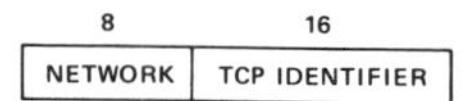

Fig. 4. TCP address.

Even though the transmitted port name field is large, it is still a compact external name for the internal representation of the port. The use of short names for port identifiers is often desirable to reduce transmission overhead and possibly reduce packet processing time at the destination TCP. Assigning short names to each port, however, requires an initial negotiation between source and destination to agree on a suitable short name assignment, the subsequent maintenance of conversion tables at both the source and the destination, and a final transaction to release the short name. For dynamic assignment of port names, this negotiation is generally necessary in any case.

SEGMENT AND PACKET FORMATS

As shown in Fig. 5, messages are broken by the TCP into segments whose format is shown in more detail in Fig. 6. The field lengths illustrated are merely suggestive. The first two fields (source port and destination port in the figure) have already been discussed in the preceding section on addressing. The uses of the third and fourth fields (window and acknowledgment in the figure) will be discussed later in the section on retransmission and duplicate detection.

We recall from Fig. 3 that an internetwork header contains both a sequence number and a byte count, as well as a flag field and a check sum. The uses of these fields are explained in the following section.

REASSEMBLY AND SEQUENCING

The reconstruction of a message at the receiving TCP clearly requires[1] that each internetwork packet carry a sequence number which is unique to its particular destination port message stream. The sequence numbers must be monotonic increasing (or decreasing) since they are used to reorder and reassemble arriving packets into a message. If the space of sequence numbers were infinite, we could simply assign the next one to each new packet. Clearly, this space cannot be infinite, and we will consider what problems a finite sequence number space will cause when we discuss retransmission and duplicate detection in the next section. We propose the following scheme for performing the sequencing of packets and hence the reconstruction of messages by the destination TCP.

A pair of ports will exchange one or more messages over a period of time. We could view the sequence of messages produced by one port as if it were embedded in an infinitely long stream of bytes. Each byte of the message has a unique sequence number which we take to be its byte location relative to the beginning of the stream. When a

[1] In the case of encrypted packets, a preliminary stage of reassembly may be required prior to decryption.

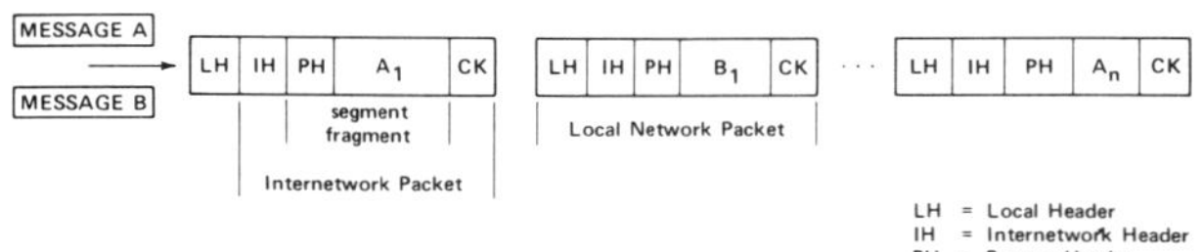

Fig. 5. Creation of segments and packets from messages.

32	32	16	16	8n
Source Port	Destination/Port	Window	ACK	Text

(Field sizes in bits)

← Process Header →

Fig. 6. Segment format (process header and text).

byte identification → sequence number

0	1	2 . . .	k . . .		
First Message		Second Message		Third Message	. . .
Segment	Segment	Segment	Segment	. . .	

(SEQ = k)

Fig. 7. Assignment of sequence numbers.

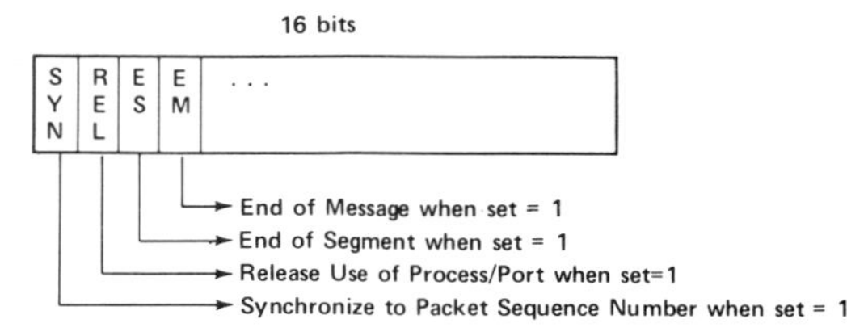

Fig. 8. Internetwork header flag field.

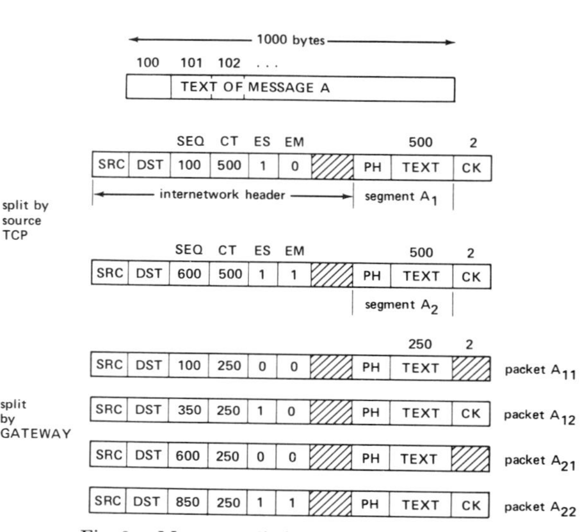

Fig. 9. Message splitting and packet splitting.

segment is extracted from the message by the source TCP and formatted for internetwork transmission, the relative location of the first byte of segment text is used as the sequence number for the packet. The byte count field in the internetwork header accounts for all the text in the segment (but does not include the check-sum bytes or the bytes in either internetwork or process header). We emphasize that the sequence number associated with a given packet is unique only to the pair of ports that are communicating (see Fig. 7). Arriving packets are examined to determine for which port they are intended. The sequence numbers on each arriving packet are then used to determine the relative location of the packet text in the messages under reconstruction. We note that this allows the exact position of the data in the reconstructed message to be determined even when pieces are still missing.

Every segment produced by a source TCP is packaged in a single internetwork packet and a check sum is computed over the text and process header associated with the segment.

The splitting of messages into segments by the TCP and the potential splitting of segments into smaller pieces by GATEWAYS creates the necessity for indicating to the destination TCP when the end of a segment (ES) has arrived and when the end of a message (EM) has arrived. The flag field of the internetwork header is used for this purpose (see Fig. 8).

The ES flag is set by the source TCP each time it prepares a segment for transmission. If it should happen that the message is completely contained in the segment, then the EM flag would also be set. The EM flag is also set on the last segment of a message, if the message could not be contained in one segment. These two flags are used by the destination TCP, respectively, to discover the presence of a check sum for a given segment and to discover that a complete message has arrived.

The ES and EM flags in the internetwork header are known to the GATEWAY and are of special importance when packets must be split apart for propagation through the next local network. We illustrate their use with an example in Fig. 9.

The original message A in Fig. 9 is shown split into two segments A_1 and A_2 and formatted by the TCP into a pair of internetwork packets. Packets A_1 and A_2 have their ES bits set, and A_2 has its EM bit set as well. When packet A_1 passes through the GATEWAY, it is split into two pieces: packet A_{11} for which neither EM nor ES bits are set, and packet A_{12} whose ES bit is set. Similarly, packet A_2 is split such that the first piece, packet A_{21}, has neither bit set, but packet A_{22} has both bits set. The sequence number field (SEQ) and the byte count field (CT) of each packet is modified by the GATEWAY to properly identify the text bytes of each packet. The GATEWAY need only examine the internetwork header to do fragmentation.

The destination TCP, upon reassembling segment A_1, will detect the ES flag and will verify the check sum it knows is contained in packet A_{12}. Upon receipt of packet A_{22}, assuming all other packets have arrived, the destination TCP detects that it has reassembled a complete message and can now advise the destination process of its receipt.

RETRANSMISSION AND DUPLICATE DETECTION

No transmission can be 100 percent reliable. We propose a timeout and positive acknowledgment mechanism which will allow TCP's to recover from packet losses from one HOST to another. A TCP transmits packets and waits for replies (acknowledgements) that are carried in the reverse packet stream. If no acknowledgment for a particular packet is received, the TCP will retransmit. It is our expectation that the HOST level retransmission mechanism, which is described in the following paragraphs, will not be called upon very often in practice. Evidence already exists[2] that individual networks can be effectively constructed without this feature. However, the inclusion of a HOST retransmission capability makes it possible to recover from occasional network problems and allows a wide range of HOST protocol strategies to be incorporated. We envision it will occasionally be invoked to allow HOST accommodation to infrequent overdemands for limited buffer resources, and otherwise not used much.

Any retransmission policy requires some means by which the receiver can detect duplicate arrivals. Even if an infinite number of distinct packet sequence numbers were available, the receiver would still have the problem of knowing how long to remember previously received packets in order to detect duplicates. Matters are complicated by the fact that only a finite number of distinct sequence numbers are in fact available, and if they are reused, the receiver must be able to distinguish between new transmissions and retransmissions.

A *window* strategy, similar to that used by the French CYCLADES system (voie virtuelle transmission mode [8]) and the ARPANET very distant HOST connection [18], is proposed here (see Fig. 10).

Suppose that the sequence number field in the internetwork header permits sequence numbers to range from 0 to $n - 1$. We assume that the sender will not transmit more than w bytes without receiving an acknowledgment. The w bytes serve as the window (see Fig. 11). Clearly, w must be less than n. The rules for sender and receiver are as follows.

Sender: Let L be the sequence number associated with the left window edge.

1) The sender transmits bytes from segments whose text lies between L and up to $L + w - 1$.

2) On timeout (duration unspecified), the sender retransmits unacknowledged bytes.

3) On receipt of acknowledgment consisting of the receiver's current left window edge, the sender's left window edge is advanced over the acknowledged bytes (advancing the right window edge implicitly).

Receiver:

1) Arriving packets whose sequence numbers coincide with the receiver's current left window edge are acknowledged by sending to the source the next sequence number

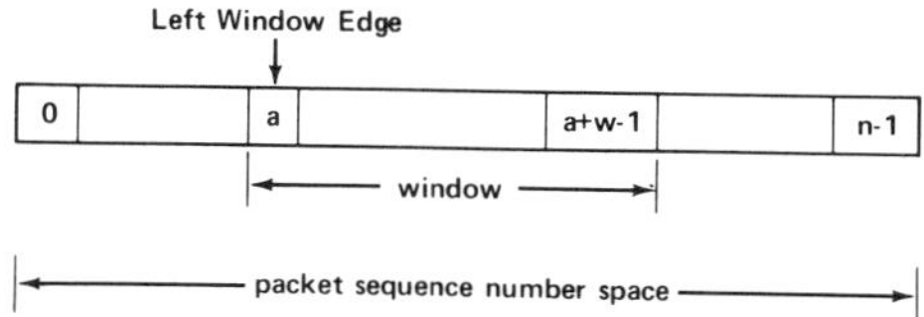

Fig. 10. The window concept.

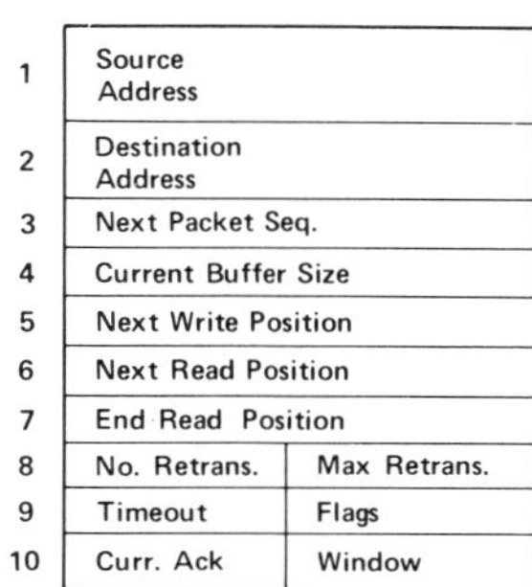

1	Source Address	
2	Destination Address	
3	Next Packet Seq.	
4	Current Buffer Size	
5	Next Write Position	
6	Next Read Position	
7	End Read Position	
8	No. Retrans.	Max Retrans.
9	Timeout	Flags
10	Curr. Ack	Window

Fig. 11. Conceptual TCB format.

expected. This effectively acknowledges bytes in between. The left window edge is advanced to the next sequence number expected.

2) Packets arriving with a sequence number to the left of the window edge (or, in fact, outside of the window) are discarded, and the current left window edge is returned as acknowledgment.

3) Packets whose sequence numbers lie within the receiver's window but do not coinicide with the receiver's left window edge are optionally kept or discarded, but are not acknowledged. This is the case when packets arrive out of order.

We make some observations on this strategy. First, all computations with sequence numbers and window edges must be made modulo n (e.g., byte 0 follows byte $n - 1$). Second, w must be less than $n/2$[3]; otherwise a retransmission may appear to the receiver to be a new transmission in the case that the receiver has accepted a window's worth of incoming packets, but all acknowledgments have been lost. Third, the receiver can either save or discard arriving packets whose sequence numbers do not coincide with the receiver's left window. Thus, in the simplest implementation, the receiver need not buffer more than one packet per message stream if space is critical. Fourth, multiple packets can be acknowledged simultaneously. Fifth, the receiver is able to deliver messages to processes in their proper order as a natural result of the reassembly mechanism. Sixth, when duplicates are detected, the acknowledgment method used naturally works to resynchronize sender and receiver. Furthermore, if the receiver accepts packets whose sequence numbers lie within the current window but

[2] The ARPANET is one such example.

[3] Actually $n/2$ is merely a convenient number to use; it is only required that a retransmission not appear to be a new transmission.

which are not coincident with the left window edge, an acknowledgment consisting of the current left window edge would act as a stimulus to cause retransmission of the unacknowledged bytes. Finally, we mention an overlap problem which results from retransmission, packet splitting, and alternate routing of packets through different GATEWAYS.

A 600-byte packet might pass through one GATEWAY and be broken into two 300-byte packets. On retransmission, the same packet might be broken into three 200-byte packets going through a different GATEWAY. Since each byte has a sequence number, there is no confusion at the receiving TCP. We leave for later the issue of initially synchronizing the sender and receiver left window edges and the window size.

FLOW CONTROL

Every segment that arrives at the destination TCP is ultimately acknowledged by returning the sequence number of the next segment which must be passed to the process (it may not yet have arrived).

Earlier we described the use of a sequence number space and window to aid in duplicate detection. Acknowledgments are carried in the process header (see Fig. 6) and along with them there is provision for a "suggested window" which the receiver can use to control the flow of data from the sender. This is intended to be the main component of the process flow control mechanism. The receiver is free to vary the window size according to any algorithm it desires so long as the window size never exceeds half the sequence number space.[3]

This flow control mechanism is exceedingly powerful and flexible and does not suffer from synchronization troubles that may be encountered by incremental buffer allocation schemes [9],[10]. However, it relies heavily on an effective retransmission strategy. The receiver can reduce the window even while packets are en route from the sender whose window is presently larger. The net effect of this reduction will be that the receiver may discard incoming packets (they may be outside the window) and reiterate the current window size along with a current window edge as acknowledgment. By the same token, the sender can, upon occasion, choose to send more than a window's worth of data on the possibility that the receiver will expand the window to accept it (of course, the sender must not send more than half the sequence number space at any time). Normally, we would expect the sender to abide by the window limitation. Expansion of the window by the receiver merely allows more data to be accepted. For the receiving HOST with a small amount of buffer space, a strategy of discarding all packets whose sequence numbers do not coincide with the current left edge of the window is probably necessary, but it will incur the expense of extra delay and overhead for retransmission.

TCP INPUT/OUTPUT HANDLING

The TCP has a component which handles input/output (I/O) to and from the network.[4] When a packet has arrived, it validates the addresses and places the packet on a queue. A pool of buffers can be set up to handle arrivals, and if all available buffers are used up, succeeding arrivals can be discarded since unacknowledged packets will be retransmitted.

On output, a smaller amount of buffering is needed, since process buffers can hold the data to be transmitted. Perhaps double buffering will be adequate. We make no attempt to specify how the buffering should be done, except to require that it be able to service the network with as little overhead as possible. Packet sized buffers, one or more ring buffers, or any other combination are possible candidates.

When a packet arrives at the destination TCP, it is placed on a queue which the TCP services frequently. For example, the TCP could be interrupted when a queue placement occurs. The TCP then attempts to place the packet text into the proper place in the appropriate process receive buffer. If the packet terminates a segment, then it can be checksummed and acknowledged. Placement may fail for several reasons.

1) The destination process may not be prepared to receive from the stated source, or the destination port ID may not exist.

2) There may be insufficient buffer space for the text.

3) The beginning sequence number of the text may not coincide with the next sequence number to be delivered to the process (e.g., the packet has arrived out of order).

In the first case, the TCP should simply discard the packet (thus far, no provision has been made for error acknowledgments). In the second and third cases, the packet sequence number can be inspected to determine whether the packet text lies within the legitimate window for reception. If it does, the TCP may optionally keep the packet queued for later processing. If not, the TCP can discard the packet. In either case the TCP can optionally acknowledge with the current left window edge.

It may happen that the process receive buffer is not present in the active memory of the HOST, but is stored on secondary storage. If this is the case, the TCP can prompt the scheduler to bring in the appropriate buffer and the packet can be queued for later processing.

If there are no more input buffers available to the TCP for temporary queueing of incoming packets, and if the TCP cannot quickly use the arriving data (e.g., a TCP to TCP message), then the packet is discarded. Assuming a sensibly functioning system, no other processes than the one for which the packet was intended should be affected by this discarding. If the delayed processing queue grows

[4] This component can serve to handle other protocols whose associated control programs are designated by internetwork destination address.

excessively long, any packets in it can be safely discarded since none of them have yet been acknowledged. Congestion at the TCP level is flexibly handled owing to the robust retransmission and duplicate detection strategy.

TCP/PROCESS COMMUNICATION

In order to send a message, a process sets up its text in a buffer region in its own address space, inserts the requisite control information (described in the following list) in a transmit control block (TCB) and passes control to the TCP. The exact form of a TCB is not specified here, but it might take the form of a passed pointer, a pseudointerrupt, or various other forms. To receive a message in its address space, a process sets up a receive buffer, inserts the requisite control information in a receive control block (RCB) and again passes control to the TCP.

In some simple systems, the buffer space may in fact be provided by the TCP. For simplicity we assume that a ring buffer is used by each process, but other structures (e.g., buffer chaining) are not ruled out.

A possible format for the TCB is shown in Fig. 11. The TCB contains information necessary to allow the TCP to extract and send the process data. Some of the information might be implicitly known, but we are not concerned with that level of detail. The various fields in the TCB are described as follows.

1) *Source Address*: This is the full net/HOST/TCP/port address of the transmitter.

2) *Destination Address*: This is the full net/HOST/TCP/port of the receiver.

3) *Next Packet Sequence Number*: This is the sequence number to be used for the next packet the TCP will transmit from this port.

4) *Current Buffer Size*: This is the present size of the process transmit buffer.

5) *Next Write Position*: This is the address of the next position in the buffer at which the process can place new data for transmission.

6) *Next Read Position*: This is the address at which the TCP should begin reading to build the next segment for output.

7) *End Read Position*: This is the address at which the TCP should halt transmission. Initially 6) and 7) bound the message which the process wishes to transmit.

8) *Number of Retransmissions/Maximum Retransmissions*: These fields enable the TCP to keep track of the number of times it has retransmitted the data and could be omitted if the TCP is not to give up.

9) *Timeout/Flags*: The timeout field specifies the delay after which unacknowledged data should be retransmitted. The flag field is used for semaphores and other TCP/process synchronization, status reporting, etc.

10) *Current Acknowledgment/Window*: The current acknowledgment field identifies the first byte of data still unacknowledged by the destination TCP.

The read and write positions move circularly around the transmit buffer, with the write position always to the left (module the buffer size) of the read position.

The next packet sequence number should be constrained to be less than or equal to the sum of the current acknowledgment and the window fields. In any event, the next sequence number should not exceed the sum of the current acknowledgment and half of the maximum possible sequence number (to avoid confusing the receiver's duplicate detection algorithm). A possible buffer layout is shown in Fig. 12.

The RCB is substantially the same, except that the end read field is replaced by a partial segment check-sum register which permits the receiving TCP to compute and remember partial check sums in the event that a segment arrives in several packets. When the final packet of the segment arrives, the TCP can verify the check sum and if successful, acknowledge the segment.

CONNECTIONS AND ASSOCIATIONS

Much of the thinking about process-to-process communication in packet switched networks has been influenced by the ubiquitous telephone system. The HOST–HOST protocol for the ARPANET deals explicitly with the opening and closing of simplex connections between processes [9],[10]. Evidence has been presented that message-based "connection-free" protocols can be constructed [12], and this leads us to carefully examine the notion of a connection.

The term *connection* has a wide variety of meanings. It can refer to a physical or logical path between two entities, it can refer to the flow over the path, it can inferentially refer to an action associated with the setting up of a path, or it can refer to an association between two or more entities, with or without regard to any path between them. In this paper, we do not explicitly reject the term connection, since it is in such widespread use, and does connote a meaningful relation, but consider it exclusively in the sense of an association between two or more entities without regard to a path. To be more precise about our intent, we shall define the relationship between two or more ports that are in communication, or are prepared to communicate to be an *association*. Ports that are associated with each other are called *associates*. 445

It is clear that for any communication to take place between two processes, one must be able to address the other. The two important cases here are that the destination port may have a global and unchanging address or that it may be globally unique but dynamically reassigned. While in either case the sender may have to learn the destination address, given the destination name, only in the second instance is there a requirement for learning the address from the destination (or its representative) each time an association is desired. Only after the source has learned how to address the destination can an association be said to have occurred. But this is not yet sufficient. If

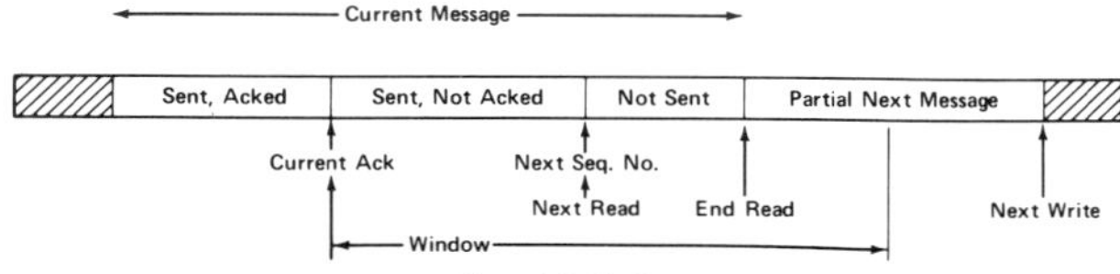

Fig. 12. Transmit buffer layout.

ordering of delivered messages is also desired, both TCP's must maintain sufficient information to allow proper sequencing. When this information is also present at both ends, then an association is said to have occurred.

Note that we have not said anything about a path, nor anything which implies that either end be aware of the condition of the other. Only when both partners are prepared to communicate with each other has an association occurred, and it is possible that neither partner may be able to verify that an association exists until some data flows between them.

CONNECTION-FREE PROTOCOLS WITH ASSOCIATIONS

In the ARPANET, the interface message processors (IMP's) do not have to open and close connections from source to destination. The reason for this is that connections are, in effect, always open, since the address of every source and destination is never[5] reassigned. When the name and the place are static and unchanging, it is only necessary to label a packet with source and destination to transmit it through the network. In our parlance, every source and destination forms an association.

In the case of processes, however, we find that port addresses are continually being used and reused. Some ever-present processes could be assigned fixed addresses which do not change (e.g., the logger process). If we supposed, however, that every TCP had an infinite supply of port addresses so that no old address would ever be reused, then any dynamically created port would be assigned the next unused address. In such an environment, there could never be any confusion by source and destination TCP as to the intended recipient or implied source of each message, and all ports would be associates.

Unfortunately, TCP's (or more properly, operating systems) tend not to have an infinite supply of internal port addresses. These internal addresses are reassigned after the demise of each port. Walden [12] suggests that a set of unique uniform external port addresses could be supplied by a central registry. A newly created port could apply to the central registry for an address which the central registry would guarantee to be unused by any HOST system in the network. Each TCP could maintain tables matching external names with internal ones, and use the external ones for communication with other processes. This idea violates the premise that interprocess communication should not require centralized control. One would have to extend the central registry service to include all HOST's in all the interconnected networks to apply this idea to our situation, and we therefore do not attempt to adopt it.

Let us consider the situation from the standpoint of the TCP. In order to send or receive data for a given port, the TCP needs to set up a TCB and RCB and initialize the window size and left window edge for both. On the receive side, this task might even be delayed until the first packet destined for a given port arrives. By convention, the first packet should be marked so that the receiver will synchronize to the received sequence number.

On the send side, the first request to transmit could cause a TCB to be set up with some initial sequence number (say, zero) and an assumed window size. The receiving TCP can reject the packet if it wishes and notify the sending TCP of the correct window size via the acknowledgment mechanism, but only if either

1) we insist that the first packet be a complete segment;
2) an acknowledgment can be sent for the first packet (even if not a segment, as long as the acknowledgment specifies the next sequence number such that the source also understands that no bytes have been accepted).

It is apparent, therefore, that the synchronizing of window size and left window edge can be accomplished without what would ordinarily be called a connection setup.

The first packet referencing a newly created RCB sent from one associate to another can be marked with a bit which requests that the receiver synchronize his left window edge with the sequence number of the arriving packet (see SYN bit in Fig. 8). The TCP can examine the source and destination port addresses in the packet and in the RCB to decide whether to accept or ignore the request.

Provision should be made for a destination process to specify that it is willing to LISTEN to a specific port or "any" port. This last idea permits processes such as the logger process to accept data arriving from unspecified sources. This is purely a HOST matter, however.

The initial packet may contain data which can be stored or discarded by the destination, depending on the availability of destination buffer space at the time. In the other direction, acknowledgment is returned for receipt of data which also specifies the receiver's window size.

If the receiving TCP should want to reject the synchronization request, it merely transmits an acknowledgment carrying a release (REL) bit (see Fig. 8) indicating that the destination port address is unknown or inaccessible. The sending HOST waits for the acknowledgment (after accepting or rejecting the synchronization request) before sending the next message or segment. This rejection is quite different from a negative data acknowledgment. We do not have explicit negative acknowledgments. If no acknowledgment is returned, the sending HOST may

[5] Unless the IMP is physically moved to another site, or the HOST is connected to a different IMP.

retransmit without introducing confusion if, for example, the left window edge is not changed on the retransmission.

Because messages may be broken up into many packets for transmission or during transmission, it will be necessary to ignore the REL flag except in the case that the EM flag is also set. This could be accomplished either by the TCP or by the GATEWAY which could reset the flag on all but the packet containing the set EM flag (see Fig. 9).

At the end of an association, the TCP sends a packet with ES, EM, and REL flags set. The packet sequence number scheme will alert the receiving TCP if there are still outstanding packets in transit which have not yet arrived, so a premature dissociation cannot occur.

To assure that both TCP's are aware that the association has ended, we insist that the receiving TCP respond to the REL by sending a REL acknowledgment of its own.

Suppose now that a process sends a single message to an associate including an REL along with the data. Assuming an RCB has been prepared for the receiving TCP to accept the data, the TCP will accumulate the incoming packets until the one marked ES, EM, REL arrives, at which point a REL is returned to the sender. The association is thereby terminated and the appropriate TCB and RCB are destroyed. If the first packet of a message contains a SYN request bit and the last packet contains ES, EM, and REL bits, then data will flow "one message at a time." This mode is very similar to the scheme described by Walden [12], since each succeeding message can only be accepted at the receiver after a new LISTEN (like Walden's RECEIVE) command is issued by the receiving process to its serving TCP. Note that only if the acknowledgment is received by the sender can the association be terminated properly. It has been pointed out[6] that the receiver may erroneously accept duplicate transmissions if the sender does not receive the acknowledgment. This may happen if the sender transmits a duplicate message with the SYN and REL bits set and the destination has already destroyed any record of the previous transmission. One way of preventing this problem is to destroy the record of the association at the destination only after some known and suitably chosen timeout. However, this implies that a new association with the same source and destination port identifiers could not be established until this timeout had expired. This problem can occur even with sequences of messages whose SYN and REL bits are separated into different internetwork packets. We recognize that this problem must be solved, but do not go into further detail here.

Alternatively, both processes can send one message, causing the respective TCP's to allocate RCB/TCB pairs at both ends which rendezvous with the exchanged data and then disappear. If the overhead of creating and destroying RCB's and TCB's is small, such a protocol might be adequate for most low-bandwidth uses. This idea might also form the basis for a relatively secure transmission system. If the communicating processes agree to change their external port addresses in some way known only to each other (i.e., pseudorandom), then each message will appear to the outside world as if it is part of a different association message stream. Even if the data is intercepted by a third party, he will have no way of knowing that the data should in fact be considered part of a sequence of messages.

We have described the way in which processes develop associations with each other, thereby becoming associates for possible exchange of data. These associations need not involve the transmission of data prior to their formation and indeed two associates need not be able to determine that they are associates until they attempt to communicate.

[6] S. Crocker of ARPA/IPT.

CONCLUSIONS

We have discussed some fundamental issues related to the interconnection of packet switching networks. In particular, we have described a simple but very powerful and flexible protocol which provides for variation in individual network packet sizes, transmission failures, sequencing, flow control, and the creation and destruction of process-to-process associations. We have considered some of the implementation issues that arise and found that the proposed protocol is implementable by HOST's of widely varying capacity.

The next important step is to produce a detailed specification of the protocol so that some initial experiments with it can be performed. These experiments are needed to determine some of the operational parameters (e.g., how often and how far out of order do packets actually arrive; what sort of delay is there between segment acknowledgments; what should be retransmission timeouts be?) of the proposed protocol.

ACKNOWLEDGMENT

The authors wish to thank a number of colleagues for helpful comments during early discussions of international network protocols, especially R. Metcalfe, R. Scantlebury, D. Walden, and H. Zimmerman; D. Davies and L. Pouzin who constructively commented on the fragmentation and accounting issues; and S. Crocker who commented on the creation and destruction of associations.

REFERENCES

[1] L. Roberts and B. Wessler, "Computer network development to achieve resource sharing," in *1970 Spring Joint Computer Conf., AFIPS Conf. Proc.*, vol. 36. Montvale, N. J.: AFIPS Press, 1970, pp. 543–549.

[2] L. Pouzin, "Presentation and major design aspects of the CYCLADES computer network," in *Proc. 3rd Data Communications Symp.*, 1973.

[3] F. R. E. Dell, "Features of a proposed synchronous data network," in *Proc. 2nd Symp. Problems in the Optimization of Data Communications Systems*, 1971, pp. 50–57.

[4] R. A. Scantlebury and P. T. Wilkinson, "The design of a switching system to allow remote access to computer services by other computers and terminal devices," in *Proc. 2nd Symp. Problems in the Optimization of Data Communications Systems*, 1971, pp. 160–167.

[5] D. L. A. Barber, "The European computer network project," in *Computer Communications: Impacts and Implications*, S. Winkler, Ed. Washington, D. C., 1972, pp. 192–200.

[6] R. Despres, "A packet switching network with graceful saturated operation," in *Computer Communications: Impacts and Implications*, S. Winkler, Ed. Washington, D. C., 1972, pp. 345–351.

[7] R. E. Kahn and W. R. Crowther, "Flow control in a resource-sharing computer network," *IEEE Trans. Commun.*, vol. COM-20, pp. 539–546, June 1972.

[8] J. F. Chambon, M. Elie, J. Le Bihan, G. LeLann, and H. Zimmerman, "Functional specification of transmission station in the CYCLADES network. ST-ST protocol" (in French), I.R.I.A. Tech. Rep. SCH502.3, May 1973.

[9] S. Carr, S. Crocker, and V. Cerf, "HOST-HOST Communication Protocol In the ARPA Network," in *Spring Joint Computer Conf., AFIPS Conf. Proc.*, vol. 36. Montvale, N. J.: AFIPS Press, 1970, pp. 589–597.

[10] A. McKenzie, "HOST/HOST protocol for the ARPA network," in *Current Network Protocols*, Network Information Cen., Menlo Park, Calif., NIC 8246, Jan. 1972.

[11] L. Pouzin, "Address format in Mitranet," NIC 14497, INWG 20, Jan. 1973.

[12] D. Walden, "A system for interprocess communication in a resource sharing computer network," *Commun. Ass. Comput. Mach.*, vol. 15, pp. 221–230, Apr. 1972.

[13] B. Lampson, "A scheduling philosophy for multiprocessing systems," *Commun. Ass. Comput. Mach.*, vol. 11, pp. 347–360, May 1968.

[14] F. E. Heart, R. E. Kahn, S. Ornstein, W. Crowther, and D. Walden, "The interface message processor for the ARPA computer network," in *Proc. Spring Joint Computer Conf., AFIPS Conf. Proc.*, vol. 36. Montvale, N. J.: AFIPS Press, 1970, pp. 551–567.

[15] N. G. Anslow and J. Hanscoff, "Implementation of international data exchange networks," in *Computer Communications: Impacts and Implications*, S. Winkler, Ed. Washington, D. C., 1972, pp. 181–184

[16] A. McKenzie, "HOST/HOST protocol design considerations," INWG Note 16, NIC 13879, Jan. 1973.

[17] R. E. Kahn, "Resource-sharing computer communication networks," *Proc. IEEE*, vol. 60, pp. 1397–1407, Nov. 1972.

[18] Bolt, Beranek, and Newman, "Specification for the interconnection of a host and an IMP," Bolt Beranek and Newman, Inc., Cambridge, Mass., BBN Rep. 1822 (revised), Apr. 1973.

Vinton G. Cerf was born in New Haven, Conn., in 1943. He did undergraduate work in mathematics at Stanford University, Stanford, Calif., and received the Ph.D. degree in computer science from the University of California at Los Angeles, Los Angeles, Calif., in 1972.

He was with IBM in Los Angeles from 1965 through 1967 and consulted and/or worked part time at UCLA from 1967 through 1972. Currently he is Assistant Professor of Computer Science and Electrical Engineering at Stanford University, and consultant to Cabledata Associates. Most of his current research is supported by the Defense Advanced Research Projects Agency and by the National Science Foundation on the technology and economics of computer networking. He is Chairman of IFIP TC6.1, an international network working group which is studying the problem of packet network interconnection.

Robert E. Kahn (M'65) was born in Brooklyn, N. Y., on December 23, 1938. He received the B.E.E. degree from the City College of New York, New York, in 1960, and the M.A. and Ph.D. degrees from Princeton University, Princeton, N. J., in 1962 and 1964, respectively.

From 1960 to 1962 he was a Member of the Technical Staff of Bell Telephone Laboratories, Murray Hill, N. J., engaged in traffic and communication studies. From 1964 to 1966 he was a Ford Postdoctoral Fellow and an Assistant Professor of Electrical Engineering at the Massachusetts Institute of Technology, Cambridge, where he worked on communications and information theory. From 1966 to 1972 he was a Senior Scientist at Bolt Beranek and Newman, Inc., Cambridge, Mass., where he worked on computer communications network design and techniques for distributed computation. Since 1972 he has been with the Advanced Research Projects Agency, Department of Defense, Arlington, Va.

Dr. Kahn is a member of Tau Beta Pi, Sigma Xi, Eta Kappa Nu, the Institute of Mathematical Statistics, and the Mathematical Association of America. He was selected to serve as a National Lecturer for the Association for Computing Machinery in 1972.

Reprinted by permission from *IEEE Transactions on Communications*
Vol. COM-22, No. 5, May 1974, pp. 637-648

Distributed Data Base Design Considerations

Resource sharing is an important feature and capability in a computer communications network. In this chapter, we deal with the sharing of file or data bases in a network. (This is also known as a distributed data base.)

Chu (p. 452) presents a mathematical model for allocating files in a network computer to achieve resource sharing. This model minimizes the total operating cost yet satisfies a set of required performance constraints. Booth (p. 457) describes various problems and design considerations associated with the use of distributed data bases in a computer communications network. Chu and Ohlmacher (p. 463) present dead lock detection and prevention mechanisms for distributed data bases.

For more reading on this subject, the reader is referred to [CAS 72], [CHU 75], [LEV 75] and [MAH 75].

Optimal File Allocation in a Multiple Computer System

WESLEY W. CHU, MEMBER, IEEE

Abstract—**A model is developed for allocating information files required in common by several computers. The model considers storage cost, transmission cost, file lengths, and request rates, as well as updating rates of files, the maximum allowable expected access times to files at each computer, and the storage capacity of each computer. The criterion of optimality is minimal overall operating costs (storage and transmission). The model is formulated into a nonlinear integer zero-one programming problem, which may be reduced to a linear zero-one programming problem. A simple example is given to illustrate the model.**

Index Terms—**Computer communication, linear integer programming, multicomputer information system, multiprocessor, nonlinear integer programming, optimal file allocation.**

Introduction

IN THE AUTOMATION of large information systems, a major portion of the planning is concerned with storing large quantities of information in a computer system. This requires study of information storage, modification, and transmission. Examples of such efforts are found in business, medical, library, and management information systems. These systems, which may consist of several geographically separated divisions (subsystems), need to process information files in common.

It is apparent that when a given information file is required in common by several computers, it may be stored in at least one of them and accessed by the others when needed. The overall operating cost related to the files is considered to consist of transmission and storage costs. The problem is the following. Given a number of computers that process common information files, how can one allocate the files so that the allocation yields minimum overall operating costs subject to the following constraints: 1) the expected time to access each file is less than a given bound, 2) the amount of storage needed at each computer does not exceed the available storage capacity.

The Model

The file allocation problem can be formulated as an integer (0 or 1) programming model.

Let X_{ij} indicate that the jth file is stored in the ith computer:

Manuscript received July 12, 1968; revised May 29, 1969. This is a generalized version of the paper entitled "Optimal file allocation in a multicomputer information system," presented at the IFIP Congress 68, Edinburgh, Scotland, August 5–10, 1968.

The author was with Bell Telephone Laboratories, Inc., Holmdel N. J. He is now with the Computer Science Department, University of the City of Los Angeles, Los Angeles, Calif.

$$X_{ij} = \begin{cases} 1 & j\text{th file stored in the } i\text{th computer} \\ 0 & \text{otherwise} \end{cases} \tag{1}$$

where

$i = 1, 2, \cdots, n$
$j = 1, 2, \cdots, m$
n = total number of computers in the multicomputer system
m = total number of distinct files in the multicomputer system.

For storing r_j redundant copies of the jth in the information system, we have

$$\sum_i X_{ij} = r_j \qquad \text{for } 1 \leq j \leq m. \tag{2}$$

To assure that the storage capacity of each computer is not exceeded, we have

$$\sum_j X_{ij} L_j \leq b_i \qquad \text{for } 1 \leq i \leq n \tag{3}$$

where

L_j = length of the jth file,
b_i = available memory size of the ith computer.

The expected time for the ith computer to retrieve the jth file from the kth computer (from initiation of request till start of reception) is denoted as a_{ijk}. The maximum allowable retrieval time of the jth file to the ith computer is T_{ij}. We required that a_{ijk} be less than T_{ij}, i.e.,

$$(1 - X_{ij}) X_{kj} a_{ijk} \leq T_{ij} \qquad \text{for } i \neq k, \qquad 1 \leq j \leq m. \tag{4}$$

When $r_j = 1$ for all j, then from (2) we know that $X_{ij}X_{kj} = 0$ for $i \neq k$. Thus (4) reduces to

$$X_{kj} a_{ijk} \leq T_{ij} \qquad \text{for } i \neq k, \qquad 1 \leq j \leq m. \tag{5}$$

Now, a_{ijk} is equal to the sum of the expected queuing delay at the ith computer for the channel to the kth computer[1] $w_{ik}^{(1)}$, the expected queuing delay at the kth computer for the channel to the ith computer $w_{ki}^{(2)}$, and the expected computer access time to the jth file t_{kj}. In most cases, the quantity t_{kj} is much smaller than $w_{ik} = w_{ik}^{(1)} + w_{ki}^{(2)}$ and can be neglected. Hence,

$$a_{ijk} \doteq w_{ik}. \tag{6}$$

[1] The number in the superscripts of $w_{ik}^{(\cdot)}$ and $w_{ki}^{(\cdot)}$ denotes the priority class of the messages that are transmitted between the ith and kth computers, which will be discussed shortly.

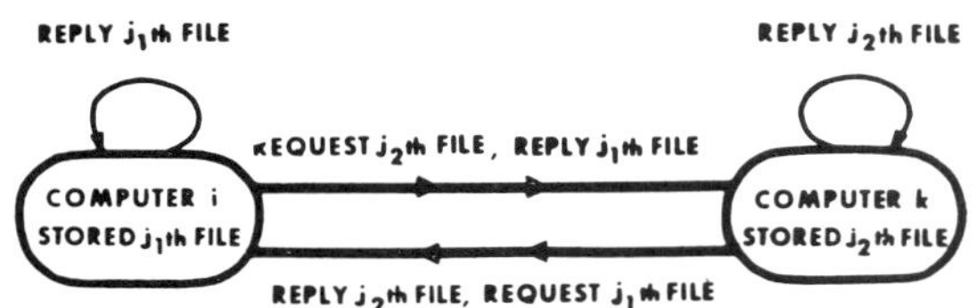

Fig. 1. Transmission paths between each pair of computers.

Next we will discuss the mechanism involved in the queuing delay. Each pair of computers is assumed to be able to transmit information in both directions simultaneously. This is known as single-channel full-duplex operation. Further, the files can be accessed by the local and remote computers at the same time. One pair of transmission paths links each pair of computers; one of these paths carries *requests* for the files from the ith computer to the kth computer, and *reply* messages (files) from the ith computer to the kth computer, whereas the other path carries *requests* for files from the kth computer to the ith computer, and *reply* messages from kth to the ith computer (Fig. 1). In most cases, the request message is much shorter than the reply message. Therefore, we shall assign a higher priority to request messages than to reply messages. Messages of the same priority are served in the order of their arrival. Assume, for example, a reply message is being transmitted on a particular transmission path at the time a new request is initiated. The request will interrupt the current reply and the computer will transmit the request first. After finishing transmission of that new request, the computer resumes transmitting the previous reply. Such preemptive-resume priority servicing faciltates optimization, since the queuing delay will be minimum if the shortest messages are serviced first [1], [2]. Recalling that the requested message length is much shorter than that of the reply message, the delay due to the request message can be neglected.[2] Under these conditions, the queuing system can be viewed as a single server queue with constant service time.

In many cases, it is reasonable to model the file accessing process as a Poisson process. Then the rate of requests from the ith computer to the kth computer (arrival rate) λ_{ik} is the sum of the rates of request of those files not stored in the ith computer but stored in the kth computer. The requested file length may be less than the entire storage file length and is defined as the length of each transaction; that is, the length of each transaction of the jth file l_j should be less or equal to the entire jth file length L_j. The average time required to transmit the reply from the kth computer to the jth computer $1/\mu_{ik}$ (i.e., service time) is dependent on l_j and λ_{ik}. Clearly, both λ_{ik} and $1/\mu_{ik}$ depend on the file allocation, yet the allocation is unknown in advance. Hence, we shall express λ_{ik} and $1/\mu_{ik}$ in terms of the X_{ij}'s:

$$\lambda_{ik} = \sum_j u_{ij}(1 - X_{ij})X_{kj} \tag{7}$$

where

u_{ij} = the request rate[3] of the entire or part of the jth file at the ith computer per unit time.

The average time required to transmit a reply message from the kth to the ith computer via a line with transmission rate R is

$$1/\mu_{ik} = \frac{1}{\lambda_{ik}} \sum \frac{1}{\mu_j} u_{ij}(1 - X_{ij})X_{kj} \tag{8}$$

where

$1/\mu_j = l_j/R$ = required time to transmit each transaction of the jth file.

Equation (8) states that $1/\mu_{ik}$ is equal to the time required for the kth computer to reply all the messages requested from the ith computer divided by the total number of requests initiated from the ith computer to the kth computer. Since the l_j's and R are constants, μ_j and μ_{ik} are also constants.

The traffic intensity from the kth to the ith computer ρ_{ik} measures the degree of congestion of the line that provides the transmission path between the kth and ith computer, or the fraction of time that the line is busy. It is defined as

$$\rho_{ik} = \lambda_{ik}/\mu_{ik} = \sum_j \frac{1}{\mu_j} u_{ij}(1 - X_{ij})X_{kj}. \tag{9}$$

Since physically it is impossible for the transmission line to be 100 percent busy, the traffic intensity is less than unity, i.e., $\rho_{ik} < 1$.

When only a single copy of the file is stored in the information system, then $X_{ij}X_{kj} = 0$ for $i \neq k$. Hence

$$\lambda_{ik} = \sum_j u_{ij}X_{kj} \qquad \text{for } i \neq k \tag{10}$$

and

$$1/\mu_{ik} = \frac{1}{\lambda_{ik}} \sum_j u_{ij} \frac{1}{\mu_j} X_{kj} \qquad \text{for } i \neq k \tag{11}$$

when all the $\mu_j = \mu$; then (11) reduces to

$$1/\mu_{ik} = 1/\mu. \tag{12}$$

The average waiting time [1], [2] from the initiation of a request at the ith computer to the receipt of the requested message from the kth computer, with the above assumptions (single server queue with Poisson arrivals and constant service time), is

[2] Preemptive priority servicing permits the assumption that $w_{ik} \doteq w_{ki}^{(2)}$. Note that the file retrieval time constraint as shown in (4) also applies to the nonpremptive priority case, but a more complex expression would be required for w_{ik} since $w_{ik}^{(1)}$ can no longer be neglected.

[3] In general, the request rate may be time dependent. In the analysis here, we are concerned with the request rate of the busy period.

453

$$w_{ik} \doteq w_{ki}^{(2)} = \frac{1}{\mu_{ik}} \frac{\rho_{ik}}{2(1-\rho_{ik})} \qquad \text{for } i \neq k \tag{13}$$

where $1/\mu_{ik}$ and ρ_{ik} are functions of X_{ij}'s as given by (8) and (9). The variance and probability distribution of w_{ik} for a specific allocation can be computed from its ρ_{ik} and μ_{ik} [1], [2].

Substituting (13) into (6) and (4), we have

$$(1 - X_{ij})X_{kj} \frac{1}{\mu_{ik}} \frac{\rho_{ik}}{2(1-\rho_{ik})} \leq T_{ij},$$

which can be rearranged into the form

$$(1 - X_{ij})X_{kj}\lambda_{ik} - 2\mu_{ik}(\mu_{ik} - \lambda_{ik})T_{ij} \leq 0. \tag{14}$$

For the special case that $\mu_{ik} = \mu$ and $r_j = 1$, (14) reduces to

$$\sum_{\substack{j_1 \\ j \neq j_1}} u_{ij}X_{kj_1}X_{kj} + 2T_{ij}\mu \sum_{j_1} u_{ij_1}X_{kj_1} + u_{ij}X_{kj} - 2\mu^2 T_{ij} \leq 0. \tag{15}$$

Finally, we shall express the operating cost (objective function) in terms of the allocation (X_{ij}'s). Suppose we know the storage cost of the jth file per unit length and unit time at the ith computer C_{ij}, the transmission cost from the kth computer to the ith computer per unit time C_{ik}', the request rate for the entire or part of the jth file at the ith computer per unit time u_{ij}, the frequency of modification of the jth file at the ith computer after each transaction P_{ij}, the length of each transaction for the jth file l_j, and the number of redundant copies of the jth file stored in the system r_j. Then the overall operating cost per unit time C for processing m distinct files required in common by n computers is

$$C = \underbrace{\sum_{i,j} C_{ij}L_jX_{ij}}_{\text{storage cost}} + \underbrace{\sum_{i,j,k} \frac{1}{r_j} C_{ik}'l_ju_{ij}X_{kj}(1 - X_{ij}) + \sum_{i,j,k} C_{ik}'l_ju_{ij}X_{kj}P_{ij}}_{\text{transmission cost}},$$

which can be rearranged into the form

$$= \sum_{i,j} D_{ij}X_{ij} - \sum_{i,j,k} E_{ijk}X_{kj}X_{ij} \quad \text{where} \quad D_{ij} > 0, \qquad E_{ijk} > 0 \tag{16}$$

when $r_j = 1$, $1 \leq j \leq m$; then $X_{kj}X_{ij} = 0$ for $k \neq i$, and $C_{ii}' = 0$. Under this case, (16) reduces to

$$C = \sum_{i,j} D_{ij}X_{ij}. \tag{17}$$

We want to minimize (16) subject to storage and access time requirements constraints given in (1), (2), (3), and (14). As X_{ij}'s take on value zero or one, the allocation problem becomes solving a nonlinear zero-one programming problem. In the next section, we shall introduce a technique to reduce the nonlinear zero-one equations to the linear zero–one equations. With this technique, the allocation problem can be then solved by standard linear zero-one programming techniques [3], [4].

Reduction of Zero–One Nonlinear Programming Problems to Zero–One Linear Programming Problems[4]

Because nonlinear programming problems are so complex, we are able to obtain a global optimal solution only for special cases (e.g., convexity). Therefore, it is desirable to reduce the nonlinear zero-one programming problems to the linear zero-one programming problems. We shall now show such a reduction, which is derived from the integer (0 or 1) property.

Suppose we want to minimize an arbitrary cost function (which need not be convex)

$$C = \min_X F(X_1, X_2, \cdots, X_k) \tag{18}$$

subject to a set of nonconvex constraint equations

$$G_i(X_1, X_2, \cdots, X_k) \leq B_i \qquad i = 1, 2, \cdots, N \tag{19}$$

where the X_i's are zero-one variables, F and G_i are polynomials of the X_i's with constant coefficients, and B_i is a constant. Clearly, $X_i^q = X_i$ (q = positive integer). Let the coefficient of the product terms in (18) or (19), $X_iX_j, \cdots, X_uX_v$, be denoted as $C_{ij\cdots uv}$.

To reduce the above nonlinear zero-one problem to a linear zero-one problem, first we consider the objective function (18). Let us define

$$X_{ij\cdots uv} = \underbrace{X_iX_j \cdots X_uX_v}_{q} \qquad q = 2, \cdots, Q \tag{20}$$

which takes value zero or one where Q is the highest degree of nonlinearity. We then represent each nonlinear term in (18) by terms of the form (20) and then examine its coefficient. If the coefficient of the nonlinear term is positive, we introduce the following constraint equation:

$$\underbrace{X_i + X_j \cdots + X_u + X_v}_{q} - q + 1 \leq X_{ij\cdots uv}. \tag{21}$$

[4] A similar but less general result has also been obtained independently by Watters [5].

If the coefficient of the nonlinear term is negative, we introduce the following constraint equation:

$$\underbrace{X_i + X_j + \cdots + X_u + X_v}_{q} \geq qX_{ij\ldots uv}. \qquad (22)$$

If all the X's in left side of (21) have value one, then $X_{ij\ldots uv}=1$. If one or more of the X's have value zero, then $X_{ij\ldots uv}$ may be either zero or one, but the coefficient of $X_{ij\ldots uv}$ in (18), $C_{ij\ldots uv}$, is positive. Thus minimizing (18) under X assures that $X_{ij\ldots uv}=0$. If we substitute (20) for each nonlinear term in (18) that has positive coefficient and introduce the additional constraint (21), then the X's in the transformed linear equations take on the same values as the original ones. Similarly, if one or more of the X's in (20) have value zero, then $X_{ij\ldots uv}=0$. If all the X's have value one, then $X_{ij\ldots uv}$ may either be zero or one, but the coefficient of $X_{ij\ldots uv}$ in (18), $C_{ij\ldots uv}$, is negative. Thus minimizing (18) under X assures that $X_{ijkl\ldots uv}=1$. If we substitute (20) for each nonlinear term in (18) that has negative coefficient and introduce the additional constraint (22), then the X's in the transformed linear equations take on the same values as the original ones. Thus, we have linearized the objective function (18).

To linearize the constraint equations, we represent the nonlinear terms in (19) by (20) and introduce its corresponding *two* additional constraint equations (21) and (22). If one or more of the X's in (20) have value zero, then $X_{ij\ldots uv}=0$; this condition is also satisfied by (21) and (22). If all the X_{ij}'s have value one in (20), then $X_{ij\ldots uv}$ is one. Similarly, from (21) $X_{ij\ldots uv}$ may be either zero or one, but from (22) $X_{ij\ldots uv}$ is one. Thus (21) and (22) assure that $X_{ij\ldots uv}=1$. Substituting (20) and introducing the additional constraint (21) and (22) for each nonlinear term in (19) satisfy all the relationships of X's. Thus, we have also linearized the nonlinear constraints equations.

With this reduction technique,[5] nonlinear zero-one programming problems may be transformed into solution of linear zero-one programming problems. Using available linear integer programming techniques [3], [4], we can obtain the global optimal solutions.

Linearization of the Objective Function and Access Time Constants

To apply the above technique to linearize the objective function (16), we let $X_{ij}X_{kj}=X_{ijkj}$. Since the coefficients of X_{ijkj} in (16) are negative, for each X_{ijkj}, we introduce the additional constraint equation

$$X_{ij} + X_{kj} \geq 2X_{ijkj}. \qquad (23)$$

Next, we shall linearize the constraint equation (15). We let $X_{kj_1}X_{kj}=X_{kj_1kj}$. For each X_{kj_1kj}, we introduce two additional constraint equations

$$\begin{cases} X_{kj_1} + X_{kj} \geq 2X_{kj_1kj} \\ X_{kj_1} + X_{kj} - 1 \leq X_{kj_1kj} \end{cases} \quad \text{for } j \neq j_1. \qquad (24)$$

In the same manner, we can linearize (14). Hence, solution to the optimal file allocation problem is reduced to: minimize (16) subject to (1), (2), (3), (14) or (15), (20), (23), and (24) which is a linear zero–one programming problem.

File Allocation in a Multiprocessor

Let us consider a multiprocessor with virtual memory system that operates in a paging environment. One of the important problems in such a system is how to allocate files to various types of available storage systems such as thin films, cores, disks, drums, data cells, tapes, etc., so that the operating cost is minimum yet the access time requirements are satisfied for each file, and the storage limitation of each storage system is not exceeded. The model developed in this paper can be directly applied to this problem by letting the distances between computers equal to zero. Clearly, under this condition, a multiple computer system becomes a multiprocessor.

Example

Consider a specific computer communication system consisting of three computers that process five information files in common, as shown in Fig. 2. These computers are located about 20 miles from each other. The transmission facility between each pair of computers has a rate of $R=5\times10^3$ char/second. The cost of each such facility is $1050 per month or $\$1.4\times10^{-7}$/char (based on 100 hours per week and 4.2 weeks per month). The first cost of storage is 35 cents per character or $\$5.8\times10^{-7}$/char second.[6] Table I gives the lengths of each file, file length for each transactions, the request rate of these files at each computer, the rate of modification of these files at each computer after each transaction, the available storage capacity of each computer, and the maximum allowable retrieval time of each file. Using the linearized model developed above and the Gomory cutting technique [3], [4] for solving the integer linear programming problem, the example was solved on the IBM 360/65. Table II lists the optimal allocation for the case of no redundant files. The computation time required for this example is about 25 seconds.

Some characteristics of the optimum allocation are worthy of note. File 4 is stored in computer 2 as it is only used by that computer. File 1 has highest request

[5] This reduction technique can be easily extended to the case when the X_i's in (18) or (19) are real numbers. In this case, we shall express each X_i in terms of binary variables X_{ij}'s as follows:

$$X_i = \sum_{l=1}^{\alpha i+\beta i} (X_{il})2^{\alpha_i - l}$$

where α_i is chosen large enough for 2^{α_i-1} to be an upper bound on the value of X_i, while β_i is chosen large enough for $2^{-\beta_i}$ to be the maximum allowable accuracy tolerance on the value of X_i. Thus (18) or (19) is reduced from a nonlinear equation to a nonlinear zero–one equation.

[6] The calculation is based on 40 months of machine life operating at 100 hours per week and 4.2 weeks per month.

TABLE I

DATA OF EXAMPLE FOR FILE ALLOCATION

File j	L_j	l_j	P_j	Computer 1		Computer 2		Computer 3	
				u_{1j}	T_{1j}	u_{2j}	T_{2j}	u_{3j}	T_{3j}
1	100×10^3	500	0.5	5	30	2	10	0	0
2	10×10^3	500	0.5	0	0	2	30	5	1
3	10×10^3	500	0.5	3	10	0	0	4	1
4	10×10^3	500	0.5	0	0	4	0.1	0	0
5	100×10^3	500	0.5	1	1	1	1	5	1

P_j = the frequency of modification of the jth file after each transaction.
L_j = length of the jth file in characters.
l_j = file length (in characters) of each transaction for the jth file.
u_i = average hourly request rate of the entire or part of the jth file at the ith computer. Request arrivals are assumed to be Poisson distributed.
T_{ij} = maximum allowable average retrieval time in seconds for the jth file to the ith computer.
C_{ij} = (storage cost) = \$0.58 $\times 10^{-8}$/char second.
C_{ik}' = (transmission cost) = \$1.4 $\times 10^{-7}$/char.
b_i = (available storage capacity of the ith computer) = 110×10^3 char for $i=1, 2, 3$.
$1/\mu = l/R$ (the time required to transmit the reply message) = 0.1 second.

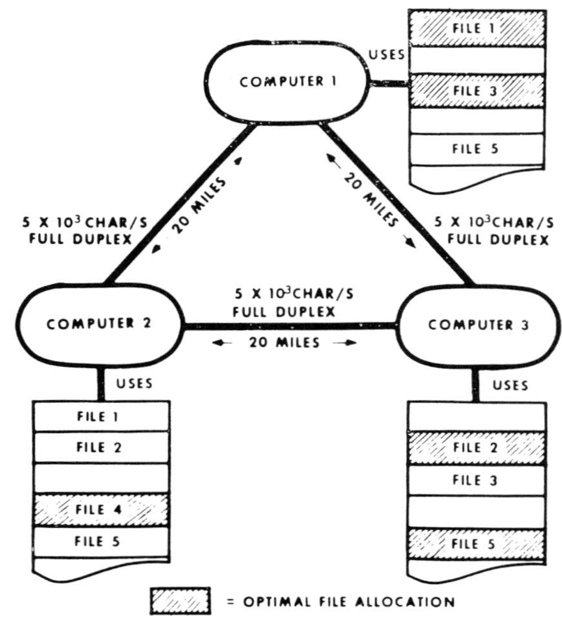

Fig. 2. A specific multiple computer system.

rate at computer 1; to minimize the transmission cost, it is stored in computer 1. For the same reason, Files 2 and 5 are stored in computer 3. Although File 3 has a high request rate at computer 3, the available storage size of computer 3 (110×10^3 char) forced File 3 to be stored in computer 1. The overall operation cost under the optimal allocation is \$3620 per month. If each file is stored at the computer where it is used, the total operating cost under such arrangement is \$6670 per month. The higher operating cost is due to the extra storage cost and the file updating cost.

CONCLUSION

The file allocation problem can be formulated into a nonlinear zero-one programming problem. By adding additional constraint equations, these nonlinear terms

TABLE II

OPTIMAL FILE ALLOCATION FOR EXAMPLE

File j	X_{ij} Computer 1	Computer 2	Computer 3
1	1	0	0
2	0	0	1
3	1	0	0
4	0	1	0
5	0	0	1

in the objective and constraint equations can be reduced to linear equations. Thus, solution of the optimal allocation requires solving a linear zero-one programming problem. The model introduced in this paper provides a common denominator for analysis and comparison of various proposed information system configurations, a tool to study the sensitivity of various parameters and constraints to the operating cost, and a method for evaluating the growth potential of information systems. However, some related problems still require further studies, such as file reliability, privacy, file partition, etc. All these problems are important considerations for optimal file allocation in multicomputer information systems.

ACKNOWLEDGMENT

The author would like to thank E. Fuchs of Bell Telephone Laboratories for his stimulating discussions.

REFERENCES

[1] D. R. Cox and W. L. Smith, *Queues, Methnen's Statistical Monographs*. London, England: Spottiswoode, Ballantyne, and Co., 1961, pp. 50–59.
[2] T. L. Saaty, *Elements of Queuing Theory*. New York: McGraw-Hill, 1961, pp. 153–161.
[3] R. Gomory, "All-integer integer programming algorithm," *Industrial Scheduling*, Muth and Thompson, Eds. Englewood Cliffs, N. J.: Prentice-Hall, 1963, pp. 195–206.
[4] J. Haldi and L. M. Isaacson, "Linear integer programming," Graduate School of Business, Stanford University, Stanford, Calif., working paper 45, December 1964.
[5] L. J. Watters, "Reduction of integer polynomial programming problems to zero-one linear programming problems," *Operations Res.*, vol. 15, pp. 1171–1174, November–December 1967.

Reprinted from Proceedings of the First International Conference on Computer Communication: Impacts and Implications. October 24-26, 1972.

THE USE OF DISTRIBUTED DATA BASES IN INFORMATION NETWORKS

Grayce M. Booth
Honeywell Information Systems, Phoenix, Arizona, U.S.A.

ABSTRACT

An overview of theories concerning distributed data base creation and use within a computer network is presented.

Alternative methods of creating a distributed data base are suggested, with notes on some of the problems associated with the more complex methods.

How to match up jobs with the correct files within the data base is discussed. Manual and software controlled methods are proposed.

The problems of allowing a single application to access files at more than one location are described. Several methods of surmounting these problems are given, with evaluations of where each method can best be used.

Finally, the problems of protecting file and system integrity when using a distributed data base are presented.

INTRODUCTION

This paper presents theoretical work concerning creation and use of distributed data bases, with emphasis on potential problems. Before these topics can be discussed, however, it is necessary to define what the term "distributed data base" means. Also, we must define an information network, which is the environment within which a distributed data base exists.

What is an information network? It is an association of elements including all or part of the following:

Information processors (data processing computers) – or IP's

Network processors (data communications computer) – or NP's

Distribution facilities (trunks, lines)

Terminals

Coupling devices

Concentrators, multiplexors, etc.

A distributed data base exists when an information network includes two or more information processors (or IP's), each of which has permanent – as contrasted to temporary or working – files attached. The permanent files attached to all IP's form a distributed data base, as shown in Figure 1.

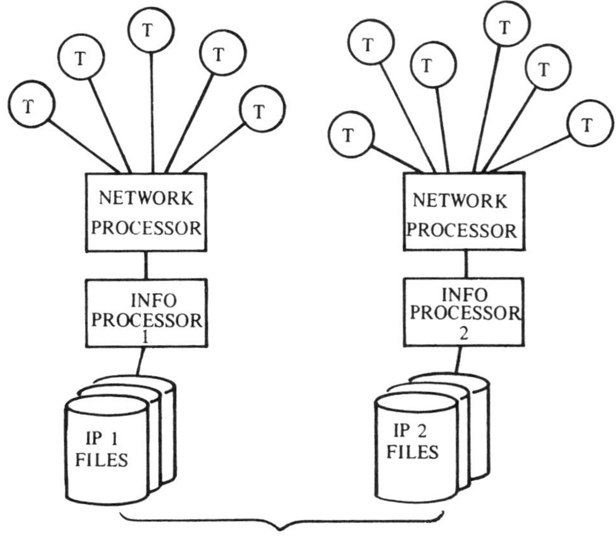

Figure 1. Typical Network

CREATING A DISTRIBUTED DATA BASE

A distributed data base can be created in any of several ways. If the data base consists of files created by individual users, and generally private to those users, its creation is implicit rather than explicit. In contrast, great care is taken when explicitly splitting an integrated file into distributed segments.

INDIVIDUAL FILES

The distributed data base which consists of individual files requires no special effort in creation. Each user creates his files at whichever IP he uses. In practice, most users access the closest IP. Files will therefore usually be located optimally in a geographic sense.

This type of distributed data base in general presents no problems. Methods of associating jobs with files in this type of data base are discussed later in this paper.

COMPANY FILES

A distributed data base which consists of company files is much more interesting to investigate. In practice, almost every information network requires some company files, as well as some users' private files.

Files which fall into this category include payroll records, order files, customer records, inventory records, and other similar data. These files do not belong to an individual user, but to the company, or to a department or division of the company.

Company files are created and controlled by a person or persons who can best be called the Data Base Manager (DBM). (This term is taken from the CODASYL Data Base Task Group Report.) The DBM is responsible for deciding file location, organization, format, and other similar factors. He may also decide who is privileged to access the file, and in what manner – inquiry, update, etc.

A distributed data base is made up of at least one, but more often multiple, files. "File" here is used to signify a logical entity; a collection of records logically related because of the owner's application(s). A data base consists of one or more files, grouped either because they are logically related or because they are all the property of a single owner – a company, government agency, or other owner.

Different methods of creating a distributed data base which includes company files are described in the following paragraphs.

GROUPING FILES. The multiple files which form a distributed data base can be separated into groups, and each group attached to one of the IP's in the information network. The method of grouping is most often geographic. Figure 2 shows an information network which spans the USA. One IP is located on the west coast, the other on the east coast.

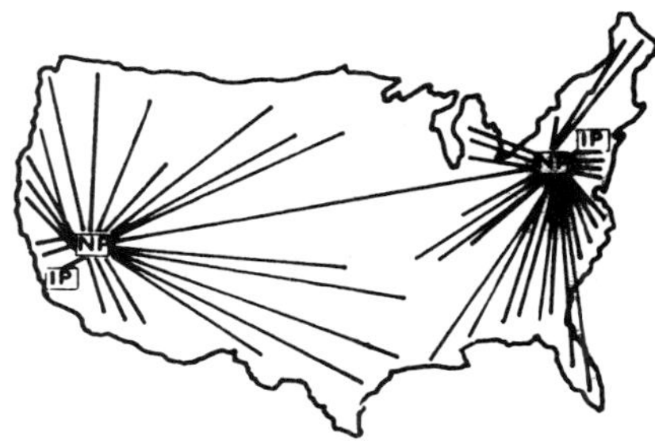

Figure 2. Nationwide Info Network

457

With this configuration, it is logical to attach files heavily used by east coast offices to the eastern IP, and attach those most used by west coast offices to the western IP. The DBM forecasts where heavy file use will originate, and causes the files to be placed there.

The main reason for geographic grouping is the cost of transmitting data to/from IP centers. In general, the shorter the transmission distance, the lower the cost. As new specialized carriers bring increasing competition into the information transmission field, line cost may become less significant. New technology will also lower communications costs. Because of these changes, processing centralization may become more attractive, since the cost penalties will be less than at present.

In the case of company files, as contrasted to private files, provision must be made for at least some use from outside of the file's area of location. In the example above, the east coast files will no doubt sometimes be accessed from west coast locations, and vice versa. In a true distributed data base such access must be allowed.

Another, less common, method of grouping files is by type. For example, all financial files might be at one location, all inventory files at another, and so on. This assumes some specialization of the IP's within the network. In this example, the financial files would be associated with the IP used for financial work.

These two methods of grouping files -- geographically or by type -- are the most common. Other methods applicable to a specific company could equally well be used. The important point is that each logical file is kept intact, but groups of files are distributed in the network.

<u>DUPLICATING FILES</u>. Within a distributed data base, it may be useful to duplicate some files at each of the IP's. Duplication may be needed for one of the following reasons:

- To increase access to the file by providing more paths to it, or more memory and/or processors capable of accessing the file.
- To provide rapid backup in case of the failure of a device, channel, or IP accessing the file.
- To decrease communications volume and/or dependencies on the communications facilities between IP's.

<u>SPLITTING FILES</u>. Still another method of creating a distributed data base is to split a logical file or files between IP's. Part of a logical file is then attached to one IP, part to a second IP, and so on.

We can ask why anyone would want to split a file. The most apparent answer is because it cannot be handled by one IP. It may be too big to be connected to a single IP, or it may be so active that its access rate cannot be supported by a single IP.

File size is not often a problem today, as mass storage technology improves. Large IP's today can support storage in the range of hundreds of billions of characters.

File access rate is more often a problem. Mass store designers seem to be building larger and larger capacity devices without increasing the device's access paths correspondingly. Load, therefore, is one reason why a logical file might be split between two or more IP's.

In this case there is no reason for the IP's to be physically remote from each other. If file activity is the only reason for file splitting, the processors can perfectly well be located in the same room.

Another reason for splitting a file is because accesses to different parts of it originate in different locations. For example, a file of all customer records for a company would form a logical entity. But customers on the west coast would originate orders from there, while east coast customers would originate their orders from the east. Communications economies might therefore, make it reasonable to locate one IP in Los Angeles and another in New York City. An even larger number of regional processing centers might be economically justified in some cases.

In split files, the file as a whole must be processed in at least some cases – perhaps for reporting purposes – and cannot always be treated in its separate parts. The real difficulties in distributed data base processing arise from split logical files of this type.

One of the problems which arises is how to catalog a split file. A separate name can be given to each segment, or the catalogs can show the same name for all segments, with some indication of the information included in each.

Although it is easy to postulate splitting a file into segments, there are a number of problems associated with doing so. Some of these problems are:

- <u>Software Complexity</u>

  Very complex software is required to handle a single logical file split across IP's. Consider, for example, an indexed sequential file split across two IP's. Where should the indices be located; in one IP, split between them, or duplicated? How can identical device addresses in both IP's be resolved in the indices? These are only two of many questions difficult to answer.

- <u>Execution Overhead</u>

  The complex software needed to handle situations of this type causes added overhead. Inter-IP messages to access data add overhead. Maintaining duplicate catalogs and/or accessing remote catalogs also increase overhead.

<u>ASSOCIATING FILES WITH JOBS</u>

In using a distributed data base, there must be a way to associate jobs or interactive executions with the file(s) needed. This can either be done under manual control or be handled automatically by the IP software.

<u>USER CONTROL</u>

In the simplest case, all file placement and job addressing for file access is manually controlled. Each user is told to address all of his input to a specific IP, usually the one closest to his terminal. When he creates files, they are therefore attached to that IP. Any jobs which subsequently use those files are also addressed to the same location.

Users of time sharing or other interactive services similarly control the location of their files. By always calling the same IP, they cause any saved files to be located there. Later access to saved files is accomplished by again calling the same IP.

If a user wishes to access another user's file, he must find out where it is located, and address his job or interaction to that IP.

Each IP needs to catalog only its own files. Little or no file movement between IP's can be allowed. If it is necessary to move a file, perhaps to balance the load between IP's, file users must be notified so that they can change the location to which they send jobs using the file.

<u>SOFTWARE CONTROL</u>

The user control described above is very simple, and is ideal for networks in which most file use is local. However, it may become unworkable if there is heavy use of files in multiple IP's accessed by a single application, and/or heavy use of files remote from the user's local IP. In cases like these, software knowledge of file location is necessary. Jobs or interactions can then be directed automatically to the correct location for execution.

<u>FULL CATALOGING</u>. One way to locate files within a network is to maintain a complete catalog of the data base at every IP. The catalog lists every file in the network, and indicates where each is physically located.

Jobs can be sent directly to the correct location. Any request for a non-existent file is spotted immediately.

The primary disadvantage is the space necessary in each IP to carry full catalogs. As a network grows, this can become a serious problem. This is particularly true if the data base is formed of a large number of small files or cataloged file segments, rather than a small number of large files.

Another disadvantage is the problem of keeping all copies of the catalog updated in parallel. For example, if a catalog change is made while one of the IP's in the network is not operational, provision must be made for recording the change later when the IP is again active.

The final disadvantage is that catalog search time for all files, including local files, may be increased by the presence of the catalogs for remote files.

INTER-IP INQUIRY. The alternative to full cataloging is to maintain only a local file catalog at each IP, and take special action if a request is received for a file not cataloged.

For a remote file, the IP software inquires within the network, and if the file exists, determines its location. If it cannot be located, the request is rejected. If the file is found, the requesting job is directed to the appropriate IP for execution.

This inter-IP inquiry may take any of several forms. All IP's can query a central IP which has a full catalog. Each IP can broadcast an inquiry to all other IP's, looking for a positive response. Each IP can pass the query to its neighbor, who can either respond affirmatively or pass the request on. If the query makes a complete circuit of the network and returns to the originating IP, the file is non-existent.

One problem is that a query may be unanswered if a remote IP is not operational. The inquiring processor may, therefore, be unable to determine whether a particular file is attached to the unavailable IP, or does not exist.

All of these query methods are perfectly feasible. To determine the most suitable in a specific network, many factors, such as frequency of non-local file use, number of files used in this way, number of IP's in the network, bandwidth of connecting communications channels, and so on, must be analyzed.

FILE NAME PREFIX USE. The file name itself can be made to indicate file location by prefixing a location code to the user assigned file name. The prefix is supplied by software when the file is created, and returned to the user as part of the official file name. He is required to use the prefixed name on all subsequent file access requests. The advantages of this method are:

- File location is obvious, and requires no processing to determine.
- The prefix can be used to manually determine file location, and so jobs can be sent to the correct IP either manually or automatically.

It has these disadvantages:

- The user must remember not only the file name but the prefix.
- File movement from one IP to another effectively causes a file name change.

FILE ACCESS METHODS

Once the assumption is made that a logical file can be split between two or more IP's, the problems of file access must be considered. Access requirements can be categorized as follows:

1. The simplest type of job requires access to a file or files connected to a single IP.
2. Another type of job retrieves or updates at one location, and also needs to retrieve a limited number of records at one or more other locations.
3. The third type is identical to number 2, except that it requires a large number of remote retrievals.
4. Another category covers jobs which retrieve or update at one IP location, and also require a limited number of updates in other location(s).
5. The final type is identical to number 4, except that a large number of remote updates is required.

It may seem unnecessary to distinguish between types 2 and 3, and between types 4 and 5, but in fact the differences are significant. Access methods which are satisfactory for small volume may be completely unacceptable for large volume situations.

Class number 1 presents no problems, so the remainder of this section will describe possible ways of providing the other types of access.

FILE TRANSMISSION

A complete copy of a file can be transmitted from its home location to another IP, so that it can be used by a job executing there. The decision to do this can be made either automatically by the operating system, or manually by the user with the file access requirement.

There are some obvious restrictions on the use of this technique. First, some limit must be set on the size of files which can be transmitted in this way. Second, if the user wishes to update the file copy which is transmitted to the remote location, care must be taken to prevent interference with any updates in the home location. This can be done by preventing update at the home IP until an updated copy is returned from the other location.

Transmission of a complete file copy has the value of simplicity. Once the file is received by the other IP, it can be cataloged normally, and the same access procedures used for all resident files can be applied to it.

Depending on the number of accesses required, this method may also reduce transmission time and overhead. Sending the entire file as a block is clearly more efficient than sending it record by record in response to individual requests. There is a break-even point at which access volume makes it less costly to send the entire file than to send individual items.

This technique allows access to multiple files, for either inquiry or update, as long as access requirements for the file allow it to be locked while remote update is in process.

SOFTWARE CONTROLLED ACCESS

The IP's operating system can provide automatic access to file data at other locations, on an individual request basis. The sequence of events to handle such an access would be roughly as follows:

- User program issues request for file data.
- The operating system discovers that the file is attached to another IP.
- An I/O request is sent to the appropriate IP, using a very high transmission priority.
- The other IP receives the request, processes it, and returns either the requested data or a denial.

To avoid delay and interference, retrieve only is normally allowed, and the file may be modified by other jobs during retrieval. Data retrieved from multiple records in the file may, therefore, be inconsistent, due to concurrent updates taking place.

This restriction is made because all other access modes (update, exclusive retrieval, etc.) have the following potential problems:

- Interference

  Jobs in each IP must wait for data to be returned from other locations. In the worst case, these jobs (although inactive) might tie up enough system resources to hamper operation. If multiple concurrent update users of the same file are executing at different locations, extensive delays might occur. Deadly embrace conditions could be caused between jobs; each of two jobs could have files locked at a different location, and the two would be mutually hung waiting for access to the other's files. Figure 3 shows this condition. (On next page)

- Software Complexity

  Also to be considered is the complicated software required, with its resulting overhead, to control the multiple update and recovery aspects. An extremely complicated mechanism is required to recognize dependencies between jobs, detect and resolve deadly embraces, and control recovery of an abnormally terminated job which was updating files at multiple locations.

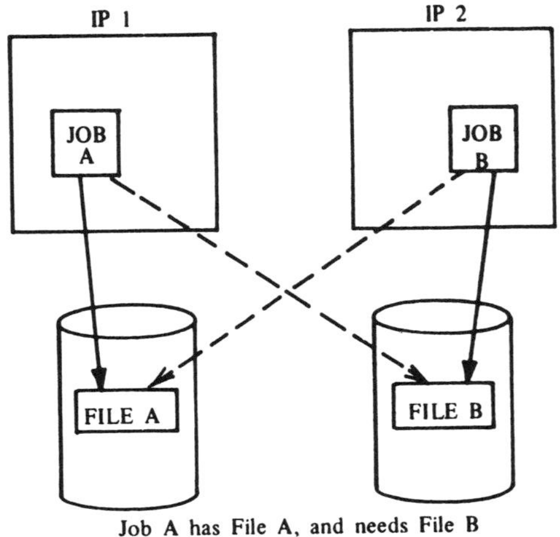

Job A has File A, and needs File B
Job B has File B, and needs File A

Figure 3. Deadly Embrace

To prevent misuse, accidental or intentional, of this mode, the user should specify, at time of file access request, the expected number of accesses. If none is specified, a default limit is applied. If accesses are attempted in excess of the limit, the job is terminated.

The idea that the operating system should provide automatic access to file data at other locations is attractive. Its most obvious advantage is simplicity from the user's point of view. In this mode, he need not worry about file separation or file location, as long as he requires only retrieve mode access.

An advantage as compared to file transmission is that only data actually accessed need be transmitted. If the access volume is below the point where transmission of the entire file becomes economical, or the file is too large to send, this mode saves transmission time and cost.

The major disadvantage is the complexity of the software required to support this mode. All necessary logic must be contained within the software system.

This type of access seems practical only where a limited number of remote inquiries is required. In all other cases the disadvantages outweigh the advantages.

APPLICATION JOB CHAINING

The following method can be used when one application requires access, particularly update access, to files attached to more than one IP.

The job which would otherwise update multiple files at multiple locations can be rearranged as a series of jobs chained together by means of a job activating scheme. Each job in such a chain can update only the files in a specific IP. As each job finishes, it activates the next job in the chain, generally in a different IP. This method requires that the analyst and/or programmer be aware of the exact file distribution among IP's.

As an example, the first job might access File A at IP #1, updating it and extracting data for reporting purposes. This data is included in a new job to be activated. This job is then directed to IP #2 for execution, where it updates Files B and C. It consolidates the information obtained during both updates. This sequence can be continued as many times as necessary to access all required files.

The last job in the chain completes any required reports, and sends them either to the originator, or to any other desired location(s). If the reports are to be printed, the final job can create and activate a reporting job in the originator's local IP, making the report available for printing there.

Using this technique, any type of access to the files at each location can be allowed. Since each job execution at each location is independent of the others, except for the passing of control, the problems of delay and interference noted under Software Controlled Access do not occur.

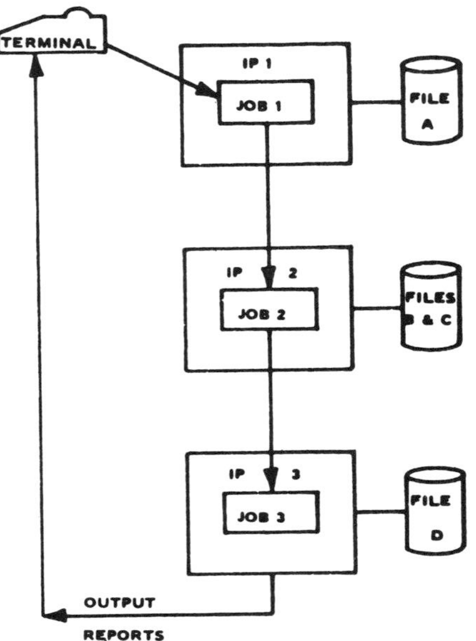

Figure 4. Job Chaining

The advantage of using job chaining to accomplish unlimited access in multiple IP's is that it provides great flexibility without causing any interference with other update users. From the operating system's point of view, it is extremely simple, since all complex logic becomes the user's problem.

There are several disadvantages to this approach. One is that the application designers/programmers must be aware of file distribution and take this into account in system design.

Second, each job in a chain is independent of its predecessors, once it is in execution. If an abnormal termination occurs somewhere in the chain, breaking the chain, it is difficult to remove the effects of preceding jobs. If, for example, a given multiple location update requires a chain of four jobs, and job number 3 terminates abnormally, the updates performed by the first two jobs remain in effect.

The termination notice resulting from a chained job can optionally be sent to the originator of the first job, who can then take appropriate action. This type of job chain requires careful design, so that a chain can be re-initiated at any point if an abnormal termination occurs.

Finally, there is no way to present an unchanging picture of data base status. The data retrieved by each job represents that part of the data base at a different point in time than the data retrieved by the other jobs. In contrast, an exclusive access job running in a single IP can obtain a completely static picture of the entire data base.

In spite of its disadvantages, this seems to be the most promising way to handle jobs which require update access to files in multiple IP's.

DELAYED AND SYNCHRONIZED UPDATING

Another mechanism which can be used to provide access to files at multiple location is delayed updating.

Delayed updating allows multiple jobs to concurrently retrieve from an apparently unchanging file. Changes made by each job are posted, not to the main file, but to a private change file. These private change files are inaccessible to any other jobs. Figure 5 shows two concurrently updating programs in the same IP. Since changes are inaccessible until they are applied to the main file, they cannot affect other jobs in concurrent execution.

Delayed update changes can be applied to the main file when each job finishes execution successfully, or more often if needed.

Multiple delayed update jobs can be run concurrently if there is a program available which can synchronize concurrent changes to the same record within the file. Such a synchronization program must of course

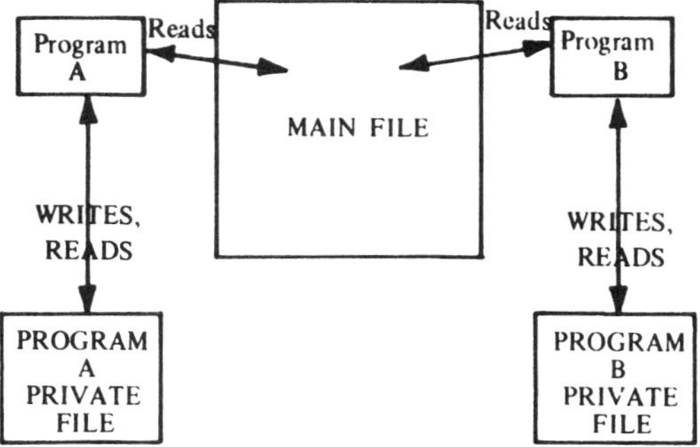

Figure 5. Delayed Update

be tailored to the format and conventions of the file type (indexed sequential, inverted, linked, etc.), and may require access to the definitions for the specific file.

As an example, a synchronization program to handle indexed sequential files would perform the following types of functions:

- Detect and delete duplicate creates or deletes of the same record.
- Detect and resolve changes to the same record. If to different fields, all are applied. If to the same field, differences are reconciled, if possible, and applied. Differences which cannot be reconciled cause one of the jobs involved to be rerun.
- Detect and resolve record creations which conflict. That is, two different records both inserted in the same available location. One of these records must be moved and the indices updated if necessary.

This is quite a complicated procedure, and may be impractical for complex file structures.

Delayed and synchronized updating can be used where duplicate file copies are maintained permanently at different locations. It can also be used when a file copy is temporarily transmitted to another IP and is updated there as well as at the original location.

This mode can also be used to allow updates to be performed in more than one IP simultaneously. Each processor would have assigned one or more record insertion areas, and each would converse with all other IP's before activating any job requiring a current file version, since this would trigger application of delayed updates.

Finally, synchronizing can be used, without delayed update, to allow simultaneous updating of multiple copies of a file, all of which are kept constantly current. Each such update requires a check throughout the network to see if synchronization is required, and a delay in further access until synchronization is accomplished, if needed. Update application can then be performed.

The ability to concurrently update one or multiple copies of the same file has many advantages. It there, at least theoretically, allows great flexibility in assigning file locations, duplicating files, etc. The interference associated with concurrent updates is reduced by confining it to the period of time necessary to actually apply updates, rather than extending it over the time of execution of all jobs involved.

Also, if updates are applied only on successful job completion, no rollback is ever required, since the main file is not changed.

It also has several disadvantages. One is that file accesses are increased, since both a pseudo and actual update access are required for every successful update. Additional overhead is caused by the necessity to search the user's change areas on each new access, to determine whether he should be given his private copy or the common copy of the requested record.

The use of delayed update also means that many file accessors will see a slightly out-of-date version of the file data. Whether or not this is significant depends on the applications involved.

Finally, the synchronization required to allow multiple concurrent delayed update users is an extremely complicated piece of software, particularly for complex file types.

The type of application for which this mode seems suited is transaction processing, where there are often numerous requests for a few accesses to a file, many of which do not involve updating. Using the methods described, rapid, economical, and reliable response can be provided by multiple copies of the file, each of which can be updated concurrently. Retrievals from each copy are delayed only while updates are being applied, but the possibility that a subsequent retrieval will encounter different values has to be tolerated. Multiple copies can provided at each of several IP's, or the number of copies at each site can be adjusted to the volume of transactions expected there.

ACCESS TO DUPLICATED FILES

Unless controlled, simultaneous access by multiple programs to duplicated copies of the same file can cause differences between the copies. Depending on file content and use, it may be possible to minimize these problems by applying the following restrictions:

- Confine updating to only one location at a time, because:
  - Only personnel there have the authority or the knowledge required to change the file.
  - Certification and coordination of changes makes updating at one place desirable.
  - Volume of changes is so low in relation to retrievals that transmission of changes to a single location, and their posting there, can be tolerated.
- Allow retrievals from a version to which the most recent updates have not been applied.

INTEGRITY ASPECTS

In an information network, file and system integrity are extremely important. File integrity protection ensures that the data content of files, and file structures, are not in any way altered or destroyed inadvertently . System integrity protection similarly protects job data and the operating system. Operating systems within network-resident IP's must provide extensive integrity protection. Some integrity problems were discussed earlier. Two other important aspects of integrity are discussed here.

REMOTE FILE UPDATE

If an application updates files in more than one IP within a network, many integrity problems arise. File integrity protection, whether local or remote, generally takes one of two forms. It may involve journaling file changes, so that the file can be restored to a prior state if needed. Or it may involve delayed updating, in which changes are posted only after known to be correct.

Since file protection involves overhead costs, it is generally optional. Files whose content is not significant, or which can easily be recreated, can be classified as unprotected. Damage to these files must be manually repaired.

Consider the case of a chain of jobs updating protected files in three separate IP's. A job in IP #1 updates File A, then activates a job in IP #2 in order to update File B. This job completes, and activates a job in IP #3 to update File C. However, this third job terminates abnormally, causing the changes to File C to be discarded. File A and File B, however, remain in their updated state.

To properly rollback both File A and File B, other updates should not be allowed until File C is known to be successfully updated. In general, this is impractical, since it restricts file access too greatly.

INFORMATION INTERCHANGE CONTROL

System integrity is involved whenever a job in execution in one IP makes an access request to another location. Because system integrity is concerned with job/system status, it is responsible for keeping track of items such as outstanding remote requests. If any IP or communica-

461

tions link failure causes loss of contact between the IP's involved, action must be taken to re-establish contact and re-synchronize all processes.

Logic is, therefore, required in all IP's to handle remote access requests received just prior to a failure of the receiver, the sender, and/or the intervening communications link. Generally, the method adopted is to ignore received requests assuming that the requesting IP will take all necessary action.

The logic to keep track of outstanding remote requests becomes more complex as the requests take longer to service. In the simplest case, a request for one record, a timer is usually sufficient to check for failure to respond. If an answer is not received in the expected time interval, a failure can be assumed in the other IP or in the communications link.

However, if a job is activated at the other location, it is difficult or impossible to determine how long the requestor should wait. A periodic handshake may be able to overcome this problem by detecting that one or the other of the IP's has failed.

SUMMARY

Information networks will be used increasingly in the decade of the 70's. This will stimulate interest in the creation and use of distributed data bases. A great deal of thought and effort will be required to solve the substantial technical problems involved, before distributed data bases can be widely used.

Reprinted by permission from *International Conference of Computer Communications*

Reprinted from the Proceedings of the ACM National Symposium, Vol. 1, Nov. 1974, pp. 156-160.

AVOIDING DEADLOCK IN DISTRIBUTED DATA BASES*

W. W. Chu[+] and G. Ohlmacher
University of California, Los Angeles

Key Words and Phrases: computer networks, deadlock, distributed data base, file, process sets

ABSTRACT

Deadlock prevention mechanisms and a deadlock protection mechanism for distributed data base systems are presented. The notion of process sets used in preventing deadlock is introduced. Examples are given to illustrate these methods for avoiding file deadlock in computer networks.

I. INTRODUCTION

When a deadlock occurs, if a job is aborted, the resulting partially completed process often represents a serious inconvenience to the user, who in many cases, must reconstruct partially altered files. For this reason, deadlock is an important consideration in the design of operating systems, even though in practice it seldom occurs. As a result, many studies of deadlock protection schemes have been reported [1-9], but the emphasis in these studies has been on centralized data base systems. In order to increase the capabilities of computer systems, remotely located computers are connected via communication links. Such a multiple computer system, or a computer network, enables the sharing of resources, such as hardware, software, and data bases. However, the efficient sharing of data bases creates many problems, such as file allocation [10], deadlock, etc. In these distributed data bases, the deadlock problem is complicated by the necessity of coordinating several computers without impeding their progress.

A deadlock exists whenever two or more processes, which are vying for the same resources, reach an impasse. When the resources required by any process can be obtained prior to starting it, deadlocks can be prevented. A deadlock prevention mechanism examines the resource requirements of all processes and allows a process to proceed only when a deadlock cannot occur. If not prevented, deadlocks can be detected and resolved by eliminating an offending process from contention. When dynamic resource allocation is implemented, deadlock detection mechanisms (which eliminate and automatically restart offending processes) are required. It is possible to combine these mechanisms so that certain resources are serviced by a detection mechanism while other resources are serviced by a prevention mechanism.

This paper examines a means of implementing two deadlock prevention mechanisms and a deadlock detection mechanism on a computer network. In addition, the notion of using process sets is introduced to improve the efficiency of one of the deadlock prevention mechanisms.

II. ACCESS CONTROL METHODS

In many cases, such as program libraries, it is necessary for two or more processes to have simultaneous access to the same file. However, a process which modifies a file cannot share access to that file with any other process at the same time. In order to provide users with this flexibility, a system must provide two methods of access to every file, either <u>shared</u> or <u>exclusive</u>. The user specifies the desired method of access when the file is requested. Using this procedure if no process has been granted exclusive access to a file, then a request for shared access to that file by any process can be granted. In the same manner, if no process has been granted either shared or exclusive access to a file, then a request for exclusive access to that file by any process can be granted. This procedure provides multiple readers <u>or</u> one writer with access to a specific file.

If it is possible for the system to conveniently generate a copy of a file when a process requires exclusive access to a file, the copy may be used for modifications while the original is maintained as a back up until the process terminates. In addition, access to the original can be granted to any process requesting shared access to that file. Consequently, shared access to a file can always be granted and requests for such access need no longer be considered by the deadlock protection mechanism. This procedure allows the system to provide multiple readers <u>and</u> one writer, with simultaneous access to a specific file.

Since most systems allocate files to a single continuous area of mass storage, it is usually inconvenient for a system to generate a copy of a file. However, for systems whose files reside on paged memory, it is possible for the system to create a copy of the file simply by making a copy of

*This research was supported in part by the U.S. Office of Naval Research, Mathematical and Information Sciences Division, Contract No. N00014-69-A-0200-4027, NR 048-129 and in part by the National Science Foundation, Grant No. GJ33007X.

+ Consultant to Advanced Development Laboratory, Xerox Palo Alto Research Center.

the page table [9] as shown in Figure 1.

When a data base has multiple copies of a file, for shared access of a file, access to any one of its copies can be granted to the requesting process; for exclusive access of a file, all of its copies must be granted to the requesting process. With such a "lock" scheme for the exclusive access, the deadlock mechanisms are not affected by the number of copies of a file.

a) Page tables after access has been granted.

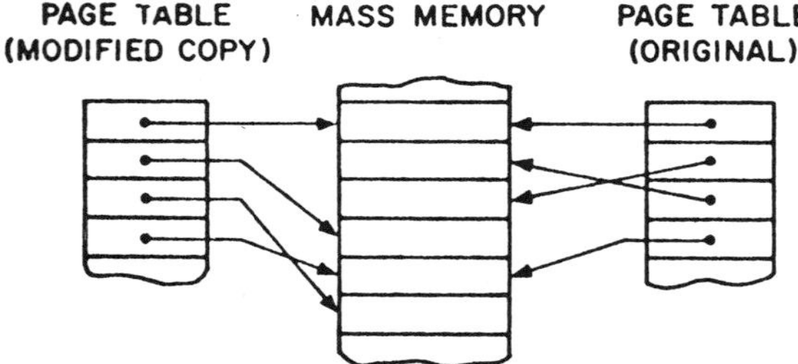

b) Page table after modifications.

Figure 1

Access Control Method for Deadlock Protection in a Paging Memory System

III. DEADLOCK PREVENTION MECHANISMS

One way to implement deadlock prevention on a computer network is to assign a node (computer) as a monitoring node, which examines the file requirements of all processes and allows a process to proceed when a deadlock cannot occur.
464 This is rather inefficient since the monitoring node has to communicate with each node to examine the file requirements before the process can be allowed to start, and the entire network can consider only one process at a time. A more efficient way to implement deadlock prevention is to assign a fixed examining path in the network by assigning every node in the network a number. Then the examining path is determined uniquely by the node numbers as shown in Figure 2. When requests for files are passed around the network according to this path, since the path is unique, each node can consider the requests for files independent of the other nodes. This improves the efficiency of the deadlock prevention mechanism.

Since the lower numbered nodes have better access to the deadlock prevention mechanism than higher numbered nodes, one way to assign the node numbers is to examine the file utilization; that is, the usage rate and the length of each file transaction for the processes at that node, and the file storage size of the node. The nodes that have higher utilization and higher file storage capability should be granted a lower numbered node.

3.1 A Simple Prevention Mechanism

Deadlock prevention mechanisms require the user to specify the files that a process requires prior to the initiation of that process. These requests are usually made through the job control language of the system. The information is used by the system to prevent a deadlock from occurring.

One means of preventing deadlock is for the system to obtain control of all the files requested by a process before initiating the process. One process at a time, the system collects the request for files and examines each one to determine if access to the file can be granted as outlined in the previous section. If all requests can be granted, the process is given access to the files and is initiated. Otherwise, the process is delayed until all processes which have access to requested files terminate. While the process is delayed, the requested files are available to other processes [1].

In a distributed data base, the system examines the requests for files to determine if all the requests are for local files. If they are, the requests are processed as outlined above. Otherwise, the requests for files are passed from node to node in the preassigned order starting with the first node. Each node examines the requests for files located at that node as outlined above. As soon as all the requests for files have been granted, the node at which the requesting process resides is so informed and the process is allowed to proceed.

The simplicity of this mechanism enables easy implementation and requires low system overhead. In addition, interactive users can avoid waiting by simply terminating a delayed process, since such a process has not been initiated. Clearly, using this simple deadlock prevention mechanism intercomputer communication is required only when remote files are requested.

3.2 Process Set Prevention Mechanism

An alternative means of preventing deadlock is to allow the process to proceed unless granting access to a file it requires may lead to a deadlock. The system collects the requests for files and initiates the process without giving it access to the requested files. The process proceeds until access to a file is required; for example, an attempt to reference a file would imply that a process required access to that file. When access to a file is required, the process is allowed to proceed if all of the processes can be completed (a process can be completed if access to all the files that it has requested can be granted, as outlined in the previous section). If a process can be completed, then the files it has access to are considered available with respect to the remaining processes. If access to the file cannot be granted, the process is delayed until some other process either terminates or releases that file [3].

In order to more efficiently determine if access to a file can be granted, processes having requests for the same file(s) can be grouped into process sets. A system may have any number of process sets, the criteria being, if a process requests exclusive access to a file, then that process and all other processes which have requested access (exclusive or shared) to that file are members of the same process set. Further, each process belongs to one and only one process set.

Let us denote F, P, and {P} as file, process and process set respectively. We then have the following properties:

1) If $eF_i \in \{P\}_I$, then $eF_i \notin \{P\}_J$ & $sF_i \notin \{P\}_J$, for $I \neq J$.
2) If $P_i \in \{P\}_I$, then $P_i \notin \{P\}_J$, for $I \neq J$

where F_i = i^{th} file, $i = 1, 2, \ldots, m$,
P_i = i^{th} process, $i = 1, 2, \ldots, n$,
$\{P\}_I$ = I^{th} process set, $I = 1, 2, \ldots, N$, $N \leq n$
e = exclusive access
s = shared access

Such a group of process sets can be formed as follows: Whenever a new process arrives all the process sets that have possession of file(s) that are requested by the new process are combined and the new process is added to the resulting process set. (Of course, if no process sets possess a file that is requested by the new process, then the new process forms a process set by itself). The rules for combining process sets are: If shared access to a file is requested by the new process, the process set containing one or more processes which have requested exclusive access to that file is combined with the new process. If exclusive access to a file is requested by the new process, all the process sets containing one or more processes which have requested access (exclusive or shared) to that file are combined, and the new process is added to the resulting process set. When a process terminates, the remaining members of the process set may be reexamined with respect to each other by the same mechanism to reform their process set or sets.

The advantage of establishing process sets is that once a process has been allocated to a set, the progress of that process is independent of all processes in other process sets. Further, in contrast with the simple deadlock prevention mechanism, a process in a process set does not require complete control of all its files. The use of process sets for deadlock prevention considerably reduces the amount of computation required to determine whether or not all the processes can be completed.

In order to simplify control of the processes, when implementing this mechanism on a distributed data base, the process sets are allocated to certain nodes. For convenience, the process set is allocated to the highest node at which a file requested in the process set is located.

Since a process set may contain processes and files from several nodes, the process set which contains a certain process may not reside at the same node as that process. Consequently, when a process requires access to a file, a request for that file must be transmitted to the node having the corresponding process set. The request is then examined according to the process set deadlock prevention mechanism.

When a system receives a process, it forms the new process set and examines the requests for files to determine if any of the requests are from remote files. If any are, the process set is passed from node to node starting with the first node and forms a process set at each node when necessary until all the files requested by the new process have been found. If all the requests are for local files, the same procedure is followed except that the new process set is started at the node that receives the process instead of the first node.

When this mechanism is used, processes are allowed to proceed until access to a file is required, subsequently files are used more efficiently, especially when they are frequently referenced. In addition, several processes could request control of, modify, and release control of a file concurrently without terminating. On the other hand, this mechanism is not easily implemented and requires considerable system overhead when continually forced to reexamine processes to determine if requests for control of files can be allowed.

As an example, consider three processes with the following requirements for files:

Process 1: Requires shared access to file A and exclusive access to files B and C.
Process 2: Requires shared access to files B and C.
Process 3: Requires shared access to file A, and exclusive access to file D.

Further, let the processes and files be distributed on the network in Figure 2 as follows:

Process 1:	Node 4	File A:	Node 1
Process 2:	Node 3	File B:	Node 2
Process 3:	Node 1	File C:	Node 3
		File D:	Node 5

When using simple deadlock prevention mechanism as described in section 3.1 the request for files of each process are passed around the network according to the preassigned order and yield the following list of processes and file requirements. Then according to the prevention mechanism we grant process 1 access to files A, B, and C, (which are underlined) and process 3 access to files A and D (which are underlined), but would delay process 2 by holding its request for file B at Node 2 until process 1 terminates.

$$\left(\begin{array}{ll} & \text{Process 1. } \underline{sA}, \underline{eB}, \underline{eC} \\ d & \text{Process 2. } sB, sC \\ & \text{Process 3. } \underline{sA}, \underline{eD} \end{array}\right)$$

s = shared
e = exclusive
d = delayed

The process set deadlock prevention mechanism, as described in this section will form the following two process sets:

Process set 1: {Process 1. sA, eB, eC; Process 2. sB, sC}

Process set 2: {Process 3. sA, eD}

Process set 1 is located at node 3, since file C is located at node 3 and node 3 is the highest node at which a file requested in process set 1 is located. Similarly, process set 2 is located at node 5 because of file D.

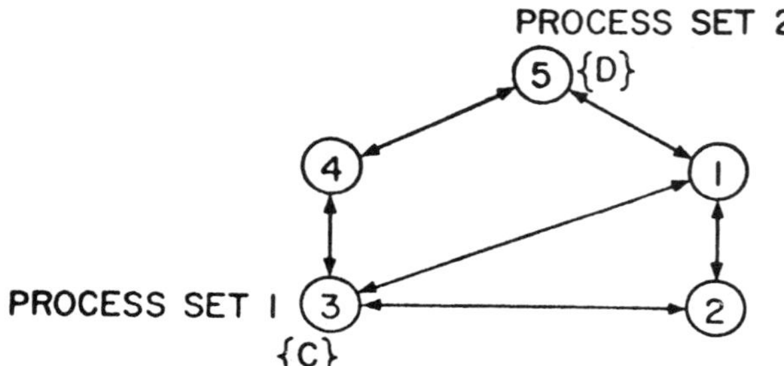

Figure 2. Deadlock Prevention in a Distributed Data Base

If process 1 requests control of files A and B and process 2 requests control of file C, then process set 1 becomes

{ Process 1. sA, eB, eC }
{d Process 2. sB, sC }

where process 2 is delayed because if process 2 were granted control of file C and then requested file B and process 1 requested file C, a deadlock would result.

Finally, if process 1 later releases control of file B, process set 1 becomes

{Process 1. sA, eB, eC}
{Process 2. sB, sC }

Process 2 is no longer delayed since process 2 can be granted access to file B. Since process sets are independent of each other process set 2 which consists of process 3 was not involved in the preceding deadlock determinations. This greatly simplifies and improves the efficiency of the deadlock prevention mechanism.

IV. DEADLOCK DETECTION MECHANISM

A deadlock detection mechanism allows the user to request access to files at any time. The system monitors these requests by maintaining two lists, a list of processes and a list of requested files as in Figure 3. Each element of the lists has a pointer which is used by the system to determine if a deadlock has occurred. When the system receives a request for access to a file, if the request can be granted, the pointer of the corresponding file is set to point to that process and the process is allowed to proceed. Otherwise, the pointer of the process is set to point to the re-
466 quested file and the file and process lists are traversed until either an open process pointer is found in which case the requesting process is delayed, or the lists return to the requesting process in which case a deadlock exists [8]. When a deadlock is detected, the system returns one of the processes involved in its initial state, releasing and restoring the files it controls. Since the files must be restored, a copy of each file or its original page table as outlined earlier must be available. The removed process is restarted at a later time [9].

The implementation of the deadlock detection mechanism in a distributed data base is accomplished by appointing one node of the network to monitor requests for files and detect deadlocks. The appointed node maintains the process and file lists, and every node is required to transmit to the appointed node information concerning the iniation and termination of each process and all requests for and releases of files. If a request for a file can be granted, the process is allowed to proceed without waiting for the deadlock detection mechanism. For the purpose of improving reliability, a second node may be appointed to monitor requests for files.

This mechanism can be easily implemented and has an advantage in that the user is not required to know in advance which files a process requires. On the other hand, even though actual deadlocks are infrequent, when they do occur, considerable system overhead must be accounted for. For example, an interactive user who is restarted must resupply all the information he had given the process, since the original information has lost its integrity. Finally, while this mechanism requires considerable inter-computer communication, even when local files are being used, processes are never delayed by this communication, since a process whose request for a file can be granted may proceed without waiting for the detection mechanism.

As an example, consider two processes which make the following series of requests for files:

Request 1. Process 1: A   Λ: null pointer
Request 2. Process 1: B
Request 3. Process 2: C
Request 4. Process 2: B
Request 5: Process 1: C

Then the process and file lists whould be formed as follows:

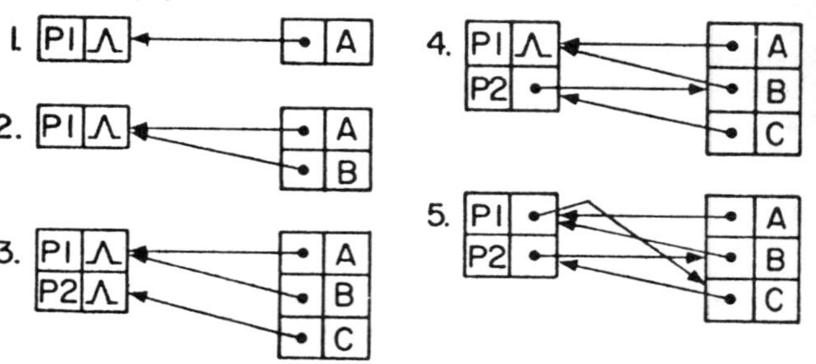

Figure 3. Deadlock Detection in a Distributed Data Base

The deadlock in request 5 is found when the loop P1-C-P2-B-P1 is detected by the mechanism. One of the processes is then returned to its initial state.

V. CONCLUSION

Three methods of protecting the user from deadlocks in a distributed data base have been presented: a simple deadlock prevention mechanism, a prevention mechanism using process sets, and a detection mechanism.

The operation of the simple prevention mechanism is straightforward and uncomplicated, and it does not require the keeping of lists or groups; thus this mechanism is easily implemented and requires less system overhead than the other mechanisms. In addition, since messages are sent to the other nodes of the network only to establish the location and availability of files, such communications are never required to handle processes using only local files. Since the simple prevention mechanism is the only deadlock protection mechanism to exhibit both of these characteristics, it is clearly superior for most applications. However, since the process set prevention mechanism provides more efficient utilization of files, and the detection mechanism provides the user with greater flexibility in that the user may request access to files at any time, in certain instances these mechanisms, are preferable.

REFERENCES

[1] Havender, J. W. "Avoiding Deadlock in Multitasking Systems," IBM Systems Journal, 7(2)74-84, 1968.

[2] Murphy, J. E. "Resource Allocation with Interlock Detection in a Multi-Task System," Proceedings of the 1968 Fall Joint Computer Conference, pp. 1169-1176.

[3] Habermann, A. N. "Prevention of System Deadlocks," Communications of the ACM, 12(7): 373-377, 385, July 1969.

[4] Berstein, A. J. and A. Shoshani. "Synchronization in a Parallel Access Data Base," Communications of the ACM, 12(11):604-607, November 1969.

[5] Coffman, E. G., Jr., M. J. Elphick, and A. Shoshani. "System Deadlocks," Computing Surveys, 3(2):67-78, June 1971.

[6] Collmeyer, Arthur J. "Database Management in a Multi-Access Environment," Computer, 4(6):36-46, November/December 1971.

[7] Shemer, J. E., and A. J. Collmeyer. "Database Sharing: A Study of Interference, Roadblock, and Deadlock," Proceedings of the 1972 ACM-SIGFIDET Workshop, 1972.

[8] Holt, Richard C. "Some Deadlock Properties of Computer Systems," Computing Surveys, 4(3):179-196, September 1972.

[9] King, P. F. and A. J. Collmeyer. "Database Sharing - An Efficient Mechanism for Supporting Concurrent Processes," Proceedings of the 1973 National Computer Conference and Exposition, June 1973, Vol. 42, pp. 271-275.

[10] Chu. W. W. "Optimal File Allocation in a Multiple Computer System," IEEE Transactions on Computers, C-18(10):885-889, October 1969.

ACKNOWLEDGMENT

The authors wish to thank Drs. J. E. Shemer and A. J. Collmeyer of Xerox Corporation for their helpful discussions during the writing of this paper.

ERRATA

P. 158, Column 2, Line 6 from top should read:
determine if any of the requests are for remote

P. 159, Column 1, Line 12 from bottom should read:
the processes involved to its initial state re-

In the design of a computer communications system, reliability and availability are fundamental considerations. The reliability of the system strongly depends on the topological layout of the communication links, as well as on the reliability and availability of the individual communication facilities and computer systems.

Computer Communications Systems Reliability

Wilkov (p. 470) surveys the various reliability criteria and their relevance to different applications. Van Slyke and Frank (p. 489) consider networks with randomly failing links and nodes. Hansler, McAuliffe and Wilkow (p. 501) provide a procedure for calculating the reliability of the communication paths between any pair of nodes in a distributed computer network.

For further reading, see [CAR 73], [CRO 73], [FRA 73], and [BOE 75].

Reprinted by permission from
IEEE TRANSACTIONS ON COMMUNICATIONS
Vol. COM-20, No. 3, June 1972

Analysis and Design of Reliable Computer Networks

ROBERT S. WILKOV, MEMBER, IEEE

***Abstract*—In the design of a computer network, one of the fundamental considerations is the reliability and availability of the communication paths between all pairs of centers in the network. These characteristics are strongly dependent on the topological layout of the communication links in addition to the reliability and availability of the individual computer systems and communication facilities. Based on graph theoretic models for computer and communication networks, many different reliability measures have been defined. Attempts have been made to characterize networks that are optimal with respect to these measures. In this paper, the most significant reliability criteria and their relevance to different applications will be discussed. Furthermore, we survey the status of current research on the different criteria. The difficulties and limitations on each reliability measure will be pointed out and what seem to be the most fruitful areas for further investigation will be indicated.**

I. Introduction

IN THIS PAPER, a computer network is modeled by a linear graph in which the nodes or vertices correspond to computer centers in the network and the edges correspond to the communication links. In the design of a computer network, one of the fundamental considerations is the reliability and availability of the communication paths between all pairs of centers in the network. These characteristics strongly depend on the topological layout of the communication links in addition to the reliability and availability of the individual computer systems and communication facilities. Graph theoretic models for computer and communication networks have previously been used in the literature to characterize maximally reliable networks based on different reliability measures. The difficulties and limitations on each of these measures will be discussed in this paper, in addition to the problem areas that appear to be fruitful for further investigation.

In studies of communication and computer networks, reliability has been defined in a number of different ways. A network has been defined to be operational in the presence of failures provided communication paths exist between certain pairs of nodes. Alternatively, a network has been considered to be operational in the presence of failures if every node could communicate with a certain percentage of the other nodes. However, these definitions would be more meaningful if they quantitatively reflected the traffic-carrying capacity of the network in the presence of failures. For example, a line-switching network,

Manuscript received December 22, 1971; revised February 24, 1972.

The author is with the IBM Thomas J. Watson Research Center, Yorktown Heights, N. Y.

subject to a given point-to-point traffic matrix, could be considered to be operational if the grade of service exceeded a certain threshold or if a specified percentage of the traffic could be carried at the original grade of service. Similarly, the operation of a message or packet switching network could be measured in terms of the mean or kth moment of the maximum end-to-end delay.

Based on several of the definitions of acceptable network operation given previously, a number of deterministic and probabilistic reliability criteria have been considered. A good reference on reliability as well as flow problems in probabilistic and deterministic networks is the recent book by Frank and Frisch [1]. The deterministic criteria were originally formulated as vulnerability measures for communication networks. In such studies, the destructive element was assumed to be an intelligent human enemy who had knowledge of the structure of the network. Therefore, the deterministic criteria indicated how difficult it was for the enemy to completely disrupt service in some part of the network by measuring the number of nodes or links that would have to fail in order to disrupt the operation of the network. In the design of networks that are optimal with respect to the deterministic measures, the aim is to maximize the number of nodes or links that must fail in order to disrupt the operation of the network, subject to fixed cost constraints. On the other hand, probabilistic criteria have been considered when randomly distributed destructive forces were expected. They were originally introduced in a military environment in which a human enemy destroyed the elements of the network in a random fashion. In a commercial environment, a natural failure probability is associated with every node and link in the network. With these probabilities specified, the analysis problem consists of determining the probability that the network is operational, according to one of the definitions discussed before. In designing maximally reliable networks, subject to fixed cost constraints, the objective is to maximize the probability that the network is operational based on a specified probability of failure for every node and link in the network.

In subsequent sections of this paper, we will survey known results and outstanding problems in the analysis and design of reliable networks based on deterministic and probabilistic criteria. This paper is intended to update and supplement the survey on survivable networks by Frank and Frisch [2]. Since much of the study of network reliability is based on graph theory, important concepts and definitions are summarized in the following section. For a comprehensive treatment of the graph theoretic concepts discussed herein, the reader is referred to Harary [3], Berge [4] or Kim and Chien [5]. Section III of this paper deals with node and edge connectivity, two of the simplest deterministic reliability measures. Section III-A treats properties of graphs and their node and edge connectivity, which are useful in network reliability studies, and in large part are not treated in [2]. Methods for determining the node and edge connectivity of a given network, which have been treated in great detail by Frank and Frisch [2], are summarized in Section III-B along with a procedure that has recently been developed. Section III-C is primarily devoted to recent results on minimizing the diameter in maximally connected homogeneous networks. In Section III-D, procedures for the realization of maximally connected nonhomogeneous networks discussed in [2] are complemented by an unpublished procedure developed by the author along with a suggested approach to minimizing the diameter in maximally connected nonhomogenous networks.

Recent results on more general deterministic reliability measures than the node or edge connectivity of a network are stressed in Section IV. In particular, based on recent graph theoretic results, a new deterministic reliability criterion related to network performance is suggested in Section IV-B. Section V deals with probabilistic reliability criteria. An attempt is made in Sections V-A and V-B to clarify and summarize some of the fundamental results on the reliability of probabilistic networks that are discussed at length in the survey by Frank and Frisch [2]. A recent deterministic reliability criterion derived from results on probabilistic networks is treated at some length in Section V-C. The remainder of this paper deals with other aspects of the reliability of probabilistic networks that are not covered in [2]. Section VI is devoted to procedures for calculating exactly the reliability of probabilistic networks. These results are combined with heuristic methods in Section VII to design highly reliable centralized networks with minimal cost.

II. Graph Theoretic Concepts and Definitions

A computer network will be modeled by a linear graph $G = (N, E)$. N is a nonempty set of n nodes that corresponds to the computer centers in the network and E is a set of b edges or branches that corresponds to the communication links. A full- or half-duplex communication link between nodes n_i and n_j corresponds to the nonoriented edge $[n_i, n_j]$. On the other hand, a simplex link from n_i to n_j corresponds to the oriented edge (n_i, n_j). In either case, n_i and n_j are said to be adjacent nodes and the associated edge is said to be incident to those nodes. The networks discussed in this paper, unless otherwise noted, are assumed to have half- or full-duplex links and therefore are modeled by graphs with nonoriented edges. We further assume, unless otherwise noted, that the graph under discussion has no parallel edges and no edges of the type $[n_i, n_i]$.

The set of nodes in $G = (N, E)$ adjacent to $n_i \in N$ will be denoted by $\Gamma(n_i)$. The degree of node n_i denoted by $d_i = |\Gamma(n_i)|$ is the number of edges incident to node n_i. It is easily established that

$$\sum_{i=1}^{n} d_i = 2b$$

and if $d = d_i$ for all i, then $d = 2b/n$ and G is called a "homogeneous" or "regular" graph of degree d. Furthermore, the two edges $[n_i, n_j]$ and $[n_j, n_k]$ are said to be adjacent in G since they have one node in common. The sequence of distinct adjacent nodes $[n_i, n_j, n_k, \cdots, n_r, n_s, n_t]$ forms a path between nodes n_i and n_t and the length of the path is equal to the number of edges on it. Any two paths between nodes n_i and n_t are said to be edge disjoint if they have no edges in common and node disjoint if they have no nodes in common except for n_i and n_t. A circuit in the graph G is a path in which the initial and terminal nodes coincide, i.e., $n_i = n_t$. The length of the circuit is the number of edges on the corresponding closed path. The minimum length of any circuit in G is known as the "girth" of the graph and is denoted by $t(G)$. Furthermore, the distance l_{ij} between n_i and n_j in G is the length of a shortest path between nodes n_i and n_j. The maximum length of any shortest path in G is known as the "diameter" of the graph and is denoted by $k(G) = \max_{i,j} l_{ij}$.

For example, a nonhomogeneous graph having 9 nodes and 16 edges is shown in Fig. 1. In this graph node 2 is of degree four and $\Gamma(2) = \{1, 7, 9, 3\}$. Edges [1, 7] and [7, 2] are adjacent and the sequence of adjacent nodes [1, 7, 2, 9] forms a path of length three between nodes 1 and 9. The paths [1, 2, 9] and [1, 7, 2, 3, 9] between nodes 1 and 9 are edge disjoint but not node disjoint since node 2 lies on both paths. On the other hand, the sequences of adjacent nodes [1, 2, 9] and [1, 8, 5, 9] are two node disjoint paths between nodes 1 and 9. The node sequences [1, 8, 7, 6, 1] and [3, 4, 9, 3] constitute circuits in the graph of length four and three, respectively. Since there is no circuit consisting of fewer than three edges, the graph has a girth of three. Considering the distances between pairs of nodes in the graph of Fig. 1, the distance between nodes 1 and 9 is two and nodes 3 and 6 are at a distance of three. After computing the distances between all pairs of nodes, we find that the graph has a diameter of three.

Any graph $G = (N, E)$ is said to be connected if there is at least one path between every pair of nodes n_i, $n_j \in N$. A subgraph G_1 of G is a graph all of whose nodes and edges are contained in G, i.e., $G_1 = (N_1, E_1)$ where $N_1 \subseteq N$ and $E_1 \subseteq E$. If $N_1 = N$, the subgraph G_1 is called a "spanning subgraph." In graph G, a maximal connected subgraph is called a "component" of G. A connected graph consists of a single component, whereas there are clearly at least two components in any graph that is not connected. A (minimal) set of edges in a graph whose removal increases the number of components by one is called a "(prime) edge cutset" and a (minimal) set of nodes, which has the same property is known as a "(prime) node cutset." We note that when a node is removed from a graph, all of the edges incident to that node are also removed. A cutset with respect to a specified pair of nodes n_i and n_j in a connected graph, sometimes called an i–j cut, is such that its removal breaks all paths between nodes n_i and n_j (results in n_i in one component and n_j in the other). The minimum number of edges in any i–j cut, denoted by C_{ij}^e, is known as the edge connectivity between nodes n_i and n_j. Similarly, the node connectivity C_{ij}^n is the minimum number of nodes in any i–j cut. Furthermore, the edge connectivity or cohesion of graph G, denoted by $C^e(G) = \min_{i,j} [C_{ij}^e(G)]$, is the minimum number of edges that must be removed in order to break all paths between some pair of nodes in G. A graph G in which $C^e(G) \geq m$ is said to be m-edge connected. The node connectivity or simply the connectivity of G is denoted by $C^n(G) = \min_{i,j} [C_{ij}^n(G)]$ and is equal to the minimum number of nodes whose removal disconnects the graph. If $C^n(G) \geq m$, then G is said to be m connected.

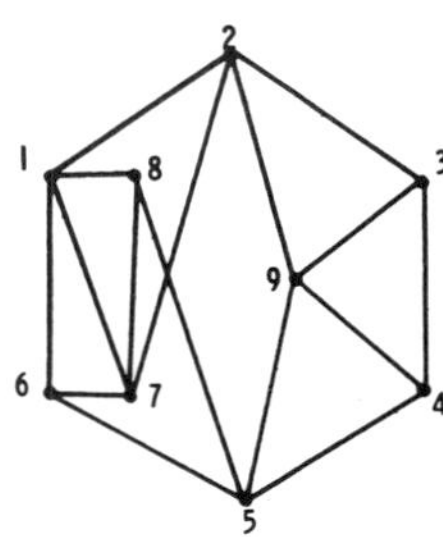

Fig. 1. Example of a nonhomogeneous graph with a node connectivity of 2 and an edge connectivity of 3.

Considering the graph of Fig. 1, the edges [2,3], [2,9], [8,5], and [6,5] form a cutset since their removal results in the two components consisting of nodes {1,8,7,6,2} and {3,4,9,5}. Nodes 2 and 5 form a node cutset since their removal results in a graph with nodes {1,8,7,6} in one component and nodes {3,4,9} in the other. From the definition in the preceding paragraph, these cutsets constitute 1–9 cuts resulting in node 1 in one component and node 9 in the other. It is easily seen in Fig. 1 that the edge connectivity C_{19}^e between nodes 1 and 9 is four and the node connectivity C_{19}^n between nodes 1 and 9 is two. Furthermore, since there are several nodes of degree three in Fig. 1, the cohesion or the edge connectivity of the graph is only three. Since the minimum size node cutset consists of two nodes, the node connectivity $C^n(G)$ of the graph is two.

In a connected graph G of b edges and n nodes, a tree T is a maximal spanning subgraph (consisting of $n - 1$ edges) that contains no circuits. The deletion of any edge from a tree clearly results in its becoming disconnected. Therefore, prime cutsets in G can clearly be formed from one edge of the tree and several edges of G not in the tree. All cutsets formed in this manner correspond to binary vectors with b components, which are linearly independent, and hence the dimension of the space of prime cutsets is $n - 1$. Furthermore, the addition of any edge to a tree forms a circuit. The circuits formed from several tree edges and one of the $b - n + 1$ edges in G–T correspond to binary vectors with b components that are also linearly independent. Hence, the dimension of the circuit space of G is $b - n + 1$, which is sometimes referred to as the nullity of the graph and is denoted by $\eta(G)$.

III. Cohesion and Connectivity as Reliability Measures

Based on a graph theoretic model for a computer network, two of the simplest deterministic reliability measures considered was the cohesion and connectivity of the graph. They were used as survivability measures for communication networks in which the network was considered to be operational if the corresponding graph was connected. In the case of computer networks, the edge or node connectivity corresponds to the minimum number of communication links or computer centers that must fail in order to disrupt communication between any operative pair of centers. This criterion is most meaningful if all centers in the net are of equal importance. Otherwise, it is desirable for certain pairs of nodes in the graphs to have a larger edge or node connectivity than others.

A. Properties of m-Connected Graphs

The cohesion and connectivity of graphs had been investigated long before network survivability was considered. Menger [6] showed that the minimum number of nodes in any i–j cut of a graph is equal to the maximum number of node disjoint paths between nodes n_i and n_j. Similarly, the edge connectivity between nodes n_i and n_j is equal to the maximum number of edge disjoint paths between that pair of nodes. The result has been extended to oriented graphs by Dirac [7]. Menger's fundamental theorem has simplified the determination of the node and edge connectivity between any pair of nodes in a graph. Furthermore, Whitney [8] demonstrated that for any graph G, $C^n(G) \leq C^e(G) \leq d^*(G)$, where $d^*(G) = \min_i (d_i)$, the minimum of the degrees of the nodes in G. The Whitney inequality cannot be improved since Chartrand and Harary [9] have shown that for all integers a, b, and c, such that $a \leq b \leq c$, a graph G exists with $d^*(G) = c$, $C^e(G) = b$ and $C^n(G) = a$.

We now recall that in any graph G having b edges and n nodes,

$$\sum_{i=1}^{n} d_i = 2b$$

and the mean degree is $2b/n$. Since $d^*(G)$ must be no greater than the mean degree of the nodes, $d^*(G) \leq \lfloor 2b/n \rfloor$, where $\lfloor x \rfloor$ denotes the largest integer no greater than x. It follows from this inequality and the Whitney theorem that

$$C^n(G) \leq C^e(G) \leq d^*(G) \leq \lfloor 2b/n \rfloor. \qquad (1)$$

This relationship between node connectivity, edge connectivity, and minimum degree follows from the fact that the maximum number of node disjoint paths between any pair of nodes n_i and n_j cannot exceed the maximum number of edge disjoint paths, which cannot exceed the minimum of d_i and d_j. Therefore, we define a "maximally connected graph" (corresponding to a maximally reliable computer network) to be a graph in which

$$C_{ij}^n = C_{ij}^e = \min(d_i, d_j), \qquad \forall\ i, j. \qquad (2)$$

Further properties of m-connected and m-edge connected graphs have been treated in the current literature on graph theory independently of network reliability or survivability studies. In the treatise by Tutte [10], 2-connected and 3-connected graphs were completely characterized. It was shown that a graph is 2-connected if and only if every two nodes lie on a circuit. Tutte characterized 3-connected graphs in terms of the wheel W_n, which consists of a circuit of $n - 1$ nodes and one node in the center adjacent to each of the nodes on the circuit. The wheel W_7 consisting of seven nodes is shown in Fig. 2.

On the more general problem, the economical design of reliable computer networks requires the realization of m-connected or m-edge connected graphs with a minimum number of edges or nodes. Along these lines, an m-connected graph has been defined by Halin [11] to be edge-critical if the deletion of any edge results in a graph that is $(m - 1)$ connected. He showed that a necessary and sufficient condition for an m-connected graph to be edge critical is that there are no more than m node disjoint paths between every pair of adjacent nodes. Furthermore, Halin [12] proved that every finite edge-critical m-connected graph contains more than $\frac{1}{2}(m + 1)^{1/2}$ nodes of degree m. An m-connected graph is node-critical if the deletion of any node results in a graph that is $(m - 1)$ connected. Lick [13] showed that in any node-critical m-connected graph G, $d^*(G) < (3m - 1)/2$. Similarly, an m-edge connected graph G has been defined to be node critical (or edge critical) if the deletion of any node (or edge) from G results in a graph that is $(m - 1)$-edge connected. Lick [13] has also shown that there is no edge-critical m-edge-connected graph in which $d^*(G) > m$. In the event that G has n nodes and $d^*(G) \geq \lfloor n/2 \rfloor$, Chartrand [14] has shown that $C^e(G) = d^*(G)$ and that the bound on $d^*(G)$ cannot be improved. A corresponding result for oriented graphs was obtained by Ayoub and Frisch [15].

We now consider homogeneous or regular graphs in which all nodes are of degree d. Such graphs are maximally connected if they are d-connected and d-edge connected. It follows from the preceding paragraph that maximally connected homogeneous graphs are node critical and edge critical. If all nodes in a communication or computer network are of equal importance, a maximally reliable network clearly corresponds to a maximally connected homogeneous graph. General procedures for constructing maximally connected homogeneous graphs are considered in Section III-C. Since almost all such graphs that have been characterized are symmetrical with respect to their nodes, the following paragraph deals with properties of node-symmetric graphs.

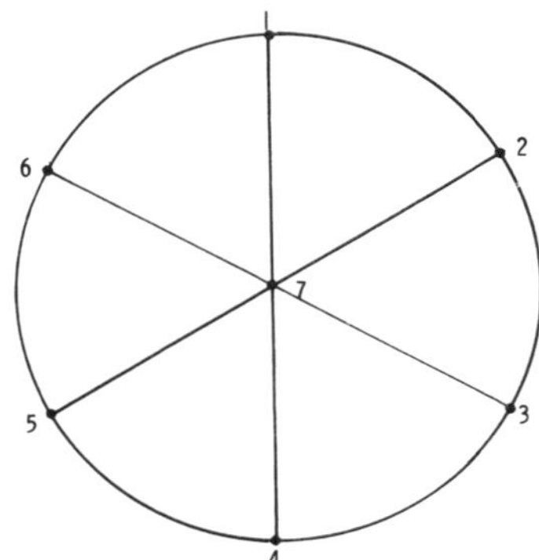

Fig. 2. 7-node wheel—a 3-connected graph.

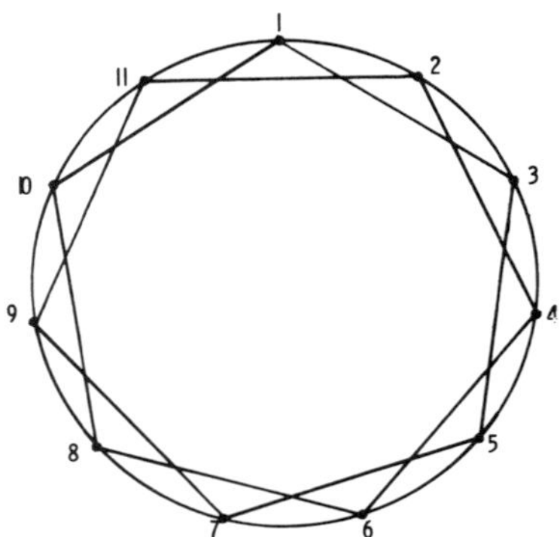

Fig. 3. 11-node starred polygon that is 4 connected.

The connectivity of node-symmetric graphs has been investigated by Watkins [16] and [17]. He defined a node-symmetric graph G to be hypoconnected if $C^n(G) < d(G)$, where $d(G)$ is the degree of every node in G. He found that hypoconnected node-symmetric graphs were difficult to characterize. However, for the set of all such graphs that are connected, Watkins has shown that the least upper bound of $d(G)/C^n(G)$ is $\frac{3}{2}$ and that the bound is never attained. Furthermore, he showed that every node-symmetric graph of degree 2, 4, or 6 is maximally connected, i.e., $C^n(G) = d(G)$. For $d(G) = 2$, the graph is a simple polygon. More generally, it has been shown by Turner [18] that the class of connected node-symmetric graphs having a prime number of nodes is identical to the class of starred polygons. Turner defined a "starred polygon" to be a graph in which nodes n_i and n_j are adjacent if and only if nodes n_{i+k} and n_{j+k} are also adjacent where $1 \leq k \leq n - 1$ and n is the number of nodes in the graph. The subscripts $i + k$ and $j + k$ are taken to be integers modulo n. The starred polygon of degree four with 11 nodes is shown in Fig. 3. This graph has four node- and edge-disjoint paths between every pair of nodes and is therefore 4-connected. In general, the starred polygons constitute a class of maximally connected node-symmetric graphs. Before proceeding with a discussion of known algorithms for realizing complete classes of maximally connected homogeneous graphs, we shall consider methods that have been developed to determine the node or edge connectivity of any given graph. These methods are required in order to analyze computer or communication network reliability based on node or edge connectivity.

B. Analyzing Network Reliability by Determining Node and Edge Connectivity

In the theory of flow networks, each edge of an oriented graph is assigned a positive number that corresponds to its capacity. Analogous to Menger's Theorem, Ford and Fulkerson [19] established that the maximum flow between any two nodes n_i and n_j is equal to the capacity of the minimum i-j cut, where the capacity of a cut is the sum of the capacities of the edges in the cut. Furthermore, they developed a labeling algorithm to find the maximum flow between any specified pair of nodes in an oriented graph. In order to apply the algorithm to a nonoriented graph G we first transform it into a symmetric oriented graph $\bar{G}$ by replacing each edge $[n_i, n_j]$ in G by the pair of edges (n_i, n_j) and (n_j, n_i) in $\bar{G}$. The capacity of each of these oriented edges in $\bar{G}$ is the same as the capacity of the original nonoriented edge in G. If all edges in G have a capacity of unity, then the maximum flow between nodes n_i and n_j in graph G is the number of edges in a minimum i-j cut, which equals the edge connectivity C_{ij}^e between nodes n_i and n_j. In order to compute C_{ij}^e for all i, j and the edge connectivity $C^e(G)$ of graph G, an algorithm was developed by Gomory and Hu [20] that required only $n - 1$ instead of $n(n - 1)/2$ iterations of the labeling algorithm.

The node connectivity C_{ij}^n between nodes n_i and n_j in an oriented graph $\bar{G}$ of b edges and n nodes can be found by splitting all of the nodes in $\bar{G}$ and inserting new oriented edges between the edges oriented toward and the edges oriented away from each node before applying the labeling algorithm. The resulting graph has $2n$ nodes and $b + n$ edges, thereby requiring twice as much computation time as the original graph $\bar{G}$. However, another labeling procedure has been constructed by Frisch [21] that enables C_{ij}^n to be calculated directly from oriented graph $\bar{G}$. In the calculation of C_{ij}^n for all i and j, Frisch [22] has shown that the flow pattern that results from applying the labeling procedure in the calculation of C_{ij}^n can be used to find the maximum flow between any other node i' and node j. This reduces the time required to calculate $C_{i'j}^n$ if C_{ij}^n has already been found. Furthermore, it has been demonstrated by Kleitman [23] that in order to verify that an n-node nonoriented graph G is m-connected, no more than $m(m - 1)/2 + m(n - m)$ out of the $n(n - 1)/2$ node pairs need be considered. This follows from the observation that to check if a nonoriented graph G is m-connected, it is only necessary to iteratively check that at the jth stage there are $m - j + 1$ node disjoint paths from any node n_j in $G_j = G - \{n_1, n_2, \cdots, n_{j-1}\}$ to all of the other nodes in graph G_j. We note that G_j is formed from graph G by deleting nodes $n_1, n_2, \cdots, n_{j-1}$ and all edges incident to these nodes. It has also been shown [23] that to verify the existence of m disjoint paths between nodes n_i and n_j in G, if one has verified the existence of m disjoint paths between

n_i and each of the k nodes in set $N_j \subset \Gamma(n_j)$ where $n_i \notin N_j$, then it is only necessary to verify that there are $(m - k)$ disjoint paths between nodes n_i and n_j in $G - N_j$.

Alternatively, a uniform approach to finding the node and edge connectivity of a connected graph in only $n - 1$ applications of a labeling algorithm has recently been developed by Frechen [24] based on the Gomory–Hu cut tree method [20]. The approach is based on transforming the given graph G into a suitable flow network N to which the latter algorithm is applied. Furthermore, applying the Ford–Fulkerson labeling algorithm to a pair of nodes n_i and n_j in N permits the identification of all edge- or node-disjoint paths between n_i and n_j in the given graph G.

C. Designing Maximally Reliable Homogeneous Networks Based on Connectivity

The results discussed above allow the analysis of the reliability of computer networks based on the node or edge connectivity of the corresponding graph. Therefore, we now consider the design of reliable computer networks in terms of the realization of maximally connected graphs having a minimum number of edges. If successful communication between all node pairs is equally important, a maximally reliable network of b edges and n nodes is one in which

$$C^n = C^e = d^* = \lfloor 2b/n \rfloor. \qquad (3)$$

The corresponding graph is obtained from a homogeneous graph of degree $2b_m/n$, where b_m is the maximum integer no greater than b such that n divides $2b_m$. In the case of oriented graphs, b_m/n edges, respectively, are oriented toward and away from each node and the node and edge connectivity is b_m/n. If $b_m \neq b$, the additional $b - b_m$ edges are then appended to the homogeneous graph between pairs of nonadjacent nodes.

The structure of two classes of maximally connected homogeneous graphs has been exhibited. One class of nonoriented graphs, introduced by Harary [25] and Hakimi [26], is such that for connectivity d even, node i is adjacent to nodes $i \pm j$ (modulo n), where $1 \leq j \leq d/2$. If n is a prime number, these graphs are examples of the starred polygons discussed in Section III-A. For these graphs, the girth is three and the diameter is $\lceil n/d \rceil$, where $\lceil x \rceil$ is the smallest integer greater than or equal to x. For d odd and n even, node i is also adjacent to node $i + n/2$ (modulo n) and the diameter has been found by the author [27] to be $\lceil n/2(d - 1) \rceil$. This class of graphs is constructed by placing the n nodes around the periphery of a circle and connecting each node to the d (for d even) or $d - 1$ (for d odd) other nodes closest to it. If d is odd, each node is also connected to the one furthest from it. The graph of connectivity 4 having 26 nodes is shown in Fig. 4(a). Since this graph is clearly node symmetric, we can obtain its diameter by finding the distance from any one node to all of the others. For any node i in Fig. 4(a), node $i + 13$ is the furthest away. In fact, the length of the shortest path

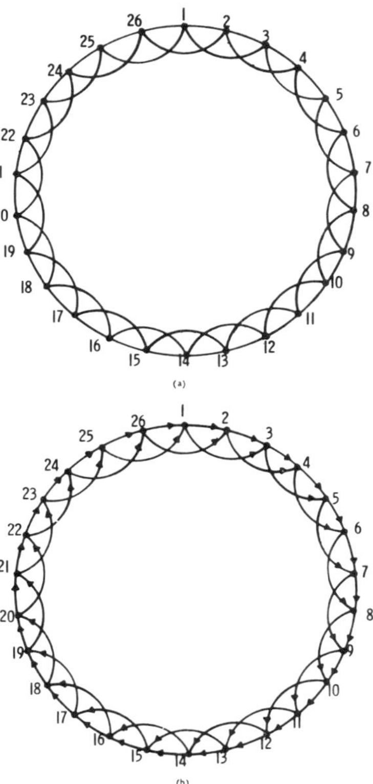

Fig. 4. Maximally connected homogeneous graphs with 52 edges and a diameter of 7. (a) Nonoriented graph of connectivity 4. (b) Oriented graph of connectivity 2.

between any pair of nodes i and $i + 13$ is 7, which is the diameter of the graph in Fig. 4(a). In order to obtain the graph of connectivity 5 having 26 nodes, edges between nodes i and $i + 13$ for $1 \leq i \leq 13$ would be added to Fig. 4(a). The corresponding class of oriented graphs has been identified by Ayoub and Frisch [28]. In the oriented graph of connectivity $\lfloor d/2 \rfloor$, every node i is adjacent to nodes $i + j$ (modulo n) where $1 \leq j \leq \lfloor d/2 \rfloor$. The oriented graph corresponding to Fig. 4(a) has a node and edge connectivity of 2 and is shown in Fig. 4(b). The diameter of this graph is still 7, as in the nonoriented case.

A class of maximally connected homogeneous bipartite graphs has been introduced by Boesch and Thomas [29]. These graphs are such that for n even, node i is adjacent to node $i + 2j - 1$ (modulo n) where $1 \leq j \leq d$. We note that a bipartite graph is one in which the set of nodes N can be partitioned into two disjoint sets N_1 and N_2 and each edge of the graph joins a node in N_1 with a node in N_2. A graph is bipartite if and only if every circuit is of even length [3]. The homogeneous bipartite graphs just mentioned have a girth of four and a diameter that has been shown [27] to be approximately $\lceil (n + 1)/2(d - 1) \rceil$. For example, the 26-node homogeneous bipartite graph of connectivity 4 is shown in Fig. 5. This graph is also node symmetric and it is easily found that it has a diameter of 5.

All of the maximally connected graphs discussed above have the property that their diameters increase very

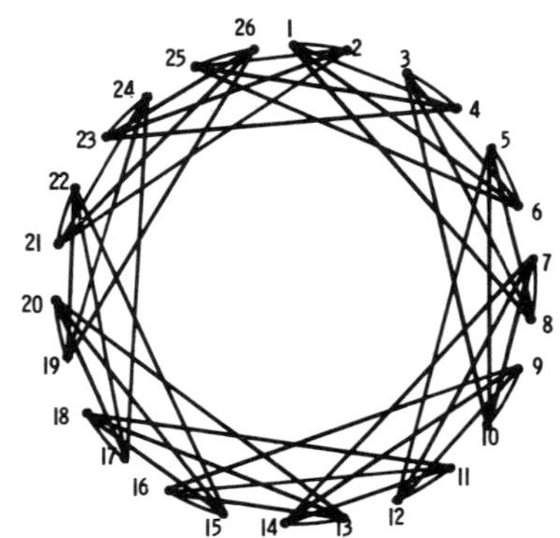

Fig. 5. Maximally connected homogeneous bipartite graph with a connectivity of 4 and a diameter of 5.

rapidly with the number of nodes, since for graphs of large computer networks $n \gg d$. Therefore, in large networks of this type, the shortest route between several pairs of nodes would have to pass through many intermediate computer centers. This is clearly undesirable in view of the processing and queueing delay associated with each node. Therefore, it is desirable in practice for the graph of a communication or computer network to have a reasonably small diameter. With this motivation, Wilkov [27], [30] has investigated maximally connected homogeneous graphs having as small a diameter as possible. In view of the fact that most of these graphs were found to have a large girth (minimum length of any circuit), properties of homogeneous graphs and their girth are considered in the following paragraph.

Homogeneous graphs having a specified girth and a minimum number of nodes have been studied by Tutte [10] and Sachs [31]. Tutte has shown that for any homogeneous graph of degree d, girth t, and diameter k, $t \leq 2k + 1$ and the minimum number of nodes n_0 is a function of d and t. Upper and lower bounds on n_0 have been exhibited by Sachs, where the lower bounds are of the form

$$n_0 \geq f(d, t) = \frac{2(d-1)^k - 2}{d-2}, \qquad t = 2k \tag{4a}$$

$$n_0 \geq f(d, t) = \frac{d(d-1)^k - 2}{d-2}, \qquad t = 2k + 1. \tag{4b}$$

The existence of homogeneous graphs of degree d, diameter k, and girth $t = 2k$ in which the number of nodes satisfies the lower bound in (4a) has been investigated by Singleton [32]. These graphs, which exist for only certain values of d and t, are subsequently referred to as "Singleton graphs." Those homogeneous graphs of diameter k and girth $t = 2k + 1$, which meet the bound in (4b), are known as "Moore graphs." They exist for very few combinations of values of d and t, as demonstrated by Hoffman and Singleton [33] and Friedman [34]. Furthermore, it has been noted in [33] that $f(d, t)$ in (4b) also specifies an upper bound on the number of nodes in any homogeneous graph G of degree d and diameter k. Therefore, if G has n nodes, $n \leq f(d, 2k + 1)$. It follows from this and (4b) that for $d \gg 2$,

$$k \geq k_0 = \left\lceil \frac{\log n}{\log d} \right\rceil. \tag{5}$$

Any n-node homogeneous graph of degree d and diameter k has a minimum diameter if $k = k_0$. For small values of d, an exact expression for k_0 is obtained from (4b). We note that k_0 is considerably smaller than the diameter of any of the maximally connected homogeneous graphs discussed above that have a large number of nodes. Furthermore, this author [30] has demonstrated that Moore and Singleton graphs are maximally connected homogeneous graphs of minimum diameter. Almost all of those that can be realized have been constructed by Tutte [10], Wilkov [27], and Longyear [35]. For example, the 26-node Singleton graph of degree 4 and girth 6 obtained in [27] is shown in Fig. 6. It has a node connectivity of 4 and diameter of 3. Unfortunately, Moore and Singleton graphs constitute only a small class of homogeneous graphs of maximum node connectivity and minimum diameter. However, more generally, if the desired number of nodes n and the node connectivity d are specified, one may proceed by constructing a homogeneous graph of connectivity d and maximum girth t_m where t_m is the largest value of t such that $f(d, t) \leq n$ in (4). It has been found [27] that the diameter of such graphs is a good approximation to the minimum value and is much smaller than the diameter of the homogeneous graphs of maximum node connectivity, which have a smaller girth. These graphs of maximum girth have only been realized in specific instances using heuristic methods.

Following an approach essentially similar to the above, the results of Trufanov [36] suggest a method for reducing the diameter of the maximally connected graphs introduced by Harary [25] and Hakimi [26]. In the construction of such graphs of even degree d, Trufanov [36] recommends that the $d - 2$ nodes on the periphery of a circle connected to each node i be selected in such a way that the maximum distance from node i to any other node is minimized. In the event that d is odd, this same rule is to be followed after node i has been connected to node $i + n/2$ (modulo n). For the 26-node graph of connectivity 4, node i is furthest from node $i + 13$ on the periphery of the circle. For all i, the distance between nodes i and $i + 13$ is minimized by also connecting node i to nodes $i \pm 7$. The resulting graph is shown in Fig. 7. It is node symmetric and is easily found to have a diameter of only 4, compared with a diameter of 7 for the corresponding graph in Fig. 4(a).

Other classes of graphs having a reasonably small diameter have been obtained, in connection with studies of logic networks, by constructing homogeneous graphs of degree d and diameter k with a large number of nodes. For those values of d and k for which Moore graphs do not exist, Elspas [37] tried to construct graphs in which the numbers of nodes were as close to the bound in (4b)

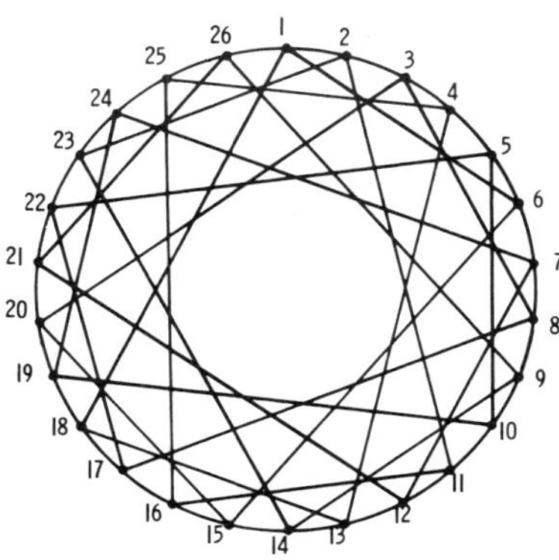

Fig. 6. Singleton graph with a connectivity of 4 and a diameter of 3.

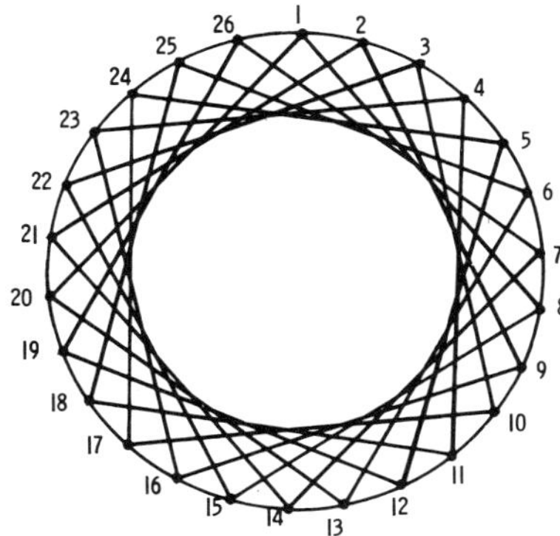

Fig. 7. Modification of the graph in Fig. 4(a) with a connectivity of 4 and a diameter of 4.

as possible. Although he was not specifically concerned with the connectivities of these graphs, several maximally connected homogeneous graphs of small diameter were constructed. Continuing with similar studies, Friedman [38] and Korn [39] exhibited a particular class of maximally connected homogeneous graphs of degree d having n nodes in which the diameter k is approximately given by

$$k = 2\left[\frac{\log (n/2)}{\log d}\right], \qquad k \text{ even and } d \gg 2 \tag{6a}$$

$$k = 2\left[\frac{\log (n/4)}{\log d}\right] + 1, \qquad k \text{ odd and } d \gg 2. \tag{6b}$$

A more general theoretical study related to the above was undertaken by Ore [40]. He defined a graph to be diameter critical if the addition of any edge decreases the diameter. Ore found general properties for m-connected diameter-critical graphs having n nodes and a diameter of k and obtained an upper bound on the number of edges in any such graph.

Requiring homogeneous graphs of degree d and diameter k to have d edge-disjoint paths each of length at most k between every pair of nodes, Quaife [41] exhibited a class of such graphs, which are also maximally node connected. Their diameter is approximately twice as large as that given in (6). A more general study of a similar nature was undertaken by Gewirtz [42]. He examined graphs of diameter k and girth $2k$ in which there are m disjoint paths of length k between every pair of nodes at a distance of k. He showed that all such graphs are regular of degree d and that they reduce to the Singleton graphs when $m = d$. Therefore, an important problem that warrants further investigation is the development of a general algorithm for constructing maximally connected homogeneous graphs with a minimum diameter.

D. Design of Maximally Connected Nonhomogeneous Networks

In the event that all nodes in a computer or communication network are not equally important, it is desirable for certain pairs of nodes to have a larger node and edge connectivity than others. In this case, as indicated previously, a maximally reliable network is one in which $C_{ij}^n = C_{ij}^e = \min (d_i, d_j)$ for all node pairs n_i, n_j. The design of such networks for specified degrees of each node or for specified node pair connectivities is much more difficult than the design of homogeneous networks. The first step taken in this direction was the discovery by Hakimi [43] of a set of necessary and sufficient conditions for a set of integers $d_1, d_2, \cdots, d_n$ to be realizable as the degrees of a nonoriented graph without parallel edges. A synthesis procedure was given in this study, but without regard to the node pair connectivities.

The realization of a matrix of node pair edge connectivities C_{ij}^e has subsequently been considered by Frank and Chou [44], [45]. In the first of these studies, for a specified $n \times n$ matrix $R = [r_{ij}]$, an algorithm was given for constructing a graph of n nodes with a minimum number of edges such that $r_{ij} = C_{ij}^e$ for all node pairs n_i, n_j. The resulting graphs were of limited practical value since parallel edges were permitted. Subsequently, allowing no parallel edges, the same authors developed a procedure for constructing a graph with $n' = \max [n, \max (r_{ij}) + 1]$ nodes having a minimum number of edges such that $C_{ij}^e \geq r_{ij}$ for $1 \leq i \leq n$ and $1 \leq j \leq n$. The edge connectivity between any of the remaining pairs of nodes is unspecified. This procedure is based on a realization of the sequence of integers $\{d_i\}$, where $1 \leq i \leq n'$. The degree of node i is given by $d_i = \max_{1 \leq j \leq n} [r_{ij}]$ for $1 \leq i \leq n$ and the degrees of the remaining $n' - n$ nodes are fixed in the course of the procedure. Unfortunately, the procedure is very cumbersome to apply and results in graphs having only a specified lower bound on the node pair edge connectivities.

Attempts at realizing nonhomogeneous networks having specified node connectivities C_{ij}^n have been less successful. Following the above approach, for a specified $n \times n$ matrix $R = [r_{ij}]$, efforts have been made by Frank and Chou [2] to construct a graph of $n' \geq n$ nodes with a minimum number of edges such that $C_{ij}^n \geq r_{ij}$ for $1 \leq i, j \leq n$. If the degrees of the nodes, as specified above, are arranged in descending order with $d_1 \geq d_2 \geq \cdots \geq d_n$, an exact algorithm has been found only in the special cases that $d_1 \geq n - 1$ or $d_1 < n - 1$ with $d_1 = d_2 = \cdots = d_{d_1+1}$. In the general case, an approximate algorithm has been developed that requires an unspecified number of extra edges. Alternatively, an approximate method for generating nonhomogeneous maximally connected networks of minimal diameter has been suggested by Wilkov [46]. This method is based on the following procedure for using a minimal number of edges to append a node to a given network without changing its connectivity or diameter.

Procedure I:

1) Let G be a graph of node connectivity d and diameter k and let n_0 be a node of maximal degree.

2) Form set $A(n_0)$ of the nodes at a distance (length of the shortest path) k from node n_0.

3) Form a graph G' consisting of the nodes in $A(n_0)$, where two nodes are adjacent in G' if the length of the shortest path between them in graph G is no greater than $k - 1$.

4) Find $T(G')$, a minimal externally stable set of G' (one of the smallest subsets of the nodes of G', which is such that every other node in G' is adjacent to at least one of the nodes in the subset).

5) Form G^* from G by connecting new node n^* to n_0 and all of the nodes in $T(G')$. If n^* is of degree less than d, connect n^* to any additional $d - 1 - |T(G')|$ nodes. Graph G^* is now of connectivity d and diameter k.

A nonhomogeneous network can be realized by iteratively using this procedure to append nodes to a homogeneous maximally connected network of minimal diameter. For example, if we wish to approximate a maximally connected network of minimal diameter having a specified number of n nodes of specified degree $\{d_i\}$, we begin by using known bounds to compute the minimum diameter denoted by k_0. We also compute the average degree (denoted by d_0) of all nodes by summing the degrees of all the nodes and dividing by n. Then the n_0 nodes of greatest importance (i.e., those of degree no less than d_0) are selected as "core" nodes. We now form a core network by constructing a maximally connected homogeneous network of n_0 nodes having the smallest degree that is necessary to attain a diameter of k_0. Procedure I is then applied to append the remaining "peripheral" nodes to the core network, using a minimal number of communication links, in such a way that the $\{d_i\}$ constraint is approximately satisfied. We conjecture, but have been unable to prove, that the resulting network is such that $C_{ij}^n = \min[d_i, d_j]$.

We note that in the above discussion, all communication links have been assumed to have the same cost. The objective has only been to minimize the number of communication links. In practical design problems, for specified geographical locations of the nodes, the cost of communication links is different between different pairs of nodes. Hence, for a given set of n nodes, there is a cost matrix $C = [c_{ij}]$ where c_{ij} is the cost of a communication link between nodes n_i and n_j. Therefore, for a specified $n \times n$ redundancy matrix $R = [r_{ij}]$, a practical design problem consists of constructing a minimum cost network, which is such that $C_{ij}^n \geq r_{ij}$ for all node pairs n_i, n_j. For other than very small values of n, it is not computationally feasible to obtain an exact solution to this problem. However, approximate solutions have been obtained using the following heuristic procedure developed by Steiglitz *et al.* [47].

Procedure II:

1) Generate a random initial solution $G^* = G$, which is such that $C_{ij}^n \geq r_{ij}$.

2) Initialize a counter to be used to keep track of edge exchanges.

3) If all edge exchanges have not been exhausted, go on to the next step. Otherwise, stop and G^* is a local optimum.

4) Perform a cost-reducing local transformation consisting of an edge exchange, i.e., if G contains edges $[n_i, n_j]$ and $[n_s, n_t]$ but does not contain edges $[n_i, n_t]$ and $[n_j, n_s]$ and if $c_{it} + c_{js} < c_{ij} + c_{st}$, then form a new network G' from G by removing the edges $[n_i, n_j]$ and $[n_s, n_t]$ and adding edges $[n_i, n_t]$ and $[n_j, n_s]$.

5) Evaluate C_{ij}^n for all node pairs in G'.

6) If $C_{ij}^n < r_{ij}$ for some node pair, go back to step 3. If $C_{ij}^n \geq r_{ij}$ for all i, j, let $G^* = G = G'$ and go back to step 2.

The computation time required for each iteration of Procedure II strongly depends on the algorithm used in step 1) to obtain an initial solution. The approach taken by Steiglitz *et al.* [47] was to iteratively realize a reasonably low-cost network G_0 of n nodes in which the degree of node n_i is $d_i \geq \max_j [r_{ij}]$. C_{ij}^n is then evaluated for all node pairs in G_0 using one of the procedures discussed in Section III-B of this paper. Edges are added to the network if $C_{ij}^n < r_{ij}$ for some node pair n_i, n_j. An alternative method for generating G_0 has been suggested by Owens [48]. His method generally results in lower cost networks and is more flexible in the number of edges required than the method used in [47]. Succeeding steps in Procedure II require a smaller amount of computation time. This is partially due to the observation [47] that when all C_{ij}^n in G are known, C_{ij}^n for all node pairs in G' can be obtained in step 5) by calculating the node connectivity between only two pairs of nodes in G'. We note that Procedure II generates a locally optimum network that is a function of the starting solution and the particular local transformation. It should be repeated for a number of different starting solutions. The final solution is the cheapest of all of the local optima that have been obtained.

IV. More General Deterministic Reliability Measures

A. Generalized Cohesion as a Reliability Measure

A more general reliability criterion than the edge connectivity or cohesion of a graph, which has recently been introduced by Boesch and Thomas [29], is the minimum number of edges that must be removed from a graph in order to isolate any subgraph of m nodes from the rest of the graph. This quantity, denoted by $\delta(m)$, corresponds to the minimum number of communication link failures that will isolate any set of m computer centers from the remaining ones. Based on this criterion, maximally reliable networks clearly correspond to graphs for which $\delta(m)$ is as large as possible for all values of m. It is to be noted that this criterion is only meaningful as a computer-network reliability measure if the probability of communication-link failures is much greater than the probability of computer-center breakdowns in the network. On the other hand, if it were more likely for computer centers to fail than for communication links to fail, we could use a criterion analogous to $\delta(m)$ for the nodes of a graph, denoted by $\delta^n(m)$.

The criteria introduced above are more general reliability measures than the edge or node connectivity of a graph since they make possible some discrimination between different failure modes in the network. It is clearly more serious for link or node failures to isolate half the nodes in the network from the other half than one node in the network from all of the others. Consequently, we would expect a highly reliable network to have a much larger value of $\delta(\lfloor n/2 \rfloor)$ than $\delta(1)$. On the other hand, edge or node connectivity reflects the minimum number of link or node failures that isolate any one part of the network from the other. Therefore, in any network of edge connectivity C^e and node connectivity C^n, $C^e = \min_m [\delta(m)]$ and $C^n = \min_m [\delta^n(m)]$.

In evaluating $\delta(m)$ for a given nonoriented graph, if we denote a subset of m nodes by M, its complement by L, and the number of edges connecting the two sets by deg (M), then

$$\deg (L) = \deg (M) = \sum_{j \in M} \deg (j) - 2b_M$$

and $\delta(m) = \min_{M:|M|=m} [\deg (M)] = \delta(n - m)$, where b_M is the number of edges in the subgraph consisting of the nodes in set M. For oriented graphs, Malek-Zavarei and Frisch [49] suggested that deg (M) can be measured by the number of edges directed away from the nodes in M toward the nodes in L and $\delta(m) = \min_{M:|M|=m} [\deg (M)]$. An upper and lower bound on $\delta(M)$ for an oriented and nonoriented graph has been exhibited [49], [29]. For a nonoriented graph G of n nodes in which $d^*(G)$ is the minimum of the degrees of the nodes,

$$\delta(m) \geq md^*(G) - m(m - 1). \tag{7}$$

This bound is met for some value of m only if G contains m nodes, each of degree $d^*(G)$, which form a completely connected subgraph. In the event that G is a completely connected graph, all nodes are of degree $n - 1$ and the lower bound in (7) is met for all values of m, i.e., $\delta(m) = m(n - m)$. The upper bound on $\delta(m)$ for a nonoriented graph G of n nodes is such that if G is homogeneous of degree $d \leq \lfloor n/2 \rfloor$,

$$d \geq \left\lfloor \frac{\delta(n - m)}{n - m} \right\rfloor + \left\lceil \frac{\delta(m)}{m} \right\rceil, \qquad m \leq n - m. \tag{8}$$

If n is even and $d = n/2$, it has been shown by Boesch and Thomas [29] that

$$\delta(m) \leq \left\lceil \frac{m(n - m)}{2} \right\rceil. \tag{9}$$

In the event that G is also bipartite, it is known as a complete bipartite graph, and equality holds in (8) and (9).

More generally, for any nonoriented homogeneous graph G of degree d having n nodes,

$$\delta(m) = md - 2 \max_{M:|M|=m} [b_M]. \tag{10}$$

G has been defined by Boesch and Felzer [50] to be $\delta(m)$ optimal if for all m it has larger values of $\delta(m)$ than any other homogeneous graph of n nodes and degree d. The calculation of $\delta(m)$ for several homogeneous graphs is given in the following example.

Example [30]: For the graph shown in Figure 4(a)

$$\delta(1) = \delta(25) = 4$$
$$\delta(m) = 4m - 2(2m - 3) = 6, \qquad 2 \leq m \leq 24.$$

For the graph shown in Fig. 5

$$\delta(1) = \delta(25) = 4$$
$$\delta(2) = \delta(24) = 6$$
$$\delta(m) = 4m - 2(2m - 4) = 8, \qquad 3 \leq m \leq 23.$$

For the Singleton graph shown in Fig. 6

$$\delta(1) = \delta(25) = 4$$
$$\delta(m) = 2m + 2, \qquad 2 \leq m \leq 5 \text{ and } 21 \leq m \leq 24$$
$$\delta(6) = \delta(20) = 12$$
$$\delta(7) = \delta(19) = 14$$
$$\delta(8) = \delta(18) = 14$$
$$\delta(m) = 16, \qquad 9 \leq m \leq 17.$$

We note from this example that the 26-node homogeneous graphs of larger girth exhibited larger values of $\delta(m)$ for all m than those of smaller girth. Consequently, using $\delta(m)$ as the reliability criterion, the homogeneous network of degree 4 and girth 6 has a much higher degree of reliability than corresponding networks of smaller girth. Similar results have been obtained for many other regular graphs. It has been shown by Boesch and Felzer [50] and Wilkov [30] that it is the variation in girth among these graphs that is largely responsible for the variation in $\delta(m)$ from one graph to another. However, it has been demonstrated [50] that maximizing the girth in a maximally connected graph is a necessary but not a completely sufficient condition for a graph to be $\delta(m)$ optimal.

In the design of maximally reliable computer networks based on the realization of $\delta(m)$ optimal graphs, only partial results are available. $\delta(m)$ optimal graphs have only been characterized in certain special cases. Among all homogeneous graphs of n nodes and degree d =

$n - n/k$, the class of complete k-partite graphs have been shown by Boesch and Felzer [51] to be $\delta(m)$ and $\delta^n(m)$ optimal. We note that a complete k-partite graph is one in which the set of nodes is evenly partitioned into k disjoint subsets $M_1, M_2, \cdots, M_k$ and every node in subset M_i is adjacent to every one of the other $n - n/k$ nodes in the graph that are not in subset M_i. Perhaps the most interesting of these is the complete bipartite graph that is of degree $n/2$ and has a girth of four. It is a special case of the Singleton graphs, which, as indicated previously, are maximally connected homogeneous graphs of minimum diameter. In general, any connected n-node homogeneous graph of maximum girth denoted by t, which is such that $\lfloor n/2 \rfloor \leq t + \lfloor (t-1)/2 \rfloor$, has been shown [50] to be $\delta(m)$ optimal. We can give the slightly sharper result that a connected n-node homogeneous graph of maximum girth denoted by t is $\delta(m)$ optimal provided $\lfloor n/2 \rfloor < 2t - 2$. This result is unpublished but has been proved by the author. Furthermore, bounds exhibited by Voss [52] on the girth of any given graph have been used by Wilkov [30] to obtain a lower bound on $\delta(m)$, which increases with the girth of the graph. In general, it has been conjectured by Boesch [53] and this author independently that Moore and Singleton graphs are $\delta(m)$ optimal. This conjecture warrants further study along with general sufficient conditions for any maximally connected graph of maximum girth to be $\delta(m)$ optimal.

B. New Reliability Measure Based on the Network Diameter

The use of $\delta(m)$ and the connectivity of a network as reliability measures is based on the assumption that the network is operational in the presence of failures provided there is at least one path remaining between every pair of nodes. However, this resulting network may have an excessively large diameter, which, as indicated previously, may result in intolerable queueing delays in routing a message through the network. Therefore, a more meaningful reliability measure for a computer network would be the minimum number of nodes or links that must fail in order for the diameter of the network to exceed a specified value. We denote by $D^e(k, \lambda)$ and $D^n(k, \lambda)$ the minimum number of edges or nodes that must be removed from a graph of diameter k in order that the diameter of the resulting graph exceed λ. Therefore, the removal of any $D^e(k, \lambda) - 1$ edges or $D^n(k, \lambda) - 1$ nodes results in a graph of diameter less than or equal to λ. A disconnected graph is assumed to have a diameter of ∞. We know of no specific attempts to analyze a network with respect to this measure. However, it is easily shown that in any network of n nodes and girth t having a node connectivity of C^n and an edge connectivity of C^e,

$$D^n(k, \lambda) \leq C^n,\ D^e(k, \lambda) \leq C^e \qquad (11)$$

and

$$D^n(k, t-2) \geq 2,\ D^e(k, t-1) \geq 2. \qquad (12)$$

Moreover, it follows from the results of Wilkov [27] and Gewirtz [42] that in Moore or Singleton graphs of connectivity d, diameter k, and girth $t = 2k + 1$ or $2k$,

$$D^n(k, t-2) = d, \qquad D^e(k, t-1) = d. \qquad (13)$$

With respect to the synthesis of networks based on the measures $D^e(k, \lambda)$ and $D^n(k, \lambda)$, let $f(n, k, \lambda, v)$ denote the minimum of the number of edges in any graph of n nodes and diameter at most k, which is such that $D^n(k, \lambda) = v + 1$ and let $g(n, k, \lambda, e)$ denote the minimum of the number of edges in any graph of n nodes and diameter $\leq k$ in which $D^e(k, \lambda) = e + 1$. The values for the functions f and g have been investigated in several special cases by Bollobas [54]. He has shown that if $n > (2 + \sqrt{2})v + 2$, then $f(n, 2, 2, v) = (v + 1)(n - v - 1)$ and the corresponding graph is a complete bipartite graph with $v + 1$ nodes in one set and $n - v - 1$ nodes in the other. If $n > (3 + \sqrt{5})(e + 1)/2$, then $g(n, 2, 2, e) = (e + 1)(n - e/2 - 1)$. The graph is obtained from the complete bipartite graph having $e + 1$ nodes in one set and $n - e - 1$ nodes in the other by appending edges between all pairs of nodes in the set of size $e + 1$. Many other special cases have also been considered, but only for v or e equal to one. In general, procedures are needed for using a minimum number of edges to construct graphs having n nodes and specified values of $D^n(k, \lambda)$ or $D^e(k, \lambda)$.

V. Probabilistic Relability Criteria

The deterministic measures discussed in the preceding sections are not completely adequate measures of computer-network reliability. In the presence of randomly distributed natural destructive forces, a reasonable indication of the overall reliability of a network is the probability of service disruption between any pair of operative centers based on a given degree of reliability for every node and link in the network. The calculation of this probability is based not only on the minimum number of link and node failures resulting in the disruption of service, but also on the total number of combinations of such failures. Therefore, based on the graph corresponding to the computer network, the above probability calculation for a given pair of nodes depends on the edges or nodes in all of the cutsets with respect to that pair of nodes. This must be reflected in any adequate computer-network reliability measure.

A. Fraction of Network Surviving Random Attack

One of the earliest studies of network reliability based on a probabilistic measure was undertaken by Baran [55]. He used Monte Carlo simulation to study the probability of communication-network survival in a military environment subject to random attacks on the network elements by a human enemy. As a measure of network survivability, he used the largest fraction of surviving nodes that could communicate with each other after an enemy attack. This study is also applicable to network reliability in which there is a certain probability of natural failure associated with each network element.

In the Monte Carlo evaluation, node and link failures are simulated and the resulting network is analyzed using deterministic methods. This is repeated for a large number of combinations of link and node failures. Using this method, d-redundant networks consisting of large uniform arrays of nodes in which each node was adjacent to d nearest neighbors were considered. Networks of several-hundred nodes with values of d greater than four or five were found to have a high degree of reliability even when individual links and nodes had a large probability of failure.

Subsequently, an analytical approach was developed by Frank [56] to evaluate the survivability of large d-redundant oriented networks in which there are d edges oriented away from each node. This approach was based on stochastic models of enemy attack. The survivability criterion used was the expected fraction of nodes that could communicate with a randomly selected node after an enemy attack. Denoting this number by γ, it has been shown [56] that as the number of nodes and hence the diameter approaches infinity,

$$\lambda = 1 - \exp\left[-d(1-p)(1-q)\lambda\right]. \tag{14}$$

In (14), d is the number of edges oriented away from each node, $1 - p$ is the probability of survival for each edge and $1 - q$ is the probability of survival for each node. In the case of finite networks, this simple expression is not valid since γ is a function of the diameter of the network. In this case, a complicated expression for $\gamma(k)$ has been obtained, where $\gamma(k)$ denotes the fraction of stations that can be reached from any given node by a path of length no greater than k.

In the design of d-redundant networks using γ as a reliability measure, for specified values of p, q, and a lower bound on γ, the asymptotic expression for γ can be used to obtain a lower bound on d. Subsequently, one can use a procedure developed by Steffen and Dent [57] for constructing a d-redundant nonoriented network with minimum cost, assuming that the cost of each communication link is a linear function of its length. Unfortunately, the networks resulting from this procedure may have cut edges and cut nodes, i.e., have a node and edge connectivity of one. This is particularly likely for small values of d. No method has been found for modifying their procedure to construct minimum cost networks without cut nodes or cut edges. In this case, it is necessary to use a heuristic procedure of the type described in Section IV.

B. Connection Probability of a Network

A comprehensive study has been made by Kel'mans [58] of the basic property of maximally reliable networks in a nonmilitary environment. In this study, it was assumed that nodes were perfectly reliable and all links failed independently with the same probability p. As a measure of reliability, he considered the probability $R_p(G)$ that the graph G was a connected graph. The connection probability $R_p(G)$ for a graph of b edges and n nodes is given by

$$R_p(G) = \sum_{i=m}^{b} A_i (1-p)^i p^{b-i} \tag{15a}$$

or

$$R_p(G) = 1 - \sum_{i=d}^{b} B_i p^i (1-p)^{b-i}. \tag{15b}$$

In these expressions, A_i denotes the number of connected spanning subgraphs of G consisting of exactly i edges and B_i denotes the number of disconnected spanning subgraphs containing exactly $b - i$ edges. Furthermore, d is equal to the edge connectivity of the graph and m denotes the minimum of the number of edges in any connected spanning subgraph and is equal to $n - 1$, the number of edges in a spanning tree. For values of p close to unity, $R_p(G)$ is clearly approximated by $A_{n-1}(1-p)^{n-1}$ where A_{n-1} is the number of trees in the graph. When p is close to zero, $R_p(G) \sim 1 - B_d p^d$, where B_d is the number of cutsets containing d edges.

Using the above relationships, it has been shown by Kel'mans [58] that there exist two graphs G_1 and G_2 such that $R_p(G_1) < R_p(G_2)$ for small values of p and $R_p(G_1) > R_p(G_2)$ for large values of p (close to unity). Consequently, the topology of maximally reliable networks depends on the magnitude of the link-failure probability. This complicates the problem of constructing optimum networks based on probabilistic reliability criteria.

With reference to the synthesis of maximally reliable networks for a specified link-failure probability p, a lower bound has been exhibited [58] on the number of edges $b(n)$ required for an n-node network to have any specified degree of reliability R_0. It has been shown that if

$$b(n) \geq \frac{n \ln n}{2\,|\ln p|}, \tag{16}$$

then there exists a value n_0, for which $R_p(G) \geq R_0$ whenever $n \geq n_0$. Furthermore, it follows that unless the average degree of each node is greater than or equal to $(\ln n)/|\ln p|$, the probability that the network is connected will decrease as the number of nodes increase, regardless of the topology of the network.

We note from the above discussion that for values of p close to unity, since $R_p(G) \sim A_{n-1}(1-p)^{n-1}$, a maximally reliable network is one with a maximum number of trees. For p close to zero, $R_p(G) \sim 1 - B_d p^d$ and the best network of b edges and n nodes has a minimum number of cutsets of size $\lfloor 2b/n \rfloor$. It has been shown by Leggett [59] that in this case it is still necessary for the network to have a maximum number of trees. In addition, a procedure has been given for constructing graphs having a maximum number of trees. It was shown that the degrees of the nodes in any graph cannot differ by more than one in order for the graph to have a maximum number of trees. Furthermore, in that study, closed form upper and lower bounds on $R_p(G)$ were exhibited. It is interesting to note that for dense graphs of n nodes and edge connectivity $C^e = d$ in which p is close to zero, the bounds take the simple form

$$1 - e^2 \sqrt{n/2}\, p^d \leq R_p(G) \leq 1 - \sqrt{2n}\, p^d. \tag{17}$$

In the event that communication links are perfectly reliable and nodes are likely to fail, network reliability has been investigated by Frank [60]. Following the approach discussed above, if all nodes fail independently with the same probability q, the connection probability $R_p(G)$ for a graph of n nodes and node connectivity $C^n = \omega$ can be expressed as

$$R_p(G) = 1 - \sum_{i=\omega}^{n} N_i q^i (1 - q)^{n-i}. \tag{18}$$

In this expression, N_i denotes the number of disconnected subgraphs of G resulting from the removal of exactly i nodes. When q is very close to zero, $R_p(G) \sim 1 - N_\omega q^\omega$, and a maximally reliable network clearly has a maximum node connectivity. Therefore for small values of q, the best network of n nodes and b edges has a minimum number of nodal cutsets of size $\lfloor 2b/n \rfloor$. It has been shown [60] that for q close to zero, the complete bipartite graph with n_1 nodes in one subset and $n_2 > n_1$ nodes in the other has a larger connection probability than any other graph of connectivity n_1 having no more than $n_1 n_2$ edges.

C. Deterministic Measures Based on Node-Pair Failure Probabilities

Further topological properties of maximally reliable networks have recently been discovered by Wilkov [61], based on a different probabilistic reliability measure. In that study, it was assumed that all communication-link failures and computer-center breakdowns are statistically independent and that each communication link fails with probability p and each computer center goes down with probability q. Then for an n-node computer network with b communication links, it follows from the two terminal network studies of Moore and Shannon [62] and Williams [63] that the probability $P_c[a, b]$ of successful communication between any pair of operating nodes a and b is approximately given by

$$P_c[a, b] = \sum_{i=0}^{b} A_{a,b}^{e}(i)(1 - p)^i p^{b-i}, \qquad p \gg q \tag{19a}$$

and

$$P_c[a, b] = \sum_{i=0}^{n-2} A_{a,b}^{n}(i)(1 - q)^i q^{n-2-i}, \qquad q \gg p. \tag{19b}$$

In these expressions, $A_{a,b}^n(i)$ is the number of combinations of i nodes such that if they are operative and the remaining $n - 2 - i$ nodes fail, there is at least one communication path between nodes a and b. $A_{a,b}^e$ is defined in a similar way. In addition, the probability $P_f[a, b]$ of a communication failure between any pair of operative nodes a and b is given approximately by

$$P_f[a, b] = \sum_{i=0}^{b} C_{a,b}^{e}(i) p^i (1 - p)^{b-i}, \qquad p \gg q \tag{20a}$$

and

$$P_f[a, b] = \sum_{i=0}^{n-2} C_{a,b}^{n}(i) q^i (1 - q)^{n-2-i}, \qquad q \gg p. \tag{20b}$$

With reference to the graph corresponding to the computer network, the coefficients $C_{a,b}^e(i)$ and $C_{a,b}^n(i)$ denote the number of combinations of i edges (nodes) such that the removal of only these edges (nodes) from the graph destroys all paths between nodes a and b. They are equal to the total number of edge (node) cutsets of size i with respect to nodes a and b.

We note that for any graph of node and edge connectivity equal to d, $C_{a,b}^n(i) = C_{a,b}^e(i) = 0$ for all $i < d$ and all node pairs a, b. Therefore, the dominant term in the expression for $P_f[a, b]$ is given by $C_{a,b}^e(d)p^d(1 - p)^{b-d}$ for $\frac{1}{2} > p \gg q$ and by $C_{a,b}^n(d)q^d(1 - q)^{n-2-d}$ for $\frac{1}{2} > q \gg q$. Since for small values of p or q (much less than one-half), these terms are reduced by increasing the value of d, it is clear that graphs of reliable networks must be maximally connected. In fact, we note that the connectivity of computer networks is analogous to the width of two terminal networks [62], [63]. Similarly, for p or q greater than one-half, the dominant term in $P_c[a, b]$ is $A_{a,b}^e(s)(1 - p)^s p^{b-s}$ for $p \gg q$ and $A_{a,b}^n(r)(1 - q)^r q^{n-2-r}$ for $q \gg p$, where s is the number of edges in a shortest path and $A_{a,b}^e(s)$ is the number of paths of length s between nodes a and b. The number r of nodes in a shortest path is equal to $s - 1$ and $A_{a,b}^n(r) = A_{a,b}^e(s)$. Furthermore, for large values of p, the dominant term in $\min_{a,b} P_c[a, b]$ is $A^e(k)(1 - p)^k p^{b-k}$, where k is the upper bound on the number of edges on the shortest path between any pair of nodes. This is the diameter of the network and is analogous to the length of the two terminal networks. Since for any network we clearly seek to maximize $\min_{a,b} P_c[a, b]$, it is necessary for computer networks to have a minimum diameter whenever p or q exceeds one-half. This is particularly likely to be true under heavy traffic conditions in which p or q denotes the probability that a communication link or computer center is near saturation. Therefore, availability considerations certainly require that computer and communication networks have a minimum diameter. In the event that $q = 0$ and that the probability of failure for each link increases exponentially with its length, it has been shown by Fratta *et al.* [64] that the above conditions still hold, subject to the definition that the length of any path is the sum of the lengths of the edges on the path.

In most computer network design problems, the value of p or q is fixed, and for all a, b, $P_f[a, b]$ varies only with the coefficients $C_{a,b}^e(i)$ and $C_{a,b}^n(i)$, which depend on the topology of the network. For a highly reliable network, $P_f[a, b]$ must be as small as possible and $P_c[a, b]$ must be as large as possible for all pairs of nodes. Therefore, $\min_{a,b} P_c[a, b]$ and $\max_{a,b} P_f[a, b]$ have been used by this author

[61] as probabilistic measures of network reliability. In that study, the structure of graphs for which the coefficients $C_{a,b}^{e}(i)$ and $C_{a,b}^{n}(i)$ are minimized for all values of i and all pairs of nodes was investigated.

We note that each node (edge) cutset of size i with respect to nodes a and b consists of a prime node (edge) cutset of size $i - j$ with respect to nodes a and b plus additional j nodes (edges) selected at random, where $0 \leq j \leq i - d$, and d is equal to the node and edge connectivity of the graph. We note that a prime node (edge) cutset with respect to nodes a and b is an $a - b$ cut which has the property that no proper subset of it is also a cutset. Letting $X_{a,b}^{n}(m)$ and $X_{a,b}^{e}(m)$ denote the number of prime node and edge cutsets of size m with respect to nodes a and b, $X^{n}(m) = \max_{a,b} X_{a,b}^{n}(m)$ and $X^{e}(m) = \max_{a,b} X_{a,b}^{e}(m)$ have been proposed by Wilkov [61] as new deterministic measures of the reliability of a given computer-network topology.

The measures $X^{n}(m)$ and $X^{e}(m)$ denote the maximum number of prime node and edge cutsets of size m with respect to any pair of nodes in the network. For small values of p or q, a maximally reliable or $X^{n}(m)$ and $X^{e}(m)$ optimal network is one for which $X^{n}(m)$ and $X^{e}(m)$ are as small as possible for small values of m. On the other hand, for values of p and q close to unity, $X^{n}(m)$ and $X^{e}(m)$ optimal networks are such that $X^{n}(m)$ and $X^{e}(m)$ are as small as possible for large values of m. Upper and lower bounds on $X^{e}(m)$ and $X^{n}(m)$ for small values of m have been exhibited [61] for the class of homogeneous graphs. The calculation of $X^{n}(m)$ for several homogeneous graphs is shown in the following example.

Example: For the graph in Fig. 4(a)

$$X^{n}(4) = \left(\frac{n-d}{2}\right)^{2} = 121$$

$$X^{n}(m) = 0, \qquad m \neq 4.$$

This is the number of prime node cutsets with respect to any pair of nodes at a distance of 7 (equal to the diameter).

For the graph in Fig. 5

$$X^{n}(4) = 2$$

$$X^{n}(6) = 316$$

$$X^{n}(m) = 0, \qquad \text{otherwise.}$$

These values are obtained with respect to any pair of nodes at a distance of 5.

For the Singleton graph in Fig. 6

$$X^{n}(m) = 2\binom{4}{i}, \qquad m = 4 + 2i$$

$$X^{n}(4) = 2, \qquad X^{n}(6) = 8, \qquad X^{n}(8) = 12$$

$$X^{n}(10) = 8, \qquad X^{n}(12) = 2$$

$$X^{n}(m) = 0, \qquad \text{otherwise.}$$

These values are obtained for any pair of nodes at a distance of 3. We note from this example that the homogeneous graph with the smallest diameter and the largest girth had the fewest small prime node cutsets. In general, it has been found that for small m, $X^{n}(m)$ and $X^{e}(m)$ optimum graphs have a maximum connectivity, a minimum diameter, a maximum girth, and a minimum number of small circuits. However, the discovery of sufficient conditions for graphs to be $X^{n}(m)$ and $X^{e}(m)$ optimal is an important unsolved problem.

With respect to the design of maximally reliable networks based on the construction of $X^{n}(m)$ and $X^{e}(m)$ optimal graphs, partial results are available. It has been shown by this author [65] that Moore and Singleton graphs are $X^{n}(m)$ and $X^{e}(m)$ optimal for small values of m. Furthermore, an iterative procedure has been developed by Wilkov [66] for approximating maximally reliable nonhomogeneous networks for small values of the node- and link-failure probability. The networks obtained from this procedure meet all the necessary conditions for the minimization of $X^{n}(m)$ and $X^{e}(m)$ for small values of m. Furthermore, the procedure generates networks that have values of $X^{n}(m)$ and $X^{e}(m)$, which are close to the lower bounds for a specified number of nodes and a specified number of edges. However, as frequently required in design problems, a method has not been found for using the procedure to construct a graph that has a minimum number of edges for a specified number of nodes and specified values of $X^{n}(m)$ and $X^{e}(m)$. In addition, the realization of minimum cost networks, which are $X^{n}(m)$ or $X^{e}(m)$ optimal, have not yet been considered.

VI. Calculation of Network Reliability

In analyzing the reliability of computer networks based on probabilistic criteria, it is frequently desirable to calculate the value of $R_{p}(G)$, $\min_{a,b} P_{c}[a, b]$, or $\max_{a,b} P_{f}[a, b]$ as given in (15), (19), and (20). It follows from (15) and the discussion in Section V-B that for a specified graph G and a specified value of the link-failure probability p, the calculation of $R_{p}(G)$ requires the examination of all connected spanning subgraphs of G. On the other hand, in the presence of link or node failures, the calculation of $\min_{a,b} P_{c}[a, b]$ for (19), for specified values of the link- or node-failure probability p or q, requires the examination of all paths in the graph between every pair of nodes. For specified values of p or q, it follows from (20) that the calculation of $\max_{a,b} P_{f}[a, b]$ requires the examination of all a–b cuts for all node pairs a, b. The solution of the three enumeration problems just mentioned is not computationally feasible for large networks. A further complication arises when all nodes and links do not have the same probability of failure or when the failures of different nodes and links are not statistically independent. Approaches that have been taken in the calculation of $R_{p}(G)$, $\min_{a,b} P_{c}[a, b]$ and $\max_{a,b} P_{f}[a, b]$ are discussed in the following.

A. Enumeration of Paths or Trees

In the case of reliability calculations for one terminal pair in a network, a decomposition procedure for the calculation of $P_c[a, b]$ has been suggested by Moskowitz [67]. Noting that every network consists of some combination of series, parallel, and bridge subnetworks, it was suggested that as a first step all series and parallel links be combined. If the k links $b_1, b_2, \cdots, b_k$ are connected in series and link b_i has a failure probability of p_i, then the failure probability p' for the series combination is given by

$$p' = 1 - \prod_{i=1}^{k} (1 - p_i), \tag{21}$$

assuming all links have statistically independent failure probabilities. If these k links were connected in parallel, the combination would fail with a probability p' given by

$$p' = \prod_{i=1}^{k} p_i. \tag{22}$$

Hence, k links connected either in series or in parallel in any network could be replaced by a single link whose reliability is given by the reliability of the combination. Furthermore, in general, it has been shown by Moskowitz [67] and Mine [68] that

$$P_c[a, b] = p_j\{P_c[a, b]\}_{p_j=1} + (1 - p_j)\{P_c[a, b]\}_{p_j=0}, \tag{23}$$

where p_j is the probability of failure for the jth link in the network and $\{P_c[a, b]\}_{p_j=1}$ denotes the probability of successful communication between nodes a and b assuming that link j fails. This theorem can be used to factor out any link in a network. It has been used to calculate $P_c[a, b]$ for a simple bridge network. Furthermore, the reliability of infinite ladder networks has also been evaluated [68] using the factoring theorem.

General algorithms have been developed by Misra [69], [70] for calculating $P_c[a, b]$ based on the combination of series–parallel edges and the iterative use of the factoring theorem for all nonseries–parallel edges. These algorithms are very effective for networks containing few nonseries–parallel edges between any pair of nodes. However, for highly nonseries–parallel graphs with b edges and n nodes, the required computation time can be shown to grow approximately as 2^{b-n}. A method has been developed by Okada [71] and Mine [68] for using the incidence and circuit matrices of a graph to find all paths between a specified pair of nodes a, b in order to compute $P_c[a, b]$. Wing and Kim [72] studied the properties of the matrix P_{ab} of all possible paths between nodes a and b in a connected and nonoriented graph G. P_{ab} has one row for each path between nodes a and b and a column corresponding to each edge in G. If G has b edges and n nodes, they have shown that the rank of P_{ab} is $b - n + 2$. Furthermore, an algorithm has been exhibited [72] for finding a submatrix of P_{ab} for a given graph G in which all rows are linearly independent. Other methods have been given by Fu and Yau [73] and Brown [74] to enumerate all paths between a specified pair of nodes. However, we note that in any graph of b edges and n nodes, there are 2^{b-n+2} possible paths between any nonadjacent pair of nodes. It is clear that the number of such paths grows very rapidly with the size of the graph.

In the event that the overall reliability of a network is to be calculated, one may proceed by finding all possible paths between each of the $n(n - 1)/2$ node pairs. Since this is clearly impractical for graphs with a large number of nodes, alternative procedures have been suggested. Following Wing and Demetriou [75], all of the $2^b - 1$ nonempty subgraphs of a graph must be examined. The probabilities of the connected subgraphs are accumulated to obtain $R_p(G)$ or the probabilities of the disconnected subgraphs can be accumulated to obtain $1 - R_p(G)$, the probability the graph is not connected. However, this procedure is clearly not feasible for graphs with a large number of edges. Therefore, Fu [76] has suggested a procedure for approximating $R_p(G)$ based on the fact that $R_p(G) \approx A_{n-1}(1 - p)^{n-1}$ when all links fail with the same probability p. If all links have a different failure probability, $R_p(G)$ can be approximated by

$$R_p(G) \approx \sum_{i=1}^{t} P[T_i],$$

where t is the number of trees in the graph and $P[T_i]$ is the probability that tree T_i exists, which is equal to the product of the probabilities that the edges on the tree are operational. We note that it is well known from classical circuit theory that the sum of the tree admittance products is equal to the determinant of the node admittance matrix AYA^t, where A is the node incidence matrix of the graph, A^t is the transpose of A, and Y is a diagonal matrix of edge admittances. Replacing the edge admittance matrix Y by an edge reliability matrix R, it follows that

$$R_p(G) \approx \sum_{i=1}^{t} P[T_i] = \det(ARA^t).$$

Hence for any graph G of n nodes with large specified edge-failure probabilities, $R_p(G)$ is easily estimated by evaluating the determinant of ARA^t, and $(n - 1) \times (n - 1)$ matrix.

B. Enumeration of Cutsets

In any graph G of b edges and n nodes, the order of the number of cutsets is 2^{n-2} whereas the order of the number of paths between any pair of nodes is 2^{b-n+2} as indicated previously. For networks having nodes of average degree greater than four, $b > 2n$ and $2^{b-n+2} > 2^{n-2}$. Consequently, such networks have a larger number of paths than cutsets. Computation time would clearly be reduced in such cases by calculating network reliability from cutsets instead of paths. It follows from the preceding section that $P_c[a, b]$ can be obtained from $P_c[a, b] = 1 - P_f[a, b]$, where $P_f[a, b]$ can be calculated from one of the expressions given in (20). Alternatively,

$$P_f[a, b] = P\left[\bigcup_{i=1}^{N} C_{a,b}{}^i\right], \quad (24)$$

where $C_{a,b}{}^i$ is the event that all edges fail in the ith prime cutset and N is the total number of prime cutsets with respect to nodes a and b. The calculation of $P_f[a, b]$ from (20) clearly requires the examination of all 2^{n-2} a–b cuts. The number of prime a–b cuts is usually much smaller. However, $P_f[a, b]$ is not readily calculated from (24) because the $C_{a,b}{}^i$ are not mutually exclusive events.

It has recently been suggested by Jensen and Bellmore [77] that

$$\sum_{i=1}^{N} P[C_{a,b}{}^i]$$

be used as an approximation to $P_f[a, b]$, where all prime cutsets for nonoriented graphs were enumerated using an algorithm they developed in [78]. This algorithm requires the storage of a large binary tree with one terminal node for each prime cutset. Similar results have been obtained by Nelson *et al.* [79] and Batts [80] for oriented graphs. However, it has been shown by Hänsler *et al.* [81], [82] that no additional computation time is required to actually compute $P_f[a, b]$ exactly. A procedure has been developed [81], [82] to iteratively calculate a minimal set of mutually exclusive events containing all prime cutsets. This procedure starts with the prime cutset consisting of the edges incident to node a. Subsequently, these edges are reconnected in all combinations and we then cut the minimal set of edges adjacent to these that lie on a path to node b. A rapid method for checking this was developed. The edge replacements are iterated until the set of edges connected to node b are reached. The procedure has been found to be particularly effective for networks of small diameter. Furthermore, it requires a very small amount of storage since each event is generated from the previous one. $P_f[a, b]$ is obtained by accumulating the probabilities of each of the mutually exclusive events. It is noted that this procedure [81] provides for correlations between certain link failures in the calculation of the probability of each event.

If one is willing to sacrifice a certain amount of flexibility in providing for correlations between certain types of link failures, a considerable improvement in the speed of the calculation of $P_f[a, b]$ is possible [83]. A recursive procedure has been developed by Hänsler [83] whereby $P_f[a, b]$ is obtained from the probability that all subsets of $\Gamma(a)$ are disconnected from b. In calculating the probability that a set of nodes A is disconnected from b, all nodes in A are coalesced into a single node, thereby reducing the resulting network. Further reductions are made by combining series and parallel combinations of links. These reductions of the network at each stage are largely responsible for the resulting savings in the necessary computation time.

It is noted that in all of the procedures discussed above for calculating the reliability of a network, nodes have been assumed to be perfectly reliable. However, almost all of the methods discussed in this section can be applied to the case that nodes fail and links are perfectly reliable. In the event that nodes and links may fail simultaneously, assuming that their failures are statistically independent, Hänsler [84] has extended his recursive procedure for calculating the probability of a communication failure between any specified pair of nodes. In order to compute $P_f[a, b]$ in this case, if node a is of degree d, he examines the 2^{2d} states of the edges incident to a and the nodes adjacent to node a. For those states in which all of the nodes in subset $A_i \subset \Gamma(a)$ can communicate with node a, he calculates the probability that set A_i is disconnected from node b as in the previous paragraph. A considerable reduction in the overall computation time results from the simplification of the resulting subnetworks as discussed above. However, it follows from the results in [84] that in the first stage of the procedure

$$\sum_{i=1}^{d} \binom{d}{i}(2^i - 1)$$

subnetworks must be considered. On the other hand, link failures alone require the processing of only 2^d subnetworks in the first stage. This is an indication of the increase in computation time required when the recursive procedure [83] discussed above is used for simultaneous link and node failures.

VII. Design of Reliable Centralized Networks

In the design of centralized computer networks, present design procedures concentrate on the allocation of channel capacities and generally provide for reliability by duplicating the communication facilities. These solutions sometimes return out to be unnecessarily expensive. Furthermore, the improvement in reliability achieved by these solutions will be reduced if there is correlation between the failures of duplicated facilities.

Kiryukhin [85] has investigated the reliability of communication systems consisting of one source of information and n receivers. As a measure of reliability, he used the expected number of receivers that could communicate with the source during any specified interval of time. Topologies having a maximum degree of reliability were sought using nonlinear integer programming. In order to obtain analytical results, the equivalent continuous variable problem was treated using Lagrange multipliers. For most interesting values of the node- and link-failure probabilities, it was shown [85] that a completely connected graph of b edges was a more reliable centralized network than a star network with a total of b duplicated facilities.

A heuristic approach to a more general centralized network problem has been investigated by Hänsler *et al.* [81]. They considered a network consisting of concentrators with different numbers of attached terminals connected to a data-processing center by full duplex communication facilities. The procedure used in this study was similar in nature to the one described by

Steiglitz *et al.* [47]. However, the feasibility conditions consisted of a specified communication failure probability for each concentrator and a specified value of the expected percentage of terminals connected to the processing center. Denoting this quantity by R, it is determined from

$$R = \sum_{i=1}^{n} N_i(1 - P_f[i, H]) \Big/ \sum_{i=1}^{n} N_i, \qquad (25)$$

where N_i is the number of terminals attached to the ith concentrator and n is the total number of concentrators. During each iteration of the heuristic procedure, the feasibility check required the exact calculation of the probability of a communication failure between each concentrator and the data-processing center. The results of this study showed that selective interconnections between the concentrators of a centralized network can significantly increase the reliability of a centralized network in comparison with a star configuration. This increase in reliability was frequently achieved without any increase in cost. For example, it was demonstrated [81] that the wheel topology shown in Fig. 2 corresponds to a highly reliable centralized network.

The wheel has been compared with a duplicated star as the topology for a line-switching network in a study by Akiyama and Hashimoto [86]. As a measure of network reliability, they used the degradation in the node-pair loss probabilities due to a failure in a single communication link. Assuming a uniform point-to-point traffic matrix and a single preselected alternate route between every pair of nodes, the node-pair loss probabilities were calculated based on classical queueing theoretic assumptions. They found that for a 1 percent call-loss probability under normal operation, the maximum of the node-pair loss probabilities increases to almost 40 percent for the star but can be kept within 20–30 percent for the wheel in the presence of a single link failure. Furthermore, the performance of the wheel would be further enhanced by more flexible procedures for route selection. Since the total line length in a wheel was less than in the duplicated star, it was concluded [86] that the wheel topology was more suitable for line-switching networks than a star with duplicated facilities. Perhaps, of greater significance is the fact that the authors considered a reliability measure that reflected the traffic carrying capacity of the network in the presence of failures.

VIII. Conclusion

Graph theoretic results have been found to be very useful in characterizing computer-network reliability. Deterministic and probabilistic measures have been considered based on different criteria for acceptable network operation. Based on the criteria that there exist paths between all pairs of nodes in order for the network to be operational, the connectivity of the corresponding graph was first considered as a reliability measure. Effective procedures have been discussed for evaluating the node-pair connectivity of any given network. A practical design procedure based on heuristic methods has been developed to construct a low-cost network satisfying any specified node pair connectivity matrix. However, we have seen that further work is necessary to extend the procedure in order that networks of minimal diameter are obtained.

A more general measure of network reliability based on cutsets has been considered. This measure $\delta(m)$ reflected the minimum size cutset that isolates any subgraph of m nodes from the rest of the graph for all values of m. It reflects acceptable network operation in a more meaningful way since it enables one to weigh the way a network is partitioned in the presence of failures. However, the network design problem with respect to this measure effectively remains unsolved. A sufficient condition for graphs to be $\delta(m)$ optimal has not yet been obtained. Nonetheless, it seems possible that a heuristic procedure could be developed for constructing low-cost networks meeting a specified lower bound on $\delta(m)$ for all values of m.

Defining acceptable operation in terms of the diameter of a network in the presence of failures, a new deterministic reliability measure has been introduced. It is based on the minimum number of failures that would result in the diameter exceeding a specified value. This measure as well as $\delta(m)$ reflect to some extent the degradation in network performance in the presence of failures. Analysis and design results available based on this new measure are sparse. An extensive amount of further work is needed in order for this new measure to be applied in a meaningful way.

Considering probabilistic reliable criteria, we have seen that the analysis and synthesis problems are much more difficult than in the deterministic case. Optimal networks can no longer be defined without specifying the value of the failure probabilities for the network elements. Furthermore, in almost all of the work to date, it has been necessary to assume that all network elements fail independently and that it is impossible for nodes and links to fail simultaneously. We have seen that the exact calculation of network reliability is very time consuming and is not feasible at all for very large networks. Therefore, it has been necessary to define probabilistic reliability criteria based on approximate calculations of the network reliability. Sparse analysis and synthesis results have been obtained based on these criteria. Furthermore, new deterministic reliability measures have recently been introduced based on probabilistic considerations. Analysis and design results obtained to date based on these measures are very encouraging. It appears that some of the inherent difficulties in probabilistic reliability calculations may be avoided by considering deterministic measures obtained from the probabilistic criteria. Specifically, further work is needed on the $N^n(m)$ and $N^c(m)$ criteria discussed in this paper. In addition, we strongly urge further investigation into other deterministic measures, which are meaningful with respect to useful probabilistic criteria.

Unfortunately, almost all of the reliability measures treated to date do not reflect the degradation in network performance that results from the failure of network elements in the presence of a specified traffic demand. Dictated by practical design requirements, this is a direction that future network reliability studies must take.

References

[1] H. Frank and I. T. Frisch, *Communication, Transmission, and Transportation Networks.* Reading, Mass.: Addison-Wesley, 1971.

[2] ——, "Analysis and design of survivable networks," *IEEE Trans. Commun. Technol.,* vol. COM-18, pp. 501–519, Oct. 1970.

[3] F. Harary, *Graph Theory.* Reading, Mass.: Addison-Wesley, 1969.

[4] C. Berge, *The Theory of Graphs.* New York: Wiley, 1962.

[5] W. H. Kim and R. T. Chien, *Topological Analysis and Synthesis of Communication Networks.* New York: Columbia Univ. Press, 1962.

[6] K. Menger, "Zur allgemeinen Kurventheorie," *Fundam. Math.,* vol. 10, pp. 96–115, 1927.

[7] G. A. Dirac, "Extensions of Menger's theorem," *J. London Math. Soc.,* vol. 38, pp. 148–161, 1963.

[8] H. Whitney, "Congruent graphs and the connectivity of graphs," *Amer. J. Math.,* vol. 54, pp. 150–168, 1932.

[9] G. Chartrand and F. Harary, "Graphs with prescribed connectivities," in *Theory of Graphs,* P. Erdos and G. Katona, Eds. New York: Academic Press, 1968, pp. 61–63.

[10] W. T. Tutte, *Connectivity in Graphs.* London: Oxford Univ. Press, 1966.

[11] R. Halin, "A theorem on n-connected graphs," *J. Combinatorial Theory,* vol. 7, pp. 150–154, 1969.

[12] ——, "On the structure of n-connected graphs," in *Recent Progress in Combinatorics,* W. T. Tutte, Ed. New York: Academic Press, 1969, pp. 91–102.

[13] D. Lick, "Critically and minimally n-connected graphs," in *The Many Facets of Graph Theory,* G. Chartrand and S. Kapoor, Eds. New York: Springer, 1969, pp. 199–205.

[14] G. Chartrand, "A graph theoretic approach to a communication problem," *SIAM J. Appl. Math.,* vol. 14, pp. 778–781, 1966.

[15] J. Ayoub and I. T. Frisch, "On the smallest branch cuts in directed graphs," *IEEE Trans. Circuit Theory* (Corresp.), pp. 249–250, May 1970.

[16] M. Watkins, "Some classes of hypoconnected vertex-transitive graphs," in *Recent Progress in Combinatorics,* W. T. Tutte, Ed. New York: Academic Press, 1969, pp. 323–328.

[17] ——, "Connectivity of transitive graphs," *J. Combinatorial Theory,* vol. 8, pp. 23–29, 1970.

[18] J. Turner, "Point-symmetric graphs with a prime number of points," *J. Combinatorial Theory,* vol. 3, pp. 136–145, 1967.

[19] L. R. Ford and D. R. Fulkerson, *Flows in Networks.* Princeton, N. J.: Princeton Univ. Press, 1962.

[20] R. E. Gomory and T. C. Hu, "Multiterminal network flows," *SIAM J. Appl. Math.,* vol. 9, pp. 551–570, Dec. 1961.

[21] I. T. Frisch, "Analysis of the vulnerability of communication nets," in *Proc. 1st Annu. Princeton Conf. Systems Science,* Princeton, N. J., 1967, pp. 188–192.

[22] ——, "Flow variation in multiple min-cut calculations," *J. Franklin Inst.,* vol. 287, pp. 61–72, Jan. 1969.

[23] D. J. Kleitman, "Methods for investigating connectivity of large graphs," *IEEE Trans. Circuit Theory* (Corresp.), vol. CT-16, pp. 232–233, May 1969.

[24] J. B. Frechen, "Graph connectivity algorithm," in *Proc. Int. Conf. Combinatorial Mathematics,* New York Acad. Sci., Apr. 1970.

[25] F. Harary, "The maximum connectivity of a graph," *Proc. Nat. Acad. Sci.,* vol. 48, pp. 1142–1146, July 1962.

[26] S. L. Hakimi, "An algorithm for construction of the least vulnerable communication network or the graph with the maximum connectivity," *IEEE Trans. Circuit Theory* (Corresp.), vol. CT-16, pp. 229–230, May 1969.

[27] R. S. Wilkov, "Construction of maximally reliable communication networks with minimum transmission delay," *Proc. 1970 IEEE Int. Conf. Communications,* vol. 6, June 1970, pp. 4210–4215.

[28] J. N. Ayoub and I. T. Frisch, "Optimally invulnerable directed communication networks," *IEEE Trans. Commun. Technol.,* vol. COM-18, pp. 484–489, Oct. 1970.

[29] F. T. Boesch and R. E. Thomas, "On graphs of invulnerable communication nets," *IEEE Trans. Circuit Theory,* vol. CT-17, pp. 183–191, May 1970.

[30] R. S. Wilkov, "On maximally connected graphs of minimal diameter," *Proc. 1970 IEEE Int. Symp. Circuit Theory,* Dec. 1970, pp. 25–26; also IBM Res. Rep. RC-2943, June 1970.

[31] H. Sachs, "On regular graphs with given girth," in *Theory of Graphs and Its Applications.* New York: Academic Press, 1964, pp. 91–97.

[32] R. R. Singleton, "On minimal graphs of maximum even girth," *J. Combinatorial Theory,* vol. 1, pp. 306–322, 1966.

[33] A. J. Hoffman and R. R. Singleton, "On Moore graphs of diameters two and three," *IBM J. Res. Develop.,* pp. 497–504, 1960.

[34] H. Friedman, "On the impossibility of certain Moore graphs," *J. Combinatorial Theory,* vol. 10, pp. 245–252, 1971.

[35] J. Longyear, "Regular d-valent graphs of girth 6 and $2(d^2 - d + 1)$ vertices," *J. Combinatorial Theory,* vol. 9, pp. 420–422, 1970.

[36] S. V. Trufanov, "Some problems of distance on a graph," *Eng. Cybern.,* pp. 60–66, Jan./Feb. 1967.

[37] B. Elspas, "Topological constraints on interconnection limited logic," *Switching Circuit Theory Logical Des.,* vol. S-164, pp. 133–147, Oct. 1964.

[38] H. Friedman, "A design for (d,k) graphs," *IEEE Trans. Electron. Comput.* (Short Notes), vol. EC-16, pp. 253–254, Apr. 1966.

[39] I. Korn, "On (d,k) graphs," *IEEE Trans. Electron. Comput.* (Short Notes), vol. EC-16, pp. 90, Feb. 1967.

[40] O. Ore, "Diameters in graphs," *J. Combinatorial Theory,* vol. 5, pp. 75–81, 1968.

[41] H. Quaife, "On (d,k,μ) graphs," *IEEE Trans. Comput.,* vol. C-18, pp. 270–272, Mar. 1969.

[42] A. Gewirtz, "Graphs with maximal even girth," *Can. J. Math.,* vol. 21, no. 4, pp. 915–934, 1969.

[43] S. L. Hakimi, "On the reliability of integers as the degrees of vertices of a linear graph," *SIAM J. Appl. Math.,* vol. 10, pp. 496–506, Sept. 1962.

[44] W. Chou and H. Frank, "Survivable communication networks and the terminal capacity matrix," *IEEE Trans. Circuit Theory,* vol. CT-17, pp. 192–197, May 1970.

[45] H. Frank and W. Chou, "Connectivity considerations in the design of survivable networks," *IEEE Trans. Circuit Theory,* vol. CT-17, pp. 486–490, Nov. 1970.

[46] R. S. Wilkov, "On the design of high speed communication networks," presented at the 5th Annu. Princeton Conf. Information Sciences and Systems, Mar. 1971.

[47] K. Steiglitz, P. Weiner, and D. J. Kleitman, "The design of minimum-cost survivable networks," *IEEE Trans. Circuit Theory,* vol. CT-16, pp. 455–460, Nov. 1969.

[48] A. B. Owens, "A starting algorithm for minimal cost survivable networks," Naval Res. Lab., Washington, D. C., Rep. 7272.

[49] M. Malek-Zavarei and I. T. Frisch, "Vulnerability of directed communication networks," in *Proc. 1970 Int. Conf. Communications,* pp. 19-35–19-39.

[50] F. T. Boesch and A. P. Felzer, "On the minimum m degree vulnerability criterion," *IEEE Trans. Circuit Theory,* vol. CT-18, pp. 224–228, Mar. 1971.

[51] F. T. Boesch and A. P. Felzer, "On the invulnerability of the regular complete k-partite graphs," *SIAM J. Appl. Math.,* vol. 20, Mar. 1971.

[52] H. J. Voss, "Some properties of graphs containing k independent circuits," in *Theory of Graphs,* P. Erdos and G. Katona, Eds. New York: Academic Press, 1968, pp. 321–334.

[53] F. T. Boesch, "A note on the generalized cohesion," in *Proc. 14th Midwest Symp. Circuit Theory,* May 1971.

[54] B. Bollobas, "Graphs of given diameter," in *Theory of Graphs,* P. Erdos and G. Katona, Eds. New York: Academic Press, 1968, pp. 29–36.

[55] P. Baran, "On distributed communication networks," *IEEE Trans. Commun. Syst.,* vol. CS-12, pp. 1–9, Mar. 1964.

[56] H. Frank, "Vulnerability of communication networks," *IEEE Trans. Commun. Technol.,* vol. COM-15, pp. 778–789, Dec. 1967.

[57] M. Steffen and W. Dent, "Construction of redundant networks with minimum distance," *J. Franklin Inst.,* vol. 289, pp. 223–231, Mar. 1970.

[58] A. K. Kel'mans, "Connectivity of probabilistic networks," *Automat. Remote Contr.*, no. 3, pp. 444–460, 1967.

[59] a. J. D. Leggett, "Synthesis of reliable networks," Ph.D. dissertation, Univ. Pennsylvania, Philadelphia, 1968.
b. J. D. Leggett and S. D. Bedrosian, "Synthesis of reliable networks," *IEEE Trans. Circuit Theory* (Corresp.), vol. CT-16, pp. 384–385, Aug. 1969.

[60] H. Frank, "Maximally reliable node weighted graphs," in *Proc. 3rd Annu. Princeton Conf. Information Sciences and Systems*, Mar. 1969, pp. 1–6.

[61] R. S. Wilkov, "Reliability considerations in computer network design," in *Proc. Int. Fed. Inform. Process. Soc. Congr. 1971*, Ljubljana, Yugoslavia, Aug. 1971.

[62] E. Moore and C. Shannon, "Reliable circuits using less reliable relays," *J. Franklin Inst.*, vol. 262, pp. 191–208, Sept. 1956.

[63] G. Williams, "The design of survivable communication networks," *IEEE Trans. Commun. Syst.*, vol. CS-11, pp. 230–247, June 1963.

[64] L. Fratta *et al.*, "Synthesis of communication networks with reliability of links exponentially decreasing with their length," in *Proc. 1971 Int. Conf. Communications*, vol. 7, pp. 3933–3937.

[65] R. S. Wilkov, "On the design of maximally reliable communication networks," in *Proc. 6th Annu. Princeton Conf. Information Sciences and Systems*, Mar. 1972.

[66] ——, "Design of computer networks based on a new reliability measure," in *Proc. Int. Symp. Computer-Communication Networks and Teletraffic*, Polytech. Inst. Brooklyn, Brooklyn, N. Y., Apr. 1972.

[67] F. Moskowitz, "The analysis of redundancy networks," *AIEE Trans.* (Commun. Electron.), vol. 39, pp. 627–632, 1968.

[68] H. Mine, "Reliability of physical systems," *IRE Trans. Circuit Theory*, vol. CT-6, pp. 138–151, May 1959.

[69] K. B. Misra and T. S. M. Rao, "Reliability analysis of redundant networks using flow graphs," *IEEE Trans. Reliability*, vol. R-19, pp. 19–24, Feb. 1970.

[70] K. B. Misra, "An algorithm for the reliability evaluation of redundant networks," *IEEE Trans. Reliability*, vol. R-19, pp. 146–151, Nov. 1970.

[71] S. Okada, "Topology applied to switching circuits," in *Proc. Symp. Information Networks*, Polytech. Inst. Brooklyn, Brooklyn, N. Y., vol. 3, pp. 267–290, Apr. 1954.

[72] O. Wing and W. H. Kim, "The path matrix and switching functions," *J. Franklin Inst.*, vol. 268, pp. 251–269, 1959.

[73] Y. Fu and S. S. Yau, "A note on the reliability of communication networks," *SIAM J. Appl. Math.*, vol. 10, pp. 469–474, 1962.

[74] D. B. Brown, "A computerized algorithm for determining the reliability of redundant configurations," *IEEE Trans. Reliability*, vol. R-20, pp. 121–124, Aug. 1971.

[75] O. Wing and P. Demetriou, "Analysis of probabilistic networks," *IEEE Trans. Commun. Technol.*, vol. COM-12, pp. 38–40, Sept. 1964.

[76] Y. Fu, "Applications of topological methods to probabilistic communication networks," *IEEE Trans. Commun. Technol.*, vol. COM-13, pp. 301–307, Sept. 1965.

[77] P. A. Jensen and M. Bellmore, "An algorithm to determine the reliability of a complex system," *IEEE Trans. Reliability*, vol. R-18, pp. 169–174, Nov. 1969.

[78] M. Bellmore and P. A. Jensen, "An implicit enumeration scheme for proper cut generation," *Technometrics*, vol. 12, pp. 775–788, 1970.

[79] A. C. Nelson, Jr., J. R. Batts, and R. L. Beadles, "A computer program for approximating system reliability," *IEEE Trans. Reliability*, vol. R-19, pp. 61–65, May 1970.

[80] J. R. Batts, "Computer program for approximating system reliability—Part II," *IEEE Trans. Reliability* (Notes), vol. R-20, pp. 88–90, May 1971.

[81] E. Hänsler, G. K. McAuliffe, and R. S. Wilkov, "Optimizing the reliability in centralized computer networks," this issue, pp. 640–644.

[82] ——, "Exact calculation of computer network reliability," to be published.

[83] E. Hänsler, "A procedure for calculating the reliability of a communication network," *Arch. Elek. Übertragung.*, vol. 25, pp. 573–575, 1971.

[84] ——, "A fast recursive algorithm to calculate the reliability of a communication network," this issue, pp. 637–640.

[85] V. V. Kiryukhin, "Optimal connecting structures in information systems," *Prob. Inform. Transm.*, vol. 1, no. 2, pp. 72–76, 1965.

[86] M. Akiyama and A. Hashimoto, "Reliability of switching networks in cases of impairment of trunk lines," *Electron. Commun. Japan*, vol. 53-A, pp. 33–43, Oct. 1970.

Robert S. Wilkov (S'62–M'69), for a photograph and biography please see page 644 of this issue.

Network Reliability Analysis: Part I

R. Van Slyke and H. Frank
Network Analysis Corporation
Glen Cove, New York

ABSTRACT

This paper considers networks with randomly failing links and nodes. In Part 1, nodes are assumed to be perfectly reliable. A combinatorial analysis is given when all links have equal reliabilities. Two general simulation methods are described. The first is particularly useful if a wide range of failure probabilities is to be considered. The second combines a combinatorial analysis with stratified sampling to yield major computational savings. Later parts will describe generalizations, decomposition methods for large networks and applications to computer network analysis.

1.1. INTRODUCTION

We consider networks whose nodes and (undirected) links are in either *failed* or *operative* states [3]. (We allow no intermediate states.) Two nodes can communicate if there is a path of operable nodes and links between them. One measure of a network's inability to support communication is the *fraction* of node pairs which are not able to communicate. It is sometimes convenient to use a simpler criterion. We say the network has *failed* if it is disconnected; that is, if there exists *any* node pair which cannot communicate. Thus, with this criterion a network would either be failed or operable.

We assume that links and nodes fail with known probabilities. There are two interpretations of the situation. A natural disaster such as an earthquake or hurricane can cause the elements to fail. One can then ask for the *expected number* of node pairs which can communicate *if* this event should occur. Alternatively, one might seek the probability the net will fail (i.e., become disconnected) as a result of the event. The

Networks, 1: 279-290

second interpretation is that elements fail and are repaired independently according to stationary random processes. If the average time each node or link is operational is known and is equal to the probability of the node or link being in the operative state at any given time, the expected number of node pairs not communicating can be interpreted as the *time average* of pairs not communicating. The alternative criterion yields the percentage of the time the network is in a failed state.

In Part 1, we consider networks with unreliable links but perfectly reliable nodes. In Section 1.2, we examine the case when all links have equal failure probabilities. This leads to strictly combinatorial analysis. In Section 1.3, we describe a convenient method to determine the components of a graph. In Section 1.4, we allow link failure probabilities to vary. A simulation method is described which is particularly useful when the network is to be analyzed for a wide range of link failure probabilities. In Section 1.5, a method is described which combines the combinatorial approach of Section 1.2 with simulation. This method yields major computational savings when compared with conventional simulation approaches.

In later parts of the paper, we first describe the generalizations of the analysis methods to the case where both nodes and links have non zero failure probabilities. Decomposition methods are then given for the analysis of large networks. Applications of the methods to analyze computer network reliability are described in detail.

1.2. COMBINATORIAL ANALYSIS

Our analysis of networks with equal link failure probabilities is based on the work of Moore and Shannon [9]. We define the *Moore-Shannon Function* h(p) to be the probability of the net being disconnected as a function of the probability p of a link failing.

490 If the network has NB links and $q = 1 - p$, there are $\binom{NB}{k}$ ways that exactly NB-k of the links can fail, and each such event has probability $p^{NB-k} q^k$. Thus, if C(k) is the number of ways exactly k remaining links can result in a disconnected net,

$$h(p) = \sum_{k=0}^{NB} C(k) \; p^{NB-k} \; q^k \qquad (1)$$

Thus, the analysis problem "reduces" to the combinatorial problem of determining how many ways k links can result in a disconnected subnet. *A priori*, we have information about the form of (1). If the network has NN nodes, it takes at least NN-1 links to connect them. Thus, $C(k) = \binom{NB}{k}$ for k = 0, 1, ..., NN-2. Similarly, if "c" is the minimum number of links which must be deleted to disconnect the network, C(NB-k) = 0 for k = 0, 1, ..., c-1. Thus, there are only NB-NN-c+2 non-trivial terms in (1) and we have:

$$\sum_{k=NB-NN+2}^{NB} \binom{NB}{k} p^{k} q^{NB-k} \leq h(p) \leq \sum_{k=c}^{NB} \binom{NB}{k} p^{k} q^{NB-k} \quad (2)$$

These bounds are apparently due to Jacobs [6]. If p is very close to 0, the last non-zero term, C(NB-c) in (1) determines the behavior of h(p). Similarly, if p is very close to 1, the first non-trivial term is most interesting. This term, C(NN-1), is simply $\binom{NB}{NN-1}$ minus the number of trees in the network. For many existing networks, c is small and C(NB-c) can often be obtained easily by enumeration. The number of trees can be obtained by formula [1; p. 139]. Thus, we find improved bounds

$$\sum_{k=NB-NN+2}^{NB} \binom{NB}{k} p^{k} q^{NB-k} + C(NN-1)\, p^{NB-NN+1} q^{NN-1} \leq h(p) \leq$$

$$C(NB-c)\, p^{c} q^{NB-c} + \sum_{k=c+1}^{NB} \binom{NB}{k} p^{k} q^{NB-k}. \quad (3)$$

The lower bound is sharp for p close to 1 and the upper bound for p close to 0. The bounds given in (3) can be further improved by using the fact that if removing a given subset of 491
k links disconnects the net, any larger subset containing the first will also disconnect the net. Similarly, if a subset of links is a connected subgraph, so is any subset containing it. This can be used to project lower bounds for C(k') given C(k) for k > k'. Similarly, upper bounds can be obtained for C(k') given C(k) for k < k'.

A general way to implement this follows from a powerful theorem by J. B. Kruskal [7]. An *abstract complex* is a finite set of points together with a class of subsets with the subset closure property; that is, if a subset belongs to the class, then so do all its subsets. For any non-negative integer n, its *r-canonical representation* is $(n_r, \ldots, n_i)$ where

$$n = \binom{n_r}{r} + \binom{n_{r-1}}{r-1} + \ldots + \binom{n_i}{i} \tag{4}$$

and n_r is as large as possible so that $\binom{n_r}{r} \leq n$, n_{r-1} is as large as possible so that $\binom{n_r}{r} + \binom{n_{r-1}}{r-1} \leq n$ and so on until equality is achieved. An *r-set* is a subset with r elements. For $r \leq r'$, $f(n; r, r')$ is the *greatest* number of r'-sets that occur in any complex having precisely n r-sets. If $r > r'$, $f(n; r, r')$ is the *smallest* number of r'-sets that occur in any complex having precisely n r-sets.

Theorem 1 (Kruskal): If $n = \binom{n_r}{r} + \ldots \binom{n_i}{i}$ is canonical, then

$$f(n; r, r') = \binom{n_r}{r'} + \binom{n_{r-1}}{r'-1} + \ldots + \binom{n_i}{r'-r+1} \tag{5}$$

with the conventions that $\binom{0}{0} = 0$, $\binom{m}{k} = 0$ for $m < 0$ or $k < 0$, or $m < k$.

If a subnet with k links is disconnected, then a subnet with only k' (for $k' < k$) of the k links is also disconnected. Thus the theorem yields:

$$C(k') \geq f(C(k); k, k') \text{ for } k \geq k' \tag{6}$$

$$C(k') \leq f(C(k); k, k') \text{ for } k \leq k' \tag{7}$$

For each C(k) that we can calculate (or get bounds on), we can get bounds on the remaining C(k') from (6) and (7). In practice, one can usually determine the first few terms C(NB-c), C(NB-c-1), ... (if necessary by enumeration), and then derive lower bounds for the remaining coefficients using (6). This yields a very good lower estimate for h(p) for p small. Good upper bounds on the coefficients are more difficult to find. C(NN-1) can be calculated by formula and upper bounds for the C(k) for k > NN-1 can be arrived at by (7). Unfortunately, the terms which are most important for small p are the ones for which the estimates from (7) are least accurate.

The estimates for C(k) implied by (6) and (7) are based only on the fact that if a network is disconnected with one set S of operative links, it is also disconnected for any subset of S. The bound does not take into account any other problem structure. We now show that while the bounds are sharp for complexes, they are not for network reliability problems.

A *matroid* $\langle S;F\rangle$ [4] is a finite set S and a non-empty family of subsets F of S satisfying:

(M1) No member of F is a proper subset of another.
(M2) If $e_1 \neq e_2$, $C_1 \in F$, $C_2 \in F$, $e_1 \in C_1 \cap C_2$ and $e_2 \in C_1 - C_2$

then there exists $C_3 \in F$ such that $e_2 \in C_3 \subset (C_1 \cup C_2) - \{e_1\}$. A *cut set* is the set of links connecting some subset of the nodes with the rest of the nodes. A *minimal cut set* is a cut set which contains no proper subset which is a cut set.

We consider matroids because of the following basic result:

Theorem 2: Let F be the family of all minimal cut sets of a network G with links S. $\langle S,F\rangle$ *is a matroid* [*1; p. 116*].

Consider (7) with k = 2, k' = 3 and C(2) = 5. Then, $C(3) \leq 2$. We now show that there exists no network such that the number of connected subnets with 2 links is 5 and with 3 links is 2. More generally, we show that $C(k) \neq 2$ for all networks with k and NB satisfying $(1/2)NB > k > 1$. This follows directly from Theorem 2 and defining property M_2 of matroids. Let $B = \{b_1, \ldots, b_k\}$ and $E = \{e_1, \ldots, e_k\}$ be non-identical sets of links which are disconnected. And let $\{\beta_1, \ldots, \beta_{NB-k}\}$ and $\{\varepsilon_1, \ldots, \varepsilon_{NB-k}\}$ be the links removed in each case. The total number of elements in $B = \{\beta_1, \ldots, \beta_{NB-k}\}$ and $E = \{\varepsilon_1, \ldots, \varepsilon_{NB-k}\}$ is $2NB-2k > NB$ since $(1/2)NB > k$. Thus for some i, $\beta_i \in E$, and since $B \neq E$, for some j, $\beta_j \notin E$. If B and E define minimal cuts, then there must exist a third minimal cut by the matroid property M2. But if E is not minimal there exists $E' \subset E$ which is minimal. But in that case there would be more than two sets* S with $|S| = NB-k$ and $S \supset E'$. On the other hand, consider the complex defined on the points 1, 2, 3, 4, 5, 6 with 3-sets (4,5,6) and (3,5,6) and 2-sets (5,6), (4,6), (4,5), (3,6), (3,5). These achieve the equality in (7).

This leads to the following interesting but yet unsolved problems. Let F be the cut sets of a finite network with NB links and NN nodes. Given there are C(k) cuts with cardinality k, what is a sharp lower bound for C(k') for $k' \geq k$ and what is

**If X is a set, $|X|$ represents the number of elements in X.*

a sharp upper bound for C(k') for k' $\leq$ k. Or more generally let $\langle S,F \rangle$ be a matroid and F' the family of all subsets of S containing a set of F. Given there are C(k) sets in F' with k elements what are sharp bounds for C(k'), k' $\neq$ k?

It should be pointed out that Leggett [8] states similar and apparently stronger bounds to those mentioned here. However, his proof seems inadequate.

1.3 DETERMINING COMPONENTS OF NETWORKS

Consider a network $G = \langle N,A \rangle$ with node set N and link set A. We wish to find the number of components of the network. A *component* is a maximal subset of nodes which can communicate with one another. Each node will be assigned a label indicating the component it is in. The notation k: = k+1 means k is replaced by k+1. We give an algorithm which while less efficient than some others for general use is particularly useful for simulation. The algorithm is as follows:

Step 0: Start with $A_o = \phi$ and assign each node a separte label. Set k = 0. Go to Step 1.
Step 1: Add a link a_k to A_k to form A_{k+1}. Suppose $a_k = (m_k, n_k)$. Examine the labels of m_k and n_k. If they are the same, repeat Step 1 with k: = k+1. If not, go to Step 2.
Step 2: Change all the node labels which are the same as the label of m_k (including m_k's label) to the label of n_k. Set k: = k+1. If $A_{k+1} = A$, stop; otherwise go to Step 1.

When the algorithm terminates, each component is listed. It is important that we can introduce the links in Step 1 in any order. Statistics such as the number of components, the number of nodes in each component, or the number of communicating node pairs can also be maintained. Initially, the number of components is NN; the number of communicating pairs NP is 0;
494 and each component contains 1 node. Each time we reach Step 2, we combine the two components, with say t_1 and t_2 nodes into a new component with $t_1 + t_2$ nodes. Also, we have $t_1 t_2$ more communicating node pairs, and thus NP: = NP + $t_1 t_2$.

Suppose we have completed the analysis for $G = \langle N,A \rangle$ using the algorithm above and that we add a link to A yielding the link set A'. We need only repeat *one* cycle of the algorithm to analyze the new network. This simplicity is of major importance. However, if we delete a link, a, from A, the situation is more difficult. If a = (m,n), m and n must initially be in the same component. We first label node m, then all nodes connected to m by a link in $A' = A - \{a\}$. In general, we label all nodes connected to a labeled node by a link in A'. If n becomes labeled, connectivity is as before. If n connot be labeled, let t_1 be the number of labeled nodes and t_0 the number of nodes in the component containing link a before its removal. Then the number of components increases by one. The old component now has t_1 elements, the new one $t_0 - t_1$ elements and $NP := NP - t_1(t_0-t_1)$.

1.4. SIMULATION METHOD I

The method we now describe can be used to solve very general reliability problems. Here, we present it in its simplest forms and in Part 2, we describe generalizations. Suppose we wish to determine either the expected number of communicating node pairs or the probability of network failure. Suppose that links fail with probability p but nodes do not fail. A direct scheme would be to choose a random number between 0 and 1 for each link. If the number is less than p, the link is removed; otherwise the link remains. If we find the number of node pairs communicating, choose another set of random numbers, compute the number of node pairs communicating and so on, the sample average would give us an estimate of the expected number of node pairs communicating for link failure probability p.

With only little extra effort, we can estimate the expected pairs communicating as a *function* of the probability of link failure. The procedure is based on a suggestion of Hammersley and Handscomb [5]. As before, we generate a random number between 0 and 1 for each link. We then determine the largest random number associated with any link, the next largest number and so on. Suppose the numbers in decreasing order are r_1, r_2, ..., r_{NB} for a given sample. Let NP_1, NP_2, ..., NP_{NB} be the number of pairs communicating after the first link, the second link, ..., and the last link have been added. Then for $1 \geq p > r_1$, the sample value for this sample is 0; for $r_1 \geq p > r_2$ the sample value is NP_1; for $r_2 \geq p > r_3$, the sample value is NP_2; and so on. The entire procedure to find the NP for all p requires one application of the algorithm to the overall network. This simple idea, which depends strongly on the form of the algorithm for finding connectivity, saves considerable computation when estimates are desired for a range of failure probabilities.

Suppose the links have different failure probabilities. If the nominal probability of link i failing is p_i, we generate a random number as before, divide it by p_i, and then for each sample we sort the resulting numbers in decreasing order as before to obtain r_1, r_2, ..., r_{NB} and NP_1, NP_2, ..., NP_{NB}. This again yields the sample mean NP as a function of p. Now p has a different interpretation. For p = 1 the corresponding link probabilities are $1 \cdot p_1$, $1 \cdot p_2$, ..., $1 \cdot p_{NB}$. For p = 1/2 link probabilities are 1/2 their nominal value, etc. By varying p we now obtain a reliability sensitivity analysis when each link failure probability is varied proportionally.

1.5. SIMULATION METHOD II

The method that follows is based on the combinatorial methods described in Section 1.2. We seek the number of ways, C(NB-k), the network can fail when k = 0, 1, ..., NB links fail. However, instead of finding upper and lower bounds on the terms, we estimate the missing terms by sampling.

To describe the procedure, consider the network in Figure 1.5.1.. Table 1.5.1. gives several important characteristics of this network.

Given only the number of nodes, the number of links, and the size of the minimum cut set, we can calculate all the C(k) except C(10), C(9), C(8), C(7). To estimate the unknown coefficients by sampling, we notice that some coefficients are more important than others. For example, the probability of a network occurring with 10 operating links is .0987 while the probability of a network with only 7 links is .00017, smaller by almost a factor of 600.

496 Our technique stems from the theory of *stratified* random sampling [2] and utilizes proportional sampling. The *strata* are those networks with no link failures, one link failure, etc. We need not consider strata for which we already have complete information. Thus, for our example, we need only consider subnets with 7, 8, 9, or 10 links.

Suppose we are allowed 100 samples. We sample each stratum a number of times proportional to the stratum's probability of occurrence. This suggests we sample: (100) (.0987)/(.0987 + .0173 + .00205 + .00017) networks with two failed links; (100) (.0173)/(.0987 + ... + .00017) networks with 3 links failed; and

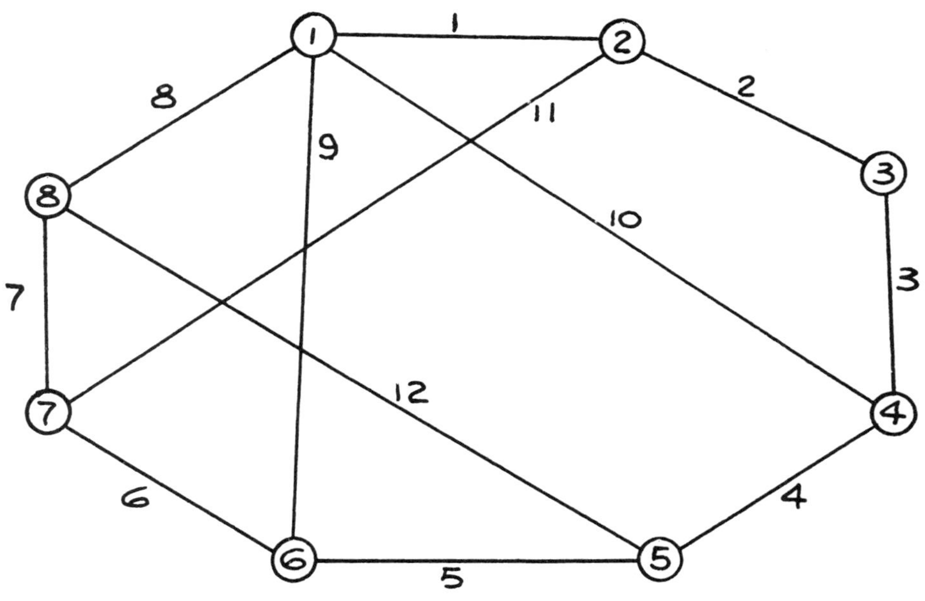

Fig. 1.5.1

Number of Links Failed k	Number of Nets Failed C(12-k)	Total Number of Nets $\binom{12}{k}$	Contribution to Net Failure Probability $C(12-k)p^k q^{12-k}$ for p - .05	Probability of Net with k Failed Links $\binom{12}{k}.p^r q^{12-k}$ for $p = .05$
0	0	1	.0	.5403
1	0	12	.0	.3412
2	1	66	.00149	.0987
3	18	220	.00141	.0178
4	124	495	.00051	.00205
5	465	792	.00009	.00017
6	924	924	.00001	.00001
7	792	792	small	small
8	495	495	.	.
9	220	220	.	.
10	66	66	.	.
11	12	12		
12	1	1	small	small
Sum	3109	2^{12}	.00353	1.000

Table 1.5.1

so on. This becomes, after rounding to integers, 83 samples for 2 link failures, 15 samples for 3 link failures, 2 samples for 4 link failures, and no samples for 5 link failures. (To simplify our calculations, we take one sample from nets with 5 links failed). Moreover, since there are only 66 possible networks with 2 failed links, we enumerate *all* 66 networks rather than sample from these 83 times with replacement.

To compare the efficiencies of the simulation methods, define a random variable X so that X = 1 with probability equal to the probability, P_f, of the network failing and X = 0, otherwise. Take n samples of X, say $X_1, X_2, \ldots, X_n$ from nets whose links have failed randomly. The variance of $\bar{X} = (X_1 + \ldots, + X_n)/n$ is $\sigma^2 = P_f(1-P_f)/n$. In an unstratified simulation, we find the variance of $\bar{X}$ obtained by examining 84 = 66 + 15 + 2 + 1 samples of the network. Thus, $\sigma_I^2 = (.00353)\ (.99647)/84 = 4.18 \times 10^{-5}$. In Simulation Method II, we first sample from 220 nets with 3 links failed 15 times with replacement. Eighteen are disconnected so P_f is 18/220 and the variance $\sigma_3^2 = (1/15)\ (18/220)\ (202/220) = .0050$. There are 495 nets with 4 links failed, of which 124 are disconnected. We take 2 samples for a variance of $\sigma_4^2 = (1/2)\ (124/495)\ (371/495) = .0938$. Finally, we take one sample from the 792 networks with 5 failed links. Of these, 456 are disconnected and thus $\sigma_5^2 = (456/792)\ (336/792) = .2749$.

The estimate $\bar{h}$ of h(p) is

$$\bar{h} = \sum_{k=0}^{12} \bar{X}_k \binom{12}{k} p^k q^{12-k}$$

where $\bar{X}_k$ is a random variable equal to the sample mean for the fraction of disconnected networks with k failed links. For k = 0, 1, all nets are connected; for $k \geq 6$ all are disconnected. We enumerate all nets for k = 2. Thus, the variance in each of these cases is 0. Then, since the variance of a constant times a random variable is equal to the constant squared times the variance of the random variable

$$\sigma_{II}^2 = [\binom{12}{3} p^3 q^{12-3}]^2 \sigma_3^2 + [\binom{12}{4} p^4 q^{12-4}]^2 \sigma_4^2$$

$$+ [\binom{12}{5} p^5 q^{12-5}]^2 \sigma_5^2 = (.00141)^2 (.005) + (.00051)^2$$

$$(.094) + (.00009)^2 (.274) \simeq 3.6 \times 10^{-8}$$

Thus, Simulation Method II is more efficient than the unstratified simulation by a factor of more than 1000 as measured by the variance for this example. In general, this will be the case when p is close to 0, since when unstratified sampling is applied in such cases, most of the samples will be connected and little information will be gained. However, in Simulation Method II, since only the first few terms of the reliability function have any significance for the result, the proportional sampling is very effective. Note that we can use the estimated coefficients from Method II to estimate h(p) for any p although for large p the variance may get large.

REFERENCES

1. Busacker, R. G., and Saaty, T. L., *Finite Graphs and Networks*, McGraw Hill, 1965.

2. Fisz, M., *Probability Theory and Mathematical Statistics*, Wiley, 1963.

3. Frank, H. and Frisch, I. T., "Analysis and Design of Survivable Networks," *IEEE Transactions on Communications Technology*, Volume COM-18, No. 5, October, 1970.

4. Fulkerson, D. R., "Networks, Frames, Blocking Systems," *Mathematics of the Decision Sciences*, Part I, pp. 303-334, American Mathematical Society, 1968.

5. Hammersley, J. N. and Handscomb, H. E., *Monte Carlo Methods*, Methuen, 1964.

6. Jacobs, I. M., *Connectivity in Probabilistic Graphs*, Report 356, Massachusetts Institute of Technology, Research Laboratory of Electronics, Cambridge, Mass., 1959.

7. Kruskal, J. B., "The Number of Simplices in a Complex," *Mathematical Optimization Techniques*, ed. R. Bellman, Berkeley: University of California Press 251-278, 1963.

499

8. Leggett, J. D., *Synthesis of Reliable Communication Networks*, PhD. dissertation, University of Pennsylvania, 1968.

9. Moore, E. F. and Shannon, C. E., "Reliable Circuits Using Less Reliable Relays," *J. of the Franklin Institute*, Volume 262, Part I, pp. 191-208, 1956.

This work was supported by the Advanced Research Projects Agency of the Department of Defense (Contract No. DAHC 15-70-C-0120).

Paper received on May 15, 1971.

Exact calculation of computer network reliability

by E. HÄNSLER

IBM Research Laboratory
Ruschlikon, Switzerland

G. K. McAULIFFE

IBM Corporation
Dublin, Ireland

and

R. S. WILKOV

IBM Corporation
Armonk, New York

INTRODUCTION

The exact calculation of the reliability of the communication paths between any pair of nodes in a distributed computer network has not been feasible for large networks. Consequently, many reliability criteria have been suggested based on approximate calculations of network reliability. For a thorough treatment of these criteria, the reader is referred to the book and survey paper by Frank and Frisch[1,2] and the recent survey paper by Wilkov.[3]

Making use of the analogy between distributed computer networks and linear graphs, it is noted that a network is said to be connected if there is at least one path between every pair of nodes. A (minimal) set of links in a network whose failure disconnects it is called a (prime) link cutset and a (minimal) set of nodes with the same property is called a (prime) node cutset. If a node has failed, it is assumed that all of the links incident to that node have also failed. A cutset with respect to a specific pair of nodes n_s and n_t in a connected network, sometimes called an s-t cut, is such that its removal destroys all paths between nodes n_s and n_t.

The exact calculation of $P_c[s, t]$, the probability of successful communication between any pair of operative computer centers n_s and n_t, requires the examination of all paths in the network between nodes n_s and n_t. More specifically, if each of the n nodes in any given network fail with the same probability q and each of the b links fail with the same probability p, then $P_c[s, t]$ is approximately given by

$$P_c[s, t]=\sum_{i=0}^{b} A^e_{s,t}(i)\,(1-p)^i p^{b-i}, \quad p\gg q. \tag{1}$$

In Eq. (1), $A^e_{s,t}(i)$ is the number of combinations of i links such that if only they are operative, there is at least one communication path between nodes n_s and n_t. On the other hand, the calculation of the probability $P_f[s, t]$ of a communication failure between nodes n_s and n_t requires the examination of all s-t cuts. For specified values of p or q, $P_f[s, t]$ is approximately given by

$$P_f[s, t]=\sum_{i=0}^{b} C^e_{s,t}(i)p^i(1-p)^{b-i}, \quad p\gg q. \tag{2}$$

For $q\gg p$, a similar expression can be given replacing $C^e_{s,t}(i)$ by $C^n_{s,t}(i)$. The coefficients $C^e_{s,t}(i)$ and $C^n_{s,t}(i)$ denote the total number of link and node s-t cuts of size i. The enumeration of all paths or cutsets between any pair of nodes n_s and n_t is not computationally possible for very large networks.

RELIABILITY APPROXIMATION BASED ON CUTSET ENUMERATION

If any network G of b links and n nodes, it is easily shown that the order of the number of cutsets is 2^{n-2}

Reprinted from AFIPS Proceedings, Vol 41, 1972

whereas the order of the number of paths between any pair of nodes is 2^{b-n+2}. For networks having nodes of average degree (number of incident links) greater than four, $b>2n$ and $2^{b-n+2}>2^{n-2}$. Consequently, such networks have a larger number of paths than cutsets. Computation time would clearly be reduced in such cases by calculating network reliability from cutsets instead of paths. In this case $P_c[s, t]$ can be obtained from $P_c[s, t]=1-P_f[s, t]$, where $P_f[s, t]$ can be calculated from Eq. (2). Alternatively,

$$P_f[s, t]=P\left[\bigcup_{i=1}^{N} \underline{C}^{i}_{s,t}\right] \tag{3}$$

where $\underline{C}^{i}_{s,t}$ is the event that all links fail in the ith prime s-t cut and N is the total number of prime cutsets with respect to nodes n_s and n_t. The calculation of $P_f[s, t]$ from Eq. (2) clearly requires the examination of all s-t cuts. The number of prime s-t cuts is usually much smaller. However, $P_f[s, t]$ is not readily calculated from Eq. (3) because the $\underline{C}^{i}_{s,t}$ are not mutually exclusive events.

Following Wilkov,[4] we shall use $P_f=\text{Max}_{s,t}P_f[s, t]$ as an indication of the overall probability of service disruption for a given computer network. For specified values of p or q, P_f depends only on the topology of the network. A maximally reliable network clearly has a topology which minimizes P_f and hence minimizes $\text{Max}_{s,t}C^{n}_{s,t}(m)$ or $\text{Max}_{s,t}C^{e}_{s,t}(m)$ for small (large) values of m when p or q is small (large). Letting $X^{n}_{s,t}(m)$ and $X^{e}_{s,t}(m)$ denote the number of prime node and edge s-t cuts of size m, $X^n(m)=\text{Max}_{s,t}X^{n}_{s,t}(m)$ and $X^e(m)=\text{Max}_{s,t}X^{e}_{s,t}(m)$ have been proposed[4] as computer network reliability measures. These measures $X^n(m)$ and $X^e(m)$ denote the maximum number of prime node and edge cutsets of size m with respect to any pair of nodes. A maximally reliable network is such that $X^n(m)$ and $X^e(m)$ are as small as possible for small (large) values of m when the probability of node or link failure is small (large).

In the calculation of $X^n(m)$ and $X^e(m)$ for any given network, all node pairs need not be considered if all nodes or links have the same probability of failure. It has been shown[5] that in order to calculate $X^n(m)$ and $X^e(m)$, one need only consider those node pairs whose distance (number of links on a shortest route between them) is as large as possible. For a specified pair of nodes n_s, n_t, $X^{e}_{s,t}(m)$ can be calculated for all values of m using a procedure given by Jensen and Bellmore.[6] Their procedure enumerates all prime link cutsets between any specified pair of nodes in a non-oriented network (one consisting only of full or half duplex links). It requires the storage of a large binary tree with one terminal node for each prime cutset. Although these cutsets are not mutually exclusive events, it has been suggested[6] that Eq. (3) be approximated by

$$P_f[s, t]\approx \sum_{i=0}^{N} P[\underline{C}^{i}_{s,t}]. \tag{4}$$

However, it is shown in the following section that no additonal computation time is required to actually compute $P_f[s, t]$ exactly.

EXACT CALCULATION OF COMPUTER NETWORK RELIABILITY

A simple procedure is described below to iteratively calculate a minimal set of mutually exclusive events containing all prime link s-t cuts. This procedure starts with the prime cutset consisting of the link incident to node n_t. Subsequently, these links are re-connected in all combinations and we then cut the minimal set of links adjacent to these that lie on a path between node n_s and n_t, assuming that the network contains no pendant nodes (nodes with only one incident link). The link replacements are iterated until the set of links connected to node n_s are reached. The procedure is easily extended to provide for node cutsets as well and requires a very small amount of storage since each event is generated from the previous one. $P_f[s, t]$ is obtained by accumulating the probabilities of each of the mutually exclusive events.

Procedure I

1. Initialization

Let: N be the set of all nodes except nodes n_s.
- C be the set of all links not incident to node n_s.
- $M_1=\{n_s\}$
- F_1 be the set of links incident to both n_s and n_t
- S_1 be the set of links incident to n_s but not n_t
- b_1 be a binary number consisting of only $|S_1|$ ones
- $i=1$

2. Let:

- T_i be a subset of S_i consisting of those elements in S_i for which the corresponding digit in b_i is unity.
- M_{i+1} be a subset of N consisting of nodes incident to the links in T_i.
- $N = N-M_{i+1}$.
- F_{i+1} be a subset of C consisting of links incident to n_t and adjacent to any member of T_i.
- S_{i+1} be a subset of C consisting of links incident to nodes in N other than n_t and adjacent to any member of T_i.
- $C = C-(S_{i+1}\cup F_{i+1})$.

3. If $S_{i+1} \neq \emptyset$, then let:
   b_{i+1} be a binary number with $|S_{i+1}|$ ones
   $i = i+1$
   Go to step 2
   Otherwise, let:
   $T_{i+1} = \emptyset$
   $$CS = \bigcup_{k=1}^{i+1} [F_k \cup \bar{T}_k \cup (S_k - T_k)],$$
   where CS is a modified cutset and $\bar{T}_k$ indicates that the links in set T_k are connected.
4. Let:
   $C = C \cup F_{i+1} \cup S_{i+1}$
   $N = N \cup M_{i+1}$
   $b_i = b_i - 1$ (modulo 2)
   If $b_i < 0$, go to step 5. Otherwise, go back to step 2.
5. Let $i = i-1$. If $i \neq 0$, go back to step 4. Otherwise, terminate the procedure.

In the calculation of $P_f[s, t]$, Procedure I performs a depth first search of the given network starting at node n_s and traversing several links at the same time. The index i indicates how far from n_s the search has progressed and b_i indicates the links traversed at the ith level of the search. During the search, set N keeps track of the nodes which have not yet been reached and C is the set of links not yet traversed. At the ith level, set F_{i+1} is a subset of the links not yet traversed which are incident to node n_t and hence must be disconnected in the formation of an s-t cut. Set S_{i+1} consists of edges in C which lie on a path to n_t but which need not necessarily be disconnected in the formation of an s-t cut. The edges in $T_{i+1} \subseteq S_{i+1}$ are those which are connected as we traverse the network toward node n_t. When set S_{i+1} is empty, the edges incident to n_t have been reached and this portion of the search is terminated with the formation of a modified s-t cut in step 3 of the procedure. The modified s-t cut is actually a group of states in the network or an event in which all links in an s-t cut are disconnected and the links in all T_i in this part of the search are connected. It is the set of connected links which makes this modified s-t cut mutually exclusive of all of the modified s-t cuts previously generated during the execution of Procedure I. In step 4, we back track one level and then continue the search by traversing a different subset of the links in S_i. After all combinations of the links in S_i have been traversed, we back track one additional level and the search continues with traversal of a different combination of the links in S_{i-1}. The procedure terminates when we have back tracked all the way up to node n_s. It is shown in the proof of the following theorem that the modified s-t cuts generated are mutually exclusive and collectively exhaustive.

Theorem I:

Procedure I generates a collectively exhaustive set of mutually exclusive modified s-t cuts.

Proof:

Part I—Prime s-t cuts

In this part of the proof, it is shown that every modified cutset CS generated in step 3 of Procedure I contains a prime s-t cut. We begin by noting that the links in $T_k (1 \leq k \leq i+1)$, traversed in the depth first search through the given network, form subnetworks containing node n_s. For any such subnetwork, set M_i contains the nodes at a distance of i from n_s. Each modified cutset CS generated by the procedure consists of all links in such a subnetwork being connected and all links in $S_k - T_k$ and F_k, that connect nodes inside the subnetwork with those outside the subnetwork, being disconnected. Node n_t is never contained in the subnetwork since any link incident to n_t must be contained in some set F_k and is therefore always disconnected.

Part II—Mutually exclusive

In order to show that the modified cutsets obtained from Procedure I are mutually exclusive, we shall demonstrate that every pair of modified cutsets disagree in the state of at least one link appended at some level j. Specifically, for any pair of distinct modified cutsets CS_p and CS_q, there exists a value of j for which if $\bar{T}_k \subset CS_p$ and $\bar{T}_k' \subset CS_q$, then $T_k = T_k'$ for $k \leq j-1$ but $T_j \neq T_j'$. This implies that during the generation of CS_p and CS_q from Procedure I, $b_k (k \leq j-1)$ was the same in both cases but the value of b_j was different. Otherwise, if CS_p and CS_q were generated from the same values of b_k for all k, then CS_p and CS_q would be identical. It is now noted that if $T_j \neq T_j'$, there exists a link e such that $e \in T_j$ and $e \notin T_j'$ which implies that $e \in (S_j - T_j')$. It follows that link e appears connected in CS_p and disconnected in CS_q.

Part III—Collectively exhaustive

We shall prove that the modified s-t cuts obtained from Procedure I are collectively exhaustive by showing that every state of the network in which nodes n_s and n_t cannot communicate is contained in one of the modified s-t cuts. We proceed by noting that in any given state of the network that includes an s-t cut, there is a maximal set of nodes N_s connected to node n_s which does not include node n_t. If set N were discarded in Procedure I, then the resulting modified s-t cuts would contain every state of the links on set N_s in which there is a path between every pair of nodes in

N_s. This follows from the fact that in the generation of all modifications of the same prime s-t cut, the deletion of set N from Procedure I would result in set S_k for all k containing every link on set N_s. As we sequence through all b_k, these links would be connected and disconnected in Procedure I in every combination in the traversal of all paths from n_s to every other node in N_s. It is now noted that any modified s-t cut generated from Procedure I that includes a connected subnetwork on N_s specifies as cut all links connecting nodes N_s to nodes in $N-N_s$, where N is the set of all nodes in the network. All links in the network connecting pairs of nodes in $N-N_s$ would be unspecified.

Taking advantage of the unspecified links, it is possible to extend one of the modified s-t cuts generated by Procedure I with set N deleted to match any specified state of the network in which nodes n_s and n_t are not connected. The effect of using set N in Procedure I is to omit several links from many of the S_k. Significantly fewer modified s-t cuts are thereby generated since the states of the redundant links joining pairs of nodes in N_s would not be specified. However, these modified s-t cuts clearly include all of those generated when set N is neglected. This is evident since each of the links on N_s not specified can be assigned a particular state in order to match a given modified s-t cut obtained from Procedure I with set N omitted. Consequently, any specified state of the network containing an s-t cut is included in one of the modified s-t cuts obtained from Procedure I. Q.E.D.

It should be noted that the collectively exhaustive set of mutually exclusive modified s-t cuts obtained from Procedure I is not minimum. This is due to the fact that for any prime s-t cut, Procedure I as given generates too many subnetworks on the set of nodes N_s connected to n_s. However, Procedure I is easily modified to eliminate the generation of any subnetworks on N_s that contain circuits. This is done by eliminating all T_i in step 2 of the procedure in which two or more links are incident to the same node. The formation of any other circuits in subnetworks on N_s is avoided through the use of set N in Procedure I. The result is that the connected links in any modified s-t cut would form trees on N_s.

It is noted that in the procedure given above, nodes have been assumed to be perfectly reliable. However, Procedure I can also be applied in the case that nodes fail and links are perfectly reliable. In the event that nodes and links may fail simultaneously, assuming that their failures are statistically independent, following Hänsler[7] we can easily modify Procedure I to obtain a collectively exhaustive set of mutually exclusive modified s-t cuts consisting of nodes and links. We would proceed by introducing a binary number b^n_i consisting of only M_i ones for each of the sets M_i in Procedure I. Analogous to T_i, in step 2 we form a set T^n_{i+1} consisting of the nodes in M_{i+1} for which the corresponding digit in b^n_{i+1} is unity. F_{i+1} and S_{i+1} in step 2 would consist of links in C incident to nodes in T^n_{i+1}. Then any modified s-t cut CS formed in step 3 of Procedure I would consist of

$$CS=\bigcup_{k=1}^{i+1}\left[F_k\cup\bar{T}_k\cup(S_k-T_k)\cup T^n_k\cup(M_k-T^n_k)\right]\cup\{\bar{n}_t\} \quad (5)$$

The only other s-t cut consists of node n_t being inoperative. The above modifications to Procedure I double the number of levels and therefore significantly increase the necessary computation time for any given network. However, the storage requirement of the modified procedure is still very small. A network of b links and n nodes would only require approximately $3b+2n$ words of storage to compute $P_f[s,t]$ in the presence of node and link failures. All modified cutsets are either printed out or their probabilities accumulated. Consequently, the exact calculation of $P_f[s,t]$ for any given network is limited only by the computer time required in view of the inherent computational complexity of the problem.

EXAMPLES OF NETWORK RELIABILITY CALCULATIONS

In this section, Procedure I will be used to obtain $P_f[s,t]$ for several networks, assuming that all nodes are perfectly reliable and all links fail with the same probability p. We shall first consider the simple network shown in Figure 1 in order to demonstrate the modified 1-4 cuts obtained from Procedure I. Figure 1

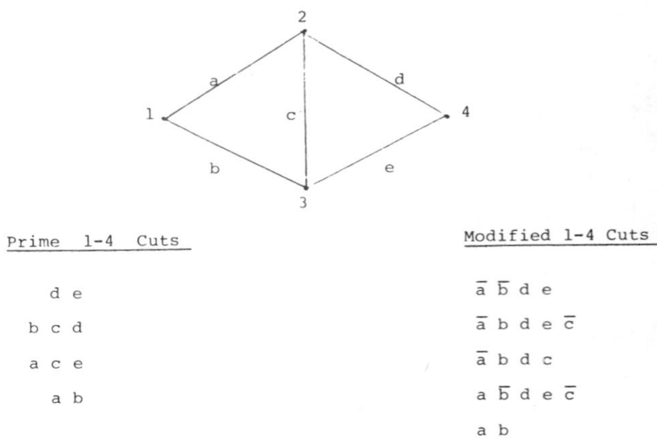

Figure 1—Example illustrating the calculation of node pair failure probability

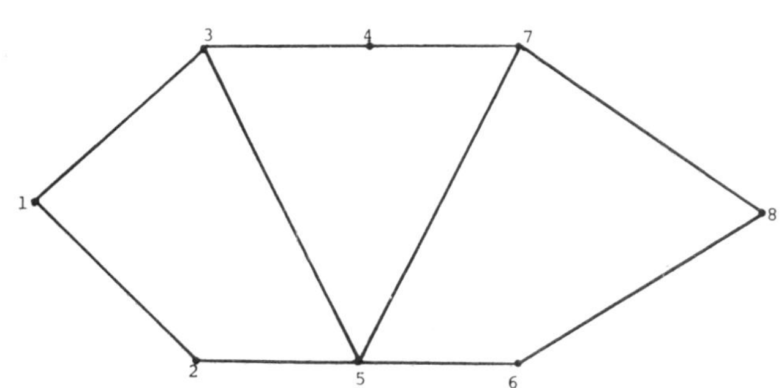

Figure 2—Example for comparison of approximate and exact reliability calculations

shows the four prime cutsets between nodes 1 and 4, which are not mutually exclusive. Also listed there are the six mutually exclusive modified 1-4 cuts obtained from Procedure I in the order in which they are obtained. Note that the second and fourth modified 1-4 cuts are not prime since link a or b has been disconnected in order for the corresponding events to be mutually exclusive.

The network shown in Figure 2 has been given by Jensen and Bellmore[6] as an example of their procedure for enumerating all prime cutsets with respect to a given pair of nodes. They listed 16 prime 1-8 cuts for the network of Figure 2. From these cutsets, $P_f[1, 8]$ was approximated by

$$P_f[1, 8] \approx 4p^2 + 8p^3 + 4p^4 \quad (6)$$

However, from the mutually exclusive modified 1-8 cuts obtained from Procedure I, $P_f[1, 8]$ is actually given by

$$P_f[1, 8] = 4p^2 + 6p^3 - 16p^4 - 32p^5 + 115p^6 - 134p^7 + 79p^8 - 24p^9 + 3p^{10} \quad (7)$$

It is clear from this example that the approximation to $P_f[s, t]$ given by Jensen and Bellmore[6] is reasonable

TABLE I—Polynomial Coefficients for P_f [9, 6] for Networks of Figure 3

Coefficient	Figure 3a	Figure 3b
c_2	3	2
c_3	6	4
c_4	−6	9
c_5	−25	−22
c_6	−25	−153
c_7	237	572
c_8	−417	−874
c_9	364	744
c_{10}	−177	−371
c_{11}	46	102
c_{12}	−5	−12

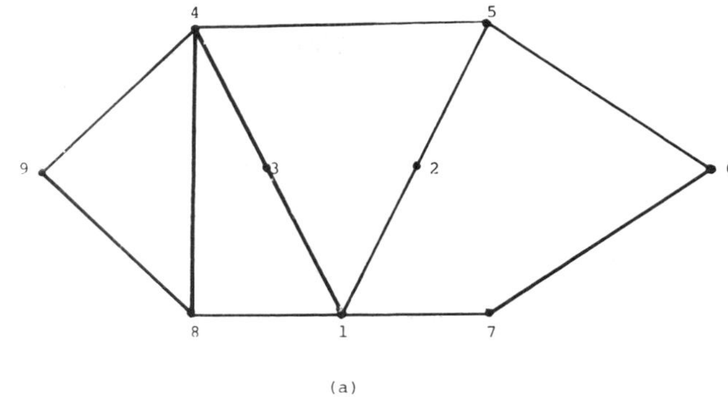

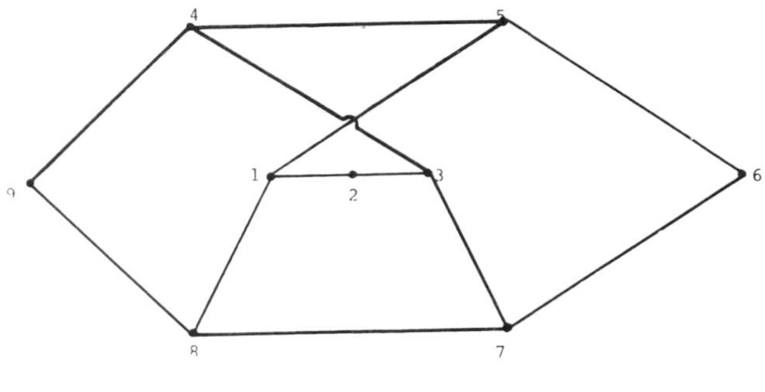

Figure 3—ARPA subnetwork topologies having 9 nodes and 12 links: (a) actual, (b) example based on $X^e(m)$

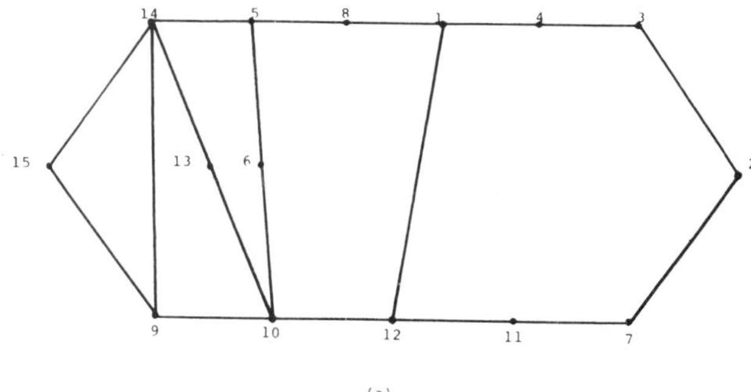

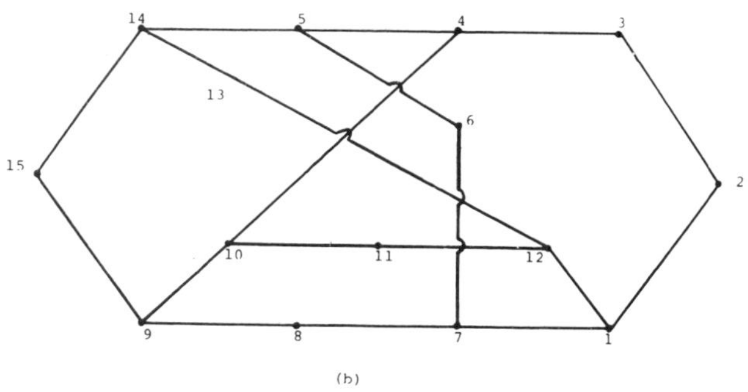

Figure 4—ARPA subnetwork topologies having 15 nodes and 19 links: (a) actual, (b) example based on $X^e(m)$

505

TABLE II—Polynomial Coefficients for P_f [15, 2] for Networks of Figure 4

Coefficient	Figure 3a	Figure 3b
c_2	12	3
c_3	5	6
c_4	−56	28
c_5	55	7
c_6	−84	−620
c_7	701	−1267
c_8	−521	20379
c_9	−6212	−77855
c_{10}	24039	171797
c_{11}	−46457	−257512
c_{12}	58369	279128
c_{13}	−51647	−224691
c_{14}	33123	135228
c_{15}	−15433	−60303
c_{16}	5121	19402
c_{17}	−1152	−4269
c_{18}	158	576
c_{19}	−10	−36

for only very small values of p since only the first coefficient in that approximation is exact.

Two topologies for 9 node and 15 link subnetworks of the ARPA network are shown in Figure 3. The network shown in Figure 3a was given by Frank, et al.[8] Figure 3b is a maximally reliable network based on $X^n(m)$ and $X^e(m)$ for small m obtained by Wilkov.[9] Assuming all nodes are perfectly reliable and all links fail with the same probability p, $P_f[9, 6]$ can be expressed as

$$P_f[9, 6] = \sum_{i=2}^{12} c_i p^i. \qquad (8)$$

The coefficients in Eq. 8 for Figures 3a and 3b are listed in Table I. They have been obtained in 18 seconds using an APL implementation of Procedure I on a 360 model 91 computer. Consistent with the results in Reference 9, Figure 3b has smaller coefficients than Figure 3a for small powers of p. Furthermore, we have found that there are a total of 2,772 cutting states with respect to nodes 9 and 6 in Figure 3b compared with 3,011 in Figure 3a. Similar results have been obtained for the 15 node and 19 link ARPA subnetwork topologies shown in Figure 4. The topology shown in Figure 4a was given by Frank, et al.[8] and Figure 4b was obtained by Wilkov[9] based on $X^n(m)$ and $X^e(m)$. The polynomial coefficients for $P_f[15, 2]$ are given in Table II. The total number of cutting states between nodes 15 and 2 is 49.7 thousand for Figure 4a and 44.9 thousand for Figure 4b.

CONCLUSION

A procedure has been given for calculating the node pair failure probability in computer networks exactly, using little more computation time than previously required to obtain an upper bound on $P_f[s, t]$. Furthermore, the storage requirement of the given procedure grows only linearly with the number of links in the given network. Unfortunately, due to the inherent computational complexity of the problem, the necessary computation time grows exponentially with the size of the given network. Nonetheless, it has been found to be computationally feasible to use the procedure given herein for networks as large as the ARPA network.

REFERENCES

1 H FRANK I T FRISCH
Communication, transmission, and transportation networks
Addison-Wesley Publishing Company Reading Massachusetts 1971

2 H FRANK I T FRISCH
Analysis and design of survivable networks
IEEE Transactions on Communication Technology Vol COM-18 1970 pp 501-519

3 R S WILKOV
Analysis and design of reliable computer networks
IEEE Transaction on Communications Vol COM-20 June 1972 pp 660-628

4 R S WILKOV
Reliability considerations in computer network design
Proceedings of IFIP Congress '71 Ljubljana Yugoslavia August 1971

5 R S WILKOV
On the design of maximally reliable communication networks
Proceedings of the Sixth Annual Princeton Conference on Information Sciences and Systems March 1972

6 P A JENSEN M BELLMORE
An algorithm to determine the reliability of a complex system
IEEE Transactions on Reliability Vol R-18 1969 pp 169-174

7 E HÄNSLER
A fast recursive algorithm to calculate the reliability of a communication network
IEEE Transactions on Communications Vol COM-20 June 1972 pp 637-640.

8 H FRANK et al
Store and forward computer networks
Third Semiannual Technical Report for ARPA Contract DAHC 15-70-C-0120 June 1971

9 R S WILKOV
Design of computer networks based on a new reliability measure
Proceedings of the International Symposium on Computer-Communication Networks and Teletraffic Polytechnic Institute of Brooklyn New York April 1972

With the growth of remote terminal devices and data banks for making information available to a wide variety of users for widely diverse applications, the problems of computer communication security and information privacy become increasingly important.

Turn (p. 510) describes privacy transformation for data base systems. Feistel (p. 523) describes cryptography and computer privacy. Chu and Neat (p. 532) proposed a new computer cryptography which used an expanded character set technique to break down the statistical parameters of the message. Such cryptography is easy to implement yet provides a high degree of privacy protection for data base applications where synchronizations can not be preserved. Winkler and Danner (p. 545) provide an overview on the data security in the computer communication environment.

Computer Communications Security

For general and additional reading on the subject of privacy transformation, the interested reader should consult [KAH 67], [GAI 56], [SIN 68], [SHA 49], [PET 67], and [SKA 69]. For further information on protection and security in computer operating systems, interested readers should refer to [EVA 67], [LAM 69], [GRA 68], [GRA 72], [POP 73], [POP 75], [BRA 75], [LIP 75], and [FAR 75].

Privacy transformations for databank systems*

by REIN TURN

The Rand Corporation
Santa Monica, California

INTRODUCTION

The term *databank* implies a centralized collection of data to which a number of users have access. A computerized *databank system* consists of the data files, the associated computer facility, a management structure, and a user community. Several classes of databank systems can be defined on the basis of the nature of the organization supported by the databank, and its activity; the nature of the data and its uses; and the structure of the associated computer facility. Such classifications have been discussed in detail elsewhere.[1]

The recent years have seen a steady increase in the establishment of databanks in all sectors of our society in the United States,[2] as well as in other countries:[3,4] in the federal, state and local governments for administrative, law enforcement, education, social welfare, health care purposes; in business and industry for supporting management, planning, marketing, manufacturing and research; in universities for administrative purposes and for supporting social research projects; and the like.

The information maintained in such databank systems includes proprietary data on the operations of industrial concerns, sales data of business establishments, and large collections of personal information on individuals. In all databank systems there is a need to control the access to the data, if for no other purpose than, at least, to assure the *integrity* of the data—that they will not be accidentally modified or erased. In many databanks containing proprietary business information, classified defense information, or confidential personal information on individuals, there is a requirement for *data security*—protection against accidental or deliberate destruction, and unauthorized access, modification or dissemination of the data.

In databanks maintaining personal information on individuals, often collected without the consent or knowledge of the persons concerned, the questions of potential violations of an individual's *right of privacy*—his right to determine for himself what personal information to share with others, arise. These, however, relate to what personal information is gathered in the first place, and thus are legal, political and ethical questions, rather than the technical questions of data security which are addressed in this paper.

Privacy transformations** represent one technique for providing data security—the mathematical/logical transformation of the protected data into forms which are unintelligible to all but the holders of the "keys" to the transformations, i.e., those who know what *inverse* transformations to apply. This capability of privacy transformations is very useful for providing data protection beyond the more conventional access control mechanisms, such as passwords in their various forms, which can be circumvented or nullified through flaws in software, wiretapping, or outright physical theft of data-carrying, demountable storage media.[5]

This paper will first briefly review the relevant characteristics of several classes of privacy transformations, then present a set of suitability criteria for databank applications, and conclude with a discussion of implementation and operational considerations.

PRIVACY AND TRANSFORMATIONS

Historically, there has always existed a requirement to prevent access to information in a message when outside of the physical control of either the originator or the intended receiver, i.e., when the message is in some communication channel. Indeed, certain classes of messages have always been subject to interception, copying, and attempts to uncover the information they contain.[6] In the computer age this threat is also extended to stored messages and data.

Shannon[7] refers to the methods of protecting information in messages and data as *secrecy systems*. There are two kinds:

- *Concealment systems* where the existence of a message is hidden, such as in the case of using invisible ink, or mixing a message with other, unrelated text.

* The research reported in this paper was supported by the National Science Foundation Grant No. GI-29943. However, any views or conclusions contained in this paper should not be interpreted as representing
510 the official position of the National Science Foundation or The Rand Corporation.

** The term "privacy transformation" is synonymous with "cryptographic transformation". It was coined in the early days of computer security research[5] to distinguish the use of cryptographic techniques in civilian and commercial systems from their use for protecting classified national defense information.

Reprinted from AFIPS Proceedings, NCC 1973

- "True" *secrecy systems* where the existence of a message is not hidden, but its *meaning* is concealed by the use of privacy transformations—encryption techniques.

In the following, only the "true" secrecy systems are considered, since concealment systems are not applicable to computerized databank systems—no one can assert that there are no data in such systems, although whether or not there is information worth protecting may be debatable.

A privacy transformation is a mapping *T(K)*, from the space *RS(A)* of all possible records of finite length which are composed of symbols from a finite alphabet, *A*, according to the vocabulary, syntax, and grammar of a natural or artificial language, *L*, into the space *ES(B)* of strings of characters from an alphabet *B*. The original, untransformed record, *R*, is called the "plaintext" and its equivalent transformed character string, *E*, the "ciphertext" or a "cryptogram." The transformation, *T*(*K*), is usually a member of a large space, *TS*, of similar transformations. The set of parameters, *K*, of the transformation *T(K)* are called the "key" which selects *T(K)* out of the space *TS*.

Several classes of privacy transformations exist and are in use. A major classification criterion is the nature of the mapping *T* itself: it may be *irreversible* (i.e., many-to-one) mapping of records into ciphertext strings, or a one-to-one mapping with a unique inverse, T^{-1}. Both classes of privacy transformations find applications in protecting confidentiality and security in databank systems.

Irreversible privacy transformations

A many-to-one privacy transformation, *T*, when applied to record space *RS(A)*, may convert more than one record into the same ciphertext string *E* in the space *ES(B)*. That is, given *E* and the knowledge of the exact transformation used, an uncertainty remains which of the possible records was transformed into *E*. Unless the intended receivers possess additional contextual information for resolving the uncertainty, many-to-one transformations are inappropriate for precise communication of storage of information.

However, there are situations in databank systems where the maintenance of the original level of information content is not required or could be reduced in the interest of protecting the confidentiality of the information. For example, statistical databank systems, such as the U.S. Bureau of Census and various social sciences research projects, collect data on individuals under the authority of a law or with the individuals' voluntary participation. The data, especially in certain social sciences research projects, may be very sensitive and may lead to considerable harm to some individuals if disclosed.[8] The threats to the confidentiality of such data include legal means—subpoenae issued by courts, grand juries, and investigative committees with subpoena power.[9]

Irreversible privacy transformations can be used in such databank systems to hide personal characteristics of individuals in the group characteristics, and by reducing the credibility of the information. The following can be used:[10,11,12]

- *Aggregation.* The irreversible transformation *T* applied to a group of data records computes the averages of various data elements in the records and, in each record of the group, replaces the original data elements with the group averages. As the size of the aggregated group of records is increased, the transformation increases the uncertainty about the original information in the records.
- *Random modification.* The transformation consists of adding a randomly varying component to the original information in the records, thereby introducing errors. If the random variables are produced by a process whose statistical characteristics are properly chosen, the statistical value of the modified records are not altered, but credibility of each individual record is now reduced and along with this, the value of such record as incriminating evidence against an individual.

A prerequisite for effective use of the above classes of irreversible privacy transformation is, of course, the original, untransformed records be totally removed from the databank. The price paid for increased data confidentiality is, however, a reduction of the future statistical utility of the data—it will not be possible to make new, precise correlation analyses between various characteristics of individuals (these have been aggregated or innoculated with errors) or to make longitudinal analyses—studies of changes in persons' characteristics or attitudes over periods of time. The confidentiality protection vs. data utility tradeoff is an important question which is still being studied.

Reversible privacy transformations

Transformations in this class are those which are usually discussed as "cryptographic transformations"—the one-to-one mappings from the record space *R(A)* into the ciphertext space *ES*(*B*) which have unique inverses. The protection provided to the data rests in keeping the key, *K*, of the transformation *T(K)* from falling into unauthorized hands, and in the expectation that the recovery of original records or the key from the ciphertext forms is a task beyond the resources and know-how of the potential interceptors.

Further classification of reversible privacy transformations, henceforth simply "privacy transformations," can be made on the basis of the mathematical or logical operations involved in applying the transformation. Four principal classes of privacy transformations used in databank systems—coding, compression, substitution and transposition, are briefly discussed below. More detailed discussions can be found in the literature.[6,13,14]

Coding

Coding is a transformation where an entire record, parts of it, words, or syllables of the language L_i used in the record space $RS(A)$ are replaced with words or groups of characters of some other (usually artificial) language L_j.[6,15] A coding transformation and its inverse are usually applied with the help of a coding dictionary (code book) or by using table look-up methods. The protection afforded depends on maintaining control over the code books and in frequent changes of codes. Besides providing confidentiality protection, coding can also provide a considerable degree of data compression in transmission or storage. The resulting economy is a main reason for the widespread use of codes in computer files.

Compression

Data compression transformations are used to reduce the redundancy in stored or transmitted data by removing repeated consecutive characters—blanks or alphanumerics, from the records. Other types of data compression transformations attempt to achieve more compact storage of records by "packing" more characters into the storage space normally occupied by a single character. The resultant, compacted data files contain records which have been distorted by the compression algorithms and which will be largely unintelligible when accessed with normal utility programs in the databank. For correct retrieval, decompression algorithms must be applied. Even though data compression is applied mainly to achieve storage or transmission time economies, the associated confidentiality protection may also be sufficient in mild threat environments.

Substitution

Substitution transformations replace single characters or groups of characters of the alphabet A_i of language L used in the record space $RS(A_i)$, with characters or groups of characters of some other alphabet B (or set of alphabets $B_1, \cdots, B_M$). That is, the transformed record is still-composed in language L, but transmitted or stored using alphabet B. Replacement of characters of English alphabet with six-bit binary codes is a very simple substitution transformation. The key K of the transformation $T(K)$ specifies a particular substitution correspondence. The protection obtained depends, in addition to protecting the key, on the number of possible substitution correspondences between alphabets A_i and B (i.e., the size of the key space) and the nature of the language L.

Substitution transformations can be subclassified as *monoalphabetic* and *polyalphabetic*. Each of these could be *monographic* and *polygraphic*. The latter classification refers to number of characters that are being substituted as a group: in monographic substitutions, single characters are substituted (independently of each other and the context of the message) with single characters (or groups of characters). In polygraphic substitutions groups of two or more characters are substituted by similar (or larger) groups.

- *Monoalphabetic substitution*. An alphabet B is chosen to correspond with the original alphabet A such that to each character in A corresponds a unique character (group of characters) in B. As will be discussed later, monoalphabetic substitutions leave the basic language statistics (average character frequency, average polygram frequencies) invariant and, thus, remain susceptible to basic cryptanalytic techniques.
- *Polyalphabetic substitution*. Here the alphabet B is actually a set of alphabets $B_1, B_2, \cdots, B_M$ which are used cyclically with period M. For example, in a monographic M-alphabetic substitution, the first character, r_1, of record R is substituted with a character of alphabet B_1, the second with a character from B_2, the M-th with a character from B_M, and the next character again from B_1. The effect of a polyalphabetic substitution is to hide the original characteristics of the language L, since a given character of alphabet A may now be transformed into M different characters of alphabets $B_1, \cdots, B_M$.

It is common to derive the alphabet B from alphabet A by making a permutation of the characters of A to correspond with the original characters. The simplest such permutation is a cyclic shift of the characters of A by a fixed number of characters, μ. This class of substitution transformations is called "Caesar ciphers." They are extremely simple to solve as, in the case of the English alphabets, a maximum of 25 trials are required to discover the "key," the number of characters that alphabet A was shifted to obtain alphabet B.

A polyalphabetic substitution transformation using M Caesar ciphers as the alphabets $B_1, \cdots, B_M$ (with repetition allowed, i.e., $B_i = B_j$, for some i and j, for several such pairs) is called a "Vigenere cipher." The key is now a set of M numbers which specify the shifts used to generate from alphabet A the alphabets $B_1, \cdots, B_M$. A special case of the Vigenere transformation is the situation where the number of alphabets, M, is larger than the number of characters in a set of records to be transformed. This transformation is called the "Vernam cipher" and it can provide a very high level of protection.[7]

Substitution transformations may be implemented in several ways. Table look-up operations are used for substitutions with alphabets B_i that are arbitrary permutations of the alphabet A. Certain *algebraic* operations, however, permit relatively simple computation of the required substitutions.[14,16,17,18,19]

In algebraic substitutions, the N_A characters of the alphabet A are set in a correspondence with the positive integers $0, 1, \cdots, N_A - 1$ (for example, $a=0$, $b \equiv 1, \cdots$, $y=25$ in the English alphabet). These form an algebraic ring under the operations of addition module (N_A) and subtraction module (N_A). Then, choosing an integer k in the range 0 to $N_A - 1$ specifies a particular substitution transformation of characters r_i of records R into characters e_i of the transformed version, E, of R:

$$e_i = r_i + k (\text{mod } N_A),$$

and the inverse transformation

$$r_i = e_i - k \ (\text{mod } N_A).$$

For polyalphabetic substitutions, a sequence of integers $k, k_O, \cdots, k_{M-1}$, are used cyclically:

$$e_i = r_i + k_j \ (\text{mod } N_A), j = i \ (\text{mod } M)$$

Polygraphic substitutions of n-character groups (n-grams) by other n-grams can be represented as sets of simultaneous linear congruences and computed by matrix operations.[16,17]

$$e_i = \sum_{j=1}^{n} c_{ij} r_j, \ i = 1, \cdots, n$$

where the elements c_{ij} of the matrix C are selected among integers in the range $0, \cdots, N_A - 1$, such that the matrix C has an inverse. If the matrix C is fixed, the substitution is monoalphabetic (in terms of n-grams). Polyalphabetic n-gram substitutions are obtained by introducing a cyclically varying parameter, t, in the matrix C.[18] The matrix $C(t)$ must have the property that its determinant is independent of the parameter t, and is a prime number modulo (N_A).

Transposition

Privacy transformations that permute the ordering of characters in the original message are called transposition transformations. The transformation may be applied to the entire message all at once, or on a block-by-block basis. The alphabet of the message remains unchanged. A common method for implementing a transposition is to write the block to be transformed in a matrix form following some rule and then rewrite in linear form using a different rule. For example, the message may be written first as rows of the matrix and then transcribed by taking the column of the matrix in some specified order.

Transposition transformations retain the character frequency statistics of the language but destroy the higher order statistics (polygram frequencies).

Composite transformations

The effectiveness of privacy transformations can be increased (although not always) by applying a sequence of transformations, $T_1(K_1), T_2(K_2), \cdots, T_S(K_S)$, such that $E = RT_1T_2 \cdots T_S$. Typically, the transformation T_i are either all substitutions, all transpositions, or a mix of these.

The case where all transformations are substitutions is called an S-loop substitution transformation:[20]

$$e_i = r_i + k_{j_1} + k_{j_2} + \cdots + K_{jS} \ (\text{modulo } N_A)$$

where $j_g = 1 \ (\text{mod } M_g), g = 1, \cdots, S$. If the periods of the polyalphabetic transformations $T_1, \cdots, T_S$, are mutually prime, the period of the composite transformation $T = T_1 \cdots T_S$ is the product of periods $M_1, \cdots, M_S$ of the component transformations.

A particularly effective composite transformation suggested by Shannon[7] is a "mixing transformation" which may consist of a sequence of n-gram substitutions and transpositions. Such mixing transformations can be highly effective in hiding the language characteristics, as well as possibly information in the ciphertext E of the nature of privacy transformations used.

SUITABILITY CRITERIA

Among a set of requirements stated by Kerckhoffs some seventy years ago[7] are:

- The cryptographic transformations used should be, if not theoretically unbreakable, unbreakable in practice;
- A knowledge by enemy of system's hardware should not compromise the protection provided to the messages;
- The key should be able to provide all the protection, it should be easily changeable;
- The application of the transformation should be simple, requiring neither complicated rules nor mental strain.

Kerckhoffs' requirements were derived for manually operated communication systems, but are also applicable in modern communication systems and computerized databanks.

The suitability of a particular class of privacy transformations for application in a communication network or in the files of a databank depends on: (1) the relevant characteristics of the particular application, (2) the inherent characteristics of the class of privacy transformations used, and (3) the technical aspects of the system that implements the application and the privacy transformation. Although the principal purpose of using privacy transformations is to provide security to information in transit or in storage, the effects of application of transformation to the utility of the system are equally important—a system may be designed to provide excellent security, but at such a cost in loss of performance that it may become useless.

Application characteristics

The characteristics that affect the effectiveness of a candidate class of privacy transformations in protecting information include the following:

a. *Value of the information.* Whether or not the value of information can be determined adequately depends largely on the nature of information involved. The most difficult to assess is personal information, the easiest to assess is business information. Information affecting national security is usually treated as invaluable and any cost in its protection is considered justifiable. Important is also the time dependency of the assessed value, and this has a direct bearing on the suitability of a class of privacy transformations. For example, if the transformations can resist a cryptoanalytic effort of reasonable intensity for T hours, and the value of the protected information is expected to decrease below a critical threshold in less than this time, the transformation will provide sufficient protection. Determination of the value of information is discussed in more detail in Section V of this progress report.

b. *Language(s) used.* The information to be protected by a privacy transformation is carried in the words of the message (or computer record) and is inextricably identified with these words and the language that provides the vocabulary, grammar, and syntax for embedding the information into the message. In natural languages the vocabulary, grammar, and syntax have evolved over periods of time with no regard to the possible application of privacy transformations. In artificial languages the need to provide protection through the use of privacy transformations can be taken into account already in the language design phase.

c. *Dimensions of the application.* The static and dynamic aspects of the application—the ranges of volumes of messages or data to be stored, processed, and/or transmitted; the required rates and maximum allowed time for operating on a message or data record; and the nature of the processing (sequential, random access, concurrent, etc.), establish criteria which must be satisfied in implementing the privacy transformation.

d. *The personnel characteristics* that affect their role in the application, control, safeguarding of the privacy transformation system: level of expertise, integrity, discipline, etc. Errors made will require repetition of processing or transmissions in providing more intercepted material for the cryptanalyst.

Inherent characteristics of privacy transformations

The most important overall criterion in selecting a privacy transformation is the *amount of security* that it can provide. In general, security appears similar to reliability—both are concerned with techniques for assuring proper operation of systems, and both require *a priori* prediction of the probability of proper operation. From the point of view of a particular implementation, however, reliable operation is a prerequisite of secure operation.

The inherent characteristics of privacy transformatio which affect the amount of security provided, and t effective operation of the application process, include:

a. *Size (cardinality) of the key space.* The protecti provided by privacy transformations depends the intruder's uncertainty concerning the transfc mation used. In general, it must be assumed th the intruder knows the particular class of transfc mations, but does not know the specific set of k parameters employed. For example, the transfc mation may be a monoalphabetic substitution, b which one? There are 26! possible permutations the English alphabet (although not all are permis ble, such as the permutation that changes only tv letters and leaves the rest the same). A large spa of *permissible* keys, each selected with the same *priori* probability is a prerequisite for any effecti secrecy system.

b. *Effect on language.* A privacy transformation pr vides protection by drastically altering the appea ance of the plaintext record (or computer record Ideally, all the characteristics of the source la guage (the plaintext language) are altered an made unrecognizable. The extent to which this achieved is one measure of the suitability of th transformations. For example, a simpl (monoalphabetic) substitution is not very effectiv for languages that have prominent differences i the average frequencies of characters. On the othe hand, simple substitution may be quite effective i enciphering numeric-data where all numerals ar essentially equally likely.

c. *Complexity.* The complexity of the privacy trans formation may contribute to the amount of securit by providing more complete scrambling of th language characteristics, but it also contributes t the cost in its application: in computer data bank where transformations are applied by softwar techniques (programs) complexity translate directly into computer time used for nonproductiv (from the point of view of the application) opera tions.

d. *Effects on dimensions.* Certain privacy transforma tions involving substitution of characters or poly grams with higher order polygrams (e.g., every character replaced by a pair of characters; digram replaced by a trigram) increase the length of the ciphertext message compared to the plaintext message. This increases the transmission time o storage space required. Coding transformations however, can be designed to reduce these requirements.

e. *Error susceptibility.* Compound transformations and super encryptions that involve several transformations applied sequentially may have very undesirable error propagation properties. Lease susceptible are monographic substitutions where error in applying the transformation to a character affects only that character and does not propagate. However, substitutions that use the ciphertext itself as the key (with appropriate translation by a few characters) are extremely susceptible to error propagation.

f. *Length of the key.* The concept of a "key" to a privacy transformation T is often used in two senses. In the case of polyalphabetic substitutions, for example, the sequence of numbers k_i added to the corresponding message characters, n_i, is called the "key." The length, N, of this sequence $k_1, \cdots, k_N$ is the "key length"; it corresponds to the period in the use of different alphabets. For the cryptanalyst who attempts to discover the key by studying intercepted ciphertext messages, longer keys mean more unknowns that must be determined, hence, providing more protection to the information. In certain implementations, however, the key sequence is produced by a computational process which is specified by only a few parameters. Here the "key" that selects the privacy transformation (i.e., the production of the sequence applied to the plaintext) is the set of parameters, rather than the sequence produced. If the cryptanalyst can attempt to solve for the parameters of this process, rather than the entire sequence produced by the process, his number of unknowns is greatly reduced. An example of this is the generation of random numbers $X_i = AX_{i-1} + B \pmod N$. A large number of X_i are produced, but there are only three unknowns: A, B, and X_0.

The various characteristics listed above are evaluated for the different classes of privacy transformations in a following section.

System implementation characteristics

The third set of characteristics that determines the suitability of a particular class of privacy transformations is associated with the system implementation of the application.

a. *Processing capability.* The processing speed of the system and the storage capacity. Availability of instructions for easy application of the privacy transformations. Availability of hardware devices or software programs. Capability to use suitable file structures.
b. *Error environment.* The error characteristics of the communication channel, or the storage medium. The availability of error detecting/correcting codes.
c. *Security environment.* The capability to provide for the security of the keys for the privacy transformations, and to protect the information in the enciphering and deciphering processes.
d. *System personnel.* These may be the same as the applications personnel. Also included are the operators, programmers, maintenance engineers of the system. Their expertise in operating the system, as well as their integrity has an important role in making the use of privacy transformations a success.

Language characteristics

As stated previously, information is communicated by using a language. Concealment of the information in a written record (on any medium such as paper, magnetic surface, electronic circuitry, etc.) through the use of privacy transformations requires that the message is transformed in such a way that any resemblance with the original form is obliterated.

Natural Languages. Investigations of the structures of natural languages[21,22] have shown that there are a number of structural and statistical characteristics of their vocabularies that, in normal usage, are relatively insensitive of the context and can be used to identify the particular language used:

a. *Single character (monograph) frequency distribution*—there is a large difference in the usage of letters in the vocabularies of natural languages. For example, on the average the letter "e" appears 100 times more often than the letter "q"; in French the letter "q" occurs 11 times as often as in English. Special vocabularies, such as family names of persons or tactical orders.
b. *Polygram frequency distribution.* The data here is normally limited to pairs of characters (diagrams) which show transitions of letters to other letters in the word structure, and triplets of characters (trigrams). For example, the two most frequent diagrams in English are "th" and "he," but "es" and "en" in French and Spanish. The two most frequent English trigrams are "the" and "ing," in French they are "ent" and "que."
c. *Starting and terminal letter frequencies.* These differ sharply from the general letter frequency distribution. For example, the letter "e" (most frequent in the general distribution) ranks 14 as a starting letter, and first as a terminal letter. The letters "v," "q," and "j" have extremely low frequencies as terminal letters. Proper names, in general, have different starting and terminal letter frequencies.
d. *Word usage frequencies.* Word frequency distributions are much more dependent on the particular application areas than the various polygraph frequencies. The first ranking words, however, tend to be prepositions and connectives which are used in the same manner in all application areas. For example, the first nine are: the, of, and, to, a, in, that, is, was. The word frequency distributions form the basis of the so-called "probable word" method of cryptanalysis.

TABLE I—Effects of Classes of Privacy Transformations on Language Characteristics

	Substitutions					
	Monoalphabetic		Polyalphabetic			
Characteristic	Simple	m-graphic	Simple	k-graphic	Transposition	Composite
Single character frequency	Invariant (changed alphabet)	Changed	Changed*	Changed*	Invariant	Changed**
k-gram frequency distribution	Invariant	Changed***	Changed	Changed	Invariant	Changed
Word frequency distribution	Invariant (within the new alphabet)		Changed	Changed	Changed	Changed**
Pattern word structures	Invariant	Changed	Changed	Changed	Changed	Changed
Syntactic structure	Invariant	Partly Changed	Invariant	Partly Changed	Changed	Changed

* Within the period of applying alphabetic transformation; over large numbers of periods, some of the characteristics may show invariance.
** Assuming a composite of transpositions and polyalphabetic substitutions.
*** Changed for certain values of k in k-grams (e.g., for k not a divisor of m).

e. *Word structure patterns* (isomorphisms). There are groups of words which have similar patterns of letter occurrences in the word (e.g., aDDeD, sEEmEd, have the pattern -xx-x-). This structural information can be used to place words in "congruence" classes, and the classes can be used in cryptanalysis.
f. *Word length frequencies*. This information also characterizes different languages and, on occasion, application areas. For example, the mean word length in English is 4.5, but 5.9 in German.

Various other statistics about word structure, word-to-word transitions, etc. can be derived. Their utility from cryptanalytic point of view depends on the specific application area. Table I presents an assessment of the effects of privacy transformations on language characteristics.

The statistical structure of a language provides a certain degree of predictability in constructing words in that language. This predictability can be measured in terms of *redundancy*—the inefficiency in the use of the available character sequences from a given alphabet as words of the language. For example, a redundancy of .75 indicates that 75 percent of the possible character-sequences (up to some relatively small length) are not used as words. In general, languages with high redundancy require more complex privacy transformations than those with low redundancy.

The sentence structure and the rules of proper usage, *syntax and grammar*, likewise, place constraints in the formation of strings of words as sentences in the message. The more rigid the syntactical and grammatical requirements imposed on the message source, the more complex privacy transformations are required to effectively diffuse the structure and increase the uncertainty of the cryptanalyst.

Artificial Languages. Application of privacy transformations to information in computerized retrieval systems involves working with so-called artificial languages (e.g., codes, query languages, and programming languages) and data. These differ significantly from the natural languages and can be expected to influence the protective effectiveness of privacy transformations in different ways.

Four levels of artificial languages can be recognized. Starting with the level most similar to a natural language there are:

a. *Query languages*. These are languages designed for user interaction with the retrieval system—to request information, choose processing options, etc. For easy interaction with the system the vocabulary of a query language statement available to the user is usually a restricted subset of natural language words, arranged with precisely specified structure in natural language sentences. For example, a request may be stated RETRIEVE ALL NAMES (ENGINEER, CALF, AGE: 30-50). Many query languages provide menus of operations that are allowed. Here the wording of the choices is, likewise, kept relatively brief. Query language statements are used mainly in communication channels linking terminals with the retrieval system computers.
b. *Higher Order Programming Languages*. Programs written in higher order languages such as FORTRAN, PL/1, ALGOL, etc. may require privacy transformations if they are considered sufficiently valuable (such as certain proprietary programs) and stored in computer accessible form. Programming languages have a *fixed vocabulary* of words selected from the natural language to specify the program structure and designate dataprocessing operations (e.g., EQUIVALENCE, DIMENSION, DO, READ, WRITE, etc.) and an open-ended *variable vocabulary* specified by the programmer for variable names, numerical values, arithmetic logi-

cal processing statements, and such. The choice of some of these words is subjective with the programmer. Often these are similar to words in the natural language (e.g., ICOUNT, JSET, II, AVALUE=BVALUE(J)+INDEX, etc.). The *character set* of a typical higher-order programming language includes many special characters (PL/1, for example, has a 60-character alphabet). The *syntactical and grammatical* rules are very rigid and must be precisely followed.

c. *Assembly languages*. An intermediate step from the higher order language designed for increasing programming ease to efficient computer-executable form—the "machine language," is an assembly language. It is obtained from a higher-order language through a compilation process. The vocabulary of an assembly language consists of mnemonic names for the instruction set of the computer (usually two- or three-letter groups) and the variable names specified in the higher order language. The format is quite rigid. Programs are sometimes stored in the assembly language form.
d. *Machine language*. A machine language program is composed of instruction codes, constant numerical values, and addresses. All of these are coded as binary numbers. The instruction words are divided into fixed length fields that contain the different codes. The sets of allowed code numbers for the various fixed fields may have different cardinalities. No resemblance with a natural language is left. The alphabet consists of binary numbers with the ranges of values specified by the field lengths. Operating programs are usually stored in the machine language form.
e. *Interpretive languages*. In some interactive computer systems programs are stored in a higher-order language only in the execution phase (e.g., the JOSS language). For this, a dictionary and various analysis programs are maintained and used. The characteristics of higher-order languages discussed above are also typical of interpretive languages.

The statistics of higher order artificial languages tend to reflect the statistics of the underlying natural language, but this similarity decreases in assembly languages, and is essentially nonexistent in machine language.

The overall effect of the limited fixed vocabulary, large character set, rigid structure and lack of syntactic ambiguity is a reduction of the effectiveness of applying privacy transformation. On the other hand, the availability of the variable vocabulary can be used to change the statistical characteristics of the language almost at will.

Data. The principal use of privacy transformations in retrieval systems can be expected to center about protection of data, both in storage and in transit. Certain categories of personal information, in particular, require a degree of confidentiality sufficiently high to warrant the use of privacy transformation.

In general, personal information records consist of the following parts:

a. Person's name, address, and other identifying characteristics. In some data files the name and address may be replaced by a code number, where the name/address and code number correspondences are maintained in some dictionary. The name and address, if included, can be expected to be in the natural language. Other characteristics may be coded.
b. General descriptive information, a mixture of proper names (e.g., the birth place, parents), codes, and numeric information.
c. Narrative information. A mixture of natural language sentences, abbreviations, and codes (e.g., the description of a person's criminal history).

The inclusion of names, abbreviations, and numerical codes can be expected to considerably change the statistics of personal data as compared with the natural language text. In particular, it may be expected that the occurrence of proper names which have no identical natural language words will tend to "flatten out" the single letter and polygram frequencies.

In records with fixed formats (i.e., where fixed length fields are provided for names, addresses, etc.) the "blank" characters will have a relative high frequency of occurrence (just as in numeric data, zeroes will be the most frequent numerals). Sorting of the files into alphabetic or numerical order, likewise, in a structural feature of data files that can weaken the effectiveness of privacy transformations.

EFFECTIVENESS AND COST

The two most important considerations in selecting a class of privacy transformations for implementation in a databank system are the *effectiveness* of the transformations in providing data security and the initial and recurring *costs* of providing this protection. These must be weighed against the estimated *value* of the protected information in order to implement a *rational* protection system—one that provides a level of data security warranted by the value of the protected information.[1]

Effectiveness measures

The effectiveness of privacy transformations is usually discussed in terms of the resources and expertise required by the "enemy" cryptanalyst to "break" the privacy transformation used, i.e., to discover the key. The following assumptions about the intruder cryptanalyst must be made:

- He knows in detail the class of transformations being used; the language (vocabulary, syntax, grammar) used in the records or programs; the general subject matter of the data. He does not know the specific key of the privacy transformations used or the exact contents of protected records, although he may know some words that are highly likely to occur.

- He is knowledgeable in computer technology, operation and use; knowledgeable in the operational procedures of the target databank; and has a digital computer at his disposal.

A necessary prerequisite for attempting to break a privacy transformation system is the availability of a sufficient amount of ciphertext. The minimum amount required for unique recovery of the record or message is called the *unicity distance* by Shannon.[7] It is a function of the size of the key space, the redundancy of the language, and the number of alphabets (key period) used in polyalphabetic substitutions, or the period of transposition transformations. For example, the unicity distance for M-alphabetic substitution transformation is $53M$ and for transposition of period M (i.e., character permutations take place in M-character groups) the unicity distance is $1.7 \log M!$. In general, it may be expected that in databank applications there will be large amounts of ciphertext available to the intruders. Note, however, that the ciphertext available must be longer than the key period, i.e., a key is used more than once to transform records or messages. In databank systems this can be expected to be the situation, as using nonrepeated keys to transform large amounts of data will be impractical from the point of key management for permitting information retrieval, and for providing security to the keys themselves.

Other information that helps the cryptanalyst includes:

- A number of different records known to be transformed with the same key—these can be used for simultaneous solution and checking of trial solutions.
- Fragments of plaintext corresponding to the available ciphertext, or paraphrased messages or records that are in the available ciphertext. These are very useful for generating trial solutions.
- Knowledge of the probable words in the records or knowledge of the key selection habits of the target databank—if keys are short, they may be *coherent*—are words of natural language or generated by some algorithmic process.
- As much knowledge of the statistical characteristics of the language used in the plaintext as possible.

Again, a great deal of this information, including plaintext fragments, must be expected to become available to the intruder. The ability of a privacy transformation system to withstand a cryptanalytic attack for sufficiently long (i.e., for the information to lose its value, or for the data to be retransformed) can be regarded as a measure of effectiveness of the transformations. There are two kinds of measures of effectiveness: information-theoretic measures and pragmatic "work-factor" measures.

Information-theoretic measures

These measures assess the theoretical effectiveness of a secrecy system against cryptanalysis where the intruder has unlimited resources and expertise available. Shannon[7] modeled the situation as follows: each message, R, and each choice of a privacy transformation key, K, has, from the point of view of the cryptanalyst, *a priori* probability associated with it. These are $p(R)$ and $p(K)$, respectively, and they represent the crytanalyst's knowledge of the situation before the message is transmitted.

After he intercepts and analyzes an intercepted ciphertext, E, he can calculate *a posteriori* probabilities of the various messages and keys, $p_E(R)$ and $p_E(K)$, respectively, that could have produced the intercepted ciphertext. *Perfect secrecy* is obtained if the $p_E(R)=p(R)$ and $p_E(K)$, i.e., the cryptanalyst has obtained no information at all from the intercepted ciphertext. Shannon shows that in order to have perfect secrecy, the number of keys must be at least as great as the number of possible messages.

As a measure of the theoretical amount of secrecy, Shannon defined *equivocation*—a statistical measure of how near to solution is an average cryptogram E of N characters. There are two equivocations, that of the key, $H_E(K,N)$, and the message equivocation, $H_E(R,N)$, where

$$H_E(K,N)=\sum_{E,K} p(E,K)\log p_E(K)$$

$$H_E(R,N)=\sum_{E,R} p(E,R)\log p_E(R)$$

where $p(E,K)$ and $p(E,R)$ are the *a priori* probabilities of cryptogram E and key K, and cryptogram E and message R, respectively. The summation is over all possible cryptograms of N letters and all keys or messages.

The equivocation functions for the key of the privacy transformation, $H_E(K,N)$, has the following properties:

- Key equivocation is an non-increasing function of N.
- For perfect systems, key equivocation remains constant at its initial value (when $N=0$).
- For non-perfect systems, the decrease in key equivocation is no more than the amount of redundancy in the N letters of the language L used in the plaintext.
- For most of the simple types of privacy transformations, equivocation becomes zero after the number of intercepted characters exceeds the unicity distance. After that point, a unique solution is theoretically possible.
- For certain privacy transformation systems, called *ideal* secrecy system, equivocation remains non-zero no matter how much ciphertext is intercepted.

These properties point out the importance of the *redundancy* in the language used in the plaintext records or language. If there is no redundancy at all, i.e., if all words are of equal length, say N, and if any combination of N characters of the alphabet used is a meaningful word of the language, the secrecy of the system will be perfect. Such properties do not exist in natural languages, but can be designed into artificial languages. However, they tend to be in conflict with present trends of making artificial languages as close to natural languages as possible.

All presently existing large databank systems have redundancy in the stored data or programs. Large amounts of ciphertext, fragments of plaintext, etc. are likely to be readily available. Although exact evaluation of initial equivocation for such databank is a complex problem and has not been attempted, it is clear that simple privacy transformation systems applied here are theoretically solvable. Nevertheless, p privacy transformation systems for databank applications can be devised to have sufficiently high levels of *practical* security, i.e., sufficiently high *work factors* for the intruders, to discourage attempts to break these systems through cryptanalysis.

Work factor measures

On the practical side, an assessment of the effectiveness of privacy transformations can be attempted in terms of the effort and resources required to break the system through crytanalysis. Such a measurement has been called the intruder's "work factor." The units of measurement can be the expected number of logical/mathematical operations. These can be converted into units of time and, subsequently, into dollars by specifying a computing capability which the intruder is expected to have available.

Several authors have examined computer-aided cryptanalysis and the effort involved.[20,23,24] Tuckerman,[20,25] in particular, has probed the computational effort involved in breaking of polyalphabetic single-loop and 2-loop substitutions under several assumptions of availability of plaintext fragments:

- For the simplest monoalphabetic substitution, the Caesar cipher, a single subtraction is sufficient if a fragment of the corresponding plaintext is available. If not, the "running down the alphabet" method can be used to generate N_A trial solutions (corresponding to the N_A characters in the alphabet) and examined for plausible plaintext. Alternately, character frequency distributions can be computed for the ciphertext and matched with the known frequencies of the language to produce solution candidates for examination. The time required on a moderately fast computer would be a few minutes at the most.
- A single-loop polyalphabetic (Vigenere) substitution of period M, can be reduced to M Caesar ciphers by a statistical analysis of the ciphertext. At least $20M$ characters of ciphertext are required. Considerable computation may be required to estimate the correct period—candidate periods are proposed, character frequency distributions computed, and correlation tests made. On a computer, however, the work is again measured in minutes or a few tens of minutes.

The 2-loop polyalphabetic substitution transformations can likewise be solved by conversion into single-loop cases and, subsequently, into Caesar ciphers. The computation required is more extensive but, by no means prohibitive. A larger hurdle to the would-be intruder is the development of programs that are needed.

Transposition transformations are solved by similar methods—by generating trial solutions, performing statistican analyses on n-grams, and using "heuristic" techniques to reduce the search space. Computational tasks, again, are not prohibitive. However, it is possible to construct complex composite transformations which require hours of computing time for their solution.

In general, the availability of digital computers and sophisticated computational algorithms has greatly reduced the protection provided in the paper-and-pencil days by the polyalphabetic and substitution transformations. Whether or not this protection is adequate in a given databank system depends on the value of protected information both to the intruder and to the owners.

Costs

The use of privacy transformations involves the initial costs of the necessary hardware or software, and the recurring costs of additional processing required and maintenance of the integrity of the privacy transformation system used.

Hardware costs are involved, in particular, in application of privacy transformations to terminal-computer communication links. Here the enciphering/deciphering device at the terminals is likely to be a hardware device. However, the logic circuitry involved is not necessarily excessive or costly since the integrated circuit prices are steadily falling. For example, the hardware involved in one, rather sophisticated ciphering/deciphering unit[26] for transforming 16-byte blocks consists of 162 TTL logic modules which could be placed on four LSI chips at a density of 280 circuits per chip. Transformation of one block requires 165 microseconds.

Software requirements, likewise, are not necessarily expensive. Programming of the mentioned transformation required some 1300 bytes of storage of 9 ms. on the IBM 360/67 computer.[26]

Other experimental data on the cost of applying privacy transformations yields similar results. The application of privacy transformations to 10-bit characters in a CDC-6600 computer[27] has shown the following percentages of processing time required for the transformations:

- Vernam type polyalphabetic substitution transformation (with one-time-only key): .66 percent to encode, .66 percent to decode.
- Polyalphabetic substitution with a short, periodic key (using table look-up technique): .25 percent to encode, 3.32 percent to decode.
- Polyalphabetic substitution with short, periodic key, using modular arithmetic for transformation: 1.94 percent to encode, 4.38 percent to decode.

As usual, there are the memory space vs. execution time overhead tradeoffs that can be applied.

The above cost figures are quite sensitive to the type of application, the computer system, and specific implementation of the transformations, and they represent only isolated data points. Estimates of decreased functional capability of a databank system due to the use of privacy transformations, as well as costs of maintaining the secrecy system integrity through providing key security, key changes, and the like, are even less available.

IMPLEMENTATION IN DATABANK SYSTEMS

Privacy transformations can be used in databank systems for protecting communications between the computer and remotely located terminals, the data stored in the files, or both. The suitability criteria for implementing privacy transformations in databanks—processing capability, error environment, security environment, and system personnel expertise—have already been discussed. These, and the specific application characteristics of the databank, provide the general criteria for selecting the type of privacy transformations to be used.

A privacy transformation system can be implemented by using hardware devices, software, or both.[26-28] Software implementation is more attractive for performing the transformations in the computer processor unit, while hardware devices appear more suitable for implementation in the remote terminals. However, the decreasing cost of hardware is making feasible the use of special privacy transformation modules also in the central processors.[26]

Application communication links and data files

The major differences in the application of privacy transformations in communication links (usually hardware switched or dedicated telephone circuits) and in data files include the following:

- In communication systems the encoding and decoding operations are done at two different locations and two copies of the key are required, while in file system application these operations are performed at the same location and only one copy of the key is needed.
- A specific communication usually involves one user, while a file may be shared between many users with different access and processing authorizations.
- In communication links, the message remains transformed for a very short time interval since encoding and decoding operations are performed almost simultaneously, in data file application this time interval may be days or months.
- The transformed records in files may be subject to selective changes at unpredictable time intervals and at unpredictable frequencies, while the message in communication link is not changed in transit.
- A change of the privacy transformation keys in a communication application is a simple replacement of the old key with the new one. In data files, this entails reprocessing the entire file of records, or maintaining an archival file of previously used keys and associated indices.
- A common-carrier communication link normally uses certain signal patterns for internal switching control. These should not appear in the ciphertext form of messages. There is no such problem in files as the control data parts.
- Communication links have higher error rates while errors in the file system are more amenable to detection and control.
- There is much less processing capability available at terminals than in the central processor.

Several other differences emerge when the implementation of one or the other of the three main classes of privacy transformations—substitutions, transpositions, composite transformations—are considered below.

Key management

The differences in the nature of communication systems and data files impact the choice of the type of privacy transformations and, in particular, the requirements for key generation, storage, logistics, and safeguarding. For example, in communication systems totally random keys can be used only once and then discarded, but in the file system they must be stored or means provided for their generation later, thus reducing the level of security such systems usually offer.

The need to store transformation keys in the data file application sets up different requirements for key possession and control than in communication links. In the latter case, individual users could be in possession of their own keys and copies stored in the processor. For file use, however, this is not desirable. The entire file, or the various classes of records in the file, should be transformed with the same key, but the keys need not be revealed to the users. Rather, the access to the file would depend on a different set of identification-authentication procedures which establish the authorization of a user to access the file and give him access to routines that retrieve or store the involved records. If the privacy transformations used have a high work factor and the key security is also high, reprocessing of the file for changing of the key need not be very frequent.

Key generation

A long key, i.e., the specification of different alphabets and their sequence, is necessary in substitution transformations where the transformation is performed by using modular arithmetic—modulo A_N addition of the key characters to the plaintext characters. As discussed previously, approximately $20M$ characters of ciphertext is needed for computer-aided solution of these transformations. If the key is sufficiently long such that this amount of ciphertext is not produced, a high degree of security is achieved (although fragments of plaintext and the language characteristics may still make breaking of the key practical). Since storage in the computer memory of very long keys is not economical, various algorithms are used to *generate* the key as required. Computation of random numbers and feedback shift-register sequence generators are among the standard key generator techniques.[29,30] A drawback of algorithmic key generation approach is that now the *real* key is not the pseudo-random sequence added to the plaintext, but the much shorter set of parameters (an initial state and a few constants) that are used to specify a particular version of the key generation algorithms. For example, only $2n$ properly selected bits are needed in a linear feedback shift-register to produce a nonrepeating sequence of 2^n bits. Also, it is possible to recover the parameters and, hence, the key by analyzing fragments of the key stream.

Another problem with key stream generators in the communication links is the need for *synchronization* of the encoding key stream at the transmitting end with the decoding key stream at the receiving end. Such synchronization may be hard to achieve and maintain in noisy communication links. Self-synchronization is definitely a property which key stream generators should possess.[31]

Transposition and composite-privacy transformations are usually called *block transformations* as they are applied to a block of plaintext simultaneously. Very complex transformations with high work factors can be obtained.[26,32] The required keys can be stored in blocks of the main memory, special read-only memories, or generated algorithmically. Assemblying of the key at the transformation application time for several independent "subkeys" can provide additional protection against key compromises. A sophisticated block transformation can be expected to involve several sequentially applied transformations on the entire block or various subblocks. Since the computation time can be substantial for the software implementation in the processor, special purpose hardware may turn out to be more economical. In terminals, the hardware implementation is the only alternative.

CONCLUDING REMARKS

The need for data security in computerized databank systems is increasing. Privacy transformations can provide protection against a variety of threats—wiretapping to obtain transmitted information or system access control information, active entry into the system through illicit terminals, disruption through insertion of illegitimate information in the communication channel, snooping in the files, theft of removable storage devices, and the like. Their use in the databank systems, both in communication links connecting remote terminals to the processor and in data files, is now economically feasible.

On the other hand, digital computers greatly simplify the cryptanalytic tasks of the would-be intruders who must be expected to have available the necessary resources and expertise. It is important, therefore, for those charged with the design of data security mechanisms in databank systems to understand the capabilities and shortcomings of privacy transformations, and to be aware of the criteria which must be applied in their selection. This paper has strived to contribute to such understanding and awareness.

However, privacy transformations are only one facet of the general problem of access control and data security. The design of a data security system providing protection commensurate with the value of protected information requires consideration of all types of available data security mechanisms, their relative advantages and disadvantages, cost-effectiveness, and the structure and operation of the databank system. The measures of the amount of security provided by different mechanisms, measures of the value of information, and the tools for tradeoff analysis, are now beginning to crystalize into a discipline of "data security engineering." It is likely that in a few years the design of data security systems will be much less an art than it is today.

REFERENCES

1. Turn, R., Shaprio, N. Z., "*Privacy and Security in Databank Systems—Measures of Effectiveness, Costs, and Protector-Intruder Interactions,*" AFIPS Conference Proceedings, FJCC, Vol. 41, pp. 435-444, 1972.
2. Westin, A. F., Baker, M. A., *Databanks in a Free Society—Computers, Record-Keeping and Privacy,* Quadrangle Books, New York.
3. Younger, K., *Report of the Committee on Privacy,* Her Majesty's Stationery Office, London, July 1972.
4. Carroll, J. M. "Snapshot 1971—How Canada Organizes Information About People," *AFIPS Conference Proceedings,* FJCC, Vol. 41, pp. 445-452, 1972.
5. Petersen, H. E., Turn, R., "System Implications of Information Privacy," *AFIPS Conference Proceedings,* SJCC, Vol. 30, pp. 291-300, 1967.
6. Kahn, D., *The Codebreakers,* Macmillan, New York, 1967.
7. Shannon, C., "Communication Theory of Secrecy Systems," *Bell System Technical Journal,* Vol. 28, pp. 654-715, 1949.
8. "ACE Study of Campus Unrest—Questions for Behavioral Scientists, *Science,* Vol. 165, July 1969.
9. Nejelshi, P., Lerman, L. M., "A Researcher-Subject Testimonial Privilege—What to do Before the Subpoena Arrives," *Wisconsin Law Review,* No. 4, Fall, pp. 1085-1148, 1971.
10. Hansen, M. H., "Insuring Confidentiality of Individual Records in Data Retrieval and Storage and Retrieval for Statistical Purposes," *AFIPS Conference Proceedings,* Vol. 39, FJCC, pp. 579-585, 1971.
11. Fellegi, I., "On the Question of Statistical Confidentiality," *Journal of the American Statistical Association,* pp. 7-18, March 1972.
12. Boruch, R. F., "Strategies for Eliciting and Merging Confidential Social Research Data," *Policy Sciences,* Vol. 3, pp. 375-397, 1972.
13. Gaines, H. F., *Cryptanalysis,* Dover Publications, Inc., New York, 1956.
14. Sinkov, A., *Elementary Cryptanalysis—A Mathematical Approach,* Random House, New York, 1968.
15. Friedman, W. F., Mendelsohn, C. J., "Notes on Code Words," *American Mathematical Monthly,* pp. 394-409, August 1932.
16. Hill, L. S., "Cryptography in an Algebraic Alphabet," *American Mathematical Monthly,* pp. 306-312, June-July, 1929.

17. Hill, L. S., "Concerning Certain Linear Transform Apparatus of Cryptography," *American Mathematical Monthly*, pp. 135-154, March, 1931.
18. Levine, J., "Variable Matrix Substitution in Algebraic Cryptography," *American Mathematical Monthly*, pp. 170-178, March, 1958.
19. Levine, J. L., *Some Elementary Cryptanalysis of Algebraic Cryptography.*
20. Tuckerman, B., *A Study of the Vigenere-Vernam Single and Multiple Loop Enciphering Systems*, IBM Corporation Report RC 2879, May 14, 1970.
21. Miller, G. A., Friedman, E. A., "The Reconstruction of Mutilated English Texts," *Information and Control*, pp. 38-55, 1957.
22. Shannon, C. E., "Predilection and Entropy of Printed English," *Bell System Technical Journal*, pp. 50-64, 1951.
23. Fiellman, R. W., *Computer Solution of Cryptograms and Ciphers*, Case Institute of Technology Systems Research Center Report SRC-82-A-65-32, 1965.
24. Edwards, D. J., *OCAS—On-Line Cryptanalytic Aid System*, Massachusetts Institute of Technology Project MAC Report MAC-TR-27, May 1966.
25. Gridansky, M. G., "Cryptology, the Computer and Data Privacy," *Computers and Automation*, pp. 12-19, April 1972.
26. Feisel, H., Notz, W. A., Smith, J. L., *Cryptographic Techniques for Machine to Machine Data Communications*, IBM Corporation Report RC 3663, December 27, 1971.
27. Garrison, W. A., Ramamoorthy, C. V., *Privacy and Security in Databanks*, University of Texas Electronics Research Center, TM 24, November 2, 1970.
28. Kugel, H. C., "Three Cipher-Decipher Programs Make Good Os/360 Demo's" *Canadian Datasystems*, pp. 38-40, April 1972.
29. Carroll, J. M., McLelland, P. M. "Fast 'Infinite-Key' Privacy Transformation for Resource-Sharing Systems," *AFIPS Conference Proceedings*, Vol. 37, FJCC, pp. 223-230, 1970.
30. Reed, I. S., Turn, R., "A Generalization of Shift-Register Sequence Generators," *Journal of the Association of Computing Machinery*, Vol. 16, pp. 461-473, July 1969.
31. Savage, J. E., "Some Simple Self-Synchronizing Digital Data Scramblers," *Bell System Technical Journal*, pp. 448-487, February 1967.
32. Skatrud, R. O., "A Consideration of the Application of Cryptographic Techniques to Data Processing," *AFIPS Conference Proceedings*, Vol. 35, FJCC, pp. 111-117, 1969.

ERRATA

1. Page 592 of original text, top of the second column. Change first sentence to read:

"The case where all transformations are additive substitutions is an S-loop additive (or Vegenere-Vernam) transformation[20]:

$$e_i = r_i + k_{1,j_1} + k_{2,j_2} \ldots + k_{S,j_S} \text{ (modulo } N_A)$$

where $j_g = i$ (mod M_g), g = 1, . . .,S."

2. Page 298. Replace the text in the first column, last paragraph ("Several authors. . ." and second column, first paragraph (ending with ". . .that are needed") with the following:

"Several authors have examined computer-aided cryptanalysis and the effort involved[20, 23, 24]. Tuckerman[20,25], in particular, has probed the computational effort involved in breaking single and multiple loop additive transformations under several assumptions of availability of plaintext. He summarized his results as follows[20]:

"Methods sometimes proposed for the encipherment of data, for security in storage or transmission, include the multiple Vigenere or Vernam systems, consisting of the successive addition of characters of clear-text to the characters from one or more periodic keys.

It is shown here that these systems are insufficiently secure.

Under the prudent assumption that an opponent can obtain or guess a limited fragment of the clear-text responsible for a known cipher-text, then all the keys, however many, can be readily determined by algebraic methods, and without even knowing the location of the fragment in the whole text, provided only that the clear-text fragment is at least as long as the sum of the lengths of the keys.

Even under the assumption that only cipher-text is known, the keys can be determined, by statistical and algebraic methods, from cipher-text of length at most 20 times the key-length for a 1-loop system, or 100 times the sum of the key-lengths for a 2-loop system.

More secure enciphering systems should therefore be used.

The above analyses are supported by actual decryptions using the time-shared, terminal-operated APL system."

3. Page 599, second column, last paragraph. Replace second sentence (". . .As discussed previously. . . of these transformations") with the following sentence

"Several key periods of ciphertext and some knowledge of the message language statistics are required for the solution of transformations where no plaintext samples are known."

4. Page 601. Correct the following references.

   a. Reference 20. Correct the organization to read:

   "IBM Research Report RC 2879, IBM Research Center, Yorktown Heights, N.Y. 10598, 14 May 1970."

   b. Reference 25. Correct the author's name to read:

   "Girsdansky, M.B."

   c. Reference 26. Correct the reference to read:

   "Feistel, H.W., A. Notz and J.L. Smith, Cryptographic Techniques for Machine to Machine Data Communications, IBM Research Report RC 3663, IBM Research Center, Yorktown Heights, N.Y. 10598, 27 December 1971."

Established 1845 SCIENTIFIC AMERICAN May 1973 Volume 228 Number 5

Cryptography and Computer Privacy

Computer systems in general and personal "data banks" in particular need protection. This can be achieved by enciphering all material and authenticating the legitimate origin of any command to the computer

by Horst Feistel

There is growing concern that computers now constitute, or will soon constitute, a dangerous threat to individual privacy. Since many computers contain personal data and are accessible from distant terminals, they are viewed as an unexcelled means of assembling large amounts of information about an individual or a group. It is asserted that it will soon be feasible to compile dossiers in depth on an entire citizenry, where until recently the material for such dossiers was scattered in many separate locations under widely diverse jurisdictions. It will be argued here, however, that a computer system can be adapted to guard its contents from everyone but authorized individuals by enciphering the material in forms highly resistant to cipher-breaking.

Traditionally those most dependent on secrecy have been military men and diplomats. Their work often calls for the element of surprise, and surprise implies secrecy. Whatever need ordinary people have had for secrecy has remained essentially an individual problem and has rarely been of public concern; lovers and thieves have solved their requirements for communications privacy as best they could. This state of affairs changed little until about the middle of the 19th century. At about that time scientific methods and modes of thought were finally enlisted to improve the techniques of cryptography. Nevertheless, the techniques employed in secret communication remained largely pencil-and-paper operations until well into this century.

Cryptographic encipherment can be achieved in two essentially different ways: by ciphers or by codes. A helpful distinction between the two is as follows. A cipher always assigns substitute symbols to some given set of alphabet letters. Being alphabetic in character, the cipher enables one to say anything that one can print on a typewriter in the particular language that can be represented by its keyboard letters. This means that with a cipher one can say things that have never been said before or even been anticipated as needing to be said. A code, on the other hand, is intrinsically semantic in character. A code can convey only meanings thought of in advance and provided for in a secret list such as a code book.

One should perhaps mention that today the word "code" is frequently used in a sense that does not imply cryptography. The word then usually has a broad meaning embracing sets of symbols with special relations. Thus one speaks of error-detection and error-correction codes, data-compression codes, codes for telecommunications purposes, commercial codes and codes involving all kinds of highly intricate electrical signals and wave forms.

In tackling the privacy problem presented by modern computers at the Thomas J. Watson Research Center of the International Business Machines Corporation we have given the central role to cipher techniques. It will not be possible here to cover the entire subject of "data bank" confidentiality and the securing of computer operations. I do hope to show, however, that certain principles underlying data encipherment and authentication of sources are pertinent to these broad problems.

In modern machine-to-machine networks of the type needed for a data bank the notion of secrecy embraces more than mere message concealment. A data bank includes a network of terminal-to-computer communications. The communications lines connecting the terminals and the computer centers are wide open not only to tapping but also to deliberate alteration and corruption of traffic. In addition to the more obvious aspects of data secrecy, one must therefore provide adequate protection against operational deception of the system. Mere error-detection will not do. The system itself must make it extremely unlikely that an unauthorized but clever and sophisticated person can either enter, withdraw or alter commands or data in such a system.

That is vitally important, because the slightest amount of false data entered in a data-bank system, whether by accident or by intent, can make much of the system's operation worthless. Computers without adequate protection are easily deceived, particularly by operators who thoroughly understand their operation. Indeed, the terminals them-

523

CLEAR	CIPHER 1	CIPHER 2
A	F	○
B	E	□
C	K	#
D	J	△
E	N	♡
F	P	∃
G	O	⋇
H	C	⧅
I	D	[illegible]
J	Y	⊗
K	U	▽
L	W	☽
M	H	⦶
N	M	⊖
O	B	∞
P	Z	m
Q	L	⬡
R	V	⧄
S	X	◎
T	G	⌂
U	T	Σ
V	R	⊠
W	S	+
X	I	⧈
Y	Q	☼
Z	A	×

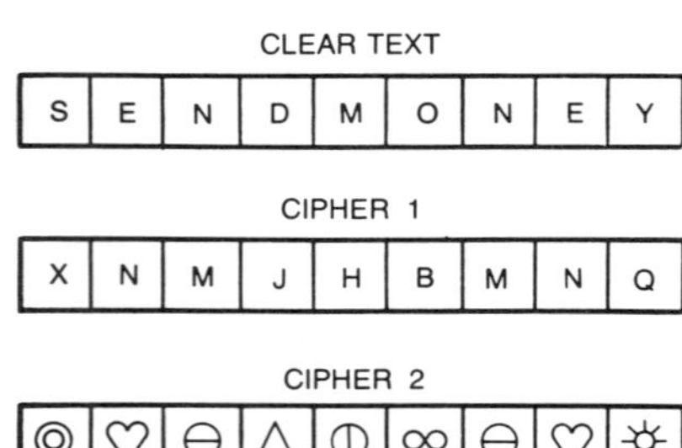

SUBSTITUTION, the basic operation in cryptography, is illustrated by two tables in which clear-text letters of the alphabet are replaced by cipher equivalents: other letters (*middle column*) or arbitrary symbols.

selves can be misused for cleverly designed data insertion. In order to preserve the purity of a data bank it will be necessary to authenticate the legitimate origin and character of any data received and to do so rapidly and with very high margins of safety.

Let us begin with the most elementary fact about ciphers: All cryptography amounts to substitution. In its simplest form a substitution can be defined by a tableau, or table. The left side lists the ordinary letters of the alphabet in "clear text"; the right side lists their cipher equivalents, the substituted values. The amateur is frequently impressed with the enormous number of possibilities of arranging such substitution, or permuting, alphabets. For the English alphabet with 26 letters there are $1 \times 2 \times 3 \ldots \times 26$ ways of writing down unique substitution alphabets. (Such a product is referred to as 26 "factorial," written 26!. Any number *n*! is the product of all the integers from 1 to *n*.)

The *n*! possible permutations of a tableau with *n* entries constitute the number of possible "keys." Now, 26! is a very large number, more than 4×10^{26}. Even so, any simple alphabetic substitution can be broken easily by frequency analysis. If the letter *Q* occurs more frequently than any other in a fairly long sample of cipher text, the analyst can be pretty sure that a cipher *Q* stands for *E*, the letter that occurs more frequently than any other in English clear text, and so on.

Nothing is gained, of course, by replacing the letters of a substitution alphabet with mysterious-looking symbols. An analyst could not care less how complicated the substitute symbols may look. He simply replaces them with a normal alphabet or number substitute of his own and proceeds with his frequency analysis. The mysterious-symbol approach does, however, demonstrate the flexibility with regard to substitute symbols. Since substitution tableaus, in spite of their well-known weaknesses, are of basic importance in cryptographic design, let us consider the possibility of introducing genuinely useful substitution symbols.

This can indeed be done. The binary number system, consisting of just two symbols, 0 and 1, is ideally suited for cryptographic processing by computers. With *n* binary digits one can generate 2^n distinct binary codes. Thus with a "block" of five binary digits one can generate 2^5, or 32, distinct combinations, or more than enough to encode the 26 letters of the alphabet [*see top illustration on opposite page*]. If we wish to name or label more items, we can increase our reservoir of distinct binary numbers merely by increasing the size of the digit block. Every time we increase the block size by one digit position we double the number of possible codes. Hence a six-digit code would provide 2^6, or 64, distinct codes, or enough to include numerals, punctuation marks and so on.

In addition to the ease with which binary digits can be represented in electronic circuitry (by on and off signals, for example) they have all the advantages of ordinary decimal numbers. Thus binary numbers can be added, subtracted, multiplied and so on, just as ordinary decimal numbers can. As we shall see, arithmetic manipulation plays a vital role in cryptographic techniques designed for computers.

Now we can introduce complexity in a fundamentally different way. Instead of using just one substitution table we can use several, in some disarranged but prearranged order. The ordering pattern constitutes a key. If we use only two tables, tagged 0 and 1, then a typical key might be 1101101. We are now dealing with multialphabetic substitution. With this new source of complexity available the question arises: Can one not now simplify the substitution tables, perhaps by making them smaller? The simplest binary substitution one can perform is on single message digits, in which case there are only two possible distinct substitution tables. Let us therefore set up two substitution tables, one for each of the two basic types of key [*see bottom illustration on opposite page*]. The table marked Key 1 simply interchanges the 0's and 1's; the table marked Key 0 preserves their identity. These are the only two possibilities. Now, it happens that the same effect can be obtained by the operation known as addition modulo 2: two digits of the same kind add up to 0, two digits of the opposite kind add up to 1. And so, in this special case, the pattern key can be called an addition key.

Before proceeding further let me explain that from here on we shall tacitly assume that the messages we wish to handle cryptographically have first been translated into a sequence of binary digits. Any kind of information, be it letters, musical sounds or television signals, can be represented by binary coding. We shall no longer worry about the original meaning of the messages. We shall deal only with their binary representation.

We are now ready to see what happens when we encipher a sequence of binary digits, let us say 0001010, into a new sequence using the two keys, Key 1 and Key 0, in some arbitrary sequence: 1101101. Remembering the rule that Key 1 interchanges 0's and 1's and that Key 0 leaves digits unchanged, we get the following:

$$\begin{array}{rr} \text{Message:} & 0001010 \\ \text{Key:} & +\ 1101101 \\ \hline \text{Cipher:} & 1100111 \end{array}$$

This represents addition modulo 2. It has the convenient property that subtraction is the same as addition, so that the message can be recovered simply by adding the sequence of digits in the key (which is known to the intended recipient) to the sequence in the cipher:

$$\begin{array}{rr} \text{Cipher:} & 1100111 \\ \text{Key:} & -\ 1101101 \\ \hline \text{Message:} & 0001010 \end{array}$$

The question immediately arises: Is this simple cipher of any practical value? Since the cipher in effect employs only two substitution tables of minimal size it is perhaps obvious that we must switch from one to the other frequently and in random fashion, that is, add a random sequence of key digits. Suppose we do. The astonishing answer is that we then have a potentially undecipherable cipher. From the viewpoint of information theory, what this cipher does is to add to each bit of message information one bit of key information (misinformation!). This is enough to completely destroy any kind of structure the original message may have had, provided that the key digits are picked at random, say by flipping a coin, and that the key sequence has the same length as the message and does not ever repeat.

Why is this system genuinely undecipherable? Actually it is no "system" at all. The basic cryptographic transformation amounts to no more than random addition of single digits. It is as trivial as that. The method derives its strength solely from the fact that for each message digit we completely and randomly change the key. This is the only class of ciphers that one can prove to be undecipherable in the absolute sense.

Even if an opponent made a brute-force attempt to break the system, for

CLEAR	BINARY EQUIVALENT	BINARY CIPHER
A	00000	00100
B	00001	01001
C	00010	10001
D	00011	01010
E	00100	00011
F	00101	10011
⋮	⋮	⋮
X	10111	11101
Y	11000	01110
Z	11001	10110

TRANSLATION TO BINARY SYSTEM is required for computer cryptography. A binary substitution-table cipher is constructed, for example, by first translating each letter of the alphabet into a five-digit binary number and then enciphering each binary equivalent.

a

KEY 0

CLEAR	CIPHER
0	0
1	1

KEY 1

CLEAR	CIPHER
0	1
1	0

b

KEY	MESSAGE 0	MESSAGE 1
0	0	1
1	1	0

c

MESSAGE		KEY		CIPHER
0	+	0	=	0
0	+	1	=	1
	+	0	=	1
1	+	1	=	0

d

$$\begin{array}{rcl} F & = & 00101 \\ \text{KEY} & = & 10110 \\ \hline \text{CIPHER} & = & 10011 \end{array}$$

$$\begin{array}{rcl} \text{CIPHER} & = & 10011 \\ \text{KEY} & = & 10110 \\ \hline & & 00101 = F \end{array}$$

BINARY SUBSTITUTION in its simplest form allows only two possibilities (*a*): in one table (*Key 0*) there is no change from clear to cipher; in the other table (*Key 1*) the cipher is the opposite of the clear. In this case of binary substitution the two tables can be represented by a single addition table modulo 2 (*b*); in this case binary substitution is equivalent to binary addition (*c*). The cipher key for addition modulo 2 is an arbitrary sequence of 1's or 0's. To encipher the binary equivalent of a message letter, one adds a key digit to each message digit (*d*). To decipher, one subtracts the key (the same as adding modulo 2).

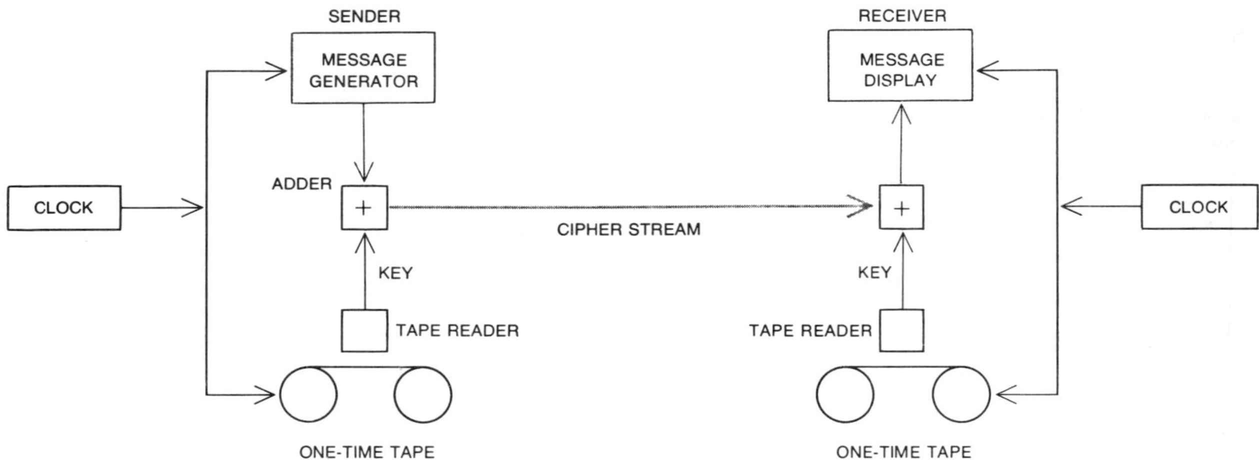

"ONE-TIME-TAPE" SYSTEM requires that the sender and the receiver have tapes carrying the same key, synchronized by clock devices. The digits of the key and of the message are added, the resulting cipher stream is transmitted and the key is subtracted (added modulo 2). For large traffic volumes a vast store of key digits must be conveyed securely to the receiver and filed there.

example by trying all the possible addition keys (2^6, or 64, in the case of our six-digit message), he would get all possible clear texts, including the one we had actually enciphered. Thus if we had enciphered the name "Tom" (which would actually take a minimum of 15 binary digits), the analyst would find among his trial decipherments all English three-letter names, such as Joe, Jim, Job and so on, including Tom, but no clue as to which name was correct. Not even a god or demon who could try all possible keys in an instant could ever establish any consistency. The system is well known and is in actual use by all major governments under various names, such as the Vernam system or "one-time pad."

In a practical system two identical tapes of random key digits are prepared; the tapes can be of any type—printed, punched, magnetic or whatever. One tape is held by the sender and the other is transmitted by "noninterceptible means," say by guarded courier, to the legitimate receiver. When the sender wants to transmit a message, he converts it first to binary form and places it in an apparatus that adds a digit, modulo 2,

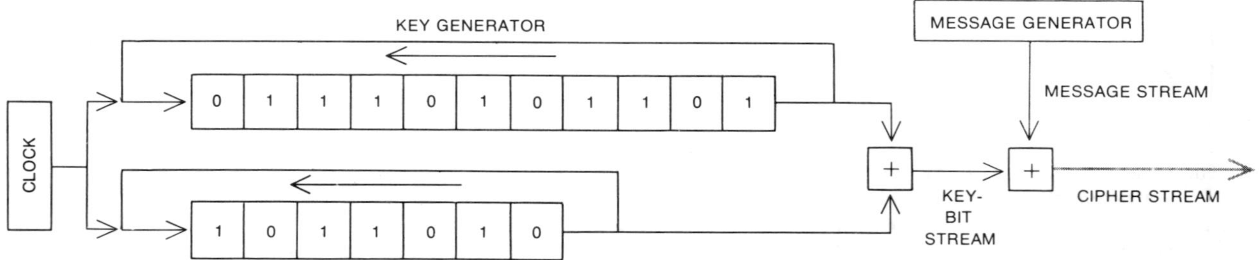

PSEUDORANDOM-TAPE SYSTEM incorporates two tape loops of key digits, or bits, that are added together to generate a "pseudorandom" key-bit stream that is in turn added to the message stream as in the one-time-tape method and is deciphered by an identically generated key at the receiver. Short tapes thus simulate long ones, but the resulting internal periodicities may be useful to an analyst.

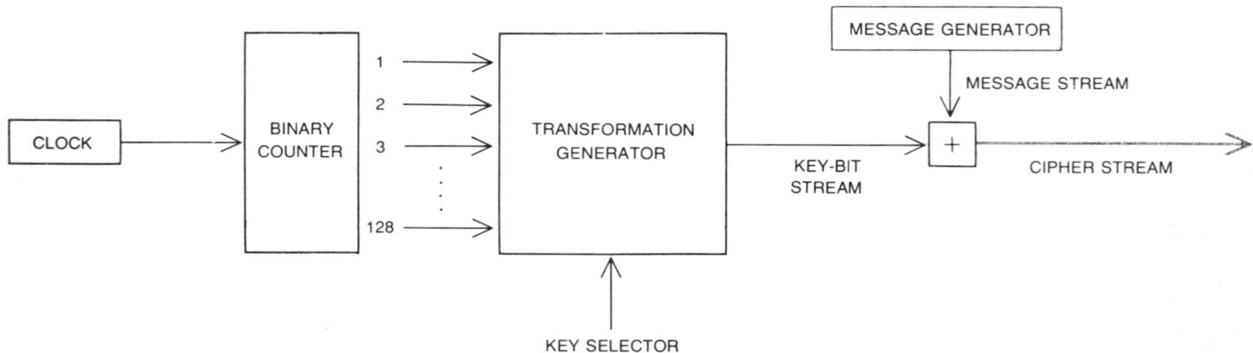

PSEUDORANDOM STREAM can be generated in more complex forms. In this generalized representation a binary counter provides the input numbers for the transformation generator, which supplies the key-stream digits to be added to the message stream.

.526

from the key tape to each message digit [*see top illustration on opposite page*]. At the receiver the coded message is recorded and run through a machine similar to the encoder that adds (subtracts) a digit, modulo 2, from the key tape to each digit of the coded message, thereby yielding the clear text. Naturally the key tape must be stepped with absolute synchronization to duplicate the encoding operation.

The fundamental drawback to the Vernam system is that for every "bit" of information transmitted the recipient needs to have in his possession in advance one bit of key information. Moreover, these bits must be in a random sequence that cannot be used a second time. For large traffic volumes that is a severe restriction. Because of this requirement the Vernam system has usually been reserved for top-secret messages.

To get around the problem of supplying the recipient with large volumes of random key digits in advance, designers and inventors have devised many ingenious schemes for generating very long pseudorandom streams of digits from several short streams according to some algorithm. The recipient of a coded message can then be provided with a generator that operates exactly like the one used to add pseudorandom digits to the original message. An algorithm of course implies systematic routines, which in turn introduce regularities for which an analyst may search.

One basic method for building such a generator is to use two or more key-bit tapes that are added, bit by bit, to yield a compounded stream. For example, the simple one-time tape can be replaced with two tape loops of prime or relative-prime lengths. In this situation the lengths have no common factors and the compounded stream has the length of the product of the component streams: two tapes of lengths 1,000 and 1,001 respectively produce a compounded stream that will not repeat for 1,000 × 1,001, or 1,001,000, digits. The tapes are circulated through an adder that makes a modulo-2 addition of the digits sampled, one from each tape [*see middle illustration on opposite page*]. The output of the adder serves as the key digit for encoding the message. It is therefore important that the compounded stream exceed the length of all the messages one expects to send over a reasonable period of time.

Since any bit-by-bit adder is linear, it is inherently weak, but it can be cryptographically strengthened in any number of ways. One can pile complication on

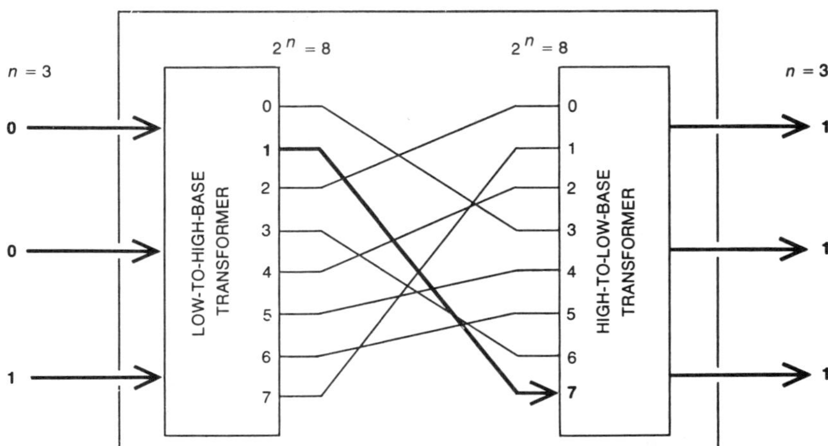

IN	OUT
000	011
001	**111**
010	000
011	110
100	010
101	100
110	101
111	001

SUBSTITUTION BOX, unlike the stream devices, is general, and includes both linear and nonlinear transformations: it does not merely add a 0 or 1 to input digits but can substitute for any input digit block any output digit block. It consists essentially of two switches. One converts a binary number of n digits into a one-digit number base 2^n; the other reconverts. The box therefore provides 2^n internal terminals that can be wired in $n!$ (n factorial, or $1 \times 2 \times 3 \ldots \times n$) different ways; in the case of this box with $n = 3$, that means 40,320 different wirings, or different tableaus like the one illustrated. A box of this kind with $n = 128$ would defeat analysis, but it is not possible to realize technologically.

complication by introducing intricate feedback arrangements, perhaps linked in some fashion to the message, or by introducing such nonlinear mathematical operations as substitutions on digit blocks of suitable size. The nonsecret cryptographic literature contains many fascinating designs for pseudorandom-stream generators, all of which can in principle be reduced to one basic scheme [*see bottom illustration on opposite page*]. One way or another they generate a pseudorandom number by performing complex mathematical operations on some ordered sequence of input numbers, thereby transforming it in a way that is supposed to confound an analyst.

The reader will be surprised and disappointed to learn that the Vernam class of ciphers—the only class that can be proved to be undecipherable in the absolute sense—is not perfect at all in another sense: it does not in itself offer protection against clever deception on nonredundant traffic. Whether a message is encoded by the use of truly random digits or by pseudorandom-stream digits, in bit-by-bit encipherment a single error that arises during transmission is confined to a single digit position; the error does not "propagate," or spread, through the rest of the message. The cipher does not introduce intersymbol dependence. When the message itself is in a "natural" language such as English text, the normal redundancy context makes it easy for a human reader to spot an occasional error. Thus if some of the five binary digits representing the letter *E* were corrupted to turn it into the binary sequence for *F* (so that, for example, SECRET came out SECRFT), a human interpreter would detect the error immediately.

The situation is quite different in a

computer environment. Here the data transmitted may often be nonredundant if, for example, they are purely numerical, and an error in a single digit can cause an avalanche of computational errors. Study of the problem has shown that simple error-detecting codes are inadequate for guarding the integrity of computer data against possible tampering by a human expert. What is required is not mere error-detection but cryptographically protected authentication. Surprisingly, this is best achieved by relying on certain principles inherent in the cipher structure itself. Rather than trying to modify the stream concept, let us take a fresh look at the basis of all cryptography: substitution on blocks of message digits.

We shall refer to any cipher that converts n message digits into n cipher digits as a block cipher. For example, a block cipher would be one that turns 00000, standing for a clear-text *A*, into, say, 11001, the cipher equivalent of *A* according to some permutation key, exactly as a tableau does. To see how such a binary transformation is performed by an electronic device let us consider a substitution on only three binary digits [*see illustration on preceding page*].

Three binary digits can represent eight items: 2^3 equals eight. The substitution device consists of two switches. The first converts a sequence of three binary digits into its corresponding value to the base eight, thereby energizing any one of eight output lines. These eight lines can be connected to the second switch in any one of 8!, or 40,320, ways. We are at liberty to decide which one of these 40,320 distinct connection patterns, or wire permutations, is to be made between the first switch and the second switch. The role of the second switch is to convert the input, presented as one digit to the base eight, back into a three-digit binary output.

If the substitution device were built to handle a five-digit binary input, it could be used to encipher an alphabet of 32 letters. The number of possible connection patterns between the two switches would then be 32!. That would seem to be an incredibly large number of keys, but the cipher produced must still be regarded as glaringly weak: it could not resist letter-frequency analysis. The weakness is not intrinsic; the device described is mathematically the most general possible. It includes, for any given input-output dimension, any possible reversible cipher that has been or ever could be invented; mathematicians would say it represents the full symmetric group. It is completely "nonsystematic": one permutation connection tells an opponent nothing at all about any other connection. The problem is not intrinsic, then, but is related to size. In spite of the large number of keys, the "catalogue" of possible inputs and outputs is too small: only 32. What is required is a catalogue so large that it is impractical for any opponent to record it. If we had a box with 128 inputs and outputs, for example, an analyst would have to cope with 2^{128} (or more than 10^{38}) possible digit blocks, a number so vast that frequency analysis would no longer be feasible. Unfortunately a substitution device with 128 inputs would also require 2^{128} internal terminals between the first and the second switch, a technological impossibility. This is a fundamental dilemma in cryptography. We know what would be ideal but we cannot achieve the ideal in practice.

Perhaps one could find a device that is easy to realize for a large number of inputs. One might, for example, build a box with, say, 128 input and 128 output terminals that are connected internally by ordinary wire crossings [*see illustration at left below*]. Such a "permutation box" with $n!$ terminals would have $n!$ possible wire crossings, each of which could be set by a different key. It could be built easily for $n = 128$. Although this provides a usefully large number of keys (128!), we are now faced with a new difficulty. By the use of special trick messages it is possible to read out the complete key to such a system in only $n - 1$ (in this case 127) trials. The trick

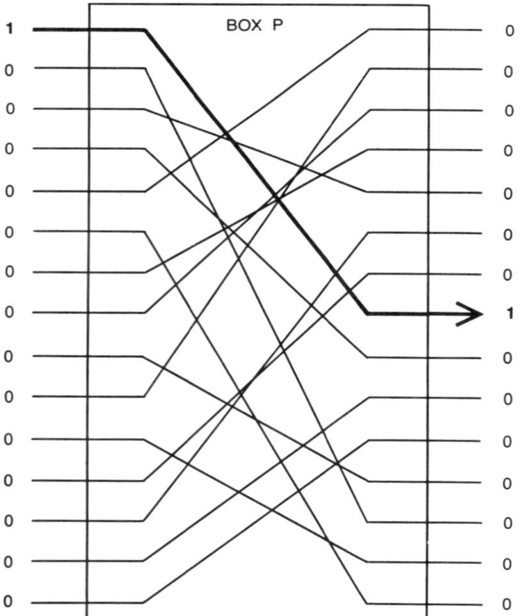

PERMUTATION BOX can handle very many terminals but it only shuffles positions of digits. An opponent can learn its wiring by feeding in inputs with single 1's and seeing where 1's come out.

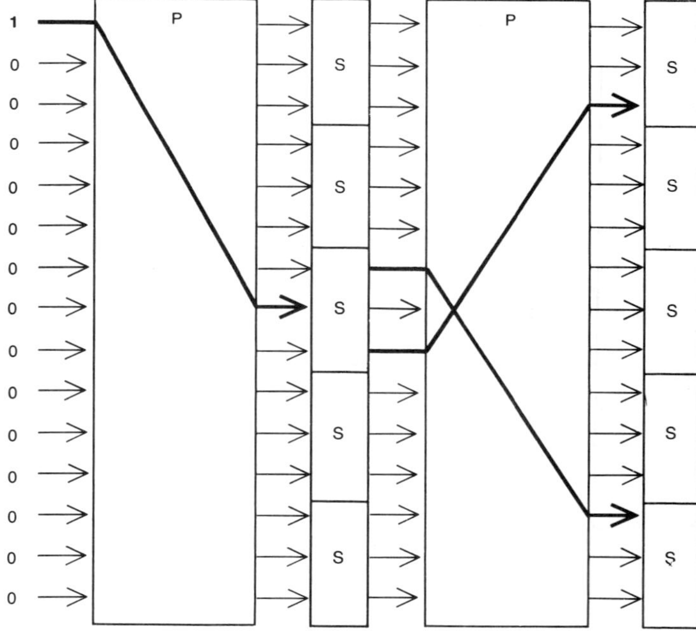

PRODUCT-CIPHER SYSTEM combines *P* boxes and *S* boxes. The *P* boxes have a large number of inputs (represented by 15 in the illustration) and the *S* boxes a number that is manageable for such

is to introduce a series of messages containing a single 1 at $n - 1$ positions; the position of the 1 in the output betrays the particular wire crossing used in the box. The flaw in the simple permutation box is again that it is a linear system.

We need a compromise that will at least approximate the features of the general system. We are led to the notion of a product cipher in which two or more ciphers are combined in such a way that the resulting system is stronger than either of the component systems alone. Even before World War I various cumbersome ciphers using several stages of encipherment were studied. The first genuinely successful example was probably the one devised by the Germans that was known as the ADFGVX system. We need only observe here that it coupled "fractionation" with "transposition." By that procedure a message was broken into segments and the segments were transposed. The important fact to note here is that the result of a product cipher is again a block cipher; the goal, of course, is that the cipher behave as much as possible as if it were a general substitution cipher.

Between World War I and World War II interest in product ciphers almost totally disappeared because of the successful development of rotor, or wired-wheel, machines, which belong to the general class of pseudorandom-stream generators. A typical rotor machine has a keyboard resembling that of a typewriter. Each letter is enciphered by the operation of several wheels in succession, the wheels being given a new alignment for each new letter according to an irregular and keyed stepping algorithm. The message is decoded by an identical machine with an identical key setting.

The modern interest in product systems was stimulated by a paper by Claude E. Shannon titled "Communication Theory of Secrecy Systems," published in the *Bell System Technical Journal* in 1949. In a section on practical cipher design Shannon introduced the notion of "mixing transformation," which involved a special way of using products of transformations. In addition to outlining intuitive guides that he believed would lead to strong ciphers, he introduced the concepts of "confusion" and "diffusion." The paper opened up almost unlimited possibilities to invention, design and research.

The manner in which the principles of confusion and diffusion interact to provide cryptographic strength can be described as follows. We have seen that general substitution cannot be realized for large values of n, say $n = 128$, and so we must settle for a substitution scheme of practical size. In the IBM system named Lucifer we have chosen $n = 4$ for the substitution box. Even though 4 may seem to be a small number, it can be quite effective if the substitution key, or wire-crossing pattern, is properly chosen. In Lucifer nonlinear substitution effectively provides the element of confusion.

We have also seen that a linear permutation box is easy to build even for $n = 128$. The number of input and output terminals is simply equal to n. Being a pure digit-shuffler, a device that merely moves digits around without altering the number of 1's in the data, the permutation box is a natural spreader of confusion, that is, it can provide optimal diffusion.

In the Lucifer system the input data pass through alternating layers of boxes that we can label P and S. P stands for permutation boxes in which n is a large number (64 or 128) and S stands for substitution boxes in which n is small (4). Whereas either P boxes alone or S boxes alone would make a weak system, their strength in combination is considerable.

One measure of strength is depicted in a device in which for simplicity the P boxes have $n = 15$ and the S boxes have $n = 3$ [*see illustration on these two pages*]. If we imagine this sandwich of boxes being "tickled" by addressing it with a specially selected input, which might consist of a number made up of

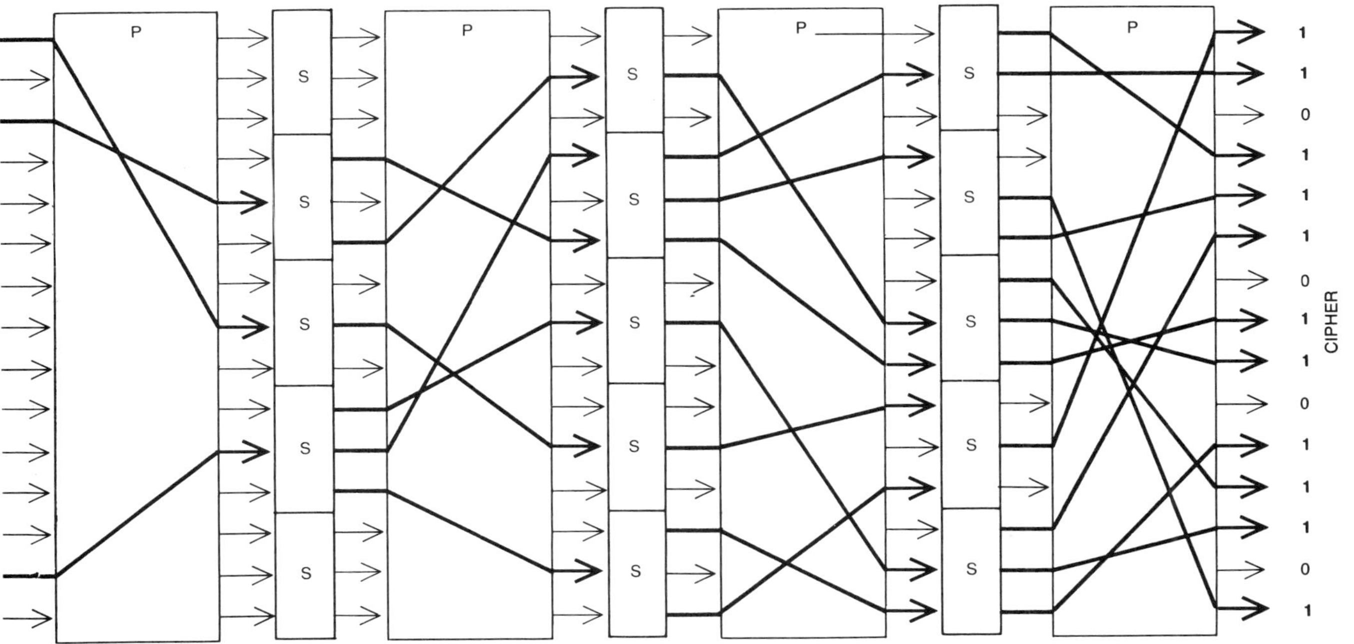

529

devices—three in this case. The *P* boxes shuffle the digits, providing "diffusion." The *S* boxes provide nonlinear substitution and thus "confusion." In this simplified example the input includes a single 1 and 14 0's. Because the *S* boxes are nonlinear, they can potentially increase the number of 1's; meanwhile the *P* boxes move the 1's around. The result can be an unpredictable avalanche of 1's.

14 0's and only a single 1, it is easy to see confusion and diffusion at work. The first box, *P*, moves the single 1 to some box S, which being a nonlinear device may convert the 1 to a three-digit output having as many as three 1's. In the diagram it actually generates two 1's. The next box, *P*, shuffles the two 1's and feeds them into two separate S boxes, which together have the potential of generating as many as six 1's. From here on the diagram is self-explanatory. As the input moves through successive layers the pattern of 1's generated is amplified and results in an unpredictable avalanche. In the end the final output will have, on the average, half 0's and half 1's, depending on the permutation keys chosen for the various *P* and S boxes.

The important fact is that all output digits have potentially become very involved functions of all the input digits. Since all the boxes are independently keyed, the avalanche and its final effect cannot be predicted. The goal of the designer, of course, is to make it very difficult for an opponent to trace the pattern back and thus to reconstruct the permutation keys on S and *P*.

In the actual Lucifer system we found it advisable to introduce a few important changes. For example, box S, being perfectly general, could be accidentally keyed to behave exactly like a *P* box, in which case the entire system would be no better than a single layer of *P*, which could be exposed by tickling. To avoid this result both S and *P* boxes are permanently keyed with permutations that are considered strong; these permanent keys will be known to anyone owning the boxes. Hence we need another keying capability, preferably one that can be represented by a binary number.

This can be accomplished by building a sandwich in which each S box has two different permanent keys and can thus be present in two different possible states, S_0 and S_1. The sequence of these states in any one sandwich constitutes a keyed pattern unknown to a potential opponent. The pattern can be represented by a binary key that in effect says which of two substitution tables is to be used, just as in the case of the two-table substitution discussed earlier [*see illustration below*]. (In the diagram there are 25 S boxes, and so the key is 25 digits long; in an actual device there would be many more S boxes and a correspondingly longer key.) The key digits can be loaded into a key register in the cryptographic device and possibly recorded magnetically in the key card assigned to the authorized user of the system. When two states of the S box are used in this way, the resulting cryptogram exhibits a sensitive intersymbol dependence that makes all output digits complicated functions not only of all message digits but also of all the digits in the key. The concept has so far proved to be resistant to penetration by mathematical analysis.

Although the strong intersymbol dependence is a necessary (but not sufficient) index of cryptographic strength, it has a dark side: it implies great sensitivity to noise or interference during transmission. The corruption of a single digit position can, through the inverse-avalanche effect, result in complete garble at the receiver. Modern communications techniques make the problem less serious, however, at least for nonmilitary uses.

Moreover, the strong interdependence among digits provides a surprising and unexpected windfall. Because the system is so sensitive and so violent in its response to changes, it is automatically an ideal agent for detecting such changes, whether generated by accident or by clever intent. And so we have now simultaneously combined high message secrecy with a tamper-proof alarm for error-detection.

To make use of this automatic feature we need only reserve space for a "password" within a given block of message digits. The password is a sequence of digits fed into the message stream automatically by the sending apparatus and does not concern the person using the system. The role of the password is to tell the receiving apparatus that the message has not been intentionally tampered with or seriously degraded by noise during transmission. The enciphering process keeps the opponent from knowing how message bits and password

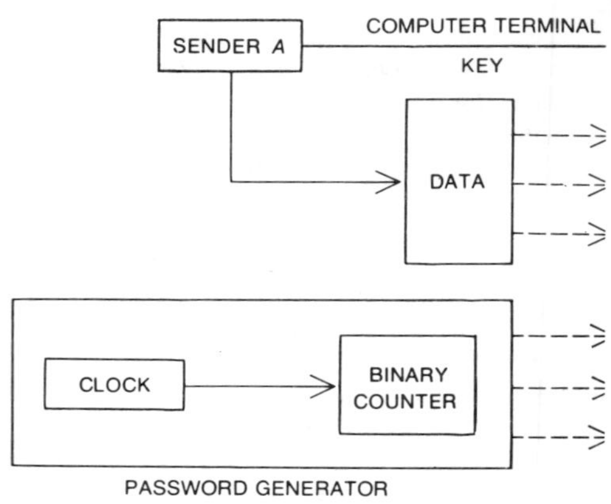

COMPLETE SYSTEM combines a password generator, a cryptographic product system such as the *P* and *S* sandwich in the preceding illustrations and error-correction. The password generator provides a fresh pass-

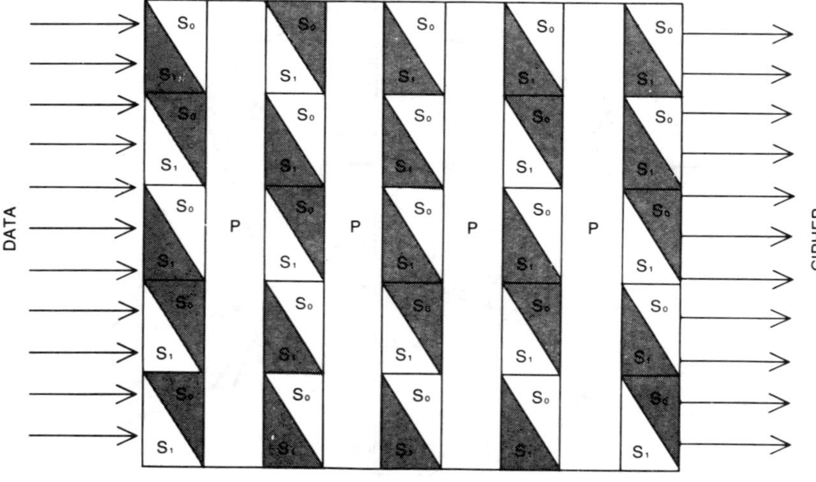

PATTERN OF S_0 AND S_1

S_1 S_0 S_1 S_0 S_0 S_0 S_1 S_0 S_1 S_1 S_1 S_1 S_1 S_0 S_1 S_1 S_0 S_1 S_0 S_1 S_1 S_1 S_0 S_1 S_0

BINARY PATTERN KEY

1 0 1 0 0 0 1 0 1 1 1 1 1 0 1 1 0 1 0 1 1 1 0 1 0

INDIVIDUAL KEYING CAPABILITY is required because the keys built into the *S* and *P* boxes are known to anyone with access to the same system. Individual keying capability can be provided as shown here. At each *S* position in the system there are two possible states, S_1 or S_0. The pattern in which they are intermixed is established by a binary key as shown.

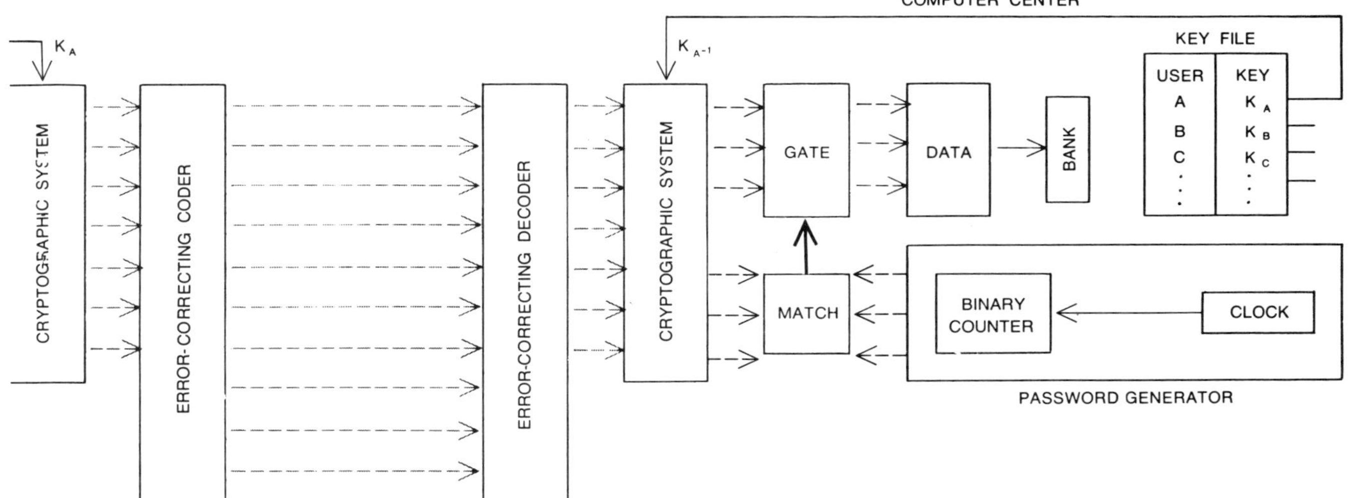

word block (*black dashes*) for each data block. The sender, using his individual key, introduces his data (*colored dashes*). Password and data digits are no longer traceable as such after being enciphered according to the key. Error-correcting digits are introduced and removed after transmission. The cryptographic system at the computer center deciphers the transmission according to the inverse of the sender's key, which has been selected from a secure file in the center, and extracts the password digits. If these match the password generated in the computer, the gate opens and the input data are admitted to the bank as being of legitimate origin.

bits are reflected in the cryptogram. If the password digits cannot be cleanly recovered by the decoder at the receiving end, the message is rejected.

The decisive role in this scheme is played by the password generator, which is required at both the transmitter and the receiver [*see illustration above*]. The password generator is really nothing more than a binary clock or counter that indicates the time or order number of the message in binary notation and combines a sequence of time digits with each block of data digits transmitted. We assume that at some initial time, say 8:00 A.M., the clocks at the two ends of the transmission channel are synchronized to the same stepping frequency.

Now let us see how the "password authentication scheme" provides privacy for the members of a centralized data-bank community who have access to a large central computer. Each member has his own private key, perhaps in the form of a sequence of binary digits recorded magnetically on a card. The keys of all members are listed in a suitably protected form at the central computer. Let us suppose that a member with Key *A* wishes to send a message to the computer. He inserts the card bearing his key in a typewriterlike terminal sitting on his desk, waits a second or two for a signal that the line is free and begins typing his message.

The message is automatically broken up into blocks of data digits (say 64) and combined at each tick of the binary clock with the password (which might also be 64 digits) that corresponds to the output of the clock at that moment. The resulting block of 128 digits is enciphered by its passing through the sandwich of *S* and *P* boxes that thoroughly mix password digits and data digits.

Since the resulting cryptogram is sensitive to transmission errors, it is fortified with an appropriate error-correcting code, which might be matched to the noise characteristics of the telephone line being used. The addition of the code lengthens the password-plus-message block by a few digits. The resulting cipher block is preceded by the address of the sender in the clear and is transmitted to the central computer. When the message arrives, the key *A* belonging to Member *A* is looked up in the listing and the inverse of Key *A* is fed into the decoder to decipher the cryptogram.

The decisive test now is whether or not the cryptogram as received will yield the same password as the one generated locally by the binary clock at the receiver. In the absence of interference, and if the cryptogram was indeed enciphered with Key *A*, the output of the decoder will consist of the data digit block and the password digit block. This is taken as sufficient proof that the cryptogram did in fact originate with Member *A*. The data are accepted as being of legitimate origin.

What happens if there is interference? If it is nothing more than sporadic bursts of noise on the transmission line, the error-correcting code will eliminate it and the message will pass the authentication test. If, however, the errors are of such a nature that they are not eliminated by the error-correcting code, even one false digit will produce an avalanche effect in the decoder and will garble the output. The passwords will no longer match. The system regards the cryptogram as being of suspicious origin and rejects the communication.

The password test would function just as reliably if someone were to record an intercepted communication and were to retransmit it when the password was no longer valid. The use of a false key, of course, is an instant cause for rejection. The system appears to be proof against any imaginable attempt to deceive it. Each binary digit invested in the password provides one bit of authentication information. If the password is n digits long, an opponent has only one chance in 2^n (or one chance in 2^{64} if $n = 64$) of generating by any means he may select a cryptogram that on decipherment will yield a password that is accidentally correct. The number 2^{64} is equal to about 10^{19}. It is not possible to authenticate more efficiently.

There is no reason why the security system described for a single link could not be expanded to provide security for all users of a network. Other cryptographic approaches are still being studied in our laboratory and elsewhere. It would be surprising if cryptography, the traditional means of ensuring confidentiality in communication, could not provide privacy for a community of data-bank users.

A NEW COMPUTER CRYPTOGRAPHY: THE EXPANDED CHARACTER SET (ECS) CIPHER

Wesley W. Chu and Charlie E. Neat
University of California
Los Angeles, California

Invited Paper

Abstract

As computer systems grow in their usage, the problem of privacy protection becomes increasingly important. This paper presents a new cryptographic technique, the ECS Cipher, for the privacy protection of programs and data in computer systems. The ECS Cipher is a new multisubstitution cipher that provides each cipher user with the capability of controlling the privacy protection for his programs and data. The algorithm for generating the ECS Cipher is presented and its implementation is described. The performance of the ECS Cipher and the costs incurred by both cipher user and intruder are discussed. An example of the ECS Cipher cost/performance for privacy protection of English clear text is given.

1. INTRODUCTION

The need for computer services has been growing rapidly. Large multi-user computer centers or computer utilities have been developed to provide these services. These centers process large amounts of proprietory data such as, manufacturing processes, marketing strategies, salary rates, and company financial status.[1] Thus, privacy protection becomes one of the most important issues now confronting computer science.

At present when users submit programs and data to the computer centers, responsibility for the privacy protection is relegated entirely to the centers. In most centers, privacy protection consists of physical security only. As a result, users have been demanding more effective protection systems and ways to measure the performance of these systems.

Non-linear pseudo-random shift registers that are used to provide perfect secrecy in many secure communications systems are seldom used for privacy protection in computer centers because of their degradation of computer performance.[2] Moreover, these devices are complex, expensive and require precise external synchronization.[3,4,5]

A few computer centers have implemented cipher systems for privacy protection that have been developed from methods used for secret writing. Most of these cipher systems are designed to mask or break down the statistical characteristics of clear text characters such as, frequency of single letters, digrams, trigrams, vowel percentages, etc. A major drawback of these systems has been their inability to provide privacy protection for large amounts of data.[6,7]

An "ideal" cipher for privacy protection in computer systems must have the following characteristics: Intruder cost performance ratio must be sufficiently high to deter potential intruders, cipher user cost performance ratio must be sufficiently low to make the cipher acceptable to each user, reduction in computer system performance (due to cipher) must be minimal, and each user should be able to select the amount of privacy protection he desires. In this paper we shall present a new cipher, the ECS Cipher[8], that has these characteristics.

We shall first describe Multisubstitution (MS)

Cipher and the ECS Cipher and their encipherments (the transformation of clear text to cipher text). Next, we present the decipherment (the transformation of cipher text to clear text using a secret formula or key) and implementation of the ECS Cipher. Finally, we present the decryption process (the transformation of cipher text to clear text without using a secret formula or key) and cost performance of the ECS Cipher.

2. ENCIPHERMENT AND DECIPHERMENT

2.1 MULTISUBSTITUTION CIPHER[9,10]

A Multisubstitution (MS) Cipher is one in which the number of Distinct Cipher Text Characters (DSTC) exceeds the number of Distinct Clear Text Characters (DKTC) in the source language alphabet. Thus, one or more DSTC are assigned to each DKTC.

MS encipherment is a two-step process as follows: 1) a DSTC subset is assigned to each DKTC and 2) the DSTC within each subset are randomly substituted for the corresponding DKTC in the clear text. Figure 1 represents a portion of an MS encipherment array produced by the first step of the encipherment process. DKTC are designated by capital letters at the tops of the columns. DSTC are the Arabic numerals representing array elements. Rows are designated by Roman numerals for convenience.

For example, in Figure 1, DSTC symbols 9 and 8 have been assigned to DKTC symbol A. The number of DSTC assigned to each DKTC is approximately proportional to the relative frequency of occurrence of each DKTC. Further, the DSTC are selected randomly without replacement from an ensemble of available DSTC for assignment to the DKTC.

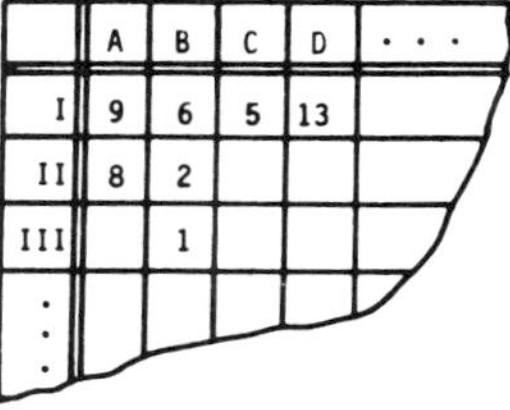

	A	B	C	D	. . .
I	9	6	5	13	
II	8	2			
III		1			
⋮					

Figure 1. A Portion of an MS Encipherment Array.

The second step of the MS encipherment process consists of random substitution of the DSTC for DKTC in the clear text. Using the DKTC and DSTC shown in Figure 1, we prepared an eighty character clear text sample from which we generated a cipher text sample for MS encipherment (Figure 2).

DKTC and DSTC n^{th}-order probabilities and frequencies can be represented in matrix form. Given an alphabet containing t distinct clear text characters, we let I^{th}, J^{th}, K^{th},... be used interchangeably to designate DKTC, where $1 \leq I,J,K,\ldots \leq t$. Let P_I and P_J be the zeroth-order probabilities that the Ith DKTC and the Jth DKTC are in a clear text sample respectively. Let $P_{I;J}$, an element of a two-dimensional matrix [P], denote the first-order probability that the Ith DKTC is followed by the Jth DKTC. In the same manner, higher-order probabilities are represented by using higher-

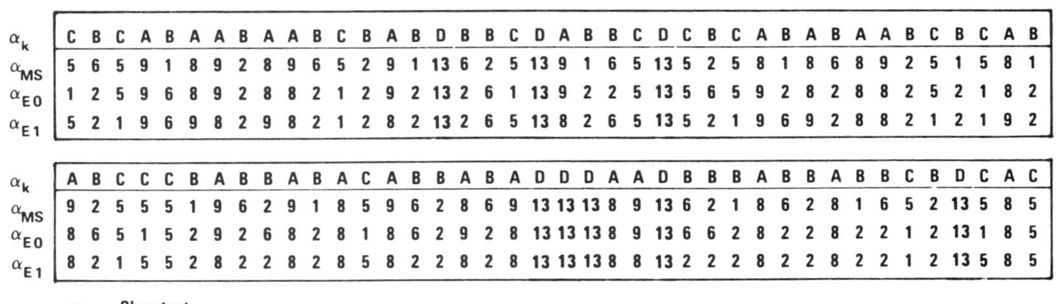

α_k	C	B	C	A	B	A	A	B	A	A	B	C	B	A	B	D	B	B	C	D	A	B	B	C	D	C	B	C	A	B	A	B	A	A	B	C	B	C	A	B
α_{MS}	5	6	5	9	1	8	9	2	8	9	6	5	2	9	1	13	6	2	5	13	9	1	6	5	13	5	2	5	8	1	8	6	8	9	2	5	1	5	8	1
α_{E0}	1	2	5	9	6	8	9	2	8	8	2	1	2	9	2	13	2	6	1	13	9	2	2	5	13	5	6	5	9	2	8	2	8	8	2	5	2	1	8	2
α_{E1}	5	2	1	9	6	9	8	2	9	8	2	1	2	8	2	13	2	6	5	13	8	2	6	5	13	5	2	1	9	6	9	2	8	8	2	1	2	1	9	2

α_k	A	B	C	C	C	B	A	B	B	A	B	A	C	A	B	B	A	B	A	D	D	D	A	A	D	B	B	B	A	B	B	A	B	B	C	B	D	C	A	C
α_{MS}	9	2	5	5	5	1	9	6	2	9	1	8	5	9	6	2	8	6	9	13	13	13	8	9	13	6	2	1	8	6	2	8	1	6	5	2	13	5	8	5
α_{E0}	8	6	5	1	5	2	9	2	6	8	2	8	1	8	6	2	9	2	8	13	13	13	8	9	13	6	6	2	8	2	2	8	2	2	1	2	13	1	8	5
α_{E1}	8	2	1	5	5	2	8	2	2	8	2	8	5	8	2	2	8	2	8	13	13	13	8	8	13	2	2	2	8	2	2	8	2	2	1	2	13	5	8	5

α_k Clear text
α_{MS} Cipher text for MS encipherment
α_{E0} Cipher text for zeroth-order ECS encipherment
α_{E1} Cipher text for first-order ECS encipherment

Figure 2. Clear Text and Cipher Text Samples.

dimensional matrices. For example, $P_{I;J;K}$ is an element of a three-dimensional matrix [P] that denotes the second-order probability that the Ith DKTC is followed by the Jth DKTC which is followed by the Kth DKTC. Likewise, n^{th}-order probabilities are denoted as $P_{\underbrace{I;J;K;\ldots}_{n+1}}$ which are elements of an n+1 dimensional space.

When an nth-order probability matrix is multiplied by the total number of characters N_c in the clear text sample, an nth-order frequency matrix [F] is obtained:

$$[F] = [P] \cdot N_c$$

F_I and F_J represent the zeroth-order frequencies of the Ith and J^{th} DKTC symbols in the clear text sample respectively. $F_{I;J}$ is an element of a two-dimensional matrix [F] that denotes the first-order frequency of the Ith DKTC followed by the Jth DKTC. In the same manner as the [P] matrix, higher-order frequencies are represented by using higher-dimensional matrices.

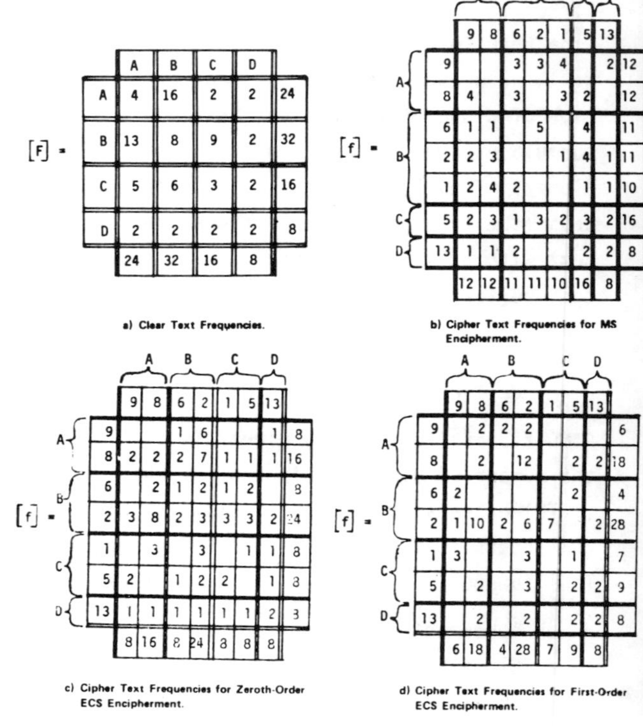

a) Clear Text Frequencies.

b) Cipher Text Frequencies for MS Encipherment.

c) Cipher Text Frequencies for Zeroth-Order ECS Encipherment.

d) Cipher Text Frequencies for First-Order ECS Encipherment.

Figure 3. Clear Text and Cipher Text Frequencies for the Example.

Zeroth- and first-order frequencies of the DKTC sequences (Figure 2) are contained in the [F] matrix (Figure 3a). The sum of the array elements in any row or column (Figure 3a) is the zeroth-order frequency of the DKTC designating that row or column. For example, the number 4 is the first-order frequency of the DKTC pair (A,A), and the number 24 at the margin of the row labeled A or the column labeled A is the zeroth-order frequency of the DKTC symbol A.

The [F] matrix (Figure 3a) has been expanded into the [f] matrix (Figure 3b) by using MS encipherment. This [f] matrix contains the zeroth- and first order frequencies of the DSTC sequences produced by the expansion. For example, the number 5 is the first-order frequency for the DSTC pair (6,2). The number 11 at the margin of the row labeled 6 and the number 11 at the margin of the column labeled 2 are the zeroth-order frequencies of the DSTC symbols 6 and 2 respectively. The sum of the nth-order frequencies of the DSTC sequences are equal to the nth-order frequency of the corresponding DKTC sequence. For example, in Figure 3b, the sum of the first-order frequencies 3, 3, 4, 3, and 3 at the intersections of rows labeled 9 and 8 with columns labeled 6, 2, and 1 is equal to 16 which corresponds to the first-order frequency of DKTC pair (A,B) in Figure 3a.

The expansion ratio ER is defined as the ratio of the total number of DSTC to the total number of DKTC. The ER for Figure 3b equals 7/4. Since three bits are needed to represent the seven DSTC and two bits are required to represent the four DKTC, the cost of base 2 representation for cipher text is 50% more than for clear text. Further, ER = 7/4 does not provide a sufficient number of DSTC to suppress all DKTC zeroth-order frequency deviations. For example, DSTC symbol 5 can be identified as belonging to DKTC symbol C because of the unique correlation of zeroth-order frequencies. In order to suppress all DKTC zeroth-order frequency deviations in this eighty character clear text sample, we would assign ten (instead of seven) DSTC to the four DKTC in numbers corresponding to the zeroth-order frequencies of the DKTC. The number of DSTC assigned to each DKTC would be 1, 2, 3, and 4; and each of the zeroth-order DSTC frequencies would be equal to 8. Distribution of the four DKTC zeroth-order frequencies between the ten DSTC in this way would cause the base 2 representation cost of the cipher text to be 100% more than for the clear text. If suppression of all DKTC n^{th}-order frequency deviations is required, the number of DSTC must be equal to the total number of clear text characters being enciphered. Therefore, this eighty character clear text sample requires eighty DSTC for the suppression of all DKTC n^{th}-order frequency deviations, and the base 2 representation cost is 250% more than for the clear text.

When the number of DSTC assigned to DKTC is equal to the number of characters in the clear text, a full expansion is being used. For example, a 2000 character sample of English clear text consisting of 26 DKTC needs 2000 DSTC to suppress all DKTC n^{th}-order frequency deviations. Eleven binary bits are required to represent the 2000 DSTC, while 5 binary bits suffice for the 26 DKTC. This constitutes a 120% increase in base 2 representation cost.

MS encipherment is based on the concept of distributing the DKTC n^{th}-order frequencies between large numbers of DSTC so that the DKTC frequency deviations can no longer be identified. When large numbers of clear text characters are being enciphered and the suppression of DKTC higher-order frequency deviations is required, base 2 representation of the cipher text produced by MS encipherment becomes too costly. To provide a cipher that is more economical than MS Cipher and more difficult to decrypt, especially for small ER values, we shall present the ECS Cipher in the next section.

2.2 THE ECS CIPHER

The basic concept of ECS encipherment is to: 1) utilize a relatively small DSTC ensemble to partially suppress DKTC n^{th}-order frequency deviations in the cipher text (this DSTC ensemble is the expanded character set and its size determines the expansion ratio), and 2) utilize DSTC n^{th}-order probabilities to control the random substitution of DSTC for DKTC in the clear text. This control of the random substitution suppresses the DKTC n^{th}-order frequency deviations that remain in the cipher text.

Let $f_{I,i}$ be the ith DSTC zeroth-order frequency of the Ith DKTC. Figure 2 shows a cipher text sample obtained from the clear text sample by using zeroth-order ECS encipherment. The DSTC zeroth-order probabilities used to control the generation of the cipher text sample were derived from the $f_{I,i}$'s shown in Figure 3c.

In ECS encipherment, the following questions must be answered: 1) For a given expansion ratio, what is the size of each DSTC subset assigned to each DKTC that will provide the maximum suppression of the DKTC n^{th}-order frequency deviations? and 2) For suppression of the remaining n^{th}-order DKTC frequency deviations in the cipher text, what are the required DSTC probabilities? An algorithm is developed to answer the above two questions and we shall call it the ECS Algorithm.

Let us describe the ECS Algorithm used to suppress DKTC zeroth-order frequency deviations. Rearrange the set of F_I into ascending order according to the value of each F_I and affix a second subscript r to denote the position of each F_I in the rearranged sequence $F_{I:r}$ for I = 1, 2, ..., t and r = 1,2,...,t, where t is the number of DKTC in the source language alphabet. Using this $F_{I:r}$ sequence, we obtain a sequence of normalized DKTC zeroth-order frequencies, $\hat{F}_{I:r}$, by dividing each term of the $F_{I:r}$ sequence by the first term $F_{I:1}$ and rounding the quotients to the nearest integer.*

*When the range of $F_{I:r}$ values is large and a small expansion ratio is required, we must partition the $F_{I:r}$ sequence into sections before performing the normalization for each section. The ECS Algorithm is then applied to each section separately.

In the example (Figure 3a), $F_{4:1} = 8$. Then the $\hat{F}_{I:r}$ sequence for I = 1,2,...,4 and r = 1,2,...4 is:

$$\hat{F}_{4:1} = 1,\ \hat{F}_{3:2} = 2,\ \hat{F}_{1:3} = 3,\ \hat{F}_{2:4} = 4$$

As we will show, the ECS Algorithm uses the $\hat{F}_{I:r}$ sequence to generate an expanded sequence of normalized DSTC zeroth-order frequencies, $\hat{f}_{I,i:r}$, which is then used to determine the $f_{I,i}$'s. We call every DSTC with a $\hat{f}_{I,i:r}$ equal to one a <u>Similis DSTC</u>. Every DSTC with a $\hat{f}_{I,i:r}$ greater than one is a <u>Summa DSTC</u>. There is at most one Summa DSTC assigned to each DKTC. The normalized zeroth-order frequency of a Summa DSTC can be the sum of the normalized zeroth-order frequencies of two or more Similis DSTC or a combination of Similis DSTC and other Summa DSTC. These relationships also apply to the $f_{I,i}$'s. For example, in Figure 3c, $f_{1,1} = f_{2,1} = f_{3,1} = f_{3,2} = f_{4,1} = 8$ are zeroth-order frequencies of Similis DSTC, while $f_{1,2} = 16 = f_{3,1} + f_{3,2}$ and $f_{2,2} = 24 = f_{1,1} + f_{1,2}$ are zeroth-order frequencies of Summa DSTC.

Let N_I be the number of DSTC assigned to the Ith DKTC. N_I can be determined from the $\hat{F}_{I:r}$ sequence as follows:

$$N_I = \begin{cases} \hat{F}_{I:r} - \hat{F}_{(\cdot):r-g} + 1 & \text{for } r > g \\ \hat{F}_{I:r} & \text{for } r \leq g \end{cases} \quad (1)$$

where r = 1,2,...,t and g = 1,2,...,t-1. $\hat{F}_{(\cdot):r-g}$ is the normalized zeroth-order frequency of the $(r-g)^{th}$ DKTC in the rearranged sequence. We use g to select the DKTC that provides the sum(s) of the DSTC zeroth-order frequencies that suppress the remaining DKTC zeroth-order frequency deviations in the cipher text. When g = 1, the smallest expanded character set is produced and when g = t-1 the largest expanded character set (full expansion) is obtained. We know that the $\hat{F}_{I:r}$ sequence is a monotonically increasing function of r, and the normalized zeroth-order frequency of every Similis DSTC is equal to 1. The term $\hat{F}_{I:r} - \hat{F}_{(\cdot):r-g} + 1$ in equation (1) is the number of DSTC assigned to the rth DKTC. All of these DSTC are Similis DSTC or all are Similis DSTC except one which is a Summa DSTC. If the Summa DSTC is present, its zeroth-order frequency is equal to the $(r-g)^{th}$ DKTC zeroth-order frequency. For $r \leq g$, all the DSTC are Similis DSTC. Therefore $N_I = \hat{F}_{I:r}$. Thus, we can use g, which determines the expansion ratio, to control the level of privacy protection.

Using the F_I values from Figure 3a and applying equation (1) with g = 1, we obtain the number of DSTC assigned to each DKTC in Figure 3c:

$$N_4 = 1,\ N_3 = 2,\ N_1 = 2,\ N_2 = 2$$

Therefore, one DSTC is assigned to DKTC symbol D and two DSTC are assigned to each of the DKTC symbols A, B, and C. A DSTC assignment occurs when a DSTC subset is assigned to a DKTC. If a DSTC subset has been assigned to each of the DKTC, we say that a DSTC ensemble assignment has been obtained. The encipherment array for this example (Figure 4) represents a DSTC ensemble assignment. The DSTC within the array are selected randomly without replacement from an available DSTC ensemble.

	A	B	C	D
I	9	6	1	13
II	8	2	5	

Figure 4. ECS Encipherment Array for the Example.

Now we show how to generate the normalized sequence of DSTC zeroth-order frequencies, $\hat{f}_{I,i:r}$, corresponding to the $\hat{F}_{I:r}$ sequence:

$$\hat{f}_{I,i:r} = \begin{cases} \hat{F}_{I:r} - N_I + 1 & \text{for } i = N_I \\ 1 & \text{for } i < N_I \end{cases} \quad (2)$$

In equation (2) if the term $\hat{F}_{I:r} - N_I + 1$ is greater than one, it is the Summa DSTC zeroth-order frequency of the N_I^{th} DSTC of the Ith DKTC; otherwise, the term is the zeroth-order frequency of a Similis DSTC which is equal to one. The $\hat{f}_{I,i:r}$ are Similis DSTC zeroth-order frequencies and equal to one for $i < N_I$.

Using the normalized sequence $\hat{F}_{I:r}$ and the N_I values computed with equation (1), we can apply equation (2) to generate the $\hat{f}_{I,i:r}$ sequence:

$$\hat{f}_{4,1:1} = 1,\ \hat{f}_{3,1:2} = 1,\ \hat{f}_{3,2:2} = 1,$$
$$\hat{f}_{1,1:3} = 1,\ \hat{f}_{1,2:3} = 2,\ \hat{f}_{2,1:4} = 1,$$
$$\hat{f}_{2,2:4} = 3$$

After obtaining the $\hat{f}_{I,i:r}$ we can delete the r subscript because the rearrangement order is no longer needed. To remove the normalization, we multiply $\hat{f}_{I,i}$ by $F_{4:1} = 8$. The resulting $f_{I,i}$'s are the DSTC zeroth-order frequencies as shown in Figure 3c. Two of many possible DSTC ensemble assignments are shown in Table 1. The first assignment has been used for the example; the second assignment was obtained from the first assignment by transposing $f_{2,2}$ with $f_{1,1}$ and $f_{1,2}$. Note the sums of the $f_{I,i}$'s for each DKTC in the two different assignments remain the same even though the partition sizes differ for the DKTC symbols A and B.

Table 1. Two DSTC Ensemble Assignments.

First assignment						Second assignment					
I	i	DKTC	DSTC	N_I	$f_{I,i}$	I	i	DKTC	DSTC	N_I	$f_{I,i}$
1	1	A	9	2	8	1	1	A	9	1	24
	2		8		16	2	1	B	8	3	8
2	1	B	6	2	8		2		6		8
	2		2		24		3		2		16
3	1	C	1	2	8	3	1	C	1	2	8
	2		5		8		2		5		8
4	1	D	13	1	8	4	1	D	13	1	8

The zeroth-order probabilities of the $(I,i)^{th}$ DSTC, $P_{I,i}$, can be computed from the $f_{I,i}$'s as follows:

$$P_{I,i} = f_{I,i} \Big/ \sum_i f_{I,i} \qquad \text{for all } I,i \qquad (3)$$

These are the $P_{I,i}$'s used for control of the substitution of DSTC for DKTC. The $P_{I,i}$'s used for the example are shown in Figure 5. For example, $P_{1,1} = 1/3$ was obtained by dividing $f_{1,1} = 8$ by $f_{1,1} + f_{1,2} = 8 + 16 = 24$.

	A	B	C	D
I	1/3	1/4	1/2	1
II	2/3	3/4	1/2	0

Figure 5. DSTC Probability Array for Zeroth-Order ECS Encipherment for the Example.

When the DSTC in the encipherment array (Figure 4) are substituted for the respective DKTC according to their probabilities (Figure 5), we obtain the cipher text sample for zeroth-order ECS encipherment (Figure 2). Equations (1), (2), and (3) constitute the ECS Algorithm for the suppression of DKTC zeroth-order frequency deviations.

In the same manner as above, we have developed the ECS Algorithm for the suppression of DKTC first-order frequency deviations. The DSTC first-order frequencies, $f_{I,i;J,j}$, for the example as shown in Figure 3d, were obtained with the first-order ECS Algorithm. The four DSTC probability arrays for the first-order ECS encipherment were obtained as shown in Figure 6. According to the immediately preceding DKTC in the clear text sequence, we select the probability array to be used for enciphering the next DKTC. When the DSTC in the encipherment array (Figure 4) are substituted for each respective DKTC according to the probabilities (Figure 6) specified by its preceding DKTC, we obtain the cipher text sample for first-order ECS encipherment (Figure 2).

A	A	B	C	D
I	1	1/8	0	1
II	0	7/8	1	0

C	A	B	C	D
I	3/5	0	0	1
II	2/5	1	1	0

B	A	B	C	D
I	3/13	1/4	7/9	1
II	10/13	3/4	2/9	0

D	A	B	C	D
I	0	0	0	1
II	1	1	1	0

• The preceding DKTC

Figure 6. DSTC Probability Arrays for First-Order ECS Encipherment for the Example.

The formulations of the ECS Algorithm for suppression of second- and higher-order DKTC frequency deviations are similar to equations (1), (2), and (3) for suppression of DKTC zeroth-order frequency deviations.

DSTC substitution can be controlled in several ways by using the DSTC probability arrays. One technique is to compute and store probability arrays for as many different orders as required. We then partition the clear text into many sections. For each of these sections, we use the probabilities computed for one of the different orders to control the random substitution of DSTC for DKTC.

2.3 ECS DECIPHERMENT

Authorized recovery of clear text from cipher text is performed with a decipherment array which can be obtained from the ECS encipherment array. The ECS decipherment array for the example is shown in Figure 7. DSTC are designated by Arabic numerals at the tops of the columns. DKTC are the capital letters representing array elements. Decipherment consists of using a DSTC to select an array element which contains the corresponding DKTC.

1	2	5	6	8	9	13
C	B	C	B	A	A	D

Figure 7. ECS Decipherment Array for the Example.

3. IMPLEMENTATION OF THE ECS CIPHER

The ECS Cipher can be implemented at interfaces within a computer system. A functional block diagram of the ECS Cipher unit is shown in Figure 8.

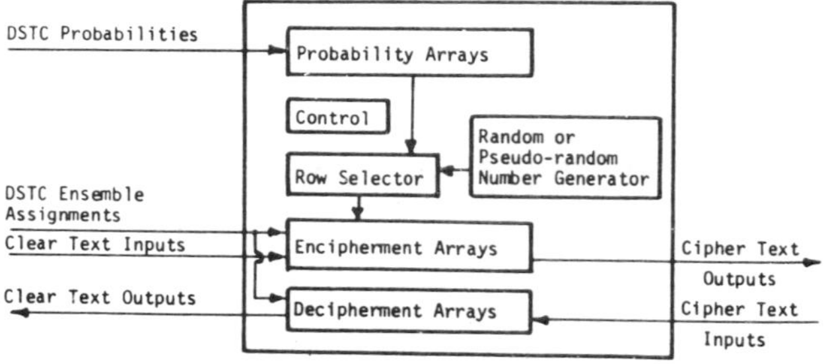

Figure 8. The ECS Cipher Unit.

The ECS Cipher unit provides parallel operations for simultaneous encipherment and decipherment. The DSTC ensemble assignment is determined during the first step of ECS encipherment and stored in computer memory. This DSTC ensemble assignment is read into the ECS Cipher unit to produce the encipherment and decipherment arrays. DSTC probabilities are computed during the second step of the ECS encipherment and stored in computer memory. These probabilities are then read into the probability arrays in the ECS Cipher unit as required and used to control the random substitution of DSTC for DKTC in the clear text. The DSTC ensemble assignment and the DSTC probabilities are erased from computer memory at job termination time. However, prior to job termination the DSTC ensemble assignment and the DSTC probabilities may be secured by the user for future use. These procedures are necessary to prevent intruders from gaining access to the DSTC ensemble assignment and/or DSTC probabilities. In multiprogrammed computer systems separate probability arrays, encipherment arrays, and decipherment arrays are provided for all jobs in the system. The clear text input (or cipher text input) is the programs and data input to the ECS Cipher unit for encipherment (or decipherment).

The Control function provides the array selection logic, the timing, and the control signals for the ECS Cipher unit. The Random or Pseudo-random Number Generator produces random numbers for selecting DSTC to be substituted for DKTC in the clear text. Using DSTC probabilities, the row selector partitions the output range of the Random or Pseudo-random Number Generator to obtain DSTC selections.

4. DECRYPTION OF THE ECS CIPHER

To evaluate the ECS Cipher cost/performance, a decryption program was developed. This program can be used to decrypt ECS cipher text that retains statistical properties of the clear text from which the cipher text was generated.

Let {S} represent the ensemble of m distinct cipher text characters used to produce the cipher text. Let us partition {S} into t disjoint subsets $\{s\}_I$ for I = 1,2,...,t; such that

$$\left| \{s\}_I \subset \{S\}, \forall I \,\middle|\, \bigcap_{I=1}^{t} \{s\}_I = \emptyset \right|$$

where $\{s\}_I$ contains m_I distinct cipher text characters for I = 1,2,...,t. Then, the total number of DSTC is:

$$m = \sum_{I=1}^{t} m_I \quad \text{and} \quad 1 \leq m_I \leq F_I'$$

where F_I' is the zeroth-order frequency of the Ith DKTC in the clear text sample used for decryption.

Let us denote the qth character in the subset $\{s\}_I$ as $\xi_{I,q}$ for $1 \leq q \leq m_I$. In the same manner, we denote the hth character in the clear text alphabet $\{K\}$ as k_h for $1 \leq h \leq t$; such that

$$\left| k_h \subset \{K\}, \forall h \middle| \bigcap_{h=1}^{t} k_h = \emptyset \right| .$$

ECS encipherment assigns an $\{s\}_I$ to each k_h for $I = 1,2,\ldots,t$ and $h = 1,2,\ldots,t$.

A DSTC ensemble assignment performed for decryption purposes is called a DSTC ensemble trial assignment. The total number of DSTC ensemble trial assignments M for an alphabet containing t distinct clear text characters is:

$$M=\binom{m}{m_1}\binom{m-m_1}{m_2}\binom{m-m_1-m_2}{m_3}\cdots\binom{m-m_1-\cdots-m_{t-1}}{m_t} \qquad (4)$$

where $m_I = 1,2,\ldots,F'_I$ for $I = 1,2,\ldots,t$.

The Ith term in equation (4) is the number of possible subsets $\{s\}_I$ that can be assigned to a particular k_h given that subsets $\{s\}_1, \{s\}_2, \ldots, \{s\}_{h-1}$ have already been assigned to $k_1, k_2, \ldots, k_{h-1}$ respectively. For the special case of substitution cipher, $m_I = 1$ for all I, m = t, and M = t!.

When an ECS encipherment array is produced, we say that a DSTC ensemble assignment is obtained. This DSTC ensemble assignment is one of the M possible DSTC ensemble trial assignments specified by equation (4) and consists of selecting each m_I for $1 \leq m_I \leq F'_I$, and assigning the particular $\xi_{I,q}$'s to form $\{s\}_I$ for $I = 1,2,\ldots,t$ and $q = 1,2,\ldots,m_I$. The intruder's decryption task is to determine which DSTC ensemble assignment from the M possible DSTC ensemble trial assignments was used to produce the ECS encipherment array. When the DSTC ensemble assignment is known, the decryption task is complete because all DSTC are identified.

Let an nth-order $k_{a,b}$ sequence be a string of n+1 characters (for n>0) taken one-by-one with order preserved from a clear text sample and consisting of $\{k_a, k_b\} \subset \{k\}_\rho \subset \{K\}$ for $a \neq b$ and $1 \leq a \leq t$ and $1 \leq b \leq t$, where $\{k\}_\rho$ is the set of DKTC with unidentified DSTC. In a similar manner, let an nth-order $\{s\}_{x,y}$ sequence be a string of n+1 characters (for n>0) taken one-by-one with order preserved from a cipher text sample and consisting of $\left|\xi_{x,u} \subset \{s\}_x, \xi_{y,v} \subset \{s\}_y\right| \subset \{s\}_\rho \subset \{S\}$ for $x \neq y$, $1 \leq x \leq t$, $1 \leq y \leq t$, $1 \leq u \leq m_x$ and $1 \leq v \leq m_y$, where $\{s\}_\rho$ is the set of unidentified DSTC.

Let F'_a and F'_b be the zeroth-order frequencies of k_a and k_b respectively in the clear text sample used for decryption. Likewise, in the cipher text sample used for decryption, let $f'_{x,u}$ and $f'_{y,v}$ be the zeroth-order frequencies of $\xi_{x,u}$ and $\xi_{y,v}$ respectively. Then the decryption procedure consists of correlating all n^{th}-order $k_{a,b}$ sequences containing the known $\{k_a, k_b\} \subset \{k\}_\rho$ with all the nth-order $\{s\}_{x,y}$ sequences containing unidentified $\left|\{s\}_x, \{s\}_y\right| \subset \{s\}_\rho$ for all $x \neq y$ where $1 \leq m_x \leq F'_a$ and $\sum_{u=1}^{m_x} f'_{x,u} = F'_a$, and $1 \leq m_y \leq F'_b$ and $\sum_{v=1}^{m_y} f'_{y,v} = F'_b$.

An $\{s\}_a$ is identified as belonging to a k_a when the $\{s\}_a$'s n^{th}-order $\{s\}_{a,y}$ sequences correlate most closely with the nth-order $k_{a,b}$ sequences used for decryption.

Notice that this sequential decryption of DKTC uses only a small fraction of the possible DSTC ensemble trial assignments specified by equation (4). This reduction is made possible because the DKTC are processed in pairs rather than all at once. This pairwise processing decrypts the DKTC one at a time and is the basic concept of the decryption process. When the encipherment order is equal to n, the required order of decryption to obtain the DSTC ensemble assignment is n+1. For example, if a zeroth-order ECS encipherment has been performed, the intruder must use first-order decryption to determine the DSTC ensemble assignment.

The functional block diagram for the ECS Cipher decryption process is shown in Figure 9. A sequential decision policy is used to determine the DKTC processing sequence that minimizes the expected decryption cost. The cipher text sample provides the nth-order $\{s\}_{x,y}$ sequences used for correlation with the nth-order $k_{a,b}$ sequences. The clear text sample, which is semantically unrelated to the cipher text sample, is the property of the intruder and provides the $k_{a,b}$ sequences. The order of decryption D is used by the intruder to specify the length of the $k_{a,b}$ sequences. $[P]_0$ is the initial zeroth-order DKTC probabilities obtained from published tables or from controlled observations of DKTC statistical behavior. The initial expansion ratio ER_0 is determined by dividing the number of DSTC in the cipher text sample by the number of DKTC in the clear text sample (same size as the cipher text sample).

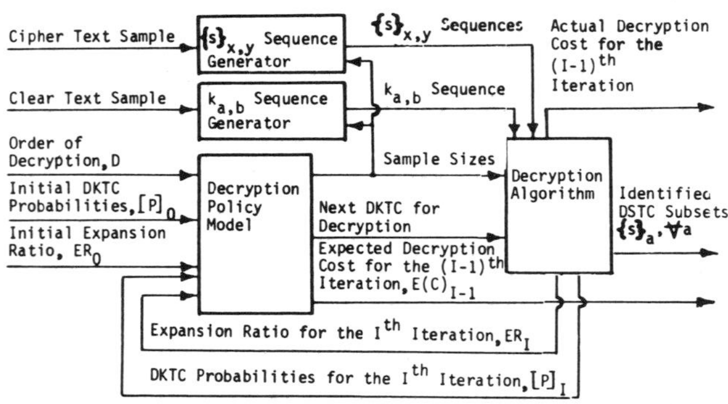

Figure 9. Decryption of the ECS Cipher.

On the first iteration, based on the value of $[P]_0$, ER_0, and D, the Decryption Policy Model* computes the cipher text sample sizes required to produce the nth-order $\{s\}_{x,y}$ sequences. The model then computes the expected decryption cost which is measured in terms of the number of DSTC trial assignments, and the DKTC processing sequence for decryption which yields minimal expected decryption cost.

The nth-order $\{s\}_{x,y}$ sequences are derived from the cipher text sample by the $\{s\}_{x,y}$ Sequence Generator. In a similar manner, the nth-order $k_{a,b}$ sequences are derived from the clear text sample by the $k_{a,b}$ Sequence Generator. These sequences are used by the Decryption Algorithm* to identify the DSTC subset $\{s\}_I$, for $1 \leq I \leq t$, in the nth-order $\{s\}_{x,y}$ sequences that correlate most closely with the nth-order $k_{a,b}$ sequences on each iteration. This identification of DSTC subsets for DKTC is the primary objective of the entire decryption procedure. The identified DSTC subsets $\{s\}_a$, $\forall a$ are the ECS encipherment array entries (DSTC ensemble assignment) that were used to generate the cipher text. The Decryption Algorithm also computes the actual decryption cost C, the updated expansion ratio ER, and the updated DKTC probabilities [P] for the next iteration.

5. COST PERFORMANCE OF THE ECS CIPHER

5.1 CIPHER USER COST

Cipher user cost is the sum of overhead cost and ECS encipherment cost. Overhead cost is the cost of the extra memory used to store the increase in computer word length needed for ECS cipher text. ECS encipherment cost is the cost of the memory needed to store the DSTC probability arrays produced by the ECS encipherment.

Recall that t is the number of DKTC in the clear text alphabet, n is the order of encipherment, and N_c is the number of clear text characters in the clear text sample used for encipherment. When $N_c \geq t^n$ and $t > n$, the number of DSTC probability arrays N_A produced with an nth-order encipherment is t^n. When $N_c < t^n$ and $t > n$, N_c is an upper bound on the number of DSTC probability arrays produced with the clear text sample. Thus,

$$N_A = \min\left[t^n,\ N_c\right] \tag{5}$$

The value of N_A depends on the distribution of nth-order DKTC frequencies in the clear text sample. Clearly, the upper bound on N_A is determined by the cipher user's choice of N_c and n.

Let N_p be the size of a probability array in bytes (eight bits/byte). Each DSTC has a probability entry in the array. Therefore, N_p is equal to the number of DSTC or $N_p = t \cdot ER$, where t is the number of DKTC and ER is the expansion ratio. Let C_s be the cost of computer memory in dollars/hour/memory increment. Then the maximum encipherment

*Due to the limited amount of space available, the lengthy descriptions of the Decryption Policy Model and the Decryption Algorithm are not presented here. These descriptions will be published in the near future.

cost is equal to the product of N_A, N_p, and C_s. For example, let t = 26 DKTC, N_c = 8000 clear text characters, and n = 1st-order = 1. Then using equation (5), we obtain N_A = 26. For an ER = 1, N_p = 26, and C_s = 10^{-5}/hour/byte, the maximum encipherment cost = $26 \cdot 26 \cdot 10^{-5} = 6.76 \times 10^{-3}$ dollars/hour. Thus the cipher user chooses N_c, n, and ER to obtain the desired privacy protection for a specified maximum encipherment cost. Table 2 shows the maximum costs of first- and ninth-order ECS encipherment of 26 character English text (plus space character) for C_s = \$$10^{-5}$/hour/byte with an 8000 character clear text sample. The encipherment cost is incurred only while clear text is being enciphered which is normally less than or equal to the user's job execution time.

Now we consider the overhead cost. Let N_b be the fraction by which the number of bytes of cipher text exceeds the number of bytes of clear text. Using eight bits/byte, the expression for N_b is:

$$N_b = \frac{1}{8} \log_2(\text{ER}) \qquad (6)$$

Let N_k be the number of bytes of clear text that is transformed into cipher text. Then the overhead cost is simply equal to the product of N_b, N_k, and C_s. For example, if we let ER = 4 in equation (6) we obtain N_b = 0.25, C_s = \$$10^{-5}$/hour/byte, and $N_k = 10^5$ bytes, the overhead cost is 0.25 dollars/hour.

5.2 INTRUDER COST

The intruders must use a decryption program to transform cipher text to clear text. Intruder cost is the decryption cost resulting from the transformation of cipher text to clear text. The decryption process described in Section 4 provides efficient decryption of the ECS Cipher text and can be used as a measure of decryption cost.

To evaluate the cost/performance of the ECS Cipher, the Decryption Policy Model shown in Figure 9 was used to obtain cumulative expected decryption cost of 26 character English text (plus space character). To keep the computer time for this evaluation to a minimum, the updated ER and updated [P] were not obtained from the Decryption Algorithm. Instead, the known DSTC ensemble assignment was used to derive the updated ER and updated [P] values. $[P]_0$ are the initial DKTC probabilities and were obtained from published tables. Expected decryption cost for each DKTC was computed for both first- and ninth-order $k_{a,b}$ sequences using expansion ratios of 1, 2, 4, and 8 as shown in Figure 10.

The average length of an English clear text string needed to produce a ninth-order $\{s\}_{x,y}$ sequence is 32 characters. When an English clear text string exceeds this length, the statistical influence between characters ceases to be of significance.[11]

The measure of decryption cost is expressed in terms of the number of DSTC trial assignments/ensemble. Each DSTC trial assignment is a possible DSTC assignment for a DKTC in the ECS encipherment array used to produce the cipher text. However, for each DKTC one and only one of the DSTC trial assignments is the DSTC assignment. Both the expected decryption cost and actual decryption cost results are shown in Figure 10. The expected decryption costs were computed with the Decryption Policy Model. The actual decryption costs were computed with the Decryption Algorithm. We found these costs to be in close agreement. Notice that the DKTC processing sequence varies with different values of ER. This is because the distribution of DKTC in fixed length clear text samples differs for each ER value. The cumulative decryption costs are the lower bound for the intruder because we assume only one 8000 character cipher text sample is needed for the decryption. In practice, several cipher text samples may be needed to

Table 2. Maximum ECS Encipherment Costs and Expected ECS Decryption Costs for an English Clear Text Sample.

	MAXIMUM ECS ENCIPHERMENT COSTS (DOLLARS/HOUR)		EXPECTED ECS DECRYPTION COSTS (DOLLARS/ENSEMBLE)	
ER	First-order encipherment	Ninth-order encipherment	First-order decryption	Ninth-order decryption
1	6.76×10^{-3}	2.08×10^{0}	8.7×10^{-1}	8.7×10^{0}
2	13.52×10^{-3}	4.16×10^{0}	8.7×10^{1}	8.7×10^{4}
4	27.04×10^{-3}	8.32×10^{0}	8.7×10^{4}	8.7×10^{8}
8	54.08×10^{-3}	16.64×10^{0}	8.7×10^{6}	8.7×10^{12}

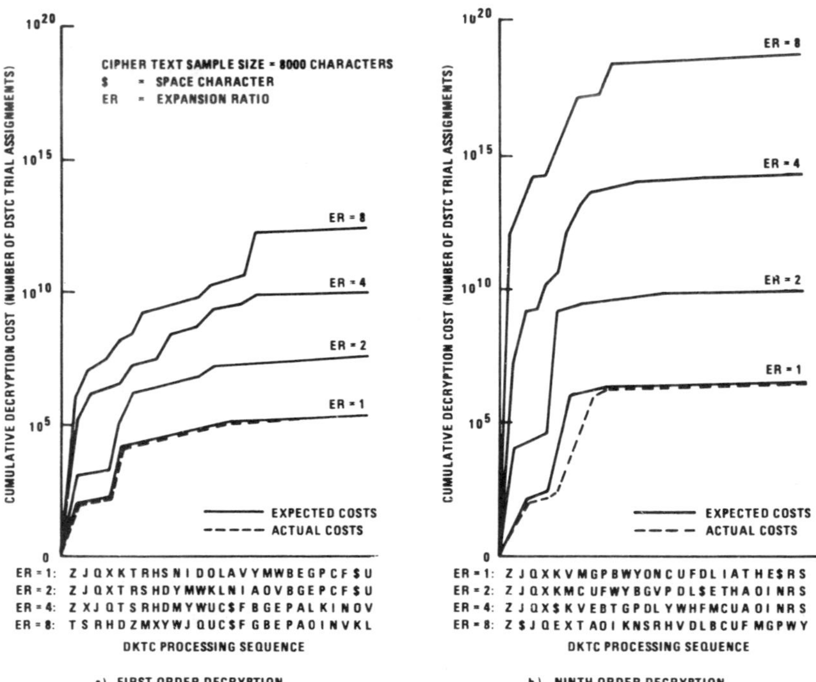

Figure 10. Decryption Costs of English Text Using the ECS Cipher.

identify all the DSTC.

The decryption cost also can be measured in terms of dollars/ensemble. For example, when using an IBM 370/165 computer, decryption of English text requires an average of 7.83 microseconds/DSTC trial assignment or approximately 65 computer instructions/DSTC trial assignment. At $400/hour for computer time, approximately 1.15×10^6 DSTC trial assignments/dollar can be performed. Using this cost data we can convert the decryption costs presented in Figure 10 into dollars/ensemble as shown in Table 2.

Comparison of ECS decryption costs with MS decryption costs reveals large cost differences. Given enough cipher text, a cipher generated with MS encipherment and using less than a full expansion can be easily decrypted.[10]

6. CONCLUSIONS

The ECS Cipher and procedures for its encipherment, decipherment, and decryption were presented in this paper. The basic concept of the ECS Cipher is to provide privacy protection by suppressing the frequency deviations of distinct clear text characters and distinct clear text character sequences within the cipher text. This is accomplished by using an expanded character set (a distinct cipher text character set that is larger than the distinct clear text character set) and using the distinct cipher text character and character sequence probabilities to control the random substitution of the distinct cipher text characters for the distinct clear text characters in the clear text. Since the ECS Cipher does not depend entirely on multisubstitution to provide suppression of the distinct clear text character frequencies in the cipher text, large expansion ratios are not required. For a specified level of privacy protection, ECS cipher text requires far less storage than that of MS cipher text. This is especially appealing for privacy protection of large data bases. The encipherment cost for the ECS Cipher is low because the cost is incurred only while clear text is being transformed into cipher text. Both the encipherment cost and the overhead cost of the ECS Cipher are functions of the amount of privacy protection desired by the cipher user. The user can choose the amount of privacy protection that he needs.

The ECS Cipher allows simultaneous encipherment and decipherment. This parallel operation is essential to prevent degradation of computer performance. The ECS Cipher permits delay between encipherment and decipherment operations without introducing operational complexity. Other systems such as those using non-linear pseudo-random shift registers require precise synchronization between encipherment and decipherment operations which can cause severe operational complexity when delayed decipherment is performed. Thus the ECS Cipher should have high potential for use in future computer centers.

NOTE: Figure 6 represents the first order probabilities of DSTC's based on the preceding DKTC. First order ECS encipherments can be implemented by using the preceding DSTC's rather than by using the preceding DKTC's. Higher order ECS encipherment can be implemented in a similar manner. For the example shown in the text (Figure 6), the number of first order DSTC probability tables increases from four to seven when preceding DSTC's are used.

7. REFERENCES

1. Ware, W. H., "Security and Privacy in Computer Systems", Proceedings of the Spring Joint Computer Conference, Vol. 30, (1967).

2. Turn, R., "Privacy transformations for databank systems", Proceedings of the National Computer Conference and Exposition, Vol. 42 (1973).

3. Golomb, S., Nonlinear Shift-Register Sequences, Memorandum No. 20-149, Jet Propulsion Laboratory, California Institute of Technology, Pasadena, California, October 25, 1957.

4. Edmonds, A. R., "The Generation of Pseudo-Random Numbers on Electronic Digital Computers", Computer Journal, No. 2, p. 181-185, (1960).

5. Baran, P., On Distributed Communications: IX. Security, Secrecy, and Tamper-Free Considerations, Memorandum RM-3765-PR, The Rand Corporation, Santa Monica, California, August, 1964.

6. Shannon, C. E., "Communication Theory of Secrecy Systems", Bell System Technical Journal, Vol. 28, No. 4 (1949).

7. Tuckerman, B., A Study of the Vigenere-Vernam Single and Multiple Loop Enciphering Systems, Report RC2879, IBM Thomas J. Watson Research Center, Yorktown Heights, New York, May 14, 1970.

8. Chu, Wesley W., "Some Recent Advances in Computer Communications", First USA-JAPAN Computer Conference Proceedings, October 3-5, 1972, Tokyo, Japan.

9. Kahn, D., The Code Breakers, The MacMillan Company, (1967).

10. Gaines, H. F., CRYPTANALYSIS, Dover Publications, Inc., New York (1956).

11. Burton, N. and J. Licklider, "Long-Range Constraints in the Statistical Structure of Printed English", American Journal of Psycology, Vol. 68, pp 650-653, 1955.

THEFT • SABOTAGE • VANDALISM • ESPIONAGE • NATURAL DISASTERS

Data Security in the Computer Communication Environment

Stanley Winkler and Lee Danner
IBM System Development Division

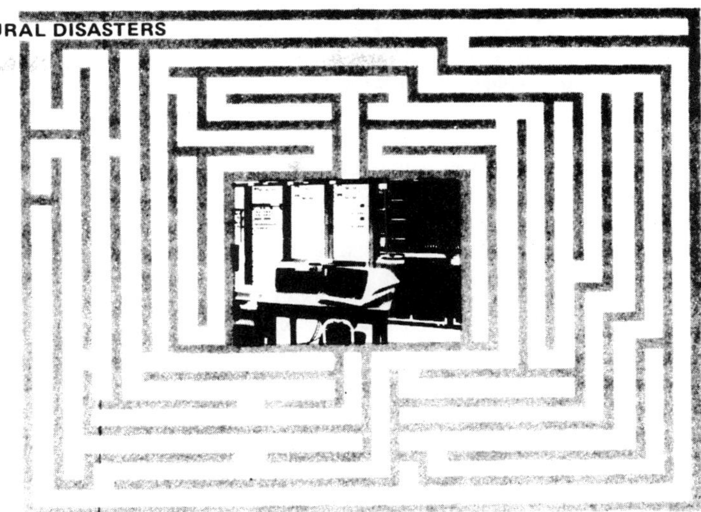

a COMPUTER reprint
Reprinted from COMPUTER.

Introduction

Data security is the protection of data against unauthorized disclosure, modification, restriction, or destruction. Recognition[1] that data in a computer system must be protected was a development brought on by three factors which caused a significant increase in the vulnerability of computer systems.

First, many more individuals obtained access to many more computer systems. The increased application of the computer to daily business practice made the computer installation a part of most organizations. Shared resources and jointly-used data became the normal mode of computer operations. Also, direct interaction with the computer, once the prerogative of the programmer or operator, became commonplace activity for the most casual of computer users.

Second, many more individuals were and are being trained in computer science. Thus the detailed knowledge of how to manipulate computer systems became readily available, instead of being confined to small isolated groups.

Third, because the amount of data which may be stored in a computer system is very large, the value of this stored information can be sufficiently large in many instances to make its theft worthwhile.

The increased vulnerability of computer systems has led to increased numbers of incidents, some of which for various reasons have remained unreported. Nonetheless, many horror stories about computer-related crimes are well-known. Some are apocryphal; others have been recorded in the computer industry trade press or publicized in daily newspapers. New techniques for committing old crimes have been developed.[2] State legislatures are considering the definition of new crimes. (Is it a crime in your state to take and use data without the knowledge and consent of the owner of that data?) Even a new profession is developing: Computer Security Manager.

As a consequence, there is growing awareness among computer users of the vulnerability of their data and the potential cost of its loss. This is in contrast to a decade ago when the major preoccupation of both computer users and designers was to make computers work better, faster, and cheaper.

Today, computer communication systems are used to meet the demand, which our societal structure has created, for much more data and for convenient and rapid access to that data. An almost explosive growth of such systems ranging from large-scale data networks (e.g., ARPA, AT&T, DATRAN, etc.) to industry-specific terminal-oriented systems (airline reservations, bank transactions, credit reporting, educational data, stock quotation, etc.) can be observed.

The computer communication environment which requires data security consists of computers, computer communication elements, a communications link, and programs for processing data and controlling the transmission of that data. For the purposes of this discussion, computer communication encompasses data processing systems with terminals, intelligent terminals, programmable data concentrators, communication preprocessors, computer-controlled switchboards (PBX's), and multiple computers arranged in networks.

Computer communication systems have those resource-sharing, multi-access, and wide-spread geographic distribution aspects which are intended to increase the accessibility of data. These aspects make such systems good potential targets for security violations and therefore have been called a security officer's nightmare. The direct conflict in goals between increased accessibility and good security, traditionally achieved by strictly limiting access to data, has increased the concern of administrators and security officers for the security of data in a computer communication environment.

The Computer Communication Environment

A computer communication environment is vulnerable to security violations in all of its programmable elements and in the communication link. The distinction between a computer communication environment and a centralized data processing system, consisting of a computer with an operator console and the customary input/output devices (tapes, disks, and printers), is the transmission link with remote peripherals. The link may be unrestricted in length and the components of the computer communication system must occupy at least two physically separate locations. Thus the environment may consist of a computer with local input/output devices and local terminals, but it must also include at least one device remotely attached through a link.

Essential to our concept of computer communication is the requirement that the data be processed as well as transmitted.[3] This rules out links which contain only repeaters, non-programmable concentrators, time-division multiplexors, and similar inflexible communication devices. Clearly, security implementation on a system is affected by whether the "processing" functions are performed through software or by hardware. The transmission process may be unrestricted in format and may be half or full duplex and communicated at bit, character, block, message, or message group level.

The transmission link in a computer communication system is often susceptible to successful attack by a determined penetrator of a system. Cryptography is frequently used to provide protection against the penetration of an otherwise secure system through the link. Difficulties arise in both the design and use of cryptographic devices. A discussion of these difficulties as well as a discussion of the general security problems for communication links are beyond the scope of this paper.

Data Security

Data security is but one of several problems encountered by the modern corporation with its extensive dependence on data processing in the conduct of its business. For some companies any interruption of the services provided by computers is a serious threat. An organization which is dependent on its computer system can suffer a large financial loss if that system is damaged or destroyed by intentional sabotage or natural disaster. The publicity attendant on bombings of computer installations has alerted many managers to that potential danger. But fire, earthquakes, or hurricanes can be almost as damaging and may be more likely to occur. To protect against dangers of this kind, *physical security,* which must include recovery plans, should be provided for the computer system.[4]

Another danger to computer systems is the irresponsible or malicious individual who is part of the computer group. Through carelessness or in anger, an employee can inflict severe damage to a computer installation by damaging its program or data libraries. Physical security measures are not effective against the "insider." Thus, *personnel security,* which really means good personnel practices, is required.

Good physical security and good personnel practices can be negated by the lack of adequate procedures. The not-so-funny story is told about the company with cipher locks guarding its computer installation and unlocked distribution boxes for the computer output in a public hallway. In a famous case where the computer was used to steal more than a million dollars from a business, the thief obtained the information he needed from a trash can in the street. *Administrative security* is a necessary part of protecting a computer system.

In addition to adequate physical, personnel, and administrative security, data in the computer system must be protected against unauthorized disclosure, modification, restriction or destruction of the types shown in Table 1. Attacks on the data security of a system may be accidental or intentional. More accidental attacks than intentional ones are reported, but any statistical summary must be suspect, because there seems to be no way to estimate unreported attacks.

Table 1. Categories of Attacks on Data Security

CATEGORY		DEFINITION
UNAUTHORIZED DISCLOSURE	EXPOSURE	The accidental disclosure of data to unauthorized persons.
	INTERCEPTION	The deliberate seizure of data by unauthorized persons.
UNAUTHORIZED MODIFICATION	ALTERATION	The accidental change of data.
	DECEPTION	The deliberate change of data.
UNAUTHORIZED RESTRICTION	INTERRUPTION	The accidental denial of proper access.
	DISRUPTION	The deliberate denial of proper access.
UNAUTHORIZED DESTRUCTION	ERASURE	The accidental expunging of data.
	ELIMINATION	The deliberate expunging of data.

The protection of the data from attack through the instruction streams or programmable portions of the computer and communication systems which comprise the computer communication environment is provided by the data security features of the system. The protection provided within the system may be accomplished through many types of implementation, but functionally it must include at least the following: a method for *identification* of a user requesting service; *authorization* techniques to establish a security relation between users and data to which they are entitled; *controlled access* methods to determine whether the user has been previously authorized to access the data and to use the requested services or programs; and a *surveillance* procedure to provide a record of all access attempts whether authorized or not. Assurance is also required that the system itself is not modified by the user to subvert the protection features. In current systems, this *integrity* of the system is usually provided through combined hardware and software facilities provided by the computer architecture and the operating system design.

These basic functions are intended to deter, prevent, or at least detect all of the attacks listed in Table 1. Clearly, complete protection or absolute security cannot be achieved, since one can never be sure that some newly-developed method of attack will not succeed in penetrating the data protection mechanism of any computer system. The practical objective of data security must be to make penetration so difficult and costly that a would-be penetrator is deterred. The minimum desired protection – which may not always be attainable – is that any attack, successful or not, be detected. A serious difficulty is that a successful attack may leave no "footprints" or evidence that the system was compromised. Unlike the theft of property, the stealing of valuable data from a computer system leaves the data in the system, apparently untouched.

Before a user is permitted to transact data processing functions on a secure system, identification and authorization must be made and recorded in the access control tables. The access control tables, often called the system security profile, when subverted, can be used to deny authorized users legitimate access to data, resources, or programs. The subverted profile can be used by a penetrator to give himself access to everything in the computer system. To prevent subversion, the programs which control the profile must be accessible only to the security office whose members are responsible for control of access to the organization's data.

In a secure system with a security profile, a user must first sign on and establish his identity. The identification problem and its solution mechanisms differ in different environments. Upon identifying the user, the system has available (from the security profile) a list of all devices, data files, programs, and other resources to which the user has been authorized.

After sign on and proper identification, the authorized user's program is given access to the system (storage is allocated, system control tables are assigned, etc.) and program execution begins. When the user program requests status information, additional system resources, input/output devices, or access to data, the request is verified through the data security functions. The operating system matches the user's identification against his security profile to assure proper authorization. Each security profile indicates security level and the type of data access. Security levels permit discriminating among devices or data with respect to sensitivity or classification of the data. It is important to assure that neither programs nor users declassify data by reading it at a high security level and outputting it at a low security level. The type of access allowed determines what users may do about the data. Some users may only read certain data; others may be authorized to both read and write the same data items. Other access types are execute-only, delete, append, etc. A request which fails a security check may cause job termination depending on the importance of the data and the procedure established for the system. Surveillance for maintenance of security is provided by recording all access requests for subsequent audit by the security office.

Each of the functional aspects of data security described above (identification, authorization, controlled access, surveillance, and integrity) will be discussed below where unique problems are introduced by a particular computer communication environment.

The Multi-terminal Computer System

One of the simplest computer communication environments contains a central processor with remote terminals (Figure 1). In the typical timesharing system which exemplifies this environment, these terminals are input/output keyboard devices, such as a typewriter or teleprinter, connected to the computer by an audio coupler and a regular voice grade telephone line. The additional security problems for timesharing systems over those problems associated with a local batch-processing computer installation arise from the "remoteness" of the terminals and the "simultaneous sharing" of the resources of the computer by many users.

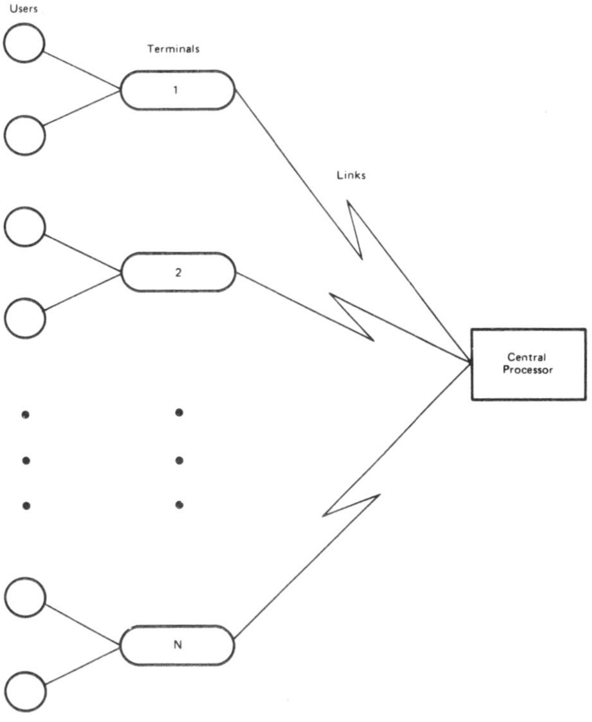

Figure 1. The Multi-terminal System

The vulnerabilities of timesharing systems appear to have been fully explored at universities which use timesharing. Large numbers of bright students, motivated to beat the system, have evolved many ingenious ways to outwit the computer. Fortunately, most students are not malicious and also like to boast of their cleverness, so their successful attacks have not been too damaging and have advanced our knowledge of security problems.

The remote location of a terminal introduces the problem of identification of the user of the system. In a local installation, the computer operator can recognize the individual who hands him a deck of cards or the signature on the form authorizing the job. If the user is remote from the central processor, the operator can no longer see him or verify a signature. Thus the need arises for a unique user ID, which identifies the user for the system. Commonly, timesharing systems require an identification followed by a

547

password. The inadequacies of passwords have been noted many times. Passwords simple enough to be easily remembered are usually also easy to compromise. Passwords also have a tendency to become known to unauthorized people. A programmer, for convenience, needs a moment with the system and borrows a password from a friend, passes it on to another friend, and as the chain of convenience enlarges, security is eroded. A good practice is to change passwords frequently, but this is rarely done because it is considered inconvenient and unnecessary.

A number of identification schemes have been suggested. One is based on storing a set of personal data which only the user would know, such as date of birth, wife's maiden name, etc., and randomly selecting a different sub-set of questions which are then matched against the pre-stored answers. Other schemes involve somewhat sophisticated hardware which recognizes magnetically encoded cards, or voice prints, or fingerprints, or signatures. There are many others; but all of these schemes have their own peculiar problems and costs. One must not assume that identification information is secure because it is not in human readable form. As so aptly stated in *Modern Data:*

> Print paper money, and thieves will use presses; issue plastic money, and thieves will use embossers; encode magnetic money, and thieves will use tape recorders.[5]

The bright side of the picture is that technical developments tend to anticipate requirements. As the need for more secure identification becomes urgent, the means to achieve it may be available.

Where terminals are connected to the computer by ordinary telephone lines, it is possible to dial up the computer from any telephone and attach a terminal equipped with an acoustic coupler. The danger in this is that it expands the area from which the computer can be attacked. One method to avoid this danger is to couple the terminal directly to the computer via a leased line. This not only reduces the flexibility of the terminal (which the user may want to connect to other computers) and increases expense, but also tends to use up the available entries to the computer and therefore provides services to only a small, fixed number of user devices. Another method is to build into the terminal a unique identification which can be recognized by the computer, but determined penetrators have successfully forged terminal identification.

The simultaneous sharing of resources produces the multi-access security problem. A user has access to the central processor while data and programs belonging to other users are available on the machine. Therefore it is necessary to control access to all "private" data in order to protect them against unauthorized disclosure, modification, restriction, or destruction. It is not sufficient to protect against direct access alone. A user, for whom *data* is not intended, may obtain it through a *program* to which he has legitimate access.

Another problem which a multi-terminal system creates is the possibility of denial of service through interruption or disruption. If one user causes the system to crash, all users are affected. The damage can range from an inconvenient delay to an irretrievable loss of essential information. In some businesses, delays in obtaining data can be as costly as complete destruction of that data. Virtual machine concepts may remove much of the danger from unintentional interruptions; but protection against disruption by prevention of crashes and quick recovery from those that occur are an important part of data security in this environment.

The protection of vital data against destruction is usually achieved by the storing of a copy in a "safe" location. This procedure is valid only if the copy is updated regularly. If data is destroyed by a systems crash or other failure, some change in the data will not have been transferred to the backup copy. If the changes have been extensive, it may be expensive to restore the data. The decision as to the frequency of updating the backup copy must be based on a risk assessment.

Simple terminals are not susceptible to penetration, but serve as entry ports into the central processor. This processor must, of course, possess the same integrity and isolation charactersitics required for security in a local, batch installation. The surveillance capability must be able to monitor and identify the terminal from which attacks against the data security of the system have been made.

The Computer System with Intelligent Terminals

A computer communication environment which incorporates a limited amount of distributed intelligence via intelligent terminals attached to a link (Figure 2) poses additional exposures beyond those discussed for remote terminals.

It is difficult to define an intelligent terminal within the spectrum of all possible distributed intelligence capabilities. At the lower limit of capability is a simple terminal which performs no actions on its own. The data stream, in either direction, is not modified, interpreted, or altered in any way by the terminal. Data is received from or sent to the terminal, in a keyboard typewriter for example, by manual keystrokes or by a stream of characters transmitted from the central computer. The minimum intelligent terminal is one which performs any function beyond the passive acceptance of impulses or keystrokes. The difficulty lies in determining the upper limits of intelligence a terminal may possess before it becomes an attached processor, and consequently a node of a computer network. For the purposes of this paper, an intelligent terminal computer communication environment may consist of special-purpose devices housed in a terminal, a programmable controller serving several terminals, or a minicomputer providing programmable control for large clusters of data entry devices or terminals. Capabilities, rather than physical or architectural characteristics, provide a better description of the environment.

Typical capabilities of an intelligent terminal are simple decisionmaking functions: deleting obviously erroneous data; collecting (or blocking) data to conserve time on the link and to reduce the number of "end of block" interrupts to the computer; multiplexing and identifying of several input or output data streams onto a single link; converting character codes from the device standard to the computer standard; and many others. Arithmetic capabilities similar to those performed by cash registers and adding machines may be included in the functional repertoire associated with an intelligent terminal.

These systems find application in many diverse businesses. One is point-of-sale recording for retail sales in stores with multiple cash registers. In this application the terminal is used as a cash register to ring up the sale, as a calculator in performing unit calculations (e.g., determining the price of two items priced at 3 for $0.79), in performing sales tax calculation, as an input terminal in recording inventory information and daily transaction totals, and as an output terminal in verifying credit. Other applications include banking, railroad rolling stock inventories, and message switching and routing.

A critical element in the attachment of an intelligent terminal into a secure data processing system is the method of implementation used to provide intelligence to the terminal. The terminal may contain hardwired or fixed program logic, it may be loaded with the intelligence in the form of a program supplied by its host computer, or it may be programmable and loadable in its field environment. Each of these three implementations presents different levels of risk to the system. In all cases, the computer in the system is assumed to be utilized for data processing functions above and beyond the support of the computer communication environment, and consequently require data security in its operating system to assure the protection of company records such as payroll information, customer lists, or mark-up percentages.

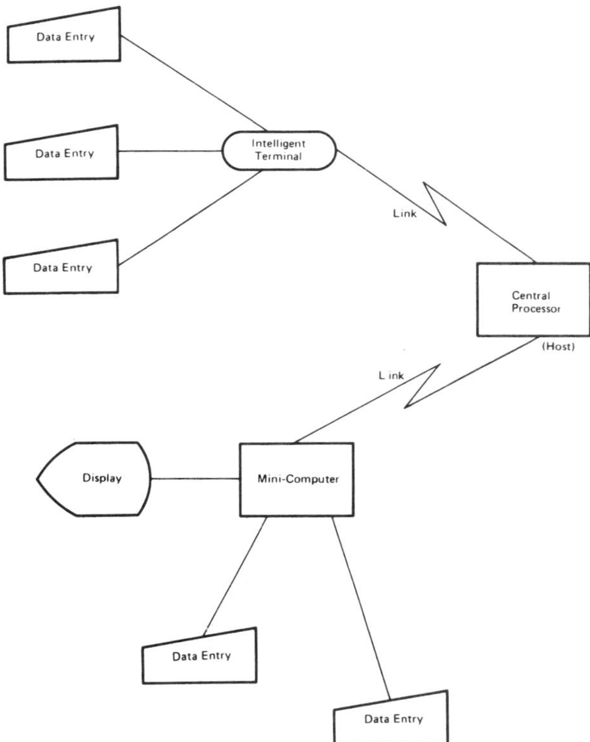

Figure 2. The Intelligent Terminal System

Intelligent terminals which are programmable and loadable only by the host computer are a lesser hazard to the security of a system than a locally programmable and loadable minicomputer used as an intelligent terminal. Three security exposures which exist in the locally programmable environment introduce the major vulnerability of the system to attack threats. The exposures are based on the possibility that the terminal may be used to

- access the information requested by other users connected through the same intelligent terminal,
- attempt to fraudulently sign on the main system by repeatedly and systematically generating passwords at computer speed, and
- deny service to all users of the main system by jamming the host computer with repeated rapid interrupt signals.

In the first case, a user loads the terminal with a program which appears normal and legitimate but which also monitors all of the activities occurring at the terminal. This program intercepts all data requested and generated by each user. It can also intercept passwords as users sign on. The hazards from a penetration of this sort are obvious. Security requires some method whereby the host processor can determine that all attached intelligent terminals perform those functions which are authorized and intended and that they do nothing else.

In the second case, a successful penetration has more potential to access the data bank of the system. Using its authorized access to the intelligent terminal, and while continuing to support the normal operation, the penetration program would commence a series of attempts to sign on the secure system. The password of a user who is authorized to access valuable data could possibly be obtained in less than a week of continuous attempts. A more insidious penetration would be to obtain the passwords of the installation security office and thus get access to the security profile and all passwords.

The third type of exposure does not penetrate the security system at the host, but disrupts the services provided to the many users of the system. With the ability in the intelligent terminal to execute a program, it is possible to generate interrupt requests to be sent to the host at computer speed rather than the maximum manual rate for which the system is designed. The cost of disruption is highest in organizations dependent on continuous computer service.

The design of a data security system must include appropriate preventive measures to protect against the three threats described above. To avoid the surreptitious introduction of monitoring type programs into an intelligent terminal, the host system must be able to check the program status of the terminal. Random interrupts of the processing at the terminal must be permitted to allow its contents to be examined without warning. Protection against the password-guessing penetrator can be accomplished through surveillance and by setting up an alarm procedure to alert the security office to the penetration attempt. Similarly, excessive interrupts can be brought to the attention of the security office through proper surveillance and alarm procedures. The denial of service to the other users of the system can be minimized by automatically disconnecting the offending device. The addition of intelligent terminals presents the designer of data security systems with additional problems, but hopefully none are insurmountable.

The Computer Network

A computer network appears as an attachment of equals to each other (Figure 3). A computer network may consist of two or more computers of equal or unequal capabilities interconnected through communication links. The functions performed by the computers in a computer network are basically those expected of an independent processor. In a computer network no one of the many nodes is necessarily predominant in terms of controlling the system or maintaining the security of the system. The nodes can be considered as stand-alone processors, each with several levels of data storage both directly addressable and addressable through input/output commands. Protection of this multiplicity of data storages introduces a new challenge to a data security system.

A computer network system also introduces the same data security problems associated with distributed intelligence. These were described in the previous section for the environment with intelligent terminals. The amount of intelligence which is distributed does not make much difference. The important aspect is the attachment of any intelligence, since all computers (including intelligent terminals) provide the basic functions of add, subtract, fetch, store, etc.

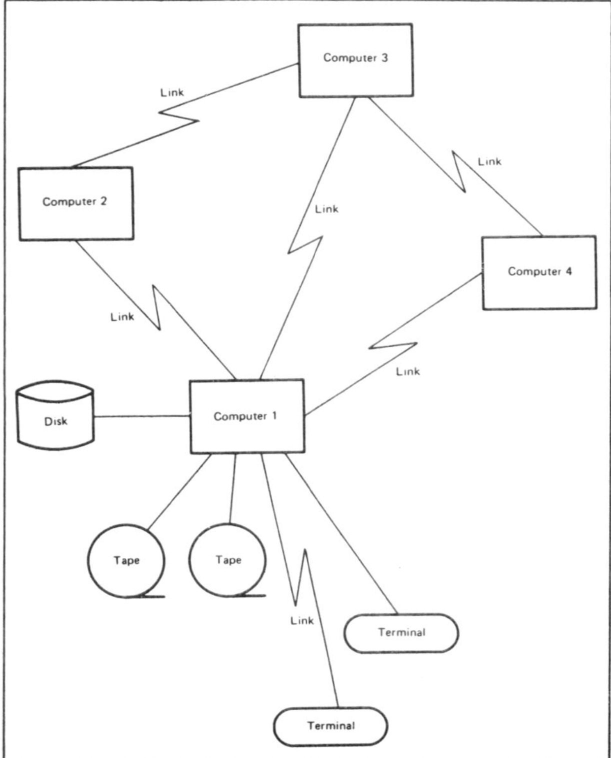

Figure 3. The Computer Network

The problems involved in the management of the data base when it is distributed in the stores of several nodes of the computer network can best be illustrated by example. Assume a user's program is running in one node of the computer network. The application has been accepted by the host computer system after identification and password have been checked against the security profile. The program now requests some data which is contained in external storage. If the data file is attached to the local system, data security features of the operating system would confirm the user's right to access the data by checking the security profile, and then allow the input/output routines of the system to supply the data requested. If the data were in the store of a different node some additional coordination would be required. Data security for the network may be implemented in at least three ways. First, all security related to a job being run on one computer can be controlled by that computer. Second, all security information about the data can be controlled by the computer containing that data. Third, all security can be controlled by one specified "security" computer in the computer network.

As a basis for evaluating the three implementations, we assume that the independent computers of the computer network run under control of their own secure operating system. Each includes the additional programs to provide the computer communication interface needed for proper network protocols[6] and data transmission interfaces.[7] The data security extensions necessary to support the data transmission interface and intersystem protocols expose the operating systems to potential data security violations.

To describe these exposures we must examine the operations required for identification and controlled access in each of the three implementations and for access requests for both local and remote data files. The three implementations and the different cases of controlled access in a computer network with data security are illustrated in Figures 4-10. Table 2 provides a guide to these figures, the implementations, and the controlled access cases.

Table 2. Guide to Figures Illustrating Methods of Implementing Security Control in a Computer Network

IMPLEMENTATION (Profile Loc.)	IDENTIFICATION	CONTROLLED ACCESS	
		Local Data	Remote Data
User Node	Figure 4	Figure 6	Figure 8
Data Node	Figure 4	Figure 6	Figure 9
Security Node	Figure 5	Figure 7	Figure 10

The identification of any user who requests service from a computer does not depend on what data files his programs may subsequently select; therefore the identification procedure is the same for the implementation with data profiles either at local or at remote nodes (see Figure 4). The first step (1)* in identification is the submission of an ID and password from the user (or terminal) to the identification module of the operating system. The module searches the security profile (2) for the submitted ID, reads the password stored in the profile (3) and compares the two in order to verify the identity of the user.

The identification of any user who requests service from a node of a computer network with all security profiles at a central security node (Figure 5) begins with the submission (1) of identification and password from the user. This information is transmitted (2) over the link to the security node for verification (3 and 4) with the information in the computer network profile. The central security node responds with a validation (5) to the operating system at the user node.

The control of access to a local data file is the same whether the data profile is stored locally or stored with the data (since it is local data). Access checking (Figure 6) is performed by accessing (1) the profile and retrieving (2) the user/data file descriptors (these transmissions may be unnecessary in systems where, for performance reasons, profiles of active jobs are held in main storage). The descriptors are checked for user authorization, type of use requested (read, write, etc.), and any other restrictions such as security level or time of day. If all access control checks are passed, the data request (3) and return of the data (4) complete the data access for this implementation.

The case where the controlled access to local data is performed at a security node (Figure 7) is the same as the local control case, but with the addition of transmissions

***Numbers in parenthesis refer to corresponding numbers in Figures 4-10.**

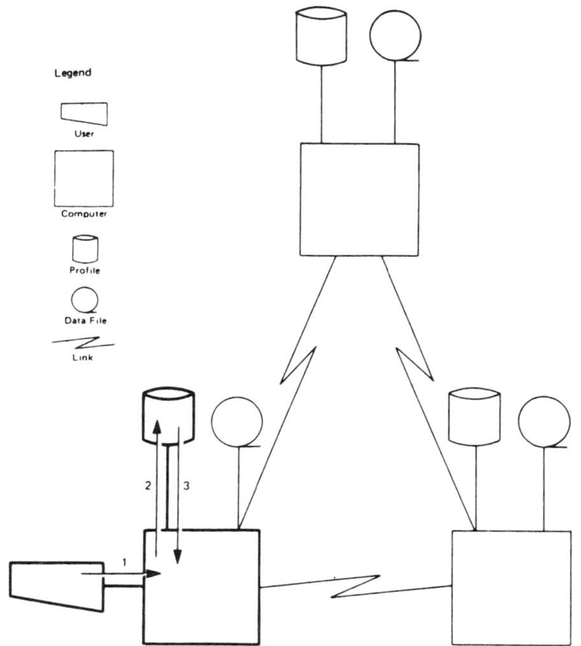

Figure 4. User Identification with User Profiles and Data Profiles at Local Node

between the nodes (1 and 4). It should be understood that even if one node of the computer network is assigned the central security function, the local operating system must assure that all system requests which require access control, surveillance logging, identification checking, or other security related functions are routed to the security system, and further that the responses from the central security system are properly interpreted.

The next three cases consider the controlled access of remote data and involve at least two nodes of the computer network for running the user programs and supplying the requested data files. When a user requests a data file stored

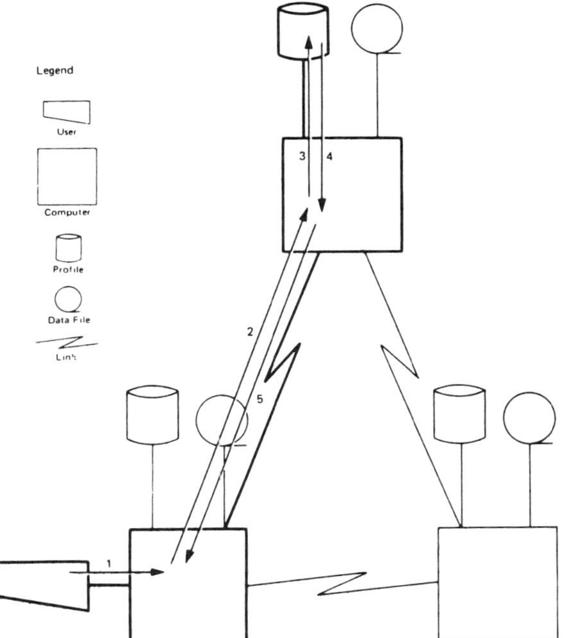

Figure 5. User Identification with User Profiles and Data Profiles at Security Node

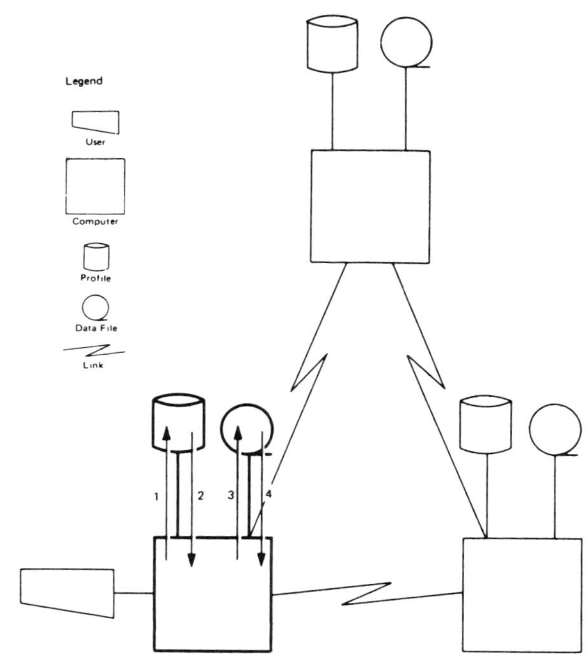

Figure 6. Controlled Access to Local Data File with Data Profile at Data (Local) Node

at a remote node and both his profile and the data profile are stored at the local node (Figure 8), the local operating system must access the local profile (1) to read (2) the authorization data. After verification of the request, a message is routed over the link (3) to the remote node containing the data file. This message must include the established computer network identification of the node making the request. The remote node queries (4) its profile to verify (5) the validity of the request. Thus the profile at each node must contain an identification description of all the nodes in the computer network. Data access (6), data input (7), and transmission over the link (8) complete the transaction.

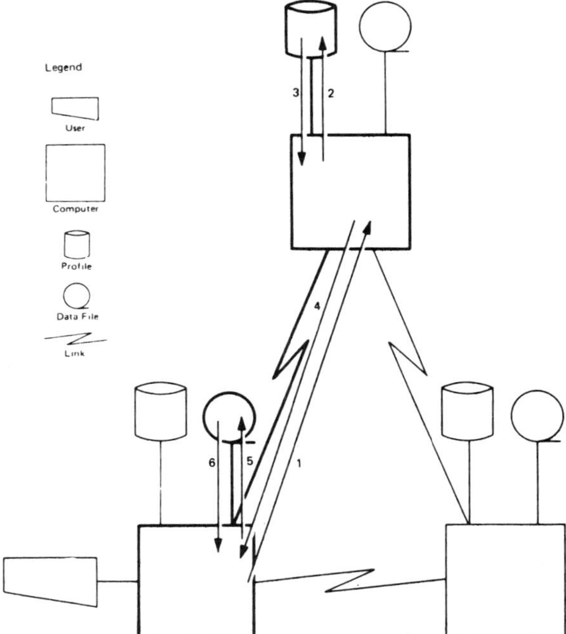

Figure 7. Controlled Access to Local Data File with User Profile and Data Profile at Security Node

Access control to a remote data file when the data profile is stored at the same node as the data file (Figure 9) requires no access control at the local node. A request is sent on the link (1) and the remote node performs profile checks (2 and 3) for both identification of the user and authorization to the requested data file. After verifying the right of access, the data is accessed (4), retrieved (5), and returned to the requestor (6).

The implementation with all access control on a specified control node of the computer network when a user requests data from a remote node is illustrated in Figure 10. In this figure, the user request (1) is shown being made to the node containing the data file, and then transmitted (2) to the security node. This transmission of the request could be made directly from the user node to the central security node. The next four steps (2-5) cause the network security profile to be accessed and the data/user authorization relationship to be verified. The data access (6), reading (7), and return (8) to the user complete the request.

Each of the above implementations of data security in a computer network has advantages and disadvantages and should be evaluated on the basis of the objectives of the computer network. Some specific goals against which the data security implementation may be evaluated are:

- The creation and maintenance of the security profile for each node and the total network must be manageable.
- Each node of the computer network may operate either as a node of the secure network or as a stand-alone processor with data security.
- A user of the computer network has controlled access to any data files for which he has been authorized.
- A user program may run on any node of the computer network. (This assumes compatible equipment and instruction sets, etc.)
- Program performance must not be unduly degraded by the data security implementation in the computer network.

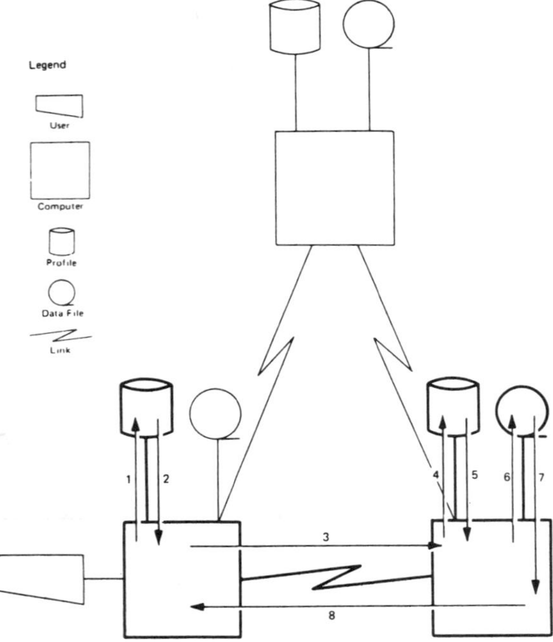

Figure 8. Controlled Access to Remote Data File with User Profile at Local Node and Data Profile at Local Node

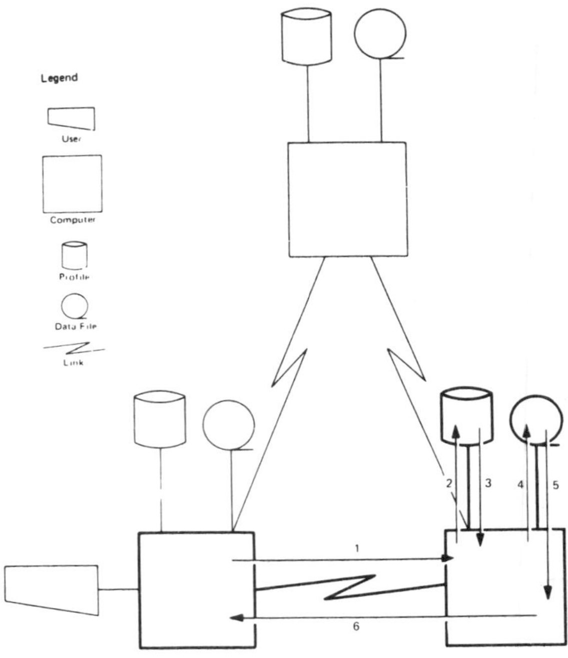

Figure 9. Controlled Access to Remote Data File with User Profile at Local Node and Data Profile at Data Node

The goal of security profile maintainability is achieved through the implementation of a central security node for the network but the ability to run independently of the computer network is lost. All three implementations allow programs to access data files at any node, and do not restrict a program to a single node. But performance for different jobs will vary with the implementation method selected.

The diversity of potential network goals and the degree to which any particular implementation of data security in a computer network may satisfy these goals cause the evalu-

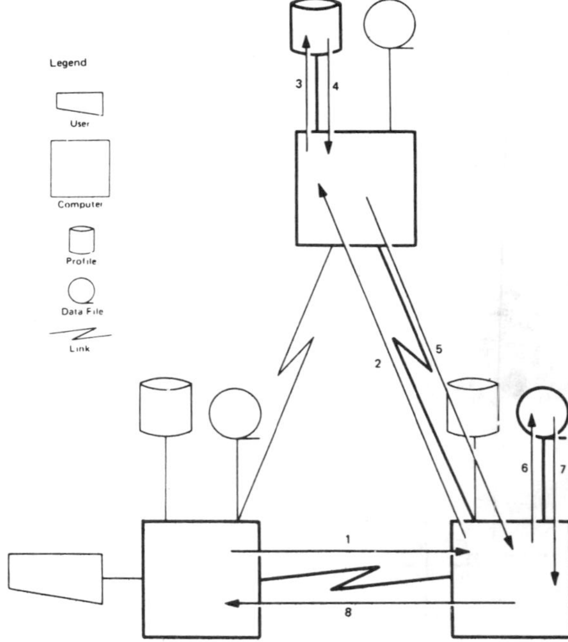

Figure 10. Controlled Access to Remote Data File with User Profile and Data Profile at Security Node

ation of any implementation to be dependent on the individual structure and specific use of the particular network. An evaluation should be made for each node of a network, and used as a basis for choosing the security implementations.

Concluding Remarks

This paper has looked at some of the questions of data security in the computer communication environment, emphasizing the problems introduced by the merging of computer and communications. There are two cliches which have appeared frequently in the literature. The first is that the weakest link in any security system is people. But people are necessary for the operation of any computer system and therefore the normal management practices for any risk situation must be invoked. The usual personnel safeguards must be applied. More importantly, the procedures adopted by the installation must avoid making it easy to violate good practice. Ignorance, apathy, and boredom are as dangerous as intentional dishonesty.

The second cliche is that defense against attack must start with awareness of the danger. Awareness is necessary but it is not sufficient.

Throughout this paper, there is repeated mention of requirements which must be placed on the operating systems of computers embedded in a computer communication environment in order to achieve some measure of data security. The paper has not addressed the feasibility of implementing these requirements, nor should it be implied that the technical solutions to this implementation are necessarily available. It should be stressed that there is a significant interrelation among the multiple disciplines involved in developing solutions to the problem. There may be gaps between the desired and feasible implementations of physical, personnel, procedural, and operational security in any installation, especially considering the different requirements that flexible data processing imposes. Different configurations, different applications, and different requirements for data security cannot be satisfied by a single general solution.

Data security in the computer communication environment is not really different from data security in general. Special problems in the computer communication environment stem from the remote location of terminals, the increased amount of resource sharing that occurs, the presence of distributed intelligence, and the existence of distributed data bases. The dispersion over wide geographic areas of many individuals capable of using the large number of devices which can access computers exacerbates the dangers. The need for data security is in direct conflict with the requirement for increased accessibility and sharing of data banks. The only certainty in this rapidly developing field of data security appears to be that technical solutions to avert known threats will be developed. With equal certainty, new threats will evolve. To paraphrase a famous saying: eternal vigilance is the price of data security. ■

Acknowledgement. Many individuals have contributed ideas and viewpoints which have shaped our thinking, and it is not possible to mention all those who have helped and influenced us. But to each of them goes our sincere thanks and appreciation. Special mention must be made of our colleagues at IBM Gaithersburg – Larry Foster, Joel Aron, Harvey Bleam, Bill Oberle, and Wayne Blackwell – for their help and encouragement. We also want to thank Prof. E. M. Glaser, Peter S. Browne, Gerald E. Short, and Willis H. Ware.

References

1. W. H. Ware, "Security and Privacy in Computer Systems," *AFIPS Proceedings,* 1967 Spring Joint Computer Conference, pp. 279-282.

2. Donn B. Parker, "The Nature of Computer-Related Crime," *Computer Communication: Impacts and Implications,* S. Winkler, ed., ICCC 1972, pp. 121-126.

3. A. F. Hartung, "Computer Communications – An Overview," *IEEE International Convention Digest,* p. 232, March 1971.

4. "The Considerations of Physical Security in a Computer Environment," IBM Data Processing Division, form G520-2700, 1972. See also "The Fire and After the Fire . . . ," IBM Data Processing Division, Form G520-2741, December 1970, and "The Considerations of Data Security in a Computer Environment," IBM Data Processing Division, Form G520-2169, July 1970.

5. "Magnetic Larceny," *Modern Data,* v. 6. Oct. 1973, p. 31.

6. D. B. McKay and D. P. Karp, "Protocol for a Computer Network," *IBM Systems Journal* 12, No. 1, pp. 94-105 (1973).

7. D. H. Frederickson, "Describing Data in Computer Networks," *IBM Systems Journal* 12, No. 3, pp. 257-282 (1973).

Stanley Winkler is a senior scientist in the IBM System Development Division, Gaithersburg, Maryland, and is a member of the Data Security Study Project Office. From 1968 to 1971, he headed the Resource Evaluation Division of OEP in the Executive Office of The President. Between 1959 and 1968, he was with IBM in various assignments including operations research, applied research, and education and training. Dr. Winkler received the Ph.D. in applied mathematics from the Courant Institute, New York University, in 1958. He is a senior member of the IEEE, a past chairman of the IEEE Engineering Management Group, and a member of the IEEE Computer Society. He is a fellow of the American Association for the Advancement of Science, a member of the ACM and a member of Sigma Xi. He is a licensed professional engineer (Arizona). He was General Program Chairman for the First International Conference on Computer Communication, October 1972 and editor of the conference proceedings, *Computer Communication – Impacts and Implications.*

Lee Danner is an advisory programmer in the IBM System Development Division, Gaithersburg, Maryland. He is currently the technical editor for the IBM Data Security Study. Previous assignments at IBM include program optimization for large systems applications, design of extensions to the OS/360 MVT control program for experimental projects, development of S/360 architectural extensions in support of special projects, and design and implementation of numerous real time command and control and diagnostic programs for the meteorological, telemetry, and radar subsystems of the Air Force Athena Program. Earlier, he was a senior systems engineer (computing) for Telecomputing Services, Inc., a project manager and senior systems analyst for Broadview Research Corporation, and a mathematician/programmer at the Lawrence Livermore Laboratory. Lee received a BS in mathematics from the University of California in 1955. He is a member of ACM.

The three papers in this chapter describe the existing and proposed services of the A.T.&T. carrier facilities for data- and computer-oriented services. The new Digital Data System which utilizes a network of digital carriers for data transmission is described. For further information on the Digital Data System, see [RUB 75].

For information about other carrier facilities such as Western Union, Datran and European data network, the interested reader should refer to [COX 72], [WOR 72], and [AND 72].

Common Carrier Facilities and Services

AT&T Facilities and Services

RICHARD T. JAMES, SENIOR MEMBER, IEEE, AND PAUL E. MUENCH, MEMBER, IEEE

Invited Paper

***Abstract*—This paper describes the U. S. telecommunications network with particular emphasis on aspects that are of importance to data- and computer-oriented services. The major portion of this network is owned and operated by the AT&T Company and the associated operating units of the Bell System as well as the independent branch of the industry. The services which the telephone network offers for data today depend in large part on transmission and switching systems which have evolved over the past decades primarily for voice transmission. An understanding of the history of the growth of the network and its facilities is useful background for the description of the current data services given later in this paper. After the current data services have been outlined, plans for AT&T's new Digital Data System, which utilizes a network of digital carriers for data transmission, will be described.**

I. Introduction

THE UNITED STATES today is provided with its telecommunications services by a vast network which has been almost a century in the making. That network, which is continually growing, services not only the voice communications needs of the country but also the data transmission needs as well. The following sections will provide some basic background on the more significant steps in the evolution of the network with emphasis on transmission, some of the fundamental considerations in using the network for data transmission, and finally a view of the next step in the evolution of the network with regard to its data transmission capabilities.

II. The Evolution of the Network

The network started to evolve in 1876—the year that the basic American telephone patents were granted. Despite the early difficulties, in the 1910–1920 decade the number of telephones connected to the network increased by an amount nearly equal to the total telephone growth prior to that decade. Except during the depression of the 1930's, growth in telephones has continued each decade since then.

Though the telephone growth was slow in the early days of the industry, the technical problems, particularly those in the transmission area, were formidable. This situation was most acute in the long-haul area because there were not really satisfactory means of amplification until the advent of the vacuum tube in 1913.

Even with the application of vacuum-tube amplifiers to the voice-frequency (VF) circuits carried on open-wire pairs, it became obvious that another approach to providing long-haul lines was essential. To handle the growth in the telephone network by adding a pair of wires (or 2 pairs—1 in each direction) per channel was clearly impractical. Thus the first carrier system, which provided 5 channels, was installed in 1918 and started a new era in long-haul transmission.

A variety of carrier systems followed leading to the introduction in 1938 of the Type J carrier systems, which were the first to exhibit some of the modern multiplex channel groupings. These systems were 12-channel systems that operated over open wire on an equivalent 4-wire basis, since different portions of the carrier spectrum were used for opposite directions of transmission.

A 2-step process was used to place the VF channels in the carrier range. They were first separately modulated to the 60–108-kHz band, and then modulated as a group to the desired portion for line transmission (for example, 36–84 kHz for one direction of transmission and 92–140 kHz for the opposite direction of transmission). The channel carriers used in the first modulation step are spaced at 4-kHz intervals. They, as well as the upper sidebands, are suppressed. This forms the "basic channel group" which is still used as the first step of modulation in many modern carrier systems (Fig. 1).

At about the same time—around 1940—the capacity of the long-haul paired cable (as opposed to open wire) plant was also expanded by the use of the Type K carrier system. Like the J systems, the K system formed the basic channel group of 12 channels as the first step of modulation. This was then modulated to the 12–60-kHz range for line transmission. This system operated on a physical 4-wire basis; different cable pairs were used for opposite directions of transmission.

Both of these systems were designed to modern 4000-mi circuit-performance objectives, and for a number of years formed the backbone of the transcontinental routes. A number of these systems are still in operation in the national network. However, their main use is now in intermediate-distance applications (800 km or so).

During the late 1940's, new methods for controlling noise and crosstalk in the cable carrier systems were developed resulting in the Type N carrier systems, introduced in 1950. The N systems, designed for intermediate and short-haul applications, are in widespread use today. The latest of these systems, introduced in 1964, is the N3 system, which has a capacity of 24 circuits compared to 12 circuits in the earlier N systems. Substantial deployment of N, primarily for intermediate-haul routes, is still occurring today.

In spite of the improvements, however, the utility of analog carrier systems using open-wire and cable pairs was obviously limited. For one thing, the circuit capacity of the carrier systems was too small and the required circuits could

Manuscript received July 26, 1972; revised August 9, 1972.
R. T. James, deceased, was with the American Telephone and Telegraph Company, 195 Broadway, New York, N. Y. 10007.
P. E. Muench is with the American Telephone and Telegraph Company, 195 Broadway, New York, N. Y. 10007.

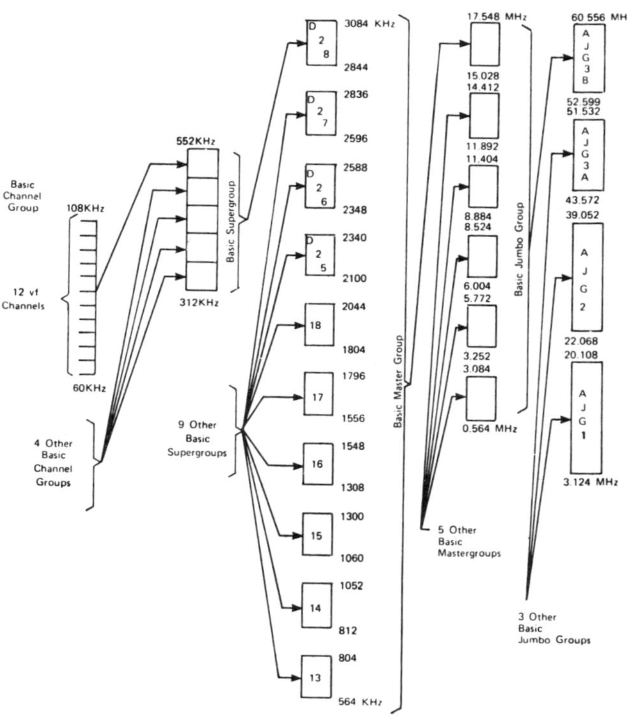

Fig. 1. Analog hierarchy.

only be obtained by adding more open-wire or cable pairs for carrier use. In the case of the open wire, this was a limited process; the resulting line structure soon became cumbersome and vulnerable. In the case of cable, the process was also limited, but due to crosstalk and noise rather than line structure. As more of the pairs in the cables were developed with carrier, the measures necessary to control noise and crosstalk became complex and expensive. Thus a new transmission medium was required.

As a transmission medium, the coaxial cable did not suffer from these limitations. Beginning in 1940 a succession of high-capacity carrier systems for long-haul transmission using coaxial cable was introduced. The first of these, the Type L1 system, had a capacity of 600 circuits per pair of coaxial tubes. It operated on a 4-wire basis; different coaxials were used for opposite directions of transmission. Another basic circuit grouping of the analog hierarchy appeared with this system, the basic supergroup (Fig. 1). This was formed by modulating 5 channel groups (60 circuits) to the 312–552-kHz range. Each supergroup was then modulated to its assigned place in the spectrum for line transmission. The L1-line spectrum extended from 68 to 3100 kHz. The repeater spacing was nominally 8 mi.

The Type L3 system, which was introduced in 1958, used the same type of coaxial cable (0.375-in diameter), but had repeaters at 4-mi intervals and provided a circuit capacity of 1800 circuits. With the L3 system another basic circuit grouping appeared, the basic mastergroup, 10 supergroups, 600 circuits. The frequency assignments of the basic mastergroup have changed slightly from the initial L3 assignments. The present standard allocation is shown in Fig. 1. Here the 10 supergroups (13–18 and D25–D28) occupy the frequency space from 0.564 to 3.084 MHz. (The spacing between supergroups 18 and D25 is greater than normal to avoid interfering with a pilot frequency on the transmission line.)

The next in the succession of Type L systems, the L4 system, was introduced in 1967. The same coaxial cable was used, but the repeater spacing was again halved (to 2 mi) and the circuit capacity was increased to 3600 circuits (6 mastergroups). The system operation is on a 4-wire basis; separate coaxials are used for opposite directions of transmission.

The latest long-haul coaxial system, the L5 system, is in the field-trial stage at the time of writing this (early 1972). It is scheduled for service early in 1974. This system provides 18 mastergroups or 10 800 circuits. It uses the same diameter coaxials as the other systems, but the repeater spacing is reduced to 1 mi.

The discussion thus far has been concerned with wire line and cable systems. It was not, however, these systems but radio systems that accounted for the majority of the carrier-circuit miles in operation at the start of this decade.

In 1946 the first commercial multichannel telephone microwave system was established between Los Angeles and Catalina Island—to provide 8 two-way circuits. With the advent of television, the development of high-capacity radio systems received added stimulation, and in 1950 the first of the modern generation TD-2 radio systems was placed in service between New York and Chicago. This system, initially designed to handle 6 two-way broad-band channels in the 4-GHz common-carrier band, saw its first use in the area of network television transmission with the first program carried being pictures of the signing of the Japanese peace

TABLE I

CARRIER CIRCUIT MILES (PERCENT OF TOTAL)

Type of Transmission	1940	1950	1960	1970
Open Wire	83	21	5	0.5
Cable (Wire)	17	50	24	13.5
Cable (Coaxial)		29	31	24.0
Radio			40	62.0

treaty. The use of TD-2 for both telephone and television transmission increased very rapidly so that today TD-2 is a major component of the nationwide telecommunications network. Today's radio systems have, of course, been greatly improved over those early ones. Modern TD-2 and TD-3 systems can carry 12 two-way broad-band channels, each of which can carry as many as 1500 telephone circuits.

Advances in microwave technology have opened the way to using other radio-frequency bands. Besides the 4-GHz common-carrier band, widespread use is made of the 6-GHz and 11-GHz bands. The TH systems operate in the 6-GHz band and provide 6 broad-band channels, each capable of carrying 1800 message circuits. In addition, a variety of short-haul radio systems, such as TJ and TL, which operate in the 11-GHz range, are widely used in the common-carrier network. Finally, it is significant to note that these radio systems use the same basic type multiplex as that used in the L systems previously discussed (Fig. 1).

In summary, then, the long-haul portion of the network has been subject to extensive changes in the last 40 years. In fact, the major portion of it has been built since 1950. The greatest area of change has been in the increasing use of radio and new high-capacity coaxial transmission media and a steady decrease in the use of the older transmission lines such as cable and open wire.

Table I shows this changing character of the long-haul plant by tabulating the percentage of carrier-circuit mileage furnished on the 4 main types of transmission lines at 10-year intervals. In this tabulation, a carrier-circuit mile is 1 mi of VF bandwidth derived from a carrier system. For example, 1 mi of a fully developed L1 system equates to 600 carrier-circuit mi.

One result of this intensive carrier development has been the steady increase in the bandwidth and complexity of the transmission systems. Fig. 2 illustrates the various bandwidths involved by showing the carrier spectra for some significant systems. The dashed bars indicate the carrier spectra of some open-wire systems. Here the largest transmission-path bandwidth was developed in the O systems (about 154 kHz). In contrast, the largest bandwidth developed by carrier systems using wire pairs in conventional cables (the N systems) is 96 kHz. These systems are shown in solid bars. (Equalization difficulties account for most of this difference.) The crosshatched bars show the coaxial carrier systems.

The carrier spectrum of the newest L system, the L5 system, starts at 3.124 MHz, just beyond the highest frequency (3.096 MHz) transmitted by the first L system. Equalization difficulties are the main reasons for not developing the L5 carrier spectrum below this point.

While the recent years of this evolution of analog systems have resulted in cost and performance improvements for data transmission, it is the more recently begun evolution of digital carrier systems that holds the most promise for major benefits to the data-communications users.

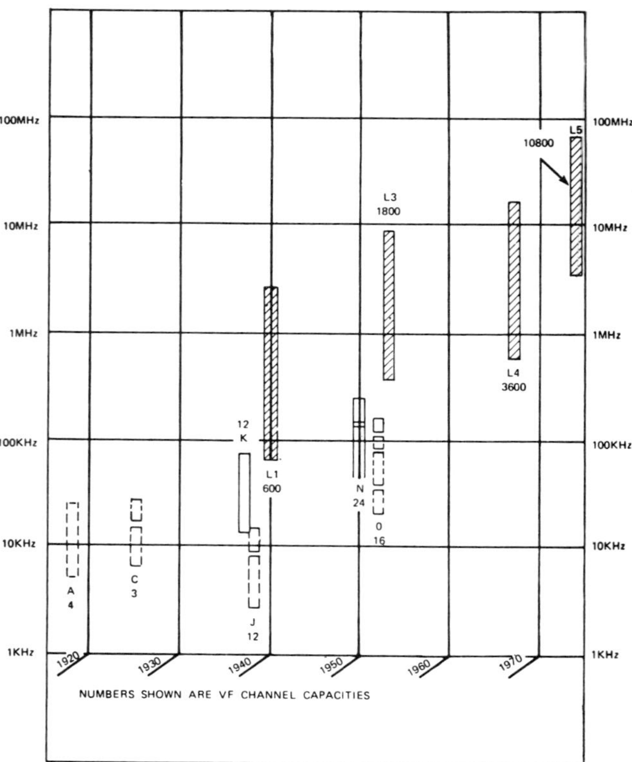

Fig. 2. Carrier system spectra.

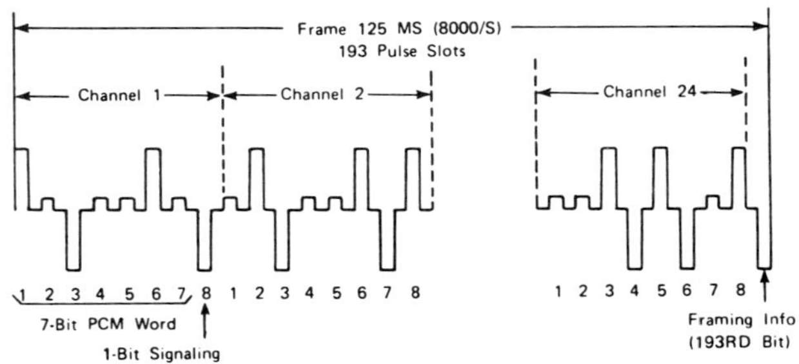

Fig. 3. T1 line format (D1 or D3 voice channel bank).

In 1962 the T1 carrier system was introduced and its use has since expanded rapidly. This system uses a line digit rate of 1.544 Mbits/s and provides 24 VF channels via a time-division multiplex. Each voice-frequency channel is sampled 8000 times/s, and the sampled amplitudes are quantized to 7-bit accuracy. As shown in Fig. 3, 1 bit is added for signaling purposes to each byte, and an overall synchronization bit is placed at the end of each frame. Thus each voice channel uses 64 kbits/s for transmission. These pulses are transmitted over wire pairs with repeaters, placed approximately at 1-mi intervals, used to regenerate and retime the wave. Because of this periodic regeneration, the effects of noise and distortion are not allowed to accumulate. Therefore, the bandwidth of the signal can be much greater than that of an analog system on the same wire-pair facility. While the T1 carrier proves economical for short-haul voice transmission, it is particularly appealing as a carrier for new data services which can take direct advantage of its digital nature and format.

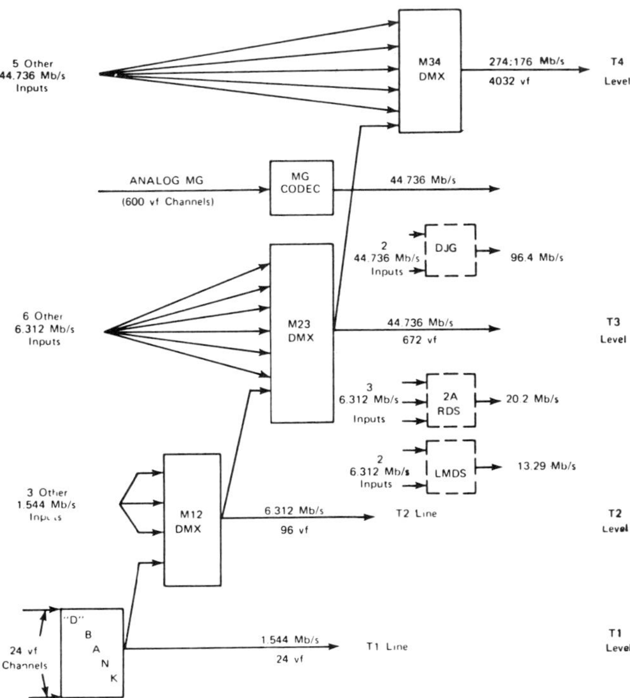

Fig. 4. Digital hierarchy.

The T1 carrier was designed as a short-haul system; it has not generally been applied for distances exceeding 50 mi (80 km). It has been widely used in urban areas as a means of economically increasing the numbers of voice channels that can be sent between central offices on existing wire cable. The T1 carrier is the lowest of a developing hierarchy of digital carrier systems. Fig. 4 attempts to show the digital hierarchy as it presently exists or will in the near future. Thus the first level of the hierarchy is the T1 level, 24 VF channels, and a bit rate of 1.544 Mbits/s.

Some intermediate levels above the T2 and T3 levels are also shown. These levels are obtained using existing analog carrier systems for digital transmission by incorporating especially designed wide-band modems for pulse transmission and regeneration. In the L4 system, for example, most mastergroups can be equipped to transmit 13.29 Mbits/s. The inputs to this are two 6.312-Mbit/s bit streams as shown. Similarly, in the L5 system a capability to transmit a 96.4-Mbit/s signal in a jumbogroup (6 mastergroups, or, equivalently, 3600 telephone channels) is envisioned. In the radio area, 3 6.312-Mbit/s bit streams can be combined in one 20.2-Mbit/s bit stream that can be transmitted over 1 radio channel.

In the L4 Mastergroup Digital System (LMDS), the line transmission system is unchanged from that of a normal L4 line. An L4 Mastergroup Digital Terminal converts the 13.29-Mbit/s digital signal into a 7-level partial-response[1] analog signal at a baud rate of 4.43 MBd. This analog signal is transmitted over the L4-line transmission system. Approximately every 300 mi, at one of the analog repeater stations, the analog signal is demodulated and then immediately remodulated and transmitted over the next line segment.

[1] This format is described in the paper by J. R. Davey in this issue.

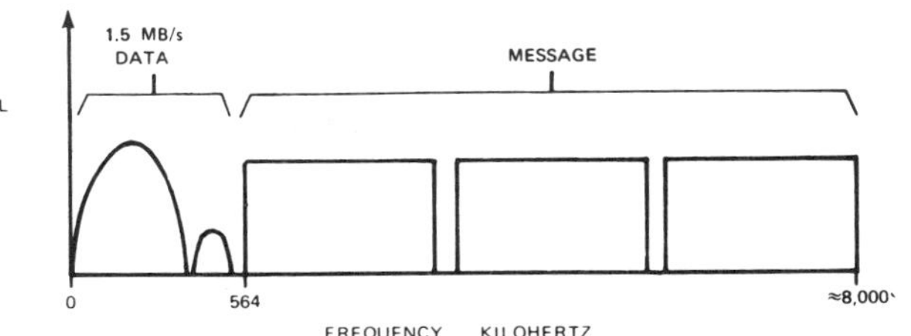

Fig. 5. Data Under Voice (DUV).

This back-to-back demodulation/modulation process provides regeneration and retiming of the digital signal. The same approach is used for the digital jumbogroup in the L5 system. Here, however, the digital signal is regenerated and retimed every 150 mi or so.

A similar scheme, but using 4-level frequency modulation, is applied to the 20.2-Mbit/s radio digital system. (This system is also called the 2A *R*adio *D*igital *S*ystem, 2ARDS.) Some special delay equalization is provided, but otherwise the radio transmission lines have the same transmission characteristics as when used for analog transmission systems. The digital signal is, however, regenerated and retimed about every 400 mi or so.

Also, as shown in Fig. 4, the T1-level 1.544-Mbit/s bit stream can be transmitted under the normal-voice baseband spectrum assignments used in radio channels. Fig. 5 shows how the radio baseband is allocated for this purpose. This radio digital system called the 1ARDS (the system has also been called the Data Under Voice or DUV System) is presently in the field-trial stage. It is expected that the main use of this system will be for the transmission of high-speed data; it is not expected that it will be used for voice transmission except under unusual circumstances.

It does not presently appear that long-haul transmission systems will be developed for all the T levels shown on Fig. 4. In view of the very substantial digital capacities of the existing long-haul coaxials and radio transmission systems, plans for further action in the long-haul areas are still fluid and under study. These plans include the 274-Mbit/s T4 digital line, an 18-GHz digital radio system, and the WT4 waveguide.

Partly as a result of this influx of digital transmission into the plant, it now appears that a system designed specially for the transmission of digital data could be implemented and would be useful and economically attractive. AT&T's plans for such a system are described later in this paper.

III. Using the Network for Data Transmission

The changes occurring by the early 1950's in the capacity to process data forewarned of the need for future data-communications capabilities [2] well beyond those of telegraph systems. Although there were no transmission and switching facilities in operation that were designed specifically for the predicted high speeds and characteristics required by the new field of data processing, it was suggested that perhaps facilities designed for voice transmission could be used. A 1955 paper by A. W. Horton and H. W. Vaughan in the *Bell System Technical Journal* evaluated existing voice facilities used for data transmission [3]. The paper reported the results of earlier studies of "high-speed" digital signaling over voice-band channels. The high speeds discussed were up to about 600 bits/s. In 1957 Malthaner described an experimental system that transmitted several hundred bits per second over channels of the switched network [4]. This work gave another evaluation of facilities, provided a first step in developing digital terminals, and was undoubtedly the precursor to today's DATA-PHONE® Service.

Needless to say, data-communications technology has progressed rapidly in the 15 years since then. Today, speeds of 4800 bits/s are achieved on the switched network, while modems operating at 9600 bits/s or even higher are being used on private lines. Nearly half a million data terminals are in service today representing an almost spectacular growth in the last decade.

This rapid growth, which is expected to continue well into the future, has brought the implementation of systems designed specifically for high-speed data transmission, as discussed in Section IV, into the range of economic feasibility. The remainder of this section will be devoted to a discussion of present-day data-transmission services (primarily voice bandwidth) provided by AT&T.

There are 2 basic classes of common-carrier channels provided by AT&T for data transmission—switched and dedicated channels. The basic switched service, Data-Phone service, uses the Switched Telecommunications Network, or, as it is often called, the Direct Distance Dialing (DDD) Network. Other switched services in which the trunks are leased on a full-time basis by a customer and are used only by his stations are also provided. The dedicated or private-line channels use the same facilities as do the switched channels, and thus share many of the transmission characteristics of Data-Phone service. In the case of private-line channels, however, since the channels are assigned in the circuit layout process rather than through the statistics of the switching and routing algorithms, they can be and are selected to meet certain minimum performance objectives.

Voice-grade private-line data channels are offered with several degrees of equalization. There are basically 5 different arrangements offered, varying from the 3002-type channel, a voice-grade channel, which in most cases requires little or no equalization, to C5 conditioning, which is the most heavily equalized arrangement offered. A more comprehensive discussion of the specifications for the 3002 voice-bandwidth channel and C-type conditioning is contained in [5].

Various configurations of private-line channels can also generally be ordered including 2-point, multipoint, or switched; and one-way (simplex), two-way alternate (half-duplex), or two-way simultaneous (duplex).

The Bell System offers a wide range of data sets (modems) [6], [7] capable of operating on the various grades of private-line conditioned channels. When these data sets are used with the recommended grade of channel, an error performance can be specified, e.g., for data sets operating at 2400 bits/s or below, a long-term average error rate of 1 error in 10^5 bits transmitted or better is specified for the system (channel plus data sets) during normal transmission conditions. If a grade of conditioning less than that recommended is used, the resulting system is maintained in 2 separate and distinct parts: 1) The Bell System data sets, and 2) the grade of channel ordered. Each will be tested and maintained to its own requirements but no attempt will be made to maintain the overall system to any specified error rate or performance level.

Similarly, when customer-provided data sets are used, the Bell System maintains the channel transmission characteristics as ordered. The customer, based on the manufacturer's recommendations, specifies the grade of channel required for operation of his data set. The Bell System does not verify these recommendations.

As is also the case in using the DDD network, the signals generated by customer-provided data sets must meet certain requirements to insure against harmful interference with other channels in the same cable or carrier systems.

Unlike dedicated channels, which can be specifically designed or conditioned to meet predetermined requirements, the DDD connections over which data are transmitted in Data-Phone Service are established on demand by connecting trunks from an oftentimes large population of facilities connecting switching centers. Thus only by treating all the trunks on all the routes between switching offices could a specific grade of conditioning be provided. The cost of such treatment would be prohibitive. Fortunately, even with all its statistical vagaries, the DDD network has been shown to be capable of supporting high-speed data transmission with acceptable error rates on a high percentage of calls.

In 1959 a nationwide data-connection survey was conducted, and the results published in a well-known paper by A. A. Alexander, R. M. Gryb, and D. W. Nast [8]. The results of this survey indicated that the switched network could adequately handle data transmission at speeds up to 1200 bits/s, with 63 percent of the calls made realizing error rates of 10^{-5} or better. It was these tests that affirmed the concept of Data-Phone Service as a workable approach to meeting the needs of the infant data-communications market.

A newer and more comprehensive description of the network as it affects data transmission is given in [9]. As discussed in that reference, the only difference between switched channels for data and those for voice involves the local subscriber loops and local central office. In the local-loop area special data-loop design rules are used to supplement basic telephone loop design. These special design rules are used whether the Bell System provides the data set or not (a piece of equipment called a Data Access Arrangement must be used in this later case). The rules are divided into 2 classifications; Type I conditioning for service at speeds of 300 bits/s and below, and Type II for speeds above 300 bits/s. Both types of conditioning impose requirements on loss, impulse noise, and message circuit noise. In addition, Type II includes requirements on slope and envelope-delay distortion.

In the area of local central-office selection, impulse noise (which originates in facilities as well as switching equipment) is probably the major transmission impairment caused by switching equipment. Work is currently in progress to further understand and reduce this impairment. Tentatively, the following can be said about impulse noise:

1) Crossbar and electronic switching systems are almost always satisfactory.

2) Step-by-step switching systems may or may not present data-transmission problems, depending upon the particular equipment involved.

3) Panel switching systems are often unsatisfactory for high-speed data service (above 300 bits/s).

® Registered service mark of AT&T Co.

The panel systems (which are found in some metropolitan areas) are gradually being replaced. For data customers who would normally be connected to a panel system or a noisy step-by-step system, a remote-exchange (RX) line is sometimes used to connect to another switching system.

Data customers using acoustically or inductively coupled data sets should be aware that these potentially noisy switching systems exist, and that unsatisfactory performance may result. When this occurs, the customer's alternative is to use a Data-Access Arrangement or Data-Phone service which will be engineered to meet data-transmission objectives.

As discussed in conjunction with private-line channels, subscribers to Data-Phone service can select from a wide variety of Bell System-provided data sets or can use customer-provided data sets connected to the network through Data-Access Arrangements. In Data-Phone service, as in private-line service, the Bell System tariff regulations specify network protection criteria which must be met by the customer-provided data-transmission equipment. These criteria are intended to protect various network services from excessive noise, intelligible crosstalk, and other forms of interference, as well as to minimize circuit interruptions, disconnections, and improper billing. In addition to the network protection criteria contained in the tariff regulations, there are hazardous-voltage limitations placed on customer-provided equipment connected to the network.

The work of Alexander, Gryb, and Nast [8], which was mentioned earlier as a key to the development of Data-Phone service, has been made obsolete by both the evolution of the plant as already described and by advances in data-set design. To provide an up-to-date picture of the transmission performance of the network, Bell Telephone Laboratories conducted a survey of toll connections during 1969 and 1970. These connections were established between Bell System and offices chosen by statistical sampling techniques. Both analog and data-transmission tests were performed, the latter at speeds ranging up to 4800 bits/s.

The results of this survey have been published in the *Bell System Technical Journal* and as a *Bell System Technical Reference* [10]. Briefly, the survey indicates improvements in the network's analog characteristics and, correspondingly, in its ability to handle data. Results of the error-rate measurements show that for operation at 1200 and 2000 bits/s, approximately 82 percent of the calls have error rates of 1 error in 10^5 bits or better. For 4800 bits/s, 50 percent of the calls had bit error rates of 10^{-5} or better. Some of these curves have been reproduced in this issue in the companion paper, "Errors and error control," by H. O. Burton and D. D. Sullivan. (As the 4800-bit/s data set used, a Bell System Data Set 203, contained a "scrambler" which results in single-line errors being transformed into bursts of errors, a more meaningful measure of performance at 4800 bits/s is the burst error rate which was 10^{-5} or better for 80 percent of the calls.) It should be mentioned that this improvement in the performance of the network is even more significant when it is realized that the transmit level was set to be −12 dBm at the serving central office in the 1969–1970 survey, whereas it was −6 dBm at the same point in the 1959 survey.

While this discussion has centered on voice-bandwidth channels, it should be pointed out that the Bell System also provides private-line channels for telegraph at speeds up to 150 bits/s and for wide-band data at speeds up to 50 kbits/s on a group and up to 650 kbits/s on a supergroup. In addition, a switched 50-kbit/s service, Data-Phone 50, is presently offered under an experimental tariff, and is available in New York, Chicago, Washington, Los Angeles, and San Francisco.

The discussion in this section has described the provision of a variety of services for data communications over analog channels (albeit, in some cases analog channels provided over digital facilities, e.g., T1). The following section discusses the Bell System's plans for providing some of these same types of services using digital facilities in their true digital form.

IV. The Digital Data System

Significant improvements in the cost of VF channels and their data carrying capabilities have resulted from the changes in plant just described. Even more promising for data transmission, however, is the rapid deployment of digital transmission systems which has occurred over the past decade. There are today over 17 million VF-channel miles of T1 in operation in the Bell System.

The T1 digital line as previously described carries 24 VF channels on a 1.544-Mbit/s bit stream. These VF channels are each in the form of a 64-kbit/s PCM signal. On the other hand, with today's degree of sophistication in modulation and equalization techniques, an analog channel can carry only 4.8 kbits/s or even in some cases 9.6 kbits/s with reasonable error rates. Thus digital voice channels, which are roughly comparable in cost to analog voice channels, provide considerably greater capacity for the digital data user.

Only a fraction of the channels' information-carrying capacity is actually used when a 64-kbit/s digital voice channel is used with standard analog modems. More specifically, the multiple transformations from digital to analog to digital produce an inefficient coding of the original data signal. While techniques to provide much more efficient utilization of these digital voice channels have been known for some time, the savings which it appears could be obtained by such efficient utilization have not in the past been realizable. The inability to realize these potential savings stems from several roots.

1) The data market itself had not developed to the point where geographic concentrations of data terminals were generally sufficient to be able to carry the costs of special-purpose multiplexing equipment.

2) While digital facilities were becoming more commonplace in the short-haul area where they had significant economic advantage for voice, long-haul digital transmission systems were still in the future, thus leaving no way to tie together these digital islands. Thus the ubiquity and economy of scale of voice channels were controlling.

In the case of wide-band (50 kbits/s or higher) data transmission, however, the potential economics of digital facilities are greater than at voice-band. In 1965 the Bell System started using a family of special-purpose T1 data terminals. The most commonly used of these, the T1WB3, uses a technique known as transition encoding or sliding-index encoding, and uses 3 64-kbit/s digital voice channels to transmit a 50-kbit/s nonsynchronous data signal. The remainder of the T1 line may be used for voice or more data channels. (A group, 12 voice channels, is required to transmit 50 kbits/s over analog facilities.) The approximate 3:1 loss of efficiency

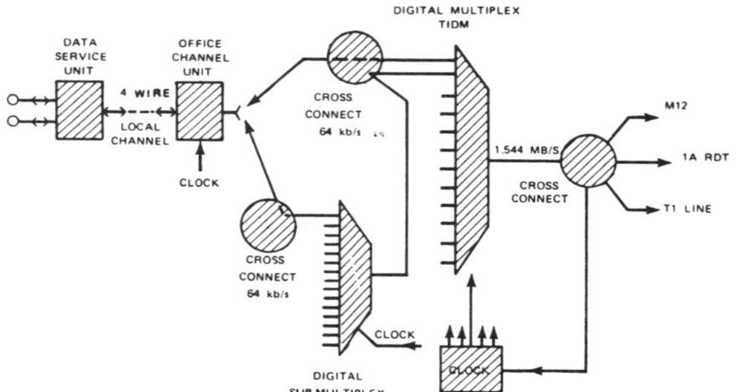

Fig. 6. Digital Data System hierarchy.

here is due to the requirement on the channel that it be able to carry nonsynchronous data over several links in tandem. The T1WB3 is used only in the short-haul section of a wide-band channel. In the absence of a long-haul digital transmission system, it is necessary to convert the transition encoded digital stream back to 50 kbits/s, and then use standard analog group-band—12 voice channels—facilities for the long haul. While the T1WB3 represents an advance in the use of digital transmission facilities in their true digital form for data transmission, a much more significant step in this evolutionary process will come with the introduction of the Bell System's Digital Data System [11] in early 1974.

The rapid expansion of the data market during the late 1960's and early 1970's, coupled with the wide availability of digital transmission facilities (T1) in the local area and the upcoming availability of long-haul digital systems such as the 1ARDS, 2ARDS, and T2, makes economically plausible the provision of a digital data system connecting major metropolitan areas of the United States.

The proposed Bell System Digital Data Service will provide private-line, synchronous, full-duplex data channels at speeds of 2.4, 4.8, 9.6, and 56 kbits/s. Initial service will be point-to-point only, and will be offered in early 1974. Shortly after the initial service date, multipoint operation will also be offered. Within 3 to 3½ years of initial service, the geographic area served will have been expanded to include about 100 major metropolitan areas.

Fig. 6 shows the major items in the Digital Data System hierarchy. Starting at the left of the figure, there is a unit located on the customer premises. This unit may be, at the subscriber's option, either a Channel Service Unit or a Data Service Unit. The former provides only the minimal functions of network protection and local-loop testing, while the latter provides conversion between the loop signals and the standard Electronics Industry Association (EIA) or CCITT interface signals as appropriate. Both the Channel Service Unit and the Data Service Unit operate over a 4-wire nonloaded loop (metallic) into a companion unit located in the serving central office. This companion unit, the Office Channel Unit, provides the transformation between the loop signal format and the cross-office signal format. Transmission on the loop is done in a bipolar baseband format similar to that used on the T1 digital line. A sufficient density of ones (pulses) on the loop must be maintained so that synchronization of the station equipment with the remainder of the network can be effected. A technique of zero suppression utilizing violations of the bipolar format is employed to insure that the required

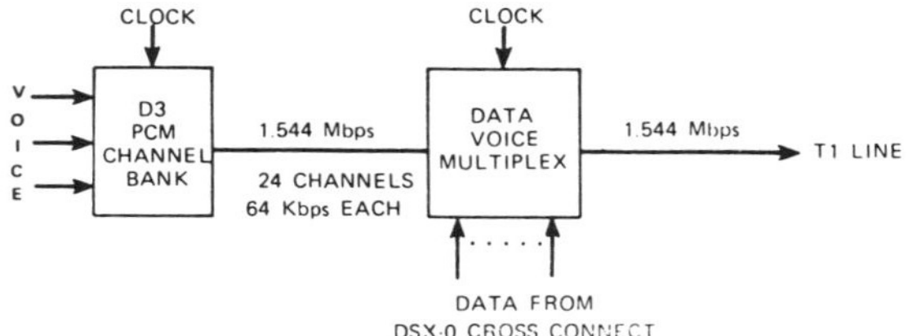

Fig. 7. Data Voice Multiplex.

one's density is provided without imposing any restrictions on the customer's data.

Within the serving central office, the Office Channel Unit is tied through a cross-connect to a time-division multiplexer. In the case of 56-kbit/s channels, a single stage of multiplexing is used as shown in the upper path in the diagram. A time-division multiplexer, called the T1DM, combines 23 such channels into a 1.544-Mbit/s bit stream suitable for transmission over T1 digital lines. In the case of the three lower speeds, as shown in the lower path in the diagram, an intermediate stage of multiplexing is used. One of three different submultiplexers (one of which combines five 9.6-kbit/s channels; another, ten 4.8-kbit/s channels; and the third, twenty 2.4-kbit/s channels) is used to derive a bit stream which is then treated as a 56-kbit/s data channel and fed into the T1DM for further multiplexing. The 1.544-Mbit/s output from the T1DM can be fed into a T1 digital line, a 1ARDT for transmission over microwave, or into an M12 multiplexer for transmission at one of the higher steps in the digital hierarchy.

As previously mentioned, the Digital Data System is a synchronous system. The synchronization is provided via a clocking hierarchy connected in a master–slave relationship over a directed tree network. The synchronization system is designed so that the Digital Data System normally operates without any losses of bit-count integrity (additions or deletions of bits—often referred to as slips). In the event of a disruption of the synchronization network due, for example, to a transmission cut, the two subnetworks formed by the cut will operate independently. The accuracy and configuration of the clocks in the network are such that the transmission path disrupted should be restored before a timing slip between these two subnetworks occurs.

Finally, in addition to the T1DM another unit shown in Fig. 7 has been designed to derive data channels from the

1.544-Mbit/s digital line. This additional unit, called a Data Voice Multiplexer and coded the T1WB4, can be used to extract individual 64-kbit/s digital voice channels from the T1 line. These 64-kbit/s channels can then be used to carry data while the remainder of the T1 line carries normal voice traffic. The 64-kbit/s channels thus derived can carry either 56-kbit/s data or submultiplexed data channels exactly as is the case with the T1DM. It should be noted that the factor-of-3 improvement in line utilization with 50–56-kbit/s data between the older T1WB3 and the new T1WB4 is due largely to the fact that the data carried by the T1WB4 is synchronous data.

The Digital Data System described above represents the latest, but by no means the last, step in the evolution of AT&T common-carrier facilities and services for data users. With the expected large-scale deployment of digital-transmission and digital-switching systems for both voice and data, the field of data communications will probably see as much change in the next two decades as it did in the entire two centuries which have passed since the earliest telegraph experiments.

References

[1] *Transmission Systems for Communications*, 3rd ed., Western Electric Co., Winston-Salem, N. C.

[2] J. L. Martin, *Teleprocessing Network Organization*. Englewood Cliffs, N. J.: Prentice-Hall, 1970.

[3] A. W. Horton, and H. W. Vaughan, "Transmission of digital information over telephone circuits," *Bell Syst. Tech. J.*, vol. 34, pp. 511–528, May 1955.

[4] W. A. Malthaner, "Experimental data transmission systems," in *1957 IRE WESCON Conv. Rec.* (San Francisco, Calif., Aug. 20–23), pt. 8, pp. 56–63.

[5] "Transmission Specifications for Voice Grade Private Line Data Channels," in *Bell Syst. Tech. Reference*, Mar. 1969 (to obtain a copy write to: Western Electric Company, Commercial Relations, P.O. Box 1579, Newark, N. J. 07102).

[6] "Bell System Data Sets," in *Bell Syst. Tech. Reference*, 1970.

[7] J. R. Davey, "Modems," this issue, pp. 1284–1292.

[8] A. A. Alexander, R. M. Gryb, and D. W. Nast, "Capabilities of the telephone network for data transmission," *Bell Syst. Tech. J.*, vol. 39, pp. 431–476, May 1960.

[9] "Data communications using the Switched Telecommunications Network," in *Bell Syst. Tech. Reference*, May 1971.

[10] "1960–70 Switched Telecommunications Network Connection Survey" (Reprints of *Bell Syst. Tech. J.* articles, Apr. 1971, pp. 1311–1405), in *Bell Syst. Tech. Reference*.

[11] R. J. Blackburn and P. E. Muench, "The Bell System's Digital Data System—An overview," in *Conf. Rec., 1972 IEEE Int. Conf. Communications*, vol. VIII, June 1972, pp. 5-1–5-5.

Reprinted by permission from *Proceedings of the IEEE*
Vol. 60, No. 11, November 1972, pp. 1254-1272

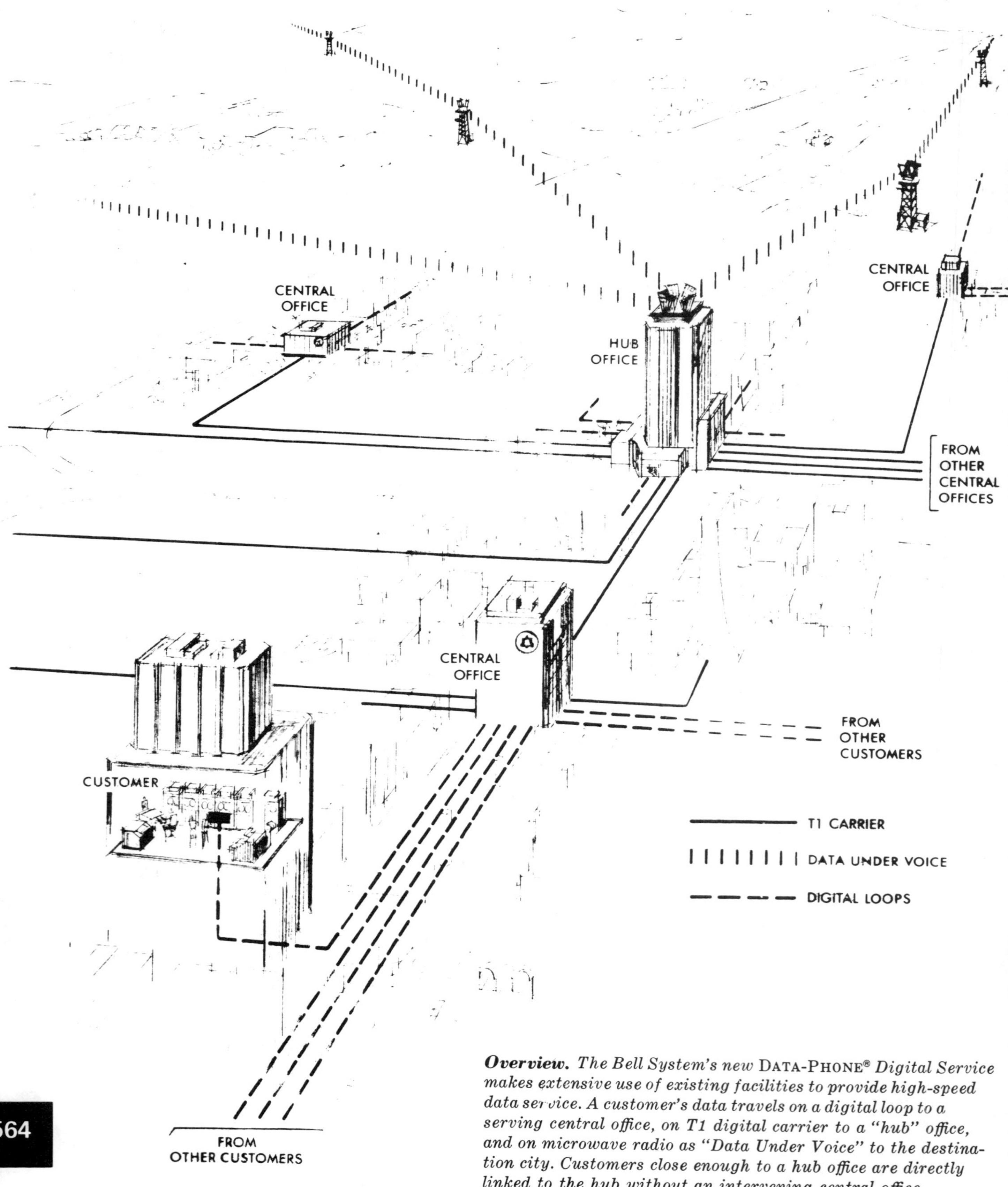

Overview. *The Bell System's new* DATA-PHONE® *Digital Service makes extensive use of existing facilities to provide high-speed data service. A customer's data travels on a digital loop to a serving central office, on T1 digital carrier to a "hub" office, and on microwave radio as "Data Under Voice" to the destination city. Customers close enough to a hub office are directly linked to the hub without an intervening central office.*

The Digital Data System launches a new era in data communications

CLARENCE R. MOSTER AND LEONARD R. PAMM

Data can be transmitted much more efficiently in digital form than in analog form. The new DATA-PHONE® *Digital Service exploits this fact by providing completely digital transmission for data, without any intervening conversion to analog form.*

ON DECEMBER 20, 1974, in New York, Boston, Philadelphia, Washington, D.C., and Chicago, the Bell System began offering interstate DATA-PHONE® Digital Service using a major new, all-digital network designed and built specifically for data communications. During 1975, 19 additional cities have been added to this network which is called the Digital Data System (DDS). Further expansion of DDS is planned so as to reach a nation-wide total of about 100 metropolitan areas during the next few years.

The introduction of DATA-PHONE Digital Service signifies a fundamental change in the way in which the Bell System can provide data transmission to its customers. With the all-digital system now made available, customers' data signals remain in their digital form while being transmitted over the dedicated DDS network. With conventional data transmission methods, customers' data signals must first be converted (modulated) into a form suitable for transmission over the largely analog channels that handle voice traffic and then, at the receiving locations, demodulated to restore the digital format required by the customers' data terminals.

DATA-PHONE Digital Service provides private line, point to point, and multipoint channels operating at customer speeds of 2400, 4800, 9600, and 56,000 bits per second (bps). Compared with transmission at these same speeds over analog circuits, transmission over the Digital Data System results in lower cost in most instances. Better performance results, too, because data signals are transmitted with a lower error rate and service is less susceptible to outages.

Although both the service and the system are new, existing business machine terminals

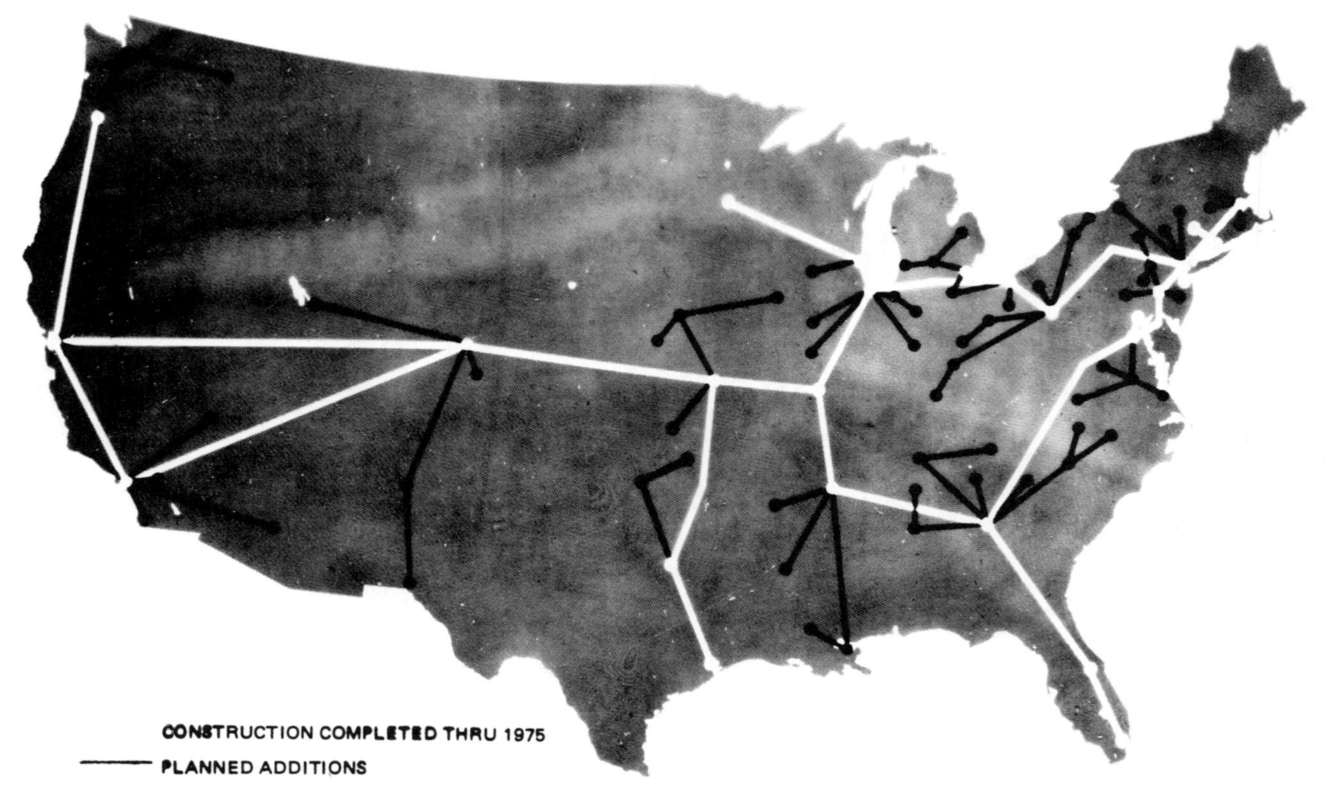

DDS network. *About 100 metropolitan areas are planned for inclusion in the* DATA-PHONE® *Digital Service network. By the end of this year, 24 cities will be linked. Less than a year ago, the network consisted of only five cities.*

can be linked to the network, without modification, through industry-standard interface connections.

Communications engineers have long known that digital transmission channels provide a technically well matched medium for the transportation of data signals that are generated and received by business machines in digital form. Furthermore, it has been recognized that significant communications economies can accrue from the use of such channels. Channel performance and cost considerations, therefore, provided the starting points for DDS planning.

Early in the DDS planning effort, it was clear to Bell Laboratories and AT&T engineers that many facilities and systems already widely deployed in the Bell System's exchange and long haul plant could be advantageously employed. Adding specially designed hardware to the existing plant would provide a functionally discrete digital data system. Among these existing Bell System plant elements are: the ubiquitous exchange cables, the extensive T1 digital carrier systems in metropolitan areas, and the nationwide network of microwave radio and coaxial cable systems. DDS architecture, then, incorporated and built upon the firm base provided by these facilities, with the fundamental aim being to realize high performance and economical channels.

Major attention has been focused on those attributes of DDS channels which significantly affect performance. Two major aspects of performance are quality of transmission and dependability of the channel. One DDS objective is to realize an average of at least 99.5 percent error-free seconds during data transmission at the highest customer speed of 56,000

At the desk. *Mike Ward, Western Electric installer, checks out a test position at a* DDS *hub office in New York City. From the test desk, a craftsperson can quickly and conveniently locate a fault without assistance from others.*

bits per second. Better performance is expected at the lower customer rates of 9600, 4800, and 2400 bits per second. Another DDS design objective is to realize at least 99.96 percent channel availability or an annual average downtime less than 0.04 percent. These stringent design objectives are aimed at establishing a new standard of performance for data transmission channels.

Basic System Architecture

A broad overview of the facilities involved in providing a point-to-point, private line service between two customers' premises with the Digital Data System is shown on page 420. The customer's station equipment communicates with the local serving office over a four-wire loop, to permit simultaneous two-way transmission, at the customer's data rate. At the serving office, the customer's signal is re-

Synchronizing. *Darryl Rosado, also of Western Electric, joins Mike Ward in checking out the hub office frequency-synchronization circuitry, which keeps both the hub office and the customers in time with a standard frequency from St. Louis.* 567

generated and then multiplexed together with other customers' signals into a 1.544 megabit per second bitstream and transmitted on the T1 carrier line to a centrally located hub office. Customers located near the hub office are served by four-wire loops brought directly into the building.

At the hub office the customer's signal is recovered from the T1 line bit stream by demultiplexing and, with other digital data traffic going to the same long haul distination, is multiplexed again. This multiplexed bundle is then transmitted on long haul digital facilities with the new Data Under Voice terminals which provide intercity digital channels operating at a speed of 1.544 megabits per second—see *The 1A Radio Digital System Makes "Data Under Voice" a Reality*, RECORD, *December 1973*, and *1A Radio Digital Terminals Put "Data Under Voice,"* RECORD, *May 1974*.

At the destination hub office, the process is reversed. The customer's signal is recovered from the digital radio channel and subsequently multiplexed onto a T1 carrier line extending to a serving office. There it is demultiplexed and placed on a loop to the distant customer's premises.

The planned DDS network is shown on page 422. Most of the intercity network facilities are provided by microwave radio systems. Expansion across the nation can be accomplished with relative ease through the addition of the Data Under Voice system to the existing transcontinental radio facilities.

The Data Under Voice terminals provide digital channels in the low-frequency part of the baseband spectrum transmitted by the radio systems and usually not used for voice transmission. Both the TD and the TH microwave radio systems can be used to derive Data Under Voice channels, providing one DUV channel for each radio channel.

Existing Network

In each of the metropolitan areas served by DDS there is a network of T1 carrier lines. About two million two-way digital voice channels are already in use for interoffice trunking in metropolitan areas. These T1 carrier lines are most important to the Digital Data System because they provide an already in-place digital transmission system for connecting serving offices to hub offices. Since each T1 line used in DDS will generally be carrying data signals from many customers, it is essential that downtime on these communications links

be minimized. To help attain that goal, each T1 line used for DATA-PHONE Digital Service is equipped with performance monitors which, in the event of a working T1 line failure, will automatically switch service to a dedicated hot standby T1 line.

A critically important function in the Digital Data System is synchronizing the far-flung network. Synchronization is achieved by means of a "tree" subnetwork in which the same data links that carry customer data are used to distribute synchronization signals throughout the network, branching tree-like all the way out to individual station units on customers' premises. A new Bell System reference frequency standard located near St. Louis sets the frequency for synchronizing the entire Bell System communications network, including DDS.

At all major (hub) offices in the network, timing supplies provide clocking signals which are synchronized with the frequency standard. These timing supplies contain highly accurate oscillators and sufficient "memory" to allow

568

'esting. *Flanked by a portable test unit, Darryl Rosado checks* ut *Digital Data System multiplex equipment.*

amiliarization. *AT&T Long Lines' Walt Korduba checks out* ewly *installed* DDS *equipment in a New York City hub office.*

free-running operation for several days in the event that the incoming synchronization is lost.

Timing supplies with less accurate free-running capability are used in noncritical distant branches of the synchronization network. All timing supplies have a sufficiently high degree of redundancy (backup units) to assure reliability.

On the Customer's Premises

For service connection to DDS on the customer's premises, Bell Laboratories engineers designed two units: a Data Service Unit and a Channel Service Unit. Both are connected by nonloaded exchange cable pairs to the nearest Digital Data System office.

The Data Service Unit accepts the customer's digital data from the data terminal across the industry-standard interface connection and converts it into bipolar signals for transmission over the four-wire loop to the serving office. From the office, the Data Service Unit receives bipolar signals which it converts into a form that can be accepted across the standard interface by the customer's data terminal. Timing is recovered from the incoming signal to give the system "clock" to the customer and to synchronize the Data Service Unit operation. The system functions performed by the Data Service Unit are simpler than those in comparable-speed modems used on analog channels; the Data Service Unit is therefore smaller and more economical than its analog counterparts—a further benefit of digital transmission.

In the Data Service Unit at the interface to the customer's data terminal and at the circuitry terminating the four-wire loop, loopback switches have been provided which can be operated either remotely or by front panel switches. The remote operation is controlled from a new testboard for DDS that provides a means of rapid and effective fault isolation.

The Channel Service Unit is a small line-interface device which only provides circuitry for properly terminating the four-wire loop and facilitating rapid, remote testing of the local channel. When using this unit, the customer receives and sends data in the same bipolar signal format as is used on the loop. The Channel Service Unit is used when signal processing to and from the bipolar line format, and retiming and regenerating incoming line signals are done by circuits in the customer's own equipment.

A complementary unit to that on the customer's premises terminates the loop at the serving Digital Data System office. This device, called the Office Channel Unit (OCU), regenerates the loop signal and prepares it for transmission through the multiplexing hierarchy. The OCU also contains a loopback switch that can be actuated remotely to facilitate fault location.

Located in the local office and the hub office are a family of new time-division multiplexers that have been developed at Bell Laboratories for the Digital Data System. One multiplexer, designed to handle the three lower customer speeds, can be configured to combine either twenty customer signals (at 2400 bps), or ten customer signals (at 4800 bps), or five customer signals (at 9600 bps) into a single bit stream of 64 kilobits per second (kbps). The output of this first-stage multiplexer is fed into a second-stage multiplexer that combines twenty-three of these 64 kbps channels into a single bit stream at 1.544 megabits per second for transmission on a T1 carrier line.

Customer's premises. *The brokerage house of Paine Webber Jackson & Curtis uses the Digital Data System to transmit data on commodities and options between Chicago and New York. At the firm's New York data center, Glenn Duffy (left), assistant vice president for data communications, and AT&T Long Lines' Gerald Tortoriello discuss the computer communication system. On the table: the Data Service Unit.*

The inherent efficiency of digital transmission for handling data signals may easily be recognized by remembering that 64 kbps is the digital capacity of a voice channel derived from the T1 system. (See *Digital Communications—A Tutorial,* RECORD, *October 1971.*) By contrast, analog voiceband channels have transmission properties which generally limit data signals to speeds no higher than 9600 bps.

Another second-stage data multiplexer, called a Data/Voice multiplexer, has also been developed (see *Mixing Data and Voice on the T1 Line,* RECORD, *February 1975*). This one can operate with a D channel bank or in a standalone mode. When operating with the D channel bank, the Data/Voice multiplexer allows 64 kbps data channels and digitized voice circuits to share a T1 line.

Each of the time-division multiplexers has protection arrangements which include performance monitors designed to detect faulty operation and command automatic switching to hot standby equipment.

The hub office, besides housing the time-division multiplexers and precision timing supplies for network synchronization and serving stations in its immediate vicinity, also carries out a number of other important functions. These include:

- Test access to individual data channels.
- Cross-connection facilities to permit efficient packing of the various customer data signals onto outgoing transmission facilities.
- Connection of the multipoint junction unit which is, broadly speaking, the digital equivalent of an analog bridge and is used to provide multipoint service. In multipoint service, many stations time-share a single circuit. The station channels are connected at the multipoint junction unit.
- Access to the long haul transmission facilities extending to other parts of the network.

Testing Facilities

Unique network testing capabilities have been built into DDS. The new testboards located in hub offices have direct access to individual customer circuits and by digital commands can remotely actuate the various loopback switches on each channel.

In the event of a customer trouble report, the testperson at the hub location receiving the report can remotely actuate loopbacks at the near-end portion of the customer's channel and, without assistance, at the far end. Doing so will enable the tester to verify a channel trouble quickly, through dynamic error performance measurements, or to isolate a fault to a particular segment of plant. Similar capabilities have been provided for testing multipoint channels.

This testing capability is intended to permit prompt and accurate responses to customer trouble reports and dispatch of the appropriate craftsperson to the proper place to repair or replace a malfunctioning unit.

Built-in features of DDS, such as the provision of signal regeneration, redundant equipment and channels, automatic switching to hot standby equipment, and rapid trouble isolation capability have all been provided in support of the stringent design objectives adopted for DATA-PHONE Digital Service.

Experience with the system points towards a new future of higher quality data transmission service as DDS expands nationwide to meet the needs of the Bell System's data customers. □

dataphone
dataphone 4800
dataphone
dataphone 2400
dataphone 4800
dataphone

NEW DEVELOPMENTS IN DIGITAL TRANSMISSION PLANNING FOR THE BELL SYSTEM

M. J. Thompson
Bell Laboratories
Holmdel, New Jersey

ABSTRACT

The rapid growth of digital transmission facilities in the Bell System serves as a continuing stimulus for new ideas and new system designs. While early digital planning focused upon PCM systems for providing the point-to-point links of a network, more recently its scope has broadened to include the time division switching of toll traffic, a family of digital data services, and analog-digital network interfaces of several kinds.

Overall system planning takes into account this broader scope as well as new developments in system architecture and component technology. This paper reports upon the status of Bell System planning with emphasis placed upon the rapidly developing area of digital terminal equipment.

INTRODUCTION

The impressive growth of digital transmission facilities in the Bell System serves as a continuing stimulus for new plans and new system designs. From time to time, descriptions have been published detailing a hierarchy of digital systems including voice-band channel banks, digital multiplexes, and digital transmission lines utilizing several transmission media.[1] As network needs are studied and as technological opportunities present themselves, planning for the hierarchy undergoes a continuing evolution. In this paper we present an overview of current plans, emphasizing the growing area of digital terminals, including interfaces with time-division switching machines and digital data networks. We begin with a summary of the digital lines.

DIGITAL LINES - WIRE PAIRS

Digital transmission lines are being developed for a variety of transmission media. Two systems for wire pairs, T1 and T2, are being manufactured, and a third, T1C, is undergoing a field trial. The twenty-four channel T1 system was introduced in 1962 and has grown rapidly to nearly two million installed voice channels, about thirty million voice-channel-miles.[2] It operates at 1.544 Mb/s (identified as the DS-1 level of the hierarchy) and is designed for single or dual cable operation up to fifty miles on pulp or PIC exchange cable, the basic medium for voice-frequency exchange trunks. The maximum repeater spacing is 6300 feet for 22-gauge pulp-insulated copper pairs.

The selection of T1 system parameters is based upon single cable operation with near-end crosstalk as the limiting type of interference. Dual cable operation circumvents this limit and permits a substantially larger number of T1 systems to share a pair of cables. More generally, there are a number of arrangements of cables, cable units, and apparatus cases which can markedly reduce if not eliminate near-end crosstalk, and these have led to two system configurations at higher bit rates. The first of these, the 96-channel T2 system, is intended for intercity transmission up to 500 miles using a low-capacitance PIC cable design (LOCAP)[3]. It operates at 6.312 Mb/s (the DS-2 level), with a maximum repeater spacing of 14,800 feet. T2 was introduced in 1972 and about 600 route miles are presently in service. The second system, T1C, matches T1 in intended transmission media, maximum length, and repeater spacing and operates at 3.152 Mb/s (DS-1C) attaining a capacity of forty-eight channels. T1C is scheduled to begin commercial service in 1976.

All three systems use pseudo-ternary codes to control dc wander, to ensure proper timing recovery, and to provide in-service performance monitoring. Automatic-line-build-out networks are used to simplify repeater installation procedures.

DIGITAL LINES - 274 Mb/s

Digital lines operating at 274.176 Mb/s (DS-4) are being developed using coaxial cable, microwave radio, and millimeter waveguide as transmission media. Each DS-4 channel carries 4032 voice circuits. The coaxial cable system, T4M, and the 18 GHz radio system, DR18, offer larger cross sections than the wire pair systems and are intended for application on metropolitan and short-haul intercity paths experiencing rapid circuit growth. The waveguide system, WT4, is intended for the classical long-haul application and provides more than twice the capacity of L5, presently the largest system in use.

The T4M digital line uses 3/8 inch coaxial tubes with up to ten working systems (and one spare) in a single sheath, resulting in a maximum cross section of 40,320 circuits.[4] Repeaters are spaced at a maximum interval of 5700 feet. A binary signal is transmitted and recovered in repeaters employing quantized (decision) feedback and automatic line buildout networks. DR-18 provides seven two-way channels (and one spare), 28,224 circuits, in the 17.7 to 19.7 GHz common carrier radio band.[5] The path loss experienced during rainstorms establishes the repeater spacing, which varies from one to five miles depending on local weather statistics. Four-phase PSK signals are transmitted, and both polarizations are employed. The WT4 waveguide system provides fifty-seven two-way channels (and three spares), in a frequency band extending from 40 to 110 GHz for a total of about 230,000 voice circuits.[6] The low attenuation of the TE_{01} circular propagation mode permits a repeater spacing of about twenty-five miles. A binary PSK signal is transmitted.

Both T4M and DR-18 will be introduced to service during 1975. The first WT4 route will enter service about 1980. As WT4 is installed, T4M and DR-18 will find applications as feeder links to waveguide routes.

DS-3 LEVEL

The six systems discussed utilize bit streams at four different rates, DS1, DS1C, DS2, and DS4. While the rates chosen are primarily a result of detailed studies of each line and its intended application, there is another important factor to be considered, the engineering and administration of system interconnection. Rates must be chosen with due regard for a multiplexing plan, and in fact another level, 44.736 Mb/s (DS-3) is required in order to satisfy two needs. The first is to provide an efficient method of interconnection with analog transmission facilities for large numbers of circuits, and the second is to establish an appropriately sized interface for implementing circuit additions and rearrangements in large terminal offices and at intermediate network branching nodes. The DS-3 level can accommodate a PCM-coded 600-channel mastergroup with nearly the same efficiency as digitally multiplexed circuits (600 circuits versus 672), and in conjunction with DS-1 can provide an efficient two-stage approach to circuit administration. The presence of DS-3 substantially reduces terminal equipment requirements and interconnection congestion at voiceband and at the DS-1 level.

MULTIPLEXING

The need for careful planning of the hierarchy can be illustrated by observing that ten functionally distinct multiplexes can be defined for interconnecting the five levels identified above. Figure 1 shows the four multiplexes actually to be used. The M12 (4:1) and M1C (2:1) provide access to T2 and T1C, and the M13 (28:1) and M34 (6:1) to the DS-4 systems. All are pulse-stuffing multiplexes[7]; the M13, however, is a departure from earlier plans which described an M12/M23 combination. The M13 is called a skip-level multiplex; viewed externally it is a single 28:1 multiplex; but its internal organization follows the essentials of the two-step approach. The consolidation of two multiplexes into one is shown in Figure 2. There is a substantial savings of interface circuitry operating at DS-2, and fewer elastic stores are required.

With the skip-level approach, the DS-2 and DS-3 levels may be interconnected by first demultiplexing to the DS-1 level. As need for this type of interconnection grows, an M23 multiplex can be added to the plan (Figure 3).

An M14 connecting DS-1 to DS-4 may appear to be a reasonable extension of the skip-level approach, but a number of difficulties are encountered with so large a multiplexing ratio (168:1). The M13/M34 approach is preferred for several reasons:

- Since per-circuit multiplexing costs dro[p] rapidly as cross section is increased, t[he] potential cost reduction associated with an M14 is small.

- More cost-effective piecewise growth of the terminal in response to circuit growth is obtained if the terminal is partitioned into a number of smaller, independently installed units.

- The physical size of an M14 would complicate the high speed common control circuits, suggesting a multistage multiplexing process.

- Faster and more cost-effective monitoring, protection switching, and sparing arrangements are possible when applied to tandem arrangements of basic multiplexing stages. In an M14, the measurement time required for detecting errors at the DS-1 ports would limit the number of points a monitor could scan to less than 168, and parallel monitors would become necessary, thus eliminating one benefit usually associated with an increased multiplexing ratio.

- With an M14, circuits must be brought to the DS-1 level for cross connection and rearrangements, as pointed out in the preceding section.

INTERFACE TERMINALS

To the multiplexing plan shown in Figure we must add the several kinds of terminals which carry signals to and from the digital network. There are four categories, terminal which convert analog signals to and from digital form, terminals that prepare bit streams for transmission over analog lines, interface equipment for digital switching, and interface equipment for digital services at speeds less than 1.544 Mb/s. There are several terminals used at the analog-digital transmission interface, and these are shown in Figure 4.

PCM CHANNEL BANKS

The basic DS-1 structure of twenty-four time-division-multiplexed 8-bit PCM words is generated for voiceband speech and data signals in the D1, D2, and D3 channel banks.[2] D1 was the first design, intended primarily for exchange applications, and was followed by D2 for toll applications. D2 introduced an 8-bit, fifteen segment, piece-wise linear companded coding law which has become a CCITT standard for 1.544 Mb/s digital channel banks The D3 bank, introduced in 1972 to replace D1 follows this standard and can be used for both exchange and toll applications. D3 is compatible end-to-end with D2 and D1D banks. D1D designates a version of D1 modified to achieve this compatibility, and the modification is easily retrofitted in existing D1 installations.

WIDEBAND DATA BANKS

Analog data services are provided at a number of rates higher than voiceband including 50 Kb/s and 230 Kb/s, corresponding to group and supergroup bandwidths. A family of data ks is available to code various combinations these signals into the DS-1 format.[9] These a signals are treated as asynchronous, and words are used to represent the time ations of transitions in the analog wave-m. Three PCM digits are required to resent one transition.

DIGITS OVER ANALOG FACILITIES

Although digital transmission over log radio and cable facilities is less icient than single-sideband frequency-ision-multiplexing for speech, it is more icient for synchronous data and for video-ne signals.[10,11] As a result a number of ital terminals have been designed for these ilities. The 1A RDT (Radio Digital minal) uses 7-level partial response ing to fit a DS-1 channel below the U600 tergroup on analog microwave radio systems pularly called DUV - Digits Under Voice).[12] 2A-RDT applies four-level FM to an entire MHz radio channel at 4 GHz and transmits ee DS-2 signals, about 19 Mb/s, which is r times the analog data capacity.[13] ally, the LMDT (L Mastergroup Digital minal) uses fifteen-level partial response ding to place two DS-2 bitstreams in the MHz band occupied by an analog master-oup on L-carrier systems.[14] The 2A RDT s been used in intercity videophone trials ile the 1A RDT and LMDT are important ements of the Bell System Dataphone® gital Service.[15]

MASTERGROUP CODING

A wideband PCM coder is planned to cilitate interconnection of the WT4 wave-ide system with other long-haul systems, l of which are currently analog. A U600-rmatted mastergroup is encoded with an bit companded coding law using a sampling equency near 5.6 MHz, after undergoing a equency translation to reduce the top seband frequency in the mastergroup.

DIGITAL TOLL SWITCHING

The No. 4 ESS Toll Switching System ilizes a synchronous, solid state, time-vision network to switch traffic among as ny as 107,000 trunks.[16] The network commodates a sequence of 128 8-bit words at ch port at the standard sampling rate of 00 samples/second. Of these time slots, 0 are assigned to carry traffic, corre-onding to five DS-1 24-channel digroups. shown in Figure 5 direct connection to gital lines at DS-1 is made through a imple interface terminal called the Digroup rminal; the elimination of channel banks is major economic breakthrough. With the igroup Terminal, T1 carrier proves in for any network environments at very short istances, even for intrabuilding trunks. ne functions of the Digroup Terminal are to ultiplex synchronously, one word at a time, he five DS-1 bit streams, to process ignaling information, and to provide certain easures of transmission performance. The igital link to the switching network operates t 16.384 Mbaud using a half-rate code to ransmit 8.192 Mb/s. This is referred to as the DS-120 level of the hierarchy. For analog trunks, a terminal called the Voice-band Interface provides the A/D conversion necessary for the DS-120 bit stream.

Time division switching requires synchronous operation. Frequency control is accomplished via master-slave synchronization of all digital switches, and phase adjustments are made in buffers contained in the Digroup Terminal. Since all traffic originates in channel banks throughout the digital network, these banks must be loop-timed rather than autonomously clocked. This capability is provided in D1D, D2 and D3. The switching office clocks are highly stable crystal oscillators which can operate through long periods of synchronization link failure with very low slip rates.

DIGITAL DATA SERVICES

The 3:1 inefficiency of transition encoding for asynchronous data may be avoided by using a synchronous technique which provides a sequence of time slots into which data signals are read. This is the basis of the Bell System's Dataphone® Digital Service[17], and the time slots are derived by subdividing the basic 8-bit codeword of the DS-1 format. Speeds of 2.4, 4.8, 9.6, and 56 Kb/s are provided. The terminal interfacing with the DS-1 level is either the T1DM, a 24-channel synchronous multiplex connecting to a 64 Kb/s level called DS-0 or the T1WB4, a terminal permitting up to twelve 64 Kb/s bit streams to be multiplexed with PCM-coded speech from a channel bank.[15] Master-slave clock synchronization is applied to DDS terminals and looped timing is used in channel banks connected to the T1WB4.

CONCLUSION

Figure 6 brings together the many types of terminals described in the preceding sections. They are grouped into three generic categories, digital transmission systems, analog/digital interfaces, and digital switching interfaces. It is apparent that overall plan-ning is becoming more complex as the role played by digital techniques expands, and it is this planning which is the key to welding the many systems into an organic whole. This paper is but a snapshot of current plans; further evolution is sure to occur, in such areas as satellite transmission and fiber optics, to mention two examples.

REFERENCES

(1) D. F. Hoth, "Digital communications," Bell Laboratories Record, Vol. 45 (Feb. 1967), pp. 38-43.

R. A. Kelley, "Multiplexing in a digital transmission hierarchy," 1968 IEEE International Convention Digest, paper 8F-3.

J. W. Pan, "Synchronizing and Multiplexing in a digital transmission hierarchy," 1971 IEEE International Convention Digest, paper 3F-2.

(2) C. W. Koman, "Basics of PCM and digital transmission in the Bell System," Proceedings of the National Electronics Conference, Vol. 28, 1973.

(3) R. B. Moore, "T2 digital line system design," Conf. Rec., 1973 IEEE Int. Conf. Communications, Vol. 9, 1973.

(4) J. M. Sipress, "T4M, A 274 Mb/s digital repeatered line for coaxial cable," Eurocon 1974 Conference Digest.

(5) J. J. Kenney and R. P. Slade, "18 GHz short hop PSK radio system experiment," Wescon, 1971.

(6) P. T. Hutchison, "A digital millimeter-wave waveguide transmission system," IEEE Trunk Telecommunications by Guided Waves Conference, 1971, London.

(7) J. S. Mayo, "An approach to digital system networks," IEEE Trans. on Communication Technology, Vol. COM-15 (April 1967), pp. 307-310.

(8) C.C.I.T.T. Recommendation G.733, Fifth Plenary Assembly, Vol. III, I.T.U., Geneva.

(9) L. F. Travis and R. E. Yaeger, "Wideband data on T1 carrier," Bell System Technical Journal, Vol. 44 (Oct. 1965), pp. 1567-1604.

(10) M. J. Thompson, "Transmitting digital signals on analog radio links," Bell Laboratories Record, April 1971, pp. 102-108.

(11) M. J. Thompson and A. B. Carlson, "Digital transmission over analog FM radio systems," Conf. Rec., 1969 IEEE Int. Conf. Communications, Vol. 5, 1969.

(12) K. L. Seastrand and L. L. Sheets, "Digital transmission over analog microwave radio systems," Conf. Rec., 1972 IEEE Int. Conf. communications, Vol. 8, 1972.

(13) C. W. Broderick, "A digital transmission system for TD-2 radio," Bell System Technical Journal, Vol. 50 (Feb. 1971), pp. 481-499.

(14) J. F. Gunn, J. S. Ronne, and D. C. Weller, "Mastergroup digital transmission on a modern coaxial system," Bell System Technical Journal, Vol. 50 (Feb. 1971), pp. 501-520.

(15) R. T. James and P. E. Muench, "AT&T facilities and services," Proc. IEEE, Vol. 60 (Nov. 1972), pp. 1342-1349.

(16) No. 4 ESS switching techniques, session presented at ICC'74.

(17) L. R. Pamm, "The Bell System's digital data system," 1974 IEEE International Convention Digest.

Reprinted by permission from *Proceedings of ICC 74*
June 1974, pp. 24a-l to 24a-4

Aside from technical considerations in designing a computer communications system, as discussed in Ch. VIII, non-technical issues such as economic, social, legal, and regulatory need to be considered. These issues will greatly influence future system design, particularly when computer communication technology matures and brings computer utility directly to the public.

Mathison and Walker discuss the modes of action of the U.S. Federal and State regulating agencies as they react to the non-technical issues and to economic factors in the computer and communications industries. Enslow discusses the economic, legal, and social considerations which should be made during the conceptual, developmental, and design phases of the construction of computing networks. Kuo addresses some of the political and economical issues about network interconnections. For further discussion of the social and economic issues, see [FAN 72], [DUN 73], [MAT 75], [GRE 75], and [KUO 75].

Social, Regulatory and Legal Issues in Computer Communications

Regulatory and Economic Issues in Computer Communications

STUART L. MATHISON, MEMBER, IEEE, AND PHILIP M. WALKER

Invited Paper

Abstract—**The rapid growth of computer communications in recent years has brought with it a number of difficult and controversial regulatory and economic problems. As the government agency responsible for the regulation of interstate common-carrier communications, the Federal Communications Commission (FCC) has been faced with many of these issues. This paper attempts to focus, in a tutorial fashion, upon four areas in the computer-communications field in which the influence of the FCC has been particularly significant. An overview of the regulatory process is given as background, after which we discuss the regulation of commercial computer-communications services, the interconnection of subscriber equipment to the telephone network, the creation of specialized communications carriers and of domestic satellite systems, and finally a number of data communications pricing problems which have arisen as a result of these developments.**

I. Introduction

IN THE computer-communications field there have been a number of important technological developments in recent years, as well as considerable innovation in the application of the new technology. These developments have created new capabilities within the industry, and have also generated new requirements among users. New market opportunities have been opened for the supply of services and equipment, and at the same time it has become technologically and economically feasible for new firms to enter certain parts of the previously tightly closed telecommunications industry. However, these advances have created a number of conflict situations between carrier and user, carrier and equipment supplier, carrier and carrier, and regulated and unregulated service firm. Generally, in the computer industry, as in other competitive industries in our free-enterprise system, these conflicts would be resolved in the marketplace. In regulated industries such as telecommunications, on the other hand, the government plays a major role in their resolution. Since the computer-communications field is at the intersection of these two industries, one regulated and the other unregulated, it is strongly affected by the actions of the regulatory agencies —especially the Federal Communications Commission (FCC), which exercises regulatory jurisdiction over all interstate common-carrier communications.

This paper attempts to focus, in a tutorial fashion, upon four areas in the computer-communications field in which the influence of the FCC has been particularly significant. An overview of the regulatory process is given as background, after which we discuss the regulation of commercial computer-communications services, the interconnection of subscriber equipment to the telephone network, the creation of specialized communications carriers and of domestic satellite systems, and finally a number of data-communications pricing problems that have arisen as a result of these developments.

The first problem areas arose in the mid-1960's, when several troublesome trends were noted among firms providing commercial computer-communications services. On the one hand, several firms offering commercial time-sharing and computer-based information services indicated an intention to also provide to the public store-and-forward message-switching services for hire—services previously provided only by regulated communications common carriers. On the other hand, several communications carriers announced plans to market computer services, both remote access and otherwise. At the same time industry observers, noting the apparent economies of scale inherent in computing systems, suggested that perhaps the remote-access "computer utility" was a natural monopoly that should, as in the case of other monopolies, be regulated. With these and other questions as an agenda, the FCC in 1966 instituted a public inquiry aimed, in part, at determining the appropriate regulatory treatment of various types of computer-communications services provided by carriers and noncarriers. Many of the issues were resolved in principle in the FCC's *Final Report and Order* issued in 1971, but the Commission's guidelines have left substantial room for interpretation.

The second major regulatory area of interest here is termed "interconnection." In the past, telephone carriers in the United States have prohibited the direct interconnection with their circuits of any devices or systems not owned by the carrier. This prohibition was adopted to protect both the physical integrity of the telephone system and also the carrier's equipment-rental revenues. Since telephone subscribers were generally satisfied with this arrangement, the regulatory agencies sanctioned it. In recent years, however, this ban on interconnection became increasingly onerous to many business-telephone users, especially where data communications was involved—for the user was forced to rent his data modem, private automatic branch exchange (PABX) system, or other terminal equipment from the carrier, even though more advanced or more cost-effective equipment was, or could have been, available from independent suppliers. Most of the computer industry respondents in the FCC's computer inquiry mentioned above strongly argued for a change in the interconnection rules (and the carriers argued against such a change), but before the Commission had time to consider the issue in that proceeding it was forced to decide it in an adjudicatory context. Thus, in its landmark *Carterfone* ruling in 1968, the FCC threw out the old interconnection prohibition and initiated the painful process of developing a new and more reasonable *modus operandi* for the industry.

The third problem area has come about as a result of advances in the state of the art in transmission. First, the development of microwave radio technology and the economics associated with it (relatively low system-investment cost, avoidance of the need for right of way, etc.) have made

Manuscript received May 9, 1972; revised July 13, 1972.

The authors are with Telenet Communications Corporation, Washington, D.C. 20006.

it possible for new firms to construct and operate intercity transmission facilities separate from those of the existing common carriers. At the same time, the development of the digital computer and the rapid expansion of computer and data-communications applications throughout our economy have created a demand for common-carrier services somewhat different from those traditionally provided by the telephone and telegraph companies. Adding to this data-oriented user demand have been rapidly growing requirements in other areas of long-haul business communications, including voice, facsimile, and record message. Given this technological opportunity and the market demand associated with it, a number of new firms known as "specialized carriers" have in the past few years proposed construction of microwave systems throughout the country and offered certain types of business and data communications services in competition with the existing carriers. These proposals were resisted by the incumbent carriers, of course, and the FCC has had to sort out the policy alternatives in the light of the public interest. Related to this has been the question of domestic communication satellites, for the development of satellite technology has made it possible for both the existing carriers and new entities as well to provide long-haul communication services through use of this attractive medium.

The fourth problem area concerns the pricing of communications services. What price-structure changes, if any, are necessary when voice-engineered communications facilities are used for handling data traffic? What type of pricing structure is appropriate for communications systems exclusively designed for data transmission? What effect will the entry of competing long-haul carriers have upon present rate levels? These, and other aspects of the rate-setting problem, are discussed in Section VI of this paper.

II. The Regulatory Process

In virtually every nation of the world, public telecommunications services are provided either by a government department or a government-owned corporation. The United States (and most of the provinces in Canada) relies instead upon private firms to supply these vital services, with the government's role limited to the formulation of broad policies, the authorization of new facilities, and the approval of services and rates. These private organizations, called common carriers, include the telephone companies (each of which has a monopoly in its geographic service area),[1] Western Union Telegraph Company (which has a monopoly on domestic telegraph service throughout the United States), several competing United States-based international telegraph companies, and a variety of small carriers providing specialized public services, such as radio paging, mobile telephone, and video transmission. To insure that these common carriers operate in the public interest, providing adequate and nondiscriminatory service at reasonable rates, the FCC exercises regulatory control over *interstate* and *foreign* carrier operations, and each state (except Texas) has a state public-utility commission which regulates *intrastate* carrier operations.

The FCC and its state counterparts perform their regulatory mission in several ways. 1) They limit entry. A firm must demonstrate public need, and its capability to satisfy that need, in order to obtain common-carrier status and be permitted to construct (or lease) facilities and offer service. 2) They bar unreasonable or discriminatory pricing policies or carrier tariff regulations. 3) They limit overall carrier profits, so that the carrier cannot take unfair advantage of his protected monopoly or near-monopoly position to exploit the public. While their authority is broad, the regulatory agencies generally operate in a passive rather than an active mode—reviewing carrier tariffs and service proposals submitted to them, but taking no initiative to plan and direct the introduction of new carrier services, the use of new technology, the choice of alternative pricing philosophies, or the setting of overall carrier priorities. These matters are ordinarily left to the carriers, with the result that most decisions reflect the interests of the carriers—which do not necessarily coincide with the public interest. For example, the Bell System has spent several hundred million dollars during the past decade developing its new Picturephone® service, considerably more than it has spent on the development of digital transmission services—although the latter may make a much more significant contribution to society in the long run.

In part, these important planning decisions are left to the carriers because both the FCC and the state regulatory agencies have inadequate budgetary and personnel resources to cover the large, complex, and growing communications-carrier industry. The FCC's Common Carrier Bureau, which has this responsibility at the Federal level, has only 11 percent of the FCC's total budget (3.3 million dollars out of 31 million dollars total in the fiscal year 1972), and some 110 professional staff (mostly lawyers, accountants, and engineers, with a handful of economists).[2] Viewed in terms of regulatory budget dollars per revenue dollar of the industry being regulated, the FCC spends only one-fifth as much to regulate the communications carriers as the Interstate Commerce Commission (ICC) and the Federal Power Commission (FPC) do to regulate the transportation and energy industries, respectively. At the state level, the regulation of telecommunications leaves even more to be desired. The state commissions typically exercise regulatory jurisdiction over many different types of intrastate public utility activities in addition to telecommunications, including gas, electricity and water service, railroads, motor carriers, etc.—and have budgets ranging from 102 000 dollars in Delaware to 10.2 million dollars in California to accomplish all this. The *total* professional staff

[1] The American Telephone and Telegraph Company (AT&T), which with its subsidiaries—23 telephone operating companies, a manufacturing and supply arm (Western Electric Co.), and an R&D arm (Bell Laboratories, Inc.)—constitutes the Bell System, is by far the largest member of the telephone industry. In 1971 Bell served 82 percent of the 125 million United States telephones in use and had revenues of 19 billion dollars, assets of 55 billion dollars, and over a million employees. (Measured by assets and employees, it is America's largest corporation by far.) Some 1700 independent telephone companies serve the remaining 18 percent of United States telephones, with 3 large holding companies [General Telephone & Electronics (GTE), United Utilities, and Continental Telephone] controlling 65 percent of that total.

® Registered service mark of the American Telephone and Telegraph Company.

[2] In December 1971 the FCC dismissed Phase II of its pending broad-scale investigation of AT&T's telephone rates, saying ". . . we do not have sufficient resources to permit adequate staffing of the hearings that would be involved or to complete the preparatory staff work required for developing a meaningful evidentiary record on these issues. This is the result of the continuing growth in the volume and complexity of regulatory problems within the common carrier field." [32 FCC 2nd 691, 692 (1971).] The Commission then listed as examples of its new regulatory responsibilities such areas as interconnection, domestic communications satellites, and specialized carriers, which are discussed elsewhere in this paper. Following severe public criticism, the FCC reinstated the investigation of AT&T, and Congress agreed to appropriate additional funds for this purpose. A substantial increase in the staff of the Common Carrier Bureau was thereby made possible, and while no decisions have yet been made regarding the temporary or permanent status of these personnel, a strong case could be made for their retention after the AT&T investigation is concluded.

TABLE I

FCC Computer-Inquiry Chronology

	1964	Western Union Telegraph Co. begins to diversify into data-processing services, aiming towards creation of a "national information utility."
	1965	Bunker-Ramo Corp. attempts to add message-switching features to its computer-based stock-quotation service, and is rebuffed by AT&T and Western Union—who refuse to furnish circuits for such a "communication" activity by a noncarrier.
Feb.	1966	IBM suggests to FCC a "primary business test" guideline for determining whether to regulate a data-processing and/or message-switching service.
June–Oct.	1966	Two international carriers, ITT Worldcom and RCA Globcom, disagree about whether their new competitive message-switching services should be tariffed as communications activities.
Nov.	1966	FCC issues *Notice of Inquiry*, asking broad range of questions concerning computer-communications policy.
Mar.	1968	Comments are filed with FCC by over 60 interested parties, including carriers, computer firms, users, and government agencies.
June	1968	FCC issues *Carterfone* decision, authorizing interconnection of customer equipment to the telephone network, and resolving one of the issues in the computer inquiry (see Section IV).
Dec.	1968	President Johnson's Task Force on Communications Policy issues its report, generally supporting the positions taken by the computer-industry respondents in the FCC inquiry.
Feb.	1969	Stanford Research Institute (SRI), under contract to the FCC, completes its analysis of the issues in the inquiry—raising more questions than it answers.
Feb.	1969	AT&T permits sharing ("joint use") of its telegraph-grade and voice-grade private-line channels, as requested by respondents in the inquiry, thus partially resolving a second issue in the inquiry.
May	1969	FCC issues *Report and Further Notice of Inquiry*, soliciting comments on the SRI study. Respondents' comments reiterate previously expressed positions, adding little to the FCC's understanding of the issues.
Aug.	1969	FCC issues *MCI* decision, approving first specialized common carrier. This action (see Section V) was motivated in part by the complaints of computer-inquiry respondents about the inadequacy of existing data-communications services.
Nov.	1969	Data Transmission Co. (Datran) files application with FCC for a nationwide digital common-carrier network incorporating features requested by computer-inquiry respondents (this, and other specialized-carrier proposals, are discussed in Section V).
Apr.	1970	FCC issues *Tentative Decision*, proposing resolution of the remaining issues in the inquiry.
Sept.	1970	FCC hears oral arguments—presentations to the Commission by some 20 interested parties.
Mar.	1971	FCC issues *Final Decision and Order* (see text).
Mar.	1972	FCC denies petitions for reconsideration submitted by several parties; court appeal of FCC's final decision remains pending.

assigned to the state commissions ranges from 1 man in Arizona to 295 in New York. Thus state regulation of telecommunications tends to be spotty, and in most states essentially ineffective.

In recent years it has become recognized that government telecommunications policy planning has been seriously deficient, and several moves have been made to improve the situation. In Canada, for example, through the Government Organization Act of 1969, a Federal Department of Communications was created to ensure the development and efficiency of communications systems and facilities, and to recommend national policies and programs in this area. The first act of the new Department was to establish a high-level fact-finding group, known as the Telecommission, to conduct a comprehensive study of the present state and future prospects of telecommunications throughout the country.

In the United States, somewhat analogous developments have taken place, although they have not yet resulted in a cabinet-level Department of Communications. In 1967 a Presidential Task Force on Communications Policy was formed to study a wide range of current issues, including computer-communication topics. And in 1970 a new Office of Telecommunications Policy (OTP) was established in the Executive Office of the President, to formulate and recommend long-range national plans and policies in telecommunications and to act as spokesman for the Executive Branch before the FCC and the Congress.

OTP is relatively small (2.5 million-dollar budget in fiscal year 1972, and some 60 total staff), but is supported by a telecommunications research staff located in the Department of Commerce, and is in a good position to exercise considerable influence in the federal regulatory and policy-making process. By taking a fresh look at traditional industry practices in the light of new technology, it appears that OTP will have a beneficial impact upon the development of regulatory practices concerning computer communications, but it is too early to draw firm conclusions. Of course, the creation of policy-analysis organizations such as OTP can be no substitute for giving the FCC adequate resources to do more of its own policy analysis and development, but at least it is a step in the right direction.

III. Regulation of Commercial Computer-Communication Services

The possible regulation of commercial computer-communication services, such as time-sharing and information-retrieval services provided by private firms and by communications common carriers, has in recent years been the subject of much discussion and controversy. Several developments that occurred in the United States in the mid-1960's highlighted the potential problems.

1) Computer time-sharing technology was emerging and a number of industry experts predicted the formation of "computer utilities" which, because of scale, would ultimately supply data-processing services to large numbers of users in much the same manner as other public utilities.

2) Common carriers were beginning to diversify into the computer services field, and Western Union in particular proclaimed its intention to become the "information utility" of the future.

3) Independent computer services firms proposed that they might offer message-switching services to their customers, in addition to data-processing or information-retrieval services.

To deal with these and other questions the FCC initiated a public inquiry in late 1966 into the "Regulatory and Policy Problems Presented by the Interdependence of Computer and Communication Services and Facilities."[3] The Commission's *Final Decision and Order* was adopted in March 1971.[4] (Table I summarizes the historical development of this proceeding.) As might be expected during the course of a 5-year proceeding, some of the issues originally addressed in the inquiry were overtaken by the course of events and became

[3] *Notice of Inquiry*, Docket 16979, 7 FCC 2nd 11 (1966).
[4] 28 FCC 2nd 267 (1971).

moot by the time of the Commission's final decision, while other issues were clearly and adequately resolved in the inquiry and reflected an unusual amount of foresight on the part of the Commission and its staff. Unfortunately, however, certain issues were only partly settled, and at the time of writing remain a source of uncertainty.

The issues addressed by the FCC, relating to the regulation of computer communications, were as follows.

1) Whether, and under what circumstances, computer-based data-processing or information services—remote-access services using communication lines, and perhaps also stand-alone services—should be regulated by the FCC (either under existing authority granted by the Communications Act of 1934, or under additional authority that would require new legislation).

2) Whether, and under what circumstances, communications common carriers should be permitted to offer data-processing services to the public.

3) Whether, and under what circumstances, computer-based store-and-forward message-switching services should be deregulated by the FCC.

4) Whether, and under what circumstances, computer-communication services combining both data-processing and message-switching functions (hybrid services) should be regulated by the FCC.

Remote-Access Computer Services

On many issues in the FCC's inquiry there was sharp disagreement between the common carriers on the one hand and the computer firms and users on the other, but regarding rate and profit regulation of computer services provided to the public there was general agreement that this was unnecessary and undesirable for the foreseeable future. These services, which do exhibit economies of scale to a point, simply do not have the *continually* increasing economies of scale that are characteristic of a "natural monopoly" (a business which, by virtue of its inherent technical characteristics, can be operated most efficiently if it enjoys a monopoly of the marketplace), such as an electric utility or a telephone company providing local exchange service. Nor do there appear to be compelling requirements to regulate computer services in order to ensure the "quality and integrity" of the product, as in the case of the pharmaceutical and banking industries. There may be reasons for imposing certain controls upon these service offerings in order to ensure the protection of individual privacy, but these would not be in the form of price and profit control as applied to common carriers.

The FCC therefore concluded that ". . . in view of all the foregoing evidence of an effective competitive situation, we see no need to assert regulatory authority over data processing activities whether or not such services employ communications facilities in order to link the terminals of subscribers to centralized computers."[5] The Commission did, however, retain the prerogative to "re-examine the policies set forth herein . . . if there should develop significant changes in the structure of the data processing industry."

Since the FCC concluded that regulation was unwarranted, it did not address the question of whether or not it had the necessary legal authority to impose regulatory controls upon these services. It appears that the only provisions of the Communications Act from which the Commission might derive such authority are the provisions dealing with common carriers. The Commission would then have to conclude that these firms were common carriers, i.e., that they offer as a for-hire service to the public at large the transportation of information that is chosen by the user. However, computer services do not simply *transmit* information; they *transform* it, and the information sent is not entirely at the discretion of the user. Although remote-access computer-service firms employ communication lines, this should no more make them common carriers than should vehicular delivery of goods make a furniture company into a regulated trucking carrier.[6] Thus the Justice Department has concluded: "It is our opinion that 'remote-access data processing' is not common carrier communications and hence, is not subject to the Commission's jurisdiction under Title II of the Communications Act."[7]

New legislation would most likely be required in order for the FCC or any other government agency to impose public utility-type regulation upon the computer-services industry. However, as stated above, such action does not appear appropriate at this time.

Common-Carrier Provision of Data-Processing Services

While the FCC has little authority over computer services in general, it does have greater authority where such services are provided by common carriers. Under the Communications Act the Commission may reasonably regulate a carrier's offering of an otherwise unregulated service in order to ensure that the carrier continues to provide its communication service in a suitable manner. The Commission has wide discretion in determining what steps are necessary to prevent diversion of the carrier's energies and resources from its public obligations. In its *Final Decision and Order* the Commission concluded it had "ample jurisdiction" to specify conditions under which common carriers may provide commercial data-processing services.

Communication carriers all over the world have shown considerable interest in diversifying into the data-processing services field. In addition to Western Union, mentioned earlier, GTE and United Utilities, Inc. have established service centers in the United States, offering a variety of on-line and batch data-processing services. (The Bell System is restricted, by its 1956 antitrust consent decree with the Justice Department, from providing other than regulated common-carrier communication services. Unless remote-access data processing is found to be a common-carrier offering—an unlikely possibility—it cannot be offered to the public by the Bell System.) In Canada, Canadian National/Canadian Pacific Telecommunications, the domestic telegraph carrier, has acquired Computer Sciences, Ltd.; and Bell Canada, serving approximately 70 percent of all Canadian telephone subscribers, has indicated its interest in providing data-processing services. In Germany, the Bundespost (the German telephone administration), in a joint effort with Nixdorf and Siemens, is offering public data-processing services. And in Japan, the Nippon Telephone and Telegraph Company offers both a public time-sharing service and a computer-based public calculator service (the latter based on the use of push-button telephones with voice answer-back).

[5] 28 FCC 2nd 291 (1970), at 298.

[6] This analogy was first suggested by S. B. Perlman, in *Legal Aspects of Selected Issues in Telecommunications.* Montvale, N. J.: AFIPS Press, 1970.

[7] *Response of the United States Department of Justice* in FCC Docket 16979 (the computer inquiry), Mar. 5, 1968, p. 64.

Carriers have been entering the data-processing services field, much to the dismay of independent computer service-bureau firms, for several reasons.

1) In order to utilize internal data-processing resources more efficiently by providing services to outside users—thus obtaining scale economies and utilizing idle capacity.

2) As a financial investment in a rapidly growing field.

3) In order to gain experience in the operation of computer-communication systems.

4) And, in some cases, to make public data-processing services widely available where this might not have otherwise occurred.

Unfortunately, the provision of data-processing services by carriers brings with it certain regulatory problems. Assuming, for example, that these services remain an unregulated activity and that no restrictions are imposed upon the manner in which the carrier provides them, the common carrier would then be: 1) offering both a regulated monopoly communications service and a highly competitive unregulated data-processing service; and 2) using common plant and personnel, at least to some degree, because of the economies that would be realized in that way. A carrier could then intentionally or inadvertently charge to the regulated communications service certain costs properly attributable to the data-processing service—forcing the communications subscriber, who has no choice in the matter, to bear a portion of the carrier's cost of providing data services.[8]

In order to minimize these cost separation and allocation problems, the FCC in its 1971 *Final Report and Order* adopted rules providing that "common carriers desiring to provide data processing services [can] do so only through affiliates utilizing separate books of account, separate officers, separate operating personnel, and separate equipment and facilities devoted exclusively to the rendition of data processing services."[9] Such subsidiaries would lease communication services from carriers (the parent company or any other carrier) under public tariffs, as would competing suppliers of data-processing services. The Commission also prohibited the data-processing affiliate from using the carrier's name and barred the carrier from obtaining any data-processing services from the affiliate.[10] While this decision, particularly the latter regulations, is being appealed[11] by several independent telephone companies, and certain modifications may result, the thrust of the decision—requiring complete separation of common-carrier communications and data-processing activities—will most likely become the *modus operandi* in the future.

Store-and-Forward Message-Switching Services

The next question addressed by the FCC was whether, and under what circumstances, public store-and-forward message-switching services should be *de*regulated. Message switching is a relatively old communications concept. Telephone answering services, for example, operate as primitive store-and-forward systems, and many readers may also be familiar with the old paper-tape store-and-forward systems supplied by AT&T and Western Union. (Many such systems are still in use.) Western Union's public-message service, the common telegram, has also relied until recent years upon a punched paper-tape reperforator network. The only new development in message switching is the fact that we are now using digital computers—specialized or general-purpose—to perform the store-and-forward function, and these computers may be programmed to provide whatever features are required by the users.

Most message-switching systems are designed and operated to provide message communications within a single organization, such as a corporation or a government agency, and are therefore private activities rather than public common-carrier undertakings. In addition to these private systems, carriers in the United States and Canada offer shared message-switching systems that provide "private" message-switching services to user organizations over shared facilities.[12] Public message-switching services are not offered by these carriers, probably because such service would seriously impact the teletypewriter exchange services (Telex and TWX) which they operate. With one exception, noncarriers have not been authorized to provide other than private intracompany message-switching services. The one exception is Aeronautical Radio, Inc. (ARINC), a nonprofit organization owned by the domestic United States airlines, which coordinates radio communications with aircraft and operates a large message-switching network for interairline communications. ARINC was granted the authority to provide certain communication services to the airlines in 1937 in order to protect the safety of life and property in the air, and has since expanded these services into one of the largest message-switching systems in the world (using communication lines leased from the carriers). A similar system is operated by the Société Internationale de Télécommunications Aéronautiques (SITA) for the international airlines.

In its computer inquiry the FCC considered the possibility that it might "deregulate" pure message-switching services, but concluded that such services are "essentially communications" in nature and "warrant appropriate regulatory treatment as common carrier services under the Act." The Commission did not explain how it reached this conclusion, but several factors appear to have been responsible. First, the respondents in the inquiry failed to put forth a sufficient argument for deregulation. However, common-carrier regulation of message switching may in certain circumstances be undesirable, for it may impede new developments and discourage or prevent the establishment of specialized systems oriented to unique requirements of different industries.

One rationale for regulation of message switching is that it provides a mechanism for ensuring compatibility among terminals, thus enabling any one user to communicate with any other user. However, if competing computer-based message-switching systems were permitted, it would be a simple matter (although a modest cost would be involved) to require such systems, where appropriate, to provide a "common interface" so that a message originating at a terminal con-

[8] In the United States the FCC and the state public-utility commissions establish profit ceilings for common-carrier services. This is accomplished by setting rates for communication services at a level that will permit the carrier to recover his operating costs for the service and earn a profit up to a fixed percentage (established by the regulatory commission) of his plant investment, or "rate base." This approach, called "rate-base regulation," encourages the carrier to capitalize as many of his costs as possible, so as to increase the size of the rate base. On the other hand, for competitive (unregulated) data-processing services, a carrier's incentive would be to minimize the costs charged to that service.

[9] 28 FCC 2nd 267, at 270.

[10] 28 FCC 2nd 267, at 272–3.

[11] In March 1972 the FCC denied all the petitions for reconsideration that had been submitted, 34 FCC 2nd 557, and at the time of this writing the matter was pending before the U. S. Court of Appeals in New York.

[12] For example, several industry-oriented systems are operated by Western Union, such as the securities-industry communications system, commonly called SICOM.

nected to system A could be relayed to a terminal connected to system B.[13] This solution would allow the essentially free development of specialized message-switching systems each serving, for example, a natural user group, such as commercial banks, credit bureaus, or stock-brokerage firms, while still providing "universal interconnectibility," where the FCC deems this desirable. Furthermore, the natural monopoly characteristic of many traditional common-carrier services is not clearly present in such systems, and thus there is no apparent need to restrict entry in order to ensure the lowest unit price to the user. Free entry, subject only to technical interconnection requirements, would stimulate competitive efforts, innovative services, and responsiveness to user requirements.

The second reason why the FCC decided not to deregulate message switching lay in its interpretation of the Communications Act of 1934—the statutory authority under which it operates. While the Commission expressed doubt that it has the authority under the Communications Act to decline to regulate a public communication service (after Congress has decided that all such services are subject to regulation), it nevertheless held that it has discretionary latitude "to refrain from subjecting a marginal activity to [its] regulatory process where it is clear that the public interest will be served by such a course." It is not altogether clear that the Act so narrowly circumscribes the FCC's discretion as to require it to impose full-blown common-carrier regulation upon a new technology that did not even exist at the time the Act was drafted; the Commission's interpretation to this effect was perhaps overly conservative. While it may be appropriate to require potential suppliers of message-switching services to apply to the Commission for authorization, it does not appear necessary or desirable in all cases for these services to be regulated as common-carrier offerings with all the trappings of tariff filings, construction permits, and profit ceilings involved. However, should it be found that the Communications Act does require such regulation, but that this is not in the public interest, it is always possible to ask Congress to amend the statute.

A third likely reason for the FCC's reluctance to consider deregulation of message switching is the adverse effect upon Western Union that such action might have. Certainly, deregulation would lead to the entry of a number of new competitors and would make life more hectic for Western Union, but as one of only a few domestic firms with experience in providing message-switching services for hire, and the only firm with several such services already in existence, the telegraph company would have a strong initial advantage over the competition. If the company is competent and willing to respond to market demands, it should then do very well in the competitive marketplace; if not, others would soon take its place as supplier of such services.

One example of a message-switching service which, if offered on a commercial basis to the public at large would, under the Commission's present rules, have to operate as a common carrier, is the computer network of the Advanced Research Projects Agency (ARPA). The ARPA network is a distributed message-switching system, consisting of approximately 30 store-and-forward mini-computers linked by high-speed 50-kbit/s communication lines leased from the carriers. Each mini-computer serves either a larger "host" data-processing computer or a group of terminals. This store-and-forward network is used to relay packets of data, in a rapid and error-free manner, from one terminal or computer center to a distant computer center.

While the question of regulating the ARPA network is somewhat academic today, since the network is a government-sponsored experimental project exclusively serving ARPA contractors, the next logical step after completion of the research stage is to consider commercial operation of the network and expansion of the user base. At that time, what effect will regulation, or the threat of regulation, have upon industry's interest in providing such services on a commercial basis? Given the uncertain commercial prospects for a communications service based upon the ARPA technology, will firms be willing to undertake such a service offering with the added uncertainties of limited profit margins, delays due to lengthy regulatory proceedings, and reduced control of one's business activities? Is it more desirable, from a public interest point of view, to authorize a single common-carrier ARPA-like network or to permit several competitive networks to go into operation? The answers to these questions are not clear. However, the possibilities for variety and innovation in services of this type suggest that they would flourish best in a competitive rather than a regulated common-carrier environment. One possible approach is to permit firms to offer ARPA-like services on a competitive basis for several years, with minimal regulatory control. If, at a later date, it appears necessary to impose a heavier regulatory hand—e.g, in order to require interconnection of several systems, or to integrate them into a single common-carrier service—this option would remain open, although there would be some penalty paid for having conducted the experiment. Subjecting such services to comprehensive common-carrier regulation from the outset seems likely to foreclose the development of a variety of public data-handling networks, tailored to the special needs of a particular industry or user group.

One illustration of the "hands-off" type of regulation that may be appropriate for firms offering message-switching services is provided by the ICC's regulatory treatment of motor-freight carriers. Firms offering transportation services to the general public on an equal basis are considered common carriers and are required to obtain a certificate of public convenience and necessity before they can provide service, and the ICC can prescribe maximum, minimum, or actual rates to be charged. This is analogous to the FCC's treatment of communications common carriers, and imposes rather strict controls upon the regulated firm. However, the ICC also recognizes another class of for-hire motor freight carriers, called "contract carriers," which provide service under individual agreements or contracts with certain organizations—specializing in the type of service offered, and typically offering such service to only a limited number of customers. Contract carriers need not prove that the public convenience and necessity *requires* their services, but only that issuance of an operating permit would be consistent with the public interest; thus it is much easier to get into business as a contract carrier. Also the ICC may only prescribe minimum rates for contract carriers, not maximum rates, and overall economic regulation of these firms is much less extensive than for common carriers. Amendment of the Communications Act may be needed to provide for such a treatment of message-switching services, but it might be well worth the effort—a sort of middle ground in which firms would be free to enter the market and offer inno-

[13] Stanford Research Institute, "Policy issues presented by the interdependence of computer and communications services," Feb. 1969, National Technical Information Service, Springfield, Va., Document no. PB 183 612.

vative and specialized services with only a minimal degree of FCC regulatory control.

Hybrid Services

Having decided in its inquiry that data-processing services would not be regulated, whether using communication lines or not, and that pure message-switching services would continue to be regulated, the FCC then addressed the question of how the in-between "hybrid" service should be treated. The Commission adopted what is known as a "primary business test," saying that:

> Where message switching is offered as an integral part of, and as an incidental feature of a package offering that is primarily data processing, there will be total regulatory forbearance with respect to the entire service whether offered by a common carrier or non-common carrier, except to the extent that common carriers offering such a hybrid service will do so through [separate] affiliates. . . . If, on the other hand, the package offering is oriented essentially to satisfy the communications or message switching requirements of the subscriber, and the data processing feature or function is an integral part of, and incidental to message switching, the entire service will be treated as a communications service for hire, whether offered by a common carrier or a non-common carrier and will be subject to regulation under the Communications Act.[14]

The following two tests were given to help apply these criteria.[14]

1) Does the service, by virtue of its message-switching capability, have the attributes of the point-to-point services offered by conventional communications carriers, and is it basically a substitute therefore? If so, this suggests that regulation may be applicable.

2) Does the message-switching feature of the service facilitate or relate to the data-processing component, or are the two components essentially independent? In order to avoid regulation, the message-switching feature must not only be secondary in importance as compared with the data-processing aspect of the service, but also the two must be closely related to one another. If the two components are functionally independent of one another, the FCC would regulate the entire service, regardless of the preponderance of the data-processing element.

Perhaps the most serious shortcoming of these rules is their vagueness. Just what is meant, in practice, by "integral" and "incidental?" As a procedural matter the FCC could not in most cases issue to a system designer a definite and confidential advance ruling, for the interests of other parties (e.g., carriers offering competing services) might be affected and these parties must be given the opportunity to present their views in an open proceeding. Therefore, the designer must either be willing to publicly disclose his plans, and thus forewarn his potential competitors, or risk his capital by implementing the system and hoping that costly and prolonged regulatory proceedings or other difficulties are not encountered at a later date. The FCC staff can, however, reduce much of the uncertainty by providing informal advisory opinions on proposed systems. Such guidance is to be encouraged, and the policy interpretations emerging from these dialogs should be publicly announced by the Commission.

The above guidelines regarding hybrid systems were tentatively established by the FCC in 1970 and finalized in 1971. Since then there have been few, if any, hybrid systems introduced, not for lack of technology or markets, but simply because of the regulatory uncertainty and the prospect of common-carrier regulation associated with the provision of hybrid services. The authors are aware of several hybrid services that are not being offered simply because of regulatory uncertainty. One can only speculate as to the number of other innovative hybrid services that have been stopped before they reached the marketplace by the same uncertainty and fear of regulation.

IV. Interconnection

One of the regulatory policy issues that has generated considerable discussion in recent years concerns the interconnection to the telephone network of subscriber-provided terminal devices and communication systems. Interconnected equipment of particular interest in the operation of computer-communication systems includes data modems, acoustic couplers, push-button telephones, augmented telephones with limited alphanumeric display capabilities, videotelephones, and advanced computer-controlled private branch exchange (PABX) systems. While telephone networks in most countries are technically quite similar, there is substantial diversity in the regulations regarding the attachment of customer equipment to the public network. Historically, the telephone companies in North America have generally prohibited such interconnection by their subscribers, which might jeopardize the telephone network if uncontrolled, and almost certainly would cut into the sales of manufacturing subsidiaries (such as AT&T's Western Electric, GTE's Automatic Electric, and Bell Canada's Northern Electric). Unlike the telephone companies in North America, overseas telephone administrations rarely own manufacturing affiliates, and, partly for this reason, interconnection of customer equipment (other than data modems) has historically been allowed. In these countries equipment certification is usually employed to safeguard the proper functioning of the public network.

Until recently the North American carriers' arguments of potential harm have been accepted without question by the FCC, the state public-utility commissions, and the federal and provincial regulatory authorities in Canada, which permitted the carriers to build a seemingly impregnable wall around their telephone network. However, the FCC's 1968 *Carterfone* decision is causing the wall to crumble in the United States, and may lead to a similar development in Canada in the near future.

Restrictive interconnection regulations, which are concerned with equipment performance and maintenance in addition to ownership, have an impact on computer-communication networks in various ways. By controlling the types of data modems allowed they determine the available data transmission speeds, the transmission error rates, and the sorts of options available to the user; by limiting the number of equipment suppliers they affect the amount of price competition and the rate of innovation; and by prohibiting the attachment of certain devices (such as acoustic couplers, which are not permitted in several countries) they affect the feasibility of certain computer-communication systems (such as systems involving the use of portable, acoustically coupled data terminals). For these reasons, interconnection policies are important in computer-communication network design and operation.

Generally, in North America and elsewhere the regulations pertaining to interconnection of customer data equipment

[14] 28 FCC 2nd 291 (1970), at 305.

have in the past been more restrictive than technically necessary. Although these regulations are, in some cases, being relaxed, change has been occurring slowly, and outdated interconnection restrictions continue to have a retarding effect upon the development of computer-communication systems.

In the United States, until the FCC's recent *Carterfone* decision, only carrier-provided modems could be connected to the dial telephone network. (User-supplied modems could be connected to channels *leased* from the carriers.) At this writing user-supplied modems may be connected to dial lines, but the use of a carrier-supplied protective coupling device called a "data access arrangement" (DAA) is required. In most other countries more restrictive policies are generally in effect. For example, in Sweden modems for use with the public network must be leased from the Swedish Telephone Administration. In Italy users must either lease modems from the local-exchange telephone company, Societa per l'Esercizio Telefonico (SIP), or purchase models that have been approved by SIP. In the United Kingdom the British Post Office Corporation (BPOC) owns and maintains all modems connected to the public switched network.

In most countries PBX and associated telephone extentions are installed and maintained by either the PTT or an independent supplier, often at the discretion of the user. For example, in the United Kingdom the following apply.

1) All small PBX's are supplied by the Post Office.

2) Larger PBX's must be purchased from one of a small number of manufacturers, mostly British. (To date only a limited number of larger models have been offered, mostly made to Post Office design regardless of supplier.)

3) All maintenance is performed by the Post Office.

In Japan and Germany users have even greater latitude. PBX equipment may be leased from the respective telephone administration, or purchased from approved independent suppliers, and it may be maintained by either.

The relationship between PBX equipment and computer-communication systems may not, at this point, be entirely clear to the reader. This is understandable, since at this point in time the relationship is minimal. However, the trend from electromechanically controlled to electronic and computer-controlled PABX systems will result in the availability of PABX equipment capable of performing certain data-communications control and storage functions normally handled within a computer mainframe, or elsewhere in a data network. For example, IBM recently introduced computer-controlled voice/data PABX systems, the models 2750 (capable of up to 700 extensions) and the 3750 (capable of up to 2000 extensions), which can terminate and interpret data entered from push-button telephones or multifrequency data terminals, accumulate these messages in buffer storage, perform code conversion, add such information as date, time, and originating-line identification, and finally transfer these messages to an interconnected general-purpose computer for processing. In essence, the voice/data PABX can operate as a rudimentary front-end communications processor. This equipment can also be programmed to provide automatic redialing of busy lines, automatic call accounting, priority access, and other features useful in the operation of data networks. IBM's voice/data PABX is, in many respects, unique. However, other computer manufacturers and communications-equipment suppliers may be expected to introduce similar product lines, and in the long term PBX equipment will play a substantially more important role in computer networks than it does today. Thus the regulations that determine what types of PBX equipment may be installed, and which manufacturing firms may supply it, will become important considerations in the design and operation of future computer-communication networks.

Historical Development of Interconnection Policy in the United States

The most dramatic changes in interconnection regulations are currently taking place in the United States. These developments are of such import that it is worthwhile recounting the events that brought these changes about.

A decade before the famous *Carterfone* ruling, the legality of the United States carriers' blanket prohibition against interconnection of customer-owned equipment was tested before the U. S. Court of Appeals, in *Hush-a-Phone Corporation v. United States*.[15] This case concerned a rubber cuplike device designed to be attached to the microphone portion of the telephone handset to provide privacy in conversation; its use on the dial network had been barred by provisions in the carrier's tariffs. Reviewing the tariff in question, a prior version of the AT&T interstate toll telephone tariff, the court found it illegal and held specifically that this ban was ". . . an unwarranted interference with the telephone subscriber's right to use his telephone in ways which are privately beneficial without being publicly detrimental." AT&T was ordered to revise its tariff to permit use of the Hush-a-Phone device, and did so—but retained the *general* interconnection prohibition in the tariff. Three years later the Carterfone struggle began.

The Carterfone was an acoustic/inductive device for interconnection of the base station of a mobile radio system (or other private communication system) with the dial telephone network. The Carter Electronics Corporation of Dallas, Tex., which developed the Carterfone, sold approximately 3500 of these devices in the United States and overseas between 1959 and 1966. The Bell System and the General Telephone System warned Carter's customers that their tariffs prohibited devices such as the Carterfone on the telephone network, and that customers who violated these tariff provisions risked having their telephone service terminated. Finally, in 1966 Carter brought an antitrust suit against the Bell System and the General Telephone Company of the Southwest. The U.S. District Court in Texas referred the case to the FCC because the Commission has primary jurisdiction in interstate communications matters.

AT&T and GTE argued before the FCC that use of the Carterfone violated their tariffs, and presented several technical arguments to support their position that the integrity of the telephone system necessitated the use of only carrier-supplied attachments, whether acoustically coupled or directly wired to the telephone network. The FCC was unpersuaded by the telephone companies' arguments and, in a unanimous opinion issued in June 1968, found that the tariff restrictions ". . . are, and have since their inception been, unreasonable, unlawful, and unreasonably discriminatory under the Communications Act of 1934."[16] The Commission further concluded:

[15] 99 U. S. App. D. C. 190, 238 F. 2d 266, D. C. Cir. (1956).

[16] *Use of the Carterfone Device in Message Toll Telephone Service*, 13 FCC 2d 420 (1968), at 426.

. . . a customer desiring to use an interconnecting device to improve the utility to him of both the telephone system and a private radio system should be able to do so, so long as the interconnection does not adversely affect the telephone company's operations or the telephone system's utility for others. A tariff which prevents this is unreasonable; it is also unduly discriminatory where, as here, the telephone company's own interconnecting equipment is approved for use. The vice of the present tariff . . . is that it prohibits the use of harmless, as well as harmful devices.

In view of the unlawfulness of the tariff, there would be no point in declaring it invalid as applied to the Carterfone and permitting it to continue in operation as to other interconnection devices. This would also put a clearly improper burden upon the manufacturers and users of other devices. The appropriate remedy is to strike the tariff and permit the carriers, if they so desire, to propose new tariff provisions in accordance with this opinion. . . . The carriers may submit new tariffs which will protect the telephone system against harmful devices, and they may specify technical standards if they wish.[17]

AT&T and GTE initially responded to *Carterfone* by seeking FCC reconsideration and later judicial review but, realizing this was fruitless, eventually withdrew their appeals and began to revise their interstate tariffs to conform with the FCC's decision.

The revised tariffs permit the attachment of customer-provided devices, such as data modems, to the dial telephone network; they also permit the interconnection of customer-provided communication systems, such as PBX switchboards, to both the dial telephone network and to "private-line" channels leased from the carriers. However, three new restrictions were imposed.

1) The tariffs require that the power and spectral energy distribution of signals entering the switched network from interconnected customer equipment stay within prescribed limits. These criteria are intended to protect network services from excessive noise, intelligible crosstalk, and other forms of interference, as well as to minimize circuit interruption, disconnections, improper billing, and voltages that might be hazardous to line maintenance personnel.

2) A "protective connecting arrangement" supplied by the telephone company for several dollars per month is required where customer-provided devices or systems are interconnected to the dial telephone network. This coupler, called a data access arrangement (DAA) or voice access arrangement (VAA), effectively isolates the line from hazardous voltages potentially generated by customer attachments, and ensures that proper signal levels are not exceeded.

3) The tariffs require that telephone-company-supplied equipment perform all "network control signaling" functions on the dial telephone network, such as dialing and hook switch connect/disconnect. An exception to this rule became effective in 1971, to permit the use of customer-owned tone-generation dialing units (but not conventional rotary dials). This requirement is intended to prevent improper network signaling that may result in frequent wrong numbers, improper billing, and wasted maintenance and administrative effort.

Many users and potential suppliers of telephone equipment objected to the new tariffs filed by AT&T, on the grounds that they are still too restrictive by requiring both telephone-company-supplied protective couplers and rotary dial equipment, and do not reflect the spirit of the *Carterfone* decision. In response to these objections, the FCC initiated informal engineering and technical conferences to assist in resolving questions raised by the tariff revisions and to ascertain the desirability and feasibility of further tariff changes. The informal conferences were conducted under the auspices of a panel appointed by the Computer Science and Engineering Board of the National Academy of Sciences (NAS). The panel reported its findings in mid-1970, concluding the following.[18]

1) Uncontrolled interconnection could cause harm to personnel, network performance, and property.

2) The use of protective couplers and signal-level criteria is an acceptable way of assuring network protection; however, the added equipment increases overall costs.

3) A program of standards and enforced certification of equipment would be another acceptable way of assuring network protection.

A subsequent report to the FCC, prepared by Dittberner Associates, a Washington-based firm of computer consultants, concluded that manufacturers of data modems and other types of interconnected customer equipment could easily build into their equipment the necessary circuitry to protect the telephone network.[19] It further found that the carriers need not have the exclusive right to provide network protective couplers. The report also concluded that a program of standards and certification of installation and maintenance *organizations* (rather than licensing of individual persons) would be an inexpensive way to extend interconnection privileges without harm to the common-carrier network.

Both the NAS and Dittberner reports to the FCC concluded that safe and reliable interconnection of subscriber equipment could be accomplished without need for the objectionable carrier-supplied access arrangement or coupler. The FCC had received many complaints from users and equipment manufacturers that the access arrangement represented a serious burden upon them—long delays were often encountered in obtaining a unit, once installed it sometimes degraded the signals passing through it, Bell kept changing its interface specifications, the device was grossly overpriced, etc.—and the Commission was eager to begin to implement an alternative program of equipment standards and certification. Because of manufacturer interest, the Commission chose the PBX area for initial consideration, with the hope that experience gained there could soon be transferred to other interconnection areas (such as data communications) as well.

In March 1971 the FCC established a PBX industry advisory committee with some 30 members representing carriers, equipment manufacturers, and users. This committee was charged with developing recommended technical standards and accompanying certification and enforcement procedures that would permit the direct interconnection of PBX equipment to the telephone network without the need for protective coupling units. Then in January 1972 the Commission formed a second industry advisory committee to address similar topics concerning answering, recording, and dialing (ARD) devices.

At the time of writing there is optimism that the FCC's PBX and ARD industry advisory committees will make significant headway in developing workable interconnection programs that willl give maximum freedom to the equipment

[17] *Use of the Carterfone Device in Message Toll Telephone Service*, 13 FCC 2d 420 (1968), at 424–425.

[18] National Academy of Sciences, Computer Science and Engineering Board, *A Technical Analysis of the Common Carrier/User Interconnections Area*, Rep. to the FCC, June 1970.

[19] Dittberner Associates, *Interconnection Action Recommendations*, Rep. to the FCC, Sept. 1970.

manufacturer and user without compromising the security of the telephone network. Such programs, if successful, can then serve as models for other types of interconnection, such as data-communications equipment. In this respect, the FCC is also considering establishment of a third advisory committee to focus on data modems, and this action appears likely in the relatively near future.

One interesting development concerning the technical and procedural aspects of interconnection has been taking place at the state, rather than the federal, level with the Rochester (N. Y.) Telephone Corporation. Rochester Telephone, serving one of the largest cities of any of the independent telephone companies, in early 1971 proposed permitting the interconnection of customer equipment on a much simpler basis than Bell and the rest of the industry currently permit. Basically, Rochester would test and certify customer-owned equipment to ensure that it met telephone-industry network-protection technical standards for signal output power and frequency. The equipment would then be interconnected on a direct electrical basis, using only a simple fuse-like device on the access line to protect the network from hazardous voltages and uncontrolled power gain. An installation charge would be made for the protective device, but there would be no recurring monthly charge such as Bell and the rest of the industry currently require for their complex VAA's and DAA's. The subscriber would also avoid the other problems associated with many of the existing access arrangements, such as potential impairment of signal quality and system reliability, complex interface relationships, and the need for a source of ac power for the access unit. The Bell System opposed the plan on its technical merits, but in August 1972 the New York Public Service Commission approved it in substance (although rejecting, for lack of cost justification, Rochester's plan to charge higher tariff rates for interconnect access lines). At the time of writing the impact of this decision was unclear, but such a program, when implemented on a limited regional basis as Rochester proposed, may provide valuable field experience for subsequent modification of interconnection procedures on a national scale.

The Impact of Carterfone

The changes brought on by *Carterfone* have been truly revolutionary, both in terms of creation of a new "interconnect" equipment industry and stimulation of innovation and lower costs in data-communications hardware. It is estimated that nearly 200 firms have entered the data-modem market since the FCC decision, in many cases bringing with them advanced technology developed for defense and aerospace applications that previously had no commercial outlet. A wide variety of new, improved, and less expensive products have been introduced. Data terminal and multiplex manufacturers can now reduce overall system costs by incorporating modems (which they can manufacture themselves or obtain in the OEM market) directly into their equipment.

The carriers have responded to this new competition by developing new products and cutting prices—much to the benefit of data-communications users. For example, the "standard" low-speed modem has been Bell's Series 103 data set, which has originate/answer capability (although many users operate in an originate-only mode) and rents for approximately 25 dollars/month. When independent suppliers began to offer originate-only units for a small fraction of that price, Bell responded by introducing the 113 data set—originate-only, for approximately half the 103 price. Interestingly, 103 units in the field were then "converted" to 113's by merely snipping a lead to disable the unneeded "answer" capability. Again, for competitive reasons, Bell in late 1971 announced plans to cut rental rates by 35 percent on its medium-speed Series 200 data sets. In spite of this vigorous competitive response by the telephone company, the number of installed VAA's and DAA's has grown rapidly, as shown in Figs. 1 and 2.

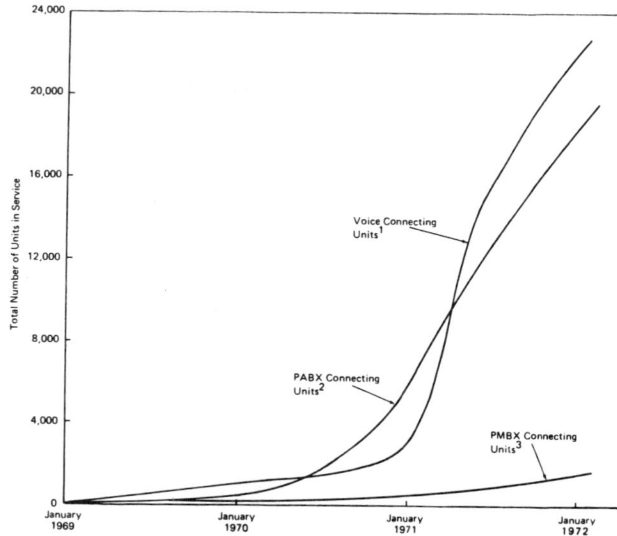

Fig. 1. Protective connecting devices furnished by the Bell System for customer-provided telephone equipment (total number of units in service).

[1] Protective interface devices for connecting customer-provided equipment to telephone company key sets or PBX's.

[2] Protective interface devices for connecting attendant position of customer-provided PABX to exchange trunk line.

[3] Protective interface devices for connecting a line from a customer-provided cord switchboard to an exchange trunk line.

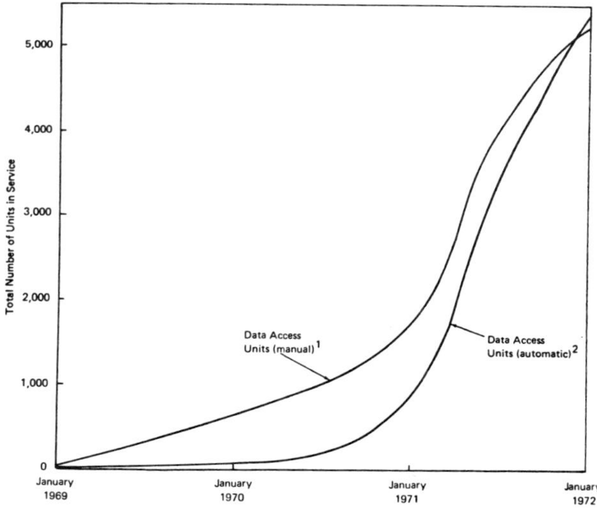

Fig. 2. Protective connecting devices furnished by the Bell System for customer-provided data modems (total number of units in service).

[1] Protective interface devices for connecting customer-provided modems to the telephone network where call origination and answering are manual.

[2] As in footnote 1, but where call origination and answering are automatic.

Similarly, in the PABX area dozens of new suppliers have begun to market customer-premises telephone equipment, introducing a wider variety of equipment types, financing plans, and service arrangements than has heretofore been available. As a result the user is apt to be better served by achieving a more optimum match between his requirements and the available types of equipment and services. So too, suppliers with special capabilities and experience have begun to apply this know-how to the development of customer-premise telephone equipment with new features and capabilities. For example, the IBM voice/data PABX mentioned earlier builds upon IBM's knowledge of stored-program control and microelectronics. Equipment that may shortly be offered by several aerospace firms builds upon experience in the design and production of highly reliable "ruggedized" military PABX systems for field use. Also, firms presently supplying PABX equipment outside of the United States—ITT, Nippon Electric (Japan), L. M. Ericsson (Sweden), Siemens (Germany), Northern Electric (Canada), etc.—are now able to introduce into the United States some of the innovations developed in foreign markets. Finally, the major United States electronics firms, such as RCA and General Electric, are slowly beginning to serve this new market, by initially distributing equipment manufactured outside the United States (by Hitachi in Japan, and Telefonbau und Normalzeit in Germany, respectively), and perhaps eventually building upon their broad capabilities in communications, electronics, and marketing to produce equipment of their own design.

Unresolved Questions

In the United States the fundamental principle has been established that the user may obtain the communications equipment on his premises from a source other than the telephone company. However, the technical and procedural details of actually interconnecting nontelephone-company equipment are still, after several years of study, under debate and subject to change.

At this writing the unanswered questions include the following.

1) If VAA's and DAA's are eliminated, what technical specifications must customer equipment meet in order to minimize any chance of service degradation on the public network?

2) Once technical standards have been established, how are they to be enforced? What organization should be responsible for ensuring compliance with the established standards? Should a government laboratory be established, comparable to the Fernmeldtechnische Zentralamt (FTZ) in Germany, or would a nongovernmental organization along the lines of Underwriters Laboratories be more appropriate?

3) Is it possible to avoid certification of each equipment model, to certify the supplying organization instead, and thus rely upon the supplier to "self-certify" each model as complying with established technical interface and reliability standards?

4) Is periodic inspection of installed customer equipment required? Must nontelephone-company installers and maintenance personnel be licensed?

As these questions are answered by the FCC, together with other interested organizations, the pace of change in the so-called "interconnect" industry is likely to accelerate and perhaps achieve the promise implied by *Carterfone* but still not fully realized.

V. Specialized Common Carriers

In 1963 a small new firm, Microwave Communications, Inc. (MCI), applied to the FCC for permission to construct a microwave radio relay system between Chicago and St. Louis in order to offer the public a variety of dedicated private-line communications services on a common-carrier basis, in direct competition with the Bell System and Western Union. Most observers saw MCI's chances of approval as practically nil, based upon the FCC's traditionally negative attitude towards competition in telephone and telegraph service, but in 1969 the Commission set a new course for itself and granted MCI a license. This decision may be of major importance to the future of data communications, for it triggered the birth of a whole new data-oriented "specialized carrier" industry and has already stimulated the established telephone carriers to introduce new data-transmission services and to generally become more innovative and responsive to the demands of their data customers. (Table II gives a history of the specialized-carrier concept.)

In pursuing its application before the FCC, MCI argued persuasively that the existing carriers were not adequately meeting all the specialized needs of business and data-communications users and that its proposed services—which included a number of new and different features tailored to these needs (see Table III)—would be in the public interest. This contention, and the specialized-carrier concept in general, received strong support from two quarters: numerous computer firms and data-communications users who submitted comments in the above-mentioned FCC computer inquiry, complaining of inadequacies in existing data-transmission services and stating their need for new ones; and the President's Task Force on Communications Policy, which issued a report endorsing competition in long-haul carrier services. On the other hand, the established carriers contended that FCC approval of a competing long-haul carrier would result in a wasteful duplication of facilities and would impair their ability to achieve maximum economies of scale. Furthermore, they said, MCI was just a "cream skimmer" trying to reap the profits of a high traffic-density route while leaving the established carriers to serve the boondocks; if this were permitted it would destroy the traditional average-cost pricing system for telephone service and would force the rates on less dense routes to rise.

Finally, after almost 6 years of delay, hearings, legal briefs, and more delay, the FCC rejected the established carriers' arguments and approved the new entrant.[20] MCI was given construction permits for its 263-mi microwave system, and after some further procedural delays the company finally constructed its system and went on the air as a full-fledged carrier on Jan. 1, 1972.

If this were all that happened, there would be little cause for more than academic interest in the computer-communications community. But the FCC's approval of MCI triggered a flood of over 1900 new microwave-station applications by several dozen firms proposing to build more than 40 000 mi of new specialized-carrier communications facilities throughout the country. All but one of the applicants (16 of whom are affiliated with MCI) proposed MCI-like analog microwave facilities that would offer a variety of business-oriented private-line communication channels, as well as

[20] *Microwave Communications Inc.*, FCC Dockets 16509 *et al.*, Decision, 18 FCC 2d 953 (1969); Petitions for Reconsideration Denied 21 FCC 2d 190 (1970).

TABLE II

Specialized-Carrier Chronology

Early	1940's	Microwave technology developed.
	1945	Microwave first used by communications common carriers.
	1959	FCC issues *Above 890* decision authorizing private microwave systems.
	1961	AT&T's bulk-discount private-line service (Telpak) counters competition of private microwave.
Dec.	1963	MCI files for authorization to construct Chicago–St. Louis microwave system, to provide a variety of private-line services on a common-carrier basis.
Spring	1967	FCC hearings on MCI application.
Dec.	1968	Interdata Communications, Inc., files with FCC for authorization to construct MCI-like microwave system between New York City and Washington, D. C.
Dec.	1968	President's Task Force on Communications Policy submits report endorsing specialized common-carrier concept.
Feb.	1969	AT&T permits sharing of its voice-grade and telegraph-grade private-line services (sharing was a service feature previously proposed by MCI).
Mar.	1969	AT&T announces Series 11 000 wide-band private-line services largely designed to compete with MCI.
Aug.	1969	FCC grants MCI construction permits (6 years after MCI's original application).
Sept.	1969	Established carriers petition FCC to reconsider its MCI decision.
Sept.–Dec.	1969	Four MCI affiliates file applications for microwave routes in various parts of the country, and a non-MCI firm files for one of the same routes.
Nov.	1969	Data Transmission Company (Datran), a subsidiary of University Computing Company, files application for nationwide common-carrier system using digital microwave and computer switching, designed exclusively for data transmission.
Jan.	1970	FCC denies established carriers' petitions for reconsideration of its *MCI* decision.
Mar.	1970	AT&T appeals FCC's *MCI* decision to the U. S. Court of Appeals.
Mar.	1970	MCI files with FCC to modify its construction permits for the Chicago–St. Louis system (largely to increase capacity).
Apr.–June	1970	Twenty-one more firms (7 MCI affiliates, 14 independent firms) file specialized-carrier route applications.
July	1970	FCC issues *Notice of Inquiry and Proposed Rule-Making* regarding specialized carriers (Docket no. 18920).
Oct.–Dec.	1970	FCC receives comments and reply comments from over 150 interested parties in Docket 18920. Another MCI affiliate files specialized-carrier application.
Jan.	1971	FCC hears oral argument in Docket 18920.
Mar.	1971	Another specialized-carrier route application is filed.
Mar.	1971	MCI and its affiliates, in a joint venture with Lockheed Aircraft Corporation, file FCC application for a domestic communications-satellite system to complement MCI's proposed terrestrial microwave network.
May	1971	FCC issues *First Report and Order* in Docket 18920, giving overall policy approval of the specialized-carrier concept.
June	1971	FCC issues *Further Notice of Inquiry* in Docket 18920, regarding allocation of frequencies for local distribution and quality and reliability of service.
July	1971	AT&T and Western Union withdraw their court appeals of the FCC's 1969 *MCI* decision.
July–Aug.	1971	Three more specialized-carrier route applications are filed.
Aug.	1971	FCC receives comments from interested parties regarding local distribution and quality of service.
Aug.	1971	Construction and system-acceptance testing of MCI Chicago–St. Louis microwave system is completed.
Oct.	1971	FCC grants construction permits to Interdata Communications, Inc., for specialized-carrier service between New York City and Washington, D. C.—the first grant under the Commission's new open-entry policy.
Dec.	1971	NARUC and the Washington State Utility Commission appeal FCC's June 1971 policy decision to the U. S. Court of Appeals.
Jan.	1972	MCI files its first tariff and begins specialized-carrier service between Chicago and St. Louis.
Apr.	1972	FCC grants construction permits to Datran for the Western half (from Palo Alto, Calif., to Houston, Tex.) of its network.
May	1972	FCC grants construction permits to MCI New York West, Inc., for a system to extend from Chicago to New York City.
July–Sept.	1972	FCC grants construction permits to a number of additional applicants, including Nebraska Consolidated Communications Corp., Western Tele-Communications, Inc., MCI Michigan, Inc., MCI New England, Inc., MCI St. Louis-Texas, Inc., and West Texas Microwave Company. Additional grants expected shortly.

TABLE III

MCI Service Features

The MCI-Carrier Applicants Intend to Offer the Following Services and Service Features Using Their Future Nationwide Network
1) Dedicated (nonswitched "private-line") channels will be provided for the transmission of voice, data, facsimile, teletype, telemetry, control, and perhaps video signals.
2) Digital and analog signal inputs will be accepted.
3) Data-transmission channels derived using time-division multiplexing (TDM) will be offered, with an error-rate objective two orders of magnitude better than that experienced on today's telephone network. Prices for such channels will be based upon actual data-transmission speed rather than channel bandwidth.
4) Multifunctional analog channels will be available in a wide variety of bandwidths (e.g., 200, 400, 600 · · · 1000 Hz; 2, 4, 6 · · · 16 kHz; 20, 24, 28 · · · 48 kHz; 64, 80, 96 · · · 240 kHz; and 288, 336, 384 · · · 960 kHz).
5) A variety of channel arrangements will be offered: Simplex (one-way transmission), full duplex (two-way), and asymmetrical (two-way with different bandwidths in each direction of transmission).
6) Channels will be available on either a part-time (day or night) or full-time (24 h/day, 7 days/week) basis.
7) Customers will be permitted to share channels (e.g., resell unused portions of their channels).
8) Customers will be permitted to interconnect their own equipment or communication systems to MCI channels, using MCI tower and shelter space for their equipment, if desired.
9) Rates will, in many cases, be substantially lower than those charged by the existing carriers for functionally equivalent service.

channels specifically designed for data transmission. The exception was the Data Transmission Company, or Datran (a subsidiary of University Computing Company), which proposed to build a nationwide all-digital switched network to offer exclusively data-transmission services on both a switched and private-line basis. Datran's network was specifically designed to provide those service features—such as rapid connect time, very short charging intervals, and low error rates—for which respondents in the computer inquiry had expressed a need. (See Table IV.)

These numerous and varied applications presented the FCC with a major policy problem, for the Commission was not sure that its MCI precedent should be extended on a nationwide basis without further analysis of the effects of such widespread competition among carriers. So the Commission in July 1970 instituted a public inquiry into the merits of the specialized-carrier concept.[21] As might have been antic-

[21] *Notice of Inquiry to Formulate Policy, Notice of Proposed Rulemaking, and Order*, Docket 18920, 24 FCC 2d 318 (1970).

TABLE IV

DATRAN SERVICE FEATURES

The Initial Service Offerings of Datran Will Include
1) The capability of establishing, within 3 s, a switched point-to-point connection between 2 compatible terminals (terminals arranged to operate at the same data-transmission speed—see below).
2) End-to-end digital channels, eliminating the need for a modem.
3) Full-duplex data transmission at speeds of 150, 4800, 9600, and 14 400 bits/s on a switched basis, and 19 200 and 48 000 bits/s on a private-line basis.
4) Likelihood of a subscriber encountering a "trunk-busy" condition during the peak hour guaranteed less than 1 in 100 call attempts.
5) A mean bit error rate of less than 10^{-7}.
6) Manual or automatic addressing by the sender.
7) Abbreviated dialing, using 1, 2, 3, or no-digit "telephone numbers." No-digit dialing would be a feature used by specialized network subscribers (such as users of credit-checking terminals) who would, upon keying a "service request" button, be automatically connected to a predetermined distant station—i.e., a "Hot Line" data service.
8) Broadcast transmission of a message to up to 6 subscribers (with compatible terminals) simultaneously.
9) Camp-on: When the called party is busy the call is held and the connection automatically established as soon as the line becomes free.
10) A separate flat charging rate for "local" and "regional" (long-distance) calls; i.e., charges are proportional to the length of a call, but other than the distinction between local and regional-type calls, rates are independent of distance.
11) Minimum charge time of 6 s for dial-up calls (as opposed to the minimum of 3 min—1 min during late evening hours—on the telephone network)
Additional Service Features, Using Store-and-Forward Message-Switching Techniques, Might Be Offered in the Future if the Market Demand Is Sufficiently Large
1) Code conversion between any 2 permissible formats.
2) Speed conversion between specified rates.
3) Expedited Information Transfer Service (EXIT), a store-and-forward message-switching service enabling the sender to specify the desired transit time for a message.

ipated from previous experience in the computer inquiry, the specialized-carrier inquiry elicited strong support for the MCI and Datran concepts from all sectors of the computer industry and from data-communications users. The established carriers, of course, continued to vigorously oppose the new competition. The same issues concerning public need, effects upon telephone rate-averaging, and duplication of facilities were debated by the FCC and resulted in the same conclusions as in the original MCI case. The Commission opted in favor of the specialized-carrier concept both to obtain the new services that these new carriers would provide and also to stimulate better performance from the existing carriers through the introduction of competition. In May 1971 its decision was issued, permitting virtually free entry of all financially and technically qualified applicants for specialized-carrier service (many of whom had filed for the same routes and thus would compete with each other as well as with Bell and Western Union), subject only to resolution of any radio-frequency interference with existing microwave systems.[22]

Several months after this overall policy decision, the FCC approved the second leg of MCI's nationwide network, giving construction permits to Interdata Communications, Inc. (an MCI affiliate) for private-line service between New York City and Washington, D.C. Then, in April 1972 the Commission granted construction permits to Datran for the first half of its nationwide digital network—the western portion, between Palo Alto, Calif., and Houston, Tex. The following month, permits were also issued to MCI New York West, Inc., for a system linking New York City and Chicago. At this writing, other specialized-carrier route approvals were expected shortly.

By the end of 1973 MCI-type specialized-carrier systems could be operational throughout the country, and by the end of 1974 Datran could have its digital network on the air. It is likely that as the various specialized carriers construct their regional microwave systems they will interconnect with each other in order to offer "through" service between different parts of the country, thus creating a nationwide network to compete with the telephone system. In addition to the microwave relay facilities that will form the backbone of this new network, other types of communications facilities may also be used.

Although the FCC has given its policy approval for the establishment of specialized carriers, a number of questions regarding this fledgling industry remain. First, particularly for Datran, is the problem of financing. Datran's nationwide switched network is estimated at 200–400 million dollar investment cost (depending largely upon the capital costs of local distribution facilities)—which is an order of magnitude greater than the capital requirements of any of the regional MCI-type private-line carriers, and far larger than the venture capital market is accustomed to handling. This fact, coupled with the high risk of the venture, may make it difficult for Datran to get off the ground. Second, once the new carriers are in operation, they face the probability of competitive price-cutting ("route pricing," which would cut prices on competitive routes and raise them on noncompetitive ones) by the established carriers; and to obtain maximum flexibility for their customers they must overcome the established carriers' resistance to permitting interconnection between the two competing networks. Local distribution also poses challenges, for telephone loops are relatively expensive, of limited bandwidth, and often available only on restricted terms from the local telephone company. As an alternative, use of CATV cable may some day be feasible, or the new carriers may elect to install their own short-haul microwave, millimeter-wave, infrared, or cable transmission facilities. However, the problems of installation delay, efficient geographic coverage, maintenance, and the like contribute to the uncertain business outlook for these firms.

While the above matters represent immediate concerns for the specialized carriers, the future establishment of domestic communication-satellite systems raises other, and broader, issues that may affect both the operations and competitive positions of specialized carriers, and also the availability and

[22] *First Report and Order*, Docket 18920 (specialized carrier inquiry), 29 FCC 2d 870 (1971).

TABLE V

Domestic Satellite Chronology

	1957	Sputnik I launched by USSR—the world's first satellite.
	1962	Congress passes Communications Satellite Act, providing for establishment of a new privately owned corporation, Communications Satellite Corporation (COMSAT), to serve as the U. S. entity in *international* satellite communications.
	1963	Syncom launched by NASA—the first geostationary synchronous satellite.
	1964	International Telecommunications Satellite Consortium (INTELSAT) formed to create international satellite communications network.
	1965	Early Bird launched—the first commercial-communications satellite and the beginning of the INTELSAT network.
	1965	American Broadcasting Company, Inc. (ABC) submits proposal to FCC for a domestic TV-distribution satellite.
	1966	FCC opens inquiry on domestic satellites, and asks broad policy questions regarding establishment of systems by nongovernment entities.
	1966	Ford Foundation submits counterproposal for a multipurpose domestic satellite, with profits to be used to support educational television.
Mar.	1967	COMSAT proposes "pilot demonstration program," with 2 satellites to be operated by COMSAT as trustee until FCC decides ownership issue.
Aug.	1967	President Johnson appoints Task Force on Communications Policy to study domestic satellites and other issues; FCC suspends action in its domestic satellite inquiry pending receipt of Task Force recommendations.
Dec.	1968	President's Task Force submits report recommending approval of a single "pilot" domestic satellite program, with COMSAT having primary responsibility.
Feb.	1969	General Electric Company proposes domestic satellite concept using time-division multiple-access (TDMA) techniques to provide new and expanded services.
July	1969	As FCC prepares to approve a pilot domestic system substantially as recommended by President Johnson's Task Force, the White House requests a delay until President Nixon's staff can study the matter and submit recommendations.
Jan.	1970	White House sends memo to FCC urging approval of all financially and technically qualified applicants for common-carrier or private domestic satellite systems—instead of a single pilot system as contemplated by FCC.
Mar.	1970	FCC issues *Report and Order* in domestic satellite inquiry, partially adopting White House recommendation and inviting all interested parties to submit domestic satellite proposals.
Mar.	1971	Before its deadline, FCC receives 8 applications for satellite systems.
May & July	1971	FCC receives comments and reply comments from the applicants and other interested parties regarding the 8 applications.
Fall	1971	NASA performs technical evaluation of the applications for FCC.
Mar.	1972	FCC's Common Carrier Bureau recommends policy of "limited open entry," consolidating in a common space segment those applicants proposing use of the same satellite technology.
May	1972	Oral argument before the Commission regarding the Bureau's recommendations.
June	1972	FCC issues ruling permitting *all* qualified applicants to provide domestic communications-satellite service, but restricts the markets that AT&T, COMSAT, and GTE satellite systems are authorized to serve.

pricing of digital data-transmission services. Over the past 7 years, the FCC has been considering, independently of its deliberations on specialized carriers, the subject of domestic communication satellites. Should a single system be constructed on a monopoly basis, or should several competing systems be authorized; and which particular organization(s) should be permitted to enter this field? These questions are beyond the scope of this paper, but Table V provides an outline of the development of domestic satellite policy in the United States during the past decade.

In June 1972 the Commission ruled—subject to possible reconsideration—that all technically and financially qualified entities may establish and operate domestic satellite systems in competition with one another. Satellite services could thus be provided to the public by the established carriers (although the FCC would initially prohibit AT&T and GTE from offering private-line services), the specialized carriers, and other new satellite operators. Two of the eight domestic satellite applications pending at the time of this writing were filed by specialized-carrier interests—MCI (in a joint venture with Lockheed Aircraft Corporation) and Western Tele-Communications, Inc. (WTCI)—and other specialized carriers, such as Datran, may obtain satellite capacity on a leased basis if they desire. Thus to the extent that domestic satellite facilities are integrated into the specialized carriers' terrestrial microwave networks, the flexibility and geographic coverage of these carriers will be increased. On the other hand, the entry of additional satellite operators will increase the amount of competition facing the terrestrial specialized carriers. (In addition to MCI and WTCI, the other satellite applicants include RCA, COMSAT, Western Union, AT&T, Fairchild Hiller, and Hughes Aircraft/GTE jointly. Not all applicants are expected to proceed with their systems, despite the FCC's open-entry policy, since the estimated traffic volume likely to be economically carried via satellite is insufficient to support that many systems.)

While the forthcoming domestic satellite systems offer a mixed blessing for the specialized carriers, they have the potential of providing data users with long-haul end-to-end digital transmission services, at costs that may be below those of terrestrial systems. RCA's domestic satellite proposal provides a good illustration of the possibilities. RCA, through two subsidiaries (RCA Global Communications, Inc., and RCA Alaska Communications, Inc.), proposes to operate a domestic communications-satellite system with 13 earth stations, 7 in the contiguous states. The company plans to provide digital transmission service, initially on a private-line basis only, among the 7 major metropolitan areas served by its earth stations in the contiguous states. High-speed transmission of data up to 64 kbits/s would be offered, with monthly tariff rates for a 64-kbit/s channel ranging from 1500 (distances below 750 mi) to 6000 dollars (coast-to-coast). The present cost of a transcontinental 50-kbit/s channel is, by way of comparison, approximately 20 000 dollars/month.

If RCA finds it economically feasible to do so, it will provide circuit-switched digital data-transmission services using exchanges specifically engineered to meet the requirements of data users. The characteristics of the proposed RCA switching equipment—fast connect time not exceeding 1 or 2 s/switching unit, probability of a trunk-busy condition not exceeding one in 100 attempts during the busy hour, etc.—are essentially the same as those proposed in the Datran system.

In terms of impact upon data communications, the advent

of the specialized carriers and the domestic satellite operators will bring about a number of important and generally beneficial results.

1) New data-communication services (many different channel sizes, rapid-connect switched service, etc.).

2) Lower error rates in data transmission.

3) Specialized-carrier and long-haul satellite prices considerably lower than today's telephone rates for functionally equivalent service.

4) Modification of certain telephone rate structures, as a response to the new competition (e.g., Western Union has already reduced its private-line rates between Chicago and St. Louis to match MCI's rates).

5) More innovation and more rapid introduction of new technology by the new and old carriers alike. [The specialized carriers have already proposed innovations such as digital microwave (Datran) and millimeter-wave local distribution (MCI).]

6) New equipment markets that are open to all suppliers and are receptive to new (especially digitally oriented) design concepts and approaches.

7) New job opportunities, with both the new carriers and their suppliers.

8) More responsiveness by the telephone companies to the needs of data-communications users.

9) Ability of the FCC to use the new carriers as a yardstick by which to measure the performance of Bell and the other telephone companies, and perhaps Western Union, in areas such as customer service, channel quality, and system costs.

Perhaps the most significant result of the entry of specialized carriers, from the point of view of the data user, is the stepped-up rate at which the Bell System will introduce all-digital data-transmission services. For example, Bell's Digital Data Service (DDS) was announced at about the same time the FCC decided, as a matter of policy, to authorize any qualified specialized carrier. Initially, DDS will provide private-line full-duplex synchronous data channels, operating at 2400, 4800, 9600, and 56 000 bits/s, on a point-to-point basis. It will be offered in approximately 24 cities by the end of 1974, 60 metropolitan areas by the end of 1975, and about 100 cities within 3 to $3\frac{1}{2}$ years from the start of service. Eventually, multipoint (polled) private-line service will also be provided.

The degree to which the individual user will be affected by or able to take advantage of these developments will obviously vary widely depending upon individual circumstances, but it is safe to predict that the overall impact of the new carriers will be substantial.

Due to limitations of space this has been a necessarily brief and superficial overview of a rather involved subject. The reader interested in a more comprehensive discussion of the specialized-carrier concept, specific features of the MCI and Datran systems, policy considerations, and outlook for the future is referred to recent papers by the authors in the Bibliography.

VI. Pricing Policies and Problems

Charges for all common-carrier communications services in the United States and Canada are formulated by the carriers and described in price schedules, called tariffs, which are subject to approval by the appropriate federal, state, or provincial regulatory authority. In most other countries, where communications services are provided either by a government department or a government-owned corporation, price schedules are established by the communications organization and may, in some cases, be subject to review by the legislature. While the rate-making principles applied in each country vary according to local circumstances, rate setting in the United States is of most relevance here, due to the advanced stage of development of United States computer communications. Also the existence of limited competition in the United States common-carrier communications industry raises pricing problems of special interest. In this section we discuss rate-making policies in the United States and regulatory problems arising from the transmission of computer data. Since a thorough analysis of rate-setting policies and problems is impossible within the limitations of this paper, our principal purpose is to identify pricing problems flowing from the transmission of computer data over the present telecommunications network and over the separate or discrete networks of the future.

Underlying Rate-Making Principles

The principal guideline under which the FCC operates in reviewing rate structures and levels, as expressed in the Communications Act of 1934, is that rates must be "reasonable and not unduly discriminatory." Thus, stated broadly, the Commission permits rate levels that provide the carrier with an adequate return upon its investment and that minimize the extent to which one class of users pays unduly high rates so that another class of users may obtain unduly low rates. The latter situation might arise, for example, where a carrier operates in both competitive and monopoly markets and may have an incentive to price below cost where competition exists and above costs where it does not. Under the Commission's interpretation of this guideline, a carrier is permitted to earn a lower rate of return on competitive services than on monopoly services—provided that the reduced charges for competitive services are compensatory in relation to the cost of furnishing these services, and that users of other services would benefit and not be burdened by the application of the reduced charges. While this principle is generally accepted as being sound in theory, the implementation of it in a particular case depends upon the availability of adequate cost information and accepted cost-allocation procedures, and it is generally in these areas where serious problems arise. For this reason, the FCC now requires carriers filing new tariffs or tariff revisions to also file detailed cost information. The effectiveness of this requirement has yet to be determined.

Local-Exchange Rates

In the United States, the term "local-exchange area" denotes a geographical region established by a telephone company—usually encompassing a city, town, or village and its environs—wherein calls between any two points are considered "local" calls and priced accordingly. A local-exchange area consists of one or more central-office districts, and a particular local tariff schedule applies to each exchange area.

The pricing of local telephone service in the United States is based upon two principles—flat-rate pricing and value-of-service pricing—that are not generally practiced outside of North America, but which have resulted in particular problems for data users and their local telephone companies. Under local flat-rate service a subscriber may place an unlimited number of local calls for a fixed monthly charge.

Outside of North America, local calls are usually priced on a message-rate basis; that is, subscribers are charged for each local call. (While virtually all local-exchange areas in the United States employ flat-rate pricing for both business and residential service, some states also offer, in large exchange areas, message-rate services for business subscribers. A few states also offer message-rate local service to residential subscribers.) Flat-rate pricing, established in accordance with the usage characteristics of voice-telephone subscribers, offers a number of advantages such as simplicity, encouragement of frequent subscriber calling, stabilization of telephone-company revenues, and elimination of the need for local call-metering equipment.

However, the usage patterns of data callers differ substantially from those of voice callers. In particular, many data users place either 1) calls with very long holding times, such as when accessing a conversational time-sharing computer system, or 2) large numbers of very short calls for inquiry or data-collection purposes. Such a user frequently imposes a different and more burdensome traffic load upon the voice-engineered telephone exchange, and the question arises, what should be done about this problem? Two alternative approaches may offer relief. First, tariff rates for data users may be modified to take into account the greater traffic burden they create; and second, new switching equipment may be provided that is engineered to handle such traffic more efficiently. Telephone companies in the United States have begun to adopt both approaches.

In an effort to distinguish data users from voice-telephone users, and to establish separate price schedules for the two classes of users, several Bell System operating companies attempted to introduce, beginning in mid-1970, a new rate classification called Information System Access Lines (ISAL) for the links between a computer and the local telephone central office. ISAL rates were to be comparable to rates for PBX trunk-line service, while computer access lines are presently tariffed at substantially lower individual business-line rates. Computer users strongly opposed the ISAL rate concept, arguing that they do not burden the telephone network any more than high-usage voice callers, and that the telephone companies were discriminating against them. In Ohio, Illinois, and the several other states where ISAL rates were proposed, the telephone company was forced to straighten these tariffs.

In California, the staff of the State Public Utility Commission also proposed a tariff specifically designed to apply to data and other nonvoice users, although somewhat different in concept from the ISAL tariffs. The proposed service, called "Exchange Data Service," would apply to all data and nonvoice terminal devices. (The ISAL tariffs would apply to computer access lines, but not to local access lines serving data terminals.) Under the proposed service, a data subscriber would be charged on a message basis for local service even in exchange areas where all other subscribers are charged on a flat-rate basis. This proposal, too, has been successfully opposed by computer-user groups.

In addition to these abortive efforts, several other separate rate classifications for data users have been introduced on an experimental basis, but these are still relatively new and not on very firm ground, and they apply to only an extremely small percentage of all data users. This approach to the problem appears to raise more problems than it solves, and hence the introduction of appropriately engineered data-oriented services promises to offer the better solution. For example, the local data line concentration services recently introduced by Bell and planned by Western Union are steps in the right direction.

The second pillar upon which the pricing of local telephone service in the United States is based is euphemistically termed "value-of-service pricing." Under this pricing philosophy, a customer is charged according to the *value* of the service to him rather than according to the actual cost of providing the service. Thus business subscribers, who use the telephone frequently and depend upon it, are charged a higher rate for a local-exchange line than are residential subscribers. Although most other countries also distinguish business from residential subscribers for pricing purposes, they do so to a lesser extent than does the United States. Germany, in fact, did not make the distinction at all until 1971.

As a result of the value-of-service pricing philosophy, data equipment that has historically been supplied exclusively by the telephone companies (e.g., data modems for the public switched network were, until the FCC's 1968 *Carterfone* decision, supplied exclusively by telephone carriers) tends to be priced substantially above cost, taking into account both equipment and maintenance expenses. As discussed in Section IV, *Carterfone* has forced the telephone companies to bring their charges for Data Phone® service more in line with actual costs. However, as discussed earlier, where nontelephone-company modems are connected to the switched telephone network the user must lease a protective connecting device, or DAA. It should be apparent that the pricing of these devices influences the extent to which true competition in data modems can exist. Therefore, charges for DAA's should properly be based upon costs, rather than value of service, and the burden of proof should rest with the telephone companies to demonstrate that this is, in fact, the case.

Long-Distance Telephone Rates

Long-distance (toll) calls are defined as calls beyond the local-exchange area. In the United States, as in other countries, the caller pays a rate roughly proportional to the distance and duration of the call. In the United States, however, automatic message accounting equipment is used to record the date, time, and called number for every toll call, and customers' monthly bills contain a detailed itemization of toll calls. In most other countries, long-distance calls are metered and customers' monthly bills indicate only the total number of metered pulses counted during that month. Also, as in most countries, a minimum charge, varying according to the time of day and day of the week, is imposed for a 3-min (in some states a 2-min or 5-min) station-to-station call. Rates increase with distance, but less than proportionately. The interstate rate is the same for equal distances anywhere in the country. The rate structure for long-distance calls within a state is basically the same as for interstate calls. However, intrastate rates for comparable distances vary widely, and they generally, although not always, exceed interstate rates.

Data users who wish to place short-duration data calls (e.g., for inquiry into a computer data base) find that the long-distance telephone rate structure discriminates against them by imposing a 3-min minimum charge. As in the case of local-exchange service, the rates and traffic engineering for

® Registered service mark of the American Telephone and Telegraph Company.

long-distance service are based upon the usage patterns of voice-telephone subscribers whose calls typically average 5 or 6 min in length. For large data users, the problem tends to be less serious than it appears because of the availability of Wide Area Telephone Service (WATS) service, discussed below. However, small users placing short calls are forced to pay a penalty because of this rate-making practice.

It is interesting to note that the Datran network (discussed above), which is designed exclusively for data usage, provides for a much shorter minimum charge time of 6 s, and a charging increment also of 6 s. This would appear to fully meet the requirements of the short-duration data caller. However, Datran's plan raises 3 questions for which the answers are not clear at present. First, since the initial or minimum charge on a switched call is designed to cover the cost of setting up the call—largely the cost of switching—and since Datran's proposed minimum charges are an order of magnitude lower than Bell's present minimum charges, will the two firms' call setup costs really be that different? If so, there are obvious implications for the design of future telephone switching plants. Secondly, on the assumption that the actual cost difference is less than the tariff rate disparity, and that Bell's rates reflect its costs (at least roughly, for a number of noncost-related factors are also involved in the setting of rates), will Datran incur a loss in handling very short-duration calls at its proposed tariff rates? If so, what volume of such calls can be expected, and what impact will this have upon the new carrier's financial viability? And third, if the actual Bell–Datran cost difference is less than the tariff-rate disparity, and if we assume Datran *can* cover its costs for short-duration calls, this suggests that Bell's rates for such calls must be substantially above its costs. Issues are then raised as to the propriety of such rates, and opportunities are presented for possible modification of the telephone minimum-rate structure for toll calls, if this would be in the public interest.

One billing arrangement for long-distance service, available in the United States and Canada, which is of particular interest to data system users is WATS. Under out-WATS, a subscriber pays a fixed charge per month and can place an unlimited number of calls from a given access line to any telephone within a designated geographic area. The rate for WATS service is a function of the size of the area covered. For this purpose, the continental United States is divided into 6 roughly concentric areas around the customer's state. A given access line may be used either exclusively to originate calls *to* telephones in selected WATS areas (out-WATS) or exclusively to receive calls *from* telephones in these WATS areas (in-WATS).

WATS service is generally used for high-volume dial-telephone traffic between one central point, such as a company headquarters or computer center, and many widely distributed remote locations. WATS service, which tends to encourage telephone usage and to reduce traffic peaks, is widely used in computer-communication systems in the United States and Canada. Often, however, subscribers use WATS lines for teleprinter-speed data transmission, most frequently at 110 or 135 bits/s, and thus grossly underutilize the voice-grade channels which this service provides.

In the early 1960's AT&T attempted to introduce Wide Area Data Service (WADS), which was basically the same as WATS, but was designed for teleprinter-speed operation and was priced accordingly. The service was rejected by the FCC for reasons unclear to the authors. Perhaps it is time for a reassessment and repricing of the WADS service, this time by Western Union, which recently purchased AT&T's TWX system.

Private-Line Rates

Private-line (leased) circuits are provided in the United States by the telephone companies and Western Union on a full-time (24 h/day, 7 days/week) basis at per-mile rates that decline as circuit length increases. Until recently, leased circuits could not be shared by different organizations (except in the case of authorized users),[23] and in most cases, outside of the United States sharing of leased circuits is still not permitted. Sharing is often considered by telephone carriers to be "resale" of circuits, a function that has historically been restricted to common-carrier organizations. The first significant departure from the historical prohibition against sharing or resale was AT&T's "joint-user" tariff provision, introduced in 1969, which permitted organizations to share telegraph-grade and voice-grade leased lines. While little actual circuit sharing has taken place to date, due primarily to the organizational difficulties of identifying and consolidating the requirements of multiple-user organizations, this development nevertheless has significant implications for data-system users. The RCA Corporation, for example, at the 1972 International Communications Association Conference proposed operating a joint-user leased-line network for major corporations, which would offer substantially improved efficiency in circuit utilization and commensurate reductions in allocated costs to the user. The participating firms would use the shared private-line facilities primarily for teleprinter service, both message and data.

A second development in private-line pricing of significance to the data-network designer—route pricing—is a natural result of the establishment of specialized common carriers, discussed above. By introducing competition into the provision of private-line services, and permitting the established carriers to depart from their traditional practice of setting interstate private-line rates at uniform levels, irrespective of location, the FCC has taken a large step toward encouraging *cost-based* pricing of long-haul private-line circuits. For example, in early 1972, shortly after MCI began providing low-cost private-line service over the heavily trafficked communications corridor between Chicago and St. Louis, Western Union proposed (subject to FCC approval) lowering its private-line rates between these cities to the same levels as offered by MCI. While the telephone companies have not, at this writing, taken similar steps, competitive pressures may ultimately force them to follow suit, and to adjust private-line rates downward (or upward) depending upon actual transmission costs over a given route.

Data network designers may find life more complicated as the uniform rate structure begins to break down, but they will probably benefit in the long run since private-line rates between major commercial and industrial centers are today priced above actual cost (and private-line rates in less populous regions are priced below costs). Life will become

[23] An authorized user is a person or firm authorized by the customer to be connected to the customer's private line, but permitted to use the private line only for communications relating directly to the customer's business.

more complicated for the FCC also, since it must carefully assess the competitive pricing responses of the established carriers to ensure that these prices are set at "compensatory"[24] levels and not at below-cost levels (subsidized by revenues from monopoly services) designed to prevent the market penetration of the new carriers.

The third and final development that will affect private-line rates is the establishment of domestic communications-satellite systems in the mid-1970's. In contrast to terrestrial networks, transmission costs via satellite are independent of distance, although unless a high level of satellite utilization is achieved the per-channel cost may be quite high. Several firms that have applied to the FCC for authorization to operate domestic satellite systems have estimated tentative rates for equivalent voice channels provided via satellite at about 1000 dollars (between any pair of earth stations located anywhere in the United States, but excluding costs associated with the earth stations themselves and connecting terrestrial links), which is approximately equal to the present private-line rate for a circuit between New York City and Chicago. Thus it appears possible that rates for longer haul private-line circuits will become less dependent upon actual distance, and will tend to be lower than present charges.

In summary, the long-term outlook for private-line rates is downward, due to increased competition from both the specialized common carriers and future domestic satellite operators. Continually declining transmission costs and economies resulting from joint usage of private-line circuits will also contribute to this general trend. While the rates for future end-to-end digital-transmission services are unknown at this time, they are likely to be lower than rates for present carrier services offering the same data-transmission speeds.[25] For the data system designer these developments will significantly improve the economic attractiveness of computer-communication systems.

VII. Conclusions

Accompanying the rapid development of the computer-communications field, there has been a sharp increase in the number of confrontations between different segments of the industry—with the established communications carriers generally on one side, and the users, equipment manufacturers, and new carriers on the other side. Because the communications field is regulated, the FCC is often the arbiter of these disputes. Unfortunately, the FCC's Common Carrier Bureau, on which such responsibilities fall, is seriously understaffed; its resources have not kept pace with its rapidly expanding workload in recent years, and the result has frequently been lengthy delays in FCC decision-making on computer-communication issues. For example, the Commission took 5 years—from 1966 to 1971—to resolve the issues in its computer inquiry. After receiving the first specialized common-carrier proposal in 1963, it delayed 8 years before deciding as a policy matter to authorize such carriers. The first application for a domestic communication satellite was filed in 1965, but 7 years passed while the Commission (and the White House, which became involved on 2 separate occasions) pondered this admittedly complex subject, finally issuing a policy decision earlier this year. Additional policy-analysis resources for the FCC, including augmentation of its Common Carrier Bureau staff, could substantially reduce regulatory delays such as these. While it may be difficult to determine the economic and social costs of such delays, they must far exceed the costs of this additional manpower.

Although slow to be completed, the FCC's computer inquiry exemplifies effective regulation—impending problems were identified in their early stages and were largely resolved before they became serious. However, the regulations regarding "hybrid" computer-communication systems (i.e., systems involving both data-processing and store-and-forward message switching) and "pure" message-switching systems offered on a commercial basis have proven to be somewhat counter-productive. That is, instead of encouraging the development of such systems they have retarded development. In this paper the authors have suggested the establishment of a new class of communications common carrier, called a "contract carrier," modeled after the concept of contract carriage in the motor-freight field. Whereas the traditional common carrier provides service to all comers, under published rate schedules that are subject to approval by the regulatory agency, the contract carrier provides service under individual agreements or contracts with certain organizations, usually a limited number. Although an operating permit must be obtained from the regulatory agency, the contract carrier need not prove that the public convenience and necessity *requires* his services. Operating in this mode, and free of cumbersome regulatory controls, many firms could provide commercial message-switching services—each service probably oriented towards a particular user group (such as the securities–brokerage industry, the credit bureaus, etc.). If undesirable fragmentation of a market occurs, the FCC could require interconnection of the systems serving this market.

In the subscriber interconnection area, as a result of the FCC's *Carterfone* decision, the user has been given greater freedom in the types of equipment he can attach to the public network. At this writing, protective coupling devices are required by the telephone companies where customer-owned equipment, such as modems and PABX units, is connected to the dial network. Efforts are under way to remove the requirement for these couplers by developing procedures and specifications for the certification of customer equipment. While it is unclear to what extent over the long run users will avail themselves of the opportunity to interconnect independently supplied customer-premise equipment, it is already apparent that the rate of innovation and the variety of equipment available is increasing significantly. Also, for the first time, price competition has been introduced into major portions of the subscriber telephone-equipment market.

While providing the user with greater flexibility, interconnection privileges impose added burdens upon the data-

[24] There is little agreement among the interested parties as to the proper definition of "compensatory" pricing. The specialized carriers argue that the proper base on which to calculate the rate of return for a communications service is "fully allocated cost;" i.e., total cost including a *pro rata* share of all overhead expenses. The established carriers, on the other hand, argue that "incremental cost" is the proper base. This debate involves both theoretical economic issues and practical questions of cost determination and joint cost allocation that are beyond the scope of this paper. The interested reader is referred to the FCC's ***Private Line/Program Transmission Proceeding***, Docket no. 18128.

[25] For example, the Bell System has developed a technique, called Data Under Voice (DUV), for carrying a 1.5-Mbit/s digital pulse stream in the unused lower spectrum of an installed microwave radio channel. The incremental cost of this approach is extremely low and the prices of future private-line digital data services may reflect this cost advantage.

equipment designer. Whereas data-equipment design was previously isolated from telephone-network considerations, this is now less so, and telephone transmission and signalling parameters are becoming matters of greater concern in data-transmission equipment engineering.

Interestingly, while the telephone companies in the United States have been relatively restrictive regarding interconnection in general, they have become more liberal than many other industrialized countries with respect to the types of data modems allowed. Perhaps this has been one factor in the somewhat sluggish growth of data transmission in several of these countries.

A final noteworthy point concerning interconnection in the United States is its likely future impact upon PABX equipment design. Nontraditional PABX suppliers, such as computer manufacturers, may now apply their skills to the development of advanced computer-controlled PABX systems. Since the orientation of these firms is quite different from that of the traditional PABX suppliers, functional design is likely to be quite different.

A pro-competition attitude is also reflected in the FCC's recent decisions regarding specialized carriers and domestic communications satellites. As a result of these major decisions, a nationwide all-digital switched data-transmission network is planned by the Datran Company, a large number of regional microwave systems offering private-line voice and data-transmission services will be built, and several domestic satellite systems will also be established. While the financial viability of many of these future systems is uncertain, they are likely to result in the provision of a wider range of data-communication services, at lower costs in some circumstances, by both the new and the established carriers.

In the pricing area several trends may be noted. First, attempts to distinguish data and voice users of telephone facilities, and to charge the data users higher rates, have been rebuffed for lack of a sufficient showing that the costs of serving data users are materially greater. Nevertheless, in the future more data users are likely to pay for their calls according to metered rather than flat monthly rates; i.e., local-exchange rates for business-telephone subscribers will become increasingly usage dependent in the United States, as they already are in most other countries.

The second pricing development of note for the data-system designer is the probable future availability of switched data service with very low-minimum per-call charges and short billing increments. The Bell System has experimented with 1-min minimum charge times, and Datran plans to employ a 6-s minimum charge time.

The final pricing trend is the downward movement of long-haul private-line rates, due in part to improvements in transmission technology, and in part to the introduction of specialized-carrier and domestic satellite competition in the long-haul area.

Bibliography

The Regulatory Process

[1] A. D. Kahn, *The Economics of Regulation*, two vols. New York: Wiley, 1970.

[2] R. A. Posner, "Natural monopoly and its regulation," *Stanford Law Rev.*, vol. 21, pp. 548–643, Feb. 1969.

[3] U. S. President's Task Force on Communications Policy, "The domestic telecommunications carrier industry," Staff Paper, 1969, National Technical Information Service, Springfield, Va., Document nos. PB 184 417 and PB 184 418.

[4] U. S. Federal Communications Commission, *Annual Reports*. Washington, D. C.: Government Printing Office.

Regulation of Computer-Communications Services

[5] FCC, *Regulatory and Policy Problems Presented by the Interdependence of Computer and Communication Services and Facilities*, Docket 16979, Notice of Inquiry, 7 FCC 2d 11 (1966); Tentative Decision, 28 FCC 2d 291 (1970); Final Decision and Order, 28 FCC 2d 267 (1971).

[6] S. L. Mathison and P. M. Walker, *Computers and Telecommunications: Issues in Public Policy*. Englewood Cliffs, N. J.: Prentice-Hall, 1970.

[7] Stanford Research Institute, *Policy Issues Presented by the Interdependence of Computer and Communications Services*, Rep. to the FCC, 1969, National Technical Information Service, Springfield, Va., Document nos. PB 183 612 and PB 183 613.

[8] M. R. Irwin, "The computer utility: Competition or regulation," *Yale Law J.*, vol. 76, pp. 1299–1320, June 1967.

[9] B. Gilchrist and M. R. Wessel, *Government Regulation of the Computer Industry*. Montvale, N. J.: AFIPS Press, 1972.

Interconnection

[10] FCC, *Use of the Carterfone Device in Message Toll Telephone Service*, Dockets 16942 and 17073, Memorandum Opinion and Order, 13 FCC 2d 420 (1968); Petitions for Reconsideration Denied, 14 FCC 2d 571 (1968).

[11] National Academy of Sciences, Computer Science and Engineering Board, *A Technical Analysis of the Common Carrier/User Interconnections Area*, Rep. to the FCC, 1970.

[12] Dittberner Associates, *Interconnection Action Recommendations*, Rep. to the FCC, 1970.

Specialized Carriers

[13] FCC, *Microwave Communications, Inc.*, Docket 16509 *et al.*, Decision, 18 FCC 2d 953 (1969); Petitions for Reconsideration Denied, 21 FCC 2d 190 (1970).

[14] FCC, Specialized Carrier Inquiry, Docket 18920, First Rep. and Order, 29 FCC 2d 870 (1971).

[15] P. M. Walker and S. L. Mathison, "Specialized common carriers," *Teleph. Eng. Manag.*, vol. 75, no. 20, pp. 41–61, Oct. 15, 1971.

[16] ——, "Regulatory policy and future data transmission services," in *Computer-Communication Networks*, N. Abramson and F. F. Kuo, Eds. Englewood Cliffs, N. J.: Prentice-Hall, in press, ch. 9.

Pricing

[17] U. S. President's Task Force on Communications Policy, "The domestic telecommunications carrier industry," Staff Paper, 1969, Appendix A: H. M. Trebing and W. H. Melody, "An evaluation of domestic pricing practices and policies," also National Technical Information Service, Springfield, Va., Document no. PB 184 417.

[18] R. H. Coase, "The theory of public utility pricing and its application," *Bell J. Econ. Manag. Sci.*, vol. 1, pp. 113–128, Spring 1970.

Non Technical Issues in Network Design– Economic, Legal, Social, and Other Considerations *

Philip H. Enslow Jr.**
Lieutenant Colonel, U.S. Army
Senior Staff Assistant

Computer networks and their communications support no longer present major technical problems. Today, many organizations are planning major networks in a very matter-of-fact way; often, however, giving little or no consideration to non-technical issues during the design phase. When operational networks are being designed, full consideration must be given to the legal, economic, social, and management factors as well as those that are purely technical.

Introduction

One of the most topical subjects of the past few years has been networks – both data communications networks as well as complete computing networks. A large number of technical studies and projects have been focused on this area; however, it is clear that many of the critical issues in network development have been overlooked or not given the attention that they require. To quote from a paper presented last year "...there is no question but that the social, political, and legal problems (rather than the technical ones) will delay the coming of the computer utility [network]."(1) Dr. Robert M. Fano recently underscored one aspect of the situation when he stated before a House of Representatives Committee hearing that there should be restrictions on the development of nationwide information networks "until we have developed adequate means for protecting individual privacy."(2) However, these voices are in the minority and even they have not fully delineated the non-technical impediments to the growth and exploitation of networks.

(*NOTE: This paper is an amplification of the paper published in the COMPCON '73 Digest and remarks made by the author at the conference.)

****Lieutenant Colonel Enslow is currently assigned as a senior staff assistant in the Office of Telecommunications Policy, Executive Office of the President, Washington, D.C. where he is program manager for policy analyses and studies in the area of data/computer communications. The opinions and conclusions expressed herein are his personally and do not reflect official OTP or government policy.**

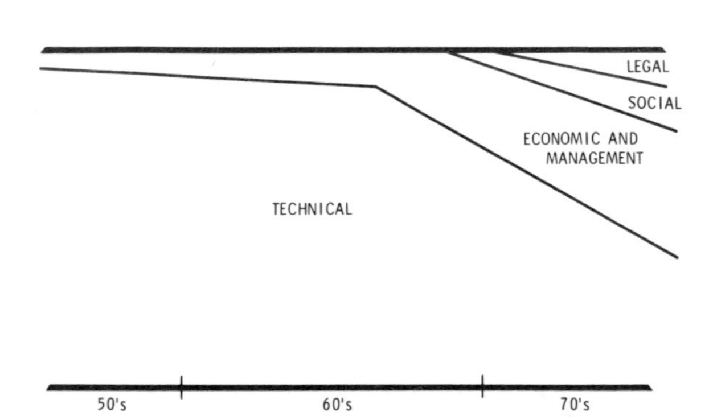

Figure 1. Changes in Influence on Network Design, Implementation and Operation

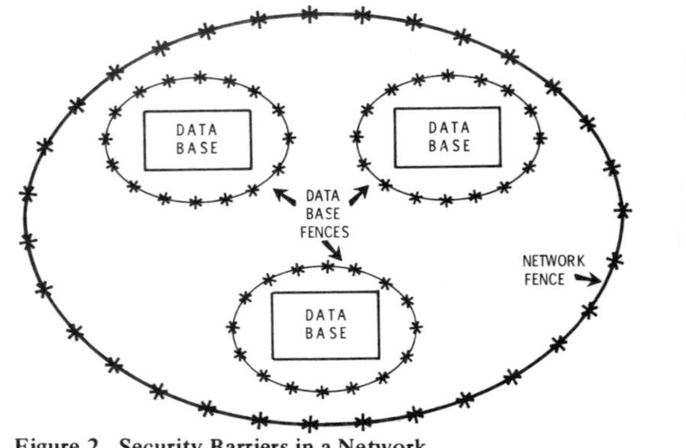

Figure 2. Security Barriers in a Network

Changes in Emphasis

As computer communications and networks have matured, there have been changes in the emphasis or the influence of different topics upon the system design. (Figure 1) The amount of consideration given to each has been based on its relative importance at that time. In the very early days of networks, the technical problems were paramount. Economics became important only *after* we determined that it *might* work. In the mid-sixties, economics became more important with management as well as operational issues being raised. And it is only recently that social implications and legal considerations have been given very much attention. The figure is an oversimplification of this, for some designers have been thinking about all of these problems for a long time; however, it probably reflects the emphasis of the *average* system designer.

One does not have to look very far for confirmation of the new trends. In October, 1972, the Computer Society and the ACM were co-sponsors of the first major meeting devoted to these and other inter-disciplinary computer-communications issues.* The "Special Issue on Computer Communications" of the *Proceedings of the IEEE* (November, 1972) reflected these changes by devoting the first two papers to social, regulatory, and economic issues; and non-technical topics are receiving more and more emphasis in the trade press.

Social Issues

Social issues cover an extremely large area. They are involved with all aspects of communications and computers. They can best be summarized by saying "What are the impacts of the system on others – both users and non-users?" There are other users of communications, other users of computers, and a large mass of non-users. The social issues are those that create any important cross-influences. Certainly, data traffic has a definite impact on other users of the communications system. Many of us did not give much thought to that factor when we started planning our systems; however, we must start doing just that. Otherwise, we may design systems not acceptable for implementation or continued use. Systems that generate excessively long holding times or have other characteristics that impair or reduce the grade of service to other customers are "socially" unacceptable and will probably result in regulatory prohibitions or economic sanctions against their continued operation. Another important social issue often associated with the applications utilizing the network is privacy. Privacy is the right to keep certain classes of information confidential. This leads into the next topic – the legal issues involved.

Legal Issues

The legal obligations and considerations involved are only beginning to be defined. Certainly one that is going to have a large impact on all uses of data communications will be the legal requirement for the protection of privacy of information. Privacy will be defined by its social aspects, but it is through the establishment of legal requirements for protection that privacy is going to obtain stature and present a major problem for network system designers. Security or controlled access must be considered in the basic system design.

The other important legal factor is the regulatory environment in which the network must operate.

Network Controlled Access

The major impact of data networks and teleprocessing systems as compared to single stand-alone systems is the greatly expanded exposure of the information. One can think of an authorized user on the data network being on the "inside" and having already passed those safeguards that protect the network as a whole. (Figure 2) Since there will be many users authorized access to the network but not to all of its resources, then each data base and other system component must have its own protection.

I recently received a response to a bibliographic search request. The computer was printing out both classified and unclassified material. There were no communication lines involved – the printer was hardwired to the multiplexor channel. Somewhere synchronization was lost on the channel and what came out were pieces of several entries intermingled. There were portions of at least three entries on a single page and one of these did not appear to even belong to my bibliography. Also lost was the security classification normally printed at the top and bottom of each page. It was not just moved, it was totally *lost*. Somehow lost during a *local* I/O operation. We have a long way to go before we are going to have confidence in the security of data networks including long-haul transmission lines. There must surely be mechanisms and procedures to guard against unauthorized entry into the system or portions thereof, as well as other closely allied problems such as the spill-over described here.

***"Computer Communication – Impacts and Implications,"** *First International Conference on Computer Communications,* **October 24-25, 1972, Washington, D.C.**

The Regulatory Environment

The regulatory environment that the network designer should assume and plan for is not at all clear. Some decisions have already been made, many more are to come.* One might well ask "Is it better to avoid the questionable areas at this time?" The answer to that is "Probably *no*" for it will be a long time before all of the issues get shaken down.

The present regulatory environment does have certain characteristics which are directly applicable to networking. Interconnection is now allowed for both customer-owned equipment as well as systems. Competition, to some degree, has been initiated. Of much more importance is the fact that the customer now has available a variety of services and sources and can expect to see even more introduced in the future as both carriers and value-added-networks respond to meet his special demands.

One of the key considerations with regulatory impact that must be considered by any data network planner is its impact on voice. What will the data traffic do to the quality of voice service? What is going to be the impact on toll revenues – the long distance DDD revenues? The planner should also consider the possible second-order effects of his network and its mode of operation.

An important regulatory issue is concerned with the separability of the communications and computation functions of the system and their regulatory status. Figure 3 shows diagramatically the Federal Communications Commission ruling on computer-communications services (Docket 16979). On the far left are stand-alone computers – "pure computing." This was specified to be unregulated. On the far right is "pure communications," dedicated circuits – obviously a regulated service. The solid line represents the "unpure" environment of hybrid services where the left terminus is characterized by simple remote computing and the right by circuit switched service. The only other point specifically identified on the chart is message switching, which is certainly a highly communications-oriented service. On the right, data processing is only *incidental* to the function of providing communications, and on the left, communications is only *incidental* to the function of providing computation. In the middle are hybrid services where both communications and data processing will be present in appreciable quantities, and it is in this area that it is not yet settled as to what will happen. Under the present FCC ruling, each hybrid service offering is to be examined by the Commission on an individual basis to determine whether or not it should be regulated. One of the things that the system designer can do to aid in this process is to consider whether or not he has separable networks. Is his network totally integrated? Are the computer network and the communications network indistinguishable or is there a distinct identifiable interface? (Figure 4) Even if this latter condition does exist, there is no assurance that the decision process will be simple; however, it will greatly simplify defining the function or functions of the sub-networks and where the system fits on the "regulatory line."

*A complete discussion of this topic is given in Mathison and Walker, "Regulatory and Economic Issues in Computer Communications," *Procs IEEE* 60:11, Nov, 72, pp 1254-1272. However, in just the short time since that article was written, significant new developments have occurred.

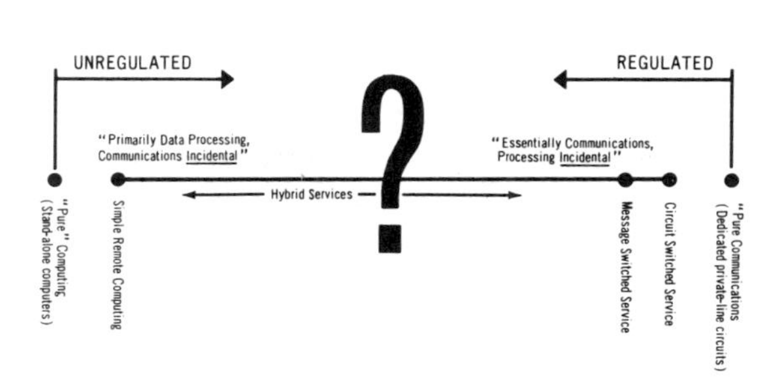

Figure 3. Regulatory Status of Computer and Communications Services (Federal Communications Commission Decision on Docket Number 16979)

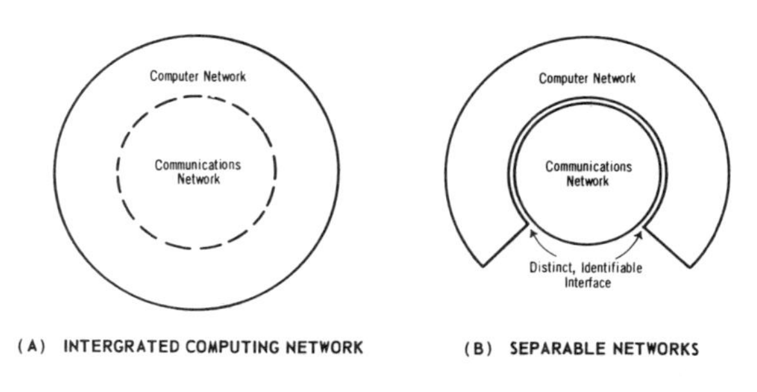

Figure 4. Separability and Identification of Sub-Networks and Their Functions

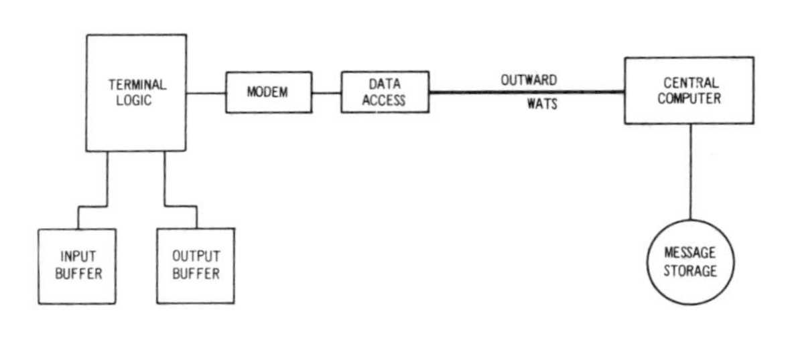

Figure 5. Use of Outward WATS Line to Automatically Poll Terminal Stations

The mere existence of this area where the regulatory implications are not clearly defined has been one of the major impediments to the commercial exploitation of networks. A clearer definition of the division between the areas must be a high priority item; however, that work in turn must await a clearer definition by the designers and implementers of the division between their sub-networks and their functions.

- GENERATION OF INQUIRY
- TRANSFORMATION TO COMMUNICATIONS FORMAT
- INTERACTION OF HOST WITH COMM CONTROLLER
- TRANSMISSION (Total Costs)
- INTERACTION OF COMM CONTROLLER WITH HOST
- TRANSFORMATION FROM COMMUNICATIONS FORMAT
- INTERPRETATION OF INQUIRY
- ACCESS TO DATA BASE
- EXTRACTION FROM DATA BASE
- TRANSFORMATION TO COMMUNICATIONS FORMAT
- INTERACTION OF HOST WITH COMM CONTROLLER
- TRANSMISSION (Total Costs)
- INTERACTION OF COMM CONTROLLER WITH HOST
- TRANSFORMATION FROM COMMUNICATIONS FORMAT
- INTERPRETATION OF REPLY

Table 1. Primary Functions in the Use of a Network System for Remote Inquiry

LOAD	COST
• PROTOCOLS	• LINES
• MESSAGE FORMATTING	• TERMINALS
• CUSTOMER TRAFFIC	• MODEMS
• ROUTING	• CONTROLLERS
• ERROR CONTROL	• REDUNDANCY
• MESSAGE CONTROL	• MAINTENANCE
• SYSTEM CONTROL	• SYSTEM DESIGN
• ACCOUNTING	• DESIGN MAINTENANCE
•	• SALES
•	• CUSTOMER TRAINING
•	• MANAGEMENT
	• BILLING
	•
	•
	•

Table 2. Communications Network Load and Cost Components

Economic Issues

It is often said that it is economics that makes the world go around and it will be the economics of the networks that will determine their future. Over time, the emphasis on cost has swung from one area to another; it is the *total* costs that are important. If anything, the raw costs of communications have received more than their proper share of attention. Terminal costs are overtaking all other hardware components; however, it is often the computational load placed on the system by the network protocols that is the most important hidden part of the "cost iceberg."

Communications costs are discussed below as well as some other aspects of the economic picture. One topic that is not covered here, for we are only just beginning to gain any appreciation of its importance, is the effect of property rights for network programs and data bases and their dollar value.

Communications Costs

The increased attention being given to communications cost and the present environment present a real challenge to the communications network designer. To provide the basic capabilities, he is faced with a wide variety of services and options such as transmission rates, disciplines, and protocols. He also must address the network design problem so that these services are obtained at the least possible cost. Recent developments such as specialized common carriers and value-added-networks catering to data transmission customers and special route prices by the regular carriers have increased the alternatives possible and made his problem even more difficult.

The costs of the increments of bandwidth that are being made available are not changing very much. The changes that are occurring are highly localized and often not significant in total system costs. The designer's approach to transmission cost reduction is to better utilize the bandwidths or the bit rates that are available, rather than to attempt to obtain an exact match to his requirement. Anyone who has looked at the problem closely has seen that communications costs are being overtaken by other costs and probably not worthy of the attention they are now receiving. The costs of the terminals used in large systems is beginning to exceed the cost of both computer equipment and communications. However, it is the *total system* costs that are important.

Often overlooked is the cost of the data base *and its use.* (Table 1) A teleprocessing system, particularly one with heterogeneous hosts and terminals, can devote a large amount of software overhead to conforming with the protocols necessary in a resource-sharing network.

Finally, in considering communications network costs, there are many factors that contribute to the total. (Table 2)

Customer Charges

There is a real problem if the charges to the customer are not consistent. He may run a program and be charged one price because it was executed on machine A. The next day, the network control switches him to machine B which has a different accounting algorithm and the price is radically different. Users are not going to be willing to accept this situation.

In a heterogeneous computing network, the question of customer charges for both communications and computation must be closely examined. All of the difficult cost allocation and consistency problems that must be solved by an accounting system for a multiprogrammed system are present as well as many others. A user's charges should reflect the demand he places on the system. It may be necessary to separate these charges between computation and communications, but in a multi-user communications network, additional thought must be given to obtaining consistent charges for executing the same program under different loading conditions.

continued page 29

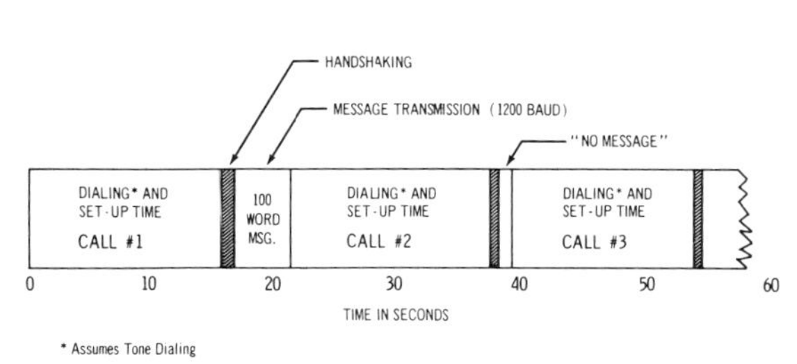

Figure 6. Outward WATS Line Utilization During Automatic Polling

Figure 7. Use of Inward WATS Line in an Automatic Contention Dialing System

Unusual Uses of Standard Communications Services

Another economic factor that must be considered is the exploitation of a current cost and service situation that may not continue. It may not continue, particularly if it degrades the service to others.

Figure 5 illustrates a possible use of an outward WATS line. When outward WATS was offered it was, of course, intended for voice traffic. In the teleprocessing application shown here, outward WATS lines are connected directly to a central computer and the computer automatically and continuously polls its terminals to see if they have any messages stored in their buffers. A typical cycle through all terminals might be 20 minutes. The WATS line is in use continuously. (Figure 6) But, more importantly, most of the time is spent in establishing the call which involves switching equipment throughout the system rather than just the use of the talking path. As you can see from the diagram, the message transmission is quite short. Similarly, utilizing inward WATS lines, the system is designed so that the terminals continuously call the computer on a contention basis trying to get through. (Figure 7) Obviously this system is most cost effective when the demand reaches the point where there are an appreciable number of busies and utilization of the computer ports is high. However, all of those attempted but uncompleted calls still tie up the long-distance dialing system and effect other DDD users, particularly at the last tandem switch serving the computer.

The system designer must evaluate his future realistically. It is unrealistic for him to believe that the public common carrier systems can continue to function effectively if such usage patterns become widespread.

Figure 8. Multiple Overlapping and Interconnected Networks

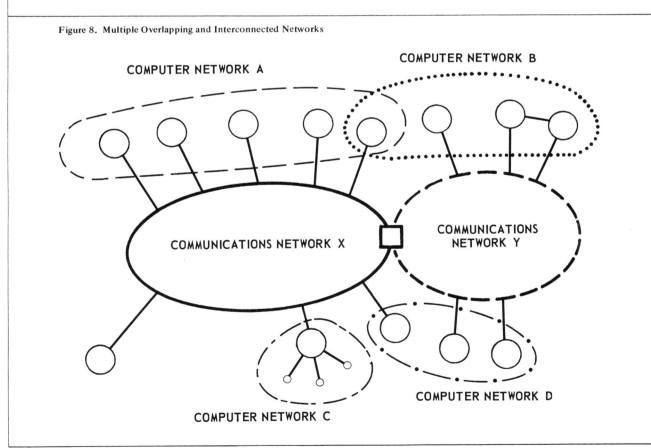

Standards

Standards are also an economic issue. The success of the voluntary standards programs in the U.S. is based on the desire for free competition in the marketplace. We are a long way from that condition in computing networks. The variations in an operation as simple as sign-on are ridiculous. And the problems of inconsistent file structuring are a much stronger deterrent to competition.

As the largest single user of computers and data processing, the Federal Government is deeply involved in fostering standards with over 200 individuals working on the various ANSI X3 committees and subcommittees. Unfortunately, participation by that sector of the computer industry most directly affected, the user, is spotty and weak. Certainly this problem deserves better attention by all concerned.

Management Issues*

The technical feasibility of networking is beginning to put pressure on management in education, government, and industry to deal with some new but fundamental policy issues. There are five important points for management to consider.

First: Communications networks facilitate large-scale sharing of computer facilities across major organizational boundaries, with the result that difficult new problems are being forced to the attention of management at *all* levels.

Second: Many organizations have grown dependent on their computer facilities. Now with networks, that dependency will be shifted to foreign (outside) computing facilities. Organizations are undergoing power structure shifts which will threaten management with rethinking their organization structures.

Third: The management problems of sharing have not been solved in pace with technical network developments. Sharing is now feasible but the management problems are unsolved. A substantial effort is required to find some way for organizations to afford the risk of becoming dependent upon foreign facilities if networking is to become acceptable.

Fourth: The role of the technician must be fully understood in relationship to the politics of the power structure shifts that are the result of networking developments. We are all confronted by some very real dangers if technicians and managers fail to play their proper roles in the effort to solve the problems posed by networks. It is vital that all the players in this drama understand their respective roles and avoid stepping on each other's lines. Imagine the problems of management in dealing with the Administration of the series of interlocking networks shown in Figure 8.

Fifth: Finally, what is the role of top management in evaluating or directing the use of a network?

Conclusions

Networks are not "on the way" – they are *here*. The technicians have done their work in providing a new method for the utilization of the capabilties of computing power. Now it remains for the lawyers, economists, and managers to do theirs so that they may be exploited to their fullest benefit.

***Based on the remarks on "The Relationship Between Technology and Management" made by Einar Stefferud at COMPCON '73.**

References

[1] Eric Harslem and John Heafner, "Aspects of Large-Scale Resource Sharing Through Network of Computers," Paper P-4833, RAND Corp., May, 1972.

[2] "News in Perspective," *Datamation*, May, 1973, p. 120.

Reprinted by permission from *Computer*
August 1973, pp. 21-30

PHILIP H. ENSLOW, JR., Lieutenant Colonel, U.S. Army, is Senior Staff Assistant, Office of Telecommunications Policy, Executive Office of the President. He is a member of the U.S. Army Signal Corps. Detailed to the Office of Telecommunications Policy in August, 1970 just as it was being formed, Lt. Col. Enslow has primary responsibility for defining, executing, and controlling OTP's programs and projects in the areas of computers and data communications as they relate to teleprocessing.

Lt. Col. Enslow graduated from the United States Military Academy in 1955. He received his Master of Science degree in Electrical Engineering in 1958, his Engineers degree in Electrical Engineering: Administration in 1960, and his Ph.D. in Electrical Engineering in 1965 from Stanford University.

At the present time, Lt. Col. Enslow is an Adjunct Professor in Computer Systems at The American University where he has been specializing in courses on Operating Systems, and a Professional Lecturer at George Washington University where he teaches systems programming. He is the author of several papers and texts in the areas of communications and computers.

Lt. Col. Enslow is a senior member of the IEEE. He is a member of the Board of Governors of the IEEE Computer Society. Within the Computer Society, he is Chairman of the Subcommittee on Operating Systems Standards, Chairman for Continuing Education, and a member of the Technical Committees on Computer Communications, Operating Systems, and Computer Architecture. He is a member of the ACM and its Special Interest Groups on Operating Systems, Data Communications, Architecture, Measurement and Microprogramming. He was Chairman of the Executive Committee for the First International Conference on Computer Communications (October 1972). He is also a member of the Society of Sigma Xi.

POLITICAL AND ECONOMIC ISSUES FOR INTERNETWORK CONNECTIONS

© Kuo, F F, University of Hawaii, Honolulu, Hawaii, USA

ABSTRACT

In this paper we will attempt to outline some of the political and economic issues which must be addressed before meaningful network interconnections can come about. The issues we discuss are: Bilateral versus Multilateral Agreements, Standards, The Viewpoint of the Common Carriers, Network Accounting, Tariffs and Excises, Privacy and Security. Our main purpose is to present the problems and issues but not to offer any solutions.

1. INTRODUCTION

With the pioneering development of the ARPA Network [1], packet switching nets such as CYCLADES [2], SITA [3], and COST-11 [4] are springing into existence. It is now possible to consider the technical, political and economic benefits of interconnecting a number of these networks to form a global system of networks. In addressing the interconnection question it is not surprising that many nontechnical or quasi-technical issues such as tariffs and excises, government policies toward telecommunications etc., are more difficult to deal with than purely technical problems, and that in many instances, the nontechnical issues prescribe the technical approaches to the problems. In this paper we will attempt to outline some of the political and economic issues which must be addressed before meaningful network interconnections can come about. Our main purpose is to present the problems and issues but not to offer any solutions.

What are the issues? In the order we will address them, they are: (1) Bilateral versus Multilateral Agreements; (2) Standards; (3) The Viewpoint of the Common Carriers; (4) Network Accounting; (5) Tariffs and Excises; and (6) Privacy and Security.

2. THE ISSUES

2.1 BILATERAL OR MULTILATERAL AGREEMENTS

In November 1971, Science Ministers of eight European countries (Britain, France, Italy, Norway, Portugal, Sweden, Switzerland, and Yugoslavia) signed an agreement in principle to proceed with the development of a European computer network known as the COST-11 Net [4]. It was expected that within two years a first prototype of the network would be operational. However, it was not until the latter part of 1973 that the technical director was appointed and sufficient funds were obtained to enable the project to begin. What accounted for the delay? Most of it could be attributed to the fact that the agreement was a multilateral agreement among nations and as such had to be approved and ratified by the PTT's of the nations involved, by the national governments, and in some instances by the parliaments of the governments. By international standards, the two-year time delay is not excessive. Some multilateral agreements take many more years to ratify.

Let us imagine a situation where the COST-11 Net is to be connected to the ARPANET and CYCLADES. A well-planned interconnection might have the structure shown in Figure 1, where each net has its own gateway computer and communication protocols and other standards are agreed to in advance. Since there are groups such as the International Network Working Group (INWG), TC6.1 of IFIP, working actively on standards for internetwork protocols [5,6,7] arriving at a set of mutually agreeable protocols is probably not a difficult task. What is much more difficult is to negotiate a political settlement between the governments of the US and France, the respective owner/operators of ARPANET and CYCLADES, and the European COST community, as well as the telecommunications carriers such as the French PTT, the British Post Office, and the international carriers ITT, RCA and Western Union International. Since this is a many-stage process, final agreement could take many years.

* This report was supported by THE ALOHA SYSTEM, a research project at the University of Hawaii, supported by the Advanced Research Projects Agency of the Department of Defense and monitored by NASA Ames Research Center under Contract No. NAS2-6700.

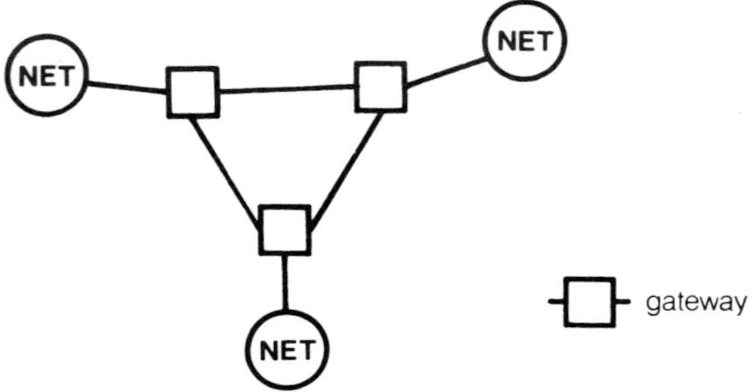

characteristics: (a) separate gateway machine
(b) standards imposed
(c) multilateral agreement required

Figure 1

A less complicated procedure for arriving at network interconnections is through bilateral agreements. It is probably less difficult to justify connecting together COST-11 and CYCLADES than connecting all three nets. In fact, since the two nets will have a common node in IRIA, near Paris, the gateway program could exist as a process in the host computer at IRIA, as shown in Figure 2. Once the bilateral

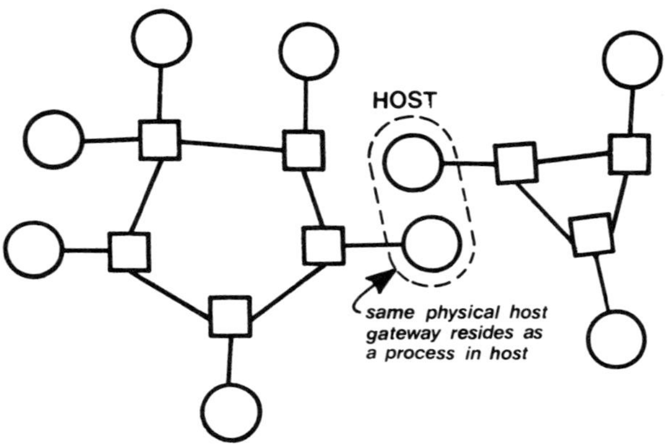

characteristics: (a) separate gateway program
(b) standards recommended
(c) bilateral agreement required

Figure 2

connection is achieved, consideration could be given to connecting other nets, such as ARPANET, in a series of bilateral agreements. Adding the third net, however, may involve as much complexity as with a multilateral agreement, since all parties must agree to the interconnections between any two of the parties. So it seems likely that bilateral agreements will only be effective for two parties and that a series of bilateral agreements may present as much if not more complications than a multilateral agreement.

To many network professionals the configuration of Figure 2 which might permit bilateral experimental connections without common protocols is a "kludge" which if permitted to grow will result in a monster. So the choice seems to be a monster now or a well-planned interconnection achieved through multilateral agreements and rational standards -- ten years from now.

2.2 STANDARDS

The issues of standards is probably the most difficult and important problem that networks people must face. There are existing networks with their own protocols and specifications. To interconnect these networks it is necessary to resolve the compatibility problems without prematurely fixing a set of standards. At the present stage of development it is difficult to determine what standards are necessary or even desirable. Various groups such as CCITT's Committee Special A, ISO/TC-97/SC-6, ANSI X3S3 and INWG (IFIP TC6.1) have been given charters to examine the issues of standards for public data networks. It is the author's view that it is important to prevent the issuance of premature standards by these groups. Packet communication networks are still in an evolutionary stage. Early standards could only freeze the development process.

2.3 THE VIEWPOINT OF THE COMMON CARRIERS

In order to interconnect any two networks, even in a bilateral agreement, it is necessary to obtain the approval and cooperation of the common carriers and the regulatory agencies of the countries in which the network resides. More often than not, this is a surprisingly difficult task. Common carriers such as the European PTT's and the US's AT&T are by their very nature slow to adapt to technological change and even slower in offering new services. It is necessary to understand this situation before one can effectively deal with it.

The common carriers in almost all cases are monopolies. They must, by law, offer a mix of services which meet the needs of society. They must plan for a consistent policy regarding standardization, long term investment, load distribution between different services, and equal treatment of customers. They have to balance their tariffs such that an overload on one service is avoided. They have to plan for new services using advanced technologies many years before the new service can be offered. In many cases technologies change radically during this period so that plans must be revised again and again to reflect the constantly changing technological-state-of-the-art.

In many countries, such as the United States, the government agency regulating telecommunications (the FCC in the case of the US) is different or distinct from the common carrier. Since telecommunications has evolved in different ways in different countries, the laws and regulations as well as tariffs governing telecommunication services are extremely varied between countries. As a result, as is the case between European countries, it is quite difficult to arrange for any telecommunication service that must cross national boundaries. We thus see that one major obstacle in the interconnection of computer networks is the fact that so far there has been insufficient interaction between the national common carriers at the periods when major new developments are planned or initiated. Due to the large scale in which innovations are planned and the resulting investments in financial and manpower resources, a reluctance to change over to another country's standards at a later stage becomes understandable.

It is this viewpoint that has blocked COST-11 from having centers in certain highly technologically sophisticated European countries. It is this viewpoint also that will effectively delay or block plans for international network connections -- no matter if the plans are technically feasible.

2.4 NETWORK ACCOUNTING

The issue of network accounting is difficult to address within a single network much less than between a number of networks. There are two kinds of costs to be accounted for -- communication costs and resource costs.

Communication Costs. In a packet-switched network, the user is charged by the number of packets he sends and not charged according to distance. This is one of the basic tenets of packet switching and this principle will be strengthened even more when packet broadcasting via satellite becomes an operational reality. When two networks are interconnected the accounting problem becomes very complex. If each net has its own charges per packet fixed, will the charge for sending a packet from one net to the other be the sum of the two individual packet charges? Some other suggested approaches are:

Charge based upon destination or source net only

Charge = Local Net Cost + Surcharge

Charge = Additive Cost/Number of Nets Traversed

Another issue is if a user limits his use of network resources to his own net, should he be required to contribute towards the gateway and internetwork management costs? Suppose one net charges by the packet, and the other has some sort of distance-dependent charge. Unless the two policies are reconciled it will be most difficult to interconnect the two nets. Also if the two nets are in different countries, the charging policies will be strongly influenced by the national PTT's and the governments' communications statutes, policies, and tariffs.

Resource Costs. The most easily identifiable resources in a computer communications network outside of the communications resources are: computers, software, memory and data bases. In some networks, remote users are often charged a different rate (usually lower) than the local user. This policy recognizes that the remote user does not have access to many of the local facilities such as keypunch, printers, software library, and consulting services. In the case when a remote user uses a computer in another network, then other factors such as tariffs, government policy, national chauvinism, etc., come into play and the computing charges are probably less dependent upon true costs than in a strictly intranetwork situation. We will discuss this issue further in the next section on tariffs and excises.

Accounting and Billing. In internetwork usage, should there be a central accounting service, or should the user receive multiple bills for the communications and computing resources used? This question deals with the issue of centralized versus distributed accounting policies. Implicit in the centralized accounting idea is the existence of a centralized internetwork control center where an internetwork financial data base might reside. This idea may not appeal to nations with strong government control of telecommunications and computing. With the distributed accounting policy, the net accounting overhead can be quite significant, and the cost of billing might exceed the cost of resources used.

2.5 TARIFFS AND EXCISES

Many countries in Western Europe and Japan have quota systems and protective tariffs on high-technology imports. A computer network that spans across national boundaries is tantamount to importing and exporting computer resources across those boundaries without physically moving the equipment. In order to interconnect two networks in two different countries, it is necessary to make all arrangements beforehand with the respective governments on such issues as: import and export of hardware, software, data bases and technological "know-how", currency import and export restrictions, and excises and duties on the transfer of non-tangible products across national boundaries. A net of nets cutting across several countries is in many respects like a multinational corporation. There is no reason why a net of nets cannot exist and be useful, but it must conform to all the restrictions which are placed by all the governments with jurisdiction.

2.6 PRIVACY AND SECURITY

Privacy and security of data bases and files are issues of paramount importance and must be guaranteed before any firm agreements for network interconnections can be promulgated. The issues are important even in an intranetwork environment; when two networks are interconnected the problems become even more complex. The following questions are pertinent:

a) Who is responsible for security and privacy and how is it done?

b) Should users be able to control message routing?

c) Should every network have the same standards for protection of data bases?

d) Should the gateways function as security guards, or should the hosts themselves assume this task?

e) What kind of overhead is tolerable in imposing interconnection security? How should this overhead be paid for?

f) Can different networks offer different levels of security and still be connected?

3. CONCLUSIONS

It is quite evident that the path to network interconnections is a long, arduous one, and that the obstacles are technical, political, and economic. In this paper we have attempted to point out a number of political and economic issues which must be addressed before meaningful interconnections can be brought about. The paper is intended to serve as an introduction to the issues. We hope that practical solutions to the problems raised here can be found and that a global net of nets can truly be realized.

4. ACKNOWLEDGEMENT

This paper owes its origin to an INWG report [8] edited by the author who served as chairman of an ad hoc committee during the INWG meeting held at the University of Hawaii, 6-7 January 1974. The committee and co-authors of the report were: Norman Abramson (University of Hawaii), Robert Blanc (National Bureau of Standards), Hartmut Grebe (Federal Republic of Germany), Juro Oizumi (Tohoku University, Japan) and Anthony Vignaux (Victoria University, New Zealand). I am most grateful to these people for supplying the ideas and discussions which made this paper possible. Indeed, if it were not for the difficult logistics of getting these people together, this paper should have been co-authored by the entire committee.

5. REFERENCES

[1] Roberts, Lawrence G.: "The ARPA Network" in *Computer-Communication Networks*, ed. Norman Abramson and Franklin F. Kuo, Prentice-Hall, Inc., 1973, pp. 485-500.

[2] Pouzin, L.: "Presentation and Major Design Aspects of the CYCLADES Computer Network," *Proceedings of the Third Data Communication Symposium*, Tampa, Florida, November 1973, pp. 80-87.

[3] Chretien, G.: "The SITA Network," *Proceedings of the NATO Advanced Study Institute on Computer-Communication Networks*, ed. R.L. Grimsdale and F.F. Kuo, Noordhoff International Publishing Co., Leyden, Holland, 1974.

[4] Barber, D.L.A.: "The European Computer Network Project, *Proceedings of the ICCC*, Washington, D.C., October 1972, pp. 192-200.

[5] Cerf, V.G. and Kahn, R.E.: "A Protocol for Packet Network Interconnection," to be published.

[6] Cerf, V.G. and Sunshine, C.: "Protocols and Gateway for the Interconnection of Packet Switching Networks," *Proceedings of the Seventh Hawaii International Conference on System Sciences - Subconference on Computer Nets*, Western Periodicals Co., January 1974, pp. 105-107.

[7] Pouzin, L.: "Interconnection of Packet Switching Networks," op. cit., pp. 108-109.

[8] Kuo, Franklin F.: "INWG Workshop Report on Political, Social and Economic Issues on Network Interconnections," *INWG Note #52, NIC Document #22030*, Stanford Research Institute, 19 March 1974.